CORPORATE BOARDS IN
LAW AND PRACTICE

University of Plymouth
Charles Seale Hayne Library
Subject to status this item may be renewed
via your Primo account

http:/primo.plymouth.ac.uk
Tel: (01752) 588588

Corporate Boards in Law and Practice

A Comparative Analysis in Europe

Edited by
PAUL DAVIES, KLAUS J. HOPT,
RICHARD NOWAK
and
GERARD VAN SOLINGE

OXFORD
UNIVERSITY PRESS

OXFORD
UNIVERSITY PRESS

Great Clarendon Street, Oxford OX2 6DP
United Kingdom

Oxford University Press is a department of the University of Oxford.
It furthers the University's objective of excellence in research, scholarship,
and education by publishing worldwide. Oxford is a registered trade mark of
Oxford University Press in the UK and in certain other countries

Published in the United States of America by Oxford University Press
198 Madison Avenue, New York, NY 10016, United States of America

British Library Cataloguing in Publication Data
Data available

Library of Congress Control Number: 2013948631

ISBN 978–0–19–870515–4

Printed in Great Britain by
CPI Group (UK) Ltd, Croydon, CR0 4YY

Preface

Corporate boards play a central role in corporate governance and are therefore regulated in the corporate law and corporate governance codes of all industrialised countries. Yet although there is a common core of rules on boards, considerable differences remain—not only in detail but sometimes also as to major issues. These differences depend partly on shareholder structure (dispersed or blockholding), and partly on path-dependent historical, political and social developments, especially employee representation on the board. More recently, with the rise of the international corporate governance code movement in particular, there is a clear tendency towards convergence, at least in terms of the formal provisions of the codes.

This book uses the functional comparative method to analyse corporate boards, their regulation in law and codes, and their actual functioning in ten European countries (Belgium, France, Germany, Italy, the Netherlands, Poland, Spain, Sweden, Switzerland and the United Kingdom). Issues addressed include: Board structure; composition, functioning and enforcement by liability rules (in particular conflicts of interest); incentive structures; and shareholder activism. The book finds convergence in these European countries due to the pressures of competition, a pro-shareholder change supported by government and institutional investors and, to a certain degree, the impact of the EU. This convergence is more evident in the codes and the ensuing practice than in the statutes. Yet considerable differences remain, in particular as a result of the failure to adopt a mandatory 'no frustration' rule for takeovers at EU-level, and diverging systems of labour co-determination. The result is an unstable balance between convergence and divergence, shareholder and stakeholder influence, and European versus national rule-making.

The information and analysis that is contained in the general and the national reports are presented in five sections and a number of sub-sections in order to facilitate search and comparison by readers. The sections correspond to the functional problems of the board, its regulation and practice in all of the ten countries covered in this book, and not the sequence and content of the different board regulations in the national company laws and corporate governance codes. In *Section 1: General Introduction* we look at the environment in which boards operate. Relevant issues include: The definition of controlled companies; the impact of ownership structures on the law; changes in the type of shareholders, such as institutional shareholders; and code developments. Without being aware of this environment it is difficult to understand special legal rules, and certainly not easy to make evaluations and comparisons. Some information on the available board models in each jurisdiction follows. In *Section 2: Authority* the focal point of the analysis is on the relationship between the board and the management of the company. How do the functions and powers of the board(s) map onto the roles of managing the company, monitoring its management, and advising its managers? How does the role of the board relate to its structure, composition and decision-making, with special emphasis on independent directors? Some of the timely issues discussed are the ways and means of monitoring, the role of the board in risk-management, diversity and quotas, appointment rights, and the relevance of a company secretary. The highly different concepts of independence concern, inter alia, the circumstances that exclude independence or make it questionable, the relevance of independence in controlled companies and companies with labour co-determined boards, and the uneasy relationship between independence and competence. Special attention is paid to the information streams in the company, both to the board and from the board, including committee work. *Section 3: Accountability* analyses the relationships between the board and the shareholders, the stakeholders (foremost labour and labour co-determination) and the creditors if the company comes under financial stress. As to the traditional principal-agent conflict between the board and the shareholders, issues covered include appointment and removal, division of powers between the board and the shareholders, liability, the growing role of institutional investors and the efforts to motivate them to engage in corporate governance (UK Stewardship Code), and remuneration as an incentive. Law in books is scarcely interesting without law in action. Company law is merely as relevant as its enforcement. *Section 4: Enforcement* deals with the enforcement of company law by civil courts, criminal courts and regulators, in particular corporate governance code commissions and stock exchanges. This is woefully neglected in many company law courses and treatises, a fact that is due to the difficult links between company law, procedural law, criminal law, and soft law. While there is much convergence in section 2 and 3, the differences as to enforcement are deep and far-reaching as regards the institutions where enforcement takes place, the methods of enforcement chosen, and in particular the actual level of enforcement. Finally *Section 5: Dynamics and Drivers of Change* is devoted to summarising the major reforms and reform trends, their causes and obstacles and, more generally, the direction boards will develop in law and practice within the ten countries and in the European Union in the foreseeable future.

This book has its origins in the decision of the Dutch legislature to open up the traditional Dutch two-tier board system and to give Dutch companies the option of having a one-tier board. Such a change is in conformity with international developments. Many countries give shareholders the choice between two—sometimes even more—board systems, most prominently France and Italy, and the European Union for the European Company (Societas Europaea). But the change also creates problems: Technical problems for company law and its interpretation and, more important, problems for companies to uncover the advantages and disadvantages of the different board systems. Answers to these problems might be found in the experiences of countries with the one-tier or the two-tier system, or countries which permit the choice between them. Gerard van Solinge and Richard Nowak (Nijmegen) came to Klaus J. Hopt (Hamburg), to discuss the consequences of the new Dutch law and the possibilities of comparative research. The three of them, later joined by Paul Davies (Oxford), brought together a group of company law experts from ten European countries with a triple requirement in mind: They should be experts in the company law of their country; they should have intimate knowledge of board practice in that country; and they should be familiar with the European and comparative dimension. This is how the Forum European Corporate Boards (FECB) was constituted in Amsterdam consisting of Peter Böckli (Basel), Paul Davies (Oxford), Guido Ferrarini (Genoa), Koen Geens (Leuven), Klaus J. Hopt (Hamburg), Alain Pietrancosta (Paris), Markus Roth (Marburg), Rolf Skog (Stockholm), Stanislaw Sołtysiński (Warsaw), Richard Nowak (Nijmegen), and Gerard van Solinge (Nijmegen), along with Marco Becht (Brussels), who as Professor of Economics gave us valuable advice. Later on Andrés Recalde Castells (Madrid), Francisco León Sanz (Huelva), and Nuria Latorre Chiner (Valencia) were invited to join the group with a report on Spain.

The work of the group started in late 2009 and continued until July 2013 with many meetings of the editors, of the whole group and of separate drafting teams in Hamburg, Amsterdam and Oxford. These meetings were most exciting comparative company law seminars discussing a host of legal and practical information, differing views on theoretical issues and practical evaluations, and all of this taking place in a very amiable and enjoyable atmosphere. Right from the beginning there was unanimous consent on using the functional comparative law method with a keen eye on economic theory and the actual practice in the different countries. The four editors of the book have also been in charge of the general report. Two of them, Paul Davies and Klaus J. Hopt, published an article on 'Corporate Boards in Europe – Accountability and Convergence', *The American Journal of Comparative Law* 61 (2013) 301–376 which, while drawing on the general report, focuses on accountability and convergence. The general report contains many more details on the various national company laws and practice, and includes exact references to the national reports and the sources cited therein.

The four editors would like to thank the members of the FECB for the diligent national reports, which are not really reports in the traditional comparative law sense, but fully-fledged articles with first-hand information on the characteristics and most recent developments of the law and practice of company boards in their respective countries. The editors would also like to thank them for devoting an unforeseen amount of time and effort for this book, and also for the marvellous friendships that have ensued. Special thanks for its generous financial support goes to the Eduard v. Schwartzkoppen Foundation in the Stifterverband für die Deutsche Wissenschaft in Essen, to Harald Schaaf who is in charge of the management of this foundation and to the Business & Law Research Centre of the Radboud University (Nijmegen), and finally to Clifford Chance Amsterdam, which hosted most of the meetings. We further thank the secretaries Jorn Wegter and Shivani Singhal for the excellent minutes they made of our meetings. We are most grateful to the editing team at the Hamburg Max Planck Institute where the book was produced in a camera-ready form with much work and enthusiasm under the coordination of Dr. Christian Eckl, in particular to Ingeborg Stahl, her successor Janina Jentz, LL.M. (Oec), M.A., and Gill Mertens, LL.B., LL.M., M.A., for editing and the language checks. Klaus J. Hopt would like to thank specifically Nina Marie Güttler, LL.B., his personal legal assistant, and Edda O'Hara, his personal secretary, who never said no when new work and challenges came up, dug out inconsistencies and reminded about dates and to-dos. Last, but not least, we would like to thank Oxford University Press, its reviewers and the team for their contribution.

Summer 2013

P. Davies, Oxford
K.J. Hopt, Hamburg
R. Nowak, Nijmegen
G. van Solinge, Nijmegen

Contents

Table of Legislation

DOMESTIC LEGISLATION

Netherlands

The Contributors

Marco Becht

Professor of Finance, Université Libre de Bruxelles (ULB), Goldschmidt Professor of Corporate Governance, Solvay Brussels School of Economics and Management; Executive Director and Fellow, European Corporate Governance Institute (ECGI); Research Fellow, Centre for Economic Policy Research (CEPR); Fellow, Center for Financial Studies (CFS), Goethe University Frankfurt; Visiting Fellow, Saïd Business School, Wadham College and Faculty of Law, Oxford (2012); Visiting Professor, Stanford University Law School (2011); Visiting Fellow, Rock Center for Corporate Governance, Stanford University (2011); Max Schmidheiny Visiting Professor of Entrepreneurship and Risk, University of St. Gallen, Switzerland (2008); Visiting Professor, Saïd Business School, Oxford (2003). He has published widely on corporate governance and the economic aspects of corporate law, including 'Bank Governance is Different', *Oxford Review of Economic Policy* 27 (2011) 3, 437–463 (with Patrick Bolton and Ailsa Roëll); 'Returns to Shareholder Activism. Evidence from a Clinical Study of the Hermes U.K. Focus Fund', *Review of Financial Studies* 22 (2010) 3093–3129 (with Colin Mayer, Julian Franks and Stefano Rossi); 'Where Do Firms Incorporate? Deregulation and the Cost of Entry', *Journal of Corporate Finance* 14 (2008) 241–256 (with Colin Mayer and Hannes Wagner).

Peter Böckli

Attorney-at-Law, Dr. iuris, Böckli Bodmer & Partner, Basel. Prof. Emeritus (tax law and business law) University of Basel. Admitted to Bar 1962, trainee and associate at the law firm White & Case in New York and Paris from 1963 to 1966. Attorney-at-Law with focus on company law, capital markets law, corporate governance and corporate taxation. Part-time Professor of Tax Law and Business Law at the University of Basel from 1975 to 2001. He is the author of numerous books and articles, including: *Swiss Corporation Law*, fourth enlarged and revised edition 2009; *Insider Trading Law and Responsibilities of the Board*; *Introduction to the International Accounting Standards IFRS/IAS*. Peter Böckli has extensive experience as chairman or member of arbitration tribunals in international cases and was a member of the board of four major Swiss public companies and several family enterprises. With two co-authors, he drafted the revised Swiss Limited Liability Company Law and, as committee head, the Swiss Code of Best Practice for Corporate Governance.

Paul Davies

Allen & Overy Professor of Corporate Law, University of Oxford, 2009–date. Previously Cassel Professor of Commercial Law, London School of Economics and Political Science, 1998–2009; Fellow and Tutor in Law, Balliol College, Oxford University, 1973–1998; Lecturer in Law, University of Warwick, 1969–1873. Visiting Professor at various times at the universities of Bonn, Bordeaux, Chinese University of Hong Kong, Leuven, Paris I, University of South Africa, Witwatersrand and Yale. Fellow of the British Academy. Honorary Queen's Counsel, Honorary Bencher of Gray's Inn. Member of the Steering Group of the Company Law Review, 1998–2001. Review of liability for misstatements to the market for the UK Treasury, 2006–2007. Has written widely in the areas of labour law, corporate law, securities law and, recently, banking law. Most recent publications *Gower and Davies' Principles of Modern Corporate Law* (12th edn., 2012, with Sarah Worthington); *Introduction to Company Law* (2nd edn., 2010); *Anatomy of Corporate Law* (2nd ed., 2009, with others); 'Corporate Boards in Europe—Accountability and Convergence', *The American Journal of Comparative Law* 61 (2013) 301–375 (with K.J. Hopt); 'Liquidity Safety Nets for Banks', *Journal of Corporate Law Studies* 13 (2013) (forthcoming).

Paul-Henri Dubois

Attorney-at-law (*Avocat à la Cour*), BCTG & Associés. Research Master Degree in business law from the University of Paris 1 Panthéon-Sorbonne, LL.M degree in corporate and securities law from the London School of Economics and MSc in Management from HEC Paris Business School. Advises French listed companies on corporate governance issues and participation in AMF consultation processes, and publishes in the area of corporate, financial and securities law.

Guido Ferrarini

Prof. Guido Ferrarini is Professor of Business Law and Capital Markets Law at the University of Genoa, Department of Law, and Director of the Centre for Law and Finance; J. D. (University of Genoa, 1972), LL.M. (Yale Law School, 1978) Dr. jur. (h.c., Ghent University, 2009). He is a founder, director and fellow of the European Corporate Governance Institute (ECGI), Brussels. He was a member of the Board of Trustees, International Accounting Standards Committee (IASC) and an independent director at several Italian blue-chip companies. Acted as advisor to the Draghi Commission on Financial Markets Law Reform, to Consob (the Italian Securities Commission) and to the Corporate Governance Committee of the Italian Stock Exchange. He has held Visiting Professor positions at several universities in Europe (Bonn, Frankfurt, Ghent, Hamburg, LSE, UCL, Tilburg and Duisenberg) and the US (Columbia, NYU and Stanford), teaching courses on comparative corporate governance and financial regulation. He is the author of many articles in the fields of financial law, corporate law and business law, and editor of several books, including the recent *Financial Regulation and Supervision: A Post-crisis Analysis* (with E. Wymeersch and K.J. Hopt).

Romain Garçon

Attorney-at-law (*Avocat à la Cour*), Freshfields Bruckhaus Deringer. Advanced Master Degrees from the University of Paris 2 Panthéon-Assas (Business law, *Magistère de Juriste d'Affaires DJCE*) and the University of Paris 1 Panthéon-Sorbonne (financial law); lecturer at the University of Paris 1 Panthéon-Assas (business law); Secretary General of the Business and Law Association (2008–2009). Advises French listed companies on corporate governance issues and publishes in the area of corporate, financial and securities law.

Koen Geens

Licentiate of Law (summa cum laude, Leuven, 1980), Master of Laws (Harvard, 1981) and Doctor of Law (Leuven, 1986). His doctoral thesis about professional regulation and ethics was awarded the biannual State Award of the Flemish Community for Law and Economics (1987) and the Baron Emile Van Dievoet Prize (1989). Since his appointment as Professor at the KU Leuven in 1986, he has taught company and tax law. Together with A. Benoit-Moury he was in charge of the codification of Belgian company law in 1999. He is currently Director of the Jan Ronse Institute for Company Law, member of the Belgian Corporate Governance Commission, editor-in-chief of the *Tijdschrift voor Rechtpersoon en Vennootschap* (Review for Legal Persons and Companies) and editor of the *International Encyclopaedia of Laws, Corporations and Partnerships*. He has authored numerous articles and contributions on company and tax law. He has also edited several international books on company law, such as (with K.J. Hopt) *The European Company Law Action Plan 2003 Revisited*, Leuven University Press, 2010.

Klaus J. Hopt

Professor and Director (Emeritus), Max Planck Institute for Comparative and International Private Law, Hamburg. 1974–95 Professor in Tübingen, Florence, Berne and Munich. Visiting Professorships in several European, American and Japanese universities, including Chicago, Harvard, NYU and Columbia. Judge, Court of Appeals Stuttgart 1981–85; Vice-President of the German Research Foundation 2002–08; member of the High Level Group of Company Law Experts, European Commission 2001–02; German Stock Exchange Experts Commission 2002–11; International Advisory Board of the Alexander von Humboldt-Foundation 2011–. Member of the German National Academy of Sciences Leopoldina (Halle); Dr. h.c. Brussels, Louvain, Paris, Athens and Tiflis). He has published widely in European corporate, capital market and financial law, including *The Anatomy of Corporate Law,* 2nd edn. 2009 (with Kraakman et al., Oxford University Press) and more recently: 'Comparative Corporate Governance: The State of the Art and International Regulation' and 'Corporate Boards in Europe – Accountability and Convergence', *The American Journal of Comparative Law* 59 (2011) 1–73, 61 (2013) 301–375.

Nuria Latorre Chiner

Holds a Doctorate in Law from the University of Valencia (1999), and is Commercial Law Professor at that University. She teaches several Masters courses at the University of Valencia and at the Polytechnic University (Valencia). Her main research fields are insurance law and companies law. She has published two monographies—*La agravación del riesgo en el Derecho de seguros* (2000) and *El administrador de hecho en las sociedades de capital* (2003)—and has co-authored a book on private insurance law which has been the basis for integrating the *International Encyclopaedia of Laws in the Insurance Law* (Ed. Kluwer Law International, 2010). She has lately centered her research on corporate management, and has published several papers on the subject in domestic and international reviews.

Francisco León Sanz

Doctorate in Law from the Universidad Complutense (Madrid) in 1992. Professor of Commercial Law since 2002 at the Universidad de Huelva. He is a member of the editors' board of several reviews (*Revista de Derecho Mercantil, Revista de Derecho de Sociedades, Cuadernos de Derecho y Comercio, Anuario de Derecho Concursal*). He has been invited to speak at several European and American Universities. Expert in Corporate and Financial Law, Capital Markets and Insolvency. He is the author of numerous doctrinal studies, as well as diverse monographies. He has worked as Of-Counsel at the law firm Pérez-Llorca (Madrid) since 2004.

Richard G.J. Nowak

Senior advisor of Clifford Chance Amsterdam, researcher at the Van der Heijden Instituut (Business & Law Research Centre) of the Radboud University Nijmegen, Substitute-judge in the Court of Appeal Arnhem. Co-author of a Dutch textbook on company law and author of publications on Dutch company law and corporate governance.

Gian Giacomo Peruzzo

Gian Giacomo holds a J.D. magna cum laude (University of Genoa) and a Ph.D. in Corporate Governance (University of Genoa). He has been Contract Professor of Financial Markets at the Genoa Law School and is a member of the Genoa Law and Finance Center directed by Prof. Ferrarini, the Genoa European Corporate Governance Training Node and a former fellow of Assonime (*Associazione fra le Società per Azioni*). His main research areas are corporate governance, capital markets and antitrust law.

Alain Pietrancosta

Professor of Law at the Sorbonne Law School. Ph.D. from the University of Paris 1 Panthéon-Sorbonne (1999). 'Concours d'agrégation' in private law (2001). Founder and director of the Masters in Financial Law program at the

Sorbonne Law School; of the *Revue Trimestrielle de Droit Financier – Corporate Finance and Capital Markets Law Review.* Founding member of the Forum Europaeum on Corporate Boards; of the *European Company Law Experts Group.* Research Associate of the ECGI. Member of the asset management commission of the French Financial Market Authority (AMF). Head of the scientific committee of the *European Association of Banking and Financial Law* (2009–2011). Professorial Fellow of the Faculty of Law of Tilburg, Anton Philips Professor 2008–2009. Co-founder of the *Paris Workshop & Lecture Series in Law & Finance.* Member of the Executive Committee of the Labex (Excellence Research Center) Financial Regulation (ESCP-Europe Business School, ENA, CNAM, ENASS, University of Paris 1). Vice-President of *Rules for Growth.* Author of *The Influence of Financial Imperatives and Market Forces on French Corporate Law,* Thomson-Transactive, 2000. Numerous publications in the fields of corporate, financial and securities law.

Andrés Recalde Castells

Professor of Commercial Law at the Universidad Autónoma (Madrid) since 2012. He studied at the University of País Vasco (San Sebastián). He has taught in the University of Alcalá de Henares, was Professor at the University of Castellón and has been invited as speaker to several European and American Universities. He is a member of the editorial board at several reviews (*Revista de Derecho Mercantil, Cuadernos de Derecho y Comercio, Revista de Derecho del Transporte*) and has published several papers on corporate law, securities markets, banking agreements, shipping law and transportation law. He has recently focused on the changes that the financial crisis has provoked in corporate law and the regulation of financial entities. He contributes to the tasks carried out to produce a new Commercial Code by the Codification General Committee. He works as Of-counsel at the law firm CMS-Albiñana&Suárez de Lezo (Madrid).

Marta Roberti

Marta Roberti holds a J.D. from the University of Genoa (2008) and a M.Sc. in Law and Finance from the University of Oxford (2013). She is finalising her Ph.D. in business law at the University of Genoa (spring 2014). She is a teaching assistant in business law and capital markets law (University of Genoa, Law Faculty). Her research fields include: business law, corporate governance, capital markets law, corporate finance and venture capital and was a visiting Ph.D. student at the University of Sydney (May–August 2012) in the fields of corporate law and venture capital. She is an attorney-at-law, admitted to the Italian Bar Association since 2011 and a member of the Oxford Business Alumni, Oxford Business Network for Private Equity and EFLN (European Financial Law Network).

Markus Roth

Professor for Civil Law, Labour Law, German and European Commercial and Business Law, University of Marburg, since 2009. 1997–2000 (research assistant) and 2002–2008 (senior research assistant) at the Max Planck Institute for Comparative and International Private Law in Hamburg; 2000–2002 assistant, University of Bremen. Research Fellow, University of Cambridge, 2008. Lectures at European, Japanese and American Universities, including Cambridge, Oxford, Bocconi, Doshisha, Kyoto, Fordham. He has published widely on German and European corporate, employment, pensions and financial law, including an 1,450 page commentary on the German supervisory board (*Großkommentar Aktiengesetz*, 2005, with K.J. Hopt) and more recently: 'Outside director liability', *Journal of Corporate Law Studies* 8 (2008) 337–372; 'Employee Participation, Corporate Governance and the Firm', *European Business Organization Law Review* 11 (2010) 51–85; 'Labor and Comparative Corporate Governance in Times of Pension Capitalism Independent Directors, Shareholder Empowerment and Long-Termism: The Transatlantic Perspective', *Fordham Journal of Corporate & Financial Law* 18 (2013) 751.

Erik Sjöman

Erik Sjöman is a capital markets and public M&A partner in Vinge, with broad experience from all types of capital markets transactions, particularly takeovers and equity offerings, and advising listed companies on all types of corporate governance and corporate law issues. He is a member of the Listing Committee of NASDAQ OMX Stockholm. He has published extensively in the field of company law and capital markets law and is the co-author of an annotated commentary on the Swedish Takeover Rules.

Rolf Skog

Secretary to the Committee on Stock Ownership and Efficiency, Ministry of Industry (1985–1990), and Secretary to the Company Law Committee, Ministry of Justice, Sweden (1991–2001). Today he serves as an expert to the Ministry of Justice in the field of company law and takeover regulation. He was the Swedish Government's negotiator on the EU Takeover Directive, and chaired the negotiations on the Statute for a European Private Company during the Swedish EU Presidency in 2009. He is also Sweden's representative to the OECD Corporate Governance Committee. He is Director General of the Swedish Securities Council, which is the Swedish equivalent of the UK Panel on Takeovers and Mergers. Twenty years ago he co-founded the Swedish Corporate Governance Forum, of which he remains managing director. In 2004 he was appointed to the European Corporate Governance Forum by the European Commission. From 2000–2009 he was Adjunct Professor of Company Law at Aarhus School of Economics, Denmark. In 2010 he was appointed Adjunct Professor of Company and Stock Exchange Law at the School of Business, Economics and Law,

University of Gothenburg. In 2006 he was visiting professor at Columbia Law School, New York. He has published extensively in the field of company law, corporate governance and takeovers. He is the co-author of annotated commentaries on the Swedish Companies Act and the Swedish Takeover Rules.

Gerard van Solinge

Professor of Company Law at the Radboud University Nijmegen since 1997; one of the leaders of the research programme Company Law of the Business and Law Research Centre and the Director of the Van der Heijden Instituut, the oldest research centre for company law in the Netherlands (established in 1966). He is also a member of the Capital Market Committee, a standing advisory committee of the AFM (Dutch Financial Markets Authority); member of the standing advisory committee of the Ministry of Safety and Justice in the Netherlands and in Curaçao (Dutch Caribbean); member of the editorial board of *Ondernemings-recht* (the leading Dutch law journal on company law). He has published numerous books, book entries and articles on corporate litigation, corporate governance, M&A (cross-border mergers, public bids, takeovers) and private international law. He is co-author of three volumes on Company Law published in the Asser Series (the authoritative treatise on Dutch private law and company law). He is an advocaat at Allen & Overy LLP in Amsterdam (member of the Amsterdam Bar since 1993).

Stanisław Sołtysiński

Professor Emeritus and former Dean of the School of Law and Administration at A. Mickiewicz University (Poznań); member of Poland's Codification Commission of Civil Law; co-author of the Polish Code of Commercial Companies (2000); member of UNIDROIT Governing Council; member of the European Company Law Experts Group, member of the EU Reflection Group on Future of Company Law (2011–2012); member of the European Model Company Act Group; member of the European Academy of Sciences (London), European Academy of Sciences and Arts (Salzburg) and Polish Academy of Science and Art (Kraków); visiting professorships in University of Pennsylvania, Goethe University (Frankfurt) and College of Europe (Brugge). Author of more than 300 publications in the field of company and civil law.

Abbreviations

AB	Aktiebolag
ACAM	Autorité de Contrôle des Assurances et des Mutuelles
ACCOM	Advisory and Controlling Committee on the Independence of the Auditor
ACP	Autorité de Contrôle Prudentiel
ADAM	Association de Défense des Actionnaires Minoritaires
ADHGB	Allgemeines Deutsches Handelsgesetzbuch
AEX	Amsterdam Exchange Index
AFEP	Association Française des Entreprises Privées
AFG	Association Française de la Gestion Financière
AFM	Autoriteit Financiële Markten
AG	Aktiengesellschaft; Die Aktiengesellschaft
AGM	Annual General Meeting
AIM	Alternative Investment Market
AktG	Aktiengesetz
ALI	American Law Institute
All ER	All England Law Reports
AMF	Autorité des Marchés Financiers
AMX	Amsterdam Midcap Index
APE	Agence des Participations de l'État
AScX	Amsterdam Smallcap Index
BaFin	Bundesanstalt für Finanzdienstleistungsaufsicht
BB	Betriebs-Berater
BCC	Belgian Companies Code
BDA	Bundesvereinigung der Deutschen Arbeitgeberverbände
BDI	Bundesverband der Deutschen Industrie
BetrAVG	Betriebsrentengesetz (Gesetz zur Verbesserung der betrieblichen Altersversorgung)
BetrVG	Betriebsverfassungsgesetz
BGBl	Bundesgesetzblatt
BGE	Entscheidungen des Schweizerischen Bundesgerichts
BGHZ	Entscheidungen des Bundesgerichtshofs in Zivilsachen
BilMoG	Bilanzrechtsmodernisierungsgesetz (Gesetz zur Modernisierung des Bilanzrechts)
BIS	Department for Business Innovation and Skills
BJR	Business Judgment Rule
BNR	Board Neutrality Rule
BOFI	Banks and Other Financial Institutions
BR	Business Review
BTDrucks	Bundestagsdrucksache
BTR	Breakthrough Rule

BV	Besloten Vennootschap
BVerfGE	Entscheidungen des Bundesverfassungsgerichtes
CA	Court of Appeal
CAC	Cotation Assistée en Continu
CBFA	Commission Bancaire, Financière et des Assurances
CCC	Code of Commercial Companies
CDC	Cuadernos de derecho y comercio
CDU	Christlich Demokratische Union
CEA	Comité des Enterprises d'Assurance
CECEI	Comité des Établissements de Credit et des Entreprises d'Investissement
CEM	Control-enhancing Mechanisms
CEO	Chief Executive Officer
CFO	Chief Financial Officer
CFSA	Consolidated Financial Services Act
CGC	Corporate Governance Code
CLR	Company Law Review
CMF	Code Monétaire et Financier
CNMV	Comisión Nacional del Mercado de Valores
CO	Swiss Code of Obligations
CRD	Capital Requirements Directive
CUBG	Código Unificado de Buen Gobierno
D&O	Directors and Officers
DB	Der Betrieb
DCC	Dutch Civil Code
DGB	Deutscher Gewerkschaftsbund
DNB	De Nederlandsche Bank
DR	Depositary Receipt
DrittelbG	Drittelbeteiligungsgesetz
DRR	Directors Remuneration Report
DTR	Disclosure and Transparency Rule
ECFR	European Company and Financial Law Review
ECGI	European Corporate Governance Institute
ESCB	European System of Central Banks
ETUI	European Trade Union Institute
ExCo	Executive Committee
FAZ	Frankfurter Allgemeine Zeitung
FCA	Financial Conduct Authority
FESE	Federation of European Securities Exchanges
FINMAG	Federal Act on the Swiss Financial Market Supervisory Authority
FRC	Financial Reporting Council
FROB	Fondo de Reestructuración Ordenada Bancaria

FSA	Financial Services Authority; Financial Supervisory Authority
FSI	Fonds Stratégique d'Investissement
FINMA	Swiss Financial Market Supervisory Authority
FSMA	Financial Services and Markets Authority
GmbH	Gesellschaft mit beschränkter Haftung
GmbHG	Gesetz betreffend die Gesellschaften mit beschränkter Haftung
IAB-IEC	Instituut van de Accountants en Belastingconsulenten – Institut des Experts-comptables et des Conseils fiscaux
IBR-IRE	Instituut van de Bedrijfsrevisoren – Institut des Réviseurs d'Entreprises
ICAC	Instituto de Contabilidad y Auditoría de Cuentas
ICFAI	Institute of Chartered Financial Analysts of India
ICGN	International Corporate Governance Network
ICS	Internal Control System
IFA	Institut Français des Administrateurs
IFRS	International Financial Reporting Standards
IMF	International Monetary Fund
InsO	Insolvenzordnung
InstitutsVergV	Instituts-Vergütungsverordnung (Verordnung über die aufsichtsrechtlichen Anforderungen an Vergütungssysteme von Instituten)
InvG	Investmentgesetz
IPO	Initial Public Offering
ISVAP	Istituto per la Vigilanza sulle Assicurazioni Private e di Interesse Collettivo
IVASS	Istituto per la Vigilanza sulle Assicurazioni
J.T.	Journal des Tribunaux
JOR	Jurisprudentie Onderneming en Recht
Journ.	Journal
KfW	Kreditanstalt für Wiederaufbau
KGaA	Kommanditgesellschaft auf Aktien
KonTraG	Gesetz zur Kontrolle und Transparenz im Unternehmensbereich
KWG	Kreditwesengesetz (Gesetz über das Kreditwesen)
LC	Ley Concursal
LID	Lead Independent Director
LMV	Ley del Mercado de Valores
LR	Listing Rule
LSC	Ley de Sociedades de Capital
LTIPs	Long-term Incentive Plans
MB	Managing Board

MEDEF	Mouvement des Entreprises de France
MitbestG	Mitbestimmungsgesetz (Gesetz über die Mitbestimmung der Arbeitnehmer)
MTFs	Multilateral Trading Facilities
NBB	National Bank of Belgium
NED	Non-executive Director
NGM	Nordic Growth Market
NJ	Nederlandse Jurisprudentie
NMA	Nederlandse Mededingingsautoriteit
NV	Naamloze Vennootschap
NZG	Neue Zeitschrift für Gesellschaftsrecht
O&F	Onderneming & Financiering
OJ L	Official Journal of the European Union, Legislation
OLG	Oberlandesgericht
OO&R	Onderneming & Recht
OPAs	Ofertas públicas de aquisição
OSNC	Orzecznictwo Sądu Najwyższego. Izba Cywilna
OSNCP	Orzecznictwo Sądu Najwyższego. Izba Cywilna Pracy i Ubezpieczeń Społecznych
OSP	Orzecznictwo Sądów Polskich
PC	Penal Code
PDG	Président-Directeur Général
PGC	Plan General de Contabilidad
PIRC	Pensions and Investments Research Consultants Ltd.
RAB	Eidgenössische Revisionsaufsichtsbehörde
RAG	Revisionsaufsichtsgesetz (Bundesgesetz über die Zulassung und Beaufsichtigung der Revisorinnen und Revisoren)
RCDI	Revista Crítica de Derecho Inmobiliario
RDBB	Revista de Derecho Bancario y Bursátil
RDM	Revista de Derecho Mercantil
RdS	Revista de Derecho de Sociedades
RGBl	Reichsgesetzblatt
RNA	Rodamco North America
RoW	Rest of the World
RUG	Rijksuniversiteit Groningen
SB	Supervisory Board
SBF	Société des Bourses Françaises
SC	Stewardship Code
SE	Societas Europaea; Société Européenne

SEAG	SE-Ausführungsgesetz (Gesetz zur Ausführung der Verordnung (EG) Nr. 2157/2001 des Rates vom 8. Oktober 2001 über das Statut der Europäischen Gesellschaft (SE))
SEK	Svensk Krona
SER	Sociaal-Economische Raad
SESTA	Federal Act on Stock Exchanges and Securities Trading
SICAV	Società d'Investimento a Capitale Variabile
SID	Senior Independent Director
SIX	Swiss Stock Exchange
SME	Small and Medium-sized Enterprises
SOU	Statens Offentliga Utredningar
SPO	Secondary Public Offering
SR	Strategic Report
StSenkG	Steuersenkungsgesetz (Gesetz zur Senkung der Steuersätze und zur Reform der Unternehmensbesteuerung)
SYSC	Senior Management Arrangements, Systems and Controls
T.R.V.	Tijdschrift voor Rechtspersoon en Vennootschap
TPP	Transformacje Prawa Prywatnego
TransPuG	Transparenz- und Publizitätsgesetz
TUB	Testo Unico Bancario
UCI	Undertaking for Collective Investment
UMAG	Gesetz zur Unternehmensintegrität und Modernisierung des Anfechtungsrechts
V&O	Vennootschap & Onderneming
VAG	Versicherungsaufsichtsgesetz (Gesetz über die Beaufsichtigung der Versicherungsunternehmen)
VOC	Vereenigde Oost-Indische Compagnie
VorStAG	Gesetz zur Angemessenheit der Vorstandsvergütung
WM	Zeitschrift für Wirtschafts- und Bankrecht, Wertpapier-Mitteilungen
WpHG	Wertpapierhandelsgesetz (Gesetz über den Wertpapierhandel)
WPNR	Weekblad voor Privaatrecht Notariaat en Registratie
WpÜG	Wertpapiererwerbs- und Übernahmegesetz
WSE	Warsaw Stock Exchange
ZGR	Zeitschrift für Unternehmens- und Gesellschaftsrecht
ZHR	Zeitschrift für das gesamte Handels- und Wirtschaftsrecht
ZIP	Zeitschrift für Wirtschaftsrecht

Part I:
General Report

Boards in Law and Practice:
A Cross-Country Analysis in Europe

PAUL DAVIES, KLAUS J. HOPT, RICHARD G.J. NOWAK
and GERARD VAN SOLINGE
FORUM EUROPAEUM CORPORATE BOARDS (FECB)[*]

* This is the general report on the research of the Forum Europaeum Corporate Boards (FECB) undertaken 2010–2012. The members of the Forum are *Marco Becht*, Brussels, *Peter Böckli*, Basel, *Paul Davies*, Oxford, *Guido Ferrarini*, Genova, *Koen Geens*, Leuven, *Klaus J. Hopt*, Hamburg, *Richard G J. Nowak*, Amsterdam, *Alain Pietrancosta*, Paris, *Markus Roth*, Marburg, *Eric Sjöman*, Stockholm, *Rolf Skog*, Stockholm, *Gerard van Solinge*, Nijmegen, *Stanisław Sołtysiński*, Warsaw. The research was later supplemented by a report on Spain by Andrés Recalde Castells, Francisco León Sanz and Nuria Latorre Chiner. Their national reports are cited by author(s), section and page in this book, or, if no specific reference is deemed to be necessary, simply by the country. The research has been generously supported by the *Schwartzkoppen-Foundation in the Stifterverband für die deutsche Wissenschaft e.V., Essen*. Cf. also P. Davies and K.J. Hopt, 'Corporate Boards in Europe—Accountability and Convergence', *The American Journal of Comparative Law* 61 (2013) 301–375. While drawing on the general report, this article is much shorter and focuses on accountability and convergence.

1. General Introduction

The board sits at the interface between the investors in the company and its senior management. That it therefore plays a crucial role in the taking of important corporate decisions may seem obvious. Nevertheless, in practice identifying the role that the board plays in the governance of the company and determining to whom it is accountable for the exercise of its powers is far from easy. Equally difficult is reaching agreement on the theories which may enable one to specify the role the board should perform, or to whom it ought to be accountable. So, at both a positive and a normative level, the role and functioning of the board are matters of continuing debate among policy makers, academics and others, and the rules relating to these matters are never stable.[1]

---

[1] As to the state of theoretical and empirical research, see R.B. Adams, B.E. Hermalin and M.S. Weisbach, 'The Role of Boards of Directors in Corporate Governance: A Conceptual Framework and Survey', 48:1 *Journal of Economic Literature* 58–107 (2010); L.A. Bebchuk and M. S. Weisbach, 'The State of Corporate Governance Research', 23(3) *Review of Financial Studies* 939 (2010); K.J. Hopt, 'Comparative Corporate Governance: The State of the Art and International Regulation', *The American Journal of Comparative Law* 59 (2011) 1; A.M. Fleckner and K.J. Hopt, eds., *Comparative Corporate Governance, A Functional and International Analysis*, Cambridge University Press, forthcoming 2013. Cf. also O.E.

cont. ...

This book focuses on the boards of publicly-traded companies and of large corporations that are not publicly-traded. It is in these companies that the distinction between the shareholders and the management of the company is most clear (as compared with a small private company, where shareholders, directors and managers may all be the same people or at least extensively overlapping groups). It appears from this general report, and from the national reports, that there are two factors which most heavily influence the role of the board in public companies. The first is the dispersed or concentrated nature of the shareholder body.[2] This may affect both what the board does and to whom it is accountable. With a dispersed shareholding body, there are strong and obvious efficiency reasons for conferring extensive powers on the board rather than allocating them to the shareholders. However, those same reasons, notably the shareholders' coordination costs, may make the accountability of the board to the shareholders problematic. By contrast, in a concentrated shareholding structure shareholders can more plausibly claim to be able to take effective decisions themselves. Even if they leave management decisions to the board, for example, in order to be able to incorporate professional management in the decision-making, large shareholders are in a much better position to hold the board accountable to them for the decisions taken. In this situation, the central question is whether large shareholders exercise their governance rights to promote only their own interests, or the interests of the shareholders as a whole.

In other words, in dispersed shareholding companies the most pressing agency problem exists between management and shareholders as a class; in concentrated shareholding companies the agency relationship between majority and minority shareholders is the most pressing issue.[3] In both cases, however, the board's role in

---

Williamson, 'Corporate Boards of Directors: In Principle and in Practice', *Journal of Law, Economics, & Organization* 24:2 (2007) 247.

[2] As to the patterns of corporate ownership, see R. La Porta et al., 'Corporate Ownership Around the World', 54 *Journal of Finance* 471 (1999); M. Faccio and L.H.P. Lang, 'The Ultimate Ownership of Western European Corporations', 65 *Journal of Financial Economics* 365 (2001); F. Barca and M. Becht, eds., *The Control of Corporate Europe*, Oxford 2001; J. Armour, H. Hansmann and R. Kraakman, in R. Kraakman et al., *The Anatomy of Corporate Law*, 2nd edn., Oxford 2009, p. 29 et seq., 305 et seq.; A.M. Pacces, *Featuring Control Power*, Rotterdam 2008; *idem*, *Rethinking Corporate Governance, The law and economics of control powers*, London and New York 2012.

[3] We use the term 'agency problem' in the sense adopted in law and economics scholarship. In this usage an 'agent' is someone who has the factual power to take decisions or undertake actions which affect, positively or negatively, the welfare of another person—the 'principal'. It is not a requirement of an agency relationship in this sense that the principal should have authorised the agent to act on the principal's behalf. Such authorisation, which is the core of the doctrinal lawyer's concept of an agency relationship, may exist in situations which the law and economics scholar views as giving rise to agency, but that element may equally not be present. Clearly, the minority shareholders (the 'principal' in law and economics terms) do not

cont. ...

the agency relationship is central, but one cannot predict *a priori* what that role will be. At one end of the spectrum the board may simply reflect the dominance of the agent in the principal–agent relationship, such as where the board is dominated by the management (in a dispersed shareholding context) or by the large shareholders (in a concentrated shareholding context). At the other end of the spectrum, the rule-maker may use the board as a mechanism for protecting the principal (the share-holders as a class or the minority shareholders, as the case may be). In this book one of our central concerns is to explore the actual and potential role for the board in mitigating the agency problems of the shareholders. To this end, we begin by analysing two issues across our jurisdictions. First, what are the powers of the board, both formally and in practice, in relation to the management of the company (the board 'authority' issue)[4] and, second, to whom is the board accountable for the exercise of its powers (the board 'accountability' issue)?[5] If the board does not have the power, both formally and in practice, to effectively control management, its utility as an instrument to mitigate shareholders' agency problems is heavily reduced, perhaps even to zero. If the board does have that control power, either in fact or potentially, but is not effectively accountable to the principal whom the rule-maker aims to protect, the board's value as a mechanism for reducing share-holders' agency costs is again heavily compromised. Thus, we need to explore both dimensions of the board's role in order to evaluate the effectiveness of the board in large companies in Europe today.[6]

Although the board has, at least potentially, an important role to play in whether the shareholdings in the company are concentrated or dispersed, the two situations give rise to very different challenges for a rule-maker seeking to reduce the agency problems of the shareholders as a class, on the one hand, and minority shareholders on the other. It is traditional to present the United Kingdom as a dispersed shareholding jurisdiction and the continental European jurisdictions as concentrated. Although this may be broadly true, it is not a wholly reliable generalisation and it ignores both the differences in the levels of concentration in the various continental jurisdictions and the lessening of concentration that is

---

normally authorise the majority shareholders to act on their behalf. See R. Kraakman et al., above n. 2, pp. 35–37.

[4] See below, part 2.

[5] See below, part 3.

[6] We use the term 'board rules' to refer to all rules relating to the board, whether taking the form of statutory rules, rules laid down by courts or the comply-or-explain recommendations of corporate governance codes. On boards, cf. P. Davies and S. Worthington in Gower and Davies, *Principles of Modern Company Law*, 9th edn., London 2012, Sections 14–18 (p. 383–686); P.C. Leyens, 'Corporate Governance in Europe: Foundations, Developments and Perspectives', in: T. Eger and H.-B. Schäfer, eds., *Research Handbook on the Economics of European Union Law*, Cheltenham (Elgar) 2012, p. 183, available at <http://ssrn.com/abstract=2176987>.

under way in some of them.[7] A linked but distinct developement is the rise of institutional shareholdings,[8] primarily insurance companies, pension funds and collective investment schemes, but also hedge funds. In concentrated shareholder jurisdictions they may constitute the mechanism whereby concentration of shareholdings is reduced,[9] but, even if that is not the case, they may provide an effective lobby group to advance the protection of minority shareholders. Equally, in dispersed shareholding jurisdictions such as the UK, institutional shareholders may provide a mechanism for reducing the collective action problems of dispersed shareholders, certainly in terms of influencing the making of board rules and perhaps also in terms of shareholder activism at investee company level. As we shall see, the rise of institutional shareholding has been a significant influence on the development of board rules in all our jurisdictions, whether dispersed or concentrated.

These remarks might seem to assume that solving shareholders' agency problems is the only appropriate role for boards. Some, however, might think that a non-accountable board,—ie. a company dominated by its managers and suffering only occasional shareholder revolts—is the most efficient form of decision-making. The German company law of 1937 (*Aktiengesetz* 1937), building on what was perceived to be the US model, is perhaps the best-known example of this model in action. However, for reasons which we explore at the end of this general report,[10] it is not a model which is widespread—perhaps will no longer exist—in an era of globalisation and a strong demand for risk capital which cannot be wholly satisfied by internally generated profits. Some substantial level of board accountability to ordinary shareholders is necessary if a company is to raise equity capital at all, or certainly at an acceptable cost.

However, whilst the board must function in a way which gives some assurance to investors that they will earn a return on their investment, it does not follow that the sole function of the board is to reduce the agency costs of shareholders. In half the Member States of the European Union, representation of the employees on the board is mandatory in the private sector of the economy. In these jurisdictions, therefore, the board has a role in facilitating the company's acquisition of labour inputs as well as inputs of capital. This is the second factor which significantly influences the authority and accountability of the board. The impact of mandatory employee representation[11] on the accountability of the board is clear enough, but it may also have an impact on the authority of the board. For example, it is conceivable that board level representation for employees is associated with boards which

---

[7] A. Pietrancosta et al., sec. 1.1, p. 178; M. Roth, sec. 1.1, p. 258.

[8] See below, sec. 3.1.4, 5.5.

[9] *Ibid.*

[10] See below, sec. 5.3.

[11] See below, sec. 3.2.1.

have less authority. Sometimes, it is argued that this hypothesis explains why in a two-tier board structure mandatory employee representation is confined to supervisory boards. However, as the national reports in this volume show, mandatory board representation for employees is not congruent with the distinction between one-tier and two-tier boards. In some countries, mandatory board representation occurs in a one-tier structure (for example, Sweden) and in others a two-tier structure is available, even though employee representation is not mandatory (for example, Italy). Although the formal distinction between one-tier and two-tier boards appears to be a defining difference for boards in the jurisdictions we study, it is doubtful whether this is in fact so in functional terms. A number of jurisdictions make a choice between one-tier and two-tier board structures available, whilst in others a single structure, whether one-tier or two-tier, is formally required but if desired is sufficiently adaptable to produce a reasonably close approximation to the other structure.

We make only passing reference to the role of boards in financial institutions, especially banks. In the light of the recent financial crisis, the corporate governance of banks has become a live issue,[12] with aspects of board composition (independence versus expertise), board function (especially risk management) and executive director remuneration being particularly contentious. We make only passing reference to this debate because the central question is whether the high and unique leverage of banks suggests that accountability to shareholders is the wrong model and that greater sensitivity on the part of boards to the interests of creditors (and the taxpayers who stand behind the depositors) is what is required. To the extent that corporate governance of banks is becoming separate from corporate governance in non-bank or non-financial companies, we do not deal with it in any depth. However, to the extent that corporate governance innovations for banks have spilled over to companies generally (for example, in the United Kingdom, with the notion of 'shareholder stewardship'), we consider them fully.

---

[12] Cf. Basel Committee on Banking Supervision, *Principles for enhancing corporate governance*, October 2010; European Commission, *Green Paper on Corporate governance in financial institutions and remuneration policies*, 2 June 2010, COM(2010) 284 final; OECD, *Corporate Governance and the Financial Crisis: Key Findings and Main Messages*, Paris, June 2009; K.J. Hopt and G. Wohlmannstetter, eds., *Handbuch Corporate Governance von Banken*, Munich 2011; K.J. Hopt, 'Corporate Governance of Banks after the Financial Crisis', in: E. Wymeersch, K.J. Hopt and G. Ferrarini, eds., *Financial Regulation and Supervision: A Post-Crisis Analysis*, Oxford 2012, p. 337; and *idem*, *Better Governance of Financial Institutions*, Cambridge University, 30 November 2012 (forthcoming *Journal of Corporate Law Studies*, autumn 2013), available at <http://ssrn.com/abstract=2212198>.

2. Authority

2.1. Functions/Power

General Description of Functions: Advice, Control, Networking—In the early days of the company, the general meeting of shareholders retained most of the powers held today by the board. But with the rise of the company, delegation by the shareholders to more professional persons became unavoidable and created the typical principal–agent control problem.[13] In the UK, this shift has been left to company law practice by way of model articles; in most other countries, it is reflected in the law.[14] The former delegation from the shareholders to the board is today mirrored in various delegations from the board to management, between two boards in the two-tier systems, within the boards to committees, and to experts outside the board. Today the functions of advice, control or monitoring, and networking are concentrated in the board. These functions are prevalent in all jurisdictions: Control has become more important *de iure* in the two-tier board systems, but also to a large degree *de facto* in the one-tier board systems because companies have grown in size and belong to groups with specialised and international business. Whether control has become more effective is quite another question; indeed, sometimes one has the impression that the reverse is true. Control is difficult and possibly less rewarding for the directors than the other functions,[15] and obscurity still clouds how boards actually fulfil their functions and what impact social and legal norms have on board behaviour.

Delegation in the one-tier and two-tier systems—At first sight the two board systems, one-tier and two-tier, look completely different as far as division and delegation is concerned. In the *two-tier systems*,[16] a strict division of powers be-

---

[13] J. Armour et al., in R. Kraakman et al., above n. 2, ch.1.

[14] For the UK, P. Davies, sec. 2.1, p. 724; for example, for Belgium, K. Geens, sec. 2.1, p. 126, sec. 3.1.2, p. 140. Under the 1873 system, the general meeting had certain exclusive powers and all residual powers, though the board was the most important *de facto* body of the company and usually by the articles of association; this order was only reversed in 1973. Very detailed company law acts are in force for example in Germany, France, the Netherlands and many other countries. Quite often there is no single company law act, but there are different acts for different forms of companies, for example for the limited liability company.

[15] Cf. K.J. Hopt, above n. 1, *The American Journal of Comparative Law* 59 (2011) 1 at 30, fn. 167.

[16] For example, Germany, Poland, as well as France, Italy and the Netherlands in their two-tier models. In the Netherlands as of 1 January 2013 the one-tier model is also formally incurporated in Dutch law, a reform aimed in particular at Anglo-American investors, R.G.J. Novak, sec. 1.3, p. 446. For a comprehensive mapping of the board structures, see most recently *Study on Directors' Duties and Liability*, prepared for the European Commission DG Markt by: C.

cont. ...

tween the management board and the supervisory board is mandatory. This functional division is bolstered by the incompatibility principle that a person cannot be a member of both boards at the same time,[17] and there is usually a prohibition against the supervisory board giving instructions to the management board.[18] The delegation of tasks is generally only possible to a certain extent within the respective board, but key decisions and certain matters—such as the remuneration of managing directors in Germany recently—are reserved to the whole board. Banks are special: Because of the particular risks involved, the two-tier system is mandatory even in some one-tier board countries such as Belgium.[19]

In traditional *one-tier systems*, the board typically has far-reaching discretion to delegate powers to managers below board level, in which case the task of the board is restricted to monitoring the management. The most liberal and flexible approach is to leave the distribution of powers, apart from appointment and dismissal rights, entirely to the board. The prototype is the UK, where the default rule is that the board of directors exercises all the company's powers but may delegate its powers to managers below board level.[20] In one-tier systems, boards can thus be seen to outsource most of their tasks and powers to a separate formal or informal executive body below board level. Sometimes one or more executive board members are represented at that level. Another question is whether

---

Gerner-Beuerle, P. Paech and E. P. Schuster, London School of Economics, London, April 2013 and the Annex to this study with 28 country reports (cited as LSE Study 2013).

[17] But the Belgian legislature, when introducing a two-tier model, provided that members of the management board may at the same time be members of the supervisory board. This provision was taken from the rules for credit institutions. K. Geens, sec. 1.3, p. 124.

[18] For Germany, M. Roth, sec. 2.1, p. 281, but there were other models for saving banks and state-owned banks (*Landesbanken*) until the Stock Corporation Act of 1937 (Aktiengesetz 1937); for Poland, following the German model, S. Sołtysiński, sec. 2.1, p. 524, but much less clear in practice. In the Netherlands it is allowed by law, but it does not occur in listed companies and it is debated in legal literature; R.G.J. Nowak, sec. 3.2.1, p. 487. Italy has different models.

[19] Belgium is somewhat complex because a two-tier model is mandatory for financial institutions; there all members are of the executive committee are members of the board of directors, but under the optional system for non-bank companies, overlap is permitted, but not required; cf. above n.14. In the Netherlands, too, the banks need to have a two-tier board, but the Netherlands are historically a two-tier board country. In Italy, financial institutions are allowed to choose between all three governance systems, but the Bank of Italy has issued rules to ensure that certain provisions from the traditional model also apply if a financial institution opts for one of the other two models.

[20] P. Davies, sec. 2.1, p. 724. In Sweden the responsibility for the day-to-day management of the company lies with the CEO, who is recognised by law as a separate corporate body; however, major decisions remain within the competence of the board. In Switzerland the management function can be—and usually is—delegated to a management board. Similarly, in Belgium, Italy, Spain and France, boards of listed companies delegate management powers to an informal executive committee.

executives are, or even must be, members of the one-tier board.[21] If the board has only non-executive members (so-called NEDs or outside directors) and its task is limited to monitoring the outsourced management, its function approximates that of a supervisory board,[22] but with the difference that the board can always revoke the delegation. The extent to which boards in one-tier systems can delegate their powers may vary from country to country, but some common characteristics can be distinguished: Certain powers cannot be delegated; the board has the right to give instructions to the body exercising the delegated powers; delegation is non-privative and revocable; and the board is obliged to monitor the exercise of the delegated powers.

Convergence—The two different models that at first sight look completely different are functionally much less different; indeed, one could say that there is considerable convergence. For Switzerland, for example, it has been stated that 'no genuine one-tier board has survived in Swiss public companies' and for Spain it has been remarked that in practice the difference between the two models 'has become barely detectable.'[23] Four observations back this convergence statement: First, the one-tier board makes use of delegation to the management to a large degree, and monitoring the exercise of the delegated powers becomes its main task. Secondly, not only the supervisory boards but also the one-tier boards are dependent on management, sometimes to the extent that management takes over. Thirdly, in the one-tier board itself there has been a certain *de facto* and *de iure* separation, not only between executives and non-executives but also between non-independent and independent directors. And lastly, there is also a convergence in the exercise of certain functions such as strategy, risk management, and internal control.

As regards the first point: Taking or participating in key decisions—and in particular monitoring and control—are matters for the board. These matters are sometimes mandatorily reserved to the board for decision, a technique that resembles the catalogue of matters reserved for approval by the supervisory board in the two-tier system.[24] One prototype is Switzerland. Swiss company law

---

[21] In some one-tier systems the board has to consist of executives and non-executives, and all senior executives are board members (UK, the Netherlands), whereas in others executives do not have to be board members (Switzerland, Sweden, Belgium and Italy). Swiss boards are even exclusively populated by non-executives.

[22] The Swiss model is sometimes referred to as 'supervisory board plus'; P. Böckli, sec. 2.1(a), p. 664.

[23] For Switzerland, P. Böckli, sec. 2.1(d), p. 667. For Spain, A. Recalde Castells et al., sec. 1.3, p. 559. Similarly for the UK, the US and the Netherlands a 'substantial convergence' has been noticed by W.J.L. Calkoen, *The One-Tier Board in the changing and converging world of corporate covernance*, doctor thesis at the Erasmus Universiteit Rotterdam 2011.

[24] See K.J. Hopt and P. Leyens, 'Board Models in Europe', *European Company and Financial Law Review* 2004, 135 at 150. German corporate law in its 1937 version, which was

cont. ...

contains a seven-point catalogue of powers that cannot be delegated, the most important of which are the determination of strategy, the appointment and removal of management, the ultimate supervision of management, the preparation of the annual accounts, and the structuring of the accounting system and financial controls.[25] In Belgian practice, many companies with a one-tier board have an informal executive committee, to which the board has given a general delegation of powers that goes beyond day-to-day management, but which does not include the determination of strategy and supervision.[26] In other countries, apart from the determination of strategy and the supervision of management, the range of delegated powers is not limited, but the board may not be deprived of all of its powers. This is also the bottom line in the UK, the most liberal country in this respect, where boards may delegate all powers to managers below board level. Yet even there the board cannot divest itself of overall responsibility for management by delegating particular functions.[27]

Secondly, it is a general practice that proposals to the board (whether one-tier or two-tier) to exercise powers that are not delegated are usually prepared at the executive level (management viz. management board), sometimes even in the form of draft resolutions. In many listed companies, board members do not have the expertise or the time to carefully study and seriously challenge management proposals. The management thus not only exercises *de iure* those powers that have been delegated to it, but also *de facto* the powers that have formally remained with the board. More generally speaking, the formal differences between the board making a decision and the board approving a decision are not as important as the way these powers are exercised in practice. It is less relevant whether the law concentrates powers in a one-tier board if that board has extensive authority and uses it to delegate those powers to management below the board level. The same is true if the law divides the powers between two boards, but the supervisory board exerts a significant *ex ante* influence by the mere fact that it has extensive approval rights.

---

carried over into the post-war laws, limited the powers of the supervisory board to approve strategic issues or to remove managing board members without cause. However, under the 2002 reforms, at least in the majority view, the supervisory board is now required to establish *ex ante* a catalogue of management decisions which require its prior consent, which must include the main elements of corporate strategy. In this case, therefore, a two-tier system moved in the direction of the *de facto* operation of the one-tier system, but the 1937 German law was always an outlier among two-tier systems by reason of its restrictive approach to the role of the supervisory board.

[25] P. Böckli, sec. 2.1(a), p. 663. In Italy there is a similar catalogue, but it does not contain the determination of strategy, Art. 2382 CC; cf. also G. Ferrarini et al., sec. 2.1(b), p. 376.

[26] For delegation to board committees, see below, sec. 2.2.2.

[27] P. Davies, sec. 2.1, p. 724. This is the effect of the company law; the UK Corporate Governance Code Section A.1.1 recommends that a list of matters which require board approval should be drawn up.

Thirdly, there are also strong separation tendencies in the one-tier systems. In the one-tier board there is *de facto* and *de iure* separation not only between executives and non-executives but between non-independent and independent directors, the latter being responsible for certain functions—in particular, control functions—which in the two-tier systems are the task of the supervisory board (see in more detail, below 2.2.3). The separation between the management board and the supervisory board is also mirrored in those one-tier board countries in which separation between the CEO and the chairman has become good corporate governance (see below 2.2.1).

Finally, as will be seen in the following, convergence can also be observed in the exercise of certain functions such as strategy, risk management, and internal control.[28]

Strategy—The power to determine the company's strategy and to monitor its implementation is one of the most important powers of the board. In most one-tier systems this power cannot be delegated to the sub-board level and has to be exercised by the entire board. But in practice, strategy proposals are usually prepared by senior management together with executive directors (if they are on the board at all), whereas the board reviews the proposal. Non-executive directors of listed companies, because of information asymmetry, may find it difficult to fully challenge the plans of the executives or even to maintain a contrary view.[29]

In two-tier systems, the management board determines the strategy, but this decision is usually subject to approval by the supervisory board, either mandatorily or in practice. This approval requirement enhances prior coordination and consultation between the two boards. Supervisory boards in two-tier models are

---

[28] P. Davies, 'Board Structure in the UK and Germany: Convergence or Continuing Divergence?', 2 *International and Comparative Corporate Law Journal* 435 (2000); J.N. Gordon and M.J. Roe, eds., *Convergence and Persistence in Corporate Governance*, Cambridge 2004; J.A. McCahery et al., *Corporate Governance Regimes, Convergence and Diversity*, Oxford 2002. As to convergence, see also below, sec. 5.1.

Cf. also European Commission, Action Plan: European company law and corporate governance—a modern legal framework for more engaged shareholders and sustainable companies, 12 December 2012, COM(1012) 740/2, point 2.1: 'In Europe, different board structures coexist. [...] The Commission acknowledges the coexistence of these board structures, which are often deeply rooted in the country's overall economic governance system, and has no intention of challenging or modifying this arrangement.' For a comprehensive appraisal of the 2012 Action Plan, see K.J. Hopt, 'Europäisches Gesellschaftsrecht im Lichte des Aktionsplans der Europäischen Kommission vom Dezember 2012', *Zeitschrift für Unternehmens- und Gesellschaftsrecht* 2013, 165–215.

[29] For the UK, P. Davies, sec. 2.1, p. 726. citing empirical studies. For Switzerland, P. Böckli, sec. 2.1(b), p. 666: 'in practice there is a tendency of strong top managers to pre-empt many decisions that belong to the Board's reserved turf by indirect and informal exertion of power in the preparatory stage of decision-making.'

increasingly seen to participate in determining the company's strategy. So again there is a functional convergence here with the one-tier board model.

Risk Management and Internal Control Systems—There is also no clear-cut division between the one-tier and two-tier systems as to risk management and internal control, not in law and even less so in practice. In some one-tier systems, the (entire) board is responsible for setting up the risk management and internal control systems, whereas the task of management is limited to implementing these systems.[30] This is also the view of the European Commission in its Green Paper of April 2011.[31] In other one-tier systems, the management is primarily responsible for setting up the systems, whereas the task of the board is limited to approving the basic guidelines and monitoring the setting, implementation and functioning of the systems.[32] This division approximates the two-tier systems, where the management board sets and implements the strategy and the supervisory board monitors the setting up and implementation,[33] although in those situations mere monitoring is usually mandatory. In the Italian traditional model the situation is more complicated, as the monitoring of the effectiveness of the company's internal control and risk management systems is also exercised by the board of (internal) auditors.[34] It should, however, be noted that the right of management to make a decision and the right of the board to approve a decision often results in co-decision in practice.

Monitoring of the internal control and risk management systems entails ensuring that a state-of-the-art risk management system is in place, checking whether the risk profile corresponds with the business profile and strategy, and reviewing how the system worked in the past period. Where the setting up and implementing of internal control systems is primarily a task of management, either by law or in practice, the board must be aware that managers often underestimate risks. Yet whether the board is in a position to effectively carry out such a check is questionable, since it is very difficult to identify unlikely risks *ex ante*.

---

[30] Italy, Sweden, Switzerland.

[31] European Commission, Green Paper, *The EU corporate governance framework*, 5 April 2011, COM(2011) 164, p. 10: 'To be effective and consistent any risk policy needs to be clearly "set from the top" i.e. decided by the board of directors for the whole organisation. It is generally recognised (note 43: From Commission interviews) that the board of directors bears primary responsibility for defining the risk profile […]'. However, the European Commission Recommendation of 15 February 2005 on the role of non-executive or supervisory directors of listed companies and on the committees of the (supervisory) board, OJ L 52/51 of 25 February 2005, mentions as a key responsibility of the board 'to monitor the procedures established for the evaluation and management of risks,' Preamble no. 14.

[32] France, Switzerland.

[33] Cf. for Poland, S. Sołtysiński, sec. 2.2, p. 525; also Germany, the Netherlands.

[34] G. Ferrarini et al., sec. 2.1(c), p. 377 et seq.

The bottom line is that detailed questions about risk can only be asked by the management. Therefore, additional monitoring steps and procedures are often built in: Within the board by a separate audit committee where particular financial expertise is required by law, sometimes by a specific risk committee,[35] and at the end by both internal and external auditors.[36]

2.2. Organisation/Internal Functioning

2.2.1. *Composition*

Size of the board and proportion of non-executive independent directors—The *size* of the board is not so relevant per se, but it is very relevant for the experience that smaller boards work more effectively due to more open discussion and better cooperation.[37] The largest (supervisory) boards can be found in German listed companies. The average number of supervisory board members in German companies is more than 17.[38] This is due to the labour co-determination regime, which requires supervisory boards of the largest companies to have 20 members. It is no wonder that this leads to exit strategies.[39] At the other end of the spectrum is the Netherlands, also with a two-tier system and a labour co-determination regime,[40] but with an average of 8.7 board members. The UK with 12.4 members approximates the European average of 12.1.[41]

The *composition* of the board in the various countries also differs, but this is more controversial. The main controversy relates, of course, to the constituency, namely labour co-determination.[42] Another question is the mix of executive and non-executive directors and the proportion of independent directors on the board.

---

[35] See below, sec. 2.2.2 under Committees.

[36] For Italy, G. Ferrarini et al., sec. 2.1(c), p. 377 et seq., and sec. 2.1.(e), p. 379 et seq. Similarly for France.

[37] K.J. Hopt, above n. 1, *The American Journal of Comparative Law* 59 (2011) 1 at 23 et seq. The different rules as to the minimum and maximum members a board may have are technical but are functionally relevant if they restrict the choice of an adequate size. Cf. also A. Boone, L. Field, J. Karpoff and C. Raheja, 'The determinants of corporate board size and composition: An empirical analysis', *Journal of Financial Economics* 85 (2007) 66; J. Coles, N. Daniel and L. Naveen, 'Boards: Does one size fit all?', *Journal of Financial Economics* 87 (2008) 329.

[38] Heidrick & Struggles, European Corporate Governance Report 2011, p. 37.

[39] See below, sec. 3.2.1.

[40] Though not so far-reaching as in Germany, see below sec. 3.2.1

[41] After Germany, France, Italy, Belgium and Spain have the largest boards with around 14 members.

[42] See below, sec. 3.2.1.

The latter question is linked to the former but is more critical. Recently, the discussion has focused less on the concept of non-executive directors and more on the (non-executive) independent director. It is even reported that in France there is no concept of executive/non-executive director.[43] In the UK, unlike earlier versions of the Corporate Governance Code, the current Code makes recommendations entirely in terms of independent non-executive directors; other non-executive directors are no longer mentioned. The same is true in Switzerland.

In the two-tier systems—at least in the German and Dutch versions—there is a mandatory neat division between the executives (only) in the management board and the *non-executives* (only) in the supervisory board, with the exception of the Italian two-tier system where the management board may consist of executives and non-executives.[44] In some one-tier system countries—for example, Belgium and the UK[45]—there is a rule that at least half of the members of the board should be non-executives, while in others there should be at least (Netherlands and Italy) or at most (Sweden) one member who is an executive director. In other countries without such requirements, the practice varies: In Belgium, the CEO is usually on the board; this is also true rather often for France and Sweden (in 40 to 50 per cent of cases); but in Switzerland it occurs more and more rarely. The EU Recommendation is satisfied if there is 'an appropriate balance.'[46]

As to the requirement, either mandatory or by code, of having *independent directors*[47] on the board, there is as much variety and even more controversy. The lead has been taken by the USA with 81 per cent independent directors in listed companies and their 'super-majority independent boards.'[48] It should be clear in the two-tier systems—though in Germany it was first disputed—that the members of the supervisory board (who cannot simultaneously be members of the management board) are non-executive by definition but certainly not per se independent; in fact, independence is usually completely contrary in the practice of Rhineland capitalism. In Germany, with its traditional reluctance against independent directors, the Corporate Governance Code only recommends that the number of independent directors be adequate as seen by the supervisory board itself and that the chairman of the audit committee should be independent and not

---

[43] A. Pietrancosta et al., sec. 2.1(g), p. 192; sec. 2.2.1(b), p. 194.

[44] The Italian Corporate Governance Code, however, envisages a management board with only executives.

[45] There should be an 'appropriate combination of executive and non-executive directors', UK Corporate Governance Code 2010, B.1 (Supporting Principles), but at the same time the board should be composed of at least 50 per cent independent non-executive directors, P. Davies, sec. 2.2.1, p. 728.

[46] EU Recommendation of 15 February 2005, above n. 31, no. 3.1.

[47] As to the criterion of independence, see below, sec. 2.2.3.

[48] L. Enriques, H. Hansmann and R. Kraakman, in R. Kraakman et al., above n. 2, p. 70.

have been a member of the management board for the last two years. In the Italian two-tier model, if the management board consists of more than four members, at least one has to be independent. Among the one-tier systems, the UK has a high level of compliance with the recommendation that half the board be independent directors.[49] But these are usually only code provisions, with recommendations that vary from at least two (Poland) to all but one as independent directors (Netherlands).[50] Switzerland has no legal rules at all, but Swiss boards are almost exclusively composed of non-executive persons.[51] The EU Recommendation again looks for a compromise by recommending a 'sufficient number' of independent directors.[52]

A critical point that is often overlooked is how to deal with companies with a controlling shareholder. For this case, the French code reduces the recommended number to one-third,[53] and in Belgium the non-independent non-executives are always in the majority.[54] According to the Heidrick and Struggles Report of 2011, which categorises labour and so-called reference shareholder representatives as non-independent board members,[55] the highest proportion of independent directors can be found in the supervisory boards of Dutch companies (75%), followed by Switzerland (62%) and the UK (61%); the other countries have between 30–50%. The lowest proportion of independent directors—due to labour representation—is in Germany (21%).[56]

Diversity, Special Qualification, Availability and Time, Multiple Board Memberships—Today it is generally agreed that diversity and qualification of its members are essential for an effective board. Diversity brings in different viewpoints, and while qualification may make better decisions, diverse qualifications improve both. Diversity can consist of very different aspects, including background, gender, age, nationality, and residency. Special qualification criteria are financial capability, knowledge of the company's business and—especially in financial institutions—integrity. Legislatures usually shy away from enacting mandatory

---

[49] Financial Reporting Council, *Developments in Corporate Governance 2011*, December 2011, p. 11.

[50] In Belgium three, in Italy one-third, and in most countries one-half (UK, Sweden, France).

[51] P. Böckli, sec. 2.1(d), p. 668 with the exceptions mentioned there.

[52] EU Recommendation of 15 February 2005, above n. 31, no. 4.

[53] Art. 8.2 of the AFEP/MEDEF Corporate Governance Code; A. Pietrancosta et al., sec. 2.2.3, p. 204.

[54] K. Geens, sec. 2.2.1, p. 127.

[55] For more detail, see below, sec. 2.2.3.

[56] Heidrick & Struggles, above n. 38, p. 43. According to the Report the proportion of independent directors in Dutch one-tier boards would be 75 per cent, but this percentage is not representative as there are only six Dutch listed companies with a one-tier board.

rules, leaving this instead at mere recommendations to the Corporate Governance Codes. This is because such rules may be discriminatory (age, nationality, and residency requirements), but more so because there is no clear evidence regarding what kind of diversity is good for a specific company.

But there are exceptions where the legislature has stepped in, quite understandably, to require financial capability for the audit committees of public companies,[57] and sometimes also for minority protection purposes, as in Italy and Poland.[58] But usually mandatory rules are for political or societal reasons. This is the case for labour representation in the board[59] as well as for gender quotas, both of which are controversial. As to *gender diversity*, the situation in Europe is indeed unsatisfactory. According to the Heidrick & Struggles 2011 Report, the average percentage of women on boards in Europe is 12 per cent. The lowest percentage of women on boards is in Italy (6%, by 2012 6.7%), while Sweden— where the issue is left to self-regulation—has a very high percentage of women on boards (29%).[60] The empirical evidence on whether companies perform better when they have women on their boards is mixed,[61] but there are other arguments even apart from fairness and equality, such as the waste of talent, the increasing need to broaden the pool of candidates in ageing societies, changes in the discussion culture of boards, and a different outlook on decision-making,

---

[57] See below, sec. 2.2.2.

[58] On the cumulative voting in Poland and the slate voting in Italy, see below, sec. 3.1.1.

[59] See below, sec. 3.2.1.

[60] Poland and Belgium are also at the lower end of the scale with 8%, followed by France and Switzerland (11%), Germany (13%) and the Netherlands (15%). Heidrick & Struggles, above n. 38, p. 39. For France the latest figure is over 25% of the boards of CAC 40 companies according to the AMF 2012 report on Corporate Governance and Executive Compensation; A. Pietrancosta et al., sec. 2.2.1(g), p. 198. For the UK the 2011 figures were 17.4% female directors in the FTSE 100 companies, Davies, sec.2.2.1, p. 733.

[61] R.B. Adams and D. Ferreira, 'Women in the Boardroom and their Impact on Governance and Performance', *Journal of Financial Economics* 94 (2009) 291; K.R. Ahern and A.K. Dittmar, 'The Changing of the Boards: The Impact on Firm Valuation of Mandated Female Board Representation', *The Quarterly Journal of Economics*, 127/1 (2012) 127 (137, the authors analyse the impact of the 2003 Norwegian law which was the forerunner of the quota regimes in Europe.) Cf. also O. Bøhren and S. Staubo, 'Does Mandatory Gender Balance Work? Changing Organizational Form to Avoid Board Upheaval' (available at <ssrn.com/abstract=2257769>— also forthcoming in the *Journal of Corporate Finance*. Cf. also D.A. Carter et al., 'Corporate Governance, Board Diversity, and Firm Value', 38(1) *Financial Review* 33 (2003); K.A. Farrell and P.L. Hersch, 'Additions to Corporate Boards: The Effect of Gender', 11(1-2) *Journal of Corporate Finance* 85 (2005); L. Rodríguez-Domínguez and J.-M. García-Sánchez, 'Explanatory factors of the relationship between gender diversity and corporate performance', *European Journal of Law & Economics* 33 (2012) 603; L. Fairfax, 'Board Diversity Revisited: New Rationale, Same Old Story?', 89 *North Carolina Law Review* 856 (2011). See more generally as to diversity A.N. Berger, T. Kick and K. Schaeck, *Executive board composition and bank risk taking*, Discussion Paper Deutsche Bundesbank No 03/2012.

including the attitude to risk-taking.[62] The latter arguments have some psychological backing, though there is still controversy. In any case, it is not yet clear what this means in terms of company performance.

Whatever the merit of these arguments may be, there is a clear trend of juridification. The importance of gender diversity is stressed in most countries, but in a number of them—such as Sweden and Poland—no targets or quotas are yet recommended or imposed. In others—such as the Netherlands and Germany—code provisions recommend that companies set targets themselves and enforce them on a comply-or-explain basis. But in the meantime, many countries have recently enacted laws to ensure increased gender diversity, or initiatives are pending, as in the Netherlands and Switzerland.[63] The minimum percentages to be reached in the next five to seven years are 30% in Belgium and the Netherlands, 40% in France and, most recently, one-third in Italy. The EU Commission followed the trend in its Green Paper of April 2011. While it recognised that companies should decide whether they want to introduce such a diversity policy, the companies should be required to consider the matter and disclose the decisions made.[64] Most recently, the Commission adopted a controversial draft for a Directive which would require companies listed on a regulated market to achieve a level of 40% of female *non-executive* directors by 2020, the requirement to be enforced by a tie-break in favour of an equally qualified female applicant. A slightly stronger version of the Green Paper approach was adopted with regard to executive directors, which would require listed companies to adopt targets for female representation but not stipulate what the target should be.[65] It remains to be seen how the problems with mandatory quotas will be dealt with,

---

[62] R.B. Adams and P. Funk, 'Beyond the Glass Ceiling: Does Gender Matter?', *Management Science* 58 (2012) 219.

[63] In the UK a government-endorsed commission recommends that FTSE-100 companies strive for 25 per cent of women in 2015. In the Netherlands as of 2013 the law requires a quota of at least 30 per cent of woman (and of men), but does not provide for sanctions, R.G.J. Novak, sec. 2.2.1(c), p. 458.

[64] EU Commission, Green Paper, above n. 31, p. 7. See previously Communication from the Commission, *Strategy for equality between women and men 2010–2015*, COM(2010) 491 final, September 2010; and its follow-up Commission Staff Working Paper, *The Gender Balance in Business Leadership*, SEC(2011) 246 final. Similarly for the UK Financial Reporting Council, above n. 49, p. 12.

[65] Proposal for a Directive of the European Parliament and of the Council of November 14, 2012 on improving the gender balance among non-executive directors of companies listed on stock exchanges and related matters, COM(2012) 614, Article 4(1); for mandatory disclosure of board diversity policy, see the Action Plan of 2012 (above n. 28), point 2.1 and Annex. Cf. for the UK Financial Reporting Council, above n. 49, p. 12. The European Commission uses disclosure and transparency as a primary method of regulation, cf. its Action Plan (above n.28), point 2.1–2.4 and Annex; cf. K.J. Hopt, above initial note*, *Zeitschrift für Unternehmens- und Gesellschaftsrecht* 2013, 165 at 186–189.

since there is stiff resistance of a number of Member States in the context of subsidiarity and constitutionality as well as because of the (still) insufficient pool of qualified women and the danger of 'golden skirts' as reported from Norway.

Another issue, though not directly involving qualification but very important for qualified board decisions, is *availability and time*, taking into consideration the fact that unlike managers board members—certainly supervisory board members—usually work part-time for the company.[66] Many corporate governance codes, including the UK, German and Spanish Corporate Governance Codes, expressly state that the directors should be in a position to devote sufficient time for the directorship. The practical demands on directors' time had already increased sharply already under normal circumstances, but this intensifies greatly during periods of crisis for the company.[67] Though it is very difficult to spell out more concrete time requirements in law or codes, one possibility would be to limit the *number of board memberships*. A number of countries still leave this to the shareholders to decide, but with proper disclosure.[68] The UK Corporate Governance Code only recommends that a full-time executive should not accept more than one non-executive directorship (and never as the chair) of a FTSE-100 company. In other countries the regulators have chosen a more interventionist approach, either by law or by code provision.[69] The limits set for multiple board memberships vary: In Germany, there is a maximum of 10 supervisory seats (by law) viz. a maximum of three in listed companies (by code, not counting supervisory seats within the same group); in French listed companies, executives may hold no more than one position as CEO and no more than five (in future possibly only three) positions as non-executive director.[70] The numbers are chosen arbitrarily and neglect the fact that companies and directors are very different. What is too much for some may be no problem for others; a well-run company may be less demanding of its non-executive directors than one which is about to break its bank covenants. If limits are considered, there should be sufficient flexibility, such as a code comply-and-explain mechanism. A special limit on interlocking directorships was recently introduced in Italy by a law forbidding board

---

[66] Other considerations for intervention are conflicts of interest and maintaining competition; cf. the rules in Germany and other countries on interlocking directorates and the prohibition to also sit on the board of a competitor of the company. See below, sec. 2.2.3.

[67] An average time estimate for Swiss board members is 200 hours per year.

[68] Sweden, Switzerland, Italy.

[69] The technique—law or codes—may have consequences for the sanctions in case of violation; see below sec. 4.1.

[70] The Dutch Corporate Governance Code, finally, has a similar provision for members of the supervisory board in listed companies, but in addition for management board members also limits the number of supervisory board memberships to two positions (not as the CEO) in listed companies. Furthermore, as of 2013 the law contains the similar, but mandatory rules for large and medium-sized listed companies. Cf. R.G.J. Nowak, sec. 2.2.1(h), p. 461 et seq.

members (and key managers) of national banks, insurance companies and investment firms to hold similar positions in competing financial institutions or groups.

In the end, what makes a person a good board member remains an open question. Diversity, special qualifications, and sufficient time are prerequisites, as we
have seen. But what counts ultimately—though the boards tend to dislike this
kind of director, and top management of course even more so—is personality, a
willingness to call into question what management presents, a feeling for the right
balance of chances and risks, and a readiness to speak up in the group and confess
that one did not understand or is not convinced of something presented by
management or considered by the majority of the board as self-evident. Standing
up against 'group think' seems to be the essential quality, and it is doubtful
whether this can be learned.

Separation of the functions of chairman and CEO—We have seen that there is
considerable convergence between the seemingly divergent one-tier and two-tier
boards. This is confirmed when one looks at the increasing corporate governance
trend toward separation—not necessarily of the boards, but of the function of the
chairman and the CEO. *Separation of roles* in one-tier models started in the UK,
where it was proposed in 2003 and recommended in the current Corporate Governance Code. As stated for the UK: 'Separation is a crucial expression of the notion
of the board's role as a monitor of the management of the company.'[71] As of 2011,
96% of the FTSE-350 companies had a separate chairman and CEO.[72] A number
of other countries have incorporated separation in their corporate governance
codes.[73] In Switzerland, the combination of chairman and CEO is not prohibited,
but it occurs very rarely as it is considered politically incorrect. The only countries
with widespread combined functions are Spain and France.[74] In France, during the
Second World War the combination of the two functions was made compulsory
and in 2012 more than 64% of CAC-40 companies with a one-tier board had
combined functions (compared to 34% in 2009), though this concentration of
power is somewhat counterbalanced by the appointment of a senior independent
director,[75] a concept that was borrowed from the UK. In Spain, twenty-five IBEX-
35 companies combined the roles. Yet the combined structure is decreasing in

---

[71] P. Davies, sec. 2.2.1, p. 731.

[72] Financial Reporting Council, above n. 49, p. 11.

[73] UK, Sweden, Italy, Belgium, and the Netherlands.

[74] 4th AFEP/MEDEF's annual report relating to the implementation of its Corporate
Governance Code by companies listed on SBF 120 and CAC 40, December 2012, p. 5; A.
Pietrancosta et al., sec. 1.3(a), p. 184, 1.3(b), p. 184. But this is considered to be a weakness in
the system, A. Pietrancosta et al., sec. 5.1(a), p. 243 et seq. For Spain, see A. Recalde Castells et
al., sec. 2.2.1(d), p. 570.

[75] See below, sec. 2.2.3.

French listed companies, probably because a clearer distinction between management and supervision is sought as a feature of good corporate governance.

In the meantime, the separation movement is developing further, both in one-tier and two-tier board countries. While continuity may be good for the company, effective monitoring may be impaired if the *retiring CEO* can move directly to be chair of the board, and in this new capacity can monitor their former management decisions. While there is empirical data indicating that if the chairman and the CEO do not get along this may have negative consequences for the company, there does not seem to be any study supporting the view that separation leads to success.[76] Nevertheless, this former practice, which was widely used in countries such as Germany, is viewed with increasing scepticism. The Combined Code and the new UK Corporate Governance Code hold this to be incompatible with good corporate governance, though this recommendation is sometimes ignored.[77] In a very controversial German company law amendment of 2009, there is even a mandatory two-year waiting period before members of the management board can move to the supervisory board, unless the general assembly of shareholders gives its consent, upon a motion of shareholders with more than 25% of the voting rights.[78] This is generally considered to be too inflexible and has led to controversies in the general assemblies of a number of German companies, such as Lufthansa in 2013. The corporate governance codes of most other countries are even more lenient, allowing a retiring CEO to become the chair with or without an explanation.[79]

Evaluation of board performance—There is a clear trend towards periodic evaluation of the board as a whole and its individual members. The EU Recommendation follows the recommendations of codes in the Member States and provides that boards should evaluate their performance annually. Still open to discussion is whether external evaluation is to be considered a requirement of good corporate governance. The UK Corporate Governance Code (for the first time in 2010), the Belgian corporate governance code and others recommend external facilitation of the annual review at least once every three years. In the UK in 2011/12 one-third of FTSE 350 companies undertook externally facilitated reviews. In Germany, despite similar proposals of practice and academia, this suggestion is viewed with reluctance; the Code just recommends that the supervisory board examine the

---

[76] Cf. K.J. Hopt, above n. 1, *The American Journal of Comparative Law* 59 (2011) 1 at 33, fn. 188.

[77] With empirical data, P. Davies, sec. 2.2.1, p. 728. The Dutch Corporate Governance Code, which does not consider a former executive non-independent nor requires the chair to be independent, recommends that a retiring CEO should not become a chairman (except in particular circumstances), both for the one-tier model and for the two-tier model: R.G.J. Nowak, sec. 2.2.1, p. 459.

[78] Section 100(2) as amended by the law of 31 July 2009.

[79] Sweden, Belgium, Italy, Switzerland, and Poland.

efficiency of its activities on a regular basis.[80] The Green Paper of the EU Commission, based on OECD research,[81] goes further and suggests board evaluation by an external service provider, for example every third year.

2.2.2. Decision-Making

Voting, separate sessions, company secretary—The decision-making rules—quorum and majority requirements, voting rights, veto and approval rights—are often mentioned in company law but generally give considerable freedom to companies to adopt the rule they find most convenient. A *quorum* requirement is rarely prescribed by law, though sometimes it is stated as a default rule. Usually it is left to the company, but not to a degree that it hinders decision-making, for example, by requiring the presence of all members or unanimity of the votes cast.[82] Usually the chairman has or can be attributed a *casting vote* in case of a tie-break. *Voting by proxy* given to another board member is allowed in most countries except Italy and, according to the prevailing view, also in Switzerland; in Germany the absent director can ask a fellow director to transmit his written vote; in Belgium a blank proxy is allowed only insofar as the director who has received the proxy does not dominate the decision-making. *Veto rights* for individual directors are usually forbidden or considered problematic; in the UK they are possible but, unlike in joint ventures, they are rarely used in large listed companies. Each director has *one vote*. Multiple voting rights for certain directors are allowed (and even set out in the law) in the Netherlands, but no director may have more votes than all other directors together.

Separate boards in the two-tier system have *separate sessions*, but it is standing practice (though not a legal right) for management board members to attend meetings of the supervisory board, except when the supervisory board discusses its own functioning or the functioning of the management board. For this reason the corporate governance codes encourage supervisory boards to hold separate sessions from time to time. In Poland, under the cumulative voting system minority representatives on the board have the right to attend meetings of the management board and to provide advisory functions at meetings.[83] If the supervisory board has different constituencies, separate sessions of the different 'benches' are standing practice, as under labour co-determination in Germany,

---

[80] German Corporate Governance Code, no. 5.6.

[81] OECD, *Corporate governance and the financial crisis: Conclusions and emerging good practices to enhance implementation of the Principles*, 24 February 2010, p. 20.

[82] For Germany, M. Roth, 2.2.2(d), p. 297; debated in Italy, G. Ferrarini et al., sec. 2.2.2(a), p. 384 et seq.

[83] Art. 390 § 2 of the Code of Commercial Companies, S. Sołtysiński, sec. 2.8, p. 530.

and is sometimes recommended by codes even for the shareholder side.[84] In the one-tier system, things are not so different: Separate informal meetings of executive and non-executive directors take place in practice. In the UK, for instance, the Corporate Governance Code encourages the independent directors to meet separately. In Italy, executive sessions of independent directors are held by 67% of all listed companies and are chaired by the lead independent director.[85] Swiss boards regularly hold separate meetings of independent directors to discuss delicate issues regarding executives or non-independent non-executives.

The *company secretary* (or board secretary) may be—but usually is not—a member of the board. The company secretary assists the board and its committees in ensuring compliance with corporate governance and internal rules and takes care of the information streams within the board and between the boards. A company secretary is mandatory in the UK and Switzerland and recommended by the Dutch and Belgian codes. The UK Corporate Governance Code states that 'the company secretary should be responsible for advising the board through the chairman on all governance matters.'[86] In Swiss public companies the company secretary acts as a 'corporate memory.'[87] In German practice the chairman of the supervisory board often has a small office staff, though the staffing of this department is provided by the management board. Some claim that the chairman should have a full office of his or her own in order to make the chairman independent of the management board.[88] This department, and sometimes the company's general counsel, fulfil the function of a company secretary.

Committees: Kind and task, composition and delegation—The role of board committees is normally to prepare the decision-making of the full board to increase the board's efficiency, but more recently also to ensure that the board's decision is free of material conflicts of interest. These tasks are delegated to the committees by the board. The rationale of avoiding conflicts of interest leads sometimes to the conclusion that the decision should be taken by the committee without referring the matter back to the full board. The use of committees was usually developed without any intervention by the legislature, which in general has been reluctant to interfere with the internal organisation and work of the board. One exception is Switzerland, where the concept of board committees was introduced in the law in 1936 and refined in 1991. But more recently, with the rise of the code movement, committee kind, composition, and delegation has

---

[84] See below, sec. 3.2.1.

[85] G. Ferrarini et al., sec. 2.2.2(e), p. 387.

[86] P. Davies, sec. 2.1, p. 727.

[87] P. Böckli, sec. 2.2.4, p.681 et seq.

[88] M. Roth, 'Information und Organisation des Aufsichtsrats', *Zeitschrift für Unternehmens- und Gesellschaftsrecht* 2012, 343 at 371.

become a matter for the codes and, in the meantime, also for the EU Commission, though only in the flexible way of a recommendation. For public interest entities, however, the Audit Directive of 2006 requires an audit committee.[89]

There are many *kinds of committees* in practice,[90] but three key committees for the most important tasks are recommended by nearly all the codes and by the EU Recommendation:[91] the nomination, remuneration, and audit committees. The most important is the audit committee, which will be treated separately below. The nomination committee has the task of selecting suitable candidates, a task that is hardly relevant in companies with a controlling shareholder, and to periodically assess the structure, size, composition, and performance of the board and its individual members. The remuneration committee makes proposals for the remuneration policy and the remuneration of the individual directors.[92] In most countries, a separate risk committee is mandatory for financial institutions, and in some countries—such as France and Switzerland—it is also used for other companies. The corporate governance codes of most countries contain separate sets of provisions for each of the three committees but allow companies to combine the nomination and remuneration committees, in which case the more stringent independence requirements for the remuneration committee apply. Whereas the German and Swiss Corporate Governance Codes are brief on committees, the French, Belgian, and Italian Corporate Governance Codes elaborate extensively on their tasks.

Committees should normally be *composed* of at least three members,[93] but companies with small boards may assign the function of the committee to the board as a whole. The codes of most countries recommend that the committees should consist only of board members, but 'the use of other structures—external to the (supervisory) board—or procedures' are allowed under the EU Recommendation, provided that they are 'functionally equivalent and equally effective.'[94] The UK model articles allow the board to delegate any of its powers to others than board committees. Under the German co-determination scheme, employee representatives are elected by the workforce, so the nomination committee

---

[89] Art. 41 of the Audit Directive of 17 May 2006, OJ L 157/87 of 9 June 2006.

[90] For example, risk committee, strategic committee, financial committee, corporate governance committee, and other ad hoc committees; cf. for Switzerland, P. Böckli, sec. 2.2.2(c), p. 675.

[91] The EU Recommendation of 15 February 2005, above n. 31, no 5, states that boards should be organised in principle in three board committees with the aim that 'a sufficient number of independent non-executive or supervisory directors play an effective role in key areas where the potential for conflict of interest is particularly high.'

[92] Yet a German law reform of 31 July 2009, Federal Gazette (BGBl.) I 2509, has provided that decisions on the remuneration of managing directors be taken by the whole board.

[93] EU Recommendation of 15 February 2005, above n. 31, Annex 1, No. 1.1; in companies with small (supervisory) boards exceptionally only two members.

[94] EU Recommendation of 15 February 2005, above n. 31, Art. 1.3.2.

is exclusively composed of shareholder representatives. In Sweden the share-holders have the exclusive right to nominate board members, but they delegate it to the committee. The Swedish Corporate Governance Code provides that the committee's members be appointed by the shareholders and that only a minority of board members may be members of the committee.

Nearly all codes contain provisions on *independent directors*,[95] but the require-ments differ considerably. The usual rule under the national codes as well as under the EU Recommendation is that the nomination and the remuneration committees[96] should consist of at least a majority of independent directors; the latter must contain only non-executives. The UK Corporate Governance Code recommends that all three key committees be dominated by independent directors, but since an amend-ment in 2006 the chairman of the board may also be a member of the committee (but routinely not the chair) if he or she was considered independent on appointment as chairman; but the UK Code sees fewer conflicts in nomination committees than in audit and remuneration.[97] The Dutch Corporate Governance Code goes further and provides that all but one board member should be independent in each committee.[98]

The *delegation of powers* to board committees as set out in the codes and the EU Recommendation is normally not a final one: The committee is expected not only to report, but also to refer the matter back to the board for the final decision. The task of the committees is only preparatory and facilitating. In the UK, though, the remuneration committee has 'delegated responsibility"—ie. decision-making power—for setting the remuneration for all executive directors, including the chairman.[99] Such far-reaching delegation is also broadly accepted in the Netherlands. Yet these are exceptions. In other countries, the delegation power of the board is limited[100] or not allowed at all.[101] The difference between committees with and without decision-making powers, however, is less important than might be thought. Where the full board makes the decision, it will normally follow the

---

[95] As to independent directors, see below, sec. 2.2.3.

[96] Stricter for the audit committee; see below, sec. 2.2.3.

[97] P. Davies, sec. 2.2.2, p. 736 et seq. In companies with a controlling shareholder, the rela-tive importance of the three committees is different. There the most critical task is certainly with the audit committee, while the controlling shareholder has its own interest in keeping the remu-neration of management in line.

[98] R.G.J. Nowak, sec. 2.2.1, p. 461. The Dutch Corporate Governance Code allows the chairman of the board and former executives to be a member of the remuneration committee, but not the chair. The Belgian Corporate Governance Code, on the contrary, recommends that the chairman of the board be the chair of the committee.

[99] But only to the extent that the shareholders are not competent to deal with remuneration questions.

[100] For example, in Germany, Switzerland, and Sweden.

[101] For example, in France, Italy, and Belgium. In exceptional cases the Belgian Company Code gives to committees the power to make binding decisions, eg., to the audit committee.

committee's recommendations since the committee is specialised and has done the work. Indeed, there may be formal pressure to adopt the committee's recommendations because failure on the part of the board to do so may have to be revealed to the shareholders' meeting.

The audit committee—A separate audit committee is today considered indispensable and is now a general feature of listed companies.[102] The *task* of the audit committee is to monitor the integrity of the company's financial information, reviewing the internal control and risk management systems at least annually, ensuring the effectiveness of the internal audit function, making recommendations as to the selection of the external auditor, and monitoring the external auditor's independence and objectivity. The audit committee has direct access to information that other board members do not have: It is entitled to meet any person in the company without the executive directors being present, it is the principal contact point for the internal and external auditors, it receives internal and external audit reports, and it should obtain timely information about any issues arising from the audit. As the head of internal control, the audit committee has a strong position against the CEO, as it will or should have the same information.

The rules on the *composition* of the audit committee take this specific task into consideration and are sometimes more demanding than for the other committees. The French and Belgian corporate governance codes are satisfied with two-thirds of the committee members, ie. a majority should be independent.[103] While the Audit Directive only requires that at least one member of the audit committee of public interest entities should be independent,[104] the EU Recommendation recommends that the audit committee be composed exclusively of non-executive directors, a majority of whom (including, in some countries, the chairman) should be independent.[105]

---

[102] In the traditional model in Italy, there is an overlap between the tasks of the audit committee (which is called internal control and risk management control committee in that model) and those of the board of auditors (which mainly performs an *ex post* control function), requiring a certain level of coordination between the two bodies. G. Ferrarini et al., sec. 2.1(c) and (d), p. 377 et seq.

[103] Both the Dutch and the Belgian Corporate Governance Codes allow the chairman of the board to be a member of the committee (but not the chair), and the Dutch Corporate Governance Code provides the same with respect to former executives. Conversely, the German Corporate Governance Code allows the chairman of the supervisory board but not a former executive to be chair of the committee.

[104] The EU Audit Directive, above n. 89, Art. 41. It allows Member States to provide that a company may refrain from instituting a separate audit committee if its functions are vested in a corporate body, such as the (entire) supervisory board. But almost all listed companies have a separate audit committee.

[105] In most countries, this discrepancy between the EU Recommendation of 15 February 2005 (above n. 31) and the EU Audit Directive (above n. 89) is maintained in the sense that the

cont. ...

The EU Audit Directive[106] provides that at least one (independent) member of the audit committee should be a *financial expert*. As of 2011 in the UK, recent and relevant financial experience is present in 92% of FTSE-350 companies.[107] The Swiss Corporate Governance Code is more demanding and provides that a majority of its members, including the chairman, should be financially literate, but does not require a 'financial expert' to sit on this committee, while in reality this is often the case.

Role of the chairman—The chairman makes or breaks the board. This is true for one-tier and two-tier systems alike. In two-tier systems the chairman is responsible for an effective interaction and information flow between the executives and non-executives—ie. between the two boards. The chairman also maintains regular contact with the CEO and consults with the CEO on strategy. The chairman has important rights in the decision-making process beyond agenda-setting and normal procedure[108]—for example, by casting a vote in case of a tied-vote or, pursuant to the German Corporate Governance Code, deciding whether a director has a conflict of interest and should be excluded from the decision-making. Sometimes the chairman also has the exclusive right to chair the shareholders' meeting. Nearly all countries provide that the chairman should be elected by the board itself, but the Swedish Code recommends election by the shareholders' meeting and in Switzerland a popular initiative seeks to introduce this mode of election. Special rules are necessary under paritary co-determination as in Germany.[109]

2.2.3. Independent Directors

Role of independent directors—The rise of independent directors goes back to the USA and is today a common feature of corporate governance laws and codes.[110] Independent directors can have two functions.[111] In dispersed ownership structures, they serve to protect shareholders against the management and must there-

---

less stringent (but mandatory) requirement of the Directive has been implemented in the law and the stricter (but not mandatory) provision of the Recommendation in the Corporate Governance Code. Technically, it suffices if the company follows the law and explains why it has not followed the Corporate Governance Code.

[106] EU Audit Directive, above n. 89, Art. 41.

[107] Financial Reporting Council, above n. 49, p. 11.

[108] See, for example, the enumeration for Sweden, R. Skog and E. Sjöman, sec. 2.1(c), p. 626.

[109] See below, sec. 3.2.1

[110] M. Roth, 'Unabhängige Aufsichtsratsmitglieder', *Zeitschrift für das gesamte Handels- und Wirtschaftsrecht* 175 (2011) 605; K.J. Hopt, above n. 1, *The American Journal of Comparative Law* 59 (2011) 1 at 25 et seq., 35 et seq. For the requirements as to number and proportion of independent directors, see already above sec. 2.1.

[111] See also Preamble no. 7 of the EU Recommendation of 15 February 2005, above n. 31.

fore be independent of the latter. In concentrated ownership structures, they serve to protect minority shareholders against strong shareholders; in order to fulfil this role, they should be independent of the latter.[112] In most countries, independent directors play a role in the review of conflict-of-interest situations in general or in related-party transactions in particular.[113]

Criteria for independence—The concept of independence is difficult and controversial, and is predominantly defined in board rules in negative terms (by the *absence* of certain relationships). In formal terms, independence can be defined by a general clause or by a catalogue that may be finite[114] or just contain major examples of independence. It is also possible to combine both approaches, which is what the European Commission has done in its Recommendation. It defines independent as being 'free of any business, family or other relationship, with the company, its controlling shareholder or the management of either, that creates a conflict of interest such as to impair his judgement.'[115] But the Recommendation has an annex which lays down a long list of far-reaching—though non-binding— criteria concerning possible threats to directors' independence.[116] Most national corporate governance codes have incorporated all or most of the Recommendation's catalogue.[117] Only in Germany and Switzerland[118] are the situations not sketched out in such a level of detail.

Specific threats to independence: shareholder and employee representatives—articularly controversial are two specific threats to independence: How to treat repre-

---

[112] See below 2.2.3 on the independence criteria.

[113] Although the conflict of interest concept is sometimes used to fill in the definition of independence in specific circumstances, it is primarily treated as a notion that regards accountability toward the shareholders and is therefore dealt with in sec. 3.1.3.

[114] The Belgian and Dutch Corporate Governance Codes do not have a catch-all provision and present the list of criteria as exhaustive, ie., if one of the listed criteria is met, the director concerned is considered non-independent, and if none of the criteria is met, the director is considered independent.

[115] EU Recommendation of 15 February 2005, above n. 31, no. 13.1.

[116] Annex II of the EU Recommendation of 15 February 2005, above n. 31, no. 1. The wording is rather unspecific: 'a number of situations are frequently recognised as relevant in helping the (supervisory) board to determine whether a non-executive or supervisory director may be regarded as independent [...]. [A] number of criteria [...] should be adopted at national level. Such criteria, which should be tailored to the national context, should be based on due consideration of at least the following situations: (a)–(i).'

[117] The Polish Corporate Governance Code simply refers to the independence criteria in the Recommendation.

[118] However, the Swiss Corporate Governance Code, para 22, contains a specific definition of independence of members of board committees: members who never were or were more than three years ago a member of the executive management and who have no or comparatively minor business relations with the company. P. Böckli, sec. 2.2.3(a), p. 679.

sentatives of a controlling or blockholding shareholder and representatives of the employees of the company or of trade unions active in the company. In both situations, the relationship between the director and the delegator and the possibility of being recalled or not prolonged by the latter are threats that endanger the independence of the director. Yet if such directors are no longer treated as independent, this weakens the influence of the controlling shareholder or the parent company in steering a subsidiary and enhances the momentum the employees and the trade unions may have over the company. The reaction in the various countries differs considerably.

Regarding shareholder representatives, the European Recommendation confines itself to treating a representative of a *controlling shareholder*[119] as not independent. Even this recommendation has up to now not been followed in all Member States, in particular in countries where controlling shareholder and family enterprises are typical. The prototype for this negative reaction was Germany,[120] though with the understandable argument that half the board of the relevant companies is filled by labour.[121] For controlled companies,[122] the French Corporate Governance Code lowers the recommended percentages of independent directors from one-half to one-third. Perhaps the clearest accommodation of the interests of controlling shareholders is to be found in Spain. Although the Spanish Corporate Governance Code recommends that a majority of the board be non-executive directors, within that group 'proprietary' directors (ie those who have a shareholding above a certain threshold) should be present in the same proportion as those shareholders who hold the total capital of the company—and sometimes the rules are more favourable to the proprietary directors.[123] In prevailing Swiss practice the representative of a large shareholder may have a conflict of interest in a concrete case, but is still considered to be independent.

---

[119] EU Recommendation of 15 February 2005, above n. 31, Annex II, no. 1 (d), control as defined in Council Directive 83/349/EEC, OJ L 193/1 of 18 July 1983.

[120] German Corporate Governance Code (2010 version), no. 5.4.2: 'A Supervisory Board member is considered independent if he/she has no business or personal relations with the company or its Management Board which cause a conflict of interests.'

[121] M. Roth, above n. 110, *Zeitschrift für das gesamte Handels- und Wirtschaftsrecht* 175 (2011) 605 at 629 et seq.

[122] French company law defines a controlling shareholder as a person who holds the majority of the voting rights, or has the power to appoint and dismiss the directors, or effectively determines the decisions of the shareholders meeting; for the text, see A. Pietrancosta et al., sec. 2.2.3(a), p. 204 et seq. For Germany there are different control concepts—a narrow one in German group annual accounts law (majority of voting rights etc. like the first French alternative) and a wide one in German group law (*de facto* control). It is not entirely clear what is meant in the 2012 revision of the German Code; see above n. 120.

[123] A. Recalde Castels et al., 2.2.1(a), p. 562.

Other countries go further than the European Recommendation and treat shareholder representatives as not independent if the shareholder is 'significant' (according to the UK) or 'major.'[124] The Swedish Corporate Governance Code recommends that at least two of the directors who are independent of the company and its management (this should be the majority) have to be independent of the major shareholders. The French Corporate Governance Code states that a board representative of a 'major shareholder' may be considered independent if the major shareholder does not 'take part in the control' of the company. Representatives of holders of at least 10% of the shares are considered non-independent in Belgium (by law) and in the Netherlands and Sweden (in the Corporate Governance Code). This 10% threshold has also been suggested by the German Corporate Governance Code Commission for the 2012 code revision, but it has been harshly critiqued in both practice and academia. In the end this threshold was adopted, but only for transparency purposes and not for the actual definition of independence.[125]

The European Recommendation provides in its Annex that *employees* and persons who were employees for the previous three years cannot be considered independent unless they have been elected to the board in the context of a workers' representation system recognised by law and provided that they do not belong to senior management.[126] As regards national rules for companies without labour co-determination, the Recommendation is generally followed. The UK, French, and Dutch Corporate Governance Codes are more severe by taking into account five previous years.

The situation in *countries with labour co-determination* at the board level is more problematic and sometimes strongly politicised. The reactions are quite different in the various countries. In the Netherlands, the Recommendation's carve-out for employee representatives is not followed because Dutch labour co-determination rules provide that employees of the company (or of another company in the group) and representatives of a union that has collective bar-

---

[124] Italian company law also contains independence rules in case of related-party transactions and takeover bids. G. Ferrarini et al., sec. 2.2.3(a), p. 388.

[125] German Corporate Governance Code (2013 version), no. 5.4.2: '[...] A Supervisory Board member is not to be considered independent in particular if he/she has personal or business relations with the company, its executive bodies, a controlling shareholder or an enterprise associated with the latter which may cause a substantial and not merely temporary conflict of interests.' The 2012 revision of the German Code has extended the definition of the independent director by treating a director which has a personal or business relationship with a controlling shareholder as not independent, provided there is a substantial and not only temporary conflict of interest. The definition of *controlling shareholder* is not fully clear (actual control as under German group law or majority of votes as in German group annual accounts law). See also above n. 120 and 121.

[126] EU Recommendation of 15 February 2005, above n. 31, Annex II no. 1 (b).

gaining rights with the company cannot be members of the supervisory board at all.[127] The works council usually nominates outside persons with a labour background. These directors are not considered to fail the independence test because of their background. For example, a former Dutch trade union chairman (and former prime minister) was appointed as a supervisory board member of ING. In *Germany*, the unions claim that there is a clear case for the co-determination carve-out of the Recommendation, and the Corporate Governance Code shies away from addressing the question at all, dealing with independence on the shareholder side only. But a growing opinion criticises the carve-out and points out the disruption of the carefully balanced constitution of the boards that are co-determined at parity. According to academia, there is a subjective standard of independence, and the trend seems to be that if it is not clear whether a person is independent, that person should be considered not independent.[128] In *Sweden*, two—or in large companies (more than 1,000 employees) three—employee representatives may be appointed by the labour union if a collective bargaining agreement is concluded between the company and that union. In general, employee representatives are not considered independent from the company, but the independence provisions in the corporate governance code apply only to directors appointed by the shareholders' meeting, and the employee representatives under the co-determination rules are appointed by the works council. The least problematic situation is in *France* where, if the company's by-laws so provide, employees may elect up to five employee representatives, who should be considered to be elected as directors under a workers' representation system in the meaning of the Recommendation,[129] unlike employee-shareholders' representatives who are elected by the general meeting of shareholders.[130]

If one looks at both issues—controlling shareholder and labour representation—it seems that it is hardly justified to treat each of these issues separately, as was done for political reasons in the EU Recommendation. It is scarcely understandable that independence from a controlling shareholder and independence of employees or union representatives should be treated differently, even more so as this splits the shareholder side, which in practice is already much less homogeneous in attitude and voting than the labour side. The balance would be

---

[127] Art. 2: 160 BW.

[128] Cf. M. Roth, above n. 110, *Zeitschrift für das gesamte Handels- und Wirtschaftsrecht* 175 (2011) 605 at 620, 630 et seq.

[129] A. Pietrancosta et al., sec. 2.2.1(c), p. 195.

[130] *Idem.* But see the most recent French reform on some mandatory labour representation on the board, below n. 276.

easier to maintain if labour also had to elect a proportion of directors who are independent, at least in a co-determination system with parity.[131]

Decision on independence—If the independence criteria are set up in the listing conditions—as, for example, in the USA[132]—the decision on independence lies with the stock exchange or, as the case may be, the stock exchange supervisory body. In many European countries, the final determination of what constitutes independence remains fundamentally an issue for the (supervisory) board itself to determine. In the United Kingdom as well as under the European Recommendation[133] it is up to the board to determine whether each director is independent in character and judgment. The aforementioned criteria are then only non-binding guidelines for the board when there are circumstances that may threaten the independence of a particular director. While this approach does something to counteract the negative character of the independence criteria in the board rules (because the board has to take a view whether the individual can in fact exercise independent judgment), the European Commission may have chosen this rule because it was well aware that the list of criteria in the annex to its Recommendation went far beyond what was the practice in the different Member States and left them an easy way out, in particular under the required independence of the director from a controlling shareholder. The recommendation that there should be an annual review of whether a person may still be regarded as independent is tightening the rule just a little.

Senior independent director—More recently there has been much discussion on the merits of a senior independent director (lead independent director) who has the task of coordinating the work and the views of the independent directors. Pursuant to the UK Corporate Governance Code, the senior independent director should provide a sounding board for the chairman, serve as intermediary for other directors and be available to shareholders if the contact through the chairman or CEO is inappropriate or has failed to resolve the issue concerned.[134] Other countries—for example, Italy[135] and Switzerland[136]—are following this concept of 'lead director.' In Italy, the presence of a lead director is recommended if the chairman is the CEO or a representative of the controlling shareholder. There the lead director cannot be a representative of a major shareholder because the

---

[131] M. Roth, above n. 110, *Zeitschrift für das gesamte Handels- und Wirtschaftsrecht* 175 (2011) 605 at 640 et seq.

[132] To this and the following, K.J. Hopt, above n. 1, *The American Journal of Comparative Law* 59 (2011) 1 at 36.

[133] European Recommendation of 15 February 2005, above n. 31, no 13.2.

[134] UK Corporate Governance Code 2010, A.4.1 and A.4.2.

[135] G. Ferrarini et al., sec. 2.2.1(d), p. 382.

[136] P. Böckli, sec. 2.2.3(b), p. 680.

director would not normally be considered independent. In Italy a lead director may be the representative of a major shareholder: this situation is similar in France, but there only if he does not take part in the control of the corporation.[137] A lead director is more relevant in one-tier systems than in two-tier systems or if the CEO and the chairman are separate, but he may also be useful in two-tier system countries like Germany.[138] To a certain degree, a lead director could function as a substitute for these separations.

Independence versus competence—The high expectations of independent directors[139] have been only partially fulfilled.[140] The economic studies do not provide clear positive data.[141] Independent directors seem to have had an impact on replacing executive directors, but this was often mainly due to pressures from institutional investors. Undeniably, independent directors have not been able to prevent huge scandals.[142] One reason for this is that they are usually nominated or selected by the CEO or executive directors with whom they have professional or personal relationships. Unless they are professional non-executive directors, they are working part-time and, while being independent, may not have the necessary know-how, either of the business sector or the actual corporation. Furthermore, the flow of information to them is often suboptimal, particularly in the case of super-

---

[137] A. Pietrancosta et al., sec. 2.2.3(b), p. 205, and sec. 5.1(a), p. 243 et seq.

[138] M. Roth, above n. 88, *Zeitschrift für Unternehmens- und Gesellschaftsrecht* 2011, 343 at 364.

[139] Cf. J.N. Gordon, 'The Rise of Independent Directors in the United States, 1950–2005: Of Shareholder Value and Stock Market Prices', 59 *Stanford Law Review* 1465 (2007).

[140] P. Davies and S. Worthington, above n. 6, § 14-76. As to the following, see K.J. Hopt, above n. 1, *The American Journal of Comparative Law* 59 (2011) 1 at 36. See also L. Enriques, H. Hansmann and R. Kraakman, in R. Kraakman et al., above n. 2, p. 66: independent directors are 'a wide-spectrum prophylactic', 'potentially valuable for treating all agency problems, but not exclusively dedicated to treating any'. See also L. Lin, 'The Effectiveness of Outside Directors as a Corporate Governance Mechanism: Theories and Evidence', 90 *Northwestern University Law Review* 898 (1996); A.B. Gillette et al., 'Board Structures around the World. An Experimental Investigation', 12(1) *Review of Finance* 93 (2008); R. Duchin et al., 'When are Outside Directors Effective?', 96 *Journal of Financial Economics* 195 (2010); R. Fahlenbrach et al., 'Why do Firms Appoint CEOs as Outside Directors?', 97 *Journal of Financial Economics* 12 (2010).

[141] Cf. L.A. Bebchuk and M. S. Weisbach, above n. 1, at 943 et seq.; cf. also R.B. Adams, B.E. Hermalin and M.S. Weisbach, above n. 1, *Journal of Economic Literature* 48 (2010) 58 at 80 et seq.; L. Guo and R. Masulis, *Board Structure and Monitoring: New Evidence from CEO Turnover*, 2012, available at <http://ssrn.com/abstract=2021468>.

[142] Eg., Enron, where the board was composed of a majority of qualified independent directors. As to Enron, see C. J. Milhaupt and K. Pistor, *Law & Capitalism*, Chicago/London 2008, p. 47 et seq.; J. C. Coffee, *Gatekeepers: The Role of the Professions in Corporate Governance*, Oxford 2006.

visory boards,[143] but also quasi two-tier boards as in Switzerland. They are also paid less than the executive directors, in particular if they are supervisory board members, and therefore may also be less motived to devote much of their time and energy to their task.[144] Therefore, in recent years, in particular after the financial crisis, the emphasis has shifted to competence.[145] The European Commission's Green Paper of April 2011 did not touch upon independence as a discussion theme and mentioned it just once as one of the 'broad set of criteria' for the selection of non-executive board members.[146] This tendency can be seen in various countries. There is also a growing interest in other governance mechanisms such as pay-performance sensitivity and the market for corporate control.[147]

2.3. Information Streams

Information is a key problem for the board in exercising its functions, in particular for monitoring. Getting sufficient and unbiased information on what is happening in the company is crucial and difficult for independent directors in one-tier systems, and even more for supervisory board members in the two-tier systems. Apart from information gained from the CEO and, of course, the external auditors, two main additional sources of information for the board can be distinguished: On the one side, access to the management information systems of the company and directly to senior non-board executives and employees; and on the other side, information from outside experts.

Although the laws of most countries give the members of (supervisory) boards the right to access all information necessary for the performance of their tasks and, less often, to pose questions to executives (also outside of board meetings), in practice when a (supervisory) board member needs information

---

[143] P. Leyens, *Information des Aufsichtsrats*, Tübingen 2006, p. 156 et seq.

[144] As a quid pro quo, their risk of being sued is much smaller.

[145] Cf. H. Hau and M. P. Thum, *Subprime Crisis and Board (In-)Competence: Private v. Public Banks in Germany*, ECGI Working Paper in Finance No. 247/2009, available at <http://ssrn.com/abstract=1627921>. See also already above sec. 2.2.1.

[146] European Commission, Green paper, above n. 31, p. 5. The following criteria are mentioned there (in this sequence): 'merit, professional qualifications, experience, the personal qualities of the candidate, independence and diversity.' Cf. also European Commission, *Feedback statement on the Green Paper on the European Corporate Governance Framework*, 15 November 2011, availablke at <http://ec.europa.eu/internal_market/company/modern/corpo rate-governance-framework_en.htm>.

[147] D. Ferreira, M.A. Ferreira and C.C. Raposo, 'Board structure and price informativeness', *Journal of Financial Economics* 99 (2011) 523 at 543: negative relation between price informativeness and board independence; stock market monitoring as a substitute for board monitoring.

from the executives, the request is usually made by the chairman to the CEO. For example, this is the case in the UK where the Corporate Governance Code makes the chairman of the board responsible for obtaining all relevant information. In France the boards of directors also obtain information almost exclusively from the CEO. Only the CEO has the right to request information directly from employees. In Sweden, the board's access to information is *de facto* often indirect and filtered by the CEO. Sometimes audit committees are seen to make these requests, as in Poland. Direct contact by non-executive board members with executives (who are not board members) is often not allowed or regarded as an unfriendly act by the executive board members.

Yet the problem with this practice is that almost all information of the board is filtered by the management. The board tends to get good information fast, but bad information late and asymmetrically. The only independent sources of information are the external and internal auditors, with whom in most cases only board members serving on the audit committee have direct and regular contact. Therefore, in some countries there are tendencies to allow a more *direct access to company information* by the board. According to the Dutch Corporate Governance Code, if the supervisory board considers it necessary it may obtain information directly from (and speak to) officers and external advisors of the company, though in practice it is usually the chairman of the supervisory board who contacts the president of the management board (CEO) if specific information is needed. Swiss law provides that board members may, upon approval of the chairman, request information directly from employees; each director may, with the consent of the chairman, inspect the company's documents. In Switzerland access by outside directors to the management information system is rare, in any event directors usually do not ask for it, except in crises. Italian law states that each director is entitled to ask executive directors to provide information in a board meeting, and in legal literature it is assumed that the same may be done outside board meetings.[148] In Germany it is controversial whether supervisory board members may put questions to employees without prior consent of the management board. In recent years this has become more accepted by academia, but it would still be considered as a mark of distrust. Some chairpersons of the supervisory board have access to the management information system, especially if they were CEO of the company previously. In German practice, it is said that about half of the supervisory board members also insist on being provided with management-independent information. For bank boards, the German Bank Supervisory Act (*Kreditwesengesetz* – KWG) as of May 2013 states expressly that the supervisory board may ask the head of the internal revision and the head of risk controlling for direct information and must only (later) inform the management board. It remains

---

[148] An important role is entrusted to the senior independent director (if appointed), who has to ensure appropriate information streams. To the lead independent director, above sec. 2.2.3.

to be seen whether this spills over the general company law. In the Netherlands board members usually do not have direct access to the management information systems, but there is usually a direct communication line from the head of compliance to the chairman of the supervisory board. Furthermore, the heads of compliance often report directly to the audit committee and the chairman has a seat in that committee. Heads of compliance probably could be summoned, on the basis of the Dutch Corporate Governance Code, to appear before the board without permission of the CEO, but it is not known whether this happens given the direct line between the head of compliance and the chairman of the board. In other countries, for example Poland, the supervisory board must request information from the management board.[149]

It is a controversial issue whether the supervisory board has access to *external advice*. Asking for external advice is a direct challenge to the management, though it might be acceptable in the context of related-party transactions. It may also be a defensive step because it allows the board to rebut a charge of mis-management. The practice appears to be that corporate governance codes give the right to get external advice, but this right is not generally used because it is seen as unfriendly; in the quasi two-tier model of Switzerland it would even be seen as hostile. However, if there is a possibility of incurring liability, the supervisory board will seek external advice. In general, the likelihood of being seen as hostile is probably lower in a two-tier model, since the role of the supervisory board is to monitor. Again, access to external advice may be contemplated more freely in the case of audit committees.[150]

3. Accountability

3.1. Board and Shareholders

3.1.1. Appointment and Removal

The appointment: general rule—Shareholders do not manage a corporation themselves but delegate this task to the board; apart from small companies, the board does not manage itself but delegates actual management to the officers of the company. As a general rule, therefore, the appointment of board members is an important task for the shareholders. In the *one-tier board system* that prevails

---

[149] But in Poland and other countries audit companies have direct access to the information in banks and other financial institutions.

[150] The Financial Reporting Council's guidance for audit committees in the UK contemplates access to external legal and accounting advice when the committee 'reasonably believes it necessary' to obtain such advice.

in the UK and many other countries,[151] the shareholders appoint and remove the directors by voting in the general assembly. This is different from the rule in the United States, where shareholders can only use the proxy fight method; but proxy fights are costly and difficult to win.[152]

In the *two-tier system*—as in Germany, for example—shareholders appoint the members of the supervisory board, which in turn appoints the members of the management board. This double delegation is not self-evident. In the Netherlands until today and in Germany before 1937, the general assembly could also appoint members of the management board. But the selection of the management is pivotal for the company, and it is argued that it is a task for which the general shareholders do not have sufficient knowledge. Today the direct appointment of the management by the shareholders is still provided for in the German limited liability company,[153] where the relationship between the shareholders and the manager(s) is close, a board is optional (apart from co-determination), and shares are not freely available in the share market or even on a stock exchange.

Perhaps for these reasons, the role of the shareholders in the appointment of the executive management (where it has this right) is usually more formal than actual. In most countries, the general assembly votes upon proposals of candidates by the board, though minority shareholders and sometimes even single shareholders may submit additional candidates, but this is rare in practice and even more rarely successful.[154] Usually the candidates proposed by the board are elected. The actual selection is therefore made by the board previously, depending on the shareholder structure either in the board itself (if shareholding is dispersed) or indirectly by instruction of the controlling shareholder. The latter is the case in groups of companies that are closely run, but not necessarily in other groups of companies. *De facto* this amounts very often to *self-recruitment of the board* via nominations to the shareholders as reported from the United Kingdom, Switzerland, Germany and the Netherlands. This leads to a serious potential principal–agent conflict between the shareholders and the board.

There are several *techniques* to mitigate this conflict situation. One is to have a nomination committee in which (truly) independent directors have the say.[155]

---

[151] On the different board systems (one-tier, two-tier, choice), see above sec. 2.1; on eligibility, see above sec. 2.2.1, also as to restrictions of a change from the management board to the supervisory board. Under certain conditions, vacant positions in the board may be filled by the court.

[152] L. Enriques, H. Hansmann and R. Kraakman, in R. Kraakman et al., above n. 2, p. 58.

[153] Similarly in the partnership limited by shares, a hybrid form between company and partnership.

[154] Voting rules may create additional difficulties for shareholders—for example, block voting instead of voting separately for the individual candidates.

[155] On the nomination committee, see sec. 2.2.2; on independent directors, see above sec. 2.2.3.

Another is to have more active shareholders, in particular institutional investors and hedge funds, who do in fact seek to exercise their formal legal rights,[156] as in the spectacular cases of Deutsche Börse in Germany in 2005 or National Express in 2011 in the United Kingdom.[157] In closely run groups of companies, the principal–agent conflict is between the minority shareholders of the parent and the subsidiary and the majority shareholder of the parent. This conflict is more difficult to mitigate. Minority representation, as in Italy, Poland and Spain, is one possible reaction of the law.[158]

The rules on *duration of office/reappointment* vary considerably. In some countries, re-election occurs annually, as in Sweden, in the United Kingdom for FTSE 350 companies and—as a consequence of the Minder referendum in March 2013—in future also in Switzerland. In other countries re-election is less frequent: At least every three years in Italy and Switzerland, four years in the Netherlands, up to five years in Germany, six years in France and Belgium (but only four years under the codes), and six years in Switzerland (though this has fallen out of use there and one year is not rare). Reduction of the period of office provided by law or codes seems to be a general tendency, though not down to one year as in the United Kingdom and in Switzerland, which in both countries was also very controversial. Yet the actual time of service seems to be becoming shorter, as clearly shown in Germany. A fixed maximum time limit for service on the board is rare. Codes may provide for an age limit, such as 70 years.

While the appointment rules are clearly correlated with the shareholder constituency, this is less clear for duration rules, as the variety of rules show. But one could venture that the function of longer periods of office for the board is to strengthen the position of the board in relation to strong shareholders—unless the shareholders have strong removal rights (see below), in which case the function of the duration rules is to determine who has to take the initiative over a removal. That protection management may derive from long periods of office is even more plausible when the managing board has the right and duty to run the company under its own responsibility, as in Germany under the so-called leader principle. A mandatory annual discharge procedure of managing and supervisory board directors may be a more long-term oriented alternative to annual re-election.

Appointment rights, cumulative voting, slate voting—The appointment of the directors by the shareholders—either directly as in the one-tier system or by delegation to the supervisory board—is only the general rule. There are a number of exceptions. The most prominent exception is mandatory *labour co-determination*

---

[156] See below, sec. 3.1.4.

[157] P. Davies, sec. 3.1.1, p. 744, n. 104.

[158] See below, sec. 3.1.1 under appointment rights.

in the board.[159] Under such a system, the board is split between the shareholder and the labour representatives, usually by two-thirds to one-third or, exceptionally as in Germany, even by half to half.

The appointment of labour representatives can be set up in different ways. The actual appointment may be up to the shareholders, but on the nomination of the works council as in the Netherlands. This nomination may be rejected by the general assembly under certain conditions, but then the works council may make new nominations. More usually the labour representatives are elected by the workforce of the company. The voting system for such an election is complicated and costly because of the sheer number of the electors and can be either by direct selection or by selection of voting delegates. The selection process is even more difficult and costly if not only the domestic workforce is entitled to vote. Reserving the labour seats on the board only to the German worker constituency is the rule in Germany, but this rule is rightly criticised and may even violate European law.[160]

Sometimes trade unions have their own seats on the board. This leads to representatives with a broader outlook beyond the company, but on the other hand this may bring in more ideological arguments depending on the history and status of the trade union movement in that country. Accordingly, one cannot generalise whether the representation of trade unions on the board adds positive diversity or has negative effects on the coherent work of the board. Sometimes leading employees (senior white-collar workers) have the right to select their own representatives. This gives credit to the particular interest of this group. This interest may lie closer to the interest of the shareholders and the board and therefore weakens the influence of the labour side in general. The old 'structure regime' of labour co-determination in the Netherlands—which consisted of self-appointing boards, nomination rights for shareholders and labour, and the control of a last instance—was given up because of major disadvantages of this system.[161]

Apart from labour co-determination, there is an argument for not mandating the appointment of directors (either the members of the one-tier board or those of the two-tier board) by shareholders alone. In several countries there is *flexibility for the articles of association* to provide otherwise. In theory the articles could provide for the appointment of all directors in another way, such as in Poland. But this would be very unusual indeed. Normally at least more than half of the directors must be chosen by the shareholders, and only the rest are chosen in

---

[159] Labour co-determination in the board and its pros and cons are discussed below, sec. 3.2.1.

[160] M. Roth, sec. 3.2.1(c), p. 335; *Report of the Reflection Group On the Future of EU Company Law*, Brussels, 5 April 2011, p. 53.

[161] L. Enriques, H. Hansmann and R. Kraakman, in R. Kraakman et al., above n. 2, p. 102 et seq., 94 et seq.

another way, as provided for in Sweden. But in listed companies non-shareholder appointments rarely occur.[162]

As to those board seats that can be filled in a way other than by general shareholder appointment, two methods are available to give single shareholders or a minority more influence. The first is *nomination rights for particular shareholders* in the articles of association. This is relatively frequent if the public company stems from a private founder who wants to maintain a secure influence even after the company has gone public. In some countries, these nomination rights can cover up to one-third of the board seats, as in the Netherlands where this is widely used. In the Netherlands, one-third of the members may be appointed by a third party (except under co-determination rules); this often occurs in listed companies. The right to make (binding) nominations, given to a shareholder, does occur more often and can—in theory—cover up to all board members. Nomination rights are also frequent in companies that are state-controlled or under the influence of the state or more local public entities, such as communities in the service sectors. An example is France. More recently, nomination rights have been used to prevent hostile takeovers—for example, when the German Krupp Foundation was recently granted three seats on the supervisory board— though often this motive is not admitted in public. While in these cases there is a formal right to nominate one or more directors, in practice there are many cases in which single shareholders are granted *ad hoc* permission to appoint a representative. This is true, for example, in family companies for different branches of family, for foreign investors with a strategic long-term investment, and for banks and other creditors during and prior to rescue situations.

In some countries—especially countries with a two-tier board—*minorities* are protected by having special legal appointment rights to the board.[163] Two forms must be distinguished: *cumulative voting* (more precisely: separate minority voting) as in Poland,[164] Spain[165] and Austria,[166] and *slate voting* as in Italy.[167] In

---

[162] For Sweden, R. Skog and E. Sjöman, sec. 3.1.1(a), p. 637. In the German partnership limited by shares (above n. 151), the partner has the role of the director and is not up for election or re-election. An indirect way of influencing the appointment of directors is to issue preference shares without voting rights.

[163] In most countries—for example, Germany—this is not possible. Sometimes it is not forbidden but very rare, as in Switzerland and in the United Kingdom, or in Belgium for listed companies. Switzerland has a mandatory legal representation of one board member for common stockholders when there is a separate class of multiple voting rights or preferred stock.

[164] S. Sołtysiński, sec. 2.8, p. 530 et seq., sec. 3.1.1, p. 533.

[165] A. Recalde Castels et al., sec. 3.1.1(b), p. 585.

[166] For Austria, see K.J. Hopt and M. Roth, *Großkommentar zum Aktiengesetz*, 4th edn., Berlin 2006, § 101 comment 57. For Spain, see A. Recalde Castells et al., sec. 3.1.1(b), p. 585, but the system is open to many questions and to a large extent diluted by the possibility of the majority to instantly also remove the directors elected by the minority.

Poland, shareholders representing at least 20 per cent of the share capital can opt for 'group' voting, which produces a result similar to cumulative voting. This permits the requisite number of shareholders to form a group which is entitled to elect one member of the board on a one share/one vote basis (though at the cost of having no role in the election of the other board members).[168] This leads to a proportional representation of the shareholder groups and is considered a powerful right of the minority shareholders. In Italy, cumulative voting is allowed for companies in general. In listed companies there is mandatory slate voting, which is a sort of cumulative voting, but it does not necessarily lead to a proportional representation of shareholders on the board. Under the slate voting system, shareholders may propose lists of candidates. At least one director is appointed from the minority slate that gets the highest number of votes and at least one director (or two, if the board members are more than seven) has to be independent according to the board of (internal) auditors' independence requirements. Thereby the majority side always gets a majority, while the minority shareholders get an average of one and a half seats.

The Italian system is considered less effective in practice than originally thought because one or two representatives on the board have no real impact. This may be different with a higher percentage of minority board members—for example, under proportional representation, or in the above-mentioned case of labour co-determination under which in most countries a third of the board is appointed by labour. But labour co-determination is also the reason why Germany, with its 50 per cent representation of labour in major companies, has ruled out a more general minority representation because it would split up[169] the shareholder side of the board even further.

---

[167] Report G. Ferrarini et al., sec. 3.1.1.1(a)., p. 392 et seq.; cf. also Assonime, *An analysis of the compliance with the Italian Corporate Governance Code (Year 2010)*, April 2011, Part 2: An analysis of slate voting in Italy, p. 76 et seq.

[168] The relevant group size is determined as follows. 'Persons, who in general meeting represent that portion of shares which is a resultant of dividing the total number of represented shares by the number of supervisory board members, may form a separate group for electing one board member, but they shall not take part in electing the remaining members.' (Art 385(5) of the Code on Commercial Partnerships and Companies.) The World Bank gives the following example of the process. 'For example: assume a company with 5 board seats. Before the AGM, a 20% block of shareholders requests group voting. At the AGM, two 20% blocks opt for group voting, and appoint one board member each. The remaining 3 board seats are elected by standard majority AGM resolution, by the remaining 60% of capital' (World Bank, *Corporate Governance Country Assessment: Poland*, Washington 2005, p. 14, fn 12.).

[169] Cf. the modern requirements for representatives with special knowledge in financial matters and for diversity, in particular a mandatory gender quota; cf. K.J. Hopt, above n. 1, *The American Journal of Comparative Law* 59 (2011) 1 at 27 et seq.

Removal—The *competence to remove directors* before the end of their term (as distinguished from disqualification[170]) lies in principal with the same body responsible for the appointment: The shareholder in the general assembly, the supervisory board for management board members, labour in codetermined boards, and the shareholder with a special nomination right. The competences for appointment and for removal differ only exceptionally, as in Poland and in the United Kingdom. This may lead to a conflict between those who appoint and those who may remove. This conflict can be solved by allowing the appointing body to re-appoint the same candidate, or in any case to appoint its own new candidates, with the consequence that both bodies will resort to a compromise. But it is also possible that the general assembly will receive the unequivocal right to dismiss any directors, irrespective of who appointed them. This is the right of the general assembly in Poland regarding management board members who are appointed by the supervisory board. Similarly, shareholders in the UK can also remove directors who were appointed by the creditors, even if this breaches a loan covenant.[171]

The *protection of directors against removal* before the end of their term varies considerably. Some protection is given by the mere fact that there must be at least a simple majority of the general assembly for the removal decision. This majority may not be reached so easily even if an activist shareholder, in practice an institutional investor or a hedge fund, pursues the removal. The coordination problem may be exacerbated by takeover and capital market rules directed against concerted action.[172] Furthermore, removal is considerably more difficult if the vote is not for the removal of a single director, but of the board as a whole under a block-voting rule or practice.

But even granted that a simple majority can be reached, the protection of directors basically varies along *three types of rules* that correspond to a more shareholder-friendly or a more board-centred system. The most shareholder-friendly rule is removal without cause and without compensation, as in Sweden. The idea of this rule is that the relationship of the director with the company and the shareholders is one of trust. This also applies to directors appointed by another party. It is another question whether in contract practice there are not termination payment clauses for such a removal. A second, still shareholder-friendly type of rule consists in the right to remove a director from office without cause, but with preservation of compensation rights under the service contract.

---

[170] As to disqualification, see above, sec. 2.2.1.

[171] P. Davies, sec. 3.1.1, p. 745. This is also the case in Switzerland.

[172] On the coordination problem, see, P. Davies, sec. 3.1.1, p. 745; see also J.M. Crespi and L. Renneboog, 'Is (Institutional) Shareholder Activism New? Evidence from UK Shareholder Coalitions', *Corporate Governance: An International Review* 18 (2010) 274 and earlier papers on ECGI. On activist institutional shareholders, see below, sec. 3.1.4. On the highly controversial concerted action problem, see *ibid.*

This seems to be the most frequent rule, as in France, Italy, Poland, and Switzerland. In the UK the service contract has been the source of substantial compensation payments to dismissed directors. In the light of complaints of 'rewards for failure', in 2013 the companies legislation was reformed so as to make compensation payments recoverable by the company unless made in accordance with a remuneration policy already approved by the shareholders or the shareholders approve the payment *ad hoc*.

The third rule is relatively rare. In countries where the position of the (management) board is rather strong, as described before for Germany, as a general rule the supervisory board may not remove the management board members before the end of the office unless there is cause. Even then removal is usually with compensation unless the service contract (as distinguished from the position as an organ of the company) has also come to an end, or damage has been caused to the company. Such a rather far-reaching protection of the management board against removal corresponds to the legal responsibility of the management board to run the company under its own responsibility. Yet in family companies and in companies belonging to a group this protection is not as strong as it may seem; under the law, good cause is also that the general assembly no longer has confidence in the managing board, unless reasons for the loss of confidence are patently unfounded. But even in case of loss of confidence, the supervisory board is not obliged to remove the managing director. As to the appointment decision, the interference of a nomination committee with independent members may help to make the appointment decision more objective. The removal of supervisory board members by the general assembly that elected them is possible without cause only by a qualified majority, in Germany a three-quarters majority. Again, this may be considered to be a certain protection against the controlling shareholder.

The removal rules, both as to competence and to legal requirements, must not only be seen in light of the shareholder constituency as mentioned before, but also under modern practice. The turnover rate for CEOs has been increasing under the pressure of global competition and technological speed. There is evidence for this not only when annual re-election is the rule, as in Sweden, but also in other countries such as Germany. Another important factor is remuneration. Even if removal is only with cause and there is no valid cause, in practice termination most often involves severance payments. So term rules may not be as relevant. This phenomenon is well known in the takeover context. Even in countries with far-reaching discretion of the board of the target company, as in the US, the takeover defences are often and easily overcome by golden handshakes and job agreements.

Banks are special, more generally regarding creditor governance, but also regarding the accountability of directors. Since financial institutions are not covered in this board project,[173] it must suffice to mention that the board of a financial institution is also, and possibly even primarily, accountable to the creditors. Accordingly, the directors of a financial institution, while still being appointed in the above-mentioned way, need to have particular competences for their office and tasks,[174] which are controlled by the bank supervisory authority. If these competences are lacking, or if it turns out later that they are not sufficient, the supervisory agency has a removal right. These supervisory intervention rights have been expanded greatly as a consequence of the financial crisis and restrict the choice of the shareholders and other parties with nomination rights very considerably. It must also be remembered that even for the shareholders of financial institutions themselves there is a fit and proper clause that is administered and enforced by the supervisory authority.

3.1.2. Division of Powers between Board and Shareholders

General division of powers—The phenomenon of more board-centric and more shareholder-centric systems already appears in the appointment and the removal decision. It is even more relevant as far as the general division of powers between the board and the shareholders is concerned. In general and as a majority rule, the company is managed and controlled not by the shareholders but by the board and, under its supervision, the officers; or in a two-tier system, by the management and the supervisory boards. Only certain key powers are reserved to the general assembly.[175] This is the case, for example, in Germany, Italy, Switzerland, the Netherlands, and Poland. The key powers are usually defined in the law either by a catch-all clause (basically: particularly important economic decisions) or by a catalogue listing so-called fundamental decisions such as charter amendments, share issuance, mergers, corporate divisions, and reincorporation. Sometimes this balance is changed somewhat by important court decisions, such as the German *Holzmüller* rule.[176] This rule went rather far regarding the requirement of approval of a management decision by the general assembly, but it was later mitigated considerably by the *Gelatine* rule,[177] which reduced the role of the shareholders to decisions affecting a very large part of the company's assets (around 80 per cent) and having a highly significant impact on the value of the shareholder rights. Definitions in the law have the advantage of better predictability,

---

[173] On financial institutions, see above, sec. 1 at the end.

[174] Cf. also above, sec. 2.2.1 as to the composition of the board.

[175] E. Rock, P. Davies, H. Kanda and R. Kraakman, in R. Kraakman et al., above n. 2, p. 183 et seq. on fundamental changes.

[176] *BGHZ* 83, 122 (1982).

[177] *BGHZ* 159, 30 = *NJW* 2004, 1860 and *BGH NZG* 2004, 375; on the controversial details, see U. Hüffer, *Aktiengesetz*, 9th edn., Munich 2010, § 119 comment 16 et seq.

whereas court decisions may create great legal uncertainty, as was indeed the case for *Holzmüller* and to a lesser degree for *Gelatine*. This division of powers in favour of the board is somewhat mitigated in a two-tier system if the management board cannot decide alone but needs the approval of the supervisory board by law, or if, as most recently in Germany, the supervisory board is permitted or required to decide that certain categories of decisions need its approval.

More shareholder-centric systems leave it to the articles of association to divide the powers between the board and the shareholders. This is the case, for example, in the United Kingdom. There the shareholders may also decide on all matters that lie within the competence of the board; they may change its decisions, even though only if a 75 per cent majority of the voting shares can be reached.[178] This basic division between the powers of the board and shareholders is sometimes complemented by a presumption for cases of doubt. This presumption applies to the board in Belgium.

This general division of powers either in favour of the board or in favour of the shareholders in more board-centered or more shareholder-friendly systems respectively, must be qualified by the role the board or the shareholders adopt. A weak board or a board under pressure from a controlling shareholder may choose to ask the general assembly to decide matters that are in the competence of the (managing) board, as is the case in Germany. This is also an option for the management board if the supervisory board refuses to give its consent when this consent is necessary. In the latter case, the decision of the general assembly must be taken by a qualified majority.[179]

On the other side, the role of shareholders is diminished by the fact that in public companies without block-holders, *absenteeism* is high, as reported for France, Germany, and Switzerland. Very often there is also a tendency for shareholders to vote in general assemblies for the board proposals even after loud criticism. Only more recently have more dissenting voting patterns been reported, for example, from France.[180] There the influence of longer term shareholders is increased by a double voting right,[181] a solution that might also be considered by the European Commission and is being discussed the Netherlands and in Switzerland. In companies with foreign shareholders, many voting rights are dormant because of the great difficulties of trans-border voting. This has rightly been criticised and proposals have been made, but a solution is not yet in sight.

---

[178] On this, see also L. Enriques, H. Hansmann and R. Kraakman, in R. Kraakman et al., above n. 2, p. 73.

[179] Sections 111(4), 119(2) of the German Stock Corporation Act (AktG).

[180] A. Pietrancosta et al., sec. 3.1.2(a), p. 210, sec. 3.1.4, p. 217 et seq.

[181] A. Pietrancosta et al., sec. 3.1.4, p. 219; cf. European Commission, Green Paper, above n. 31, at 164 sub 2. Shareholders.

Instructions to the board—The shareholders may be tempted to give specific instructions to the board to change its business policy or its attitude toward certain transactions. Shareholders and directors have different incentives: In general, the former tend to be more short-term and more risk-prone (because they may hold diversified portfolios); the latter are more risk-averse because of their investment of human capital in their firm only (though not so in the case of perverse incentives, end games, or pyramid building).[182] The general division of powers between the board and the shareholders is also reflected when it comes to giving instructions to the board. In board-centric systems such as Germany and Switzerland as well as in Poland, the shareholders cannot give instructions to the board. The management board or the board of directors, respectively, runs the company on its own responsibility. If the shareholders want the management board to follow another business policy and make or refrain from a certain transaction, they may—and in the case of a controlling shareholder, they will—have their way in the end only by removing the board, in Germany first the supervisory board and then via its intervention the management board as well. It should be remembered though that this strong position of the (management) board exists only in the stock corporation, not in the limited liability corporation, where in Germany instruction powers and removal are powers of the shareholders.

In other systems instructions are possible. This is the case, for example, in Sweden and in the Netherlands, and in the United Kingdom only with a supermajority. Yet instructions to the board are not easy to come by. Much depends on the shareholder constituency as well as on the size of the company. In large companies, instructions are unusual—even if legally possible—because it is just too complicated to bring them about unless there are relevant multiple voting rights. Therefore, the easier way may still be the removal of directors. This is certainly true in the United Kingdom because of the aforementioned super-majority requirement.

A milder form of interference as a binding instruction is an *advisory vote* of the general assembly. As a general rule, the general assembly may discuss all matters relevant to the company as long as it does not interfere with competences that are reserved to the board. Such a discussion is always possible when the general assembly passes the resolution to discharge the directors. But apart from discharge resolutions, the general assembly[183] can also pass other resolutions of an informative or advisory character. More recently, discussion and advisory

---

[182] Cf. K.J. Hopt, *Corporate Governance of Banks,* above n. 12, p. 348. For directors, liability also has an impact. For shareholders, the problem of short-termism has raised concern, in particular after the financial crisis; see sec. 3.1.4 on institutional investors.

[183] H. Fleischer, 'Konsultative Hauptversammlungsbeschlüsse im Aktienrecht', *Die Aktiengesellschaft* 2010, 681.

resolutions are even mandated by law for remuneration,[184] for example, in the United Kingdom, Germany, Italy, and other countries. Such a mandatory say-on-pay is an interesting legal technique that practically constrains the discretion of the board while still leaving it the final decision.

3.1.3. Liability Rules (Special Issues)

Duty of care—As an agent of the shareholders (and under certain jurisdictions, also of labour and other stakeholders), the board has a duty of care when fulfilling its task. Because this study is not a handbook for board members, the obvious details of what the directors have to do and refrain from doing need not be covered in detail. A list of the duties can be found in the reports on each jurisdiction and in the LSE Study on Directors' Duties and Liability for the European Commission of April 2013.[185] It suffices to mention three points that are more generally relevant.

First, the standard of care is an *objective* one nearly everywhere. A director cannot excuse his or her actions by pointing to a personal lack of knowledge or experience. This is also the standard under general civil law with its concepts of *pater familias* or reasonable man. Up to 2006 there was an exception in the United Kingdom,[186] but this has been changed into an objective standard that requires the director to achieve the level of competence that a reasonable person in the director's position would adhere to.[187]

Secondly, the general duty of care is concretised by case law and legal commentaries in each of the jurisdictions. This could lead to the impression that liability of directors for violating their duty of care in one of their many concrete forms is a great risk and would lead to many court cases. Yet in practice the number of cases in which directors are actually held liable for violation of their duty of care are limited. A major factor for this is *de iure* or *de facto* the *business judgment rule*, which exists in many countries. It is sometimes laid down expressly in the company statute, as in Germany, while in other countries—such as Italy or the United Kingdom—the courts decide accordingly. The legal definition of the duty of care, if there is any, varies considerably from one jurisdiction to another. The German definition is as follows: There is no violation of the duty of care if the director who makes a business decision may reasonably

---

[184] See below, sec. 3.1.5.

[185] For example, for France, A. Pietrancosta et al., sec. 3.1.2(b), p. 194; for Switzerland, the 'seven-points' catalogue, see P. Böckli, sec. 2.1(a), p. 664. For details on the substantive provisions on directors' duties in 28 countries, see the LSE Study 2013 (above n. 16), part 2.

[186] The idea was probably shareholder supremacy or an enlightened shareholder approach. If the shareholders want to entrust their affairs to an 'amiable lunatic', they should be free to do so without holding him liable if things go wrong.

[187] P. Davies, sec. 3.1.3, p. 747.

believe that he or she acts, on the basis of adequate information, in the interest of the company.[188] While this and other definitions of the business judgment rule lead to many difficult interpretation problems,[189] the heart of the rule is that (managing) directors can only make business decisions with uncertain consequences, since by definition business implies foresight and risk-taking. If directors were liable in cases where the foresight proved to be wrong or the risk materialised, they could no longer perform their profession. The business judgment rule gives them a safe haven. This necessity to avoid judicial hindsight is acknowledged by company law judges in all countries, regardless of whether or not a formal legal business judgment rule exists.

Yet this safe haven has important limits. The most important are the rather strict informational duties. To ensure that they receive adequate information, directors must meet increasingly severe organisational duties, including setting up an internal control system or more recently, as a spillover from the law of financial institutions, installing some sort of a risk management system.[190] Reports from Switzerland indicate that the legal demands for the duty of care by Swiss courts are stricter than those of the Delaware Court of Chancery.[191] In a liability suit, the question of who has the burden of proof may be decisive. Some company laws, such as the German one, lay the burden of proof on the director. Furthermore, far-reaching documentation duties may come into play, as in Germany and even in Switzerland, where court rulings have not yet endorsed the fondness of legal writers for the business judgment rule.

Thirdly, the requirements of the duty of care rise dramatically if the company runs into difficulties and *financial distress*. Then the directors must see whether the company can still be rescued, or whether the risks for the creditors of continuing operations are too high. In the latter case, they may violate special legal duties, such as under the unlawful trading rule in the United Kingdom or similar rules in Germany, France, Italy and Belgium.[192]

---

[188] Section 93(1) sentence 2 of the German Stock Corporation Act (AktG). See M. Roth, sec. 3.1.2(b), p. 320.

[189] See the intense debate and controversies in Italy, G. Ferrarini et al., sec. 3.1.2(c), p. 397 et seq.; and Germany, M. Roth, sec. 3.1.2(b), p. 321 and K.J. Hopt and M. Roth, above n.166, comments on Section 93(1) sentence 2, 4 new version.

[190] Cf. European Commission, Action Plan 2012 (above n. 28) point 2.1 and Annex: 'Disclosure of board diversity policy and of risk management arrangements'; M.T. Moore, 'The evolving contours of the board's risk management function in UK corporate governance', *Journal of Corporate Law Studies* 10 (2010) 279.

[191] P. Böckli, sec. 3.1.2(b), p. 687. Cf. *idem*, 'Die Schweizer Verwaltungsräte zwischen Hammer und Amboss', *Schweizerische Juristen-Zeitung* 106 (2010) No. 1, p. 1, No. 2, p. 25.

[192] K.J. Hopt, above n. 1, *The American Journal of Comparative Law* 59 (2011) 1 at 42 et seq. with references. See also below, sec. 3.3.

Conflicts of interest—While the duty of care circumscribes the general professional behaviour of the directors, there are special situations in which the directors may be tempted by particular circumstances not to act in the interest of the shareholders. There the *duty of* loyalty comes in.[193] The directors are dealing with other people's money. They are trustees of these other people, expressly as in the United Kingdom and in the USA, or *de facto* as they are held to obey similar standards as trustees in many other countries. The temptation not to act in the interest of the shareholders is particularly strong if there is a *conflict of interest*[194] between the interest of the shareholders and of the directors themselves, or third parties with whom the directors have close relations or owe conflicting duties. This temptation is even more acute and the interests of the shareholders are even more endangered if, as is often the case, the conflict of interest situation is not apparent to the shareholders, or if it is known only theoretically but not for the concrete case.

This strong principal–agent conflict between the shareholders and the board[195] is addressed in all jurisdictions, but what they consider a *conflict of interest* varies considerably. Some jurisdictions, such as the United Kingdom and the USA, go very far, while most European continental countries circumscribe a conflict of interest more narrowly. Some are content with a general clause, while others enumerate a whole catalogue of situations that may lead to a conflict of interest for the directors. European law uses both ways of defining director independence. The general clause defines independence, a similar concept, as 'free of any business, family or other relationship, with the company, its controlling shareholder or the management of either, that creates a conflict of interest such as to impair his judgment.'[196] A number of Member States leave it like this or make an exception for certain conflicts, such as the German Corporate Governance Code

---

[193] The question whether the duty of loyalty encompasses the duty of care as it is recently brought forward can be left aside in this context.

[194] P. Davies and S. Worthington, above n. 6, §§ 1693 et seq.; K.J. Hopt, 'Conflict of Interest, Secrecy, and Insider Information of Directors, A Comparative Analysis', *European Company and Financial Law Review* 2013, 167, available at <http://ssrn.com/abstract=2178 152>; J. Farrar and S. Watson, 'Self-dealing, Fair Dealing and Related Party Transactions— History, Policy and Reform', *Journal of Corporate Law Studies* 11 (2011) 495. The question whether the duty of loyalty encompasses the duty of care can be left aside in this context.

[195] For the two other principal–agent conflicts (minority shareholder/controlling shareholder, shareholders/other stakeholders), see J. Armour, H. Hansmann and R. Kraakman, in R. Kraakman et al., above n. 2, p. 35 et seq.

[196] European Recommendation of 15 February 2005, above n. 31, no. 13.1. But there are differences: 'Independence' in relation to self-dealing is assessed at the transaction level, not the enterprise level, as it is under the Corporate Governance Codes. Thus, an 'independent' director (under the Corporate Governance Codes), who contracts with his company is not indepndent for the purposes of the transaction rules. Equally, an executive director who is not involved in the transaction is independent for the purposes of the transaction rules, but would be under Corporate Governance Codes.

until 2012 as far as the controlling shareholder is concerned.[197] The European Recommendation in its Annex II enumerates eight situations (without excluding others) in which independence may not exist. The conflict of interest situations are indeed so manifold that enumerations may help to exemplify the problem, but they are unsatisfactory if conclusive. Insofar, a general clause that leaves room for interpretation by the courts is more effective.[198] Sometimes it is clear that even the mere appearance of a conflict of interest creates distrust of the share-holders and should be avoided.[199] On the other hand, the conflict of interest must be financial as opposed to merely emotional,[200] though here there are also border-line cases, such as more reputation or societal functions.

The *techniques* to deal with conflicts of interest differ considerably. The old rule is to avoid the conflict of interest entirely, such as by a *substantive* prohibition rule. For example, self-dealing—a special conflict situation treated in more detail below—would be forbidden irrespective of possible good reasons for it. As to appointment decisions, a similarly strict rule requires that certain or even all positions in key committees be reserved for independent directors. Yet as far as transactions are concerned, the strict prohibition or exclusion of conflict of interest is not practicable. Therefore, *procedural* techniques have been developed. As a minimum, conflicts of interest have to be disclosed. Disclosure is usually to the board or, as a more strict solution, to the shareholders, either in the general assembly and/or in the annual report. Yet mere disclosure is usually considered insufficient—authorisation may be required. Here again the solutions differ: Normally authorisation is by the board (as a whole or only by the independent directors) and sometimes authorisation is by the general assembly (*ex ante* or, as in the United Kingdom, *ex post*; 'whitewash' in Italy). In its Action 2012 the European Commission announced an initiative aimed at improving shareholders' control over related-party transactions, possibly through an amendment to the shareholders' rights Directive.[201] The requirement of calling in outsiders is more

---

[197] This was true only as far as the independence of the directors is concerned; the conflict as such is dealt with by the German law on groups. As to the 2010 version, see notes 120 and 121, but see now the 2013 version, above n. 125.

[198] Cf. the Dutch Supreme Court in the *Bruil* case of 29 June 2007 and the provisions of the new Dutch law on management and supervision as of 2013, R.G.J. Nowak, sec. 3.1.3(a), p. 479 et seq.

[199] For Sweden, R. Skog and E. Sjöman, sec. 3.1.3(a), p. 639: 'appearance of propriety'.

[200] For Belgium, K. Geens, sec. 3.1.3(a), p. 141. Cf. K.J. Hopt, 'Self-Dealing and the Use of Corporate Opportunities and Information: Regulating Directors' Conflict of Interest', in K.J. Hopt and G. Teubner, eds., *Corporate Governance and Directors' Liabilities*, Berlin/New York 1985, p. 285 at 314 et seq.

[201] European Commission, Action Plan (above n. 28), point 3.2 and Annex.

severe (for example, the statutory auditor as in Belgium), as is asking for the fairness opinion of an independent expert (as in Switzerland and Italy).[202]

Particular problems arise as to whether the conflicted directors may *continue to make decisions* in the company. There are various degrees of incapacitation. The interested director may not participate in the decision of the board on the approval of the conflicted transaction. This is clear-cut. According to some views, the director may also not participate in the discussion on this matter. In more severe cases of conflict of interest, the interested director must abstain from the conflicted activity more broadly; for example, the director cannot serve on the board of a competitor of the company. If the conflict is serious and permanent, there is no other way for the director than stepping down or being ousted.[203]

These general definitions, rules, and techniques may be modified for *specific situations*. Three of these are covered below: related-party transactions, corporate opportunities, and inside information. But there are others, including *institutional conflicts of interest*, which by definition cannot or need not be avoided. One example is the conflicts of interest for representatives of labour, and even more so for trade union representatives in the board.[204] Another example is multiple directorships by part-time directors.[205] But less complicated conflict of interest situations may also arise for which there may be special rules. Examples are *loans* to a director, which in many jurisdictions are prohibited or need special authorisation by the whole board. Another example is *sideline jobs* of a director, which again must be authorised by the board, either because (executive) directors

---

[202] In Belgium related-party transactions between a controlling shareholder and its listed company are dealt with by a committee of three independent directors and an independent expert, K. Geens, sec. 3.1.3(b), p. 142. This is not necessary for conflicts of interest of directors. For Switzerland, see P. Böckli, sec. 3.1.3(c), p. 690; for Italy, see G. Ferrarini et al., sec. 3.1.3.2., p. 400. On fairness opinions more generally, see H. Fleischer, 'Die Fairness Opinion bei M&A-Transaktionen zwischen Markt und Recht', in: S. Grundmann et al., *Festschrift für Klaus J. Hopt zum 70. Geburtstag*, vol. 2, Berlin 2008, p. 2753.

[203] Cf. the Swiss Corporate Governance Code para. 16 subpara. 2 (second sentence), P. Böckli, sec. 3.1.3(c), p. 690; similarly for Germany K.J. Hopt, 'Interessenwahrung und Interessenkonflikte im Aktien-, Bank- und Berufsrecht, Zur Dogmatik des modernen Geschäftsbesorgungsrecht', *Zeitschrift für Unternehmens- und Gesellschaftsrecht* 2004, 1 at 31 et seq.; idem, 'Prävention und Repression von Interessenkonflikten im Aktien-, Bank- und Berufsrecht', in: *Festschrift für Peter Doralt*, Vienna 2004, p. 213 et seq.

[204] For example, if the board deals with labour conditions, if a labour representative takes part in a strike against the company, or if the trade union member organises the strike, etc. See K.J. Hopt, n. 203, *Zeitschrift für Unternehmens- und Gesellschaftsrecht* 2004, 1 at 35 et seq.; M. Roth, Book Review, *Zeitschrift für das gesamte Handels- und Wirtschaftsrecht* 173 (2009) 717 at 720 et seq.

[205] For example, if transactions between the two companies take place, or if one is a bank of which the company is a client, or if a takeover takes place between the two companies. See K.J. Hopt, 'Takeovers, Secrecy and Conflicts of Interest: Problems for Boards and Banks', in: J. Payne, ed., *Takeovers in English and German Law*, Oxford 2002, p. 33.

should give their full capacity for work to the company or because conflicts of interest may arise. The latter is particularly true if the other employing company is a competitor; in that case, working for it is usually prohibited. If the businesses only overlap to a small extent, the board may or may not authorise the service contract with the other company. The latter cases are usually specifically dealt with in the contract of the director, for example, by a no-competition clause as reported from many countries such as Germany, Switzerland, and Poland.

The whole area of regulation of conflicts of interest is in flux. Traditionally, the civil law countries concentrated more on the duty of care, while the United Kingdom, the United States, and other common law countries have always been more rigid regarding conflicts of interest of directors.[206] More recently the attitude has also been changing in the continental European countries, partly because of more case law and partly because of new legislation. The European Commission is aware of and about to regulate the conflicts of interest of directors.[207] In 2011 the German Corporate Governance Commission declared that one of its main focuses for 2012 would be conflicts of interest and, as mentioned before, the new version of the rule in the Code as of 2013 is stricter. This raises the question why this was different to begin with and why this has now begun to change and converge. One hypothesis is again the different shareholder structures. In a system with dispersed ownership, the basic principal–agent conflict is between the shareholders and the board. The former trust the latter only if conflicts of interest are dealt with satisfactorily. If there are controlling shareholders, detailed conflicts of interest rules for the board are less relevant for the minority and outside shareholders than protection against the majority. For this protection, special rules restraining controlling shareholders (whether acting as shareholders or directors) or an outright law of groups are needed. With increasingly dispersed ownership and the rise of institutional investors in continental European countries, the attention given to directors' conflicts of interest is also rising. Additional factors play a role, including the general influx of Anglo-American legal practice in the process of internationalisation.[208]

---

[206] But in the limited liability company, the conflict of interest rule for the manager (whose equivalent in the stock corporation is the management board) was always more apparent and more strictly regulated.

[207] Cf. European Commission, Green Paper, *Corporate governance in financial institutions and remuneration policies*, Brussels 2 June 2010, COM(2010) 284 final sub 3.1.: The question of conflicts of interest. Cf. also Report of the Reflection Group, above n. 160, ch. 4: Groups of companies.

[208] J. von Hein, *Die Rezeption US-amerikanischen Gesellschaftsrechts in Deutschland*, Tübingen 2008; P. Böckli, 'Osmosis of Anglo-Saxon Concepts in Swiss Business Law', in: *Festschrift für Thomas Bär und Robert Karrer*, Zurich 1997, p. 9 et seq. For the 2013 version, see above n.125.

Related-party transactions and self-dealing—Related-party transactions constitute a specific group of conflicts of interest. In a broad sense, related-party transactions comprise the appropriation of corporate opportunities by a director as
well as securities transactions by a director on the basis of inside information
obtained from the company.[209] In economic terms this is indeed so, but corporate
opportunities present special problems, and insider dealing is not confined to
directors. Accordingly, both are treated here separately from related-party transactions. The prototype of related-party transactions by directors is *self-dealing,* ie.
transactions between the director and the director's company. These transactions
may be direct or indirect, either by a go-between or in the context of a group of
companies. The definitions vary; sometimes they are shaped after or refer to
groups of company rules or international accounting standards (IAS).[210] The
principal–agent conflict in such transactions is particularly striking because the
director acts on both sides, thereby putting the director in a position in which he
as an incentive to shape the price and the contractual conditions in his own interest to the detriment of the shareholders.

The *techniques* used are very different. In some countries such as the
Netherlands[211] the need for special rules apart from conflicts of interest is denied
completely; in other countries there are rules in the Corporate Governance Code
or at the stock exchanges.[212] In virtually all jurisdictions there must be full disclosure to the whole board. This is easy and low-cost but open to mutual back
scratching.[213] Therefore, in the United Kingdom approval by the shareholders is
required in four cases: For substantial property transactions, for loans to directors,
and for two cases relating to the remuneration of directors. However, the Listing
Rules go further and require shareholder approval for all related-party transactions. In some countries such as Belgium[214] and Italy[215] the fairness rules, both
procedural and substantive, are so much stricter and detailed that it may be
appropriate to give a flavour of this even in this general report. In Italy there must
be full transparency, not only to the board but also to the shareholders. The board
that authorises the transaction must follow a strict procedure; in particular, it must
act on the advice of a committee consisting of a majority of independent
directors. For transactions of greater importance, all members must be indepen-

---

[209] See, for example, L. Enriques, G. Hertig and H. Kanda, in R. Kraakman et al., above
n. 2, p. 154.

[210] For example, Italy, G. Ferrarini et al., sec. 3.1.3.2, p. 400 et seq.

[211] This is the position of the Dutch government in response to the Green Paper of the
European Commission on corporate governance. See R.G.J. Nowak, sec. 3.1.3(b), p. 480.

[212] For Sweden, R. Skog and E. Sjöman, sec. 3.1.3(b), p. 639.

[213] P. Davies, sec. 3.1.3, p. 749.

[214] K. Geens, sec. 3.1.3(b), p. 142 et seq.

[215] G. Ferrarini et al., sec. 3.1.3.2, p. 400 et seq.

dent. The committee has the right (in Belgium it is required) to be assisted at company expense by outside independent experts; it must motivate its decision by pointing out the interest of the company in the relevant transaction and the substantive fairness of the deal. In Italy, in transactions of greater importance the opinion of the committee is binding on the board. In Belgium, the statutory auditors must certify the correctness of the factual information on which the advice of the committee and the decision of the board are based. The result of so many procedural obstacles may finally be the same as a substantive prohibition.

As the practice in various countries shows, regulating the self-dealing of directors is particularly relevant in two cases. First, self-dealing between directors and the company seems to happen more frequently *in smaller companies,* such as the limited liability company (GmbH) in Germany, probably because of the more personalised relations there. At least case law is clearly less rare for such companies. Second, self-dealing is frequent but less transparent *in groups of companies,* not only between the different companies belonging to the group, but also as far as contracts with directors in the group are concerned. In countries with a more developed law of groups such as Germany, related-party transactions—both by member companies and by members of the organs of the various group members—are covered by special group law provisions. For example, the transaction must be at arms' length and must be disclosed in the group dependence report. Yet enforcement and effectiveness are not beyond doubt.[216]

There seems to be a *tendency toward more strictness* vis-à-vis related-party transactions and self-dealing. In some countries, specific rules have been set up by the supervisory agency; in some other countries, company law reform will come up with stricter rules. It is to be noted that the reforms have been of an essentially procedural character rather than focused on court review of the fairness of the transaction. If fairness review plays a part in the procedure, it is provided by outside professionals, for example, investment banks. Although effective courts or other bodies are required to enforce the strengthened procedures, that role is less demanding for them than substantive review of fairness. The procedural bias of the European reforms, even in the UK, may reflect a traditional reluctance to give such open-ended tasks to courts and thus the failure of courts to emerge which have an expertise in this activity.[217]

Corporate opportunities—Corporate opportunity is a different conflict of interest. While in self-dealing the director enters into a transaction with the director's company, in a corporate opportunity situation the director takes away from the company and for the director a business opportunity that 'belongs' to the company. Among the conflict of interest situations, it is the clearest case of misap-

---

[216] See, for example, Italy: G. Ferrrarini et al., sec. 3.1.3.2(e), p. 405.

[217] Cf. R. Gilson and A. Schwartz, *Constraints on Private Benefits of Control: Ex Ante Control Mechanisms Versus Ex Post Transaction Review,* ECGI—Law Working Paper 194/2012.

propriation or even outright 'theft' by the director. Of course, it is not theft in the technical sense of criminal law, and its contours are controversial.

A corporate opportunity is usually *not defined* by written law. In many countries, such as Belgium, Sweden, or Poland, there is no rule against the use of corporate opportunities, though there are transparency rules, as in Belgium, and sometimes there is recent doctrine and occasional case law. Also, in European countries where the corporate opportunity doctrine is established, such as Germany, the Netherlands and Spain, this has been developed only relatively late and by case law. The reasons for this may be similar to those mentioned above for the duty of loyalty and conflicts of interest in general. But an additional reason may be that here the fact patterns are manifold, and more factual inquiry and flexible reactions by the courts may be needed.

The *technique* used for dealing with corporate opportunities is for once clear-cut. Disclosure alone is not enough. Approval by the board is necessary and usually sufficient; consent by the shareholders is an exception. In the United Kingdom this is the default rule for public companies. If the rules are more sophisticated, interested directors may not vote, as stated by law and partly by listing rules as in the United Kingdom. The *sanction* is also clear. If a corporate opportunity has been appropriated by the director for himself or herself, the company has a damage claim. In addition, the company may have the right to require the director to hand over the product of his or her disloyal action to the company, as in Switzerland, at least in theory, or even suffer outright disgorgement of all personal profit, as in Germany and the UK. The latter sanction gives to the company more than it would have had if it had made use of the opportunity itself, and even more than if it had decided not to make use of it at all. But this overreaching sanction is known to both common and civil law and is intended to work as a deterrent.

As seen for self-dealing, the practical relevance of the corporate opportunity rule appears foremost in two cases: in *smaller companies* as with the German GmbH, and in *groups of companies*, even though in the latter the problems are less the appropriation of a corporate opportunity by directors to themselves than the attribution of corporate opportunities by the parent to itself or other members of the group. In these cases, fair appropriation should be dealt with by special group law provisions finding the right balance between the interest and expectation of the parties involved and the need for a consistent group policy by the parent, *inter alia* for tax reasons, cheaper production possibilities, and similar considerations.

Also in the case of corporate opportunities, a *certain tendency toward more strictness* is perceptible. It is reported that United Kingdom case law is even stricter than in the United States.[218] Yet this tendency is not so clear as in the other cases of conflict of interest; it is perceptible only in certain countries, and in particular by courts that may have to face hard cases. It is true that hard cases make bad law, but sometimes one has the impression that the court may not have fully evaluated the economic consequences of a strict decision. In Germany, for example, the Federal Court of Justice (*Bundesgerichtshof*) had to decide a case in which the manager of a GmbH was an expert in a particular area and worked as a director in this business for a company. He got an offer to open his own business in the field together with a partner who promised to bring in the capital. The manager terminated his contract correctly and started the new company. The *Bundesgerichtshof* overturned the decision of the court of appeals and held that this was a corporate opportunity of the company and that the ex-director had to disgorge his profit.[219] Whether or not this case was decided correctly, extending the doctrine of corporate opportunities too far may have undesired economic consequences, such as tying the director too strongly to the company, hampering new start-ups, and stifling competition and innovation.

Inside information—Insider law is an important and broad part of capital markets law today that goes far beyond the prohibition of insider dealing by board members, though originally the latter was at the heart of the insider dealing problem. This was the case in the United States, where insider law started before spreading all over Europe and beyond. When the European Union started to introduce insider dealing provisions, it first started with a proposal for the European Company to prohibit insider dealing by the directors of such a company. But today board members—like many other persons inside and outside the company—are prohibited from using inside information by acquiring or disposing of, for their own account or for the account of a third party, financial instruments to which that information relates.[220] Therefore, this specific conflict of interest will not be covered here in more detail. Three short observations concerning the board must suffice.

Firstly, the economic thesis brought forward by Manne and others and still maintained by some economists[221] today that board members should be allowed to engage in insider trading is unconvincing. Allowing insider trading by com-

---

[218] Cf. the case *Bhullar v. Bhullar*, [2003] 2 BCLC 2241, CA.; P. Davies, sec. 3.1.3, p. 747 text at n. 116.

[219] Bundesgerichtshof, 23 September 1985, *Neue Juristische Wochenschrift* 1986, 585 as to Court of Appeals of Stuttgart. It must be disclosed that at that time Hopt was a part-time judge in the lower court and referee of this case. Cf. the extensive UK law on this topic permitting directors to take preliminary steps towards setting up a competing business whilst in office but not to initiate it. See P. Davies and S. Worthington, above n. 6, Section 16-170.

[220] Taken from the proposal for a European Regulation on insider dealing and market manipulation (market abuse) of 20 October 2011 Art. 7 para 1.

[221] J. Macey, *Corporate Governance*, Princeton/Oxford 2008.

pany insiders to bring out information to the public is second best to outright disclosure rules as they exist today all over Europe as part of the market abuse regime of the European Union. Under certain circumstances—for example, if negative information is dealt upon and the market is misled—such an incentive may even become perverse. It is also not true that the possibility of making insider profits as part of the remuneration of directors is a proper incentive. Because of its uncertainty, it never really was.

Secondly, insider trading has negative effects for the market since it adds to the costs of the transaction because the market intermediaries will make up for the risk of insider trading by raising the spread of their offers. The insider laws of most countries, as well as the listing rules of the stock exchanges and code provisions, react against this danger by the prohibition of insider dealing and severe sanctions. Today these sanctions are criminal sanctions in the United States and in most of the Member States of the European Union as well as in Switzerland.[222] While the existence and nature of civil sanctions—for example, liability for damages—is controversial and there are very few civil law cases of insider trading, there is agreement on the specific sanctions for board members. By insider dealing they violate their duties to obey the law, they may break board secrecy, and under certain circumstances they may inflict actual damage on their company.[223] The usual civil law sanctions apply in cases of board member liability, including damages, disgorgement of profit, and dismissal from office. But it is true that there are a high number of undetected violations and that serious difficulties of enforcement exist as in other cases of white-collar criminality. Spectacular recent insider cases in the United States and elsewhere may just be the tip of the iceberg, though draconian prison sentences may have a deterrent effect.

Thirdly, the real problems of inside information of board members are not so much the prohibition against using inside information by the directors themselves or persons close to them; this prohibition is generally accepted. They are the requirement by law and stock exchange rules to disclose inside information as soon as possible, and certain restrictions on passing on inside information even to major shareholders and third parties. The requirement to disclose inside information as soon as possible has continuously been extended, even to situations where the transaction is still pending and the supervisory board has not yet given its consent.[224] This is, of course, very difficult for companies to handle. On the

---

[222] See now the proposal of a European directive on criminal sanctions for insider dealing and market manipulation of 20 October 2011, COM(2011) 654 final.

[223] Cf. the famous case *Diamond v. Oreamuno* 248 N.E. 2d 910, 24 N.Y. 2d 494, 301 N.Y.S. 2d 78 (1969).

[224] The European Court of Justice will have to decide this in the pending *Daimler* case, which the *Bundesgerichtshof* referred to in 2011. The problem is mitigated by the fact that under the present law the company is allowed under certain narrow circumstances and under its own responsibility to postpone the disclosure if the transaction is still pending. The actual
cont. ...

other hand, passing on inside information to major shareholders before important decisions, and to potential investors in M&A, takeover, and rescue situations, may be rendered more difficult by insider law.[225] The practice works with confidentiality agreements but faces legal uncertainties. As will be mentioned for takeover regulation below, the rules on inside information and early disclosure should not be construed as impeding shareholder engagement[226] and useful projects and transactions of the company, though they tend to do so.

Takeovers—Similar to insider dealing law, the regulation of takeovers has become a very important part of capital markets law.[227] Even though there are many duties of the board—both of the bidder company and much more so of the target company, and not only during the takeover but also before and afterwards[228]—these duties cannot be described here because this cannot be done seriously without the full context of takeover law. Again, two observations concerning the board under the heads of accountability must suffice. One concerns board neutrality, or more precisely the prohibition for the board of the target to frustrate a bid; the other relates to the mandatory opinion of the board of the target company for its shareholders.

As a frequent consequence of a takeover, in particular a hostile takeover, the management of the target is replaced by a new management team. This threat is a powerful incentive for directors to avoid this, either by sound performance that would drive up the stock price and make takeovers more costly and less probable, or by defensive actions either before or at least during the takeover bid period. Takeovers are therefore an important instrument of accountability of the board. This instrument may be more important than the possibility of removal because of the collective action problem mentioned above,[229] and more important than the duties of care and loyalty that may be enforced finally only by lengthy lawsuits

relevance and meaning of the ECJ's decision is highly controversial, cf. for example M. Nelemans and M. Schouten, *Takeover Bids and Insider Trading*, August 2012, available at <http://ssrn.com/abstract=21473960>; L. Klöhn, 'Das deutsche und europäische Insiderrecht nach dem Geltl-Urteil des EuGH', *Zeitschrift für Wirtschaftsrecht* 2012, 1885; G. Bachmann, 'Ad-hoc-Publizität nach "Geltl"', *Der Betrieb* 2012, 2206.

[225] Cf. for Switzerland P. Böckli, sec. 3.1.3(e), p. 692 et seq.

[226] P. Davies, sec. 3.1.3, p. 747 et seq.

[227] P. Davies and K.J. Hopt, in R. Kraakman et al., above n. 2, ch. 8 on Control Transactions.

[228] For example, K.J. Hopt, 'The Duties of the Directors of the Target Company in Hostile Takeovers – German and European Perspectives', in: G. Ferrarini, K.J. Hopt and E. Wymeersch, eds., *Capital Markets in the Age of the Euro – Cross-Border Transactions, Listed Companies and Regulation*, The Hague et al. 2002, p. 391.

[229] See above, *sec.* 3.1.1.

with an insecure outcome.[230] According to some observers, the disciplining force of takeovers can even be considered 'the most effective corporate governance mechanism.'[231] It is therefore hardly surprising that the question of what defences are allowed against takeovers is most controversial in all countries. Usually the board can arrange defensive actions relatively freely before the takeover. But frustrating an upcoming or pending bid is forbidden by the anti-frustration rule in the United Kingdom and some other countries, including Switzerland and—with the exception of reciprocity—France and Spain. This rule requires mandatory shareholder approval for frustrating actions after the bid is made or is imminent. The European Commission was not able to introduce a similar rule in the 13th Directive on a mandatory basis, but had to allow the Member States to opt out of the board neutrality rule as well as of the encompassing breakthrough rule and to introduce a reciprocity exception. This is what many Member States chose. As a consequence, boards in Germany, the Netherlands, Belgium, Poland, and other countries have wide possibilities for shielding themselves from being held accountable by means of unfriendly takeovers.[232] In takeover situations, the target board will often form a coalition with labour because the interest of the directors to stay in office and the interest of labour not to be subject to restructuring lay-offs often run parallel. This effect is enforced if there is labour co-determination in the board. Seeking a white knight always remains possible, but usually the board of the target company retains broad discretion to pass on relevant information only to the white knight while holding it back from the bidder. The Dutch Code provides that if a competitive bidder requests the management to give information on the company, it has to discuss this request with the supervisory board immediately. In Switzerland and the UK competitive bidders have to be treated alike. This has the effect of strengthening the accountability of the board.

In case of a takeover bid, the target board has the right and duty to give its opinion on the bid and the reasons for it, including its views on the effects of the bid on all the company's interests, specifically employment.[233] This is perfectly

---

[230]   P. Davies, sec. 3.1.3, p. 747.

[231]   J. Macey, *Corporate Governance, loc. cit.*, p. 40 table 3.1 as to the effective and not-so-effective mechanisms. See also the list given by the High Level Group of Company Law Experts, *Report on Issues Related to Takeover Bids*, European Commission, Brussels 10 January 2002, Annex 4: Overview of most important barriers to takeover bids. Cf. also K.J. Hopt, *Europäisches Übernahmerecht*, Tübingen 2013, p. 230 et seq.

[232]   P. Davies et al., 'The Takeover Directive as a Protectionist Tool?', in: U. Bernitz and W.G. Ringe, eds., *Company Law and Economic Protectionism*, Oxford 2010, p. 105. But see now the German Corporate Governance Code (2013 version), no. 3.7 last para: 'In the case of a takeover offer, the Management Board should convene an extraordinary General Meeting at which shareholders discuss the takeover offer and may decide on corporate actions.'

[233]   Art. 9 para 5 of the 13th Directive. Particular problems arise for two-tier boards and regarding dissenting views of individual board members.

legitimate under the accountability perspective as well, because as mentioned initially, the board is the trustee of the shareholders, and possibly labour and other stakeholders. This opinion may be tainted by self-interest, but this must be taken into account; it is mitigated by the fact that reasons must be given. It is up to the shareholders and their intermediaries to judge the conflicting views of the target and the bidder boards.

One of the reasons for the fundamentally different policies described above is again shareholder constituency. In the United Kingdom, with its dispersed share-holders, institutional investors play a primary role in the development and satis-factory practice of the anti-frustration rule. In countries where families and con-trolling shareholders in groups of companies prevail, institutional shareholders have a much lesser role, although it is increasing. It is true that controlling share-holders and block-holders are much less threatened by unfriendly takeovers, which may explain why the anti-frustration rule exists without much ado even in some continental European countries with strong block-holders, such as Spain. But still they have an interest in keeping the directors they have chosen directly or indirectly in office. So in many continental European countries, the British rule is not very much in vogue. This is particularly so in the wake of the financial crisis, which has led to a wave of protectionism, as shown by the example of Italy with its three successive different versions of the anti-frustration rule.[234] The actual situation of takeovers as an instrument of accountability of the board is therefore the result of difficult tensions between industry, labour, government, regulators, and the financial press. Under these circumstances, the pending reform of the 13th Directive cannot be expected to take up this problem, and even less so to replace the present option and reciprocity system by the British anti-frustration rule.[235]

3.1.4. *Institutional Investors*

As seen before in many countries, accountability of the board by the threat of takeovers is reduced considerably because of the many defences that may legally be installed. But even where takeovers are frequent, they primarily concern only listed companies. Even more relevant, they concern not only those in which the directors are doing a bad job, but also others where the company is flourishing. Therefore, the attention of corporate governance and the accountability of the board has recently again centred on the shareholders to watch over the board. While the controlling shareholder and also the block-holders have their own incen-

---

[234] G. Ferrarini et al., sec. 3.1.3.5, p. 406 et seq.

[235] As is clear from the Commission's response to the review of the operation of the Direc-tive which it commissioned (COM(2012) 347 final). See K.J. Hopt, 'Stand der Harmonisierung der europäischen Übernahmerechte', in P.O. Mülbert et al., eds., *10 Jahre Wertpapiererwerbs-und Übernahmegesetz* (WpÜG), Frankfurt 2011, p. 42; *idem, Europäisches Übernahmerecht*, Tübingen 2013, above n. 231.

tive to monitor the board, in companies with dispersed shareholding the only shareholders to be called on are the institutional investors, since rational apathy prevails for the other shareholders.[236] In some countries like the United Kingdom, institutional shareholders make up a clear majority of the shareholders of listed companies, while since the 1960s individual share ownership has dropped from 50 per cent to under 20 per cent.[237] Institutional shareholding is also prevalent in some other European countries, such as Sweden with 85 per cent of the total share-holding in listed companies,[238] in France with 40 per cent of the CAC 40 com-panies,[239] and similarly for the top-tier Swiss listed companies. In other European countries, institutional investment is still lagging behind because of special factors: In Italy because of prevailing block-holder control[240] and in Germany in particular because of labour's dependence on the state old age retirement and pension system rather than on its own saving and investing. Yet in many DAX 30 companies, foreign shareholding, and in particular foreign institutional shareholding, is very considerable—for example in Deutsche Börse AG, where the large private German banks sold out their shareholdings some years ago under a changed tax system. More generally, the Rhineland capitalism with its close intertwining of German industry and banks has been disappearing over the years. However, these figures and statistics should be read with caution because they group together the different kinds of institutional investors that may have very different short-term or long-term investment policies.[241] Institutional investors may be pension funds such as CalPERS (California Public Employees' Retirement System), insurance com-panies, mutual funds (UCITs), sovereign wealth funds, and banks. Typical insti-tutional investors hardly ever hold larger blocks. Usually they stay with only up to five per cent, but they may combine forces for the purpose of influencing the companies in which they have invested. Their investment horizon is traditionally not short-term, though more recently there has also been a trend for institutional

---

[236] On institutional shareholders, see the introductory remarks in R. Kraakman et al., above n. 2, p. 83, 92,106, 108, 181 et seq.

[237] See the tables in D. Prentice, 'The United Kingdom', in: S. Bruno and E. Ruggiero, eds., *Public Companies and the Role of Shareholders*, Alphen aan den Rijn 2011, p. 197 at 206 et seq.: B. Cheffins, *Ownership and Control: British Business Transformed*, Oxford 2008; R. Crespi-Cladera and L. Renneboog, *Corporate Monitoring by Shareholder Coalitions in the UK*, ECGI Finance Working Paper No. 12/2003. In the US, institutional shareholders already held 61.2% of the whole share capital in 2005: The Conference Board, *U.S. Institutional Investors Continue to Boost Ownership of U.S. Corporations*, 22 January 2007.

[238] R. Skog and E. Sjöman, sec. 3.1.4, p. 641.

[239] For France, see A. Pietrancosta et al., sec. 3.1.4, p. 217.

[240] G. Ferrarini et al., sec. 3.1.4, p. 407 et seq.

[241] P. Davies, sec. 5(b), p. 781 et seq. See also for Belgium, K. Geens, sec. 3.1.4, p. 148 et seq.; for the Netherlands, R.G.J. Nowak, sec. 3.1.4, p. 484 et seq.; for Switzerland, P. Böckli, sec. 3.1.4, p. 695 et seq.

investors to have shorter time horizons in their investment policies. This is different on the one side from private equity, which is clearly longer term with an exit policy of between three to five years, and on the other side activist hedge funds,[242] with a special business model that is clearly short-term, looking for a quick rise of the stock price and immediate exit afterward.

The United Kingdom has been the first country to try to activate institutional shareholders for taking up a role in the internal corporate governance of companies.[243] The Stewardship Code, which stems from the Financial Reporting Council, recommends on a comply-or-explain basis that institutional investors take an active role by developing a policy on intervention in portfolio companies (not just in relation to voting but including active steps to change management policy and remove recalcitrant directors), and reporting periodically on their stewardship and voting activities. Other countries, such as France,[244] have followed or are considering following this path and are putting pressure on the institutional investors, though up to now legislatures have not yet enacted mandatory legal rules. They have only threatened to do so if disclosure and self-regulation do not work.[245] As to the practice of many institutional investors to rely for their own voting on the advice of proxy advising firms, legislative intervention is on the way in the European Union and several European countries,[246] although others, like Switzerland, have begun to try self-regulation.

Whether the hopes placed in institutional investors as active shareholders to play an important role in holding directors accountable will materialise is still open to doubt. Traditionally there have been special rules only for controlling or major shareholders, especially in group law. But as institutional investors hold

---

[242] Cf. J. Armour and B. Cheffins, *The Rise and Fall (?) of Shareholder Activism by Hedge Funds*, ECGI Law Working Paper No. 136/2009.

[243] See P. Davies, sec. 3.1.4, p. 752 et seq. The Stewardship Code is available at <http://www.frc.org.uk/corporate/investorgovernance.cfm>. Cf. P. Davies and S. Worthington, above n. 6, §§ 15–25 et seq., 15–30; B. Cheffins, 'The Stewardship Code's Achilles' Heel', *Modern Law Review* 73 (2010) 1004; D. Arsalidou, 'Shareholders and Corporate Scrutiny: the Role of the UK Stewardship Code', (2012) 9 *European Company and Financial Law Review* 342.

[244] A. Pietrancosta et al., sec. 3.1.4, p. 217. For the Netherlands, see R.G.J. Nowak, sec. 3.1.4, p. 484 et seq. For Belgium, see K. Geens, sec. 3.1.4, p. 148 et seq. For Spain, A. Recalde Castells et al., sec. 3.1.4, p. 599: legal rules for mandatory voting in listed companies, but not always effective.

[245] For example, in the United Kingdom, the Companies Act 2006 contains a reserve power for the government; see P. Davies, sec. 3.1.4, p. 755. Cf. also European Commission, Green Paper, above n. 31, at 164 sub 2.3 and 2.4 as to institutional investors, and European Commission, Action Plan 2012 (above n. 28), point 2.4 and Annex: Disclosure of voting and engagement policies as well as voting records by institutional investors, possibly to be integrated in the Shareholders' Rights Directive.

[246] *Idem* sub 2.5. Proxy advisors. See also as to Switzerland, P. Böckli, sec. 3.1.4(a), p. 695.

only small blocks of shares, these rules are not applicable; worse, other rules work as an obstacle for more activism, such as the concerted actions rule under the disclosure and takeover regime of the European Union, as well as in Switzerland. In addition, the prudential rules for insurance companies and investment funds to behave as prudent investors, to pay minimum interest and, in the case of open funds, to take back the shares at any time set an incentive to these institutions to follow the market and not to do worse than the market, rather than being criticised if activism does not pay out. The most relevant point is the lack of incentive for institutional investors to become active, because this implies costs. They lack manpower, and if they have a large portfolio—sometimes many hundreds of different investments—economically it may just not make sense for them to become active in all these companies.[247] It is doubtful whether the incentives that are discussed make a substantial change, such as double voting rights for more long-term shareholders as they exist in France and are considered by the European Commission, or similar measures such as bonuses for attending the general assembly or loyalty dividends. Therefore, while there is clearly a rise of activism on the part of institutional investors in many countries, high expectations that their accountability problems can be solved by better self-regulation, or even by turning self-regulation into hard law of disclosure and similar duties, may turn out not to be well-founded.

3.1.5. Remuneration (as Incentive)

Remuneration of directors and officers is a hot topic in many European countries, though the excesses known from the United States and the United Kingdom have not yet spilled over into many continental European countries. The starting point is that many corporate governance codes, for example in the UK, positively recommend a substantial element of variable pay in directors' remuneration and the linking of the amount of that payment to the achievement of shareholder-oriented goals. There is, of course, no legal obligation on the company to remunerate its directors in this way. The codes' perspective is that of remuneration as an incentive to induce directors to promote the interests of the shareholders. However, following a public outcry in many countries over the distributional consequences of this approach (excessive remuneration, in particular over exorbitant exit pay), most recently in Switzerland, recent reforms of corporate law and codes have been enacted to place limits (usually procedural) on the make-up of directors' remuneration packages. The pros, cons, and ways of directors' remuneration have been discussed at length in economic and legal literature.[248] Many of these

---

[247] As to these issues, see for the United Kingdom, P. Davies, sec. 3.1.5, p. 758 et seq.

[248] G. Ferrarini, N. Moloney and M. C. Ungureanu, *Understanding Directors' Pay in Europe: A Comparative and Empirical Analysis*, ECGI Law Working Paper No. 126/2009; G. Ferrarini et al., 'Executive Remuneration in Crisis: A Critical Assessment of Reforms in

cont. ...

remuneration reforms have had a strong populist bent—but also a distributional and societal side (societal cohesion and trust in the economic system)—that goes beyond board and company law concerns. For all these reasons, the board remuneration problem is treated here only succinctly under the aspect of remuneration as an incentive for directors. Remuneration as a positive incentive—traditionally stock options to align the interest both of the company and the directors in performance and higher stock price of the company's shares—supplements the measures already discussed for holding directors accountable, most of which work with negative incentives. However, if variable remuneration is not aligned with the interests of the shareholders, and in some jurisdictions also the other stakeholders, remuneration may work as a perverse incentive.[249]

Remuneration rules can cope with the incentive problem, both negative and positive, by using *two basic techniques:* By changing the competence for deciding on remuneration; and by rules for the structure, content, or limits of remuneration. As to the first, under the traditional arrangements remuneration of the managing board members in the two-tier board is decided upon by the supervisory board, while in the one-tier system the board decides on the remuneration of officers. Remuneration of the executive members of the board is decided by the remuneration committee alone or the full board; in companies with a controlling shareholder, it is decided indirectly by that controlling shareholder. Only for stock options and the like is the general assembly responsible because of the danger of dilution of the shares.[250] Since remuneration is mainly a problem for the management board members viz. the executive directors, the problem is one of the board not living up to the expectation of the legislatures and the general public.

Europe', *Journal of Corporate Law Studies* 10 (2010) 73; Y. Hausmann and E. Bechtold-Orth, 'Changing Remuneration Systems in Europe and the United States – A Legal Analysis of Recent Developments in the Wake of the Financial Crisis', 11 *European Business Organization Law Review* 195 (2010); R. Thomas and J. Hill, eds., *Research Handbook on Executive Pay*, Elgar 2012; L. Enriques, H. Hansmann and R. Kraakman, in R. Kraakman et al., above n. 2, p. 75 et seq. For figures, see Heidrick & Struggles, *European Corporate Governance Report 2011, Challenging board performance*, p. 45 et seq.

[249] During the financial crisis remuneration rules and practices for directors and officers of financial institutions contributed to the crisis. It is argued that it was the linkage to the shareholders' interests in dividends and more risk-taking that caused remuneration to operate in a perverse way in financial institutions. As a consequence of the crisis, remuneration rules for financial institutions have been considerably tightened and subjected to certain supervisory and enforcement competences of the supervisory agencies. This latter field is excluded from this study, though some spillovers are already recognisable. See the literature above, sec. 1 at the end.

[250] In the United Kingdom, two additional special cases are reserved to shareholder decision: compensation for loss of office in connection with a takeover, or transfer of a business and long-term service contracts. The Listing Rules provide shareholder approval also for long-term incentive plans (ltips). See P. Davies, sec. 3.1.5, p. 758 et seq.

Since self-regulation does not work well in this field—not even in the United Kingdom, the stronghold of self-regulation[251]—in many countries the legislatures have stepped in and made changes to the *competence* of the board. In many countries the remuneration committee[252] must comprise a majority of independent directors. This is also a recommendation of the European Commission. More recently, various countries such as Germany, Italy, and Sweden as well as the European Commission are following the British example[253] and giving the general assembly a say-on-pay,[254] so that fixing pay ceases to be prerogative of the board and its committees. However, say-on-pay typically involves only a consultative vote on the remuneration system and structures without a real competence to get down to the remuneration in individual service contracts, though there is a tendency towards a binding vote on the company's remuneration system (to be held at least at three-yearly intervals) as in the UK since 2013. In some other countries, such as France, say-on-pay is discussed but is not on the reform agenda. Interestingly enough, some minority shareholders' associations are not in favour for fear that compensation largely approved by the general assembly might be more difficult to challenge. On the contrary, in other countries, such as Switzerland, the public pressure was so strong that in the so-called *Abzocker* (rip off) referendum of the people on 3 March 2013 it was decided that the general meeting should fix the remuneration instead of a mere advisory say-on-pay.[255] This might lead to a bandwagon effect as seen already in the reform plans of the German government (right in time before the autumn election in 2013). Termination payments are seen with particular scepticism in Germany, France and the UK, for example.

---

[251] P. Davies, sec. 3.1.5, p. 759: 'an example of the failure of non-legislative rule-making'.

[252] See above, sec. 2.2.2.

[253] An annual advisory vote was introduced in the UK in 2002 on both overall executive pay policy and the remuneration of individual directors, and reforms in 2013 have introduced a three-yearly binding vote on pay policy, ie. future payments made in breach of the policy will be recoverable by the company from the payee and directors authorising such payments will be liable to the company for losses caused, even if they were not the recipients of the payments; Enterprise and Regulatory Reform Act 2013, Part 6. Even the former advisory system produced adverse shareholder votes, especially—but not only—in financial companies where shareholders (rightly) feared intrusive regulation if shareholder activism was not seen to work.

[254] In 2010 in Germany 27 of the DAX 30 companies practised the say-on-pay at the general meeting. See also M. Roth, sec. 3.1.2(c), p. 322. In Germany as well as in many other countries equity-based remuneration plans need to be approved by the general assembly. See further J. Lieder and P. Fischer, 'The Say-on-Pay Movement—Evidence from a Comparative Perspective', (2011) 8 *European Company and Financial Law Review* 376.

[255] P. Böckli, sec. 3.1.5, p. 697, and sec. 5, p. 708. As to the referendum proposal and the counterproposal of the Swiss Parliament which was voted down, see P. Forstmoser, '"Say on Pay": Die Volksinitiative "gegen die Abzockerei" und der Gegenvorschlag des Parlaments', *Schweizerische Juristen-Zeitung* 108 (2012) No. 14, p. 337.

Clawbacks exist or are discussed in many countries, including Germany, the Netherlands, and Poland. These rules are also extended to pension payments.

In most countries, there are also *substantive rules* as to directors' remuneration and the structure of the compensation packages concerning a link to performance and sometimes to sustainability. The requirements concern the following in particular: An adequate relationship between the remuneration and the tasks and performance of the director and the financial situation of the company; sometimes particular reasons for remuneration beyond the normal level of comparable companies or in the business sector; the orientation of remuneration toward the long-term development of the company (for variable remuneration elements more than a one- or two-year basis); the possibility for the board to reduce remuneration unilaterally in case of extraordinary developments; and more generally, the reduction of remuneration to an adequate level if the company gets into difficulties.[256]

The results expected from these remuneration rules and techniques and their reform were disappointing. The disclosure requirements,[257] probably the earliest reaction of law and codes, proved to have some effect, not the least of which was raising public envy. Sometimes it even had the perverse effect of driving up the overall payment level through the disclosure of individual remuneration packages. Say-on-pay also had fewer effects than expected apart from some spectacular cases in the United Kingdom, for example. This is because of the natural propensity of shareholders to more risk-taking in contrast to the risk-averseness of creditors, which is the main reason why corporate governance and creditor governance for financial institutions are fundamentally different. The role of employees in countries with labour co-determination was weak, too, in the famous German *Mannesmann* case. Not only the chairman of the board, Ackermann, but also the trade union boss waved through the high bonuses even though the takeover had already been successfully completed.[258] Maybe the technique of holding the supervisory board personally responsible for not complying with the remuneration rules may bring some help. In the parallel case of the liability of the supervisory board for not filing suit against the management board under certain conditions after the *ARAG/Garmenbeck* rule of the German Federal Court of

---

[256] All this can be found, for example, in Art. 87 of the German Stock Corporation Act (AktG) as of 31 July 2009. See also the list of the French AFEP/MEDEF Corporate Governance Code, A. Pietrancosta et al., sec. 3.1.5(a), p. 221. Cf. L. A. Bebchuk and J. M. Fried, 'Paying for Long-Term Performance', 158 *University of Pennsylvania Law Review* 1915 (2010).

[257] See, for example, the Directors' Remuneration Report as of 2006 in the United Kingdom. See also G. Ferrarini et al., sec. 3.1.5, p. 409, as to Italy.

[258] C. J. Milhaupt and K. Pistor, above n. 142, ch. 4: 'The Mannesmann Executive Compensation Trial in Germany', p. 69 et seq.

Justice (*Bundesgerichtshof*),[259] the liability suits brought by the supervisory board against members of the management board have certainly increased, in particular after the financial crisis. In sum, the problem is still unsolved, and it remains to be seen whether a more effective technique can be found, short of more radical reforms propagated by popular envy and populist reform proposals in Switzerland and other countries and in the end numerically fixed ceilings.[260]

3.2. Board and Stakeholders

3.2.1. Board and Employees

Techniques of representing employee interests in the company—Traditionally, employee interests have been taken care of by contract and labour law, either in the individual contracts between the company and the employee or collectively by collective agreements.[261] But there are also various techniques of representing employee interests in the company itself. The three main techniques are as follows: Firstly, charging the board to aim not only at the shareholders' interest but also at the interest of the employees; secondly, providing for a works council at the plant level and sometimes additionally at the group level with information, consultation, and co-determination rights; and thirdly, giving the employees a number of seats on the board.

While the classical shareholder-oriented approach still prevails in the United States[262] and in Europe—for example, in Sweden and more recently again in Belgium[263]—it is obvious that the long-term success of the company requires that the board should not neglect the interests of the employees. Many countries charge the board to do so either by law or by corporate governance code provisions, but the degree to which employee interests are to be taken into

---

[259] *BGHZ* 135, 244 = *NJW* 1997, 1926. On liability of directors and the problems of enforcing it, see K.J. Hopt, above n. 1, *The American Journal of Comparative Law* 59 (2011) 1 at 42 et seq.

[260] For Switzerland, see above, n. 255. P. Böckli, sec. 5(b), p. 710: '[…] distinct risk it will result in inadequate, burdensome and restrictive legislation.' Yet asking the board to consider the relationship between the compensation of the executives (management board) and that of senior management and the staff overall, as recommended by the German Corporate Governance Code (2013 version), no. 4.2.2 para 2, seems reasonable.

[261] In the UK, the function of employee representation has been performed by trade unions through collective bargaining, though its importance has been diminishing; P. Davies, sec. 3.2.1, p. 761.

[262] K.J. Hopt, above n. 1, *The American Journal of Comparative Law* 59 (2011) 1 at 28 et seq.

[263] For Sweden, R. Skog and E. Sjöman, sec. 3.2, p. 644; for Belgium after the Fortis takeover, K. Geens, sec. 1.1, p. 121 et seq., sec. 3.2.3, p. 154 et seq.

consideration varies. Under the enlightened shareholder approach as practised in Switzerland and even expressly provided in the UK in 2006, the board has to steer the company in the interest of the enterprise as a whole. This includes the interest of the employees, though in the takeover context the ultimate decision on the bid rests with the shareholders. But the members' interests are paramount, and there is no balancing of interests.[264] The German rule goes further. Based on the concept of the 'enterprise per se' as developed in the Weimar Republic, today it is widely agreed that the management board has to act in the interests of the enterprise, ie. the combined interests of the shareholders, the employees, and the general public. It is up to the management board to balance these interests, which gives the board wide discretion and accordingly weakens the board's account-ability.[265] Yet the limits of discretion are reached when the company gets into financial difficulties.[266] An intermediate solution has been proposed in the Netherlands: The shareholder interest normally prevails over the interest of the other stakeholders, unless these would be disproportionally harmed.[267]

The technique of charging the board with taking care of the employees' interests has a serious weakness. Under none of its various forms, including the German enterprise rule, was there a right of the employees to enforce the rule. Therefore, the second technique of installing a special body for taking care of employees' interests is more effective. Works councils are provided for in an EU directive[268] and are widely known beyond the EU Member States as well. The works council protects the interests of the employees, usually at the plant level; sometimes there is provisions for special group works councils. The formation, rights, and duties of the works council are regulated in detail in the labour law of the respective countries. While there are also individual information rights of employees, information rights and sometimes consultation rights on more general work matters such as lay-offs and pending takeovers are concentrated in the works council. Sometimes the works council has specific rights of action, such as having an expert appointed by the court to report on specific transactions.[269] In Belgium the works council has a veto right over the appointment of the external

---

[264] P. Davies and S. Worthington, above n. 6, p. 16–25 et seq.

[265] M. Roth, sec. 3.2.1(a), p. 331, but the business judgment rule is directed to the company, not the enterprise. Some authors instead favour a shareholder-value concept, eg., P. Mülbert, 'Shareholder Value aus rechtlicher Sicht', *Zeitschrift für Unternehmens- und Gesellschaftsrecht* 1997, 129, but this was before the financial crisis. Balancing of interests also in the Netherlands, R.G.J. Nowak, sec. 1.1, p. 431 et seq., and Poland, S. Sołtysiński, sec. 3.2, p. 538 et seq.

[266] M. Roth, sec. 3.2.3, p. 340.

[267] R.G.J. Nowak, sec. 1.1, p. 435.

[268] Council Directive 97/74/EC of 15 December 1997, OJ L 10/22 of 16 January 1998.

[269] Cf. for France, A. Pietrancosta et al., sec. 3.2.1, p. 224; see also for the Netherlands, R.G.J. Nowak, sec. 3.2.1, p. 489.

auditor.[270] In the Netherlands the works council of a public company has the right to give its (non-binding) opinion in the general assembly on some key decisions and has the right to make binding recommendations with respect to one-third of the supervisory board members.[271] Labour co-determination via a works council is often considered to be more important for the employees than co-determination in the board since it is more specifically geared toward labour interests.

Forms of co-determination at board level—Actual co-decision of the employees on the strategy and other matters of the company beyond immediate labour interests is provided by co-determination at the board level. Such far-reaching labour co-determination presupposes that conflicts between capital and labour can be solved within the board by information, discussion, and compromise. If there is a tradition of confrontation between the employers and the trade unions as in Italy and Spain,[272] or if there is a strong tradition of collective bargaining as in the UK,[273] or if there are other path-dependent reasons as in Belgium and Switzerland, co-determination at board level does not exist. In some other countries, in particular formerly socialist countries such as Poland,[274] it is to be found only in state enterprises and companies with state participation, ie. partially privatised companies.

The forms of co-determination at board level vary considerably. Most often the co-determination laws provide for one-third of the board to be elected by labour. This is the case for many EU Member States.[275] In some countries, such as Sweden, under certain circumstances labour gets up to two or three seats on the board.[276] A parity form of boardroom co-determination exists only in Germany and, in a co-optative form, until 2004 in the Netherlands. This might suggest that the old rules in the Netherlands provided for parity representation,

---

[270] K. Geens, sec. 3.2.1, p. 151.

[271] R.G.J. Nowak, sec. 3.2.1, p. 488; see below on co-determination at board level.

[272] For Italy, G. Ferrarini et al., sec. 2.2.1(b), p. 381: not even put on the political agenda. Similarly for Spain, A. Recalde Castells et al., sec. 2.2.1(b), p. 568, but there is regulation of labour co-determination for the Societas Europaea.

[273] For the UK, P. Davies, sec. 3.2.1, p. 761 though this tradition has been declining.

[274] S. Sołtysiński, sec. 3.2, p. 538.

[275] T. Baums and P. Ulmer, eds., *Unternehmens-Mitbestimmung der Arbeitnehmer im Recht der EU-Mitgliedstaaten/Employees' Co-Determination in the Member States of the European Union*, Heidelberg 2004. For the beginnings, cf. K.J. Hopt, 'Labor Co-determination in Europe', *Journal of Comparative Business and Capital Market Law* 6 (1984) 216.

[276] R. Skog and E. Sjöman, sec. 3.2.1, p. 644. In France, one or more directors must be elected among the employee-shareholders when the shares held by a listed company's staff and by the staff of affiliated companies represent more than 3% of the company's share capital. But most recently a mandatory requirement for French companies having more than 5,000 permanent employees was introduced to have 1 or 2 (depending on the size of the board) board members (with deliberative voting rights) representing employees, Code de commerce Art. L. 225-27-1. Cf. also A. Pietrancosta et al., sec. 2.2.1(c), p. 194.

whereas labour in fact only received the same right of (non-binding) recommendation as the general assembly; in practice, this right was only used in bigger companies. In all 113 companies (large and small) investigated in 1995 there was on average only one member of the supervisory board member (out of 5, 7 or 9 in total) who the works council regarded as a labour representative.[277]

In the Netherlands the old regime (*structuur regime*) proved to have negative effects, though there had been exceptions for international groups of companies.[278] Therefore, it was given up in favour of a one-third parity regime under which the shareholder meeting appoints the members of the supervisory board, with the employees' one-third appointed upon a 'binding' recommendation of the works council. The shareholder meeting can reject the recommended candidate but cannot appoint a person of its own choice; instead, it must wait for another recommendation. Employees of the company or its subsidiaries and members of trade unions who have negotiated the employment conditions with the company cannot be members of the supervisory board.[279]

The German co-determination regime is an outlier since it is at parity, more exactly at quasi-parity since the shareholder-elected chairman has a double voice. Yet this voice is hardly ever used because of its very negative consequences for the working climate in the company and possible clashes with the unions.[280] This far-reaching co-determination system is path-dependent and has its origins in the post-World War I (1922) and post-World War II (1950/1952/1976) eras when the forces of capital and labour had to jointly rebuild Germany's industry after the two wars. The extent of the co-determination depends on the legal form of the company and its size (from more than 500 employees up: one-third parity with about 3,000 companies; from more than 1,000 employees up: one-half parity with about 40 companies). The employee representatives are elected either directly or indirectly by the workforce but, in violation of EU law,[281] only by the German workforce. Some board seats are reserved for representatives of the trade unions. This far-reaching co-determination regime and its accompanying vested interests are so deeply rooted in the country that Germany has held up EU efforts to harmonise some company law for decades, most recently with the European Private Company (SPE), and until now all the many efforts of reform within Germany have failed.

---

[277] R.G.J. Nowak, sec. 3.2.1, p. 488.

[278] If the majority of the employees of the group are employed abroad, R.G.J. Nowak, sec. 3.2.1, p. 487

[279] R.G.J. Nowak, sec. 3.2.1, p. 490. An employee representative is not considered to be independent if that employee is employed by the company or one of its subsidiaries; see above, sec. 2.2.3 on independent directors.

[280] To this and the following, see M. Roth, sec. 3.2.1., p. 331 et seq.

[281] See M. Roth, above n. 160; Reflection Group, above n. 160.

This leads to the question of voluntary, fall-back, or mandatory rules. Some states in which board-level co-determination is voluntary provide in the by-laws for upper limits of one-third or one-half.[282] In Sweden, labour co-determination is basically up to the trade unions, which under certain circumstances have the right to present up to three representatives, provided that there is no co-determination if the company is not bound by a collective agreement.[283] The EU provides for a complicated and burdensome bargaining system in the European Company, but it protects national labour co-determination, particularly in Germany, by mandatory fall-back rules if a compromise between the representatives of the company and labour cannot be reached. In other states, and particularly in Germany, labour co-determination is mandatory. This lack of flexibility has led not only to reform proposals by industry and academia, but also to exit strategies. The most common way of exit is the choice of the legal form of the European Company.[284] An empirical study for the European Commission found that this exit possibility, restricted as it is, is a major reason for choosing the legal form of the European Company, certainly in Germany.[285] Mandatory parity labour co-determination also explains why the founders of a European Company in Germany shy away from opting for a one-tier board instead of a two-tier board.[286]

Impact of co-determination at board level —The most challenging, controversial, and least empirically confirmed question is what impact co-determination has at board level.[287] Apart from a problematic impact on the size of the board, felt most under parity co-determination in Germany,[288] and of the costs and the slowing down of the decision-making process, much of the information from companies and trade unions remains anecdotal and is very often contradictory.

---

[282] One-third in France, A. Pietrancosta et al., sec. 3.2.1, p. 224 et seq.

[283] R. Skog and E. Sjöman, sec. 3.2.1, p. 644 et seq.

[284] M. Roth, sec. 3.2.1(c),(d), p. 335 et seq.

[285] European Commission, *Study on the operation and the impacts of the Statute for a European Company (SE)* of 9 December 2009 (Ernst & Young), and European Commission Report of 19 November 2010, available at <http://ec.europa.eu/internal_market/company/se/index_en.htm>.

[286] For details, see M. Roth, sec. 3.2.1(e), p. 338 et seq.

[287] See K. Pistor, 'Corporate Governance durch Mitbestimmung und Arbeitsmärkte', in: P. Hommelhoff, K.J. Hopt and A. v. Werder, eds., *Handbuch Corporate Governance*, 2nd edn., Cologne 2009, p. 231 at 236 et seq. on economic and sociological theories and at 246 et seq. on empirical studies. See also K.J. Hopt, above n. 1, *The American Journal of Comparative Law* 59 (2011) 1 at 54. See further L. Fauver and M.E. Fuerst, 'Does good corporate governance include employee representation? Evidence from German corporate boards', (2006) 82 *Journal of Financial Economics* 673, suggesting that the strongest evidence for an efficiency impact of employee representation on corporate performance exists in relation to less than parity co-determination.

[288] M. Roth, sec. 3.2.1(d), p. 336 et seq.

As to possible impacts on the company and its corporate governance, the impact on the information streams is most probable. The presence of employee representatives on the board may improve the information available to the board because the information the board—namely, the supervisory board—gets is filtered by the management—namely, the management board. The employee representatives are usually members of the works council, and as such they have thorough information about what is going on at the grassroots level of the company. But information goes both ways. Some seats of the labour side, at least in Germany, are filled directly by trade unions, and most of the other employee representatives are trade union members. The labour constituency and the trade unions expect to be informed by their representatives. While there is a mandatory rule on boardroom secrecy, in practice this is often not respected. Even inside information slips out to employees and trade unions, though the European Court of Justice has clearly stated that co-determination cannot justify such a leak.[289] The danger of such leaks may make the management reluctant to inform the (supervisory) board of inside information. Whether an increased flow of (non-inside) information about corporate strategy to trade unions reduces the likelihood of management and union misunderstanding their respective positions in collective bargaining is rather speculative.

Another impact on decision-making is probable insofar as labour issues are more likely to be brought to the board from the workforce in the company as well as from the trade unions. This may be helpful because critical labour issues may be discussed and solved at the board level instead of looming unsolved or coming up only during collective bargaining. But there is also a *quid pro quo*: The management and the board may omit or delay decisions that would be useful for the company, such as more investment in foreign countries that would have consequences for the workforce at home.[290] On the other hand, if measures—even drastic ones—need to be taken in the interest of the company, this may even be facilitated by co-determination, as the experience of rescues, layoffs, and closedowns of companies after German reunification has shown. Some expect that co-determination will enable better board control over management risk-taking and management remuneration. But experiences from the financial crisis and cases like the *Mannesmann* case[291] cast doubt on this. Nevertheless, recent decisions in

---

[289] European Court of Justice, *Grongaard and Bang*, 22 November 2005 – C-384/02, European Court Reports 2005, I-09939; see K.J. Hopt, 'Insider- und Ad-hoc-Publizitätsprobleme', in H. Schimansky, H.-J. Bunte and H.-J. Lwowski, eds., *Bankrechts-Handbuch*, vol. II, 4th edn., Munich 2011, § 107 comment 58 et seq.

[290] Anecdotal evidence on Volkswagen and Brazilian subsidiaries.

[291] C. Milhaupt and K. Pistor, above n. 142, p. 69 et seq.

Germany about the compensation of directors have been taken away from the remuneration committees and mandatorily assigned to the board as a whole.[292]

Co-determination may have a distorting impact on the board. Co-determination, at least co-determination at parity, leads to a division between two camps ('benches'). Employee members regularly meet previously in caucus and tend not to split up in discussing and voting, unless there is a special representative for leading employees. This has been different on the shareholder side, though the German Corporate Governance Code recommended that they also have separate pre-meetings.[293] The distorting effect may be even stronger if the unions have their own representatives on the board. While the unions tend to have a broader view that may be useful for the board in some cases, they may bring in labour interests from outside the company that may not be in the interest of the company and the shareholders. On the whole, this polarisation by encouraging separate 'benches' or sides is rather negative.[294] Whether this distorting effect can be avoided by having independent directors is doubtful, even if the employee side were to have independent directors as well.[295]

Co-determination may also have an effect on external corporate governance, ie., on the takeover market. Indeed, co-determination is sometimes considered to be one of the many structural obstacles to the development of a lively takeover market. This is because both management and labour have an incentive to fight off (hostile) takeovers that may result in installing new management and cutting down labour costs and jobs at home.

Consequences of co-determination beyond the company are even more anecdotal and speculative. Co-determination in Germany is said to have contributed to a more peaceful climate between capital and labour, to fewer strikes, and to better cooperation of both sides in the interest of the economy as a whole. Some have called co-determination an early social monitoring system.[296]

---

[292] K.J. Hopt, above n. 1, *The American Journal of Comparative Law* 59 (2011) 1 at 34 and 54. This has led to an increased influence of trade unions, though this has not been emphasised in the reform discussion. The trade unions obviously were in favour of this reform since it gives them more bargaining power on the boards for other issues.

[293] The German Code Commission has been criticised for this and in its May 2012 amendments has abolished this recommendation and merely states that this can be done.

[294] M. Roth, sec. 3.2.1(d), p. 335.

[295] See above, sec. 2.2.3 on independent directors.

[296] K.J. Hopt, 'Labor Representation on Corporate Boards: Impacts and Problems for Corporate Governance and Economic Integration in Europe', *International Review of Law and Economics* 14 (1994) 203 at 212.

3.2.2. *Board and Creditors*

Duties of the board toward creditors—Creditors are usually not protected by board rules but rather by general company law such as capital maintenance rules, restrictions on distributions and shareholder loans,[297] and in particular by insolvency law.[298] Many of the shareholder protection rules also serve creditor interests. This is true for information, for example, in particular the annual accounts and the information rights of shareholders. Banks are special. Banking law—ie. not the private but the supervisory law for banks—is geared toward creditor protection and creditor governance, not really for shareholder protection and corporate governance.[299]

Unlike shareholders, creditors typically do not have rights of their own against the company before insolvency. Companies or banks protect their creditor interests by private contracting[300]—for example, by loan covenants and similar clauses and instruments. Sometimes they have special information rights; for example, when debt securities are admitted to trading on a regulated market, there are information requirements for issuers.[301] Exceptionally, creditors do have rights of their own, namely when their interests are particularly threatened as in the case of a merger or a capital reduction.[302] They may also have the right to sue the board members[303] or to enforce the company's rights via a derivative suit if the company fails to do so, or they may have the right to call capital if the company has uncalled capital.[304]

Representation on the board—Sometimes creditors take a seat on the board—more often only on the supervisory board—to protect their credit or investment. This has been typical for certain countries and certain periods, as in Germany during the era of Rhineland capitalism, which is fading away.[305] But for the most

---

[297] For the UK, P. Davies, sec. 3.2.2, p. 761 et seq.; for Italy, G. Ferrarini et al., sec. 3.3, p. 415; for Switzerland, P. Böckli, sec. 3.2.2, p. 699.

[298] From a principal–agent conflict approach, see J. Armour, G. Hertig and H. Kanda, in R. Kraakman et al., above n. 2, ch. 5, p. 115 et seq.

[299] See on banking governance, above n. 12. For Belgium, K. Geens, sec. 3.3, p. 155 et seq.

[300] For the UK, P. Davies, sec. 3.2.2, p. 761 et seq.

[301] Cf. Art. 18 of the Transparency Directive 2004/109/EC of 15 December 2004, OJ L 390/38 of 31 December 2004.

[302] For France, A. Pietrancosta et al., sec. 3.2.2, p. 225; for Belgium, K. Geens, sec. 3.2.2, p. 151 et seq.; for Poland, S. Sołtysiński, sec. 3.2, p. 538 et seq. These rights do not block the transaction but concern additional guarantees or reimbursement.

[303] For Italy, G. Ferrarini et al., sec. 3.2.2, p. 413.

[304] For Belgium, K. Geens, sec. 3.2.2, p. 152.

[305] For Germany, M. Roth, sec. 3.2.2, p. 339; formerly also in Switzerland, P. Böckli, sec. 3.2.2, p. 699.

part, creditors are unwilling to take up this role as long as the company is solvent since they rely on their secured loans, on general company law, and on the reputation of the company. Taking a seat on the board may also imply additional risks for creditors because of lender liability or board member liability, for example. Of course, the situation changes when the company is in financial distress.[306] but even then a board seat may seem especially fraught with liability risks.

3.2.3. Board and Other Stakeholders

Enlightened shareholder approach—Stakeholders other than employees and creditors are usually not protected by board rules and company law but by other laws, in particular information and social accounting. But in some countries that provide for a stakeholder-oriented approach for the board, the board has to consider as a matter of law not only employees' and creditors' interests, but more broadly the interests of other stakeholders and the 'public interest.' In the UK, for example, the core duty of loyalty requires directors to also have regard, when promoting the success of the company for the benefits of its members, to the impact of the company's operations on the community and the environment.[307] Similarly in Germany, since 1937 the board must take the public interest into account, balancing it with the interest of the shareholders and employees.[308] Since 2009 in listed companies, the boards have to look for a sustainable creation of value and take a long-term perspective in setting the remuneration of directors. The balancing of interests by the board reaches its limits when substantial money is diverted from the business, though the limits on charitable gifts (a general practice), art collections (a not unusual practice, for example the famous art collection of the Deutsche Bank), and contributions to political parties are generally not clearly set. In many countries, corporate social responsibility has gained attention in business practice,[309] though often only as far as this promotes business interests.

No stakeholder rights—Since stakeholders do not have rights to enforce against the board, the actual impact of these rules is limited, but the trend is to give them more teeth. This applies to the sustainability information[310] if it is part of the annual report and as such has to be audited. The European Commission is

---

[306] See below, sec. 3.3.

[307] P. Davies, sec. 3.2.3, p. 762 et seq.

[308] M. Roth, sec. 3.2.3, p. 340 et seq.

[309] For Belgium, for example, see K. Geens, sec. 3.2.3, p. 154 et seq.

[310] For the UK, see P. Davies, sec. 3.2.3, p. 762: The annual report of quoted companies in the UK must contain information about environmental matters and social and community matters in its business review part (from 2013 re-named 'strategic report'). For France, A. Pietrancosta et al., sec. 3.2.3, p. 225. For Spain, A. Recalde Castells et al., sec. 3.2.3, p. 605; in Spain, there has been a State Council on the Social Responsibility of Enterprises since 2008.

becoming more active in the field of social responsibility[311] and, as in corporate governance, is considering coming up with more transparency and legal duties, though this is widely criticised.

3.3. Board and Creditors: Changing Roles in Financial Distress

Increasing duties and liabilities of the board in and before financial distress— When the company gets into financial difficulties, things become more difficult for the board. Not only must the board become more active to solve the difficulties or to negotiate a work-out before outright insolvency,[312] but the board must also inform the shareholders. For the EU Member States this is specified expressly as a legal duty if more than half the capital of the company is lost.[313] The board must also carefully consider whether it may go on with its business. Otherwise, in many countries the directors run the risk of becoming liable to those creditors who have contracted with the company after the critical moment. When this moment is reached, the weighing of the positive and negative prospects of the company and the amount of time the board has to look for a rescuer who might bring in fresh money is generally controversial.[314] In addition, the doctrines concerning this liability and their relevance in practice vary considerably, such as wrongful trading in the UK[315] and similar actions in France, Belgium, Germany, and other countries.[316]

---

[311] European Commission, Proposal for a Directive of the European Parliament and of the Council amending Council Directives 78/660/EEC and 83/349/EEC as regards disclosure of non-financial and diversity information by certain large companies and groups, 16 April 2013, COM(2013) 207 final. Cf. also O. de Schutter, 'Corporate Social Responsibility European Style', *European Law Journal* 14 (2008) 203.

[312] In Switzerland, the entire leadership functions may quickly concentrate in one person: the Chairman/CEO; P. Böckli, sec. 3.3, p. 700 et seq. In the Netherlands, the notion of intensified supervision by the board in financial distress has been developed by the courts; R.G.J. Nowak, sec. 3.3, p. 490 et seq. On directors' duties and liabilities in the vicinity of insolvency, see LSE Study 2013 (above n. 16), part 4.

[313] Art. 17 of the Second Council Directive, the so-called Capital Directive.

[314] See J. Armour, H. Hansmann and R. Kraakman, in R. Kraakman et al., above n. 2, at 134 et seq.

[315] P. Davies, sec. 3.2.2, p. 762 et seq.; F. Steffek, 'Wrongful Trading—Grundlagen und Spruchpraxis', *Neue Zeitschrift für das Recht der Insolvenz und Sanierung* 2010, 589; *idem, Gläubigerschutz in der Kapitalgesellschaft, Krise und Insolvenz im englischen und deutschen Gesellschafts- und Kapitalmarktrecht*, Tübingen 2011, ch. 4, p. 259 et seq.

[316] K.J. Hopt, above n. 1, *The American Journal of Comparative Law* 59 (2011) 1 at 43 et seq.; Forum Europaeum Group Law, 'Corporate Group Law for Europe', *European Business Organization Law Review* 1 (2000) 165 at 245 et seq. for the UK, France, Belgium, and Germany. For Italy, G. Ferrarini et al., sec. 3.3, p. 415; for the Netherlands, R.G.J. Nowak, sec. 3.3,

cont. ...

Once the company is insolvent and the insolvency procedure has begun, things change completely. The receiver takes over and usually the board no longer has any say. In some states and under special circumstances, the debtor may remain in possession and the board can go on under the supervision of the creditors or, as in Switzerland, a court-appointed trustee.

Increasing creditor rights—It has been said that with insolvency of the company, the creditors become the quasi-owners of the company, and indeed from that moment on the creditors have the say rather than the shareholders. This implies that the creditors, who usually do not actively intervene before the financial distress,[317] receive rights of their own that differ according to the different kinds of insolvency and similar proceedings.[318] Apart from their personal claim, the creditors' rights are exercised through committees, such as a steering and restructuring committee.[319] In some jurisdictions, the creditors already have certain intervention rights before outright insolvency, including information rights[320] or the right for a creditor to ask for the dissolution of the company or to open insolvency proceedings.[321]

4. Enforcement

It is a truism that a rule is only as good as its enforcement—though that tells us little about what level of enforcement is needed to make a rule effective in practice.[322] However, enforcement can take two different forms. In the more traditional form enforcement means resort to a third party to secure the imposition of some sanction for breach of the rule. That third party may be a body which itself will not initiate action but needs to be moved into action by someone who has an interest in the enforcement of the rule. A court typically falls into this category and is considered in section 4.1. The third party may be prepared to initiate action of its own accord. A regulator typically falls into this category; see section 4.2 below. Alternatively, the rule may be of a self-enforcing character, ie. those whose interests the rule is there to protect may be able to take action that is

---

p. 490 et seq.; for Sweden, R. Skog and E. Sjöman, sec. 3.3, p. 646. Cf. also for Switzerland, P. Böckli, sec. 3.3, p. 700.

[317] See above, sec. 3.2.2.

[318] For example, for France, A. Pietrancosta et al., sec. 3.3, p. 226 et seq.

[319] For Switzerland, P. Böckli, sec. 3.3, p. 700; cf. also for France, A. Pietrancosta et al., sec. 3.3, p. 226 et seq.

[320] See above, 3.2.2, n. 301 (Transparency Directive).

[321] For Belgium, K. Geens, sec. 3.2.2, p. 153; for Germany, § 13 of the Insolvency Law: application by the debtor or by a creditor.

[322] On enforcement by private and by administrative remedies, see P. Davies and S. Worthington, above n. 6, §§ 17–18 and LSE Study 2013 (above n. 16), part 3.

wholly under their own control to enforce the rule, without invoking a third party. For example, in the law of contract a party may respond to the counterparty's breach of contract by (lawfully) refusing to perform its side of the bargain, and in some circumstances that may be an adequate enforcement of the rule for the innocent party. We consider analogous situations in relation to board rules in 4.3.

4.1. Civil Courts

Minority shareholder actions—In all the countries considered board decisions are potentially subject to review by the courts by reference to general standards pertaining to the board's competence in discharging its functions and its 'loyalty' (eg. the avoidance of conflicts of interest). The content of these standards has been considered above. Typically, there is a potential liability in damages to the company on the part of the directors for breach of these duties, and complaints about breaches lie to the relevant civil court. However, in all jurisdictions it is reported that the level of civil litigation is low when the company is a going-concern, though somewhat higher when the company is insolvent and control of the company has passed to a person acting on behalf of the creditors.[323]

In the case of going-concern companies, the crucial issue concerns the barriers to and incentives for litigation on the part of non-controlling share-holders. The board is unlikely to initiate litigation, although if it is a new board installed after the sale of the company, it may do so. A controlling shareholder may be implicit in the breach of duty or, if it is not, have other remedies at its disposal, so that it will not be interested in securing a decision to sue the directors from the general meeting. So, where there is a controlling shareholder, initiation of suit by a minority shareholder against the directors in effect constitutes a form of minority shareholder protection. Where shareholdings are dispersed, the collective action problems of the shareholders may prevent the general meeting from taking action. Here, enforcement of directors' duties by a minority share-holder may operate so as to protect the shareholders as a class against management. Thus, in both types of shareholding structure, it is highly significant whether a minority shareholder, in law and in practice, is in a position either to act on behalf of the company to enforce its rights (the 'derivative' action) or cause the company itself to act to enforce its rights. We will use the term 'minority shareholder action' to refer to both types of suit.

In all jurisdictions there are still considerable obstacles to minority share-holder actions. In the past, law-makers have been suspicious of the motives of minority shareholders, with only limited stakes in the company, who wish to see

---

[323] These propositions are confirmed for the EU as a whole by the LSE Study 2013 (above n. 16) part 3.

the company's rights enforced. They have therefore set high standing rules, usually expressed in terms of a percentage of the company's equity, for access to the minority suit. In the past a standing requirement of 10% was common and it still remains at that level in Sweden.[324] Generally, however, standing requirements have been reduced in recent reforms, often to the 1% level.[325] Even in these jurisdictions, however, the level of minority shareholder actions is reported to be low. There are two possible explanations for the lack of impact of the reduction of the standing requirements. One is that even 1% of the capital of a large publicly traded company is a large amount.[326] The alternative is that there are other barriers to minority shareholders' actions even if the standing criteria are met. The fact that levels of litigation are low even in countries where a single shareholder may sue[327] suggest that the non-standing barriers are significant.

In some jurisdictions, the costs rules are a big disincentive to sue. If the suing shareholder bears the costs of the litigation but recovery is by the company, this creates a strong disincentive to litigation, especially if the costs rule in question is that the loser pays the winner's costs.[328] However, the costs disincentive is not present in all jurisdictions. If the minority shareholders' action takes the form of the company being forced to litigate, the costs will fall on the company. Even in a derivative action it is possible to make the company liable for the costs of the action, including cases where the action is unsuccessful.[329] The final point is that, even if standing and costs considerations are put on one side, the financial incentives for a

---

[324] R. Skog and E. Sjöman, sec. 4.1.1(c), p. 648. For an overview, see M. Gelter, 'Why Do Shareholder Derivative Suits Remain Rare in Continental Europe?', 37 *Brooklyn Journal of International law* 843 (2012).

[325] This the requirement in Germany—subject to restrictions (see section 148 AktG—for extensive discussion of the reform process, see H. Hirt, *The Enforcement of Directors' Duties in Britain and Germany*, Peter Lang, 2004, ch. 6.3 to 6.5) and in Belgium (K. Geens, sec. 4.1.1, p. 157). Italy (G. Ferrarini et al., sec. 4.1.1(b), p. 417) has a 2.5% rule, whilst Poland (S. Sołtysiński, sec. 4.1.3, p. 542) allows any shareholder to sue if the company has not acted within a year of the injury. In the UK, a single shareholder can initiate the procedure but effective control lies with the court which, at the beginning of the litigation, must decide whether it is in the interests of the company for the litigation to proceed.

[326] In some cases there is an alternative monetary qualification threshold which may be easier to meet, such as holding shares of a nominal value of at least €1.25 million in Belgium, though this is still a stiff hurdle. More easy to meet is the German alternative monetary threshold of €100,000.

[327] This is the case in Switzerland (P. Böckli, sec. 4.1.1(a), p. 701 and Poland (S. Sołtysiński, sec. 4.1.3, p. 542). In the UK, the 2006 reforms permit a single shareholder to sue, provided a court approves the litigation. The operation of this judicial filter is still being tested in litigation (P. Davies, sec. 4.1.2, p. 767).

[328] A. Pietrancosta et al., sec. 4.1.1(a), p. 232.

[329] As in the UK. Contingent fee litigation is another cost-shifting device, but that is underdeveloped in Europe.

minority shareholders' suit are limited: The effort falls on the minority shareholder but the recovery goes to the company so that the shareholder benefits only to the extent of his or her (*ex hypothesi*) limited interest in the capital of the company.[330] Contrary to the traditional view, therefore, the problem may not be that minority shareholders are over-incentivised to sue but that they are under-incentivised. However, positive encouragement of minority shareholder suits, for example, by facilitating the funding of litigation by lawyers through contingent fees, is underdeveloped in Europe. Despite recent reforms it can be said that the traditional suspicion that liability suits brought by minority shareholders are likely not to be in the interests of the company as a whole still sets limits to policy makers' willingness to encourage such suits.[331] The US notion of the individual shareholder as the company's 'private attorney-general' has not taken root.

Direct actions—The financial incentives for shareholders to sue might be transformed if the duties mentioned above were owed directly to the shareholders who would therefore have a direct, rather than indirect, interest in any recoveries from the directors. The universal rule, however, is that directors' duties are owed to the company and recovery goes to the company. Only if the loss suffered by the individual shareholder is separate from the loss suffered by the company and, sometimes, if there is in addition a breach of a separate duty owed by the director to the individual shareholder is a direct action permitted.[332] Thus, direct actions are rare and, by extension, representative (or class) actions which aggregate the rights of individual shareholders are uncommon in the area of directors' duties (in contrast to the securities law area).

Insolvency—The general duties of directors continue to apply as the company nears insolvency. In addition, many jurisdictions now have additional rules and procedures for establishing the negligence liability of directors of insolvent com-

---

[330] It may also act as a disincentive to minority shareholders' litigation that, outside the UK, liability for breaches of the loyalty duties is often confined to damages for the harm caused to the company and that disgorgement of the profit made by director, where the company has suffered no harm, is not clearly available as a remedy.

[331] E.P.M. Vermeulen and D.A. Zetzsche, 'The Use and Abuse of Investor Suits—An Inquiry into the Dark Side of Shareholder Activism', *European Company and Financial Law Review* 1 (2010) comparing Germany and the Netherlands; C.A. Paul, 'Derivative Suits under English and German Corporate Law', *European Company and Financial Law Review* 81 (2010) comparing Germany and the UK. This approach may explain why in some countries—France, Italy—shareholders can 'piggyback' a civil claim on a criminal prosecution, eg. for abuse of the corporate assets. Control of the criminal process by the public authorities reduces the scope for opportunistic behaviour by minority shareholders, ie. the risk of 'gold-digging' suits—though it creates other problems.

[332] Referred to as the 'no reflective loss' principle in the UK. See also A. Pietrancosta et al., sec. 4.1.1(a), p. 232.

panies.[333] The level of litigation to enforce the personal liability of directors in insolvency is reported to be higher than in the case of going-concern companies. This can be understood to flow from the fact that litigation (now on behalf of creditors rather than shareholders) is centralised in the hands of the person in charge of the insolvency and is not left to disorganised creditors. Moreover, the person in charge of the insolvency, accountable to the creditors, is less likely to suffer from the conflicts of interest which might have prevented the board from initiating suit. Even so, it is not clear that the levels of litigation against directors in insolvency are significantly higher. This may be because the person in charge of the insolvency has to fund the litigation and will be willing to do so only in rather clear cases, for otherwise the creditors may end up worse off than before.[334]

Litigation in the two-tier system—In a two-tier board system there is the additional possibility that litigation against the management could be brought by the supervisory board as well as by the shareholders, collectively or individually. However, there is a disincentive for the supervisory board to bring litigation against the management board in that it may implicitly reveal its own failures in supervising that body. Hence the decision of the *Bundesgerichtshof* in the *ARAG/ Garmenbeck* case is significant because it in effect deprived the supervisory board's decision not to sue of the protection of the business judgment rule and exposed it to a more rigorous level of judicial scrutiny. Even so, the supervisory board retains some discretion in weighing up the corporate interest in litigation. Greater litigation by supervisory boards against management boards has followed the *ARAG/Garmebeck* decision, and in particular since the financial crisis, but, though it is hard to get empirical data beyond the financial press and anecdotal evidence, supervisory board litigation has not yet fundamentally altered the overall picture of low levels of litigation to enforce liability against directors.

D&O insurance—Directors and Officers (D&O) insurance (ie. insurance paid for by the company but protecting the director against liability to the company for breach of duty) is generally permitted, though often with some restrictions— either in law or in practice—on its cover against criminal liability or civil liability

---

[333] P. Davies, sec. 3.2.2, p. 762; A. Pietrancosta et al., sec. 4.1.1(a), p. 233; P. Böckli, sec. 4.1.1(a), p. 701; R.G.J. Nowak, sec. 4.1.1(a), p. 493; K. Geens, sec. 3.2.2, p. 154. In 2002 the High Level Group of Company Law Experts (Final Report, Brussels, 2002) recommended a Community rule along these lines and the Commission is currently exploring this possibility.

[334] Thus, some form of litigation funding is probably necessary to unlock the full potential of litigation against directors on behalf of creditors. In the aftermath of the financial crisis, a number of funds have been established in the UK to finance litigation (by no means only against directors) in exchange for a proportion of the proceeds, to the extent that an Association of Litigation Funders has been established and a semi-official voluntary Code of Conduct has been adopted (available at <http://www.judiciary.gov.uk/about-the-judiciary/advisory-bodies/cjc/third-party-funding#headingAnchor1>).

for intentional wrongdoing.[335] In principle, one would expect D&O insurance to increase the incidence of litigation and also the rate of settlement of litigation. The presence of a defendant who is assured of being able to meet the damages claim is an incentive to litigation, but both claimant and defendant director have an incentive to settle within the limits of the insurance coverage, with regard to both its financial and its substantive limits.[336] Nevertheless, D&O insurance appears not to have been effective to overcome the barriers to litigation to enforce directors' duties noted above, suggesting that the standing and funding restrictions operating on the claimant are still substantial.

Shareholder release—Clauses in the articles or elsewhere giving blanket exemptions to directors in respect of potential breaches of duty to the company are of doubtful legality in all our jurisdictions.[337] Even the release of directors voted on at the annual general meeting has little impact on the incidence of subsequent litigation because it does not bar action in relation to facts which were not fully disclosed at the time. Heavily discussed in the UK, though less so elsewhere, are the conditions under which shareholders *ex post* on the basis of full disclosure may relieve the directors of liability.[338]

The court as regulator—An interesting hybrid model for the court has emerged in the Netherlands, with some echoes in Belgium,[339] in the shape of the Enterprise Court.[340] This court still needs to be moved into action by someone involved in the company, though the range of litigants is wide, including minority shareholders

---

[335] In 2009 Germany (M. Roth, sec. 4.1.1(b), p. 343) introduced a mandatory deductible for D&O insurance, which seems likely to be ineffective.

[336] Thus, if the insurance excludes wilful misconduct, the settlement of a claim based on intentional wrongdoing may still be covered by the insurance if intentional wrongdoing is not admitted in the settlement. To some extent, this analysis depends upon the defendant's insurer regarding it as more important to retain the company's D&O insurance business than to minimise its losses in a particular case. If the company is not very sensitive to the premium levels, settling rather than fighting the case may be the financially more attractive course for the insurer, because it will be able to recover its pay-out through future premium increases.

[337] By contrast, Delaware law permits blanket exclusion in the company's statutes of liability in damages for breach of duty where bad faith is not alleged (DGCL §102(b)(7)). Thus, successful negligence litigation in Delaware requires a showing of bad faith, a demanding hurdle. On the other hand, directors in Europe, at least to date, may obtain a functionally equivalent protection from the low incidence of litigation, as discussed above.

[338] P. Davies, sec. 4.1.1, p. 766. This is normally permitted but subject to the disenfranchisement of the interested directors.

[339] K. Geens, sec. 4.1.3, p. 162 et seq.

[340] R.G.J. Nowak, sec. 4.1.3, p. 498. It should be noted that the Netherlands has no formal derivative action, but the Enterprise Court procedure somewhat reflects the UK judicial control model for derivative claims (above n. 325), with the important difference that the EC plays a much more active role than any UK court would contemplate.

and the works council, and the basis of complaint is mismanagement of the company. However, the court does not engage in the backward-looking process of assessing whether a director is liable for mismanagement; in fact, it does not have power to impose liability on a director, which is a matter for the ordinary courts. Instead the Enterprise Court acts as an investigative body, operates quickly and can impose a wide range of forward-looking interim measures relating to the conduct of the company, in extreme cases even before it has decided whether to open an investigation. The de-coupling of wide-ranging remedial powers from any conclusive finding of illegality (mismanagement) is what makes this procedure a hybrid. The Enterprise Court is not primarily engaged in redressing past wrong-doing but is determining the appropriate governance regime for the company in the future.[341] It operates as an investigative body, but one with enforcement powers rather than simply a reporting function. In the *Stork* case (2007),[342] in a dispute between activist shareholders and the management of the company the court ordered the reversal of a share issue (thus favouring the activists) and appointed three new members to the company's supervisory board with control over the company's strategy (thus disappointing the activists who had wanted the supervisory board removed). It is difficult to believe this mechanism could be transplanted to another jurisdiction. It requires the judges—usually two of the five judges are chartered accountants or similar professionals—to have a particular set of skills, for which their training does not normally equip them, in order to determine effective ways of running companies. Each and every decision of the Enterprise Court, not being grounded in an interpretation of the law, puts the court's reputation at risk, for example, if the court's solution is publicly seen not to work. These problems are only partially mitigated by including accountants and or similar professionals amongst the judges.

4.2. Criminal Courts and Regulators

In the above section on civil courts, we saw that it was a crucial limitation on their effectiveness that the court will not act unless moved to do by someone having the necessary standing. Some enforcement bodies, however, will act of their own

---

[341] For further analysis, see J McCahery and E Vermeulen, *Conflict Resolution and the Role of Corporate Law Courts*, ECGI Law Working Paper 132/2009. The requirement for a finding of illegality is what distinguishes the apparently equally wide-ranging 'unfair prejudice' procedure in UK law from the EC. The UK procedure is used mainly to enforce the implicit (informal but nevertheless real) prior understandings among incorporators setting up or operating a small company. Therefore it has little application to public companies: P. Davies, sec. 4.1.2, p. 766 et seq.

[342] A brief account of the case in English can be found at <http://www.eurofound.europa.eu/eiro/2007/02/articles/nl0702039i.htm>.

motion. This does not mean that they will act in every possible case where enforcement action could be regarded as plausible. Limitations of resources mean that action is likely to be taken only if the case fits within certain pre-determined policy parameters which body has established. Nevertheless, where action is taken, the costs of it fall on the public purse or on the regulated industry in general (depending on how the enforcement body is funded) rather on a particular claimant or the particular company, as in the case of a claim to a civil court.

Looking at matters from this perspective, it seems sensible to put together in this section both regulators and the criminal courts. In both cases the decision to take action does not rest with the complaining shareholder, but rather with the public authorities, in the shape of either the enforcement arm of the regulator or the prosecuting authorities.

4.2.1. Criminal Law

With one exception, the criminal law does not play an important direct role in the enforcement of directors' duties of care and loyalty to the company. The exception is Poland which until recently provided severe criminal penalties on board members for acting to the detriment of the company or aiding an illegal act by the company.[343] These provisions were actively enforced by the public authorities, though there were few successful prosecutions. In 2011 the criminal provisions were substantially reduced in scope. Elsewhere, criminal prosecutions play a lesser, though sometimes very visible, role in relation to the general duties of directors, for example, in respect of the bonus paid in the aftermath of the *Mannesmann* takeover in Germany.[344] In France, using the assets or powers of the company in a way which is harmful to the company and serves the personal interests of the director or a third party is a criminal offence,[345] and this offence obviously covers a central element of the director's general duty of loyalty. Of course, all systems penalise fraud or theft committed in connection with the conduct of a company's business, though levels of enforcement may not be high.

4.2.2. Administrative Bodies

Whilst administrative (regulatory) bodies are well established and active in financial markets, they are much less prominent in enforcing the duties of directors to their companies, which are regarded as essentially matters of private,

---

[343] S. Sołtysiński, sec. 4.1.4, p. 542 and 5.1, p. 544.

[344] M. Roth, sec. 4.1.1(f), p. 347—*BGHSt* 50, 331. A certain tension has arisen between the criminal and the civil courts in Germany as to the appropriate approach to breaches of the fiduciary standard (*Untreue*).

[345] A. Pietrancosta et al., sec. 4.1.1(a), p. 235. Such prosecutions sometimes seem to be motivated by political considerations.

not public, concern. The main general exception[346] to this statement is the role of the Insolvency Agency in the UK whose task is to seek the disqualification of directors of insolvent companies whose conduct has shown them to be unfit to be in charge of companies whose shareholders have limited liability.[347] Although liability to disqualification is a common feature of European laws on directors' duties, the UK is an outlier in the resources it devotes to the enforcement of these rules. However, in the context of this study which concentrates on public and, indeed, listed companies, the exception is only partial. The driving force behind the introduction of this provision in the 1980s was the problem of under-capitalised small companies, ie. it is an *ex post* technique for dealing with an issue which minimum capital rules address from an *ex ante* perspective. How-ever, since the concept of 'unfitness' is very general, the mechanism is occa-sionally used against directors of public companies who have mismanaged those companies in a serious way. Thus, the directors of MG Rover Group Ltd, an economically significant company which collapsed in 2005, were disqualified from being directors of a limited liability company for periods of three to six years as a result of their conduct leading up to the collapse.[348]

4.3. Self-Regulation

Because corporate governance codes are at the heart of much board regulation today, so self-regulation has also become central to the enforcement of board rules. Although the obligation to comply-or-explain is embodied in some appropriate piece of hard law or stock exchange rule, compliance or otherwise with the substantive provisions of the corporate governance code is policed on a self-regulatory basis.[349] The expectation is that those to whom the comply-or-explain

---

[346] In particular areas the duties of directors may be subject to regulatory control, for example in relation to takeovers (where the Takeover Directive (2004/25/EC) Art. 4 requires such regulation) or the annual reporting requirements.

[347] P. Davies, sec. 4.2(a), p. 769 et seq.

[348] Department for Business, Innovation and Skills, *Press Release*, 9 May, 2011. The dis-qualification was preceded by a report of inspectors, appointed by the government under provi-sions in the companies legislation to investigate the circumstances of the collapse. This investi-gative power could be regarded as a method of enforcement (since it may result in reputational loss for those investigated) or a method of facilitating formal enforcement action, either by the public authorities or shareholders. However, the government rarely appoints investigators.

[349] There is an intermediate question of whether those who draw up the code are free to change it and thus change the obligations of the subject companies (as in the UK) or whether the legislation creating the comply-or-explain obligation also specifies the version of the code which is to be applied (as Belgium), so that changes in the code need the endorsement of the legislature before they become applicable to companies. In practice, there may not be much functional difference between the two situations because even in the former case there will be

cont. ...

disclosure is made, principally the shareholders but conceivably other groups able to influence management behaviour, will assess the quality of the non-compliance explanations. They will find them convincing or otherwise, and, if otherwise, either exercise their governance rights to try and change the directors' behaviour or dispose of the stock in the market, actions which in either case will put pressure on the management to comply with the substantive provisions of the code[350] or to provide more convincing explanations of their non-compliance.

The rationale for self-regulation, rather than court or regulator enforcement in this area, is that corporate governance codes enter into very sensitive and detailed areas of board operation and it is unlikely that in these areas the rule-maker is capable of producing a single solution which is best for all companies. On efficiency grounds, some degree of flexibility for companies is required.[351] On the other hand, the line between matters which substantively are to be dealt with in hard law and those which are to be dealt with in codes is necessarily contestable, as witness the current debate over whether the goals for women directors should be stated in legislation or a code and the general tendency for some of the provisions on directors' remuneration to move over time from the corporate governance code to legislation. The movement from code to legislation is particularly noticeable in relation to code provisions on remuneration. Because of the political saliency of these issues, governments find it difficult to refrain from using legislation in this area and thus to hand the regulation of the area over to others.[352]

In all the jurisdictions there is a high level of compliance with the substantive recommendations of the code. This may indicate that the drafters of the code have done a good job identifying practices which suit the majority of companies or at least that the companies see no merit in fighting the recommendations.[353] However, the quality of the explanations for non-compliance, which is crucial to the self-regulatory process, is sometimes criticised.[354] If the explanation of non-compliance is inadequate, this constitutes a breach of the comply-or-explain obligation. Those responsible for policing this rule seem disinclined to enforce

informal consultation between government and those responsible for the code before changes are made.

[350] Except in France, where plurality reigns, there is only a single code in each jurisdiction for listed companies.

[351] S. Arcot and V. Bruno, *One Size Does Not Fit All, After All: Evidence from Corporate Governance* (2007). Available at SSRN: http://ssrn.com/abstract=887947.

[352] See, for example, Hopt, above n. 1, *The American Journal of Comparative Law* 59 (2011) 1 at 16, n. 66, giving three examples, two in the remuneration area.

[353] In so far as companies comply with a provision of the code for fear that something worse will be enshrined in legislation, we are not talking about self-enforcement but compliance 'in the shadow of the law', where the adverse reaction is anticipated to come from government rather than shareholders or other stakeholders in the company.

[354] P. Davies, sec. 4.2(b), p. 774; K. Geens, sec. 4.3.2, p. 168 et seq.

the rule by imposing sanctions against particular companies, perhaps fearing that the line between judging the completeness of the explanation and judging its persuasiveness will be difficult to draw. However, in some jurisdictions there is an annual survey of the quality of the explanations, which may help to improve the usefulness of the explanations to shareholders.[355] The technique of comply-or-explain may be at a cross-roads. The European Commission expressed the view that 'in the majority of cases' the explanations given for non-compliance are 'not satisfactory'[356] and expressed scepticism in principle about the operation of the mechanism where there is a controlling shareholder.[357] Further, whilst stating that the first problem should be addressed in a way which does not undermine the comply-or-explain approach,[358] the Commission seemed open to the trend, noted above, of moving provisions from codes to legislation where there is popular pressure for reform.[359] These criticisms from the Commission prompted various soft law initiatives among the Member States to improve the quality of the non-compliance explanations, and in its Company Law and Corporate Governance Action Plan of December 2012[360] the Commission expressed itself happy with these actions and committed itself at Union level only to 'an initiative, possibly in the form of a Recommendation' to improve the quality of the explanations.

5. Drivers of Change

5.1. Introduction

The earlier parts of this chapter—and the national reports contained in this volume—indicate not only the current state of board rules in the various jurisdictions, but also provide some information on the changes which have occurred in recent years. There has been a substantial development in legal scholarship seeking to identify and evaluate the drivers of change in corporate

---

[355] R.G.J. Nowak, sec. 4.3, p. 501 et seq.; A Pietrancosta et al., sec. 4.2(a), p. 239. In the UK the Financial Reporting Council, which is responsible for the substance of the Code, was recently moved to issue a paper designed to increase companies' understanding of what constitutes a good explanation: Financial Reporting Council, *What constitutes an explanation under comply-or-explain?* (February 2012).

[356] European Commission, Green Paper, *The EU corporate governance framework*, COM (2011) 164, p. 3. The document of the Financial Reporting Council, referred to in the previous note, was in part a response to this scepticism.

[357] *Ibid.* 2.7.

[358] *Ibid.* 3.

[359] *Ibid.*

[360] See also the Action Plan discussed above in n. 28.

law. A particularly important, but controversial, theory predicts that market forces will produce significant change in corporate laws and that the direction of those changes will be towards the convergence of company laws into a common model.[361] The market forces pointed to in this theory are the pressures of competition released by globalisation, ie. the reduction in the barriers to trade in both goods and services. Globalisation has clearly had profound effects on economies around the world, but its specific effect on corporate law is hypothesised to be that jurisdictions with company laws which do not provide for the combination of productive inputs in the most cost-effective way will come under pressure to change their company laws so as to accord with a model which minimises the costs of production. Entrepreneurs in jurisdictions with 'inefficient' company laws will lobby their governments to reform those laws so that the costs of production are minimised. Governments will have an incentive to respond to such lobbying, since more efficient laws may encourage inward investment or otherwise increase the tax revenue and employment opportunities within the jurisdiction.[362] Since the corporate constituency which benefits most from cost-reducing corporate laws are the shareholders, as residual claimants, this theory suggests that company laws in general, and board rules in particular, will move in a shareholder-friendly direction.[363]

There are a number of qualifications which must be made to this theory. Firstly, as its authors themselves concede, their theory does not clearly specify a timescale over which convergence on the cost-reducing form of company law will be achieved. It is a theory which proposes a direction of travel in corporate law reform rather than a timetable for that reform. Secondly, the traditional comparative lawyer's qualification must be made: The theory supports view that company laws will converge on functionally efficient models, not necessarily that

---

[361] The literature on this issue is now extensive, but the original argument is best put in H. Hansmann and R. Kraakman, 'The End of History for Corporate Law', (2001) 89 *Georgetown Law Journal* 439. See also H. Hansmann, 'How Close is the End of History?', (2006) 31 *Journal of Corporate Law* 745.

[362] 'Company law can help business or it can hinder it. Company law can encourage entrepreneurship, promote growth, enhance international competitiveness and create conditions for investment and commitment of resources, whether of savings or employment. Or it can frustrate entrepreneurs, inhibit growth, restrict competitiveness and undermine the conditions for investment.' (Company Law Review Steering Group, *Modern Company Law: Final Report*, 2001, para 1 (UK).)

[363] Since shareholders will be the beneficiaries of market-driven change, they have the strongest incentive to lobby for it. Indeed, shareholders may lobby more strongly than bodies representing managers, who may wish to oppose certain pro-shareholder reforms if these will increase the chances of managers losing their jobs. So managers may appear, at least on some reform issues, as incumbents opposing change rather than lobbyists for change. However, managers may support pro-shareholder reforms if those reforms enable the company to compete more effectively in international markets.

they will converge doctrinally, though some degree—perhaps a even high degree—of doctrinal convergence is to be expected as well.[364] Thus, in one jurisdiction court-enforced standards may be more important in securing board sensitivity to shareholder desires than in another where strong governance rights for shareholders exist. This may reflect effective procedures for the enforcement of legal standards in the one jurisdiction and low collective action costs for shareholders in relation to their governance rights in the other. But both techniques may be equally effective in securing board responsiveness to shareholder interests.

However, further arguments against the convergence theory are more far-reaching. Political forces are important even under the market theory, because lobbying by firms suffering from inefficient company law is seen as a crucial mechanism whereby legal change is brought about. However, and this is the third argument, the political process may just as easily throw up obstacles to the reform of company law as provide a channel for its implementation. Incumbents may lobby against reform if their current benefits from an unreformed system are greater than they can expect from a reformed one.[365] Managers may not welcome changes which make them more accountable to shareholders, for that may threaten their job tenure. Equally, controlling shareholders benefitting from high private benefits of control may resist reform aimed at encouraging institutional investment. Moreover, incumbents, because they are already entrenched, may have some natural advantages in the lobbying process, so that it is not obvious that the reformers will always win. The balance of power as between reformers and incumbents will naturally vary from jurisdiction to jurisdiction and from time to time.

We may imagine that, for most voters most of the time, company law rules are a matter of indifference, so that their reform is indeed a matter of lobbying and counter-lobbying by those interest groups to whom the rules do matter. However, in times of crisis, such as the collapse of Enron and other companies at the beginning of the century or the more recent financial crisis, company laws (or at least certain parts of them) may become salient for elected politicians because voters do perceive that these rules matter. At such times, the balance in the corporate law debate may shift in favour of the reformers,[366] but the political pressures may also move the reforms in a populist direction, so that the question of the efficiency of company law in cost-reduction terms becomes submerged in

---

[364] R. Gilson, 'Globalizing Corporate Governance: Convergence of Form or Function', (2001) 49 *The American Journal of Comparative Law* 329, arguing that the adaptivity or otherwise of a corporate governance system will determine the extent to which the convergence which occurs is functional or formal.

[365] In other words, the incumbents do better from having a larger slice of a smaller pie than a smaller slice of a larger pie. Of course, whether this is so—or is perceived to be so—in any particular case is an empirical matter.

[366] P. Davies, 'Enron and Corporate Governance Reform in the UK and the European Community', in J. Armour and J. A. McCahery, eds., *After Enron*, Oxford/Portland 2006, p. 415.

other issues. Moreover, populist movements tend to have characteristics which vary from one polity to another, so that reforms driven by such concerns may not enhance the convergence of company laws overall, though on certain specific issues—such as women on the board or directors' remuneration—that may indeed be the result.

However, the strongest challenge to the theory of convergence of company laws via the pressures of competition comes for the 'varieties of capitalism' literature.[367] At the heart of this literature lies the concept of complementarities, ie. that a feature of a corporate governance system may have greater impact in lowering the costs of production in the presence of some other element of the environment (its 'complement') than if the complement is not present. To take a simple example, a rule permitting the shareholders by ordinary resolution at any time and for any reason to remove the members of the board will have a different impact if the shareholdings in the company are concentrated than if they are completely atomised. This argument gives rise to the possibility that differently constructed company law systems may be equally efficient because they are constructed around different complements. In the example, company law needs to address the agency problems of the minority shareholders, where shareholdings are concentrated, and the agency problems of shareholders as a class where shareholdings are dispersed. The resulting company law rules are likely to look very different, but they may represent equally efficient equilibria. One might try to find convergence here on the basis that both systems of company law seek to make the board responsive to the needs of non-controlling shareholders (who are the shareholders as a whole in the one case or only the minority shareholders in the other). However, the fact remains that the provisions of the company laws in the two systems will be different, functionally as well as formally, and any attempt to impose the rules of the one system on the other would be likely to increase the costs of production so long as the latter's shareholder structure remained unchanged.

A more challenging example is set by company law rules which reduce the responsiveness of the board to shareholder influence but can be regarded as complementary to rules and institutions which encourage firm-specific human capital investments by employees. It is conceivable that such rules raise the company's cost of capital (because of the reduced shareholder influence over management) but reduce the company's costs of production overall, because the company's labour costs are reduced to a greater extent than its capital costs are increased. Whether this is empirically the case in any particular jurisdiction may be difficult to demonstrate.[368] For example, the empirical literature on the

---

[367] P. Hall and D. Soskice, eds., *Varieties of Capitalism*, Oxford 2001.

[368] J. Addison, C. Schnabel and J. Wagner, 'Works Councils in Germany: their effects on establishment performance', (2001) 53 *Oxford Economic Papers* 659, suggesting that the distributional effects of works councils in favour of employees and away from shareholders are not inconsistent with an overall reduction in the costs of production.

German institutions of employee voice suggests that strong works councils are not inconsistent with an overall reduction in companies' costs of production, whilst even mandatory board level representation, if structured in a particular way, can have positive efficiency effects.[369]

The 'varieties of capitalism' literature thus suggests that differences in corporate law are likely to persist, even under the competitive pressures of globalisation, where the corporate law rules are complements to other differences in the productive arrangements in a particular jurisdiction. In fact, to change the corporate law rule in such a case might lead to a less efficient outcome. Thus, if corporate law rules in jurisdiction A, diluting the responsiveness of the board to shareholder interests, are a complement to institutions giving employees a strong voice in the governance of the enterprise, then changes increasing the influence of the shareholders on the board might both increase the levels of conflict within the board and render employees less likely to make human capital investment in the company. So, the equilibrium position within jurisdiction A is one where the shareholders' influence is diluted in order to maintain high levels of human capital investment.

However, it does not follow that this equilibrium is as successful in reducing the overall costs of production as the equilibrium which obtains in jurisdiction B, where the corporate law rules give shareholders a strong influence over the board and the employees have only limited governance rights. Let us suppose that the institutions overall in jurisdiction B do in fact produce lower costs of production than those in jurisdiction A. In this situation, a convergence theorist might argue that, under the pressures of competition, jurisdiction A will change both its rules on the board's responsiveness to shareholders and its rules on employee governance rights. However, the costs of making both changes in jurisdiction A are likely to be greater than the single change needed in jurisdiction B, where employee governance rights are not entrenched, to increase shareholder influence on the board. This is because there is likely to be greater opposition to the change in jurisdiction A by incumbents (ie. the employees) and because of the transitional costs of moving from a cooperative to a liberal model of company organisation. Thus, one might predict that jurisdiction A will increase the responsiveness of the board to shareholders only where the gains from such a move will be much higher than in jurisdiction B, where more modest gains will induce this move because the costs of reform (both political and financial) are less.[370]

---

[369] L. Fauver and M. Fuerst, 'Does good corporate governance include employee representation? Evidence from German corporate boards', (2006) 82 *Journal of Financial Economics* 673, suggesting that the efficiency gains are more likely if the representation is set at a less than parity level and if the employee representatives are not union appointees.

[370] For an analysis along these lines of the impact of globalisation on German corporate governance, see A. Börsch, *Global Pressure, National System*, Cornell U P, 2007.

Overall, the above theories suggest that over relatively short periods of time it will be difficult to predict the pace of change in corporate law and perhaps even its direction. The purpose of the next sections is to consider what light is shed on the theories just discussed by the experiences analysed in this book.

5.2. Board Composition

The spread of corporate governance codes across the EU, based on the UK model, is an apparently strong piece of evidence of changes in corporate law in a shareholder friendly direction. In the 1990s and 2000s corporate governance codes were adopted in all the jurisdictions covered in this volume (and indeed more broadly in the EU).[371] At a very general level, the pro-shareholder orientation of the codes was indicated in many cases by their endorsement of shareholder value as a proper goal of board activity, in the form of references to 'enlightened shareholder value'. Only in the UK, however, does the enlightened shareholder value, which unusually was embodied in the companies' legislation, give absolute priority to the interests of the shareholders.[372] Elsewhere, enlightened shareholder value is construed as a theory in which shareholder interests are given primacy, unless a proposed course of action would have a seriously adverse impact on non-shareholder interests.[373] In other cases, without specific reference to the enlightened shareholder value, the promotion of the long-term value of the company is regarded as legitimating pro-shareholder policies, but without ignoring stakeholder interests, because in the long-term these two sets of interests were perceived as reasonably well aligned.[374]

More important than the general statements contained in the codes were the particular board reforms which were recommended as best practice. Here the recommendations of the British code were highly influential. From the first British code of 1992 (the 'Cadbury Code') and throughout its subsequent iterations, that Code placed great weight on increasing the number and function of the independent non-executive directors ('independent directors'). In the UK context this was a pro-shareholder reform because it lessened the managerial agency costs of the then-dominant shareholder group, the long-only institutional shareholders, who were not block-holders but did have sufficiently large shareholdings to have a strong interest in the proper governance of portfolio companies. The current

---

[371] Weil/Gotshal/Manges, *Comparative Study of Corporate Governance Codes on behalf of the European Commission*, 2002.

[372] P. Davies, sec. 3.1.4, p. 752 and 3.2.3, p. 762.

[373] R.G.J. Nowak, sec. 1.1(f), p. 435; R. Skog and E. Sjöman, sec. 1.1(d), p. 622; S. Sołtysiński, sec. 3.2, p. 538.

[374] M. Roth, sec. 3.2.3, p. 340; G. Ferrarini et al., sec. 1.3, p. 373.

version of the British Corporate Governance Code recommends that half the directors should be independent and that they should dominate the audit, remuneration and appointment committees.[375]

The adoption by the other jurisdictions of the independent director model is surprising, since in those other jurisdictions the dominant form of shareholding is blockholding or concentrated shareholding. The presence of independent directors on boards (ie. board composition rules) is hardly needed to make directors responsive to controlling shareholders, who can use appointment and removal rights effectively for this purpose. On the contrary, rules requiring independent directors on the board are likely to dilute the influence of block-holders, especially if the board must contain employee representatives who do not count towards the independence requirement, so that the latter applies exclusively to the shareholder-appointed board members. Independent directors might operate in this context as protectors of non-controlling shareholders, but this is again to underline their dilution of the influence of block-holders.

It is significant that, in but one of our jurisdictions, the UK recommendation for a majority of independent directors was softened in one way or another.[376] In Germany, at least until recently, the recommendation is simply that 'the Supervisory Board shall include what it considers an adequate number of independent members',[377] without specifying a specific number of independent directors.[378] In fact, no code other than the UK one recommends a majority of independent directors.[379] A common way to formulate the requirement is to specify the composition rules in terms of non-executive directors, rather than independent non-executive

---

[375] P. Davies, sec. 2.2.1, p. 728 and 2.2.2, p. 734.

[376] The exception is the Netherlands, whose Corporate Governance Code recommends that all but one of the members of the supervisory board should be independent. However, there is no controlling shareholder in most of the Dutch companies listed on Euronext Amsterdam, so that the problem discussed in the text does not arise or does not arise in an acute form. See R.G.J. Nowak, sec. 1.1, p. 431 et seq. It is also notable that the independence principle also applies to the employee representatives, who in the Netherlands are not permitted to be employees of the company or employees of the union with representation rights within the company.

[377] German Corporate Governance Code, no. 5.4.2. This still falls short of recommending a particular proportion of independent directors.

[378] Since the supervisory board has to state and publish concrete aims for its composition and, since the 2012 revision, has to do this *inter alia* taking into consideration the number of independent supervisory board members, there is also an expectation that the actual number should be published, no. 5.4.1 sections 2 and 3 of the Code. But it remains to be seen how this section will be construed in practice.

[379] France is a partial exception to this statement. The AFEP/MEDEF code recommends that half the directors should be independent in a widely held company, but only one-third in a closely held one: A. Pietrancosta et al., 2.2.3(a), p. 203 et seq.

directors, as in Spain.[380] Alternatively, independence from shareholders may be omitted as one of the criteria for 'independence'.[381] As is expressly noted in some of the national analyses, the recommendations on board composition do not in fact prevent a controlling shareholder from appointing a majority of the board who are linked to that controlling shareholder.[382] The Polish experience is particularly instructive. The Polish Corporate Governance Code of 2002 recommended a majority of independent directors on the supervisory board, but by 2010 that recommendation had been reduced to a reference to two members. This was a response to complaints by controlling shareholders.[383]

This adaptation of the UK Code when adopted in continental jurisdictions could be explained as reflecting the ability of incumbents, powerful blockholding shareholders, to resist developments which threaten their position. Alternatively, it could be seen as functional. If the goal is the sensitivity of management to the interests of the shareholders, it would be contradictory to weaken the influence of large shareholders over boards.[384] In principle, minority protection can be addressed in other ways.[385] Or the continental codes might reflect some scepticism, expressed in all the national studies, about the ability of independent directors to exercise effective control over the management of companies.

However, this account does raise the question of why corporate governance codes spread to continental Europe at all if the UK model was designed to address a managerial agency problem for shareholders which is not typical in continental Europe. One possible answer is that the effect of globalisation was to increase successful companies' demand for risk capital and to promote the relaxation of obstacles to cross-border investment. Consequently, a code may have been seen as a necessary element in a policy of attracting foreign, especially US, portfolio investment. Codes drawn up from this perspective might then be as much concerned with explaining the domestic arrangements to foreign investors as with changing those arrangements. There seems to have been a strong element

---

[380] This allows significant shareholders as directors to count towards the non-executive requirement. See A. Recalde Castels et al., ch, 2.2.1(a), p. 567.

[381] In Switzerland, where the majority of directors are 'independent' in practice, though the Swiss Corporate Governance Code does not require this: 'a representative of a *large shareholder* on the Board does not, by that fact alone, lose "independence" from the Company'. P. Böckli, sec. 2.2.3(a), p. 679.

[382] R. Skog and E. Sjöman, sec. 2.2.3, p. 634 (where the nomination committee and plurality voting requirements tend in the same direction); K. Geens, sec. 2.2.1, p. 127 et seq. ('If there is a controlling shareholder, non-independent non-executives are always in the majority').

[383] S. Sołtysiński, sec. 2.5, p. 528.

[384] See A. Pietrancosta et al., sec. 2.2.3(a), p. 204, where the distinction made between the more demanding independence requirements for widely held companies and the less demanding ones for closely held companies can be seen as functional.

[385] See the discussion below concerning related-party transactions.

of this function when codes were adopted initially.[386] However, over time the parts of the Code containing actual recommendations have grown considerably, whilst the explanations of domestic law have been criticised as being sometimes too imprecise or even wrong and more generally as unnecessary today.[387] Of course, codes in continental jurisdictions never were simply information-giving mechanisms. They were concerned as well, today perhaps primarily, with providing assurance to foreign investors that the local corporate governance arrangements were credible. An enhanced role for independent directors was important in providing this assurance, even if the recommendation did not extend to the level of half the board.

5.3. Board Function and Board Structure

The introduction of independent directors was associated in the UK and the US with a change in the function of the board, ie. from advising to monitoring (or, better, from advising only to monitoring and advising). In the absence of regulation, in a dispersed shareholding model the board is chosen by the management. Being beholden to the management for their places, the non-executive members of the board are valuable because of the advice which they may provide from a perspective not well represented in the management or because of networking contacts they have which management does not have, but they are not well placed to monitor management. By contrast, the code movement proposed the injection of independent non-executive directors into the board in order to strengthen its monitoring function (as well as to provide advice). The board, afforced by the independent directors, should both participate in the setting of corporate strategy and review its implementation. The UK Corporate Governance Code is particularly emphatic on the monitoring role of the board, partly because the functions of the board are not specified in legislation and partly because this monitoring was what the institutional shareholders were pushing for.[388]

In a blockholding structure directors who owe their places to controlling shareholders are unlikely to shirk from monitoring, if that is what the controlling share-

---

[386] In its introduction, the German Code states: 'The Code aims at making the German Corporate Governance system transparent and understandable. Its purpose is to promote the trust of the international and national investors, customers, employees and the general public in the management and supervision of listed German stock corporations.'

[387] K.J. Hopt, 'Der Deutsche Corporate Governance Kodex: Grundlagen und Praxisfragen', in: *Festschrift für Hoffmann-Becking*, Cologne 2013, p. 563. But in a lecture for the 2012 German Corporate Governance Code Conference in Berlin, H.-C. Hirt from the UK pension fund Hermes remarked that this function may still be useful at least for US and other non-EU Member States investors.

[388] P. Davies, sec. 2.2.3, p. 738 et seq.

holder wishes them to do.[389] Shareholder-friendly reform in such a case is likely to consist in the removal of legal or regulatory obstacles to the board acting in a monitoring role, if such obstacles exist. The best example of this is probably Germany. German corporate law in its 1937 version, which was carried over into the post-war laws, limited the powers of the supervisory board to approve strategic issues or to remove managing board members without cause, whilst the presence of employee representatives in significant numbers on the supervisory board created the possibility of strategic alliances between the managing board and those representatives to dilute the influence of the shareholder representatives on the supervisory board. However, under the reforms of 2002, at least in the majority view, the supervisory board is now required to establish *ex ante* a catalogue of management decisions which require its prior consent, which catalogue includes the main elements of corporate strategy. The law's prior formulation that management is solely a matter for the management board, and with it the implication that strategy setting is a matter for the management board alone, remains, but that statement is in fact now qualified as a result of the 2002 reforms.[390]

The French board structure reforms of 2001 can perhaps be viewed in the same light. Under the traditional mandatory single-tier form power was concentrated, under the reforms of 1940, in a single person as chairman and managing director (*président-directeur général*—PDG), but the 2001 reforms allowed the board to decide that the general management of the company would not be assumed by its chairman.[391] This change can be seen as facilitating the operation of a monitoring board by removing the all-powerful PDG, even if the reform did not prohibit the traditional arrangement, which therefore still continues in some companies.[392]

What is striking, however, about the national analyses is that the distinction between one-tier and two-tier boards today has little impact on the ability of the board or supervisory board to perform a monitoring function. In the one-tier system this is because, except for the traditional French system, they are very flexible and allow extensive delegation of functions to management, perhaps in the form of a management board or perhaps more informally, whilst strategy remains with the board.[393] As for the two-tier systems, the German Act of 1937,

---

[389] Where employees are strongly represented on the board, the block-holder may prefer to do the monitoring directly rather than via the board.

[390] M. Roth, sec. 2.1(c) , p. 282.

[391] A. Pietrancosta et al., sec. 13, p. 184. A two-tier option had been introduced as early as 1966.

[392] A. Pietrancosta et al., table at p. 185, shows that about half the SBF 120 and CAC 40 companies continue to combine the functions of chair and CEO, whilst the other half have either separated the functions within a one-tier model or have adopted a two-tier board (which necessarily involves separation).

[393] P. Davies, sec. 2.1, p. 724; P. Böckli, sec. 1.3, p. 662; R. Skog and E. Sjöman sec. 1.3, p. 623; K. Geens, sec. 1.3, p. 124; G. Ferrarini et al., sec. 2.1(b), p. 376; A. Recalde Castells et al., sec. 2.2.2(b), p. 573.

now in any case amended as indicated above, was an outlier in aiming to exclude the supervisory board from strategy; the more typical approach puts involvement in the setting of strategy into the task of 'supervision'.[394]

It may be that the perception that there is a relatively weak link between board structure and board function has encouraged the development in some jurisdictions of a choice of board structures.[395] This approach is reflected in the Community provisions on the SE, which require Member States to make the choice between one-tier and two-tier structures available to SEs incorporated in their jurisdictions, even if that choice is not made available to national public companies.[396] Equally, it is not clear that the efficiency of the monitoring function is linked to board structure (in the absence of specific legal rules hindering monitoring by the board or supervisory board). In both cases, proposals for strategy will lie within the realm of management and the ability of independent directors effectively to challenge those proposals when they are considered by the board or supervisory board will depend heavily on the expertise and personalities of those independent directors.

5.4. Minority Shareholders

The main agency problem for shareholders in concentrated shareholder jurisdictions exists between controlling and non-controlling shareholders. The risk that minority shareholders run is that of a non-pro rata distribution of the revenues of the company as between controlling and non-controlling shareholders. An obvious technique for extracting such private benefits of control is the self-dealing transaction, ie. a transaction between the company and, directly or indirectly, the controlling shareholder, in which the terms of the transaction are skewed against the company. In a number of our jurisdictions reforms were implemented in recent years designed to protect minority shareholders against extraction of value from the company in this way. In general what is required is disclosure of the conflict to the board *ex ante* (and to the shareholders *ex post*), non-participation by an interested director in the decision on the transaction, sometimes allocation of the decision to a committee of independent directors,

---

[394] S. Sołtysiński, sec. 2.2, p. 525; M. Roth, sec. 1.3(b), p. 276; R.G.J. Nowak, sec. 2.1(c), p. 452 et seq.

[395] A. Pietrancosta et al., sec. 1.3, p. 183 et seq.; G. Ferrarini et al., sec. 1.3, p. 373 (both jurisdictions now providing three choices); R.G.J. Nowak, sec. 1.3, p. 446 (suggesting the introduction of a one-tier alternative in 2011 was aimed at encouraging Anglo-US investors); S. Sołtysiński, sec. 5.3, p. 547 (a future possibility). The trend is more general; see K.J. Hopt, above n. 1, *The American Journal of Comparative Law* 59 (2011) 1 at 22 et seq.

[396] Council Regulation (EC) No 2157/2001 of 8 October 2001 on the Statute for a European company (SE), Art. 38.

with liability in damages to the company in the case of non-compliance. The most elaborate recent innovations are to be found in the Italian reforms of 2010,[397] but other jurisdictions have also made changes in this area in recent years, either through the companies legislation or through the corporate governance code.[398] In Poland, where domestic companies are dominated either by foreign shareholders or the Polish state, the introduction of a group rule based on the French *Rozenblum* doctrine has been recently mooted but is proving very controversial.[399] Most recently the European Commission has announced in its Action Plan of 2012 the intention to improve the information available on groups and to recognise the concept of 'group interest'.[400]

An alternative form of minority shareholder protection is to guarantee minority shareholder representation on the board. The moves in corporate governance codes towards requiring even a minority of independent directors on the board go some way in this direction, because independent directors may be more sensitive to the interests of minority shareholders than directors aligned with management or controlling shareholders. However, only Italy, Austria, Spain and Poland guarantee minorities representation at board level in some circumstances.[401] It seems fair to state that protection of minority shareholders has proceeded further in relation to high-risk transactions[402] than in relation to a guaranteed presence on the board. This may be a functional arrangement since minority representation at board level may lead to high levels of intra-board conflict.

---

[397] G. Ferrarini et al., sec. 3.1.3.1 and 2, p. 399 et seqq.

[398] R.G.J. Nowak, sec. 3.1.3(a) and (b), p. 479 et seq.—the Corporate Governance Code and the Law on management and supervision (to enter into force in 2013); R. Skog and E. Sjöman, sec. 3.1.3, p. 639—stock exchange rules for related-party transactions; P. Böckli, sec. 3.1.3(c), p. 690—legislative reform proposed; K. Geens, sec. 3.1.2, p. 140—reforms dating from 1995. The European Commission's Company Law and Corporate Governance Action Plan (above n. 28) moots the notion of amendments of the Shareholder Rights Directive to generalise these reforms across the Union. This is another example of rules in codes or stock exchange rules being moved into the sphere of 'hard' law (if the Commission's recommendations are accepted).

[399] S. Sołtysiński, sec. 5.2, p. 545.

[400] See above n. 28 and K.J. Hopt, *Zeitschrift für Unternehmens- und Gesellschaftsrecht* 2013, 165 at 209–212.

[401] S. Sołtysiński, sec. 2.8, p. 530—cumulative voting can be triggered by those holding at least 20% of the share capital; G. Ferrarini et al., sec. 3.1.1, p. 392—slate voting (in practice a minority with an average 2.3% holding can submit a slate but only one or two minority directors are elected in this way). Cf. already above, sec. 3.1.1 under appointment rights.

[402] But even here rules on corporate opportunities are either lacking or underdeveloped, outside the UK.

5.5. Shareholder Activism

This book is a study of boards, not shareholders, but just as the functioning of the board turns on its relationship with management, so also it turns on its relationship with the shareholders. There is a complex double relationship here. On the one hand, shareholders who have pushed for policies which make the board more sensitive to their interests may come under pressure from government to use that influence to improve the management of the company. On the other, governments which want shareholders to improve the governance of companies, so that they can reap the financial benefits (taxes, jobs) arising from more competitive companies, do not want shareholders to engage in activities which will cause them political problems.

In the case of controlling shareholders, they already had access to the instruments—appointment and removal rights—necessary to secure their influence over the board, and their 'locked in' status gave them an incentive to promote the efficient running of the company. So, the first aspect of the double relationship has arisen only in jurisdictions with significant institutional shareholders, which have formed a constituency which has pushed for more influence over boards. However, institutional shareholders are not normally locked into any particular company and so can choose exit rather than the exercise the newly acquired influence over the board.[403] This provides the context for the second aspect of the relationship. Institutional shareholders have been an obvious target for governments wishing to promote the efficient running of companies but not wishing to do that job themselves. However, from an institutional shareholder's point of view, engagement policies run the risk of reducing the institutional shareholders' freedom of action (notably by making the exit option politically suspect). Governmental pressure on institutional shareholders to engage with investee companies has proceeded furthest in the UK, with its Stewardship Code (2010),[404] and in the Netherlands with similar but so far self-regulatory efforts.[405]

---

[403] The institution may find it difficult to dispose immediately of a substantial holding in publicly traded company without adverse price consequences, but it is better placed to run the holding down over a period of time.

[404] P. Davies, sec. 3.1.4, p. 752. See also *The Kay Review of UK Equity Markets and Long-Term Decision-Making, Final Report,* July 2012.

[405] R.G.J. Nowak, sec. 3.1.4, p. 484—the Eumedion *Code of Best Practices for Engaged Share Ownership* (30.6.2011). In France, a semi-official group has proposed something similar: A Pietrancosta et al., sec. 3.1.4, p. 217—proposal from the *Club des Juristes.* For the USA see S. Gillan and L. Starks, 'The Evolution of Shareholder Activism in the United States', *Journal of Applied Corporate Finance* 19 (2007) 55.

When governments propose deeper shareholder engagement with companies, for example as in the UK and the Netherland as well as the European Union,[406] they are thinking probably about engagement by long-only institutional share-holders, whose interests in the long-term success of the company coincide broadly with those of other stakeholders. However, shareholder engagement could also be attractive to more short-term shareholders, notably activist hedge funds. There is a strong argument that such funds, which take only minority stakes in companies, can be successful only if they attract the support of long-only shareholders, so that the dichotomy between activist and institutional share-holder engagement is a false one. Activist shareholders, it can be argued, provide the mechanism whereby long-only investors overcome their collection action problems. Nevertheless, whilst long-only shareholders typically engage with in-vestee company management in a reactive way, in order to preserve the value of investments made for non-activist reasons, activist hedge funds are pro-active, ie. they invest in order to reap benefits from changing the policies of the incumbent management. They tend to concentrate on proposing immediate and fairly radical changes to existing corporate strategy in order to increase the value of the com-pany, with aim of exiting it after the changes have borne fruit. Interventions by activist shareholders can thus be seen a qualitatively different from interventions undertaken by long-only shareholders, even if the former type of intervention is dependent upon the support of the institutions. Activists' interventions are more likely to be resisted not only by incumbent management but also by other stake-holders, especially employees. Governments tend not to welcome such forms of engagement, because they are politically unpopular, but it is difficult to craft laws which facilitate long-term but not short-term engagement.[407] The tensions in this area are well illustrated by Dutch experience, where reforms of 2004 making it easier for minority shareholders to influence management are currently proposed not only to be reversed but also to be replaced by more constraining rules than existed before 2004, in the light of only limited, but politically unpopular, use of such rights by activist shareholders.[408] Thus, governmental support for increased governance rights for non-controlling shareholders is not without limits.

[406] European Commission, Green Paper, above n. 31, ch. 2, and Action Plan 2012 (above n. 28), point 3.1–3.5: Engaging Shareholders, and point 2.4 on institutional investors; cf. also Report of the Reflection Group, above n. 160, ch. 3.

[407] Incentives to long-termism are an alternative approach that has been adopted in France and in the Netherlands. See, for a general proposal, P Bolton and F Samama, *L-Shares: Rewar-ding Long-term Investors* (available at <http://cgt.columbia.edu/papers/Bolton_Samama_L-Shares-Rewarding_Long-Term_Investors/>).

[408] R.G.J. Nowak, sec. 1.1(h), p. 437 and 5(a), p. 503 (as of 2013). A similar but less extreme story can be told about France where 2001 reforms promoting shareholder activism were supplemented by2010 reforms prohibiting opaque 'empty voting' and restricting activism by hedge funds (A. Pietrancosta et al., sec. 3.1.4, p. 218 et seq.).

5.6. Successful Resistance to Pro-Shareholder Changes

In all the above cases some change favourable to shareholders occurred, but it was not always as extensive as pro-shareholder reformers would have wished nor did the reforms always take root in the legal system in question. Nevertheless, the above might be regarded as evidence of a movement in the direction of more shareholder-friendly board rules. However, the most effective technique for making the board sensitive to the interests of the shareholders is probably the threat of a hostile takeover bid, ie. an offer from a bidder made directly to the shareholders of the company (and thus over the heads of target management) to acquire their shares. The possibility of a hostile takeover creates a strong incentive for managements of all companies subject to this threat at all times to act in the interest of the shareholders who might otherwise be susceptible to a takeover offer.[409] Again, the feature of board rules most likely to make the board less sensitive to the interests of the shareholders is a substantial mandatory presence of employee representatives on the board. How have these features of corporate law changed in recent years?

Mandatory employee representation at board level—In none of our jurisdictions having such arrangements were the board representation rights of employees significantly reduced over the past two decades. The jurisdictions with the strongest systems are Germany and the Netherlands. In both there were proposals from normally influential groups for reduction of the employees' representation rights and in the Netherlands the issue even reached the official agenda, but no reform occurred.[410] On the other hand, none of the existing regimes for employee representation at board level was significantly strengthened in this period.[411] It is difficult to know whether the better explanation for the 'stickiness' of the rules on board level representation is to be found in the opposition of politically important incumbents (notably organised labour) or in a complementarities story under

---

[409] In other words, it is the *ex ante* effect of the takeover threat which is crucial rather than the *ex post* effect if a bid is launched. Of course, hostile bids may also be motivated by industrial re-construction ('synergies') rather than managerial discipline goals.

[410] R.G.J. Nowak, sec. 5, p. 503; M. Roth, sec. 3.2.1(d), p. 335 et seq.

[411] The Dutch 'structure regime' was reformed in 2004, but the impact of the reform is unclear. Before that, the supervisory board (under the 'structure' regime) was a self-perpetuating body, but with the works council and the shareholders having equal rights to recommend or oppose proposed members of the supervisory board. In theory this might lead to parity of representation but in practice the level of employee representation was thought by those involved to be much lower. In 2004, the system was reformed so as to give the works council, in effect, appointment rights over one-third of the board, which rights are normally exercised. So, in practice there may have been an increase in the board influence of the works council, but that influence is now clearly capped at one-third of the supervisory board seats. See R.G.J. Nowak, sec. 3.2.1, p. 488.

which greater protection for employee interests in strategic decision-making facilities firm-specific human capital investments by employees. Equally, there is in our jurisdictions no example in recent years of the introduction of board level representation in jurisdictions previously without it or (arguably) significant extension of existing regimes.[412]

Hostile takeovers—The European Commission wished to impose a pro-shareholder solution which would have sidelined target management in takeover bids, thus facilitating hostile bids, but the Takeovers Directive of 2004 was eventually agreed only on the basis that the matter was left, almost entirely, to the Member States. At Member State level, the main pattern was one of states continuing as before with whatever policies they had in relation to such bids, with some move towards allowing target management a bigger defensive role where there was no 'reciprocity' between bidder and target.[413] The 'stickiness' of the rules on hostile takeovers again admits of an efficiency and a 'political' explanation. Making hostile takeovers difficult permits companies to commit to rewarding firm-specific human capital investments by employees, and thus can be argued to be a complement to rules requiring mandatory representation of employees at board level. Even in jurisdictions without mandatory board representation for employees, management will be in a better position to commit to employees if it is not subject to the threat of a hostile bid. The political explanation suggests that the views of incumbents, especially incumbent managers, were crucial in determining the rate and direction of change in the rules on hostile takeovers. In general, managers might be expected to oppose more liberal rules on hostile

---

[412] In 2013 France introduced a limited extension of its provisions for the mandatory representation of employees on the board with full voting rights. The new rules are confined to companies with at least 5000 workers in France (or 10,000 worldwide) and provide for the appointment of one or two (depending on the size of the board) worker directors, cf. the 1000-worker threshold for parity representation in Germany. The default selection method is direct election by the workers (but, as in Germany, only by the French workers). Nevertheless, this is a not unimportant change since the previous French rules provided only very limited opportunities for worker directors with full voting rights. See A. Pietrancosta et al., sec. 2.2.1(c), p. 194. One may speculate that this reform responds to a post-financial crisis environment which is less accepting of a liberal view of economic relations.

[413] Reciprocity refers to the situation where the bidder is subject to a ban on taking defensive actions (if it would be a takeover target). The reciprocity principle allows a target normally not permitted to take post-bid defensive action to do so if the bidder is not subject to a board neutrality rule. The Directive was interpreted as permitting Member States that imposed a board neutrality rule to make it subject to a reciprocity exception. For the spread of reciprocity exceptions to the prohibition on defensive action by targets, see P. Davies, E.-P. Schuster and E. van de Walle de Ghelcke, 'The Takeover Directive as a Protectionist Tool?', in U. Bernitz and W.-G. Ringe, eds., *Company Law and Economic Protectionism*, Oxford 2010, p. 105, available as ECGI – Law Working Paper No. 141/2010 at: <http://ssrn.com/abstract=1554616> or <http://dx.doi.org/10.2139/ssrn.1554616>.

takeovers, though in some jurisdictions they might support them if they expected to be more often bidders than targets.[414]

The potential downsides of excluding hostile bids are clear: less managerial discipline and a lesser possibility of synergistic changes of control occurring. However, if shareholdings are concentrated in jurisdictions where the hostile bid is not facilitated, both these potential downsides are reduced. As we have mentioned above, concentrated shareholders are well placed to remove underperforming management themselves through the exercise of their governance rights (rather than relying on a bidder to do so). Further, where shareholdings are concentrated, a synergistic bid will turn on the decision of the shareholders, since the board, appointed by those shareholders is not likely to operate contrary to their interests. In other words, the rules on hostile takeovers are irrelevant if the shareholders and the directors are, in effect, the same people. However, even in jurisdictions with predominantly concentrated shareholdings, there will be some companies with sufficiently dispersed shareholdings that a decision by the shareholders cannot be expected always to be the same as a decision by the board, so that in these cases the rules on hostile takeovers do matter. In the jurisdictions studied there is evidence of some decrease in the levels of concentration amongst the largest publicly traded companies.[415] Consequently, the question of whether post-bid defensive action is permitted without shareholder approval is likely to become more, not less, important in the future.

5.7. Politics Re-setting the Board Rules Agenda

When company law rules become salient for voters, the prospects for alignment between the government's interests and those of the shareholders are reduced. Across all our jurisdictions the issue of executive remuneration has become salient for voters and all report changes designed to address the issue. So long as the remuneration changes are aimed at addressing the agency costs of shareholders, government and shareholder interests are aligned, but it is less clear that they are if the thrust of the regulation is to reduce the absolute level of remuneration. Remuneration committees dominated by independent shareholders, strict criteria for performance-related pay, a greater role for the shareholders in setting pay policy and even longer vesting periods for performance related pay and the clawing back of bonuses if subsequent performance is poor (all common)

---

[414] P.C. Culpepper, *Quiet Politics and Business Power*, Cambridge 2011, arguing that the interests of incumbent managers were predominant in determining the stance of takeover rules in France, Germany and the Netherlands, but explaining the more liberal stance of French takeover law by reference to the internationalist ambitions of French managers.

[415] M. Roth, sec. 1.1(a), p. 258; A. Pietrancosta et al., sec. 1.1(e), p. 180.

are not necessarily contrary to the interests of shareholders, though all risk constraining the company's freedom to structure pay in an optimal way. Outright limits on payments are more questionable from a shareholder's point of view, even when they are expressed in general terms.[416] Change is this area is usually presented as addressing agency costs (market failure) but it is far from obvious that this is always true, for some of the pressure on governments to act arises from distributional rather than efficiency concerns.

Remuneration has always been a topic addressed in companies legislation and corporate governance codes, so that its 'politicisation' does not bring a new issue into the area of board rules but simply re-frames an old question in a new, but particularly pressing, way. By contrast, the currently much discussed issue of quotas for women on boards brings in a new issue. It is doubtful whether voters much care about this particular issue, but there is a high degree of political support for gender-equality policies. What we have here is a link being made between one area of governmental policy (equality) into another (board rules) which those whose focus is solely on the formulation of board rules would probably not have made, but governments under political lobbying may do. The opportunity to make the link was presented when it was perceived that corporate governance failed in the financial crisis.[417] The argument for more women on the board is sometimes presented as one for improving corporate performance. In fact, the evidence that having more women on boards improves board performance is weak, though the contrary is often confidently asserted.[418] By contrast, the argument that more women on boards would promote the objectives of equality legislation is more robust, ie. the issue is essentially distributional rather than about efficiency.[419]

5.8. Convergence

The supporters of the convergence thesis can derive some comfort from the above analysis. Their hypothesis that the pressures of global competition would drive

---

[416] M. Roth, sec. 3.1.5, p. 329—requirement that remuneration be based on the 'sustainability' of the company. Or when expressed in structural terms, such as the proposal for financial companies that variable pay should not exceed a multiple of one of fixed pay (or two if shareholders consent).

[417] In fact it is far from clear that the boards of non-financial institutions did 'fail' in the recent financial crisis. See B. Cheffins, 'Did Corporate Governance "Fail" During the 2008 Stock Market Meltdown?', (2009) 65 *Business Lawyer* 1.

[418] See above, sec. 2.2.1 n. 60.

[419] M. McCann and S. Wheeler, 'Gender Diversity in the FTSE 100: The Business Claim Explored', (2011) 38 *Journal of Law and Society* 542; L. Fairfax, 'Board Diversity Revisited: New Rationale, Same Old Story?', (2011) 89 *North Carolina Law Review* 856.

board rules in a shareholder-friendly direction is supported in particular by the recent reforms to the rules on board composition (emphasising the role of independent directors) and the strengthening of the controls on related-party transactions. By contrast, board rules have not moved in favour of other stakeholders, especially employees, in recent decades. Both the changes which did occur and those which did not are in strong contrast to, for example, the reforms to board rules which occurred in the 1970s, when many jurisdictions introduced or strengthened provisions on mandatory board representation for employees, whilst pro-shareholder change was difficult to detect.

However, the limits to the pro-shareholder changes to board rules which occurred over the past two decades are also striking. Mandatory board representation for employees made little or no progress, but equally it was not in retreat—at least not at the level of the formal rules,[420]—whilst managers and employees were able to resist the emergence of a vibrant market in corporate control. The above account might suggest that the role of politics in mediating the pro-shareholder impact of globalisation is important. Pro-shareholder change was supported by government, partly because it encouraged the inward flow of equity capital, but also because boards were seen as insufficiently accountable and prone to error, as in the *Parmalat* and *Ahold* cases at the beginning of the century or as in the example of executive remuneration. But pro-shareholder change might meet effective opposition from non-shareholder groups, notably managers and employees, and that set limits to its development.

For the future, it is not clear that the same level of political support for pro-shareholder change will be forthcoming. The recent financial crisis is perceived in some quarters to have shown that shareholders are not capable of controlling boards or even that the shareholders played an unacceptable role in urging boards to pursue reckless courses of action. Whether this will prove to be a passing phase of analysis or whether the pressures for pro-shareholder change will permanently weaken remains to be seen.

6. Conclusion

6.1. Board Decision-Making and Shareholder Decision-Making

The board of directors is the central constituent of the governance arrangements in public companies. In fact, the board is a mandatory part of the constitutional

---

[420] The pressures of product market competition have probably diluted the effective level of influence of employees in relation to corporate policy. See G. Jackson, M. Höpner and A. Kurdelbusch, 'Corporate Governance and Employees in Germany: Changing Linkages, Complementarities and Tensions', in H. Gospel and A. Pendleton, eds., *Corporate Governance and Labour Management*, Oxford 2005.

arrangements for public companies in all jurisdictions. This is in contrast, for example, to the partnership where the default rule is that decisions are taken by a majority of all the partners, though the partners may, and in larger partnerships normally do, introduce by agreement a governing body consisting of some sub-set of the partners. Why is the board mandatory in companies? Looking at it from the perspective of the shareholders, one answer might be that it permits specialisation as between investors and managers. Those whose skills are as investors are enabled to put money into the business without having to take on the burden of managing it, and vice versa. Even from a shareholder perspective, this view is not wholly convincing, since a permissive default rule, as found in partnerships, rather than the mandatory rule found in companies would also permit specialisation.

A stronger argument might be that, in companies with many shareholders, the efficiency arguments against shareholder decision-making and in favour of decision-making by a small group are so overwhelming as to justify a mandatory rule. Shareholder decision-making in core management areas is likely to be slower, less expert and less committed than decision-making by the board.[421] However, this argument would suggest, not only that the board be a mandatory element in the constitutional structure of the company, but also that the core management decisions be compulsorily allocated to it. As we saw in 2.1 above, this result has long obtained in all our jurisdictions, normally by legislative stipulation of the board's functions. However, the efficiency arguments in favour of allocating core management issues to the board are so strong in public companies that it is doubtful whether a different arrangement would exist from what is now found even if both the functions of the board and its very existence were left to default, rather than mandatory, rules.[422]

Even though the arguments for taking core management decisions away from the shareholders are strong in a public company, nevertheless shareholder decision-making in such companies has a significant role to play. Corporate decisions

---

[421] Slower because the shareholder body is more difficult to convene; less expert because the only consistent requirement to be a shareholder in a public company is the ability to pay for the shares; and less committed because the shareholder body is a large one so that the incentive to invest resources working out the right decision is weak, except for a controlling shareholder.

[422] A small piece of evidence in this direction can be found in the United Kingdom. UK company law, betraying the influence of the partnership on its origins, is something of a hybrid: the board is mandatory but the specification of its functions is left very largely to the articles (ie. to the shareholders). In practice, the articles specify the board functions which are found in the legislation in other countries. The official 'model' articles, which apply in default of contrary agreement among the incorporators, take this approach. So, the 'steady state' result is the same. However, the possibility of removing functions from the board, even if remote, may provide greater accountability to shareholders. See below. The greater formal flexibility in the UK legislation may reflect the fact that the UK Companies Act applies to all sizes of company—including private, even very small private—companies, where separation of board and shareholder decision-making is often meaningless.

which can have, at least potentially, an impact on the rights of the shareholders, such as alterations of the company's constitution or mergers, require shareholder approval, even when wide general management powers are delegated to the board. Unlike in Delaware, shareholders in Europe normally have the formal power to initiate such changes as well, though they exercise it rather infrequently. The second traditional use of shareholder decision-making, even under extensive delegation to the board, is to deal with directors' conflicts of interest. A loss of efficiency in decision-making may appear to be a price worth the shareholders paying if the benefit is a reduced level of diversion of value to the managers themselves. Nevertheless, the loss of efficiency is a real one, so that shareholder decision-making is normally required in conflict situations only where alternative, board-level solutions have been tried and proved inadequate. A prime and on-going example is that of directors' remuneration. Board-level solutions, in the way of remuneration committees controlled by independent directors, having proved inadequate to moderate executive pay, the move towards advisory or even binding shareholder votes on executive pay is now well under way across Europe.[423] By contrast, the general rules on self-dealing[424] still display a greater reluctance to move to shareholder decision-making and they concentrate instead on identifying a robust form of non-conflicted decision-making at board level, for example, through the use of board committees and independent outside advice (though disclosure to the shareholders is normally an important element of these rules).[425] This may be in part because, in a company with a controlling shareholder, moving the issue from board to shareholders may not change much—unless interested shareholders are disqualified from voting.[426]

Neither of these exceptions makes a serious inroad into the principle of excluding shareholders *de facto* from core management decision-making in public companies. Corporate constitutions and legislation are sparing in the allocation of rights to shareholders, so that management decisions only infrequently impinge on

---

[423] See above, sec. 3.1.5. The European Commission's Company Law and Corporate Governance Action Plan 2012 (above n. 28) contemplates amending the Shareholder Rights Directive to give shareholders across the Union a say-on-pay—though it is unclear whether that 'say' is to be advisory or binding. See above, sec. 3.1.5.

[424] See above, sec. 3.1.3.

[425] See the discussion of Belgium and Italy, above sec. 3.1.3 notes 214 and 215. In blockholder jurisdictions shareholder approval of related-party transactions may be meaningless, so that transparency and outside evaluation assume greater importance.

[426] Contrast the UK, where controlled public companies are uncommon and where shareholder approval of conflicted transactions is required in certain high-risk cases under the Companies Act and in all but *de minimis* cases by the Listing Rules. Even so, directors may regard the uncertainty and disclosure associated with shareholder approval as a prohibition on related-party transactions—and that may not be in the company's interests if the director is the best supplier of the good or service in question.

the rights, as opposed to the interests, of shareholders.[427] Other than mergers and similar corporate restructurings, the main area where shareholders have veto rights is in relation to the issuing of shares or the various forms of capital reduction.[428] As to conflicts of interest, since the purpose of excluding shareholders from management decisions is to enhance the efficiency of corporate decision-making, rather than to permit directors or controlling shareholders acting through the board to divert corporate benefits to themselves, removing or qualifying board decision-making in such cases is in principle unobjectionable. However, the notion of excluding shareholders from management decisions is challenged if there is a rule requiring shareholder consent for board initiatives simply on the grounds of their economic significance to the company. In our jurisdictions, only the UK clearly has such a rule and even then, it is not to be found in the companies legislation but in the Listing Rules, which have been particularly subject to the influence of institutional shareholders.[429] The German *Holzmüller* rule,[430] although applying to all public companies, is but a pale-reflection of the UK Listing Rule because, as now understood, it applies only to decisions having a much bigger economic impact on the company than the UK rule and because, though rather unclearly, it is still tied to the notion of an infringement of shareholder rights.

Overall, the proposition that shareholder decision-making is an inefficient way of taking core managerial decisions is well supported by our work.

6.2. Board Decision-Making and Management Decision-Making

Although there is a strong efficiency argument for not placing core management decisions with the shareholders of public companies, it is not obvious that a board of directors is needed to achieve this result. The shareholders could, and in

---

[427] See above, sec. 3.1.2.

[428] The classical concerns of company law with share issues and reductions are captured in the Second Company Law Directive. Of course, creditor protection is a central concern of this Directive, but it also promotes equal treatment of shareholders through, for example, pre-emption rights or requirements for shareholder approval of the terms of share buy-backs. For a critique of the Second Directive, see for example European Company Law Experts, *Response to the European Commission's Consultation on the Future of European Company Law*, May 2012, 4(b), available at <http:/ssrn.com/abstract=1912548>.

[429] J. Armour and D.Skeel, 'Who Writes the Rules for Hostile Takeovers and Why?—The Peculiar Divergence of U.S. and U.K. Takover Regulation', (2007) 95 *Georgetown Law Journal* 1727 at 1770–1772, especially at fn. 210. Further, the rule applies only to companies which have chosen a Premium Listing on the Main Market of the London Stock Exchange. The idea underlying the requirement of shareholder approval is that economically large decisions raise as much investment as management issues.

[430] See above, sec. 3.1.2.

private companies in some jurisdictions do, choose the senior managers of the company but the law creates no board of directors. What advantages accrue as a result of a mandatory rule constituting a board? It could be that the identification of a group of senior managers as the 'board of directors' facilitates the imposition of liability on the senior management of the company for the conduct of the company's affairs. This is particularly important in relation to the duty of care, including the establishment of appropriate systems for evaluating and monitoring risk, and fiduciary duties.[431] Attaching such liability to those who are directors of the company removes any doubt about which managers are subject to this liability.[432] Of course, this strategy will work only if a substantial number of senior managers are members of the board (or of one of the boards). When, as often in the US, the board contains only a single manager (the CEO), the identification problem re-surfaces—and is expressed in the need to identify 'officers' to whom these liabilities may be attached, as well as directors. By contrast, in Europe the board of a public company[433] (or one of the boards) generally contains all the senior managers to whom it is necessary to attach duties of care and loyalty in order appropriately to constrain managerial decision-making.[434]

Apart from identification, there are two linked functions which a board facilitates. One is the introduction into management decision-making of areas of expertise which are not represented among the managers themselves. This is sometimes referred to as the 'advisory' or 'networking' function of the board. For example, a banker on the board of a manufacturing company may be able to provide corporate finance expertise which its managers do not have. Or an outsider might have extensive experience in dealing with a problem which the company is facing for the first time, for example, coping with a declining market or to pushing into foreign countries. Of course, such expertise could be 'bought in' via a long-standing relationship with a particular bank or auditing or legal firm or other supplier of the needed expertise. Management consultancy, also, could provide expertise in the design of corporate strategies without involving a board appointment.

The second function is that of monitoring the management of the company. Here the requirement for a board is probably vital for the effective discharge of

---

[431] See above, sec. 3.1.3.

[432] Of course, in the absence of a board and at the cost of some uncertainty, it would not be impossible to produce some general formula indicating which senior managers were to carry these liabilities.

[433] Contrast the private company, where a board may not always be necessary (eg. the GmbH in Germany—see n. 440 below) or where the hard and soft law requirements as to its composition may be minimal (as with the private company in the UK).

[434] However, sub-board senior managers will normally be categorised as agents or employees of the company to whom fiduciary duties can be attached, if necessary, though generally fiduciary duties of a less wide-ranging character than those attached to senior managers who are directors.

the monitoring function. By placing the board above the managers, whom the board appoints, the task of monitoring is facilitated, both because of the formal subordination of the managers, as managers, to the board and because of the greater status of the board members. Nevertheless, it is wrong to see the tasks of advising and monitoring as fully separate. An effective monitor will need the respect of the managers and that respect will be grounded in part in the monitor's understanding of the company's business and his or her ability contribute to the development of corporate strategy in a way which the managers regard as persuasive. If it comes to a serious conflict between management and monitor over corporate strategy, a monitor who has the respect of management will have a much better chance of carrying his or her point of view.

As we saw in section 2.2.1 above, board rules, especially those contained in corporate governance codes, have been reformed over recent decades so as to emphasise the monitoring role of the board or supervisory board, thus underlining the centrality of the board in the company's constitutional arrangements. Particular emphasis has been on increasing the proportion and functions of independent directors, enhancing the role of the board as against the management and the role of board committees dominated by independent directors, and the separation of the roles of the most senior manager and the chair of the board. Nevertheless, there is virtually no reliable empirical evidence that these reforms have improved corporate performance across the economy. Even in the narrow area of conflicts of interest, remuneration committees have a poor record for reigning in managerial excesses.[435] The lack of firm empirical support for the monitoring role of the board (or supervisory board), coupled with the spill-over from the financial crisis, has produced a swing of the pendulum back towards the advising end of the spectrum, through the now conventional contrast between independence and expertise.[436] Whether a more expert but less independent set of non-executive directors will be more successful in raising corporate performance remains to be seen. It may be that the inherent limitations on the position of the non-executive director (or member of a supervisory board), notably their dependence on the management for pertinent information, mean that expectations about their impact, whether as independents or experts, have become unrealistic.

Whether the non-executive members of the board (or supervisory board) are chosen for their independence or expertise, there is no doubt that the board today operates in a more professional way than previously. Proper induction for new board members, devotion of adequate time to the board role and periodic evaluation of the effectiveness of the board, perhaps involving external facilitators, are becoming standard.[437] The days of the 'figurehead' board of directors are long

---

[435] See above, sec. 3.1.5.

[436] See above, sec. 2.2.3 at notes 139 et seq.

[437] See above, sec. 2.2.1 at notes 79 and 80.

gone,[438] but the actual and potential contribution of the board to the effective running of the company (as opposed to dealing with crises such as the sudden departure of the CEO or an unwanted takeover offer) has not be securely identified.

6.3. Board Accountability

Since the essence of board decision-making is the centralisation of management decisions in the hands of a small group of expert people, the issue of the accountability of the board for the decisions it makes clearly arises. Three views of this issue can be identified, each of which has been dominant at different times in the history of the public corporation. The classical view is that the board should be accountable to the shareholders as the 'owners' of the company, as it would have been put in the nineteenth century, or as the residual claimants on the company's revenues, as contemporary law and economics scholars put it. The strength of that accountability could be calibrated at different levels but on this view it should not be negligible.

The second view is that the importance of the issue of accountability has been exaggerated. Effective development of the company's business in the medium-term will be best achieved by isolating the board from strong accountability to the shareholders. This view was well articulated in the German Companies Act 1937, which sought formally to exclude the board from strong accountability to the shareholders. This policy was based upon an analysis of contemporary US experience, though the basis for shareholder weakness in the US was rather different. In the US, and in the immediate post-war period in the UK, management autonomy stemmed not so much from rules designed to keep the shareholders at arm's length as from the inability of dispersed shareholders to overcome their coordination problems so as effectively to exercise the governance rights conferred upon them by the law. In either case, however, on this view of management accountability managers are kept up to the mark by influences other than shareholder pressure, perhaps the pressures of a competitive product market, perhaps formal or informal pressure from the state—or even trade unions.[439]

---

[438] Contrast the instructive nineteenth century UK case of *Re Cardiff Savings Bank* [1892] 2 Ch100 where the aristocratic Marquis of Bute was held not to have fallen below the required standard of care even though he had attended only one board meeting of the company in the whole of his adult life. However, the bank had appointed the Marquis president of the bank when he was a mere six months old. This hardly suggests that the bank expected sage business advice from its new, and indeed leading, board member, but rather wanted him merely as a figurehead. Therefore, by subsequently suing the Marquis for negligence it was the bank that sought to depart from the expectations embodied in the appointment.

[439] Cf. C.A.R. Crosland, *The Future of Socialism*, London 1956, p. 276, arguing that in the 1950s the shareholder primacy of British company law offered no serious impediment to

cont. ...

The third view is that accountability should run, not only to shareholders but also to other stakeholders in the company, especially the employees. Accountability to non-shareholder stakeholders is promoted by making the board a mandatory part of the company's constitution,[440] because the board can then be the body into which the representatives of, for example, the employees are inserted.[441] Although theoretically extendable to all non-shareholder stakeholders, in practice one finds board rules being used to provide board membership for employees only—perhaps because of the political influence of trade unions, perhaps because employees are better organised than other stakeholders, perhaps because employees are more firmly locked into the company than other stakeholders. Without board membership, some accountability to non-shareholder stakeholders can be provided through other mechanisms, for example, the formulation of directors' duties, but these mechanisms by themselves tend to have only a weak impact.

Of the three views mentioned above, the second view (management autonomy) is only weakly reflected in current company law systems, although the premises underlying it are often deployed to argue for not imposing very rigorous forms of accountability to shareholders. The last survivor of this view, the Dutch 'structure' regime,[442] was reformed in 2004 so as to replace the principle of a self-perpetuating board with the more familiar arrangement of directors appointed by the shareholders (two-thirds) or the employees (one-third).[443]

The third view (accountability to employees as well as shareholders) represents probably the great dividing line in corporate governance systems in Europe, which are split roughly equally between those with mandatory rules for employee representation in private sector companies and those without. In most jurisdictions—Germany is an outlier—employee representation does not extend beyond one-third of the board seats. The evidence in favour of the efficiency of such representation is mixed,[444] and it is notable that rules requiring such representation were normally put in place in the aftermath of a period of social upheaval—in Germany after the First and the Second World Wars[445] and most recently in the

socialist reforms because dispersed shareholders were incapable of exercising their governance powers and government and trade unions were the real influence on corporate management.

[440] Thus, in German private companies, where a board is in principle optional, a board is required if that private company is subject to co-determination because of the number of workers it employs. See above, sec. 3.2.1.

[441] The arguments against management decisions being taken directly by the employees are as strong as those against the decisions being taken by the shareholders directly. See above.

[442] See above, sec. 3.2.1 at n. 278.

[443] R.G.J. Nowak, sec. 3.2.1, p. 487.

[444] See above, sec. 3.2.1.

[445] See above, sec. 3.2.1.

early 1970s after the social unrest in Europe of the late 1960s.[446] Since that time, this form of accountability has made no further significant progress.

The first and classical view (accountability to shareholders) has made progress over the past few decades. Inherent in the very concept of an independent director, as someone who is independent of management, is a greater sensitivity to the interests of the shareholders. Beyond that, a number of initiatives have been launched across all our jurisdictions which strengthen board accountability to shareholders as a class, to minority shareholders or to creditors[447] as insolvency looms, although it is as yet unclear how significant or long-lasting they will turn out to be.[448] Perhaps the most significant change in relation to the classical view is the slow departure from the equally classical notion that the votes and other rights attached to shares are property rights to be exercised as their holder wishes. Institutional shareholders are coming under indirect pressure, as with the Stewardship Code in the United Kingdom, to exercise their rights in the public interest (ie. to secure change in underperforming companies rather than to dispose of their shares). Engagement may be in the interests of those whose funds the institutions invest, but there may be pressure to 'engage' whether that is so or not.

6.4. Overall

Because of the strong arguments in favour of delegated decision-making to a board in public companies, the board sits at the centre of the public company's corporate governance arrangements. But what the board is required to or actually does, and therefore how it should most appropriately be composed and structured, can change significantly in response to the economic environment in which the company operates,[449] the structure of its shareholdings[450] and the salience of poli-

---

[446] In this period even the UK toyed with mandatory rules on employee representation at board level. See the *Report of the Committee of Inquiry on Industrial Democracy,* Cmnd 6706, 1977 (often referred to as the Bullock Committee after its chairman), proposing a system of quasi-parity co-determination for the largest British companies.

[447] See above, sec. 3.3. On the residual claimant theory the substitution of creditor interests for shareholder interests in the vicinity of insolvency is fully explicable, since, once the shareholders' equity has disappeared irretrievably, the creditors are the residual claimants. The difficulties of applying the theory arise in the twilight zone before that point is reached when a particular risky project might, if successful, restore the shareholders' equity to a positive figure but, if unsuccessful, might make the creditors worse off.

[448] See above, sec. 3.1.1

[449] For example, the need for equity capital to fund expansion in a globalised economy.

[450] For example, the partial re-concentration of shareholdings in the hands of institutional shareholders in dispersed shareholding jurisdictions or the decline of blockholding in concentrated shareholder jurisdictions.

tical concerns.[451] That the social and economic functions of a continuing insti-tution change, sometimes quite radically, is not a new insight,[452] but, in the case of the board, it suggests that assessment of the board's role and reform of board rules, are likely to be a continuing feature of corporate law. The search for an ideal role for the board which, once identified, will never need to be altered is as elusive as the search for the Holy Grail.

[451] For example, social unrest in the late 1960s or responses to austerity in the wake of the recent financial crisis.

[452] K. Renner, *Die Rechtsinstitute des Privatrechts und ihre soziale Funktion* (1929); English: *The Institutions of Private Law and their Social Function*, Transl. by A Schwarzschild, with an introduction by Otto Kahn-Freund, London 1949.

Part II:
National Reports

Corporate Boards in Belgium

KOEN GEENS

1. Introduction

The main legal sources for corporate governance in Belgium are the Belgian Companies Code (*BCC – Wetboek van vennootschappen/Code des sociétés*) and the Corporate Governance Code (the 2009 Code).

The BCC is the result of the 1999 coordination of all Belgian company law legislation (the third such reform since 1873) by means of the Act of 7 May 1999 together with the Royal Decree of 30 January 2001.

The original version of what became the 2009 Code dates back to 2004–2005 and was drafted by the Corporate Governance Commission, a private foundation. It was restated after public consultation in 2009.

The Corporate Governance Code is not binding as such, but is to be followed on a comply-or-explain basis. The Act of 6 April 2010 and the Royal Decree of 6 June 2010 point out that—pursuant to European Directive 2006/46—Belgian listed companies are required to opt for a corporate governance code recognised by Royal Decree and must report and explain any exceptions they make to complying with the chosen code. The Royal Decree of 6 June 2010 then recognised the 2009 Code as the only code to which listed companies may refer.

Under Belgian law, listed companies are required to prepare and publish both a Corporate Governance Charter and a Corporate Governance Statement. The Charter contains the general policy and the detailed plan of the corporate governance structure of the company. It is published on the website of the company and its content is regulated by the 2009 Code. The Statement forms part of the annual report of the company and refers to the Corporate Governance Code applied. It must indicate any rules or parts of the 2009 Code which are not being complied with by the company, and explain the reasons for such non-compliance.

1.1. The Environment in which Boards Operate

Even in 2011, the shareholding structure of most Belgian listed companies was mostly of a concentrated nature. This is largely a consequence of the choices made by the legislature in 1934.[1] It should nonetheless be noted that there are important exceptions which confirm the rule: Ironically, the ownership of Société Générale de Belgique, the largest holding company in Europe at the time with 1,200 subsidiaries, was totally dispersed when Carlo De Benedetti launched his raid; today, Umicore is one of the few leading listed industrial companies which is not backed by a dominant shareholder. Most of the time, institutional share-holders only invest in Bel-20 companies, ie. the 20 listed companies with the largest capitalisation. Foreign shareholders acquiring control of a listed company usually delist their target. Many of the larger Belgian companies have been delisted for that reason over the last ten years. All in all, there are no more than 120 listed companies on Euronext Brussels (about 20 of them primarily listed abroad). The influence of foreign stock corporation law is rather limited, although the origin of Belgian company law is found in the French *Code de commerce* (1807). The Dutch control-enhancing mechanism of *certificering* (fiduciary ownership) is however often used by the controlling shareholder of a listed company, without the certificates themselves being listed (article 503 ff. BCC). US law inspired the Belgian registration mechanism (article 533 BCC).

The governance/agency problem in Belgian companies is therefore mostly not of the Anglo-American type: Ownership and control usually coincide, and manage-ment suffers from too much rather than too little control. This has traditionally re-sulted in a large board of non-executive directors on which the majority share-holders are represented and on which no executive management members other than the CEO have a seat. Minority shareholders and free float have to trust in the majority to govern the company in the best interests of all shareholders and not just in the interest of the majority. However, since 1995, listed companies need three independent directors whenever they envisage taking a decision on a transaction that relates to their controlling shareholder, eg. when a loan contract is entered into between the parent company and its listed subsidiary (see below section 2.2.3, *Criteria*).

Besides majority–minority and shareholder–management agency problems, there is also a third agency problem—that between *shareholders* of the company

---

[1] See K. Geens and C. Clottens, 'One share one vote', in *The European Company Law Action Plan Revisited: Reassessment of the 2003 Priorities of the European Commission* (ed. K. Geens, K. Hopt), Leuven University Press, 2009, 145. One peculiarity of the 1873 system (see below sec. 1.3 and 2.1) was a voting restriction which was formulated in terms of a maximum number of shares (20%) rather than a maximum number of votes. Shares with multiple voting rights (as counting was done per share and not per vote) were therefore very popular until the legislature imposed the 'one share one vote' principle in 1934. Together with the narrow banking system im-posed in the same year, this principle led to the holding and pyramid capitalism that was very successful until 1990 (although the voting restriction had been somewhat reformulated in 1934, it was ineffective against concerted action and was abolished in 1991). Even today, Albert Frère's Groupe Bruxelles Lambert is the largest private shareholder in GDF Suez and in Total [formerly TotalFinaElf].

and *other stakeholders* of the company, eg. creditors, employees, buyers and suppliers. An important question in this regard concerns the corporate interest: Does
this corporate interest also include the interest of other stakeholders or only the
interest of the shareholders? After an emphasis on the interests of the other
stakeholders in the 1960s and 1970s, the focus was recently shifted to the shareholders' interest. No company's judicial history has shown this shift more clearly
than the Brussels Court of Appeal cases with regard to *Société Générale de
Belgique* and *Fortis*. During the raid by Carlo De Benedetti and Suez on Société
Générale de Belgique in 1988, the focus was clearly on a broadly defined corporate interest, encompassing all stakeholders. This was already less the case in 1998,
when Fortis and ABN AMRO fought their battle for Société Générale de Banque
(the principal subsidiary of Société Générale de Belgique). The Court concentrated even more on the shareholders' interest in 2008 when it was asked to rule on
the transfer of the assets of Fortis to the Dutch State and to BNP Paribas.

1.2. Financial Institutions

Already back in 1971, more than 30 years before the BCC made this possible for
public limited liability companies (see below section 1.3, *Executives vs. non-
executives*), it became mandatory for credit institutions to establish a separate
Executive Committee (*comité de direction/directiecomité*), which has the residual
powers. The Board of Directors of a credit institution is only allowed to supervise
the Executive Committee, to determine general policy and to exercise some
reserved powers (eg. presenting the annual accounts to the general meeting for
approval). All members of the Executive Committee also have to be members of
the Board of Directors (but of course not all members of the Board have to be
member of the Executive Committee). The Banking, Finance and Insurance
Commission (*Commission Bancaire, Financière et des Assurances/Commissie
voor het Bank-, Financie- en Assurantiewezen*) (CBFA)[2] initiated this principle of
an autonomous Executive Committee in order to guarantee the independent
exercise of the banking profession in the interest of the deposit-holders—or at
least to enable the Executive Committee to take into account the 'public interest'
character of a bank without being unduly influenced by the controlling shareholder
(*l'autonomie de la fonction bancaire/autonomie van de bankfunctie*). The Board
of Directors in a Belgian credit institution is in that respect the intermediary, but
also the buffer, between the shareholder(s) and the Executive Committee. Until
recently, the CBFA demanded that shareholders, the Board and the Executive
Committee sign a protocol with the CBFA in which they undertook to respect
banking autonomy. Since 2007 the obligation to sign a governance memorandum

---

[2] This name is no longer used; see following page.

has been in place, pursuant to a CBFA Circular. In this Circular, the CBFA set out ten principles of good governance for credit institutions. Three of these principles related to the relationships between the different bodies and organs of the bank, the selection of the board members and their tasks, and the rules regarding the effective 'leadership' of the bank.

In the Act of 2 July 2010, the 'Twin Peaks model' was adopted in Belgium (see below section 4.2, *FSMA*). The CBFA was renamed the FSMA (Financial Services and Markets Authority) as of 1 April 2011: It continues to be responsible for consumer protection and market supervision. Its micro-prudential tasks are now carried out by the National Bank of Belgium (NBB), which prior to 1 April 2011 already exercised macro-prudential control together with the CBFA/FSMA.

The company law concerning the duty to establish an audit committee, and the exemption from such duty, also applies to credit institutions (see below section 2.2.2(a), *Composition*). However, the NBB may exempt a credit institution from this duty if there is an audit committee at group level. In a public communication, the NBB announced that it would only allow rare exemptions, *inter alia* where this would be justified by the relationship between the activity levels of the group and the individual credit institution in terms of size and nature. The NBB will be more lenient when it comes to the composition of such a separate audit committee, in terms of the number of independent directors it is required to have and the possibility for external persons who are non-directors to be part of it.

The function of statutory auditor in a credit institution, as foreseen in the Belgian Companies Code, may only be entrusted to one or more auditors or audit firms accredited by the NBB. The appointment of an accredited statutory auditor in credit institutions and the renewal of the mandate are subject to the prior (revocable) approval of the NBB.

When (re)appointing a director or a member of the senior management, the credit institutions have to inform the NBB. The NBB has to be provided with all relevant information and documents which will allow it to assess whether or not the person to be (re)appointed has the required professional integrity, expertise and appropriate experience to carry out his or her function. The (re)appointment has effect as from the NBB's advice, which is non-binding when (re)appointing non-executive directors and binding when (re)appointing executive directors or members of the senior management.

Any person acquiring more than 10%, 20%, 30% or 50%, of the shares or voting rights in a credit institution, alone or in concert, should notify such acquisition to the NBB. The same rule applies when, as a consequence of an intended sale by such a person, his participation would fall below one of those thresholds. In the case of an acquisition in excess of a threshold, a mere notification is not sufficient. The candidate shareholder has to undergo a very severe 'fit and proper test', and the formal approval of the proposed acquisition by the NBB is required. It may thus object to the proposed acquisition, and even force the sale of shares which were acquired without awaiting formal approval.

The credit institutions themselves also have to inform the NBB upon becoming aware of any acquisitions or disposals which cause holdings to exceed or fall below one of the thresholds mentioned.

1.3. Available Board Models

History—Belgian company law finds its origin in the French *Code de commerce* of 1807–1808. However, an entirely 'Belgian' company law was adopted in 1873 (Book I, title IX *Code de commerce*): The main novelties were: (i) A new set of rules with regard to the public limited liability company (*naamloze vennootschap/société anonyme*); and (ii) the creation of the French inspired cooperative society (*coöperatieve vennootschap/société cooperative*).

The Belgian legislature of 1873 only recognised the one-tier system: There was no management body other than the Board of Directors. That tradition is still very much alive today.

1979 reform plans— In 1979, after thirty years of learned study by a Scientific Committee, the Belgian government envisaged imposing an obligatory two-tier system on all *sociétés anonymes*, inspired by the banking model (see above section 1.2). The difference would have been that the members of the Executive Committee would have had no seat on the Board of Directors, whereas in a Belgian credit institution, each member of the Executive Committee has to be part of the Board. The 1979 draft bill, which besides an obligatory two-tier system also proposed a whole new company law code, was never enacted because priority was given to the transposition of the European Directives. Parts of the draft bill of 1979 were recycled in the Acts of 18 July 1991 and 13 April 1995. The inconsistencies resulting from this recycling process led to the codification of 7 May 1999 (see Introduction).

2002 reform—The Corporate Governance Act of 2 July 2002 provided for an optional two-tier system, once again largely inspired by the banking model. However, members of the Executive Committee were permitted, but not required, to be members of the Board of Directors (see preceding paragraph and section 1.2 above). All *sociétés anonymes*, whether listed or not, could now opt for the creation of a separate management body—the 'Executive Committee' (*directiecomité/comité de direction*), which has the residual powers.

The Board of Directors (see *Aufsichtsrat, Raad van Commissarissen*) had reserved only the competencies to determine the general policy, to supervise management and to exercise clearly-defined exclusive powers (eg. in relation to the annual accounts). Other than these reserved matters, the company cannot limit the powers of the Executive Committee vis-à-vis third parties, even when such limitations are provided for in the articles of association. Only a few listed companies use this two-tier model: We counted six among the twenty largest listed Belgian companies,[3] and two of those are credit institutions—for the latter, the two-tier system is quasi-obligatory (see above section 1.2).

The reasons for this hesitation are probably fear: (i) On the part of the Board members regarding losing power and competence; (ii) on the part of the share-holders about losing their grip on a management which would become too autonomous in an independent Executive Committee; (iii) on the part of the CEO, about losing his/her exclusive connecting ('pivotal') function between the Board and the operational management; and (iv) on the part of managers as regards incurring greater responsibility or losing their employee status.

In reality, however, many companies operate with some kind of informal Executive Committee, which does not follow the lines of the legal two-tier system, and does not suffer from its binding third-party effects. It comes down to a general (as opposed to *ad hoc*) delegation of powers by the Board of Directors which go beyond the day-to-day management, but which are not as broad as the residual powers reserved to the legally recognised Executive Committee in the two-tier system. These informal Executive Committees, and the general delegation of powers they benefit from, have no sound legal basis. Indeed, this practice entails the Board of Directors relinquishing its own powers in a general way, without having recourse to a proper control system.

Executives vs. non-executives in a single tier—The lack of a two-tier system is somehow mitigated by the role played by independent non-executive directors on the remuneration, nomination and audit committees (see below section 2.2.2(a)). In most of these committees, a majority of independent directors is required, and at least a majority—if not all—of its members should be non-executive directors. The more transparent division of tasks and allocation of responsibilities within the one-tier Board which results from this may compensate for the disadvantages of having a single tier.

Societas Europaea—Belgium has few SEs. Belgian law allows for the choice between the one-tier and two-tier structure (article 896 ff. BCC).

---

[3] And about 11 out of all listed companies, ie. some 8%. See M. Wyckaert and K. Geens, 'Het gebruik van het facultatief duaal systeem in Belgische beursgenoteerde vennootschappen', *T.R.V.*, 2010, 527.

2. Authority

2.1. Functions/Powers

Distribution of powers—The general meeting was sovereign in the 1873 system—which meant that it had both certain exclusive powers and all residual powers. In fact, however, it was the Board of Directors which was the most important body in the company. Indeed, the hierarchy between the general meeting and the Board of Directors was mostly inverted by the articles of association. It was not until exactly one hundred years later that the legislature reversed the powers (see below section 3.3.1, *Legal person*).

The Board of Directors does not have to engage in the operational or executive management of the company. It can limit itself to the determination of the company's strategy (possibly after deliberation of strategic options that are suggested by the management) and to the supervision of the implementation of that strategy by the management. To that extent, the Board appoints the people that it sees fit to implement the company's strategy in practice. During Board meetings the Board will be kept informed on how the outlined strategy is being put into practice.

Pursuant to article 522§1, 3rd paragraph BCC, the Board can decide to set up, under its authority one or more advisory committees, the composition and assignments of which it can freely determine. The Board can thus create an *ad hoc* committee of independent directors to advise on a certain matter. As of 2009, 'large' listed companies[4] are obliged to establish an audit committee and a remuneration committee within the Board of Directors. These committees are composed of non-executive directors (see sections 2.2.2(a) and 2.2.2(b) below).

Internal control and risk management—Article 96§2, 3° BCC provides that listed companies must include in their annual report a corporate governance statement which describes, *inter alia*, the internal control and risk management mechanisms of the company. 'Large' non-listed companies[5] also need to put in place

---

[4] In this context there is a special definition of 'large' (different from the general definition in the next footnote) which is derived from the Prospectus Directive (see n. 5, which is an Annual Accounts Directive definition): *Sociétés anonymes*, even if listed, are not obliged by the BCC to establish a remuneration committee or an audit committee if they meet at least two of the following criteria: (i) an average number of employees not exceeding 250 during the financial year concerned; (ii) a balance sheet total of EUR 43,000,000 or less, and (iii) annual net revenues of EUR 50,000,000 or less.

[5] According to the BCC, a company (whether listed or unlisted) is 'large' (for all purposes other than those mentioned in n. 4) if it employs 100 employees, or if more than one of the following thresholds was exceeded during the last and second-last financial year:
- Average number of employees during one year: 50;
- Annual revenues (excluding value-added tax): EUR 7,300,000;

cont. ...

mechanisms of internal control and risk management. This subsidiary part of the duty of care is monitored by the Board, the audit committee (see section 2.2.2(a) below) and, in the last instance, by the external auditor.

Auditors. A peculiarity of the 1873 system was the requirement to appoint one or more *commissaire(s)* who—in the latter case—met as the board of *commissaires.* Their role was styled by the legislature as a kind of auditor, but not professionally trained. In theory, their task was to verify the annual financial statements; in practice, the position of *commissaire* was a step in the *cursus honorum* leading automatically to a seat on the Board of Directors.

The general audit profession was only recognised by the Belgian legislature in 1953. It was inspired by the model of the bank auditor (1934) and by a study of the profession which the Brussels professor Van Ryn carried out in London in 1945. The new profession led to the disappearance of the 1873 *commissaire,* first in listed companies (1953), and eventually also in the unlisted *sociétés anonymes* (1985) (see also below section 2.2.2(a), *Tasks,* and 4.2, *ACCOM*).

The works council has a veto right when it comes to the nomination and appointment of the auditor. Where there is no consensus between the works council and the Board of Directors, the general meeting cannot appoint an auditor, and will have to leave the matter to the court. This joint auditor appointment is the closest Belgium has ever come to co-determination (see below section 3.1.5, *New legislation*).

2.2. Organisation/Internal Functioning

2.2.1. Composition

Number—According to article 518 BCC, the Board of Directors of a *société anonyme* must consist of at least three directors.[6]

The Belgian Companies Code does not explicitly impose requirements as to the number of non-executive directors on the Board of Directors. However, in a listed company with one or more controlling shareholders, at least three directors should be independent in order to render the related-parties procedure possible (see below section 2.2.3, *Criteria*). Moreover, the need for a listed company to have audit and remuneration committees consisting exclusively of non-

---

   – Balance sheet total: EUR 3,650,000.

  [6] However, if the company is incorporated by two persons or if, at a general meeting of shareholders, it is established that the company does not have more than two shareholders, the Board of Directors may consist of only two members (until there are again more than two shareholders). If the Board consists of only two members, any clause in the articles of association granting the casting vote to the chairman in deadlock situations is suspended (article 518§1, Sec. 3 BCC).

executives, and the fact that controlling shareholders usually want a majority on the Board, result in boards rarely numbering less than 8 to 10 members. Belgium has a tradition of large boards, since major shareholders insist on representation by several board members with entitlement to *tantièmes*. As corporate governance rules point in the opposite direction, habits have recently changed. At any rate, executives rarely account for more than one board member, the CEO. If there is a controlling shareholder, non-independent non-executives are always in the majority.

Specialisation of board members—The 2009 Code requires the Board of Directors to be (i) small enough to ensure efficient decision-making and (ii) large enough to ensure that experience from different fields of expertise is present within the Board of Directors (2009 Code, article 2.1, guideline). At least half of the members should be non-executive (2009 Code, article 2.3). Although the Board is conceived as a collegiate body, article 3.3 of the 2009 Code emphasises the complementarity that should exist between the executive and the non-executive directors. In the guidelines under article 3.3 of the 2009 Code, it is pointed out that the main role of the executive directors is to provide the Board of Directors with all relevant business and financial information, while the main role of the non-executive directors is to critically question and to assist in the elaboration of the strategy and the main policies of the company. This is the way the 2009 Code copes with the disadvantages of the one-tier system: One collegiate body wherein executive directors and non-executive directors each have a different role to play.

Interim vacancies—If, for whatever reason, the minimum number of directors required by law (3, sometimes 2) or by the articles of association are no longer in office, the remaining directors have the right to fill the vacancy provisionally. In such a case, the next general meeting may either ratify the appointment made or choose another director (article 519 BCC). Either way, the new director completes the term of office of the replaced person (article 519 BCC).

Number of mandates—To ensure that non-executive directors who are not active in the company on a full-time basis spend a sufficient amount of time in the execution of their duties, the 2009 Code provides that non-executive directors must not take up more than 5 mandates in listed companies. The nominees have to inform the company of their external commitments and should only accept an appointment as a non-executive director if they reserve a sufficient amount of time for their new duties (2009 Code, article 4.5).

Expertise—Once they are active in the company, directors must continue to improve their skills and their knowledge of the company in order to fulfil their duties within the Board and its committees. The company should facilitate this continuing education (2009 Code, article 4.10). There are special expertise and knowledge requirements for some members of the audit and remuneration committees (see below sections 2.2.2(a) , and (b), *Composition*).

2.2.2. Decision-making

Consensus and voting rights—Consensus of the Board as a whole is the usual decision method. No distinction is made between executive and non-executive members of the Board, and they cannot act or vote separately.

As a general rule, when there is no consensus with regard to a decision, each director has one vote. In case of deadlock, the articles of association may give the casting vote to the chairman.

The use of multiple voting rights at Board level is controversial among Belgian legal scholars. Supporters argue that, since the BCC does not contain any prohibition, multiple voting rights are valid as long as collegial functioning is maintained—a criterion which is not easy to test. Opponents suggest that multiple voting rights devalue the *intuitu personae* character of Board membership which would require equality. Practitioners have found a safe way out by drafting clauses in the articles of association which require a qualified majority for certain Board decisions.

In addition to the rules concerning the composition and powers of the Board of Directors, the 2009 Code also contains certain procedural provisions regarding decision-making within the Board of Directors. These rules relate to the convening formalities for Board meetings, the rights and duties of the chairman, the rights and duties of the individual directors, the appointment of a corporate secretary, and a rule concerning the minutes of meetings of the Board of Directors.

Convening rules—Since the Belgian Companies Code remains silent in this regard, most companies have arranged for convening rules in the articles of association or in the Board charter. On top of these arrangements, the 2009 Code recommends that the agenda should not only include the topics as such but should also distinguish clearly between topics for decision and topics for discussion or information only (2009 Code, article 2.6, guideline). Furthermore, the Code emphasises the importance of timely communication of accurate and clear information before every meeting, and if necessary, in between meetings (2009 Code, article 2.7).

Chairman—The Belgian Companies Code is not explicit about the role, rights and duties of the chairman of the Board. However, the 2009 Code devotes much more attention to this important function: The chairman should create confidence within the Board of Directors to stimulate open discussion, constructive criticism and support for the resolutions of the Board (2009 Code, article 2.5). In addition, the chairman should encourage effective interaction between the Board and the management (2009 Code, article 2.5, guideline). The chairman sets the agenda, after consultation with the CEO, and ensures compliance with all procedures for preparation, discussion and approval of resolutions (2009 Code, article 2.6). He chairs the meeting and ensures that sufficient discussion takes place before resolutions are passed (2009 Code, article 2.7, guideline). Article 2.8 of the 2009 Code states that the Board should convene as many times as required in order for it to effectively fulfil its duties. It can be assumed that it is the responsibility of the chairman to monitor this.

Independent and professional judgment—According to the 2009 Code, every director, whether executive or non-executive, should make decisions on the basis of independent judgment (2009 Code, article 3.1), and should thoroughly study the information received and ask for clarification if needed in order to gain and retain a good understanding of the key elements of the corporate activity (2009 Code, article 3.2). In addition, the 2009 Code prohibits the directors from using the information at their disposal for any purposes other than accomplishing their duty as directors and obliges them to act discreetly when they are in the possession of confidential information (2009 Code, article 3.4, guideline).

Belgian courts assess director liability in the light of the standard of the diligent professional. Although this standard is demanding, it will be softened by a kind of business judgment rule *à la belge*, ie. if the judge finds that a professional in similar circumstances of time and place could reasonably have formed the same opinion, he will not declare the director liable. So full and professional diligence is the absolute and severe standard, but its retroactive application makes room for a somewhat milder assessment.

Proxy voting—There is a general prohibition against one director or group of directors dominating the Board of Directors (2009 Code, article 2.2). This means that, where the articles of association allow directors to take a mandate from another director (since a directorship is in principle *intuitu personae*), the 2009 Code, agrees with this practice to the extent that it does not result in one director dominating the decision-making within the Board of Directors.

Specialised committees—The law allows for the creation of specialised committees within the framework of the Board of Directors and even provides a detailed set of rules for 'large'[7] listed companies with regard to two committees that they must establish: the audit committee and the remuneration committee. Listed companies which are not 'large' are exempted from establishing these committees subject to (i) the Board playing the role of the committee; (ii) the company having at least one independent director; and (iii) the condition that, if the chairman of the Board is an executive director, another non-executive director chairs the Board while it is acting in the capacity of the audit or remuneration committee.

Powers of committees—In general, the powers of the committees are purely advisory.[8] As these specialised committees usually deal with confidential and/or

---

[7] See definition in n. 4.

[8] In exceptional instances, though, the BCC gives them almost the power to take binding decisions (eg. article 133 §6: the audit committee may 'decide' (*beslissing/délibération*) that the
cont. ...

highly specialised topics, it is sometimes hard to see the difference between their preparing a Board decision and their taking a decision only to be ratified by the Board. The standard compromise is that the Board decides, but is not completely informed about all factual elements and written documents which underpin the decision for reasons of secrecy (remuneration, nomination) or technicality (audit).

a) Audit Committee

Composition—The audit committee is regulated by the Belgian Companies Code and it is mandatory in 'large'[9] listed companies (article 526*bis* BCC).

The Belgian Companies Code provides that this committee is exclusively composed of non-executive directors. At least one member should be independent. One of the independent directors must possess a sufficient degree of expertise in the field of accounting and audit. This should be stated in the annual report (article 96, 9° BCC).

On top of the legal provisions, the 2009 Code prescribes that the committee must consist of at least three members, all non-executive, more than half of whom must be independent (2009 Code, article 5.5 and Annex C, article 5.2/4). The chairman of the Board of Directors can be member of the audit committee, but cannot chair the committee (2009 Code, Annex C, article 5.2/3).

Tasks—According to the Belgian Companies Code, the audit committee has the following minimum duties: (i) Monitoring of the process of financial reporting; (ii) monitoring of the effectiveness of the system of internal control and risk management of the company; (iii) monitoring of internal audit and its effectiveness, if internal audit exists; (iv) monitoring of the legal control of the annual accounts and the consolidated annual accounts; and (v) assessment and monitoring of the independence of the statutory auditor and, as the case may be, of the auditor verifying the consolidated accounts. The audit committee regularly reports to the Board of Directors on the accomplishment of its tasks.

The 2009 Code describes in greater detail the four important aspects of a company's audit and the committee's duties in this regard:

> *Financial reporting*—In its supervision of the financial reporting process, the committee must investigate the correctness, completeness and consistency of periodic financial information before it is published by the company. In particular, it investigates the relevance and consistency of the accounting principles applied by the company and, as the case may be, the group. The management should inform the committee of the principles applied for significant and unusual transactions, the accounting treatment

---

auditor can still be considered as independent although his firm receives in total more than 200% of the strict audit fee because of related services).

[9] For a definition of 'large', see n. 4 above.

of which can be subject to different approaches. The audit committee must review all problems of financial reporting with management and with the statutory auditor(s) (2009 Code, Annex C, article 5.2/11-13).

At least once every year the committee must investigate the effectiveness of internal control and risk management systems to ensure that significant risks are identified, managed and published in accordance with the framework approved by the Board of Directors (2009 Code, Annex C, article 5.2/14). The committee must also investigate 'whistle-blowing' procedures allowing personnel to report irregularities in the financial reporting or in other matters in a confidential way (2009 Code, Annex C, article 5.2/16).

Internal audit—A listed company must establish an independent internal audit function, adapted to the characteristics of the company. Should the company not have established such a function, at least once a year it should investigate whether it would be useful to do so. The committee must review the programme of work of the internal auditor, bearing in mind the complementary roles of the internal auditor and the statutory auditor. The committee receives the internal audit reports, or at least a periodic summary thereof. Furthermore, the committee assesses the effectiveness of the internal audit and makes recommendations about the selection, appointment and dismissal of the head of internal audit and the internal audit budget. It will also monitor the receptiveness of managers to recommendations of the audit committee (2009 Code, Annex C, article 5.2/17-19).

External audit—In relation to the external audit, the committee makes recommendations on the selection, appointment and conditions for the hiring of the statutory auditor. The committee's proposal must be included in the agenda of the shareholders' meeting which will decide on the appointment of the auditor, upon the proposal of the Board of Directors (2009 Code, Annex C, article 5.2/20-21 and article 134 BCC). The committee must also verify the independence of the auditor. In this context, each year the external auditor confirms his independence to the committee, informs the committee of additional audit and non-audit services provided by the auditor and his firm to the company, and discusses with the committee how this might endanger his independence (article 526*bis*§6 BCC and 2009 Code, Annex C, article 5.2/22). For the same purpose, the auditor provides the committee with a report on an annual basis describing all relations between himself and the company or the group to which it belongs (2009 Code, Annex C, article 5.2/23). In the same context, the committee must prepare a policy document distinguishing between additional non-audit services that are (i) allowed as such; (ii) allowed, but only after investigation by the committee; and (iii) not allowed as such (2009 Code, Annex C, article 5.2/24). Indeed, since the Corporate Governance Act of 2 August 2002, in the aftermath of the

Enron scandal, the BCC and its Royal Decree contain provisions narrowing the scope of non-audit services one and the same audit firm may perform within one company (articles 133–134 BCC; see also above section 2.1, *Auditors,* and below section 4.2. *ACCOM*).

Charter—The 2009 Code provides that the role and the rules of the committee are described by the Board of Directors in its Charter (2009 Code, article 5.1). In addition, the audit committee is convened at least four times per year and it reviews its rules regularly, assesses its own effectiveness and reports to the Board of Directors about its functioning (2009 Code, Annex C, article 5.2/28). The audit committee has at least two meetings per year with the internal auditor and the external auditor to discuss all matters related to its rules and to the audit process, and in particular relating to weaknesses in the internal controls (2009 Code, Annex C, article 5.2/29).

b) *Remuneration Committee*

Composition—The remuneration committee is regulated by the BCC, and its creation is obligatory in 'large'[10] listed companies. It consists exclusively of non-executive directors, the majority of which should be independent. The Board of Directors must see to it that the remuneration committee has the necessary expertise with regard to remuneration policy. The chairman of the committee can be the chairman of the Board or another non-executive director (2009 Code, article 5.5 and Annex E, article 5.4/1).

With regard to discussion in the committee concerning the remuneration of the executive directors, of the members of the Executive Committee, of the other executive directors of the company and of the persons in charge of the day-to-day management of the company, the main representative of their body (eg. the chairman of the Executive Committee) must be called upon to assist the committee (article 526*quater* §7 BCC).

The term for membership of the committee must not be longer than the term of a director, which has a maximum length of four years under the 2009 Code (2009 Code, article 4.6).

Powers—The remuneration committee only has advisory powers and duties. The Board of Directors (and the shareholders, if the remuneration of the directors is at stake) has the final decision-making power regarding the remuneration policy of the company. The main role of the committee is to prepare the decision process on the remuneration of the directors and the executive managers. More specifically, it should give its advice on the remuneration policy and individual remuneration, on variable remuneration, on long-term incentives, whether or not

---

[10] For a definition of 'large', see n. 4 above.

related to remuneration in shares or other securities, on arrangements for early termination and, as the case may be, on proposals to be presented to the shareholders' meeting (2009 Code, Annex E, article 5.4/3). In addition, it presents a remuneration report to the Board of Directors (2009 Code, Annex E, article 5.4/4) and advises on contracts of appointment of the CEO and other members of the executive management (2009 Code, article 7.17). The committee can also make recommendations relating to the granting of higher severance payments for the CEO or another member of the executive management (2009 Code, article 7.18).[11] The BCC contains a rather detailed set of rules with regard to variable remuneration and severance payments, as well as with regard to their limitation.

Charter—According to article 526*quater* §6 BCC, the remuneration committee must convene at least twice per year and in general whenever its duties so require. Moreover, it reports regularly to the Board of Directors on the accomplishment of its duties. Apart from these obligations under the BCC, the 2009 Code requires the committee to regularly evaluate its own rules and charter and to make recommendations to the Board of Directors regarding its own functioning (2009 Code, Annex E, articles 5.4/5-8). If required, an expert can be present at the meetings of the committee (2009 Code, article 5.5, guideline).

c) Nomination Committee

Composition—The nomination committee is one of three specialised teams a company should establish according to principle 5 of the 2009 Code (2009 Code, article 5.3). It is never mandatory by law.

The nomination committee consists of at least three members, the majority of whom must be independent, non-executive directors. The meetings of the committee are chaired by the chairman of the Board or by another non-executive director (2009 Code, Annex D, article 5.3/2). The 2009 Code allows the nomination committee and the remuneration committee to be merged, subject to the condition that the composition of the combined committee complies with the stricter requirements of the remuneration committee (see above) (2009 Code, article 5.4, guideline). Such a merger becomes less straightforward in those listed

---

[11] The BCC imposes a minimum set of tasks. As a minimum, the remuneration committee should take charge of:
- proposing the remuneration policy for directors, members of the Executive Committee, other executive directors of the company and persons in charge of the day-to-day management of the company;
- proposing the individual remuneration of directors, members of the Executive Committee, other executive directors of the company and persons in charge of the day-to-day management of the company;
- preparing the annual remuneration report;
- explaining the remuneration report during the statutory shareholders' meeting.

companies which are required by law to have a remuneration committee. The term for membership of the committee must not be longer than the term of a directorship, which has a maximum length of four years under the 2009 Code (see above).

Powers—In general, the role of the nomination committee is to advise and assist the Board of Directors in the appointment of directors, of the CEO and of the other members of management. More specifically, the tasks of the committee are to develop appointment procedures, to periodically evaluate the size and composition of the Board, to search for and nominate candidates for the position of director, to advise on appointment proposals made by the shareholders and to deal with questions of succession and continuity (2009 Code, Annex D, article 5.3/4). It should be noted that the final responsibility lies with the Board and the actual appointment of directors is done by the shareholders' meeting after nomination by the Board.

Charter—The 2009 Code does not go into any great detail about the functioning of the nomination committee, except to say that it should convene at least twice per year and as often as its duties require (2009 Code, Annex D, article 5.3/6). Rules on the functioning of the nomination committee can be included in the Charter drawn up by the Board of Directors and regularly re-evaluated by the committee itself (2009 Code, Annex D, article 5.3/6).

2.2.3. Independent Directors

Number—The BCC and the 2009 Code contain the same criteria concerning independence. The BCC lists these criteria in the framework of the mandatory preliminary reporting on related-parties transactions between a listed company and its controlling shareholder: At least three independent directors, assisted by an independent expert, should report on such transactions and their impact on the corporate interest to the full Board before the Board makes any decision with regard to such transactions (see below section 3.1.3(a), *Procedure*). But this does not imply that every listed company should have three independent directors. From reading the exemption granted to small listed companies from the duty to establish an audit committee or a remuneration committee, one might even conclude that the BCC requires no independent director at all. Indeed, such exemption is available subject to several conditions, including the requirement for the company to have at least one independent director (see above section 2.2.2(c), *Powers*). The 2009 Code is abundantly clear, however, and requires a minimum of three independent directors for any listed company.

Task—Besides their role in the framework of related-party transactions, independent directors should constitute the majority on the specialised committees (see above section 2.2.2(a)–(c)). There is no requirement that the chairman of the Board should be independent (see above section 2.2.2, *Chairman*). In a related-party transaction, the committee of independent directors is chaired by an independent director. However, under Belgian corporate governance practice, there is no specific role attributed to the most 'wise' of the independent directors.

Criteria—Unlike the European Recommendation,[12] the BCC and the 2009 Code do not provide a catch-all clause guaranteeing the independence of the directors in all circumstances. The nine requirements are exhaustive.[13] This leads to a rather formal concept of independence: If the criteria do not apply, one is independent; otherwise, one is not independent. The reading and interpretation of the criteria becomes excessively important.

The main purpose of these nine requirements is to ensure independence from (i) the company; (ii) the main shareholders of the company or their management; and (iii) the management of the company:

- The director has not been an executive member of the Board of Directors, a member of the Executive Committee or a day-to-day manager in the company (or any of its affiliated companies) for a term of five years prior to his or her election;
- The director has not been a non-executive director for more than three consecutive terms; the period within which he holds these consecutive mandates may not exceed twelve years;
- The director has not been a member of the managerial staff (*personnel de direction/leidinggevend personeel*) of the company (or of an affiliate of the company) during a term of three years prior to his or her election;
- The director does not receive and has not received any remuneration or other significant financial advantage from the company (or any of its affiliated companies), other than the profit share (*tantièmes*) and remuneration received in his or her capacity as a non-executive director or as a member of the supervisory body;
- The director does not own any corporate rights (*droits sociaux/maatschappelijke rechten*) that represent 10% or more of the share capital, the corporate funds or a class of shares of the company. If the director has corporate rights which represent less than 10% of such rights, taken together with rights in the same company held by companies over which the director has control, these may not represent 10% or more of the share capital, the corporate funds or a class of shares of the company; or the disposal of these shares, or the exercise of the rights attached thereto, may

---

[12] Commission Recommendation 2005/162/EC of 15 February 2005 on the role of non-executive or supervisory directors of listed companies and on the committees of the (supervisory) board.

[13] The old article 524 BCC listed some specific situations in which a director cannot be regarded as independent, but also contained a catch-all provision: A director may not have any relationship with the company that is likely to encumber his independence. This catch-all clause was removed by the Act of 17 December 2008.

not be subject to agreements or unilateral commitments entered into by the director. In any event, the director cannot represent a shareholder who meets the conditions set forth in this criterion;

- The director does not and, during the past financial year did not, have a significant business relationship with the company (or any of its affiliated companies), either directly or as a partner, shareholder, member of the Board of Directors or member of the managerial staff of any company or person that maintains such a relationship;
- The director is not, and has not been at any time during the past three years, a partner or an employee of the company's current or former statutory auditor or of a company or person affiliated therewith;
- The director is not an executive director of another company in which an executive director of the company is a non-executive director or a member of the supervisory body, and has no other significant ties with executive directors of the company through his or her involvement in other companies or bodies;
- The director's spouse, unmarried legal partner and relatives (via birth or marriage) up to the second degree do not act as a member of the Board of Directors, a member of the Executive Committee or a day-to-day manager or member of the managerial staff of the company (or any of its affiliated companies), and meet all of the requirements set out above.

This independence is a continuous requirement. If a director no longer complies with one of the criteria, he should immediately inform the other directors thereof.

Remuneration—According to the criteria mentioned in the preceeding paragraphs, independent directors should in principle not receive any variable remuneration, ie. based on performance of the director or the company itself. This is stated more clearly in the 2009 Code (principle 7.7). This implies at first sight that a company may explain why it nonetheless wishes to reward independent directors partially on a variable basis. Since the Act of 6 April 2010, such an explanation is no longer sufficient. Moreover, prior approval of the variable remuneration by the general meeting is required (article 554 BCC).

2.3. Information Streams

Right to information—Directors have the right to collect information. Besides sheer necessity, the ultimate legal basis for this right is their joint and several liability for violations of the articles of association and the Belgian Companies Code. Directors are released from liability for any breach in which they had no part if (i) they were not negligent (eg. absent without justification) and (ii) they denounced the breach at the first general meeting after they became aware thereof (article 528 BCC). A director can therefore only conduct his own defence successfully if a right to information is granted to him. In general, the directors are required to obtain the information through a request presented to the chairman, who in turn obtains the information from the management. Although non-executive directors could contact one another on an informal basis, the legislature by no means encourages any such separate meetings.

Right to advice—Moreover, a director has a right to independent expert advice, for which the expenses are borne by the company (2009 Code, article 2.7, guideline). For this professional advice to be granted, compliance with internal procedures is required, and access to such advice can thus be limited. A similar right to professional advice is granted to the committees of the Board of Directors. In this instance, no internal procedures have to be complied with. The only formality is that the chairman of the Board should be informed of this request for information (2009 Code, article 5.6).

Corporate secretary—With a view to adequately assisting the Board in ensuring compliance with internal rules and corporate governance, the Board appoints a corporate secretary—who is not necessarily a member of the Board. The corporate secretary should ensure the efficient flow of information within the Board of Directors and its committees on the one hand, and between the executive directors and non-executive directors on the other hand. The directors should have access to the corporate secretary, in practice mostly in order to call upon the secretary's legal knowledge. An important duty of the secretary is drafting the minutes of the Board under the supervision of the chairman (2009 Code, article 2.9, guideline).

3. Accountability

3.1. Board and Shareholders

3.1.1. Appointment and Removal

Majority rule/minority directors—In no circumstances may the directors be designated by the articles of association, although they may be appointed at the time of incorporation of the company in the last—'temporary'—section of the deed of incorporation. While the company is being operated as a going concern, however, they are appointed (and dismissed) by the general meeting under majority rule.

In companies with a controlling shareholder, directors are in fact appointed by that shareholder. However, a clause of binding nomination can be inserted in the articles of association in order to allow minority shareholders to propose one or more candidates for membership (eg. the State participating in financial institutions in distress). Within these limits, the general meeting retains its power of decision; more than one candidate should therefore be proposed per vacancy.

Cumulative voting is never applied in listed companies. There is no tradition whatsoever of having employee representatives on the Board.

Term—The maximum term for a directorship provided for by law is six years (article 518§3 BCC). The 2009 Code reduces this to four years (2009 Code, article 4.6). *Because the law allows* is certainly not a sustainable argument to justify non-compliance for a term longer than four years. A director is always re-eligible no matter how long he has held office previously (article 520 BCC). It is true that there is a rule that an independent director loses his independence when serving more than three consecutive terms as a non-executive director (article 526*ter* 2° BCC). He may, however, continue to serve as a non-executive.

Ad nutum revocability—Directors may be removed from office at any time, also during the term for which they were appointed, by a simple majority vote of the general meeting (this is known as termination *ad nutum*; article 518§3 BCC). The company has no obligation whatsoever to substantiate the reasons for dismissing a director. In the *société anonyme,* this *ad nutum* rule is of public order. Any provisions in the articles of association which deviate from this rule are therefore null and void.

The revocability *ad nutum* of the mandate to act as a director also implies that one cannot hold the office of a director as an employee, for the sole reason that labour law provides considerable protection against unilateral and immediate dismissal. Moreover, the lack of the potential exercising of permanent authority over such a director (which is considered to be one of the conditions for an employment relationship under Belgian labour law) is another reason why a director, in this capacity, cannot be considered to be an employee.

Vacancy—If, for whatever reason, the minimum number of directors required by law (3, sometimes 2) or by the articles of association are no longer in office, the remaining directors have the right to fill the vacancy provisionally. In such a case, the next general meeting ratifies and makes a definitive appointment (article 519 BCC). In the event of a premature vacancy, a newly appointed director serves for the period of the person he replaces (article 519 BCC).

Legal person—A legal person can be appointed as a director, a day-to-day manager or as a member of an Executive Committee. The rules in this matter were inspired by French law (article 210-5 *Code commercial*). Most of the time, the purpose of this is to facilitate tax optimisation schemes for directors who do not wish to hold office in their own name.

The legal person which is nominated as a director or as a member of the Executive Committee must designate a natural person (known as the 'permanent representative') to exercise the function in its name and on its behalf (article 61§2

BCC).[14] This person must be a shareholder, director or employee of the legal person/director and must meet any conditions or restrictions the company's articles of association prescribe with regard to its directors or members of the Executive Committee.

The permanent representative must satisfy the same requirements and will be liable as if he were performing the task in his own name and on his own behalf, notwithstanding the several liability of the legal person thus represented.

The obligation to appoint a permanent representative does not apply to a legal person which becomes a day-to-day manager. Therefore, if a legal person is a director and at the same time charged with the day-to-day management of the company, it can only appoint a permanent representative for the function of director.

3.1.2. *Division of Powers between Board and Shareholders*

Supremacy of the board—The general meeting was sovereign in the 1873 system—which meant that it had both certain exclusive powers and all residual powers. But in fact it was the Board of Directors which was the most important body in the company. Indeed, the hierarchy between the general meeting and Board of Directors was inverted by the articles of association in most cases. It was not until 1973, exactly one hundred years later, that the legislature reversed the powers: the Board now has the residual powers, whereas only certain exclusive powers are reserved to the general meeting. The Board can therefore do anything necessary or useful with the purpose or the aims of the company in mind, ie. anything that can be considered as being in the interests of the company. Moreover, this hierarchy cannot be inverted by the articles of association—or, at least, the company cannot invoke vis-à-vis third parties any contractual modification of the legal distribution of powers.

3.1.3. *Special Issues:*

a) *Conflicts of Interest—General Remarks*

General—In Belgium, two different types of conflicts of interest are governed by law: Conflicts of interest where a director has a conflicting interest in a decision to be taken by the Board of Directors (article 523 BCC) and conflicts of interest in the case of related-party transactions in which parent companies are involved with their listed subsidiaries (article 524 BCC).

---

[14] At one point in time, thus system was also applied to audit firms exercising the function of *commissaire*. Since the Act of 18 January 2010, although an audit firm should still appoint a natural person as its permanent representative, the latter is no longer personally liable (article 132 BCC).

Conflict of interest of a director—Article 523 BCC concerns Board decisions in which one of the directors has a conflicting interest. Only decisions or trans-actions of the Board of Directors in which the director has, directly or indirectly, a conflicting *financial* (as opposed to a purely emotional) interest fall within the scope of this article.

The Belgian Companies Code provides for a similar mechanism in the event of a conflicting interest for a member of the Executive Committee where the company has opted for a two-tier system (article 524*ter* BCC).

The first exemption under article 523 concerns decisions or transactions taking place between companies where one company holds, directly or indirectly, 95% of the votes attached to the securities issued by the other, or between companies where at least 95% of the votes attached to their securities are held by a third company.

The second exemption relates to decisions or transactions taking place in the ordinary course of business of the company (usual transactions) under arm's length conditions.

Procedure—The director involved should alert his colleagues and inform them about the conflict before the Board decides upon the matter. The notification should be included in the minutes. Finally, the statutory auditor of the company must at some point in time be informed about the conflict of interest (possibly after the decision, but at any rate before he prepares his opinion—see below).

In listed companies, the conflicted director cannot take part in the decision-making. Somewhat awkwardly, in a non-listed company, the conflicted director may participate in both the decision-making and the voting.

The conflict of interest has to be published in the annual report of the com-pany: A description of the conflict of interest must be included in the minutes of the meeting and must be reproduced in the annual report. More specifically, the minutes should describe the nature of the decision or transaction. The minutes must also include a justification of the decision taken, ie. the reason why the decision could be taken despite the fact that there was a conflict of interest. Thirdly, the financial consequences of the resolution for the company must be analysed.

In addition, the statutory auditor must describe, in his opinion on the annual accounts, the financial consequences of the decision in which a conflicting interest was present. This, of course, must also be published in the annual report.

The sanction for non-compliance with article 523 BCC is twofold. First, there is a potential liability for the directors of the company. In addition to the general ground for directors' liability (article 528 BCC), there is a specific liability for non-compliance 'on the merits': The law provides for liability even if the formal article 523 procedure has been applied in cases where the conflicted directors cause an unreasonable disadvantage to the company (article 529 BCC). Secondly, the company may demand that the resolution passed in breach of article 523 should be declared void, even with third-party effect if the counterparty of the company acted *mala fide*, ie. if it can be proven that it was or should have been aware of the conflict of interest.

In addition to the legal provisions of article 523 BCC, the 2009 Code requires the Board of Directors to put in place a policy with regard to transactions or other contractual relations between the company, including its affiliates (*verbonden vennootschappen/sociétés liées*) on the one hand, and its directors on the other hand, although these transactions or relations do not fall within the scope of article 523 BCC. This policy must be part of the Corporate Governance Charter of the company, and the circumstances in which this mechanism was applied must be described in the Corporate Governance Statement in the annual report (2009 Code, article 3.6).

The 2009 Code does not enumerate the transactions or relations which fall within the scope of this provision. Examples include a conflicting interest of a director which is not of a financial nature or a financial interest of the director which is aligned with the interest of the company.

The 2009 Code also provides for arrangements in case of conflicts of interest with managers rather than directors. Members of the executive management should order their affairs in such a way that no direct or indirect conflicts of interest can arise between them and the company. This means that transactions between the company and its management should always occur at arm's length (2009 Code, article 6.8). This 2009 Code policy is primarily relevant to companies without an Executive Committee, to which the equivalent of article 523 BCC for members of the Executive Committee does not apply (article 524*ter*).

b) Related-Party Transactions

Application and exemptions—Under article 524 BCC, certain related-party transactions of a listed company must be reviewed beforehand by a committee of three independent directors—assisted by an independent expert—before being decided upon by the Board of Directors.[15] In the end, however, it is not the committee of independent directors that takes the decision, but the Board of Directors, after being informed of the opinion of the committee. Nevertheless, the Board will rarely deviate from the opinion of the committee, as it would be obliged to publicly substantiate its reasons for doing so.

This article 524 BCC procedure has to be complied with (i) when the Board of Directors of a listed company takes any decision or executes any transaction pertaining to any relationship with an affiliated company other than its subsidiaries; or (ii) when a subsidiary of a listed company takes any decision or executes any transaction pertaining to any relationship with an affiliated company other than one of its own subsidiaries (or than the listed company itself).

---

[15] K. Geens and M. Wyckaert, 'Conflicts of interest: can a director serve himself or his kin?', in *VOC 1602-2002: 400 years of Company Law*, Kluwer Legal Publishers, 2005, 387–427.

Moreover, it should be noted that for decisions or actions which concern the relationship between a non-listed Belgian subsidiary of the listed company and a company affiliated with the listed company, approval in accordance with article 524 BCC is required from the listed parent company, even though the company itself is not directly involved in the decision-making.

Two types of decisions or transactions fall outside the scope of article 524, however. The first exemption is the transaction or decision which takes place in the ordinary course of business ('usual transactions') under arm's length conditions. The second exemption concerns transactions or decisions of minor importance. This *de minimis* rule relates to decisions that represent less than 1% of the consolidated net assets of the listed company.

Procedure—If article 524 BCC applies, the transaction or decision has to be reviewed beforehand by a committee of three independent directors, which must be assisted by one or more independent experts (lawyer, auditor, investment banker) designated by the committee and paid for by the company. The report drafted by the committee, with the aid of the expert, describes the nature of the transaction or decision, its advantages and disadvantages both for the company and for its shareholders, and estimates the patrimonial consequences of the transaction. Based on this evaluation, the committee assesses whether or not the decision or transaction may cause a disadvantage to the company which, in the light of its policy, is manifestly abusive (*kennelijk onrechtmatig*/*manifestement abusive*). If the committee comes to the conclusion that the decision or transaction is not manifestly abusive but could still harm the company, it should indicate the compensating advantages.

Thereafter, the Board of Directors will discuss and vote on the decision, basing its deliberations on this report. The minutes of the meeting must specify the fact that the special procedure of article 524 BCC was complied with and, as the case may be, on which grounds the advice of the committee of independent directors was not (or not entirely) followed.

The statutory auditors are also informed, as they have to certify the correctness of the factual information contained in the advice of the committee and in the minutes of the Board of Directors.

A summary of the decision must be included in the annual report of the Board, together with the advice of the committee and the certification of the facts and figures by the statutory auditors.

The sanctions for non-compliance with these shareholders' conflict of interest rules are largely comparable to those applicable to the directors' conflict of interest rules. First, there is a potential liability for the directors for non-compliance with the Belgian Companies Code. This general ground for directors' liability (article 528 BCC), is supplemented by a specific liability in cases where—notwithstanding formal compliance with article 524 BCC—the transaction or decision has resulted in an illegitimate financial disadvantage for the company to the benefit of another company within the group (article 529 BCC). Secondly, the company can demand that the resolution passed in breach of article

523 be declared void with third-party effect if the counterparty acted *mala fide*, ie. it was or should have been aware of the conflict.

Related-party transactions and the Executive Committee—Although the legislature intended to apply article 524 also to the decisions of the Executive Committee in a company which had opted for the two-tier system, it is as yet unclear how the procedure for intra-group conflicts of interest should be applied in that situation: Should it be applied by the Executive Committee itself, or does the decision or transaction fall under the powers reserved for the Board by virtue of its related-party nature? This uncertainty can be avoided by inserting a clause in the articles of association stating that the transfer of powers to the Executive Committee does not include decisions which would entail an intra-group conflict of interest.

c) Corporate Opportunities

There is no corporate opportunities doctrine in Belgian law. The issue of corporate opportunities was examined by an expert commission in the framework of the Corporate Governance Act of 2002. The commission concluded, however, that it would be extremely difficult to lay down rules on how corporate opportunities could be distributed in a group of companies. Furthermore, every rule would be hard to enforce, as many parent companies of Belgian subsidiaries are situated outside Belgium and minority shareholders would often not know which opportunities had arisen. For these reasons, the legislative commission concluded that no rules on corporate opportunities should be drafted as such, but recommended mandatory disclosure of potential corporate opportunities.

Therefore, article 524§7 BCC now obliges a listed company to notify in its annual report any significant limitations or burdens, or preservations of such limitations or burdens, which its parent company imposed or requested in the previous financial year. By means of this public notification, investors can take a better-informed decision, and may indeed put the Board under pressure not to accept these burdens and limitations too readily.

If a company does not comply with the corporate opportunities rule, the directors may be held liable for damages claimed by shareholders and third parties arising from such non-compliance.

d) Inside Information

Principle—All directors have a right to information. However, this right is limited because the information is only received and can only be used in the execution of their function (2009 Code, article 3.4). A director always has to act according to the corporate interest. Each director must treat the information received in his capacity of director with caution, given the confidential nature of the information concerned (2009 Code, article 3.4, guideline).

Criminal law—Different criminal law provisions can be relevant in this context. Under article 309 of the Belgian Criminal Code, it is a punishable offence for any person to deceitfully communicate trade secrets of the company he is or has been working for.

In this context, insider trading merits special attention. Directors of the issuer of the financial instrument concerned or of an affiliated company are forbidden to use their knowledge upon acquiring or selling the financial instrument (articles 25 and 40 Act of 2 August 2002). Punishment of directors for insider trading presupposes that they know or ought to know that the information concerned can be regarded as privileged. In addition to criminal penalties, sanctions of a purely administrative nature can also be imposed—the latter by the FSMA.

The 2009 Code requires the Board of Directors to take the necessary measures to ensure effective and efficient execution of the Belgian rules on market abuse (2009 Code, article 3.7).

The main rules in Belgium on market abuse are found in the Act of 2 August 2002[16] and the Royal Decree of 5 March 2006. The most crucial is the duty for the issuer of financial instruments to immediately publish insider information from the moment it comes into possession of such information. Under certain strict conditions—secrecy required in the company's interest while not misleading the market—the issuer can, on its own responsibility, delay the publication of such information, provided that (i) it can guarantee non-disclosure and (ii) it immediately informs the FSMA of the existence of privileged information. Furthermore, issuers must establish and keep up to date a list of insiders; in practice, this list is often requested by the FSMA shortly after completion of an important transaction such as a takeover bid or an IPO/SPO.

The issuers must ascertain that every insider understands his duties in this context. To that effect, the Board of Directors must prepare a dealing code for transactions in shares of the issuer for the personal account of directors and key management personnel (2009 Code, Annex B). The dealing code should also provide for transfer restrictions with regard to securities of the issuer during periods preceding the publication of financial results (closed periods) and during other sensitive periods (prohibited periods). Compliance with the dealing code is verified by a compliance officer. In addition, transactions in securities of the issuer by executive personnel or persons closely related to such persons should be notified to the FSMA shortly after completion of the transaction. The FSMA publishes these notified transactions on its website.

Duty of discretion and loyalty—The information a director receives when carrying out his tasks is protected by a general duty of discretion and loyalty. A director can only use this information in the interests of the company.

---

[16] On the supervision of the financial sector and financial services.

Director 'de facto' representing a shareholder—Special problems arise when a director represents *de facto* the interests of a (minority) shareholder at Board level without the shareholder itself being a director. Some authors suggest that these directors are at liberty to provide 'their' shareholders with information which they obtained as a director; others maintain that even under these circumstances the communication of privileged information qualifies as a violation of the insider trading laws (see below section 3.1.4, *Information streaming*). At any rate, this possibility is limited. Information may not be shared when such communication would violate a rule of public order. Moreover, the Board of Directors could decide that some information is of a highly confidential nature and therefore must not be communicated. Finally, the access to information is merely functional: A director may only share his information with 'his' shareholders in order to ensure the optimal exercise of his mandate. He cannot communicate the information solely in the personal interest of the represented shareholder.

When a legal person has a seat on the Board of Directors, its permanent representative (article 61§2 BCC) has the same right to information as the legal person whom he represents. The permanent representative is responsible for this information as if he holds the mandate personally, but can—quite para-doxically—freely communicate about this information 'within' the legal person since it is this legal person which holds the directorship.

e) Takeover Situations

Board document—Since the transposition into Belgian law of Directive 2004/25 on takeover bids, the Board of the target company must draw up and make public a document setting out its opinion of the bid and the reasons on which it is based, including its views on the effects of implementation of the bid on all the company's interests—specifically employment—and on the bidder's strategic plans for the target company and their likely repercussions on employment and the locations of the company's places of business. The Board of the target company must at the same time communicate that opinion to the works council. When the Board of the target company receives in due course a separate opinion from the works council on the effects of the bid on employment, that opinion must be appended to the document (Article 9(5) of Directive 2004/25/EC).

Passivity and breakthrough rules; opt-out and opt-in—In addition, Directive 2004/25/EC on takeover bids provides for a rule of passivity of the Board of Directors in relation to post-bid or defensive mechanisms: the Board must not act in a way that could frustrate the takeover bid, unless it acts with the prior consent of the general shareholders' meeting.

Belgium has made use of the possibility under Article 12 of the Directive to opt-out of the rules set forth in Articles 9 and 11. Therefore, Belgian companies whose shares are admitted to trading on a regulated market are only subject to the rule of passivity if they opt-in.

Such opting-in has to be formalised in the company's articles of association, must be published in the Annexes to the Belgian State Gazette, and must also be notified without delay to the FSMA, as well as to the supervisory authorities of Member States in which the company's relevant securities are admitted to trading on a regulated market or where such admission has been requested.

Besides the possibility for companies to opt-in, the Directive also provides for a possibility to only opt-in under the condition of reciprocity: The Board will then only be bound by the rule of passivity if the bidding company has also opted-in on that rule. This matter is governed by article 47 of the Belgian Takeover Act of 1 April 2007.

At present, almost none of the Belgian listed companies have decided to opt-in, not even under the condition of reciprocity.

Belgium made an absolutely similar opt-out choice, and at the same time created a similar opt-in possibility with regard to the so-called 'breakthrough rule' under Article 11 of the Directive.

Defensive mechanisms—In general, the Board of Directors can thus take defensive measures, but must always act in the interest of the company. As stated above (1.1), this interest was initially construed in case law as a broad conglomeration of the interest of all stakeholders, whereas more recently it has been more strictly limited to the interest of the shareholders. The issuance of authorised shares up to a maximum of 10% of the capital is the most popular defensive mechanism. It can only be used if the prior authorisation (*in tempore non suspecto*) of the general meeting specifically envisages its use in the event of a takeover bid, and if such authorisation is not older than three years (article 607 BCC). Another frequently used mechanism is a share buyback authorised by the general meeting—up to 20%, in the face of a 'serious threat' (article 620§1 BCC). Crown jewels (substantial assets or liabilities) can only be transferred or acquired after the launching of a bid (i) if the transfer or acquisition is decided upon by the general meeting itself or is the result of the exercise of an option granted to a third party by the general meeting *in tempore non suspecto,* and (ii) if this option was duly registered at the Commercial Court (article 556–557 BCC). The exercise of the option may be conditional upon the success of the bid. More generally, change of control clauses can only be invoked against the bidder subject to the same conditions, ie. approval by the general meeting and registration at the Commercial Court. A final mechanism is the 'poison warrant'. This is issued in favour of a befriended person (ie. a potential white knight) by the general meeting *in tempore non suspecto* (article 605, 1° BCC). It can only be exercised at the average stock price of the last thirty days before such exercise (article 598 BCC), and the shares issued in exchange should be nominative and held by the holder of the option for a minimum of twelve months (article 500 BCC).

3.1.4. *Institutional Investors*

Hybrid group—Institutional shareholders are a hybrid group. After the banking crisis of 1929, the banks had to disinvest, and were replaced by the holding companies. Investment funds (UCIs) were regulated in 1957. As from 1993, the investment ban was lifted for financial and insurance institutions. Hedge funds recently joined the group of institutional investors and have played an important role in several takeover bids.

Specific laws—Institutional investors' conduct (as a shareholder) is very often regulated by specific laws. For example:

The Act of 20 July 2004 obliges undertakings for collective investment (UCIs) to spread their holdings over different companies: They may not acquire a holding of securities in a company if that holding would enable the UCI to influence the company's management or its appointment, taking into account the shareholding structure and the dispersion of ownership. The Act of 20 July 2004 also prohibits UCIs from entering into voting agreements or committing themselves to use their voting rights as instructed by a person that is not participating in the shareholders' meeting. Furthermore, a UCI cannot commit itself not to sell its securities or to grant pre-emptive rights, nor can it conclude any agreement that would impede its management autonomy (article 67 of the Act of 20 July 2004).

Credit institutions may have shareholdings, other than those which they have acquired or subscribed to with a view to trading (ie. with a view to offering them for resale), in (i) (foreign) credit institutions; (ii) Belgian stockbroking firms and securities institutions; (iii) (foreign) insurance companies; and (iv) (foreign) companies principally engaged in carrying out financial transactions or providing financial services. In other cases, a credit institution may have shareholdings (financial assets), provided that no single shareholding exceeds 15% and total shareholdings do not exceed 45% of the institution's own funds (article 32 of the Act of 29 June 1993 and the Royal Decree of 17 June 1996). In special cases, however, the NBB may authorise shareholdings to be held notwithstanding and/or in excess of these conditions and limitations (article 32).

Behaviour—In the past, as a result of the above-mentioned rules which led to a dispersion of investments and made an active involvement impossible, institutional investors were unwilling to have discussions with management and, for example, did not exercise their voting rights; they attended shareholders' meetings, or they abstained from voting whenever a conflict between their voting behaviour and the interest of their investors might arise.

Institutional investors in the 2009 Code—Recognising the important role institutional investors (can) play in the governance of a company, the 2009 Code contains some provisions specifically related to major and institutional shareholders.

Given the reliance on market monitoring to enforce the flexible comply-or-explain approach of the 2009 Code, its authors found that shareholders, and in particular institutional shareholders, play an important role in carefully evaluating a company's corporate governance and that the Board of Directors should endeavour to ensure that institutional shareholders consider carefully all relevant factors drawn to their attention (Preamble 2009 Code under 6) (2009 Code, article 8.12).

In addition to article 10 of the Takeover Directive (Directive No 2004/25), the 2009 Code also recommends that the identity of the company's major shareholders should be disclosed in its Corporate Governance Charter, together with a description of their voting rights and special control rights, and, if they act in concert, a description of the key elements of existing shareholders agreements. The company should also disclose other direct and indirect relationships between the company and major shareholders (2009 Code, article 8.4).

Beyond that, the Board of Directors should have the controlling shareholder(s) make considered use of its/their position and respect the rights and interests of minority shareholders. The Board also should encourage the controlling shareholder(s) to respect the 2009 Code and should ask institutional shareholders and their voting agencies for explanations concerning their voting behaviour (2009 Code, articles 8.11 and 8.5, guideline).

Information streaming from director to shareholder—Another interesting question is whether and to what extent a director can stream up certain information to a major shareholder that he (*de facto*) represents. The corollary of the director's right to collect information is at any rate his duty of confidentiality (see section 3.1.3(d), *Director;* 2009 Code, article 3.4, guideline). In principle, therefore, a director cannot keep the shareholder he (*de facto*) represents informed with regard to major events within the company. The reasonableness of such a prohibition can, however, be questioned, considering the specific situation such directors face.[17] It can be easily by-passed—and the information stream secured—by appointing the shareholder itself as director, and not one of its executives (see section 3.1.3(d), *Duty*).

As the 2009 Code provides for a general recommendation to treat all shareholders equally (2009 Code, article 8.1), a solution can be found in organising information sessions which all shareholders are invited to attend (see 2009 Code, article 8.2 and 8.3). Alongside the legally recognised shareholders' information rights (eg. the right to ask questions at the general shareholders' meeting (article 540 BCC) and the right to receive the main corporate reports before each general shareholders' meeting), such sessions are a useful way of ensuring that all the shareholders are given the opportunity to be informed on an equal basis.

---

[17] The risk of falling within the scope of the legislation on market abuse should also be taken into account (eg. see articles 25–40 the Act of 2 August 2002). The exception allowing for the communication of privileged information when this is required by one's profession could be invoked (see section 3.1.3(d)). To be sure, this exception is conditional upon the information being communicated to the market immediately afterwards. However, this condition can be avoided if such public communication would militate against the interest of the company, when the secrecy of the information can be guaranteed without misleading the market. In such a case, the FSMA ('stock watch') should be alerted to the fact that privileged information exists.

3.1.5. Remuneration (as an Incentive)

New legislation on severance payments—The Act of 6 April 2010 introduced some new rules: The limitation of severance payments and a new mechanism in relation to variable remuneration for management.

Severance payments to top management and top executives are limited to an amount equal to 12 months' (fixed as well as variable) remuneration. The limit is 18 months if there is a duly reasoned recommendation from the remuneration committee. However, subject to prior approval by the shareholders' meeting, and under the same condition, severance payments exceeding these amounts are valid. This principle only applies with certainty to contractual severance payments. It certainly does not only limit the rights granted by the Employment Contracts Act of 3 July 1978. If, on the other hand, such rights would be the consequence of a settlement agreement providing for amounts in excess of the minimum under the Act (3 months per 5 years of seniority), it would seem wise to seek the approval of the general meeting. In any case, requests for severance payments equivalent to in excess of 18 months' remuneration have to be presented to the works council or the employee representatives. These bodies can submit a non-binding recommendation to the shareholders' meeting.

New rules on variable remuneration—The new article 520*bis* BCC provides for new rules on variable remuneration of executive directors. The criteria for performance-based remuneration must be explicitly included in the contractual documentation. If these criteria are not met, the variable part of the remuneration must not be paid, and the shareholders' meeting has no authority to overrule this. Furthermore, non-compliance can entail director's liability due to violation of the Belgian Companies Code.

The Act of 6 April 2010 also provides for a mechanism to render variable remuneration dependent on long-term rather than short-term targets (article 520*ter* BCC). Share-related remuneration needs to run through a vesting period, meaning that shares are only permanently acquired or options can only be exercised after a period of 3 years. However, one can overrule this mechanism in the articles of association or by means of explicit approval by the shareholders' meeting.

A second measure to increase the focus on long-term targets is the extension of the period over which performance assessment of managers takes place. To achieve this, article 520*ter* BCC provides for a spreading mechanism which compares the fixed remuneration of a given year to the maximum variable remuneration the executive may be entitled to over the next three years. The mechanism applies as soon as variable remuneration exceeds 25% of total remuneration. In that case, 50% of the variable remuneration needs to take into account the performance over the next year; 25% of the variable remuneration should relate to performance over a period of a minimum of two years and the remaining 25% to performance over a period of a minimum of three years. Consequently, only half of the variable remuneration may be awarded on the basis of criteria relating to performance in the next year. Again, one can overrule this mechanism in the articles of association or with the explicit approval of the shareholders' meeting.

The above-mentioned rules only apply to executive directors. For independent directors, the Belgian Companies Code (unlike the 2009 Code, article 7.7) allows for variable remuneration—but only to the extent that preliminary approval has been given by the shareholders' meeting (article 554 BCC) (see section 2.2.3).

3.2. Board and Stakeholders

3.2.1. Board and Employees/Labour Co-Determination

Works council—Unlike Germany and the Netherlands, Belgium is not familiar with using corporate structures as a means of co-determination for employees. There was some ideological discussion in the 1970s about the use of an obligatory two-tier system and the integration therein of workers participation, but no changes came about as a result of this.

The participation of workers and employees is governed by labour law and is essentially realised through the creation of a works council in all economic entities with more than 100 employees (Act of 20 September 1948). The works council should be provided with certain basic information (eg. articles of association), periodic information (annual accounts) and occasional information (eg. relating to a merger or takeover) regarding the company (Royal Decree of 27 November 1973 and Collective Labour Agreement No. 9 of 9 March 1972).

In addition, the employer must consult the works council in certain circumstances which are set forth by the Act of 1948 (training, new technologies).

Auditor appointment—Furthermore, the works council has the power to co-determine certain issues (eg. appointment of auditors, annual vacation, public holidays). The works council has a veto right when it comes to the appointment of the auditor in 'large'[18] companies. If there is no consensus between the works council and Board of Directors, the general meeting cannot appoint an auditor, and will have to leave the matter to the court. This joint auditor appointment is the closest Belgium has ever come to co-determination (see above section 2.2.1, *Number*).

3.2.2. Board and Creditors

Applicable legislation and going-concern hypothesis—Creditors have no specific role in company law, not even in banking law[19]—except to some extent in situa-

---

[18] For the definition, see n. 5 above.

[19] Of course, micro-prudential supervision of banks is all about the protection of depositaries, but no specific role is provided for creditors.

tions of financial distress (see below section 3.3). Indeed, company law itself provides only for a set of rules related to capital maintenance in case the company is confronted with discontinuity problems (see below). There is of course more specific bankruptcy-like legislation which allows for the judicial reorganisation of a business enterprise whose valuation as a going concern is no longer justified due to the threat of discontinuity (article 28 BCC). Company law, for that matter, only urges management to value the enterprise then on the basis of the liquidation hypothesis (article 38 Royal Decree 30 January 2001), as this allows the statutory auditor, notwithstanding his duty of professional secrecy, to alert the President of the Commercial Court if he has reason to believe that the going-concern hypothesis is jeopardised (ie. that the continuity of the business enterprise is no longer guaranteed) (article 138 BCC). The Commercial Court may then at its own discretion start proceedings under the Act on the Continuity of Enterprises of 31 January 2009[20] or the bankruptcy legislation.

Undercapitalisation—The founders of an undercapitalised company may be held personally and severally liable for all or part of the net debt. The action is brought by the liquidator before the Commercial Court. It requires the bankruptcy to have occurred within three years of the inception of the company, as well as proof that the undercapitalisation contributed to the bankruptcy—no strict causal relationship is required. To prevent such undercapitalisation, the founders of a company should make a financial plan before incorporating the company. Even if the term of three years has lapsed, tortious liability of the founders or directors remains possible in respect of undercapitalisation to the extent that such undercapitalisation may qualify as negligence under the standard of *bonus pater familias* (article 1382 Civil Code). In that case, a causal relationship between the undercapitalisation and the bankruptcy should be established.

Uncalled capital—Capital can be called by the Board of Directors at any time unless the shareholder negotiated a term upon promising his contribution. The unpaid part of the consideration must otherwise be paid up at the first request of the company. If the negotiated term for full payment has not yet lapsed, it can be invoked by the shareholder against the company as well as against any creditors of the company who, by means of the so-called 'indirect claim' (article 1166

---

[20] This new Act of 31 January 2009 contains a range of (Chapter 11-like) instruments which give the Commercial Court the opportunity to reorganise an enterprise in financial difficulties. For example, where evident and serious shortcomings of the debtor threaten the continuity of the enterprise, any interested party may ask the court to designate a judicial trustee (*gerechtsmandatari/mandataire de justice*) (article 14 of the Act on the Continuity of Enterprises). This trustee may substitute the debtor, and thus also its Board of Directors. The court is free to determine the content and the term of the trustee's mandate. The debtor itself may also request the appointment of a judicial trustee.

Civil Code), could initiate a request for payment in full, representing as such the company (article 199 BCC).

Capital reduction—In the event of a real capital reduction, creditors will lose part of their collateral as a result either of assets leaving the company to reimburse the shareholders, or, if the capital has not yet been fully paid up and its reduction functions as a waiver, of fewer funds being available—eg. through an indirect claim. For this reason, article 613 BCC grants the creditors of the company the right to request security (eg. a lien or mortgage) if their claim has not yet become due and payable at the time of the publication of the capital reduction decision in the Annexes to the Belgian Official Gazette (*Belgisch Staatsblad, Moniteur belge*). Effective reimbursement of the capital reduction is therefore not possible until two months after such publication. The company may grant the security requested or it may pay the discounted value of the outstanding claims. If the company chooses not to do so, the President of the Commercial Court may either grant the security requested or dismiss the claim altogether if he believes the company's solvency and liquidity are adequate.

Merger/split-up—In scenarios of reorganisation (merger or split-up) where a debt is being transferred, creditors of any company participating in the transaction may request additional security for the payment of their debts if they fear that the company acquiring the debt will not be able to pay (articles 684 and 766 BCC). The rules and conditions are identical to those applied in the case of a capital reduction (see preceeding paragraphs). Since the consent of bondholders is not required for a merger or a split-up, they have the same rights as any other creditor in this respect. If deceitful intent can be proven, an action based on Article 1167 of the Civil Code (*actio pauliana*) is, of course, always possible.

Loss of capital—In the event that a company's net assets fall below 50% of its initial paid-up capital, its Board of Directors should convene a general meeting within two months of that event (article 633 BCC). The general meeting may then either approve the restructuring measures proposed by the Board, or decide to liquidate the company. The latter decision requires an attendance quorum of half of the capital[21] and a majority of 75%.

If after such restructuring the net assets would further decrease below one quarter of the initial paid-up capital, a minority of one quarter at the general meeting can decide to wind up the company.

If the net assets fall below the statutory minimum amount for the share capital of a limited liability company, any interested party (eg. a creditor, a competitor) may request the court to dissolve the company (article 634 BCC). Although this request cannot be denied by the court in the event that this threshold has been

---

[21] This quorum is no longer required at a second meeting called immediately after the first where it was not attained.

crossed, the court may decide to grant the company a grace period to rectify the situation.

Director's liability after bankruptcy and wrongful trading—Directors whose gross negligence contributed to the bankruptcy of the company may be held jointly and severally liable by the Commercial Court for part of the net debt (article 530 BCC). The liquidator is not required to demonstrate a strict causal relationship. Fiscal fraud and money laundering are *per se* cases of gross negligence which are presumed, without any possibility of rebuttal, to have contributed to the bankruptcy. Since liquidators used this instrument only on rare occasions, the Parliament wanted to allow individual action in respect of tax and social security contributions, and extended this privilege to all creditors.[22] Even now there is little case law on the subject.

More generally, a director can be liable for continuing to trade in a situation where a reasonably diligent person would realise that insolvency is inevitable. Under Belgian law, this sanction also applies to persons who in strictly legal terms have no directorship, but exercise the function *de facto* (eg. a controlling shareholder). The same rule may apply to a controlling holding company, or to a major creditor or bank which, by keeping its credit lines open, creates the appearance of solvency.

3.2.3. Board and Other Stakeholders

Corporate interest—It is generally agreed that the Board must act in the corporate interest. However, as we discussed above, it is disputed whether this corporate interest also includes the interest of other stakeholders or only the interest of the shareholders. After an emphasis on the interest of the other stakeholders in the 1960s and 1970s, the focus was recently shifted to the shareholders' interest (see above section 1.1). Of course, following on from the focus on corporate governance, corporate social responsibility is also becoming more important in Belgium.

Soft law—The 2009 Code provides the guideline that '[i]n translating values and strategies into key policies, the Board should pay attention to corporate social responsibility, gender diversity and diversity in general'. Moreover, the Buysse Code II, which is the Belgian corporate governance code for non-listed enterprises, strongly encourages stakeholder management. The Buysse Code II recommends that 'enterprises design their strategy so as to sustainably increase their attractiveness to all stakeholders, both internal and external'. In addition, it provides for explicit recommendations as to the company's relations with bankers, clients, suppliers, governmental bodies, external advisors, interest groups, and

---

[22] Creating in this way serious concursus problems: Indeed, the losses incurred should be compensated on an equal basis, while the new version of article 530 BCC allows an individual creditor to pursue his sole interest.

even competitors. Almost all listed companies publish charters on their website setting out the priorities in their action vis-à-vis the general interest, how they contribute in their own enterprise to sustainable growth, and which social or environmental projects at home or abroad receive their specific attention.

Hard law—Although not explicit, there is also hard law encouraging the company (and/or the Board of Directors) to take into account the interest of stakeholders. We already referred to the role of the works council in a number of instances, which is also explicitly mentioned in the Belgian Companies Code (see section 3.2.1).

Other examples can be given:

In the document referred to in 3.1.3 and which the Board of Directors has to draw up in response to a takeover bid prospectus, it has to take into account the interest of the company, ie. the interest of the shareholders, of the employees and workers and of the creditors (Act of 1 April 2007).

In cases where manifest and serious misconduct that has contributed to the company's bankruptcy, directors can be held severally liable for all or part of the company's liabilities (article 530 BCC). This liability does not require proof of a causal relationship in the strict sense, and underlines the social responsibility of directors.

In the (former) Economic Expansion Act of 30 December 1976, there was a duty to inform the government before transferring a branch of a company with net assets over EUR 2,500,000, when the transfer included more than one-third of the share capital.

The Economic Recovery Act of 27 March 2009 (*Economische Herstelwet/Loi de relance économique*) and the Royal Decree of 22 April 2009 extend employers' obligations to assist the redeployment efforts of workers who lose their jobs in the framework of a collective redundancy. Under this legislation, any company employing over 20 workers and announcing a collective redundancy is obliged to create or to affiliate with an employment cell, which must organise outplacement assistance for the workers.

3.3. Changing Roles in Financial Distress[23]

Resolution and sale of bank assets and liabilities by Royal Decree—The stakeholdings of depositaries in financial institutions is never felt more clearly than in times of financial distress. The biggest Belgian bank, Fortis Belgium, was sold during to BNP Paribas the financial crisis of 2008. Of course, this share purchase

---

[23] Belgian law does not provide for any exception to the mandatory takeover bid rules in the case of a target in serious financial difficulties (see Article 5(4), second paragraph of Directive No 2004/25). See K. Geens, 'Post financial crisis regulation in Belgium', *European Company Law Review*, 2011, Volume 8/Issue 5, 208.

agreement was executed by the Board of Directors of Fortis Holding (a listed company). The Board did so at the instigation of the Belgian State without prior approval of the general meeting although the corporate governance charter of Fortis Holding seemed to require such approval—and although admittedly such approval was certainly not required by the Belgian Companies Code itself.

Since difficult litigation arose from this government-induced sale, an Act was passed on 2 June 2010 allowing the King to adopt in similar circumstances in the future, at the request of—or at least subject to the prior advice of—the NBB, any measure related to assets or liabilities linked to the shares issued by a 'system relevant' insurance company, credit institution or clearing and settlement house. The King can only proceed to these measures if (i) the entity's policy or its financial position could jeopardise the successful meeting of its engagements, or the entity does not provide sufficient guarantees as to its solvency, liquidity or profitability, or if its administrative or accounting organisation or internal structure shows serious gaps; and (ii) this situation could affect the stability of the Belgian or European financial system (making it a so-called 'system relevant' or systemic institution).[24]

The measure may have the Belgian State or any other public or private Belgian or foreign legal entity as the counterparty. Owners of assets or holders of rights subject to the measure will receive compensation in the manner determined in the King's decision. If the State is not the beneficiary of the expropriated assets and liabilities, the affected persons are entitled to the price agreed between the State and the third party buying the assets or liabilities, in line with a distribution formula determined in the King's decision.

The forced sale of assets cannot cause the existing agreements between the entity concerned and third parties to be altered or to be terminated, nor can it give one of them the right to unilaterally terminate such agreement.

Determination of the 'price'—A second Act dated 2 June 2010 makes the decree ordering the measure subject to a mandatory judicial review similar to the review one would expect in the case of an expropriation. The civil Court of First Instance of Brussels must determine whether the measure is in line with the law and whether the compensation seems fair. During this procedure, the institution and the owners may be heard. Once the court's positive decision is published, the decree enters into force. No appeal can be lodged against this judgment. Nevertheless, within two months, a procedure to reconsider the compensation can be launched separately before the same court, but it will not have any effect with regard to the transfer of property.

---

[24] For financial institutions to be systemic, a balance sheet total of EUR 150 billion is required or a market share of over 10%.

Exceptional board powers—As indicated (see above in this section), the legislation of 2 June 2010 was to a large extent inspired by the fear that a requirement for prior approval by the general meeting would hinder the Board or the government in taking the measures which the stability of the financial markets urgently required. Therefore, not only the Belgian Government, but also the Board of a 'systemic' credit institution, a 'systemic' insurance institution or a 'systemic' investment services institution, may take—without prior approval of the general meeting—any exceptional measures, even beyond the limits of the articles of association, which are required by the gravity of the situation, ie. if (i) the institution's policy or its financial position could jeopardise the successful meeting of its engagements, or the institution does not provide sufficient guarantees as to its solvency, liquidity or profitability, or its administrative or accounting organisation or internal structure shows serious gaps; and (ii) this situation could affect the stability of the Belgian or international financial system.

4. Enforcement

4.1. Courts

4.1.1. Personal Liability Claims

Liability grounds—Directors, as well as members of the Executive Committee and day-to-day managers, are responsible for the performance of the duties entrusted to them and are individually liable to the company for any shortcomings in their management and administration. The extent of this duty of care is determined based on the professional skills which can reasonably be expected of a normally prudent and reasonable director facing the same factual circumstances (see above section 2.2.2, *Independent and professional judgment*).

Directors and members of the Executive Committee are jointly and severally liable to the company or third parties for any loss resulting from a breach of the provisions of the Belgian Companies Code or of the company's articles of association. The presumption can be rebutted if the directors succeed in proving that: (i) They did not participate in the violation; (ii) they were not or could not reasonably have been expected to be in a position to prevent it; and (iii) they properly informed the first general meeting held after they gained knowledge of such violation. Similarly, members of the Executive Committee must report to the next meeting of the Board of Directors in order to escape liability.

In principle, non-executive directors bear the same liability risk as executive directors. Of course, a non-executive director will find it easier to prove that he was not or could not reasonably have been expected to be aware of wrongful acts—which, of course, is only helpful if he informs the general meeting as soon as possible after discovery. Recent case law indicates that scrutiny is more precise with regard to non-executives who are member of the audit committee.

Release/discharge—Directors can be discharged vis-à-vis the company by a special vote (*kwijting/décharge*) of the shareholders in the annual general meeting. The discharge is only valid if the annual accounts prepared and presented by the Board do not contain any omission or misstatement, and if breaches of the BCC or the articles of association for which discharge is envisaged have been specifically mentioned in the convening notice for the meeting. The discharge only releases the directors of their liability vis-à-vis the company, but not from their liability vis-à-vis third parties.

Since the legislature 'forgot' to act on rules on the discharge (*quitus*) in the relationship between the Board of Directors and the Executive Committee, it makes sense to provide for this aspect in the articles of association.

Majority, individual and minority action—As the director is contractually liable vis-à-vis the company, the authority to decide whether or not to start proceedings against the directors rests with the general meeting.

Individual shareholders can only instigate an action against the director if he inflicted direct damage upon the shareholder personally—from which other shareholders did not suffer, or at least not to the same extent.

In order to compensate for failure by majority shareholders to commence proceedings against the Board of Directors, minority shareholders can institute a 'minority action' in their own name, but for the account of the company. Such minority actions can only be brought by one or more shareholders holding, collectively or individually, securities representing not less than (i) 1% of the voting rights within the company, or (ii) a portion of the nominal capital over EUR 1,250,000. Shareholders who voted in favour of a discharge of the directors do not benefit from this possibility, unless the discharge is subsequently shown to be invalid. A negative vote is not required, however; it is sufficient for them to have abstained or been absent. All damages to be paid by the director(s) will be paid to the company, and not to the individual claimant(s). Conversely, if the claim is rejected by the courts, the claimant(s) will have to bear all expenses personally.

Case law shows few minority actions, mostly due to the fact that the proceeds will at any rate be paid to the company, while—at least until final victory is secured—the lawyer's fee must be borne by the claimant.

Exoneration, indemnification and insurance—Under Belgian law, parties to an agreement may stipulate clauses that limit or exclude their liability. Such exoneration clauses are not unlawful, but are to be construed in a restrictive manner. This rule also applies to directors of companies.

However, there are some exceptions to the general rule of validity of an exoneration clause: (i) It must not cover deception, fraud or intentional fault; (ii) it must not have the effect of rendering the agreement void of meaning or purpose; and (iii) a specific regulation may prohibit the application of exoneration clauses in certain sectors. A general exoneration clause whereby a company waives, in advance, its right to submit a claim against its directors is therefore null and void under Belgian law, since such a clause would totally change the nature of a directorship and render ineffective the power of the general meeting to control and to grant discharge.

A company may hold the directors harmless against liability claims brought against them by third parties if such engagement is not contrary to the interest of the company. In principle, such 'hold harmless' engagement should not prevent the company from reclaiming afterwards, from its directors, the amounts it has paid. The indemnification guarantee can be granted by the Board of Directors, since it does not as such limit the power of the general meeting to grant discharge or to file a claim.

Directors can be insured against the liability risk. The company may pay the insurance premium, because the insurance is in the company's interest (eg. in the event that it should have to sue its directors or hold them harmless). The insurance policy only covers the civil—contractual and extra-contractual—liability of directors. Moreover, the insured hazard can be limited to an exhaustive account of faults, or the amount of cover may be 'capped'. In all events, the director must not be insured against fraud or an intentional fault but may be insured against gross negligence.

4.1.2. Nullification of Resolutions of the General Meeting and Board of Directors

Formal irregularity—Article 64 of the BCC contains a general regulation with regard to the grounds for nullity of decisions made by the general meeting of companies. The BCC also provides for the procedure and consequences of the nullity of those decisions (articles 178–180). These rules apply *mutatis mutandis* to the decisions of the Board of Directors.

The general grounds for nullification because of a formal irregularity can be found in Article 64, 1° BCC. A decision can be declared null and void because of any formal irregularity if the claimant can show that the irregularity had an influence on the outcome of the decision process. This is the case, for example, if there is a violation of the rules which guarantee the participation of all shareholders or directors, or which guarantee their correct information.

Exceptions to the formal irregularity rule—There are two exceptions to the general grounds for nullification: (i) Fraud (article 645, 2° BCC), and (ii) the ground for nullification because of any other reason mentioned in the Companies Code (article 64, 5° BCC), which includes the mere absence of written reports required for certain corporate law transactions (eg. a contribution in kind, or a capital increase with exclusion of preferential rights (see articles 181, 447, 559, 560, 602, 633 and 780 BCC). In the latter instance, there is no need to prove that the irregularity had an influence on the outcome of the decision process.[25] In the former instance, fraud means that artificial devices were used to prevent (i) the presence of a shareholder, director or auditor at the general meeting, or (ii) the truth being brought to the attention of the shareholders (eg. falsification of the annual accounts).

Abuse and ultra vires—Not only formal irregularities but also intrinsic flaws in a decision can lead to annulment of the decision. Decisions will be declared null and void on account of abuse of power or use of power beyond one's capacity, ie. *ultra vires* (article 64, 3° BCC). These nullity grounds, which find their origin in administrative law, must be interpreted as a 'residual category' containing all material irregularities in addition to those provided by article 64, 1°, 2°, 4° and 5° BCC, which are the result of a specific violation of the law or of the articles of association.

Examples of *ultra vires* actions are: (i) The violation of the power of other representative bodies in the company—more specifically, the exclusive powers of the Board of Directors by the general meeting, or vice versa; (ii) the transfer of some of the exclusive powers of a representative body to another representative body; (iii) a decision which no representative body in the company has the authority to take (eg. forcing the shareholders to transfer their shares); (iv) decisions taken in violation of certain majority requirements imposed by the Company Code or by the articles of association; or (v) decisions taken in violation of provisions in the articles of association with regard to the division of profits.

Abuse of power can be defined as any circumstance 'in which the power of a representative body or the power of a majority at the general meeting is being used to sacrifice the interest of the company for private interests which are outside the company structure'.[26] This covers abuse both of a majority position and of a minority position.

Listed companies—Article 64, 4° BCC, referring *inter alia* to the Act of 2 March 1989 (see also articles 514–516, 534 and 545 BCC), contains additional grounds for nullification specific to general meetings of listed companies. If a person holds a number of securities in a Belgian listed company in excess of a certain threshold, he must—according to the existing disclosure legislation—immediately[27] send a notification to the company and the FSMA (Act of 2 May 2007). When voting rights attached to securities were not duly notified, and therefore

---

[25] The general rule applies, however, if the report is incomplete, incorrect or submitted too late.

[26] J. Ronse, *Preadvies over de nietigheid van besluiten van organen van de naamloze vennootschap*, Zwolle, W.E.J. Tjeenk Willink, 1966, p. 25.

[27] Within four trading days (article 12 Act of 2 May 2007).

suspended by law[28] or by the President of the Commercial Court, the use of these rights notwithstanding such suspension will render the decision of the general meeting null and void—at least if the claimant can prove that the legally required attendance quorum or majority would otherwise not have been attained (article 516§4 BCC).

Confirmation—The person who has confirmed the decision cannot claim nullity of that decision afterwards, unless the nullity would result from the violation of a rule of public order (article 178BCC). According to Belgian law, confirmation is a unilateral legal act through which one waives the right to claim nullity. It can be given explicitly if it is stated in a formal way. This need not be done in writing—eg. the approval, without reservation, of the decision in the general meeting, provided that it was well-informed approval (article 178§2 BCC). The confirmation is implicit, however, if it can be derived, without any reasonable doubt, from what a person does or does not do, that he has the intention of waiving the nullity (eg. a shareholder participating without reservation in a general meeting, even though the meeting was irregularly convened).

Regularisation—Regularisation means that the general meeting renders a deficient decision valid, by repairing the grounds for nullity. Regularisation can be accomplished (i) by meeting the formal requirements which were previously lacking, or (ii) by taking a new decision, retroactively replacing the former decision considered as invalid. In principle, regularisation is only possible for formal irregularities, since it aims to correct a specific decision. In other words, if a decision is intrinsically irregular, this irregularity cannot simply be corrected by taking the same decision, because the content needs changing. Although, in principle, such regularisation must be decided by the general meeting before the nullity claim is brought, it is not to be excluded that a judge might allow for a certain regularisation period.

Peremptory time limit—The term within which the claim for annulment of a decision is to be brought lapses six months after its publication, ie. within six months of the day the decision can be invoked against third parties (article 198§2, Sec. 3 BCC; however, see article 551§3 BCC).[29] This special time limit is only applicable to the nullity grounds of article 64 BCC and as a rule does not apply to decisions of the Board of Directors. Other actions for nullity are mostly time-barred after a period of ten years (article 2262*bis* Civil Code).

---

[28] Eg. when the breaching of a threshold was notified later than 20 days before a general meeting (article 545 BCC).

[29] The term starts as of the vote when nullity is claimed for a decision which would not have been taken without the nullity of certain votes (article 551§3 BCC).

Procedure—According to Belgian law, the nullity verdict with regard to a decision of the general meeting must always be rendered by the Commercial Court. Pending such a verdict, the decision of the general meeting is to be considered valid. However, the nullity of a decision can be invoked during a judicial procedure as a means of defence, ie. as an exception.

To initiate an action for the annulment of a decision, the claimant must have a legitimate and personal interest in the action (articles 17 and 18 Judicial Code). Obviously the individual shareholders are the most interested parties in this matter. Although it is not unanimously accepted that the company has the right to initiate a claim itself, it can certainly invoke the nullity as a means of defence. Directors and auditors may claim the nullity of a decision to revoke them. Third parties will in general only have a sufficient interest to initiate an action where a rule of public order was violated (*openbare orde/ordre public*).

Article 179§1 BCC confirms the general rule that the claim for nullity must be directed against the company. Otherwise the action will be inadmissible. In the event of a claim for nullity regarding a merger decision, the action must be directed against all the companies involved, including those which have been wound up by the merger and artificially survive for the sole purpose of this nullity claim (article 682, 1° BCC).

Consequences of the annulment—The annulment has retroactive effect *erga omnes* and in principle leads to the nullity of all decisions or transactions based on the annulled decision. The rights acquired by third parties only remain intact if they acted in good faith while being unaware that the decision was flawed by an irregularity. On the other hand, a judgment denying the nullity claim only has consequences *inter partes*—ie persons not involved in the procedure can still invoke nullity at a later point in time.

4.1.3. Special Procedures and Issues

Commercial Court/Injunction proceeding before the President of the Commercial Court—The normal court for companies is the Commercial Court, even when the company is not a *commerçant* in the strict sense of the word. The Commercial Court is composed of a professional judge and two lay magistrates. There are 27 commercial courts in Belgium, one per *arrondissement*. Appeal is brought before five Courts of Appeal (Brussels, Antwerp, Hasselt, Liège, Mons). The highest instance is the Court of Cassation in Brussels.

The most frequently used judicial procedure in Belgian company law practice is the (interim) injunction proceeding before the President of the Commercial

Court.[30] This specific procedure makes it possible to obtain an (interim) decision in a rather short time.

Most of the time, the decision of the President is *ad interim,* ie. provisional (eg. suspension by the President); it should therefore not harm or preclude the definitive outcome upon which another judicial body will decide (eg. a decision as to nullity or validity by the Commercial Court). This procedure is generally called *en référe/in kort geding.* All sorts of interim injunctions and/or orders can be requested through the (interim) injunction proceeding: for example the appointment of a 'judicial trustee' (*gerechtelijke mandataris/mandataire de justice*), an ad hoc director, a depositary (*bewaarnemer/dépositaire*) or a sequestrator (*sekwester/séquestre*); the convening of a general shareholders' meeting; or the stay of execution of a resolution of the general meeting pending a judicial decision with regard to the validity of such resolution.

In some exceptional instances, company law itself gives the President alone the power to render a definitive decision: (*het kort geding/la procedure en référé*). Various examples can be found in the Belgian Companies Code (BCC):

- The appointment of an auditor if the general shareholders' meeting fails to appoint one (article 131 BCC);
- The procedure for dispute resolution (articles 636–644 BCC (see below, *Dispute resolution*);
- Creditor protection in the case of a capital reduction (article 613 BCC) (see above section 3.2.2, *Uncalled Capital*);
- Valuation of shares without voting rights when acquiring own shares (article 626 BCC);
- Creditor protection in the case of merger or split-up (article 684 BCC) (see above section 3.2.2, *Capital reduction*).

Brussels Court of Appeal.—The Brussels Court of Appeal plays an important role in takeover bid situations (see above section 3.1.3(d)) in respect of any claim on the merits or for interim measures which are (partially) based on or related to the takeover bid legislation (article 41 Act of 1 April 2007). As such, it is also the judge in appeals against decisions of the FSMA. If, for instance, the FSMA finds no grounds to order a mandatory bid, the Brussels Court of Appeal may confirm or revise that decision. The same Court is the only Belgian court where relief can be sought from decisions of other Belgian regulatory authorities, eg. in competition law matters (appeals against the Belgian Competition Council), or in the sector of regulated industries (telephone, post, electricity, etc.).

Arbitration—In company law, parties frequently opt to refer their dispute to arbitrators and to handle their dispute outside the courts: arbitrators with

---

[30] As stated, there is a commercial tribunal for each of the 27 Belgian *arrondissements*; this means that there are also 27 Presidents.

appropriate knowledge and expertise can be appointed. Arbitration is often quicker and more flexible than judicial proceedings; moreover, the arbitral award and the proceedings are generally confidential. Although arbitration was mandatory for conflicts between shareholders in the 1808 Commercial Code, nowadays it is much more often seen as a means of resolving post-acquisition problems rather than normal company law disputes. For the latter, the President of the Commercial Court has become the 'natural' or normal judge, partly because of the swiftness of the *référé* proceedings (see above section 4.1.3, *Commercial Court*), and partly because the relationship between arbitration and the parts of company law which are considered as *ius cogens*, or of public order, remains unclear. The annulment of an arbitral decision for violation of public order is rarely sought. If it is, the civil court has jurisdiction.

Dispute resolution/general—In case of serious conflicts between shareholders in non-listed public and private limited liability companies, the BCC provides for dispute resolution before the President of the Commercial Court. The decision of the President is *comme en référé/zoals in kort geding*) (see above section 4.1.2, *Procedure*), ie. summary proceedings with a definitive, non-provisional outcome (subject, of course, to appeal).

Shareholders holding more than a certain percentage of the shares or the voting securities and having valid reasons can file a request with the President of the Commercial Court seeking the exclusion of another shareholder to whom these reasons can be attributed, ie. seeking to force that shareholder to transfer its shares (and other voting securities in its possession) to the claimant(s). This request cannot be made by the company itself, or by a subsidiary of the company. It can only validly be filed by shareholders holding, individually or collectively, (i) either 30% of all the voting rights; (ii) or 20% of the voting rights if the company has issued securities with voting rights that do not represent the capital; (iii) or 30% of the capital of the company.

Any shareholder who has valid reasons can file a demand with the President of the Commercial Court seeking an exit, ie. to force other shareholders—to whom these reasons can be attributed—to purchase its shares.

The 'valid' reasons (*justes motifs*) needed to force exclusion or an exit do not require negligence on the part of the defendant. It suffices that a situation has arisen which requires their separation in the interest of the company. Valid reasons include serious default on meeting certain obligations, abuse of a majority or minority position, serious conflicts which cannot be resolved, or incapacity to act.

Dispute resolution/procedure—Alongside the shareholder to whom the aforementioned 'valid' reasons can be attributed, the company itself must also be summoned to appear before the President of the Commercial Court of the *arrondissement* (district) where the company has its registered seat.

As of that day, the summoned shareholder is no longer allowed to transfer the shares or grant certain security rights without the approval of the President or of the other parties. The President can decide to suspend the rights attached to the shares, except for the dividend right. If the President decides that there are 'valid reasons', he will order the defendant to transfer or buy the shares for a certain price which he determines, usually after receiving thorough and adversarial expert advice. If there are any rights (eg. pre-emption rights) attached to these shares, the President must ensure that these rights are respected. The President can, however, decide to exercise a company-specific (articles of association) or contractual right of approval in the interest of the shareholders. He must also indicate which pre-emption rights can be exercised and the price thereof.

The shareholders—whether obtaining the exclusion or forced to buy—are jointly liable for the payment of the price for the transferred shares.

Dispute resolution is rather frequently used with success in small and medium-sized companies (SMEs), much more than in the Netherlands although the Dutch first 'invented' the procedure.[31] Due to the nature of the process, the legal quality of dispute resolution decisions is variable. The procedure is not concerned with liability. It is more along the lines of asking: Are there enough good reasons to make a divorce desirable? On the other hand, the high price to be paid in larger enterprises makes a positive outcome less likely. Judges generally realise that the financial burden of such an outcome would eventually be borne by the company itself.

Squeeze-out—Article 513 BCC states that any shareholder owning at least 95% of the votes attached to all the securities issued by a *société anonyme* can make an offer to the remaining shareholders in order to acquire the remaining shares. If the bidder(s) follow(s) the prescribed equal treatment and publicity rules, all the shares become his/their property upon termination of the takeover bid-like procedure, at least if the company was listed before the squeeze-out (Act of 1 April 2007 and Royal Decree of 27 April 2007). If the company was not listed, the shareholders have the explicit option not to accept the bid (art. 219 Royal Decree of 30 January 2001). After a successful takeover bid leaving the bidder and the shareholders in concert with him with more than 95% of the voting rights, the bidder can take the company private by launching a squeeze-out at the bid prices using the same prospectus, within three months. Under the same percentage and time limit conditions, remaining minority shareholders can request a sell-out in respect of their own shares only.

4.2. Regulators

The Accounting Standards Commission—(Commissie voor Boekhoudkundige Normen/Commission des Normes Comptables) advises the Government (mandatorily) and the Parliament (optionally) on all annual account and bookkeeping

---

[31] B. Tilleman and G. van Solinge, 'De uittreding en uitsluiting', *T.P.R.*, 2000, 625.

regulations. Companies and enterprises in general can request the opinion of the Commission in specific matters (article 13 of the Act of 17 July 1975 on the bookkeeping of enterprises). Of course, the Commission itself can also take the initiative to issue recommendations. The opinions and recommendations of the Commissions are published annually.

IBR-IRE, IAB-IEC—Auditors, accountants and tax consultants exercise their profession under the supervision of the Institute of Auditors and the Institute of Accountants and Tax consultants (*Instituut van de Accountants en de Belastings-consulenten/Institut des Experts-comptables et des Conseils fiscaux*). The institutes monitor the training and the continuing influx of auditors, accountants and tax consultants. The Institute of Auditors prepares technical standards which prescribe the process according to which auditors should go about their different monopoly tasks (article 30 Act of 22 July 1953). The technical standards and professional regulations for these three professions have to be submitted for prior advice to the High Council of Economic Professions (*Conseil Superieur des Professions Economiques/Hoge Raad voor Economische Beroepen*), an independent government body with separate legal personality.

ACCOM—In the context of the major debates in 2001 with regard to auditor independence and the related rules, the Belgian legislature has substantially strengthened the independence rules with regard to the auditing function (see above sections 2.1 and 2.2.2(a), *Tasks/Eternal audit*). The Advisory and Controlling Committee on the Independence of the Auditor (*Advies- en controlecomité op de onafhankelijkheid van de commissaris/Comité d'avis et de contrôle de l'indépendance des commissaires*) was established under the same law—the Corporate Governance Act of 2 August 2002. The committee has a twofold mission. It has to (i) give preliminary advice at the request of an auditor; and (ii) monitor compliance with the rules for the independence of auditors.

FSMA—Pursuant to the Act of 2 July 2010 and the Royal Decree of 3 March 2011, the 'Twin Peaks model' was adopted in Belgium. As of 1 April 2011, the former Banking, Finance and Insurance Commission was renamed the Financial Services and Markets Authority (FSMA) and is responsible for financial consumer protection and financial market supervision. Its micro-prudential tasks with regard to financial, insurance and investment service institutions are now carried out by the National Bank of Belgium (NBB), which already co-exercised macro-prudential control. The FSMA indirectly monitors compliance by listed companies with the Corporate Governance Code while supervising the financial information they have to provide to the market (see also section 4.3.1 below).

4.3. Self-Regulation

4.3.1. Corporate Governance Codes

The Corporate Governance Commission—This Commission is the main actor in the field. It is a private foundation and was established on 22 January 2004 by the Federation of Belgian Enterprises (*Verbond van Belgische Ondernemingen/ Fondation des Entreprises Belges*), Euronext Brussels, and some private individuals. This commission has about 20 members: Besides the parties mentioned, the listed companies themselves, the audit sector, the FSMA, the CRB (Central Council for the Enterprise) and the legal sector are represented. The main duty of this commission is to ensure that the 2009 Code remains relevant for listed companies and to regularly update the Code based on industry practice, new legislation, and international standards.

Its original purpose was to draft a single reference code for Belgian listed companies. After public reassessment, a second edition of the Code was published in 2009. The aim of the committee is to contribute to the development of corporate governance by regularly monitoring enforcement of the 2009 Code, submitting suggestions for amendments, and issuing positions on any regulatory initiative or other initiative pertaining to corporate governance.

The only reference code admitted—The Belgian legislature pointed out in the Act of 6 April 2010 and the Royal Decree of 6 June 2010 that Belgian listed companies—pursuant to European Directive 2006/46—have to opt for a Corporate Governance Code recognised by Royal Decree. The 2009 Code was then recognised by Royal Decree of 6 June 2010 as the only one to which such listed companies may—and thus must—refer.[32] It is obvious that in order to be relevant—ie. to have the same binding force, from now on every change to the 2009 Code will have to be ratified by means of new approval of the Code by Royal Decree.

Comply-or-explain—Listed companies are required to publish a Corporate Governance Statement in their annual report. They must refer therein to the 2009 Code, indicate any parts of this Code with which they do not comply, and explain the reason for any such non-compliance. The 2009 Code does not prescribe how the company should explain non-compliance; as a result, explanations regarding non-compliance often tend to be very concise. A better approach, no doubt, would be to explain why, in a given situation, non-compliance with a certain rule is more in keeping with the underlying principle than compliance. The 2009 Code recommends that the shareholders' meeting and the Board of Directors should start a discussion in cases of non-compliance with the Code if the shareholders'

---

[32] However, the new law also encompasses Belgian companies which are only listed abroad. For such companies, this may create the need to combine two corporate governance codes.

meeting does not agree with the explanation given by the Board of Directors (Preamble to the 2009 Code under 6, 2009 Code, article 8.13).

The question to what extent the rules of the 2009 Code now have binding effect has to be answered in the light of the fact that the law itself, and no longer the market alone, requires an explanation for each case of non-compliance.[33] Although the difference may seem minor, it is substantial from a purely legal point of view. Indeed, violation of the comply-or-explain rule—a rule now mandatory by law—is now a violation of the Belgian Companies Code. This being the case, the directors are jointly and severally liable (article 528 BCC) (see above section 4.4.1, *Liability grounds*). An insufficient explanation of non-compliance might constitute a basis for directors' liability if the company, an individual shareholder or a third party can demonstrate a causal relationship between the absence or insufficiency of an explanation and a loss incurred by that party allegedly arising as a result. Such a relationship is not unlikely if a company forgets altogether to indicate the fact that it is not complying with a certain rule. In that case, the appearance of compliance is indeed created, and this could cause a third party who relied on such compliance to sustain a loss.

4.3.2. Does the Comply-or-Explain System Produce Effective Results?

Compliance study (respect/naleving) on the 2009 Code—A recent study carried out by FSMA in December 2010[34]—and thus before the entry into force of the Act of 6 April 2010 (see above section 4.3.1)—shows that the companies examined often fail to indicate whether or not a provision of the 2009 Code is applicable to them. For instance, they do not explicitly state whether or not the non-executive directors receive performance-related remuneration, whether or not the members of the management benefit from pension schemes, or whether or not share options are part of the remuneration package, etc.

The FSMA also found that a number of the examined provisions of the 2009 Code are not being properly observed. This is the case for the provisions relating to the characteristics of the internal control and risk management systems, the evaluation of the Board and Board members, the procedure for the development of a remuneration policy, and the determination of the level of remuneration.

In addition, significant progress needs to be made as regards compliance with the provisions relating to the basic and variable remuneration of the CEO and the other members of the management, the information on pension schemes and other components of the remuneration, and the information on shares and share options.

---

[33] K. Geens, 'What if you don't explain why you don't comply?', in *Corporate Governance: carcan ou clé du succès*, Brussels, Bruylant, 2010, 1–44.

[34] French version: <www.CBFA.be/fr/publications/stu/pdf/study38.pdf>; Dutch version: <www.CBFA.be/nl/publications/stu/pdf/study38.pdf>.

Nevertheless, compliance is being observed for other provisions of the 2009 Code. Almost all the companies examined identify the corporate governance code they apply.[35] Regarding remuneration, the provision relating to the amount of the remuneration of non-executive directors is being complied with particularly well.

A more recent FSMA-study made in December 2012[36] shows improvement with regard to the provisions relating to the remuneration report for which the comply-or-explain rule in the annual financial reports was no longer possible. More than 86% of the declarations of corporate governance in 2011 contained a separate remuneration report. This implies an increase of 39 percentage points compared to 2009. About 98% (compared to 84% in 2009[37] and 89% in 2010[38] of the remuneration reports contained information on an individual basis with regard to the remuneration of non-executive directors and 88% (in comparison with 61% in 2009 and 70% in 2010) contained information concerning the basic and variable remuneration of the CEO (on an individual basis) and the other members of the management (on a global basis).

Observance of the comply-or-explain rule—The FSMA found that, for a number of provisions of the 2009 Code, (eg. the procedure for the development of a remuneration policy, and the determination of the level of remuneration, and the information on pension schemes) not one of the companies they examined explained why it did not comply. Non-compliance with other provisions was explained by some companies (eg. the internal control and risk management systems and evaluation). The most frequently occurring explanation relates to the absence of individual information on the remuneration of the CEO and on the performance-related remuneration of non-executive directors.

In its study, the FSMA states that it has the impression that some provisions of the 2009 Code have simply escaped the attention of the companies they examined. It recommends that (listed) companies should determine, for each of the rules in the 2009 Code, whether or not is it applicable and, if it is not applied despite being applicable, to explain explicitly why the provision in question is not being complied with. It is often difficult to qualify a certain text as the company's explanation for not complying with the 2009 Code.

Finally, the FSMA recommends that (listed) companies should refer in the Corporate Governance Statement to the relevant parts of the Corporate Govern-

---

[35] By Royal Decree of 6 June 2010, the Belgian Federal Government has designated the 2009 Code as the mandatory corporate governance code for Belgian listed companies.

[36] Study No. 42: French version: <www.fsma.be/~/media/Files/fsmafiles/studies/fr/study42.ashx>; Dutch version: <www.fsma.be/~/media/Files/fsmafiles/studies/nl/study42.ashx>.

[37] Study No. 38: French version: <www.fsma.be/~/media/Files/fsmafiles/studies/fr/study38.ashx>; Dutch version: <www.fsma.be/~/media/Files/fsmafiles/studies/nl/study38.ashx>.

[38] Study No. 40: French version: <www.fsma.be/~/media/Files/fsmafiles/studies/fr/study40.ashx; Dutch version: <www.fsma.be/~/media/Files/fsmafiles/studies/nl/study40.ashx>.

ance Charter and, if at all possible, bundle the information together in one document (see Introduction).

5. The Dynamics of Change: Peculiarities, Novelties and Expectations

Holding capitalism—Belgium has only a few peculiarities which are worth mentioning. The 'one share one vote' principle and the narrow banking system were both imposed in 1934. Their coincidence led to 'holding capitalism' which was very successful until 1990. Even in 2011, the shareholding structure of most Belgian listed companies is of a concentrated nature. Ironically, the ownership of Société Générale de Belgique, the largest parent company in Europe in 1988 with 1,200 subsidiaries, was totally dispersed when Carlo De Benedetti launched his raid. Today there are a few leading listed industrial companies which are not backed by a dominant shareholder. There is little scientific proof that holding capitalism slowed down the—external—growth of large listed companies so that they failed to find in due course the right 'global size'. Nor is there convincing proof that holding capitalism allowed the creation of internal growth and order so that an international acquisition path became easier. Empirically, at first sight, both theses could credibly be pleaded in Belgium.

One-tier, optionally two-tier system—The one-tier board is the standard. A two-tier system is only obligatory in credit institutions and insurance companies, the reason being the autonomy that management requires to serve the public interest. Co-determination is unknown in Belgium except for the strange rule—again a Belgian peculiarity—that the works council has a veto right when it comes to the appointment of the auditor (see above sections 2.1 and 3.1.5). The Corporate Governance Act of 2 July 2002 provided for an optional two-tier system, largely inspired by the banking model. All public limited liability companies, whether listed or not, may now opt for the creation of a separate management body (*'comité de direction'*) which has the residual powers (see above section 1.3). Only the competencies to determine the general policy, to control management and to exercise well-determined exclusive powers were reserved to the Board of Directors (see *Aufsichtsrat, Raad van Commissarissen*). Only a few listed companies use this two-tier model: we counted 11 or 12 of them at the beginning of 2010 (of which 6 were among the top 20 listed companies), which is no more than 8% of all listed companies in Brussels. It is unclear whether a free choice between a one-tier and a two-tier system is helpful for listed companies. It is also not known how investors consider the multiple choices that can be made within each system. The fact that the general policy is a competence explicitly reserved by the Company Code to the Board creates the perception that it is the Board which eventually determines the strategy of the company.

Majority rule, but independent directors institutionalised—The governance/agency problem in Belgian companies is therefore mostly not of the Anglo-American type: Ownership and control usually coincide, and management suffers from too much rather than too little control. This has traditionally resulted in a large board of non-executive directors on which the majority shareholders are represented and on which no executive management members other than the CEO have a seat. Minority shareholders and free float shareholders have to trust in the majority to govern the company in the best interest of all shareholders and not just in the interest of the majority. However, since 1995, listed companies need three inde-pendent directors whenever they envisage taking a decision on a transaction which relates to their controlling shareholder, eg. when a loan contract is entered into between the parent company and its listed subsidiary (see above section 3.1.3(a)). This procedure is often applied, and helps a great deal in making the relationship between a listed company and its controlling shareholder more transparent.

Directors revocable ad nutum (at will)—Another Belgian peculiarity is that the directors may be removed from office at any time, also during the term for which they were appointed, by a simple majority vote of the general meeting (termina-tion *ad nutum*, article 518§3 BCC). In the public limited liability company, this *ad nutum* rule is of public order. Any provisions in the articles of association which deviate from this rule are therefore to be considered null and void.

Corporate Governance Code— Belgian corporate governance rules are framed by the Belgian Corporate Governance Commission, a private organisation. The 2009 Corporate Governance Code was made the only recognised reference code by the Belgian Government in a Royal Decree dated 6 June 2010. Comply-or-explain is now also a legally binding rule. Whenever the 2009 Code changes, a Royal Decree will be required to make it binding on listed companies. Moreover, a large number of traditional governance matters have been incorporated in the law itself: The definition of independent directors (see above section 2.2.3), the audit and remuneration committees (see sections 2.2.2(a), (b)) as well as variable remuner-ation and severance pay issues (see section 3.2.2.). The addition of these measures and mechanisms make it very doubtful that the driving force behind corporate governance these days is still market-controlled self-regulation. The general meeting of shareholders was given more specific governance com-petencies than ever before, eg. with regard to remuneration (sections 2.2.3 and 3.1.5) or takeover bids (section 3.1.3(e)).

Novelties and expectations—Belgian company law in recent times has done no more than follow the European path and the international waves of corporate governance and remuneration. Rather than launching major reforms, successive governments have adopted a tax law approach in corporate matters: Every year, piecemeal changes are inserted in the Belgian Companies Code, buried in Acts containing very detailed and wide-ranging provisions concerning budgetary matters and programmes. As a result, there is a risk that fragmentation, lobbying and inconsistency will set the tone. Very recently the Belgian Parliament imposed Norwegian-inspired quotas for more equal male and female representation on boards of directors.[39]

Legal scholars have been pleading the case for making Belgian company law reliable and logical:[40] Only three types of corporations/partnerships instead of twelve; abolition of the distinction between commercial and civil law companies; and clearer differentiation of corporations from associations and foundations. Such an overhaul would be most welcome given the present-day state of competition, especially when—as a consequence of the 2009 Stockholm Programme—the place of incorporation (and not the real seat) eventually becomes the sole criterion for determining applicable company law in Europe.[41]

6. Selection of Literature in English

Articles

Bertrand, A. and Coibion, A., 'Shareholder Suits against the Directors of a Company, against other Shareholders and against the Company itself under Belgian Law', *ECFR* 2009, 270–306.

Cools, S. 'The Real Difference in Corporate Law between the United States and Continental Europe: Distribution of Powers', *Delaware Journal of Corporate Law* 2005, 697–766.

Cools, S., 'Europe's Ius Commune on Director Revocability', *ECFR* 2011, 199–234.

Geens, K. and Wyckaert, M., 'State Competition: the Belgian Case for Reform', *European Company Law* 2012, 270–275.

Lee, J., 'Minority shareholders' enforcement of corporate governance in takeovers: an English law perspective on the Belgian Fortis case', *RPS* 2009, no. 7008, 391–419.

Lee, J., 'Regulatory Regimes and Norms for Directors' Remuneration: EU, UK and Belgian Law Compared', *EBOR* 2012, 599–637.

---

[39] Act of 28 July 2011. Within 5 years, one-third of the directors in Boards of listed companies should be women.

[40] K. Geens, 'Ten years after : de la Belgique au Delaware', *J.T.*, 2011, 178; *T.R.V.*, p. 3.

[41] *The Stockholm Programme – An open and secure Europe serving and protecting the citizens*, European Council, 10/11 December 2009, *OJ*-2010, C 115, 16; Communication from the Commission of 20 April 2010 (COM(2010)171 final), 25. See also K. Geens, 'The Stockholm Promise', *European Company Law*, 2010/5.

Books and contributions

Fassin, Y., Leverau, A. and Van den Berghe, L., 'Corporate governance and initial public offerings in Belgium', in: A. Zattoni & W. Judge (eds.), *Corporate Governance and Initial Public Offerings*, Cambridge, Cambridge University Press, 2012, 64–88.

Geens, K., 'On corporate governance, shareholder structures and company law', in: J. Stuyck & F. Abraham (eds.), *Financial services and financial markets in Europe. Changes and adjustments,* Leuven, Leuven University Press, 2000, 203–229.

Geens, K. and Clottens, C., 'Belgian monograph on Corporations and Partnerships', in: *International Encyclopaedia of Laws. Corporations and Partnerships,* Mechelen, Kluwer, 2012.

Hopt, K., Kanda, H., Roe, M.J., Wymeersch, E. and Prigge, S., *Comparative Corporate Governance: the State of the Art and Emerging Research,* Oxford, Clarendon, 1998.

Laga, H., and Parrein, F., 'Corporate governance in a European perspective', in K. Geens and K.J. Hopt (eds.), *The European Company Law Action Plan Revisited,* Leuven, Leuven University Press, 2010, 79–143.

Wymeersch, E., Jakhian, G. and Caeymaex, B., 'Belgium—Rights of minority shareholders', in: E. Perakis, *Rights of Minority Shareholders: General and National Reports,* Brussels, Bruylant, 2004, 163–223.

Working papers

Van der Elst, C., *Belgian Bank Governance Before and After the Financial Crisis,* University of Ghent Financial Law Institute Working Paper 2010/10.

Wameersch, E., *Corporate Governance Codes and Their Implementation,* University of Ghent Financial Law Institute Working Paper 2006/10.

Studies

Grant Thornton, *Review of Annual Reports 2010 of Euronext Brussels listed companies,* 2011. Available at <www.guberna.be>.

Guberna, *Remuneration of non-executive directors,* 2012. Available at <www.guberna.be>.

OECD, *Corporate governance: a survey of OECD countries,* OECD, 2004.

Corporate Boards in France

ALAIN PIETRANCOSTA, PAUL-HENRI DUBOIS and ROMAIN GARÇON

1. General Introduction[1]

1.1. Environment in which Boards Operate

a) Legislative and Regulatory Framework

The rules governing boards, directors' duties and corporate governance are mainly contained in the French Commercial Code[2], and companies' by-laws.

In addition, more specific regulations apply to listed companies, in particular certain provisions of the French Monetary and Financial Code (the *CMF*)[3], the regulations of the French Financial Market Authority (the *AMF*)[4] and non-binding recommendations made by professional associations such as the Association of French Private-Sector Companies (the *AFEP*)[5] and the French Business Confederation (the *MEDEF*)[6] corporate governance code for listed companies.

b) Public and Private Companies

Under French law, only certain forms of companies, in particular joint-stock companies (*sociétés anonymes*), limited partnerships with share capital (*sociétés en commandite par actions*) or real-property investment partnerships (*sociétés civiles de placement immobilier*) are allowed to make a public offering or list their securities. Although the distinction between public or listed companies and private companies under French law does not result in a *summa divisio* with two separate regimes, the former are subject to numerous additional rules set by the Commercial Code, the CMF and the AMF, as well as recommendations issued by professional associations and organisations.

c) Principal Agent Conflicts

Agency theory reflects a shareholder-centred perspective and can be defined as a contract whereby the shareholders (the *Principal*) appoint a manager (the *Agent*)

---

[1] This report focuses on French joint-stock companies (sociétés anonymes), which are the most commonly used structures for large business in France. Therefore, other specific forms of companies that may also be listed entities, such as limited partnerships with share capital (sociétés en commandite par actions), will not be covered by this study. (According to the 4th AFEP/MEDEF Annual Report dated December 2012 relating to the implementation of its corporate governance code by companies listed on SBF 120 and CAC 40 (p. 5), only 3% are limited partnerships with share capital.)

[2] Code de Commerce.

[3] Code Monétaire et Financier.

[4] Autorité des Marchés Financiers.

[5] Association Française des Enterprises Privées.

[6] Mouvement des Entreprises de France.

and delegate to him a part of their authority to manage the company. As the Agent is responsible for the company's day-to-day management and therefore is generally better informed than the Principal, various conflicts may arise between them.

As we will see, even though the shareholdings of French listed companies appears relatively concentrated, French law has developed several mechanisms to reduce such conflicts of interest and enables shareholders to enhance their control over their Agent by aligning his interest with the Principal's. For example, besides the use of optional securities or the allocation to managers of stock-options, in order to encourage the Agent to properly manage the company so as to exercise his rights, the Commercial Code and corporate governance codes require the setting up of specific committees of the board of directors to deal with the more sensitive issues (remuneration, nomination, risk and audit). In addition, French law provides for a certain degree of transparency and requires managers to disclose their remuneration[7] and all transactions undertaken in relation to the securities held in their companies.

d) Relevance of Institutional Shareholding

Institutional investors, such as investment companies, insurance companies, mutual funds, pension funds and investment banks, are entities that are devoted to holding and managing assets, either for clients or for themselves. This category of investors collects considerable cash reserves that are invested in the securities markets.

Even though private pension funds do not really exist in France, institutional investors play an important part in French securities markets: Approximately 40% of the shares of CAC 40 French companies are held by institutional investors, of which 20% are from the euro zone.

Consequently, the individual shareholders' interests in the market capitalisation of Euronext France companies are residual: According to the Federation of European Securities Exchanges (FESE), such interest amounted to 6.7% in 2007, less than half the European average.

Although institutional investors usually hold minority shareholdings in French public companies, they play an important and increasing role in the supervision and the strategy of such companies through relational investing or by participating in shareholders' meetings.[8]

---

[7] In listed companies, only a specific part of manager remuneration must be disclosed (please refer to sec. 3.1 for further information).

[8] See below.

Tableau 1 Le patrimoine des secteurs institutionnels fin 2009

(en milliards d'euros ; évolution en %)

	Ensemble de l'économie nationale	Ménages (a)	Sociétés non financières	Sociétés financières	Adminis-trations publiques	Évolution du patrimoine de l'économie nationale	
						2007-2008	2008-2009
Actifs non financiers (ANF)	**12 147**	**6 768**	**3 748**	**247**	**1 385**	**- 0,4**	**- 2,4**
Constructions et terrains	10 061	6 282	2 324	211	1 245	- 0,7	- 2,6
dont : Logements	*3 794*	*3 143*	*547*	*51*	*53*	*4,5*	*1,9*
Autres bâtiments et génie civil	*1 928*	*185*	*889*	*69*	*784*	*5,0*	*1,3*
Terrains bâtis	*4 340*	*2 954*	*888*	*91*	*408*	*- 6,3*	*- 7,8*
Machines et équipements	610	48	506	15	41	3,2	0,1
Stocks	378	39	323	–	16	3,3	- 9,3
Autres actifs produits	232	131	82	8	11	4,1	1,9
Autres actifs non produits	866	268	512	13	73	- 2,0	0,2
Actifs financiers (AF), hors produits dérivés	**20 235**	**3 832**	**4 913**	**10 616**	**873**	**- 6,0**	**6,6**
Numéraire et dépôts	4 218	1 115	315	2 680	108	11,4	- 4,1
Titres hors actions hors produits dérivés	2 919	63	100	2 699	57	5,4	2,5
Crédits	3 450	24	839	2 527	60	8,3	3,3
dont crédits des sociétés financières accordés aux ANF	*2 252*	*–*	*–*	*2 252*	*–*	*7,4*	*2,5*
Actions et titres d'OPCVM	6 232	915	2 687	2 223	407	- 28,8	18,8
Provisions techniques d'assurance	1 506	1 485	20	1	1	0,7	8,5
Ensemble des actifs (A) = (ANF) + (AF)	**32 382**	**10 600**	**8 661**	**10 863**	**2 258**	**- 3,8**	**3,0**
Passifs financiers (PF), hors produits dérivés	**20 225**	**1 324**	**6 847**	**10 212**	**1 842**	**- 4,4**	**6,2**
Numéraire et dépôts	4 679	–	–	4 608	71	11,8	- 6,8
Titres hors actions hors produits dérivés	3 051	–	361	1 337	1 352	12,1	9,5
Crédits	3 261	1 023	1 675	334	230	7,4	1,8
dont crédits bancaires accordés aux ANF	*2 066*	*1 007*	*864*	*–*	*195*	*7,7*	*1,9*
Actions et titres d'OPCVM (Passif en actions)	5 914	7	3 935	1 972	–	- 28,7	19,7
Provisions techniques d'assurance	1 510	–	–	1 510	–	0,7	8,5
Solde des produits dérivés (S)	**- 43**	**- 1**	**- 5**	**- 37**	**–**	**ns**	**ns**
Patrimoine financier net = (AF) - (PF) + (S)	**- 33**	**2 507**	**- 1 939**	**367**	**- 968**	**(b)**	**(b)**
Patrimoine (ou valeur nette) = (A) - (PF) + (S)	**12 115**	**9 275**	**1 809**	**614**	**417**	**- 3,2**	**- 1,8**
Fonds propres = (Patrimoine net) + (Passif en actions)			**5 744**	**2 585**			

(a) Y compris entrepreneurs individuels et institutions sans but lucratif au service des ménages (ISBLSM)
(b) Le patrimoine financier net de l'économie nationale s'élève à + 247 milliards d'euros en 2007, - 110 milliards d'euros en 2008 et - 33 milliards d'euros en 2009.
« ns » correspond à « non significatif ».
« - » correspond à un actif non détenu.
Sources : INSEE, Banque de France, comptes nationaux base 2000

e) Ownership of French Listed Companies

Capital concentration remains rather high in the French market (families remain important, representing 48% of controlling block-holders[9]), although the number of companies classified as having a broad shareholding continues to grow (increasing from 21% to 37% between 1996 and 2006).

Foreign control is said to be the second most prevalent form of ownership in France (20%, compared to 70% for domestic block-holders).

---

[9] On the higher profitability of family firms listed on the French stock market, see the study of the Centre de Recherche sur l'Entreprise Familiale et Financière de Bordeaux, summarised in *Les Echos*, 29 November 2004, p. 4.

Indeed, the French financial market attracts a large number of non-resident investors. At the end of 2009, non-residents owned 42.3% (€404.5 billion) of the total market capitalisation of CAC 40 French companies (€955.4 billion).[10] Non-French European and US investors own 17% and 15.6% respectively of CAC 40 companies and remain the major investors.

f) Specific Characteristics of Environment

The French State holds minority or majority stakes in a number of public companies through the French Government Shareholding Agency (the *APE*)[11], an organisation belonging to the Department of Treasury (*Direction générale du Trésor*) within the Ministry for the Economy. Therefore, the APE is designed to act as a shareholder for the French Government in order to develop its assets and maximise the value of its stakes.

The APE invests in a wide range of companies and assets from minority stakes to State-controlled large entities. Its portfolio comprises a total of 70 entities.

On 31 August 2012, the combined market capitalisation of the French State's portfolio of quoted shareholding amounted to €60 billion (compared to €69 billion at 1 September 2011), representing 10% of the total market capitalisation of CAC 40 companies (compared to 11% at 1 September 2011).[12]

Company	French government interest (%)	Value € bn
Air France – KLM	15.9	189
RATP	100	N/A
SNCF	100	N/A
Aéroport de Bordeaux-Mérignac	100	N/A
Aéroport de la Côte d'Azure	100	N/A
Aéroport de Lyon	100	N/A
Aéroport de Montpellier Méditerranée	100	N/A
Aéroport de Toulouse Blagnac	100	N/A
Aéroport de la Réunion – Roland Garros	100	N/A
Aéroport de Strasbourg	100	N/A
Aéroport de Paris	52.1	2,734
ATMB	91.3	N/A
SFTRF	99.9	N/A
Grand port maritime de Dunkerque	100	N/A
Grand port maritime du Havre	100	N/A
Grand port maritime de Marseille	100	N/A

---

[10] 'La détention par les non-résidents des actions des sociétés françaises du CAC 40 à fin 2009', Julien Le Roux, *Bulletin de la Banque de France*, n°180, 2ᵉᵐᵉ trimestre 2010.

[11] Agence des participations de l'Etat.

[12] *The French State as shareholder*, report dated 30 October 2012, p. 5 (English version): *Rapport sur l'Etat Actionnaire 2012*. Available at <http://www.ape.minefi.gouv.fr/sections/rapports_sur_l_etat/rapport_de_l_etat_ac9656>.

Company	French government interest (%)	Value
Grand port maritime de Nantes Saint-Nazaire	100	N/A
Port autonome de Paris	100	N/A
Grand port maritime de Rouen	100	N/A
RFF	100	N/A
Areva	88.7	744
EDF	84.4	29,351
GDF Suez	39.11	17,13
DCI	49.9	N/A
DCNS	63.6	N/A
EADS	14.96	2,964
GIAT Industries – Nexter	100	N/A
Safran	30.2	2,922
SNPE	100	N/A
Thalès	27.08	1,435
FSI	100	N/A
Imprimerie Nationale	100	N/A
LFB	100	N/A
La Monnaie de Paris	100	N/A
Renault	15.01	1,190
France Télécom	26.95	4322
La Française des Jeux	72	N/A
Groupe la Poste	100	N/A
Arte France	100	N/A
Audiovisuel extérieur de la France	100	N/A
France Télévisions	100	N/A
Radio France	100	N/A
Dexia	23.3	31
Semmaris	56.73	N/A

Source: <www.ape.minefi.gouv.fr>[13]

In addition, the French government together with the *Caisse des Dépôts et Consignation*[14] decided to establish the Investment Strategic Funds (*Fonds stratégique d'investissement – FSI*) in 2008 to support the development of midcap and public companies. Through its investments, the FSI intends to stabilise the ownership of the developing or public companies and improve their corporate governance.

As a major shareholder, the French government plays an important role in such public companies by promoting transparency and participating in their management through a significant number of its representatives who are appointed as directors. Indeed, two representatives of the French government sit on the FSI's board of dir-

---

[13] *The French State as shareholder*, report dated 30 October 2012, p. 42 (French version). *Rapport sur l'Etat Actionnaire 2012*. Available at <http://www.ape.minefi.gouv.fr/sections/rapports_sur_l_etat/rapport_de_l_etat_ac9656>.

[14] A public group with a statutory base, which is a long term investor serving general interest and the economic development of the country.

ectors and one-third of directors of public companies where the APE holds more than 50% are appointed by the French government (eg. Aéroports de Paris and EDF).

1.2. Financial Institutions

In terms of corporate governance, financial institutional are subject to a series of specific provisions. For instance, French law[15] requires certain entities (credit institutions, insurance and reinsurance companies, and entities whose securities are admitted to trading on a regulated market) to establish a specialised audit committee to monitor the preparation and control of accounting and financial information. Pursuant to article L. 823-19 of the Commercial Code, this committee acts under the exclusive responsibility of the board of directors.

In addition, the French Parliament passed a law on banking and finance regulation, dated 22 October 2010,[16] which, among many other things, regulates rating agencies. This Act also requires banks and insurance companies to set up a compensation committee and a risk committee. The boards of such companies would set the size, the number and the qualifications of the committee's members. At least one member of that committee has to be independent and skilled in accounting and auditing.

France was the first country to implement the G20 Pittsburgh statements regarding financial supervision and compensation in banks for professionals whose activities have a significant impact on the company risk profile. Through a Decree dated 13 December 2010,[17] French law now requires that 40% of variable bonuses (and up to 60% for the highest remunerations) should be paid over a three-year period, and that 50% of variable compensation should be paid in shares or equivalents.

1.3. Available Board Models (Including Board Models in SEs)

Under French law, joint stock companies may have two different forms of corporate governance structure. Their by-laws may provide for governance with either a unitary structure (one-tier model) or a dual structure (two-tier model).

---

[15] Ordinance dated 8 December 2008 resulting from European directive CE 2006/43 dated 17 May 2006 (Ordonnance n° 2008-1278 du 8 décembre 2008 transposant la directive 2006/43/CE du 17 mai 2006 et relative aux commissaires aux comptes).

[16] Loi n° 2010-1249 du 22 octobre 2010 de régulation bancaire et financière.

[17] Arrêté en date du 13 décembre 2010 modifiant diverses dispositions réglementaires relatives au contrôle des rémunérations des personnels exerçant des activités susceptibles d'avoir une incidence sur le profil de risque des établissements de crédit et entreprises d'investissement ainsi que diverses dispositions de nature prudentielle.

a) One-tier Model

Historically, French company law was based on a one-tier model. This requirement for French joint-stock companies to set up a board of directors originated from a law dated 16 November 1940[18]. Such requirement was then confirmed by a law dated 24 July 1966[19] (henceforth referred to as the 1966 Company Act).

The unitary structure is the most widely-used form of governance and consists of a board of directors (*conseil d'administration*) headed by a chairman (*président*), who may also be the chief executive officer (*CEO*) (*directeur général*) of the company.

French law allows the board of directors of a company to choose whether the same or different persons should hold the offices of CEO and chairman.

However, in terms of corporate governance, it is usually considered best practice[20] to appoint two different persons. Having a separate CEO and chairman promotes independence in the control of the management of the company and increases transparency for the shareholders and the market.

Nevertheless, in practice 64% of CAC 40 companies have elected to appoint a single person as chairman and CEO (compared to 34% three years ago).[21]

b) Two-tier Model

The dual structure, directly inspired by the German legal system, originates from the 1966 Company Act and provides for an alternative structure to the board of directors having both the managing and supervising functions. By promoting a stricter division between the management and its supervision, the dual structure was considered to be more respectful of corporate governance practices.

Typically, dual structures correspond to family-owned companies in which representatives of the controlling family sits on the supervisory board, while the company's managers sit on the managing board.

The two-tier model consists of a managing board (*directoire*), composed of up to five members who run the company, and a separate supervisory board (*conseil de surveillance*) that oversees the managing board.

The managing board's members and its chairman are appointed by the supervisory board. The managing board can be dismissed by the shareholders at a general meeting, unless this power is granted to the supervisory board by the

---

[18] Loi du 16 novembre 1940 Sociétés Anonymes.

[19] Loi n°66-537 du 24 juillet 1966 sur les sociétés commerciales.

[20] Proxinvest *Principes de gouvernance et politique de vote*, p. 18 and AFG *Recommandations sur le gouvernement d'entreprise 2012*, p. 16.

[21] 4th AFEP/MEDEF Annual Report relating to the implementation of its corporate governance code by companies listed on SBF 120 and CAC 40, dated December 2012 (p. 5).

company's by-laws. The supervisory board members are appointed and dismissed by the shareholders at a general meeting.

Since the 2001 New Economic Regulation Act[22] allowed one-tier model companies to adopt a system of management composed of a separate chairman and CEO, the distinction between the two governance structures has become less important.

Dual structures are not very common in France, where joint-stock companies are usually small and non-listed and for which the two-tier system appears expensive and complicated to operate due to the presence of two separate bodies.

Of the two governance structures, French companies have largely opted for the one-tier model, although the percentage of two-tier model companies is higher among listed companies.

Governance structure chosen by SBF 120 and CAC 40 companies from 2009 to 2011

		SBF 120			CAC 40		
		FY2009	FY2010	FY2011	FY2009	FY2010	FY2011
SA with a one-tier structure	CEO/chairman combined functions	47%	50%	55%	40%	50%	64%
	CEO/chairman separated functions	30%	27%	24%	37%	30%	16%
SA with a two-tier structure		19%	18%	16%	17%	17%	17%
Societas Europaea		-	-	-	-	-	-
Limited partnership with share capital (*sociétés en commandite par actions*[23])		4%	5%	3%	6%	3%	3%
Total		100%	100%	100%	100%	100%	100%

Source: AFEP/MEDEF[24]

In 2011, more than 80% of CAC 40 companies operate under the one-tier model. Due to the financial crisis, listed companies with two-tier structures tend to adopt highly concentrated governance structures for efficiency reasons. As an example, on 29 April 2010 Axa, a French listed insurance company, approved the change of its governance structure to a one-tier model and provided the following justifications:

'This unitary board structure was implemented in order to enhance the efficiency and reactivity of the Group's governance processes and has been carefully designed to ensure an ap-

---

[22] Loi n° 2001-420 du 15 mai 2001 relative aux nouvelles régulations économiques.

[23] For instance, Bonduelle, Hermès International, Lagardère, Michelin, Groupe Steria.

[24] 3rd and 4th AFEP/MEDEF Annual Reports relating to the implementation of its corporate governance code by companies listed on SBF 120 and CAC 40, dated November 2011, p. 6 and December 2012, p. 5.

propriate balance of powers. In the uncertain market, regulatory and competitive environment coming out of the financial crisis, greater reactivity and increased efficiency in the Group's governance processes were considered critical to the Group's continued future success.'[25]

c) Board and Societas Europaea[26]

Presentation—Under French law, the Societas Europaea (SE) is governed by the provisions of the Directive dated 8 October 2001[27], transposed into French law on 26 July 2005 by the Commercial Code (article L. 229-1) and in the Labour Code (*Code du travail*) (article L. 2351-1).

France was the third most popular country in terms of incorporation of SEs in 2007 with seven incorporations.[28]

583 European Companies (SEs), established in 21 countries

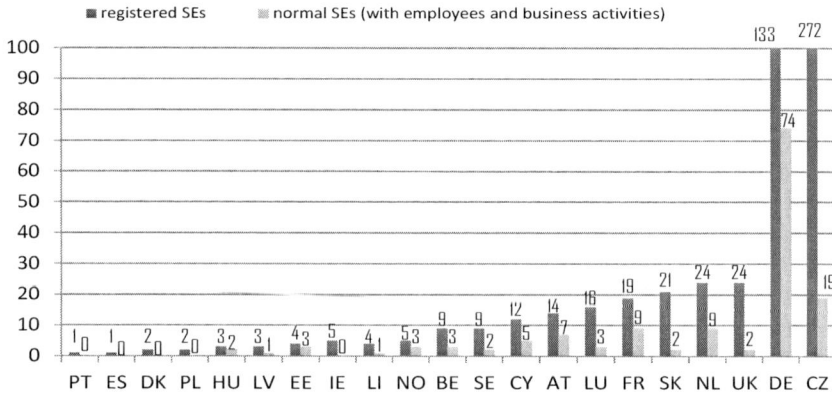

Data source: ETUISE Factsheets Website, http://ecdb.worker-participation.eu (20 May 2010)

Source: 'Overview of current state of SE founding in Europe', p. 4.

However, France has become less attractive and the growth of SE incorporations in other countries accelerated between 2007 and 2010. Indeed, only 19 out of a total of 618 SEs are presently incorporated in France (in particular Innovatis SE, Viel et Compagnie-Finance, Scor SE).

[25] Axa, Registration document, *Annual Report 2010*, p. 112. Available at <http://www.axa.com/lib/fr/library/ran/groupe/7866.aspx>.

[26] Since Oplustil/Teichmann, *The European Company – all over Europe* (Berlin, December 2003).

[27] Directive 2001/86/EC of 8 October 2001 supplementing the Statute for a European company with regard to the involvement of employees.

[28] See C. Cathiard, 'Société européenne, fusions transfrontalières: 'bilan de la pratique et perspectives d'avenir', *Journ. societies,* December 2007, p. 58.

As a general principle, the rules applicable to the organisation and management of SEs are similar to those applicable to a French joint-stock company (*société anonyme*). Therefore, SEs can be organised with a unitary (one-tier model) or a dual structure (two-tier model) of governance. Moreover, the SE regime largely refers to the applicable domestic law of the company.

The SE particularly involves its employees in its organisation and its management. According to the Directive and the French Labour Code, a special negotiating group must be created to enable the employees to take part in the creation of such a company and in the establishment of its governance processes.

Boards in labour co-determination regimes—Two important features of French law are that (i) representatives of the Works Council are involved in proceedings of the board in an advisory capacity; and (ii) in listed companies, employee shareholders holding in excess of 3% of the share capital may appoint one or more directors among them.[29]

In addition, employees of the company may elect employees' representatives as directors to sit on the board, if the company's by-laws so permit.

Other employees may also, in their individual capacities, be elected to the board of directors or to supervisory boards, up to certain limits.[30]

2. Authority

2.1. Functions/Powers

a) Introduction

Under the one-tier system, the board of directors' role lies both in the determination of the strategy of the company and in the monitoring of the management by examining significant decisions and requesting information when appropriate. The CEO manages the company on a day-to-day basis.

Under the two-tier system, the supervisory board merely has supervision powers and is forbidden from intervening in the management of the company, which is under the sole responsibility of the managing board.

b) General Powers for Supervision and Management

Under the one-tier system, the board of directors has the general authority to determine the strategic orientation of the company's business and ensures its implementation. The board of directors is a collegial body representing all

---

[29] Article L. 225-23 of the Commercial Code.

[30] See sec. 2.2.1(c) for further information.

shareholders that must act in the interests of the company. It may deal with all matters relating to the conduct of the company's business and decide all relevant issues through its deliberations. Within this framework, the board of directors not only advises and monitors the management of the company by the CEO but also sets the strategic targets of the company. In order to ensure that these targets are complied with by the CEO, the board of directors may get involved in the management of the company, including if necessary by dealing with any questions having a substantial impact of the company and/or requiring a report on financial and accounting questions from an expert appointed at the sole discretion of the board.[31] If the directors fail to do so, they could be held liable for losses sustained by the company.

The respective powers of the board of directors and its chairman are defined very broadly, which is often criticised for generating confusion and potential conflicts. Nevertheless, in practice, such broad definitions allow the company to adjust the directors' roles to specific situations and circumstances.

It should also be noted that French law requires the board to decide whether the chairman of the board also acts as CEO or if this role should be granted to another individual. From a corporate governance point of view, the board of directors is considered to be in a better position to monitor the CEO when the CEO is not also the chairman of the board.

Under the two-tier system, the supervisory board oversees the work of the managing board and may undertake any review procedure it considers useful. However, unlike the managing board or the board of directors, the supervisory board has no management power over the company except for the specific powers set forth in the section hereunder.

c) *Specific Powers for Supervision and Management*

The board of directors has the power to appoint and remove the CEO and the chairman of the board of directors, which is a strong means of supervision. This power is reinforced if it is decided that the powers of the CEO are exercised by an individual other than the chairman of the board, making the chairman more independent from the management.

The board of directors can carry out the investigations and the verifications which it considers appropriate. Therefore, the company's chairman or the CEO is required to provide all documents and information requested by the board. The investigations of the board of directors facilitate its supervision of the implementation of the company's strategic plan.

The AFEP/MEDEF Corporate Governance Code recommends that transactions with genuine strategic importance should be submitted to the board

---

[31] The board of directors can freely appoint an expert without the CEO's consent (TC Bordeaux, *ordonnance de référé*, 2 January 2003).

of directors, after review by an ad hoc committee if appropriate. The internal rules of the board of directors should, in particular: (i) Specify the cases in which prior approval by the board is required; (ii) contain the principle that any material transaction outside the scope of the firm's stated strategy is subject to prior approval by the board; and (iii) determine the means by which the board is informed of the corporation's financial situation, cash position and commitments.

Also, in accordance with the Commercial Code, the board of directors under the one-tier system is entitled to convene the shareholders' general meetings, and to draw up the yearly financial statements and the annual management report. In addition, the board may implement the company's share capital increases or reductions decided by the general meeting.

The role of the supervisory board in monitoring the management is similar to the role of the board of directors. It is in particular responsible for reviewing the annual financial statements and the annual management report of the managing board and has the power to convene shareholders' meetings.

Pursuant to the Commercial Code, the supervisory board also appoints the members of the managing board and may be authorised by the by-laws to dismiss them. It may also grant to one or several managing directors the power to represent the company in its relations with third parties. The supervisory board also has authorisation powers originating from French law (related-party transactions,[32] assignments of real property, of equity holdings, provisions of sureties, security, avals and guarantees) and by-laws.[33]

As already pointed out, the limit of the supervisory board's power is that it does not have the same management role as the board of directors. This may be considered preferable from a corporate governance standpoint, as it renders the supervisory board more independent in its control of management.

d) Tasks of Chairman of the Board of Directors, CEO and Managing Board

The chairman organises and manages the board of directors and ensures the proper functioning of the company's decision-making bodies. He may also be the CEO and benefit from the powers attached to this position.

The CEO is responsible for the company's general management and represents the company vis-à-vis third parties. Subject to the legal powers granted to the shareholders and the board of directors, and to the extent permitted by the company's corporate purpose, he has extensive powers to act in all circumstances on behalf of the company. Nevertheless, his powers may be limited by the company's by-laws and by the board of directors, although such limitations are ineffective vis-à-vis third parties.

---

[32] See sec. 3.1.3(b) below for further information.
[33] Article L. 225-68 of the Commercial Code.

Pursuant to article L. 225-35 of the Commercial Code, the company is bound by the decisions of its board of directors taken outside the company's corporate purpose, unless it can prove that the third party knew that the specific action was outside the corporate purpose or, given the circumstances, the third party could not have been ignorant of that fact.

Under the two-tier system, subject to the legal powers granted to the supervisory board or to the shareholders, and to the extent permitted by the company's corporate purpose, the managing board carries out the day-to-day management of the company and has the most extensive powers to take decisions in all circumstances on behalf of the company. More specifically, and in accordance with the Commercial Code, the managing board convenes the general meeting, prepares the annual financial statements, prepares the annual management report and, if authorised by the general meeting, may increase or reduce the share capital of the company and issue securities.

The managing board is a collegial body whose chairman is appointed by the supervisory board. The chairman of the managing board and, if so decided by the supervisory board,[34] other members of the managing board acting as managing directors (*directeurs généraux*), represent the company in relation to third parties. The title of chairman does not bestow greater powers than those which are held by other managing board members.

Restrictions on the powers of the managing board by the by-laws or via board resolutions are unenforceable against third parties.

e) Allocation/Delegation/Assignment of Tasks

Subject to the powers granted to the chairman of the board of directors, French law does not specifically allocate or assign duties to a particular office or body. As the board of directors and the supervisory board are collegial bodies, their powers do not belong to their members individually but are exercised by the entire board.

However, specific authorisations may be granted to directors or members of the supervisory board and, according to case law, delegations to directors and members of the supervisory board are allowed. Under no circumstances may the board may be deprived of all its powers.

Also, unless otherwise provided for in the by-laws and with the consent of the supervisory board, allocation and division of tasks within the managing board is allowed. As each decision (even if taken individually) is deemed to be taken by the entire managing board, the allocation of tasks has no impact on the collective responsibility of the board.

---

[34] Article L. 225-66 of the Commercial Code.

Therefore, the managing board must be permanently informed of all decisions taken by its members and the entire managing board remains responsible for decisions taken by any of its members.

f) Board Committees

In both the unitary and dual structures, the board of directors and the supervisory board may delegate responsibility for specific issues to committees whose members may or may not be directors or supervisory board members. These committees cannot be involved in the company's management or indirectly limit the statutory powers of the relevant board or the CEO.

The AFEP/MEDEF Corporate Governance Code recommends that the number and structure of the committees should be determined by the board of directors or by the supervisory board. The review of the accounts, the monitoring of internal auditing, the selection of statutory auditors, the compensation policy and the appointments of directors should be subject to preparatory work by specialised committees of the board.

Audit committees, required by French law since 2008,[35] are to be composed of members of the board of directors or members of the supervisory board who have no management functions. At least one member of that committee must be independent and have skills in accounting and auditing.

In order to carry out their tasks, the committees may contact the main executives of the company, after informing the chairman of the board and subject to reporting back to the board on such discussions. They may also request external technical studies relating to matters within their competence.[36]

In accordance with corporate governance codes of conduct, many listed companies have voluntarily created other committees (strategic, labour, nomination and/or compensation committees, etc.).[37]

---

[35] See the Ordinance n° 2008-1278 dated 8 December 2008, which implemented Directive 2006/43/EC of the European Parliament on statutory audits of annual accounts and consolidated accounts.

[36] These studies will be paid by the company.

[37] For instance, the supervisory board of Vivendi has set up four specialised committees (the strategic committee, the audit committee, the human resource committee, and the corporate governance committee). Other listed companies, such as Danone, have created a social responsibility committee which is responsible for reviewing the main risks to the company arising from environmental matters and evaluating the impact of socially responsible investments for the company.

g) Internal Control and Risk Management: Responsibility of the CEO, Managing Board, Supervisory Board, Executive Directors and Non-Executive Directors

The concept of executive and non-executive directors does not exist under French law, which merely refers to directors with or without an employment contract. Corporate governance codes prefer the concept of independent and non-independent directors.[38] Independent directors are seen as a neutral control on the management of the company as they are supposed to have no relationship (professional, financial, personal, family) with the company and its representatives and as such are supposedly better able to control the management.

There is, however, no specific responsibility arising from the fact of being designated either as an independent or non-independent director and no difference between the responsibility borne by the members of the supervisory board and of the board of directors regarding internal control of the company. It is only when management is concerned, for instance with determining the strategy of the company, that the role of the board of directors may result in a greater responsibility than that of the supervisory board.

Also, article L. 225-37 of the Commercial Code requires the chairman of the board of a listed company to report on the composition, preparation and organisation of the work of the board, as well as on the internal control and risk management procedures established by the company. The same requirement is applicable to supervisory boards (article L. 225-68 of the Commercial Code).

h) Control by or Reporting of Auditors

Statutory auditors play an important role in the control of French companies. Article L. 225-218 of the Commercial Code requires that all joint-stock companies appoint at least one statutory auditor, and at least two if they are required to issue and publish consolidated financial statements due to the crossing of certain thresholds. The statutory auditors must not have any stake in the company they audit, nor in any company which is part of the company's group. Consequently, they may not have any connection with the company that is personal (ie. any family connection with an individual having a decisive position in the company), financial (eg. owning shares, bonds or debts) or professional (resulting in a common commercial interest). The statutory auditors may not provide the company with any services other than the certification of its financial statements. Any statutory auditors violating these rules face criminal sanctions.

The statutory auditors are appointed for six financial years by the shareholders' meeting further to a proposal from the board in which the CEO, if a member of the board, does not take part. The audit committee must make a recommendation regarding this appointment. The AMF must be informed of the

---

[38] See sec. 2.2.1(b) for further information.

proposed appointment and may make any comments it deems appropriate, which are communicated to the shareholders' meeting. The statutory auditors must, within three months following the close of the financial year, issue a transparency report (article R. 823-21 of the Commercial Code) including in particular a description of their internal quality control and notification systems relating to the independent practices of their audit firm.

2.2. Organisation/Internal Functioning

2.2.1. Composition

a) Size of the Board: Average Size, is it Workable?

In the one-tier model, the board of directors must have at least three but no more than eighteen directors. A law dated 15 May 2001[39] reduced the maximum number of directors on the managing board from twenty-four to eighteen, but provided for temporary exceptions in the event of a merger.

According to article L. 225-17 of the Commercial Code, a company's by-laws may set a fixed or variable number of directors within the statutory limits. Some companies prefer to choose a variable number to give them more flexibility to run their business, whereas others set a fixed number of directors.

The average number of members of board of directors depends on the size of the companies. Midcap companies usually have fewer directors, six on average, whereas SBF 120 and CAC 40 companies have an average number of twelve and fourteen directors respectively.

The following table shows the 2009, 2010 and 2011 figures:

	SBF 120			CAC 40		
	2009	2010	2011	2009	2010	2011
Average number of directors	12.2	12.7	12.5	14.1	14.5	14.4

Source: AFEP/MEDEF [40]

In the two-tier model, the managing board of a listed company consists of up to seven members (compared to five for an unlisted company). Nevertheless, only one member may be appointed if the company's share capital is less than

---

[39] Loi n° 2001-420 du 15 mai 2001 relative aux nouvelles régulations économiques.

[40] 3rd and 4th AFEP/MEDEF Annual Reports relating to the implementation of its corporate governance code by companies listed on SBF 120 and CAC 40, dated November 2011, p. 12 and December 2012, p. 11.

€150,000. In any case, the managing board must only be composed of natural persons.

The number of supervisory board members is set in the by-laws, but it must be between three and eighteen (twenty-four following a merger). Members of the managing board cannot be appointed as supervisory board members.[41]

According to the AMF,[42] the average number of members of the supervisory board in listed companies remained consistently at thirteen in 2008 and 2009.

b) Proportion of Executive Directors and Non-Executive Directors

As discussed above, the concept of executive or non-executive directors, referring to board members who occupy—or who do not occupy—a top management position in the company, does not exist under French law. In its approach to corporate governance, French law-makers have preferred the notion of independent directors and non-independent directors. By definition, an executive director cannot be an independent director, but all non-executive directors do not necessarily qualify as independent directors.[43]

In dual structures, members of the managing board have executive functions by definition, although they are not necessarily employees of the company. Members of the supervisory board merely have monitoring functions even though the law or a company's by-laws may occasionally grant them a decision-making role.

French corporate law only provides for a maximum number of directors or supervisory board members bound to the company by a contract of employment, which should not exceed one-third of the serving directors or members. It should be noted that, for this purpose, directors or supervisory board members elected by the employees or representing the employee shareholders are not included in the number of directors bound to the company by a contract of employment.

c) Labour Representatives on the Board

According to French law, employees may appoint representatives to the board as follows:
- two Works Council representatives (with an advisory voting right) in companies with more than 50 employees;[44]
- up to five (compared to four in private companies) representatives elected by the company's employees, if the company's by-laws so provide.

---

[41] Article L. 225-74 of the Commercial Code.

[42] 2010 AMF Report on corporate governance and directors' compensation, p. 24.

[43] For a full definition of independent director, please refer to sec. 2.2.3.

[44] Works Council representatives only attend board meetings and are not considered as directors.

Such representatives are not taken into account for the minimum and maximum number requirements[45] but cannot exceed one-third of the total number of other members of the board.

In addition, when the shares held by a listed company's staff and by the staff of affiliated companies represent more than 3% of the company's share capital, one or more directors are to be elected among the employee-shareholders, by the general meeting of shareholders on a proposal from these employee-shareholders.[46] Such directors are not counted when calculating the minimum and maximum numbers of directors.

Employee-elected members, other than Works Council representatives, have the same status, duties and liabilities as directors appointed by a general meeting and thus have deliberative rights. As provided by the AFEP-MEDEF Code, regardless of their personal qualities or abilities each director should consider themselves as representing all shareholders and act accordingly in the performance of their duties. Failure to do so would give rise to personal liability. Consequently, all directors must act in the shareholders' and the company's interest without instead promoting the specific interest of employees or other stakeholders.

As regard CAC 40 companies, more than 13 listed companies in which employees hold more than 3% of their share capital have elected employee directors (AXA, BNP Paribas, Bouygues, Cap Gemini, Danone, Vinci[47]).

d) Special Qualification Requirements

In the one-tier model, French law does not require specific qualifications for directors except for the composition of the audit committee which must be composed of at least one independent director with accounting and auditing skills.

However, the AFEP/MEDEF Corporate Governance Code recommends appointing 'directors who are, naturally, honest, but also competent, who understand the corporation's operations, are concerned with the best interests of all shareholders, and are sufficiently involved in the definition of strategy and in discussions, to play an active part in collegial decision making, in order to subsequently support any decisions effectively'.[48]

Since the law 2008-776 dated 4 August 2008,[49] directors are no longer required to hold a specific number of shares (unless otherwise provided by the

---

[45] Article L. 225-27 of the Commercial Code.

[46] Article L. 225-23 of the Commercial Code.

[47] The employees shareholding respectively represent 9% and 18.30% of Vinci and Bouygues share capital.

[48] See AFEP/MEDEF Corporate Governance Code dated April 2010, article 6.1, p. 11.

[49] Loi n° 2008-776 du 4 août 2008 de modernisation de l'économie.

company's by-laws). However, both the AFEP/MEDEF and the Middlenext corporate governance codes provide for a code of ethics applicable to directors stating that directors of listed companies should hold a fairly significant number of shares.

In addition, regarding State-owned companies,[50] representatives of the State may be appointed as directors. As noted above, in public companies mainly owned by the APE (more than 50%), one-third of directors are appointed by the French government (eg. Aéroports de Paris and EDF).

In the one-tier model, the same restrictions apply to members of the supervisory board. Moreover, it will be recalled that a managing board member cannot simultaneously sit on the supervisory board of the same company and vice versa. One person cannot hold more than one seat on a managing board at the same time, except in unlisted or controlled companies.

The AFEP/MEDEF Corporate Governance Code recommends that when a senior executive is appointed as chairman of the managing board, his employment contract should be terminated. Such a recommendation applies to the CEO as well as the chairman of the board of directors and the managing board.

Out of the twenty-one listed companies that re-appointed their CEO, chairman of the board of directors, or chairman of the managing board in 2009, (i) fourteen complied with this recommendation by terminating the employment contract, and (ii) seven maintained such a contract, justifying this decision by the in-house long-term experience of the person concerned.[51] In 2012, fifteen listed companies do not comply with this recommendation.[52]

e) *Chairman: (Independent) Non-Executive or CEO?*

In the one-tier model, according to article L. 225-47 of the Commercial Code the board of directors elects a chairman from its members, who must be a natural person. The chairman is appointed for a term which cannot exceed his term of office as a director (maximum of six years). Furthermore, the by-laws must specify an upper age limit for those performing the office of chairman which, in the absence of an explicit provision, is fixed at sixty-five years.

The board decides whether the roles of chairman and CEO are separated or held by the same person. A graph published by the AMF in 2010[53] indicates the changes in the corporate governance structure that took place in 2009 and those that took place or were announced in 2010.

---

[50] In particular in companies where the French State owns more than 10% of the share capital.

[51] 2010 AMF Report on corporate governance and compensation of executive directors, dated 12 July 2010, p. 54.

[52] 2012 AMF Report on corporate governance and compensation of executive directors, dated 11 October 2012, p. 12.

[53] See 2010 AMF Report on corporate governance and directors' compensation, p. 19.

In 2010, 22% of listed companies made a change in their governance structure. Four listed companies which had previously separated their chairmen from their CEO have now chosen to combine these roles under the authority of a single individual (Axa, Saint-Gobain, Total and Vinci). Conversely, two listed companies have opted for a separation (Crédit Agricole and Sanofi-Aventis). In 2011, L'Oréal and France Telecom decided to follow the reunification trend. In 2012, 64% of CAC 40 companies have elected to appoint a single person as chairman and CEO.[54]

In the two-tier model, the supervisory board elects a chairman and a deputy chairman from its members, who are responsible for calling and conducting its meetings. They hold their position throughout the term of office of the supervisory board and must be natural persons, failing which their appointments would be null and void.[55] The supervisory board also elects the chairman of the managing board, who represents the company.

As a general rule, members of a board of directors or the managing board (including the chairman), do not need to be shareholders. However, the AFEP/MEDEF Corporate Governance Code recommends that such members hold a fairly significant number of shares.[56]

f) Requirements Relating to other Board Functions

Under French law, a natural person can only hold one position as CEO of a French (listed or unlisted) company[57] and cannot hold more than five offices of director at any one time, although directorships with a parent company and its unlisted subsidiaries count as one directorship.[58] Legislative bills dated 19 October 2010[59] and 24 March 2011[60] intend to reduce the number of directorships to three, including in foreign companies.

Any natural person who breaches this rule must resign from one of his directorships within three months of being appointed. Otherwise, he would be deemed to have resigned either from his new directorship or from the directorship which no

---

[54] See sec. 1.3(a) and (b) for further information.

[55] Article L. 225-81 of the Commercial Code.

[56] Article 17 of the AFEP/MEDEF Corporate Governance Code.

[57] However, article L. 225-54-1 of the Commercial Code allows a second position of CEO in specific cases (in controlled or unlisted companies).

[58] Pursuant to article L. 225-21 of the Commercial Code, 'this shall not apply to directorships or supervisory board membership of companies which are controlled by the company of which that natural person is director'.

[59] Proposition de loi n° 2871 de M. Jacques Domergue limitant le cumul de mandats sociaux dans les sociétés cotées.

[60] Projet de loi du 24 mars 2011.

longer meets with the required conditions, and must return any compensation received.[61]

Although a director cannot enter into an employment contract with the company, an employee can become a director and continue working as an employee under certain conditions.

In addition, the AFEP/MEDEF Corporate Governance Code also recommends that: (i) directors should not hold more than four other directorships in listed companies including foreign corporations not affiliated with its group;[62] and (ii) the senior executive's employment contract should be terminated[63] upon his appointment as CEO.

g) Gender Diversity, Non-French Nationals on the Board

An increasing number of French listed companies have recently been adjusting their corporate governance practices, in an effort to increase the representation of women at corporate level.

A law dated 27 January 2011[64] on gender diversity calls for a more balanced gender representation in the governing bodies of French listed companies. Article L. 225-18-1 of the French Commercial Code requires each gender to represent at least 40% of the membership of boards of directors (or supervisory boards) of listed companies within six years of the statute's enactment (with an intermediary quota of 20% within three years). In addition, in the case of listed companies with boards of eight members or more the difference between the number of male and female board members would not be allowed to exceed two.

Appointments made in violation of the quota requirements would be considered null and void. If each gender is not represented on the board of directors or the supervisory board at the time of the statute's enactment, at least one gender representative would have to be appointed at the time of the first renewal of the term of a director or supervisory board member to occur after the date of the enactment.

Interestingly, probably in an attempt to pre-empt or prevent further legislation, the AFEP/MEDEF recommended on 19 April 2010 that French listed companies increase the representation of women in their governing bodies by adopting, in almost exactly the same form, the proposed law on gender diversity into the AFEP/MEDEF Corporate Governance Code for French listed companies. This

---

[61] This breach does not affect the validity of the deliberations in which the member participated.

[62] Article 7 of the Middlenext Corporate Governance Code also provides for such recommendation.

[63] Article 19 of the AFEP/MEDEF Corporate Governance Code.

[64] Loi n° 2011-103 du 27 janvier 2011 relative à la représentation équilibrée des femmes et des hommes au sein des conseils d'administration et de surveillance et à l'égalité professionnelle.

code serves as a benchmark for nearly all French listed companies in determining their governance policies.

Several CAC 40 companies had already anticipated the enactment of these quotas by the French Parliament. The AMF notes that at the end of the 2012 annual meeting season, the proportion of women directors on the board of CAC 40 companies was over 25% (compared to 15% in 2010 and 11.4% in 2009).[65] Of 576 directorships in 2010 (compared to 562 in 2009), 88 are held by women (compared to 59 in 2009).[66] Furthermore, it should be noted that according to a poll half of shareholders prefer appointing women based on their merits and experience rather than imposing quotas.

More recently, a poll issued by Capitalcom[67] notes that the proportion of women directors on the board of CAC 40 companies was still increasing in 2011 over 20%: 105 women currently hold 119 out of 573 directorships. In addition, the proportion of women on board committees increased from 46% in 2010 to 60% in 2011. Nevertheless, the board of a small number of listed companies is still exclusively composed of men.[68]

The following table and graph, published in 2011 and 2012 by the AFEP/and the AMF, confirms the positive trend promoting gender diversity in the composition of boards of directors or supervisory boards.

---

[65] 2012 AMF Report on corporate governance and directors' compensation, p. 9.

[66] 2010 AMF Report on corporate governance and directors' compensation. For example, PPR which in 2009 had just one woman serving on its board of directors, decided during its general shareholders' meeting held on 19 May 2010 to appoint three additional women to its board, thereby increasing its size from 11 to 14 members, of which nearly 30 per cent will be women. Similarly, Vivendi decided during its general shareholders' meeting dated 29 April 2010 to appoint three women to its supervisory board, increasing female representation to one-third. Other CAC 40 companies that have recently appointed one or more women to their corporate boards are Schneider Electric, Saint Gobain, Air Liquide, GDF Suez, Total, LVMH (with the appointment of Bernadette Chirac), Lafarge, Vallourec, Alcatel Lucent, Renault, Sanofi-Aventis and BNP Paribas.

[67] Press release dated 22 June 2011.

[68] 2011 AMF Report on corporate governance and directors' compensation, p. 7.

Proportion of women on boards of listed companies from 2009 to 2012 (excluding directors elected by employees)

SBF 120				CAC 40			
General meetings				General meetings			
2009	2010	2011	2012	2009	2010	2011	2012
9.1%	12.5%	17.2%	21.9%	11.3%	16.3%	21.1%	25.2%

Source: AFEP/MEDEF [69]

Number of women elected as directors of listed companies following the 2011 general meetings

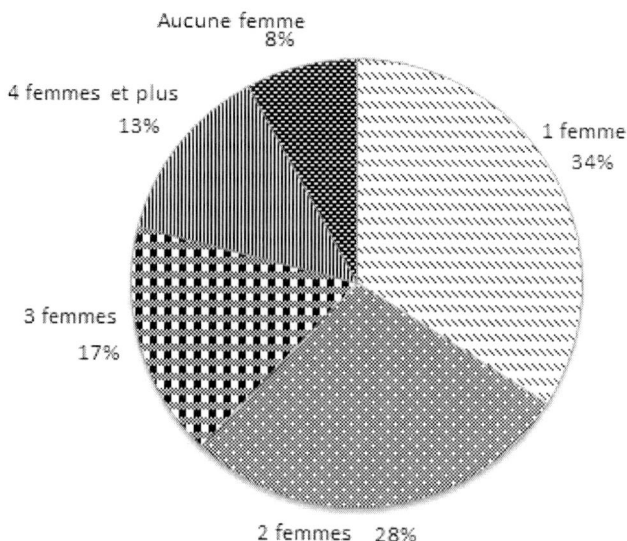

Source: AMF [70]

Regarding the directors' nationality, non-French nationals represent approximately 20% of members of the board of directors or supervisory boards of CAC 40 companies.[71]

---

[69] 3rd and 4th AFEP/MEDEF Annual Report relating to the implementation of its corporate governance code by companies listed on SBF 120 and CAC 40, dated November 2011, p. 19, and December 2012, p. 17.

[70] 2011 AMF Report on corporate governance and directors' compensation, p. 46.

[71] 2012 AMF Report on corporate governance and directors' compensation, p. 9.

h) Evaluation of Board Performance

According to French law, in companies whose financial securities are admitted to trading on a regulated market the chairman of the board is required to report on the composition, preparation and organisation of the work of the board, as well as internal control and risk management procedures established by the company, especially those relating to preparing and processing accounting and financial information.[72] The report should indicate any restrictions and limitations imposed by the board on the CEO's powers, and describe the mechanisms for the participation of shareholders in the annual meeting.

The AFEP/MEDEF Corporate Governance Code also recommends that the board of directors or the supervisory board evaluate its own ability to meet the shareholders' expectations and consider its how best to perform its duties. Such evaluation should aim to: (i) assess the way in which the board operates; (ii) check that important issues are properly prepared and discussed; and (iii) identify the actual contribution of each director to the board through his knowledge and his involvement.[73]

According to the Code, the evaluation should be conducted on an annual basis by dedicating one of the items on the agenda of a general meeting to a debate concerning the board of directors' operations (basic evaluation). Furthermore, the Code recommends that a formal evaluation should be completed at least once every three years.

Most public companies comply with this recommendation. More than 85% of listed companies (86% of SBF 120 companies and 97% of CAC 40 companies) implement the AFEP/MEDEF's recommendation and disclose it in their annual reports.

The following table indicates the proportion of compliant listed companies.

---

[72] Article L. 225-37 of the Commercial Code.

[73] See Article 9.2 of the AFEP/MEDEF Corporate Governance Code dated April 2010, p. 15.

	SBF 120			CAC 40		
	2009	2010	2011	2009	2010	2011
Companies complying with the recommendation	86%	82%	89%	97%	81%	92%
Basic evaluation	35%	19%	25%	20%	14%	22%
Formal evaluation	51%	63%	64%	77%	67%	70%

Source: AFEP/MEDEF [74]

2.2.2. Decision-making

a) Veto Rights/Approval Rights for Non-Executives

There are no veto rights, approval rights or any specific rights granted to non-executive or independent directors under French law. The regime applicable to French joint-stock companies is very strict in relation to the rules governing the decisions of board meetings and does not provide for specific rights.

Under the one-tier model, a board meeting may only be held if at least half of the directors are present. Decisions are taken by a majority vote of the directors, each director having one vote. The chairman of the meeting has a tie-breaking vote, unless otherwise stipulated in the by-laws. The by-laws may only depart from these rules by requiring a higher majority.[75]

This means in particular that they cannot:
- provide for a lower majority requirement;
- grant a decisive vote to any other director than the chairman of the meeting;
- grant multiple voting rights to any director;
- deprive directors of their voting right outside the cases set by law (eg. the director interested in a 'related-party transaction' is prohibited by law from voting on its approval).[76]

These rules are also applicable to supervisory board decisions.[77]

---

[74] 3rd and 4th AFEP/MEDEF Annual Reports relating to the implementation of its corporate governance code by companies listed on SBF 120 and CAC 40, dated November 2011, p. 24 and December 2012, p. 22.

[75] Article L. 225-37 of the Commercial Code.

[76] See sec. 3.1.3(b) for further information.

[77] Article L. 225-82 of the Commercial Code.

b) Role of the Chairman of the Board

The powers of the chairman of the board of directors are quite limited, as the CEO is the manager of the company. The chairman organises and leads the work of the board, for which he is accountable before the general meeting. He ensures the proper functioning of the board and of the other corporate bodies, and ascertains that directors are able to fully carry out their tasks.[78] In particular, he ensures that directors are given all the information they need.

The chairman chairs board meetings (if he is not present, the meetings will be chaired by a director designated by the board). If the by-laws do not provide otherwise, the chairman is the only member of the board empowered to convene the meeting (even though the CEO may require that the chairman convene a board meeting on a specific agenda at any moment and directors representing at least one-third of the board may also require the chairman to convene a board meeting if there has not been one for more than two months).

When the chairman is also CEO, his powers are much broader as he also has the powers described in section 2.1.

The powers of the chairman of the supervisory board appear more limited than the powers of the chairman of the board of directors because article L. 225-81 of the Commercial Code only grants the supervisory board chairman the power to convene the supervisory board meetings and lead the discussions of the supervisory board. However, the main distinction between them lies in the different powers granted to the boards they chair as the board of directors is involved in the management of the company, whereas the supervisory board's role is limited to the control of the managing board.

c) Board Committees

The decision-making rules of board committees are broadly defined by the by-laws or the internal rules of the board.

There is no legal requirement that members of committees should be independent, except for rules governing audit committees in listed or regulated companies, which, as noted above, require that at least one member must be independent.[79]

However, the AFEP/MEDEF Corporate Governance Code recommends that at least two-thirds of the audit committee's members should be independent directors and that the committee should not include any executive director. It also provides that a majority of the remuneration committee's members should be independent directors, with no executive director.

---

[78] Article L. 225-51 of the Commercial Code.

[79] See sec. 2.1(f) for further information.

Under French law, committees only have a consultancy role. They cannot be granted a decision making power competing with the powers, or reducing the responsibilities, of the CEO, the management board, or the board of directors and supervisory boards, which the committees are only supposed to assist. Consequently, committee recommendations should not be systematically adopted or dilute the board's role.

2.2.3. Independent Directors

a) Origin and Numbers

A report published in July 1995 (the Vienot Report) introduced the concept of independent directors for listed companies in France. The Vienot Report has been supported by several studies and working groups,[80] which all recommend that a minimum number of independent members should be appointed to the board of directors or to the supervisory board.

There are no legal obligations regarding independent directors (except for the rules discussed above regarding audit committees, where at least one member must be independent[81]). However, the corporate governance codes of best practice recommend their appointment to guarantee the overall independence of the board. In practice, numerous listed companies have appointed independent directors in recent years.

The AFEP/MEDEF Corporate Governance Code further recommends that independent directors should account for half of the board in widely-held corporations without controlling shareholders, whereas they should account for at least a third in closely controlled companies.[82] Even though the AFEP/MEDEF code does not refer to French corporate law to define the concept of 'control', the Commercial Code provides that a company is deemed to control another company:

1. when it directly or indirectly holds a fraction of the capital that gives it a majority of the voting rights at that company's general meetings;
2. when it alone holds a majority of the voting rights in that company by virtue of an agreement entered into with other partners or shareholders and this is not contrary to the company's interests;
3. when it effectively determines the decisions taken at that company's general meetings through the voting rights it holds;

---

[80] See the Second Vienot Report published in 1999: *Rapport du Comité sur le gouvernement d'entreprise presidé par M. Marc VIENOT juillet 1999,* or the Bouton Working group in 2003: Rapport du groupe de travail preside par Daniel Bouton 'Pour un meilleur gouvernement des enterprises côtées', 22 septembre 2002.

[81] See sec. 2.1(f) and 2.2.2(c) for further information.

[82] Article 8.2 of the AFEP/MEDEF Corporate Governance Code.

4. when it is a partner in, or shareholder of, that company and has the power to appoint or dismiss the majority of the members of that company's members of the board of directors, managing board or supervisory board; or

5. when it directly or indirectly holds a fraction of the voting rights above 40% and no other partner or shareholder directly or indirectly holds a fraction larger than its own.

In addition, two or more companies acting jointly are deemed to jointly control another company when they effectively determine the decisions taken at its general meetings.

According to the AMF,[83] the average percentage of independent directors on boards of CAC 40 companies is 60%. The following table indicates the percentage of compliant listed companies.

	SBF 120			CAC 40		
	2009	2010	2011	2009	2010	2011
Widely-held companies	76%	75%	76%	82%	86%	79%
Controlled companies	63%	71%	74%	71%	63%	57%

Source: AFEP/MEDEF [84]

b) Qualification and the Comply-or-explain Rule

Unlike French law, the AFEP/MEDEF Corporate Governance Code defines the concept of independence and provides for one of its strictest definitions: a director is independent:

'when he has no relationship of any kind whatsoever with the corporation, its group or the management of either that is such as to colour his judgment. Accordingly, an independent director is to be understood not only as a non-executive director, ie. one not performing management duties in the corporation or its group, but also as one devoid of any particular bonds of interest (significant shareholder, employee, other) with them.'[85]

Even though conflict of interest is used by the corporate governance code to ensure independence of directors, no definition of such concept exists under French law. The Commercial code only provides specific examples of conflict of interest, in particular through related-party transactions. Accordingly, the French

---

[83] 2012 AMF Report on corporate governance and directors' compensation, p. 8.

[84] 3rd and 4th AFEP/MEDEF's annual report relating to the implementation of its corporate governance code by companies listed on SBF 120 and CAC 40, dated November 2011, p. 15 and 16 and December, p. 14 and 15.

[85] Article 8.1 of the AFEP/MEDEF Corporate Governance Code.

Institute of Directors (*Institut Français des Administrateurs*) has recently made several proposals to define the concept of conflict of interest applicable to directors.[86] In addition, in April 2011, the AFEP/MEDEF ethics committee issued a guide designed to help directors to prevent and deal with conflict of interest, in particular directors with vested interests (eg. directors appointed by employees or by certain shareholders in accordance with a shareholders' agreement) are more clearly exposed to conflict of interest.

In order to prevent a conflict of interest, several criteria must be satisfied for a director to qualify as an independent director. A director must not be: (i) An employee or the CEO of the company or of a company in which the corporation holds a directorship; (ii) a customer, supplier or investment or commercial banker of the company; (iii) related by close families ties to the CEO; or (iv) an auditor of the corporation having held office within the previous five years or a director of the corporation having held office within the previous twelve years.[87]

'As regards directors representing major shareholders of the corporation or its parent, these may be considered as being independent, provided that they do not take part in control of the corporation. In excess of a 10% holding of stock or votes, the Board, upon a report from the appointments committee, should systematically review the qualification of a director as an independent director, having regard to the make-up of the corporation's capital and the existence of a potential conflict of interest'.[88]

The Board of Directors must, upon the motion of the appointments committee, review individually the position of each of its members on the basis of these criteria, then notify its conclusions to the shareholders in the annual report and to the shareholders' meeting at the time of the particular director's appointment. The characterisation as an independent director should be discussed and reviewed every year by the board of directors or the supervisory board prior to the publication of the annual report.[89]

However, the Board of Directors may consider that, although a particular director meets all of the above criteria, he or she cannot be held to be independent owing to the specific circumstances of the person or the company, its ownership structure or for any other reason. Conversely, the Board may consider that a director who does not meet the above criteria is nevertheless an independent director.[90]

---

[86] Note de synthèse de la commission Déontologie de l'IFA: *Administrateurs et conflits d'intérêts*, November 2010.

[87] Article 8.4 of the AFEP/MEDEF Corporate Governance Code.

[88] Article 8.5 of the AFEP/MEDEF Corporate Governance Code.

[89] Article 8.3 of the AFEP/MEDEF Corporate Governance Code.

[90] Article 8.3 of the AFEP/MEDEF Corporate Governance Code.

For example, in 2009, Lafarge justified the appointment of Michel Pébereau (chairman of the board of directors of BNP Paribas) as independent director in order to prevent any potential conflict of interest. According to Lafarge's Annual Report for 2009, 'the Board reviewed the

cont. ...

In practice, approximately 15% of directors defined as independent by the board do not comply with the AFEP/MEDEF recommendations.

As at the date of this report, there is not a significant number of professional independent directors in France even if certain organizations and associations (IFA, *Association des Administrateurs Professionnels Indépendants Associés*) have recently developed specific training.

2.3. Information Streams

a) Information Streams from the Company through the Company's Management Information System to the Executives. Information Streams from Executives (MB) to Non-Executives (SB) and the Role of the Company Secretary

According to article L. 225-35 of the Commercial Code, the board of directors carries out the inspections and verifications which it considers appropriate. The chairman or the CEO has a duty to give to the members of the board of directors all documents and information needed to perform their duties. The AFEP/MEDEF Corporate Governance Code further specifies that the internal rules of the board should set the procedure according to which this information is provided. It should specify what information is to be delivered, which depends on the specific purpose of the board meeting, and when it should be provided.

Such information provided by the chairman or the CEO is essential for the directors insofar as they are liable for mismanagement of the company.[91]

According to article L. 225-68 of the Commercial Code, the supervisory board may carry out the verifications and the inspections it considers useful and may request any document it considers necessary for the accomplishment of its duties. These rules governing directors' information rights also apply to members of the managing board who must be provided with the necessary information within the stated time limit, before the management board meetings.

However, it is usually considered under French law that a director or a member of the supervisory board may not request information directly from an employee, as it is only the CEO and the managing board that manage the company and have the power to give orders to employees. However, if the

relationship between Lafarge and BNP Paribas, one of the Group's corporate and investment banks, of which Michel Pébereau is Chairman. The fact that Lafarge can rely on a pool of banks competing with one another prevents the possibility of a relationship of dependency on BNP Paribas. Likewise, the fees that BNP Paribas receives from the Group account for an infinitesimal percentage of the bank's revenues and do not create a situation of dependency for Lafarge. In the light of these factors, and given the independent thinking that Michel Pébereau has shown in his capacity as Director, the Board has decided to consider him for the position of independent Director'.

[91] See sec. 3 for further information.

information is urgently required (article 872 of the French Civil Proceedings Code) or if the refusal to communicate the information will lead to harm that is obviously wrongful (article 873 of the French Civil Proceedings Code), a director may ask the presiding judge of the Commercial Court, acting in summary proceedings, to order that the relevant documents be delivered to them.

The violation of the rights to information of the directors triggers the nullification of the corresponding board decisions.

Because the board of directors and supervisory board almost exclusively receive information from the CEO or the managing board, and because such information may be incomplete in particular in relation to bad news, internal control proceedings have been put in place for French listed companies.

Finally, it should be noted that there is no requirement for a company secretary to be appointed under French law. In practice, when they exist, it is unusual for company secretaries to sit on the boards of directors.

b) Supervision of Risk Management/Internal Audit Control/External Auditors

As stated above, article L. 225-37 of the Commercial Code requires the chairman of the board of directors of a listed company to report on the composition, preparation and organisation of the work of the board, as well as on the internal control and risk management procedures established by the company. This report specifically includes the procedures relating to the preparation and the setting up of accounting and financial information.

Listed companies are required to set up a specialised audit committee to monitor the preparation and control of accounting and financial information. The external auditor, appointed by the general meeting of shareholders, controls the accuracy and veracity of such reports. Even though many listed companies decided to set up a single committee gathering the audit and risk functions, some companies have established separate audit committees and risk committees (Alstom, Alcatel, Natixis…).

The chairman's report should indicate any restrictions applied by the board on the powers of the CEO.

In the two-tier model, the same rules apply to the chairman of the supervisory board who is required to issue such a report. Moreover, it should be noted that the managing board is required to present quarterly reports to the supervisory board in addition to the annual reports on the company's financial accounts.

Also, in order to improve understanding of internal control mechanisms, in July 2010 the AMF published a new reference framework to help companies develop their internal control systems and ensure that they are operating effectively.

The AMF recommends that all companies use its reference framework. It remains to be seen whether this will have a further impact. However, an AMF report dated 7 December 2010 on corporate governance and internal control of French midcap companies listed in France points out that 50% of the mid-cap companies refer to a reference framework, of which 87% refer to the AMF reference framework.

3. Accountability

3.1. Board and Shareholders

3.1.1. *Appointment and Removal*

a) *Appointment of Board Members*

Board members (other than those elected by employees) are appointed at the ordinary general meeting. However, in the event of a merger or spin off, appointment may be made by an extraordinary general meeting.

The term of their office is determined by the by-laws, but may not exceed six years. According to the AFEP/MEDEF Corporate Governance Code, the term of a director's office should not exceed four years, so that the shareholders are called to vote with sufficient frequency.[92] Most listed companies comply with this recommendation. Out of a sample of 60 listed companies, the AMF has determined that only 10 companies do not comply with this requirement.[93]

Where there are vacancies due to death, dismissal or resignation, the board can elect a director. This decision must be ratified by the general meeting.

Supervisory board members are appointed under the conditions described above, whereas managing board members are appointed by the supervisory board.

b) *Removal of Board Members*

Directors can be removed *ad nutum* from office and replaced by the general meeting of shareholders with immediate effect, even though their removal was not on the agenda of the general meeting.

The dismissed director has no right to compensation but may be awarded damages if the dismissal is deemed to be abusive. Golden parachutes may also be granted if duly approved.[94]

Supervisory board members can be dismissed under the same conditions as directors. Managing board members are dismissed by a general meeting—or, if the by-laws so provide, by the supervisory board—under the same conditions. Managing board members are entitled to be paid damages by the company if the decision dismissing them is not justified. According to case law, a majority shareholder may remove a member of the managing board who would express divergent opinions on the operation of the business without awarding him any damages.

---

[92] Article 12 of the AFEP/MEDEF Corporate Governance Code.

[93] 2012 AMF report on corporate governance and directors' compensation, p. 9.

[94] See sec. 3.1.3(c) for further information.

3.1.2. Division of Powers between Board and Shareholders

a) Rights and Powers

The powers of the directors, chairman of the board of directors, CEO, members of the management and supervisory boards are set out in the Commercial Code and the company's by-laws.

In the one-tier structure, members of the board of directors collectively determine the company's general business strategy and ensure its implementation. Subject to powers granted to shareholders and to the extent permitted by the company's corporate purpose, the board of directors may get involved in any matter concerning the company's business.[95]

In the two-tier structure, the managing board has the most extensive powers to act in all circumstances on behalf of the company, subject to the powers granted to the supervisory board and the shareholders. The supervisory board monitors the work of the managing board (in particular the preparation of the annual financial statements and the annual management report) and may thus proceed with any review procedure it considers useful.[96]

The distinction between the one-tier and the two-tier structures is often less pronounced in practice. Indeed, in the one-tier structure, the personality, shareholding, skills, reputation and expertise of the CEO should be taken into consideration insofar such features enable him to dominate the board of directors. As in the two-tier structure, the importance of large shareholders' representatives sitting on the supervisory board may limit managing board members' powers or ability to act.

Shareholders are consulted on the major decisions of the company through ordinary and extraordinary general meetings. In that respect, only extraordinary general meetings are entitled to amend the company's by-laws and therefore decide, in particular, to increase the share capital, extend the corporate purpose or the term of the company. Other decisions such as the approval of financial statements and related party agreements, the allocation and calculation of dividends, and the appointment or dismissal of directors are made by ordinary general meetings.

General meetings are no longer simple recording chambers. In recent years, dissenting opinions have increased. In 2012, the percentage of dissenting shareholder votes at general meetings amounted to approximately 5.9% (compared to 6.3% in 2010), ie. the second highest dissenting rate in Europe. According to Proxinvest,[97] in 2012 shareholders of French listed companies refused to adopt 50

---

[95] See sec. 2.1 for further information.

[96] See sec. 2.1 for further information.

[97] Proxinvest, *2012 general meetings of French listed companies.* Proxinvest, *Agence de conseil de vote:* Available at <www. Proxinvest.com>.

resolutions recommended by the board of directors (compared to 44 in 2011 and 64 in 2010), in particular resolutions relating to the appointment of CEOs or allocation of golden parachutes and stock options to managers.

b) Duties

Directors and members of the supervisory board owe several duties directly to the company, and consequently, to all interested parties (such as shareholders, employees, creditors) who may suffer the adverse effects of the breach of such duties.

Directors and members of the managing board must:

(i) comply with French company law and the company's by-laws;
(ii) take decisions in the interests of the company (they can therefore be held liable for mismanagement of the company in respect of their actions or omissions which are contrary to the company's interests, or if they conduct the business in a careless, negligent or fraudulent manner, eg. by presenting inaccurate accounts);
(iii) act in good faith and exercise reasonable care, skill and diligence (they must act as a reasonably diligent person. The two-prong test used to determine whether this standard has been met analyses the actions of the relevant person on the basis of the general knowledge, skill and experience that may reasonably be expected to be attributed to a person carrying out the same functions and the general knowledge that such person actually possesses);
(iv) avoid conflicts of interest;[98]
(v) disclose any interest in a proposed transaction or arrangement with the company (directors and members of the managing board must disclose any interest, whether direct or indirect, in a transaction or arrangement that the company is proposing to enter into, or that it has already entered into. Once declared, a prior authorisation procedure must be followed.)[99]

c) The Say-on-Pay Rule

The say-on-pay rule is usually considered an instrument of corporate governance, whereby the company's shareholders are entitled to cast a non-binding vote on the compensation granted to managers. Unlike under English and American law, French law does not provide for such a general rule but requires the shareholders' authorisation in specific cases, in particular for the allocation of stock-options and performance shares to managers of listed companies.[100] Although the AMF, IFA and Proxinvest are now promoting the introduction of such a concept under

---

[98] See sec. 3.1.3 for further information.

[99] *Ibid.*

[100] See sec. 3.1.3 for further information.

French law, the say-on-pay rule is not unanimously supported, even among minority shareholders associations, which fear that compensations largely approved in general meetings will be more difficult to challenge. In August 2012, a public consultation was launched by the authority of the Directorate General of the Treasury (*direction générale du Trésor*) to collect the views of professional bodies and associations on a potential introduction of the say-on-pay rule into French law. More recently, a French listed company has voluntarily decided to implement such a rule for the next shareholders' general meeting to be held in the first quarter of 2013.[101]

3.1.3. Special Issues

a) Conflicts of Interest—General Remarks

Avoiding conflicts of interest lie at the heart of corporate governance. As a general rule, directors' decisions must comply with the company's interests: Otherwise, they may incur liability for mismanagement. Directors must avoid situations where their interests conflict, or may possibly conflict, with the company's interests, unless authorised by the board.

Many corporate governance rules, either legal or arising from the various corporate governance codes, aim to prevent conflicts of interest. Related-party transactions regulated by legal provisions are based on simple and straightforward criteria: the identity of the signatories and the characteristics of the transaction. Therefore, the concerned directors can easily be excluded from the corresponding vote without any risk that their directors' rights may be violated on a discretionary basis.

However, the AFEP/MEDEF Corporate Governance Code provides for rules of best practice for directors intended to prevent a risk of conflict of interest. For instance, a director should ensure that he holds a fairly significant number of shares in the company so that his interests are aligned with the interests of the company. He should also keep in mind that he represents all of the shareholders and that he should act in the company's interest.

The AFEP/MEDEF Corporate Governance Code also takes a wider stance and recommends that the directors report any conflict of interest to the board, a notion which goes far beyond that of related-party transactions, whether actual or potential, and refrain from taking part in any vote on such resolutions.[102] The purpose of these rules is consequently less precise and straightforward than the legal provisions mentioned above, which is why recommendations are in this case more appropriate.

---

[101] Publicis, press release dated 28 November 2012.

[102] Article 17 of the AFEP/MEDEF Corporate Governance Code.

The AMF issued a recommendation in 2012 that information should be provided to the board in respect of the management of conflicts of interests mentioned in the AFEP/MEDEF Corporate Governance Code.[103]

According to the AMF, following a review of a sample of 60 companies listed on Euronext Paris, all of said companies now deal with the conflicts of interests one way or another and only two of them do not issue any specific representation on the potential or actual conflicts of interests of the members of their boards.[104]

These recommendations are largely taken up by the internal rules of listed companies, which often contain additional provisions. For instance, they may provide for the appointment of a lead director or a vice-chairman who will be in charge of overseeing potential conflicts of interest and to whom conflicted directors may refer. According to the AMF, one-third of the sample of 60 companies mentioned above had appointed observers (*censeurs*) to their board.[105]

According to the AFEP/MEDEF Corporate Governance Code, directors should ensure that they are aware of all the obligations arising from their appointment, and in particular should review the by-laws and internal board rules of the company.

More recently, the MEDEF ethic committee issued some guidelines applicable to managers, directors and employees to prevent conflicts of interest.[106]

b) Related-party Transactions

Considering the risk of abuse of related-party transactions, French law decided to regulate them at an early stage. In accordance with its *ratio legis*, the regulation of related-party transactions depends on the types of transactions concerned.

Indeed, certain transactions that are likely to raise a severe conflict of interest or significantly alter the assets of a company may not be entered into by a director with his company. According to article L. 225-43 of the Commercial Code, directors who are not legal entities are prohibited from contracting loans from the company in any way, as well as from having the company guarantee their commitments towards third parties.

On the contrary, French law does not require any specific process for agreements relating to ordinary transactions conducted under normal conditions, in the ordinary course of business and on an arm's length basis.

---

[103] AMF Recommendation n° 2012-02.

[104] 2012 AMF Report on corporate governance and directors' compensation, p. 43.

[105] 2012 AMF Report on corporate governance and directors' compensation, p. 9.

[106] 'Prévenir et gérer les conflits d'intérêts dans les sociétés', lettre Omnidroit dated 16 March 2011.

All other related-party transactions are subject to prior approval by the board. They are, according to articles L. 225-38 and L. 225-86 of the Commercial Code, as follows:

– any agreements entered into, either directly or through an intermediary, between the company and its CEO, one of its deputy executive officers, one of its directors (or when applicable, a member of the supervisory board or of the managing board), one of its shareholders holding more than 10% of the voting rights or, in the case of a corporate shareholder, the company which controls it; and

– any agreements entered into between the company and another company, if the company's CEO, one of its deputy executive officers or one of its directors (or when applicable, a member of the supervisory board or of the managing board) is the owner, an unlimited liability partner, a manager, a director or a member of that company's supervisory board or, more generally, is in any way involved in its management.

– French law extends the scope and the definition of the conflicted person to include persons who are party to:

   · transactions in which one of the persons mentioned above may have an indirect interest because 'connected' persons are involved; and

   · agreements entered into by the company and one of the persons above through an intermediary. The concept of intermediary is broadly construed under French law.

c) Decision-making Procedures

In the event of a related-party transaction, the conflicted director must inform the board of directors. The transaction is subsequently submitted to the board of directors, which must decide on it before the company enters into the transaction.

The conflicted director may not vote on the approval of the transaction. The chairman of the board must inform the statutory auditor of the signing of the transaction, on which the statutory auditor must issue a report.

At the next annual general meeting, the shareholders must vote on the transaction, with any interested shareholder not having the right to vote. Such shareholders' vote is an illustration of the agency theory whereby shareholders exercise their control over self-interested agreements entered into by their agent.

If the transaction has not been approved by the board, it may be declared null and void by a court upon the request of the company or a shareholder, provided that it can be demonstrated that the performance of such a transaction results in a loss for the company. The interested person may also be held liable for the loss suffered by the company as a result of the performance of the related-party transaction.

The transaction remains in force even if not ratified by the annual general meeting, except in the event of fraud. However, the interested person and the members of the board who approved the transaction may be held liable if a loss results from the company's performance of the transaction.

These rules are equally applicable to companies with a supervisory board.

d) Corporate Opportunities and Inside Information

Inside information is defined under French law (article 621-1 of the general regulation of the AMF[107]) as any information that is of: (i) a precise nature; (ii) that has not been made public; and (iii) which, directly or indirectly, concerns the listed company and which, if it were to be made public, would be liable to have a significant impact on the trading price of the securities.

On a personal basis, the director of a listed company must refrain from trading in that company' securities:

– during the period between the date when he has knowledge of inside information and the date when this inside information is made public;

– during the 15-day period before the date of publication of the company's annual consolidated financial statements as well as the date of publication of its interim financial statements (half-yearly and quarterly, if any). In practice, this duty to abstain starts once the director has knowledge of any draft of annual, half-yearly or quarterly financial statements of a listed company in so far as financial statements contain price-sensitive information.

Insider dealing is punished both as an administrative offence (article L. 621-15 of the CMF[108] and article 622-1 of the general regulation of the AMF) and as a criminal offence (article L. 465-1 of the CMF). In order to help monitor their dealings, directors and managers are required to notify the AMF of their purchase or subscription of the company's securities.

Regarding the shareholders, directors have a duty of confidentiality and secrecy. Article L. 225-37 of the Commercial Code provides that the directors, as well as any persons attending board meetings, are bound to keep confidential all confidential information provided by the chairman of the board. This duty also applies to any employee or executive who may take part in certain board meetings. The violation of this duty is not a criminal offence but the director may be held personally liable for any harm done to the company. In practice, this duty is also restated in the internal rules of the board.

Consequently, if a shareholder is a member of the board of directors, he should not deal in the company's shares if he has knowledge of any inside information or if he has any such knowledge in the 15-day period preceding the publication of financial statements. If the shareholder is not directly appointed but has had one of its representatives appointed, such representative should not

---

[107] Article 621-1 du Règlement Général de l'Autorité des Marchés Financiers.

[108] Article L. 621-15 du Code monétaire et financier.

provide the shareholder with any inside information. In particular, in the event of a new issuance of securities, or if the company is preparing to make fundamental changes, or if a public tender offer is being negotiated, such events are likely to have a significant impact on the trading price of the securities, and the shareholders—including those who have a representative appointed to the board—should not be informed of the contemplated transaction if it has not yet been made public. At the very least, shareholders should not deal in the shares of the company during that period.

e) *Takeover Situations*

In the event of a takeover, the board must consider the merits of the offer and provide shareholders with its opinion on the consequences of the offer for the company, its shareholders and its employees. In order to assist it in discharging this obligation, the target board will generally seek financial advice, although it is not under an obligation to do so. In addition, the practice has developed for the target company's directors to include a recommendation to target shareholders to accept or reject the offer.

The target company must request a formal fairness opinion from an independent expert in certain situations. These include situations where the offer is likely to give rise to conflicts of interest within the target's board or to threaten the equality of treatment of shareholders, or in the event of a squeeze-out procedure. The general regulation of the AMF includes a non-exhaustive list of situations that the AMF views as constituting a conflict of interest and accordingly where a fairness opinion is required.

These include in particular where:

- the target company is already controlled by the bidder;
- there are a number of ancillary transactions related to the main bid that are likely to have a significant impact on the offer price; and
- the management of the target company or the person that controls it have entered into an agreement with the bidder that is likely to affect their independence.

The ability of the target company's board of directors (as well as its managers) to take defensive measures during an offer period is very limited. Unless reciprocity[109] applies, they are prohibited from taking any action to frustrate the takeover without specific shareholder approval during the offer period. In addi-

---

[109] Reciprocity is the principle according to which the board of directors of a target company is released from the restrictions from taking frustrating action described above in the event that the target company is the subject of a hostile bid from a company that is itself not subject to the same or equivalent restrictions. Where reciprocity applies, the target board may take any frustrating action that has been expressly approved as such by a general meeting of its shareholders in the previous 18 months.

tion, previous authorisations granted by shareholders and previous decisions taken that may frustrate the offer and that have not been fully implemented (such as authorisations to issue new shares or shareholder warrants given to the board of directors by the shareholders' meeting before the filing of the offer) are suspended during the offer period unless specifically renewed during such period.

Furthermore, the terms of any agreement that could affect the outcome of a takeover offer must be disclosed to the AMF and made public.

3.1.4. *Institutional Investors*

Institutional investors play an important role in listed companies. Approximately 40% of the shares of CAC 40 French companies are held by institutional investors, among which 20% belong to the euro zone.[110]

Regarding their involvement in the company's business and management, institutional investors may be divided into two main categories: passive or active. The majority of institutional investors are passive shareholders whereas only a minority of them—defined as active investors—attend general meetings, exercise their voting rights and initiate discussions with the management.

Specific institutional investors as portfolio management companies of collective security investment institutions (*sociétés de gestion d'organismes de placement collectif de valeurs mobilières*) must comply with certain corporate rules relating to the exercise of their voting rights in the companies that they manage. Both the CMF and the AMF require such companies to explain and justify their voting policies. Indeed, article L. 533-22 of the CMF requires that if such entities do not exercise their voting rights, they should explain their reasons to their shareholders, and articles 314-100 and 314-102 of the AMF general regulation provide that portfolio management companies must:

'draw up a document titled "voting policy" which sets out the terms and conditions on which they intend to exercise the voting rights attached to the securities held by collective investment institutions that they manage';

and

'within four months of the end of the financial year, report on how they have exercised their voting rights in the past year'.

According to the French Association of Financial Management (*Association Française de la Gestion Financière* – *AFG*), more than half of portfolio manage-

---

[110] See sec. 1.1(d) and (e) for further information.

ment companies pursue a policy of active dialogue with issuers, and more than 85% exercised their voting rights in 2010.[111]

In addition, following the Walker Report,[112] which recommended that the Financial Reporting Council adopt the Institutional Shareholders' Committee's recommendations in the 'Stewardship Code', a French working group—*le Groupe de Travail de la Commission Europe du Club des Juristes*'[113]—proposed a code of best practices applicable to French institutional investors.

Such recommendations seek to increase the role and the importance of institutional investors in the monitoring of listed companies. More specifically, the working group recommends that such investors:

(i)   disclose their voting policy within a reasonable time before general meetings of shareholders;

(ii) disclose their proxy advisors and their recommendations; and

(iii) should not exercise their voting rights if they do not bear the economic risk of the shares.

More generally, shareholder activism is currently increasing in France due to the high absenteeism rate[114] at shareholders' meetings, the increasing number of foreign institutional investors (in particular hedge funds[115]) and professional proxy advisors (RiskMetrics/Deminor, Proxinvest, AFG) that provide institutional investors with corporate governance advice and convenient voting mechanisms.[116]

According to InvestorSight's report based on a sample of 203 French and foreign listed companies (including CAC 40 companies), 33% of such companies had been concerned by shareholder activism in 2007 (compared to 20% in 2006).[117]

Over the years, French laws have implemented several provisions promoting the development of shareholder activism and minority shareholders. In 2001, the New Economic Regulation Act[118] lowered the threshold for minority shareholders

---

[111] AFG *2010 AGM voting results*, p. 1 and 3—*Etudes sur l'exercice des droits de vote en 2010.* Available at <http://www.afg.asso.fr>.

[112] David Walker, *A review of corporate governance in UK banks and other financial industry entities, Final Recommendations,* dated 26 November 2009. Available at <http://web archive.nationalarchives.gov.uk/+/http:/www.hmtreasury.gov.uk/d/walker_review_261109.pdf>.

[113] Composed of representatives of the AMF, listed companies, lawyers and notary.

[114] According to a poll issued by Capitalcom, such absenteeism should decrease because 89% of shareholders are willing to exercise their voting right in 2011.

[115] See sec. 1.1(e) for further information.

[116] See, M. Tonello, 'The Professionalization of Shareholder Activism in France', *The Conference Board,* on 13 March 2011, Harvard Law School Forum on Corporate Governance and Financial Regulation. Available at <http://blogs.law.harvard.edu/corpgov/2011/03/13/the-professionalization-of-shareholder-activism-in-france/> .

[117] In particular, Atos Origin, Valeo, Strafor Facom, Société du Louvres, Rhodia, Sidel and Vivendi.

[118] Loi n° 2001-420 du 15 mai 2001 relative aux nouvelles régulations économiques.

to convene a general meeting, submit draft resolutions to the agenda of general meetings, require the appointment of an expert charged with presenting a report on management transactions, submit written questions to the chairman of the board of directors or to the managing board on any matter of such a nature as to threaten the continued operation of the company or the dismissal of statutory auditors, from 10% to 5%—and even lower than that to 5%, or 1% depending on the company's share capital—if minority shareholders gathered in associations. The 2003 Financial Security Act[119] also strengthened the powers of associations of investors, but without giving them real resources to grow, and required portfolio management companies to explain and justify their policies.[120] In addition, since the implementation of the EU Directive 2007/36 dated 11 July 2007 relating to the exercise of shareholders' voting rights in listed companies,[121] any person who actively engages in the collection of proxies must disclose his voting policy.

As a general rule, French law encourages the good form of counter-powers in listed companies by rewarding faithful shareholders (including institutional investors) through the allocation of preferred dividends or double voting shares.[122] Two-thirds of listed companies implement double voting policies, whereas only a few listed companies allocate preferred dividends (L'Oréal, Air Liquide).

In the meantime, the law on banking and financial regulation dated 22 October 2010[123] introduced article L. 225-126 in the Commercial Code to prohibit opaque empty voting and regulate certain active minority shareholders (in particular hedge funds), which are especially creative in decoupling voting rights from economic ownership through stock loan agreements. Consequently, French law requires shareholders temporarily acquiring a number of shares representing more than 2% of the voting rights of a listed company to disclose their identity and the number of shares acquired to the company and the AMF at least three days before the shareholders' general meeting.

The following table shows the main examples of shareholder activism in France in the last decade.

[119] Loi n° 2003-706 du 1er août 2003 de sécurité financière.

[120] See above.

[121] Through Ordinance n° 2010-1511 dated 9 December 2010 and Decree 2010-1619 dated 23 December 2010. Ordonnance n° 2010-1511 du 9 décembre 2010 portant transposition de la directive 2007/36/ CE du 11 juillet 2007 concernant l'exercice de certains droits des actionnaires de sociétés cotées; Décret n° 2010-1619 du 23 décembre 2010 relatif aux droits des actionnaires de sociétés cotées.

[122] Such shares with double voting rights may only be allocated to shareholders whose shares have been registered in their name for at least two years. Conversion into bearer form or sale of the shares dissipates their additional voting rights.

[123] Loi n° 2010-1249 du 22 octobre 2010 de régulation bancaire et financière.

Targeted firm	Year	Issues	Activism stages	Type of activists (percentage of share-holding, when available)
Vivarte	2000	Alter business strategy: achieve operational efficiency Improve governance: oust CEO	Public	*Raider:* Guy Wyser Pratt and Atticus (33%)
Alstom	2004	Improve governance: lawsuit against excessive executive remuneration	Public and penal action	*Investor association:* APPAC
	2008	Environmental, Social and Ethical Issues	Public	UNPRI Sudan Engagement Group; Hermes EOS
Arcelor	2006	Alter business strategy: carry out M&A Improve governance: rescind takeover defenses	Private	*Investor associations:* ADAM, APPAC, Goldman Sachs, Several hedge funds
	2007	Other policies: stop unequal treatment of shareholders	Threat of legal action	SRM
Suez	2006	Alter business strategy: opposed to the merger between Suez and Gaz de France (spin-off)	Public and judicial	ADAM; *Raider:* Albert Frère; Knight Vinke (1%)
	2008	Alter business strategy: obtain focus (spin-offs, dismantle)	NA	NA; Centaurus; Pardus
Atos Origin	2007	Alter business strategy: obtain focus (spin-offs, dismantle) Improve governance: oust CEO and nominate independent board members	Public	ADAM; Pardus (10.04%); Centaurus (12.3%)
Carrefour	2008	Alter business strategy: obtain focus (spin-offs, dimantle)	Public	*Raider:* Arnault Gropp, Blue Capital (12,9%)
Valéo	2007	Improve governance: nominate board members	Public	Guy Wyser Pratt; Pardus (19.7%)
	2008	Alter business strategy: obtain focus (business restructuring)	Private	Pardus (18.54%)
Accor	2008	Improve governance: oust CEO and nominate board members Alter business strategy: obtain focus (spin-offs, dismantle)	Public	Arnault Group; *Private equity fund:* Eurazeo; Blue Capital (10.7%)
Saint-Gobain	2008	Improve governance: change board members	Private	Wendel Investment (18%)

Source: Carine Girard and Stephan Gates, 'The Professionalization of Shareholder Activism in France', The Conference Board, February 2011, Volume 3, Number 4.

More generally, the AMF notes that in France the government has played a key role as majority or minority shareholder. For instance, it voted against the approval of the non-competition indemnity of the former CEO of Air France and against the golden parachute of the former CEO of Safran.

3.1.5. *Remuneration (as Incentive)*

French law deals with the compensation of directors of French companies under three regimes: General compensation, stock options and performance shares, and termination payments.

a) General Compensation

The remuneration of the members of the board of directors and of the supervisory board is determined by the ordinary general meeting. In both cases, the remuneration must be a fixed fee that the board of directors or the supervisory board distributes freely to each director or member. Approximately 90% of SBF 120 companies determine the compensation of their directors according to their assiduity and their involvement in the committees of the board.[124] According to Proxinvest, such members are paid less than most of their counterparts in Europe.[125]

	Midcap	SBF 120	CAC 40
Remuneration of directors in 2009 (Euros)[126]	14.300	28.000	64.000

By contrast, the remuneration of the chairman of the board of directors, the supervisory board, the CEO and the members of the managing board are set respectively by the board of directors and the supervisory board. This remuneration, which may be fixed or variable according to certain performance criteria, is not considered as a related-party transaction. Therefore, the interested directors may vote upon it and the general meeting is not required to vote upon it.

According to the AMF, the remuneration paid in 2011 to the CEOs and general managers of CAC 40 companies can be divided in the following quarters:

- One quarter of CEOs/general managers were paid between €719,000 and €1,538,000 (compared with €591,000 to €1,189,000 in 2010),
- A second quarter of CEOs/general managers were paid between €1,538,000 and €2,096,000 (compared with €1,189,000 to €1,620,000 in 2010),
- A third quarter of CEOs/general managers were paid between €2,096,000 and €2,959,000 (compared with €1,620,000 to €2,497,000 in 2010), and
- A fourth quarter of CEOs/ general managers were paid between €2,959,000 and €4,532,000 (compared with €2,497,000 to €4,048,000 in 2010).[127]

---

[124] *Le Figaro*, 'les conseils d'administration du CAC 40 plus transparents', 7 December 2010.

[125] Nevertheless, in 2009: (i) Arcelor Mittal, Danone; and (ii) Alcatel-Lucent, LVMH, Sanofi-Aventis, ST Microelectronics had respectively allocated more than €115,000 and €80,000 to their directors.

[126] *Le Monde*, 'mieux payés, les administrateurs contrôlent insuffisamment les risques', 21 October 2010, and *Les Echos*, 'CAC 40: la rémunération des administrateurs en forte hausse', 22 September 2010.

[127] 2012 AMF Report on corporate governance and directors' compensation, p. 67.

The AFEP/MEDEF Corporate Governance Code has set some guiding principles for the determination of the compensation of the CEO. The board of directors or the supervisory board should therefore take into account the principles of:

- comprehensiveness (the board must set all components of the remuneration, fixed and variable, stock-options, performance shares);
- balance (between each compensation component);
- benchmark (the compensation must be assessed within the context of a business sector and the benchmark of the European or global market);
- consistency (with the compensation of other officers and employees of the company);
- clarity of the rules (which must be simple, stable and transparent); and
- reasonableness (the remuneration must also take into account the company's general interest, market practices and officer performance).[128]

Based on these principles, the AFEP/MEDEF Corporate Governance Code gives various recommendations regarding both the fixed and variable parts of the compensation of the CEO. Also, it recommends that a remuneration committee with a majority of independent directors—of which the CEO may not be a member—should be created to make recommendations to the board as to the determination of the remuneration of the directors of the company. More recently, the Court of Appeal of Versailles condemned the former CEO of Vinci for the conditions under which he obtained his remuneration and prepared the ground for his retirement.[129]

b) Stock Options and Performance Shares

According to the AFEP/MEDEF, 52.4% of SBF 120 companies and 63.9% of CAC 40 companies granted stock options in 2011. Of these, 93.9% of the stock options granted by SBF 120 companies and 100% of the stock options granted by CAC 40 companies were granted without any discount.[130]

A total of 66.7% of SBF 120 companies and 69.5% of CAC 40 companies granted performance shares.[131]

---

[128] Article 20.1 of the AFEP/MEDEF Corporate Governance Code.

[129] In its decision dated 24 May 2011, the Court of Appeal of Versailles condemned the first criminal of 'abuse of power' committed by the former CEO of Vinci (a CAC 40 company) and imposed a fine of €375,000. According to the Court, the former CEO ousted three members of the compensation committee and used his position to influence the board of directors to increase the variable part of his remuneration.

[130] 2012 AFEP/MEDEF Annual Report, p. 45 and 47.

[131] 2012 AFEP/MEDEF Annual Report, p. 50.

The granting of stock options or performance shares is not subject to authorisation under the related-party transaction procedure. However, to avoid potential conflicts of interest, it is strictly regulated.

The grant of stock options to the board of directors or supervisory board must be authorised by the shareholders meeting. To prevent insider dealing in listed companies, stock options may not be granted ten days before or after financial statements are published or when the corporate bodies of the company hold inside information. The price of the option is also regulated as it may not amount to less than 80% of the average stock price for the twenty trading days preceding the day when the option is granted.[132]

The AFEP/MEDEF Corporate Governance Code has added more onerous recommendations to these legal provisions. In particular, options and performance shares should be conditional upon performance targets and should not be awarded to a director who is leaving office. They should not represent a disproportionate percentage of the aggregate of all compensation options and shares awarded to each director. Regarding the price, the recommendations are more demanding than the legal provisions, as the AFEP/MEDEF code provides that no discount should be applied to the award of stock options.

c) *Termination Payments*

According to the AFEP/MEDEF, 56.2% of SBF 120 companies and 50% of CAC 40 companies provided for termination payments in 2011.[133]

Any commitment by a listed company to pay a termination fee (a 'golden parachute') to a director in the event that he ceases to be a director is subject to authorisation under the related-party transaction procedure.[134]

Also, article L. 225-42-1 of the Commercial Code, which is only applicable to listed companies, prohibits remuneration, indemnities and any other kind of advantages to be paid in the event of termination of the mandate of a director, if they are not subject to conditions based on the performance of the beneficiary as a manager of the company.

The AFEP/MEDEF Corporate Governance Code recommends choosing strict performance conditions. A director should not be entitled to an indemnity unless his departure is imposed on him and due to a change of control or a change of strategy by the company. In any event, the termination payment should not exceed two

---

[132] Article L. 225-177 of the Commercial Code.

[133] 2012 AFEP/MEDEF Annual Report, p. 57.

[134] Article L. 225-42-1 of the Commercial Code.

years' compensation[135] (fixed and variable). Additional pension schemes may be offered by the company, but should avoid giving rise to any abuse.[136]

3.2. Board and Stakeholders

3.2.1. *Board and Employees/Labour Co-determination*

French law gives rights to employees directly or indirectly through the Works Council, the applicable rules under the one-tier and two-tier models being very similar.

The Works Council has enhanced rights to receive information. It is to be informed and consulted on all questions regarding the organisation, the management and the general business of the company, and in particular on any actions that are likely to affect the headcount, the duration of the working week, or employment conditions (articles L. 2323-6 *et seq.* of the Labour code[137]). The Works Council must also be informed of any proposed takeover offer.[138] However, as with directors and any other persons invited to attend board meetings, the Works Council members are bound to secrecy with regards to information of a confidential nature presented as such by the chairman of the board.[139]

According to article L.225-231 of the Commercial Code, the Works Council may also apply to the court for an expert to be appointed and charged with a report on specific transactions.

Regarding the governance of the company, the by-laws can provide that up to five directors be elected directly by the company's employees or by the employees of the company together with the employees of its subsidiaries whose registered offices are located in France, as long as this number does not exceed

---

[135] Article 20.2.4. of the AFEP/MEDEF Corporate Governance Code.

[136] Article 20.2.5. of the AFEP/MEDEF Corporate Governance Code.

[137] Articles L 2323-6 et seq., Code du Travail.

[138] Under French law, the target company's Works Council or group Works Council must be informed of any proposed takeover offer. The bidder must send a copy of the final offer document (approved by the AMF) to the target company's Works Council within three days of publication. In the absence of a Works Council or group Works Council, direct contact must be made with the target group's employees.

The obligation to convene a meeting of the relevant Works Council falls primarily on the management of the target company and arises on the day of the filing of the offer document with the AMF. At this meeting, the Works Council may decide to convene a further meeting with the bidder and will give its opinion on the nature (hostile or recommended) of the offer. If the bidder fails to attend a meeting organised by the Works Council, the voting rights attached to the target shares it owns or acquires are suspended until it does so.

[139] Article L. 225-37 of the Commercial Code.

one-third of the rest of the directors (article L. 225-27 of the French commercial code). Similar rules are applicable to members of the supervisory board.

On the other hand, in order to avoid directors being subordinated to the CEO, French law provides for specific conditions under which a director may be an employee of the company. A director who is incumbent is barred from becoming an employee of the company. Conversely, an employee may become a director and still remain an employee only under certain conditions (mainly if the employment contract was entered into before the appointment as a director and if it corresponds to real employment). The total number of directors who are also employees cannot exceed one-third of the directors (article L. 225-22 of the Commercial Code).

In order to allow the employees to be involved in the business of the company, French law also provides for financial rights. In particular, it provides for a profit-sharing scheme consisting of the issuance of shares in favour of the employees in order that they benefit from the profits realised by the company (article L. 3332-1 et seq. of the Labour code).

3.2.2. Board and Creditors

The impact of creditors on the governance of companies listed in France is limited. The rights of creditor, when a company is *in bonis* only exist under French law when specific transactions affect the substance of the company. For instance, in the event of a merger, unsecured creditors may oppose the proposed merger of the company concerned. As such, they cannot stop the merger but the Commercial Court may request the reimbursement of their claims or the taking of guarantees over the company's assets (article L. 236-15 of the Commercial Code).

3.2.3. Board and Other Stakeholders

The corporate social responsibility of companies—and in particular listed companies, given their importance—is increasingly taken into account under French law. According to article L. 225-102-1 of the Commercial Code, the board of directors must set forth in its annual report information on the way the company takes into account the social and environmental consequences of its business. In particular, following the Commercial Code, the report must include information detailing any redundancies, the working time organisation and the use of sub-contracting by the company. Also, the report must give an account of the consumption of water, energy and raw materials by the company, as well as on the treatment of wastes and on valuation, certification and the amount of related provisions booked.

The French Parliament has recently increased the amount of information required by passing a law in July 2010[140] providing that the report must also include information relating to the sustainable development policies implemented by the company.

3.3. Changing Roles in Financial Distress

3.3.1. Preventative Proceedings

The Commercial Code provides for two preventative proceedings: voluntary arrangement (*mandat ad hoc*) and conciliation proceedings (*procédure de conciliation*). The main characteristics of these preventative proceedings are that: (i) They are confidential; (ii) they do not necessarily involve all of the debtor's creditors; (iii) they are informal and flexible; and (iv) no rescheduling or waiver of debt may be imposed on the creditors without their consent.[141]

In the *mandat ad hoc* and in the conciliation proceedings, a company that experiences difficulties (whether financial, commercial or otherwise) but is not insolvent may request that the presiding judge of the Commercial Court appoints either a *mandataire ad hoc* or initiates a conciliation proceeding and appoints a *conciliateur*. The task of the *mandataire ad hoc* and the *conciliateur* is to facilitate, through negotiations, the conclusion of an agreement resolving the debtor's difficulties (eg. through debt forgiveness, debt rescheduling and/or new loans) between the debtor and one or more of its willing creditors. Both proceedings are similar, although the Commercial Court is more involved in the conciliation proceedings.

In both proceedings, the petition to the court is made by the management, ie. the CEO and the president of the managing board, who are not specifically required by law to consult the board of directors and the supervisory board. Still, with such a decision having a substantial impact on the company and its strategy, management should request the approval of the board or risk being held liable for any harm to the company.

Once the *mandataire ad hoc* and the *conciliateur* are appointed, the management of the company retains full powers to run the business, and shareholders exercise their prerogatives as usual. The *mandataire ad hoc* and the *conciliateur* have no coercive powers over the company. Their role is only to facilitate negotiation with creditors.

---

[140] Loi n° 2010-788 du 12 juillet 2010 portant engagement national pour l'environnement; article L 225-102-1 du Code de Commerce.

[141] A debtor may however request the court to reschedule a portion of its debts for up to two years pursuant to Article 1244-1 et seq. of the French Civil Code.

The Works Council must be informed and consulted on matters concerning the organisation, management and general operation of the company.[142] Hence, it must be informed and consulted when the management petitions the court to appoint a *mandataire ad hoc* or to initiate conciliation proceedings.

3.3.2. Insolvency Proceedings

The Commercial Code provides for three types of insolvency proceedings:[143] (i) Safeguard proceedings (where the company is not yet insolvent); (ii) reorganisation proceedings; and (iii) liquidation proceedings.

a) Safeguard Proceedings

Safeguard proceedings (*procédure de sauvegarde*) can only be commenced at the request of companies that are not insolvent according to the French test of illiquidity (ie. unable to pay their debts as they fall due). The request is made by the legal representative of the company, ie. the CEO or the president of the managing board. As in preventative proceedings, even if not specifically required by law, the board should be consulted on a decision that has such a significant impact on the company.

Safeguard proceedings are overseen by court-appointed key officials. These include the creditors' representative (*représentant des créanciers*), who has authority to act on behalf of and in the collective interest of creditors; and the judicial administrator (*administrateur judiciaire*), whose role is to assist the company in preparing a safeguard or reorganisation plan and who has authority to oversee, or assist in all or part of, the management of the debtor's affairs (in safeguard or reorganisation proceedings).

The CEO or the managing board of the company draws up a safeguard plan with the help of the judicial administrator. Such a plan may provide for (partial or total) waivers of debts and/or a rescheduling of debts, a change of control (ie. a total sale of the debtor company's business), and/or a sale of certain business units. It will be submitted to the court once approved by creditors.

The business is continued and operated by the existing management who will also draw up a restructuring plan with the help of the judicial administrator. Consequently, the company is still managed in the interest of the shareholders and not in the interest of the creditors. However, the court may limit the management's powers by giving specific missions to the judicial administrator. His role is either to supervise the management (*a posteriori*), or to assist, which

---

[142] Article L.2323-6 of the Labour Law Code.

[143] Within the meaning of Article 2(a) of EU Regulation 1346/2000 of 29 May 2000 on Insolvency Proceedings.

implies that the management may not make certain types of decisions without the judicial administrator's approval (double signature).

Based on the economic and social analysis undertaken by the judicial administrator, the management—with the help of the judicial administrator—develops a plan that must determine the prospects of the company's profitability and ways to honour the claims of the creditors.

The creditors are consulted on the safeguard plan. In particular, for companies having more than 150 employees and an annual turnover in excess of €20 million, for the purposes of negotiating the safeguard plan the judicial administrator will be required to organise two creditors' committees, the credit institutions committee (*comité des établissements de crédit*) and the main suppliers' committee (*comité des principaux fournisseurs*). Also, if the company has issued notes, whether in France or abroad, all note holders are consulted on the plan in one single general meeting (irrespective of the law applicable to the notes, currency, terms, number of series or other factors distinguishing various issues of notes).

If both committees and the general meeting of note holders approve the company's proposals, the court then officially approves the safeguard plan if it is found compatible with the interests of all the company's creditors. Such court decision makes the plan binding on the dissenting committee members and note holders.

Employees are also involved in the safeguard plan. The Works Council must be consulted before the management petitions the court for the opening of safeguard proceedings. The judicial administrator will have to inform the Works Council on payment schedules for claims. Finally, in order to approve the safeguard plan, the judge must consult the Works Council and the Works Council has a right to appeal the judgment approving, modifying or rejecting the safeguard plan.

In the event that the court does not approve a plan by the end of the observation period, and if the court refuses to extend it (or following extensions the maximum possible period has elapsed), the court may commence reorganisation or liquidation proceedings if no recovery of the business is possible.

b) Reorganisation Proceedings

When a company is insolvent, the legal representative of the company, ie. the CEO or the president of the managing board, is bound to inform the Registrar of the Commercial Court. As for the other insolvency proceedings, it should consult the board of directors or the supervisory board about such decisions. A judicial administrator is appointed. Following an observation period, the court may:

- approve a continuation plan (*plan de continuation*) if the judicial administrator determines that there should be a reorganisation of the company's business. A continuation plan is similar to a safeguard plan and most rules

applicable to the approval of a safeguard plan also apply to the approval of a continuation plan;[144] or
- approve a sale of all or part of the debtor's business to a third party through a sale plan (*plan de cession*), which is in essence an asset sale. As a general rule, and subject to certain exceptions, the purchaser of the business does not therefore assume the debtor's liabilities. On-going contracts deemed necessary to the continuation of the business are transferred to the purchaser; or
- order the commencement of liquidation proceedings.[145]

Most rules applicable to the approval of a safeguard plan apply equally to the approval of a continuation plan. In both continuation and sales of assets plans, the company retains its existing management with the assistance of the court-appointed judicial administrator. The directors remaining at the head of the company, the interest of the shareholders still prevail over the interests of the creditors, although the judicial administrator's role is to ensure that the interest of the company and of all stakeholders is taken into account.

However, in contrast with the safeguard proceedings, in both continuation and sales of assets plans:
- if the management has been grossly negligent, the court may order that the administrator replaces the debtor's management; in any case, as from the beginning of the plan the directors are barred from selling shares and any securities giving right to shares of the company that they hold directly or indirectly. Such shares and securities are transferred to a blocked account until the plan is adopted or after the closing of all transactions provided by the plan; and
- if the condition of the company requires, the Commercial Court may order that the directors sell their shares and securities giving rights to shares for a price set by an expert appointed by court.

Where the assets of the debtor are sold under a sale plan, creditors are paid out of the proceeds of such sale, the employees being paid first (ring-fenced):[146]

The Works Council must be consulted, as in safeguard proceedings. It is also consulted when the management or the judicial administrator decides to cease part of the business' activity.

In addition, the Works Council has a right of appeal against the judgment approving, modifying or rejecting the continuation plan.

---

[144] See sec. 3.3.2(a) for further information.
[145] See sec. 3.3.2(c) for further information.
[146] Article L.622-17 II of the Commercial Code.

c) Liquidation Proceedings

The company immediately ceases trading on the day of the opening judgment of liquidation proceedings. However where the company's assets may be sold as a going concern, the court may authorise the temporary continuation of the company's operations for up to three months (renewable once).

Where there are no prospects of recovery, the court orders the commencement of liquidation proceedings (*liquidation judiciaire*), and appoints a liquidator whose role is to take over the administration of the debtor's estate and dispose of its assets to pay off its creditors.

Creditors are paid out of the proceeds of such sales; however, the employees are paid first (using the ring-fenced assets) (article L. 641-13 II of the Commercial Code).

When the court decides to convert any proceedings into liquidation or when liquidation is inevitable from the onset, the Works Council must be consulted.

When the court decides to sell part of the business, the Works Council must also be consulted.

In addition, the Works Council has a right of appeal against the judgment opening liquidation proceedings.

d) Sanctions on Management in Insolvency Proceedings

As stated above, if the condition of the company so requires, the management of the company may be transferred to a judicial administrator, and management's shares in the company may be blocked or even sold pursuant to court decision. In addition to these measures, the directors may also be sanctioned on three grounds:

- Firstly, they may be required by court to reimburse part or all of the liabilities of the company if they committed management misdeeds;
- Secondly, they may be forbidden to manage a company or a business for a number of years in case of certain misconduct; and
- Thirdly, they may be convicted of *banqueroute*, a criminal offence, in particular if they endeavoured to artificially delay the insolvency of the company.

3.3.3. Recent Reform: the Law on Banking and Financial Regulation 2010

a) Specific Proceedings with Financial Creditors: Accelerated Financial Safeguard

The law on banking and financial regulation dated 22 October 2010[147] introduced a new procedure: the accelerated financial safeguard (*sauvegarde financière accélérée*), inspired in part by the American pre-packaged restructuring plan.

---

[147] Loi n° 2010-1249 du 22 octobre 2010 de régulation bancaire et financière.

The proceedings only concern financial creditors and note holders, excluding public and other private creditors. Most rules applied to the safeguard procedure are also applicable to the accelerated financial safeguard, including those relating to the management.

The goal of the new procedure is to obtain the agreement of a majority of financial creditors and note holders and to force the safeguard plan on un-cooperative creditors.

The advantage of the procedure is that it remains informal and confidential in relation to the non-financial creditors, who are not involved in the negotiation. Thus, the economic value of the company is preserved and the chance of re-covering claims in the long term is higher. Maintaining economic value is especially important for creditors whose claims will be converted into equity in the share capital of the company.

The new proceedings are most relevant to companies that are heavily in debt due to complex financial arrangements (covenants).

b) Changes to the 'Normal' Safeguard Proceedings brought about by the 2010 Reform

The above changes also apply to reorganisation proceedings pursuant to the Commercial Code.

Furthermore the ordinance of 18 December 2008[148] introduced the possibility for a creditor to convert its claims into equity of the distressed company. Until the reform, this ability was limited to credit institution creditors and to the general assembly of note holders. From 22 October 2010, outside of committees or when no committees exist due to company's size, creditors may be offered such a conversion. Creditors are consulted individually. The court must formally approve the conversion agreement, in order to ensure that the interests of the other creditors are preserved.

However, the shareholders must still approve the increase of share capital.

---

[148] Ordonnance n° 2008-1345 du 18 décembre 2008 portant réforme du droit des entreprises en difficulté.

4. Enforcement

4.1. Courts

4.1.1. Personal Liability Claims

a) Liability of Executives and Non-Executives

Directors and members of managing or supervisory boards may incur civil and criminal liability. Although this study focuses on such liability, please note that tax law, securities law (misleading information, insider trading, share price manipulation, etc.), health and safety regulations, and environmental and anti-trust law might also impose liability on the chairman of the board of directors, the members of the managing board or even ordinary directors.

The cases of market abuse should be singled out for discussion as they are heavily punished under French law both as criminal and administrative offences. The banking and financial law dated 22 October 2010[149] raised the amount of the administrative fine incurred for a market abuse from a maximum of €10 million to a maximum of €100 million (while inexplicably leaving the amount of the corresponding criminal offence at the level of €1.5 million). By contrast, the directors found guilty of such offences are seldom held liable for the losses suffered by the victims. Only a dozen liability claims have been judged by French courts, these claims usually being ancillary to criminal claims. French courts have only recently endeavoured to extend victims' rights to compensation.

aa) Civil Liability

CEOs, members of the managing board and directors can be held liable in civil law towards the company and/or the shareholders for any breach of company law or the by-laws, and for mismanagement. Traditionally, because of legal and practical constraints such actions are rarely used, in particular for *in bonis* companies. However, the growth of shareholder activism and the recent developments of case law in favour of managers' civil liability, in particular directors' civil liability, may increase the number of actions brought by the company or the injured shareholder.

One-tier model

Grounds for liability—In the one-tier model, directors' legal duties cover in particular the requirements for convening board or shareholders meetings,[150] the

---

[149] Loi n° 2010-1249 du 22 octobre 2010 de régulation bancaire et financière.

[150] For instance: to give proper notice of a meeting compliance with quorum and majority rules; to ensure that the board does not perform any acts falling outside the company's objects; and to perform certain publicity and filing formalities.

obligation for the board to prepare annual, half-yearly and quarterly financial statements within certain specified deadlines and the conditions for the payment of dividends.

Furthermore, directors must comply with the company's by-laws and are under a duty to act in good faith and in the interests of the company with appropriate diligence, care and skill.[151] They can, therefore, be held liable for mismanagement of the company in respect of any acts or omissions they have committed that are contrary to the interests of the company, or if they run the business in a careless, negligent or fraudulent manner (eg. by presenting inaccurate accounts, failing to supervise the work of the CEO, etc.).

Finally, it should be noted that, in the event of the company's insolvency, in certain circumstances the directors who have mismanaged the company may be held liable for all or part of the company's debts (*action en responsabilité pour insuffisance d'actif*). Indeed, the liquidator appointed by the insolvency court in a company's liquidation proceedings may bring an action for mismanagement against one or more of the company's directors if it is established that such mismanagement contributed to the loss in value of the company's assets. Liability for mismanagement therefore requires evidence that the defendant was an officially-appointed director, or acted as a shadow director, and mismanaged the company in such capacity (thus contributing to the loss in value of the company's assets).

Proceedings determining directors' liability and avoidance of liability on the basis of division of responsibility—As directors' duties are owed primarily to the company, the company itself can sue its directors, the chairman of the board or the CEO (or former directors, chairmen and CEOs) if it has suffered a loss as a result of their actions or omissions. The company may sue a director, the chairman of the board or the CEO either directly (ie. acting through its legal representatives) or through a derivative action brought by a shareholder acting on behalf of the company. Such derivative action is known as the *ut singuli* action. Such action is rarely brought in practice, as the financial costs incurred are only born by the claimant shareholder, who will not receive any compensation even if he succeeds.

Directors, chairmen of the board and CEOs can also be liable to shareholders or third parties, eg. creditors or employees. However, the loss suffered by the shareholder or the third party must be distinct from that suffered by the company itself. In addition, following a very recent judgment, shareholders can directly sue such directors,[152] whereas third parties must demonstrate that the wrongful act or negligence was separable from the directors' functions (*faute séparable des fonc-*

---

[151] Article L. 225-251 paragraph 1 of the Commercial Code.

[152] Judgment n° 294 dated 9 March 2010, Cour de cassation – Chambre commerciale, financière et économique.

tions) (ie. wilful misconduct that is particularly serious and incompatible with the normal exercise of their duties).

Except where the relevant wrongful act or negligence is attributable to a particular director, all board members are jointly and severally liable for any wrongful action or negligence of the board.

Directors may seek to avoid liability for a decision of the board by proving that they were not present at the meeting or that they did not approve the decision of the board that resulted in the loss.[153] A vote against the decision may not be sufficient (the dissenting director should ensure that the objections raised are clearly reported in the minutes of the board meeting). Furthermore, subject to certain conditions, the delegation of powers may be a way for directors, chairmen of the board and CEOs to mitigate their potential liability.

The statute of limitations in respect of claims against directors, chairmen of the board and CEOs is generally three years from the date of the action or omission resulting in the loss, or from the date it is revealed (if concealed).

Two-tier model

According to article L. 225-256 of the Commercial Code, members of the managing board are subject to the same civil liability as described above for directors.

Unlike the managing board or the board of directors, supervisory board members have no liability for managerial actions and their consequences insofar as they have no management power over the company (subject to decisions made in relation to powers specifically granted to them by the Commercial Code or the company's by-laws).

However, supervisory board members may be criminally liable for negligent or tortious acts committed by them in their personal capacity in the performance of their duties.[154]

bb)   Criminal Liability

One-tier model

Directors, chairmen of the board and CEOs may also be held criminally liable, in particular where they are offenders, co-offenders or accomplices to a criminal offence. Several criminal offences are applicable to directors.

Under French law, directors are prohibited from:
 (i) voting for the distribution of an unauthorised dividend;
 (ii) failing to prepare the financial statements or the annual report on the
      company's operations as required by law, or publishing accounts which

---

[153] Judgment dated 30 March 2010, Cour de cassation – Chambre commerciale, financière et économique, Fonds de garantie des dépôts c/Sté Caribéenne de conseil et d'audit.

[154] Article L. 225-256 of the Commercial Code.

they know to be inaccurate or not to represent a true and fair view of the company's financial position;

(iii) using assets of the company in a manner that is contrary to the interests of the company and that serves a personal interest or the interests of a third party;

(iv) misusing their powers or voting rights in a manner that is contrary to the interests of the company and that serves a personal interest or the interests of a third party; or

(v) approving the grant of financial assistance to a holding company to finance the acquisition by the holding company of shares in the company, or granting security to a lender in order to secure a loan issued to the holding company for the same purpose.[155]

The criminal offences referred to in paragraphs (i) to (iv) above can give rise to up to five years' imprisonment and/or a fine up to €375,000.[156]

The criminal offence referred to in paragraph (v) is punishable by a fine of up to €9,000.

The statute of limitations in respect of criminal action against directors, chairmen of the board and CEOs is generally three years from the date of the action or omission resulting in the loss, or from the date it is revealed (if concealed).

Two-tier model

Under French law,[157] the rules governing the criminal liability of directors, chairmen of the board and CEOs apply to managing and supervisory board members.

Therefore, supervisory board members may be criminally liable for negligent or tortious acts committed in their personal capacity in the performance of their duties. Moreover, according to article L. 225-257 of the Commercial Code, they may be held liable for criminal offences committed by managing board members if they are aware of such offences and fail to report them to the general meeting.

b) Protection from Liability: Contractual Release from Liability and D&O Insurance

French companies do not indemnify their directors or their managing board members for liabilities incurred in connection with the exercise of their duties. However, it has become common practice for French groups to cover the civil liability of their directors and officers through specific insurance policies. Such directors' and officers' policies (D&O policies) are directly subscribed by the company for the benefit of its directors and officers.

---

[155] Article L. 225-216 of the Commercial Code.

[156] Article L. 242-6 of the Commercial Code.

[157] Articles L. 242-30, L. 245-17 and L. 247-9 of the Commercial Code.

It had been questioned whether the payment of D&O policy premiums by a company is legally permissible in France. However, it is now well established that such a payment is valid and deemed compliant with the corporate interest of the company.

These policies protect the directors and officers of a company from the financial consequences of civil liability that they may incur towards third parties during the course of the exercise of their duties. D&O policies also cover legal costs incurred in investigating, preparing for and attending hearings for civil or criminal actions.

D&O policies do not cover any liability relating to criminal acts (although the civil consequences of a criminal action may be covered). Exclusions will vary, but the following are generally excluded from the scope of D&O policies:

- gross negligence (*faute lourde*);
- wilful misconduct (*faute intentionnelle*);
- criminal fines and penalties of all types;
- disputes relating to the compensation of directors and officers;
- disputes between the company and its directors and officers; and
- claims and proceedings brought by the company against one of its directors or officers directly or through a derivative action brought by a shareholder action on behalf of the company.

These policies mainly benefit directors, chairmen of the board, CEOs and members of the managing board of a French joint-stock company. D&O policies often exclude actions against directors which aim to recover the company's debts in the event of its insolvency (*action en responsabilité pour insuffisance d'actif*).

Legal entities acting as directors do not benefit from D&O policies. However, individuals who represent these legal entities (as a legal or permanent representative) would be covered.

Directors and officers whose term of office expires during the course of the D&O policy continue to benefit from the policy in relation to any actions, claims and legal actions arising out of, related to or in connection with the exercise of their duties as directors or officers. In the event of the death of a director or an officer, the guarantee passes to their heirs or successors. A D&O policy may also extend to *de facto* officers (*dirigeants de fait*).

4.1.2. *Nullification of Resolutions*

Nullification of resolutions is governed by Article L. 235-1 of the Commercial Code and concerns both general meetings and board resolutions. Indeed, French law provides specific grounds for nullification depending on whether the resolution in question would amend the companies' by-laws.

The nullification of resolutions amending the company's by-laws results from a breach of specific provisions clearly identified in the Commercial Code (known as 'express provisions'). Such a regime mainly concerns decisions of extraordinary general meetings (as they are empowered to amend the by-laws) or resolutions made by the board of directors or the managing board on behalf of share-holders (in practice, the extraordinary general meeting usually delegates its powers to the board to complete a capital increase).

Regarding other resolutions (appointment of directors, approval of board of directors etc.), the Commercial Code requires the breach of an 'imperative' provision. In such a case, since the imperative feature does not expressly result from the law, the court must construe the provision in question and decide whether it considers it as imperative. Most board resolutions are governed by this regime. For example, the nullification of a board decision may result from an irregular composition of the board or from the breach of directors' information rights.

In addition, please note that the nullification of a resolution is retroactive, but that neither the company nor the shareholders may oppose such nullification toward *bona fide* third parties.

4.1.3. Special Procedures and Issues

a) The 'Class Action' in France

The class action can be defined as 'the right of one member of a group of persons to pursue for all without the prior consent of each'.[158] Unlike inter alia American, English and Swedish law, French law does not provide for such a procedure.

However, its introduction is currently supported by the French Senate committee on finance[159] (*la Commission des finances du Sénat*)[160] and a draft bill was introduced on 22 December 2010 in that respect.[161] Although such draft bill would limit the scope of the collective action to consumer and antitrust law, the AMF recently issued a report promoting its extension to financial law.[162]

French law nevertheless provides legal instruments to defend a collective cause. Indeed, the French Consumer Code,[163] the CMF[164] and the Commercial Code enable specific associations to act on behalf, and for the benefit of, consumers, shareholders or investors.

---

[158] W.B. Fisch, 'Analogons to the class action: group action in France and Germany', 27 *American Journal of Comparative Law*, 51 [1979].

[159] The French Senate committee on finance issued a report dated May 2010.

[160] Which proposes a collective action relating to consumer law and to specific breaches of financial law.

[161] However, please note that such draft bill would limit the scope of the collective action to consumer and antitrust law.: Projet de loi n° 202 (2010-2011) de M. Richard Yung, and Projet de loi n° 201 (2010-2011) de M. Laurent Beteille.

[162] The AMF's Report on indemnification of loss suffered by savers and investors, 25 January 2011.

[163] Article L 421-1 du Code de Consommation.

[164] Article L.452-1 of the CMF.

According to the CMF, properly approved associations (by the public ministry and the AMF), whose purpose is the protection of investors in relation to transferable securities or financial products, may bring legal proceedings in any jurisdiction in order to compensate collective losses. If, in their capacity as investors, several natural persons have suffered individual damage having a common origin through the actions of the same person, any such association may, if it has been instructed by at least two of the investors concerned, sue for damages before any court on behalf of those investors.[165] However, the power so to act cannot be solicited via a public appeal on television or radio, nor via a poster campaign, tracts or personalised letters. It must be given in writing by each investor.

In practice, only one association has been approved and, so far, has not brought such a collective action.

As a general rule, ordinary associations actively defend their members and regularly bring legal proceedings. In the Vivendi case,[166] an association for the defence of minority shareholders (*ADAM*) brought a claim against Vivendi's CEO for a breach of US stock exchange regulations.

b) Securities Litigation

Securities litigation (mainly market abuse) is mainly brought before the AMF, the French securities regulator created in November 2003 from the merger of three national regulatory authorities, and sometimes before criminal jurisdictions (please note that cumulative actions are allowed).

As an independent public authority, the AMF regulates and polices French financial markets in order to protect savings and investments. It is empowered to conduct inspections and investigations into possible breaches of the obligations imposed by the laws or regulations or by professional rules intended to protect investors from insider trading, price rigging and dissemination of false information, including financial or even corporate governance comply-or-explain statements,[167] and any other breach likely to jeopardise investor protection or the proper operation of the market.[168]

Following such investigations, the AMF's Sanction Committee (*Commission des sanctions*) can initiate sanction proceedings against legal or natural persons who infringe French regulations (in particular the AMF general regulation) or that fail to fulfil their professional obligations. Financial penalties can go up to €100

---

[165]   Article L.452-2 of the CMF.

[166]   CA Paris, 2ᵉ ch., 28 April 2010, n°10/01643, SA Vivendi.

[167]   See Alain Pietrancosta, 'Enforcement of corporate governance codes: A legal perspective', *Festschrift für Klaus J. Hopt, Unternehmen, Markt und Verantwortung*, De Gruyter, 2010, p. 1109.

[168]   Article L.621-14 of the CMF.

million or ten times the amount of any profit realised; the sums are paid to the public treasury (*trésor public*).[169]

4.2. Regulators

Regulators also play an important role in the enforcement of corporate law. Under French law, two regulators may require listed companies to comply with corporate legal provisions.

a) The French Financial Markets Authority (AMF)

The AMF effectively contributes to the enforcement of corporate law through its general regulations and the issuance of reports.

Listed companies are legally required to provide a statement on corporate governance in their annual reports that indicates which corporate governance code the company voluntarily applies and explain why such company fails to apply a code.

In this respect, according to Article L. 621-18-3 of the CMF, the AMF has a statutory duty to draw up an annual report based on information on corporate governance and internal control published by corporate entities having their registered offices in France and whose financial securities are admitted to trading on a regulated market.

The AMF has already issued seven reports on corporate governance and executive compensation in listed companies. More recently, the regulator issued two new reports relating to the practices in small and medium-capital companies (with special reference to the new Middlenext code)[170] and to the indemnification of losses suffered by savers and investors.[171] As a general rule, such reports reflect a further improvement in French companies' corporate governance practices.

Therefore, by issuing corporate governance codes and monitoring their implementation, both private entities and the AMF respectively contribute to the enforcement of corporate law. Even though such division of tasks produces effective results, the AMF recently stated its wishes to extend its powers beyond the monitoring function, by playing a more active role in the formulation of corporate governance rules.

---

[169] Article L.621-15 of the CMF.

[170] AMF report, 7 December 2010.

[171] The AMF Report on indemnification of loss suffered by savers and investors, 25 January 2011.

b) The Prudential Control Authority (ACP)

The ACP was set up by an ordinance dated 21 January 2010 from the merger of the four previous banking and insurance licensing and supervisory authorities.[172]

As an independent administrative authority operating under the auspices of the French Central Bank (*Banque de France*), the ACP's mission is to provide stability for the financial system (supervision of prudential ratios) and to protect banking and insurance customers (supervision of business practices).

The ACP supervises the banking and insurance sectors by: (i) Monitoring credit, investment, payment institutions, banking intermediaries and insurance companies; and (ii) issuing recommendations.

For instance, in its annual report for 2009, Natixis indicates that its audit committee

'monitors the implementation of actions based on the conclusions of assignments by the Internal Audit department and Banking Commission [the predecessor of the ACP]; for this purpose, it may receive reports from the Internal Audit department and the Banking Commission concerning Natixis and its subsidiaries'.[173]

4.3. Self-Regulation

4.3.1. Corporate Governance Codes

The current corporate governance codes in force in France are the result of numerous reports and recommendations issued over the last few years.

In the last decade, several working groups have published successive reports to promote corporate governance in French listed companies and to propose non-binding codes of best practices for listed companies. The Vienot Report, published in 1995, was the first in a long series of such reports. These reports aim to strengthen the managing board's powers, improve transparency and promote specialised committees, especially audit, nomination and compensation committees.

In September 2002, the AFEP and MEDEF issued a report which focused on increasing the importance of board committees and on promoting the independence of board members.

These numerous initiatives resulted in business associations and organisations issuing several corporate governance codes. The AFEP/MEDEF Corporate Gov-

---

[172] The banking regulator (*Commission bancaire*), the insurance firms and mutuals regulator (*Autorité de contrôle des assurances et des mutuelles* – ACAM), and the two authorities responsible for the licensing of banking firms (*Comité des établissements de credit et des entreprises d'investissement* – CECEI) and insurance firms and mutuals (*Comité des enterprises d'assurance* – CEA).

[173] Natixis, 2009 Annual Report, p. 25.

ernance Code[174] is the most popular, but the French Institute of Directors (*Institut Français des Administrateurs – IFA*) has also made several proposals relating to the role of independent directors, audit committees and internal audit. The French Association of Financial Management (*Association Française de la Gestion Financière – AFG*) has contributed to this movement by publishing its *Recommendations on Corporate Governance*.[175] In addition, the MiddleNext organisation published a code of corporate governance in December 2009 designed for small and midcap companies. More recently, the MiddleNext Organisation, together with similar English and German associations, have identified thirteen common guidelines applicable to European small and midcap companies.

Although these corporate governance codes are not binding, French law n° 2008-649 of 3 July 2008, transposing Directive (2006/46/EC) of 14 June 2006, amending the 4th and 7th Company Law Directives, has introduced the comply-or-explain rule. Indeed, pursuant to article L. 225-37 of the Commercial Code:

'If a company voluntarily applies a corporate governance code drafted by a business representative organisation, the company's chairman's report should identify any provisions it has chosen not to apply and give the reason for doing so. The report should also indicate where the code can be consulted. If a company does not apply such a corporate governance code, the report should indicate the rules that it applies in addition to the statutory requirements, and explain why it chose not to apply any of the provisions of this corporate governance code.'

This regime lends strong weight to the enforcement of corporate governance codes.[176] According to the AMF, following a review of a sample of 60 companies listed on Euronext Paris, companies systematically refer to a corporate governance code. All of them refer to the AFEP/MEDEF Corporate Governance Code, 60% set aside some of the code's provisions, with 80% of those not complying providing an explanation for such divergence.[177]

Even though most listed companies apply the AFEP/MEDEF Corporate Governance Code, small and midcap companies tend to refer to the MiddleNext code. Of 30 small and midcaps companies identified by the AMF (7 listed on Compartment B and 23 listed on Compartment C of Euronext Paris), 27 used to apply the AFEP-MEDEF and recently adopted the MiddleNext code. Such a code differs from the AFEP-MEDEF corporate governance code on several points (directors with or without employment contracts, number of independent directors

---

[174] 2010 AMF Report on corporate governance and compensation of executive directors, dated December 2008, renewed in April 2010, December 2011 and October 2012.

[175] AFG, Recommendations on Corporate Governance, January 2012.

[176] See Yann Paclot, 'La juridicité du Code AFEPP-MEDEF de gouvernement d'entreprise des sociétés cotées', *Revue des sociétés* 2011 p. 395.

[177] AMF news release, dated 12 July 2010, on its 2010 report on corporate governance and directors' compensation.

limited to one or two members (for boards of directors composed of at least five members), optional setting up of specialised committees) and better corresponds to the smaller size of midcap companies by giving them more flexibility.[178]

4.3.2.   Does the System of Comply-or-explain Produce Effective Results?

As a general rule, listed companies usually comply with French corporate governance codes. The AFEP/MEDEF's second annual report dated November 2010 indicates that most SBF 120 and CAC 40 companies mostly comply with its recommendations.

Indeed, 100% of listed companies disclose the required information relating to managers' compensation (criteria of performance, allocation of termination payments), and provide internal rules or a code of ethics applicable to the board of directors.

In addition, the level of compliance of such companies can also be illustrated by the following table on members of the board of directors:

Information relating to directors (disclosed in the companies' annual reports)[179]

Information disclosed	SBF 120		CAC 40	
	2010	2011	2010	2011
Beginning of director's office	100%	100%	100%	100%
Term of director's office	99%	100%	100%	100%
Age of directors	98%	97%	100%	100%
Role of directors	100%	100%	100%	100%
Offices held in other companies	100%	100%	100%	100%
Number of shares held by directors	97%	96%	100%	100%
Biography of directors	92%	95%	94%	97%

However, although such results appear very encouraging, some weaknesses still remain and need to be resolved.[180]

---

[178] Even though the MiddleNext code provides more flexible rules on board committees than the AFEP/MEDEF code, it restricts the number of office directors to 4 compared to 5 in the AFEF/MEDEF code. For further information, please refer to Catherine Malecki, 'Le premier regard de l'AMF sur la pratique du Code de gouvernement d'entreprise de MiddleNext', *Bulletin Joly Bourse*, March 2011 n°3 p. 197.

[179] 2nd AFEP/MEDEF Annual Report, dated November 2012, p. 17.

[180] See below.

5. The Dynamics of Change

5.1. Reform Movements/Current Trends

a) Weaknesses in the System

Compliance with corporate governance codes—Listed companies' compliance with corporate governance principles remains incomplete.

For instance, out of a sample of 60 companies reviewed by the AMF, 40% do not comply with the required ratio of two-thirds of independent directors within the audit committee.[181] The AMF is also asking for more transparency from listed companies on the roles, experience and competence of independent[182] or lead directors, and more detailed information on the implementation of the comply-or-explain rule. The French Financial Market Authority also recommends that companies should precisely define the tasks of board chairmen.

For their part, shareholders tend to question the efficiency of the board of directors and expect more information on their criteria of selection, roles and compensation. According to a 2011 poll,[183] 62% of shareholders consider that the boards do not properly exercise their functions (compared to 82% in 2010).

The composition and diversity of French boards of directors or supervisory boards also needs to be improved. Although listed companies have attempted to diversify the composition of their boards,[184] most directors still graduate from the same prestigious business, engineering, or top civil servant schools. The directors who hold the highest number of directorships have graduated from the National School of Administration (*École Nationale d'Administration*).[185] Ninety-eight individuals represent 43% of all directors of CAC 40 companies. In addition, according to the OFG Research's analysis carried out on the basis of 70 listed companies, 48 directors still hold simultaneously at least three directorships and some directors hold up to seven directorships (beyond the recommendations of the AFEP/MEDEF Corporate Governance Code). In addition, more than 90

---

[181] See 2012 AMF Report on corporate governance and internal control, 11 October 201, p. 58.

[182] The AMF highlights the need to provide detailed and sufficiently clear explanations about the application of the independence criteria in the AFEP/MEDEF code, especially the criteria on business relations: 'not to be a customer, supplier, investment banker or commercial banker that is material for the corporation or its group, or for a significant part of whose business the corporation or its group accounts'.

[183] See Capitalcom, *6ème baromètre annuel*, 16 March 2011.

[184] In 2009, boards of listed companies comprised: 24% non-residents, 11.4% women and 3% academics and professors.

[185] See 2009 Ernst & Young's Report *Panorama des pratiques de gouvernance des Bigcaps françaises*, p. 12 and in particular the composition of CNP Assurance's board of directors.

directors hold an office in other CAC 40 companies. Even though the AFEP/
MEDEF Corporate Governance Code recommends that directors should not agree
to hold more than four additional directorships in listed corporations, several
directors exceed the required limits.

The striking image below shows the multiple connections which exist
between the boards of CAC 40 companies.

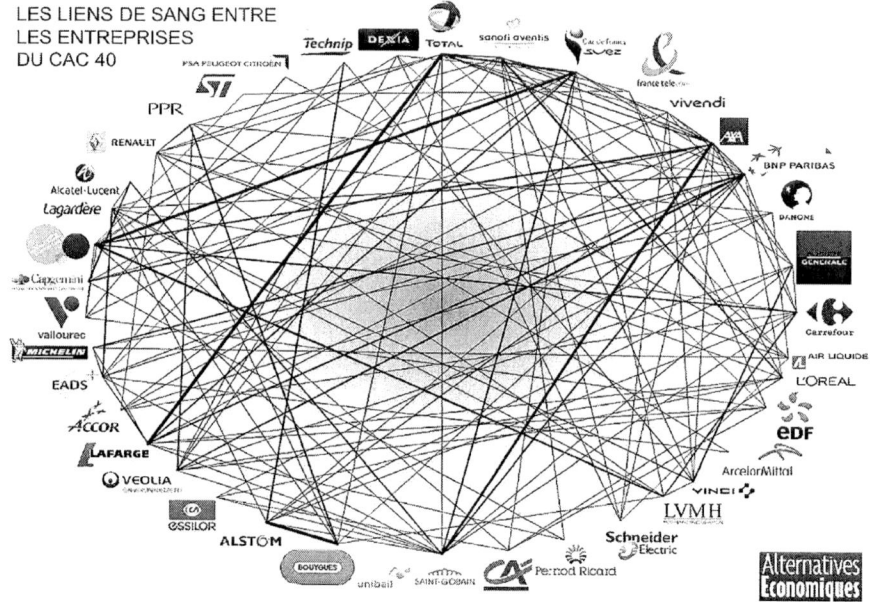

LES LIENS DE SANG ENTRE LES ENTREPRISES DU CAC 40

In 2010, all CAC 40 companies (except Unibail Rodamco) had at least one director in common.

*Concentration of power with the chief executive of French listed companies and
appointment of a 'senior independent director'*—A growing number of CAC 40
companies, which had previously adopted a system of management by a separate
chairman and CEO, are now choosing to combine these roles under the authority
of a single individual,[186] while counterbalancing this concentration of power with
the appointment of a senior independent director (sometimes also referred to as a
vice chairman or reference director). However, some two-tier model companies[187]
also decided to appoint such an individual.

---

[186] See sec. 1.3 for further information.

[187] See Schneider (available at: <http://www2.schneider-electric.com/sites/corporate/en/fi
nance/general-information/corporate-governance/supervisory-board.page>) and Vallourec, avail-

cont. ...

The concept of a senior independent director, which originates from the UK's Combined Code of Corporate Governance (the Combined Code), does not exist under French law. An increasing number of corporate boards of CAC 40 companies are nevertheless adopting the role with a view to conforming to best practices in corporate governance. Furthermore, the trade association representing the French asset management industry (the *Association Française de la Gestion Financière*) recommended in January 2010 that companies that do not have a separation of powers: (i) Explain to their shareholders why the two functions are not separated; and (ii) appoint an independent lead director who would monitor conflicts of interest and report on them at the general meeting.

Many listed companies (Accor, Axa, Carrefour, Lafarge, LVMH, Renault, Schneider, Technip, Vallourec, Veolia Environnement, Vinci, Société Générale) proceeded with appointments reflecting this trend, some of them drawing inspiration from the British model and the definition of senior independent director set out in the Combined Code. For instance, the senior independent director should be available to shareholders if they have concerns that the normal channels of contacting the chairman, chief executive or finance director have failed to resolve the issue or where such channels are inappropriate; and non-managing directors should meet without the chairman present at least annually, under the leadership of the senior independent director, in order to appraise the chairman's performance.

At Axa, the lead independent director has a number of specific powers including the capacity:

- to require the chairman and CEO to convene full meetings of the board of directors on a specific agenda at any time;
- to convene meetings of the non-executive directors at any time without the attendance of the chairman and CEO and the deputy CEO;
- to attend and participate in all meetings of Board Committees (regardless of whether or not he is a Committee member);
- to inform the chairman and the board of directors about any potential conflicts of interest;
- to report to Axa's shareholders' meetings with respect to all corporate governance related matters.

Remuneration: transparency and performance criteria—In its 2012 annual report on corporate governance and executive compensation, the AMF notes some progress in the corporate governance of listed companies. However. it emphasises the standardisation of explanations on changes of governance structures, showing a lack of details on the characteristics of the relevant companies. For instance, it emphasises the fact that being a director of a company for more that twelve years

able at: <http://www.vallourec.com/fr/groupe/gouvernance/conseil-de-surveillance/ConseildeSur veillance.aspx>).

cannot only be justified by the mere professional experience of the relevant individual.

In addition, the AMF underlines the progress made in respect of the determination and transparency of the remuneration of CEOs/chairmen of the managing board and reasserts its recommendations.

On the information to be published on remuneration, the AMF states that companies provide increasingly precise and specific explanations.

In relation to stock-options and performance shares, the AMF reminds that their allotment should be subject to serious and demanding performance criteria, which should relate to both internal and external factors.[188]

In relation to pension schemes, the AMF considers that significant progress must still be made (37% of the 60 companies reviewed were satisfactory in 2011, compared to 30% in 2009).

The AMF finally recommends that professional associations amend their governance codes to take into account all forms of pension schemes, miscellaneous fees, retention plans, cash incentives, and all types of ad hoc variable remunerations, that they do not yet oversee.

b) Forthcoming Bill/Regulations

A legislative bill[189], relating to the establishment of compensation committees in listed companies, was debated in the Senate on 20 October 2009. The bill requires listed companies to set up a compensation committee composed of members of the board of directors or members of the supervisory board (who have no management functions) among which one member must be independent. Such committee would issue recommendations on the compensation policies applicable to legal representatives (*mandataires sociaux*), in particular for the definition of their variable remunerations.[190]

Also, legislative bills dated 19 October 2010[191] and 24 March 2011 intend to reduce the number of directorships that a natural person may hold, including in foreign companies.

In addition, please note that the introduction of a class action mechanism is currently being debated in France. Draft bills[192] and reports[193] have recently been issued to support its establishment in French law.[194]

---

[188] Rémunération dans les sociétés anonymes – Proposition de loi n° 47 (2009–2010) dated 20 octobre 2009.

[189] Rémunération dans les sociétés anonymes – Proposition de loi n° 47 (2009–2010) dated 20 octobre 2009.

[190] Note that the AFEP/MEDEF Corporate Governance Code already recommends the establishment of such a committee (please refer to section 3.1.5 for further information).

[191] Proposition de loi N° 2871 de M. Jacques Domergue limitant le cumul de mandats sociaux dans les sociétés cotées.

5.2. Summary of Main Findings

French listed joint-stock companies may have two different forms of corporate governance, based either on a one-tier system or a two-tier system. The unitary structure consists of a board of directors (*conseil d'administration*), headed by a chairman and a chief executive officer (*directeur général*) who runs the company. The dual structure, directly inspired by the German legal system, consists of a managing board (*directoire*) composed of up to five members who run the company, and a separate supervisory board (*conseil de surveillance*) that oversees the managing board. If the unitary structure is by far the most widely-used form of governance of ordinary French joint-stock companies, the idea of a clearer distinction between the management and the supervision functions has progressively made its way as a sound corporate governance practice for listed companies. As a result, the traditional management structure combining the roles of CEO and chairman of the board of directors under the authority of a single individual is decreasing and only corresponds to half of listed companies.

In this framework, corporate governance has also changed over recent years through amendments to the French Commercial Code and the French Monetary and Financial Code.[195] Recommendations by professional associations have also played an increasing role. Although the corporate governance codes are not binding, European directives have introduced the comply-or-explain rule that lends strong weight to their enforcement. Such recommendations deal, in particular, with board composition and the proportion of independent directors, board committees, conflicts of interest, and evaluation of board members and their remuneration. Laws have been passed recently to reinforce these recommendations, in particular requiring the setting up of audit committees and by providing for strict rules on remuneration.

However, French listed companies not only need to improve their corporate governance, in particular regarding diversity in the composition of their boards (board members still tend to be graduates from the same schools, with a strong majority of males), but also the characteristics of their remuneration and the transparency of the information related to remuneration. Shareholders have recently expressed resentment regarding directors of distressed companies being granted substantial sums of money, in particular as 'golden parachutes' (see recent Société Générale and Thomson cases). This illustrates that issues remain regarding the composition and operation of boards of directors which are still not

---

[192] Draft bill dated 22 December 2010.

[193] In particular, the AMF Report on indemnification of loss suffered by savers and investors, 25 January 2011.

[194] See sec. 4.1.3(a) for further information.

[195] Code monétaire et financier.

able to efficiently control their CEOs. The fact that CEOs increasingly also hold the positions of chairman of the board, and the connections between the boards of listed companies, may render the board's control even more difficult to exercise.

5.3. List of Key Issues

'Soft law' and legal requirements—Corporate governance is increasingly ruled by recommendations issued by professional associations, which are set out in corporate governance codes, in particular the AFEP/MEDEF Corporate Governance Code. Although these codes are not binding, the comply-or-explain rule lends strong weight to their enforcement. It should also be noted that an increasing number of laws have been passed to reinforce these recommendations. There is an interesting dynamic between hard law, soft law, comply-or-explain and public and private supervision. A number of factors influence these changes, in particular, increasingly important holdings by foreign investors in French listed companies and the tendency for the capital of such companies to be more widely-held than before.

One-tier/two-tier system—A large majority of listed companies have chosen the one-tier system with a CEO and a board of directors and have decided that the CEO should also be the chairman of the board of directors. The economic crisis has further reinforced this trend. This is not best practice in corporate governance. To counterbalance the power of the CEO-chairman, companies tend to appoint a senior independent director (sometimes also referred to as a vice chairman or reference director).

Executive and non-executive directors/independent and non-independent directors—The concept of executive or non-executive director, referring to board members who occupy, or who do not occupy, top management positions in the company, does not exist under French law, which merely refers to the distinction between directors with or without an employment contract. In addition, in its approach to corporate governance French law prefers the notion of independent directors as opposed to directors who are not independent. By definition, an executive director cannot be an independent director, but all non-executive directors do not necessarily qualify as independent directors. The AFEP/MEDEF Corporate Governance Code recommends that independent directors account for half of the board in widely-held corporations without controlling shareholders, whereas they should account for at least a third in closely controlled companies. It also recommends that when an employee becomes a director, his employment contract may be terminated.

Board committees—The setting up of board committees (audit committee, compensation committee, nomination committee, accounting committee) is recommended by the AFEP/MEDEF Corporate Governance Code. It should be noted that the Commercial Code has now reinforced this recommendation by imposing the establishment of an audit committee and rules regarding its members.

Decision-making process—Decisions are taken by a majority vote of the directors. The by-laws may only depart from this rule by requiring a higher majority. In particular, they cannot grant multiple voting rights to a director nor deprive a director of his voting right.

Conflicts of interest—In addition to the approval procedure applicable to agreements entered into by the company and its directors, the AFEP/MEDEF Corporate Governance Code recommends that directors report any conflicts of interest they are aware of to the board. This recommendation is widely taken up in boards' internal rules.

Remuneration of the CEO/chairman of the board—The AFEP/MEDEF Corporate Governance Code gives a number of recommendations relating to fixed and variable remuneration, the granting of stock-options and performance shares, and the termination payments the CEO receives. The Commercial Code has recently taken into account these recommendations in particular in relation to golden parachutes, by prohibiting any termination payments that are not based on the performance of the beneficiary as a manager of the company. Remuneration and transparency practices are still in need of improvement, in particular in relation to pension schemes, stock-options and performance shares.[196]

Board composition and diversity—Although listed companies have attempted to diversify the composition of their boards, most directors still originate from the same prestigious business, engineering, or top civil servant schools. The directors who hold the highest number of directorships have graduated from the National School of Administration (*École Nationale d'Administration*), with a majority of male directors.

On the gender diversity front, the French Parliament has passed a law, dated 27 January 2011,[197] which calls for a more balanced gender representation in the governing bodies of French listed companies. To prepare the entry into force of this bill, an increasing number of listed companies have recently been adjusting their corporate governance practices, in an effort to move to a balanced representation of men and women on their boards.

Multiple connections between the boards of CAC 40 companies—More than 90 directors hold an office in other CAC 40 companies. Even though the AFEP/

---

[196] See *Société Générale* case (Daniel Bouton), *Valeo* case (Thierry Morin) and *Thomson* case (Frank Dangeard).

[197] Loi n° 2011-103 du 27 janvier 2011 relative à la représentation équilibrée des femmes et des hommes au sein des conseils d'administration et de surveillance et à l'égalité professionnelle.

MEDEF Corporate Governance Code recommends that directors should not agree to hold more than four additional directorships in listed corporations, several directors exceed the required limits.

New law on banking and financial regulation for the setting up of compensation and risk committees—The Law of 22 October 2010 on banking and financial regulation requires that banks and insurance companies set up a compensation committee and a risk committee.

Setting up of a code of good practice by the AMF on insider dealing—In November 2010, the AMF issued a code of good practice on the prevention of insider dealings committed by legal representatives of listed companies. It recommends that its provisions be integrated into the non-binding corporate governance codes issued by professional associations. In particular, companies are advised to issue ethics codes, appoint a compliance officer, set out closed periods during which directors may not buy or sell a company's shares and ensure that directors use trading plans when they deal with their company's shares.

6. Selection of Literature

AFEP/MEDEF, *Corporate Governance Code,* April 2010.

AFEP/MEDEF, *Annual Report,* December 2012.

AFG, *Recommandations sur le gouvernement d'entreprise,* 2012.

AFG, *Exercice des droits de vote par les sociétés de gestion en 2010,* 8 February 2011.

AMF, *Report on corporate governance and internal control,* 11 October 2012.

AMF, *Report on corporate governance and compensation of executive directors,* 11 October 2012.

Cathiard, C., 'Société européenne, fusions transfrontalières: bilan de la pratique et perspectives d'avenir', *Journ. societies,* December 2007, p. 58.

Ernst & Young, *Panorama des pratiques de gouvernance des Bigcaps françaises,* 2009.

Ernst & Young, *Panorama des pratiques de gouvernance des sociétés cotées françaises,* 2009.

Fisch, W.B. 'Analogons to the class action: group action in France and Germany', 27 *American Journal of Comparative Law,* 51 (1979).

IFA, *Note de synthèse de la commission Déontologie de l'IFA: Administrateurs et conflits d'intérêts,* November 2010.

IFA, 'Relations entre Direction Générale et Conseil d'administration sur les sujets de communication financière', *Recueil de Bonnes Pratiques,* September 2010.

Le Roux, J., 'La détention par les non-résidents des actions des sociétés françaises du CAC 40 à fin 2009', *Bulletin de la Banque de France,* n°180, 2nd Semester 2010.

Omnidroit, lettre 'Prévenir et gérer les conflits d'intérêts dans les sociétés', 16 March 2011.

Paclot Y., 'La juridicité du Code AFEPP-MEDEF de gouvernement d'entreprise des sociétés cotées', *Revue des sociétés* 2011, p. 395.

Pietrancosta, A., 'Enforcement of corporate governance codes: A legal perspective', *Festschrift für Klaus J. Hopt, Unternehmen, Markt und Verantwortung,* De Gruyter, 2010, p. 1109.

Proxinvest, *Principes de gouvernance et politique de vote*, 2012.

Proxinvest, *2012 general meetings of French listed companies. Proxinvest, Agence de conseil de vote: www. Proxinvest.com.*

Tonello, M. 'The Professionalization of Shareholder Activism in France', The Conference Board, on 13 March 2011, *Harvard Law School Forum on Corporate Governance and Financial Regulation*. Available at <http://blogs.law.harvard.edu/corpgov/2011/03/13/the-professionalization-of-shareholder-activism-in-france>.

Wolker, D., *A review of corporate governance in UK banks and other financial industry entities,* Final Recommendations, dated 26 November 2009. Available at <http://webarchive.nationalarchives.gov.uk/+/http:/www.hmtreasury.gov.uk/d/walker_review_261109.pdf>.

Corporate Boards in Germany

MARKUS ROTH[*]

---

[*] I thank Martin Wilhelm for language revision.

1. General Introduction[1]

German boards traditionally serve as a role model[2] in the international and interdisciplinary corporate governance debate.[3] Since most listed companies are incorporated under the German Stock Corporation Act (*Aktiengesetz* – AktG),[4] a two-tier system with a mandatory division of powers between a management and a supervisory board[5] applies. Roughly, the control function is attributed to the supervisory board while the management board runs the affairs of the company. The German Corporate Governance Code[6] stresses the co-operation of the two boards, which are balanced and linked to each other.[7] Although the two boards are generally composed of different persons, the members of the management board routinely attend the meetings of the supervisory board at full length.[8] The supervisory board is excluded from managing the company but has veto rights and the duty to advise the management board.[9]

The typical supervisory board of a larger German firm is not (super)majority independent[10] in international terms, but subject to a co-determination system with up to (quasi-)parity board level employee representation, which is unique worldwide. In larger enterprises with more than 2,000 employees in Germany the

---

[1] This report states the law as at the beginning of 2013, but the amended version of the German Corporate Governance Code which was approved on May 13, has been taken into account.

[2] For German corporate governance in the 1990s, see K.J. Hopt, 'The German Two-Tier Board: Experience, Theories, Reforms' in Hopt et al (eds.), *Comparative Corporate Governanc The State of the Art and Emerging Research* (Oxford, Clarendon Press 1998) 227. For a more technical description in English, see J.J. du Plessis and I. Saenger, 'The Supervisory Board as Company Organ' in J.J. du Plessis et al, *German Corporate Governance in International and European Context*, 2nd edn. (Heidelberg, Springer 2012) 91.

[3] For a current analysis K.J. Hopt, 'Comparative Corporate Governance: The State of the Art and International Regulation', *American Journal of Comparative Law* 59 (2011) 1.

[4] Aktiengesetz (AktG), 6.9.1965, BGBl (Federal Gazette) I 1089: Stock Corporation Act, English translations by Norton Rose LLP (2011, available at <www.nortonrose.com/files/german-stock-corporation-act-2010-english-translation-pdf-59656.pdf >) and Wirth et al, *Corporate Law in Germany*, 2nd revised edn. (Munich, C.H Beck 2010).

[5] Sections 76–94, 95–116 Stock Corporation Act (AktG), see below 2.1, 2.2.2.

[6] German Corporate Governance Code, as amended on 13 May 2013 (German Corporate Governance Code 2013) and promulgated in the Federal Gazette on 10 June 2013 (BAnz AT 10.6.2013 B3).

[7] German Corporate Governance Code, Chapter 3.

[8] See below 2.2.2(c), 2.2.2(e), 2.3(e).

[9] Section 111(4)2 Stock Corporation Act, see below 2.2.2(b).

[10] For supermajority independent boards in the US, see J.F. Gordon, 'The Rise of Independent Directors in the United States, 1950–2005: Of Shareholder Value and Stock Market Prices', *Stanford Law Review* 59 (2007) 1465, 1476; for the German boards, see below 2.2.3.

Co-Determination Act 1976[11] applies, employees must be represented by half of the number of the board's members.[12] Co-determination also contributes to German boards being the largest, at least in major European countries,[13] with up to twenty members.[14] Moreover, co-determination indicates that the interests of stakeholders are also taken into account. While the stakeholder approach is widely accepted in German literature, the modern view, also in Germany, is best described as an enlightened shareholder value approach.[15]

The two-tier system and large boards due to co-determination are still characteristic for larger enterprises. This will not change in the short term, although the European Company is the fastest growing form of incorporation for listed companies. In Europe, Germany is the country which hosts the most Societas Europaea (SE), meaning European Companies with at least five employees.[16] The success of the European Company can be explained in part also by the more flexible co-determination regime than in Germany and the availability of the one-tier board. The European Company influences German business law in general. Academics are calling for a more flexible co-determination regime, also incorporating staff employed in other European countries.[17] Recently, the one-tier board has been proposed to apply to stock corporations incorporated under the German Stock Corporation Act.[18]

Ownership structure and corporate governance is subject to international developments, and both have changed in recent years.[19] The majority of the German blue chips (DAX 30 companies) have a dispersed ownership. The German Corporate Governance Code stresses the co-operation between the boards. The interaction of institutional investors and supervisory directors is still subject to

---

[11] Gesetz über die Mitbestimmung der Arbeitnehmer (Mitbestimmungsgesetz – MitbestG), 4.5.1976, BGBl I 1153. English translation by S. Lingemann, R. von Steinau-Steinrück and A. Mengel, *Employment & Labor Law in Germany*, 3rd edn. (Munich, C.H. Beck, 2012), 380-405.

[12] Section 7(1) Co-Determination Act (MitbestG), see below 2.2.1(c), 3.2.1(a).

[13] Heidrick & Struggles, *Challenging board performance* (2011) 37.

[14] Section 7(2) Co-Determination Act (MitbestG), see below 2.2.1(b).

[15] See below 3.2.1(a).

[16] ETUI (European Trade Union Institute), *Overview of current state of SE founding in Europe*, 1 October 2012: 105 out of 223 'normal' SE; see below 1.1(e).

[17] Arbeitskreis 'Unternehmerische Mitbestimmung' (G. Bachmann, T. Baums, M. Habersack, M. Henssler, M. Lutter, H. Oetker and P. Ulmer), 'Entwurf einer Regelung zur Mitbestimmungsvereinbarung sowie zur Größe des mitbestimmten Aufsichtsrats', *Zeitschrift für Wirtschaftsrecht* 2009, 885; see below 3.2.1(d), 5.3(a).

[18] German Jurists Forum 2012, Business Law Section, see below 1.3(d).

[19] See below 1.1(a).

debate. Direct contact between institutional shareholders and supervisory directors is viewed with reluctance, at least by some in practice and academia.[20]

1.1. Environment in which Boards Operate

a) Ownership Structure

Corporate governance in Germany—the environment in which boards operate and especially the ownership structure—has been subject to changes in the last century. The current system is best described as a *duality of dispersed ownership and family controlled firms*. Before World War I, the stock market in Germany was even more predominant than in the US.[21] After World War II, the 'German Inc.' corporate governance system (*Deutschland AG*), which was dominated by banks (*Hausbanken*) and blockholdings even in German blue chips,[22] evolved due to capital shortage and political pressure.[23] Since the 1990s, the blockholdings, cross-ownerships and personal ties among the largest firms have been declining, leaving most DAX 30 companies with a dispersed ownership structure and a high proportion of foreign institutional investors.[24] The German Government facilitated the dissolution of equity ties among German firms by removing taxes on selling stock of other firms in 2000.[25] Allianz and Munich Re gave up their inter-

---

[20] Such contacts are recommended in the UK; UK Corporate Governance Code 2012, Code Provisions E.1.1, E.1.2, see below 2.3(c).

[21] R.G. Rajan and L. Zingales, 'The great reversals: the politics of financial development in the twentieth century', *Journal of Financial Economics* 69 (2003) 5, 15.

[22] See K.J. Hopt, 'Two Tier Board' in Hopt et al (eds.), *Comparative Corporate Governance* (see n. 2) 246; S. Prigge, 'A Survey of German Corporate Governance', in Hopt et al (eds.), *Comparative Corporate Governance* (see n. 2) 943.

[23] M.J. Roe, 'Legal Origins, Politics, and Modern Stock Markets', *Harvard Law Review* 120 (2006) 460, 502; W. Gerke, F. Mager and T. Förstermann, 'Die Rolle von Finanzintermediären bei der Corporate Governance im Wandel', in P. Hommelhoff, K.J. Hopt and A. von Werder (eds.), *Handbuch Corporate Governance,* 2nd edn. (Stuttgart and Cologne, Schäffer-Pöschel and Otto Schmidt 2009) 503, 506.

[24] For data, see the BaFin database on 'Bedeutende Stimmrechtsanteile an inländischen Gesellschaften, die zum Handel an einem organisierten Markt zugelassen sind', DAI Factbook, Deutsche Bundesbank *Statistik über Wertpapierinvestments* (June 2012) 28: market value of domestic equity €1,105,140 million, foreign investors: €521,006 million and the recent study of K. Fehre, M.S. Rapp, B. Schwetzler and M.O. Sperling, 'The Disappearing "Deutschland AG" – An analysis of block holdings in German large Caps', *Problems and Perspectives in Management* 9:4 (2011) 46, (<http://ssrn.com/abstract=1100582>), cited data from websites of BaFin, Deutsche Börse, other German stock exchanges and the DAX 30 companies (December 2012 and January 2013).

[25] Gesetz zur Senkung der Steuersätze und zur Reform der Unternehmensbesteuerung (Steuersenkungsgesetz – StSenkG), 23.10.2000, BGBl (German Federal Gazette) I 1433.

locking participation and Deutsche Bank, like the other banks and insurance companies, diversified its investments by selling significant stakes in German stock corporations such as Daimler. This led to the disintegration of the traditional 'Rhine capitalism' practiced in Germany.[26]

Today two-thirds of the DAX 30 companies have a dispersed ownership structure. Of these, fourteen companies have no significant shareholder holding ten per cent or more;[27] two companies have only international investors, such as Berkshire Hathaway (Warren Buffet)[28] or Blackrock,[29] holding more than ten per cent of the capital; and in four companies the majority of the share capital is in dispersed ownership and the company is not controlled by a family or foundation.[30] One DAX 30 company is at least *de facto* controlled by another DAX 30 company.[31] The enduring dominance of family-owned firms and the presence of controlling shareholders in most other firms are best illustrated by the fact that the number of companies in dispersed ownership in the DAX 30 is almost identical to the number of companies in dispersed ownership among the hundred largest German enterprises.[32] Not even the majority of the hundred biggest German firms in terms of revenues are in dispersed ownership but have a foreign majority stockholder (twenty-six), are family owned (twenty-one) or owned by the state (thirteen).[33] Non-listed family-owned companies (especially medium-sized ones) play an important role in German business. In Germany, there is comparably little pressure for diversification due to inheritance tax and only a moderate tax incentive for

---

[26] For case studies dating back to the 1980s, see W. Streeck and M. Höpner (eds.), *Alle Macht dem Markt?, Fallstudien zur Abwicklung der Deutschland AG* (Frankfurt, Campus 2003).

[27] Adidas, Allianz, BASF, Bayer, Daimler (Kuwait 7.6%, Renault and Nissan 3.1%), Deutsche Bank, Deutsche Börse, Deutsche Lufthansa, Eon, Infinion (Dedge & Cox 9.95%, Capital Group 8.02%, Blackrock 5.08%), Kali + Salz: Meritus Trust 9.98%, Blackrock 5.08%, Linde, SAP (from the founders: Plattner 9.95%, Tschira 7.58%, Hopp 6.13%), Siemens (Siemens family around 6%); only selected shareholdings close to ten per cent are stated here.

[28] Munich Re: Berkshire Hathaway (Warren Buffet): 11.2%.

[29] Lanxess: Blackrock 10.08%.

[30] In these companies the majority of the share capital is in dispersed ownership: Commerzbank (Soffin/Federal Republic of Germany 25.00%), Deutsche Post (Kreditanstalt für Wiederaufbau 25.5%), Deutsche Telekom (KfW 16.87%, Federal Republic of Germany 14.83%, Blackstone 4.40%), RWE (RWE Beteiligungsgesellschaft 16.00%, Blackrock 5.31%.

[31] Fresenius Medical Care (Fresenius 35.69%), formerly also MAN: Volkswagen controls 75% of the voting shares in MAN.

[32] Identified by the German Monopolies Commission. In its report of June 2012, the German Monopolies Commission names a total of 21 companies with the majority of shares in dispersed ownership (largest companies not according to market capitalisation but to value creation), *Neunzehntes Hauptgutachten der Monopolkommission 2010/2011*, BTDrucks (German Parliamentary Papers) 17/10365, p. 29, 153 et seq.

[33] Monopolies Commission (see n. 32) 29, 165.

investments in equity-linked private pension products.[34] The number of directorships of managing directors of the 100 largest German enterprises in the
supervisory board of other companies among such enterprises declined by over fifty
per cent from 1996 to 2008 (external supervisory directorships by managing
directors from banks and insurance companies fell by eighty per cent),[35] while cross
holdings among the 100 largest German firms dropped from 143 to 37.[36] Until the
1990s, bank representation was a characteristic of German corporate governance.[37]

Family ownership in traditional and new industries is also prevalent for listed
companies.[38] Families and foundations control (at least *de facto*) a third of the
DAX 30 companies.[39] Founder directors are not as important as in the US;[40] SAP
is the only founder-director-company in the DAX 30. It is also the only company
having no ties to old business families or predecessor-companies founded in
World War II or earlier. Generally, traditional industrial firms (MAN[41] can be
traced back to 1758), banks and other financial institutions (bofi) dominate the
DAX 30 but not the MDAX. In some privatised companies, such as Deutsche
Post, Deutsche Telekom and Volkswagen, the State[42] still holds substantial shareholdings directly or via the state owned bank, *Kreditanstalt für Wiederaufbau*
(*KfW*). Just before the financial crisis, there was a trend towards (*de facto*)
controlling stakes in other industrial DAX 30 companies by family owned
firms.[43] Also due to the outbreak of the financial crisis, some acquirers got into

---

[34] For the UK, see B.R. Cheffins, *Corporate Ownership and Control, British Business
Transformed* (Oxford, OUP 2008) 346–349 and S.A. Bank and B.R. Cheffins, 'Tax and the
Separation of Ownership and Control', in W. Schön (ed.), *Tax and Corporate Governance*
(Heidelberg and Berlin, Springer 2008) 111, 115–145.

[35] Monopolies Commission (see n. 32) 180.

[36] Monopolies Commission (see n. 32) 171.

[37] K.J. Hopt, 'Two Tier Board', in Hopt et al *Comparative Corporate Governance* (see
n. 2) 245–246.

[38] The Quandt and Klatten families in BMW, traditionally the Haniel and Schmidt-
Ruthenbeck families with recently extended stakes in Metro (now MDAX), and recently the
Porsche and Piëch families in VW (both families have invested in Porsche Holding SE).

[39] Beiersdorf, BMW, Fresenius, Fresenius Medical Care, HeidelbergCement, Henkel, Merck,
Metro, ThyssenKrupp, and Volkswagen.

[40] For the US, see F. Li and S. Srinivasen, 'Corporate governance when founders are directors', *Journal of Financial Economics* 102 (2011) 454.

[41] This has recently become a Volkswagen subsidiary but is still listed on the MDAX.

[42] The Federal Republic—in the case of Volkswagen, the state of Lower Saxony.

[43] Porsche holds fifty per cent of the voting rights of VW; VW holds 75 per cent of MAN;
Schaeffler holds 75 per cent of Continental.

financial trouble.[44] However, even taking these instances into account, there is little pressure from hostile takeovers.[45]

Until now, Germany has a small basis of shareholders, still in decline after the financial crisis[46] and low market capitalisation as compared to gross domestic product.[47] That was different before World War I when the ratio of market capitalisation to gross domestic product in Germany was higher than that of the US.[48] The reservation about equity may be rooted in the volatility of German equity, which is traditionally high.[49] Unlike in the UK, where Keynes promoted investments of life-insurance companies in equity,[50] German life-insurance companies and occupational pension providers are reluctant about equity investments.[51] This is also driven by the investment rules in the Insurance Supervision Act[52] that also covers pension funds and *Pensionskassen*.[53] The absence of German institutional investors in the equity market and the presence of international institutional investors have shaped the ownership structure since the dissolution of the old Deutschland AG. Virtually all German DAX 30 companies in dispersed

---

[44] Porsche Holding SE had to sell the manufacturer to VW, while Schaeffler and Continental had to restructure their debt.

[45] But some first hostile takeover attempts were successful after being transformed into friendly takeovers or mergers: Mannesmann by Vodafone as the world largest ever merger, Continental by Schaeffler and the merger between Thyssen and Krupp.

[46] Only 8.2 million people in Germany (12.6% of the population) hold equities either directly or indirectly via investment funds (DAI Kurzstudie 1/2011) down from 12.9 million in 2001.

[47] According to Deutsche Börse (Cash Market, monthly statistics, December 2011, 41) the total market capitalisation of all domestic equity was €912,490 million (Deutsche Bundesbank *Statistik für Wertpapierinvestments*, June 2012: €1,105,140 million), and gross domestic product was about €2,570,000 million at the end of 2011 (Statistisches Bundesamt, *Statistisches Jahrbuch 2012*, 317).

[48] For the great reversals, see Rajan and Zingales (n. 21).

[49] *Global Investment Returns Yearbook 2008*, Synopsis, 4: highest volatility of industrialised countries between 1900 and 2007.

[50] J.M. Keynes, 'Zur Entwicklung der Anlagen britischer Lebensversicherungsgesellschaften von 1900 bis 1965', *Zeitschrift für die gesamte Versicherungswissenschaft*, 1927, 32, 39. Keynes was also an advisor for life-insurance companies.

[51] Direct equity holdings were 0.5% of the assets of all insurance companies, BaFin Annual Report 11, 112.

[52] Gesetz über die Beaufsichtigung der Versicherungsunternehmen (Versicherungsaufsichtsgesetz – VAG), 12 May 1901, version of 17 December 1992, BGBl 1993 I 2, English translation by the German Federal Financial Supervisory Authority (BaFin), 2007, available at <www.bafin.de/SharedDocs/Aufsichtsrecht/EN/Gesetz/vag_010512_va_en.html>.

[53] For a critical view, see M. Roth, *Private Altersvorsorge – Eine Gesamtschau des Betriebsrentenrechts und des Rechts der individuellen Vorsorge* (Tübingen, Mohr Siebeck 2009), 298–301.

ownership (or without a family or a foundation as dominating shareholder) have a majority foreign (institutional) shareholder.[54]

b) Shareholder vs. Stakeholder Model

Germany was the pioneer of the stakeholder model,[55] which also helped to contain the effects of the financial crisis for the German labour market.[56] After World War I, the idea of an enterprise per se,[57] consisting of more than the company itself, formed the intellectual basis for the unique German co-determination system.[58] Incorporating other interests than just the interests of the shareholders into the decision-making is still seen as good corporate governance: According to the German Corporate Governance Code, the company is to be managed in the interest of the enterprise, meaning to take into account the interests of the shareholders, of the employees and of other stakeholders, with the objective of the sustainable creation of value.[59]

In its foreword, the German Corporate Governance Code[60] refers to the interest of the enterprise and states that it 'clarifies' the obligation of the management board and the supervisory board to ensure the continued existence of the enterprise and its sustainable creation of value in conformity with the prin-

---

[54] As an airline, Deutsche Lufthansa is legally required to have a domestic shareholder basis; Commerzbank has such a basis due to state aid in the financial crises. Infinion does not report on domestic and foreign investors. For 2006, 2008 and 2011 Deutsche Bank reports a majority of domestic shareholders, for 2007, 2008 and 2010 a majority of foreign shareholders. Not all shareholders are identified for BASF; a majority of foreign shareholders is likely.

[55] For the historical development of co-determination, see T. Raiser, 'The theory of Enterprise law in the Federal Republic of Germany', *American Journal of Comparative Law* 36 (1988) 111; F.A. Mann, 'The New German Company Law and Its Background', *Journal of Comparative Legislation and International Law* 19 (1937) 220, 223–227. Recent survey by N. Raabe, *Die Mitbestimmung in deutschen Aktiengesellschaften, Theorie und Wirklichkeit in deutschen Aktiengesellschaften* (Berlin, Erich Schmidt 2011); O. Sandrock and J.J. du Plessis, 'German System of Supervisory Codetermination by Employees', in J.J. du Plessis et al, *German Corporate Governance in International and European Context*, 2nd edn. (Heidelberg, Springer 2012) 149–196.

[56] At least until 2012.

[57] M. Roth, 'Employee Participation, Corporate Governance and the Firm: A transatlantic view focused on Occupational Pensions and Co-determination', *European Business Organization Law Review* 11 (2010) 51, 62.

[58] K.J. Hopt, 'Labor representation on corporate boards: Impacts and problems for corporate governance and economic integration in Europe', *International Review of Law and Economics* 14 (1994) 203.

[59] Point 4.1.1 German Corporate Governance Code.

[60] Foreword (2), German Corporate Governance Code.

ciples of the social market economy.[61] The management board is responsible for independently managing the enterprise, with the objective of sustainable creation of value and in the interest of the enterprise, thus taking into account the interests of the shareholders, its employees and other stakeholders.[62] Such other stakeholders are customers, suppliers and the public.[63]

For company law, it is disputed whether the Stock Corporation Act (AktG) follows the shareholder value or the stakeholder-approach. Despite mandatory co-determination, the Stock Corporation Act no longer explicitly refers to non-shareholder interests.[64] Reflecting the international discussion, the shareholder value approach is preferred by at least some German commentators.[65] Hinting at shareholder primacy, the German business judgment rule refers not to the interests of the enterprise (comprising the interests of the stakeholders) but to the best interests of the company.[66] Given the mixed views in academia[67] and the pronouncement of the German Corporate Governance Code to give a correct interpretation of the Stock Corporation Act,[68] it is appropriate to state that German company law follows an enlightened shareholder value approach.[69]

c) Principle-Agent Conflicts

Due to the mixed ownership-structure, German stock corporation law has to address not only agency conflicts between shareholders and directors but also—

---

[61] For incorporating also interests of the employees, see the report of Gerald Spindler for the Boeckler Foundation: G. Spindler, *Unternehmensinteresse als Leitlinie des Vorstandshandelns – Berücksichtigung der Arbeitnehmerinteressen und Shareholder Value* (Böckler-Stiftung, 2008).

[62] Point 4.1.1. German Corporate Governance Code.

[63] A. von Werder, in H.M. Ringleb et al, *Deutscher Corporate Governance Kodex*, 4th edn. (Munich, C.H. Beck 2010) 353.

[64] See also below 3.2.1(a).

[65] For the shareholder value-approach, see B. Dauner-Lieb, 'Aktuelle Vorschläge zur Präsenzsteigerung in der Hauptversammlung', *Wertpapier-Mitteilungen* 2007, 9, 13; P.O. Mülbert, 'Shareholder Value aus rechtlicher Sicht', *Zeitschrift für Unternehmens- und Gesellschaftsrecht*, 1997, 129, 147; *idem.*, *Festschrift Röhricht* (Munich, C.H. Beck 2005) 421.

[66] See in detail below 3.2.1.

[67] In favour of also incorporating the interests of stakeholders, see M. Kort, *Groß-kommentar Aktiengesetz*, 4th edn. (Berlin, De Gruyter 2002), Section 76 nos. 52–75; G. Spindler, *Münchener Kommentar Aktiengesetz*, 3rd edn. (Munich, C.H. Beck 2008), Section 76 no. 65, 82–87; H.J. Mertens and A. Cahn, *Kölner Kommentar zum Aktiengesetz*, 3rd edn. (Cologne and Berlin and Bonn and Munich, C. Heymans 2009), Section 76 no. 15; U. Hüffer, *Aktiengesetz*, 10th edn. (Munich, C.H. Beck 2012, Section 76 no. 12.

[68] According to Foreword (10)7 of the German Corporate Governance Code, parts of the Code not marked with the terms 'shall' or 'should' are neither presumptions nor a recommendation but contain descriptions of legal regulations and explanations.

[69] M. Roth, 'Employee Participation' (see n. 57) 63.

and in many companies even more importantly[70]—conflicts between dominant and minority shareholders as well.[71] Concerning the agency conflicts between directors and shareholders, the two-tier board system leads to an intermitted agency problem: Supervisory directors act as agents for the shareholders, and management directors as agents for the supervisory directors.[72] For the supervisory directors, remuneration is set by the general meeting or the articles of incorporation,[73] while the remuneration of the managing directors is set by the supervisory board.[74]

The principle–agent conflict between the majority shareholders and the minority shareholders is subject to the German law on groups of companies (*Konzernrecht*) and the Securities Acquisition and Takeover Act.[75] The *Konzernrecht* is rooted in the Stock Corporation Act;[76] therefore, the statutory *Konzernrecht* deals with stock corporations,[77] while for limited liability companies (GmbHs) the *GmbH-Konzernrecht* was developed by the courts.[78] The concept of *Konzernrecht* was introduced by the 1965 Stock Corporation Act and is based on the concept of treaties between the parent and the dependent company. The German *Konzernrecht* is a surprising result of a legal transplant, the exclusion of the shareholders from the management of the company:[79] To secure the influence of dominating or sole shareholders on the management, it is necessary to conclude a special control contract (*Beherrschungsvertrag*); doing this is also fa-

---

[70] For the debate on investor protection, see La Porta et al, 'Legal Determinants of External Finance', *Journal of Finance* 52 (1997) 1131.

[71] K.J. Hopt, 'Comparative Corporate Governance' (see n. 3) 5.

[72] P.C. Leyens, *Information des Aufsichtsrats* (Tübingen, Mohr Siebeck 2006) 22, refers to a multi-level agency model (*mehrstufiges Agentenmodell*).

[73] Section 113 Stock Corporation Act.

[74] Section 87 Stock Corporation Act.

[75] Wertpapiererwerbs- und Übernahmegesetz (WpÜG), 20 December 2001, BGBl I 3822, English translation by the German Federal Financial Supervisory Authority (BaFin), available at <www.bafin.de/SharedDocs/Aufsichtsrecht/EN/Gesetz/wpueg_en.html?nn=2821360>.

[76] Sections 15–22, 291–328 Stock Corporation Act.

[77] R. Kraakman et al, *Anatomy of Corporate Law,* 2nd edn. (Oxford, OUP 2009) 176; G. Wirth et al, *Corporate Law in Germany,* (see n. 4), 207–218; M. Dearborn, 'Enterprise Liability: Reviewing and Revitalizing Liability for Corporate Groups', *California Law Review* 97 (2009) 195, 215–221; C.E. Decher, S. Kalss and K.J. Hopt, 'Das Konzernrecht des Aktiengesetzes – Bestand und Bewährung', 'Alternativen zum deutschen Aktienkonzernrecht' and 'Konzernrecht – Die europäische Perspektive', *Zeitschrift für das gesamte Handels- und Wirtschaftsrecht* 2007 (171), 126, 146 and 199.

[78] See V. Emmerich and M. Habersack, *Aktien- und GmbH-Konzernrecht,* 6th edn. (Munich, C.H. Beck 2010).

[79] See below 1.3(b).

voured by tax law.[80] Also, the German Corporate Governance Code has a perspective on groups of companies. The Code refers to the term 'enterprise' if it refers to the group of companies and not to the listed company alone.[81]

d) Specific Environment

German public and listed companies are regulated primarily by the Stock Corporation Act (AktG)[82] which applies to all stock corporations and partnerships limited by shares.[83] German company law distinguishes stock corporations (*Aktiengesellschaften, AG*, newly also in the form of European Companies (*Societas Europaea, SE*), partnerships limited by shares (*Kommanditgesellschaft auf Aktien, KGaA*) and limited liability companies (*Gesellschaften mit beschränkter Haftung, GmbH*).[84] For all these company forms, there is extensive literature and exchange between academia and practice. Besides several journals focusing on company law,[85] there are also (multi-volume) commentaries on the Stock Corporation Act[86] and handbooks on the supervisory board.[87] The exchange between

[80] For a recent account, see B. Haar, 'Corporate Group Law', in J. Basedow et al (eds.), *Max Planck Encyclopaedia of European Private Law* (Oxford, OUP 2012).

[81] Foreword (11) German Corporate Governance Code. This differentiation is mostly omitted in the report.

[82] Aktiengesetz (AktG), 6 September 1965, BGBl I 1089; for translations, see n. 4.

[83] Partnerships limited by shares were the nucleus of German stock corporation law; they are now regulated in Sections 278–290 Stock Corporation Act.

[84] Family-held corporations which do not intend to offer stocks or debentures (*Schuldverschreibungen*) to the public may be incorporated as stock corporations. On the other hand, limited liability companies incorporated as a GmbH may also offer debentures to the public.

[85] *Zeitschrift für Unternehmens- und Gesellschaftsrecht* [ZGR], *Zeitschrift für das gesamte Handels- und Wirtschaftsrecht* [ZHR], *Die Aktiengesellschaft* [AG], *Neue Zeitschrift für Gesellschaftsrecht* [NZG] devoted primarily to company law; of substantial relevance also *Betriebs-Berater* [BB], *Der Betrieb* [DB], *Zeitschrift für Wirtschafts- und Bankrecht, Wertpapier-Mitteilungen* Teil IV [WM] and *Zeitschrift für Wirtschaftsrecht* [ZIP].

[86] Multi-volume commentaries for the Stock Corporation Act: *Großkommentar Aktiengesetz, Kölner Kommentar Aktiengesetz* and *Münchener Kommentar Aktiengesetz*, two-volume commentaries by G. Spindler and E. Stiltz (Spindler/Stilz, *Supervisory Board* by G. Spindler, 2nd edn. Munich, C.H. Beck, 2010), K. Schmidt and M. Lutter (Schmidt/Lutter, *Supervisory Board* by T. Drygala, 2nd edition, Cologne, Otto Schmidt 2010) and R. Godin and S. Wilhelmi, single-volume commentaries by U. Hüffer (10th edn. Munich, C.H. Beck 2012) and others. Recent works on the supervisory board in the *Großkommentar Aktiengesetz*, 4th edn. by K.J. Hopt and M. Roth (Berlin, De Gruyter 2005) for the German business judgment rule, Section 93 new version, 2006) and in the *Münchener Kommentar Aktiengesetz* (3rd edn. Munich, C.H. Beck 2008) by M. Habersack, in 2013 followed by the most recent work of H.J. Mertens and A. Cahn in the *Kölner Kommentar Aktiengesetz* (3rd edn. Cologne, Carl Heymanns).

academia and practice takes place at regular conferences,[88] publications by practitioners[89] and via citations of academics in court rulings.[90]

The limited liability company (*GmbH*) is regulated in the Limited Liability Company Act (*GmbHG*);[91] the Societas Europaea (*Europäische Gesellschaft, SE*), in the European Regulation and in the German SE-Implementation Act.[92] The close corporations incorporated as limited liability companies (*GmbH*) were subject to a major reform in 2008,[93] driven by company law competition within the EU.[94] One of the main fields of the discussion in advance was the capital requirement for close corporations.[95] In the end, the provisions concerning minimum capital were left unchanged but a so-called 'enterprise company' (*Unternehmergesellschaft*) was introduced in the German Limited Liability Company Act

---

[87] M. Lutter and G. Krieger, *Rechte und Pflichten des Aufsichtsrats*, 5th edn. (Cologne, Otto Schmidt 2008), and J. Semler and K. von Schenck, *Arbeitshandbuch für Aufsichtsratsmitglieder*, 3rd edn. (Munich, Vahlen 2009).

[88] ZGR/ZHR conferences take place every year.

[89] Not only publishing but also editing commentaries: W. Goette (former chief justice in the company law chamber of the German Federal Court of Justice) in the *Münchener Kommentar Aktiengesetz*, and E. Stiltz (Higher Regional Court Stuttgart, Spindler/Stiltz).

[90] This discourse between courts and academia began in the 19th century. See H. Wiedemann, 'Ein Diskurs zwischen Rechtsprechung und Rechtslehre', *Recht der Arbeit* 1999, 5, 6.

[91] Gesetz betreffend die Gesellschaft mit beschränkter Haftung, 20 April 1892, RGBl 477, in the version from 20 May 1898, RGBl 846; English translation by B.W. Meister, M. Heidenhain and J. Rosengarten, *The German Limited Liability Company*, 7th edn. (Munich, C.H. Beck 2010).

[92] Council Regulation (EC) No 2157/2001 of 8 October 2001 on the Statute for a European company (SE), OJ L 294/1; Gesetz zur Ausführung der Verordnung (EG) Nr. 2157/2001 des Rates vom 8. Oktober 2001 über das Statut der Europäischen Gesellschaft (SE) (SE-Ausführungsgesetz – SEAG), 22 December 2004, BGBl I 3675.

[93] Gesetz zur Modernisierung des GmbH-Rechts und zur Bekämpfung von Mißbräuchen (MoMiG), 23 October 2008, BGBl I 2026; for the Governmental Draft, see U. Noack and M. Beurskens, 'Modernising the German GmbH – Mere Window Dressing or Fundamental Redesign?', *European Business Organization Law Review* 9 (2008) 97; for the initial proposal of the Ministry of Justice, see U. Seibert, 'Close Corporations – Reforming Private Company Law: European and International. Perspectives', *European Business Organization Law Review* 8 (2007) 83.

[94] U. Seibert (*ibid.*) 84; U. Kornblum, 'Bundesweite Rechtstatsachen zum Unternehmens- und Gesellschaftsrecht (Stand 1.1.2012)', *GmbH-Rundschau* 2012, 728, 729 specifies 12,553 Ltd and 3,585 Ltd & Co KG companies, a drop of about 20 per cent from the previous year respectively.

[95] See the conference reports by H. Eidenmüller and W. Schön, *European Business Organization Law Review* 7 (2006) 1 and M. Lutter (ed.), *Legal Capital in Europe* (Berlin, De Gruyter 2006), for the proposal to reduce the minimum capital in the draft of the Ministry of Justice (no longer in the governmental draft); U. Seibert (see n. 93) 86–87.

(GmbHG).[96] An enterprise company (*Unternehmergesellschaft*) may be founded with one Euro and is therefore the German equivalent to other continental one-Euro limited liability companies.[97]

The German Stock Corporation Act increasingly distinguishes between listed, non-listed and public companies.[98] A representative of the German Ministry of Justice declared that non-listed, public and listed stock corporations will also be dealt with differently in new reforms.[99] Due to European company law, the publicly traded companies issuing shares or bonds on regulated markets are newly introduced as a fourth type. Since all publicly companies have to declare whether they comply with the German Corporate Governance Code, this is relevant for corporate governance.[100] Publicly traded companies are companies whose transferable securities are admitted to trading on a regulated market of any Member State within the meaning of Article 4(1)(14) of Directive 2004/39/EC.[101]

e) Number of (Listed) Companies

The most popular company form providing limited liability is the limited liability company (*Gesellschaft mit beschränkter Haftung* – GmbH). About one million companies with limited liability are incorporated in the legal form of a *GmbH*.[102] Of about 16,000 to 17,000 stock corporations in Germany,[103] roughly 1,000 are

---

[96] Section 5a Limited Liability Company Act; for a discussion, see Noack and Beurskens (see n. 93) 111.

[97] For a recent comparative study, see E. Wymeersch, 'Comparative Study on the Company Types in Selected States', *European Company and Financial Law Review* 2009, 71. According U. Kornblum (see n. 94), in 2010 there were 23,369 Unternehmergesellschaften (UG) and 1,384 UG & Co KG companies (limited partnerships with an Unternehmergesellschaft as sole general partner); these figures (almost) doubled in 2011 to 44,361 UGs and 2,951 UG & Co KGs, and tripled in 2012 to 64,371 UGs and 4,477 UG & Co. KGs, U. Kornblum, 'Bundesweite Rechtstatsachen zum Unternehmens- und Gesellschaftsrecht (Stand 1.1.2011)', *GmbH-Rundschau* 2011, 692, 693.

[98] According to U. Seibert, *Verhandlungen des Deutschen Juristentages* (German Jurists Forum) 2008 N. 126, 127, in general this differentiation is not made for all provisions of the German Stock Corporation Act but in detail within every reform. Such a general reform was rejected by the German Jurists Forum in 2008.

[99] U. Seibert, *German Jurists Forum 2008* (see n. 98) n. 126, 127.

[100] Since 2009, publicly traded companies are subject to the comply-or-explain requirement of Section 161 Stock Corporation Act (required to state whether the stock corporation fulfils the German Corporate Governance Code).

[101] Gesetz zur Modernisierung des Bilanzrechts (Bilanzrechtsmodernisierungsgesetz – BilMoG), 25 May 2009, BGBl I 1102 [Act to Modernise Accounting Law].

[102] U. Kornblum (see n. 94) 723 specifies 1,071,908 GmbHs.

[103] According to the statistics of the German Central Bank, *Bundesbank Kapitalmarkt-statistik*, August 2011, 46: 12,764 in June 2011, down from about 16,000 in 2004 (companies

cont. ...

listed or traded in the over-the-counter market.[104] Unlike the stock corporation itself, the European Company (Societas Europaea, SE) is becoming more important in Germany. This can best be illustrated by the fact that Germany hosts the greatest number of operating European Companies;[105] half of the European Companies in operation (small companies having more than five employees and larger companies have more than 250 employees) are registered in Germany.[106] The importance of the Societas Europaea for listed companies is growing steadily.[107] In December 2012, more than 30 Societas Europaea of German origin were listed companies (listed in the regulated market or at least traded in the over-the-counter market), among them currently four of the DAX 30 companies (Allianz, BASF, Fresenius Medical Care and E.ON); other prominent SE in Germany are Porsche Holding SE, MAN (formerly in the DAX), SGL Carbon, Wacker Neuson and Puma.[108] Of the DAX 30 companies incorporated as SE, in 2010/11 Fresenius Medical Care transformed into a SE & Co KGaA, having a Societas Europaea as sole partner of a partnership limited by shares (*Kommanditgesellschaft auf Aktien, KGaA*). In a partnership limited by shares (*KGaA*), the personally liable partners may fulfil the functions of the management board.[109] Even if the personally liable

with securities number). Reporting that there are about 17,000 stock corporations, W. Bayer and T. Hoffmann, 'Statistiken zur AG – Eine kritische Bestandsaufnahme', *AG-Report 2010*, 283, 286 (16,998) and U. Kornblum (see n. 94) 729 (16,705 companies in the companies' register), with an on-going negative tendency.

[104] Deutsche Börse, *Cash Market: Monthly Statistics* – December 2011, 40: 999.

[105] Ernst & Young, *Study on the operation and the impacts of the Statute for a European Company (SE)*, 9 December 2009, 180: 68 non-shelf SE in April 2009. According to data of the European Trade Union Institute (ETUI) in September 2009, more than half of the European Companies (78 of about 150) were of German origin; see <www.etui.org> or <www.worker-participation.eu>.

[106] *Commission Staff Working Document*, Brussels 17 November 2011, SEC(2010) 1391 final, 3, Annex 1 and 29 (as of 25 June 2010). For June 2012, ETUI reports 100 German SE out of 213 'normal' SEs with more than five employees.

[107] H. Eidenmüller et al, 'How Does the Market React to the Societas Europaea?', *European Business Organization Law Review* 11 (2010) 35, counted 17 SEs in mid-2009 and M. Roth, 'Employee Participation'. (see n. 57) 20 SEs in early 2010.

[108] 27 Societas Europaea are traded in the regulated market: ADVA Optical Networking SE, Aixtron SE, ALBA SE, Allgeier SE, Allianz SE, BASF SE, Bilfinger SE, DVB Bank SE, E.ON SE, Fresenius SE & Co KGaA, GfK SE, Global PVQ SE, IMW Immobilien SE, Klöckner & Co SE, MAN SE, Masterflex SE, mybet Holding SE, Nordex SE, Porsche Automobil Holding SE, Pulsion Medical Systems SE, Puma SE, SCA Hygiene Products SE, SGL Carbon SE, Solon SE, Surteco SE, Tipp24 SE, Wacker Neuson SE. Three companies, Mensch und Maschine Software SE, Impreglon SE and STEICO SE are traded in the Entry Standard, with net SE, one company is traded in the Quotation Board, a newly introduced segment for the open market. At least two further companies are now traded in Hamburg (Hoffmann AHG SE and Recyc Commodities SE) and one company in Stuttgart (Impreglon).

[109] Section 283 Stock Corporation Act.

partner is not a natural person, employee representatives in the supervisory board do not participate in the election of managers. Besides Fresenius Medical Care, three other DAX 30 companies are incorporated as KGaA.[110] Puma, a MDAX-company controlled by the French luxury group PPR, newly transformed into a European company, was the first co-determined company to choose a one-tier board. Q-Cells is the first European Company that had to file for insolvency proceedings.

The transformation into a European Company, a partnership limited by shares or a foreign legal form, might also be on the agenda for other listed companies in the near future. The Corporate Governance Principles of the Hermes Pension Fund calls for the conversion of German stock corporations into European Companies to allow for the representation of workers employed in other European countries or abroad.[111] Even in the light of the fact that some companies, such as Air Berlin, have been transformed into foreign legal forms, there is no European Delaware.[112] A prominent role for listed companies with ties to Germany may be played by Dutch company law: Quiagen, a German tech-company,[113] and EADS, a European holding company, are incorporated as *naamloze vennootschap* (NV), and Deutsche Börse and NYSE Euronext Group intended to merge into a Dutch-based international holding company.

f) Influence

German Corporate Governance is influencing the international corporate governance debate. In the 1970s, Melvin Eisenberg explicitly referred to Germany in proposing the switch from the advising to the monitoring board,[114] which had taken place in the meantime, and gave rise to the independent director paradigm.[115] The separation of CEO and chairman of the board may also have been derived from the German separation of the supervisory board and the management board, since members of German management boards are banned from

---

[110] Fresenius, Henkel, Merck.

[111] Hermes Equity Ownership Services, *Hermes Corporate Governance Principles* – Germany: Supervisory board, employee representation, August 2011.

[112] R.M. Buxbaum, 'What would the Delaware of the European Community look like? Comparative Aspects of Regulatory Competition in Company and Capital Market Law', *RabelsZeitschrift* 74 (2010) 1, Dammann, 'Freedom of Choice in European Corporate Law', *Yale Journal of International Law* 29 (2004) 477.

[113] Formerly represented at the German Governmental Commission of the Corporate Governance Code by P. Schatz; for the current composition, see below 4.2.1.

[114] M.A. Eisenberg, *The Structure of the Corporation, A Legal Analysis* (Little Brown and Company, Boston 1976).

[115] Eisenberg (see n. 114) 170–177, for the two-tier board as an alternative 177–185; Gordon (see n. 10) 1563.

being members of the supervisory board of the same company.[116] European corporate governance standards as such were cited in the US by pension funds that lobbied for the Dodd-Frank Act,[117] allowing, as practised in Europe, the shareholders to nominate directors, to call for a separation of the CEO and the president of the board and giving the shareholders a say-on-pay.

On the other hand, Germany modernised its company by incorporating and transforming ideas first from French law (*conseil de surveillance*),[118] then from the UK and the US.[119] The influence of US law goes back to the 1920s when Walter Hallstein, later to become the first president of the European Union, wrote his post-doctoral thesis on (at that time) modern company law.[120] In the 1937 Stock Corporation Act, the law of capital increase and also the 'leadership principle' were legal transplants from US company law.[121] The most prominent examples for the second half of the 20th century and in the beginning of the 21st century are the business judgment rule and capital market law regulations.[122] Nowadays, UK company law has regained its predominance for Germany. This is largely because European regulations, directives and recommendations since the 1990s are rooted in UK company law; but it is also due to the pragmatic view on modern corporate governance issues found in the City Code on Takeovers, the UK Corporate Governance Code, the UK Companies Act, the UK Insolvency Act

---

[116]   Section 105 Stock Corporation Act.

[117]   Referring to European standards, see the Council of Institutional Investors, *US Financial Regulatory Reform: The Investors' Perspective*, July 2009, C. Corporate Governance, recommendations 2.

[118]   See below 1.3(b).

[119]   For the initial relevance of French company law, see A. Deutsch, 'Die Aktiengesell-schaft im Code de Commerce von 1807 und ihre Vorbildfunktion für die Entwicklung in Deutschland', in W. Bayer and M. Habersack (eds.), *Aktienrecht im Wandel,* Vol 1, (Mohr Siebeck, 2007) 46; the limited liability company (GmbH) was inspired by the English close corporation.

[120]   W. Hallstein, *Die Aktienrechte der Gegenwart* (Munich, Vahlen 1931). Foreword by the German Ministry of Justice and the predecessor of the Max Planck Institute of Comparative and Private International Law (Kaiser-Wilhelm-Institute).

[121]   See M. Roth, 'Möglichkeiten vorstandsunabhängiger Information des Aufsichtsrats', *Die Aktiengesellschaft* 2004, 1, 4; M. Roth, 'Private Altersvorsorge als Aspekt der Corporate Governance', *Zeitschrift für Unternehmens- und Gesellschaftsrecht* 2011, 516, 532; and M. Roth, 'Information und Organisation des Aufsichtsrats', *Zeitschrift für Unternehmens- und Gesellschaftsrecht* 2012, 343, 377; generally J. von Hein, *Die Rezeption des US-amerikanischen Gesellschaftsrechts* (Tübingen, Mohr Siebeck, 2008).

[122]   For the reception of the business judgment rule, see K.J. Hopt, 'Die Haftung von Vor-stand und Aufsichtsrat – Zugleich ein Beitrag zur corporate governance-Debatte', *Festschrift Mestmäcker* (Baden-Baden, Nomos 1996) 909, 914 ff.; for investor protection, *idem.*, *Kapital-anlegerschutz im Recht der Banken* (Munich, C.H. Beck 1975).

and in the UK courts. Prominent examples are the takeover regulation, the comply-or-explain principle and the say-on-pay.

1.2. Financial Institutions

a) The Influence of Financial Institutions After the Financial Crisis of the 1920/30s

The German financial industry has heavily influenced the German corporate governance system as a whole. During the woes following the financial and economic crisis of 1929, the strict separation of management and control was promoted by (former) representatives of banks and insurance companies.[123] Johannes Zahn, working for the association of private banks, wrote an influential monograph on leadership in stock corporation law.[124] Zahn's ideas were supported by Walter Kißkalt,[125] CEO of Munich Re at that time, who served as the chairman of the law commission preparing the new 1937 Stock Corporation Act.[126] Kißkalt was appointed by the Minister of Business Affairs, Kurt Schmitt, formerly CEO of Allianz.[127]

The mandatory exclusion of shareholders and supervisory directors from managing the company in the 1937 German Stock Corporation Act and the exclusion of the general meeting from appointing and dismissing managing directors[128] ended the traditional, more flexible German model of corporate governance that had been in place since 1870.[129] This, like the whole debate on modernising German stock corporation law in the 1920s, had been influenced by US company law.[130] The move towards the 'leadership principle' and the intro-

---

[123] M. Roth, 'Corporate Governance' (see n. 121) 531–534.

[124] J.C.D. Zahn, *Wirtschaftsführertum und Vertragsethik im neuen Aktienrecht* (Berlin, De Gruyter, 1934). Zahn was later CEO of HSBC Trinkhaus.

[125] W. Kißkalt, in W. Schubert (ed.), *Akademie für Deutsches Recht, Protokolle der Ausschüsse, Aktienrecht* (Berlin, De Gruyter 1986) 20.

[126] W. Kißkalt, 'Reform des Aktienrechts', *Zeitschrift der Akademie für Deutsches Recht* 1 (1934) 20; for a major influence of Kißkalt in the Acadamy of German Law, see M. Stolleis, *Gemeinwohlformeln im nationalsozialistischen Recht* (Berlin, Schweitzer 1974) 152.

[127] Allianz was a Munich Re foundation in 1890 and at that time still strongly tied to Munich Re.

[128] See below 1.3(b).

[129] The Reform Act of 1884, Art 225 (3) Commercial Code (Allgemeines Deutsches Handelsgesetzbuch, ADHGB), explicitly mentions the possibility to give more power than mere control to the supervisory board.

[130] See above 1.1(f).

duction of a mandatory minimum capital contribution[131] for stock corporations was aimed at saving the stock corporation as a legal form in Germany.[132] Ironically, it is for savings banks and Landesbanken owned by the state(s), by cities or by administrative districts, that the laws of the states prescribe a management board and a board of directors.[133]

b) Corporate Governance of Financial Institutions

Besides this early spill-over of governance standards for financial institutions[134] to all stock corporations, German company law contains special provisions for the corporate governance of banks and other financial institutions. The Federal Financial Supervisory Authority (*BaFin*) may dismiss members of the supervisory board who do not have sufficient expertise to fulfil their duties.[135] In the aftermath of the financial crisis, the requirement of special expertise is extended from the members of the management board to the members of the supervisory board. Before the new provisions on the skills of supervisory directors were enacted in the Banking Act (KWG),[136] a German-based study demonstrated the effects of bad corporate governance, attributed mostly to the lack of knowledge of non-executive directors[137] in state owned banks.[138] Furthermore, the Federal Financial Supervisory Authority may participate in meetings of the supervisory board; banks have to give notice of the meeting and the agenda.[139] Risk com-

---

[131] This alone cut the number of stock corporations into half, M. Roth, 'Besondere Regeln für geschlossene und börsennotierte Gesellschaften, Überlegungen aus Anlass des 67. Deutschen Juristentags 2008', in *Festschrift Hopt* (Berlin, De Gruyter 2010) 1261, 1274.

[132] At least some in the Nazi party pressed for the elimination of all stock corporations. Explicitly refusing to give up the stock corporation as a legal form, see W. Kißkalt (see n. 126) 248.

[133] For example, the de facto regime for all German stock corporations until the 1937 Stock Corporation Act.

[134] For a mandatory two-tier board as appropriate corporate governance for financial institutions, see the Swiss report by Peter Böckli in this volume.

[135] Section 36 (3) Banking Act (KWG); Section 7a (4) Insurance Supervision Act (VAG).

[136] Gesetz über das Kreditwesen (Kreditwesengesetz – KWG), 9 September 1998, BGBl I 2276. English translation by the German Central Bank (Bundesbank, July 2009), available at <www.bundesbank.de/Redaktion/EN/Downloads/Core_business_areas/Banking_supervision/P DF/banking_act.pdf?__blob=publicationFile>.

[137] State-owned banks have a two-tier structure with either a supervisory board or a board of directors and a management board; see above 1.2(a).

[138] H. Hau and M. Thum, 'Subprime crisis and board (in-)competence: private versus public banks in Germany', *Economic Policy* 24 (2009) 701.

[139] Section 44(4, 5) Banking Act.

mittees of the supervisory board are common among German banks, and they are required by some state laws for state-owned savings banks.[140]

German insurance companies are subject to the Insurance Supervision Act (VAG).[141] In the aftermath of the financial crisis personal skills are also required for supervisory board members.[142] The Federal Financial Supervisory Authority may dismiss members of the supervisory board who do not have sufficient expertise to fulfil their duties.[143] Also, the Federal Financial Supervisory Authority may participate in meetings of the supervisory board of insurance companies, and notice of the meeting and the agenda is to be given.[144] For investment funds, the Investment Act[145] (*Investmentgesetz* – InvG) requires in a recently amended provision[146] that one supervisory director of an investment fund has to be independent.[147]

c) The CRD IV Transposition Bill 2012

Further changes to the corporate governance of financial institutions with possible spill-overs to general company law and corporate governance will take place under the CRD IV Transposition Bill.[148] The CRD IV Transposition Bill was introduced into parliamentary proceedings in October 2012 by the German government for the purpose of transposing the proposed Directive[149] and imple-

---

[140] Section 15(3) Saving Banks Act North Rhine-Westphalia (Sparkassengesetz Nordrhein-Westfalen).

[141] Gesetz über die Beaufsichtigung der Versicherungsunternehmen (Versicherungsaufsichtsgesetz – VAG), 17 December 1992, BGBl 1993 I 2.

[142] For members of the management board, Section 7a(1) Insurance Supervision Act.

[143] Section 7a(4) Insurance Supervision Act (VAG).

[144] Section 83(1) Insurance Supervision Act (VAG).

[145] Investmentgesetz (InvG), 15 December 2003, BGBl I 2676, English translation by the German Financial Supervisory Authority (BaFin), 2011, available at <www.bafin.de/SharedDocs/Downloads/EN/Aufsichtsrecht/dl_invg_en.html>.

[146] M. Roth, *Private Altersvorsorge* (see n. 53) 216; also to the U.S. Investment Company Act 1940.

[147] Section 6(2a) Investment Act (InvG).

[148] Entwurf eines Gesetzes zur Umsetzung der Richtlinie 2012/.../EU über den Zugang zur Tätigkeit von Kreditinstituten und die Beaufsichtigung von Kreditinstituten und Wertpapierfirmen und zur Anpassung des Aufsichtsrechts an die Verordnung (EU) Nr. .../2012 über die Aufsichtsanforderungen an Kreditinstiutute und Wertpapierfirmen (CRD IV-Umsetzungsgesetz), BTDrucks 17/10974, Bill by the German Government, 15 October 2012. See T.O. Brandi and K. Gieseler, 'Der Aufsichtsrat in Kreditinstituten', *Neue Zeitschrift für Gesellschaftsrecht* 2012, 1321.

[149] Proposal for a Directive of the European Parliament and of the Council on the access to the activity of credit institutions and the prudential supervision of credit institutions and investment firms, COM(2011) 453 final.

menting the Internal Governance Guidelines of the European Banking Authority.[150] The Act of Parliament[151] provides for the establishment of a risk committee, an audit committee, a nomination and a remuneration oversight committee dependent on the size, quality, scope, complexity and riskiness of the affairs of the company.[152] According to the notes of the governmental draft, a company with a supervisory board or board of directors of less than ten members is exempted from the establishment of such committees without needing the consent of the Financial Supervisory Authority.[153]

So far, German financial institutions need not have a risk committee or a remuneration committee of the supervisory organ. The risk committee advises the supervisory board or the board of directors on the actual and future overall risk appetite of the company, and supports the supervisory organ in monitoring the implementation of the risk strategy by senior management.[154] The risk committee and the president of the remuneration oversight committee have direct access to senior officers of the company—the risk committee to the head of internal control and risk compliance,[155] and the remuneration oversight committee to the head of internal control and the head of the divisions responsible for setting the remuneration policy.[156] The management must be informed of such contacts.[157] The remuneration oversight committee[158] supervises the adequacy of the remunerations systems of the management board and specific senior managers, prepares the resolutions of the supervisory board or the board of directors concerning the remuneration of the management board—in this regard with special focus on risk and risk management and the long-term interests of shareholders, investors, other stakeholders and the public interest—and ensures that the internal control division and other relevant divisions are adequately involved in setting-up the remuneration system.[159] At least one member of the remuneration control com-

---

[150] European Banking Authority, EBA Guidelines on Internal Governance (GL 44), London, 27 September 2011.

[151] The German Bundestag voted for the CRD IV-Transposition Bill in the version proposed by the Financial Committee, German Parliamentary Papers 17/13524, on 17 May 2013.

[152] Section 25d(7)-(12) Banking Act proposed by the CRD IV-Transposition Bill.

[153] BTDrucks (Parliamentary Papers) 17/10974, p. 110.

[154] Section 25d(8)(2) Banking Act proposed by the CRD IV-Transposition Bill.

[155] Section 25d(8)(6) Banking Act proposed by the CRD IV-Transposition Bill.

[156] Section 25d(12)(7) Banking Act proposed by the CRD IV-Transposition Bill.

[157] Section 25d(8)(7), (12)(8) Banking Act proposed by the CRD IV-Transposition Bill.

[158] A remuneration committee (at management level) is also required by Section 6 of the Verordnung über die Aufsichtsrechtlichen Anforderungen an Vergütungssysteme von Instituten (Instituts-Vergütungsverordnung – InstitutsVergV), 6 October 2010, BGBl (Federal Gazette) I 1374.

[159] Section 25d(12)(2) Banking Act proposed by the CRD IV-Transposition Bill.

mittee has to have expertise in risk management and risk control;[160] the remuneration control committee should interact with the risk committee and seek internal and external advice.[161]

The audit committee has to support the supervisory board or the board of directors in monitoring the internal audit process, the efficiency of risk management, especially internal control, the external audit process and the rectification of shortcomings identified by the auditor.[162] The nomination committee has more competences than under the German Corporate Governance Code.[163] It prepares not only the nomination of the supervisory directors but also that of the managing directors, and regularly assesses the structure, size, composition and performance of the management board and the supervisory board, the respective directors and the rules for hiring senior management.[164] The nomination committee may use all resources it deems adequate and may hire external advisors.[165] Rules on electing and suspending employee representatives in the supervisory board or in the board of directors are not affected.[166]

1.3. Available Board Models

a) The German Two-Tier System as One of the Basic Corporate Governance Models

The two-tier system, which divides the administration of German stock corporations into a management board and a supervisory board, is one of the basic corporate governance models in the world. In many surveys, it serves as a contrast to the one-tier board in the US and in UK.[167] However, another line of literature stresses the convergence of these two systems.[168] While in the US the

---

[160] Section 25d(12)(3) Banking Act proposed by the CRD IV-Transposition Bill.

[161] Section 25d(12)(5) Banking Act proposed by the CRD IV-Transposition Bill.

[162] Section 25d(9)(2) Banking Act proposed by the CRD IV-Transposition Bill. The president of the audit committee has direct access to the head of internal control and risk compliance, and the management is to be informed of such contacts: Section 25d(9)(2) Banking Act proposed by the CRD IV-Transposition Bill.

[163] Below 2.2.2(g).

[164] Section 25d(11)(2) Banking Act proposed by the CRD IV-Transposition Bill.

[165] Section 25d(11)(3) Banking Act proposed by the CRD IV-Transposition Bill.

[166] Section 25d(11)(4) Banking Act proposed by the CRD IV-Transposition Bill.

[167] K.J. Hopt, 'Two-Tier Board' (see n. 22) 228.

[168] R. Kraakman et al, *The Anatomy of Corporate Law* (Oxford, OUP 2004) 40 (2nd edn., with focus on independent directors).

advisory board has developed into a monitoring board,[169] dominated by independent non-executive directors, the German supervisory board, which the law explicitly requires to monitor (control) the corporate affairs, is also obliged to advise the management board, according to the German Federal Court of Justice and academia.[170] The German Corporate Governance Code therefore adopted the view that the different board models (one-tier and two-tier) are converging and states that the two systems are 'equally successful'.[171] Practical differences remain, *inter alia*, on the number of meetings held. According to a recent study, the average frequency of board meetings is 9.4 (in 2009: 9.6) per annum in Europe, but only 5.9 (5.8) in Germany,[172] the lowest number of all the European countries examined.

b) The Evolution of the German Two-Tier System for Stock Corporations

The traditional German board model is a mandatory two-tier board (supervisory board and management board) for German stock corporations incorporated under the Stock Corporation Act (AktG). This model can be traced back to the first rules for stock corporations at the national level in the Commercial Code of 1861 (*Allgemeines Deutsches Handelsgesetzbuch, ADHGB*).[173] The Prussian Stock Corporation Act 1843,[174] the Draft Commercial Code of 1848/9[175] and the Draft for a Prussian Commercial Code lacked provisions for a supervisory board or a board of directors (*Verwaltungsrat*), but concentrated on the management board, the *Vorstand*. In the discussion of the Prussian Draft, following the French Act on Partnerships Limited by Shares,[176] the *Verwaltungsrat*, which was prescribed for

---

[169] J.F. Gordon (see n. 10) 1518, referring to M.A. Eisenberg, *The Structure of the Corporation: A Legal Analysis* (Boston and Toronto, Little, Brown and Company 1976).

[170] See above 2.1(a), 2.2.2(b).

[171] Foreword (9) German Corporate Governance Code 2012, omitted in 2013.

[172] Heidrick & Struggles, *Challenging board performance* (2011), 26, second lowest number by Austria, 6.0, for 2009: boards in turbulent times, 2009, 6, naming for the survey only Austria with a lower number (5.6).

[173] K.J. Hopt, 'Ideelle und wirtschaftliche Grundlagen der Aktien-, Bank- und Börsenentwicklung im 19. Jahrhundert', in H. Coing and W. Wilhelm (eds.), *Wissenschaft und Kodifikation im Privatrecht', Bd. 5, Geld und Banken* (Frankfurt, Vittorio Klostermann, 1980) 128, 152, idem., in N. Horn and J. Kocka (eds.) *Recht und Entwicklung der Großunternehmen im 19. und frühen 20. Jahrhundert* (Göttingen, Vandenhoeck & Ruprecht 1979), 227, 231.

[174] See Baums (ed.), *Entwurf eines allgemeinen Handelsgesetzbuches für Deutschland (1848/9)* (Heidelberg, Recht und Wirtschaft 1982).

[175] See Baums (ed.), *Gesetz über die Aktiengesellschaften für die Königlich Preußischen Staaten vom 9. November 1843* (Aachen, Scientia 1981).

[176] Loi 17 juillet 1857 relative au sociétés en commandite par actions.

partnerships limited by shares,[177] was renamed the *Aufsichtsrat* (supervisory board, which in French law is called *conseil de surveillance*),[178] and a new section on the supervisory board for stock corporations was added.[179] The supervisory board has been mandatory since the switch from the state allowance system to the legal system that established stock corporations in 1870.[180]

As long as the stock corporation was regulated in the Commercial Code (first *Allgemeines Deutsches Handelsgesetzbuch* (*ADHGB*), later *Handelsgesetzbuch* (*HGB*) *1897*), ie. from 1861 until 1937, the articles of incorporation could, and usually did, give more powers to the supervisory board than the mere control function as required by mandatory law:[181] In practice, the supervisory board was a *de facto* board of directors. Since the reform of 1884, the German Commercial Code explicitly allowed the company statutes to give more power to the supervisory board than the mere supervision function.[182] Comparable regulations are still in place today in Poland[183] and in the Netherlands.[184] The traditional Danish corporate governance regime might be regarded as a statutory version of the German practice until 1937.[185]

The supervisory board has been excluded from the management of the company, in other words from running the affairs of the company, since the 1937 Stock Corporation Act.[186] Neither the exclusion of the general meeting[187] nor the exclusion of the supervisory board[188] from managing the company were required or practised in the Weimar Republic[189] but enacted in the 1930s.[190] As mentioned

---

[177] Initially called silent companies.

[178] Protocols, 399, motion A, referring to Articles 5, 7–11, 14, 15 of the French Act and arguing that the limited partners are excluded from running the affairs of the company.

[179] Art. 204 in the first draft, Art 210 in the second draft. Art. 225 Commercial Code (ADHGB) 1884.

[180] Hopt/Roth, *Großkommentar Aktiengesetz* (see n. 86), Section 111 no. 2.

[181] See A. Pinner, *Staub Handelsgesetzbuch*, 14th edn. (Berlin, De Gruyter 1932), Section 246 Commercial Code no. 10.

[182] Art 225(3) Commercial Code; for the notes of the governmental draft, see W. Schubert and P. Hommelhoff, *Hundert Jahre modernes Aktienrecht* (Berlin, De Gruyter 1985) 460; also below 2.2.1.

[183] Stanislaw Sołtysiński, report on Poland in this volume.

[184] Section 57(5) Dutch Civil Code Book 2.

[185] Former Section 59(1)3 Danish Companies Act, now section 111 (1) Danish Companies Act 2009.

[186] Section 95(5) 1937 Stock Corporation Act.

[187] Now section 119(2) Stock Corporation Act.

[188] Now section 111(4)1 Stock Corporation Act.

[189] For extensive comparative work, see the monograph of Hallstein (above n. 120) and the first issues of *Rabels Journal*. On the German discussion, see W. Schubert, *Die Aktienrechts-*
cont. ...

earlier,[191] representatives of the financial industry played a central role in the formulation of the current corporate governance regime. Johannes Zahn, at that time legal counsel of the association of private banks in Germany, proposed to transplant US corporation law into the traditional German company law by introducing the so called 'leadership principle', which primarily focuses on the exclusion of the general meeting from management decisions.[192] Adopting this terminology at that time was helpful to make sure that the stock corporation as a legal form was not abolished, as some National Socialists had pleaded.[193]

c) Alternative Board Models

For German stock corporations, a one-tier board is available only by transforming the company into a European Company (SE)[194] or a foreign stock corporation. In practice, most German firms opting for a one-tier board choose the legal form of a European Company. While large firms, and especially the DAX 30 companies, have two boards (management board and supervisory board),[195] in 2011 more than forty per cent (before 2011, about half) of the co-determination free German SE[196] had a board of directors.[197] For larger companies with more than 500 employees in Germany, the choice of the one-tier board system is subject to practical restrictions due to mandatory co-determination. According to the unions, but also most academics, quasi-parity co-determined supervisory boards are to be transformed into quasi-parity co-determined boards of directors.[198] This enhance-

---

reform am Ende der Weimarer Republik (Berlin, De Gruyter, 1987) and initially the 34th German Jurists Forum, Cologne 1926.

[190] Text and Notes by F. Klausing, *Gesetz über die Aktiengesellschaften und Kommandit-gesellschaften auf Aktien* (Berlin, Heymanns 1937).

[191] See above 1.2.

[192] J.C.D. Zahn (see n. 124), referring to *Lamb v. Lehmann*, Supreme Court of Ohio, 143 Northeastern Reporter 276, 278 (1 April 1924), and *Manson v. Curtis*, Court of Appeals of New York, 119 Northeastern Reporter 559, 562 (23 April 1918).

[193] M. Roth, 'Information' (see n. 121) 377.

[194] Generally, more SE are set up in countries which allow only the two-tier system; see Report from the Commission to the European Parliament and the Council, *The application of Council Regulation 2157/2001 of 8 October 2001 on the Statute for a European Company (SE)*, COM(2010) 676 final, 5.

[195] Heidrick & Struggles, *Challenging board performance* (2011), 11.

[196] With no employee representatives in the supervisory board or board of directors, ETUI, *Overview of current state of SE founding in Europe*, 1 December 2011, p. 7, 10.

[197] See below 3.2.1(e).

[198] H. Oetker, in M. Lutter and P. Hommelhoff (eds.), *SE-Kommentar* (Cologne, Otto Schmidt 2008) Section 35 SEBG no. 9–14; A. Feuerborn, in *Kölner Kommentar zum Aktien-gesetz* Band 8/2 (Cologne, Carl Heymanns 2010), Section 35 SEBG no. 21–28; for the unions' perspective, R. Köstler, 'Die Mitbestimmung in der SE', *Zeitschrift für Unternehmens- und*

cont. ...

ment of co-determination will regularly conflict with shareholders' interests.[199] Since until recently no co-determined SE of German origin has installed a one-tier board,[200] it is at least doubtful whether the majority view is in line with the *effet utile* doctrine of the European Court of Justice.[201] Puma, being the first third-parity co-determined company, is an exception due to its listing with a 75.12 per cent shareholder (PPR SA), holding first five out of nine—and as of December 2012 four out of eight—directorships on the board.[202] The one-tier system is to be seen in the tradition of strong mandatory regulation in German company law,[203] since there are thirty statutory sections for the one-tier board alone.[204] A few companies with their centre of business in Germany are incorporated in another EU jurisdiction,[205] but as yet there is no competition for legal forms such as that for limited liability corporations (*GmbH*); the latter led to the introduction of the *Unternehmergesellschaft* in 2008.[206] The possibility of incorporating under US law due to the German-US Friendship Treaty[207] is used by some US firms for their German subsidiaries.

The Limited Liability Company Act (*GmbHG*) does not require a supervisory board for close corporations incorporated as *GmbH*. However, the establishment of a supervisory board is mandatory if the limited liability company (*GmbH*) is

---

Gesellschaftsrecht 2003, 800, 803. Today even the majority view in academia might be to refer to the same proportion of non-executive directors (see sources in n. 737).

[199] See below 2.2.3(c).

[200] M. Roth, 'Employee Participation' (see n. 57) 83.

[201] K.J. Hopt, 'Europäisches Gesellschaftsrecht und deutsche Unternehmensverfassung – Aktionsplan und Interdependenzen', *Zeitschrift für Wirtschaftsrecht* 2005, 461, 471; M. Roth, 'Die unternehmerische Mitbestimmung in der monistischen SE', *Zeitschrift für Arbeitsrecht* 2004, 431, 444–445; *idem.*, 'Employee Participation' (see n. 57) 83.

[202] Representatives of PPR S.A. are Palus, Pinault, Hymel, Friocourt, plus one more shareholder representative (Ohlsson) and three employee representatives.

[203] F. Kübler, 'A Shifting Paradigm of European Company Law?', *Columbia Journal of European Law* 11 (2005) 219, 234.

[204] Gesetz zur Ausführung der Verordnung (EG) Nr. 2157/2001 des Rates vom 8. Oktober 2001 über das Statut der Europäischen Gesellschaft (SE) (SE-Ausführungsgesetz – SEAG), 22 December 2004, BGBl I 3686: Sections 20–49.

[205] To name in this regard are Air Berlin, the second largest German aviation company (SDAX), and TUI (MDAX). Air Berlin is incorporated as a UK public limited company (plc). TUI is supposed to concentrate on its travel business, which is directed by its UK subsidiary TUI Travel plc, listed on the London Stock Exchange. Gagfah (a real estate company, listed in the MDAX) is incorporated as a S.A. in Luxembourg.

[206] See above 1.1(d).

[207] Treaty of Friendship, Commerce and Navigation between the Federal Republic of Germany and the United States of America, BGBl (Federal Gazette) II, 1956, 487; German Federal Court of Justice, Bundesgerichtshof, 29 January 2003, VIII ZR 155/02, Amtliche Sammlung (BGHZ) 153, 353.

subject to co-determination due to the One Third Participation Act[208] or the Co-Determination Act 1976.[209] The limited liability company has one or more managing director(s) (*Geschäftsführer*). A board of directors, which combines the tasks of the managing directors and the supervisory board, is allowed but is not common in practice.

d) *German Jurists Forum 2012: One-Tier Board for German Stock Corporations*

In September 2012 the German Jurists Forum proposed the introduction of a one-tier board for German stock corporations incorporated under the German Stock Corporation Act.[210] Such choice reflects not only the growing importance of the Societas Europaea in Germany,[211] but also a European trend. Despite the fact that in most Member States there are only a small number of European Companies, a growing number of Member States offer both models for all stock corporations under the national regime.[212]

The resolution of the German Jurists Forum builds on the report of Mathias Habersack, which generally deals with state and parastatal interventions into corporate governance.[213] Former German Jurist Forums rejected such a proposal.[214] The Habersack report pointed especially to the choice offered by the European Company.[215] In fact European Companies not subject to co-determination use the monistic board system.[216] For stock corporations incorporated under the German Stock Corporation Act, the choice of a one-tier board might initially be limited to companies not subject to co-determination.[217] Provisions for the

---

[208] Gesetz über die Drittelbeteiligung der Arbeitnehmer im Aufsichtsrat (Drittelbeteiligungsgesetz – DrittelbG), 18 May 2004, BGBl I 974. English translation by Lingemann et al, (see n. 11) 409–417. The One-Third Participation Act applies if the company has more than 500 employees in Germany: Section 1(1) One Third Participation Act.

[209] The Co-Determination Act 1976 applies if the company has more than 2,000 employees in Germany: Section 1(1) Co-Determination Act (MitbestG).

[210] German Jurists Forum, Business Law Section, Resolution 19.

[211] See above 1.1(e).

[212] For such choice, see the General Report in this volume.

[213] M. Habersack, *Staatliche und halbstaatliche Eingriffe in die Unternehmensführung*, Gutachten E of 69th German Jurists Forum in Munich 2012.

[214] The last German Jurists Forum to decline such a choice was held in 2008: Business Law Section, Resolution 19.

[215] Habersack (see n. 213) E 71, 103 (proposal 12).

[216] See below 3.2.1(e), 6.

[217] M. Roth, 'Wirtschaftsrecht auf dem Deutschen Juristentag 2012', *Neue Zeitschrift für Gesellschaftsrecht* 2012, 881, 885; these companies account for more than 90 per cent of all German stock corporations.

European Company are based on the two-tier model, but to offer a real choice, there should be a 'true' one-tier board.

2. Authority

2.1. Functions and Powers

a) General Description of Functions of the Supervisory Board

The primary functions of the supervisory board are to control the business affairs of the company,[218] to advise the management board[219] and to appoint and dismiss the members of the management board.[220] The supervisory board also proposes the auditor to be appointed by the general meeting and instructs him as to the financial statements.[221] The supervisory board has to make proposals for all items on the agenda of the general meeting[222] and report to the general meeting.[223]

Traditionally, a strong networking function has characterised the practical work of German supervisory boards.[224] This network of supervisory directorships was an integral part of the *Deutschland AG* corporate governance system. Due to the general corporate governance debate, restrictions on the number of directorships in the supervisory board of listed firms, and especially the growing reluctance of banks to send managing directors onto the supervisory boards of customers, this kind of networking is in decline.[225]

---

[218] Section 111(1) Stock Corporation Act.

[219] Bundesgerichtshof, 25 March 1991, II ZR 188/89, Amtliche Sammlung (BGHZ) 114, 127; Bundesgerichtshof, 4 July 1994, II ZR 197/93, BGHZ 126, 340, 344; see also above 2.2.2(d).

[220] Section 84 Stock Corporation Act.

[221] See section 124(3) Stock Corporation Act for the proposal to the general meeting; and section 111 (2) 3 Stock Corporation Act for the instruction. The latter provision includes the power to act on behalf of the company although not explicitly mentioned in Section 112 Stock Corporation Act.

[222] Section 124(3)1 Stock Corporation Act.

[223] Section 171 Stock Corporation Act.

[224] K.J. Hopt, 'Two-Tier Board' (see n. 22) 243; focusing on banks K. Krenn, 'Von der „Macht der Banken" zur Leitidee des deutschen Produktionsregimes: Bank-Industrie-Verflechtungen am Beginn des 20. Jahrhunderts', *Zeitschrift für Unternehmensgeschichte*, 2008, 70 ff.; *idem., Alle Macht den Banken? Unternehmensverflechtungen im deutschen Produktionsregime, 1896–1933* (Wiesbaden, Springer 2012).

[225] See also above text to n. 35.

b) Division of Powers between Management and Supervisory Board

The daily business affairs of the stock corporation are exclusively handled by the management board, which leads the company independently.[226] In performing the control of the business of the company, the supervisory board has to respect that the management board is responsible for managing. The supervisory board itself may not direct the management board and is excluded from managing the company.[227]

However, the division of powers is not strict. The German Corporate Governance Code stresses the cooperation between management and the supervisory board more strongly than traditional doctrine. According to the Code, the management board and the supervisory board cooperate closely for the benefit of the company.[228] Also, according to the Stock Corporation Act, the supervisory board itself or the articles of incorporation have to determine that certain types of transactions by the company need the consent of the supervisory board.[229] The annual financial statement is approved by the management board with assent of the supervisory board, unless the management board and the supervisory board delegate the approval to the general meeting.[230]

c) Strategy

Strategy is developed (at least in principle) by the management board.[231] Building on mandatory provisions in the Stock Corporation Act,[232] the German Corporate Governance Code states that the management board is responsible for independently managing the company and developing its strategy.[233] On the other hand, advising the management board is seen as a main duty of the supervisory board.[234] According to the Corporate Governance Code, the management board and the supervisory board cooperate closely for the benefit of the company.[235] The management board coordinates the company's strategic approach with the supervisory board and discusses the current state of strategy implementation with

---

[226] Sections 76, 77 Stock Corporation Act.

[227] Section 111(4) 1 Stock Corporation Act.

[228] Point 3.1 German Corporate Governance Code.

[229] Section 111(4)2 Stock Corporation Act.

[230] Section 172 Stock Corporation Act.

[231] Kort, *Großkommentar Aktiengesetz* (see n. 67), Section 76 no. 36.

[232] Sections 76, 77 Stock Corporation Act.

[233] Points 4.1.1 and 4.1.2 German Corporate Governance Code.

[234] Hopt/Roth, *Großkommentar Aktiengesetz* (see n. 86), Section 111 no. 61.

[235] Point 3.1 German Corporate Governance Code.

the supervisory board at regular intervals.[236] For transactions of fundamental importance, the articles of association or the supervisory board specify provisions requiring the approval of the supervisory board. Such transactions include decisions or measures which fundamentally change the asset, financial or earnings situations of the company.[237]

The supervisory board or the statutes of the company may require the consent of the supervisory board for the strategy of the company. Since 2002,[238] the Stock Corporation Act imposes a duty on the supervisory board to establish a consent requirement.[239] The majority view in academia is that this establishes a duty for a catalogue of transactions and affairs of the company which have to be consented to (strategy, plant closures, mergers, acquisitions etc.).[240] The minority view holds that it is sufficient to require consent when the management board intends to commit a breach of duty.[241] Furthermore, it is proposed that formal consent by the supervisory board should be required for the strategy.[242]

d) Supervision

The supervisory board has to monitor the running of the affairs of the company.[243] This is a core duty of the supervisory board explicitly stipulated in the legislation and one of the primary functions of the supervisory board. However, according to the German Federal Court of Justice and academia, the supervisory board also has to give advice to the management board.[244] Stressing the relevance of control for the future prospects of the company, the German Corporate Governance Code names advice first and states that the supervisory board must regularly advise and supervise the management board in the management of the company.[245] In academia it is disputed whether only the members of the manage-

---

[236] Point 3.2 German Corporate Governance Code.

[237] Point 3.3 German Corporate Governance Code.

[238] Gesetz zur weiteren Reform des Aktien-, und Bilanzrechts, zu Transparenz und Publizität (Transparenz- und Publizitätsgesetz), 19 July 2002, BGBl I 1588.

[239] Section 111(4)2 Stock Corporation Act.

[240] M. Lutter and G. Krieger, *Rechte und Pflichten des Aufsichtsrats,* 5th edn. (Cologne, Otto Schmidt 2008) no.104.

[241] Hopt/Roth, *Großkommentar Aktiengesetz* (see n. 86), Section 111 no. 605–631.

[242] Lutter/Krieger, *Rechte und Pflichten des Aufsichtsrats* (see n. 240), no. 109, 113.

[243] Section 111(1) Stock Corporation Act.

[244] See above 2.1(a).

[245] Point 5.1.1(1) German Corporate Governance Code.

ment board or also the employees of the company are to be monitored by the supervisory board.[246]

While supervision is one primary task of the supervisory board, there are also monitoring duties for the management board.[247] Supervision by the management board is apparently needed for (senior) employees. Due to the concept of common responsibility for the management board, there should also be supervision of the fellow managing directors.

e) Internal Control and Risk Management

The supervisory board as a whole has to also monitor risk management, internal control and the external auditor.[248] This is part of the general duty of the supervisory board to monitor the business of the company.[249] The Stock Corporation Act contains a duty of the management board to provide the supervisory board with information on the affairs of the company.[250] The audit committee, if established, has to monitor risk management, internal control and the external auditor.[251]

According to the German Corporate Governance Code, the supervisory board must set up an audit committee that, in particular, handles the monitoring of the accounting process, the effectiveness of the internal control system, risk management system and internal audit system, the audit of the annual financial statements (in particular, the independence of the auditor, the additional services rendered by the auditor, the issuing of the audit mandate to the auditor, the determination of auditing focal points and the fee agreement) and—unless another committee is entrusted therewith—compliance.[252] The management board has to inform the supervisory board[253] and it has to consult the chairman of the supervisory board on the risk situation and the risk management of the company.[254]

---

[246] For an opinion that the employees should be monitored, see M. Roth, 'Möglichkeiten vorstandsunabhängiger Information des Aufsichtsrats', *Die Aktiengesellschaft* 2004, 1, 5; it is generally accepted that at least the supervision of the employees by the management board has to be monitored, see Hopt/Roth, *Großkommentar Aktiengesetz* (see n. 86), Section 111 no. 251–259.

[247] K.J. Hopt, *Großkommentar Aktiengesetz,* 4th edn. (Berlin, De Gruyter 1999), Section 93 no. 107.

[248] For the duties of the supervisory board as a whole and delegable tasks, see Hopt/Roth, *Großkommentar Aktiengesetz* (see n. 86), Section 111 no. 210–231, 476–487.

[249] Section 111(1) Stock Corporation Act.

[250] Section 90 Stock Corporation Act.

[251] Section 107(3)(2) Stock Corporation Act.

[252] Point 5.3.2(1) German Corporate Governance Code.

[253] Point 3.4(2) German Corporate Governance Code.

[254] Point 5.2(4) German Corporate Governance Code.

f) Auditor

In German corporate governance, the general meeting appoints the auditor.[255] The supervisory board proposes the auditors for appointment by the general meeting and contracts with the auditor appointed by the general meeting.[256] The auditor has to attend the meeting of the supervisory board dealing with the annual accounts or a meeting of the audit committee.[257]

g) Representation of the Company

As a general rule, the stock corporation is represented by the management board.[258] As against the members of the management board, it is the supervisory board, and not the chairman of the supervisory board,[259] that represents the company.[260] According to the German Federal Court of Justice, the same applies vis-à-vis former members of the management board.[261] Although not explicitly stated in the German Stock Corporation Act, the company is also represented vis-à-vis the auditor by the supervisory board.[262]

2.2. Organisation and Internal Functioning

2.2.1. Composition of the Boards

a) Size of the Supervisory Board

The size of the supervisory board is subject to the Stock Corporation Act and the co-determination regimes which allow between three and twenty-one members.[263] For companies subject to quasi-parity co-determination, the Co-Determination Act 1976 provides for a board of twelve, sixteen or twenty supervisory directors, depending on the number of employees in Germany.[264] German blue chips

---

[255] Section 119(1) no. 4 Stock Corporation Act.

[256] Section 111(2)3 Stock Corporation Act.

[257] Section 171(1)2 Stock Corporation Act.

[258] Section 78 Stock Corporation Act.

[259] Hopt/Roth, *Großkommentar Aktiengesetz* (see n. 86), Section 112 no. 71.

[260] Section 112 Stock Corporation Act.

[261] Bundesgerichtshof, 16 February 2009, II ZR 282/07, *Neue Zeitschrift für Gesellschaftsrecht* 2009, 466; Hopt/Roth, *Großkommentar Aktiengesetz* (see n. 86), Section 112 no. 25–37.

[262] Hopt/Roth, *Großkommentar Aktiengesetz* (see n. 86), Section 112 no. 58.

[263] Section 95(1)-(3) Stock Corporation Act.

[264] Section 7(1)1, 2 Co-Determination Act (Mitbest).

therefore have by far the largest boards in Europe.[265] German stock corporations reincorporating as European Companies usually choose smaller boards; BASF and Allianz reduced the size of the supervisory board from twenty to twelve members.[266] This is considered to be one of the driving forces for choosing the form of a European Company.[267]

b) Number of Non-Executives (Supervisory Directors) and Executives (Managing Directors)

The supervisory board is mandatory and composed only of non-executive directors (NEDs). Since the reform of the Commercial Code (HGB) in 1884, members of the management board may not simultaneously be members of the supervisory board.[268] The aim of that reform was to avoid the management board and the supervisory board being appointed so as to build a *de facto* board of directors[269] by staffing both boards (partly) with the same persons. Nevertheless, German company law at that time explicitly gave the supervisory board more competences,[270] thereby transforming the supervisory board into a *de facto* board of directors.[271] This two-tier structure is still predominant for savings banks and Landesbanken.[272] Initially, the supervisory board was to be staffed only with outside directors, given the definition of the inside director having his primary employment within the company.[273] Employees could not be appointed as supervisory directors until co-determination was introduced.[274] The exclusion of employees from being supervisory directors was removed in the 1950s to allow co-determination and also higher levels of co-determination than required by law.[275]

---

[265] Heidrick & Struggles, below n. 281.

[266] K.J. Hopt, 'Comparative Corporate Governance' (see n. 71) 53.

[267] Ernst & Young, *Study on the operation and the impacts of the Statute for a European Company (SE)*, 9 December 2009, 246.

[268] Section 225a Commercial Code (Allgemeines Handelsgesetzbuch, ADHGB 1884).

[269] Notes to the governmental draft, see Schubert and Hommelhoff (see n. 182) 461.

[270] Art 225 (3) Commercial Code (ADHGB 1884).

[271] Notes to the governmental draft, see Schubert and Hommelhoff (see n. 182) 461.

[272] See above 1.2.1, 1.3(b).

[273] M. Becht, P. Bolton and A. Roëll, 'Corporate Law and Governance', *Handbook of Law and Economics*, Volume 2 (Amsterdam, Elsevier 2007) 829, 877.

[274] First after World War I, then after World War II, see below 3.2.1(b). For a different co-determination model, see the Dutch report.

[275] Section 84(2) no. 3 Betriebsverfassungsgesetz, 11 October 1952, BGBl I 681, 694 (cited as BetrVG 1952).

However, even during the Weimar Republic, the Works Council was allowed to appoint one or two employee representatives to the supervisory board.[276]

The number of supervisory board members is regulated in the Stock Corporation Act,[277] in the Co-Determination Act 1976 (quasi-parity co-determination for companies with more than 2,000 employees in Germany)[278] and in the Act on Co-Determination in the Coal, Iron and Steel Industry.[279] Due to co-determination, large companies have a supervisory board of twelve to twenty members.[280] Therefore, the average board size in the DAX 30 companies is 17.1 (in 2009: 17.7), the highest in Europe.[281] For companies not subject to the Co-Determination Act 1976 or the coal, iron and steel co-determination regime, the Stock Corporation Act applies.[282] The Stock Corporation Act provides for a supervisory board of three to twenty-one; the number of supervisory directors has to be a multiple of three.[283] That rule was introduced in the 1950s when co-determination was mandatory in principle for all stock corporations regardless of the number of employees.[284] This was not reversed when the co-determination regime for stock corporations was adjusted to the co-determination regime for limited liability

---

[276] Betriebsrätegesetz, 4 February 1920, RGBl 147, Section 70, supplemented by by the Gesetz über die Entsendung von Betriebsratsmitgliedern in den Aufsichtsrat, 15 February 1922, RGBl 209; for the interpretation G. Flatow and O. Kahn-Freund, *Betriebsrätegesetz*, 13th edn. (Berlin, Springer 1931).

[277] Section 95 Stock Corporation Act: between 3 and 21 members, the number has to be divisible through three.

[278] Section 7(2) Co-Determination Act (MitbestG).

[279] Gesetz über die Mitbestimmung der Arbeitnehmer in den Aufsichtsräten und Vorständen der Unternehmen des Bergbaus und der Eisen und Stahl erzeugenden Industrie, English translation by the Federal Ministry of Economics and Technology (BMWI), available at <www.bmwi.de/English/Redaktion/Pdf/__Archiv/labour-law/act-on-co-determination-in-the-coal-iron-and-steel-industry>, Section 4(1) Act on Co-Determination in the Coal, Iron and Steel Industry (Montan-MitbestG). For more detail, see below 3.2.1.

[280] Section 7(2) Co-Determination Act (MitbestG) 1976: 12, 16 or 20 members; the higher the number of employees, the higher the minimum number of supervisory directors.

[281] According to Heidrick & Struggles, *Challenging board performance* (2011) 37; *idem.*, *Boards in turbulent times* (2009) 12, European average 11.8.

[282] Section 95 Stock Corporation Act.

[283] The supervisory board may therefore have three, six, nine, twelve, fifteen, eighteen or twenty-one members.

[284] Only family owned companies (*Familiengesellschaften*) with no more than 500 employees were excluded.

companies (*GmbH*) in 1994.[285] Today, the One-Third Participation Act applies only for 'new' companies with more than 500 employees in Germany.[286]

The number of directors in the management board is not subject to restrictions in the Stock Corporation Act.[287] The German Corporate Governance Code provides for a management board comprising several persons and the appointment of a chairman or spokesman;[288] the Co-Determination Act allows for an *Arbeitsdirektor* (a managing director responsible for the employees).[289] The management board is (at least in most cases) smaller than the supervisory board. It is common practice in Germany that all members of the management board are executives. Whether the transformation of the management board into a board of directors subject to control of the supervisory board fits into the legal framework of the current Stock Corporation Act[290] should be subject to further discussion.[291]

c) Employee Representation

Due to mandatory employee representation in large German companies, a stakeholder-oriented composition of the board prevails.[292] Three models of employee representation can be distinguished: the third-parity co-determination according to the One-Participation Act in companies with more than 500 employees; the quasi-parity co-determination with a decisive vote of the chairman of the supervisory board according to the Co-Determination Act 1976 in companies with more than 2,000 employees; and parity composition with an independent member according to the special co-determination regime in the coal, iron and steel industries.[293] The German co-determination system allows only for the

---

[285] Gesetz für kleine Aktiengesellschaften und zur Deregulierung des Aktienrechts, 2 August 1994, BGBl I 2911; for the increase the numbers of AGs since 1994 (now falling) above 1.1(e) and M. Roth, *Festschrift Hopt* (see n. 331) 1264.

[286] This number is in principle necessary if the company was registered on or after 10 August 1994, Section 1(1) no. 1 One-Third Participation Act (DrittelbG).

[287] Section 76(2)1 Stock Corporation Act; it may be one or more managing directors.

[288] Point 4.2.1 German Corporate Governance Code; assuming that two managing directors fulfil this provision, see H.M. Ringleb in Ringleb et al (see n. 63) no. 664.

[289] Section 33 Co-Determination Act (MitbestG).

[290] For a suggestion to explicitly allow appointing managing directors with an advisory function, see the Notes of the Company Law Reform Act 1884, Schubert/Hommelhoff (see n. 182) 461.

[291] For China, see D.C. Clarke, 'The Independent Director in Chinese Corporate Governance', *Delaware Journal of Corporate Law* 31 (2006) 125.

[292] In more detail, see below 3.2.1(b).

[293] Section 4(1) One-Third Participation Act (DrittelbG), Section 7(1) Co-Determination Act (MitbestG) and Section 4(1) Act on Co-Determination in the Coal, Iron and Steel Industry (Montan-MitbestG). For numbers, see below 3.2.1(b).

representation of employees employed in Germany,[294] a provision which is strongly criticised.[295] Co-determination is not only mandatory for the supervisory board in companies that employ more than 500 (2,000) employees. Holding companies incorporated as a stock corporation or a limited liability company with subsidiaries employing more than 500 (2,000) employees also have to include employee representatives on their supervisory board.[296] About 1,500 companies are subject to third-parity co-determination (695 stock corporations)[297] and about 700 companies are subject to quasi-parity co-determination (280 stock corporations).[298] Also taking into account parity co-determination, about 1,000 stock corporations in Germany are subject to co-determination.

Employee representation is in principle limited to the supervisory board. However, in companies with more than 2,000 employees in Germany, an *Arbeitsdirektor* must be appointed.[299] The *Arbeitsdirektor* is often a member of a union which is represented in a company.[300]

d) Special Qualification Requirements and Training of Supervisory Directors

In implementing the auditor directive, one member of the supervisory board of publicly traded companies must be a financial expert.[301] Employee representatives are not subject to special qualification requirements. The literature emphasises that all supervisory directors must have sufficient expertise to fulfil their

---

[294] For a reform proposal, see below 3.2.1(d).

[295] N. Raabe (see n. 55) 333; H.J. Hellwig and C. Behme, 'Gemeinschaftsrechtliche Probleme der deutschen Unternehmensmitbestimmung', *Die Aktiengesellschaft,* 2009, 261; *idem.*, 'Zur Einbeziehung ausländischer Belegschaften in die deutsche Unternehmensmitbestimmung', *Zeitschrift für Wirtschaftsrecht* 2009, 1791 and 'Gemeinschaftsrechtswidrigkeit und Anwendungsvorrang des Gemeinschaftsrechts in der deutschen Unternehmensmitbestimmung', *Zeitschrift für Wirtschaftsrecht* 2010, 871; V. Rieble and C. Latzel, 'Inlandsmitbestimmung als Ausländerdiskriminierung bei Standortkonflikten', *Europäische Zeitschrift für Arbeitsrecht* 2011, 145. Currently, German companies have reincorporated as SEs, M. Roth, 'Employee Participation' (see n. 57) 72.

[296] Section 5 Co-Determination Act (MitbestG), Section 2 One-Third Participation Act (DrittelbG).

[297] W. Bayer and T. Hoffmann, 'Drittbeteiligung der Arbeitnehmer im Aufsichtsrat', *AG-Report* 2010, 151, 153.

[298] Data for end of 2010 available at <www.boeckler.de>.

[299] Section 33 Co-Determination Act (MitbestG).

[300] The Arbeitsdirektor does *not* represent the interests of the employees: M. Henssler, in P. Ulmer, M. Habersack and M. Henssler, *Mitbestimmungsrecht,* 2nd edn. (Munich, C.H. Beck 2006), Section 33 Co-Determination Act no. 29: primarily the interest of the enterprise.

[301] Section 100(5) Stock Corporation Act.

duties.[302] For the financial industry, the expertise of supervisory directors is also now subject to control by the Federal Financial Supervisory Authority (BaFin).[303] Since the amendments to the German Corporate Governance Code in 2012, the Code contains a special provision on the training of supervisory directors. The members of the supervisory board are themselves responsible for taking the necessary training and further education measures required for the performance of their tasks. They should be supported by the company appropriately.[304]

e) Independence and Expertise Requirements for the Chairman

In Germany, there is no general independence requirement for the chairman of the supervisory board at the time of appointment.[305] However, according to the German Corporate Governance Code, if a former member of the management board is to be elected as the chairman of the supervisory board, this exception must be justified at the general meeting.[306] Generally, a quorum of shareholders with 25 per cent of the voting rights of the company is needed to elect a member of the management board (current or in the last two years) as supervisory director and they must present a motion to elect the (former) member of the management board as supervisory director.[307]

For the chairman of the management board, neither the Stock Corporation Act nor the German Corporate Governance Code contains specific requirements. According to the Stock Corporation Act, the functions of the CEO and the chairman of the supervisory board may not be combined.[308] Both the chairman and the CEO must have the expertise to fulfil the respective function in the management or in the supervisory board.

f) Restrictions with Respect to Similar Functions in Other Companies

The number of supervisory board directorships is restricted by both the Stock Corporation Act and the German Corporate Governance Code. The Stock Corporation Act limits the total number to ten seats in (non-group) supervisory

---

[302] J. Semler, *Münchener Kommentar Aktiengesetz,* 2nd edn. (Munich, C.H. Beck 2004), Section 100, no. 66–74.

[303] Section 36(3) Banking Act, Section 7a(4) Insurance Supervisory Act; see above 1.2.

[304] Point 5.4.5(2) German Corporate Governance Code.

[305] For such a requirement, see UK Corporate Governance Code A.3.1.

[306] Point 5.4.4(2) German Corporate Governance Code refers indirectly to memberships in the last two years.

[307] Section 100(2)1 no. 4 Stock Corporation Act, Point 5.4.4(1) German Corporate Governance Code.

[308] Section 105 Stock Corporation Act.

boards.[309] For managing directors of listed companies, the German Corporate Governance Code restricts supervisory directorships to three in other non-group listed companies.[310] Furthermore, every member of the supervisory board must take care that they have sufficient time to perform their mandates.[311]

Some other restrictions with respect to similar positions in other companies are to be seen in the light of independence requirements and conflicts of interest. A member of the management board of a controlled company may not be appointed as supervisory director in a controlling company.[312] By law it is forbidden to hold an interlocking directorship, ie. to be legal representative of another corporation whose supervisory board includes a member of the management board of the company.[313]

The German Corporate Governance Code provides that supervisory directors must not exercise directorships or similar positions or advisory tasks for important competitors of the company.[314] In academia, it is contested whether the election of someone also serving in the supervisory board of a competitor is void.[315] According to the majority view, such person may be dismissed for not being able to fulfil their duties.[316]

g) Expertise Requirements and Gender Diversity

The Stock Corporation Act contains no overall principles for the composition of the supervisory board or the composition of the management board. Besides the principle of shared responsibility of all directors in the respective boards,[317] the Stock Corporation Act provides only that directors must be natural persons.[318] Academic opinion also suggests that directors should have adequate skills and

---

[309] Section 100(2)1 no. 1 Stock Corporation Act; seats with the function of a chairman count for two seats but five seats in supervisory boards of the same group do not count.

[310] Point 5.4.5(2) German Corporate Governance Code.

[311] Point 5.4.5(1) German Corporate Governance Code.

[312] Section 100(2)1 no. 2 Stock Corporation Act.

[313] Section 100(2) 1 no. 3 Stock Corporation Act.

[314] Point 5.4.2(3) German Corporate Governance Code.

[315] For this view, see M. Lutter, 'Bankenvertreter im Aufsichtsrat', *Zeitschrift für das gesamte Handels- und Wirtschaftsrecht* 145 (1981) 224, 236 ff.; idem., in 'Die Unwirksamkeit von Mehrfachmandaten in den Aufsichtsräten von Konkurrenzunternehmen', *Festschrift Beusch* (Berlin, De Gruyter 1993) 509; Lutter/Krieger, *Rechte und Pflichten des Aufsichtsrats* (see n. 240) no. 22.

[316] Hopt/Roth, *Großkommentar Aktiengesetz* (see n. 86), Section 100 nos. 78–85.

[317] Sections 76, 77, 111 Stock Corporation Act.

[318] Sections 76(3) 1, 100(1) Stock Corporation Act.

experience.[319] Overarching principles are stated in the German Corporate Governance Code.[320] The overall principles for the composition of the supervisory board
were rewritten in 2009 and 2010. Since 2010, there has been more emphasis on
the focus on diversity on the management board; in particular, the appointment of
women was added.[321] In 2011, there was no change to the German Code, also to
prevent further political pressure towards a quorum on board diversity in the German Corporate Governance Code. In 2010, non-compliance was rather high.[322]

In 2009, the German Corporate Governance Code stated that for nominations
for the election of members of the supervisory board, care must be taken that the
supervisory board is at all times composed of members who have the required
knowledge, abilities and expert experience to properly complete their tasks.[323]
Furthermore, attention must be paid to the international activities of the company,
potential conflicts of interest, specifying an age limit for the members of the
supervisory board, and diversity.[324] Since June 2010, the German Corporate Governance Code states that the supervisory board has to be composed in such a way
that its members as a group possesses the knowledge, ability and expert
experience required to properly complete its tasks.[325] The supervisory board must
specify concrete objectives regarding composition which, whilst considering the
specifics of the company, must take into account the international activities of the
company, potential conflicts of interests—since 2012 also the number of independent supervisory directors,[326]—an age limit specified for the members of the
supervisory board, and diversity. These concrete objectives must, in particular,
stipulate an appropriate degree of female representation.[327]

The overall principle for the composition of the management board is that
when appointing the management board, the supervisory board must also respect
diversity and, in particular, aim for an appropriate consideration of women.[328]
The management board must comprise several persons and have a chairman or

---

[319] Hopt/Roth, *Großkommentar Aktiengesetz* (see n. 86), Section 100 no. 20, arguing that it is
not a requirement for the validity of the appointment; see now the corporate governance of banks,
which also gives BaFin the power to check the skills of supervisory directors; see above 1.2.

[320] Point 5.4.1 German Corporate Governance Code.

[321] Point 5.1.2(1)2 German Corporate Governance Code.

[322] A. von Werder and J. Böhme, 'Corporate Governance Report 2011', *Der Betrieb*, 2011,
1285, 1345: 83%.

[323] Point 5.4.1(1) German Corporate Governance Code 2009.

[324] Point 5.4.1(2) German Corporate Governance Code 2009.

[325] Point 5.4.1(1) German Corporate Governance Code.

[326] Independent within the meaning of Point 5.4.2 German Corporate Governance Code
(not a controlling shareholder).

[327] Point 5.4.1(2) German Corporate Governance Code.

[328] Point 5.1.2(1) (2) Corporate Governance Code.

spokesman.[329] By-laws must govern the work of the management board, in particular the allocation of duties among individual management board members, matters reserved for the management board as a whole, and the required majority for management board resolutions.[330]

According to a recent study by Heidrick & Struggles, German boards have one of the smallest proportions of foreign directors in Europe.[331] The proportion of women on the boards is slightly above the European average;[332] this is due to co-determination. The One-Third Participation Act requires that the number of female employee representatives is comparative to the ratio of female employees in Germany.[333] For the union-representatives in quasi-parity co-determined companies, the union for the metal and electronic industry (IG Metall) recently implemented a quorum of thirty per cent for women.[334] Among the shareholder representatives, the proportion of women is low. The German Government has pressed for improvements, most recently in the response to the report of the Government Commission German Corporate Governance Code in February 2011,[335] but is currently divided as to how to proceed.

h) Evaluation of Supervisory Board Performance

According to the German Corporate Governance Code, the supervisory board must examine the efficiency of its activities on a regular basis.[336] Evaluation is a recommendation with a high compliance rate expected but not reported.[337] No

---

[329] Point 4.2.1(1) German Corporate Governance Code.

[330] Unanimity or resolution by majority vote, Point 4.2.1(2) German Corporate Governance Code.

[331] According to Heidrick & Struggles, *Challenging board performance* (2011) it is 11%, versus the European average of 24%. Only Spain has less non-national directors (10%), according to Heidrick & Struggles, *Boards in turbulent times* (2009), also referred to by the green paper (6): *Boards in turbulent times*, 2009, 13: 8%, European average 23%.

[332] Apparently 13% (11%) versus 12% (10%) in Europe, Heidrick & Struggles, *Challenging board performance* (2011) 39; *idem.*, *Boards in turbulent times* (2009) 15.

[333] Section 4(4) One-Third Participation Act (DrittelbG); there is a similar practice for companies subject to the Co-Determination Act 1976 (MitbestG).

[334] *Frankfurter Allgemeine Zeitung (FAZ)*, 14 February 2011, 13.

[335] Stellungnahme der Bundesregierung zum Bericht der Regierungskommission Deutscher Corporate Governance Kodex vom November 2010, (1).

[336] Point 5.6 German Corporate Governance Code.

[337] A. von Werder and J. Böhme (see n. 322) 1285 and 1345 and A. von Werder and T. Talaulicar, 'Kodex Report 2010: Die Akzeptanz der Empfehlungen und Anregungen des Deutschen Corporate Governance Kodex', *Der Betrieb* 2010, 853, 860 report no data, apparently referring to data in the annual reports; Heidrick & Struggles, *Challenging board performance* (2011) 29–30 (60% for Germany).

external control is required; yet it is employed in practice, at least by some boards. As a result of the Green Paper on corporate governance, further action might be on the agenda, even though not mentioned explicitly in the Action Plan.[338]

2.2.2. Decision-making

a) Direction of the Management Board and Agenda-setting in the Supervisory Board

As mentioned above,[339] in Germany the company is directed by the management board. The management board sets the strategy and is responsible for the daily business affairs. The management board determines the discussions and decisions of the supervisory board *inter alia* in its reports.[340] The preparation and conduction of the supervisory board meetings has to reflect the limited time for individual items on the agenda of the supervisory board and the possible enhancement, or at least preservation of, corporate value through challenging the view of management. In setting the agenda, the supervisory board is not entirely dependent on management: The chairman of the supervisory board not only meets regularly with the management board,[341] and therefore has a more in-depth view of the company; he might also use other information channels,[342] enabling him to set an agenda which might promote a fruitful discussion, prevent wrongdoing and limit questionable business decisions by the management, but also provide new insights by supervisory directors for the management.[343]

b) Veto Rights of the Supervisory Board (Non-Executive Directors) and the Right to Advise the Management Board

The Stock Corporation Act states that the articles of association or the supervisory board itself has to require the consent of the supervisory board for certain transactions.[344] This excludes the use of blanket clauses, such as 'all significant transactions'. Rather, the transactions covered by the reservation of approval must be determined according to specific features.[345] Examples of such reservations of

---

[338] *Action Plan: European company law and corporate governance – a modern legal framework for more engaged shareholders and sustainable companies*, Brussels, 12 December 2012, COM(2012) 740 final.

[339] See above 2.1(b).

[340] See below 2.3(a).

[341] See below 2.2.2(f).

[342] See below 2.3.

[343] On the co-operation of the boards, see above 2.1(a).

[344] Section 111(4)2 Stock Corporation Act. See already above 2.1(b), (c).

[345] Hopt/Roth, *Großkommentar Aktiengesetz* (see n. 86), Section 111 no. 643.

approval specified[346] are, *inter alia*, budget planning and investment planning, their adjustment and transgression. In the literature, there are a great deal more specifications.[347] The dominant view in academia is that ad hoc consent requirements do not meet the criteria of the German Stock Corporation Act;[348] therefore, such catalogues are of relevance for practice.

Possibly an even more powerful tool to influence the management of the company is the supervisory board's right to advise the management board in managing the company. While veto rights are seldom applied and serve as fleet in being in normal business, the right to advise may add real value by challenging, and possibly improving, management board decisions. Advice could be provided by the chairman who regularly meets with the management board,[349] but is primarily given by the supervisory board.[350] The Federal Court of Justice assumes a duty of the supervisory board to advise the management board.[351] In conducting its advisory function, the supervisory board is not restricted to investigating whether the acts of management were lawful.[352] In giving advice, the supervisory board must apply its own business discretion[353] and may develop solutions not

---

[346] Lutter/Krieger, *Rechte und Pflichten des Aufsichtsrats* (see n. 240), no. 109.

[347] Lutter/Krieger, *Rechte und Pflichten des Aufsichtsrats* (see n. 240), no. 109, referring further to the formation of subsidiary companies and branches domestically and abroad, provided their task goes beyond that of distribution; acquisition and disposal of companies or parts of companies exceeding x Euros; acquisition and disposal of immovable property exceeding x Euros; raising of loans exceeding x Euros; extension of loans exceeding x Euros; adoption and adjustment of employee option plans, regardless of how these are structured; admission of new products and productions, including their function; appointment and dismissal of management board members and managing directors in substantial subsidiary companies. There is also a group of company perspective: the management board is obligated to adopt the same rights to reserve approval in substantial subsidiary companies. This is in conjunction with its duty to grant its approval in those subsidiaries only after the supervisory board's approval. The conclusion of company-internal collective wage agreements and works agreements can also be subject to supervisory board approval. In this respect, no approach is evident which derives inherent limits of this right from the trade unions' right to free collective bargaining or from the competences accorded to the bodies under the industrial relations law.

[348] See above 2.1(c).

[349] See above 2.2.2(f).

[350] For notification duties of the management board correlated to advice of the supervisory board, see below 2.3(a).

[351] Bundesgerichtshof, 25 March 1991, II ZR 188/89, Amtliche Sammlung (BGHZ) 114, 127; Bundesgerichtshof, 4 July 1994, II ZR 197/93, BGHZ 126, 340, 344.

[352] This is the minimum standard for control. On its reach, see Hopt/Roth, *Großkommentar Aktiengesetz* (see n. 86), Section 111 no. 301–305.

[353] Hopt/Roth, *Großkommentar Aktiengesetz* (see n. 86), Section 111 no. 276

considered by the management board, choose the most suitable alternative or estimate the profitability of projects developed by management.[354]

c) *Supervisory Directors Acting as a Group*

Following the long-time view of the German Corporate Governance Code, which corresponds with comparative literature,[355] the one-tier and the two-tier systems are converging;[356] yet differences remain due to the respective institutional settings. The main difference between the two systems is that by definition supervisory directors act as a group. With managing and supervisory directors, German corporate governance defines two groups. When resolutions of the supervisory board are needed, only members of the supervisory board may vote. The supervisory board has to be composed in such a way that its members *as a group* possess the knowledge, ability and expert experience to properly complete its tasks.[357] In a one-tier board, committees staffed with independent directors might form similar groups and therefore be seen as an 'amalgam' of a supervisory board.[358] Compared with traditional German supervisory boards, such practice shifts monitoring from the board as a whole to its committees. Nevertheless, internationally there are generally fewer 'executive meetings', comprising all non-executive (independent) directors, than meetings of a German supervisory board.[359]

For the practical differences between the one-tier and the two-tier board models, it is to be stressed that members of the management board in Germany regularly attend the meetings of the supervisory board in full length. The difference between one-tier boards and two-tier boards could therefore be seen as the mandatory partition of the directors into two groups of directors in the setting of a board meeting, attended by both executive and non-executive directors. Behavioural science might give further insights to the understanding of the two basic corporate governance models. A stronger group feeling of supervisory directors might explain why German policy makers are reluctant to recommend committees.[360]

---

[354] Hopt/Roth, *Großkommentar Aktiengesetz* (see n. 86), Section 111 no. 290, 306–308.

[355] For this view, see text to n. 358 below.

[356] German Corporate Governance Code 2012, Foreword (9): one-tier and two-tier systems converge and are equally successful, omitted in 2013.

[357] Point 5.4.1(1) German Corporate Governance Code.

[358] R. Kraakman et al (see n. 168) 40, 2nd edn., (see n. 77) with greater focus on independent directors.

[359] Heidrick & Struggles, *Challenging board performance* (2011) 26, reports 5.9 meetings of the supervisory board; see above 1.3(a).

[360] See 2.2(f).

d) Majority

The Stock Corporation Act states that the supervisory board makes decisions by resolution.[361] To be competent, as an overall default rule, at least half of the members of the supervisory board have to attend the meeting.[362] Practical problems occur in small boards since at least three members must vote on the resolution.[363] Since the number of supervisory directors has to be divisible by three,[364] the board cannot act if it has less than six members (ie. three members) and one member is absent or excluded from resolutions due to a conflict of interest. In the latter case, the German Federal Court of Justice allows the fellow supervisory director to take part in the resolution in which he has to abstain.[365] This pragmatic view helps but cannot solve every problem.

The divisibility-by-three principle, meant to ensure third-parity co-determination, has effectively lost its rationale since the overwhelming majority of German stock corporations are now co-determination-free.[366] All small and medium-sized companies founded in 1994[367] and later with less than 500 employees in Germany are not subject to the One-Third Participation Act.[368]

For resolutions in the supervisory board, the general rule is that a simple majority of votes is sufficient for a resolution to pass.[369] The articles of association may set a higher quorum (for certain matters) but may not require unanimous consent.[370] Higher standards may not take the risk of hindering the affairs of the company; therefore, in companies subject to quasi-parity co-determination, higher quorums are ruled out.[371] Multiple voting rights violate the principle of same duties, same rights, that is applicable to supervisory directors.[372] However, the

---

[361] Section 108(1) Stock Corporation Act.

[362] Section 108(2)1 Stock Corporation Act. The articles of incorporation generally may provide a higher or more lenient quota, but not in (quasi-)parity co-determined companies; for details, see Hopt/Roth, *Großkommentar Aktiengesetz* (see n. 86), Section 108 no. 71–96.

[363] Section 108(2)3 Stock Corporation Act.

[364] Section 95 Stock Corporation Act.

[365] Bundesgerichtshof (BGH), 2 April 2007, II ZR 325/05, ZIP 2007, 1056 (assuming a duty of the interested supervisory board member to participate).

[366] Above 2.2.1(c).

[367] Registration on 10 August 1994 or later.

[368] Section 1(1) no. 1 One-Third-Participation Act (DrittelbG).

[369] Hopt/Roth, *Großkommentar Aktiengesetz* (see n. 86), Section 108 no. 30.

[370] Hopt/Roth, *Großkommentar Aktiengesetz* (see n. 86), Section 108 no. 36–38.

[371] Hopt/Roth, *Großkommentar Aktiengesetz* (see n. 86), Section 108 no. 35.

[372] No explicit regulation in the Stock Corporation Act or court decisions, but considered as common sense in academia.

chairman of the supervisory board in quasi-parity co-determined companies has a deciding vote.[373]

In the management board, the default rule is that it must act unanimously in running the affairs of the company.[374] The articles of association or the regulation of the management board may not provide that one member of the management board may make a decision against the wishes of the majority of the management board.[375]

e) Separate Sessions

Taking the two German boards together, the supervisory board and the management board serve as a segregated board of directors: the Stock Corporation Act speaks of the administration of the company by the members of the management and the supervisory board.[376] As mentioned,[377] the members of the management board usually participate in meetings of the supervisory board and attend the meetings in full length. The members of the management board have no legal right to participate in the meetings of the supervisory board and could be excluded without cause.[378]

The German Corporate Governance Code provides for 'executive sessions' of the supervisory board in which the management board does not take part.[379] Unlike the listing requirements of the Nasdaq, which allow for two executive sessions,[380] there is no explicit number or minimum requirement. The German Corporate Governance Code provides only that, if necessary, the supervisory board must meet without the management board,[381] but is open to regular executive sessions.[382] It is not specified when executive sessions are to be seen as necessary.[383] Before the 2012 amendments of the German Corporate Governance

---

[373] Section 29(2) Co-Determination Act (MitbestG).

[374] Section 77(1) 1 Stock Corporation Act.

[375] Section 77(1) 2 Stock Corporation Act.

[376] Section 120(2) Stock Corporation Act.

[377] At 2.2(b).

[378] Hopt/Roth, *Großkommentar Aktiengesetz* (see n. 86), Section 109 no. 27.

[379] Point 3.6(2) German Corporate Governance Code.

[380] Nasdaq Listing Rules 5605(b)(2) and IM 5605-2.

[381] Point 3.6(2) German Corporate Governance Code.

[382] A. von Werder, in Ringleb et al (see n. 63) no. 412 (good reasons for regular executive sessions, one or two sessions per year).

[383] A. von Werder, in Ringleb et al (see n. 63) no. 411: it is up to the supervisory board to decide when an executive session is necessary.

Code, executive sessions were phrased as mere suggestions, though the company did not have to disclose deviations from the Code.[384]

While separate sessions of the employee representatives on the supervisory board are common practice, the holding of separate sessions by the shareholder representatives, which the Corporate Governance Code prior to the 2012 amendment suggested, was contested.[385] The rationale in favour thereof might have been to provide an institutionalised mechanism for control by the shareholder representatives. It is reported that the shareholder representatives addressed strategic questions and critique in informal sessions with members of the management board, not in the sessions of the supervisory board.[386] Since the 2012 amendment, the German Corporate Governance Code provides for separate sessions of employee and shareholder representatives merely as a possibility.[387]

f) Role of the Chairman of the Supervisory Board

Appointing a chairperson of the supervisory board has been a mandatory requirement of German company law since 1937.[388] According to the current Stock Corporation Act, the supervisory board has to elect a chairman and at least one deputy chairman[389] The deputy has only the rights and the duties of the chairman if the latter is incapacitated,[390] eg. cannot attend the meeting of the supervisory board.[391] In quasi-parity co-determined companies, the chairman is usually a shareholder-representative and the deputy chairman is an employee-representative. The Co-Determination Act provides for a two-thirds majority for the first vote to elect the chairman and the vice chairman.[392] If there is no such majority,

---

[384] Foreword (10) German Corporate Governance Code.

[385] Thinking in subgroups splits the board, see even A. von Werder, in Ringleb et al (see n. 63), no. 406; therefore practice is reluctant and the compliance rate is low, see A. von Werder and T. Talaulicar (see n. 337) 860, below n. 716.

[386] T. Baums and K.E. Scott, 'Taking Shareholder Protection Seriously? Corporate Governance in the United States and Germany', *American Journal on Comparative Law* 53 (2005) 31, 55.

[387] M. Roth, 'Deutscher Corporate Governance Kodex 2012', *Wertpapier-Mitteilungen* 2012, 1985, 1990.

[388] Section 92 (1) 1937 Stock Corporation Act. Calling for more extensive regulation of the role of the chairman, K. von Schenck, 'Der Aufsichtsrat und sein Vorsitzender – Eine Regelungslücke', *Die Aktiengesellschaft*, 2010, 649.

[389] Section 107(1)1 Stock Corporation Act.

[390] Section 107(1)3 Stock Corporation Act.

[391] Hopt/Roth, *Großkommentar Aktiengesetz* (see n. 86), Section 107 no. 155.

[392] Section 27(1) Co-Determination Act (MitbestG).

in a second vote, the shareholder-representatives elect the chairman and the employee-representatives elect the deputy-chairman.[393]

The chairman sets the agenda of the supervisory board meeting.[394] This, and the practice that the chairman of the supervisory board is in close contact with the chairman of the management board,[395] designates him to be the central player in the supervisory board. The Co-Determination Act 1976 allows for a decisive vote in quasi-parity co-determined companies.[396] The chairman also decides whether a member should be excluded from participating in a meeting or from decision-making due to a conflict of interests.[397] In academia, it is disputed whether the supervisory board as a whole may overrule procedural decisions of the chairman.[398] The better arguments are for the view that the supervisory board as a whole makes the final decisions.

According to the German Corporate Governance Code, the chairman of the supervisory board coordinates the work within the supervisory board, chairs its meeting and attends to the affairs of the supervisory board externally.[399] Until the revision in 2013, the chairman of the supervisory board should also chair the committees that handle contracts with members of the management board and prepare the supervisory board meetings.[400] The chairman of the supervisory board shall regularly maintain contact with the management board, in particular with the chairman or spokesman of the management board, and consult with him on strategy, business development and risk management of the company. The chairman of the supervisory board will be informed by the chairman or spokesman of the management board without delay of important events which are essential for the assessment of circumstances and development and for the management of the company. The chairman must then inform the supervisory board and, if required, convene an extraordinary meeting of the supervisory board.[401]

---

[393] Section 27(2) Co-Determination Act (MitbestG).

[394] Hopt/Roth, *Großkommentar Aktiengesetz* (see n. 86), Section 107 no. 103.

[395] For recommendation 5.2(4) of the German Corporate Governance Code, see above 2.3(a).

[396] Section 29(2) Co-Determination Act (MitbestG) 1976.

[397] Hopt/Roth, *Großkommentar Aktiengesetz* (see n. 86), Section 108 no. 66.

[398] For such a view, see Hopt/Roth, *Großkommentar Aktiengesetz* (see n. 86), Section 107 no. 93–97, Section 108 no. 66.

[399] Point 5.2(1) German Corporate Governance Code.

[400] Point 5.2(2) German Corporate Governance Code 2012.

[401] Point 5.2(4)2, 3 German Corporate Governance Code.

g) Committees of the Supervisory Board

According to the Stock Corporation Act,[402] the supervisory board may nominate —and in practice does set up—committees of the board.[403] The German Corporate Governance Code states that depending on the specifics of the company and the number of its members, the supervisory board must form committees with sufficient expertise. They serve to increase the efficiency of the supervisory board's work and the handling of complex issues. The respective committee chairmen report regularly to the supervisory board on the work of the committees.[404] The audit committee is mentioned in the Stock Corporation Act[405] but is not mandatory, since the supervisory board as a whole may fulfil the function of the audit committee.[406]

As special committees, the German Corporate Governance Code names only the audit committee[407] and—with limited tasks—the nomination committee;[408] but not a remuneration committee,[409] which is usually required by international Corporate Governance Codes and listing rules. The German Corporate Governance Code explicitly stated that the supervisory board can refer other factual issues to one or more committees for handling (naming the company's strategy, compensation of the members of the management board, investments, financing)[410] and can arrange committees to prepare supervisory board meetings and to take decisions in place of the supervisory board.[411] In DAX 30 companies, the appointment and the remuneration of managing directors is overseen by a presidential or personal committee.[412] A mandatory risk committee and a remuneration oversight committee ought to be introduced for banks.[413]

---

[402] Section 107(3) Stock Corporation Act.

[403] Heidrick & Struggles, *Challenging board performance* (2011), reports that with an average of 4.5 committees this is the highest number in Europe, 17; this is contrary to the focus of the role of the board as a whole, see below n. 423.

[404] Point 5.3.1 German Corporate Governance Code.

[405] Section 107(3) 2 and 107(4) Stock Corporation Act.

[406] Art 4(2) Directive 2006/43/EC.

[407] Point 5.3.2 German Corporate Governance Code.

[408] Point 5.3.3 German Corporate Governance Code.

[409] The possibility is mentioned in Point 4.2.2. On financial institutions, see above 1.3(c).

[410] Point 5.3.4 German Corporate Governance Code 2012, omitted in 2013.

[411] Section 107 (3) Stock Corporation Act, Point 5.3.5 German Corporate Governance Code 2012 explicitly mentioned this.

[412] M. Roth, 'Information und Organisation' (see n. 121) 358–360.

[413] For reform proposed in 2012, see 1.3(c) above.

According to the German Corporate Governance Code,[414] the task of the audit committee is in particular to handle issues of accounting, risk management and compliance, the necessary independence required of the auditor, the issuing of the audit mandate to the auditor, the determination of auditing focal points and the fee agreement.[415] The chairman of the audit committee must have specialist knowledge and experience in the application of accounting principles and internal control processes. He should be independent and not be a former member of the management board of the company whose appointment ended less than two years previously.

The task of the nomination committee[416] is to propose suitable candidates for the supervisory board for recommendation to the general meeting.[417] This proposal is for the election of the representatives of the shareholders;[418] employee representatives are elected by the employees.[419] Therefore, the committee must be comprised only of representatives of the shareholders. According to the 'same rights, same duties' doctrine applied to employee representatives in German supervisory boards, the German Federal Court of Justice as a general rule calls for an adequate representation in the committees.[420] The preparation of the appointment of managing directors is not mentioned in the German Corporate Governance Code.

A remuneration committee is not explicitly mentioned and therefore not recommended by the German Corporate Governance Code. If established, it is not necessarily separated from a nomination committee. Both tasks may even be combined in an executive committee of the supervisory board, being comprised of the chairman and the deputies. According to the Code, the supervisory board can delegate preparations for the appointment of members of the management board to a committee, which also deals with the terms of employment contracts, including compensation.[421] Such committees are quite common, at least among blue chips.[422] The Stock Corporation Act now declares remuneration to be a matter for the whole board,[423] which is reflected in the Code.[424]

---

[414] For financial institutions, see above 1.3(c).

[415] Point 5.3.2 German Corporate Governance Code.

[416] For financial institutions, see above 1.2(c).

[417] Point 5.3.3 German Corporate Governance Code.

[418] Section 124(3) 4: the proposal for the general meeting may be given by the majority of the shareholder representatives.

[419] See below 3.1.1(c).

[420] Bundesgerichtshof, 17 May 1993, II ZR 89/92, BGHZ 122, 342, 355.

[421] Point 5.1.2(4) German Corporate Governance Code.

[422] M. Roth, 'Information und Organisation' (see n. 121) 358–360.

[423] Section 107(3)2 Stock Corporation Act was amended by the Gesetz zur Angemessenheit der Vorstandsvergütung (VorstAG), 31 July 2009, BGBl I 2509.

[424] Point 4.2.(2), (3) German Corporate Governance Code.

Recent reform strengthened the role of the board as a whole[425] by further re-stricting topics delegable to committees for decision. According to the Stock Corporation Act, the supervisory board as a whole has to decide on the appointment and remuneration of the managing directors, on the appointment of the chairman of the supervisory board, on advance payments of distributable profits, on by-laws of the management board, on the examination of the annual financial statement and the annual report and on the examination of the report with affiliated companies.[426] Besides the explicit regulation in the Stock Corporation Act, academia assumes unwritten competences for the board as a whole.

2.2.3. *Independence of Supervisory Directors*

a) *Number and Regulation of Independent Directors*

Independent directors are still viewed with reluctance by many German practitioners and academics.[427] This is (at least until now) reflected by the German Corporate Governance Code, which recommends no explicit number or quorum of independent directors but only to an 'adequate number' of independent directors.[428] According to the widespread view in academia, employee represen-tatives are not independent; therefore, the independence requirement only applies vis-à-vis the shareholder representatives. In balancing experience and inde-pendence, the German Corporate Governance Code places experience above all else.[429] This provision was left unchanged in 2012; in the same year the Govern-mental Commission first published proposals for strengthening the independence of German supervisory boards,[430] then conducted the first consultation in the history of the German Corporate Governance Code, and finally implemented a modest reform.

Independent directors can only be found in German supervisory boards, not in management boards. Management boards, according to the current understanding of the Stock Corporation Act, are composed solely of executive directors. The number of independent directors in German supervisory boards is comparably low. According to the data of Heidrick & Struggles, twenty-one per cent of

---

[425] Recent economic literature suggests for the one-tier board that monitoring by the whole board increases firm value: I.F. Brigg and N.K. Chidambaran, 'Board meetings, committee structure, and firm value', *Journal of Corporate Finance* 16 (2010) 533.

[426] Section 107(3)2 Stock Corporation Act.

[427] See J. Lieder, 'The German Supervisory Board on Its Way to Professionalism', *German Law Journal* 11 (2010) 115, 131–138, referring to studies concerning the performance of inde-pendent boards, 134.

[428] Point 5.4.2(1) German Corporate Governance Code.

[429] Point 5.4.1 German Corporate Governance Code.

[430] Proposals from the plenary session of 17 January 2012.

supervisory directors are independent (2009: thirty per cent), forty-nine (2009: forty-eight) per cent are employee representatives, five per cent are former executive directors, eight (2009: four) per cent are reference shareholders and nineteen (thirteen) per cent are other non-independent directors.[431] The variation in these figures, and especially the number of the other non-independent directors, is rather high since whether or not directors are independent (and who they are) is not disclosed by the firms.[432] Related to shareholder representatives, about forty-two (sixty) per cent of such supervisory directors are independent. German audit, nomination and remuneration committees have by far the lowest proportion of independent directors.[433] The reluctance towards independent directors is rooted also in the relevance of family-controlled and dependent firms.[434]

German company law provides some mandatory requirements for supervisory director independence. In the Stock Corporation Act, there is the explicit requirement for an independent member of the supervisory board[435] and of the audit committee (if established);[436] this is derived from the EC Directive on statutory audits of annual accounts and consolidated accounts.[437] More provisions of the German Stock Corporation Act deal indirectly with independence. A member of the supervisory board may not be a member of the management board,[438] or a legal representative of a subsidiary[439] and may not hold an interlocking directorship.[440] A person who was member of the management board of a listed company has to be proposed with a quorum of twenty-five per cent of the shareholders to be elected as member of the stock corporation.[441]

---

[431] Heidrick & Struggles, *Challenging board performance* (2011) 42; *idem.*, *Boards in turbulent times*, 2009, 31.

[432] Heidrick & Struggles, *Boards in turbulent times* (2009): none of the German companies provide information, see 31; if the case is not clear, directors are categorised as 'other non-independent'.

[433] Heidrick & Struggles, *Challenging board performance* (2011) 44.

[434] M. Habersack, 'Der Aufsichtsrat im Visier der Kommission', *Zeitschrift für das gesamte Handels- und Wirtschaftsrecht* 168 (2004) 373, 377, 379.

[435] Section 100(5) Stock Corporation Act.

[436] Section 107(4) Stock Corporation Act.

[437] Directive 2006/43/EC of the European Parliament and of the Council of 17 May 2006, Art 41 (1).

[438] Section 105 Stock Corporation Act.

[439] A supervisory director in this function would be supervised by the managing director he himself supervises: Section 100 (2) 1 no. 2 Stock Corporation Act.

[440] Section 100(2)1 no. 3 Stock Corporation Act.

[441] Section 100(2)1 no. 4 Stock Corporation Act.

Independent directors are regulated in the German Corporate Governance Code in a way that is arguably different from the European recommendation.[442] The German Corporate Governance Code does not contain a list with independence requirements and provides only for an 'adequate number' of independent supervisory directors: the supervisory board must include what it considers to be an adequate number of independent members.[443] Independence is not the key requirement in the overall rule for the composition of the supervisory board.[444] The only explicit independence criterion is for the chairman of the audit committee.[445] This is about to change due to proposals of the Governmental Commission. According to these proposals, the supervisory board will define the number and reveal the names of the independent directors, and the number of independent directors must be reasonable. In this context, the guidelines of the international proxy advisor ISS is of relevance: ISS requires a third of the supervisory board to be independent;[446] therefore in quasi-parity co-determined companies, two-thirds of the shareholder representatives have to be independent.

The ISS policy will potentially lead to dysfunctional boards with international and diverse shareholder representatives and a monolithic bloc of employee representatives from Germany.[447] The policy should be revised, also due to the 2012 reforms of the German Corporate Governance Code.[448] Even if the EU recommendation on independent directors is not fully implemented in the German Code, the instances excluding independence now explicitly include being (a representative of) a controlling shareholder. Correctly understood, the adequate number of independent directors should be defined in line with international standards. Therefore, in large listed firms (DAX 30 and MDAX), half of the shareholder representatives should be independent;[449] one or two representatives are sufficient for smaller listed companies.[450] Also, more lenient quotas should be acceptable for family-controlled and dependent firms.[451]

---

[442] Point 5.4 German Corporate Governance Code.

[443] Point 5.4.2(1) German Corporate Governance Code.

[444] Point 5.4.1 German Corporate Governance Code.

[445] Point 5.3.2(3) German Corporate Governance Code.

[446] ISS, *2012 European Proxy Voting Summary Guidelines,* 19 December 2011, 8.

[447] M. Roth, 'Information' (see n. 121) 352, 380.

[448] ISS, *2013 European Corporate Governance Policy Updates,* does not provide for such a change.

[449] M. Roth, 'Unabhängige Aufsichtsratsmitglieder', *Zeitschrift für das gesamte Handels- und Wirtschaftsrecht,* 175 (2011) 605, 636.

[450] For this differentiation, see the UK Corporate Governance Code 2012, Code Provision B.1.2 (2): A smaller company should have at least two independent non-executive directors.

[451] For the French rules, see 2.2.3(d) (below) and the French report in this volume.

In the German Corporate Governance Code, more emphasis is given to knowledge than independence. The German Code states that the supervisory board has to be composed in such a way that its members (as a group) possess the knowledge, ability and expert experience required to properly complete its tasks.[452] It should be mentioned that there is also a developing market for professional supervisory board members in Germany.[453] Since these professional supervisory directors will generally meet the independence criteria, the numbers mentioned above have to be interpreted also with regard to professional independent directors.

The strong emphasis on the qualification of supervisory directors[454] and the market for professional supervisory directors have to be taken into account for the interpretation of the comparably low proportion of independent directors in Germany. Further factors are the mandatory co-determination regime, which heavily affects the composition of the board, and the tradition of appointing the former president of the management board (*Vorstandsvorsitzender*), which serves as equivalent of the CEO as president of the supervisory board (*Aufsichtsratsvorsitzender*). Last but not least, the prominent role of family-owned (listed) companies should be kept in mind.

b) *Definition of Independence*

The independent director is not defined in the Stock Corporation Act. For the independence criterion in the German Stock Corporation Act, introduced to implement the revised auditor directive,[455] academia draws on the European Commission Recommendation of 15 February 2005 on the role of non-executive or supervisory directors of listed companies and on the committees of the (supervisory) board.[456] Also in the German Corporate Governance Code, independent directors are not yet defined in detail as in the European recommendation or in the UK Corporate Governance Code, but a short list of (non) independence criteria is proposed by the Code Commission.

According to the former wording of the German Corporate Governance Code,[457] a supervisory board member is considered independent if he or she has

---

[452] Point 5.4.1(1) German Corporate Governance Code.

[453] A professional chairman of the supervisory board was explicitly discussed in the notes of the governmental draft of the Gesetz zur Kontrolle und Transparenz im Unternehmensbereich (KonTraG), BTDrucks 13/9712, 16.

[454] J. Semler, *Münchener Kommentar Aktiengesetz* (see n. 302), Section 100 no. 66–74 with specific requirements in no. 76–85.

[455] Section 100(5) and 107(4) Stock Corporation Act.

[456] U. Hüffer, 'Die Unabhängigkeit von Aufsichtsratsmitgliedern nach Ziffer 5-4-2 DCGK', *Zeitschrift für Wirtschaftsrecht* 2006, 637.

[457] Point 5.4.2(2) German Corporate Governance Code 2010.

no business or personal relations with the company or its management board that cause conflicts of interests. Academia was split on whether the EU recommendation can also be used to sharpen the independence requirements in the German Code.[458] The split is likely to prevail because in 2012 the Commission merely added the requirement of independence from controlling shareholders and enterprises linked to controlling shareholders,[459] but refrained from introducing a concrete list with independence criteria. Not more than two former members of the management board must be members of the supervisory board and members of the supervisory board must not exercise directorships or similar positions or advisory tasks for important competitors of the company.[460]

According to the German Corporate Governance Code 2012, the supervisory board must include a reasonable number of independent members. A supervisory board member is considered independent if they have no business or personal relations with the company, its management board, a controlling shareholder or an enterprise connected to the controlling shareholder, which may cause a material conflict of interests.[461] A more stringent standard applies to proposed candidates. For nominees to be elected as supervisory directors by the general meeting, the supervisory board must also disclose significant shareholdings, that is, where the proposed candidate directly or indirectly holds ten per cent of the voting shares of the company.[462]

The list of independence criteria[463] proposed by the Commission in January 2012[464] was heavily criticised in the consultation conducted until March 2012,[465]

---

[458] M. Roth, 'Unabhängige Aufsichtsratsmitglieder' (see n. 449) 628. Assuming a clearly distinct German definition: M. Lutter, 'Die Empfehlungen der Kommission vom 14.12.2004 und vom 15.2.2005 und ihre Umsetzung in Deutschland', *Europäische Zeitschrift für Wirtschaftsrecht* 2009, 799, 804.

[459] Point 5.4.2(2) German Corporate Governance Code 2012.

[460] Point 5.4.2(3) German Corporate Governance Code.

[461] Point 5.4.2(1), (2) German Corporate Governance Code.

[462] Point 5.4.1(4), (6) German Corporate Governance Code.

[463] The proposal that was *not implemented in the Code* read as follows: 'As a rule, a supervisory board member cannot be assumed to be independent if in particular he/she
- receives or has in the past two years received material additional compensation from the company in addition to the compensation received as a supervisory board member;
- has been a member of the company's management board in the past two years;
- holds 10 per cent or more of the company's shares or is a statutory representative of another company which holds such a stake;
- can be considered to be a close member of the family of any of the management board members as defined in the applicable accounting rules;
- maintains or has in the past year maintained material business relations with the company to a substantial extent—directly or indirectly as a partner, shareholder, management board member or managing director of an enterprise which has such business relations with the company;

cont. ...

and was therefore not included in the amendments to the German Corporate Governance Code of 2012. The lack of such a list is not only critical in the light of the European recommendations on independence but also due to German court practice of holding resolutions of the general meeting voidable if the board failed to explain deviations from the German Corporate Governance Code.[466] To reduce legal uncertainty in relation to the lack of a German list, a reference to the list contained in the EU recommendation on independent directors is advisable.[467]

c) Independence of Employee Representatives

It is further contested whether employee representatives are independent. Unions claim that the employees of the company sitting on the board as employee representatives and the union delegates representing the employees in the supervisory board are independent.[468] Decisions by the courts are not apparent. Most academics deny the independence of employee representatives.[469] This classification is based primarily on the conflicts of interest of employee representatives.[470] Equally important is that only outside directors, not having their primary employment within the company or corporate group, are qualified to be independent supervisory directors.[471]

   – is a partner of the company's auditor or is or has in the past three years or less been the responsible auditor for the company.'
This does not have any effect on the special conditions arising from co-determination, eg. on employee representatives due to the Co-Determination Act (MitbestG) or the One-Third Participation Act (DrittelbG).

[464] Proposal from the plenary session of 17 January 2012, German Corporate Governance Code Point 5.4.2(1)3, not enacted.

[465] See, *inter alia,* Handelsrechtsausschuss des Deutschen Anwaltsvereins (Business Law Committee of the German Lawyers Association), 'Stellungnahme zu den Änderungsvorschlägen der Regierungskommission Deutscher Corporate Governance Kodex vom 1.2.2012', *Neue Zeitschrift für Gesellschaftsrecht* 2012, 335, 337: overregulation and lack of legal certainty due to the list.

[466] See below 4.1.2.

[467] M. Roth (see n. 387) 1987.

[468] R. Köstler (see n. 198) 803 f.

[469] See Hopt/Roth, *Großkommentar Aktiengesetz* (see n. 86), Section 100 no. 90.

[470] For this conflict, see also below 3.1.3.1(a).

[471] For the definition of inside and outside directors, see R. Adams, B.E. Hermalin and M.S. Weisbach, 'The Role of Boards of Directors in Corporate Governance: a Conceptual Framework & Survey', *NBER Working Paper No.14486*, November 2008, 25.

The EU recommendation on independent directors[472] is somewhat ambiguous in formulating that employee representatives need not to be declared non-independent.[473] Employee representatives might feel independent of the management board but they have strong ties with the corporation itself. In Germany, employee representatives enjoy no explicit statutory protection from dismissal[474] and are only therefore likely to vote for maintaining as many jobs as possible.[475] Due to mandatory co-determination and classifying employee representatives as non-independent, far less than half of all supervisory directors are independent in Germany.[476] The provisions on independence in the German Corporate Governance Code do not affect employee representatives. Companies may restrict the quota for independent directors in respect of shareholder representatives.[477]

d) Independent Directors in Groups of Companies

The traditional reluctance towards independent directors is also rooted in its effects on running the affairs in groups of companies,[478] a characteristic of corporate Germany.[479] The German *Konzernrecht* offers the possibility to integrate companies without a merger.[480] In this respect, it should be stated[481] that German companies often transform their business by buying new technologies via share deals. This explains why most DAX firms are industrial companies with modern technical expertise but have predecessors dating back to before World War II.

Until the recent reform of the German Corporate Governance Code in May 2012, many academics in Germany treated majority shareholders or their repre-

---

[472] Commission Recommendation of 15 February 2005 on the role of non-executive or supervisory directors of listed companies and on the committees of the (supervisory) board, OJ L 52/51.

[473] Annex II, 1(b) of the EU-recommendation.

[474] For the works council, such a provision is given in Section 15 Protection Against Unfair Dismissal Act (Kündigungsschutzgesetz), 25 August 1969, BGBl I 1317, English translation by Lingemann et al (see n. 11), 178–198.

[475] Nevertheless, general anti-discrimination rules apply.

[476] Heidrick & Struggles, see above n. 432.

[477] M. Klein, 'Die Änderungen des Deutschen Corporate Governance Kodex 2012 aus Sicht der Unternehmenspraxis', *Die Aktiengesellschaft* 2012, 805, 809, also hints at the possibility of declaring employee representatives to be independent.

[478] Explicitly M. Hoffmann-Becking, 'Organe: Strukturen und Verantwortlichkeiten, insbesondere im monistischen System', *Zeitschrift für Unternehmens- und Gesellschaftsrecht* 2004, 355, 360.

[479] See above 1.1(c).

[480] Audi, the VW-subsidiary, has for decades been a listed company as such.

[481] In general, see above 1.1(a).

sentatives as independent.[482] That view was based on the German law of groups of companies, the regulated *Konzernrecht*, the German Corporate Governance Code did not explicitly require independence from (major) shareholders.[483] Staff and members of the governmental commission treated controlling shareholders as independent, basing this claim on an interpretation of the Code.[484] Such a view is contrary to the EU recommendation on independent directors[485] and is therefore isolated in the European Union.

Since 2012, the German Corporate Governance Code provides that a supervisory director also has to be independent from a controlling shareholder and an enterprise linked to the controlling shareholder.[486] Moreover, in respect of nominations to the general meeting the supervisory board must also disclose whether such candidates directly or indirectly hold a significant part of the shares of the companies, meaning at least ten per cent.[487] Since 2012, the supervisory board must also declare the number of independent directors it assumes to be adequate.[488] The objectives on the number of independent directors and the status of implementation must be disclosed in the corporate governance report.[489]

In the European Union, a more adequate approach than lessening the requirements for independence (as practised in Switzerland and the US)[490] is to reduce the number of independent directors. In line with modern European corporate governance standards, for example in France,[491] it should also be regarded as 'adequate' under the German Corporate Governance Code where a third of the shareholder representatives are independent.[492]

---

[482] Habersack (see n. 434) 377, stressing positive aspects in the control of managers by a controlling shareholder; U. Wackerbarth, '*Investorvertrauen und Corporate Governance*', Zeitschrift für Uhnternehmens- und Gesellschaftsrecht 2005, 686, 717–720.

[483] Point 5.4.2 German Corporate Governance Code.

[484] Kremer, in Ringleb et al (see n. 63) no. 1038; subseq., M. Lutter (see n. 458) 804, and M. Lehmann and C. Manger-Nestler, 'Die Vorschläge zur neuen Architektur der europäischen Finanzaufsicht', *Europäische Zeitschrift für Wirtschaftsrecht* 2010, 87.

[485] Commission recommendation of 15 February 2005 on the role of non-executive or supervisory directors of listed companies and on the committees of the (supervisory) board, OJ L 52/51, 13.1.

[486] Point 5.4.2(2) German Corporate Governance Code.

[487] Point 5.4.1(4), (6) German Corporate Governance Code.

[488] Point 5.4.1(2)1 German Corporate Governance Code.

[489] Point 5.4.1(3) German Corporate Governance Code.

[490] Nasdaq IM-5605. Definition of Independence – Rule 5605(a)(2); 22 Swiss Code of Best Practice, no. 22.

[491] Corporate Governance Code of Listed Companies, December 2008, 8.2.

[492] M. Roth, 'Unabhängige Aufsichtsratsmitglieder' (see n. 449) 636.

2.3. Information Streams

a) Information Streams in General

The Stock Corporation Act allows for passing of information by the management board to the supervisory board and a corresponding duty of the managing directors.[493] Due to the duty of the supervisory directors to monitor the management board, courts and academia assume a duty of the supervisory directors to ask for information necessary for the monitoring.[494] In line with this view, and based on early German company law, the German Corporate Governance Code states that providing sufficient information to the supervisory board is the joint responsibility of the management board and supervisory board.[495] In practice, about half of the supervisory board members also insist on receiving management-independent information.[496]

The management board informs the supervisory board regularly, without delay and comprehensively, about all issues important to the company with regard to strategy, planning, business development, risk situation, risk management and compliance. The management board points out deviations of the actual business development from previously formulated plans and targets, indicating the reasons for such deviations.[497] The supervisory board must specify the management board's information and reporting duties in more detail. The reports of the management board to the supervisory board are, as a rule, to be submitted in writing (including in electronic form). Documents required for decisions, in particular the annual financial statements, the consolidated financial statements and the auditors' report, are where possible to be sent to the members of the supervisory board in due time before the meeting.[498]

Between meetings, the chairman of the supervisory board shall regularly maintain contact with the management board, in particular with the chairman or spokesman of the management board, and consult with him on issues of strategy, planning, business development, the risk situation, risk management and compliance by the company. The chairman of the supervisory board will be informed by the chairman or spokesman of the management board without delay of important events which are essential for the assessment of the situation, development and management of the company. The chairman must then inform

---

[493] Section 90 Stock Corporation Act.

[494] Hopt/Roth, *Großkommentar Aktiengesetz* (see n. 86), Section 111 no. 170–190.

[495] Point 3.4(1) German Corporate Governance Code.

[496] BDO Deutsche Warentreuhand in Kooperation mit Der Aufsichtsrat, *Aufsichtsrats-Panel* 07-2010, 30 April 2010.

[497] Point 3.4(2) German Corporate Governance Code.

[498] Point 3.4(3) German Corporate Governance Code.

the supervisory board and, if required, convene an extraordinary meeting of the supervisory board.[499]

A company secretary as in the United Kingdom and in the Netherlands is neither mentioned in the Stock Corporation Act nor in the German Corporate Governance Code. In German practice, however, there are some bureaux of the supervisory board, which serve as a tool for the chairman to collect information and to administer the affairs of the supervisory board.[500] The staffing of these bureaux by the management board and not by the supervisory board[501] is a questionable practice.

A management information system is not addressed by the Stock Corporation Act or the German Corporate Governance Code. Explicit legal rules exist only for risks threatening the existence of the company. The management board must take suitable measures, in particular surveillance measures, to ensure that developments threatening the continuation of the company are detected at an early stage.[502] However, there is a common understanding that in order to fulfil its duty of care the management board has to take suitable measures.[503] Internal control and risk management are to be supervised by an audit committee (if established)[504] and are required by the Federal Financial Services Authority (BaFin).

b) Interrogation Rights of Supervisory Directors (Non-Executives)

Besides the concept of passing information by the management board to the supervisory board,[505] the Stock Corporation Act contains some management-independent information rights of the supervisory board. The supervisory board may inspect and examine the books and records of the company and its assets, in particular cash, securities and merchandise.[506] The supervisory board may also

---

[499] Point 5.2(4) 1–3 German Corporate Governance Code.

[500] Hopt/Roth, *Großkommentar Aktiengesetz* (see n. 86), Section 111 no. 530–533; Heidrick & Struggles, *Challenging board performance* (2011) did not include data due to insignificance, 24.

[501] D. Feddersen, 'Neue gesetzliche Anforderungen an den Aufsichtsrat', *Die Aktiengesellschaft* 2000, 385, 395.

[502] Section 91(2) Stock Corporation Act.

[503] K.J. Hopt, *Großkommentar Aktiengesetz* (see n. 247), Section 93 no. 107.

[504] For best practice, see AKEIÜ der Schmalenbach-Gesellschaft für Betriebswirtschaft e.V., *Der Betrieb* 2011, 2102, suggesting, *inter alia*, an integration of risk management and internal control.

[505] Section 90 Stock Corporation Act.

[506] Section 111(2)1 Stock Corporation Act.

commission individual members or—with respect to specific assignments— special experts to carry out such inspections and examinations.[507]

In German academia, there is debate as to whether the supervisory board may talk to employees without the prior consent of the management board and, at least if there is general consent by the management board, also request an answer.[508] The traditional view is that only the management board may provide access to employees;[509] the information of the supervisory board was therefore seen as a weakness in the German system.[510] Recently, the majority of academics also allow for questions to employees without prior consent of the management board.[511] In practice, this view is endorsed by the former legal counsel of Deutsche Bank;[512] recent reforms give direct access to some senior officers, at least for banks.[513] Interrogation rights towards employees should be subject to an information regime agreed upon by the management and the supervisory board; if no such agreement is in place, direct interrogation will be seen as a sign of distrust by supervisory directors of managing directors and will rarely be used in order to avoid a rift between the boards. According to another line of argument, co-determination serves as an information channel from employees to the outside directors in German supervisory boards.[514]

[507] Section 111(2)1 Stock Corporation Act.

[508] According to M. Lutter, 'Der Aufsichtsrat im Konzern', *Die Aktiengesellschaft* 2006, 517, 520, this opens Pandora's box; for another view, see M. Roth, 'Möglichkeiten vorstands-unabhängiger Information des Aufsichtsrats', *Die Aktiengesellschaft* 2004, 1, and Hopt/Roth, *Großkommentar Aktiengesetz* (see n. 86), Section 111 no. 502–529.

[509] For the view to allow direct contacts, see Hopt/Roth *Großkommentar Aktiengesetz* (see n. 86), Section 111 no. 245, 538.

[510] P.L. Davies, 'Struktur der Unternehmensführung in Großbritannien und Deutschland – Konvergenz oder fortbestehende Divergenz?', *Zeitschrift für Unternehmens- und Wirtschafts-recht* 2001, 268.

[511] Hopt/Roth, *Großkommentar Aktiengesetz* (see n. 86), Section 111 no. 502–529; M. Habersack *Münchener Kommentar Aktiengesetz* (see n. 86), Section 111 no. 68; M. Roth, 'Vorstandsunabhängige Information' (see n. 508); P.C. Leyens, *Information des Aufsichtsrats* (see n. 72) 182–199; S.H. Schneider, *Informationspflichten und Informationseinrichtungs-pflichten im Aktienkonzern* (Berlin, Duncker & Humblot 2006) 102–108; B. Kropff, 'Zur Information des Aufsichtsrats über die das interne Überwachungssystem', *Neue Zeitschrift für Gesellschaftsrecht* 2003, 346, 350, for the former dominant German view, M. Lutter and G. Krieger, *Rechte und Pflichten des Aufsichtsrats* (see n. 240) no. 246 with further references.

[512] Marsch-Barner, 'Zur Information des Aufsichtsrates durch Mitarbeiter des Unterneh-mens', *Festschrift Schwark* (Munich, C.H. Beck) 2009, 219.

[513] See above 1.2(c).

[514] G. Hertig, 'Codetermination as a (Partial) Substitute for Mandatory Disclosure?', *European Business Organization Law Review* 7 (2006) 123, 130.

As mentioned above,[515] there is no provision for a company secretary either the Stock Corporation Act or the German Corporate Governance Code. A so-called *Aufsichtsratsassistent* was discussed in the 1990s,[516] but was not included in the corporate reform of that time.[517] Presently, such a requirement is again under discussion and there is a suggestion that it should be at least incorporated in the German Corporate Governance Code.[518] In practice, there are some bureaux of the supervisory board and assistants of the supervisory board.[519]

c) Source of Information

Members of the management board are the primary source of information for the supervisory board.[520] In a case concerning auditors, the German Federal Court of Justice spoke of natural tendencies of self-justification.[521] This illustrates the problem of the monitor obtaining primary information by the monitored.[522] Nevertheless, it is not an option to exclude management from informing the supervisory board. Furthermore, it is difficult to determine the appropriate quantity and quality of information or to decide whether too much or too little information is worse. Therefore, the institutional precautions to lessen the problem of information primarily by the controlled should be addressed.

The most common institutional settings to provide management-independent information to the supervisory board are auditors and internal control. Since 1998, the supervisory board gives instructions to the auditor.[523] The auditor is obliged to take part in a meeting of the supervisory board or the audit committee.[524] The audit committee, recommended by the German Corporate Governance Code, is also

---

[515] See above 2.3.

[516] Entwurf eines Gesetzes zur Steigerung der Effizienz von Aufsichtsräten und zur Beseitigung der Machtkonzentration bei Kreditinstituten infolge von Unternehmensbeteiligung, BT-Drucks 13/9716 (Bundesrats-Entwurf), providing a new Section 111a Stock Corporation Act.

[517] Gesetz zur Kontrolle und Transparenz im Unternehmensbereich (KonTraG), 27 April 1998, BGBl I 786.

[518] P.C. Leyens, *Information des Aufsichtsrats* (see n. 72) 437.

[519] Hopt/Roth, *Großkommentar Aktiengesetz* (see n. 86), Section 111 no. 530.

[520] See above 2.3(a).

[521] Bundesgerichtshof, 25 November 2002, II ZR 49/01, BGHZ 153, 32, 42: 'Natürliche Selbstrechtfertigungstendenzen' (natural tendency to justify own acts).

[522] Hopt/Roth, *Großkommentar Aktiengesetz* (see n. 86), Section 111 no. 505.

[523] Section 111(2)3 Stock Corporation Act, amended by the Gesetz zur Kontrolle und Transparenz im Unternehmensbereich (KonTraG), 27 April 1998, BGBl I 786.

[524] Section 171(1)2 Stock Corporation Act.

linked to the internal control-unit of the company.[525] Routine meetings of the audit committee with the head of the internal control are considered good corporate governance.[526] Furthermore, some chairmen of the supervisory board may use the management information system, especially if they had been CEO of the company previously. According to a study from 2004, every seventh supervisory board had access to the management information system.[527]

A point of controversy of recent origin is whether the supervisory directors, or at least its chairman, should be allowed to have direct contacts with shareholders. Due to the division of powers between the two boards, contacts with shareholders are to be attributed primarily to the management.[528] It has even been argued by some that only the management board should be allowed to have contacts with third parties, such as the Federal Financial Supervisory Agency.[529] This is in general correct in respect of the representation of the company, but not for informal contacts. The fact that the chairman of the supervisory board appears on business letters of the company[530] suggests that the supervisory board's function is not restricted to a merely internal role.[531] At the very least, contacts with shareholders are allowed.[532]

d) Joint or Separate Meeting of Supervisory Board and Management Board (Executives and Non-Executives)

Due to the fact that managing directors usually attend the meetings of the super-visory board, the German Corporate Governance Code also contains a provision recommending executive sessions without the management board.[533] Such executive sessions must take place 'if necessary'.[534] Regular sessions are not obligatory but seen as good corporate governance, at least by some.[535]

---

[525] Point 5.3.2 German Corporate Governance Code; more to the point, see Section 107(3)2 Stock Corporation Act.

[526] Hopt/Roth, *Großkommentar Aktiengesetz* (see n. 86), Section 107 no. 318.

[527] Deloitte, *Entwicklung der Aufsichtsratspraxis in Deutschland*, 2004, 8: 16%.

[528] On the division of powers, see above 2.1(b).

[529] M. Dreher and H. Häußler, 'Die Aufsicht über Versicherungsunternehmen durch die BaFin und die Überwachungsaufgabe des Aufsichtsrats', *Zeitschrift für Unternehmens- und Gesellschaftsrecht* 2011, 471, 504–506.

[530] Section 80 Stock Corporation Act.

[531] M. Roth, 'Information und Organisation' (see n. 121) 370.

[532] M. Roth, 'Information und Organisation' (see n. 121) 368–369.

[533] Point 3.6 (2) German Corporate Governance Code.

[534] See above n. 383.

[535] See above 2.2(d).

3. Accountability

3.1. Boards and Shareholders

3.1.1. *Appointment and Removal*

a) *Appointment and Removal of Supervisory Directors*

The members of the supervisory board who represent the shareholders are elected by the general meeting[536] by proposal of the shareholder representatives in the supervisory board[537] or by proposal of shareholders.[538] The German Corporate Governance Code recommends that the supervisory directors are elected by single votes.[539] Prior to the Code, it was common practice to elect the supervisory directors based on lists. In academia, some even argue that single voting is mandatory.[540] Minority representatives are not provided for by the Stock Corporation Act or the German Corporate Governance Code. It is even contested whether cumulative voting is in line with German company law.[541]

One third of the members of the supervisory board may be appointed by specific shareholders if the articles of incorporation allow for such a privilege. In co-determined companies, appointment rights are limited to one third of the shareholder representatives.[542] Currently under discussion is whether such a provision might be contrary to the freedoms provided by the Treaty on the Functioning of the European Union.[543] Appointment rights are questionable, especially in quasi-parity co-determined companies, since they function as a poison pill.[544]

Former members of the management board (in the last two years before election) may be elected or appointed as a member of the supervisory board of a listed company only if a quorum of shareholders holding more than 25 per cent of the voting rights presents a motion for the former member of the management

---

[536] Section 101(1)1 Stock Corporation Act.

[537] Section 124(3) Stock Corporation Act.

[538] Section 127 Stock Corporation Act.

[539] Point 5.4.3(1) German Corporate Governance Code.

[540] For the discussion, see Hopt/Roth, *Großkommentar Aktiengesetz* (see n. 86), Section 101 no. 44–61.

[541] See Hopt/Roth, *Großkommentar Aktiengesetz* (see n. 86), Section 101 no. 57–61, 62–66.

[542] Section 101(2) Stock Corporation Act.

[543] F. Möslein, 'Inhaltskontrolle aktienrechtlicher Entsendungsrechte – Europäische Anforderungen und Ausgestaltung im deutschen Aktienrecht', *Die Aktiengesellschaft* 2007, 770.

[544] See M. Roth, 'German Takeover Law after the implementation of the European takeover directive, Corporate Finance and Capital Markets Law Review', *Revue Trimestrielle de Droit Financier* 2007, 26, 28.

board.[545] The supervisory board does not have the power to appoint members, even in case of emergency; but it is possible to elect substitute directors where one of the supervisory directors has stepped down.[546] If the remaining supervisory directors do not form a quorum of the board or directors are missing for more than three months, supervisory directors may be appointed by the court.[547]

The members of the supervisory board may be dismissed by the general meeting or by the court.[548] If there is no resolution of the general meeting with a three-quarters majority, dismissal of supervisory directors is only possible by the courts for good cause (*wichtiger Grund*). The good cause-requirement dates back to the enactment of the 1937 Stock Corporation Act, which aimed especially to protect the management directors from interference into their decision-making.[549]

b) Appointment and Removal of Managing Directors

The members of the management board are appointed by the supervisory board.[550] Until 1937 German stock corporation law was more flexible in this respect; the general meeting could also appoint members of the management board.[551] Today, appointment of the managers by the general meeting is possible only for corporations incorporated as limited liability company (*GmbH*). According to the Limited Liability Company Act, the general meeting appoints the (managing) directors.[552] A supervisory board is mandatory for limited liability companies (*GmbH*) that are subject to co-determination. If the employees may elect half of the members of the supervisory board,[553] the supervisory board also appoints the managing directors in a limited liability company (*GmbH*).[554]

---

[545] Section 100(2) no 4 Stock Corporation Act, amended by the Adequate Management Remuneration Act 2009.

[546] Section 101(3) Stock Corporation Act.

[547] Section 104(2) Stock Corporation Act.

[548] Section 103 Stock Corporation Act.

[549] The standard of review is somewhat stricter than for managing directors, where some *de facto* assume an *ad nutum* revocability; see below 3.1.1(b).

[550] Section 84 Stock Corporation Act.

[551] A. Pinner, *Staub Aktiengesetz* (see n. 181), Section 231 Commercial Code no. 16.

[552] Section 46 no. 5 Limited Liability Company Act (GmbHG).

[553] Co-determination Act (MitbestG) 1976 and Act on Co-Determination in the Coal, Iron and Steel Industry (Montan-MitbestG).

[554] The Stock Corporation Act prescribes a *Vorstand* (management board, Section 76–94 Stock Corporation Act), while German close corporation law allows for one or more directors (*Geschäftsführer*).

The German Stock Corporation Act requires good cause for the removal of managing directors.[555] This provision protects the independence of the management board but the standard of review is not too restrictive. The Stock Corporation Act itself specifies the withdrawal of confidence by the general meeting as constituting good cause;[556] therefore international literature assumes *ad nutum* revocability.[557] The removal itself has to be effected by the supervisory board.[558]

c) Employee Representatives

Members of the supervisory board who represent the employees[559] are appointed by the employees;[560] in the coal, iron and steel industry they are appointed by the general meeting according to the proposal of the employees.[561] Each co-determination regime provides for special guidelines on how to proceed with the election of employee representatives. The Co-Determination Act 1976 provides for special rights for senior employees (*leitende Angestellte*)[562] and for unions active in the company.[563] In quasi-parity co-determined companies, one senior employee is to be elected. Unions may propose two or three candidates for election that do not have to be employees in the company.[564] Union leaders therefore generally have one or more mandates in the supervisory boards of major German companies.

Contrary to Dutch co-determination law, where an election of an employee of the company as employee representative would be void,[565] as a general rule employee representatives in Germany have to be employees of the company.[566] In German practice union representatives acting as employee representatives ac-

---

[555] Section 84(3)1 Stock Corporation Act.

[556] Section 84(3)2 Stock Corporation Act.

[557] S. Cools, 'Europe's Ius Commune on Director Revocability', *European Company and Financial Law Review* 2011, 199, concerning La Porta et al her contribution 'The Real Difference Between in Corporate Law Between the United States and Continental Europe: Distribution of Powers', *Delaware Journal of Corporate Law* 30 (2005) 697.

[558] Kort, *Großkommentar Aktiengesetz* (see n. 67), Section 84 nos. 160–167.

[559] On the *Arbeitsdirektor*, see above 2.2.1(b).

[560] Co-Determination Act (MitbestG) 1976 and One-Third Participation Act (DrittelbG).

[561] Section 101 Stock Corporation Act.

[562] Section 15(1)2 Co-Determination Act (MitbestG).

[563] Section 7(2), 16 Co-Determination Act (MitbestG).

[564] Section 7(2) Co-Determination Act (MitbestG).

[565] See Dutch report in this volume.

[566] Section 7(2) Co-Determination Act (MitbestG), Section 4(2) One-Third Participation Act (DrittelbG).

cording to the Co-Determination Act 1976[567] are senior union functionaries. This is contrary to Dutch law, which bars those union representatives who deal with collective agreements from being elected, and contrary to Dutch practice, where there is reluctance to nominate union officers. Independent employee representatives are provided for only in the coal, iron and steel co-determination regime,[568] influenced by the British rule in North Rhine-Westphalia after World War II. Employee representatives bargaining for collective agreements are barred only from participating in supervisory meetings dealing with such bargains.[569]

d) Duration of Term

The terms of supervisory and managing directors may not exceed five years respectively. For members of the management board, the German Stock Corporation Act explicitly refers to the period of five years.[570] For supervisory directors, there is only a *de facto* reference to a five-year period. The members of the supervisory board may not be appointed for a period of time extending beyond the adjournment of the shareholders' meeting resolving on ratification of the acts of management for the fourth fiscal year following the commencement of their respective term of office. The fiscal year in which such term of office commences must not be taken into account.[571] According to a recent decision, the term of office ends even when the company delays the shareholder meeting.[572] These limitations for the terms also apply to renewals.[573]

3.1.2. Division of Powers between Boards and Shareholders

a) Division of Powers

Original German company laws treated the general meeting as the primary body.[574] It was only in the 1937 Stock Corporation Act that Germany restricted

---

[567] Section 7(2) Co-Determination Act (MitbestG).

[568] Section 4, 8 Act on Co-Determination in the Coal, Iron and Steel Industry (Montan-MitbestG).

[569] All employee representatives are excluded from decisions on collective bargains; see Hopt/Roth, *Großkommentar Aktiengesetz* (see n. 86), Section 109 no. 24.

[570] Section 84(1)1 Stock Corporation Act.

[571] Section 102 Stock Corporation Act.

[572] Higher Regional Court (Oberlandesgericht, OLG) Munich, 9 November 2009, 31 Wx 136/09, *Wertpapier-Mitteilungen* 2010, 357.

[573] For members of the management board, see Section 84(1)2 Stock Corporation Act; for members of the supervisory board this is generally accepted in academia, Hopt/Roth, *Großkommentar Aktiengesetz* (see n. 86), Section 102 no. 42–49.

[574] H. Fleischer, 'Kompetenzen der Hauptversammlung', in W. Bayer and M. Habersack (eds.), *Aktienrecht im Wandel* (Tübingen, Mohr Siebeck 2007) 430, 435.

the powers of the shareholders and excluded the general meeting from giving instructions to the boards of the company.[575] The right of shareholders to give instructions to the board is today one of the characteristics of the limited liability company (*GmbH*).[576] For stock corporations, instructions have played no role in practice.[577] Of practical importance was the right to appoint and dismiss members of the management board.[578]

Although no longer the primary body of the company in all respects, fundamental decisions for the company still fall within the competence of the general meeting.[579] The powers of the shareholders provided for in the German Stock Corporation Act are, *inter alia*, shareholder resolutions at the annual or extraordinary general meeting for the appointment and removal of supervisory directors, annual discharge of managing and supervisory directors, the appointment of the auditors, the decision over distributable profits, amendments of the articles of association, increase or decrease of capital and the dissolution of the company.[580] Mergers and transitions into another legal form are subject to resolutions of the general meeting, provided for in the Reorganisation Act. Unwritten powers concern other fundamental decisions, such as selling the main activity of the company, despite the fact that the famous *Holzmüller* doctrine[581] was developed further.[582]

b) Rights and Duties of Directors

Liability of managing and supervisory directors is provided for by the Stock Corporation Act.[583] Members of the management and of the supervisory board are liable for their own mistakes. A division of tasks shields directors from liability only if there is no duty to oversee the fellow director, no actual knowledge of wrongdoings of another director and no reason for investigations. Some tasks are

---

[575] See above 1.2.

[576] For the limited liability company, see W. Zöllner in *Baumbach/Hueck GmbHG*, 20th edn. (Munich, C.H. Beck 2013) Section 46 no. 89–91.

[577] See W. Kißkalt (see n. 125) 47 f.

[578] See A. Pinner, *Staub Handelsgesetzbuch* (see n. 181), Art. 246 Commercial Code no. 10.

[579] For a transatlantic view on shareholder rights, recently A. Hellgart and A. Hoger, 'Transatlantische Konvergenz der Aktionärsrechte – Systemvergleich und neuere Entwicklungen', *Zeitschrift für Unternehmens- und Gesellschaftsrecht* 2011, 38.

[580] Section 119(1) Stock Corporation Act specifies many but not all competences of the general meeting.

[581] Bundesgerichtshof, 25 February 1982, II ZR 174/80, BGHZ 83, 122 (Holzmüller).

[582] Bundesgerichtshof, 26 April 2004, II ZR 155/02, BGHZ 159, 30 (Gelantine) and Bundesgerichtshof, 26 April 2004, II ZR 154/02, *Zeitschrift für Wirtschaftsrecht* 2004, 1001.

[583] Sections 93, 116 Stock Corporation Act.

so important that the whole board (management board, supervisory board or both) has to decide on them. All directors have to ensure that the whole board deals with tasks of utmost importance for the company or tasks prescribed by special legislation to fall in the responsibility of the whole board.[584]

The German business judgment rule was codified in 2005 for members of the management board[585] but is of relevance also for supervisory directors.[586] The introduction aimed to counterbalance facilitating actions by shareholders by lowering the quorum.[587] A German business judgment rule was already applied *de facto* by the German Federal Court of Justice in the *ARAG/Garmenbeck* decision[588] but reformulated by the legislature. The German business judgment rule stipulates that there is no breach of duty if the director makes a business decision and could reasonably believe he is acting on an informed basis and in the best interests of the company.[589] The German Corporate Governance Code translates the German business judgment rule into English in the following way: In the case of business decisions an infringement of duty is not present if the member of the management board or supervisory board could reasonably believe, based on appropriate information, that he or she was acting in the best interest of the company.[590]

For the reception of the US business judgment rule in Germany, the Corporate Governance Principles of the American Law Institute (ALI) were crucial.[591] Nevertheless, there are fundamental differences between the German business judgment rule and the US prototype. First, the German rule is codified while the US rule is not. Second, the US business judgment rule, as developed by the

---

[584] Hopt/Roth, *Großkommentar Aktiengesetz* (see n. 86), Section 111 no. 115, but it is also possible to delegate topics of fundamental importance, Hopt/Roth, *Großkommentar Aktiengesetz* (see n. 86), Section 107 no. 399.

[585] Section 93 Stock Corporation Act.

[586] Section 116 Stock Corporation Act, referring to the rules for managing directors in Section 93 Stock Corporation Act.

[587] See below 4.1.3.

[588] Bundesgerichtshof, 21 April 1997, II ZR 175/95, BGHZ 135, 244, 253–254 (*ARAG/Garmenbeck*); see H. Henze, 'Entscheidungen und Kompetenzen der Organe in der AG: Vorgaben der höchstrichterlichen Rechtsprechung', *Betriebs-Berater* 2001, 53, 57; W. Goette, 'Organisationspflichten in Kapitalgesellschaften zwischen Rechtspflicht und Opportunität', *Zeitschrift für das gesamte Handels- und Wirtschaftsrecht* 175 (2011) 388, 395 (n. 31); both are former Federal Court of Justice judges in the Senate responsible for company law.

[589] M. Roth, 'Outside Director Liability: German Stock Corporations Law in Transatlantic Perspective', *Journal of Corporate Law Studies* 8 (2008) 337, 349.

[590] Point 3.8(1)(3) German Corporate Governance Code.

[591] The German Federal Federal Court of Justice (Bundesgerichtshof) in *ARAG/Garmenbeck* based its decision on the US business judgment rule; see H. Henze, 'Leitungsverantwortung des Vorstands – Überwachungspflicht des Aufsichtsrats', *Betriebs-Berater* 2000, 209, 215. Henze was the judge in the company law chamber at the time.

courts, is a presumption that the directors acted in good faith,[592] while the majority view in German academia is that the directors have to prove that they did not
violate their duties.[593]

German courts apply strong standards of review in the monitoring context.[594]
According to the German Federal Court of Justice, there is no business discretion
for decisions of the supervisory board that belong to its control function.[595] The
relatively strong willingness to second-guess the monitoring of the supervisory
board in company affairs is mirrored by a dozen cases of supervisory director
liability since 1979,[596] which have recently been criticised by practitioners.[597] A
more modern approach might give German firms discretion to exercise control as
long as the supervisory directors act in good faith.[598] In the US, courts are very
reluctant to hold non-executive and independent directors liable.[599] The Delaware
Supreme Court decided in *Stone* that a non-executive director is liable in the
monitoring context only if he ignored red flags.[600] A director ignoring red flags
cannot be presumed to be acting in good faith.

c) Say-on-Pay

The say-on-pay is explicitly mentioned in the Stock Corporation Act since 2009.[601]
The shareholders' meeting of a listed company may make a resolution on the
approval of the compensation scheme. The resolution must not give rise to any

---

[592] *Aronson v. Lewis* 473 A.2d 805, 812 (Del. 1984).

[593] See below 4.1.1(e).

[594] Recently highlighting this problem, M. Hoffmann-Becking, 'Das Recht des Aufsichtsrats zur Prüfung durch Sachverständige nach § 111 Abs. 2 Satz 2 AktG', *Zeitschrift für Unter-
nehmens- und Gesellschaftsrecht* 2011, 136, 145–148, which favours giving up information
rights of supervisory directors to shield them from liability.

[595] Bundesgerichtshof, 21 April 1997, II ZR 175/95, BGHZ 135, 244 (*ARAG/Garmenbeck*).

[596] M. Roth, 'Outside Director Liability' (see n. 589) 342.

[597] K. von Schenck (see n. 388) 653–657 (concerning the chairman, von Schenck is Of
Counsel at Clifford Chance); M. Hoffmann-Becking (see n. 594) 145 (Hoffmann-Becking is
senior partner at Germany's leading law firm, Hengeler Mueller).

[598] Referring to Stone, see M. Roth, 'Outside Director Liability' (see n. 589) 365–367,
arguing for economic discretion of supervisory directors; see already M. Dreher, 'Das Ermessen
des Aufsichtsrats', *Zeitschrift für das gesamte Handels- und Wirtschaftsrecht* 158 (1994) 614.

[599] For reluctance in the UK, see *Re Continental Assurance Co. of London Plc,* [2007]
2 BCLC 287, 360 = [2001] B.P.I.R 733 (Ch.), (no. 110): 'I do not base my decision on what I
say now, but I cannot refrain from remarking that, if the non-executive directors were liable to
pay millions of pounds to the liquidators in this case, it is hard to imagine any well-advised
person ever agreeing to accept appointment as a non-executive director of any company'.

[600] *Stone ex rel. AmSouth Bancorporation v. Ritter*, 911 A.2d 362, 369 (Del.Supr. 2006).

[601] Section 120(4) Stock Corporation Act. For the VorstAG, see below n. 673.

rights or obligations; in particular, the obligations of the supervisory board in respect of the remuneration of the management board[602] must remain unaffected. In June 2013 a mandatory and binding say-on-pay on the remuneration system[603] was passed by the German Bundestag, scheduled to com into force in 2014.[604]

d) Spill-over from the Regulation of Financial Institutions

Director primacy and the mandatory division of powers in German corporate governance were driven by members of the German financial industry after the financial crisis of 1929.[605] The German corporate governance system as a whole might therefore be seen as an early spill-over from financial regulation. In contrast to that, the spill over from bofi corporate governance to the corporate governance system as a whole in the current financial crisis has (up to now) been moderate. The only regulatory reaction of this kind[606] was the extension of the limitation period for the liability of directors from five years to ten years.[607] This new provision in the aftermath of the 2008 financial crisis is aimed at financial institutions but, despite critique, is implemented as an overall rule in the Stock Corporation Act. Another recent proposal provided that there should be a minimum period for limitation of directors' liability of three years after the directors have left office.[608]

e) Annual Discharge of Managing and Supervisory Directors

The annual discharge of managing and supervisory directors is a German peculiarity.[609] The annual discharge is a central feature for director accountability in Germany. With the discharge, the general meeting backs the administration of the company by the managing and supervisory directors.[610] The discharge has no effect on future or current liability claims against directors.[611] According to

---

[602] Section 87 Stock Corporation Act.

[603] Section 120(4) Stock Corporation Act, reversed, not yet in force.

[604] Management Board Remuneration Control Act, resolution of 27 June 2013 (according to recommendation 17/14214) is not subject to approval by the upper house (Bundesrat) but might be further discussed and only thereafter might be published in the Federal Gazette.

[605] See above 1.2.

[606] For the VorstAG, see below n. 673.

[607] Section 93(6) Stock Corporation Act; for the notes Referentenentwurf, see <www.bmj. bund.de/files/-/4612/RefE_Bankenrestrukturierung.pdf>.

[608] T. Baums, ILF working paper 119 (07/2010), 'Managerhaftung und Verjährung', *Zeitschrift für das gesamte Handels- und Wirtschaftsrecht,* 174 (2010) 593.

[609] Sections 119(1) no, 3, 120(1) Stock Corporation Act.

[610] Section 120(2)1 Stock Corporation Act.

[611] Section 120(2)2 Stock Corporation Act.

general principles of German director liability law, stock corporations may not waive liability claims against directors in the first three years after they arise.[612] The denial of the discharge or low quotas backing the administration of the company therefore serves as a tool to express dissatisfaction. A recent example was low quotas for the chairman of Deutsche Bank, where the UK pension fund Hermes and other institutional investors expressed discomfort with the way the succession of the former CEO was handled.

3.1.3. *Special Issues:*

3.1.3.1. *Conflicts of Interest—General Remarks*

a) *Definition of Conflict*

From a comparative perspective, academics describe the German law on conflicts of interest as inadequate.[613] There is no overall rule in the Stock Corporation Act or in the German Corporate Governance Code which defines conflicts of interest and states how to deal with them. Special conflicts regulated in the Stock Corporation Act are loans for members of the management and the supervisory board and for advisory and other service contracts with supervisory directors. As is the case for concluding service contracts,[614] the practice of extending loans from the company to members of the management and supervisory board or their relatives requires the approval of the supervisory board.[615]

The German Corporate Governance Code mentions the non-competition obligation of managing directors[616] and that management board members and employees may not, in connection with their work, demand or accept from third parties payments or other advantages for themselves or for any other person, nor are they allowed to grant third parties unlawful advantages.[617] As a general rule,[618] the Code states that members of the management board and the supervisory board are bound by the company's best interests. No member of the management board or the supervisory board may pursue personal interests in his decisions or use business opportunities intended for the company for himself.

---

[612] Section 93(4)3 Stock Corporation Act.

[613] T. Baums and K.E. Scott (see n. 386) 70.

[614] Section 114 Stock Corporation Act.

[615] Sections 89, 115 Stock Corporation Act. Simply referring to the law in this respect, see the German Corporate Governance Code, Point 3.9 German Corporate Governance Code.

[616] Point 4.3.1 German Corporate Governance Code, based on Section 88 Stock Corporation Act.

[617] Point 4.3.2 German Corporate Governance Code.

[618] Points 4.3.3, 5.5.1 German Corporate Governance Code.

Each member of the supervisory board must inform the supervisory board of any conflicts of interest, in particular those which may result from a consultant or directorship function with clients, suppliers, lenders or other third parties.[619] In its report, the supervisory board must inform the general meeting of any conflicts of interest which have occurred, together with their treatment. Material conflicts of interest and those which are not merely temporary in respect of the person of a supervisory board member must result in the termination of his mandate.[620]

Academia applies general principles of civil law for detecting and dealing with conflicts of interest.[621] It remains doubtful what this means for employee representatives in the supervisory board,[622] since German co-determination law gives rise to conflicts of interests by installing employees of the company and union representatives on the supervisory boards.[623] Employee representatives are expected to represent the interests of the employees, which may conflict with the interests of the shareholders and the company.[624]

b) Decision-making Procedure

The decision making procedure concerning conflicts of interest is not explicitly regulated in the Stock Corporation Act and only outlined in the German Corporate Governance Code. The Stock Corporation Act implies that the chairman of the supervisory board decides on the existence of a conflict of interests since the chairman may exclude supervisory directors from committee meetings if they are not also member of the respective committee of the supervisory board. [625] Academia therefore supposes that it is primarily the decision of the chairman to decide whether a conflict of interest exists; whether the board may overrule the decisions of the chairman in this respect is contested.[626]

If a conflict of interest arises, supervisory directors may be excluded from the discussion in the supervisory board and/or the decision-making itself. According to the German Corporate Governance Code, the supervisory board not only has to

---

[619] Point 5.5.2 German Corporate Governance Code.

[620] Point 5.5.3 German Corporate Governance Code.

[621] Hopt/Roth, *Großkommentar Aktiengesetz* (see n. 86), Section 100 no. 131–178.

[622] M. Roth, 'Buchrezension, Marcus Lutter and Gerd Krieger, *Rechte und Pflichten des Aufsichtsrats*, 5th edn. 2008 und Tobias Brouwer, *Zustimmungsvorbehalte des Aufsichtsrats im Aktien- und GmbH-Recht*, 2008' *Zeitschrift für das gesamte Handels- und Wirtschaftsrecht* 173 (2009) 717, 720–721.

[623] For Dutch practice, see 3.1.1(c) and the Dutch report in this volume.

[624] M. Habersack, *Münchener Kommentar Aktiengesetz* (see n. 86), Section 100 no. 66.

[625] Section 109(2) Stock Corporation Act.

[626] Hopt/Roth, *Großkommentar Aktiengesetz* (see n. 86), Section 107 no. 93–97, Section 108 no. 66.

report where a conflict of interest occurred, but also how this conflict was handled.[627] Due to pressure by the German Federal Court of Justice, German blue chips now report at least some conflicts.[628] The Federal Court of Justice has held resolutions of the general meeting concerning the discharge of directors to be voidable since the supervisory board did not report conflicts of interest and their treatment.[629]

According to the German Corporate Governance Code,[630] all members of the management board must disclose conflicts of interest to the supervisory board without delay and inform the other members of the management board thereof. All transactions between the company and the members of the management board, as well as persons they are close to or companies they have a personal association with, must comply with the standards customary in the sector. Important transactions must require the approval of the supervisory board. Members of the management board may take on external activities, especially supervisory board mandates outside the company, only with the approval of the supervisory board.[631]

3.1.3.2. *Related-party Transactions*

Related party transactions are only partly explicitly mentioned for management and supervisory directors but subject to the law for groups of companies (*Konzernrecht*) in the German Stock Corporation Act and the German Corporate Governance Code.[632] Already in 1979, the influence of a supervisory board chairman who pressed the management board to enter into a transaction in favour of a company affiliated to him, led to liability of the chairman in the *Schaffgotsch* decision of the German Federal Court of Justice.[633]

As to related party transactions other than for groups of companies, the Stock Corporation Act deals only with credits to members of the management board, the supervisory board or affiliated persons,[634] and with service contracts of supervisory directors.[635] Requiring the consent of the supervisory board also for

---

[627]   Point 5.5.3(1) German Corporate Governance Code.

[628]   Daimler (2010), Deutsche Bank (2009, employee representatives), Deutsche Börse (2009), Deutsche Telekom (2010); Metro (2009).

[629]   See in detail under enforcement, below 4.1.2.

[630]   Point 4.3.4 German Corporate Governance Code.

[631]   Point 4.3.5 German Corporate Governance Code.

[632]   For potentially upcoming reform due to the Action Plan, see below 5.2.

[633]   Bundesgerichtshof, 21 December 1979, II ZR 244/78, *Neue Juristische Wochenschrift* 1980, 1629.

[634]   Sections 89, 115 Stock Corporation Act, see above n. 615.

[635]   Section 114 Stock Corporation Act.

service contracts is explained by the need to limit back scratching between members of the management board and members of the supervisory board.[636] The doctrinal approach stresses that it is up to the general meeting to decide on the remuneration of supervisory directors.[637] The Austrian Stock Corporation Act (derived from the German 1937 Stock Corporation Act) now goes further, requiring the consent of the supervisory board for all related party transactions of supervisory directors.[638]

The law for groups of companies (*Konzernrecht*) allows for an annual report on transactions among affiliated companies (report on control relationships) which has to be examined by independent auditors.[639] The report is not disclosed to the shareholders but only to the supervisory board. This leads to enforcement issues.[640]

The German Corporate Governance Code deals with related party transactions of managing directors in the above-mentioned way.[641] Related party transactions are to be handled at arm's length. The Code refers to 'standards customary in the sector' for all transactions between the company and the members of the management board as well as persons they are close to or companies with which they have a personal association.[642]

3.1.3.3. Corporate Opportunities

According to German doctrine, directors and officers are prohibited from using corporate opportunities.[643] This is rooted in the duty of loyalty of managing and supervisory directors.[644] However, court rulings are rare.[645] The German Corporate Governance Code explicitly prohibits using corporate opportunities. No supervisory director may seize business opportunities intended for the (affiliated) company for personal use.[646]

---

[636] T. Baums and K.E. Scott (see n. 386) 41.

[637] Hopt/Roth, *Großkommentar Aktiengesetz* (see n. 86), Section 114 no. 5.

[638] Section 95 no. 11 Austrian Stock Corporation Act.

[639] Sections 312–314 Stock Corporation Act.

[640] T. Baums and K.E. Scott (see n. 386) 40.

[641] Above 3.1.3.1.

[642] Point 4.3.4 German Corporate Governance Code; referring to the enterprise, but the Code also refers to all companies affiliated to the company.

[643] H. Merkt, 'Unternehmensleitung und Interessenkollision', *Zeitschrift für das gesamte Handels- und Wirtschaftsrecht* 159 (1995) 423.

[644] M. Roth, *Unternehmerisches Ermessen und Haftung des Vorstands* (Munich, C.H. Beck 2001) 61.

[645] For cases see H. Merkt (see n. 643) 425–428.

[646] Point 5.5.1(2) German Corporate Governance Code.

3.1.3.4. Inside Information

The German Stock Corporation Act prescribes the provision of information regarding the company's affairs to shareholders in the general meeting. Upon request either during or before the general meeting, the management board has to provide information to shareholders, in so far as the information is related to a resolution on the agenda of the general meeting.[647] If information is given to one shareholder by reason of his status as a shareholder outside the general meeting, other shareholders have a right to get the same information at the general meeting if they ask for it.[648] For state owned (not listed) companies, a new provision will be introduced.[649] Furthermore, the insider-regulation based on European directives applies.[650]

3.1.3.5. Takeover Situations

According to German company law, the management board does not choose the shareholders, leading to a board neutrality rule pursuant to the Stock Corporation Act.[651] In contrast, the German Takeover Act allows frustrating actions of the management board if conducted with the consent of the supervisory board.[652] Germany therefore opted out of the European board neutrality rule.[653] In doing so, general standards of company law were not changed. This is relevant for director's liability. The German business judgment rule provides a safe harbour for uninterested and therefore independent decisions. Whether such an independent decision was conducted will be questionable, at least in most cases.[654]

3.1.4. Institutional Investors

In contrast to countries with more developed private pension markets, in Germany the stock capitalisation ratio to GDP is low; the same is true of total

---

[647] Section 131(1) Stock Corporation Act.

[648] Section 131(4) Stock Corporation Act.

[649] Referentenentwurf eines Gesetzes zur Änderung des Aktiengesetzes ('Aktienrechtsnovelle 2011'), proposal to amend Section 394 (possibility to specify the duty of non-disclosure in the articles of incorporation for state-owned stock corporations).

[650] Gesetz über den Wertpapierhandel (Wertpapierhandelsgesetz – WpHG), 9 September 1998, BGBl I 2708.

[651] K.J. Hopt, *Großkommentar Aktiengesetz* (see n. 247) Section 93 no. 122; *idem.*, 'Europäisches und deutsches Übernahmerecht', *Zeitschrift für das gesamte Handels- und Wirtschaftsrecht* 161 (1997), 368, 391, 411.

[652] Section 33 (1) 2 German Securities Acquisition and Takeover Act (WpÜG).

[653] Art 12 Takeover Directive.

[654] Cases where a modified business judgment rule is applied, as in Delaware, are not apparent.

pension fund assets in proportion to the stock market capitalisation.[655] The minor role of the stock market correlates with the minor importance of institutional investors of German origin.[656] This is due to the German pension system focusing on state pensions (pay as you go), low holdings of life insurance companies in equity because of restrictions by the German Insurance Supervision Act[657] and a low proportion of occupational pensions, combined with the allowance of balance-sheet (book-reserve) backed occupational pensions by the German Occupational Pensions Act.[658] The latter is subject to change in practice due to the pressure of rating agencies, which heavily influence the capital structure of companies[659] and due to (international) accounting standards.[660] Listed companies with a dispersed ownership structure fund their pension promises with separate assets in proportions that are comparable internationally.[661] Since institutional investors of German origin are still a rare breed, initiatives for good corporate governance are associated with foreign institutional investors, especially the UK Hermes Pension Fund.[662]

[655] According to figures of the OECD, Pensions Outlook 2008, 64, only 6.5%, compared to 113.1% in the Netherlands, 61.9% in the UK and 39.8% in Switzerland.

[656] M. Roth, 'Corporate Governance' (see n. 121) 530.

[657] Versicherungsaufsichtsgesetz (VAG), see n. 52).

[658] Gesetz zur Verbesserung der betrieblichen Altersversorgung (Betriebsrentengesetz – BetrAVG), 19 December 1974, BGBl I 3610. English translation by Lingemann et al (see n. 11) 207–252). Critical, M. Roth, *Private Altersvorsorge* (see n. 53) 298–301.

[659] *Ibid.* 58–59.

[660] The new IAS 19 standard will further enhance transparency but also lead to greater volatility for defined benefit contributions. Also the Commercial Code (HGB) provides for matching of pension obligations and pension assets.

[661] TowersWatson, *DAX-Pensionswerke 2011,* April 2012, 8, 9, 26: average of 66%. Excluding former state owned companies and Thyssen/Krupp with its poison pill, this average rises to over 76%. Formerly state-owned and family-owned companies tend to have lower ratios: Deutsche Telekom: 12%, VW: 28%, Deutsche Post: 56% (formerly state owned), VW: Porsche, Piech, Katar, 28%, Fresenius: 43%, Metro: 49%, Merck: 55%, Henkel: 79%, MAN: 81% HeidelbergCement: 82%, BMW: Quandt und Klatten: 83%, Beiersdorf: Herz, 83% (family-owned), Thyssen/Krupp: 20% (poison pill, foundation as major shareholder with appointment rights for the supervisory board in a quasi-parity co-determined company). These companies have a funding ratio of only 48.4% overall, the former state-owned companies Deutsche Post, Deutsche Telekom and Volkswagen together with poison pill-shielded Thyssen-Krupp of only 31.7%.

[662] Hermes, *Corporate Governance Principles – Germany*, September 2009, current version from Hermes Equity Ownership Services, *Hermes Corporate Governance Principles – Germany*: Supervisory board, employee representation, August 2011.

3.1.5. *Remuneration (as Incentive)*

The remuneration of supervisory directors is determined by the articles of incorporation or the general meeting.[663] If no remuneration is provided for in the articles of incorporation or in a resolution of the general meeting, supervisory directors accepting their directorship have to fulfil their duties without remuneration. Average remuneration of supervisory directors in Germany was low until the 1990s,[664] attributable partly to co-determination.[665] Since the same-duties same-rights doctrine applies to all supervisory directors, employee representatives receive the same remuneration as shareholder representatives. The widespread practice that employee representatives keep only a modest deductible for themselves, while having to give the rest to the Boeckler Foundation associated with the Confederation of the German Unions (*Deutscher Gewerkschaftsbund, DGB*),[666] is subject to critique.[667]

The level of supervisory director remuneration today is comparably high in large German firms and therefore not a key problem. Average remuneration in 2011 was €93,000 (in 2009: €110,000) according to Heidrick & Struggles,[668] the fourth (in 2009: second) highest in Europe (average €77,000, in 2009: €83,000), with a rather high proportion of performance-based remuneration.[669] The structure of the compensation, especially to what extent and in which form performance-related pay is good practice and in line with the German Stock Corporation Act, is subject to debate.[670] There was a (modest) trend towards companies no longer complying with the recommendation of the Code for performance-based compensation of supervisory directors,[671] and since 2012, performance-related compensation for supervisory directors is mentioned as a mere possibility in the Code.[672]

In the aftermath of the financial crisis of 2008, there are stricter standards for the remuneration of managing directors in listed companies: The incentive struc-

---

[663] Section 113 Stock Corporation Act.

[664] Average: DM 16,900, about €8,500.

[665] Hopt/Roth, *Großkommentar Aktiengesetz* (see n. 86), Section 113 no. 11, 14, 57.

[666] See Hopt/Roth, *Großkommentar Aktiengesetz* (see n. 86), Section 113 no. 11.

[667] Hopt/Roth, *Großkommentar Aktiengesetz* (see n. 86), Section 113 no. 7, 129.

[668] Heidrick & Struggles, *Challenging board performance*, 2011, 47; *idem. Boards in turbulent times* (2009) 16.

[669] Of which the basic fixed fee of €40,000 in 2009 constitutes only 57% of the total remuneration; by comparison, the European average is 83%. In 2011 average basic remuneration in Germany was €41,000 (total €93,000), in Europe €53,000 (total €77,000).

[670] Hopt/Roth, *Großkommentar Aktiengesetz* (see n. 86), Section 113 no. 35–48.

[671] See, *inter alia* (in 2011) Siemens.

[672] Point 5.4.6(2)2 German Corporate Governance Code: if enacted, it shall be oriented toward sustainable growth of the company.

ture has to be structured towards the sustainable development of the company.[673] Sustainability, as a legal term, was only incorporated in the Stock Corporation Act following the recent financial crisis. Its dictionary meaning is long-standing, long continuing to have an effect, lasting.[674] Sustainability, often attributed to 19th century German forestry,[675] therefore requires at least long-term incentives. However, incentives for German managers are medium-term.[676] The Stock Corporation Act and the German Corporate Governance Code subject variable remuneration only to a multi-year assessment; according to a recent study, variable remuneration is free from restrictions for five years.[677] Pension payments which might give long-term incentives are often of minor importance. As an example, the total pension rights of the former CEO of Deutsche Bank, Josef Ackermann, accounted in 2009 for just half of his latest yearly remunerations.[678]

The supervisory board elects the members and decides on the remuneration of the management board.[679] According to new legislation passed in the aftermath of the financial crisis,[680] the supervisory board can no longer delegate the decision on remuneration to a committee and the general meeting may give an advisory vote (say-on-pay) concerning the remuneration of the members of the management board. The Stock Corporation Act explicitly provides for this (only) for listed companies.[681]

---

[673] Section 87(1)2 Stock Corporation Act, implemented by the Gesetz zur Angemessenheit der Vorstandsvergütung (VorstAG), 31 July 2009, BGBl I 2509.

[674] For the German term *nachhaltig*, see Wahrig, *Deutsches Wörterbuch*.

[675] G. Thüsing and G. Forst, 'Nachhaltigkeit als Zielvorgabe für die Vorstandsvergütung', *Gesellschafts- und Wirtschaftsrecht* 2010, 515 with further references.

[676] Section 120(4) Stock Corporation Act.

[677] Point 4.2.3 German Corporate Governance Code incorporates Section 87(1)2 Stock Corporation Act without adjustments for sustainability. For restrictions, see Allen & Overy, *Die Vorstandsgehälter der DAX30-Unternehmen, Analyse der Vergütungssysteme*, January 2011.

[678] Compensation Report of Deutsche Bank 2009: Annual remuneration of Josef Ackermann totalled €9,551,530, and the balance of pension accounts is €4,459,769.

[679] Sections 84, 87 Stock Corporation Act.

[680] Gesetz zur Angemessenheit der Vorstandsvergütung (VorstAG), 31 July 2009, BGBl I 2509.

[681] Section 120(4) Stock Corporation Act.

3.2. Boards and Stakeholders

3.2.1. *Boards and Employees and Labour Co-determination*

a) *The Enlightened Shareholder Value Approach*

Internationally, academia assumes a correlation of the rise of the shareholder value approach and the independent director paradigm.[682] Whether a shareholder value or a stakeholder approach is appropriate and to be followed by the boards is hotly debated in Germany.[683] The traditional, and widely accepted doctrine of the 'enterprise per se',[684] formed the legal ground in Germany for including not only the interests of the shareholders;[685] it also gave impetus to the co-determination regimes after World War I and World War II. According to the 1937 Stock Corporation Act,[686] the management board had to consider the interests of the shareholders, of the employees and of the public (*Unternehmensinteresse*, interest of the enterprise).[687] This provision was not transformed into the 1965 Stock Corporation Act but, according to the governmental draft, seen as 'self-evident'.[688]

Considering the interests of stakeholders was the dominant view until the mid-1990s. Now, academia is split.[689] The German business judgment rule[690] refers not to the interest of the enterprise (doctrine of the enterprise as such) but to the interest of the company.[691] Since the German Corporate Governance Code still sees the stakeholder approach as the appropriate interpretation of the Stock

---

[682] J.N. Gordon (see n. 10), M. Roth, 'Unabhängige Aufsichtsratsmitglieder' (see n. 449) 605.

[683] M. Roth, 'Employee Participation' (see n. 57) 51.

[684] A. Riechers, *Das 'Unternehmen an sich': die Entwicklung eines Begriffs in der Aktienrechtsdiskussion des 20. Jahrhunderts* (Tübingen, Mohr Siebeck 1996).

[685] For the EU, see Commission document *Towards a Single Market Act – for a highly competitive social market economy*, COM(2010) 608 (final), 27.

[686] Section 70(1) 1937 Stock Corporation Act.

[687] F.A. Mann, 'The New German Company Law and Its Background', *Journal of Comparative Legislation* 19 (1937) 220, 227.

[688] B. Kropff, *Aktiengesetz 1965* (Düsseldorf, Institut der Wirtschaftsprüfer 1965); notes to the governmental draft of the Stock Corporation Act 1965, 97.

[689] For a shareholder value concept, see P.O. Mülbert, 'Shareholder Value aus rechtlicher Sicht', *Zeitschrift für Unternehmens- und Gesellschaftsrecht* 1997, 129; for the traditional concept, see G. Spindler, *Münchener Kommentar Aktiengesetz*, Section 76 no. 65; see also above 1.1.b, (n. 67).

[690] Section 93(1)2 Stock Corporation Act.

[691] See M. Roth, 'Outside Director Liability' (see n. 589) 337.

Corporation Act[692] and co-determination is still in place, a pure shareholder value approach might overstate the role of the shareholders in German corporate governance. The assessment that German company law follows an enlightened shareholder value approach is appropriate.[693] The directors are bound primarily by the interests of the shareholders but may (and should) give attention to the interests of other stakeholders as well.

b) Evolution and Forms of Co-determination, Works Councils

First forms of co-determination at board level were introduced after World War I by the Works Councils Act 1920 and the Act on Appointment of Works Council Members in the supervisory board of 1922.[694] These forms of employee participation[695] were abolished by the Nazis in the National Works Act, but reintroduced after World War II. The first employee representative scheme was the parity co-determination in the coal, iron and steel industry in the British zone after World War II, accepted by the employers to maintain these industries. The special regime for these industries was adopted by West Germany after the foundation of the Federal Republic of Germany.[696] The third-parity co-determination regime was introduced in 1952.[697] The quasi-parity co-determination for companies with more than 2,000 employees was introduced in 1976.[698] Since reunification in 1990, the West-German co-determination regime was also introduced in the former East Germany. East Germany therefore is one of the very few regions in former communist Eastern Europe with mandatory co-determination for all companies. Of the companies in East Germany, a considerable proportion has chosen the European Company.[699]

As for corporate governance of firms incorporated in accordance with the German Stock Corporation Act, there is no flexibility in the German co-determination system. Negotiations for tailor-made employee representation are provided only for the European Company. Efforts to expand the SE-model to stock

---

[692] Betriebsrätegesetz, 4 February 1920, RGBl 147; Gesetz über die Entsendung von Betriebsratsmitgliedern in den Aufsichtsrat, 15 February 1922, RGBl 209, Commentary by G. Flatow and O. Kahn-Freund, 13th edn. (Springer, Berlin 1931). See also above 1.1(b).

[693] See M. Roth, 'Employee Participation' (see n. 57) 63, above 1.1(b).

[694] *Ibid.* 62, with further references.

[695] Financial participation was proposed (Crome partiarische Rechtsgeschäfte, 1897) but has not been successful in practice.

[696] Co-Determination Act of 1950 (MitbestG), renamed in 1976, now Act on Co-Determination in the Coal, Iron and Steel Industry (Montan-MitbestG).

[697] Works Councils Act 1952 (Betriebsverfassungsgesetz – BetrVG 1952), since 2004 One-Third Participation Act (DrittelbG).

[698] Co-Determination Act (MitbestG) 1976.

[699] Mensch und Maschine, Q-Cells, <unitedprint.com>.

corporations incorporated under German law have been blocked by the unions.[700]
The Stock Corporation Act contains a formal procedure to find the respective co-
determination regime, ie. to decide whether the One-Third Participation Act, the
Co-Determination Act 1976, the coal, iron and steel industry co-determination
regime or no co-determination regime is to be applied.[701] If the management board
does not apply another co-determination regime and no interested party calls for a
new regime which is then found applicable by a court, the old co-determination
regime, or lack thereof as the case may be, remains in place.

The most common form of co-determination with about 1,500 companies is
the third-parity co-determination.[702] The One-Third Participation Act is applicable
to all stock corporations and limited liability companies (*GmbH*) with between
500 and 2,000 employees employed in Germany.[703] More than 700 companies are
subject to quasi-parity co-determination pursuant to the Co-Determination Act
1976.[704] It provides the same number of directors representing the shareholders
and the employees; however, the chairperson—who is supposed to be (and in
practice is) a shareholder nominee—has a decisive vote.[705] The decisive vote
applies to a second vote if there was no decision of the supervisory board in the
first vote due to a tie. However, it is rarely—if ever—used in practice. A special
regime is in place for the coal, iron and steel industry (parity co-determination).
Such parity co-determination in companies with more than 1,000 employees in
Germany with an independent member to be elected from employee and shareholder representatives applies to about 40 companies.[706]

Employee representatives may not disclose the information given in supervisory meetings to the employees. Meetings have to be kept confidential, which is
particularly mentioned in the Stock Corporation Act due to concerns about
employee representatives talking in the works council or in public.[707] It is primarily
within the competence of the management board to decide on giving information to

---

[700] See for the German unions, D. Hexel, 'Podiumsdiskussion', *Beilage zu Zeitschrift für Wirtschaftsrecht* 48/2009, 35, 36, above 3.2.1(a).

[701] Sections 97–99 Stock Corporation Act. For the various co-determination regimes, see above 2.2.1(c).

[702] See above n. 297.

[703] Section 1 (1) One-Third Participation Act (DrittelbG).

[704] See above n. 298. The Co-Determination Act (MitbestG) applies to stock corporations and limited liability companies (GmbH) with more than 2,000 employees in Germany.

[705] Section 29(2) Co-Determination Act (MitbestG).

[706] For independent directors representing employees, see above 2.2.3(c).

[707] Section 116(2) Stock Corporation Act, introduced in 2002 with the Gesetz zur weiteren Reform des Aktien- und Bilanzrechts, zu Transparenz und Publizität (Transparenz- und Publizitätsgesetz – TransPuG), 19 July 2002, BGBl I 2681.

third parties. The supervisory board as a whole may overturn such a decision belonging to its own competences,[708] but not a single supervisory director.

Employee participation in business decisions is not limited to the supervisory board.[709] Besides the unique German co-determination via employee represent- ation at board level, the Works Constitutions Act[710] also applies, implementing not only works councils. In companies with more than 100 employees in Ger- many, a business committee is to be established,[711] which consults with the em- ployer in economic affairs.[712] The members of the business committee are ap- pointed by the works council.[713]

c) The European and International Dimension of Co-determination

Doubts concerning the current German co-determination regime arise especially in relation to the international (or at least European) dimension of the German co- determination system. Even today, German Co-Determination Acts apply only with respect to the representation of employees in Germany. This might have been state of the art when the foundations of the German co-determination system were laid, after the Second World War and until the 1970s. Within the European Union and due to globalisation, such preferential treatment of the home country is hardly acceptable.[714]

Co-determination is mandatory for stock corporations incorporated under the Stock Corporation Act and limited liability companies incorporated according to the Limited Liability Company Act (*GmbH-Gesetz*). Some other forms, such as cooperatives, may be subject to co-determination, but not foundations and partner- ships with at least one natural person as partner. Furthermore, companies incor- porated in foreign jurisdictions, for example UK listed companies like Air Berlin (plc & Co) or Dutch *naamloze vennootschap* (Qiagen NV), are not subject to the German co-determination regime, even if the centre of business is in Germany. Some US firms made use of the US-German Friendship Treaty and are incorpor- ated as US (Delaware) corporations. Some prominent German companies have

---

[708] Hopt/Roth, *Großkommentar Aktiengesetz* (see n. 86), Section 116 no. 241.

[709] For the Arbeitsdirektor, according to Section 33 Co-Determination Act (MitbestG) 1976; see 2.2.1(c).

[710] Betriebsverfassungsgesetz (BetrVG), 15 January 1972, BGBl I 13, version of 25 September 2001, BGBl I 2518, English translation by Lingemann et al (see n. 11) 261–370.

[711] Section 106(1) Works Constitution Act (BetrVG).

[712] Section 106(1) Works Constitution Act (BetrVG), catalogue of affairs in Section 106 (3) Works Councils Act.

[713] Section 107 Works Constitution Act (BetrVG).

[714] See already above 2.2.1(c).

foundations as holding companies or at least major shareholders, for example Aldi, Bertelsmann, Bosch, Fresenius, Fresenius Medical Care, Lidl and ThyssenKrupp.

d) Corporate Governance and Current Reform Proposals

Co-determination was excluded from the Baums Commission[715] and is still mostly barred from the German Corporate Governance Code. The only provision explicitly addressing co-determination is now one of the most contested in the Code—the recommendation of separate meetings of shareholder and employee representatives to prepare for a meeting of the supervisory board.[716] Meetings of the employee representatives were common.[717] However, due to the risk of impairing the work atmosphere in the supervisory board as a whole, it is doubtful and there is much criticism about transplanting this practice to the shareholder nominees. The critique states that this provision cements the banks in the supervisory board.[718]

Inspired by the implementation of the Societas Europaea, in 2004 the German industry and employer associations (BDA/BDI) demanded a more flexible co-determination-regime by the introduction of negotiated solutions. Furthermore, the BDI/BDA proposed that, instead of quasi-parity co-determination, third-parity co-determination should be the rule for the supervisory board; for the board of directors in a one-tier system, there should be a separate body for employee participation.[719] Such a reform would facilitate the establishment of (super)majority independent boards;[720] an alternative would be to allow employee representation by non-employees and non-union functionaries.[721]

From an economic perspective, the difference between third-parity co-determination and quasi-parity co-determination is seen as merely symbolic for the influence of employee representatives; but in third-parity co-determination it is easier for employee representatives to work constructively in the interests of the enterprise.[722] Today, lessening co-determination via reductions of the quota

---

[715] Government Corporate Governance Commission, Baums (ed.), *Bericht der Regierungs-kommission Corporate Governance* (Cologne, Otto Schmidt 2001); this is to be distinguished from the current Government Commission German Corporate Governance Code, below 4.3.1.

[716] Point 3.6 (1) German Corporate Governance Code; the compliance rate was just over 50% for all listed companies (54%, 88% for the DAX 30 companies), A. von Werder and T. Talaulicar (see n. 337) 860. Since 2012, the Code only mentions the possibility of separate meetings of shareholder and employee representatives.

[717] Hopt/Roth, *Großkommentar Aktiengesetz* (see n. 86), Section 110 no. 79.

[718] See Hopt/Roth, *Großkommentar Aktiengesetz* (see n. 86), Section 110 no. 80.

[719] BDA/BDI *Bericht der Kommission Mitbestimmung, Mitbestimmung modernisieren*, Berlin, November 2004; see also M. Roth, 'Unternehmerische Mitbestimmung' (see note 201).

[720] M. Roth (*ibid.*) 456–461.

[721] M. Roth, 'Unabhängige Aufsichtsratsmitglieder' (see n. 449) 640–642.

[722] N. Raabe (see n. 55) 334.

for employee representatives is not on the agenda but other reform options have also failed, at least until now.

In 2006, the German Jurists Forum discussed the co-determination regime but, for the first time in its 150 year history, did not vote for special recommendations.[723] Also, a Government Commission that dealt with the reform of the co-determination regime could not come up with a joint proposal of the whole group, since the members representing employees and employers could not agree whether to strengthen or loosen the German co-determination regime. The remaining group, composed of the former law professor and politician Kurt Biedenkopf, the former President of the German Federal Labour Court (*Bundesarbeitsgericht*) Helmut Wissmann and the sociologist Wolfgang Streek, proposed also incorporating a negotiation solution for stock corporations, incorporated in accordance with the German Stock Corporation Act.[724] Likewise, Raiser, in his expert report for the German Jurists Forum, pleaded for allowing negotiations with regard to a tailor-made co-determination statute of German stock corporations.[725] Economists of the Kronberger Kreis put forward similar reform proposals.[726]

In 2009, a number of law professors formed a committee (*Arbeitskreis 'Unternehmerische Mitbestimmung'*) and developed a governmental-style draft of a reform act.[727] They refer explicitly to the European Company and propose to implement a similar regime also into the Co-Determination Act 1976. The Corporate Governance Principles of Hermes, the largest UK pension fund, which also offers services for other private pension entities, encourages German listed companies to convert their legal status into a European Company to address concerns about the current German co-determination regime.[728] The proposal calls for a more flexible regime, also including employees in other Member States of the European Union and reducing the mandatory size of big German supervisory boards.

The mandatory size under the Co-Determination Act 1976 of twelve, sixteen or twenty members is too large to be in line with conventional economic wis-

---

[723] German Jurists Forum (Deutscher Juristentag), Stuttgart 2006.

[724] Kommission zur Modernisierung der deutschen Unternehmensmitbestimmung, *Bericht der wissenschaftlichen Mitglieder* [Kurt Biedenkopf, Wolfgang Streek, Hellmuth Wissmann], Dezember 2006, available at <www.boeckler.de>.

[725] T. Raiser, *Unternehmensmitbestimmung vor dem Hintergrund europarechtlicher Entwicklungen*, Verhandlungen des 66. Deutschen Juristentages Stuttgart 2006, Vol. I, Part B (Munich, Beck 2006) B 15.

[726] Kronberger Kreis, *Unternehmensmitbestimmung ohne Zwang* (2007).

[727] Arbeitskreis 'Unternehmerische Mitbestimmung' (G. Bachmann, T. Baums, M. Habersack, M. Henssler, M. Lutter, H. Oetker and P. Ulmer), 'Entwurf einer Regelung zur Mitbestimmungsvereinbarung sowie zur Größe des mitbestimmten Aufsichtsrats', *Zeitschrift für Wirtschaftsrecht* 2009, 885.

[728] Hermes Equity Ownership Services, *Hermes Corporate Governance Principles, Germany, August 2011*: Supervisory board – Employee Representation.

dom[729] and is therefore subject to critique. Larger boards are only seen as being more effective for conglomerates.[730] A minimum of twelve members applies to companies with more than 2000 employees in Germany, a minimum of sixteen members applies to companies with more than 10,000 employees in Germany; companies with more than 20,000 employees in Germany have to establish a supervisory board with twenty members.[731] Companies like BASF and Allianz reduced the size of their supervisory board from twenty to twelve by reincorporating as European Companies.[732]

e) Co-determination for a One-tier Board

According to data of the European Commission from June 2010, of the 73 German companies with more than five employees operating as European Companies, 25 installed the monistic board structure and 48 installed the dualistic board structure.[733] For an analysis of these figures, it has to be taken into account that of the 30 European Companies with board-level employee representation, 25 are of German origin, and that no co-determined Societas Europaea of German origin chose the one-tier system.[734] Looking only at the SE not subject to a co-determination agreement, about half of the European Companies of German origin in operation implemented the one-tier system.[735]

In practical terms, choosing a monistic board seems not to be a choice for co-determined German Stock Corporations being transformed into a Societas Europaea. All four DAX 30 companies incorporated as SE have a two-tier board. The prevailing view is that employees may nominate the same proportion of representatives in a one-tier board as in a two-tier board,[736] and not only the same proportion of non-executive directors.[737] Therefore, according to the majority

---

[729] M.C. Jensen and W.H. Meckling, 'Theory of the firm: Managerial behavior, agency costs and ownership structure', *Journal of Financial Economics* 3 (1976) 305.

[730] J.L. Coles, N.D. Daniel and L. Naveen, 'Boards: Does one size fit all', *Journal of Financial Economics* 2008, 329.

[731] Proposing reductions, Arbeitskreis 'Unternehmerische Mitbestimmung' (see n. 727).

[732] For the effects of such transitions on the supervisory board's size, see 2.2.1(a).

[733] Commission Staff Working Document, Brussels 17 November 2010, SEC(2010) 1391 final, Annex 4, 23 and 24 (as of 25 June 2010).

[734] SE Europe, *Overview of the current state of SE founding in Europe*, Update 20 May 2010.

[735] The EU reported a thin majority of one-tier boards, ETUI a thin majority of dual boards (as of June 2011, increasing in December 2011, above 1.3(c); the current overview (1 October 2012) contains no such data.

[736] R. Köstler (see n. 198) 803.

[737] Suggesting this, M. Jacobs, *Münchener Kommentar Aktiengesetz*, 3rd edn. (Munich, C.H. Beck 2012), Section 35 SEBG no. 23; M. Henssler, 'Unternehmerische Mitbestimmung in
cont. ...

view, a company with a supervisory board subject to third-parity co-determination would also be subject to third-parity co-determination in the board of directors, and a company with a supervisory board subject to (quasi-)parity co-determination would be subject to (quasi-)parity co-determination in the board of directors.[738] While this might be acceptable for third-parity co-determined companies being a subsidiary (eg. Puma as the first co-determined company which converted into a SE),[739] it is hardly acceptable for quasi-parity co-determined or holding companies.

From a comparative corporate governance perspective, the possibility of nominating a large number of independent directors on a one-tier board is crucial. In Germany, a majority or a super-majority independent board is difficult, and in large firms even impossible, to implement within the current co-determination regime. Even considering market failure, therefore, the allowance of the SE-style negotiation regime is more appropriate today than it was after World War II and in the 1970s. From a European point of view, the possibility of choosing a form of co-determination which represents not only employees employed in Germany but also employees in Europe seems to be inevitable, not only for European Companies (SE).[740] A modern co-determination regime should also include employees employed outside the European Union, independent employee representatives (at least as an option) and the choice to implement co-determination at the national level only (therefore establishing a holding company free of co-determination).

3.2.2. Boards and Creditors

Due to creditor protection being one of the traditional features of the German Stock Corporation Act,[741] it is accepted that managing and supervisory directors may also take into account the interests of the creditors.[742] However, taking account of the interests of the creditors is seldom mentioned, even by protagonists

---

der Societas Europaea – Neue Denkanstöße für die 'Corporate Governance"-Diskussion', *Festschrift Ulmer* (Berlin, De Gruyter 2003) 193, 210; J. Reichert and S. Brandes, 'Mitbestimmung der Arbeitnehmer in der SE – Gestaltungsfreiheit und Bestandsschutz', *Zeitschrift für Unternehmens- und Gesellschaftsrecht* 2003, 767, 792; C. Teichmann, 'Gestaltungsfreiheit im monistischen Leitungssystem der Europäischen Aktiengesellschaft', *Betriebs-Berater* 2004, 53, 56–57.

[738] See 1.1.3(c).

[739] The controlling shareholder in Puma, the French luxury producer PPR, holds 75.12% of the shares.

[740] See above 2.2.1(c)

[741] M. Lutter (ed.), *Legal Capital in Europe* (see n. 95).

[742] Stressing the priority of shareholder interests, see L. Klöhn, 'Interessenkonflikt zwischen Aktionären und Gläubigern der Aktiengesellschaft im Spiegel der Vorstandspflichten', *Zeitschrift für Unternehmens- und Gesellschaftsrecht* 2008, 110, 155.

of the interest of the enterprise (enterprise per se). The German Corporate Governance Code names only the interests of the shareholders, the employees and 'other stakeholders'.[743]

Historically, there was a strong representation of banks in the supervisory boards of German industrial companies.[744] Since the 1990s, these personal ties have been loosening.[745] Deutsche Bank now prohibits chairmanships in non-group supervisory boards for members of the management board.[746] According to a recent study, bank representatives in a supervisory board lead to lower market capitalisation of the controlled firms.[747] Bank managers may not use their knowledge derived from outside supervisory boards; meetings have to be kept confidential.[748]

3.2.3. Boards, Other Stakeholders and Sustainability

Taking into account the interests of the public was explicitly mentioned in the 1937 Stock Corporation Act. According to the governmental draft of the current 1965 Stock Corporation Act, such a view is self-evident and therefore no longer mentioned.[749] According to the German Corporate Governance Code, looking for sustainable creation of value is the objective of managing and supervisory directors.[750] For managing directors, the long-term perspective is to be taken as the leading principle for remuneration in listed companies.[751] Corporate social responsibility is accepted[752] and promoted by some firms with a code of responsible conduct for business.[753]

---

[743] Point 4.1.1 German Corporate Governance Code.

[744] K.J. Hopt, 'Two-Tier Board' in Hopt at al (see n. 2) 246.

[745] Monopolies Commission, see above n. 35.

[746] Terms of reference for the management board of Deutsche Bank, 2 February 2011, VI (1).

[747] I. Dittmann, E.G. Maug and C. Schneider, 'Bankers on the Boards of German Firms: What They Do, What They are Worth, and Why They are (Still) There', *Review of Finance* 14 (2010) 35.

[748] Section 116(2) Stock Corporation Act: The supervisory board members are particularly bound to maintain confidentiality as to confidential reports received or confidential consultations, see Hopt/Roth, *Großkommentar Aktiengesetz* (above n. 86), Section 116f no. 215–278.

[749] Kropff *Aktiengesetz 1965* (see n. 688), notes to the governmental draft of the Stock Corporation Act 1965, 97.

[750] Foreword (2) German Corporate Governance Code.

[751] Section 87 Stock Corporation Act. For performance-related remuneration of supervisisory directors, the same applies according to Point 5.4.6(2)2 German Corporate Governance Code.

[752] P.O. Mülbert, 'Soziale Verantwortung von Unternehmen im Gesellschaftsrecht', *Die Aktiengesellschaft* 2009, 766.

[753] The signatories include Deutsche Bank and BASF.

Also for the German system there is the pragmatic view that in the long run shareholder value and the stakeholder approach converge.[754] In particular the German Corporate Governance Code takes such a long-term view.[755] Since the German corporate governance system was traditionally seen as taking a long-term perspective due to bank holdings[756] and co-determination, this view best describes the focus of the management and the supervisory board in administering the company.[757] However, the continued existence of the company should not be overstated. In academia, a well-established line of argument states that the management may not put the existence of the company at risk.[758] Such a view is doubtful. Doing business may (and usually does) require management to put the existence of the company at risk to some degree.[759]

The public has a special interest in detecting long-term trends and minimising systemic risks. The European Commission addresses such problems as demographics and climate change within its new agenda, Europe 2020.[760] Taking into account environmental matters is considered good business practice, especially by German firms.[761] Hindering prosperity in the long run, Germany faces huge demographic challenges.[762] Also, German managers see the shrinking population as one of the biggest long-term systemic risks for German firms. Improved compatibility of family and work and diversity, especially enhancing the parti-

---

[754] Hopt/Roth, *Großkommentar Aktiengesetz* (see n. 86), Section 93 no. 27, Section 111 no. 104.

[755] Foreword (2) German Corporate Governance Code: The Code clarifies the obligation of the Management Board and the Supervisory Board to ensure the continued existence of the enterprise and its sustainable creation of value in conformity with the principles of the social market economy (interest of the enterprise).

[756] For tax restrictions to sell shares until 2000, see text to n. 5 above.

[757] M. Hellwig, *Jahrestagung des Vereins für Socialpolitik,* Thünen-Vorlesung 2010.

[758] H.J. Mertens and A. Cahn, *Kölner Kommentar Aktiengesetz* 3rd edn. (Cologne, Heymanns 2010) Section 93 no. 86; M. Lutter, 'Die Business Judgment Rule und ihre praktische Anwendung', *Zeitschrift für Wirtschaftsrecht* 2007, 841, 845; *idem.*, 'Bankenkrise und Organhaftung', *Zeitschrift für Wirtschaftsrecht* 2009, 197, 199.

[759] For another view, see Hopt, *Großkommentar Aktiengesetz* (see n. 247), Section 93 no. 82; Hopt/Roth, *Großkommentar Aktiengesetz* (see n. 86), Section 93 new version no. 36; Fleischer, *Spindler/Stilz Aktiengesetz* (see n. 86), Section 93 no. 81; M. Roth, *Unternehmerisches Ermessen* (see n. 644) 110 f; T. Drygala 'Die Pflicht des Managements zur Vermeidung existenzgefährdender Risiken', *Festschrift Hopt* 2010, 541; T. Florstedt, 'Zur organhaftungsrechtlichen Aufarbeitung der Finanzmarktkrise', *Die Aktiengesellschaft* 2010, 315.

[760] Europe 2020, *A strategy for smart, sustainable and inclusive growth*, Brussels, 3 March 2010, COM(2010) 2020 final.

[761] Munich Re, Allianz; see M. Roth, 'Corporate Governance' (see n. 121) 548–549.

[762] Standard & Poor's, *Global Aging 2010: The Irreversible Truth,* also incudes data for Germany.

cipation of women, and the efforts to enhance labour participation of the elderly have to be seen in this respect.[763] Long-term investors, such as pension funds and life-insurance companies, have to minimise systemic risks for their long-term beneficiaries.

3.3. Changing Roles in Financial Distress

In times of financial distress, the supervisory board becomes more active. This is also derived from the legal duty to oversee the management of the company.[764] This duty obliges the supervisory board to take a closer look at management board decisions in times of financial distress. Besides the duty to monitor, the supervisory board has to advise the management board and, if needed, to remove members of the management board and to appoint new ones. Defining precise standards is difficult. Johannes Semler, a former managing director of AEG and subsequently supervisory director of Daimler, proposed an escalating duty of the supervisory board.[765] In normal times, he conceded an accompanying supervision; if first signs of decline occur, there should be a supporting supervision; and in times of crisis there should be a shaping supervision. This view is seen as too restricting; literature now distinguishes only between normal and special situations.[766]

4. Enforcement

4.1. Courts

4.1.1. *Personal Liability Claims*

a) *General Remarks*

Overall, the interpretation of the German Stock Corporation Act by the courts and academia is rather pragmatic. With its *ARAG-Garmenbeck* decision, the German Federal Court of Justice[767] laid the foundation for the introduction of the German business judgment rule.[768] In addition, by establishing the duty of the supervisory

---

[763] Some investors explicitly refer to progress in German labour participation.

[764] Hopt/Roth, *Großkommentar Aktiengesetz* (see n. 86), Section 111 no. 313–321.

[765] J. Semler, *Leitung und Überwachung* 2nd edn. (Cologne, Heymanns 1996) no. 232; *idem, Münchener Kommentar Aktiengesetz* (see n. 302), Section 111 no. 61–63.

[766] M. Habersack, *Münchener Kommentar Aktiengesetz* (see n. 86), Section 111 no. 46, Hopt/Roth, *Großkommentar Aktiengesetz* (see n. 86), Section 111 no. 317.

[767] Bundesgerichtshof, 21 April 1997, II ZR 175/95, BGHZ 135, 244.

[768] See above 3.1.2(b).

board to advise the management board, the courts[769] have promoted the transformation of the German supervisory board function from monitoring ('controlling') to advising the management board.[770] In a recent decision concerning breach of trust (*Untreue*) in criminal law, the German Constitutional Court took a law and economics approach.[771] Nevertheless, there are some rigid views on the duties of supervisory directors and a substantial number of court rulings have held supervisory directors of different legal forms liable for breach of duties.

b) Release and Indemnification

The Stock Corporation Act forbids contractual release from liability;[772] German company law knows no Delaware-style rule in this respect. The company may not waive or compromise a claim earlier than three years after the claim has arisen, and then only if the general meeting gives its consent, and provided no minority, whose holdings of shares amounts to no less than one-tenth of the share capital records a formal objection in the minutes.[773] The foregoing time limit must not apply if the person liable for damages is insolvent and enters into a compromise with his creditors in order to avoid or terminate insolvency proceedings.[774]

Insurance is permitted and common for listed companies, both for members of the supervisory and the management board (D&O insurance, directors' and officers' liability insurance).[775] It is common practice that the company pays the premium and also insures against damages of the company itself. Since 2002, directors must pay a part of the damage. Such participation was provided for first in the form of 'a suitable deductible' if the D&O insurance premium is paid by the company. This suitable deductible should be paid directly by the management and supervisory directors but was not defined by the German Corporate Governance Code.[776] Compliance rates were low.[777]

---

[769] Bundesgerichtshof, 25 March 1991, II ZR 188/89, BGHZ 114, 127.

[770] According to Point 5.1.1 German Corporate Governance Code, the task of the supervisory board is to advise and to supervise the management board.

[771] Bundesverfassungsgericht, 23 June 2010, 2 BvR 2559/08, 2 BvR 105/09, 2 BvR 491/09, Amtliche Sammlung, BVerfGE 126, 170, 228. The court stated that the prevailing normative view assuming that the risk for losses is a loss as unconstitutional and ruled that an economic perspective is to be taken.

[772] Section 93(4)3 Stock Corporation Act.

[773] Section 93(4)3 Stock Corporation Act.

[774] Section 93(4)4 Stock Corporation Act.

[775] See H. Ihlas, *D&O: Directors and Officers Liability*, 2nd edn. (Berlin, Duncker & Humblot 2009).

[776] Point 3.8(2) German Corporate Governance Code 2002.

Such deductibles are now mandatory.[778] In 2009, the German Stock Corporation Act was amended by the Adequate Management Remuneration Act (VorStAG).[779] Now, if the company takes out a D&O insurance policy for the management board, a deductible of at least ten per cent of the loss up to at least the amount of one and a half times the fixed annual compensation of the management board member must be agreed upon.[780] The German Corporate Governance Code recommends a similar deductible must be agreed upon in any D&O policy for the supervisory board.[781]

c) Insolvent Trading

German executive directors have to file for insolvency proceedings within three weeks after there is a cash-flow or balance-sheet insolvency.[782] In 2008, the corresponding provision was moved from the Stock Corporation Act[783] into the German Insolvency Code (InsO), covering all legal forms, whether German or foreign juristic persons or partnerships without a natural person as personally liable partner.[784] The liability arising for violation of the duty to file for insolvency proceedings in case of insolvency might be briefly addressed as insolvent trading.[785] Such a term also covers the liability of corporate directors for payments after insolvency.[786] Losses occurred by payments after insolvency are

---

[777] A. von Werder and T. Talaulicar (see n. 337) 855: 78% of the DAX 30 but only 45 of all listed companies complied, which was the only recommendation with a compliance rate under 50%.

[778] Section 93(2)3 Stock Corporation Act.

[779] Gesetz zur Angemessenheit der Vorstandsvergütung (VorstAG), 31 July 2009, BGBl I 2509.

[780] Also Point 3.8(2)(1) German Corporate Governance Code.

[781] Point 3.8(2)(2) German Corporate Governance Code.

[782] For the special balance-sheet insolvency, see recently Federal Court of Justice (Bundesgerichtshof) 5 February 2007, II 234/05, BGHZ 171, 46 and 9 October 2006, 303/07, *Wertpapier-Mitteilungen* 2006, 2254.

[783] Dating back to the ADHGB 1884 (Art. 240), there were special provisions especially in the Stock Corporation Act, Section 92(2) and in the Limited Liability Corporation Act (GmbHG), Section 64(2).

[784] Section 15a Insolvency Code (InsO). For the notes: governmental draft of the Act on Modernisation and on Prevention of Malpractice in the Limited Liability Company Law (MoMiG), BTDrucks 16/6140.

[785] The legal term insolvent trading is laid down in the Australian Corporation Act and imposes liability on directors for trading when the company is insolvent either on a cash-flow or on a balance-sheet basis, Section 588G Corporations Act 2001.

[786] Section 9 (2) Stock Corporation Act.

easier to calculate and therefore of significant practical importance.[787] If the debtor's assets do not cover his existing liabilities, the company will meet the balance-sheet test when it is highly likely that the company will continue to exist.[788] In 2012 the German parliament made this balance-sheet test permanent after it had been introduced on an interim basis after the financial crisis.[789]

It is an expression of the flexibility inherent to German methodology and court practice that a modified business judgment rule[790] is applied to the German insolvent trading provision.[791] German practitioners, scholars and, at least to a certain degree also courts, do so even without an explicit reference to a 'reasonable' standard as in the English wrongful trading provision.[792] The German Federal Court of Justice ruled in the 1970s that after the company became balance-sheet insolvent, the management board was allowed to try to save the company after a diligent investigation of the probable outcome of such an attempt and if such an attempt could be regarded by the directors as making sense.[793] In a later decision in the 1990s, the Federal Court of Justice ruled that there is a limited discretion in judging whether a going concern is probable.[794] The former president of the Company

---

[787] K. Schmidt, 'Übermäßige Geschäftsführerrisiken aus § 64 II GmbHG, § 130a III HGB?', *Zeitschrift für Wirtschaftsrecht* 2005, 2177.

[788] Section 19 Insolvency Code (InsO).

[789] Gesetz zur Einführung einer Rechtsbehelfsbelehrung im Zivilprozess und zur Änderung anderer Vorschriften of 5 December 2012, BGBl I 2418; see the notes BTDrucks 17/11385 (to Art. 18), basing this on a study by Georg Bitter and Christoph Hommerich, *Die Zukunft des Überschuldungsbegriffs*, Abschlussbericht, 15 May 2012.

[790] For a modified business judgment rule concerning accounting decisions, see W. Müller, 'Bilanzentscheidungen und business judgment rule', *Liber americorum Happ* (Cologne, Heymanns 2006) 179, 198 f; H. Fleischer in Spindler/Stilz. *Aktiengesetz* (see n. 86), Section 93 no. 68.

[791] M. Roth, *Unternehmerisches Ermessen* (see n. 644) 150ff, 210ff; H. Henze, 'Entscheidungen und Kompetenzen der Organe in der AG: Vorgaben der höchstrichterlichen Rechtsprechung', *Betriebs-Berater* 2001, 53, 57; see also H. Fleischer, 'Erweiterte Außenhaftung der Organmitglieder im Europäischen Gesellschafts – und Kapitalmarktrecht – Insolvenzverschleppung, fehlerhafte Kapitalmarktinformation', *Zeitschrift für Unternehmens- und Gesellschaftsrecht* 2004, 437, 458–459; G. Spindler, 'Prognosen im Gesellschaftsrecht', *Die Aktiengesellschaft* 2006, 677, 687.

[792] The Higher Regional Court (OLG) Saarbrücken denied liability in a case where the company was probably continuing its business operations 18 months after balance-sheet insolvency, 30 November 2000, 8 U 71/00, *Neue Zeitschrift für Gesellschaftsrecht* 2001, 414, 415.

[793] Bundesgerichtshof, 9 July 1979, II ZR 118/77, BGHZ 75, 96 = *Neue Juristische Wochenschrift* 1979, 1823.

[794] Bundesgerichtshof, 6 June 1994, II ZR 292/91, BGHZ 126, 181, 199 = *Neue Juristische Wochenschrift* 1994, 2020, 2024.

Senate of the Federal Court of Justice declared this as a case of business discretion (*unternehmerisches Ermessen*).[795] Of course, this discretion is a limited one.

d) Liability of Supervisory Directors in Insolvency

Most cases of supervisory director liability occur in insolvency proceedings.[796] As in the US, the insolvency of a company is part of a 'perfect storm' leading to supervisory director liability.[797] Of practical importance are loans to parent companies or to third parties without securities,[798] but other forms of wrongdoing are also in the focus of insolvency administrators.[799] Until recently,[800] there have not been any reported cases in which external directors of listed or non-listed stock corporations were held liable by the courts for not placing the company into insolvency proceedings within the three-week window period.

e) Burden of Proof

Unlike in the US,[801] the German Stock Corporation Act contains a presumption that the managing directors culpably violated their duties. In academia, it is contested whether this reversal of the burden of proof in the Stock Corporation Act[802] is subject to culpability only or also to the breach of duty itself. Although German civil law distinguishes between violating duties (*Pflichtverletzung*) and culpably violating duties (*Verschulden*), the extension of the presumption to the

---

[795] W. Goette, 'Leitung, Aufsicht und Haftung – zur Rolle der Rechtsprechung bei der Sicherung einer modernen Unternehmensführung', *Festschrift 50 Jahre Bundesgerichtshof* (Cologne, Heymanns 2000) 123, 137; *idem.*, 'Haftung' in P. Hommelhoff, K.J.Hopt and A. von Werder (eds.), *Handbuch Corporate Governance*, 2nd edn. (Stuttgart and Cologne, Schäffer-Pöschel and Otto Schmidt 2009) 713, 732.

[796] M. Roth, 'Outside Director Liability' (see n. 589) 342: in all cases decided after the *ARAG/Garmenbeck* decision of the German Supreme Court, the companies were insolvent.

[797] For the perfect storm in the US, see B.S. Black, B.R. Cheffins and M. Klausner, 'Outside Director Liability', *Stanford Law Review* 58 (2006) 1055.

[798] Regional Court (Landgericht) Dortmund, 1 August 2001, 20 O 143/93, *Die Aktiengesellschaft* 2002, 97; German Federal Court of Justice, *Die Aktiengesellschaft* 2007, 167.

[799] For cases, see M. Roth, 'Outside Director Liability' (see n. 589) 342.

[800] Recently, Bundesgerichtshof, 16 March 2009, II ZR 280/09, *Wertpapier-Mitteilungen* 2009, 851, for limited liability companies, see Bundesgerichtshof, 20 September 2010, BGHZ 187, 60 = *Wertpapier-Mitteilungen* 2010, 1947 (Doberlug) with note M. Habersack, 'BGH, Urteil vom 20.9.2010, II ZR 78/09', *Juristen-Zeitung* 2010, 1191; J. Schürnbrand, 'Überwachung des insolvenzrechtlichen Zahlungsverbots durch den Aufsichtsrat', *Neue Zeitschrift für Gesellschaftsrecht* 2010, 1207; J. Thiessen, 'Haftung des Aufsichtsrats für Zahlungen nach Insolvenzreife', *Zeitschrift für Unternehmens- und Gesellschaftsrecht* 2011, 275.

[801] *Aronson v. Lewis* 473 A.2d 805, 813 (Del. 1984).

[802] Section 93(2)2 Stock Corporation Act.

breach of duty is the majority view.[803] According to this view, German stock corporation law presumes that a director did not act with due care if facts show that there was possibly of wrongdoing.[804] For directors who have left the company, and therefore for most cases in practice, the majority view is that this presumption cannot be held since former directors do not have access to documents which might be in favour of their legal position.[805]

f) Cases

There are cases of supervisory director liability across all legal forms.[806] Litigation was not common for (listed) companies but is becoming more important both for managing and supervisory directors. In the general meeting season 2012, with Siemens, Infinion and Telekom, quite a number of blue chips have votes to accept settlements for compensation and pension payments on the agendas of the general meetings.[807] Actions against former management directors[808] and other cases, such as a demand for a fine against the former chairman of the supervisory board of Siemens, are a novelty.

Payments of supervisory directors from listed companies to settle liability claims were rare, as are court cases. The famous *Mannesmann* case which involved the CEO of Deutsche Bank, Josef Ackerman, was a criminal law case.[809] The *Mannesmann* case was compared with the famous *Disney* decision concerning the remuneration of Michael Ovitz.[810] While the amount paid to Ovitz was higher, there was an *ex ante* contractual ground in the contract before Ovitz

---

[803] U. Hüffer *Aktiengesetz* (see n. 86), Section 93 no. 16. Minority view in Hopt/Roth, *Großkommentar Aktiengesetz* (see n. 86), Section 93nF no. 69; W.G. Paefgen, 'Grundlagen, Anwendungsbereich und Formulierung einer Business Judgment Rule im künftigen UMAG', *Die Aktiengesellschaft* 2004, 245, 258.

[804] For the majority view, see G. Spindler, *Münchener Kommentar Aktiengesetz*, (see n. 67), Section 93 no. 162–171.

[805] M. Foerster, 'Beweislastverteilung und Einsichtsrecht bei Inanspruchnahme ausgeschiedener Organmitglieder', *Zeitschrift für das gesamte Handels- und Wirtschaftsrecht* 2011, 221, 245–247.

[806] M. Roth, 'Outside Director Liability' (see n. 589) 342.

[807] Section 93(4)3 Stock Corporation Act: no waiver or compromise in the first three years after the claim arose.

[808] According to the press, state banks (Bayern LB and Sachsen LB) are demanding €200 million and €60 million from their former managing directors; MAN is demanding €237 million, *Financial Times Deutschland*, 1 February 2011, 20.

[809] Bundesgerichtshof, 21 December 2005, 3 StR 470/04, BGHSt 50, 331.

[810] F.A. Gevurtz, 'Disney in a Comparative Light', *American Journal Comparative Law* 55 (2007) 453; stressing the differences in the cases, see D. Donald, 'Approaching Comparative Company Law', *Fordham Journal of Corporate and Financial Law* 14 (2008) 83, 101.

took office and not *ex post*, as in the Mannesmann case. There appear not to be any cases of independent director liability.[811]

4.1.2. Nullification of Resolutions

For nullification of the resolutions of the general meeting, there are special provisions in the Stock Corporation Act distinguishing between voidable and void resolutions.[812] This legal regime is in general subject to critique[813] since as under German contract law[814] a successful challenge to a voidable resolution is supposed to nullify it *ex tunc*.[815] A practical consequence of the German regime for the nullification of resolutions of the general meeting is the emergence of so-called predatory shareholders (*räuberische Aktionäre*), who may block resolutions from being registered and therefore from being executable.[816] There are special provisions concerning the election of supervisory directors; for example, the election of a supervisory director holding already ten seats in other supervisory boards is void.[817]

German courts developed the nullification of the vote on discharge of supervisory and managing directors as a specific sanction for not being committed to the corporate governance declaration of the supervisory and the management board.[818] In two decisions (*Deutsche Bank* and *Springer*), the German Federal Court of Justice nullified such resolutions of the general meeting since, in its report to the general meeting, the supervisory board did not report on conflicts of interests and its treatment of the conflict.[819]

---

[811] Since the independent directors are not a yet category of German stock corporation law, they are not easily detectable.

[812] Sections 241, 243 Stock Corporation Act.

[813] Arbeitskreis Beschlussmängelrecht, *Die Aktiengesellschaft* 2008, 617 (members: V. Butzke, M. Habersack, P. Hemeling, R. Kiem, P.O. Mülbert, U. Noack, C. Schäfer, E. Stiltz, J. Vetter).

[814] Section 142 Civil Code (BGB).

[815] Section 248 Stock Corporation Act does not deal with *ex tunc* or *ex nunc*; academia favours *ex tunc*, U. Hüffer, Aktiengesetz (see n. 86), Section 248 no. 6.

[816] On the abuse of rights, see U. Hüffer, *Aktiengesetz* (see n. 86), Section 245 no. 22–27a.

[817] Section 250 Stock Corporation Act; for voidable resolutions, see section 251 Stock Corporation Act.

[818] For critique, see below 4.3.1.

[819] Bundesgerichtshof, 16 February 2009, II ZR 185/07, BGHZ 180, 9 (*Kirch/Deutsche Bank*); Bundesgerichtshof, 21 September 2009, II ZR 174/08, BGHZ 182, 272 (*Springer*, also called *Umschreibungsstopp*); for sanctions on incorrect declarations of compliance, see A. Kiefner, 'Fehlerhafte Entsprechenserklärung und Anfechtbarkeit von Hauptversammlungsbeschlüssen', *Neue Zeitschrift für Gesellschaftsrecht* 2011, 201.

In Germany, it is generally accepted that resolutions of the supervisory board can also be nullified. In the *ARAG/Garmenbeck* case, the German Federal Court of Justice nullified the resolution of the supervisory board not to sue managing directors.[820] The procedure to nullify resolutions of the supervisory board is developed independently from the provisions concerning the resolutions in the general meeting.[821]

4.1.3. Special Procedures and Issues

For intra-company claims, the management board sues the members of the supervisory board, while the supervisory board sues current and former members of the management board.[822] Shareholder action, in the form of appointment of special auditors and (minority) rights to sue management and supervisory directors,[823] was reformed in 2005[824] but still plays no role in practice.[825] A minority of one per cent of the shareholders or representing a capital of one per cent could file a petition for suing the supervisory or management directors.[826]

Intra-company law suits are subject to the general judicial system which comprises three instances. There are specialised chambers for commercial affairs in the first instance (Regional Court, *Kammer für Handelssachen am Landgericht*), specialised chambers in most areas at the Court of Appeals (*Oberlandesgericht*) and a specialised chamber for company and partnership law at the German Federal Court of Justice (*Bundesgerichtshof*). The German Jurists Forum proposed reducing litigation to two instances[827] aiming for faster settlement of conflicts and to build even more specialised courts. In particular, *Spruchverfahren* often take eight or ten years to be resolved.[828] Building chambers at the courts

---

[820] Bundesgerichtshof, 21 April 1997, II ZR 175/95, BGHZ 135, 244 (*ARAG/Garmenbeck*).

[821] Hopt/Roth, *Großkommentar Aktiengesetz* (see n. 86), Section 108 no. 136–140.

[822] This leads to problems if the former member of the management board is, or later becomes, a supervisory director.

[823] Sections 142–149 Stock Corporation Act.

[824] Gesetz zur Unternehmensintegrität und Modernisierung des Anfechtungsrechts (UMAG), 22 September 2005, BGBl I 2802.

[825] For recent reform proposal for Germany, see K.U. Schmolke, 'Die Aktionärsklage nach § 148 AktG', *Zeitschrift für Unternehmens- und Gesellschaftsrecht* 2011, 398; for Austria, G. Eckert, K. Grechnig and A. Stremitzer, in S. Kalss (ed.), *Vorstandshaftung in 15 europäischen Ländern* (Vienna, Linde 2005) 95, 136–149.

[826] Section 148(1) Stock Corporation Act.

[827] Resolution of the German Jurists Forum 2008; M. Roth, 'Börsennotierte und geschlossene Aktiengesellschaften, Die Rechtsform Aktiengesellschaft „ausspalten"?', *Anwaltsblatt* 2008, 580, 584; idem., *Festschrift Hopt* (see n. 131) 1277–1278.

[828] J. Wittgens and J. Redeke, 'Zu aktuellen Fragen der Unternehmensbewertung im Spruchverfahren', *Zeitschrift für Wirtschaftsrecht* 2007, 2015, 2020.

staffed with specialised judges might, as in the US in Delaware, attract firms to have their legal seat in that jurisdiction.[829]

A German peculiarity is the so called *Spruchverfahren*, which is a special procedure aimed to fix the 'real value' of a company. The *Spruchverfahren* is regulated in a special Act[830] and gives shareholders appropriate compensation for the exclusion from the company in a squeeze-out as well as for incorrect pricing in a merger or for losses arising in the formation of a group of companies. Arbitration is restricted due to mandatory company law.[831]

4.2. Regulators

Supervisory agencies as regulators are of relevance especially for banks and other financial institutions. The Federal Financial Supervisory Agency (BaFin) has the power to intervene in the corporate governance of supervised firms.[832] The leading German stock exchange, Deutsche Börse, played some role in developing the first German takeover regulations,[833] and in the Neuer Markt,[834] which was destined to stay in Frankfurt after the failed merger with the London Stock Exchange. Since then, Deutsche Börse is not an active norm-setter; the German Corporate Governance Code is enacted by a government commission, seen as self-regulating. The merger with NYSE Euronext that is currently on the agenda might lead to a more active role in the future.

---

[829] The legal seat and centre of business must not correlate: Gesetz zur Modernisierung des GmbH-Rechts und zur Bekämpfung von Missbräuchen, notes to the governmental draft, BTDrucks 16/6140, 29.

[830] Gesetz über das gesellschaftsrechtliche Spruchverfahren (Spruchverfahrensgesetz – SpruchG), 12 June 2003, BGBl I 838.

[831] Section 23(5) Stock Corporation Act.

[832] See above 1.2(b).

[833] K.J. Hopt, 'The duties of directors in target companies in hostile takeovers – German and European perspectives', in Ferrarini et al (eds.), *Capital Markets in the Age of the Euro* (Oxford, OUP 2002) 391.

[834] M.O. Kersting, 'Der Neue Markt der Deutsche Börse AG', *Die Aktiengesellschaft* 1997, 222.

4.3. Self-regulation

4.3.1. *German Corporate Governance Code*

Since 2002, the Stock Corporation Act[835] has required listed companies to report on whether the company follows the recommendations of the German Corporate Governance Code.[836] The German Code is published in the Electronic Federal Gazette (*elektronischer Bundesanzeiger*)[837] and on the website of the Government Commission German Corporate Governance Code.[838] The first version of the German Code and some further changes of the Stock Corporation Act itself were prepared by the Baums Commission.[839] The Code is reviewed annually in May or June by the Government Commission German Corporate Governance Code;[840] the announcement of the Ministry of Justice in the Electronic Federal Gazette is published in July or August. The publication in the Electronic Federal Gazette is relevant for the declaration to comply (or to explain non-compliance) of the companies:[841] if companies do not want to comply with new provisions, they have to provide an explanation.

The Government Commission German Corporate Governance Code used to have 12 members and in January 2013 had 14 members—four active and former members of the management boards of the industry (currently of Daimler, BASF, SAP and Fraport);[842] four members of the financial services industry, recently including the gate-keepers;[843] two members representing employees and private investors;[844] and four (previously two) academics.[845] The meetings of the Com-

---

[835] Gesetz zur weiteren Reform des Aktien-, und Bilanzrechts, zu Transparenz und Publizität (Transparenz- und Publizitätsgesetz), 19 July 2002, BGBl I 1588.

[836] Section 161 Stock Corporation Act, establishing a comply-or-explain principle. There is no alternative code.

[837] See <www.ebundesanzeiger.de>.

[838] See <www.corporate-governance-code.de>.

[839] Named Government Commission Corporate Governance. For the development, see M. Lutter, 'Deutscher Corporate Governance Kodex', in P. Hommelhoff, K.J. Hopt and A. von Werder (eds.), *Handbuch Corporate Governance*, 2nd edn. (Stuttgart and Cologne, Schäffer-Pöschel and Otto Schmidt 2009)123, 126.

[840] Foreword (13) German Corporate Governance Code.

[841] Section 161 Stock Corporation Act.

[842] M. Gentz [now ICC], M.D. Kley [former CEO, now chairman of the supervisory board], H. Kagermann [now president of acatech] and S. Schulte [only current CEO].

[843] K.P. Mueller, current chairman of the government commission, former CEO of Commerzbank; C. Strenger of the investment fund group of Deutsche Bank (DWS); H.F. Gelhausen of Price WaterhouseCooper; D. Weber-Rey of Clifford Chance as the first woman.

[844] D. Hexel, vice chairman of the German Unions (DGB) and U. Hocker, Deutsche Schutzvereinigung Wertpapierbesitz.

mission are not held in public. The fact that the review of the Code does not include views of the interested public in a formalised procedure,[846] the general standard in Germany, is subject to criticism.

In the amendment in 2010, emphasis was given to diversity in the boardroom. Diversity should be enhanced not only in the supervisory board but also in the management board. Until recently, the management boards of the DAX 30 companies were in the hands of men only. The outlook for further changes to the German Code is difficult; some voices are calling for a regulatory pause. Since its enactment in 2002 until 2010, the German Corporate Governance Code was changed almost every single year.[847]

The Code was left unchanged for the second time in 2011. This was due to critique from both practice and academia concerning political pressure for a quota on diversity in boardrooms.[848] Furthermore, it was argued that there should be a regulatory pause, not a reform in permanence, with future changes being subject to public discussion, as is the case for the UK Corporate Governance Code.[849] The German Corporate Governance Commission has responded positively to this criticism and declared that it will change its policy.[850] The first public consultation has been conducted in order to prepare the amendments for 2012, also in 2013, such a consultation takes place.

4.3.2. *Does the System of Comply-or-explain Produce Effective Results?*

In Germany, the comply-or-explain principle is embedded in a dense corpus of mandatory company law for stock corporations. Management boards and supervisory boards are regulated in forty sections of the Stock Corporation Act.[851] The compliance with the recommendations and suggestions of the German Corporate Governance Code is reviewed regularly by the economist Axel von

---

[845] A. von Werder, economist, newly B. Weber di Mauro (economist, second woman), A.K. Achleitner (economist, third woman) and T. Baums, law professor and former chairman of the preparing governmental Commission Corporate Governance.

[846] M. Hoffmann-Becking, 'Zehn kritische Thesen zum Deutschen Corporate Governance Kodex', *Zeitschrift für Wirtschaftsrecht* 2011, 1173, 1175–1176.

[847] For former versions of the Code, see <www.corporate-governance-code.de>.

[848] See M. Hoffmann-Becking, 'Zehn kritische Thesen zum Deutschen Corporate Governance Kodex', *Zeitschrift für Wirtschaftsrecht* 2011, 1173, 1176; T. Kremer, 'Der Deutsche Corporate Governance Kodex auf dem Prüfstand: bewährte Selbst- oder freiwillige Überregulierung', *Zeitschrift für Wirtschaftsrecht* 2011, 1177; C. Gehling, 'Diskussionsbericht zum "Deutscher Corporate Governance Kodex – Eine kritische Bestandsaufnahme"', *Zeitschrift für Wirtschaftsrecht* 2011, 1181 with a list of participating practitioners and law professors.

[849] See the discussion report of C. Gehling (*ibid.*).

[850] Press release, 4 May 2011.

[851] Sections 76–116 Stock Corporation Act.

Werder (member of the Government Commission German Corporate Governance Code) together first with Till Talaulicar[852] and now Jenny Böhme;[853] since 2012, a detailed report is also published by economists from the Handelshochschule Leipzig.[854] The compliance rate for the DAX 30-companies is for most recommendations higher than ninety per cent;[855] over all, in 2009, the compliance rate is ninety-six per cent for recommendations and eighty-five per cent for suggestions,[856] in 2011 for recommendations 98 per cent.[857]

In terms of acceptance, most recommendations are efficient, even taking into account that in smaller firms, compliance rates are lower.[858] This does not mean that complying improves the value of the firms. Studies on the effects of compliance to the recommendations of the German Code show mixed results.[859] Complying with the provisions of the German Corporate Governance Code enhances trust. The enforcement of the German Corporate Governance Code by the German Federal Court of Justice via nullification of resolutions at the general meeting[860] is subject to critique[861] and even provoked the question whether this could cause demands for the revocation of the Code.[862]

In its 2012 reform, the German Corporate Governance Commission amended the Foreword of the Code by stating that a well-explained deviation from the Code might be good corporate governance.[863] This is to be seen in the context of

---

[852] A. von Werder and T. Talaulicar (see n. 337) 853.

[853] 'Corporate Governance Report 2011' *Der Betrieb* 2011, 1285 and 1345; 'Corporate Governance Report 2012', *Der Betrieb* 2012, 869.

[854] C.R.G. Kohl, M.S. Rapp and M. Wolff, *Kodexakzeptanz 2012, Analyse der Entsprechenserklärungen zum Deutschen Corporate Governance Kodex*, April 2012, Handelshochschule Leipzig, Center for Corporate Governance.

[855] In detail, A. von Werder and T. Talaulicar (see n. 337) 853; Kohl/Rapp/Wolff (see n. 854).

[856] A. von Werder and T. Talaulicar (see n. 337) 854.

[857] Kohl/Rapp/Wolff (see n. 854) 5.

[858] A. von Werder, A. Pissarczyk and J. Böhme, 'Größere Kodexakzeptanz im General Standard?', *Die Aktiengesellschaft* 2011, 492.

[859] Studies published in English by E. Nowak, R. Rott and T.A. Mahr, 'The (Ir)relevance of Disclosure of Compliance with Corporate Governance Codes – Evidence from the German Stock Market', (Swiss Finance Institute Research Paper Series N°06, 11, April 2006, available at <http://ssrn.com/abstract=891106>, and C. Andres and E. Theissen, 'Setting a Fox to Keep the Geese: Does the Comply-or-Explain Principle Work?', *Journal of Corporate Finance* 14 (2008) 289.

[860] See above 4.1.2.

[861] R. Kiem cited in *FAZ*, 24 February 2011, 11.

[862] N. Bröcker, 'Selbstbindung mit Anfechtungsrisiko – Was sind die richtigen Sanktionsmechanismen für den Deutschen Corporate Governance Kodex?', *Der Konzern* 2011, 313, 321.

[863] Foreword (11)4, now Foreword (10)4 German Corporate Governance Code 2013.

the public discussion on an *Abweichungskultur* (deviation culture).[864] Further, like the Stock Corporation Act,[865] since 2012 the German Corporate Governance Code explicitly calls for a justification of the deviation from the Code.[866]

5. The Dynamics of Change

5.1. Diversity

Currently, diversity is the hottest debate in German corporate governance.[867] In its response to the Report of the Government Commission on German Corporate Governance, the government stressed that politicians expect to see improvements on the participation of women in supervisory and management boards.[868] The method of implementing stronger participation is not yet clear. German company leaders, politicians and even the government are split over the question whether a legal rule as in Norway, the Netherlands and France should be enacted. Some commentators doubt whether the Corporate Governance Commission had a mandate to include diversity into the German Code;[869] but also whether a legal quorum for women would be in line with the German Constitution[870] and the European anti-discrimination rules[871] is questioned.

---

[864] H.-M. Ringleb, T. Kremer, M. Lutter and A. von Werder, 'Die Kodex-Änderungen vom Mai 2012', *Neue Zeitschrift für Gesellschaftsrecht* 2012, 1081, 1082 with further references on the discussion.

[865] Section 161(1)1.

[866] Foreword (11)2, now Foreword (11)2 German Corporate Governance Code 2013.

[867] G. Bachmann, 'Zur Umsetzung einer Frauenquote im Aufsichtsrat', *Zeitschrift für Wirtschaftsrecht* 2011, 1131; K. Langenbucher, 'Zentrale Akteure der Corporate Governance: Zusammensetzung des Aufsichtsrats', *Zeitschrift für Unternehmens- und Gesellschaftsrecht* 2012, 314; J. Redenius-Hövermann, 'Zur Frauenquote im Aufsichtsrat', *Zeitschrift für Wirtschaftsrecht* 2010, 660; C. Schubert and G. Jacobsen, 'Personelle Vielfalt als Element guter Unternehmensführung – die Empfehlung des Corporate Governance Kodex und die Rechtsfolgen ihrer unzureichenden Berücksichtigung', *Wertpapier-Mitteilungen* 2011, 726; D. Weber-Rey and F. Handt 'Vielfalt and Diversity im Kodex – Selbstverpflichtung, Bemühenspflicht und Transparenz', *Neue Zeitschrift für Gesellschaftsrecht* 2011, 1.

[868] Stellungnahme der Bundesregierung zum Bericht der Regierungskommission Deutscher Corporate Governance Kodex, November 2010, (1).

[869] P.O. Mülbert and A. Wilhelm, 'Grundfragen des Deutschen Corporate Governance Kodex und der Entsprechenserklärung nach § 161 AktG', *Zeitschrift für das gesamte Handels- und Wirtschaftsrecht* 2012, 286.

[870] G. Spindler and K. Brandt, 'Zulässigkeit einer Gleichstellungsquote im Aufsichtsrat der börsennotierten AG', *Neue Zeitschrift für Gesellschaftsrecht* 2011, 401, 404–405; more flexible in this regard is H-J. Papier and M. Heidebach, 'Die Einführung einer gesetzlichen Frauenquote

cont. ...

For a better understanding of the German discussion on diversity, it should be kept in mind that the German supervisory board is already highly politicised.[872] Taking into account quasi-mandatory co-determination in big companies, implementing the proposal of a 40 per cent quota made by the Green Party[873] would restrict shareholders to free choice for only three directors out of ten. This might explain why the industry, to hinder further action, took the German Corporate Governance Code itself on the agenda.[874] Even if a repeal of the German Corporate Governance Code is highly unlikely, due to this pressure, 2011 was the first year since 2004 in which the German Corporate Governance Code was not changed.

Until the Commission launches the proposal for a directive,[875] the German discussion had largely ignored the European initiatives;[876] shortcomings in the compatibility of family life with career for women have been cited, and better conditions in neighbouring countries have been stressed.[877] Empirical research shows a correlation between the absence of women on supervisory boards and their exclusion in German supervisory board networks; it also showed that supervisory board networks with a woman in one supervisory board tend to

für die Aufsichtsräte deutscher Unternehmen unter verfassungsrechtlichen Aspekten', *Zeitschrift für Unternehmens- und Gesellschaftsrecht* 2011, 305.

[871] J.H. Bauer, 'Frauenquote', *Betriebs-Berater,* Die erste Seite, no. 48 (2011); more flexible in this regard is K. Brandt and A. Thiele 'Zulässigkeit einer Gleichstellungsquote im Aufsichtsrat unter Berücksichtigung der Rechtsprechung des EuGH', *Die Aktiengesellschaft* 2011, 580.

[872] For co-determination, see M. Roe, *Political Determinants of Corporate Governance* (Oxford, OUP 2003) Chapter 4, 29–37, referred to in the country analysis, 71–82.

[873] Bündnis 90/Die Grünen, Entwurf eines Gesetzes zur geschlechtergerechten Besetzung des Aufsichtsrates, BTDrucks 17/3296.

[874] T. Kremer, who comments the Code (in Ringleb/Kremer/Lutter/von Werder (see n. 63 and 848) was chief compliance officer of ThyssenKrupp and is now managing director of Deutsche Telekom.

[875] Proposal for a Directive of the European Parliament and of the Council on improving the gender balance among non-executive directors of companies listed on stock exchanges and related measures, Brussels, 14 November 2012, COM(2012) 614 final.

[876] Green paper, The EU corporate governance framework, Brussels, 5 April 2011, COM(2011) 164 final, 6–7, Questions (5), (6); Commission Communication Strategy for equality between women and men COM(2010) 491 final, 7: initiatives to improve the gender balance in decision-making; comparative overview in Commission Staff Working Paper, *The Gender Balance in Business Leadership*, SEC(2011) 246 final.

[877] M. Peltzer, 'Der Bericht der Corporate Governance Kommission an die Bundesregierung', *Neue Zeitschrift für Gesellschaftsrecht* 2011, 281, 283.

install women in the other boards.[878] Since the literature on positive economic effects of women in boardrooms is US-based,[879] where—as in Germany— seventeen per cent of the directors are women,[880] a more cautious and evolutionary approach might be appropriate for future decisions about diversity. For quite a long time in the debate, a self-binding declaration of larger companies seemed to be the most likely policy option,[881] promoted by the CDU party[882] which later decided to campaign for a binding quota of 30 per cent in the 2013 parliamentary elections.

The DAX 30 companies declared in October 2011 that they will enhance the proportion of women in higher management;[883] all but two gave self-binding declarations, mostly with goals for significant improvements. From currently between 7.6 per cent and 28.5 per cent, the quota (for 2015 to 2020) must be between 10 per cent and 32 per cent; the company which has today the highest ratio plans to enhance the quota by one to two percentage points per year.

5.2. Independence, Conflicts of Interest and Remuneration

An opportunity to strengthen the independence of shareholder representatives and deal with conflicts of interests[884] presented itself as part of the recent proposal by the Government Commission German Corporate Governance Code,[885] but only initial changes on independence were adopted.[886] Until the amendment in 2012, the German Corporate Governance Code did not request a declaration of independence and even now is unclear on whether a declaration for individual directors is required.[887] To bring it in line with the European recommendation on inde-

---

[878] J. Oehmichen, M.S. Rapp and M. Wolff, 'Einfluss der Aufsichtsratsstrukturen auf die Präsenz von Frauen in Aufsichtsräten', *Zeitschrift für betriebswirtschaftliche Forschung* 62 (2010) 503, 523.

[879] See, *inter alia*, D.A. Carter, B.J. Simkins and W. Simson, 'Corporate Governance, Board Diversity, and Firm Value', *Financial Review* 38 (2003) 33.

[880] Spencer Stuart, *Board Index 2012*, 3.

[881] A study for the Ministry for Family, Elder, Woman and Youth to be presented by Weller (University of Freiburg).

[882] Christlich Demokratische Union, 25. Parteitag der CDU Deutschlands, *Beschluss Starkes Deutschland. Chancen für Alle!, Kompetenzen von Frauen besser nutzen*.

[883] See <www.spiegel.de/politik/deutschland/0,1518,792261,00.html>.

[884] T. Baums and K.E. Scott (see n. 386) 72.

[885] Government Commission German Corporate Governance Code, Report November 2010, Proposal of January 2012.

[886] See above 2.2.3(b).

[887] For such transparency, Roth (see n. 387) 1988.

pendence, not only should controlling shareholders or their representatives be explicitly disqualified on independence grounds,[888] but a list with specifics disqualification grounds for independence should also be included in the Code.[889] An example for considering the specific situation in groups of companies is found in France, where the ratio of independent directors is lowered for groups.[890] Implementing a (super)majority independent board as practised in the US and in UK is not possible in Germany due to co-determination. Despite the European recommendation, the majority of scholars deny independence of employee representatives due to their conflicts of interest.[891] Due to the unique German co-determination regime, the corporate governance standards applied by international proxy advisors ought to be reviewed.[892]

The discussion of the announced proposals by the Action Plan on European Company Law and Corporate Governance 2012 might raise the awareness of independence and conflicts of interests. According to the Action Plan, shareholder control over related party transactions is to be improved, possibly through an amendment to the shareholders' rights directive.[893] The European Corporate Governance Forum proposed even shareholder approval of related party transactions.[894] Volkswagen introduced a committee for related party transaction;[895] the Stock Corporation Act provides for dependent companies the control by the supervisory board and an auditor,[896] but not for the approval by shareholders.

In 2013, the revision of the German Corporate Governance Code focused on the remuneration of managing directors.[897] In this respect, long-termism and pensions of managing directors were on the agenda. Any further action needs to take account of upcoming European initiatives. In the Action Plan, the European Commission announced its intention to propose the improvement of transparency but also the introduction of a mandatory shareholder vote on the remuneration policy and the remuneration report.[898]

---

[888] For this, see above 2.2.3(b).

[889] M. Roth (see n. 387) 1987.

[890] One third, normally the majority, see above 2.2.3(d).

[891] See above 2.2.3(c).

[892] For ISS, see above 2.2.3(a).

[893] Action Plan, COM(2012) 740 final, 3.2, p. 10.

[894] European Corporate Governance Forum, Statement on Related Party Transactions for Listed Entities, 10 March 2011.

[895] Committee for Major Shareholder Business Relationships.

[896] Section 314 Stock Corporation Act, see above 3.1.3.2.

[897] Regierungskommission Deutscher Corporate Governance Kodex, Press release 14 June 2012: structure of management remuneration as topic for the next year.

[898] Action Plan, COM(2012) 740 final, 3.1, p. 9.

5.3. Co-determination and the Stock Corporation Act:
A More Flexible Governance Regime?

a) Modernising Co-determination

Co-determination is still a subject of discussion,[899] but a reform is not on the agenda in the short term. If the trend towards European Companies, partnerships limited by shares and foreign legal forms prevails,[900] this may change in the medium or long-term. Assuming a reform is on the agenda, the size of co-determined supervisory boards should be reduced and representation of non-German employees should at least be encouraged.[901] A corresponding proposal by law professors[902] was rejected by the unions.[903] Of practical importance is the shift to the European Company, which also formed the basis of the latest reform proposal,[904] aiming, *inter alia*, to introduce negotiations upon the co-determination regime. Reincorporating German stock corporations as a European Company might be on the agenda of international institutional investors. This is requested by the English pension fund Hermes as long as the German co-determination system is not reformed.[905] Reducing the proportion of employee representatives on the board was discussed at the time of the implementation of the SE Directive.[906] Appointing independent employee representatives should no longer be limited to the coal, iron and steel industry.[907] Independent employee representative in all co-determined companies would be in line with modern corporate governance standards;[908] they may also be better able to represent the interests of all employees than country-specific employee nominees.

---

[899] At the German Jurists Forum of 2006, it is said that it was the only time in 150 years that it did not vote for recommendations (the theme was co-determination).

[900] Seven out of thirty DAX 30 companies are incorporated as SEs and/or partnership limited by shares (above 1.1.e): with Bilfinger, EADS, Gagfah, Klöckner & Co, MAN, Puma, SGL Carbon; furthermore seven out of fifty MDAX companies are incorporated as SEs or in a foreign legal form. Therefore, about 16% of the 80 top-indexed companies are not incorporated as German stock corporations.

[901] T. Baums and K.E. Scott (see n. 386) 72.

[902] Arbeitskreis 'Unternehmerische Mitbestimmung' (see n. 727).

[903] D. Hexel, 'Podiumsdiskussion', *Beilage zu Zeitschrift für Wirtschaftsrecht* 48/2009, 35, 36.

[904] Arbeitskreis 'Unternehmerische Mitbestimmung' (see n. 727).

[905] Hermes Equity Ownership Services, *Hermes Corporate Governance Principles – Germany*: Supervisory board, employee representation, August 2011.

[906] BDA/BDI Bericht der Kommission Mitbestimmung, *Mitbestimmung modernisieren*, Berlin, November 2004.

[907] Sections 3, 7 Act on Co-Determination in the Coal, Iron and Steel Industry (Montan-MitbestG), building on provisions developed in the British zone after World War II.

[908] M. Roth, 'Unabhängige Aufsichtsratsmitglieder' (see n. 449) 640–642.

b) The One-tier Board as an Option for German Stock Corporations

In line with the recent developments in Europe, German stock corporations should be able to choose a one-tier board.[909] The practical need for such an option is shown by the Societas Europaea and its success in Germany. Among the SE of German origin not subject to co-determination, about half of the operating SE opted for the one-tier system.[910] Other continental jurisdictions already allow such a choice under their national stock corporation laws. Until the enactment of the 1937 Stock Corporation Act, German supervisory boards were *de facto* boards of directors. Due to the modern corporate governance debate, a one-tier board of directors should also be possible outside the financial industry.[911]

5.4. Long-termism (Action Plan and the Stock Corporation Act)

The European Commissions' Green Paper focuses on (long-term) shareholders and their long-term commitment.[912] Following this line of argument, the Action Plan aims to encourage and facilitate long-term shareholder engagement.[913] However, concrete tasks associated with long-termism are limited. The Action Plan refers to employees' interest in the sustainability of the company and therefore announces appropriate action to encourage employee share ownership in Europe.[914] The extension of the reporting requirements to non-financial aspects should encourage companies to adopt a sustainable and long-term strategic approach to their business.[915] To let companies benefit from remuneration policies which stimulate longer-term value creation, better shareholder oversight of the remuneration policy must be provided.[916] The reference in the Action Plan to a later Green Paper on long-term financing of the European economy[917] provides

---

[909] K.J. Hopt, 'Comparative Corporate Governance' (see n. 3) 23.

[910] See above 3.2.1(c).

[911] The current German Corporate Governance system might be seen as an early spill-over of financial (self-regulation), see above 1.2, 1.3(b). For the suggestion by the German Jurists Forum, see above 1.3(d).

[912] Green Paper (see n. 876), 9, 10–18, questions 10, 13–23.

[913] Action Plan: European company law and corporate governance – a modern legal framework for more engaged shareholders and sustainable companies, Brussels, 12 December 2012, COM(2012) 740 final, p. 15.

[914] Action Plan, COM(2012) 740 final, 3.5, p. 11.

[915] Action Plan, COM(2012) 740 final, 2.1, p. 6.

[916] Action Plan, COM(2012) 740 final, 3.2, p. 9.

[917] Green Paper, long-term financing of the European economy, Brussels 25 March 2013, COM(2013) 150 final.

the most compelling link between corporate governance and long-termism in the Action Plan, which will possibly provide further input on how long-term shareholder engagement can be encouraged and how appropriate corporate governance arrangements might support long-term financing.[918]

As a result of German private pension regulation, long-term institutional shareholders of German origin are rare.[919] Life insurance companies have had to sell their equities in the downturn of the stock market since 2000. Despite some reforms since 2001, occupational pensions still play a minor role for pensions overall. Even with more political backing, pension funds and *Pensionskassen* might not enjoy the same importance as in the Netherlands, Switzerland and the UK. In the latter countries, pension funds have gained importance before occupational pension promises shifted from defined benefits to defined contributions. This shift was propelled by rating agencies and international accounting rules, such as the new IAS 19 Standard. Automatic enrolment into occupational pension plans suggested by the German Jurists Forum in 2004 and implemented in the UK Pensions Act 2008 could also improve occupational pensions and create domestic institutional shareholders in Germany.[920] After the tax reform in 2001, German banks and insurance companies lost this role.[921]

The lack of national institutional long-term investors in Germany sets it apart not only from the UK but also from other Rhineland-capitalism models such as Switzerland and the Netherlands.[922] Building such institutional investors today is difficult, given the worldwide trend from defined benefit to defined contribution occupational pensions. Since the volatility of pension obligations will be enhanced by new accounting rules (IAS 19), traditional pensions will not be an option. Modern life-cycle investment models might serve better. Such models could provide for asset allocation in long-term holdings of equity[923] with an reinvestment of dividends in bonds, both contributing to corporate finance of employers as well as return on investment and security interests of employees.

---

[918] Action Plan, COM(2012) 740 final, 1., p. 5.

[919] Looking for more such shareholder activism Green Paper (see n. 876), 11–16, 18.

[920] M. Roth, 'Corporate Governance' (see n. 121) 547–548; *idem.*, *Private Altersvorsorge* (see n. 53) 2009. For a recent proposal of such a reform, see also the German Occupational Pensions Association, AbA – Arbeitsgemeinschaft für betriebliche Altersversorgung e.V., *Dialog pro Betriebsrente, Memorandum für eine Neujustierung der Altersversorgung in Deutschland,* October 2011, 3.3 (opting out).

[921] See above 1.1(a).

[922] Also in Austria and France, private pension institutions invest more in equity than their German counterparts.

[923] Proposing higher dividends for such holdings, see the Reflection Group, *On the Future of EU Company Law*, Brussels, 5 April 2011, 3.2.3., Long term ownership, Recommendation 1b, 47.

Long-termism will be of crucial importance for the future corporate governance debate.[924] At company level, long-termism is traditionally the focus of German company law,[925] today also due to the management compensation rules. According to the Stock Corporation Act, the remuneration of the management board has to be aligned with the sustainable development of the company.[926] This is not yet adequately implemented in practice.[927] The German Corporate Governance Code generally refers to the sustainable development of the company.[928] Since contract and corporate governance are generally understood as tools to minimise systemic risks,[929] this enhances the accountability of companies for the society as a whole.

5.5. Tailor-made Corporate Governance Rules?

The duality of family-owned firms and firms in dispersed ownership could be reflected by more tailor-made corporate governance rules. Recent economic literature suggests that the capital markets reward companies with dispersed ownership gain for complying with the German Code, while family-owned firms are disadvantaged if complying fully.[930] The Green Paper hints in this direction

---

[924] See M. Roth, 'Labor and Comparative Corporate Governance in Times of Pension Capitalism Independent Directors, Shareholder Empowerment and Long-Termism: The Transatlantic Perspective', *Fordham Journal of Corporate & Financial Law*18 (2013), 751.

[925] See G. Bachmann, 'Der "Europäische Corporate Governance-Rahmen"', *Zeitschrift für Wirtschafts- und Bankrecht, Wertpapier-Mitteilungen* 2011, 1301, 1308; critical towards stewardship codes, also H. Fleischer, 'Zukunftsfragen der Corporate Governance in Deutschland und Europa: Aufsichtsräte, institutionelle Investoren, Proxy Advisors und Whistleblowers', *Zeitschrift für Unternehmens- und Gesellschaftsrecht* 2011, 155, 164–167; towards shareholder engagement, M. Peltzer (see n. 877) 962–963, 965–966, 967. On the annual discharge of managing and supervisory directors, see above 3.1.2(e).

[926] See above 3.1.5.

[927] Seemingly assuming that sustainability and long-termism are not treated as synonyms and long-term means just several years (see the notes to the parliamentary draft, BTDrucks 16/13433, 10). According at least to some and correctly understood, sustainability is more than just long-termism, D. Kocher and L. Bednarz 'Mehrjährigkeit der variable Vorstandsvergütung im Lichte der Nachhaltigkeit nach dem VorstAG', *Der Konzern* 2011, 77, 82; see also K.S. Hohenstadt and M. Kuhnke 'Vergütungsstruktur und variable Vergütungsmodelle für Vorstandsmitglieder nach dem VorstAG', *Zeitschrift für Wirtschaftsrecht* 2009, 1981, 1982.

[928] German Corporate Governance Code, Foreword (2): sustainable creation of value.

[929] F. Möslein, 'Contract Governance und Corporate Governance im Zusammenspiel', *Juristen-Zeitung* 2010, 72, 73.

[930] D.E. Jahn, M.S. Rapp, C. Strenger and M. Wolff, 'Der Deutsche Corporate Governance Kodex: Compliance-Erfahrungen 2002–2009', available at <http://ssrn.com/abstract=1723152>, published in *Zeitschrift Corporate Governance* 2011, 64.

by distinguishing between large and SME companies.[931] Further empirical and comparative legal research is needed with a focus on large companies which are not in dispersed ownership. Truly implementing independent directors into German corporate governance will not be possible without a tailor-made rule in the German Corporate Governance Code. In the US and in France, there is some relief for family-owned and other controlled firms.

According to the amendment of the Foreword[932] of the 2012 German Corporate Governance Code, a well justified deviation from a Code recommendation might be in the interest of good corporate governance. The German Corporate Governance Commission is discussing a so called 'deviation culture', which is yet to be applied to concrete examples and might be better brought to life by modifying the recommendations of the Code according to specific attributes of the companies. Some rules might be attributed only to firms listed in specific stock exchange indices[933] or controlled companies;[934] some special flexibility might be given to small and medium enterprises, founder (family) firms or even family-owned firms in general.

6. Conclusion

The main characteristics of the German system are the two-tier board, co-determination, duality of dispersed ownership and family firms, also for blue chips, and some company law principles which might promote long-termism. A one-tier board is already available for European Companies (SE), which play a significant and still growing role especially for listed companies. In line with the growing number of countries which also allow a choice between a one-tier and a two-tier system under national company law, in September 2012 the German Jurists Forum also proposed the introduction of a one-tier model under German stock corporation law.

For a stock corporation incorporated under the German Stock Corporation Act, the two-tier structure is mandatory. The Stock Corporation Act provides for a division of powers between the management and the supervisory board. While the management board runs the affairs of the company independently, the supervisory board is excluded from management but has to advise the management board and may determine that certain transactions need its consent. Such an exclusion from the management shows no apparent negative effects, but the two-tier board is to be

---

[931] Green Paper (see n. 876), 3–4, question (1).

[932] Foreword (11)4, now Foreword (11)4 German Corporate Governance Code 2013.

[933] UK Corporate Governance Code 2012, Code Provision B.1.2(2), see above 2.2.3(a).

[934] France, Corporate Governance Code of Listed Companies, December 2008, 8.2; see above 2.2.3(d).

seen altogether as a balanced system. Supervisory directors acting as a group might even enhance the quality of control in challenging the management.

Germany's co-determination regime makes adoptions of some corporate governance principles necessary. In quasi-parity co-determined boards, a majority independent board is not possible. Even governance principles (as from the ISS), which call for a third of all members to be independent, lead to potential dys-functional boards with united employee representatives and diverse shareholder representatives. The practice has adapted itself to that system. The main legal problem is the representation of only employees within Germany; even employ-ees in other countries of the European Union are not covered, which is causing the conversion of many German Stock Corporations to European Companies. Due to quasi-parity co-determination in the supervisory board, a co-determination system for one-tier boards is difficult to establish.

For the European discussion on long-termism, some German corporate gover-nance features ought to be considered, such as annual discharge of directors instead of annual re-election, sustainability as an element in managing director remuneration and limiting the insurability of director liability.

7. Selection of Literature in English

Legislation

Aktiengesetz (AktG), 6.9.1965, BGBl (Federal Gazette) I 1089: [German] Stock Corporation Act, English translations by Norton Rose LLP (2011, available at <www.nortonrose.com/files/german-stock-corporation-act-2010-english-trans lation-pdf-59656.pdf>) and Wirth et al *Corporate Law in Germany*, 2nd revised edn. (Munich, C.H Beck 2010).

Capital market and supervisory law in English translation of the German Federal Financial Supervisory Authority (BaFin) available at http://www.bafin.de/EN/ DataDocuments/datadocuments_node.html.

German Corporate Governance Code, as amended on May 13, 2013 (German Corporate Governance Code 2013), to be valid after announcement in the Federal Gazette. Current and all former versions of the German Corporate Governance Code available at <www.corporate-governance-code.de>.

Hermes Equity Ownership Services, *Hermes Corporate Governance Principles – Germany*: Supervisory board, employee representation, August 2011.

Labor Law including Acts on co-determination in Germany, english translation by S. Lingemann, R. von Steinau-Steinrück and A. Mengel, Employment & La-bor Law in Germany, 3rd edn. (Munich, C.H. Beck, 2012), 380–405.

Literature

T. Baums and K.E. Scott, 'Taking Shareholder Protection Seriously? Corporate Governance in the United States and Germany', *American Journal on Comparative Law* 53 (2005) 31.

R.M. Buxbaum, 'What would the Delaware of the European Community look like? Comparative Aspects of Regulatory Competition in Company and Capital Market Law', *RabelsZeitschrift* 74 (2010) 1.

I. Dittmann, E.G. Maug and C. Schneider, 'Bankers on the Boards of German Firms: What They Do, What They are Worth, and Why They are (Still) There', *Review of Finance* 14 (2010) 35.

D. Donald, 'Approaching Comparative Company Law', *Fordham Journal of Corporate and Financial Law* 14 (2008) 83.

L. Fauver and M.E. Fuest, 'Does Good Corporate Governance Include Employee Participation? Evidence from German Corporate Boards', *Journal of Finance* 82 (2006) 673.

K. Fehre, M.S. Rapp, B. Schwetzler and M.O. Sperling, 'The Disappearing "Deutschland AG" – An analysis of block holdings in German large Caps', *Problems and Perspectives in Management* 9:4 (2011) 46, (available at <http://ssrn.com/abstract=1100582>).

M. Gelter, 'Why Do Shareholder Derivative Suits Remain Rare in Continental Europe?', *Brooklyn Journal of International Law* 37 (2012) 843.

G. Gorton and F.A. Schmid, 'Capital, Labour and the Firm: A Study of German Codetermination', *Journal of the European Economic Association* 2 (2004) 863.

H. Hau and M. Thum, 'Subprime crisis and board (in-)competence: private versus public banks in Germany', *Economic Policy* 24 (2009) 701.

K.J. Hopt, 'Comparative Corporate Governance: The State of the Art and International Regulation', *American Journal of Comparative Law* 59 (2011) 1.

K.J. Hopt, 'Labor representation on corporate boards: Impacts and problems for corporate governance and economic integration in Europe', *International Review of Law and Economics* 14 (1994) 203.

K.J. Hopt, 'The German Two-Tier Board: Experience, Theories, Reforms' in Hopt et al (eds.), *Comparative Corporate Governance – The State of the Art and Emerging Research* (Oxford, Clarendon Press 1998) 227.

K.J. Hopt, 'The duties of directors in target companies in hostile takeovers – German and European perspectives' in Ferrarini et al (eds.), *Capital Markets in the Age of the Euro* (Oxford, OUP 2002) 391.

K.J. Hopt and P. Leyens, 'Board Models in Europe – Recent Developments of Internal Corporate Governance Structures in Germany, the United Kingdom, France and Italy', *European Company and Financial Law Review* 1 (2004) 135.

K.J. Hopt and M. Roth in K.J. Hopt and H. Wiedemann (eds.), Großkommentar zum Aktiengesetz [Commentary on the German Stock Corporation Act], §§ 95–116 [on the German supervisory board), 1.450 pages, 2005.

U. Hüffer, Aktiengesetz, Kommentar, [Commentary on the German Stock Corporation Act] 10th edn. 2012.

J. Lieder, 'The German Supervisory Board on Its Way to Professionalism', *German Law Journal* 11 (2010) 115.

F.A. Mann, 'The New German Company Law and Its Background', *Journal of Comparative Legislation and International Law* 19 (1937) 220.

H. Merkt, Germany, 'Internal and external corporate governance' in A. Fleckner and K.J. Hopt (eds.), *Comparative Corporate Governance*, (Cambridge, Cambridge University Press 2013) 521.

E. Nowak, R. Rott and T.A. Mahr, 'The (Ir)relevance of Disclosure of Compliance with Corporate Governance Codes – Evidence from the German Stock Market', (Swiss Finance Institute Research Paper Series N° 06, 11, April 2006, available at <http://ssrn.com/abstract=891106>

J.J. du Plessis et al, *German Corporate Governance in International and European Context*, 2nd edn. (Heidelberg, Springer 2012).

S. Prigge, 'A Survey of German Corporate Governance', in Hopt et al (eds.), *Comparative Corporate Governance – The State of the Art and Emerging Research* (Oxford, Clarendon Press 1998) 943.

T. Raiser, 'The theory of Enterprise law in the Federal Republic of Germany', *American Journal of Comparative Law* 36 (1988) 111.

M. Roth, 'Employee Participation, Corporate Governance and the Firm: A transatlantic view focused on Occupational Pensions and Co-determination', *European Business Organization Law Review* 11 (2010) 51, 62.

M. Roth, 'Outside Director Liability: German Stock Corporations Law in Transatlantic Perspective', *Journal of Corporate Law Studies* 8 (2008) 337.

E.P.M. Vermeulen and D. Zetzsche, 'The Use and Abuse of Investor Suits – An Inquiry into the Dark Side of Shareholder Activism', *European Company and Financial Law Review* 7 (2010) 1.

Corporate Boards in Italy

GUIDO FERRARINI, GIAN GIACOMO PERUZZO
and MARTA ROBERTI

1. General Introduction

The Italian legal framework relating to listed companies has experienced major developments in the last 20 years, including a thorough overhaul of financial markets regulation in 1998[1] and of company law in 2003.[2] In addition, a Corporate Governance Code was adopted in 1999 and later revised in 2002, 2006 and 2011.[3] Moreover, the law on savings of 2005 attempted to strengthen shareholders' protection in listed companies after the *Parmalat* scandal.[4]

Therefore, boards of listed companies need to be analysed from the perspective of a complex system of company law rules, capital markets law provisions and soft-law instruments (subject to comply-or-explain). Since corporate ownership is generally concentrated in Italy, the agency costs that arise between block-holders and minority shareholders are at the core of most regulatory developments, as shown by the requirement of 'slate voting' for the election of directors (which entitles minority shareholders to appoint some board members: see 3.1.1 below) and the new regime of related parties transactions (directed to curb wealth expropriation by controlling shareholders: 3.1.3.2 below).

Three different board models are available under Italian Law: The traditional model (consisting of a board of directors and a board of auditors), the one-tier model (a board of directors and an audit committee of independent directors) and the two-tier model (a supervisory board and a management board). However, the last two governance structures are not widespread amongst Italian listed companies. The average number of directors in the boards is 10, but it varies depending on the business sector. The majority of directors are non-executive (about half are independent) and most listed companies have a minority director. Italian boards generally delegate the day-by-day management of the company to one or more members. Nearly all listed companies have established board com-

---

[1] The Consolidated Financial Services Act of 1998 (CFSA), Legislative Decree n. 58 of 24 February 1998 (*Testo unico delle disposizioni in materia di intermediazione finanziaria*, Decreto Legislativo n. 58 del 24 febbraio 1998).

[2] The reform is based on the Law n. 366 of 3 October 2001 (*Delega al Governo per la riforma del diritto societario*, Legge n. 366 del 3 ottobre 2001), which delegated to the Italian Government the power to adopt one or more legislative decrees (among them the Legislative Decree n. 6 of 17 January 2003 – Decreto Legislativo n. 6 del 17 gennaio 2006, *Riforma organica della disciplina delle societa' di capitali e societa' cooperative*, in attuazione della Legge n. 366 del 3 ottobre 2001) including new rules on business companies and co-operatives; criminal and administrative violations concerning business companies; civil procedure, financial and banking law matters. See G. Ferrarini, P. Giudici and M. Richter, 'Company Law Reform in Italy: Real Progress?' *Rabels Zeitschrift* (2005) 69, p. 658.

[3] Codice di autodisciplina, 2011, (available at <www.borsaitaliana.it/borsaitaliana/regola menti/corporategovernance/corporategovdec2011.en_pdf.htm>).

[4] Law n. 262 of 28 December 2005 (Legge n. 262 del 28 dicembre 2005, *Disposizioni per la tutela del risparmio e la disciplina dei mercati finanziari*).

mittees with advisory and preparatory functions, such as the remuneration committee, the internal controls (audit) committee and the nomination committee, as recommended by the Corporate Governance Code.

1.1. Environment in which Boards Operate.

The number of Italian listed companies (266 in 1990; 282 in 2005; 272 in 2010; 262 in 2011)[5] is small with respect to the total number of joint-stock companies in Italy (8,448 in March 2010);[6] however, the capitalisation of listed companies has grown considerably over time (from 11.2% of GDP in 1992 to 30.7% in 1997, 49.4% in 2005, 47.8% in 2007, 27.6% in 2010 and 20.7% in 2011).[7] Most listed companies are small and medium-sized enterprises (SMEs). The small number of listed companies is partly due to the relatively high regulatory and compliance costs arising from stock exchange listing, but also arises from deeply engrained attitudes of entrepreneurs, who often prefer to shun the transparency required by stock exchange listing and the accountability to a wide shareholder constituency. In an effort to attract SMEs, the Italian Exchange has established an alternative market (AIM Italia-Mercato Alternativo del Capitale), which does not involve a formal listing of the shares and the relevant regulatory burdens (this market, however, is not yet significantly developed).[8]

Starting in the 1990s, the Italian stock market developed mainly along the following lines:

- a decrease in the number of non-financial companies, as a result of the dismantling of pyramidal groups, however the presence of which is still relevant;
- the Government's retreat from the corporate sector through massive privatisations, although public shareholdings are still important especially in public services.[9] In particular, the Government privatised some major

---

[5] Assonime, *An analysis of the compliance with the Italian corporate governance code year 2011* (2012) p. 7. Assonime is a long-established business association and think-tank set up by companies in different branches of activities (industry, finance, services and public utilities). See <www.assonime.it>.

[6] Data from the Register of Companies.

[7] Borsa Italiana, *Market Review* (1992, 1997, 2005, 2007, 2010 and 2011). See also M. Bianchi and M. Bianco, *Italian Corporate Governance in the Last 15 Years*, ECGI Finance Working Paper n. 144/2006, p. 6 (available at <www.ecgi.org/wp>).

[8] 'AIM Italia – Mercato Alternativo del Capitale' was created recently (1 March 2012) by the aggregation of the two previous operating alternative markets, AIM Italia and MAC, into a single market.

[9] Assonime, *Principi di riordino del quadro giuridico delle società pubbliche* (2008) (available at <www.assonime.it>); A. Irace, *Il ruolo degli investitori istituzionali nel governo*

cont. ...

corporations (including Telecom Italia and Istituto Nazionale delle Assicurazioni, both of which underwent hostile takeovers at the end of the 1990s) and reduced its holdings in other blue-chip companies which remained under state control (ENI, ENEL and Finmeccanica);

– increasing presence of institutional investors in listed companies, albeit not at the pace of international developments, and of foreign investors, particularly in large companies;[10]

– persistent involvement of private investors in the capital of listed companies.[11]

Nonetheless, most Italian listed companies have concentrated ownership (often family ownership), so that the separation between ownership and control is uncommon.[12] Shareholders' agreements are widely adopted to enhance control and pyramidal groups are not rare.[13] Joint-stock companies, both listed and non-listed, generally belong to groups.

The boards of Italian listed companies consist of a relatively high number of members (an average of 15.6 in the financial sector and 9.4 in other sectors).[14] Interlocking directorates are frequent, particularly for blue-chip companies.[15] A recent

---

delle società quotate, Giuffrè, Milan (2001), p. 111 ff.; R. Weigmann, 'Dall'intervento dello Stato nelle imprese alle privatizzazioni' in V. Buonocore and G. Racugno (eds.) *Privatizzazioni e regioni,* Giuffrè, Milan (2003), p. 17. See also F. Guerrera (ed.) *Le società a partecipazione pubblica,* Giappichelli, Turin (2010).

[10] M. Bianchi and M. Bianco, *Relazioni proprietarie tra banca e impresa: alcune evidenze empiriche* presentation at SIDE (2007), p. 5 (available at <www.side-isle.it/ocs/viewpaper. php?id=52&cf=1>).

[11] Bianchi and Bianco, see n. 7 above, p. 8 ff.

[12] M. Bianchi, M. Bianco and L. Enriques, 'Pyramidal groups and the separation between ownership and control in Italy', in F. Barca and M. Becht (eds.) *The Control of Corporate Europe,* Oxford University Press, Oxford (2001), p. 2 ff.; L. Enriques, 'Corporate Governance Reforms in Italy: What has been done and what is left to do?', *European Business Organization Law Review* (2009) 10, p. 477.

[13] M. Belcredi and S. Rigamonti, 'Ownership and board structure in Italy', presentation at EFMA Annual Meeting (2008) (available at <www.efmaefm.org/0EFMAMEETINGS/EFMA %20ANNUAL%20MEETINGS/2008-athens/Rigamonti.pdf>); Bianchi and Bianco, 'Italian Corporate governance in the last 15 years', see n. 7 above, p. 6 ff.

[14] Assonime, see n. 5 above, p. 36.

[15] P. Santella, C. Drago and A. Polo, *The Italian Chamber of Lords sits on listed company boards: An empirical analysis of Italian Listed Company Boards from 1998 to 2006* (2007), p. 5 ff. (available at <http://ssrn.com/abstract=1027947>); R. Santagata, 'Interlocking directorates ed interesse degli amministratori di società per azioni', *Rivista delle Società* (2009), p. 310 ff. See also Autorità Garante della Concorrenza e del Mercato, *La corporate governance di Banche e Compagnie di assicurazione* – IC36 (2009); (available at <www.agcm.it>).

reform prohibited interlocking directorates for competing banks, financial firms and insurance companies operating in the same product and geographic market.[16]

The cross-ownership of banks and firms (as measured on the one side by the ratio between the sum of the market value of shares held by banks in non-financial firms and by the latter in banks, and the total market value of the share capital of banks and non-financial companies on the other) increased rapidly between 2000 and 2006 (from 1.7% to 4.8%). The observed growth mainly concerns the participation of non-financial companies in banks.[17] Banks still play a major role, with 26 of them listed (out of a total of 799 banks in the country).[18] According to the Bank of Italy,[19] financial intermediaries, banking foundations, insurance companies, non-financial companies and investment funds were the main shareholders of the 10 largest banking groups at the end of 2008. The degree of cross-ownership between the 4 largest groups (Intesa Sanpaolo, Unicredit, Mediobanca and Ubi Banca) was considerable (6% of their share capital), as well as the shares held by common shareholders (3% of the capital).

1.2. Financial Institutions

Banks are subject to the provisions carried by the Consolidated Law on Banking[20] and the Bank of Italy's regulations, including the Supervisory instructions for banks[21] and the New regulations for the prudential supervision of banks[22], which implement the Basel II framework (the Basel Capital Accord and Community Directives 2006/48/EC and 2006/49/EC). Banks' corporate governance is also subject to the Bank of Italy's supervisory measures, among which the Super-

---

[16] See Decree Law n. 201 of 6 December 2011, Art 36 (Decreto Legge n. 20 del 6 dicembre 2011, *Disposizioni urgenti per la crescita, l'equità e il consolidamento dei conti pubblici* (c.d. Salva Italia) convertito dalla legge n. 214 del 22 dicembre 2011).

[17] In fact, 7% of all relevant shareholders of banks are non-financial; 3.2% of all relevant shareholders of non-financial companies are banks. See Bianchi and Bianco, see n. 7 above, p. 9.

[18] *Annual Report for 2008*, Bank of Italy, 29 May 2009, p. 234 (available at <www.bancaditalia.it/pubblicazioni/relann/rel08/rel08it/>).

[19] *Ibid.*

[20] *Testo Unico Bancario, Decreto Legislaltivo n. 385* of 1 September 1993 and subsequent amendments (TUB).

[21] *Istruzioni di vigilanza per le banche*, Circular n. 229 of 21 April 1999 and subsequent updates (Italian version available at <www.bancaditalia.it>).

[22] *Nuove disposizioni di vigilanza prudenziale per le banche*, Circular n. 263 of 27 December 2006, as amended (Italian version available at <www.bancaditalia.it>).

visory Provisions Concerning Bank's Organization and Corporate Governance'[23] and the Provisions on remuneration and incentive policies and practices concerning Banks and Banking Groups[24]. Insurance Companies are subject to similar rules carried by the Insurance Code.[25]

1.3. Description of Available Board Models

The Civil Code now includes the concept of 'monitoring board' (Art. 2381), while the Corporate Governance Code specifies that the board of directors should pursue the goal of shareholder value creation from a medium-long term perspective (Art. 1)[26]. The traditional governance model—made up of a board of directors and a board of auditors—is the one commonly adopted by listed companies. The one-tier and two-tier models, introduced by the 2003 reform, are rare in practice.

There is no example of Societas Europaea (SE) incorporated in Italy,[27] despite the fact that the legislation applicable to SEs in this country is one of the most attractive, as argued by Ernst & Young in a report on the operation and impact of the European Company Statute (2008/S 144-192482) commissioned by the European Commission.[28] The question has been asked whether the 'traditional'

---

[23] *Disposizioni di vigilanza in materia di organizzazione e governo societario delle banche* of 4 March 2008 and subsequent amendments (Italian version available at <www.banca ditalia.it>).

[24] *Politiche e prassi di remunerazione e incentivazione nelle banche e nei gruppi bancari* of 31 March 2011 (Italian version available at<www.bancaditalia.it>).

[25] Italian Insurance Code, Legislative Decree n. 209 of 7 September 2005 (Decreto Legislativo n. 209 del 7 settembre 2005, *Codice delle assicurazioni private*). It is aimed at replacing and unifying most of the existing legislation regulating insurance and re-insurance companies, intermediaries and contracts. The Code includes completely new regulation on reinsurance business, insurance mediation and indemnification of insured under motor insurance policies. It also contains new provisions with respect to access into the Italian market, insurance groups, investments, bancassurance, disclosure obligations and protection of policyholders. The role of the Italian Insurance Regulatory Authority (*Istituto per la Vigilanza sulle Assicurazioni Private e di Interesse Collettivo* – ISVAP) is significantly strengthened by the Insurance Code. ISVAP is replaced by the Institute for the Supervision on Insurances (*Istituto per la Vigilanza sulle Assicurazioni* – IVASS) as from 1 January 2013. Nevertheless, IVASS will hold the same functions and powers as ISVAP. Another important regulation concerning internal control, risk management and compliance systems and implementing the Insurance Code is the Regulation n. 20 of 26 March 2008 published by ISVAP.

[26] Regio Decreto n. 262 of 16 March 1942, *Approvazione del testo del Codice Civile*.

[27] There is only a branch office of the company Galleria di Base del Brennero – Brenner Basistunnel BBT SE, although its main headquarters is located in Innsbruck.

[28] Final Report, 9 December 2009, p. 146 ff. (available at <http://ec.europa.eu/internal_ market/consultations/docs/2010/se/study_SE_9122009_en.pdf>).

Italian board structure should be described as either a unitary or dual structure or a *tertium genus* from the Societas Europaea perspective (in the latter case it could not be adopted by an SE based in Italy, as the relevant EC Regulation only allows for either a one-tier or a two-tier governance system). In our opinion, the traditional system can still be regarded as one-tier, despite the presence of the board of auditors.[29] In fact, as explained below, the board of directors includes both members with executive functions and members with a supervisory (non-executive) role. It is therefore identical to the board of directors in the unitary model and different from the management board in the classic two-tier structure. The monitoring function of the statutory auditors in the traditional system complements the supervisory activities carried out by the non-executive directors.[30] As a result the board of auditors cannot be equated to the supervisory board in the two-tier structure. For example, no deliberative powers can be attributed to the statutory auditors with respect to either corporate strategy or individual transactions.

2. Authority

2.1. Functions/Powers

a) *General Description of Functions and Powers*

Joint-stock companies are entitled to choose one of three governance systems, with the variations permitted by the enabling provisions of each model.[31] The traditional system is the default model, which applies if the articles of association do not provide otherwise (Art. 2380 Civil Code ff.). It includes two corporate organs, in addition to the general meeting of shareholders: the board of directors (*consiglio di amministrazione*) and the board of auditors (*collegio sindacale*). Moreover, listed companies must appoint an external auditor, choosing the same amongst registered audit companies. The annual general meeting (AGM) appoints the board of directors and the board of auditors, as well as the registered auditing company. In the abstract language of the Civil Code, the board of directors takes

---

[29] See, for a different view, G.A. Rescio 'La Società Europea tra diritto comunitario e diritto nazionale', *Rivista delle Società* (2003), p. 967 ff., defining the traditional Italian structure as a dual structure from the perspective of the EC Regulation.

[30] Ferrarini, Giudici and Richter, see n. 2 above, p. 676.

[31] F. Ghezzi and C. Malberti, 'Corporate law reform in Europe: The Two-tier Model and the One-tier Model of Corporate Governance in the Italian Reform of Corporate Law – between Hypothetical Bargain and Regulatory Competition', *European and Financial Law Review* (2008), pp. 1–47; M. Ventoruzzo, 'La composizione del consiglio di amministrazione delle società quotate dopo il d. lgs. n. 303 del 2006: prime osservazioni', *Rivista delle Società* (2007), p. 205.

care of the company's administration (*amministrazione*), while the board of auditors is in charge of the control activities (*controllo*) and the external auditors audit the company's accounts (*controllo contabile*).

The two-tier system (Art. 2409-octies Civil Code ff.) also includes two organs, in addition to the general meeting: the supervisory board (*consiglio di sorveglianza*) and the management board (*consiglio di gestione*). In addition, a registered audit company must be appointed as an external auditor. The general meeting appoints the supervisory board, which nominates the management board. In contrast to other models such as the German system, no workers' representation is foreseen for the supervisory board. The external auditors are appointed by the general meeting. In the language of the Code, the management board runs the corporation (*amministra*), while the supervisory board monitors (*controlla*) the organisation and management of the same, in addition to performing other duties that in the traditional model are entrusted either to the board of directors (such as approving corporate strategy, if allowed by the articles of association) or to the AGM (such as approving the financial statements).

The one-tier system (Art. 2409-sexiesdecies Civil Code ff.) also consists of two bodies: the board of directors (*consiglio di amministrazione*) and the audit committee (*comitato per il controllo sulla gestione*). In addition, a registered audit company must be appointed by the general meeting as an external auditor. The general meeting appoints the board of directors, which selects the audit committee's members from its independent directors (unless the articles of association attribute the relevant power to the AGM). In the language of the Code, the board of directors manages the company (*amministra*), while the audit committee monitors (*controlla*) the organisation and the management of the company.

Only few Italian listed companies have opted for one of the alternative governance structures. To our knowledge, only three listed companies have adopted the one-tier system and seven the two-tier system;[32] the remaining companies (96.3% of the total) have the traditional model still in operation. Two of the largest banks (Intesa Sanpaolo and UBI) opted for the two-tier system after a series of mergers, which were no doubt eased by the possibility of distributing a substantial number of seats in the two boards (management and supervisory board) of the new entity to the directors of the merging banks. However, banks are subject to the Bank of Italy's Supervisory Provisions Concerning Banks Organization and Corporate Governance' of 4 March 2008. This aims to neutralise the impact of the choice of one of the new governance models from a supervisory perspective by extending the requirements foreseen for the traditional system to the unitary and dual systems.

---

[32] Assonime, see n. 5 above, schedule 1.

b) Strategy and Supervision

Under the traditional model, the management of the company is generally entrusted to the board of directors. Directors can perform any activity that is linked to the corporate purpose, save for the few tasks attributed to the general meeting by the law (or by the articles of association, to the extent allowed).[33] Directors do not need to be shareholders (Art. 2380-bis Civil Code). The board can delegate some of its functions (if permitted either by the articles or the general meeting) to an executive committee and/or to one or more directors (delegated directors)[34] who are then authorised to manage the company (Art. 2381 Civil Code). To the extent that board functions are delegated, the board has a monitoring role. When one or more managing directors and/or an executive committee are appointed, they have the power to propose the company's strategy to the board of directors for consideration.[35] In the practice of banks and financial companies, the articles often entrust to the executive committee (or the chairman of the board) tasks pertaining to the board of directors such as in the case of an emergency.[36]

Delegated directors have to make sure that the organisational, administrative and accounting structures are adequate for the nature and size of the company. They must report to the board of directors and to the board of auditors, at least every six months, on the general course of the company's business, on its projected development and on major transactions entered into by the company or

[33] See F. Bonelli, *Gli Amministratori di S.p.A. dopo la riforma delle società*, Giuffrè, Milan (2004), p. 11; A. De Nicola, 'Commento all'articolo 2381', in P. Marchetti, L.A. Bianchi, F. Ghezzi and M. Notari (eds.) *Commentario alla riforma delle società. Amministratori*, Egea, Milan (2005), p. 95; V. Calandra Buonaura, 'I modelli di amministrazione e controllo nella riforma del diritto societario', *Giurisprudenza Commerciale* (2003) I, p. 535. After the 2003 reform, boards of directors can also resolve on issuing debentures, if the law or the articles do not provide otherwise (Art 2410 Civil Code) and on constituting a dedicated asset within the company, if the articles do not provide otherwise (Art 2447-ter/2 Civil Code). If allowed by the articles, the board can also resolve on other issues foreseen by Art 2365 Civil Code, such as the creation or suppression of branches; the designation of directors with a general power of attorney; the reduction of the company's capital in the event of exit of a shareholder; amendments of the articles in conformity with new provisions of law; the transfer of the company's seat in the national territory; and the merger with wholly or ninety per cent owned subsidiaries.

[34] See P. Abbadessa, 'Profili topici della nuova disciplina della delega amministrativa' in P. Abbadessa and G.B. Portale (eds.) *Il nuovo diritto delle società – Liber amicorum Gian Franco Campobasso*, UTET, Turin (2006) II, p. 491; L. Nazzicone, 'Comment of Art 2381 Civil Code', in L. Nazzicone and S. Providenti (eds.) *Società per azioni, Amministrazione e controlli*, Giuffrè, Milan (2003), p. 28 and ff.; G.M. Zamperetti, *Il dovere di informazione degli amministratori nella governance delle società per azioni*, Giuffrè, Milan (2005), p. 309 ff.

[35] Assonime, see n. 5 above, p. 23: an executive committee was found in 44 (out of 262) companies of the sample, more frequently in financial companies.

[36] De Nicola, see n. 33 above, p. 121.

its subsidiaries (Art. 2381/5 Civil Code). In listed companies, the reporting to the board of auditors must take place quarterly (Art. 150 CFSA, on which see 2.3 below). When an executive committee is appointed, non-executive directors can sit on the committee because the powers are delegated to the committee and not to its individual members. Moreover, non-executive directors monitor the general course of the company's business and assess the adequacy of the organisational, administrative and accounting structure of the company on the basis of the information received from the executive directors. In addition, they examine the company's strategic, operational and financial plans (Art. 2381/3 Civil Code). Further details on the role of the board of directors and its monitoring functions are foreseen by the Corporate Governance Code (Arts. 1 and 2).

The board determines the limits and scope of its delegated powers;[37] it may always give instructions to the delegated organs (ie. executive directors and executive committee) and it may adopt resolutions in areas included in the delegated powers. The board evaluates the activities of the delegated organs on the basis of the information they provide periodically. Each director can ask the delegated organs to provide specific information about the company's management in a board meeting.

In the alternative models, the corporate strategy is approved by the management board—or the supervisory board, if the articles so provide—in the two-tier system and by the board of directors in the one-tier system. The management board can also delegate its functions to one or more of its members, in which case the same rules apply as for the board of directors in the traditional system. As a result, the management board could include both executive and non-executive directors, just like the board of directors in the other two systems. However, the Corporate Governance Code envisages a management board made up of executive directors (comment to Art. 10), while suggesting that the supervisory board should be empowered to make decisions on strategic transactions and industrial and financial plans. The one-tier system is subject to the rules on boards of directors foreseen for the traditional system.

c) The Monitoring Role of the Board of Auditors

In the traditional governance system, the board of auditors performs monitoring tasks over the company's management and organisation. For listed companies, these monitoring functions are further specified with reference to the company's

---

[37] Art 2381/4 Civil Code foresees the functions which cannot be delegated, such as drawing up of the annual accounts, drawing up of a consolidation or merger or de-merger programme, the reduction of capital pursuant to losses and the reduction of capital below the legal minimum, the issue of one or more convertible debentures up to a specified amount and for a maximum of 5 years, the power to increase the capital stock one or more times up to a specified amount and for a maximum period of 5 years.

compliance with the law, the articles of association and the principles of correct corporate management; to the adequacy of the company's organisational structure, internal control system and administrative and accounting system; and to the arrangements for implementing corporate governance codes. Moreover, the board of auditors of listed companies must report to the *Commissione Nazionale per le Società e la Borsa* (Consob) on any irregularity found in the performance of its monitoring activities (Art. 149 CFSA).

Similar monitoring functions are allocated to the supervisory board in the two-tier system and to the audit committee in the one-tier system. The audit committee's competencies are similar to those of the board of statutory auditors (Art. 2409-octiesdecies Civil Code and Art. 149/4-ter CFSA).[38] As a result, the board of auditors does not completely disappear in the unitary model of governance. Rather, it is replaced by an audit committee which closely resembles the board of auditors to the extent that many rules are common. This could be regarded as an example of path dependency limiting convergence towards international standards. Also most of the supervisory board's functions in the two-tier system are similar to those of the board of auditors, but others are typical of the shareholders' meeting in the traditional system (Art. 2409-terdecies Civil Code and Art. 149/4-bis CFSA).

d) Internal Control System

Boards of directors, including independent directors, play an important role in the area of internal controls. The Civil Code requires the board to assess the adequacy of the organisational structure of the company including the internal control system (Art. 2381/3). Under the Corporate Governance Code, the board of listed companies defines the guidelines of the internal control system and evaluates its adequacy and effectiveness (Art. 7). The board of auditors plays an important role in the monitoring of the internal control system as established by the board of directors (Art. 149 CFSA). In listed companies, according to the Corporate Governance Code (Art. 7), the risk management and internal control committee (hereinafter 'internal control committee'), which is made-up exclusively of independent non-executive directors (or at least of a majority of independent directors), assists the board in performing the tasks concerning the establishment and monitoring of an internal control system. The activities of this committee partly overlap with those of the board of auditors, requiring practical coordination between the two committees.[39]

---

[38] The audit committee is also entrusted with some functions pertaining to the board of directors in the traditional system (see Art 2409-octiesdecies/5 Civil Code).

[39] G. Ferrarini, 'Funzione del consiglio di amministrazione, ruolo degli indipendenti e doveri fiduciari' in M. Bianchini and C. Di Noia (eds.) *I controlli societari. Molte regole, nessun sistema*, Egea, Milan (2010), pp. 49–65; G. Ferrarini, 'Controlli interni e strutture di
cont. ...

When defining the guidelines of the internal control system, the board of directors also identifies the main risks concerning the issuer. As stated in the Corporate Governance Code, the director in charge of the internal control system has to identify the main business risks and report on them to the board of directors. The officer responsible for the internal control system (typically the internal auditor) reports his or her evaluations to the board of directors (in particular to its internal control committee), so as to enable the board to assess the risk management procedures to achieve an acceptable overall risk profile (Art. 7).

The board of directors must describe the essential elements of the internal control system in the annual report on corporate governance, expressing its evaluation on the overall adequacy of the same, especially with regard to the main characteristics of risk management systems (Art. 123-bis/2 CFSA and Comment to Art. 7 Corporate Governance Code). The Corporate Governance Code provisions are also applicable to the supervisory board in the two-tier system and to the board of directors in the one-tier system. Nevertheless, an internal control committee does not need to be established in the one-tier system, as the audit committee already performs similar functions.

e) External Auditors

The Legislative Decree n. 39 of 27 January 2010 has implemented Directive 2006/43/EC on the statutory audits of annual and consolidated accounts.[40] Accordingly, new rules are foreseen with regard to the qualifications required for the licence to audit activities; programs of continuing education; auditors' independence; public disclosure and public oversight. On the whole, the new rules enhance the role and powers of public authorities in this area.[41]

Public-interest entities (including listed companies) must appoint either an auditing firm or individual professionals qualified to provide auditing services in order to carry out the external audit. They have to be entered in the special register that is kept—for the time being—by Consob.[42] The implementing Decree identifies the 'internal and accounting control committee' foreseen by the European Directive with the board of auditors in the traditional model; with the

---

governo societario' in Abbadessa and Portale (eds.), see n. 34 above, p. 3; P. Montalenti, 'Il sistema dei controlli interni nelle società di capitali', *Le Società* (2005), p. 294; P. Montalenti, 'Corporate governance, consiglio di amministrazione, sistemi di controllo interno: spunti per una riflessione', *Rivista delle Società* (2002), p. 803.

[40] Decreto Legislativo n. 39 del 27 gennaio 2010, *Attuazione della direttiva 2006/43/CE, relativa alle revisioni legali dei conti annuali e dei conti consolidati, che modifica le direttive 78/660/CEE e 83/349/CEE, e che abroga la direttiva 84/253/CEE.*

[41] See P. Giudici, 'La nuova disciplina della revisione legale', *Le Società* (2010), p. 533.

[42] In fact, according to Art 6 of the Legislative Decree n. 39/2010, the Ministry of Economy and Finance and the Ministry of Justice, after having heard Consob, are entitled to establish new regulations pertaining to the 'registration of external auditors in a public register'.

supervisory board in the two-tier system and with the audit committee in the one-tier system.[43] These bodies are entrusted with the monitoring of (a) the financial reporting process; (b) the effectiveness of the company's internal control, internal audit, and risk management systems; (c) the statutory audit of the annual and consolidated accounts, and (d) the independence of the audit firm, and in particular the provision of additional services to the audited entity (Art. 19 Legislative Decree n. 39/2010).

The external auditors are appointed by the general meeting upon a proposal by the company's control committee. The external auditors should verify throughout the financial year that the company's accounts are kept properly and corporate transactions are reported correctly in the accounting records. They must give their opinion on the company's annual and consolidated accounts in the annual report, and are entitled to obtain documents and information needed to carry out the audit from the company's directors and may carry out examinations, inspections and controls (Art. 14 Legislative Decree n. 39/2010). They should inform Consob and the board of auditors without delay of any reproachable behaviour found in the performance of their duties (Art. 155 CFSA). Detailed provisions are also foreseen in order to assure independence, objectivity and responsibility of external auditors and to avoid 'revolving door' phenomena between auditing firms and their clients (See Arts 10, 13, 14, 15, 16, 17, 18, 19 and 20 Legislative Decree n. 39/2010).

2.2. Organisation/Internal Functioning

2.2.1. Board Composition

a) Size of the Board

The boards of listed companies generally consist of a relatively large number of members. This may hinder their effectiveness in practice. Further, in the case of blue chips, interlocking directorates often make boards less independent.[44]

The proportions of non-executive directors (70% of all members) and independent directors (nearly 50% of NEDs) are acceptable in theory, considering that most listed companies have controlling shareholders or block-holders (who generally appoint NEDs that cannot qualify as independent). However, the inde-

---

[43] Art 19 of Legislative Decree n. 39/2010 is quite confusing in foreseeing that the *internal and accounting control committee* has to be identified with the board of auditors (traditional system), the audit committee (one-tier system) and the supervisory board (two-tier system). Nevertheless, this body has to be kept distinguished from the internal control committee that is the control committee established within the board of directors of listed companies.

[44] Santagata, see n. 15 above; Santella, Drago and Polo, see n. 15 above.

pendence of boards and their professional qualifications and engagement are often criticised as inadequate.[45]

The articles of association fix the number of directors. When they indicate a minimum or maximum number of directors, the precise number is determined by the general meeting. The board of directors appoints the chairman from amongst its members, unless the chairman is appointed by the general meeting (Art. 2380-bis Civil Code).

In the traditional system (Art. 147-ter/4 CFSA), the board includes both executive and non-executive directors (at least one NED must be independent, or two if the board comprises more than seven members). In the two-tier model, the supervisory board consists of non-executive (supervisory) directors, who must also comply with independence requirements, while the management committee can include both executive and non-executive members (when there are more than four members, at least one must be independent). In the one-tier model, the audit committee's members must be independent, while the board of directors consists both of executive and non-executive directors, of which one third at least must be independent.

The Corporate Governance Code (Comment to Art. 2) recommends that shareholders evaluate the professional characteristics, the experience, including managerial competencies and the gender of the candidates in relation to the size of the issuer, the complexity and the specificity of the business sector in which the issuer operates, as well as the size of the board of directors. It also foresees that the number, authority, competence and time availability of non-executive directors should be such as to ensure that their judgment has a significant impact on board decisions. In practice, the number of non-executives generally exceeds that of executives. Assonime shows that on average executive directors make up 2.8 per board (29.8% of all members), while NEDs are 7.3 70.2% of all).[46] In the few cases of two-tier models, out of 52 members of management committees, 32 are executive and 20 non-executive (8 independent).[47] Supervisory board members are all independent.

b) *Labour Representatives*

There are no labour representatives in the boards of Italian companies. The concept of codetermination has always been rejected both by the entrepreneurs and by the unions, so that it was never put on the political agenda. Also a limited participation of workers on boards was generally excluded and is never practised. On the whole, Italian unions prefer a confrontational approach to labour issues,

---

[45] F. Denozza, 'L'amministratore di minoranza e i suoi critici', *Giurisprudenza commerciale* (2005) I, p. 767.

[46] Assonime, see n. 5 above, schedule 13.

[47] Assonime, see n. 5 above, p. 38.

while entrepreneurs prefer to keep boards for controlling shareholders and block holders, save for a limited number of independent directors.

c) Special Qualification Requirements

The articles of association can stipulate requirements as to the integrity, expertise and independence of directors, also by reference to those established by codes of conduct issued by either business associations or exchanges[48] (Art. 2387 Civil Code for the traditional system; Art. 2409-undecies for the two-tier system and Art. 2409-noviesdecies for the one-tier system). To our knowledge, only a few examples exist of similar clauses in practice. A notable example is the articles of association of Parmalat, which require a majority of independent directors and specify the applicable independence requirements.[49]

The CFSA sets specific integrity and independence requirements for the directors of listed companies (Art. 147-quinquies and Art. 147-ter/4) as well as professional, independence and integrity requirements for auditors (Art. 148/4). Special requirements are set for investment firms, asset management companies and SICAVs[50] (Art. 13 CFSA); insurance companies (Art. 76 Italian Insurance Code) and banks (Art. 26 TUB).

d) Requirements for Chairman/CEO

No independence requirements are set for the chairman in the traditional system. However, the Corporate Governance Code recommends that the roles of chairman and CEO be kept separate (Comment to Art. 2). Assonime (2012) reports that in 59% of the listed companies the chairman has delegated powers; a higher percentage is found for SMEs and non-financial companies.[51]

If the chairman is either the CEO or a controlling shareholder, the board should appoint a Lead Independent Director (LID) (Art. 2 Corporate Governance Code). At the FTSE-Mib companies, a LID is also appointed upon request from a majority of independent directors, save for a contrary resolution of the board (which should be motivated and made public in the issuer's corporate governance report). The LID should cooperate with the chairman in ensuring a good flow of information to the board and convene meetings of independent directors when appropriate (Art. 2 Corporate Governance Code and the relevant comment). The appointment of LIDs is on the rise: According to Assonime (2012), 37% of the

---

[48] For example, The Corporate Governance Code, see n. 3 above.

[49] Clauses n. 6.2 and 12 of Parmalat's articles of association.

[50] *Società d'Investimento a Capitale Variabile* (Investment Company with Variable Capital).

[51] Assonime, see n. 5 above, p. 40 and schedule 15.

companies analysed appointed an LID, mostly in cases where the chairman is a controlling shareholder (whether CEO or not).[52]

The CFSA provides that the chairman of the board of auditors in the traditional system (Art. 148/2-bis and 148/3) and that of the audit committee in the one-tier system (Art. 148/4-ter and 148/4-ter) are appointed by the general meeting from the directors elected by the minority shareholders. A similar provision, which is clearly designed to reinforce the monitoring powers of minority shareholders, does not apply to the chairman of the supervisory board in the two-tier system (Art. 148/4-bis).

e) *Restrictions with Respect to Similar Positions in Other Companies: Limits on the Cumulus of Directors' Offices*

Recently Italian law has approved a bill pertaining to interlocking directorships: Article 36, Decree Law n. 201 of 6 December 2011 provides that a member of the administrative or control body or a top manager of banks, financial firms and insurance companies cannot hold a similar position in a competing firm.[53]

The Corporate Governance Code generally states that directors should accept a board seat only when they can devote sufficient time to the performance of their duties, also taking into account the number of seats held by the same as either directors or statutory auditors in other listed companies (Art. 1.C.2,3,4). The board should evaluate each individual case on the basis of the information received, record this information annually and include it in its corporate governance report. The board should also set internal guidelines fixing the maximum number of offices that a director can hold.

Furthermore, the Consob Regulation on issuers n. 11971 of 14 May 1999[54] provides that statutory auditors may not hold a similar position in more than five listed issuers (Art. 144-terdecies CSFA). The articles of association may fix a lower threshold. Consob Regulation (Annex 5-bis) also requires disclosure to Consob and the Italian Exchange of the offices held by statutory auditors in other companies. The limit of 5 offices is also applicable to members of the supervisory board (in the two-tier system) and the audit committee (in the one-tier system).

Assonime (2012) shows that the average number of offices held by a director is 3.26; 32% of directors do not declare other offices and 16% have only one other position. However, a minority of directors hold a high number of offices:

---

[52] Assonime, see n. 5 above, schedule 15.

[53] Decreto Legge n. 201 del 6 dicembre 2011 convertito dalla legge n. 214 del 22 dicembre 2011, *Disposizioni urgenti per la crescita, l'equità e il consolidamento dei conti pubblici*.

[54] Regolamento Consob n. 11971 del 14 maggio 1999 *di attuazione del decreto legislativo 24 febbraio 1998, n. 58, concernente la disciplina degli emittenti*

26% of the sample hold at least 5 additional seats and 8% at least ten (one director stands out of the group with 68 offices held).[55]

f) Expertise Requirement and Gender Diversity; Foreigners on the Board

The Italian Parliament recently approved a law on gender diversity fixing a compulsory percentage (at least one third) of the less represented gender (presently women) within the board and the 'control organs' of listed companies.[56] The new law applies to the board of directors (Art. 147-ter/1 ter CSFA) and to the board of auditors (Art. 148/1-bis); to the supervisory board (Art. 148/4-bis) and to the management board, if constituted by at least three members (Art. 147-quarter/1 bis) and to the board of directors in the one-tier system. It does not apply to the audit committee (Art. 147-ter/1-ter).

Assonime (2012) shows that the number of female directors was much lower than now required under the new law: only 182 of 2,728 directors of listed companies were female (6.7% of the total).[57] These new gender rules apply from the first renewal of the administrative and auditing bodies of companies listed in regulated markets after one year from the date of commencement of the new law (July 2012), reserving for the less-represented gender, for the first mandate in appli-cation of the law, a quota of at least one fifth of the directors and auditors elected. There is currently low level of participation of foreign directors on Italian boards.

g) Evaluation of Board Performance

The Corporate Governance Code (Art. 1) recommends that boards evaluate, at least once a year, their size, composition and performance (including that of their committees). Assonime (2012)[58] reports that more than half of the listed companies (mainly large issuers) reported on self-evaluation conducted by their boards relative to their own performance. There is no evidence of differences across the sectors.

2.2.2. Decision-Making Process

a) Veto/Approval Rights for Non-Executives

The Civil Code (Art. 2388) foresees two conditions for the validity of board resolutions. First, a majority of board members must participate in the meeting,

---

[55] Assonime, see n. 5 above, p. 33.

[56] Law n. 120 of 12 July 2011 (Legge n. 120 del 12 luglio 2011, *Modifiche al testo unico delle disposizioni in materia di intermediazione finanziaria, di cui al decreto legislativo 24 febbraio 1998, n. 58, concernenti la parita' di accesso agli organi di amministrazione e di con-trollo delle societa' quotate in mercati regolamentati).*

[57] Assonime, see n. 5 above, p. 44 and schedule 16.

[58] Assonime, see n. 5 above, p. 32 and schedule 7.

unless the articles of association require a greater number. Second, the majority of those present must vote for the resolution, unless the articles require a special quorum. It is debated whether the articles can require either the presence of all members or the unanimity of those present for the validity of resolutions.[59] Proxy-voting is not allowed in boards, while means of telecommunication (such as teleconferencing and videoconferencing) may be used (Art. 2388).

The law does not grant veto or approval rights to non-executive directors. Nevertheless, board resolutions that are in breach of the law and/or the articles can be challenged in court by directors who either did not take part in the meeting or dissented from the resolution, and by the board of auditors. A judicial action must be brought within ninety days from the date of the resolution. Shareholders are entitled to challenge those resolutions that negatively affect their rights. However, the rights acquired by third parties in good faith through execution of the resolution are preserved. The same rules apply to the board of directors in the one-tier model and to the supervisory and management boards in the two-tier model (Art. 2409 undecies, quaterdecies and noviesdecies).

b) Delegation of Tasks Within the Board

Tasks can be delegated to one or more managing directors entrusting the same with the day-to-day management of the company, and/or to an executive committee (Art. 2381 Civil Code).[60] Assonime (2012) found an executive committee in 42 companies (out of the 262 analysed).[61] This committee is more common in financial companies.

c) Role of the Chairman of the Board

Unless otherwise provided in the articles, the main tasks of the chairman are to convene the board, fix and coordinate the agenda of the meetings, including ensuring that adequate information is given to all directors (Art. 2381 Civil Code).[62] According to the Corporate Governance Code, the chairman has a key role in the organisation and functioning of the board (Arts. 1 and 2). The chairman should also take care to ensure the participation of NEDs to educational programs directed to improve their knowledge of the relevant business and its

---

[59] Most legal scholars object to the validity of similar clauses, which are supported by some authors. See, for all, G.F. Campobasso, *Diritto commerciale*, II, UTET, Turin (2011) p. 372.

[60] See F. Barachini, *La gestione delegata nella società per azioni*, Giappichelli, Turin (2008), p. 210 ff.; Bonelli, see n. 33 above, p. 42 ff.; A. Zanardo, *Delega di funzioni e diligenza degli amministratori nelle società per azioni*, CEDAM, Padua (2010), p. 92 ff.

[61] Assonime, see n. 5 above, p. 10.

[62] P.M. Sanfilippo, 'Il Presidente del consiglio di amministrazione nelle società per azioni' in Abbadessa and Portale (eds.) see n. 34 above, p. 454 ff.

perspectives, and of the regulation applicable to the same. The board usually appoints a Secretary to assist the chairman in the performance of the relevant tasks.[63]

d) Committees

The Corporate Governance Code foresees the creation of board committees with preparatory and advisory functions (Art. 4), including a remuneration committee, an internal control committee and a nomination committee.[64]

The internal control committee (Art. 7) is made up exclusively of independent NEDs, or NEDs with a majority of independents; however, all members should be independent when the issuer is under the control of another listed company. At least one member should be an expert in accounting and finance or in risk management. The committee gives opinions to the board of directors on the definition of the guidelines of the internal control and risk management system; the evaluation of the adequacy of the same; the description of the main features of the system in the corporate governance report and the approval of the plan drafted by the person in charge of the internal audit. It also gives an opinion to the board on the appointment and removal of the person in charge of the internal audit (7.C.1). The committee also plays the function of assisting the board of directors in the exercise of several specific tasks; among them, it conducts a preliminary analysis of the draft balance sheet and half-yearly report, before approval of the same by the board (7.C.2). However, the committee's role is different from that of the board of auditors, which is defined as the 'control committee' vis-à-vis the auditors (see above 2.1.3). For the rest, the Corporate Governance Code recommends that the internal control committee co-ordinates its functions with those of the board of auditors. The Code also provides that an internal control committee should not be established in the one-tier system, given that the law already requires an audit committee within the board. With regard to the two-tier system, the Code suggests to apply its provisions pertaining to board committees to the supervisory board (Art. 10).

Assonime (2012)[65] found that 89.7% of the companies analysed had an internal control committee in place. The committee mostly consisted of between 2 and 9 members. In most cases the committee consisted of NEDs, with a majority of independents in 93% of the cases. In 83% of the cases at least one member was

---

[63] See De Nicola, see n. 33 above, p. 79 ff. The chairman is responsible for the minutes, which he has to sign, as a part of his coordination function: D.U. Santosuosso, *La riforma del diritto societario*, Giuffrè, Milan (2003), p. 136.

[64] The creation of one or more of these committees can be avoided and their functions can be played directly by the board of directors when the requirements foreseen by Art 4.C.2 of the Corporate Governance Code are satisfied.

[65] Assonime, see n. 5 above, p. 90 ff. and schedule 40.

a financial expert. The number of meetings in a year varied between zero and 53, while the average participation to meetings was high: 76% (511 directors) are always present; 97% of the members attended at least half of the meetings.

The remuneration committee (Art. 7) is made up exclusively of independent NEDs, or NEDs, with a majority of independents; however, all members should be independent when the issuer is under the control of another listed company, and at least one member must be an expert in finance or in compensation policies. The committee should assist the board in defining the remuneration policy for directors and directors entrusted with strategic tasks. It should formulate proposals on the various types of compensation and on the performance targets for variable pay. The committee should periodically reassess the remuneration policy criteria and their implementation and submit general recommendations to the board. The committee should report to the AGM on its activity.

Assonime (2012)[66] found that 85% of the companies examined had established a remuneration committee, generally consisting of 3 members. In 96% of the cases, all members were NEDs, with a majority of independents in 90% of the committees and a totality of independents in 32% of the same. The number of meetings in a year varied between zero (in 16 companies) and a maximum of 21. The average attendance rate was fairly high: 87% of directors (521 directors) have always been present; 97% of them attended at least half of the meetings; low attendance is extremely rare.

The nomination committee (Art. 5) has to consist of a majority of independent directors, and is entrusted with an advisory role as to the best composition of the board. The committee is entrusted also with other functions, such as proposing candidates to the board for the replacement of deceased directors or directors who left office voluntarily and to the shareholders' meeting for the appointment of independent directors, and assessing the size and composition of the board. Assonime (2012) found that a nomination committee was established in 43 companies (16%).[67] This low percentage may be better understood in light of the slate voting requirement (see 3.1.1 below) which deprives the board of any real influence on the selection of its members, leaving the same to the (majority and minority) shareholders who submit the slates to the general meeting (a possibility not recognised to the board).

e) Executive Sessions

Executive sessions of the board (meetings in which only NEDs participate) are increasing, but cannot yet be considered general practice. Assonime (2012) found that 71% of the companies analysed held executive sessions chaired by the Lead

---

[66] Assonime, see n. 5 above, p. 78 ff. and schedule 30.
[67] Assonime, see n. 5 above, p. 55 ff. and schedule 20.

Independent Director.[68] These sessions, however, cannot take formal decisions that are binding for the company.

2.2.3. Independent Directors

Independence requirements are found both in hard law and soft law.[69]

a) Mandatory Requirements

Under the CFSA, the board of directors must at least comprise either one or two independent directors, depending on whether the board members are a maximum of seven or more (Art. 147-ter/4). The independence requirements are those set for statutory auditors by Article 148/3. However, the articles may refer to additional requirements established by codes of conduct issued either by exchanges or trade associations, a possibility that is almost never used in practice.

In the two-tier model, supervisory directors should comply with the independence requirements provided for statutory auditors in the traditional system (Art. 148/4-bis), in addition to those possibly foreseen by the articles of association (Art. 2409-duodecies Civil Code). The management committee, if constituted by more than four members, should include at least one independent director (Art. 147-quarter CFSA). This requirement is better understood by recalling that the management committee is regulated similarly to the board of directors in the traditional system and is allowed to include both executive (delegated) and non-executive directors (see 2.2.1(a) above). In the one-tier model, at least one third of the directors must comply with the independence requirements foreseen for statutory auditors (Art. 2409-septiesdecies Civil Code). Moreover, the audit committee should exclusively consist of independent directors (Art. 2409-octiesdecies Civil Code).

Consob sets out specific rules for independent directors with regard to related parties transactions (see 3.1.3 below) and takeover bids (Consob Regulation on issuers Art. 39, 39-bis and Annex 2).[70]

---

[68] Assonime, see n. 5 above, p. 43.

[69] See M. Belcredi, 'Amministratori indipendenti, amministratori di minoranza e dintorni', *Rivista delle Società* (2005), p. 853; G. Ferrarini, 'Ruolo degli amministratori indipendenti e Lead Independent Director' in Assogestioni, *La Corporate Governance e il risparmio gestito* (2006; available at <www.assogestioni.it/index.cfm/3,140,624/assog_quad_27.pdf>), p. 35; R. Lener, 'Gli amministratori indipendenti' in G. Scognamiglio (ed.) *Profili e problemi dell'amministrazione nella riforma della Società*, Giuffrè, Milan (2003), p. 115; D. Regoli, 'Gli amministratori indipendenti' in Abbadessa and Portale (eds.), see n. 34 above, p. 385 ff.; R. Rordorf, 'Gli amministratori indipendenti', *Giurisprudenza Commerciale* (2007) I, p. 152.

[70] Art 39-bis of the Consob Regulation on issuers provides that before publishing the issuer's statement, the NEDs who are not related parties to the bidder render an opinion about

cont. ...

b) Comply-or-explain

Under the Corporate Governance Code, an adequate number of NEDs should be independent and comply with the independence criteria stated by Article 3.C.1. The board should periodically assess their independence and communicate the results of its assessment to the market (Art. 3.P.2). The Code also specifies that the number and competence of independent directors should be adequate in relation to the size of the board and to the business of the issuer, and sufficient to enable the constitution of committees within the board (Art. 3.C.3). The board of auditors should review the assessment criteria and the procedures followed by the board of directors for evaluating independence and the results should be notified to the market (Art. 3.C.5). The independent directors should meet at least once every year without the other directors attending the meeting (Art. 3.C.6).

The Code specifies the independence criteria by stating that 'an adequate number of non-executive directors should be independent, in the sense that they do not maintain, nor have recently maintained, directly or indirectly, any business relationship with the issuer or persons linked to the issuer, sufficiently significant as to influence their autonomous judgment' (Art. 3.P.1). A number of examples are subsequently indicated of situations in which a director should not be considered as independent. However, the possibility of defining a director as independent in similar cases is not excluded, provided the reasons for doing it are clearly explained to the market. The board should evaluate the independence of NEDs having regard to substance rather than form (see the comment to Art. 3.C.1). In a communication of March 2010,[71] the Corporate Governance Committee recommended that companies inform the market about 'whether they adopt criteria for the evaluation of independence different from those specified in the Code (also with specific reference to individual directors) and about the quantitative and/or qualitative criteria used in evaluating the relevance of directors' relationships'.[72]

Stricter requirements are foreseen for issuers admitted to the Star segment of the Italian Exchange according to the relevant Rules, which make some of the Corporate Governance Code provisions mandatory.[73]

---

the offer and the adequacy of the compensation offered by the bidder. If the NED is a related party to the bidder, he cannot render the opinion mentioned above.

[71] Borsa Italiana, 3 March 2010, 'The Corporate Governance Committee adopts new principles about remuneration and a recommendation about the disclosure of independence requirements' (available at <www.borsaitaliana.it/borsaitaliana/regolamenti/corporategovernance/cor porategovernance.en.htm>).

[72] See Assonime, 'L'indipendenza dei componenti degli organi di amministrazione e controllo nelle società per azioni', *Rivista delle Società* (2010), p. 195.

[73] Star is an Index of the Italian Stock Exchange to which small-medium capitalisation companies are admitted. Star issuers must apply specific provisions of the Corporate

cont. ...

Assonime (2012)[74] found an average number of 3.7 independent directors per board, corresponding to 36% of the total number of directors. In two-tier structures, the proportion of (supervisory) directors complying with the Corporate Governance Code independence requirements is greater than in traditional governance structures.[75] Some independent directors also sit in management boards. Most companies declared to comply with the Corporate Governance Code's criteria on independence. Only 26 companies (10% of the sample) stated that either one or more criteria had not been complied with, and provided an explanation.[76] However, almost all of these companies (25 cases) reject the criterion by which independence would be lost by a director sitting for more than 9 years on the same board.[77]

Nonetheless, the practical impact of independent directors is often below expectations. This is due to well-known information asymmetries between executive and independent directors, but also to the fact that the latter either lack the professional competences needed for their office or do not devote sufficient time to the same.[78] There is also a trade-off between independence and experience, so that more independent boards may be less effective at monitoring the managers.[79]

2.3. Information Streams

Italian law regulates two types of information streams in listed companies: the first runs between executive and non-executive directors; the second between board of directors and board of auditors (see 2.1.3 above). Other information streams exist between the board and the general meeting and between the company and the market. We focus here on the first two streams.

i) All directors must perform their duties in an informed way (Art. 2381/6 Civil Code). Moreover, each director is entitled to ask the delegated organs (ie. executive directors and executive committee) to give specific information about

---

Governance Code listed by Art 2.2.3. of the 'Rules of the markets organised and managed by Borsa Italiana S.p.A.'.

    [74] Assonime, see n. 5 above, p. 37 and schedule 13.

    [75] Assonime, see n. 5 above, schedule 14.

    [76] Assonime, see n. 5 above, p. 48.

    [77] *Ibid.*

    [78] Belcredi, see n. 69 above, p. 868 ff.; Regoli, see n. 69 above, p. 385 ff.

    [79] Lener, see n. 69 above, p. 134.

the company's management in board meetings.[80] As already stated (2.1(b) above), the delegated organs have to make sure that the organisational, administrative and accounting structures are adequate for the nature and size of the company. They must also report to the board of directors at least every six months on the trends and perspectives of the company's business and on the transactions of major relevance for the company (Art. 2381/5). On the other hand, the non-executive directors should: Evaluate the adequacy of the organisational, administrative and accounting structure of the company on the basis of the information received from executive directors; examine the strategic, industrial and financial plans of the company, if any; and evaluate the general trend of the company's business on the basis of the information received from the delegated organs.

The Corporate Governance Code specifies that in carrying out their tasks, directors should review the information received from the delegated organs, and ask the same for clarification, elaboration or supplements that may be necessary or appropriate for a complete and correct evaluation of the facts submitted to the board (Comment to Art. 1). The chairman of the board of directors should use his or her best efforts to ensure that the material information and documents for enabling the board to take decisions are available to its members according to adequate procedures and timing.

A strategic role in ensuring appropriate flows of information is also recognised for the Lead Independent Director (if appointed) and to internal compliance programs, which are in some cases mandatory (eg. for banks), while in others they are optional (ie. Legislative Decree n. 231 of 8 June 2001[81]) on criminal liability of legal entities, including business corporations.[82]

The chairman must ensure that pre-meeting information is supplied in a timely and accurate manner, provided that all the measures for ensuring confidentiality of the information and data so supplied are adopted (see Comment to Art. 1 Corporate Governance Code). The board should promote initiatives

---

[80] Zamperetti, see n. 34 above, p. 333; Abbadessa, see n. 34 above, p. 506. An author argues that directors are entitled to ask the officers directly for information (V. Salafia, 'Amministratori senza deleghe fra vecchio e nuovo diritto societario', *Le Società* (2006), p. 292), get access to data and make inspections (Campobasso, see n. 59 above, p. 376 f). However, all are of the opinion that non-executive directors are also entitled to ask delegated directors for information outside of board meetings and that delegated directors have to report to the board the questions submitted and relevant answers (Barachini, see n. 60 above, p. 154 f; Zanardo, see n. 60 above, p. 107).

[81] Decreto Legislativo n. 231 dell'8 giugno 2001, Disciplina della responsabilità amministrativa delle persone giuridiche, delle società e delle associazioni anche prive di personalità giuridica, a norma dell'articolo 11 della legge n. 300 del 29 settembre 2000.

[82] For conflicts that might arise in the internal control system, see P. Montalenti, 'Struttura e ruolo dell'organismo di vigilanza nel quadro della riforma del diritto societario' in Bianchini and Di Noia (eds.), see n. 39 above, p. 85 ff.; Ferrarini, 'Controlli interni e strutture di governo societario', see n. 39 above, p. 17 ff.

directed to enhance shareholders' participation to general meetings and make access to relevant corporate information easier to the extent required for the exercise of their rights (Art. 9 Corporate Governance Code).

ii) Strong information powers are attributed to the board of auditors, according to its monitoring functions (Arts. 150 and 151 CFSA). With regard to alternative systems, the law entrusts the supervisory board and the audit committee in the one-tier system with information powers and duties that are similar to those foreseen for the board of auditors (Arts. 150, 151-bis and 151-ter). In addition, the directors must promptly inform the board of auditors, in the manner laid down in the articles of association and at least every three months, of the activities carried out and the transactions of greatest significance for the company's profitability, financial position or assets and liabilities executed by the company or its subsidiaries (Art. 150/1). The management board has a similar duty to report to the supervisory board. In the one-tier system, it is up to the delegated directors (or executive committee) to report to the management control committee.

3. Accountability

3.1. Board and Shareholders

3.1.1. Appointment and Removal

3.1.1.1. Traditional Structure

a) Board of Directors

The general meeting appoints the directors, except for the first directors who are appointed by the founders when the company is formed (Art. 2383 ff. Civil Code). Only individuals can be appointed as directors (to the exclusion of legal entities).[83] The term of appointment cannot be for more than three fiscal years and expires on the date of the AGM convened for the approval of the financial statements relative to the last year of appointment. Directors can be re-elected.

Board members of listed companies are elected on the basis of slate voting, which should assure that also minority shareholders are represented on the board of directors. In fact, at least one director must be elected from the minority slate that receives more votes, provided that it has no link—even indirect—with the majority slate, ie. the slate which obtained the highest number of votes in the general meeting (Art. 147-ter CFSA).[84] The articles of association should

---

[83] Campobasso, see n. 59 above, p. 349.

[84] See also Consob, 'Nomina dei componenti gli organi di amministrazione e controllo', Communication DEM/9017893 of 26/02/2009. About boards elections and shareholder activism

cont. ...

establish the minimum share participation required for the presentation of a slate, in a measure not exceeding one-fortieth of the share capital or the different threshold fixed by Consob in its Regulation on issuers, taking into account capitalisation, floating shares and ownership structure. The slates must indicate which candidate directors comply with the independence requirements established by the law and the articles (Art. 147-ter CFSA; Art. 144-quarter ff. Regulation on issuers). Assonime (2012) reports that the average quorum required to submit a slate for the board of directors (and the board of statutory auditors) is 2.3%.[85]

Directors can be removed by the general meeting at any time, but removal without cause entitles the removed director to recover damages from the company (Art. 2383 Civil Code). A director can resign from the office by sending a written notice to the board and to the chairman of the board of auditors. The resignation is effective immediately, provided that a majority of directors remain in office; otherwise, the resignation takes effect only from the time when the majority of the board has been reconstituted through the appointment of new directors and acceptance by the same (Art. 2385). Moreover, in the case of vacancy of a seat, it is possible for the board to co-opt a new member by resolution approved also by the board of auditors; if a vacancy of the majority of seats occurs, the remaining directors shall call a general meeting (Art. 2386). The articles of association can also provide that the entire board will be terminated as a result of the cessation of one or more directors (this is the so called *simul stabunt simul cadent* clause).

The articles can also reserve the appointment of an independent director to the holders of hybrid financial instruments (Art. 2351/5). In companies with participation by the state or public bodies, the law or the articles can empower the state or public body to appoint one or more directors (Art. 2449/4).[86]

In cases of serious mismanagement, the tribunal can replace the board by appointing a judicial administrator, who will remain in office for the time needed to adopt the required measures, under the special investigation procedure foreseen by Article 2409/4.

---

see M. Belcredi, S. Bozzi and C. Di Noia, 'Boards elections and shareholder activism: the Italian experiment', in M. Belcredi and G. Ferrarini (eds.), *Boards and shareholders in European Listed Companies. Facts, Context and the Post-Crisis Reforms*, Cambridge University Press, forthcoming.

[85] Assonime, see n. 5 above, schedule 21.

[86] See F. Ghezzi and M. Ventoruzzo, 'La nuova disciplina delle partecipazioni dello Stato e degli altri enti pubblici nel capitale delle società per azioni: fine di un privilegio?', *Rivista delle Società* (2008), p. 683 ff.

b) Board of Auditors

Statutory auditors are appointed by the general meeting, except for the first auditors who are appointed by the company's founders. The articles of association specify the number of ordinary members (no less than three) and that of alternates (no less than two) who will constitute the board. In listed companies, at least one auditor is elected from a minority slate (Art. 148 CFSA), similarly to the position for minority directors. The auditors stay in office for three fiscal years. The general meeting can remove the same only for just cause, but the relevant resolution must be approved by the Court after hearing the auditor in question (Art. 2400 Civil Code). This regime is directed to protect statutory auditors' independence. In the case of death, resignation or forfeiture of an auditor, the senior alternate auditor replaces the same until the next general meeting where the board must be re-integrated. If the board of auditors cannot be completed with alternate auditors, a general meeting shall be called to appoint the new auditors (Art. 2401 Civil Code).

3.1.1.2. Alternative Systems

The Civil Code includes a number of articles referring to alternative systems; for the rest, the provisions concerning the traditional system apply. Moreover, the slate voting requirement for listed companies is applicable to the supervisory board and to the board of directors in the one-tier system, where the chair of the audit committee must be a minority director.[87]

a) One-Tier System

Unless the articles of associations state otherwise, the general meeting sets the number of directors (at least three in listed companies), appoints the same and can remove them at any time. At least one-third of board members must comply with the independence requirements set out in the law for auditors and, if foreseen by the articles, those provided for in the codes of conduct issued by trade associations or regulated markets (Art. 2409-septiesdecies Civil Code and Art. 148/3 CFSA). The board selects the members of the audit committee (*comitato per il controllo sulla gestione*) from amongst the directors who comply with independence requirements (Art. 2409-octiesdecies Civil Code). All committee members must further comply with the integrity and professional requirements foreseen by the law (also applicable to the statutory auditors and to the members of the supervisory board).[88] At least one member must be a

---

[87] See Ghezzi and Malberti, n. 31 above, p. 22.

[88] See also CFSA (Art 148/4). and the Ministry of Justice in concert with the Ministry of the Treasury, Budget and Economic Planning Decree n. 162 of 30 March 2000 (Ministro della Giustizia di concerto con il Ministro del Tesoro, del Bilancio e della Programmazione Eco-

cont. ...

registered auditor (Art. 2409-octiesdecies/3 Civil Code) and one, who is the committee's chairman, must have been elected in the minority slate (Art. 147-ter CFSA).

The board is empowered to remove the audit committee members from office, but removed members stay in office as directors. No court approval is required, compared to what is required for the board of auditors in the traditional system. In the case of death, removal or forfeiture of a committee member, the board replaces the member with another independent director (Art. 2409-octiesdecies/4 Civil Code).

b) Two-Tier System

The supervisory board members are appointed by the general meeting (save for the first ones who are appointed by the company's founders) and can be removed by the general meeting at any time. However, the board members are entitled to damages for unjustified removal. The supervisory board (Art. 2409-duodecies Civil Code) consists of at least three members who are not necessarily shareholders; one of them must be a registered auditor and another must have been elected from a minority slate (Art. 148/4-bis CFSA). All members must comply with the integrity and professional requirements set out by the law (and by the articles, if any).[89] The chairman of the board is appointed by the general meeting. Supervisory directors can be re-appointed, unless otherwise set out in the articles. Should one member die or resign, the general meeting should promptly replace the director.

The management board must include at least two members, not necessarily shareholders, who are appointed by the supervisory board, except for the first members who are appointed by the company's founders (Art. 2409-novies Civil Code). If the management board has more than four members, at least one must satisfy the independence requirements established for the board of auditors and, if the articles of association so provide, the additional requirements established in codes of conduct adopted by the company (Art. 148/3 CFSA).[90] The board members must also possess the integrity requirements set out by the law (Art. 147-quinquies CFSA).

Members of the management board cannot also be members of the supervisory board. They are appointed for a term of at least three years until the date of the meeting of the supervisory board convened for the approval of the financial statements pertaining to the last fiscal year of their office. If one or more mem-

---

nomica, Decreto n. 162 del 30 marzo 2000, *Regolamento recante norme per la fissazione dei requisiti di professionalita' e onorabilita' dei membri del collegio sindacale delle societa' quotate da emanare in base all'articolo 148 del decreto legislativo 24 febbraio 1998, n. 58.*

[89] *Ibid.*

[90] See CFSA (Art 147-quarter).

bers leaves office earlier, the supervisory board should promptly replace the director. Current members can be re-elected to the management board (unless otherwise provided by the articles) and dismissed by the supervisory board at any time; however, they are entitled damages if their dismissal proves unjustified.

c) Cumulative Voting

Cumulative voting is allowed for companies in general. However, in listed companies the slate voting system is mandatory (Art. 147-ter/3 CFSA). This system is functionally similar to cumulative voting, with different mechanisms. Under cumulative voting, each share votes for only one candidate director, so that minority shareholders can be represented on the board in proportion to their shareholdings. Under slate voting, shareholders are entitled to submit a list of candidate directors and vote for the list. Like cumulative voting, this would in principle allow for a proportional representation on the board. However, slate voting as adopted in Italy only requires at least one director to be appointed from the minority slate getting the highest number of votes. Therefore, the representation of shareholders on the board is not proportional, as the majority slate always get a majority of the board, with minority directors covering an average of 1.5 seats.

3.1.2. Division of Powers between Board and Shareholders

a) Rights and Powers

The board of directors is solely empowered to manage the company. The same is true for the management board in the two-tier system.[91] On the other side, the general meeting cannot resolve management issues. The articles of association can only permit certain management actions on the authorisation of the general meeting (Art. 2364/1 n. 5 Civil Code), which however will not relieve the directors from liability in case of wrongdoing. Moreover, the law specifically requires the authorisation of the general meeting for some actions, such as purchasing assets from founders, promoters and shareholders (Art. 2343-bis Civil Code), purchasing own shares (Art. 2357), and suing directors and statutory auditors for damages (Art. 2393).

b) Duties

Directors are subject to a duty of care when carrying out their responsibilities. They are required to fulfil the obligations set out by the law and by the articles of

---

[91] There is debate on whether shareholders should be entitled to vote on issues that are strategic for the company: see G.B. Portale, 'Le competenze gestorie "non scritte" dell'assemblea di società per azioni' in Abbadessa and Portale (eds.), see n. 34 above, p. 3 ff.

association with the diligence required by their office and their professional competence (Art. 2392 Civil Code). In addition, the actions of directors should be based on being fully informed about the company and its business (Art. 2381/6). Directors are bound by a duty of loyalty as specified by Article 2390 (forbidding directors to act, either directly or indirectly, in competition with the company's business), Article 2391 (regulating self-interested transactions) and Article 2391-bis (regulating related parties transactions).[92]

Other rules set out specific duties for directors, such as the duty to call the general meeting (Art. 2366 Civil Code); the duty to draw up the annual accounts [Art. 2423 ff; the CFSA includes further duties as to financial reporting (Art. 154-ter) and disclosure of information to the public (Art. 114)]. Directors are under a duty to keep the company's books as listed in Article 2421 of the Civil Code and file with the registrar all the documents required by the law; a duty to comply with the company's tax and social security duties; a duty to call an extraordinary meeting if the net assets of the company fall below its legal capital by more than one third (Art. s. 2446 and 2447 Civil Code) and a duty to timely ascertain any cause of company's dissolution and take the appropriate actions (Arts. 2485 and 2486 Civil Code).

c) Business Judgment Rule (BJR)

Italian law does not include any specific provision preventing judges applying hindsight to decisions made by directors.[93] However, courts[94] and scholars[95] share the opinion that judges must abstain from engaging in a substantive review of

---

[92] Italian law does not define the fiduciary duties of directors in detail. Therefore, the duty of care and the duty of loyalty are broad concepts subject to interpretation by the courts. See also Art 9 Corporate Governance Code (conflict of interest) and 1.P.2. ('directors have to act pursuing the priority of creating value for shareholders'). See, G. Ferrarini, 'Valore per gli azionisti e governo societario', *Rivista delle Società* (2002), p. 462.

[93] Zanardo, see n. 60 above, p. 241; but see I. Kutufà, 'Adeguatezza degli assetti e responsabilità gestoria' in *Amministrazione e controllo nel diritto delle società Liber Amicorum Antonio Piras*, Giappichelli, Turin (2010), p. 727.

[94] Among judgments: Court of Cassation, 12 August 2009, n. 18321, *Danno e responsabilità* (2010) p. 241 with comment of B. Di Palma; Court of Cassation, 24 March 2004, n. 5718, *Rivista del notariato* (2004) p. 1571 with comment of C. Chirilli; Court of Cassation, 28 April 1997, n. 3652, *Le Società* (1997) p. 1389 with comment of A. Figone; Trib. Palermo, 13 March 2008, *Giurisprudenza commerciale* (2010) II, p. 121 with comment of M. Cordopatri.

[95] *Ex multis* M. Dellacasa, 'Dalla diligenza alla perizia come parametri per sindacare l'attività di gestione degli amministratori', *Contratto e impresa* (1999), p. 209; G. Cabras, *La responsabilità per l'amministrazione di società di capitali*, UTET, Turin (2002), p. 34 f; M. Franzoni, *Art 2380-2396. Società per azioni. Dell'amministrazione e del controllo. Parte I. Disposizioni generali. Degli amministratori*, in F. Galgano (ed.) *Commentario del Codice civile Scialoja-Branca*, Zanichelli, Bologna (2008), p. 467 ff.; for criticism, see R. Weigmann, *Responsabilità e potere legittimo degli amministratori*, Giappichelli, Turin (1974), p. 188 ff.

business decisions. Nonetheless, the scope and criteria of the BJR have been intensely debated and still raise controversy.

Scholars have discussed, in particular, whether directors must not only be careful, but also skilled. Those who reject the skill requirement generally argue that directors can be sued for their actions only if they do not follow a correct decision-making process.[96] The scholars supporting the skill requirement propose a weak version of the BJR, under which courts should consider both the decision-making process and the substance of decisions, and hold directors liable in the case of egregious and irrational mistakes.[97]

Courts have followed both approaches.[98] When reviewing business decisions, judges hold directors liable for decisions which are too risky[99] or for the incorrect evaluation of assets that they were buying or selling for the company (the case of *La Centrale* is the most famous and controversial in this area).[100] In more recent

---

[96] Bonelli, see n. 33 above, p. 61 ff.; Cabras, see n. 95 above, p. 31 ff. Nonetheless, this opinion acknowledges that macroscopic mistakes can be evidence of directors' careless behaviour: Bonelli, see n. 33 above, p. 66 f, n. 118.

[97] Weigmann, see n. 95 above, p. 148; V. Allegri, *Contributo allo studio della respon-sabilità civile degli amministratori*, Giuffrè, Milan (1979) p. 172 ff.; Dellacasa, see n. 95 above, p. 210; Franzoni, see n. 95 above, p. 467 ff.; see also P. Montalenti, 'Gli obblighi di vigilanza nel quadro dei principi generali sulla responsabilità degli amministratori di società per azioni' in Abbadessa and Portale (eds.), see n. 34 above, p. 839.

[98] For the opinion admitting the review of egregious decisions caused by macroscopic errors: Trib. Milan, 28 March 1985, *Fallimento* (1985), p. 1287 with comment of M. Baglioni; Court of Appeal Milan, 21 January 1994, *Le Società* (1994), p. 923, with comment of V. Salafia; Trib. Milan, 2 March 1995, *Giurisprudenza italiana* (1995) I, c. 706, with comment of E. Desana; Trib. Reggio Emilia, 12 June 1996, *Diritto fallimentare* (1996) II, p. 718, with comment of G. Ragusa Maggiore; Trib. Milan, 10 February 2000, *Giurisprudenza commerciale* (2001) II, p. 339, with comment of A. Tina (as *obiter dictum*, because directors were sued—and not condemned—for self-dealing); Trib. Milan, 29 May, 2004, *Giurisprudenza italiana* (2005) II, p. 2333, with comment of G. Cottino. For the opinion that takes into account only the decision-making process: Court of Appeal of Milan, 30 March 2001, *Giurisprudenza com-merciale* (2002) II, p. 200, with comment of R. Ventura; Trib. Milan, 3 September 2003, *Giurisprudenza italiana* (2004) p. 350.

[99] Trib. Milan, 28 March 1985, see n. 98 above; Trib. Reggio Emilia, 12 June 1996, see n. 98 above.

[100] Trib. Milan, 26 June, 1989, *Giurisprudenza commerciale* (1990) II, 127, with comment of F. Arrigoni, confirmed on appeal, even if with a different motivation based on the fact that the acquisition conflicted with the company's interest: Court of Appeal Milan, 16 June 1995, *Le Società* (1995), p. 1562, with comment of L. De Angelis. However, in many cases in which judges reviewed business decisions and held directors liable for their egregious behaviour there was also clear evidence that directors were involved in self-dealing transactions: Trib. Milan, 28 March 1985, see n. 98 above; Court of Appeal Milan, 21 January 1994, see n. 98 above; Trib. Milan, 2 March 1995, see n. 98 above; Trib. Milan, 29 May 2004, see n. 98 above. See also the cases cited by F. Bonelli, see n. 33 above, p. 69. In similar cases, therefore, the duty of

cont. ...

times, since the 1990s an approach has prevailed that only requires a correct deci-sion-making process.[101] However, there may be second-guessing and courts have some discretion in assessing the adequacy of the decision-making process.[102]

As a result, the conceptual difference between the two approaches is less im-portant than the standard of conduct applied by judges in individual cases. Indeed, courts—notwithstanding the approach adopted—have recently followed a rather mild standard of conduct, no doubt less demanding than that adopted in the case of *La Centrale*.[103] In other words, case law appears to have endorsed a strong version of the BJR which has offered directors extensive protection from liability for their business decisions.

d) Say-on-Pay

See below 3.1.5.

3.1.3. Special Issues

3.1.3.1. Conflict of Interest—General Remarks[104]

Italian law tries to prevent conflicts of interest through a strategy of disclosure and board deliberation. Article 2391/1 of the Civil Code provides that a director must inform the other directors and the board of auditors of any interest that the director may have, with respect to a given transaction, on his or her account or on account of third parties. Any interest must be disclosed, despite the fact that it may not give rise to a conflict. Moreover, the nature, terms, origin and extent of

loyalty rather than that of care was at stake, with the irrational decision deriving from a fraudulent plan of directors against the company.

[101] See the judgments cited at n. 98 above regarding the opinion that takes into account only the decision-making process.

[102] Indeed, judges may hold that directors should have collected more information before taking an action that resulted in damages to the company and/or that the correct analysis of similar information would have led to a different course of action. See A. Rossi, 'Responsabilità degli amministratori verso la società per azioni' in S. Ambrosini (ed.) *La responsabilità di am-ministratori, sindaci e revisori*, Giuffrè, Milan (2007), p. 16.

[103] Court of Appeal Milan, 30 March 2001, see n. 98 above; Trib. Parma, 3 November 1999, *Nuova giurisprudenza civile commentata* (2001), p. 220, with comment of C. Conforti. The former case dealt with the acquisition of control in a listed company. The plaintiffs claimed that the directors of the acquiring company could have discovered the weak financial conditions of the target had they gone through a due diligence process, rather than basing their decision on market values and a fairness opinion. The Milan Court of Appeal held that the directors had behaved correctly. In the latter case, the Court rejected the claim that making an investment made in the absence of a business plan was for the directors careless and irrational.

[104] Zamperetti, see n. 34 above, p. 326. See also, L. Enriques, *Il conflitto d'interessi degli amministratori di società per azioni*, Giuffrè, Milan (2000) *passim*.

the interest must be specified before the board takes a resolution on the transaction at issue. If the interest concerns the managing director, the managing director cannot execute the transaction and this must be resolved by the board.

Furthermore, the board resolution must adequately explain the reasons for the transaction and for the company's interest in the same (Art. 2391/2). In the event of non-compliance with the directors' duties just reviewed, or if the board resolution was adopted with the decisive vote of the interested director, the resolution can be challenged within ninety days by either the other directors or by the board of auditors, if there could be damage to the company resulting from the transaction. A director who voted for the resolution cannot challenge the resolution unless the interested director did not properly disclose his or her interest in the transaction to the board. In any case, the rights of third parties are preserved if they are acquired in good faith as a result of the resolution being taken (Art. 2391/3).

Directors are liable to the company for damages deriving from their action or inaction (Art. 2391/4) such as for damages resulting from the sale or the purchase of an asset if the price agreed is below (or above) the market value. Moreover, breach of the duty of disclosure and other duties set out in Article 2391/1 may give rise to criminal liability of directors (and members of the management board) of listed companies and financial intermediaries (Art. 2629-bis).

3.1.3.2. *Related-Parties Transactions*

Consob has adopted a Regulation on related-party transactions[105] pursuant to Article 2391-bis Civil Code and Articles 113-ter, 114, 115 and 154-ter CFSA.[106] This new regime applies to Italian companies having their shares either listed on regulated markets (in Italy or other EU countries) or widely distributed among the

---

[105] Regulation n. 17221 of 12 March 2010, later amended by Resolution n. 17389 of 23 June 2010 (*Regolamento Consob n. 17221 del 12 marzo 2010 recante disposizioni in materia di operazioni con parti correlate*). Then in September and November 2010 Consob issued two communications (DEM/10078683 of 24 September 2011 and DEM/10094530 of 15 November 2010) in order to better explain its discipline. The Regulation enactment has been preceded by two drafts issued for consultation (Consob, *Disciplina regolamentare di attuazione dell'Art 2391 bis Codice Civile in material di operazioni con parti correlate*, 9 April, 2008 and 3 August 2009; available at <www.consob.it>). The previous regulatory framework (that applied only to listed companies) did not require any special procedure for related-parties transactions; it mainly focused on disclosure issues: see P. Montalenti, 'Le operazioni con parti correlate' *Giurisprudenza Commerciale* (2011) I, p. 323; M. Miola, 'Le operazioni con parti correlate' in *Amministrazione e controllo nel diritto delle società. Liber Amicorum Antonio Piras*, see n. 94 above, p. 632 f. The Corporate Governance Code has been adopting progressively stronger measure for related-parties transactions. See generally Assonime, *La disciplina della Consob in material di operazioni con parti correlate*, Circ. nr. 38 of 6 December 2010, p. 9 ff. (available at <www.assonime.it>).

[106] The aforementioned CSFA rules regard transparency and accounting information duties and will be explained in the next paragraphs.

public. Article 2391-bis was introduced by the 2003 company law reform with wording echoing Article 9 of the Corporate Governance Code. However the wording is more general and is mainly focused on the standards of procedural and substantive fairness, which in turn derives from US jurisprudence on related party transactions.[107]

Article 2391-bis of the Civil Code requires Consob to adopt measures ensuring that related parties transactions are performed in a transparent manner and in compliance with substantive and procedural fairness.[108] Moreover, the control organ (board of auditors, supervisory board or audit committee) must supervise compliance with the relevant criteria and report to the AGM. Two types of information flows are included in the new Regulation: There must be disclosure within the company by directors who must take an informed decision, and there must be disclosure to the market through disclosure by the company to investors.[109] The definitions of 'related party' and 'transactions with a related party' (Annex I) are derived from IAS 24.[110]

a) Procedures

Each company must adopt detailed procedures to ensure the transparency and fairness of related party transactions (Art. 4 of the Regulation). These procedures must identify the transactions of greater importance and the cases of exemption.[111] Furthermore, they must establish the time and manner of the information to the board. The procedures are adopted by the board of directors (in the two-tier system, by the management board) on the advice of a special committee of independent directors[112] or of one of the existing committees, provided that its

---

[107] Montalenti, see n. 105 above, p. 321.

[108] Assonime, see n. 105 above, p. 11. About Art 2391-bis Civil Code see M. Ventoruzzo, 'Comment of Art 2391-bis' in Marchetti et al (eds.) n. 33 above, p. 501 ff.

[109] D. Regoli, 'L'informazione delle e sulle operazioni con parti correlate, in V. Cariello (ed.) *Le operazioni con parti correlate*, Giuffrè, Milan (2011) p. 141. As Regoli argues, there is also a third aspect regarding information: intra group information. On this topic, see P. Ferro-Luzzi, 'Le operazioni con parti correlate infragruppo' in Cariello (ed.) in this note p. 3.

[110] It is the version provided by Art 6, Regulation (EC) No. 1606/2002: see Assonime, see n. 105 above, p. 12.

[111] Art 4/8 provides that entities with a controlling interest and any other entities specified in Article 114/5 CSFA (members of the board of directors, the members of the internal control body, managers and persons who hold a major holding pursuant to Article 120 CSFA or who are parties to a shareholders' agreement pursuant to Article 122 CSFA) that are related-parties of the companies, shall provide them with the necessary information to enable identification of related-parties and transactions with the same.

[112] In case of two-tier system the committee can be comprised of independent management and supervisory board members (Art 4/3).

members are all independent.[113] The procedures must be published on the issuer's website. Also any dissenting opinion (expressed by either a board or committee member or by an independent expert) must be disclosed.[114] The procedures must be made known by the board in the annual management report (Art. 2391-bis Civil Code).

The Regulation foresees two types of procedures depending on whether the transactions are of greater or lesser importance under a given threshold (Art. 7 and 8 of the Regulation).[115] For transactions of greater importance, the committee must consist solely of independent and unrelated directors. Moreover, the committee (or one or more of its members) must be involved in the negotiation of the relevant transaction and receive timely information on the same. The committee should also have the possibility of requesting additional information and providing comments to the executive directors and the officers in charge of the transaction.[116] For transactions of less importance, the committee should include non-executive and unrelated directors, with a majority of independents.[117] In addition, the committee and the board or other body delegated to approve the transaction must be provided with full and appropriate disclosure in advance (Art. 7/1 of the Regulation).[118]

For both types of transactions the committee is entitled to be assisted, at the expense of the company, by one or more independent experts of its own choice.

---

[113] Assonime, see n. 105 above, p. 60 f; M. Richter jr, Regole delle procedure per le operazioni con parti correlate e modificazioni statutarie conseguenti, in V. Cariello (ed.) see n. 109 above, p. 48.

[114] Consob, Com. 10094530 of 15 November 2010, see n. 105 above.

[115] The operations are considered of greater importance when one of the following ratios is greater than 5% (Annex 3): equivalent-value relevance ratio; asset relevance ratio; or liabilities relevance ratio.

Procedures may define criteria for identifying transactions for smaller amounts to which the provisions of the Regulation shall not apply (Art 13/2). This option aims to exempt those related-parties operations that prime facie do not present any dangerous situation for investors: see Consob, Com. 10078683 of 24 September 2011, see n. 105 above, p. 19.

[116] Despite the different terms adopted by Art 7 and Art 8, information delivery is the same for transactions of both greater and lesser importance: see Regoli, n. 109 above, p. 151.

[117] Whenever at least two unrelated and independent directors (in transactions of lesser importance) are not available (three in transactions of greater importance), specific internal controls—equivalent to those set forth as if the minimum number of independent directors were available—shall be established to protect the substantial correctness of the transaction (Art 7/1d). Statutory board, an independent expert (only for transactions of lesser importance) or the available independent directors (only for transactions of greater importance) represent equivalent control: see Consob, Com., 10078683, n. 105 above, 15.1 and 15.2. Assonime, see n. 105 above, p. 71, criticises the involvement of the control body into managerial issues.

[118] Regoli, see n. 109 above, p. 147 f, argues that there should be a person responsible for information delivery (who should be the CEO or the general manager).

The committee should in both cases express its opinion on the company's interest to the relevant transaction and on the substantive fairness of the transaction.[119] However, the committee's opinion is binding on the board only for transactions of greater importance, and the board can only approve those transactions after it has received a positive opinion by the committee.[120] The procedure that can be followed to overcome a negative opinion of the committee (Art. 8/2 and 13/3 of the Regulation) is called 'whitewash'. The board may go on with the related party transaction notwithstanding disagreement by the committee, provided that the general meeting passes a resolution authorising the transaction at issue with the vote of the majority of the unrelated shareholders (whitewash). This whitewash mechanism must be set out in the articles of association.[121]

In all cases, the resolution approving the transaction must offer adequate reasons in writing on the interest of the company in the relevant transaction and its substantive fairness.[122] Similar rules apply to transactions requiring either the approval or the authorisation of the general meeting (Art. 11 of the Regulation). All related party transactions must be fully disclosed, at least quarterly, to the board of directors and the board of statutory auditors.

As to the two-tier system, Annex 2 of the Regulation includes special criteria, partly diverging from those examined above.[123] The committee is formed within the supervisory board, except in cases where the management board includes one or more independent members. However, the committee's opinion is always non-binding, as all types of transactions fall within the competence of the manage-

---

[119] According to Assonime, see n. 105 above, p. 67, the committee's valuation takes into account both the procedural fairness and the decision itself and does not involve the whole board as Art 2380-bis Civil Code requires. Assonime criticises this solution, because, especially in transactions of greater importance, the decision to approve or reject an operation is up to only some of the board members (those who are part of the committee). In contrast, Montalenti 'Le operazioni con parti correlate', see n. 105 above, p. 331, affirms that the committee can only check the procedural fairness but because of the business judgment rule it is not entitled either to make any suggestion or to value the transaction's convenience.

[120] In transactions of greater importance, companies are allowed to apply other methods of transaction approval (different from the committee approval) that ensure a decisive role by a majority of independent and unrelated directors (Art 8/1c). For example the decision can be made by the board provided particular majority requirements are met in which the vote of the independent directors is determinant: see Assonime, see n. 105 above, p. 79.

[121] P. Abbadessa, 'Assemblea ed operazioni con parti correlate (prime riflessioni)' in Cariello (ed.) see n. 109 above, p. 19; Assonime, see n. 105 above, p. 86; Montalenti, see n. 105 above, p. 333.

[122] In transactions of lesser importance, in case that the transaction has been concluded by a director or officer as bodies delegated by the board pursuant Art 7, the procedure can request him to draw the reasons upon which the decision was made: Assonime, see n. 105 above, p. 73.

[123] See V. Cariello, 'Operazioni con parti correlate e sistema dualistico' in Cariello (ed.), see n. 109 above, p. 61.

ment board. Should the management board approve the transaction after receiving a negative opinion from the committee, the transaction is subsequently put to a non-binding resolution of the general meeting to be convened without delay.

b) Exemptions

There are several exemptions. Some apply automatically, while others depend on a decision by the issuer. Moreover, exemptions relate to procedures, transparency and accounting. An example of an automatic exemption involves directors' remuneration, whenever directors' fees are fixed by the general meeting and do not include financial instruments. Cases of optional exemption are the remuneration policy for directors based on financial instruments approved by the general meeting; transactions involving smaller amounts; regular transactions completed in market-equivalent or standard terms (subject to some of the transparency and the whole accounting information duties), and transactions within a group, provided that other related parties do not have a significant interest in the company which is a counterparty to the transaction.[124]

c) Disclosure Duties

In the event of transactions of greater importance, the company must publish an information document after the transaction has been approved (Art. 5/1 of the Regulation). If the transaction is also price sensitive, the issuer must disclose further information about the related party's name and nature and the procedure adopted. Moreover, the issuer should disclose whether an exemption applies and whether the transaction was approved despite the contrary opinion of independent directors (Art. 6).

d) Banks

Special rules apply to banks, including non-listed banks. After having launched two consultation documents about banks and bank groups' risky activities and conflicts of interest,[125] in December 2011 the Bank of Italy adopted a Regulation

---

[124] Montalenti, see n. 105 above, p. 339 affirms that this exemption should not be allowed only if the related party to the issuer is significant not in general, but only if it is significant to a certain operation. Ferro-Luzzi, see n. 109 above, p. 9 ff. points out the differences between the companies' group discipline and related-party transactions discipline; M Maugeri, 'Le opera-zioni con parti correlate nei gruppi societari' *Rivista di diritto commerciale* (2010) I, p. 889 ff. who describes the several combinations that can arise between the holding and its subsidiaries in managing related parties transactions.

[125] Banca d'Italia, *Documento per la consultazione disposizioni in materia di attività di rischio e conflitti di interesse delle banche e dei gruppi bancari nei confronti di soggetti collegati*, June 2011. The first consultation document *Attività di rischio e conflitti di interesse delle banche e dei gruppi bancari nei confronti di soggetti collegati* was published in May 2010.

concerning related party transactions.[126] The aim is to align banking regulation with Consob Regulation on related party transactions. However, some of the proposed criteria concern prudential supervision of banks, touching upon issues not covered by Consob. Among the most important differences between the regulation by Consob and by the Bank of Italy is that the latter does not provide that the opinion of the committee is binding on the board in approving transactions of greater importance.

e) Enforcement

The enforcement of the new regime on related party transactions remains an open issue. Indeed, there is no specific sanction for the breach of the new Regulation by an issuer, except for the beach of disclosure rules.[127] However, non-compliance with procedural rules may have an impact on civil liability and it may provide a reversal of the burden of proof concerning the fairness of the transaction. In particular, a court could place this burden on the defendant directors requiring them to prove that the transaction was fair despite non-compliance with procedural rules.[128]

3.1.3.3. Corporate Opportunities

Article 2391/5 of the Civil Code provides that directors are liable for losses which may be incurred by the company for conduct by directors from the use for their own benefit, or the benefit of third parties, of data, information and business opportunities known in connection with their appointment (misuse of their corporate opportunities). Nevertheless, the law does not offer a definition of 'corporate opportunities', and has left this definition to the courts and scholars.[129]

---

[126] Bank of Italy, 'Attività di rischio e conflitti di interesse nei confronti di soggetti collegati', Section V, Chapter V, Circolar n. 263/2006 (*New regulations for the prudential supervision of banks*) as amended on 12 December 2011 (available at <www.bancaditalia.it/vigilanza/normativa/norm_bi/circ-reg/vigprud>).

[127] Montalenti, see n. 105 above, p. 340.

[128] Corte di Cassazione, 24 August 2004, n. 16707, *Giurisprudenza Commerciale* (2005) II, p. 246, with comment of D. Monaci.

[129] F. Barachini, 'L'appropriazione delle corporate opportunities' in Abbadessa and Portale (eds.), see n. 34 above, p. 607 ff.; Bonelli, see n. 33 above, p. 155; F. Bonelli, La *responsabilità degli amministratori di società per azioni*, Giuffrè, Milan (1992) p. 93; L. Solimena, *Il conflitto d'interessi dell'amministratore di società per azioni nelle operazioni con la società amministrata*, Giuffrè, Milan (1999), p. 151 ff.; M. Ventoruzzo, 'Comment of Art 2391-bis' in Marchetti et al (eds.), see n. 33 above, p. 490 ff.

3.1.3.4. Inside Information[130]

Article 181 CFSA defines inside information as 'information (i) of a precise nature, (ii) which has not been made public, (iii) is related, directly or indirectly, to one or more issuers of financial instruments or one or more financial instruments and (iv) is likely to have a significant effect on the prices of those financial instruments if made public'. Inside information has to be disclosed to Consob and the public without delay (Art. 114, in accordance with the procedure foreseen by Consob Regulation on issuers (Art. 66 ff). The exploitation of inside information is punishable as insider trading with criminal sanctions (Art. 184) and administrative sanctions (Art. 187-bis).

3.1.3.5. Takeover Situations[131]

Italy has implemented the Takeover Directive (2004/25/CE) in three steps. The first step towards implementation was under the Prodi government, which made both board neutrality and breakthrough rules mandatory for all listed companies. The second step was under the Berlusconi government, which reversed this law in favour of pure optionality—wherein the rules would only apply if the companies opted into their effect. This reversal was officially motivated by the global financial crisis of 2009 and the need to protect corporations from takeovers. The third step was also made by the Berlusconi government with Legislative Decree n. 146/2009. This reintroduced board neutrality as a default rule—a rule which listed companies can exclude in their charter.

Currently, Article 104 CFSA prohibits managers from undertaking actions that may result in frustration of the bid, other than the search for other bids, unless duly authorised by a resolution of either the ordinary or extraordinary share-

---

[130]	F. Annunziata, *La disciplina del mercato mobiliare*, Giappichelli, Turin (2010), p. 396 ff.; R. Costi, *Il mercato mobiliare*, Giappichelli, Turin (2008), p. 286.

[131]	See R. Costi and L. Enriques, *Il mercato mobiliare*, in G. Cottino (ed.) *Trattato di diritto commerciale*, VII, CEDAM, Padua (2004), p. 114; L. Enriques, 'A dieci anni dal Testo Unico della Finanza: il ruolo delle Autorità di vigilanza' *Giornale di diritto amministrativo* (2009), p. 329 ff., arguing that abolition of the board neutrality rule could remove a disincentive for entrepreneurs to open their companies to the stock market); G. Ferrarini and G. Miller, 'c Simple Theory of Takeover Regulation in the United States and Europe', *Cornell International Law Journal* (2009) 42(3), p. 301 ff., and *Rivista delle Società* (2010), p. 680 ff.; M. Gatti, *Opa e struttura del mercato societario*, Giuffrè, Milan (2004), p. 210; C. Mosca, 'Comment of Art 104 CSFA', in P. Marchetti, L.A. Bianchi (eds.) *La disciplina delle società quotate nel Testo Unico della finanza, D. Lgs. 24 febbraio 1998, n. 58*, Giuffrè, Milan (1999), p. 259; F. Venturini, ' Milan, concerto e derivati nelle ultime modifiche alla disciplina OPA' *Le Società* (2010), p. 433. See, also for criticism, M. Ventoruzzo, 'Un nuovo giro di giostra per la passivity rule', *La Voce*, 6 October 2009 (available at <www.lavoce.info>).

holders' meeting.[132] This rule applies from the time the bid is notified to Consob to the time the bid is completed or expires. Nevertheless, directors, management board members, supervisory directors and general managers are responsible for all actions taken despite the approval of the general meeting. The articles of association may deviate, in total or in part, from this provision, but the company must notify the relevant articles to Consob and to the competent authorities in the Member States where their securities are either admitted to listing on a regulated market or where admission to listing has been requested. The same provisions must also be promptly disclosed to the public.

Under Article 104-bis, the articles of association can adopt the neutrality rule foreseen by the European Directive. As a result, during the bid period limitations on the transfer of securities foreseen in the articles of association have no effect on the bidder. Likewise, in cases where a shareholders' meeting is called under Article 104, limitations on voting rights set out in the articles or in the shareholders' agreement have no force or effect on the bidder. If the bidder acquires 75% of the voting shares, limitations on voting rights do not apply at a shareholders' meeting following the close of the bid called to amend the articles or remove or replace directors.

Article 104-ter incorporates the reciprocity rules set out by the European Directive. As a result, both the neutrality rule and the breakthrough rule, even when applicable in principle, do not apply if the bidder is not subject to the same or equivalent provisions.

However, most Italian firms are family controlled and therefore subject to a low risk of unfriendly takeovers. In general, concentrated ownership is an effective pre-bid defence, which may explain why Italy, at least initially, was ready to adopt both board neutrality and the breakthrough rules.[133] Indeed, most potential targets had no reason to fear these rules and therefore did not mobilise sufficient opposition against them, which left potential bidders sufficient room for political action. Subsequent reforms which relaxed the previous regime were motivated by the willingness to protect some large companies governed by controlling minorities (including the state) from unwanted takeovers, which were made easier by the fall in stock market values after the global financial crisis.

3.1.4. *Institutional Investors*

Although the Italian legal environment can be considered as more favourable to institutional investor activism than that of other European countries—especially after the legal changes prompted by the 1998 financial markets reform and the

---

[132] On the rationale of this provision, which was adopted for the first time in 1998 in anticipation of the European Directive, see G. Ferrarini, 'A chi la difesa delle società bersaglio?' *Mercato, concorrenza, regole* (2000) p. 140 ff. and Ferrarini, see n. 92 above, p. 463 ff.

[133] Ferrarini and Miller, see n. 131 above, p. 323.

implementation of directive 2007/36/EC on shareholders' rights[134]—institutional investors are not active in the governance of Italian companies. Indeed, both Italian and foreign institutional investors[135] tend to have a low voting turnout and mainly rely on 'exit' rather than 'voice'.[136] This phenomenon may derive, in part, from the predominance of mutual fund management companies belonging to banking groups and from the ownership structure of Italian listed companies (generally controlled by block-holders).[137]

Institutions' voting rights depend on the type of portfolio management undertaken. In the case of individual portfolio management, the power to vote for the financial instruments included in the portfolio may be conferred on the investment firm, bank or asset manager by means of a written proxy for each general meeting, in compliance with the limits and procedures established by the Ministry of the Treasury, Budget and Economic Planning through regulation (Art. 24/1 CFSA).[138] In the case of collective portfolio management, asset management companies and SICAVs exercise the voting rights attached to the financial instruments under management on behalf of investors, except as otherwise stated by law (Arts. 40/2 and 50). Furthermore, asset management companies and SICAVs shall adopt and publish in their prospectuses an efficient voting strategy for participating companies, so as to protect their investors (Art. 32 of Consob – Bank of Italy Regulation of 29 October 2007[139]).

---

[134] Implemented by Legislative Decree n. 27 of 27 January 2010 (Decreto Legislativo n. 27 del 27 gennaio 2010, *Attuazione della direttiva 2007/36/CE, relativa all'esercizio di alcuni diritti degli azionisti di società quotate*).

[135] P. Santella, E. Baffi, C. Drago and D. Lattuca, 'A comparative analysis of the legal obstacles to institutional investors activism in Europe and in the US' (2009) (available at <http://papers.ssrn.com/sol3/papers.cfm?abstract_id=1137941>) shows that only 13% of the investors in Italian listed companies are represented by foreign investors.

[136] See V. Calandra Buonaura, 'Intermediari finanziari e corporate governance' *Giurisprudenza Commerciale* (2009) I, p. 876, and *Id.,* 'Le fondazioni bancarie come investitori di lungo periodo', *Banca Impresa Società* (2010) p. 375.

[137] See Calandra Buonaura, 'Intermediari finanziari e corporate governance', see n. 136 above and *Id.,* 'Le fondazioni bancarie come investitori di lungo periodo' see n. 136 above; M. Bianchi and L. Enriques, 'Corporate Governance in Italy after the 1998 reform: what role for institutional investors?', *Quaderni di Finanza Consob* (2001) n. 23; Santella et al, see n. 135 above, p. 16.

[138] Ministry of the Treasury, Budget and Economic Planning Decree n. 470 of 11 November 1998 (Ministro del Tesoro del Bilancio e della Programmazione Economica, decreto n. 470 del 11 novembre 1998, *Regolamento recante norme per l'individuazione dei limiti e le modalità dell'esercizio dei diritti di voto degli strumenti finanziari in gestione presso imprese di investimento, banche, società di gestione del risparmio o agenti di cambio*).

[139] *Regolamento Consob-Banca d'Italia del 29 Ottobre 2007 in materia di organizzazione e procedure degli intermediari che prestano servizi di investimento o di gestione collettiva del risparmio, adottato dalla Banca d'Italia e dalla Consob con provvedimento del 29 ottobre 2007*

cont. ...

3.1.5. Remuneration

The remuneration of directors is central to the corporate governance discussion, particularly after the global financial crisis. The remuneration contract is typically regarded as a remedy for the agency costs of dispersed ownership, but may also protect minority shareholders against the abuses by controlling shareholders in blockholding governance.[140] According to Assonime, the average remuneration of listed companies' directors was €219 thousand in 2010, down 7% from 2009 (€235 thousand) due to a bonus drop (from €34 thousand to €21 thousand), connected to the negative scenario in previous years.[141] In 2011 the average remuneration rose to €226 thousand.[142] Assonime also shows that remuneration for office (Chairman, CEO) amounts to approx. 53% of directors' total compensation and 'other fees' account for approximately 36%, while bonuses are 10% of the total (down from 14% in 2009, a result no doubt influenced by the economic crisis) and non-monetary benefits are almost negligible (1%).[143]

e successivamente modificato con atti congiunti Banca d'Italia-Consob del 9 maggio 2012 e 25 luglio 2012.

[140] For an analysis of the executive pay contract in the context of dispersed and block holding systems see G. Ferrarini and N. Moloney, 'Executive Remuneration in the EU: The Context for Reform', *Oxford Review of Economic Policy* (2005) 21, p. 304; G. Ferrarini, N. Moloney and Ungureanu, *Understanding directors' pay in Europe, a comparative and empirical analysis* (2009) (available at <http://ssrn.com/abstract=1418463>).

[141] The average remuneration varies considerably according to firm size (it is €434,000 in FTSE Mib) and—to a lesser extent—to industry (it is €299,000 in financial versus €200,000 in non-financial firms). The average compensation also varies according to the directors' role: the 326 directors qualified as Managing Directors get the highest average remuneration (€672,000); Chairmen who are not also MDs (approx. 214 people) receive on average €555,000, whereas other executive directors (approx. 225 directors) and non-executive members of the executive committees (approx. 58 people) receive, on average, €340,000 and €131,000 respectively. The majority of directors (approx. 1,736 people) belongs to categories (non-executive and independent) receiving, on average, a remuneration lower than € 80,000. Furthermore, the average compensation declined in almost all categories (except non-executives, whose remuneration increased 8%) and the higher drop involved executive directors (the remuneration of MDs decreased 9% from 2009).

[142] Assonime, see above, n. 5 p. 89.

[143] According to Assonime, *An analysis of the compliance with the Italian corporate governance code year 2009* (2010), p. 13, the recourse to stock-based incentive plans is rather frequent: 123 companies (44% of the total) have at least one such plan in place; unsurprisingly, stock-based incentive plans are more frequent among large firms (86% in S&P) and in the financial sector (58%, while only 42% of non-financial firms have adopted such plans). Stock option plans account for 80% of the total; the rest are stock grants (40 cases) and phantom stock options or Stock Appreciation Rights (SARs: 25 cases). The choice of a particular instrument is arguably connected to the differential tax treatment (more favourable to stock options, at least until recently). Stock grants are more frequent in the financial sector (47%; 10% amongst non-financial firms) and for larger firms (41% in S&P companies; lower than 10% elsewhere). Such

cont. ...

Article 2389 of the Civil Code provides that directors' remuneration is fixed either at the time of their first appointment by the founders or subsequently by the shareholders' general meeting. It also specifies that the remuneration of directors for corporate offices foreseen by the articles (such as the compensation for the chairman and for the managing director) is decided upon by the board of directors following consultation with the auditors.

Under the new Article 6 of the Corporate Governance Code, executive remuneration should be fixed at an amount sufficient to attract, maintain and motivate directors endowed with the professional skills necessary to manage the issuer successfully.[144] Article 6 also recommends setting an adequate balance between fixed and variable remuneration and suggests that the latter should be linked to the issuer's economic performance and possibly to non-economic goals indicated in advance by the board of directors.[145] The Code also provides that non-executive directors should not be paid a remuneration related to the economic results of the issuer and should not be assigned either stock options or equity based remuneration plans, unless it is so decided by the shareholders' meeting, which should also give the relevant reasons.[146] The remuneration should be proportional to the engagement required from each director, taking into account participation in board committees, if any. The Code also recommends the creation of a remuneration committee, made up of non-executive directors, the majority of which are independent (see above 2.2.2(d).[147] Such committee also plays an important role in the remuneration process, as it formulates proposals to

plans are almost always based on common stock of the listed company. The option to get the shares through a buy-back is provided (for at least one plan) by 48% of the companies (it is more frequent in larger firms).

[144] Art 6 Corporate Governance Code as amended by the Corporate Governance Committee of Borsa Italiana S.p.A., in order to implement the recommendations issued by the EU Commission: 2009/385/EC complementing recommendations 2004/913/EC and 2005/162/EC as regards the regime for the remuneration of directors of listed companies, and 2009/384/EC on remuneration policies in the financial services sector. The new text of Art 7 also aims to guarantee more transparency as to remuneration of managing directors.

[145] See Art 6 P.2 of the Corporate Governance Code. The Code also provides for the establishment of upper limits for variable components of remuneration; that the non-variable component shall be sufficient to reward the director when the variable component was not delivered because of the failure to achieve the performance objectives specified by the Board of Directors; that such performance objectives shall be predetermined, measurable and linked to the creation of value for the shareholders in the medium-long term; that the payment of a significant portion of the variable component of the remuneration shall be deferred for an appropriate period of time and that termination payments, which should not exceed a fixed amount or fixed number of years of annual remuneration, shall not be paid if the termination is due to inadequate performance.

[146] See Art 6.C.2 of the Corporate Governance Code.

[147] See Art 6.P.3 of the Corporate Governance Code.

the board with regard to executive directors' compensation policy and periodically evaluates the criteria for establishing their remuneration.[148] However, it is the board that should define the general remuneration policy concerning executive directors, approve the annual remuneration report and submit it to a shareholders' vote at the annual general meeting.

Issuers are asked to voluntarily apply, subject to comply-or-explain, the principles and related application criteria contained in new Article 6 by the end of 2011, disclosing the relevant information in the report on corporate governance to be published in 2012. Nevertheless, the Rules of the Market issued by the Italian Stock Exchange[149] provide that one of the admission requirements to listing on the Star Sector (reserved to issuers with high profile corporate governance and disclosure systems) is the proper compliance with Article 6 on directors' remuneration. In practice, remuneration policies are generally described in a section of the annual report on corporate governance and ownership structure, which must also specifically provide detailed information on agreements between companies and directors envisaging indemnities for the event of resignation or dismissal without just cause, or termination of the employment contract as a result of a takeover bid.[150]

Furthermore, Article 123-ter CFSA[151] recently implemented the European Commission's recommendations on executives' pay, requiring that a 'report on remuneration policies for directors' be approved by the board and disclosed to the market annually. This report must be drafted according to the criteria stated by para 3 and 4 of the same Article,[152] as further specified by Consob (the relevant

---

[148] More specifically, Article 6.C.5 of the Corporate Governance Code provides that the Remuneration Committee shall periodically evaluate the adequacy, overall consistency and actual application of the general policy adopted for the remuneration of executive directors, other directors who cover particular offices and key management personnel. It also submits to the Board of Directors proposals for the remuneration of executive directors and other directors who cover particular offices as well as for the identification of performance objectives related to the variable component of that remuneration. It monitors the implementation of decisions adopted by the Board of Directors and verifies, in particular, the actual achievement of performance objectives.

[149] See Art 2.2.3m of the Rules of the Market, managed by The Italian Stock Exchange (Borsa italiana s.p.a.), adopted by the shareholders general meeting on 16 July 2010, approved by Consob in Resolution 17467 of 7 September 2010 and in force since 8 November 2010.

[150] See Art 123-bis, para 1, i CFSA.

[151] This article has been introduced by the Legislative Decree n. 259 of 30 December 2010 (Decreto Legislativo del 30 dicembre 2010, n. 259, *Recepimento delle Raccomandazioni della Commissione europea 2004/913/CE e 2009/385/CE in materia di remunerazione degli amministratori delle società quotate*), implementing the European Commission recommendations n. 2004/913/CE and 2009/385/CE on directors' remuneration in listed companies.

[152] More specifically, para 3 provides that the annual 'report on remuneration policies of directors' must include the company's policy on the remuneration of the members of the

cont. ...

regulation is still to be issued). The annual general meeting must vote on these remuneration policies, but its vote is not binding for the company (para 6 of Art. 123-ter).[153] In addition, Article 114-bis establishes that compensation plans based on financial instruments in favour of directors, executives and employees should be approved by the general meeting and publicly disclosed every year, in accordance with the terms and conditions envisaged in Article 123-ter. Consob regulates disclosure of further information concerning the implementation of these plans (see Art. 84-bis and 84-quater Regulation on issuers).

Therefore, the remuneration governance matrix also includes the shareholders' voice. On the one hand, the shareholders are engaged in the pay-setting process with respect to equity-based compensation, which needs their prior approval; on the other hand, the 'say on pay' mechanism, supported by effective disclosure, engages the shareholders in the monitoring of remuneration policies, and is an effective remuneration governance mechanism.[154]

With regard to the two-tier system, the Civil Code provides that, unless otherwise foreseen by the articles, supervisory boards set the remuneration of the members of management boards.

Banks have been subject to special rules concerning executive pay since 2008.[155] Recently, the Bank of Italy issued a new regulation implementing the provisions on remuneration policies of Directive 2010/76/EC (CRD III), which in turn reflect the international principles and standards fixed by the Financial Stability Board.[156] On the one hand, such rules aim to reduce directors' incentives

---

administrative bodies, with reference to at least the following year, and the procedures used to adopt and implement this policy. Moreover, according to para 4, the second section of the Report must provide an analytical explanation of the remuneration effectively paid or in any case attributed to such directors, in nominative form for the members of the boards of directors and auditors and for the general managers and in aggregate form for managers with strategic responsibilities.

[153] See Consob Communication n. DEM/11012984 of 24 February 2011, *Requests of disclosure pursuant to Article 114, paragraph 5 of Italian Legislative Decree no. 58 of 24 February 1998 on indemnities in the case of early termination – Recommendations on succession planning and disclosure of remuneration as established by Art 78 of Regulation n. 11971 of 1 May 1999 and subsequent amendments (Regulation on issuers)* (available at <www.consob.it>). More specifically, the Commission intervened on a temporary basis on some areas considered as particularly sensitive and which are already concerned by current regulation, in order to improve transparency on remuneration at the time of the shareholders' meetings called to approve the financial statements for 2010. Such action aims to encourage better information to the public on indemnities due in the event or early termination and on the disclosure of remunerations as requested by Art 78 of the Consob Regulation on issuers.

[154] Ferrarini, Moloney and Ungureanu, see n. 140 above, p. 11 ff.

[155] Bank of Italy, *Supervisory Provisions Concerning Bank's Organization and Corporate Governance* of 4 March 2008, see n. 23 above.

[156] Bank of Italy, *Provisions on remuneration and incentive policies and practices concerning Banks and Banking Groups* of 31 March 2011, see n. 24 above. In order to

cont. ...

to take excessive risk and to align their compensation with prudent risk-management practices; on the other, they also focus on detailed methods that must be used to provide an effective disclosure and shareholders' supervisory oversight of the adopted remuneration policies.

Insurance companies are not yet subject to a uniform European regime regarding executive pay, comparable to that now in force for banks. Nevertheless ISVAP, the Italian Supervisory Institute for Private and Collective Insurances,[157] recently issued a regulation reflecting both the European Commission's recommendations and the international principles on sound compensation practices.[158] Not only do such provisions describe the decision-making process regarding the adoption of remuneration policies, which must involve the shareholders' meeting, the board of directors and the remuneration committee, but they also provide more specific criteria to establish directors' compensation and to ensure the balance between fixed and variable remuneration.

3.2. Board and Stakeholders

3.2.1. Board and Employees/Labour Co-determination

Italian firms do not have labour representatives either on boards of directors or supervisory boards (see 2.2.1(b)).

3.2.2. Board and Creditors

Directors have a duty to preserve corporate assets, which are the main guarantee for creditors, and are liable for damages deriving from breach of this duty (Art. 2394/1 Civil Code). Creditors can bring the relevant action before a court whenever the corporate assets prove insufficient to satisfy their claims (Art. 2394/2). In practice, directors are sued for damages only when a company becomes insolvent.[159] In fact, the insolvency receiver generally brings a similar action under Article 146 of Bankruptcy Law (Royal Decree of 16 March 1942, n. 267).

---

implement such Provisions, the Ministry of Economy and Finance Decree n. 676 of 27 July 2011 (Decreto del Ministro dell'Economia e delle Finanzia n. 676 del 27 luglio 2011, *Sistemi di remunerazione e incentivazione nelle banche e nei gruppi bancari*) allows Bank of Italy to issue more specific regulations concerning the public disclosure of the remuneration and incentive systems adopted by banks and banking groups (so-called 'Third Pillar').

[157] ISVAP is replaced by IVASS as from 1 January 2013. See n. 25 above.

[158] Regulation n. 39 of 9 June 2011, *Regulation on remuneration policies in Insurance Companies* (Regolamento n. 39 del 9 giugno 2011 relativo alle politiche di remunerazione delle imprese di assicurazione) (available at <www.isvap.it>).

[159] See Bonelli, see n. 33 above, p. 204; Bonelli, see n. 129 above, p. 184 and 212; Campobasso, see n. 59 above, p. 384.

3.2.3. *Board and Other Stakeholders*

The prevailing scholarly opinion supports a contractual view of the corporation, which identifies the company's interest with the interests of shareholders, mainly considered from a long-term perspective. Nevertheless, specific provisions also establish directors' duties to creditors (see Art. 2394 Civil Code on liability to creditors), other companies in the group (Art. 2497 ff) and investors in general (disclosure duties foreseen by CFSA for listed companies).[160]

Stakeholders other than creditors are not specifically protected under company law.[161] However, the articles of associations, labour agreements and ethics codes[162] (adopted by the board for directors and employees of the company) may take the interests of other constituencies into account.[163] Moreover, environmental concerns are taken care of under general private law (ie. Art. 844 Civil Code), criminal law (ie. Art. 674 Criminal Code) and specific laws including the Environmental Code.[164]

---

[160] See R. Costi, 'Relazione di sintesi', in AA.VV., *L'interesse sociale tra valorizzazione del capitale e protezione degli stakeholders. In ricordo di Pier Giusto Jaeger*, Giuffrè, Milan (2010) p. 189; F. Denozza, 'L'interesse sociale tra "coordinamento" e "cooperazione"' *ibid.*, p. 41; P. Montalenti, 'Interesse sociale e amministratori' *ibid.*, p. 81; R. Sacchi, 'L'interesse sociale nelle operazioni straordinarie' *ibid.*, p. 152; R. Weigmann, 'I doveri di collaborazione degli azionisti' *ibid.*, p. 63; G. Ferrarini, see n. 92 above, p. 462; L. Van den Berghe, *International standardisation of good corporate governance*, Kluwer Academic Publishers, Dordrecht (1999) p. 42. S. Rossi, 'Luci e ombre dei codici etici d'impresa', *Rivista delle Società* (2008) p. 23 ff., highlights that codes of conduct of some large companies set forth provisions for protecting stakeholders. However, it may be inappropriate to speak of stakeholders' rights, as stakeholders are not entitled to enforce the relevant provisions: Denozza, 'L'interesse sociale tra "coordinamento" e "cooperazione"' in this note p. 39.

[161] See F. Denozza, see n. 160 above, p. 41.

[162] See P. Montalenti, see n. 160 above, p. 99.

[163] See *Governance e responsabilità sociale, Analisi sull'applicazione dei codici etici d'impresa in Italia*, in I quaderni di Unipolis (2009; available at <www.fondazioneunipolis.org/wp-content/uploads/2011/07/Ricerca-Codici-Etici.pdf>).

[164] Legislative decree n. 153 of 3 March 2006, as amended by the Legislative Decree n. 128 of 29 June 2010 (Decreto Legislativo n. 153 del 6 marzo 2006,. *Modifiche al Decreto del Presidente della Repubblica n. 495 del 16 dicembre 1992,*). See also European Directive 2004/35/CE of the European Parliament and of the Council of 21 April 2004. For the analysis of the 'environmental liability action'. See also: U. Salanitro, *Il danno ambientale*, Aracne Editrice, Roma (2009); F. Giampietro, 'La responsabilità per danno all'ambiente in Italia: sintesi di leggi e giurisprudenza messe a confronto con la direttiva 2004/35/Ce e con il T.U. ambientale', *Rivista della giurisprudenza ambientale* (2006), p. 19 ff., p. 31 ff.

Furthermore, depositors at banks are protected under banking regulation, which also foresees discrete duties for directors aimed at assuring the stability of banks and the financial system.[165]

3.3. Changing Roles in Financial Distress

When a company is in financial distress, special duties arise for the board of directors.

i) When the share capital is reduced by more than one third as a result of losses, directors must call the shareholders' meeting without delay to take proper actions. A report on the financial situation of the company must be submitted to the meeting. If the losses are not reduced to less than one-third within the following fiscal year, the shareholders' meeting must reduce the company's capital (Art. 2446 Civil Code).

If the capital is reduced below the minimum amount required by law (€120.000), the board of directors must call a shareholders' meeting without delay. This meeting will resolve on the reduction of the share capital and the reintegration of the same to at least the minimum amount required by the law (Art. 2447), otherwise the company will be dissolved. In the case of dissolution, directors are jointly and severally liable for the damages incurred by the company, its members, creditors and third parties in the event of a delay or omission in taking the actions reported above.

ii) The Bankruptcy Law, introduced by the Royal Decree n. 267 of 16 March 1942 sets out the procedures directed to mitigate the financial distress of undertakings and avoid bankruptcy.[166] A company can submit a re-organisation plan, which also prevents the claw back of agreements, payments and warranties executed by the company in accordance with the same. Directors have to draw up the plan and carry out its provisions (Art. 67/3). A company can also make recourse to the preventive creditors' settlement procedure (Art. 160). In this case, directors stay in office, but a Commissioner is appointed by the Court. As an alternative, the company can file a debt restructuring plan which has to be approved by creditors representing at least 60% of the amount of credits and endorsed by the Court (Art. 182-bis).

---

[165] See Bank of Italy, TUB, Title VI; *Id.*, 'New regulations for the prudential supervision of banks', *Circular* n. 263/2006 (as lately amended); *Id.*, Supervisory bulletin n. 7 of July 2007, p. 3 (for the *compliance* function; available at <www.bancaditalia.it>); *Id.*, *Supervisory Provisions Concerning Bank's Organization and Corporate Governance* of 4 March 2008; *Id.*, *Final Remarks*, 31 May 2008, pp. 17–19 (available at <www.bancaditalia.it/interventi/inte gov/2008/cf/cf07/cf07_considerazioni_finali.pdf>); see also Consob – Bank of Italy Regulation of 29 October 2007, see n. 139 above.

[166] *Regio Decreto n. 267 del 16 marzo 1942, Disciplina del fallimento.*

4. Enforcement

4.1. Courts

4.1.1. *Personal Liability Claims*

a) *Directors' Liability*

Directors can be held personally liable towards the company (Art. 2392-2393-2393-bis Civil Code), the creditors (Art. 2394) and one or more shareholders or third parties (Art. 2395). Article 2392, concerning the 'liability to the company', provides that directors are jointly and severally liable for damages deriving from non-compliance with their duties, except for functions vested solely on either the executive committee or one or more directors.[167] This does not mean that non-executive directors (delegated directors) are relieved from liability when individual directors are tasked with specific functions (such as delegated directors) or an executive committee is appointed. Rather, they shall be liable when at fault in performing their monitoring duties.[168]

---

[167] Bonelli, *Gli amministratori di S.P.A. dopo la riforma delle società*, see n. 33 above, p. 159 ff.; Campobasso, see n. 59 above, p. 377; De Nicola, see n. 33 above, p. 545; L. Nazzicone and S. Providenti, *Amministrazione e controlli nella società per azioni*, Giuffrè, Milan (2010) p. 267.

[168] See C. Malberti, F. Ghezzi and M. Ventoruzzo, 'Comment of Art 2380 Civile Code' in Marchetti et al (eds.), n. 33 above, p. 17. According to Art 2392 Civil Code, as formulated before the 2003 company law reform, directors were jointly and severally liable if they do not monitor the general course of the company's business (C. Di Nanni, *La vigilanza degli amministratori sulla gestione nella società per azioni*, Jovene, Naples (1992)). Courts enforced this rule strictly, especially in bankruptcy cases, often holding non-executive directors liable without properly investigating whether the latter had been in a position to ascertain and contrast directors' mismanagement (in particularly, financial statement manipulation: see M. Cassottana, *La responsabilità degli amministratori nel fallimento di s.p.a*, Giuffrè, Milan (1984)). Article 2392 Civil Code, as presently in force, does not include a duty to monitor the general course of the company's business (see above 2.1(b)). Some scholars argue therefore that the duty to monitor non-executive directors was repealed by the company law reform (Bonelli, *Gli amministratori di S.P.A. dopo la riforma delle società*, see n. 33 above, p. 159), while others state that a similar duty is still in force (G. Mosco, 'Comment of Art 2392 Civil Code' in G. Niccolini and A. Stagno d'Alcontres (eds.) *Società di capitali*, Jovene, Naples (2004) p. 601; V. Giorgi, *Libertà di informazione e dovere di riservatezza degli amministratori nei gruppi di società*, Giappichelli, Turin (2005) p. 34). Most scholars, however, acknowledge that non-executive directors, under their duty to act in an informed way, have to conduct further investigations if they believe that the information submitted to them by the executive directors is either insufficient or inadequate (Barachini, see n. 60 above, p. 153; Ferrarini, 'Controlli interni e strutture di governo societario', see n. 40 above, p. 25; Zamperetti, see n. 34 above, p. 331). This opinion was accepted by the Supreme Court of Cassation (criminal section): Corte di Cassazione, 22 September 2009, n. 36595, *Le Società* (2010) p. 386 with comment of

cont. ...

Moreover, directors are jointly and severally liable if, knowing of a conduct prejudicial to the company, they omit doing what is in their powers to prevent the same and either remove or reduce its harmful consequences (Art. 2392/2). The liability does not extend to the director who, not being at fault, has his dissent entered in the minute book of the board without delay and gives immediate notice in writing to the chairman of the board of auditors (Art. 2392/3). Specific instances of liability are those of directors breaching their duty not to compete with the company (Art. 2390/2), self-interested directors (Art. 2391/4) and directors appropriating corporate opportunities (Art. 2391/5).

In the two-tier system, members of the management board are subject to the same duties and liabilities as directors in the traditional system (see Art. 2409-undecies making reference to Art. 2394 and Art. 2395). Article 2409-terdecies provides that supervisory directors are jointly and severally liable with the management board's members for the damages caused by the wrongful acts or omissions of the latter, if the same damages could have been avoided through proper exercise of supervisory functions.

The rules foreseen for the traditional system are also applicable to the one-tier approach (Art. 2409-noviesdecies).

b) Liability Suits[169]

The company can sue directors for damages only following to a resolution of either the shareholders' meeting (Art. 2393/1 Civil Code) or the board of auditors (Art. 2393/3). Shareholders holding at least one-fifth of the share capital or one-fortieth in the case of companies making recourse to the capital markets (such as listed companies) can bring a derivative action against the company's directors (Art. 2393-bis).

In the two-tier system, the company can sue the members of the managing board for damages following to a resolution of either the shareholders' meeting (as provided by Art. 2393/1 cited above) or the supervisory board (Art. 2393/2). Moreover, the shareholders can sue the managing board's members for damages to the company by promoting a derivative action under Article 2393-bis.

A company can waive its right to sue directors for damages or settle similar claims, provided that the waiver or settlement is explicitly approved by the

---

P. Chiaraviglio; *Id.,* 24 May 2007, n. 23838, *Giurisprudenza commerciale* (2008) II, p. 369, with comment of R. Sacchi.

[169] Bonelli, *Gli amministratori di S.P.A. dopo la riforma delle società,* see n. 33 above, p. 191 ff.; Campobasso, see n. 59 above, p. 382 ff.; L. Enriques and F. Mucciarelli, 'L'azione di responsabilità da parte delle minoranze' in Abbadessa and Portale (eds.), see n. 34 above, p. 859; G. Ferrarini and P. Giudici, 'La legge sul risparmio, ovvero un pot-pourri della corporate governance' *Rivista delle Società* (2006), p. 573; Nazzicone and Providenti, *Amministrazione e controlli nella società per azioni,* see n. 167 above, p. 290; A. Picciau, 'Comment of Arts. 2392, 2393, 2393-bis, 2394-bis Civil Code', in Marchetti et al (eds.) see n. 33 above, p. 574.

shareholders' meeting and the relevant resolution is not voted down by a minority of shareholders representing at least either one-fifth of the share capital or one-twentieth in the companies making recourse to the capital markets, including listed companies (Art. 2393/6). Otherwise, the waiver or settlement has no legal effect. However, the shareholders' meeting cannot approve a waiver from liability *ex ante,* with reference to the future conduct of directors.[170] Similarly, an agreement by which shareholders undertook not to vote for a resolution authorising a liability suit against a director was declared null and void by the Court of Cassation,[171] for shareholders cannot dispose of a right of the company by private agreement.

According to Article 34 of Legislative Decree n. 5 of 17 January 2003,[172] liability actions against directors of listed companies cannot be subject to alternative dispute resolution, including arbitration.[173]

On the whole, the system just described does not perform satisfactorily for lack of effective enforcement. Civil suits are brought almost exclusively in the case of bankruptcy.[174] The introduction of the derivative suit has not led to significant changes yet (see below 4.1.3(b)). Also public enforcement is often ineffective.

Company law does not foresee specific criteria for the allocation of the burden of proof in directors' liability suits. However, courts identified similar criteria in accordance with private law principles. In general, the plaintiff company should allege the directors' breach of a general or specific duty, prove that damages

---

[170] Bonelli, see n. 33 above, p. 19; A. Tina, *L'esonero da responsabilità degli amministratori di S.P.A.*, Giuffrè, Milan (2008) p. 150.

[171] Corte di Cassazione, 27 April 1994, n.7030, *Giurisprudenza Commerciale* (1997) II, p. 99 with comment of F. Camilletti.

[172] *Decreto Legislativo n. 5 del 17 gennaio 2003, Definizione dei procedimenti in materia di diritto societario e di intermediazione bancaria e creditizia, in attuazione dell'articolo 12 della legge n. 366 del 3 ottobre 2001.*

[173] In fact, listed companies' articles of association cannot foresee arbitration clauses. See F. de Santis, 'Comment of Art 34' in G. Arieta and F. de Santis (eds.) *Commentario dei processi societari*, UTET, Turin (2007), p. 881 ff. It is worth noticing that different points of view exist among scholars. See, P.L. Nela, 'Comment of Art 34' in S. Chiarloni (ed.) *Il nuovo processo societario*, Zanichelli, Bologna (2004), p. 929 ff.

[174] See G. Ferrarini and P. Giudici, 'Scandali finanziari e ruolo dell'azione privata: Il caso Parmalat' in F. Galgano and G. Visintini (eds.) *Mercato finanziario e tutela del risparmio*, CEDAM, Padua (2006), p. 261 ff. (English version: 'Financial Scandals and the Role of Private Enforcement: The Parmalat Case' in J. Armour and J.A. McCahery (eds.) *After Enron: Improving Corporate Law and Modernising Securities Regulation in Europe and the US*, Hart Publishing, Oxford (2006) p. 159 and ECGI Law Working Paper n. 40/2005 (available at <www.ecgi.org>).

ensued and establish causation. Defendant directors must prove either that they performed their duties or that no damage was caused to the plaintiff company.[175]

c) Directors' Crimes

Under Article 32-bis of the Criminal Code, a person is disqualified from acting as a director when sentenced to prison for not less than six months for crimes committed through abuse of powers or breach of duties relative whilst exercising an office. Penal sanctions for directors' crimes are found in the Civil Code and in the CFSA. Amongst the corporate crimes, the following can be mentioned.

(i) *Civil Code*—false statements in balance sheets, reports or other communications prescribed by the law (Art. 2621 and Art. 2622); unlawful reimbursement of capital contributions (Art. 2626); unlawful distribution of profits and reserves (Art. 2627); unlawful transactions on own shares or controlling a company's shares (Art. 2628).

(ii) *CFSA*—unlawful acquisition of shares (Art. 172); failure to dispose of shareholdings when required by the law (Art. 173); false statements in prospectuses (Art. 173-bis); insider trading (Art. 184); market manipulation (Art. 185).

In the case of directors' crimes, the company can also be found criminally liable under Legislative Decree n. 231/2001, which foresees the 'administrative responsibility' of legal entities and corporations for crimes committed in their interest or to their benefit.

d) D&O Insurance

In recent years, directors and officers (D&O) liability insurance has become relatively popular also in Italy, particularly in the case of listed companies.[176] According to the majority of scholars, D&O liability insurance falls under Article 1917 of the Civil Code on civil liability insurance and is subject to the relevant rules.[177] D&O insurance policies cover the liability of directors, statutory auditors and supervisory directors towards the company, shareholders, creditors and third parties. Dishonest or fraudulent acts (*dolo*) cannot be covered, but most policies cover civil and criminal legal defence costs before the civil and criminal courts.

Several types of D&O insurance coverage are found in practice, depending on whether the relevant policy is underwritten by either an individual director or

---

[175] Bonelli, see n. 33 above, p. 162; Campobasso, see n. 59 above, p. 383; De Nicola, see n. 33 above, p. 546; Nazzicone and Providenti, see n. 167 above, p. 278.

[176] U. Tombari, 'L'assicurazione della responsabilità civile degli amministratori di società per azioni', *Banca borsa e titoli di credito* (1999) I, p. 180.

[177] See D. Regoli, 'Le polizze assicurative professionali: nuovi profili' in P. Montalenti (ed.) *Responsabilità societarie e assicurazione: amministratori, sindaci e revisori*, Giuffrè, Milan (2009), p. 103; Tombari, see n. 176 above, p. 198.

auditor (stand-alone policy)[178] or by the company itself for the benefit of all directors and members of control bodies, statutory auditors or supervisory directors (global coverage).[179] It is also possible to underwrite policies in which only one category of officers is insured (ie. executive directors, non-executive directors or statutory auditors). Presently, global coverage represents the most common form in Italian practice; however, scholars suggest that after the 2003 company law reform attention should be focused on specific category policies.[180]

D&O insurance is a perk for directors and statutory auditors, so that the insurance premium is disclosed as part of their remuneration (see Consob Regulation on issuers, Annex n. 3 C, Scheme n. 1).[181] From a company law perspective, Article 2389 of the Civil Code applies (see above 3.1.5), providing that in the traditional governance system the remuneration of board members is fixed by the shareholders' meeting, whereas executive remuneration is fixed by the board.[182]

With regard to external auditors, Article 161/4 CFSA foresees that they either provide an adequate guarantee issued by banks, insurance companies or intermediaries or must execute an insurance policy against civil liability for professional negligence or errors, including a guarantee for employees' breach of duty.[183]

4.1.2. Nullification of Resolutions

Board resolutions that were adopted in breach of the law or the articles of association can be challenged either by the board of statutory auditors or by absent or dissenting directors within ninety days from the date of the meeting. Individual shareholders can challenge board resolutions that are prejudicial to their rights (Art. 2388 Civil Code).[184]

---

[178] These stand-alone insurance coverages are generally offered by insurance companies only if professional coverage (*polizze di responsabilità professionale*) has already been stipulated between the vested person and the insurance company itself. This coverage is generally granted with regard to internal and external auditors.

[179] Regoli, see n. 177 above, p. 122.

[180] Regoli, see n. 177 above, p. 124; L. Tessore, 'Le coperture assicurative della responsabilità di amministratori, sindaci e revisori nel mercato italiano' in Montalenti (ed.), see n. 177 above, p. 131.

[181] Electronic document available at <www.consob.it>. Also, Tombari, see n. 176 above, p. 180.

[182] Accordingly, the general meeting has to approve D&O insurance coverage for directors (or the articles of association may authorise this type of insurance). De Nicola, see n. 33 above, p. 546; Tombari, see n. 176 above, p. 186

[183] The text of article 161 CSFA has been repealed by Art 40 Legislative Decree n. 39/2010, nevertheless it continues to be applicable until the Ministry of the Economy and Finance publishes the Regulation foreseen by Art 5 of Legislative Decree n. 39/2010.

[184] See A.P. Massamormile, 'Invalidità delle delibere consiliari' in Abbadessa and Portale (eds.), see n. 34 above, p. 520 and 562.

4.1.3. Special Procedures and Issues

a) Class Actions

Article 140-bis of the 'Consumer Code'[185], introduced class actions in Italy.[186] Class actions are aimed to protect 'homogeneous individual rights of consumers' (both as individuals and as members of associations). Accordingly, each class member can bring an action for damages and repayments either individually or through associations or committees.

Article 140-bis provides that the following consumer rights are enforceable through a class action:

i) contract rights of a plurality of consumers and users who are in the same position vis-à-vis the same company;

ii) identical rights of final consumers of a given product towards its manufacturer, even in the absence of a direct contractual relationship;

iii) identical rights to damages deriving to consumers and users from unfair commercial practices or anti-competitive behaviour'.

It is controversial whether these provisions also apply to securities litigation. Scholars disagree both on defining the relationship between issuers and investors (consumers) as 'contractual' and on the possibility of identifying an 'unfair commercial practice' in the distribution of securities.[187] So far, we are not aware of cases in which the Italian Courts have applied Article 140-bis to securities litigation.

---

[185] *Decreto Legislativo n. 206 del 6 settembre 2005, Codice del Consumo.*

[186] As amended by Art 49 of Law n. 99 of 23 July 2009 (Legge 23 luglio 2009, n. 99. *Disposizioni per lo sviluppo e l'internazionalizzazione delle imprese, nonché in materia di energia*). See, G. Alpa, 'L'Art 140-bis del codice del consumo nella prospettiva del diritto privato', *Rivista trimestrale di diritto e procedura civile* (2010) p. 379 ff.; R. Lener, 'L'introduzione della class action nell'ordinamento italiano del mercato finanziario', *Giurisprudenza Commerciale* (2005) I, p. 269; S. Menchini, A. Motto, 'Art 140-bis of Legislative Decree n. 206 of 6 September 2005', *Nuove leggi civili commentate* (2011), p. 1413; M. Palmieri, 'Azione di "classe" e tutela degli investitori: prospettive italiane' *Banca impresa società* (2007), p. 227; M. Rescigno, 'L'introduzione della class action nell'ordinamento italiano. Profili generali', *Giurisprudenza Commerciale* (2005) I, p. 407.

[187] Alpa, see n. 186 above, p. 164; P. Giudici, 'Representative litigation in Italian capital markets: Italian derivative suits and (if ever) securities class actions' *European Company and Financial Law Review* (2009) 6, p. 13; P. Giudici, *La responsabilità civile nel diritto dei mercati finanziari*, Giuffrè, Milan (2008) p. 241; P. Giudici, 'La responsabilità nei mercati finanziari' paper presented at the conference on *Class action: il nuovo volto della tutela collettiva in Italia*, Courmayeur, October 2010, on file with the author.

b) Derivative Actions[188]

As already mentioned (see above 4.1.1(b)), the Civil Code regulates derivative actions (Art. 2393-bis). Accordingly, members of listed companies representing at least one-fortieth of the company's capital (or the lower percentage established by the articles) can sue directors for liability in the company's interest.

However, no derivative actions have yet been brought in practice. The following appear to be the main obstacles to the diffusion of derivative actions: (i) The concentrated ownership structure of Italian listed companies and the limited role played by institutional investors as shareholders; (ii) the lack of economic incentives, given that contingent-fee agreements not allowed; and (iii) the lack of appropriate rules on discovery and information rights for minority shareholders.[189]

c) Securities Litigation

In general, securities suits against issuers and directors are infrequent. Only a few cases have been brought for prospectus liability and liability for false or misleading information in the secondary markets.

A specific regime for prospectus liability was introduced in 2007 and is included in Article 94 CFSA.[190] Previously, prospectus liability was mainly grounded on the pre-contractual liability provision set forth in the Civil Code (Art. 2337), as also held by the courts in some cases.[191]

Other judgments held either issuers or directors liable for misstatements in the secondary market, in connection with the disclosure of official documents containing false or misleading information. In these cases, the provision on

---

[188] L. Enriques and F. Mucciarelli, 'L'azione di responsabilità da parte delle minoranze' in Abbadessa and Portale (eds.) see n. 34 above, p. 859; Ferrarini and Giudici, see n. 169 above, p. 597; Ferrarini and Giudici, see n. 174 above, p. 260; Giudici, 'Representative litigation in Italian capital markets', see n. 187 above, p. 2; Giudici, *La responsabilià civile nel diritto dei mercati finanziari*, see n. 187 above, p. 157; D. Latella, *L'azione sociale di responsabilità esercitata dalla minoranza*, Giappichelli, Turin (2007), p. 209; Nazzicone and Providenti, see n. 167 above, p. 290; Picciau, see n. 169 above, p. 574.

[189] Ferrarini and Giudici, see n. 169 above, p. 597; Ferrarini and Giudici, see n. 174 above, p. 260.

[190] Giudici, *La responsabilià civile nel diritto dei mercati finanziari*, see n. 187 above, p. 217 ff.; M. Ventoruzzo, *La responsabilità da prospetto negli Stati Uniti d'America tra regole del mercato e mercato delle regole*, Egea, Milan (2003).

[191] See Trib. Milan, 11 January1988, *Giurisprudenza Commerciale* (1988) II, p. 585, with comment of G. Ferrarini. More recently, see, Trib. Milan, 25 July 2008; Trib. Milan, 24 March 2009. See, G. Ferrarini, *La responsabilità da prospetto. Informazione societaria e tutela degli investitori*, Giuffrè, Milan (1986); G. Ferrarini, 'Sollecitazione del risparmio e quotazione in borsa' in G.E. Colombo and G.B. Portale (eds.) *Trattato delle società per azioni*, UTET, Turin (1993) X, p. 289.

directors' liability towards individual shareholders and creditors was also applied (Art. 2395 Civil Code).[192]

Only one case concerns civil liability for insider trading, a theme which is still controversial in Italy.[193]

4.2. Regulators

The *Commissione Nazionale per le Società e la Borsa* (Consob) is the securities markets regulator. Consob is a public body, consisting of an independent commission made up of five full-time members, assisted by staff, along the model followed by other securities authorities, the SEC in particular. Consob is tasked with investor protection in securities markets. It exercises regulatory and supervisory functions, mainly in the following areas: (i) Investment inter-mediaries, with particular reference to the fairness and transparency of business conduct (see Art. 5 CFSA); (ii) issuers of financial instruments, including listed companies, with particular reference to prospectuses and disclosure (see Art. 91 CFSA making reference to efficiency and transparency of markets as regulatory goals); (iii) takeover bids and the market for corporate control; (iv) trading venues, including regulated markets, multilateral trading facilities and systematic internalisers; and (v) market abuse.

The Bank of Italy, in addition to being a central bank within the European System of Central Banks (ESCB), is empowered by the TUB to act as the regulator and supervisor of the banking system. Therefore, banks that are listed companies are supervised both by Consob, as listed issuers, and the Bank of Italy, which also regulates and supervises the corporate governance of banks (whether listed or not). Moreover, banks are supervised by Consob to the extent that they provide investment services to clients. Similarly, insurance undertakings constituted as listed companies are supervised both by Consob and the *Istituto per la vigilanza sulle assicurazioni private e di interesse collettivo* (ISVAP), an independent public authority tasked with the supervision of insurance firms under the Insurance Code.

---

[192] See Trib. Milan, 21 October 1999, *Giurisprudenza Italiana* (2000) I, c. 554. Although in this case the information exchange regarded both primary and secondary markets.

[193] See Trib. Milan, 14 February 2004, *Foro italiano* (2004) I, c. 1581. For a complete analysis of liability actions in Italian capital markets— including the possibility of claiming for damages in the case of not launching a mandatory takeover bid – see Giudici, *La responsabilià civile nel diritto dei mercati finanziari*, see n. 187 above, p. 300; see also E. Macchiavello and G.G. Peruzzo, 'Mancato lancio di OPA obbligatoria: il puzzle SAI-Fondiaria alla luce di alcune esperienze europee', *Giurisprudenza Commerciale* (2008) I, p. 908.

4.3. Self-Regulation

The first edition of the Corporate Governance Code was published in 1999, a year after the CFSA, which in fact did not deal with boards of directors, implicitly leaving the subject matter to self-regulation. The relevant initiative was taken by the Italian Stock Exchange, which promoted the formation of a Corporate Governance Committee consisting of the CEO of some listed companies and of representatives of the main business associations. A second edition of the Code was published in 2002, a third one in 2006 and the latest one in 2011, reflecting changes brought about by the company law reform (no doubt influenced by previous editions of the Code, which inspired the formation of some of the new provisions on boards). The Corporate Governance Committee is assisted by a group of experts, a working group and a secretariat established at the Italian Exchange. The Code includes 10 articles, each stating some principles, implementing criteria and an official comment.

Adoption of the Code and compliance with the same by listed companies are subject to comply-or-explain.

All 262 Italian listed companies considered by Assonime (2012)[194] disclosed their reports on corporate governance and ownership structure to the public. The level of compliance with the recommendations of the Code is rather high (95%).[195]

5. The Dynamics of Change

As shown in this paper (see above 2.1(a)), there are three different board models available under Italian law: the traditional model (consisting of a board of directors and a board of auditors), the one-tier model (a board of directors and an audit committee of independent directors) and the two-tier model (a supervisory board and a management board). However, the latter two governance structures are not widespread among Italian listed companies (262 companies in all), 96.2% of which still had the traditional model in place at the end of 2011.[196]

The number of directors varies depending on the business sector: an average of 10 members, 15.6 in the financial sector and 9.4 in the other.[197] The majority of directors are non-executive directors (70%);[198] about half are independent

---

[194] Assonime, see n. 5 above, p. 21 ff.

[195] *Ibid.*, p. 21.

[196] *Ibid.*, schedule 1.

[197] *Ibid.*, p. 36.

[198] *Ibid.*, p. 37.

directors (36% of the total).[199] The law makes it mandatory for listed companies to empower minority shareholders to appoint at least one director (Art. 148 CSFA). Most listed companies have a minority director.[200]

Italian boards generally delegate the day-by-day management of the company to one or more members. However, boards can delegate powers to an executive committee appointed from their members (Art. 2381 Civil Code). In practice, boards in financial companies often appoint a similar committee (57%), in addition to delegating individual powers to one (or more) of their members.[201]

Nearly all listed companies have established board committees with advisory and preparatory functions, such as the remuneration committee, the internal controls (audit) committee and the nomination committee, as recommended by the Corporate Governance Code. The Code also recommends separating the role of chairman from that of the CEO, a recommendation that is followed by 70% of Italy's listed companies.[202]

Interlocking directorates are frequent, particularly in the case of blue chip companies, which are interconnected through a web of directors.[203]

The following issues remain open:

Executive remuneration—The main issues concerning executive remuneration regard disclosure and the formulation of appropriate remuneration policies. Both aspects are currently under review, together with the issue of 'say-on-pay'. Banking regulation is more advanced as a result of international and European developments after the global financial crisis.

Minority directors—Board elections are based on slate voting. At least one board member should be elected from the minority slate that obtains the largest number of votes. Clearly, the minority slate must not be linked in any way with the majority shareholders who presented or voted their own slate. This requirement, however, is difficult to enforce, and it may threaten the whole concept of minority directors.

Information streams from executive to non-executive directors—Even though non-executive directors are entrusted with powers to require information from executive directors and the latter have to report to the board, practice shows a limited flow of information to non-executives (this is partly due to the typical Italian concentrated ownership structure).

---

[199] *Ibid.*, p. 37.

[200] *Ibid.*, p. 13.

[201] *Ibid.*, p. 31. In non-financial companies the percentage is 11%.

[202] *Ibid.*, p. 42 and schedule 15.

[203] Santella, Drago and Polo, see n. 15 above.

Composition of boards—The composition of Italian boards raises some concerns. The proportion of non-executive directors (70% of all members) and that of independent directors (nearly 50% of NEDs) are acceptable in theory, considering that most Italian listed companies have controlling shareholders or block-holders. However, the true independence of independent directors and their professional qualifications and engagement are often criticised as inadequate.

The Corporate Governance Code defines independence analytically in conformity with international best practices. However, enforcement of the relevant requirements is far from satisfactory. Independence could be enhanced through enforcement of Consob's Regulation on related-party transactions. This implies a monitoring of independence by the securities supervisor, at least to the extent that compliance with the relevant requirements is disclosed. Nonetheless, it is doubtful that a public authority might place sufficient emphasis on substance rather than form when monitoring the independence of directors.

Moreover, Italian boards are often too large, which hinders their efficiency in practice. In the case of blue chips companies, boards are also too interlocked, which will casts doubts on their independence.

Monitoring of internal controls—The governance of internal controls is often criticised for its sheer complexity.[204] In the traditional model, both the board (assisted by the internal controls committee) and the statutory board of auditors monitor the internal control systems. The duties and responsibilities of the two boards overlap, with the risk of hindering their effectiveness. In addition, the functions of the internal controls committee are similar to those of the board of statutory auditors, making it necessary in practice for two bodies to co-operate. Similarly, in the two-tier system it is not clear which are the respective functions of the management board and the supervisory board with respect to internal controls. The one-tier system partially avoids this complexity but there is still resistance to its adoption in practice.

The weakness of public and private enforcement—A series of financial scandals showed that even the recent corporate reforms are based on shaky foundations to the extent that both public and private enforcement are weak. This is evidence of path dependency, as the weakness of private enforcement largely depends on the notorious dysfunctions of the Italian judicial system, which appear difficult to cure.[205]

---

[204] Bianchini and Di Noia (eds.) *I controlli societari. Molte regole, nessun sistema*, see n. 39 above.

[205] Ferrarini and Giudici, 'Scandali finanziari e ruolo dell'azione privata: Il caso Parmalat', see n. 174 above, p. 246 ff.; G. Ferrarini, 'Corporate Governance Changes in in the 20th Century: A view from Italy' in K.J. Hopt, E. Wymeersch, H. Kanda, T. Baum (eds.) *Corporate Governance in Context Corporations, States, and Markets in Europe, Japan, and the US*, cont. ...

6. Selection of Literature

AA. VV., *Amministrazione e controllo nel diritto delle società, Liber amicorum Antonio Piras,* Giappichelli, Turin, 2010.

Belcredi M., Ferrarini G., *Boards and Shareholders in European Listed Companies. Facts, Context and Post-Crisis Reforms,* Cambridge University Press, Cambridge (UK), forthcoming.

Bonelli, F., *Gli amministratori di s.p.a.: dopo la riforma delle società,* Giuffrè, Milan, 2004.

Buonocore, V., 'Adeguatezza, precauzione, gestione, responsabilità: chiose sull' Art. 2381, commi terzo e quinti, del codice civile', *Giurisprudenza commerciale,* 2006, I, 5.

Bruno, S., *Il ruolo dell'assemblea di s.p.a. nella corporate governance,* CEDAM, Padua, 2012.

Cariello, V., *Il sistema dualistico,* Giappichelli, Turin, 2012

Cariello, V. (ed.), *Le operazioni con parti correlate,* Giuffrè, Milan, 2011

Enriques, L., *Il conflitto d'interessi degli amministratori di società per azioni,* Giuffrè, Milan, 2000.

Ferrarini, G., 'Controlli interni e strutture di governo societario', in: Abbadessa and Portale (eds.), *Il nuovo diritto delle società, Liber amicorum, Gian Franco Campobasso,* UTET Giuridica, Turin, 2007, p. 3.

Gezzi, F., Malberti C., 'The Two-Tier Model and the One-Tier Model of Corporate Governance in the Italian Reform of Corporate Law', *European Company and Financial Law Review,* 5 (1), 2998, 1.

Meruzzi, G., *I flussi informativi endosocietari nelle società per azioni,* CEDAM, Padua, 2012.

Montalenti, P., 'Amministrazione e controllo nelle società per azioni: riflessioni sistematiche e proposte di riforma', *Rivista delle società,* 2013, p. 42.

Riolfo, G., 'Il sistema monistico nelle società di capitali e cooperative', in *Trattato di diritto commerciale e di diritto pubblico,* v. 53, Cedam, Padua, 2012.

Sacchi, R. (ed.), *L'interesse sociale tra valorizzazione del capitale e protezione degli stakeholders,* Giuffrè, Milan, 2010.

Zamperetti, G., *Il dovere di informazione degli amministratori nella governance della società per azioni,* Giuffrè, Milan, 2005.

Oxford University Press, Oxford (2005), p. 57 ff.; Ferrarini and Giudici, see n. 169 above, p. 597 ff., p. 606 ff.; Enriques, see n. 12 above.

Corporate Boards in the Netherlands

RICHARD G.J. NOWAK

1. Introduction

Dutch corporate law is historically based on the two-tier board model. In this model, there is a formal and personal division between the management board (*bestuur*), whose tasks are the day-to-day management and the strategy of the company, and the (optional) supervisory board (*raad van commissarissen*), whose tasks are supervising and advising the management board. The supervisory board may not engage in the management of the company and its members may not simultaneously be members of the management board. In the second half of the 20th century, the one-tier board model of corporate practice was imported from the UK. On 1 January 2013, the one-tier board model became law. Most listed Dutch companies have a traditional two-tier board. At the end of 2012, of a total of 88 listed companies, eight companies had a one-tier board, four of which were created in 2012. The two best known companies with a one-tier board are Unilever and Heineken Holding. Apart from the obvious advantages and disadvantages which are inherent in each of the two models, Dutch economic research and legal literature have yet not found an objective reason why it would be preferable for companies to have either of the models.

In this paper, the basic model is the traditional two-tier board model, after which we will address the one-tier board model.

1.1. Environment in which Boards Operate

a) Listed Companies

Dutch company law deals with two types of companies divided by shares: public limited liability companies (*naamloze vennootschappen*; hereinafter: 'public companies') and private limited liability companies (*besloten vennootschappen met beperkte aansprakelijkheid*; hereinafter 'private companies'). Shares of public companies may be listed and traded on the Dutch stock exchange Euronext Stock Exchange Amsterdam ('Euronext').[1]

b) Ownership Structure

Public companies listed on Euronext are listed in one of three indices according to trading volume: AEX (Amsterdam Exchange Index), AMX (Midcap) and AScX (Smallcap) (together: 'listed companies').[2] In December 2012, the three indices totaled 88 companies, the AEX index had 25 companies, and the total market capitalisation more than quadrupled the market capitalisation of AMX and

---

[1] Private companies may offer debentures (*obligaties*) to the public.

[2] Furthermore, there is a group of approximately 70 locally traded companies.

AscX together. The focus in this report is on AEX companies incorporated in the Netherlands ('AEX companies').

The following tables give a general impression of the ownership structure of AEX companies in the period 1995–2010 and the size of the holdings.

Table 1: Ownership structure of AEX companies[3]

	1995	2003	2010
Foreign investors	37%	69%	76% US and Canada: 39.1% UK and Ireland: 14.9% Belgium and Luxembourg: 11.8% France: 9.7%.[4]
Dutch institutional investors[5]	24%	12%	8%
Dutch non-financial enterprises	19%	–	11%
Dutch private investors	19%	11%	5%

Table 2: Major shareholders in AEX companies[6]

Size of shareholding	Percentage of AEX companies in which these holdings occur in 2010
> 30% ('controlling interest')	19%
10–30%	19%
5–10%	52%
1 < 5%	10%

These tables show that foreign shareholdings in Dutch AEX companies has more than doubled in the past 15 years, whereas Dutch institutional investors have de-

---

[3] Source: <www.eumedion.nl>.

[4] Source: IMF. See also R. Abma and R. Munsters in S.C. Peij et al (eds.), *Handboek Corporate Governance* (2010).

[5] Such as banks, insurance companies and pension funds.

[6] Source: R. Abma and R. Munsters, in S.C. Peij et al (eds.), *Handboek Corporate Governance* (2010), based on the register of Authority Financial Markets. Companies that have listed depositary receipts of shares (see below) are not taken into account.

creased their shareholdings in AEX companies from 24% to 8%.[7] Further, AEX companies are dominated by Anglo-American investors.

Dutch listed companies are said to have a dispersed ownership structure. However, this qualification mainly applies to AEX companies; Midcap and Smallcap companies usually have (more) larger shareholders. Even some AEX companies have large shareholders. In 2010, 19% of the AEX companies had shareholders with substantial holdings between 10–30% and more than half of the AEX companies had one or more shareholders having 5–10% or of the shares. However, compared to ownership structures which are characterised as concentrated, the ownership structure of AEX companies may be characterised as dispersed.

The State holds shares in a number of non-listed companies, mostly public utilities (infrastructure and financial services) and in two financial institutions.

c) The Concept of 'Control' and 'Controlling Shareholder'

The concept of control and controlling shareholder mainly occurs in rules with respect to groups of companies. In Art. 2:24a Dutch Civil Code ('DCC') 'subsidiary' is defined as a company in which another company can exercise the majority of the voting rights and appoint and dismiss the majority of the board members. In the Financial Supervision Act, (*Wet financieel toezicht*) a controlled entity is defined as a 'subsidiary' or a company in which a person has control (*overwegende zeggenschap*, 'predominant say') within the meaning of the Take-over Directive.

As far as ownership structure in listed companies is concerned, the concept is to delineate the mandatory bid threshold: A company is obliged to make a bid if it acquires a 'predominant say', which is defined as 30% or more of the voting rights. This threshold is used in practice in a broader sense to indicate a shareholder which normally would have control of the company.[8]

One could further speak of control in an indirect sense in those provisions that mandatorily require a supermajority, eg. the provisions on merger, demerger and decrease of share capital, which require a majority of two-thirds of the votes cast if the quorum is less than 50% of the issued share capital. In Dutch practice, the question whether and to which extent certain shareholders may exert control

---

[7] It should be noted, however, that in the last decade Dutch institutional investors have outsourced parts of their investment activities to large US capital management companies, who may have increased their holdings in AEX companies. See R. Abma, De verander(en)de rol van de private aandeelhouder binnen de vennootschap, in N.E.D. Faber et al (eds.), *De kredietcrisis*, Serie OO&R, Vol. 54 (2010) and R. Abma and R. Munsters in S.C. Peij et al (eds.), *Handboek Corporate Governance* (2010), pp. 201–236.

[8] In legal literature, the concept of major shareholder is sometimes used to indicate a shareholder having more than 10% of the votes. In the Financial Supervision Act, a holding of 5% of the shares or the votes is defined as a substantial interest.

depends to a large degree on majority and quorum requirements in the articles of association. The concept of control, therefore, has a dynamic rather than a static meaning. As far as shareholder decisions may be adopted by simple majority, it can be said that a shareholder has control if he has more than half of the votes represented at the shareholders' meeting. In 2012, the participation degree at shareholders' meetings of AEX companies was 63.7% of the votes, so a shareholding of 32% is usually decisive.[9]

d) Degree of Participation in Shareholder Meetings; Voting Agencies

The average degree of participation in shareholder meetings of AEX companies increased from 45% in 2008 to 63.7% in 2012.[10] Proxy voting is often used; the majority of institutional investors give a proxy or send in their vote prior to the meeting. In the past five years, encouraged by the corporate governance code and public debate, there has been an increase of awareness among institutional investors[11] to actively monitor their most important portfolio companies and attend shareholder meetings. The influence of voting advisory agencies such as ISS/RiskMetrics on major institutional investors has increased accordingly,[12] although it should not be overestimated.[13] Partisan proxy solicitation is possible (though not regulated), but not used on a large scale.

e) Takeover Bids

In the period 2003–2008, public bids on companies listed on Euronext Amsterdam, took place about ten times per year. After 2008 public bids became less frequent, eg. on Super de Boer, Smit International, Océ, Dim Vastgoed (2009), Draka (2010), Gamma, VastNed, Crucell (2011), TNT Express, Fornix Biosciences, KPN (2012). There were a few hostile takeover bids, the *cause celèbre* being the friendly takeover bid on ABN-Amro by Barclays that was followed by a competitive hostile bid by the consortium of Royal Bank of Scotland, Fortis and Banco Santander. In the end, the board of ABN-Amro did not recommend nor

---

[9] Please note that the attendance rate is not broken down into blocks of shareholdings.

[10] Source: Eumedion, *Evaluatie ava-seizoen 2012*, <www.eumedion.nl> and the Compliance report 2012 (see n. 13) even mentions 69%.

[11] Co-ordinated by their representative Eumedion.

[12] See the conclusions of the compliance report of the Monitoring Commission, *Corporate Governance Code Compliance Report 2010*, <www.corpgov.nl>. See further sec. 4.3.

[13] See the conclusions of the compliance report of the Monitoring Commission Corporate Governance Code December 2011 and December 2012, *Compliance Report 2011* and *Compliance Report 2012*, respectively) <www.corpgov.nl>, in particular *Compliance Report 2012*, pp. 39–42, and Eumedion, *Evaluatie ava-seizoen 2012*, pp. 11–13.

advise against either of the bids. A recent hostile bid was the bid for Koninklijke KPN by América Movil in 2012.

f) Stakeholder Model: the Standard of 'Interest of the Company'

Dutch company law is stakeholder-oriented.[14] This entails that the members of the management board and the supervisory board have to be guided by the interests of the company and its purpose (also called corporate interest, *vennoot-schappelijk belang*).[15] This standard applies to all members of the management board and the supervisory board, even if they are employee, shareholder or creditor nominees. Board members are not appointed in order to foster the interests of specific groups and are not bound by instructions of any party or group.[16] The standard of the interest of the company is considered to be the result of weighing the interests of all parties involved in the company ('stakeholders'), in particular the company's shareholders, employees, creditors and, to a lesser extent, the public interest. For companies organised in a group of companies, the interest of the group is an important (though not *per se* decisive)[17] element, which should be included in the weighing of the interests of the company by the board of every group company.[18] The standard has a dynamic nature and its content depends on the specific circumstances of the company. Two tendencies have become discernible in the past decade. First, as a general rule, the standard refers to the company's long term interest. Second, a view was proposed fairly recently stating that the interest of the shareholders should normally prevail above the interests of the other parties involved, unless these interests would be dis-proportionately harmed.[19] This view of 'qualified predominance' of the interest of shareholders, when weighing all interests that together form the interest of the

---

[14] See Asser/Maeijer/Van Solinge and Nieuwe Weme 2-II* (2009), no. 394 and Van Schilfgaarde/Winter (2009) no. 71.

[15] See Art. 2:140 DCC and 2:129 par. 5 DCC; and Principle II.1 of the corporate governance code. See also M.J. van Ginneken and L. Timmerman, 'De betekenis van het even-redigheidsbeginsel voor het ondernemingsrecht', *Ondernemingsrecht* 2011/123, p. 604.

[16] Asser/Maeijer/Van Solinge and Nieuwe Weme 2-II* (2009), nos. 489 and 560.

[17] See Enterprise Court 13 March 2003, *JOR* 2003/85 (*British Steel/Hoogovens*): the Enterprise Court ruled that it belongs to the tasks of the supervisory board of a group company (in particular with labour co-determination) to pay attention to the question whether the interests of that group company are sufficiently considered and valued by the board of the ultimate parent company. Conversely, the board of the ultimate parent is not free to automatically subordinate the interest of a group company to the interest of the group as a whole.

[18] See Asser/Maeijer/Van Solinge and Nieuwe Weme 2-II* (2009), no. 827.

[19] See L. Timmerman, 'Grondslagen van geldend ondernemingsrecht', *Ondernemingsrecht* 2009/1. Against this view: the responses of H.J. de Kluiver 'Vennootschappelijke repliek op Timmermans grondslagen', and J.M. Blanco Fernández, 'Grondslagen: reactie op de oratie', in *Ondernemingsrecht* 2009/1.

company (in Dutch legal literature sometimes referred to as enlightened share-holder value), is gaining weight.[20]

These two tendencies come together in the corporate governance code, which states that it is based on the principle, accepted in the Netherlands, that a company is a long-term alliance between the various parties involved in the company. The management board and the supervisory board have overall responsibility for weighing up these different interests, generally with a view to ensuring the continuity of the enterprise, while the company endeavours to create shareholder value in the long term. Shareholders as such are not obliged to be guided by the standard of interest of the company, but the larger the shareholder's stake in the company, the bigger their responsibility towards the company, the minority shareholders and the other stakeholders (CGC, preamble).

In takeover situations, there is no 'reconfiguration of board rules' in this respect: the board is obliged to continue weighing the company's interest in the way described above.[21]

g) Influence of Work Force

Public and private companies which meet certain quantitative criteria, are subject to a mandatory regime of labour co-determination (*structuurregime*). This regime entails that there is a mandatory supervisory board, consisting of at least three persons, who are appointed by the shareholders' meeting following a binding nomination by the supervisory board, whereby the works council has the right to make a binding recommendation with respect to one-third of the number of supervisory board members.[22] Of all listed companies about 30% were subject to labour co-determination regimes in 2010. In comparison, in 1996 about 60% of all listed companies mandatorily applied co-determination rules.[23]

h) Agency Conflicts; External Pressures

As described above, AEX companies have a dispersed ownership structure, which makes them vulnerable to unsolicited takeovers. There are few controlling share-holders, and board members are usually not shareholder nominees. This means that the first agency conflict is permanently present. Listed companies have a long-standing tradition to protect themselves against hostile takeovers and undesired influence on the company's strategy. In 2004, the shareholder-oriented

---

[20] See L. Timmerman, *Ondernemingsrecht* 2009/1, p. 6–7.

[21] Supreme Court 13 July 2007, *JOR* 2007/178 (*ABN AMRO/Lasalle*).

[22] See further sec. 2.2.2.

[23] C.F. van der Elst, A. de Jong, M.J.G.C. Raaijmakers, 'Een overzicht van juridische en economische dimensies van de kwetsbaarheid van Nederlandse beursvennootschappen', *Report to the Social and Economic Council of the Netherlands* (SER) (2007), p. 56.

Dutch corporate governance code came into effect. In the same year, the law granted a number of important rights to the shareholders' meeting, in particular the right to approve board decisions of major importance and the right for holders of 1% of the issued share capital to put items on the agenda of a shareholders' meeting.[24] The right to put items on the agenda was a major boost for shareholder activism. Activist shareholders started using this right in order to influence the company's strategy. A well-known example was the investment fund TCI, who requested the board of ABN Amro to put the issue of strategy on the agenda of the annual shareholders' meeting in 2007, which eventually led to the split-up of ABN-AMRO.[25] This event marked the end of the expansion of shareholders' rights and a return to protection of companies.[26]

i) Investigation Proceeding before the Enterprise Court

The investigation proceeding before the Enterprise Chamber of the Court of Appeal in Amsterdam (*Ondernemingkamer van het Gerechtshof te Amsterdam*) ('Enterprise Court') is another strong tool in the hands of activist shareholders. Shareholders having a certain percentage of shares can institute proceedings against a company with the Enterprise Court in order to request the Enterprise Court to start an investigation into the company's affairs with the aim to declare that the company has been mismanaged. The Enterprise Court has far-reaching powers and its case law has very significant influence on the corporate governance discussion in the Netherlands. See further section 4.1.3.

j) Protective Devices

Traditionally, Dutch listed companies seek protection, not only against undesired takeover bids, but also against activist shareholders. Protective devices came under pressure when the Anglo-American concepts of the level playing field and shareholder value gained ground in the Netherlands in the late 1980s.[27] This led in 1989 to the listing rule prohibiting listed companies having more than two protective devices.[28] This rule was abolished in December 2007, but most companies kept the devices they had.[29] The criticism against protective devices faded away

---

[24] For NV's, the threshold will be increased to 3% in the course of 2013.

[25] A similar course of action was followed by the hedge funds Paulson and Centaurus in respect of Stork: see below under 'Protective devices'.

[26] See further sec. 5.

[27] See for literature from this period: Asser-Maeijer 2-II (1994), nos. 411–412 and Asser/Maeijer/Van Solinge and Nieuwe Weme 2-II* (2009), no. 634.

[28] Annex X of the Euronext Rule Book II.

[29] The reason given for their abolishment was that the introduction of the takeover rules made them superfluous. See NYSE Euronext Amsterdam Notice 2007-051.

after 2007, when it became clear that activist shareholders were using the set of new rights granted to them in full.[30] In 2012, the interest for protective devices seems to have diminished: four companies abolished their protective devices (TNT Express, NSI, Grontmij, Mediq), whereas in three IPO's no protective devices were utilised (Ziggo, Core Laboratories, DE Masterblenders).

The use of ad hoc protective devices is allowed by the Dutch Supreme Court, but only if they are temporary and proportionate[31] and if it is likely that the continuity of the company's policy (including its strategy) or the interest of the company or its stakeholders is threatened[32] (so-called RNA standard).[33] The notion 'temporary' is vague by nature, but case law has set out that a period of six months may in principle be considered reasonable.[34] Permanent protective devices (such as an option to take shares; depository receipts; priority shares—see below) cannot, by their nature, be subject to the RNA standard.[35] Such devices appear from the company documents and characterise the company as a company with a 'non-open' structure. Dutch legislation implementing the Takeover Directive gives companies the choice of protecting themselves or providing in the articles of association that they will not invoke any protective devices in case of a

---

[30] See further Asser/Maeijer/Van Solinge and Nieuwe Weme 2-II* (2009), nos. 636 f. and B.F. Assink, 'Ondernemingsbestuur en risicobeheersing op de drempel van een nieuw decennium: een ondernemingsrechtelijke analyse', *preadvies van de Vereeniging Handelsrecht* (2009), pp. 15–51.

[31] According to the RNA decision, as the aim of the protection is to maintain the *status quo* in order to create the possibility of deliberations between all parties involved.

[32] Not only by an intended hostile takeover, but also by a shareholder's intention to change the company's strategy or dismiss members of the board.

[33] This standard was developed in Supreme Court 18 April 2003, *JOR* 2003/110, *NJ* 2003, 286 (*RNA* (*Rodamco North America*)). RNA did not have structural protective devices (it had a so-called open structure) but launched an incidental protective device (the issue of ordinary shares to a foundation) as a response to an unfriendly takeover bid (not being a public bid). It is broadly assumed that the RNA standard also applies to other shareholder actions which are likely to inflict serious damage to the company's interest, inter alia an agenda proposal to dismiss board members or to change the strategy. See further Asser/Maeijer/Van Solinge and Nieuwe Weme 2-II* (2009), no. 635 and, extensively, M.J. van Ginneken, *Vijandige overnames: de rol van de vennootschapsleiding in Nederland en de Verenigde Staten,* PhD thesis, Serie IvO, Vol. 79 (2010), Chapter 10.

[34] See also Art. 2:359c (withdrawn later) in the initial proposal implementing the Takeover Directive, which provided for a 'breakthrough' for a bidder having acquired 75% of the shares after the lapse of 6 months upon the announcement of the bid. An indication of a longer period could be seen in the provision that a foundation exercising a call option for high voting preference shares is exempted from the obligation to make a mandatory bid for a period of two years. See Art. 5:71 par. 1 sub c Wft.

[35] See Asser/Maeijer/Van Solinge and Nieuwe Weme 2-II* (2009), no. 635 and Maeijer, comment to Supreme Court 18 April 2003, *NJ* 2003/286 (*Rodamco N.A.*).

hostile bid[36] (*board neutrality rule*).[37] To date, no company listed at Euronext Amsterdam has chosen the latter option.[38]

Pursuant to the corporate governance code, the board has to provide an overview in the annual report of all existing protective devices and all protective devices which can be activated against a takeover, and indicate in which circumstances these devices can be exercised.[39]

Below follows a brief description of the most common methods for AEX companies to protect themselves against hostile bids and activist shareholders who demand a change of strategy or dismissal of board members.

Table 3: Protective devices of AEX companies [40]

	High voting preference shares	Depository receipts	Priority shares	Labour co-determination regime[41]
AEX companies	61.9%	14.3%	9.5%	30%

High voting preference shares—This is the most common protective device. It was put in action in a number of high profile cases that were brought before the Enterprise Court.[42] Typically, the company grants a foundation a call option to acquire high voting preference shares of up to 50% of the issued share capital. The foundation has a board consisting of independent board members.[43] The foundation's object usually is to promote the long-term interest of the company and its enterprise. If a hostile bidder or activist shareholder appears, the foundation exercises the call option, which neutralises the voting power of the bidder or

---

[36] Or that they will dismantle any protective devices when the bidder has acquired 75% of the issued share capital.

[37] Art. 2:359b DCC.

[38] See further Asser/Maeijer/Van Solinge and Nieuwe Weme 2-II* (2009), nos 644–657.

[39] CGC IV.3.11.

[40] Status end 2010. Source: Eumedion <www.eumedion.nl>. Total exceeds 100% because of combinations.

[41] Mandatory and voluntary. Source: own research.

[42] *Inter alia*, Enterprise Court 17 January 2007, *JOR* 2007/42 (*Stork*) and Supreme Court 9 July 2010, *JOR* 2010/228 (*ASMI*).

[43] The mandatory bid rules are not applicable if the board is independent (Art. 5:71 par. 1 sub c Wft). The notion of independence is not defined, but probably the definition of Art. 2:118a par. 3 DCC (for foundations holding DRs) applies: if at least half of the total number of votes can be cast by persons who are not (former) board members or employees or advisors of the company or a group company. See further Asser/Maeijer/Van Solinge and Nieuwe Weme 2-II* (2009), no. 627 under e.

activist shareholder. In the *Stork* case,[44] two hedge funds, Centaurus and Paulson, holding 32% of the shares in Stork,[45] communicated to the board in 2007 that they wished to split-up the company, but that they did not want to announce a takeover bid. When the board refused to consider the split-up, the funds used their right to put the dismissal of the entire board on the agenda of the shareholders' meeting.[46] The foundation exercised the option to receive preference shares with a number of voting rights equal to that of the funds jointly.[47] Most listed companies have granted the option to a foundation decades ago. But there are companies that installed this protective device only recently: in 2009, for example, Midcap company Delta Lloyd—a former subsidiary of Aviva—granted a call option during its IPO, to be exercised 'to resist undesired influence on and pressure to change the strategy.'[48]

Non-voting depository receipts of shares ('certificaten') ('DRs')—A number of companies have not listed their shares but DRs. This entails that ordinary[49] shares are issued to a foundation, which issues DRs to the public and pays the received dividends on to the holders of the DRs.[50] The board of the foundation consists of independent members.[51] The foundation is the legal owner of the shares and has the right to vote on the shares. Companies usually grant DR holders a proxy or the right to give instructions to the foundation how to vote on the shares, except in takeover situations. The listing of DRs was, therefore, used as a protective device. In 2004, this practice was laid down in the law, including the foundation's right to refuse granting a proxy when a public bid is announced or when the use

---

[44] Enterprise Court 17 January 2007, *JOR* 2007/42 (*Stork*).

[45] The Takeover Directive was not yet implemented in the Netherlands at that time.

[46] Stork was a company with labour co-determination: see sec. 3.1.1 for dismissal requirements in such companies.

[47] However, the founding documents provided that the foundation may (only) exercise the call option in case of a hostile takeover bid. The Enterprise Court established that the intention of Centaurus and Paulson to dismiss the board could not be interpreted as such, and cancelled the preference shares issued to the foundation. No Supreme Court appeal was lodged against this decision.

[48] Source: Eumedion, *Evaluatie ava-seizoen 2010* <www.eumedion.nl>.

[49] Some AEX companies have listed DRs of preference shares. These preference shares themselves can also be considered as a protective device because of the fact that the voting rights attached to them are based on their nominal value and not on the real market value. The corporate governance code seeks to address this distortion by providing that the voting rights on these shares have to be based on the real value of the capital contribution (CGC IV.1.2). In order to avoid the applicability of this provision, a few companies have listed DRs of these shares, whereby an independent foundation exercises the voting rights on the shares.

[50] Asser/Maeijer/Van Solinge and Nieuwe Weme 2-II* (2009), no. 658.

[51] For example, if at least half of the total number of votes can be cast by persons who are not (former) board members or employees or advisors of the company or a group company. See further Asser/Maeijer/Van Solinge and Nieuwe Weme 2-II* (2009), no. 674.

of the voting right by DR holders is, in the opinion of the foundation, essentially in contradiction with the interests of the company.[52] The corporate governance code, however, provides that holders of DRs should be granted a proxy under all circumstances. Some companies declared in their corporate governance statement that they would (advise the foundation to) comply with this provision; other companies stated that they would use the right given by law to refuse proxies in the above-mentioned circumstances.[53]

In the years after 2004 a number of companies abolished the protective character of DRs, but since 2007, as a result of actions by activist shareholders, some companies are considering reintroducing DRs as a protective device.[54] By the end of 2012, about 25% of the AEX companies still used DRs as a protective device. ING stated in 2009 that it would postpone the decision to cancel the DRs until the annual meeting of 2013. In 2012, ASML issued DRs to new investors in the framework of an innovation programme.

Labour co-determination regime—The labour co-determination regime can serve as a protective device, given the fact that in a co-determined company the shareholders' meeting can only appoint members of the supervisory board pursuant to a nomination by the supervisory board. The most recent case in which the shareholders were halted by the supervisory board was the intended sale by Merck/MSD of its research division Organon, which it acquired from Schering-Plough in 2009. In 2010, the supervisory board refused to give its approval for the lay-off of the company's employees[55] and initiated a proceeding before the Enterprise Court, which was withdrawn when agreement between the works council and the supervisory board was reached.[56] A company can also voluntarily

---

[52] Art. 2:118a DCC. See Asser/Maeijer/Van Solinge and Nieuwe Weme 2-II*(2009), nos. 675–676.

[53] See, *inter alia*, F.J.P. van den Ingh and R.G.J. Nowak in N.E.D. Faber et al (eds.), *Libellus amicorum Prof. Mr. S.C.J.J. Kortmann* (2007), pp. 87–102; and J. de Koning Gans and W.J. Oostwouder, 'Herwaardering van certificering als beschermingsconstructie' *O&F* 2010 (18) 4.

[54] This development is also mirrored in legal doctrine, where the critical attitude towards DRs as protective device that could still be seen in 2007, changed into an understanding and even approving attitude. See recently J. de Koning Gans and W.J. Oostwouder, *O&F* 2010 (18) 4, pp. 60–74 and the articles referred to therein. See for a more critical judgement recently D.F.M.M. Zaman, 'Beschermingsstichtingen als aandeelhouder', *Tijdschrift voor Onderne-mingsbestuur* (2010-6), pp. 150–156.

[55] Art. 2:164 par. 1 under j DCC.

[56] A similar case took place in 2003, when the supervisory board of Hoogovens (later renamed Corus), a subsidiary of British Steel, refused to approve the sale of a division of Hoogovens to Pechiney. British Steel started an investigation proceeding, but the Enterprise Court rejected the claim (Enterprise Court 13 March 2003, *JOR* 2003/85).

opt for the application of the labour co-determination regime.[57] In the last decade, voluntary application of the labour co-determiniation regime as a protective device has decreased while shareholder influence has increased. In 2009, the management of TNT NV, an AEX company, proposed to voluntarily continue the co-determination regime (which was no longer mandatorily applicable), but the shareholders' meeting rejected the proposal.[58] However, the device remains on the radar of company boards. In December 2012, AEX company Corio announced that it will dismantle its co-determination regime in 2013.

Appointment and removal protection—The law allows the articles of association to provide that, for example, the supervisory board[59] has the right to make binding nominations for the appointment of members of the management board and the supervisory board and that only a supermajority of shareholders can set aside the binding nomination (Art. 2:133 DCC). See further section 3.1.1.

Priority shares—The articles of association may provide that specific governance rights may be granted to the meeting of holders of shares of a particular class. Such governance rights may include the right to issue shares, to make binding nominations for appointment of board members[60] and to approve board decisions on certain matters. This device is less effective than devices pursuant to which an *amicus societatis* receives the majority of the voting power.

Holding/pyramid structure—There is only one example of a company with a pyramid structure: Heineken. Through a majority share in a joint venture, the Heineken family holds a 50.57% interest in Heineken Holding NV, and Heineken Holding NV holds a 50.005% interest in Heineken NV. Both companies are listed.

Right to put items on the agenda subject to board initiative or approval—The majority of listed companies has provided in the articles of association that the shareholders' meeting may only take certain decisions (eg. capital increase) on the initiative of the management board and/or upon approval by the supervisory board. This seems to be in contradiction with the mandatory right of holders of a certain percentage of shares to request the board to put draft resolutions on the agenda of the shareholders' meeting, as set out in the Shareholders Directive.[61] A slightly different technique is sometimes used by providing that if an agenda item is proposed by the board, a decision on this item requires a simple majority, whereas a

---

[57] Provided it has a mandatory works council. See Art. 2:157 DCC and Asser/Maeijer/Van Solinge and Nieuwe Weme 2-II* (2009), no. 534.

[58] See *Eumedion*, Report 2010, <www.eumedion.nl>.

[59] The right to make binding nominations can also be given to the holder of priority shares (see above).

[60] This right may also be given directly to the (supervisory) board, see below.

[61] Jo. Art. 2:114a DCC.

decision on an agenda item proposed by a shareholder requires a supermajority. It goes without saying that if the provision mentioned first is in contradiction with mandatory law, the same applies to this provision.

Response period—The corporate governance code states that if a shareholder intends to request the board to put an item on the agenda that may lead to a change of the company's strategy, the board will be given the possibility to invoke a reasonable time period to consult with these and other shareholders in order to respond to the request. This response period may not be longer than 180 days and the shareholder has to 'respect' such response period.[62] In general, shareholders as such are not bound by the corporate governance code (with the exception of institutional investors). The Dutch Civil Code provides as a rule of mandatory law that a shareholder request to put an item on the agenda has to be honoured when it is submitted 60 days before the shareholders' meeting.[63] In its Compliance Report 2010[64] the monitoring committee reported that 69% of the interviewed institutional investors considered a response period of 60 days or shorter to be reasonable.[65] In its Compliance Report 2011 the monitoring committee stated that shareholders should, on the basis of the standard of reasonableness and fairness, respect the response period invoked by the board pursuant to the Code. However, in a survey 60% of the insitutional investors indicated they would not.[66]

Some companies have tried to make the 180-day period binding for their shareholders. For example, before the annual meeting of 2011, the board of AEX company TNT had issued a statement saying that it took for granted that the shareholders would observe a response period of 180 days if invoked by the board. However, the shareholders objected and the board was forced to withdraw the statement.

---

[62] CGC IV.4.4 and II.1.9. See also Eumedion, *Handboek Corporate Governance* (2013), p. 25. Available at <www.eumedion.nl/nl/public/kennisbank/handboeken/eumedion_handboek_cg_2013.pdf>.

[63] Art. 2:114a DCC. In legal literature, it is assumed that the board cannot reject a shareholder request that was submitted 60 days before the shareholders meeting on the ground that the board wishes to use a (longer) response period. See *inter alia* R.G.J. Nowak, 'Aangepaste corporate governance code vastgesteld' *Ondernemingsrecht* 2009/9, p. 39, M. Kroeze, NJB 2008, 1736 p. 2155. The minister stated that a response period of 180 days probably is contrary to the Shareholders Directive, which requires one uniform convocation period. TK 2008–2009, 31 083, no. 30, p. 12. These are two different things, however.

[64] See <www.corpgov.nl>.

[65] Compliance Report 2010, p. 56. See also sec. 4.3.

[66] Compliance Report 2011, p. 41.

k) Regulatory Environment

Dutch company law for public and private limited liability companies is mainly regulated in Book 2 of the Dutch Civil Code ('DCC'). Book 2 also contains some provisions that apply only to public companies which are listed on a regulated market or multilateral trading facility in the EEA or a comparable system outside the EEA.[67] The law on private companies was created in the Dutch Civil Code in the 1970s by copying most of the existing rules for public companies.[68] Many restrictions prescribed by the Second Directive for public companies, such as the financial assistance prohibition, were thus copied into the law for private companies without an obligation to do so.[69] Dutch company law has no separate set of rules regulating groups of companies (*concernrecht*), but case law and legal doctrine have developed a few rules on specific issues, such as piercing the corporate veil, identification, and a the duty of care of the parent company towards the creditors of its subsidiary.

The Dutch corporate governance code applies to Dutch public companies (i) whose shares or depositary receipts for shares have been admitted to trading on a regulated market or a comparable system; and (ii) with a balance sheet value exceeding €500 million whose shares or depositary receipts for shares have been admitted to trading on a multilateral trading facility or a comparable system.

Financial Supervision Act (*Wet financieel toezicht*)—In the past decade, largely necessitated by the coming into effect of the Transparency Directive, the Prospectus Directive and the Market Abuse Directive, a vast and rapidly increasing body of regulatory legislation has been enacted with respect to the (supervision of) publication of information by listed companies.[70] By far the most important law in this respect is the Financial Supervision Act (*Wet financieel toezicht*). It provides for a wide range of rules, varying from rules on (voluntary and mandatory) public bids to various disclosure obligations, such as the obligation of companies to publish price-sensitive information, the obligation of shareholders to notify certain percentages of shareholdings in listed companies, as well market abuse rules.[71] The *Euronext Amsterdam listing rules* apply to companies listed on Euronext.[72]

---

[67] Art. 2:114a (right to put items on the agenda) and 2:118a DCC (proxy to DR holders).

[68] See further Asser/Maeijer/Van Solinge and Nieuwe Weme 2-II* (2009), no. 6.

[69] See Asser/Maeijer/Van Solinge and Nieuwe Weme 2-II* (2009), no. 10.

[70] See the PhD thesis of J.B.S. Hijink, *Publicatieverplichtingen voor beursvennootschappen*, Serie IvO Vol. 74 (Deventer, Kluwer 2010).

[71] See on market abuse the PhD thesis of G.T.J. Hoff, *Openbaarmaking van koersgevoelige informatie*, Serie VHI Vol. 107 (2011).

[72] See sec. 4.3.

1.2. Financial Institutions[73]

Financial institutions are not the main focus of this report. Licensing and supervision of financial institutions is regulated in Chapter III of the Financial Supervision Act. Licenses are granted by the Dutch Central Bank (*De Nederlandsche Bank*). The policy of a financial institution has to be determined by persons who have the necessary expertise and whose reliability is beyond doubt (Art. 3:8 Financial Supervision Act).

A corporate governance code for banks was adopted by the Dutch Association of Banks in September 2009.[74] As with the corporate governance code for all listed companies, the Banking corporate governance code is the result of self-regulation by the sector and is based on the comply-or-explain principle. The Banking corporate governance code contains principles which are based on the Dutch corporate governance code of 10 December 2008, but focuses on the function and control of risk management in connection with the level of risk appetite. The corporate governance code for all listed companies also applies to listed financial institutions to the extent that the Banking corporate governance code does not deviate from it.

In the fall of 2008, the State acquired, by way of expropriation, the Dutch part of the Fortis Group, consisting of Fortis Bank en Fortis Verzekeringen (Fortis Insurances; later renamed ASR Nederland).[75] The shares acquired by the State were later transferred to an independent trust-like foundation, in which the State has certain veto rights.[76] In 2011, the Minister of Finance stated that he would strive for an exit for these two companies within four or five years,[77] but this intention was not repeated in 2012.

A law on special measures for financial institutions entered into force in 2012. It enables the Dutch Central Bank, *inter alia*, to separate good assets from bad assets within an unstable financial institution, and the Minister of Finance to expropriate outstanding shares of financial institutions if the stability of the financial system as a whole is threatened.

---

[73] See for a recent document on the governance of financial institutions:, Research Newsletter (Vol. 8/Summer 2010), *European Corporate Governance Institute*, available at <www.ecgi.org/research/research_newsletter/vol8.pdf/>.

[74] *Corporate governance code Banken* <www.commissiecodebanken.nl/scrivo/asset.php?id=541086>. See also the report of the Parliamentary Committee under presidency of MP De Wit: <www.tweedekamer.nl/images/Eerste_rapport_onderzoekscommissie_financieel_stelsel_118-206529.pdf> p. 14 f.

[75] Fortis, as part of a consortium with RBS and Banco Santander, had acquired a part of ABN-AMRO, which part was transferred to the State in 2008. As of 1 April 2010, the Dutch part of Fortis and the Fortis part in ABN-Amro were merged into ABN AMRO Bank NV (a subsidiary of the holding ABN-AMRO Group NV). ASR Nederland (the former insurance branch of Fortis) is a separate, direct holding of the State.

[76] TK 2010-11, 32 000, no. 2.

[77] Letter of the Minister of Finance, no. BFI/2011/00013 U.

1.3. Description of Available Board Models

Historically, Dutch company law is based on a two-tier board model. There is a formal and personal division between the management board (*bestuur*) and the supervisory board (*raad van commissarissen*). A supervisory board is usually used in listed companies[78] and is mandatory in (i) companies with labour co-determination; (ii) financial institutions;[79] and (iii) in a *Société Européenne* (SE) with seat in the Netherlands.

In legal practice, the one-tier model was imported from Anglo-American legal culture in the second half of the 20th century.[80] The former Koninklijke Olie NV (better known as Shell), and Unilever have had a one-tier board for decades.[81] The one-tier board model was formally incorporated in Dutch law as per 1 January 2013. One of the reasons for doing so was to better accommodate the Dutch legal system to the needs of foreign (in particular Anglo-American) investors, whose traditional board model is the one-tier model.[82]

The two-tier board is the reference point in Dutch company law. As of 1 January 2013, the law contains only a few specific provisions about one-tier boards; in all other matters the rules for two-tier boards should be applied correspondingly (see further below). The corporate governance code also contains a few provisions relating to one-tier boards.[83]

In past years, more than one-third of listed companies have established an Executive Committee (ExCo), consisting of all members of the management board and members of the higher management level. The latter are usually in the

---

[78] There is no provision explicitly stating that listed companies (not having a one-tier board) must have a supervisory board, but the corporate governance code takes it for granted that all listed companies have one.

[79] See at the end of this paragraph.

[80] See for a recent comparison between the UK, US and the Dutch one-tier board model: J.W.C. Calkoen, *The One-Tier Board The one-tier board in the changing and converging world of corporate governance: a comparative study of boards in the UK, the US and the Netherlands*, Serie IvO Vol. 107 (2011).

[81] It should be noted that these companies were dual headers with the other head in a country whose law has the one-tier system as a standard. Reed Elsevier NV has approximated the one-tier model by creating a combined meeting of the management board and the supervisory board.

[82] The Minister of Justice in the Explanatory Memorandum, TK 2008–2009, 31 773, no. 3, p. 1.

[83] Composition and functioning of the board should be such that a proper and independent supervision by the non-executives is safeguarded; the chairman may not be a (former) executive; only non-executives may sit on the committees; the majority of the board members has to consist of independent non-executives (CGC III.8).

majority.[84] Its activities and competence are usually only summarily described (if at all) in the company documents. The supervisory board is usually informed by the CEO about the ExCo's activities. Interestingly, the ExCo members of the higher management level often participate in meetings of the supervisory board.[85]

Companies with labour co-determination at board level were initially excluded from the scope of the first draft incorporating the one-tier board model into Dutch law. The minister stated that, except in the case of SEs, it was impossible or undesirable to create the possibility of a one-tier board in the labour co-determination regime (which provides for a separate supervisory board with employee representatives) as this would weaken the position of the employee representatives. But when the market parties, including the labour unions,[86] stated that they had no objections, the minister opened the possibility for labour co-determined companies to opt for a one-tier board.[87]

The law simply states that the co-determination rules with respect to the supervisory board (or its members) apply correspondingly to a one-tier board and its members. This corresponding application triggers the same type of questions as with one-tier boards in general. When the relevant provisions are applied correspondingly, the one-tier board as such should be identified with the company's management board (*bestuur*). This means that, as a general rule, all provisions concerning the management board in the Dutch Civil Code apply to the entire one-tier board (including the non-executives). Another question is whether the rules with respect to the supervisory board should be applied correspondingly to the entire board[88] or to the group of non-executives.[89] These questions have to be answered by taking into account the specifics of each provision.

[84] The average management board consists of 2.5 members, whereas the average number of higher management level represented in the ExCo is 6.5 members.

[85] *Compliance Report 2012*, p. 32.

[86] In its comments on the draft, FNV, the largest labour union stated that the usefulness of Dutch company law, which is an important reason to introduce the one-tier board, will be served if the one-tier board can also be used by companies with labour co-determination, available at <http://home.fnv.nl/02werkgeld/arbo/wetgeving/medezeggenschap/Bestuur_en_toezicht.htm>.

[87] See the Minister's justification in the Explanatory Memorandum, TK 2008–2009, 31 763, n° 3, p. 4.

[88] This corresponding application leads to problems in cases where the DCC provides that the management board has to submit a proposal or document to, or receive approval from, the supervisory board. See the interpretation of corporate governance code II.1.8 below. See further R.G.J. Nowak, 'Tegenstrijdig "Belang in het wetsvoorstel Bestuur en toezicht"', *Ondernemings-recht* 2008/16, p. 590.

[89] A related question is whether a provision with respect to members of the management board or supervisory board applies correspondingly to the members of the entire one-tier board or only to the executives or non-executives.

The SE Regulation gives SEs the right to choose between a two-tier board (with mandatory supervisory board) and a one-tier board.[90] As a consequence, EU Member States which had only one model, had to provide for legislation offering both models for SEs. Dutch law implementing the SE Regulation provides that in a one-tier model, the board consists of at least three members. Although one of the first SEs was established in the Netherlands in 2004, there was not much interest in them subsequently. As per 25 June 2010, there were 21 SEs with their seat in the Netherlands, of which 13 did not have employees.[91] As per December 2012, there is one listed company that has the form of a SE: Unibail Rodamco. It has a two-tier board and is not subject to the labour co-determination regime.

A financial institution (incorporated as a public company) is obliged to have a supervisory board with at least three members.[92] As to the question whether financial institutions can have a one-tier board (and delegate the required supervision to the non-executives), there is no indication of an answer in the applicable regulations or the parliamentary documents. The Banking corporate governance code contains separate rules for the management board and the supervisory board. The corporate governance code, applicable to all listed companies, contains a specific provision stating that these rules apply accordingly to one-tier boards. The Banking corporate governance code does not contain a similar provision, but it may be argued that the corresponding application in the corporate governance code applies. If this is correct, there is no reason to object to a one-tier board in financial institutions. The European Commission Green Paper on corporate governance in financial institutions states in this respect:

'The term "board of directors" in this Green Paper essentially refers to the supervisory role of directors in a company which, in a dual structure, generally falls within the scope of the supervisory board. This Green Paper does not prejudice the role attributed to different company bodies under national legal systems.'[93]

The response of the Dutch Government is not entirely clear: It states that in the Green Paper no difference is made between one-tier and two-tier boards and that the Netherlands 'pursuant to its starting point' (*naar uitgangspunt*) will interpret questions on the board of directors as pertaining to the supervisory board.[94]

---

[90] Council Regulation (EC) No. 2157/2001 on the Statute for a European Company (SE).

[91] Source: *Report from the Commission to the European Parliament and the Council,* COM(2010) 676 final dated 17 November 2010, Annex p. 14. See also Ernst & Young Study on the operation and the impacts of the SE, prepared on behalf of the European Commission, 9 December 2009, p. 152. For an updated overview of all SEs in the European Union, retrieved from <http://ecdb.worker-participation.eu/index.php>.

[92] Art. 3:19 Financial Supervision Act.

[93] Green Paper COM(2010) 284 final, note 15 on page 6.

[94] Letter of the Minister of Finance to the Lower House dated 23 July 2010 (FM/2010/4820 M), p. 3.

2. Authority

2.1. Functions/Powers

a) General Description of Functions

The law does not describe the tasks and functions of the management board and the supervisory board, but the corporate governance code contains a number of provisions to that effect. In a two-tier model, the task of the management board is to manage the company, which means, among other things, that it is responsible for achieving the company's aims, the strategy and associated risk profile, the development of results and corporate social responsibility issues that are relevant to the enterprise.[95] The management board is also responsible for complying with all relevant legislation, for managing the risks associated with company activities and for financing the company. The management board has to submit to the supervisory board for approval the operational and financial objectives of the company, the strategy that should lead to achieving the company's objectives, and the parameters to be applied in relation to the strategy. The management board is accountable for these responsibilities to the supervisory board and to the shareholders' meeting and it provides the supervisory board with all information necessary in time for the exercise of its the duties.[96] The task of the supervisory board is, briefly speaking, to supervise the management board's activities and give advice to the management board.

The board in a one-tier model has, *grosso modo*, the same tasks and duties as the management board and the supervisory board taken together. There is ample freedom in allocating the tasks which the two separate bodies have in a two-tier board, between the executives and non-executives of a one-tier board (but see below for specific prohibitions). The most important differences probably are that supervision in a one-tier board is not exercised by a separate body and that the non-executives formally have a co-originating role in respect of the development of the stategy and the performance of other board tasks.

b) Delegation of Tasks within the Board

Delegation of board tasks[97] to board members is allowed under Dutch law[98] and is commonly used in practice. Tasks are usually delegated in board regulations or by means of board resolutions. The core task of the management board, ie. determining the company's general policy (including its financial policy and its

---

[95] See CGC II.1.

[96] See 1.1.2.

[97] Here used as synonym for division, allocation and assignment of tasks.

[98] Art. 2:9 DCC.

strategy), cannot be delegated to board members, but has to be performed by the entire management board; and the core task of the supervisory board, ie. the supervision on the general policy of the company, cannot be delegated to board members, but has to be performed by the entire supervisory board.[99] Other tasks may, in principle, be delegated to one or more board members.[100] The delegation should be revocable; the board may decide that it wants to perform the delegated task as a collective and revoke the delegation.[101] If a task is delegated to one or more board members, the prevailing opinion probably is that they can also take (board) resolutions with respect to that task.[102]

[99] However, supervision on the company's financial policy is usually delegated to the audit committee.

[100] See A.M.H.W. Strik, 'Grondslagen bestuurdersaansprakelijkheid', PhD thesis, Serie IvO Vol. 73 (2010), pp. 91–92; B.F. Assink, *Preadvies Vereeniging Handelsrecht* (2009), pp. 140–141; S.H.M.A. Dumoulin, 'De positie van niet-uitvoerend bestuurders in het monistisch bestuursmodel' *Ondernemingsrecht* 2005/8, p. 269 (of whom only Assink mentions strategy). P. J. Dortmond, *De one tier board in de Nederlandse vennootschap*, Serie IvO Vol. 40 (2003), p. 121, argues that if the law (mandatorily) requires a board decision, the decision has to be made by the board members collectively. As an example he mentions the board decision to (de)merge. The same line of reasoning seems to be used in Asser/Maeijer/Van Solinge and Nieuwe Weme 2-II* (2009), no. 501, where it is argued that the powers which the law mandatorily gives to the supervisory board in a co-determined company cannot be delegated to an individual member of the supervisory board. It is not clear, however, whether the authors have in mind only the decision-making with respect to these tasks of also the actions preceding the decision-making.

[101] See, for example, Van Schilfgaarde/Winter (2009), no. 42, who state that every board member may always request that a matter that is allocated to a board member, be resolved by the entire board.

[102] See, *inter alia,* Asser/Maeijer/Van Solinge and Nieuwe Weme 2-II* (2009), no. 417; M. van Olffen, *inrichting one tier-vennootschap bij of krachtens de statuten*, in Serie IvO Vol. 67 (2009), p. 41 with further references; A.G. van Solinge, in *Liber amicorum Sjef Maeijer* (1988), p. 310; cfr. Preamble 10 of Recommendation 2005/162/EC on the role of non-executive or supervisory directors. However, in the parliamentary discussions in 2009 on the one-tier model the Minister of Justice expressed the opinion that without a specific provision in the law board members to whom a certain task is delegated, cannot take board resolutions with respect to that task (TK 2008–2009, 31 763, no. 3 p. 17). This view was contradicted by M. Van Olffen, 'Inrichting van de one tier vennootschap bij of krachtens de statuten', *Ondernemingsrecht* 2012/89, p. 486; Dumoulin, *Ondernemingsrecht* 2005, p. 268, stated that allocation of tasks cannot include the power to take (board) decisions with respect to these tasks, but in *Ondernemingsrecht* 2012, p. 493 states (referring to Van Olffen) that under current law it is generally held that delegation of decision-making is possible. Seemingly hesitant: De Kluiver, in P. Essers et al (eds.), *Met recht, Liber Amicorum voor Theo Raaijmakers* (2009), pp. 253–254; and Dortmond, *Ondernemingsrecht* 2005, p. 264. The matter is also disputed in other jurisdictions; see K.J. Hopt, 'Comparative Corporate Governance: The State of the Art and International Regulation', *The American Journal of Comparative Law*, 2011, Vol. 59, p. 32.

A delegation of tasks does not detract from the collective responsibility of the board for the proper performance of all of the board's tasks.[103] All board members are, in principle, responsible and liable for improper performance of a task, whether or not delegated. This implies that board members to whom a particular task is not delegated, should monitor the performance of that task by the board member to whom the task is delegated. However, a delegation of tasks may offer an escape from personal liability.[104] The law states (with respect to both one-tier and two-tier boards) that the tasks which are not delegated to one or more board members are incumbent upon all board members.

The above-mentioned general rules also apply to the one-tier model.[105] As in a two-tier model, the prevailing view is that the (entire) board should always be able to revoke a delegation of tasks.[106] The law further explicitly provides that board members can take decisions with respect to tasks delegated to them.[107] The nature of the one-tier board implies that the tasks of a more managerial character, in particular the day-to-day management (*dagelijks bestuur*), will usually be delegated to the fullest extent to the executive(s).[108] This entails that the tasks of the non-executives will probably be concentrated on supervision.[109] The law contains specific provisions in respect of the following tasks: The supervision of the performance of (all) board members cannot be 'withheld from the non-executives'; and the determination of the remuneration of executives and the

---

[103] This is the prevailing view. See further D.A.M.H.W. Strik, PhD thesis, Serie IvO Vol. 73 (2010), pp. 87–94, with references to dissenting opinions (including her own opinion). Strik points out that the precursors of Art. 2:9 DCC contained the opposite principle: no responsibility and liability for those board members to whom the relevant task is not allocated.

[104] See further sec. 4.4.1.

[105] See, *inter alia*, D.A.M.H.W. Strik, 'Aansprakelijkheid van niet-uitvoerende bestuursleden: you cannot have your cake and eat it', *Ondernemingsrecht* 2003, p. 373; probably also S.H.M.A. Dumoulin, *Ondernemingsrecht* 2005, p. 269.

[106] See, *inter alia*, S.H.M.A. Dumoulin, *Ondernemingsrecht* 2012, p. 494; A.F. Verdam, 'Collectieve en indidviduele bestuursverantwoordelijkheid', in J.B. Huizink et al (eds.), *Hoe verder met collegiaal bestuur in Nederland? Bestuurstaak, bestuursverantwoordelijkheid en bestuurdersaansprakelijkheid volgens het nieuwe artikel 2:9 BW* (2011), p. 33. The fact that the law prescribes that the delegation of tasks be laid down in the articles of association (Art. 2:129a par. 1 DCC) does not necessarily entail that the delegation cannot be withdrawn. It may be argued that the principle of collective responsibility entails that the full board always has the right to revoke the delegation.

[107] Art. 2:129a par. 4 DCC.

[108] See inter alia P.J. Dortmond, in *Nederlands ondernemingsrecht in grensoverschrijdend perspectief*, Serie IvO Vol. 40 (2003), p. 118 and S.H.M.A. Dumoulin, *Ondernemingsrecht* 2012, p. 492.

[109] See S.H.M.A. Dumoulin, *Ondernemingsrecht* 2012, p. 491.

nomination of board members cannot be 'delegated to the executives'. All other tasks of the board can be delegated to the executives.[110]

c) *Strategy*

The determination of the company's strategy falls within the competence of the management board, supervised by the supervisory board; it does not fall within the competence of the shareholders (meeting).[111] The corporate governance code provides that the role of the management board is to manage the company, which means, among other things, that it is responsible for the strategy. The management board is responsible for weighing up the different interests with respect to the company's strategy, whereas the supervisory board has to supervise this process. The management board submits the proposed strategy to the supervisory board for approval. The supervisory board discusses the strategy at least once a year.[112]

In a landmark decision of 2010, the Dutch Supreme Court has significantly reduced the playing field of activist shareholders by ruling—against the direction hitherto taken by the Enterprise Court—that it is up to the management board, under supervision of the supervisory board, to decide if and to what extent it is desirable to consult shareholders on matters of strategy, and that the duties of the supervisory board do not as such include an obligation to mediate in conflicts between the management board and shareholders in matters of strategy.[113] This is in contradiction with the UK corporate governance code, which provides that the chairman of the board should discuss governance and strategy with major shareholders.[114]

Although decisions on strategy, therefore, do not belong to the competence of the shareholders' meeting, it is possible to put the issue of strategy on the agenda of the shareholders' meeting for discussion purposes,[115] as is also acknowledged by the corporate governance committee:

'If the dialogue [between the board and the shareholders] fails to produce a result, shareholders are of course entitled to exercise their statutory rights (right to put items on the agenda and right to call an extraordinary meeting of shareholders) in order to express the views they have on the strategy.'
(corporate governance code, Account of the Committee, no. 45).

---

[110] Explanatory Memorandum, TK 2008–2009, 31 763, no. 3, p. 15. See also B.F. Assink, *Preadvies* (2009), p. 140–141.

[111] See, *inter alia,* Supreme Court 17 January 2007, *JOR* 2007/42 (*Stork*) and 13 July 2007, *JOR* 2007/178 (*ABN Amro*).

[112] CGC Principle II.1, Preamble no. 9, II.1.2 and III.1.8.

[113] Supreme Court 9 July 2010, JOR 2010/228 (*ASMI*).

[114] See also the advice of the Attorney-General Timmerman in the *ASMI* case.

[115] See further sec. 1.1(j), *Response period.*

In a one-tier model, determination of the strategy belongs to the core tasks of the (entire) board. It may be assumed that the determination of the strategy cannot be delegated to the executives, or, in other words, the (co-)determination may not be withheld from the non-executives. This assumption is further backed by the corporate governance code which states, with respect to two-tier boards, that the strategy set out by the management board needs the approval of the supervisory board. A corresponding application of this provision leads to the conclusion that the task of the non-executives is to co-determine the strategy.

d) Supervision

In a two-tier model, the core task of the supervisory board is to supervise the management and policy (including the strategy and the internal control and risk management systems) of the management board and the general affairs of the company and its enterprise.[116] The supervision also extends to the functioning, quality and continuity of the management. Further, the supervisory board monitors the way the management board fulfils its task with respect to financial reporting. The supervisory board is guided by the interests of the company and its enterprise, and takes into account the relevant interests of the company's stake-holders. The supervision is not only *ex post* but also entails the monitoring *ex ante* of the general line of policy in the long term.[117] At least once a year the supervisory board discusses the company's strategy and the main risks of the business, the result of the assessment by the management board of the design and effectiveness of the internal risk management and control systems, as well as any significant changes thereto.[118]

A commonly used technique to structure supervision is to make management board decisions subject to the approval of the supervisory board.[119] The Dutch Civil Code provides that decisions of the management board may be made subject to approval of the supervisory board or the shareholders' meeting. The bottom line is the principle that the management board has to have a minimum autonomy in order to be able to properly perform its tasks. Legal literature explains this principle by stating that not all management board decisions in all

---

[116] See for the accountability of the management board towards the supervisory board: H. Bahlmann, in M.J. Kroeze et al (eds.), *Verantwoording aan Hans Beckman* (2006), pp. 1–10. See for accountability in a one-tier board: H. Honée, in M.J. Kroeze et al (eds.), *Verantwoording aan Hans Beckman* (2006), pp. 215–224. See for the accountability of the supervisory board, in particular when it does not agree with the policy of the management board: P. Verdam, in P. Essers et al (eds.), *Liber amicorum Th. Raaijmakers* (2009), pp. 507–518.

[117] See corporate governance code par. III.1 and V.1 and Asser/Maeijer/Van Solinge and Nieuwe Weme 2-II* (2009), no. 487.

[118] CGC III.1.8; see also Art. 2:141 par. 2 of the DCC.

[119] See further sec. 2.2.2.

fields may be made subject to approval of the supervisory board and/or the shareholders' meeting.[120] In practice, usually a number of key decisions are made subject to approval.[121]

Given the historical roots of the two-tier model in the Netherlands, in particular the issue of how supervision works in a one-tier model, has given rise to debate in legal literature. The law provides that the supervision of the performance of tasks by board members cannot be delegated to the executives.[122] The Explanatory Memorandum states:

'In any case the non-executives should supervise the executives, but also each other. Also the executives have to take action when it comes to their knowledge that one of them does not properly perform his task. Supervision, therefore, is not exclusively a matter of the non-executives.'[123]

To a certain extent, this concept of internal supervision of board members of each other applies in every two-tier and one-tier board, but in the one-tier board model there is obviously more emphasis on internal supervision and on the duty of a board member to inform the other board members *ex ante* of the performance of the tasks delegated to him. Thus, the principle of collective responsibility shifts from decision-making to internal supervision on the (preparation and) decision-making of those to whom a task has been delegated.[124]

With respect to companies with labour co-determination, Dutch law mandatorily subjects a number of key decisions of the management board to the approval of the supervisory board, such as issue of shares, listing of shares and entering into or terminating a co-operation with another entity which is of significant importance to the company. Obviously, this approval requirement is meaningless in a one-tier model. Therefore, the law provides that the above-mentioned board decisions require a positive vote of the majority of the non-executives.[125]

e) Representation of the Company

The Dutch Civil Code provides that the management board (*bestuur*) as a body and any member individually are authorised to represent the company vis-à-vis third

---

[120] Asser/Maeijer/Van Solinge and Nieuwe Weme 2-II* (2009), no. 415.

[121] Often the list is copied of management board decisions which are subject to supervisory board approval in the labour co-determination regime (Art. 2:164 DCC).

[122] S.H.M.A. Dumoulin, *Ondernemingsrecht* 2012, p. 492 states that the text of the law permits that the task of supervising the way board members perform their task can be taken away from the executives.

[123] TK 2008–2009, 31 763, no. 3, p. 26.

[124] See further H.J. de Kluiver, in P. Essers et al (eds.), Met Recht. *Liber amicorum Theo Raaijmakers* (2009), p. 258 and the literature mentioned therein.

[125] Art. 2:164a par. 4 DCC. See further sec. 2.2.2(a).

parties. The articles of association may, however, provide that individual members are not so authorised, but certain combinations of them, or a combination of a board member and another person, may have this authority. The representation regime has to be filed with the trade register. If the company is represented in conformity with the information set out in the trade register, third parties are protected, as a general rule, against any deficiencies in the representation.

The law does not contain special provisions regarding representation in a one-tier model. This means that the articles of association may provide that (apart from the entire board) any combination of one or more executives and/or non-executives have the power to represent the company.

f) Internal Control and Risk Management;[126] *Auditors*

The rules on internal control and risk management are laid down in the corporate governance code. The company is obliged to have an internal risk management and control system that is suitable for the company. In the annual report the management board has to provide: A description of main risks related to the strategy of the company; a description of the design and effectiveness of the internal risk management and control systems; a description of any major failings therein; and a statement to the effect that these systems have worked properly in the reporting year and that they provide a reasonable assurance that the financial reporting does not contain any errors of material importance (so-called 'in control statement').[127]

The external auditor is appointed by the shareholders' meeting.[128] The corporate governance code provides that the supervisory board has to nominate a candidate for this appointment, having taken advice from the audit committee and the management board. The external auditor examines the annual accounts and reports his findings to both the management board and the supervisory board. He attends the meeting of the supervisory board at which the financial statements are adopted.[129] The external auditor also attends the shareholders' meeting at which the financial statements are to be adopted and may speak at that meeting;[130] the shareholders' meeting may ask him questions about the annual accounts.[131] The internal auditor operates under the responsibility of the management board. His main task, as the third line of defense, is to evaluate the effectivity of the internal control framework, ie. risk management and internal control processes. The

---

[126] See extensively on liability for improper risk management: D.A.M.H.W. Strik, *Pre-advies Vereeniging Handelsrecht* (2009), pp. 201–370.

[127] CGC II.1.3-5.

[128] Art. 2:393 par. 1 DCC.

[129] CGC V.2, V.4 and V.4.1

[130] Art. 2:117 par. 5 DCC and CGC V.2.1.

[131] CGC V.2.1.

internal auditor may also investigate matters that have been notified by a whistleblower. He usually co-operates with the external auditor and sometimes performs a part of the tasks of the external auditor. The powers, functions and tasks of the internal auditor are usually laid down in an *audit chart*.[132] The internal auditor has direct access to the external auditor and to the chairman of the audit committee.[133]

2.2. Organisation and Internal Functioning

2.2.1. Composition

a) Size of the Board

There are no requirements as to the size of the management board or the supervisory board, with the following exceptions. Under the labour co-determination rules the supervisory board has to consist of at least three persons. Applying this rule to the one-tier model, this means that the board should consist of at least three non-executives. Further, the law implementing the SE provides that if an SE has a one-tier board, it should consist of at least three members.[134] Finally, a financial institution is obliged to have a supervisory board with at least three members.[135] As for one-tier boards the law prescribes that they have to consist of one or more executives and one or more non-executives, so that at least one executive and one non-executive should sit on the board. The corporate governance code provides that the majority of members have to be non-executives.

In AEX companies the number of members of the management board varies from 2 to 6. The number of members of the supervisory board, including companies subject to the labour co-determination rules, varies from 5 to 11. The average number of supervisory board members of Dutch listed companies was 8.7 in 2010, against a European average of 12.1.[136] One-tier boards tended to be slightly larger than the management board and the supervisory board together:

---

[132] On audit charts see L. de Bruijn, 'Corporate governance en de internal auditor', *Onder-nemingsrecht* 2011/85, pp. 428–432.

[133] CGC V.3.1-3.

[134] Art. 13 of the Law implementing the SE (*Wet van 17 maart 2005 tot uitvoering van verordening (EG) Nr. 2157/2001 van de Raad van de Europese Unie van 8 oktober 2001 betreffende het statuut van de Europese vennootschap (SE)*, Stbl. 2005/150, on the basis of Art. 43 of the Regulation on the Statute for a European company (SE), OJ L 294/1.

[135] Art. 3:19 Financial Supervision Act.

[136] Heidrick & Struggles, Challenging board performance, *Corporate governance report 2011*, p. 37, available at <www.heidrick.com/PublicationsReports/PublicationsReports/HS_EuropeanCorpGovRpt2011.pdf>.

one-tier boards had on average 11.4 members, whereas the two boards in a two-tier model had a joint average of 9.9 members.[137] The board of Unilever NV consists of 10 non-executives and 2 executives; the board of Heineken Holding consists of 8 non-executives and 2 executives.

b) Overall Principles for Composition[138]

A member of the management board cannot at the same time be a member of the company's supervisory board.[139] A member of the supervisory board (and a non-executive in a one-tier board) must be a natural person.[140] The corporate governance code provides that the supervisory board has to be composed in such a way that its members can operate critically and independently in relation to each other, the management board and party interests. It further provides that the supervisory board should prepare a profile of its size and composition, taking account of the nature of the business, its activities and the desired expertise and background of the supervisory board members.[141] The supervisory board should aim to have a mixed composition.[142] At least one member of the supervisory board should be a financial expert with relevant knowledge and experience of financial administration and accounting for listed companies or other large legal entities. At least once per year, the supervisory board discusses its own func-tioning (including the functioning of the committees) and the functioning of the members of the management board without the members of the management board being present.[143]

c) Diversity

As of 1 January 2013, the law contains a provision stating (with respect to both one-tier and two-tier boards) that the composition of the management board and

---

[137] SpencerStuart, *Netherlands Board Index 2010*, p. 14, available at <http://content.spencerstuart.com/sswebsite/pdf/lib/NLBI_FINAL2010.pdf> The proportion of executives (2.2) vs. non-executives (9.2) differed from that of management board members (3.4) vs. supervisory board members (6.5): in one-tier boards less than one fourth of the directors is an executive, in two-tier boards more than one-third is a member of the management board.

[138] See further the report of the Universities of Groningen and Utrecht of November 2010: *Samenstelling en functioneren van de raden van commissarissen van Nederlandse beurs-genoteerde vennootschappen in 2009*, available at <www.corpgov.nl>.

[139] This follows from the system of Dutch company law, which is based on the two-tier model. See further Asser/Maeijer/Van Solinge and Nieuwe Weme 2-II* (2009), nos 486 and 493.

[140] Art. 2:140 and Art. 2:129a par. 1 DCC.

[141] The law obliges supervisory boards of co-determined companies to compose a profile for the members of the board (Art. 2:158 par. 3).

[142] III.3 CGC.

[143] CGC III.2, III.3, III.3.1 and III.1.7.

the supervisory board should be balanced in terms of gender representation and specifies that at least 30% of the members of the boards (if natural persons) should consist of women and at least 30% of men.[144] No sanction is imposed in case of non-compliance.

The proportion of women on boards of Dutch listed companies in 2010 was higher than the European average (15% versus 12% in Europe).[145] The Compliance Report 2010 shows that in 2009 the supervisory boards of AEX companies consisted of 137 men and 28 women, but that there were six companies without women on the board, so that the average of the remaining AEX companies was higher than 15%.[146]

On 14 November 2012, the European Commission launched a proposal for a Directive on improving the gender balance among non-executive directors of listed companies, providing for a minimum of 40% of each gender.[147] A majority of the Dutch Parliament has declared that it is against the proposal on the ground that it is in contradiction with the principle of subsidiarity.[148]

d) The Chairman of the Board[149]

There is no description of tasks of a chairman of the management board in the Dutch Civil Code nor in the corporate governance code. The corporate governance code provides that the chairman of the supervisory board ensures the proper functioning of the supervisory board and its committees, and acts as the main contact for the management board and for shareholders regarding the functioning of the board members. In his capacity of chairman, he ensures the orderly and efficient conduct of the shareholders' meeting. He is also the person to whom

---

[144] See on this provision M. Lückerath-Rovers/S. Paans, 'De haalbaarheid van het quota wetsvoorstel', *Ondernemingsrecht* 2011/31, pp. 160–164.

[145] Heidrick & Struggles, *Corporate Governance Report 2011*, p. 39.

[146] *Compliance Report 2010*, p. 42.

[147] COM(2012) 614 final, 2012/0299 (COD).

[148] Upper House and Lower House of Parliament, Letter to the president of the European Commission dated 18 December 2012. The percentage of non-Dutch members in supervisory boards of Dutch listed companies in 2010 is still comparatively high but has decreased from 54% in 2008 to 47% in 2010. The European average is 24%. Heidrick & Struggles, *Corporate Governance Report 2011*, p. 37. From the *Compliance Report 2010* it appears that this percentage has significantly decreased in 2009 to approx. 30% (*Compliance Report 2010*, p. 44). It is not clear how these data relate to the Heidrick & Struggles' data for 2010.

[149] See on the functions of the chairman: S. Schuit, *The Chairman makes or breaks the Board* (in Dutch) (2010).

See on separation of the functions of chairman and CEO: R. Kraakman, 'One Cheer for the Two-Tier Board', in *Liber Amicorum Theo Raaijmakers* (2009), pp. 277–278.

board members have to report a possible conflict of interest.[150] The chairman of the supervisory board may not be a former member of the management board.[151] There is no rule stating that the chairman has to be independent. Usually, the chairman of the supervisory board is appointed by the supervisory board from amongst its members. The chairman of the management board is usually appointed by the supervisory board or by the joint meeting (see below) of the supervisory board and the management board.[152]

In the one-tier model the law provides that the chairman of the board may not be an executive director.[153] The corporate governance code contains a broader restriction by providing that the chairman of a one-tier board may not be *or have been* in charge of the daily affairs of the company.[154]

e) Company Secretary

The supervisory board is assisted by a company secretary. The company secretary ensures that correct procedures are followed and assists the chairman with the organisation of the supervisory board. He is, either on the recommendation of the supervisory board or otherwise, appointed and dismissed by the management board, subject to approval of the supervisory board.[155] In practice, in two-tier systems the company secretary is secretary to the management board in the first place. He plays a pivotal role in enhancing information streams and contacts between board members and management.[156] A recent questionnaire shows that company secretaries increasingly fulfil the role of an unappointed chief governance officer.[157]

---

[150] CGC II.3.2, III.4 and III.6.1. See further Asser/Maeijer/Van Solinge and Nieuwe Weme 2-II*(2009), no. 500.

[151] CGC III.4.2.

[152] See further J. Dop, J.W. de Groot, 'Checks and balances bij de aanwijzing van de bestuursvoorzitter', *WPNR* 2006/6671, pp. 459–464.

[153] M. van Olffen, in Serie IvO, Vol. 67 (2009), p. 44, remarks that, as a consequence, executives may not participate in the board resolution appointing a non-executive as chairman. It is not clear why this would be the case.

[154] Art. 2:129a DCC and CGC III.8.1, respectively.

[155] CGC III.4.3. See also Asser/Maeijer/Van Solinge and Nieuwe Weme 2-II*(2009), no. 502.

[156] See S. Schuit, *The Chairman makes or breaks the Board* (2010), p. 63.

[157] See M.L. Lückerath, 'Report on the role of the company secretary', Vol. 16 and B. van Leeuwen, 'Rapport over de rol van de (directie)secretaris bij corporate governance' *Ondernemingsrecht* 2011/118, p. 590–591.

f) Joint Meetings of Management Board and Supervisory Board

The members of the management board often participate (without voting power) in meetings of the supervisory board, but they have no legal right to enforce such participation.[158] The CEO almost always attends supervisory board meetings and the CFO is also often present. However, supervisory boards regularly have a separate meeting prior to the joint meeting. Conversely, supervisory board members seldom participate in management board meetings.[159]

g) Committees of the Supervisory Board

Dutch company law has no mandatory rules on committees.[160] The corporate governance code provides that if the supervisory board consists of more than four members, it appoints from among its members an audit committee, a remuneration committee, and a selection and appointment committee. The purpose of the committees is to prepare the decision-making of the supervisory board. No more than one member of each committee may be non-independent within the meaning of corporate governance code.[161] If the supervisory board contains four members or less, the board itself may exercise the functions of these committees.

The audit committee supervises the activities of the management board with respect to, *inter alia*, the operation of internal risk management and control systems, the provision of financial information by the company and compliance with recommendations of the internal and external auditors.[162] The audit committee may not be chaired by the chairman of the supervisory board nor by a former member of the management board.[163] The Dutch Decree implementing the

---

[158] The average number of meetings of one-tier boards of AEX companies was 8 in 2010, whereas the average for combined management and supervisory board meetings was 8.8. See SpencerStuart, *Netherlands Board Index 2010*, p. 24.

[159] See *Compliance Report 2012* p. 31. The Dutch Civil Code provides that the articles of association may create a combined meeting (*gemeenschappelijke vergadering*) of the management board and the supervisory board, which the law identifies as a separate body of the company (apart from the two boards) and to which certain powers may be conferred. See, for example, Reed Elsevier NV, where the joint meeting may subject categories of decisions of the management board to its approval. This brings into mind the one-tier board as a sort of combined meeting of executives and non-executives. See also P.J. Dortmond, Serie IvO Vol. 40 (2003), pp. 115–116.

[160] See further Asser/Maeijer/Van Solinge and Nieuwe Weme 2-II* (2009), no. 494.

[161] CGC III.2.1.

[162] See further H. Langman, 'De audit-commissie', *Ondernemingsrecht* 2005/89, pp. 259–263.

[163] CGC III.5.4 and 6.

Audit Directive[164] prescribes that at least one member of the audit committee must be independent and declares most provisions of the corporate governance code relating to the audit committee applicable. The Audit Directive allows Member States to provide that a company may refrain from instituting a separate audit committee if it designates a corporate body (the entire supervisory board) to perform the tasks of that committee. The Decree contains a provision to that effect.[165] It should be noted once more that the corporate governance code prescribes (on a comply-or-explain basis) that only one supervisory board member may be non-independent. The remuneration committee may not be chaired by the chairman of the supervisory board nor or by a former member of the management board of the company or by a supervisory board member who is a member of the management board of another listed company. No more than one member of the remuneration committee may be a member of the management board of another Dutch listed company.[166] Risk committees can be found in financial institutions but not often in (other) listed companies. Other committees that may be established are the strategy committee and the merger committee.

h) Restrictions with Respect to Similar Positions in Other Companies

As of 1 January 2013, the number of memberships of two-tier boards and one-tier boards in NVs, BVs and foundations of a certain size[167] is limited by law in the following ways:

A person cannot be appointed as managing director or executive director: (i) If he or she is a supervisory director or non-executive director in more than two other such entities; or (ii) if he or she is the chairman of the supervisory board or the one-tier board of another such entity. A person cannot be appointed as supervisory director or non-executive director if he or she is a supervisory director or non-executive director in more than four other such entities, whereby the position of chairman of the supervisory board or one-tier board counts twice. The limitations do not apply to advisory positions, or to any positions with non-Dutch entities. Supervisory/non-executive directorships within a group are counted as one.[168]

---

[164] Directive 2006/43/EU and Decree of 26 July 2008, Official Journal 2008/323, implementing Directive 2006/43/EU of 17 May 2006 regarding the control of annual and consolidated accounts.

[165] Audit Directive Art. 41 par. 5 and Decree (see previous note) Art. 2 par. 3.

[166] CGC III.5.11 and 12.

[167] At least two of the following criteria have to be met: (i) Asset value exceeding €17,500,000 according to the balance sheet; (ii) the financial year's net turnover exceeding €35,000,000; (iii) number of employees in the financial year on average 250 or more.

[168] Art. 2:132a and 2:142a DCC.

The consequence of non-observance of these rules is that the last appointment is invalid. In order to mitigate this far-reaching consequence, the law provides that the invalidity of the appointment does not affect the validity of the resolutions taken. This awkward solution was apparently inspired by French law.

The corporate governance code contains similar provisions. It provides that a member of the management board of a listed company may hold no more than two supervisory board positions (not being that of chairman) in other listed companies; and a member of the supervisory board may hold no more than four other supervisory board positions (a chairmanship counting twice).[169] The acceptance by a management board member of such a position requires the approval of the supervisory board. Other important positions held by a management board member have to be notified to the supervisory board.[170]

i) Disqualification of Directors

There are no rules regarding disqualification of directors. The Ministry of Justice, in the framework of the incorporation of a company or an amendment of its articles of association, tested whether its directors had a criminal record, but this test was abolished as of 1 January 2011. The government has announced that it will launch a legislative proposal on disqualification in 2013.

2.2.2. Decision-Making

a) Majorities, Multiple Voting Rights, Decisive Vote

Apart from a few mandatory rules, companies are free to choose their own decision-making rules. They have to be laid down in the articles of association or in board regulations.[171] As for quora and majorities, the general principle is that resolutions can be adopted without a quorum and with a simple majority of votes cast, unless the articles of association or board regulations provide otherwise.[172] This principle is explicitly set out in the law in respect of shareholder resolutions.[173] The articles or board rules may provide for any quorum or supermajority requirement, including unanimity of all the members of the board, even if such

---

[169] CGC III.3.4.

[170] In one-tier boards, the notification and approval provisions should probably be applied correspondingly in the following manner: if a member of a one-tier board wants to accept a position as member of a supervisory board or as non-executive in a one-tier board, he needs to notify or receive approval from the entire board.

[171] Provided that the articles of association state that board regulations may be adopted. Asser/Maeijer/Van Solinge and Nieuwe Weme 2-II* (2009), no. 420.

[172] Asser/Maeijer/Van Solinge and Nieuwe Weme 2-II*(2009), nos 365–366.

[173] Art. 2:120 par. 1 DCC.

requirement impedes the decision-making process.[174] The law explicitly allows multiple voting rights with respect to board resolutions, the bottom line being that one board member alone must never be able to cast more votes than the other members together.[175] Multiple voting rights are seldom used in listed companies, one of the few examples being Ahold, but this system was withdrawn a few years ago. The situation of a tie-vote is not regulated with respect to management and supervisory board resolutions. With respect to shareholder resolutions the law provides that in case of a tie-vote the proposal is rejected,[176] unless the law or the articles provide for another solution; this solution may be that a third party is requested to take the decision.[177] As to tie-votes in boards, it is generally held that the chairman of the board may be given a decisive (casting) vote, or that another corporate body (such as the supervisory board) may take the decision.[178] It is then a small step to assume that the chairman of that other corporate body may also take the decision.[179] If the chairman of the board is given a decisive vote in case of a tie-vote, he may not have as many votes as all other board members together. This is a consequence of the rule that one board member must never be able to cast more votes than the others together.

As for the one-tier model, an earlier discussion draft of the law contained a provision stating that the executives together cannot cast more votes than the non-executives together.[180] This provision was abolished without further explanation. It is not clear whether this opens the possibility of giving the group of executives more voting power than the group of non-executives.[181] The corporate govern-

---

[174] This is not different under the labour co-determination regime. The labour representatives in the supervisory board, having one-third of the seats/votes, may even obtain a veto position if a particular supermajority is prescribed.

[175] Art. 129 par. 2 and Art. 2:140 par. 4 DCC; see also Asser/Maeijer/Van Solinge and Nieuwe Weme 2-II* (2009), no. 419.

[176] But if it concerns the election of persons, the outcome is decided by lot.

[177] Art. 2:120 par. 1 DCC.

[178] See the Policy rules of the Ministry of Justice (*Departementale richtlijnen*), formally abolished in 2001 because of procedural changes, but materially still containing the prevailing view.

[179] See further G. van Solinge and R.G.J. Nowak, 'Bestuursbesluiten na afschaffing van het preventief toezicht', *Ondernemingsrecht* 2002/14, pp. 434.

[180] Preliminary draft Art. 2:129a par. 3, as published on the website of the Ministry of Justice. The draft explanatory memorandum, p. 18, gave the following justification: In case of discord in the board the opinion of those who are in general more focused on long-term interest, should prevail. For criticism on this justification, see M. van Olffen, Serie IvO no. 67 (2009), p. 46. At another place the draft explanatory memorandum also confusingly implied that the draft Bill stated that the non-executives should have more votes than the executives.

[181] The same effect can, of course, be reached by appointing (in deviation from the corporate governance code) more executives than non-executives. S.H.M.A. Dumoulin, 'De positie van niet-uitvoerend bestuurders in het monistisch bestuursmodel' *Ondernemingsrecht* 2005/91,

cont. ...

ance code seems to prohibit this by providing that the majority of the members of the one-tier board has to consist of non-executives.[182] Also here, it is probable (but not entirely clear) that the underlying idea is that the executives together should not be able to cast more votes than the non-executives together.

The above rules with respect to quorum, majorities and tie-vote also apply in companies with labour co-determination. Multiple voting rights can also be used in co-determined companies. However, the mandatory rule that gives the works council the right to nominate one-third of the members of the supervisory board, cannot be circumvented by giving the other members more voting rights. The provision should therefore be understood as follows: The works council has the right to nominate one-third of the members or so many members as represent one-third of the total number of votes.

b) *Veto Rights and Approval Rights*

Veto rights and approval rights both aim to give certain board members the power to block a board decision that otherwise could have been taken. There are three types of veto and approval rights that can be created in a board under Dutch law. The first requires unanimity of all existing board members: In that case, each board member has a veto right. The second type is attained by granting multiple voting rights: If a board member is granted as many votes as all other board members have together (which is allowed), he *de facto* has a veto right. The final type of veto is by providing that a decision can only be validly adopted if a particular (group of) board member(s) is not against it or is in favour of it. The last type is known as veto right *stricto sensu*. It was used by the Dutch State when during the financial crisis it had to make credit facilities available to ING, Aegon and SNS. In return for these facilities, the State required two persons to be appointed as supervisory board members. The board regulations provided them with a veto right in respect of certain decisions. Although this construction was criticised in legal literature, most authors acknowledge its validity.[183] Another form of approval right (with the effect of a veto right) is the right of another corporate body (eg. the supervisory board or the shareholders' meeting) to approve decisions of the management board. According to Dutch law, decisions

---

p. 269 points out (conversely) that multiple voting rights can be used to obtain a majority of votes of non-executives who are a minority in number. However, normally the non-executives are in the majority. For the use of multiple voting rights in one-tier boards see also P.J. Dortmond, Serie IvO Vol. 40 (2003), p. 121.

[182] CGC III.8.4.

[183] See, with further references, R.G.J. Nowak and J. Wegter, 'Overheidscommissarissen in financiële instellingen', in N.E.D. Faber et al (eds.), *De kredietcrisis*, Serie OO&R, Vol. 54 (2010), pp. 121–138.

of the supervisory board cannot be made subject to the approval of any other corporate body or person.[184]

The above-mentioned three types of veto and approval rights can also be used in the one-tier model. The question arises whether decisions on issues belonging to the competence of (the group of) executives can be made subject to a veto of the group of non-executives in the same way as where in a two-tier model decisions of the management board can be made subject to approval of the supervisory board. This question should be answered in the affirmative.[185] It is clear that if this technique is used too abundantly, the result will be a board within a board. The rule in two-tier boards, that decisions of the supervisory board cannot be made subject to the approval of any other corporate body or person, has in a certain sense disappeared in the one-tier model, as board decisions may be subjected to approval of the shareholders' meeting.

With respect to companies with labour co-determination, the law provides in the two-tier model that the supervisory board has a mandatory right of approval of certain important decisions of the management board.[186] There was some conceptual difficulty incorporating this mandatory approval right in the one-tier model. The minister initially stated that in a one-tier board the management board decisions concerned have to be taken by all board members (both executives and non-executives) and, therefore, there would be no need for an additional approval right of the non-executives.[187] However, in terms of checks and balances the supervisory board of a two-tier co-determined company would in that case have a better position than the non-executives in a one-tier board, as a supervisory board can block the relevant management board decisions by withholding the required approval. Therefore, an amendment was proposed to the effect that the relevant management board decisions require the 'approval' (ie. the vote) of the majority of the non-executives.[188] The Minister of Justice strongly advised against it, stating that if one opts for a one-tier board, one should not create a board within the board. The amendment was nevertheless adopted.

---

[184] Asser/Maeijer/Van Solinge and Nieuwe Weme 2-II*(2009), no. 499.

[185] See also below under 'Companies with labour co-determination: One-tier model'.

[186] Art. 2:164 DCC.

[187] TK 2008–2009, 31 763, no. 3, p. 21.

[188] TK 2009–2010, 31 763, no. 15.

2.2.3. Independent Directors[189]

The supervisory board can only perform its tasks properly if it is sufficiently independent in relation to the different interests of the company. This independence from interests of specific parties or groups is underlined by the rule laid down in the law stating that the supervisory board has to act solely in the interest of the company and its enterprise.[190] This implies that independent directors should be independent from all stakeholders, not only from management.[191] The rule applies to all board members, whether or not qualifying as non-independent. A board that exclusively consists of representatives of the parent company or of the various other partial interests, is not recommended. Independence and knowledge of the board as a whole should always prevail.[192]

The corporate governance code provides that the composition of the supervisory board should be such that its members are able to act critically and independently of one another, the management board and any particular party interest.[193] It further specifies that all supervisory board members, with the exception of not more than one person, have to be independent. The code contains a catalogue of situations similar to the criteria in Annex II of the Recommendation on non-executive directors.[194] A supervisory board member is deemed to be non-independent if they, or their spouse or other life companion, foster child or relative by blood or marriage up to the second degree:

a) has been an employee or member of the management board of the company including associated companies[195] in the five years prior to the board member's appointment;

b) personally receives financial compensation from the company, or a company associated with it, other than the compensation received for the

---

[189] See extensively: N.J.M. van Zijl, *The Importance of Board Independence. A Multi-disciplinary Approach*, PhD thesis, Erasmus University Rotterdam 2012. See for a comparison between US and Dutch independency requirements, M.J. van Ginneken, 'De onafhankelijke commissaris' *Ondernemingsrecht* 2012/134, pp. 719–727 (based on his inaugural lecture, Rotterdam University, May 2012). Van Ginneken pleads for less stringent independency requirements and more powers for independent directors in order to enhance the trustee-relationship.

[190] Art. 2:140 par. 2 DCC. See further H.H. Kersten, 'De onafhankelijke toezichthouder', *Ondernemingsrecht* 2004, 43, p. 130.

[191] See also M.J. van Ginneken, *Ondernemingsrecht* 2012 (see n. 189), p. 724.

[192] Asser/Maeijer/Van Solinge and Nieuwe Weme 2-II* (2009), no. 509. See further M.J. Kroeze, 'Onafhankelijkheid van commissarissen', *Ondernemingsrecht* 2005/92, p. 273 and H.H. Kersten, Ondernemingsrecht 2004, pp. 129–136.

[193] CGC III.2.

[194] See for criticism M.J. Kroeze, *Ondernemingsrecht* 2005, pp. 274–275.

[195] As referred to in Art. 5:48 of the Financial Supervision Act.

work performed as a supervisory board member and in so far as this is not in keeping with the normal course of business;

c) has had an important business relationship with the company, or a company associated with it, in the year prior to the appointment. This includes the case where the supervisory board member, or the firm of which he is a shareholder, partner, associate or advisor, has acted as advisor to the company (consultant, external auditor, civil notary and lawyer) and the case where the supervisory board member is a management board member or an employee of any bank with which the company has a long-standing and important relationship;

d) is a member of the management board of a company in which a member of the management board of the company which he supervises is a supervisory board member;

e) holds at least ten percent of the shares in the company (including the shares held by natural persons or legal entities which cooperate with him under an express or tacit, oral or written agreement);

f) is a member of the management board or supervisory board—or is a representative in another way—of a legal entity which holds at least ten percent of the shares in the company, unless such entity is a member of the same group as the company; or

g) has temporarily managed the company during the previous twelve months due to the fact that management board members have been absent or unable to discharge their duties.[196]

In takeover situations, the requirement that the supervisory board should have a sufficient number of independent members also applies as long as the company still has minority shareholders after a succesful takeover bid.[197]

In the first years, the corporate governance monitoring committees reported that a significant minority 13–15% of the companies deviated from (ie. 'explained' the non-compliance of) this code provision. The Compliance Report 2010 stated that in 2009 all listed companies met the requirement of having at most one non-independent member (in the meaning of the corporate governance code) on the supervisory board.[198] In 2010, 75% of the non-executive (supervisory) directors in Dutch listed companies were independent.[199] The Compliance

---

[196] CGC III.2.2.

[197] See Supreme Court 14 September 2007, *JOR* 2007/239 (*Versatel III*).

[198] *Compliance Report 2010*, p. 41.

[199] Heidrick & Struggles, *Corporate governance report 2011*, p. 42. Less than 1% are employee representatives, 4% are former executive directors, 2% are reference shareholders and 8% are other non-independent directors. Assuming that also in 2010 all listed companies met the companies met the requirement of having at most one non-independent member, there is an inconsistency, as 75% independent directors means, in boards counting eight members, that two board members are non-independent.

Reports 2011 and 2012 no longer address this issue, probably because it seems that the companies state that they are in full compliance in this respect.[200]

As for the one-tier model, the corporate governance code states that it applies correspondingly to non-executives. However, the code further provides that the majority of the board has to consist of non-executive members who are independent within the meaning of the code.[201] This means that if, for example, a board consists of 15 members, at least 8 of them must be independent (non-executives). Therefore, if this one-tier board of 15 members would consist of 13 non-executives, 5 of them do not have to be independent. This rule is far less strict than the rule that only one member of a supervisory board may be non-independent.[202]

The Dutch Civil Code mandatorily provides that in co-determined companies the following persons cannot be a member of the supervisory board: Persons employed by the company or a subsidiary; and persons employed by trade unions involved in establishing the employment conditions of the persons employed by the company.[203] The independence requirements of the corporate governance code apply in full. In principle, under the labour co-determination rules a large shareholder is also not excluded from membership of the supervisory board.[204]

The requirement of all but one board member having to be independent is far more severe than any other European country's corporate governance code pre-scribes. To understand the background of this requirement, its history is briefly set out below. In December 2003, the Tabaksblat Committee published a separate 'Account of the Committee's work' together with the first corporate governance code. This account does not form an official part of the CGC and, therefore, does not appear in official editions of the corporate governance code.[205] In the Account, the Tabaksblat Committee defends this requirement by stating that the presence of more than one non-independent member in the supervisory board is difficult to reconcile with the statutory tasks of the supervisory board. The relevant *passus* of the Account is quoted here in full because it sheds some light on the creation of this surprisingly rigid rule:

---

[200] Some companies smuggled in this respect by stating that although a particular director would qualify as non-independent according to the CGC criteria, the company considers him or her independent because he or she is perfectly able to make an independent judgment.

[201] CGC III.8.4.

[202] See further N.J.M. Van Zijl, *The Importance of Board Independence: A multi-disciplinary Approach*, PhD thesis, Rotterdam University, Serie IvO no. 90 (Deventer, Kluwer 2012), pp. 226–227.

[203] Art. 2: 160 DCC.

[204] See further Kersten, *Ondernemingsrecht* 2004, p. 131, note 17 for references to the Explanatory Memorandum of the law introducing the labour co-determination regime.

[205] Remarkably, the account is published as a part of the CGC on the Committee's website <www.corpgov.nl>.

'42. Many companies have criticised the provision that only one person within the supervisory board need not be independent as well as the criteria applied to determine whether a person qualifies as independent. It is alleged that the independence criteria and the rule that only one supervisory board member need not be independent would place the Netherlands out of line with international practice. In addition, the independence criteria are said to be arbitrary and too rigid. The provision of one "dependent" supervisory board member at maximum could cause the loss of a lot of experience if supervisory board members who are closely involved with the company are denied membership of the supervisory board. The small listed companies asked the committee to relax the requirements in relation to their supervisory boards.

43. The independence criteria were selected with reference to the British Combined Code and the criteria named in the report entitled "A Modern Regulatory Framework for Company Law in Europe" of the EU High Level Group of Company Law Experts. In its communication published on 21 May 2003 entitled "Modernising Company Law and Enhancing Corporate Governance in the European Union – A Plan to Move Forward", the European Commission announced its intention to apply these criteria in a soon-to-be published recommendation on the independence of supervisory board members and non-executive directors. These independence criteria would, at the very least, have to be incorporated into the national corporate governance codes. The committee is thus acting in anticipation of this European obligation. The argument that the provision of at maximum one dependent supervisory board member is too stringent cuts no ice. In discharging its role, supervisory board members shall be guided by the interests of the company and its affiliated enterprise. These interests should outweigh any sectional or individual interest. In discharging its role, supervisory board members should not serve particular interests. When a company is dominated by a major shareholder, the supervisory board members should for example also take the interests of the minority shareholders into account. The presence of more than one non-independent member in the supervisory board is difficult to reconcile with the statutory tasks of the supervisory board.'[206]

In legal literature, the requirement has been much criticised as being unnecessarily severe and counter-productive.[207] It was also (probably justly) held that the requirement does not represent a common principle of good governance in the time before the corporate governance was published (nor thereafter).

---

[206] Account of the Committee of the corporate governance code of 2004, No. 42 (translation provided by the Committee, except for the last sentence). The Account of the CGC of 2008 no longer contains this *passus*.

[207] Most recently, M.J. van Ginneken, *Ondernemingsrecht* 2012 (see n. 189), p. 724.

2.3. Information Streams[208]

The members of the management board often participate in meetings of the supervisory board. The management board has the obligation to provide the supervisory board in a timely manner with all information necessary for the performance of its functions.[209] The members of the supervisory board have the duty to ask the management board for all information necessary to fulfil their duties as a member of the supervisory board. The duty to ask for information follows directly from the duty to properly perform the supervisory task. In a number of mismanagement proceedings, the Dutch Supreme Court (ruling in appeal) has elaborated on the required degree of activity of the supervisory board by investigating, in the cases concerned, the moment at which and the extent to which the supervisory board should have asked for information with more urgency and should have monitored the performance of tasks by the management board in a more active manner.[210]

The corporate governance code provides that the supervisory board and its individual members each have their own responsibility for obtaining all information from the management board (and the external auditor) that the supervisory board needs in order to be able to properly perform its monitoring task. If the supervisory board considers it necessary, it may directly obtain information from (and speak to) officers and external advisors of the company.[211] In practice, it is usually the Chairman of the supervisory board that contacts the President of the manangement board (CEO) if specific information is needed. It is the Chairman who is responsible for effective information streams from the management board to the supervisory board. Informal contacts between the Chairman (or other members of the supervisory board) and members of the management board occur more or less frequently, depending on the culture in a given company. Contacts between the Chairman and executives under management board level occur less often.[212] The company secretary plays an important role in these matters.

---

[208] See for the issue of relying on information by management board members: M. Mussche, *Vertrouwen op informatie bij bestuurlijke taakvervulling*, PhD thesis 2011, Serie IvO Vol. 83. See for information provided to the supervisory board by the auditor sec 2.1. See for information streams in companies in financial distress sec. 3.3.

[209] Art. 2:141 DCC and corporate governance code II.1. See further Asser/Maeijer/Van Solinge and Nieuwe Weme 2-II* (2009), no. 492; see for the reporting obligations of the management board to the supervisory board: Bahlmann, in M.J. Kroeze et al (eds.), *Verantwoording aan Hans Beckman* (2006), pp. 1–10 and Honée, *ibid.*, pp. 215–223.

[210] See in particular Supreme Court 8 April 2005, JOR 2005/119 (*Laurus*).

[211] CGC III.1.9.

[212] See S. Schuit, *The Chairman makes or breaks the Board* (2010), pp. 61–64.

3. Accountability

3.1. Board and Shareholders

An important standard is the standard of reasonableness and fairness.[213] In company law this standard is expressed in Art. 2:8 DCC, which states that, *inter alia*, the board(s) and the shareholders have to act toward each other in accordance with the standard of reasonableness and fairness. Resolutions of the board and the shareholders' meeting which are contrary to this standard are voidable.[214]

3.1.1. *Appointment, Suspension and Dismissal of Directors*

a) *General Remarks*

The members of the management board and the members of the supervisory board are appointed, suspended and dismissed by the shareholders' meeting.[215] For appointment, suspension and dismissal in co-determined companies, see below. In an SE with seat in the Netherlands and with a two-tier board, the members of the management board are appointed, suspended and dismissed by the supervisory board, unless the articles of association vest this power in the shareholders' meeting.[216] The articles of association may provide that up to one-third of the members of the supervisory board may be appointed by a third party.[217] This option is not available if the labour co-determination regime is applicable.

Dismissal under Dutch company law is at will (without good cause), albeit that all resolutions of the board and the shareholders' meeting have to be in accordance with the standard of reasonableness and fairness, and that resolutions adopted contrary to this standard are voidable.[218] This may be the case if the board member involved has had no proper opportunity to defend himself against the intended dismissal or to present his view on the intended dismissal. The grounds for the dismissal do not play a role when judging whether the resolution

---

[213] Formerly known as 'good faith'. See Art. 6:2 and 6:248 DCC for this standard in the relationship between debtor and ceditor and between parties to an agreement. See for the relation between this standard and the broader standard of proportionality: M.J. Van Ginneken and L. Timmerman, 'De betekenis van het evenredigheidsbeginsel voor het ondernemingsrecht' *Ondernemingsrecht* 2011/17, pp. 601–618.

[214] Art. 2:15 par. 1 under b DCC. See further sec. 4.1.2.

[215] Art. 2:132/134 and Art. 2:142/144 DCC.

[216] Art. 11 UitvW SE-Verordening.

[217] Art. 2:143 DCC.

[218] Art. 2:15 par. 1 under b.

was adopted contrary to the standard of reasonableness and fairness,[219] but are relevant when testing, in the context of a claim for damages, whether the termination of the employment agreement was reasonable.[220]

The resolution to dismiss a board member has direct effect and terminates (in case of a management board member) the employment agreement. Since 1 January 2013, the law provides that the legal relationship between a listed company and a member of the management board cannot be qualified as an employment agreement.[221]

b) Binding Nomination

The articles of association may provide that appointment of members of the management and/or supervisory board can only take place on the basis of a binding nomination of a person mentioned in the articles of association.[222] Usually this right is granted to the supervisory board, which means that this facility is used as a protective device.[223] The binding nomination may always be rejected by the shareholders' meeting with a majority of two-thirds of the votes cast, if such majority represents more than half of the issued share capital.[224] Upon rejection, the shareholders' meeting is free to propose and vote for its own candidate. However, the articles of association, stretching up the nomination right, sometimes provide that upon rejection the supervisory board is entitled to make another binding nomination. A variation of this technique is to provide that a resolution appointing a candidate who is proposed by a shareholder, needs a larger majority than a candidate proposed by the board. A corresponding provision then usually exists in case of removal.[225] With respect to suspension and dismissal, the law provides for the same ceiling to the protection: If the articles of association require a certain supermajority in conjunction with a quorum, this requirement may not be higher than a majority of two-thirds of the votes cast, and

---

[219] This is different in case of companies subject to labour co-determination, where supervisory board members may be dismissed by the Enterprise Court, but only in case of negligence and for other important reasons (Art. 2:161 para. 2 DCC).

[220] See further Asser/Maeijer/Van Solinge and Nieuwe Weme 2-II* (2009), no. 426 and 435.

[221] Art. 2:132 par. 3 DCC.

[222] Art. 2:133 DCC.

[223] See further sec. 1.1(j).

[224] Art. 2:133 par. 2 and Art. 2:142 par. 2 DCC.

[225] It may be argued that this 'unequal treatment' is allowed because it is in line with the possibility of allowed unequal treatment in the form of binding nominations (provided that the supermajority is not larger than that for rejection of the binding nomination).

such two-thirds majority may not be required to represent more than half of the issued share capital.[226]

The corporate governance code, however, recommends a lower ceiling for the rejection of a binding nomination: The shareholders' meeting may reject the nomination by a simple majority of votes. A quorum requirement may be connected to this simple majority, but it may not exceed one-third of the issued share capital. If such a quorum requirement is not met, but a simple majority is in favour of the resolution, the code provides that a new meeting may be convened at which the resolution may be passed by a simple majority of the votes cast, regardless of the proportion of the capital represented at the meeting. The same applies to quorum requirements for dismissal (but not for suspension). [227] According to the Compliance Report 2010, 19 listed companies deviated from the corporate governance code in this respect and used the maximum ceiling of protection permitted by the law.[228]

c) Suspension of Management Board Members by Supervisory Board

Both the shareholders' meeting and also the supervisory board have the right to suspend management board members, unless the articles of association provide otherwise. The shareholders' meeting can always lift the suspension.[229]

d) Inability of Board Members; 'Substitute Directors'

In case of temporary or permanent inability[230] of a member of the management board or supervisory board to perform his functions, the other members continue to act as the board, but the articles of association may contain specific provisions in this respect. The supervisory board does not have the authority to formally appoint (either temporarily or otherwise) a new board member in case of inability of an existing board member.[231] In case of inability of the entire management board, the articles have to provide how management will be temporarily per-

---

[226] Art. 2:134 par. 2 and Art. 2:144 par. 2 DCC. This raises the question which combinations of higher majority and lower quorum requirements (and v.v.) are allowed; see W. Westbroek and A.A. Schulting, *Departementale Richtlijnen Commentaar*, Par. 6, note 10, Rechtspersonen (losbladig) (1986).

[227] CGC IV.1.1.

[228] *Compliance Report 2010*, p. 19.

[229] Art. 2:147 DCC. This is different if the full co-determination regime is applicable—see below.

[230] Temporary inability comprises absence without contact possibilities and severe illness, whereas permanent inability means resignation, dismissal and death.

[231] Except in co-determined companies with the so-called full regime, where the supervisory board has the power to appoint the members of the management board.

formed until the shareholders' meeting is able to appoint new management board members.[232] Usually the articles provide that one or more members of the supervisory board will temporarily perform the tasks of the management board. It is not possible to appoint 'substitute directors' in the sense that the 'real' board member and the substitute board member are (appointed) board members at the same time. However, it is possible to appoint a person in advance as per the next term and probably also under the condition precedent that a current board member ceases to be board member before his term ends.[233]

e) Term

The law does not prescribe a minimum or maximum term of appointment. Under the labour co-determination rules a supervisory board member has to resign after four years, but he can be re-elected.[234] The corporate governance code provides that members of the management board are appointed for a term of four years, which may be extended for another period of four years.[235] Members of the supervisory board are appointed for a term of four years, which may be extended for two other periods of four years. The situation that the term of all supervisory board members end in the same year must be avoided.[236] According to the Compliance Report 2010, 50% of the listed companies deviated in 2009 from the term for management board members.[237]

In a one-tier model, the above rules apply correspondingly. Pursuant to the law the shareholders' meeting has to appoint board members either as an executive member or as a non-executive member. The (entire) board has at all times the right to suspend executive members, whereby the executive concerned abstains from the discussions and voting. The right to make nominations for the appointment of board members may only be granted to non-executives, not to executives.[238] As in the two-tier model with respect to supervisory board members, the articles of association may provide that up to one-third of the non-

---

[232] Art. 2:134 par. 4 DCC.

[233] Probably in this sense (with respect to members of the supervisory board): Asser/Maeijer/Van Solinge and Nieuwe Weme 2-II* (2009), no. 493, although in no. 484 they seem to agree with the ministerial Guidelines (now abolished) that an appointment under a condition precedent is not admitted.

[234] Art. 2:161 DCC.

[235] CGC II.1.1.

[236] CGC III.3.5-6. See further Asser/Maeijer/Van Solinge and Nieuwe Weme 2-II* (2009), nos. 431 and 506.

[237] *Compliance Report 2010*, p. 22.

[238] Art. 2:132 par. 1, Art. 2:134 par. 1 and Art. 2:129a par. 1 DCC.

executives may be appointed by a third party, unless the labour co-determination regime is applicable.[239]

f) Companies with Labour Co-Determination

Companies with labour co-determination have different and complicated rules for appointment, suspension and dismissal of board members. The members of the management board are appointed, suspended and dismissed by the supervisory board in the so-called full co-determination regime; this power may not be restricted by any binding nomination.[240] In the so-called mitigated co-determination regime, the members of the management board are appointed, suspended and dismissed by the shareholders' meeting.[241] In the latter case, the supervisory board has the right to suspend members of the management board (unless the articles provide otherwise), but the shareholders' meeting can always lift the suspension.[242]

The members of the supervisory board are appointed by the shareholders' meeting on the basis of a 'binding' nomination of the supervisory board itself. The works council has the right to nominate one-third of the members.[243] The nomination may be rejected by the shareholders' meeting with a simple majority representing at least one-third of the issued share capital; if there is a majority that votes for rejection but does not represent at least one-third of the issued share capital, a new meeting must be convened in which the quorum requirement does not apply.[244] Upon rejection, the shareholders' meeting is not free to nominate its own candidate: the supervisory board has the right to make a new binding nomination (in case of a rejected works council nominee: on the basis of a new nomination by the works council). Deviation in the articles of association from these nomination and appointment rules is possible by agreement between the supervisory board, the works council and the shareholders' meeting.[245]

---

[239] Explanatory Memorandum in respect of Art. 2:134 DCC.

[240] Art. 2:162 DCC. In the mitigated regime, the articles may provide that appointment of management board members takes place on the basis of a binding nomination. See further sec. 3.2.1.

[241] Art. 2:155 DCC. See for the notion of mitigated regime sec. 3.2.1.

[242] Art. 2:147 DCC.

[243] For this reason supervisory boards of co-determined companies often have a total number of members divisible by three minus one, eg. 5 (resulting in 20% labour members), 8 (25% labour members) or 11 (37% labour members).

[244] This rule was inserted by amendment with the explanation that the quorum requirement is an important impediment for the exercise of the right of dismissal by the shareholders meeting (TK 2002-2003, 28 179, no. 42).

[245] Art. 2:158 DCC.

A member of the supervisory board may only be suspended by the supervisory board. Subsequently, the board has to file an application with the Enterprise Court for his dismissal.[246] A member of the supervisory board may only be dismissed by the Enterprise Court. Dismissal takes place at the request of the supervisory board or by a person designated by the shareholders' meeting or the works council, and only when the member has neglected his tasks or in case of other serious reasons or significantly changed circumstances.[247]

The supervisory board may be dismissed collectively by the shareholders' meeting. The resolution may be adopted by a simple majority of votes, which majority has to represent at least one-third of the issued share capital.[248] The works council has to be informed of the proposed resolution at least 30 days before the day of the shareholders' meeting. The resolution has to contain the reasons for the dismissal.[249] After the dismissal of the entire supervisory board, the Enterprise Court appoints one or more interim members of the supervisory board. This interim board appoints a new full board within the period stipulated by the Enterprise Court.[250] The *Stork* case is the only instance so far in which two activist shareholders (the hedge funds Centaurus & Paulson) requested the dismissal of the entire supervisory board on the ground that they did not agree with the company's strategy.[251] When Stork issued high voting preference shares by way of protective device, the hedge funds initiated proceedings before the Enterprise Court. The Enterprise Court ordered the protective device to be lifted by way of immediate relief but at the same time, at the request of the works council, prohibited the voting on the dismissal of the board at the forthcoming shareholders' meeting on the grounds that the actions of the hedge funds were contrary to the standard of reasonableness and fairness.[252] Recently, in a remarkable decision the President of the Amsterdam District Court ordered the listed football club Ajax to convene a shareholders' meeting with the sole agenda

---

[246] Art. 2:161 par. 3 DCC.

[247] Art. 2:161 par. 2 DCC.

[248] This quorum requirement is a rule of mandatory law, given the purpose of the requirement (to avoid that an incidental majority of the shareholders meeting could dismiss the entire supervisory board). See De Monchy et al, De nieuwe structuurwet (2004), p. 85. Therefore, a smaller quorum may not be provided in the articles of association, nor a provision to the effect that if the required quorum was not reached, a second meeting may be held without a quorum requirement.

[249] If the resolution contains no or insufficient reasons for the dismissal, it is voidable. See further Asser/Maeijer/Van Solinge and Nieuwe Weme 2-II* (2009), no. 587.

[250] Art. 2:161a.

[251] See further 1.1 under 'Protective devices'.

[252] Supreme Court 17 January 2007, *JOR* 2007/42 (*Stork*). See further Asser/Maeijer/Van Solinge and Nieuwe Weme 2-II* (2009), no. 558.

item the dismissal of the entire supervisory board.[253] The decision was quashed by the Court of Appeal.[254]

In co-determined companies with a one-tier board, the provisions with respect to the appointment, suspension and dismissal of the members of supervisory board apply correspondingly to the non-executives of a one-tier board.[255] The corresponding application leads to the following rules:[256]

1. Executives in the full co-determination regime are appointed, suspended and dismissed by the non-executives;
2. Executives in the mitigated co-determination regime are appointed, suspended and dismissed by the shareholders' meeting;[257]
3. Executives may (also) be suspended by the entire board;[258]
4. There have to be at least three non-executives,
5. Non-executives are appointed by the shareholders' meeting based on a 'binding' nomination of the non-executives;
6. The works council has the right to nominate one-third of the non-executives;
7. Non-executives may be suspended by the group of the non-executives;
8. Non-executives have to resign after four years;
9. Individual non-executives may be dismissed by the Enterprise Court;
10. The group of non-executives may be dismissed collectively by the shareholders' meeting.

3.1.2. Division of Powers between the Board and the Shareholders' Meeting

The law mandatorily confers certain powers upon the shareholders' meeting and certain other powers upon the board(s).[259] Powers which the law gives neither to the shareholders' meeting nor to the board(s) may be attributed to either of them in the articles of association.[260] In order to avoid doubt as to whether a particular power belongs to the board or the shareholders' meeting, the law provides that all

---

[253] Voorzieningenrechter Rechtbank Amsterdam 12 December 2011, *JOR* 2012/7, with comment by R.G.J. Nowak.

[254] Gerechtshof Amsterdam 7 February 2012, *JOR* 2012/76, with comment by J.M. Blanco Fernández.

[255] Art. 2:164a DCC.

[256] See also Asser/Maeijer/Van Solinge and Nieuwe Weme 2-II* (2009), no. 558.

[257] This is an omission in the law; see R.G.J. Nowak, *Ondernemingsrecht* 2013/1.

[258] Art. 2:134 par. 1.

[259] See Asser/Maeijer/Van Solinge and Nieuwe Weme 2-II* (2009), nos. 319–321 for the shareholders meeting, nos. 389–392 for the management board and nos. 486–488 for the supervisory board.

[260] Asser/Maeijer/Van Solinge and Nieuwe Weme 2-II* (2009), no. 321.

powers which the law or the articles of association do not attribute to the board or to others fall within the competence of the shareholders' meeting.[261] In practice, this attribution of residual competence works the other way round.

Certain powers the law confers upon the shareholders' meeting may be delegated to the board, in particular the power to issue shares and to exclude preemptive rights of existing shareholders, as well as the power to buy back shares. In practice, these powers are delegated for a period of 18 months and the delegation is renewed at every annual shareholders' meeting. Certain powers cannot be delegated (eg. capital decrease and amendment of the articles of association).

The most important powers which the law confers on the shareholders' meeting are:
- appointment and dismissal of board members;
- changes in the company's articles of association;
- changes in the company's capital and governance structure (other than by way of amendement of the articles of association)
- approval of legal merger and demerger;
- approval of board decisions with very substantial impact (see below); and
- bankruptcy and liquidation of the company.

In 2004, a new provision was incorporated in the Civil Code, giving the shareholders' meeting the right to approve board decisions with respect to an important change of the identity or the character of the company or its enterprise.[262] The provision lists three categories of decisions which are subject to shareholder approval in any case (but the list is not exhaustive). The provision was used by the parties who wanted to prevent ABN Amro from selling its subsidiary LaSalle Bank to Bank of America. The Enterprise Court blocked the sale, but in the appeal proceedings the Supreme Court concluded that the LaSalle sale, with a purchase price of €11 billion, did not qualify as a board decision falling under the scope of the mandatory approval right because it did not constitute an important change of the company's character and because the rule has to be interpreted in a restrictive way.[263]

The articles of association may provide that the management board has to act in accordance with the instructions of the supervisory board or the shareholders' meeting regarding the general policy to be followed by the company.[264] There has been much debate on the question of whether a shareholder may give specific,

---

[261] Art. 2:107 DCC.

[262] Art. 2:107a DCC.

[263] Supreme Court decision in the *ABN AMRO/LaSalle* case, HR 13 July 2007, *JOR* 2007/178.

[264] Art. 2:129 par. 4 DCC.

concrete instructions to board members.[265] The prevailing view seems to be that board members, depending on the circumstances and the nature of the desired policy, cannot refuse to act pursuant to an instruction of the shareholders' meeting if certain conditions are met, such as the parent company compensating the subsidiary for damages caused by the execution of the instruction, or the absence of disproportionate damage to the interests of the creditors.[266] It has been argued in literature that giving instructions to the management board is not in accordance with the supervisory task of the supervisory board.[267] If one assumes that it is, it is questionable whether the right to give instructions to the executives can be granted to the non-executives in a one-tier board.[268] Instruction rights do not occur in the articles of association of AEX companies.

3.1.3. Special Issues

a) Conflicts of Interest

There are two (similar) sets of conflict of interest rules: Mandatory rules in the Dutch Civil Code (for all public and private companies) and comply-or-explain rules in the corporate governance code (for listed companies). Listed companies have to comply with both sets.

As of 1 January 2013, new conflict of interest rules were introduced in the Dutch Civil Code entailing that if one of the members of the management board or the supervisory board has a possible conflict of interest with the company, he or she has to inform the other board members thereof and may not participate in the deliberations and the decision-making on the issue concerned. If all members of the management board are conflicted, the power to adopt the resolution is transferred to the supervisory board; and if all members of the supervisory board are conflicted, the authority to adopt the resolution is transferred to the share-holders' meeting, unless the articles of association provide otherwise.[269] Non-observance of these rules results in the resolution concerned being voidable. The definition of conflict of interest is given by the Supreme Court and is very casuistic: There is a conflict of interest in the meaning of the law if a director, as a consequence of a direct or indirect personal interest which is not congruent with the interest of the company, taking into account all circumstances of the case at

---

[265] The law governing private limited companies (BVs) allows the shareholders meeting and the supervisory board to give specific instructions to the management board (Art. 2:239 par. 4).

[266] L.Timmerman, 'Instructierecht', *Ondernemingsrecht* 2001/16, p. 477. See also Asser/Maeijer/Van Solinge and Nieuwe Weme 2-II* (2009), no. 831 (with further references).

[267] See further Asser/Maeijer/Van Solinge and Nieuwe Weme 2-II* (2009), no. 413.

[268] Affirmative: J.P. Dortmond, Serie IvO Vol. 40 (2003), p. 121.

[269] Art. 2:129/239 par. 5 and Art. 2:140/250 par. 6.

hand, could not have deemed himself capable to safeguard the interest of the company with the required integrity and objectivity.[270] It is the court that judges *ex post* whether a director had a conflict of interest in a specific situation. The board has to strive for maximum transparency and accountability in the internal decision-making process, as the Supreme Court and also the Enterprise Court have underlined in many decisions.[271] The law does not give a special role to independent directors (disinterested directors) in conflicts.

The corporate governance code contains *grosso modo* the same procedural rules for conflicts of interest but it does not provide a definition. It only refers to conflicts of interest 'which are of material significance for the company or for the board member concerned'. It also states that there is in any case a conflict of interest in the following circumstances: When the company intends to engage in a transaction with a legal entity in which he personally has a material financial interest; where a member of the management board has a family relationship with him; or where he is member of the management or supervisory board.[272] If a board member thinks he has a conflict of interest with the company that is of material significance for the company or for the board member, he has to report this to the chairman of the supervisory board. The supervisory board (not the chairman) determines whether there is a conflict of interest. If so, the board member concerned has to abstain from the discussion and the voting on the relevant item, and the decision of the management board to enter into the trans-action concerned is subject to approval of the supervisory board. The code gives no rules for cases in which all board members have a conflict of interest. The transaction has to be concluded on customary terms and must be published in the annual report.[273] Non-observance of these rules does not lead to the resolution concerned being voidable, but to an obligation for the board to explain the non-observance in the annual report.

b) *Related-Party Transactions*

Related-party transactions fall within the scope of the conflict of interest rules, both pursuant the Civil Code rules and the corporate governance code rules. Furthermore, pursuant to the code, transactions of material significance between the company and a person holding 10% or more of its shares, are subject to approval of the supervisory board.[274] The EC Green paper posed the question to

---

[270] Supreme Court 29 June 2007, JOR 2007/169 (*Bruil*).

[271] See also Asser/Maeijer/Van Solinge and Nieuwe Weme 2-II* (2009), nos. 402–403; 410.

[272] CGC II.3.2 and III.6.2.

[273] See further Asser/Maeijer/Van Solinge and Nieuwe Weme 2-II* (2009), nos. 428–429 and 412.

[274] II.3.1-4 and III.6.1-2 CGC.

Member States whether they are of the opinion that minority shareholders should be better protected against transactions of the company with related parties.[275] The Dutch government answered that no special rules on related-party transactions are needed, as 'it is not necessary to protect one particular group against damages caused by acting in case of a conflict of interest. Dutch law already contains sanctions against acting in case of a conflict of interest.'[276]

c) *Corporate Opportunities and Non-Compete*

The corporate governance code provides that a management board member: Will not enter into competition with the company; will not demand or accept (substantial) gifts from the company for himself or for his spouse, partner, children or close blood relatives; and will not provide unjustified advantages to third parties to the detriment of the company. Furthermore, he will not take advantage of business opportunities to which the company is entitled for himself or for his spouse, partner, children or close blood relatives.[277] The concept of corporate opportunities has been further developed in case law and legal literature.[278]

d) *Inside Information*[279]

The Financial Supervision Act (*Wet financieel toezicht*), implementing, *inter alia*, the Market Abuse Directive, contains a number of provisions with respect to inside information. Non-compliance with these provisions constitutes a criminal offence. Only the most important provisions are briefly mentioned here. Firstly, board members[280] are prohibited from using inside information by concluding a transaction relating to a large range of listed financial instruments (including shares) of the company concerned.[281] Inside information is defined as information

---

[275] Green Paper COM(2010) 284 final dated 5 April 2011. See also the ECGF statement on related-party transactions dated 10 March 2011.

[276] Letter of the minister of Justice to the Lower House dated 31 May 2011, 22 112, no. 1181, p. 5.

[277] CGC II.3.1.

[278] See inter alia A.F. Verdam, *Corporate opportunities, Over de toeëigening door functionarissen van aan de vennootschap toebehorende business opportunities* (1995), and more recently D.R.A. Goris, 'Corporate opportunity leer aanvaard?', *V&O* 2006/11, pp. 213–216.

[279] See extensively the PhD thesis of G.T.J. Hoff, *Openbaarmaking van koersgevoelige informatie*, Serie VHI Vol. 107 (2011).

[280] And holders of 10% or more of the issued share capital or the voting rights.

[281] Art. 5:56 Financial Supervision Act. The element of knowledge (conscious use) of inside information that was introduced in Dutch law was modified by a decision of the Court of Justice, stating that if a person with inside information concludes a transaction in financial instruments to which the inside information pertains, this entails that this person uses the inside

cont. ...

related to the company which is not published but which, were it published, could have had a significant impact on the share price of the financial instruments. Secondly, board members are prohibited from passing inside information to other persons or recommending or persuading other persons to conclude transactions in respect of the financial instruments concerned.[282] Issuers are obliged to keep insider lists and issue insider regulations. The corporate governance code provides that the management board or, where appropriate, the supervisory board should provide all shareholders and other parties in the financial markets with equal and simultaneous information about matters that may influence the share price.[283]

e) Takeover Situations[284]

Apart from detailed rules regulating the procedure for public bids,[285] Dutch law does not provide much guidance as to how boards should act in takeover situations. Two main rules apply to boards in a takeover situation. Firstly, there is no reconfiguration of board rules, which means that the board is obliged to continue to act in the interest of the company and its stakeholders.[286] Secondly, there is no mandatory passivity rule,[287] which means that the board may oppose the takeover attempt if it thinks the takeover is not in the interests of the company. Of course, shareholder interest plays a central role in takeover situations, in particular the question whether the shareholders are offered a fair price. If the board is of the opinion that the offered price is too low, ie. if the board thinks that the long term shareholder value (when the company's current stategy is continued) is higher than the offered price, it may decide not to support the bid.[288] Obviously, the

---

information (proof to the contrary being admitted). Court of Justice 23 December 2009, JOR 2010/70.

[282] Art. 5:57 Financial Supervision Act.

[283] CGC IV.3.

[284] See in particular the PhD thesis on hostile takeovers by M.J. van Ginneken, Serie IvO Vol. 79 (2010).

[285] These rules, most of them based on EU directives, contain, *inter alia,* dislosure, notification and publication requirements and time limits for all stages of a public bid. They are not dealt with here, nor are the mandatory bid rules or the squeeze-out procedure.

[286] See sec. 1.1. There is a certain tension here, because the intention of creating shareholder value in the long term, as emphasised in the Preamble of the corporate governance code, cannot be realised for the existing shareholders when they accept the bid. See M.W. Josephus Jitta and B.R. van der Klip, *De rol van het bestuur en de raad van commissarissen bij een openbaar bod,* Serie IvO Vol. 46 (2008), p. 307.

[287] The law implementing the Takeover Directive has made the passivity rule optional for companies. See Art. 2:359b DCC and sec. 1.1.

[288] See further M.W. Josephus Jitta and B.R. van der Klip, *De rol van het bestuur en de raad van commissarissen bij een openbaar bod,* Serie IvO Vol. 46 (2008), pp. 313–317.

board has to explain such a decision. The absence of support may be expressed either in the form of a neutral advice or in the form of negative advice. Depending on the circumstances, negative advice may be supported by the exercise of a protective device.

Most Dutch listed companies have one or more protective devices in place (or are subject to the labour co-determination rules, which can also function as a protective device). With respect to the two most used protective devices—high voting preferences shares and depositary receipts of shares—the decision to use the device lies with the (independent) board of the foundation that holds the option, or the shares, respectively.[289] In case of a hostile bid, the company's board will inform the board of the foundation about the situation and will give its opinion, but the foundation's board has its own responsibility to do what it believes to be in the interest of the company.

Change of control clauses may lead to conflicts of interest in takeover situations. The same applies to management incentive plans and private equity leveraged buy-outs. The law and the corporate governance code do not contain specific rules for conflicts in takeover situations (nor do the takeover rules), but the general conflict rules apply, entailing that board members who have a conflict of interest, may not participate in the decision-making process. The Enterprise Court has ruled that the mere fact that board members have a financial interest in the takeover, does not preclude them from participating in the negotiations, nor from taking the strategic decisions resulting in the takeover. Further, the Enterprise Court ruled that the mere fact that board members would receive a new board position after the takeover provides insufficient grounds for a presumption of a conflict of interest.[290] The Minister of Justice has emphasised that board members in a takeover situation should be aware of a possible conflict of interest, especially if a board member receives an allowance or bonus if the bid is successful.[291]

With respect to change of control clauses, the corporate governance code provides that they have to be published upon conclusion of the agreement with the board member.[292] In takeover situations, the law requires that the amount of all allowances in connection with the execution of the bid per member of the board has to be published in the bid document.[293]

The corporate governance code provides that in case of a takeover bid the management board board ensures that the supervisory board is closely involved in

---

[289] See further sec. 1.1.

[290] Enterprise Court 17 April 2008, *JOR* 2008/154 (*ABN AMRO*).

[291] Explanatory Memorandum, TK 2008–2009, 31 763, no. 3, p. 12. See further Josephus Jitta and Van der Klip, *De rol van het bestuur en de raad van commissarissen bij een openbaar bod*, Serie IvO Vol. 46 (2008), p. 322–326, and, in the same book, Leijten, p. 341–371.

[292] CGC II.2.14.

[293] Annex A, § 2, part 9 Besluit Openbare Biedingen, Stbl. 2007/329.

the process in a timely manner. Furthermore, if a takeover bid is made and a competitive bidder requests the board to receive access to company information, the management board has to discuss this request with the supervisory board without delay. The supervisory board should have a (pro-)active, independent attitude, especially given the fact the members of the management board usually have substantial financial interests in case of a succesful bid.[294]

As stated, in takeover situations, the requirement that the supervisory board should have a sufficient number of independent members continues to apply as long as the company still has minority shareholders after a succesful takeover bid. If this requirement is no longer met, the Enterprise Court may appoint one or more supervisory board members to protect the interests of the non-accepting minority before and during the squeeze-out procedure.[295]

3.1.4. *Institutional Investors*

The corporate governance code contains a number of provisions directed at institutional investors holding shares in listed companies. The code defines institutional investors as pension funds, insurance companies, investment institutions and asset managers. Since 2007, pension funds, life insurance companies, investment institutions and premium pension institutions are obliged to state in their annual report whether they have complied with these provisions.[296] Institutional investors act primarily in the interests of the ultimate beneficiaries or investors and are accountable to them. They are obliged to publish their policy relating to the exercise of voting rights for shares they hold in listed companies annually; the manner in which they have implemented their policy on the exercise of the voting rights in the year under review; and, at least once a quarter, the manner in which they have voted as shareholders at the shareholders' meeting of the companies concerned.[297]

In the last few years, institutional investors have been under pressure to become more active shareholders in the companies in which they hold shares. The majority of pension funds and many other institutional investors have set up Eumedion, an influential organisation monitoring the performance of listed companies and representing institutional investors as shareholders at shareholder meetings. The participants are not only Dutch but also foreign institutional investors, including some of the largest foreign asset management funds. Dissatisfaction with a company's policy is thus regularly shown by (succesfully) opposing resolutions regarding directors remuneration and annual release of

---

[294] CGC II.1.10-11.

[295] See Supreme Court 14 September 2007, *JOR* 2007/239 (*Versatel III*).

[296] Art. 5:86 Financial Supervision Act.

[297] CGC IV.4.1-4.

liability of directors. In 2011, Eumedion adopted a set of *Best practices for engaged share ownership* for its participants.[298] As of 1 January 2012, the Best Practices have to be observed by the participants on an apply-or-explain basis. The Best Practices are in line with international guidelines for institutional investors, such as the *UK Stewardship Code* and the ICGN *Statement of Principles on Institutional Shareholder Responsibilities*. Eumedion participants are requested to cast informed votes at shareholder meetings, as well as to monitor their investee companies' activities in the field of risk management, disclosure and remuneration policy, and to support the company in respect of good governance and consulting other shareholders and stakeholders where appropriate.

3.1.5. *Remuneration (as Incentive)*

The Dutch Civil Code provides that the shareholders' meeting has to set a policy for the remuneration of the management board. The remuneration of individual members of the management board is determined, taking into account the remuneration policy, by the shareholders' meeting or, if the articles so provide, by the supervisory board. In the latter case approval of the shareholders' meeting is still required insofar as the remuneration contains shares or the right to take shares in the company.[299] With respect to members of the supervisory board, the Dutch Civil Code only provides that the shareholders' meeting may determine their remuneration.[300]

Pursuant to the corporate governance code, the supervisory board determines the remuneration of the individual members of the management board, taking into account the remuneration policy as established by the shareholders' meeting.[301] If a variable remuneration component conditionally awarded in a previous financial year would, in the opinion of the supervisory board, produce an unfair result due to extraordinary circumstances during the period in which the predetermined performance criteria have been or should have been achieved, the supervisory board has the power to adjust the result downwards or upwards.[302] Further, the supervisory board may recover from the management board members any

---

[298] Best practices for engaged share-ownership intended for Eumedion participants, adopted on 30 June 2011, see <www.eumedion.nl/en/public/knowledgenetwork/best-practices/best_practices-engaged-share-ownership.pdf>.

[299] Art. 2:135 DCC. In the *one-tier model*, the task of determining the remuneration for executives cannot be delegated to executives and executives do not participate in the decision-making with respect to their remuneration (Art. 2:129a DCC).

[300] Art. 2:145 DCC.

[301] CGC, unnumbered provision following II.2.9.

[302] CGC II.2.10.

variable remuneration awarded on the basis of incorrect financial or other data (claw back).[303]

In 2009, the Minister of Finance decided to put similar rules into law. A bill[304] containing rules on the claw back of bonuses for managing directors was adopted by the Lower House of the Dutch Parliament in December 2012 and will probably enter into force in the course of 2013. The rules will apply to all public limited companies and financial institutions (no matter what their legal form) such as banks, insurance companies and investment companies. The bill provides that the corporate body that is authorised to determine the remuneration of managing directors, ie. the supervisory board or the shareholders' meeting, may adjust the agreed bonus (ie. the variable part of the remuneration), to a suitable amount if payment of the agreed bonus would be unacceptable pursuant to the standard of reasonableness and fairness. In case of a public bid this rule applies to the bonus that becomes unconditional as a result of the bid. The bill further provides that the company is authorised to reclaim a bonus to the extent it has been paid on the basis of incorrect information regarding the fulfillment of conditions for payment of the bonus, or regarding the underlying circumstances on which the payment was made subject. Finally, the bill contains a provision entailing that the value of listed shares held by a company's management board members, will be frozen in takeover situations, in case of merger and demerger and major acquisitions and disposals.[305] This means that upon establishing the market value of the shares four weeks before and four weeks after the relevant event, any increase in the value of their shares between these dates will be deduced from the directors' remuneration.[306]

The corporate governance code provides that the company may not grant its management board members any personal loans, guarantees or the like unless in the normal course of business and on terms applicable to the staff as a whole, and after approval of the supervisory board. Remission of loans may not be granted.[307]

The average remuneration of a managing director of a Dutch listed company in 2010 was €64,000 per month (European average €77,000), including a high basic fixed fee of €53,000.[308]

---

[303] CGC II.2.11.

[304] *Voorstel van wet tot wijziging van boek 2 van het Burgerlijk Wetboek en de Wet op het financieel toezicht in verband met de bevoegdheid tot aanpassing en terugvordering van bonussen en winstdelingen van bestuurders en dagelijks beleidsbepalers en deskundigheids-toetsing van commissarissen.*

[305] Art. 2:135 par. 7 DCC, sentences 4 and 5.

[306] TK 2009–2010, 32 512, no. 2 and TK 2011–2012, 32 512, no. 9.

[307] CGC II.2.9.

[308] Heidrick & Struggles, *Corporate Governance Report 2011*, p. 47.

3.2. Board and Stakeholders

3.2.1. *Board and Employees*[309]

Public and private companies which meet certain quantitative requirements, are subject to a mandatory regime of labour co-determination (*structuurregime*). These quantitative requirements are: (i) Issued share capital of at least €16 million; (ii) mandatory works council in the company or in a subsidiary of the company; and (iii) at least 100 employees of the company or a subsidiary are employed in the Netherlands. Exemptions exist for group companies of a co-determined company, for management and service companies and for international holding companies if the majority of employees of the group is employed abroad. A company to which the co-determination regime does not apply mandatorily can adopt it voluntarily if the company has a mandatory works council.[310]

The most important elements of the labour co-determination regime are:

(i) There is a mandatory supervisory board, which has the right to nominate its own members; the shareholders' meeting can reject the nomination, but cannot appoint a person of its own choice;

(ii) The works council has the right to nominate one-third of the members of the supervisory board;

(iii) The supervisory board appoints the members of the management board (so-called full co-determination rules);

(iv) The supervisory board has the statutory right to approve certain important management board decisions.[311]

Labour co-determination at board level was instituted by law in 1971. The law introduced a mandatory supervisory board which appointed its own members (co-optation), whereas the shareholders' meeting and the works council were granted the right to recommend a member and to object, by appeal to the Enterprise Court, against an appointment proposed by the supervisory board.[312] The labour union CNV had pleaded that the works council should, as in Germany, have a

---

[309] For a comparison between the German and the Dutch labour co-determination rules, see M.M.G.B. van Drunen, *Funktionsdefizite in Regelungen zum Aufsichtsrat im deutschen und im niederländischen Recht* (Doctoral Dissertation) Humboldt University (Berlin, Berliner Wissenschafts-Verlag 2010) pp. 88–131.

[310] Art. 2:153 and 2:157 DCC.

[311] See Art. 2:158, 161, 162 and 164 DCC.

[312] The objection could only be made if the supervisory board did not comply with the notification requirements or if it was to be expected that the person nominated would be unsuited to fulfilling the task of supervisory board member or that appointment would result in the board not being duly constituted. See Art. 2:158 (old) DCC.

(third parity or) parity representation in the supervisory board.[313] The minister stated that his objection to this mechanism was that it could jeopardise harmony within the board, and he followed the advice of the Social Economic Council.[314] The right of recommendation was more actively used in larger companies, but the right of objection was not often used, probably because the supervisory board usually had informal meetings with the works council before it would nominate a candidate.[315] Statistical research in 1995 demonstrated that formal and binding agreements were not often made, but that the works council of the 113 companies (both listed and not listed) involved in the questionnaire on average considered (only) one member of the seven or more members of the supervisory board as having special affinity with the interests of the work force (*vertrouwenscommissaris*, trusted supervisory director).[316]

In 2004, a major overhaul of the labour co-determination regime took place entailing that the supervisory board members are appointed by the shareholders' meeting on a binding nomination of the supervisory board. The works council received the right to make a binding recommendation with respect to one-third of the number of supervisory board members. The supervisory board must propose the recommended person to the shareholders' meeting, but may object if it is to be expected that the person nominated is unsuited to fulfil the task of supervisory board member or that his appointment results in the board not being duly constituted. In that case, it has to try to reach agreement with the works council on a suitable candidate. The supervisory board's binding nomination can be rejected by the shareholders' meeting, but the supervisory board has the right to make a new nomination; the shareholders' meeting cannot appoint a person of its own choice.[317]

The standard of corporate interest fully applies to labour nominees.[318] Of course, labour nominees will carefully weigh the interest of the employees in particular. Labour nominees are bound by the same confidentiality rules as the other members of the supervisory board, so they may not pass information on confidential matters discussed in the supervisory board meeting to the labour unions. Employees of the company or its subsidiaries and members of trade

---

[313] In 1984, the Social Economic Council published an evaluation (SER advice no. 1984/06), in which it concluded with the smallest majority that the co-determination regime could be continued in the then existing form. The largest possible minority, however, pleaded for a system of parity appointment of supervisory board members.

[314] Explanatory Memorandum, 10 751, Tweede Kamer 1970–1971, no. 3, p. 9.

[315] Asser-Maeijer 2-III (2000), no. 368; Stichting MNO, *Resultaat onderzoek voordracht leden raad van commissarissen*, 2006, p. 10–11.

[316] R.H. van het Kaar, *Ondernemingsraad en vertrouwenscommissaris* (1995) pp. 48 and 103.

[317] Art. 2:158 DCC.

[318] Asser/Maeijer/Van Solinge and Nieuwe Weme 2-II* (2009), no. 560.

unions who have negotiated the employment conditions with the company, cannot be members of the supervisory board.[319] The corporate governance considers an employee nominee as independent if he is not employed by the company itself or one of its group companies.[320]

In recent years, works councils of most AEX companies have used their right to make binding recommendations for one-third of the members of the supervisory board.[321]

The works council has a number of other rights with respect to important board decisions. It has the right to approve certain important decisions with respect to labour issues[322] and to give advice on a catalogue of important issues such as transfer of a part of the company's enterprise and important investments.[323] The works councils of public companies have the right to give their (non-binding) opinion on a number of important decisions of the shareholders' meeting.[324] A company employing more than 50 employees is obliged to notify the trade unions when it becomes involved in the preparation of a merger or takeover. [325] Trade unions have the right to institute proceedings against a company with the Enterprise Court in order to request the Enterprise Court to start an investigation into the company's affairs with the aim of declaring that the company has been mismanaged.[326]

---

[319] Art. 2:160 DCC.

[320] CGC III.2.2 under a.

[321] See for an evaluation on how the works council has used this right in the period 2004–2009: Rienk Goodijk, *Ontwikkelingen in de relatie tussen OR en (voordrachts)commissarissen*, RUG 2009.

[322] See article 27 of the Works Council Act. (*Wet op de ondernemingsraden*) A decision taken without the works council's approval is invalid.

[323] See article 25 of the Works Council Act. If the company takes a decision contrary to the works council's advice, the works council may institute a proceeding before the Enterprise Court. The Enterprise Court can rule that the company may not pursue its decision, but rights acquired by third parties cannot be prejudiced.

[324] Art. 2:107a par. 3 (sale of substantial parts of the company's enterprise or assets) Art. 2:134a (appointment and dismissal of directors) and Art. 2:135 par. 2 DCC (remuneration policy of directors). The works council has to be given the opportunity to give its view in a timely manner before the convocation of the shareholders meeting and is entitled to explain its view at the shareholders' meeting.

[325] Art. 4 SER-Besluit Fusiegedragsregels 2000. The trade unions should be notified before a public announcement about the merger or takeover is made.

[326] Art. 2:347 DCC.

3.2.2. Board and Creditors

Creditors of the company have a contractual relationship with the company, not with the board or its members. The board members have to act in the interests of the company. The concept of the interests of the company is the result of weighing the interests of the shareholders, the work force and the creditors. Creditors contending that the board has underweighted their interests have to fall back on an action based on wrongful act.[327] A special action is the *actio pauliana* (voidable preference), allowing creditors under certain circumstances to nullify a transaction between the company and a third party if the company (the board) and the third party knew or could have known that the transaction would cause detriment to one or more creditors.[328]

3.2.3. Board and Other Stakeholders

The public interest (society at large, general interest) is often considered as forming part of the bundle of interests that together form the interests of the company; it should, therefore, be taken into account by the board when weighing these interests.[329] In recent years, sustainability has become a very important aspect in entrepreneurial activities as a result of increasing corporate social responsibility.[330] Sustainability has become an issue that the board takes into account when weighing all relevant interests. The corporate governance code explicitly mentions corporate responsibility as an issue that is relevant to the enterprise.[331]

3.3. Changing Roles in Financial Distress[332]

When a company is in financial distress, the management board and the supervisory board face three types of problems. Firstly, they have a problem with the company's creditors, whose claims are at risk. Secondly, they have a problem with the shareholders, who will want to have a say in any restructuring measures.

---

[327] See sec. 4.1.1.

[328] Art. 3:45 par. 2 DCC. See also par. 3.3 (Changing roles in financial distress) and par. 3.1.3 under a (Conflicts of interest).

[329] See Van Schilfgaarde/Winter (2009) no. 5.

[330] See recently the Phd thesis of T.E. Lambooy, *Corporate Social Responsibility: Legal and semi-legal frameworks supporting CSR developments*, Serie IvO Vol. 77 (2010).

[331] CGC II.1.

[332] See in particular M. Olaerts, *Vennootschappelijke beleidsbepaling in geval van finan- ciële moeilijkheden: de positie van bestuurders en aandeelhouders*, PhD thesis, Antwerpen 2007.

And lastly, they have a problem between themselves, as there is (or should be) intensified supervision by the supervisory board.

The relations with the creditors concern the company's solvency. If the company has ceased to pay its debts when they fall due, an insolvency proceeding should be initiated. In that case, the board is obliged to immediately inform the shareholders' meeting, which has the authority to instruct the board to file a bankruptcy request.[333] Further, the board has to consider whether the company will be able to repay new debts when it enters into new obligations. If the board knows or ought to know that the company will not be able to meet its obligations and that it will have no recourse, it has to refrain from entering into new agreements, failing which they may be held personally liable vis-à-vis creditors on the basis of wrongful act. In case law criteria have been developed for liability of board members in this type of situations.[334]

The relations with the shareholders (and other stakeholders) concern the measures the company has to take in order to escape the situation of financial distress. The problem is that when the company is in crisis, the board immediately wants to implement far-reaching restructuring measures which usually will be subject to approval of the shareholders' meeting.[335] The law does not provide for special decision-making rules on the brink of insolvency.[336] Therefore, shareholder approval is also required in a crisis situation.[337] The only escape is the generally accepted opinion that the approval of the shareholders' meeting may be requested after the board has adopted the relevant resolution, but even then the board would have to refrain from carrying out its decision until the approval is granted.[338]

The notion of intensified supervision by the supervisory board in a company in financial distress has been developed in case law. As soon as the supervisory board notices that the financial position of the company is quickly deteriorating, its members have to play a more active role, by asking the management board more questions and requesting more information and requesting more frequent

[333] Art. 2:136 DCC. The articles of association may delegate this authority to the board.

[334] See, *inter alia*, Supreme Court 8 December 2006, JOR 2007/38 (*Ontvanger/Roelofsen*); 6 October 1989, *NJ* 1990, 286 (*Beklamel*); 3 April 1992, *NJ* 1992, 411 (*Van Waning/Van der Vliet*).

[335] In the articles of association or by law: Art. 2:107a DCC (see Supreme Court decision in the *ABN AMRO/Lasalle* case, HR 13 July 2007, JOR 2007/178).

[336] Apart from Art. 2:108a DCC, which contains an obligation for the board to convene a shareholders' meeting if the value of the company's assets has become less than half of the issued and paid-up share capital.

[337] See also M. Olaerts, *Vennootschappelijke beleidsbepaling in geval van financiële moeilijkheden: de positie van bestuurders en aandeelhouders*, PhD thesis, Antwerpen 2007, no. 3.4.

[338] See, ia, Asser/Maeijer/Van Solinge and Nieuwe Weme 2-II* (2009), no. 323.

(eg. weekly) meetings with the management board.[339] If the position of the company further deteriorates, the supervisory board is obliged to intervene.[340] An intervention can take the form of developing and proposing alternatives for the strategy of the management board or requesting the management board members to step down.

4. Enforcement

4.1. Courts

Typically, litigation before the ordinary courts takes place at three levels: District Court (*Arrondissementsrechtbank*), Court of Appeal (*Gerechtshof*) and Supreme Court (*Hoge Raad*). A procedure conducted at all three levels can last 5–8 years (not including a referral of the case by the Supreme Court back to a Court of Appeal). If the damage claimed is too complex to calculate, the court that has awarded the claim may refer the case to a special court proceeding to establish the amount of damages. An example of such procedures are claims on the basis of personal liability of directors (see below). The special court proceeding with the Enterprise Court (*Ondernemingskamer van het Gerechtshof te Amsterdam*) is in fact a proceeding in one factual instance (with only the Enterprise Court establishing the facts), with appeal to the Supreme Court.[341]

An important standard which permeates all Dutch civil law is the standard of reasonableness and fairness. In company law (as part of civil law) this standard is laid down in Art. 2:8 par. 1 DCC, which states that the board and the shareholders have to act vis-à-vis each other and *inter se* in accordance with the standard of reasonableness and fairness. This open standard, which is developed in a long tradition of Supreme Court case law, plays an important role in all fields of Dutch law, especially in the law of obligations and in company law. It gives the court a certain interpretative (and corrective) flexibility when applying rules laid down in the law, in the articles of association and in agreements.[342]

---

[339] See also Supreme Court 8 April 2005, *JOR* 2005/119 (*Laurus*).

[340] If the company is a group company, the same applies to the (management board of the) parent company, which has the obligation to manage the group: see Asser/Maeijer/Van Solinge and Nieuwe Weme 2-II* (2009), no. 828.

[341] See sec. 4.1.3.

[342] The standard of reasonableness and fairness has a far-reaching application in its so-called derogative effect: A provision in the law, articles of association, regulations or resolution which governs the relationship between board and shareholders, or each of them *inter se*, will not be applied if this would in the given circumstances be unacceptable according to the standard of reasonableness and fairness (Art. 2:8 par. 2 DCC). This application of the standard can even set aside rules of mandatory law.

4.1.1. Directors' Liability

a) Introduction

There is abundant case law on personal liability of directors since the introduction of legislation vesting personal liability in case of bankruptcy in 1987.[343] This gave the administrator of an insolvent company a stronger position to initiate litigation against board members on the basis of personal liability for improper performance of their task.

A well-known case of personal liability litigation in bankruptcy was the claim the administrators instituted against the members of the management board and supervisory board members in the bankruptcy of *Ceteco NV* in 2000.[344] The District Court in Utrecht ruled that the board members were personally liable for improper performance of their functions.[345] The amount of damage would have to be established in another court proceeding, but the District Court ruled, at the request of the administrators, that the board members would have to make an advance payment of €50 million in the aggregate. An appeal was lodged with the Court of Appeal of Arnhem, but the appeal was withdrawn in 2009 shortly before the court's decision, probably because the matter was settled with the board members' D&O insurers. Court decisions with respect to failing supervision are less frequent. A famous case was the *Casino* transaction by the listed supermarket chain Laurus. The Enterprise Court ruled that the supervisory board had improperly performed its supervisory task because it had not properly monitored the transition of the chain to one formula, but the decision was quashed on formal grounds by the Supreme Court.[346] In legal literature it is assumed that the Enterprise Court's criteria for establishing personal liability of supervisory board members are still valid.

b) Directors' Liability vis-à-vis the Company

Each board member is under a duty towards the company to properly perform his or her tasks. He is personally and jointly (with his fellow board members) liable for improper performance of tasks that fall within the competence of the board, regardless of who actually caused the improper performance of tasks.[347] According to Supreme Court case law, liability arises in the event of manifestly

---

[343] See Asser/Maeijer/Van Solinge and Nieuwe Weme 2-II* (2009), nos. 445–448.

[344] A company listed on Amsterdam Euronext, which later became subsidiary of Hagemeyer.

[345] Rechtbank Utrecht 12 December 2007, JOR 2008/10.

[346] Supreme Court 18 January 2006, JOR 2006/46.

[347] Art. 2:9 and Art. 2:149 DCC. See Asser/Maeijer/Van Solinge and Nieuwe Weme 2-II* (2009), no. 445; Van Schilfgaarde/Winter (2009) no. 47; J.B. Huizink (ed.), *Rechtspersonen* (losbladig) (Groene serie) (2005) Art. 2:9 DCC, Notes 3–4a.

improper performance of the director's duties for which a serious reproach (*ernstig verwijt*) can be made against the relevant director.[348] In determining whether a serious reproach can be made against the director, all circumstances have to be taken into account, including:

- the nature of the company's activities and the general risks resulting from these activities;
- the delegation (allocation) of tasks within the board to certain directors[349] as well as the company's internal guidelines and regulations to which the directors must adhere;
- the information that was or should have been available to the director at the moment he improperly performed his duties; and
- the due care that would be taken by a director who is qualified for his duties and who performs these duties conscientiously.

It should be noted that the concept of a business judgment rule (ie. the standard of review of the board's business judgments as developed in Delaware case law) is not used by the courts as a standard to establish personal liability. Although its introduction was pleaded in literature in the last years,[350] this view has not yet gained common ground.[351]

In case of bankruptcy, the board members are jointly and severally liable for all of the company's debts that remain unpaid after the realisation of the company's assets, if the board has manifestly failed to perform its duties properly, and this is an important cause of the company's insolvency.[352] The board members can (under the rules of Art. 2:138 DCC) only be held liable for improper performance of tasks in the three year-period preceding the company's insolvency.

The board's manifest failure to perform its duties properly is assumed by law if the members of the board have acted as no reasonable and sensible directors would have acted under the same circumstances.[353] The board must have made a

---

[348] See the landmark cases: Supreme Court 10 January 1997, *JOR* 1997/29 (*Staleman/Van de Ven*) and Supreme Court 29 November 2003, *JOR* 2004/2 (*Schwandt/Berghuizer Papierfabriek*) and Asser/Maeijer/Van Solinge and Nieuwe Weme 2-II* (2009), nos. 446–448.

[349] With respect to delegation of tasks, the prevailing opinion in literature is that it cannot set aside the principle of collective responsibility and personal liability for the proper performance of all board tasks. See further D.A.M.H.W. Strik, PhD thesis, Serie IvO Vol. 73 (2010), pp. 87–94.

[350] See in particular B.F. Assink, *Rechterlijke toetsing van bestuurlijk gedrag*, PhD thesis 2007, Serie IvO Vol. 59 (2007) with further references.

[351] See Asser/Maeijer/Van Solinge and Nieuwe Weme 2-II* (2009), no. 448, Van Schilfgaarde/Winter (2009) no. 47.

[352] Art. 2:138 DCC and Art. 2:149 DCC.

[353] HR 8 June 2001, *JOR* 2001/171 (*Gilhuis qq/Bestuurders Panmo*).

serious mistake which goes well beyond the limits of acceptable risk in the ordinary course of the business concerned.[354] The manifestly improper performance of tasks by board members, as well as the causal link with the company's insolvency, have to be proved by the administrator; proof to the contrary is allowed.[355]

If liability has arisen, an individual board member may disculpate himself and escape from joint and several liability by proving that the improper performance of tasks was not attributable to him personally and that he did not refrain from taking measures to avert the consequences of the improper performance. In establishing whether this is the case, the court may take into account that there was a delegation of tasks and that the tasks that were improperly performed, or were delegated to other members of the board.[356]

The shareholders' meeting may grant board members a *release from liability* (*decharge*) when adopting the annual accounts.[357] This release is *ex post* and may even cover wilful conduct (*opzet*). Also the company itself may grant board members a release from liability (indemnification, *vrijwaring*). This release is mostly *ex ante* and cannot cover improper performance of tasks in the meaning of Art. 2:9 and 2:138 DCC as this would be in contradiction with mandatory company law.[358] The company can also indemnify the directors against third party claims instituted against directors in person under civil law (eg. on the basis of wrongful acts), administrative law or penal law. The indemnification may be set out in an agreement with each director, or in the company's articles of association.

D&O insurance can cover the same types of liability as an indemnification, but there may be differences. It may cover personal liability for claims instituted by third parties and/or claims instituted by the company. It may have a less strict

---

[354] See Asser/Maeijer/Van Solinge and Nieuwe Weme 2-II* (2009), no. 457, Van Schilfgaarde/Winter (2009) no. 48.

[355] If, however, the board members have not complied with their obligations to maintain proper administration in relation to the company's accounts and activities and to publish the company's annual accounts in a timely manner, the law provides that the board members are deemed to have failed to perform their duties properly; proof to the contrary is not allowed. It is then assumed that such improper performance constituted an important cause of the company's insolvency, but here proof to the contrary is allowed. Asser/Maeijer/Van Solinge and Nieuwe Weme 2-II* (2009), no. 459; Van Schilfgaarde/Winter (2009) no. 48.

[356] Asser/Maeijer/Van Solinge and Nieuwe Weme 2-II* (2009), nos. 445–446 and the case law mentioned there. See also the new wording of article 2:9 DCC.

[357] See Art. 2:101 par. 3 DCC. The release is restricted to what appears from the annual accounts or can be deduced from them. Courts tend to become more critical towards releases of liability when dealing with personal liability claims based on Art. 2:9 DCC, see,Supreme Court 15 June 2010, JOR 2010/227 (*De Rouw*).

[358] Van Schilfgaarde/Winter (2009) no. 47.

scope than an indemnification by the company, it may be limited in time, claim filing period or maximum amount, and it may contain all kinds of exclusions and restrictions.[359]

It is broadly assumed that, as a principle, in a one-tier model both executive directors and non-executive directors are liable in the same manner and to the same extent as members of the management board in a two-tier model, with the same possibilities of disculpation, including the defence that a particular (executive or non-executive, as the case may be) task was not delegated to them.[360]

c) Directors' Liability vis-à-vis Third Parties

The most common form is liability is based on a wrongful act. In principle, improper performance of tasks vis-à-vis the company does not constitute liability vis-à-vis third parties, such as shareholders or creditors. As far as shareholders are concerned, their damages are deemed to be identical with the damage suffered by the company.[361] However, in more recent case law the Supreme Court has ruled that in specific circumstances a board member may be liable vis-à-vis a shareholder if the board member's acts were specifically wrongful vis-à-vis that shareholder.[362] A board member may in specific circumstances be liable for wrongful act vis-à-vis creditors (or other third parties) if he can be personally made a sufficiently serious reproach (*voldoende ernstig verwijt*).[363] In a number of decisions the Supreme Court has distinguished two main types of cases: A board member has either entered into a contract with a third party on behalf of the company, or caused or not prevented the company from taking on legal or contractual obligations, where he knew or ought to have known that the company will not be able to meet its obligations and that it will have no recourse.[364]

---

[359] See most recently on release of liability in combination with D&O insurance, Meerdink and Horeman, *Tijdschrift voor de Ondernemingsrechtpraktijk* 2011, pp. 150–158.

[360] See, *inter alia,* L. Timmerman, Serie IvO Vol. 67 (2009), pp. 25–28 and B. Wezeman, *ibid.*, p. 93; D.A.H.M. Strik, PhD thesis, Serie IvO Vol. 73 (2010), pp. 123–130; F.J. Oranje (ed.), *Het nieuwe BV-recht voor de praktijk*, Preadvies KNB (2008), pp. 81–82; M.M. Seinstra, '*Het dualistische en het monistische bestuursmodel: een vergelijking*', O&F 2008/4, pp. 60–62; T.M.L. van Es, 'Het aansprakelijkheidsregime van non-executives in een one tierbestuursstructuur', *V&O* 2007/3, p. 50.

[361] Supreme Court 2 December 1994, *NJ* 1995, 288 (*Poot/ABP*).

[362] Supreme Court 20 July 2008, JOR 2008/260 (*Willemsen/NOM*). See further Asser/Maeijer/Van Solinge and Nieuwe Weme 2-II*(2009), nos. 451 and 216, where the authors see a certain convergence between the requirements for liability for improper management and liability for wrongful act.

[363] See Asser/Maeijer/Van Solinge and Nieuwe Weme 2-II* (2009), no. 469.

[364] See, *inter alia*, Supreme Court 8 December 2006, JOR 2007/38 (*Ontvanger/Roelofsen*); 6 October 1989, *NJ* 1990, 286 (*Beklamel*); 3 April 1992, *NJ* 1992, 411 (*Van Waning/Van der Vliet*). See for a specific case in which it seems that the serious reproach condition does not have

cont. ...

The personal liability of board members for misleading financial information can be regarded as a special form of liability based on a wrongful act.[365] A high profile case was the investigation proceeding with the Enterprise Court against *Fortis*, in which the investigators concluded that Fortis had given misleading information with respect to the issue of shares to finance the acquisition of ABN-Amro.[366] Another important case was the IPO and secondary offering of shares of of *World Online*, in which the Supreme Court in a milestone decision ruled that World Online, ABN Amro and Goldman Sachs committed a wrongful act on the basis that the prospectus contained misleading information and omissions; and World Online and World Online's leading officer and shareholder had given misleading information to the press shortly before and after the subscription of the offered shares.[367]

4.1.2. Nullification of Resolutions

Resolutions of the shareholders' meeting, the management board and supervisory board that are in contradiction with the rules set out in the law and the articles of association concerning the division of powers and quorum and voting requirements are void *ab initio*.[368] If a resolution is taken in contradiction with the rules regulating the preparatory stage of decision-making, such as convocation, agenda and place of the meeting, it is not void but voidable (with retroactive effect). Resolutions are also voidable if they are adopted contrary to the standard of reasonableness and fairness.[369] Furthermore, resolutions are void or voidable pursuant to the general civil law rules for voidance of legal acts.[370] A resolution can only be voided by the court. The law provides for several techniques of

to be met: Supreme Court 23 November 2012, LJN: BX5881 (the director has acted contrary to a duty of care he personally had via-à-vis the third party; the basis was not a reproach made against him for improper performance of his tasks as director as a consequence of which the company acted contrary its duty of care vis-à-vis the third party).

[365] Art. 2:139/150 DCC. See further Asser/Maeijer/Van Solinge and Nieuwe Weme 2-II* (2009), no. 470.

[366] Enterprise Court 24 November 2008, *JOR* 2009/9 and 16 June 2010. The Enterprise Court can only rule that the company has been mismanaged, after which separate personal liability proceedings against its directors have to be initiated.

[367] Supreme Court 27 November 2009, *JOR* 2010/43. See on this decision and the (indirect) causal connection between damage and misleading information: B.J. de Jong, 'Liability for misrepresentation – European Lessons on causation from the Netherlands', *ECFR* (2011), 352–375.

[368] Art. 2:14 DCC. See Van Schilfgaarde/Winter (2009) nos 93 and 95; Huizink, Losbl. Rp (2005), Art. 2:14 DCC, Note 2.

[369] Art. 2:15 DCC par. 1 sub b. Van Schilfgaarde/Winter (2009) nos 94, 96 and 98; Huizink, Losbl. Rp. (2005), Art. 2:15 DCC, Notes 2–8.

[370] See Van Schilfgaarde/Winter (2009) no. 91–97.

ratification of void and voided resolutions. As a general rule, the invalidity of a resolution only has internal effect and does not affect the validity of subsequent legal acts (transactions) between the company and third parties. If the resolution itself also contains a legal act with a third party, the possible voidness of the resolution does not affect the legal act unless the party involved knew or should have known the reason of the voidness.[371]

4.1.3. *Investigation Proceeding before the Enterprise Court*[372]

Shareholders and holders of depository receipts (in a public company or in a private company), either alone or acting together, may request the Enterprise Court to start an investigation into the company's affairs in order to establish whether the company has been mismanaged. Decisions of the Enterprise Court in this matter are subject to appeal before the Dutch Supreme Court. The Supreme Court only tests whether the decision is in accordance with the law.

This proceeding is open as of 1 January 2013 to the following: With respect to companies with an issued share capital of €22.5 million or less, it is open to shareholders having ten per cent or more of the issued share capital or having a shareholding with an aggregate nominal value of at least €225,000; in companies with an issued share capital of more than €22.5 million it is open to (a) holders of one per cent of the issued share capital and (b) in the case of a company listed on Euronext to holders of shares representing one per cent of the issued share capital or a market value of at least €20 million. As of 1 January 2013, the company itself is also authorised to file such a request, enabling the board to request the investigation of shareholder conduct leading to the company being mismanaged.[373]

The Enterprise Court usually handles cases with a panel of five persons, three judges and two laymen, such as chartered accountants, economists or similar professionals. It has a flexible agenda and can be approached at very short notice in urgent matters. Furthermore, since 1994, it has the power to order interim measures when requested by the parties concerned in any stage of the proceeding. It may do so even if the decision whether an investigation will be ordered is postponed (although the Supreme Court has ruled that the Enterprise Court

---

[371] Art. 2:16 par. 2 DCC. Example: a resolution of the board giving a power of attorney.

[372] See extensively Asser/Maeijer/Van Solinge and Nieuwe Weme 2-II* (2009), nos 726–812 and E.P.M. Vermeulen/D.A. Zetzsche, *The Use and Abuse of Investor Suits – An Inquiry into the Dark Side of Shareholder Activism*, ECFR (2010).

[373] Before that, listed companies granted a 'friendly' foundation the right to institute a proceeding before the Enterprise Court. The proceeding would be based on the argument that the mismanagement was caused by the activist shareholder not acting in accordance with the standard of reasonableness and fairness.

should do that only when there are serious reasons).[374] These interim measures may deviate from mandatory law. Although they are of a temporary nature, they may have irreversible consequences. The Enterprise Court may, for example, suspend the voting rights of shareholders, cancel a convened shareholder meeting, suspend board members and temporarily appoint new board members, if appropriate with a casting vote. In the *Inter Access* case, for example, after a very careful examination of the situation, the Enterprise Court granted the board the power to issue new shares, which led to dilution of the existing shareholders. The Supreme Court rejected an appeal against this decision.[375]

If the Enterprise Court rules that the company has been mismanaged, it may impose the following measures:[376]

1. Suspension or nullification of a resolution of the board or the shareholders' meeting (eg. a release from liability of the board members);
2. Suspension or dismissal of one or more board members;
3. Temporary appointment of one or more board members;
4. Temporary deviation from specific provisions of the articles of association;
5. Temporary transfer of shares to a trustee; and/or
6. Liquidation of the company.

A decision of the Enterprise Court stating that the company has been mismanaged does not as such constitute personal liability of the company's directors. In practice, however, many conflicts end with a decision by the Enterprise Court without personal liability claims against directors being filed. In order to establish personal liability, the District Court has to be addressed, which is formally not bound by the decision and facts established by the Enterprise Court.[377]

4.2. Regulators

AFM (Autoriteit financiële markten, Financial Markets Authority)—The AFM supervises the conduct of the entire financial market sector. The AFM operates in two areas: financial services and capital markets. The AFM ensures that financial services are provided to consumers with due care and supervises the fair and

---

[374] Supreme Court 14 December 2007, JOR 2008/11 (DSM). See further Asser/Maeijer/Van Solinge and Nieuwe Weme 2-II*(2009), no. 769.

[375] Supreme Court 25 February 2011, JOR 2011/115 (*Inter Access*).

[376] Art. 2:356 DCC.

[377] The Enterprise Court further is the competent court to order, at the request of an interested party, a listed company to amend its annual accounts or annual report if they are not in conformity with the applicable EU rules. It is also the competent court in squeeze-out proceedings. Art. 2:447 f., Art. 2:92a and 2:359c DCC.

efficient operation of capital markets. The consequences of the implementation of the Market Abuse Directive as of 1 October 2005 included an expansion of the ban on market manipulation and the delegation to the AFM of the supervision of the publication of price-sensitive information by listed companies. The AFM enforces the regulations governing the issue of securities, public offers, financial reporting and audit entities, by granting or cancelling permits and/or imposing administrative measures such as fines and public warnings.

DNB (De Nederlandsche Bank; the Dutch Central Bank)—The DNB also supervises the financial market sector, but is responsible for so-called prudential supervision. Prudential supervision addresses the question whether participants in the financial markets can rely on their contracting parties being able to meet their financial obligations. As regulator, the DNB deals with monetary policy and a stable financial network; as advisor it gives economic advice to the government; and as supervisor it continuously monitors financial institutions (banks, pension funds and insurers, investment firms, collective investment schemes, money transaction offices and trust companies). The DNB's supervision focuses on financial health and operational management, administrative organisation and internal control. The DNB also tests the expertise and integrity of directors and other persons who determine the financial institution's policy. The provisions of financial services is subject to authorisation by the DNB. If an institution is in trouble, the DNB can choose from a wide range of supervisory tools, such as the appointment of a 'silent administrator', who could co-run the institution's operations behind the scenes. In 2012, a law entered into force enabling state intervention in financial institutions whose *déconfiture* would jeopardise the financial system. The law gives the DNB far reaching powers to nationalise the shares in listed financial institutions in certain circumstances.

NMa (Nederlandse Mededingingsautoriteit; Dutch Competition Authority)—The NMa monitors effective competition and contributes to proper functioning of markets. The NMa enforces compliance with the Competition Act in all markets. It takes care of general competition enforcement as well as industry-specific regulation. The NMa assesses merger proposals in order to avoid the emergence of concentrations obstructing the proper functioning of markets. The NMa acts against infringements and solves competition problems, by imposing sanctions for infringements of competition law and by implementing alternative enforcement instruments to effect changes in market behavior. The NMa has full authorisation to enter private premises without prior consent of the resident. Also, the NMa may impose fines on board members and directors who exert *de facto* leadership or give instructions in case of infringements of the Competition Act.

4.3. Self-Regulation

The corporate governance code has become the most important instrument of self-regulation for Dutch companies listed on a regulated market in or outside the EEA.[378] These companies are obliged to comply with the code's provisions or to explain why one or more provisions are not complied with.[379] The comply-or-explain statement (also called corporate governance statement) of the board forms part of the annual report.[380] The corporate governance code further specifies that the main characteristics of the company's corporate governance structure are set out in a separate chapter of the annual report. Under that chapter the company has to explicitly state to what extent it follows the code's best practice provisions and if not, why it deviates from them. Any deviation should be properly explained. Any material change in the company's governance structure or in the compliance with the code should be submitted for discussion to the shareholders' meeting as a separate agenda item. The shareholders should be prepared to enter into a dialogue with the company if they do not accept the company's explanation of a deviation.[381]

The external auditor investigates whether the annual report is drawn up in accordance with applicable rules.[382] The auditor's investigation in this respect is limited to establishing whether the annual report contains the corporate governance statement; the auditor does not (have an obligation to) investigate the contents of the statement.

The first version of the corporate governance code was drafted in 2003 by a government endorsed corporate governance committee, called the Tabaksblat Committee. A monitoring committee was established in order to review compliance with the corporate governance code once per year and to propose amendments to the code every five years. The present corporate governance monitoring committee consists of seven members, most of whom hold positions in (supervisory) boards in Dutch listed companies.

The Compliance Report 2010 shows that the following provisions were most frequently not complied with: Claw-back clause; maximum appointment period;

---

[378] De Nederlandse corporate governance code, *Official Gazette* 2009, 18499.

[379] Pursuant to the Royal Decree of 23 December 2004, *Official Gazette* 2004/747, as amended by Royal Decree of 10 December 2009, *Official Gazette* 2009/545. Technically, these Royal Decrees are based on Art. 2:391 par. 5 DCC, which provides that further provisions can be prescribed by Royal Decree with respect to the contents of the Royal Decree, in particular the compliance with a code of conduct designated in that Royal Decree.

[380] Art. 2:391 par. 5 DCC. The annual report also has to contain a so-called 'in control statement'; see further II.1.5 CGC and sec. 2.1.

[381] See Principle I and best practice provisions I.1 and I.2 CGC.

[382] Art. 2:393 par. 3 DCC.

maximum compensation for dismissal; 5 years lock-up period for shares; and composition and functioning of the three committees. The most frequent explanations for the non-compliance were: Observance of existing agreements; the non-compliance is of a temporary nature; the company is in the process of implementing compliance; or the company applies another rule in this field.[383] The committee made a number of observations. The influence of voting advisory agencies such as ISS/RiskMetrics on major institutional investors has increased substantially. All of the responding asset management funds said they used a voting advisor. Most institutional investors took off-the-shelf advice, only asset managers asked for customised voting advice.[384] Secondly, in 43% of the shareholder meetings where the respondents had voting power, institutional investors had sent in their vote prior to the meeting. Thirdly, the number of Dutch persons in the supervisory board of AEX companies has increased to 101, compared to 64 non-Dutch (mainly American) board members.[385]

The Compliance Report 2011 shows that the same provisions were most frequently not complied with as those mentioned in the Compliance Report 2010.[386] Further, the report suggests that the influence of voting advisory agencies might be less important than assumed in the 2010 report, at least as far as the interviewed foreign asset managers are concerned: They stated that they usually took only proxy services, not voting advice, and if they did, it was based on a customised voting policy. From Eumedion statistics relating to the annual shareholders' meetings in 2011 it further appeared that in a considerable number of cases voters voted against ISS advice.[387] From Eumedion research over 2012 it furthermore appered that a large number of proposals which received a positive advice of voting agencies were approved but with a very substantial percentage of voters (30–40%) voting against.[388] The Compliance Report 2012 contains detailed research on voting advice in the years 2011 and 2012. The report states that the results of the research seem to suggest that voting agencies have had no decisive influence on the voting outcome and that investors seem to use their own insights when casting their vote. At the same time, according to the Compliance Report 2012 the companies have the idea that the voting agencies ISS and Glass

---

[383] *Compliance Report 2010*, p. 18.

[384] *Ibid.*, p. 56.

[385] *Ibid.*, p. 44.

[386] It does not quantify deviations per provision as does the *Compliance Report 2010*, so that reference is made to the latter when deviations are indicated.

[387] For example, in the case of AEX company *Wessanen* ISS advised to vote *for* the proposed delegation of the power to issue shares and to exclude the pre-emptive rights and 65% of the shareholders voted *against* the proposed resolutions.

[388] Eumedion, *Evaluatie ava-seizoen 2012*, pp. 11–14. This was confirmed in the *Compliance Report 2012*, p. 41.

Lewis have a (very) substantial influence on the voting decisions of investors.[389] These differences in perception will keep the issue on the agenda.

Another source of self-regulation is the listing rules provided by Euronext Amsterdam. Euronext as market operator has issued rules providing the framework for the organisation of the European markets of NYSE Euronext.[390] The Euronext Rulebooks for the regulated markets currently consist of two books: Book I contains the harmonised rules (cash and derivatives), including rules of conduct and enforcement rules that are designed to protect the markets, as well as rules on listing, trading and membership; Book II contains all rules of the individual markets that have not been harmonised, *inter alia* the Euronext Amsterdam rules. The Euronext rules do not contain rules regarding the governance of listed companies (with the exception of rules for companies with listed depositary receipts of shares). In the listing agreement between Euronext and the company, the latter agrees to comply with the listing rules. If the company does not comply with the listing rules, Euronext can rescind the agreement and, ultimately, cancel the listing of the company.[391]

5. The Dynamics of Change

a) The Pendulum of Shareholder Activism

In the last decade, boards of Dutch listed companies have seen shareholder influence grow. Important new powers were granted to shareholders in 2004 and the Enterprise Court with its low threshold and far reaching powers has become a dangerous weapon for activist shareholders. The notorious *Dear board* letter of TCI in 2007 requiring the split-up of ABN-Amro was the culmination of shareholder activism and at the same time marked the turning of the tide. As from 2008, companies started to reinstall the protective devices they were in the process of dismantling and the legislature announced the preparation of legislation restricting shareholder rights. When the Dutch Parliament discussed the timepath for privatisation of the nationalised ABN-Amro Bank in 2011, it was suggested that a protective device be put in the Bank's articles of association.

The agenda of this counter-movement has led a number of legislative proposals which were adopted by Parliament in 2012:[392]

---

[389] *Compliance Report 2012*, pp. 41 and 42.

[390] Available at <www.euronext.com/fic/000/055/290/552902.pdf>.

[391] See for a procedure between Euronext and CSM: Supreme Court 25 June 1999, *JOR* 1999/176.

[392] These laws will probably enter into force on 1 July 2013, except the increase of the threshold for initiating an investigation, which entered into force on 1 January 2013.

- The threshold for putting items on the agenda of the shareholders' meeting is increased from 1% to 3% of the issued share capital.
- A shareholder exercising his right to put items on the agenda of the shareholders' meeting, is obliged to fully disclose his long and short economic interests in the company.
- The lowest shareholding notification threshold is decreased from 5% to 3% of the issued shares.
- Listed companies are given the possibility of identifying their shareholders.
- The threshold for initiating an investigation proceeding at the Enterprise Court was increased to shareholdings with a market value of at least €20 million (or 1% of the issued share capital).

b) Functioning of the Board

The supervision by the supervisory board proved to be insufficiently hands-on in the period of shareholder activism. Reporting obligations, corporate governance rules and performance related remuneration became more and more important instruments to monitor and influence board behaviour. However, the financial crisis undermined investors' confidence in these instruments.[393] The efforts to strive for parallel interests of directors and shareholders by way of remuneration in the form of shares, and the improvement of the market for corporate control, have not led to a decrease of corporate governance problems in listed companies.[394] In recent years, the legislature and investors have put increasing emphasis on qualifications and availability of supervisory board directors. In particular, investors are more critical about automatic reappointments and they often require publication of the frequency of each director's absence at board meetings and of the most important conclusions of the board's self-assessment.[395]

c) Labour Co-determination

In the past two decades, many authors have pleaded for the abolition of labour co-determination at board level (and instead for strengthening the works council's rights under the Works Council Act). These voices gained strength in 2004, when important shareholder rights were incorporated in the Dutch Civil Code. The Minister of Justice promised at that time to consider abolition of the co-determination regime. However, since the increase of shareholder activism in the

---

[393] See further R. Abma, 'De verander(en)de rol van de private aandeelhouder binnen de vennootschap', in N.E.D. Faber et al (eds.), *De kredietcrisis*, Serie OO&R Vol. 54 (2010).

[394] See, *inter alia*, Abma and Munsters in S.C. Peij et al (ed.), *Handboek Corporate Governance* (2010).

[395] See Eumedion, *Evaluatie ava-seizoen 2012*, pp. 6–8.

years thereafter, abolition of labour co-determination at board level is no longer on the agenda. On the contrary, the monitoring committee corporate governance code has suggested allowing companies to increase the maximum supermajority requirements for dismissal of supervisory board members in companies subject to labour co-determination.

The co-determination regime is a two-tier model almost by nature, but the law enables co-determined companies to opt for a one-tier board. Technically, there are still some questions to answer, but the implementation of the one-tier board in co-determined companies will probably not lead to serious problems, although it remains to be seen whether many co-determined companies will move over to a one-tier board model.

d) Reform of Law for Public Companies

A general reform of the laws governing public companies is not currently on the agenda, although the Minister of Justice has stated that he will consider an overhaul following the implementation of the Bill introducing a fundamental and far reaching liberalisation of the rules governing private companies, which has entered into force on 1 October 2012. Legal authors have repeatedly requested the Minister to consider to what extent these rules could also be applied to public companies (insofar as permitted by EU legislation).[396]

e) Litigation

The Enterprise Court is very popular amongst active shareholders. The recent increase of the threshold for bringing investigation proceedings to the Enterprise Court will probably lead to a decrease of cases brought before this court. Enterprise Court decisions are often used to assess the chances of personal liability proceedings against individual board members. If the Enterprise Court rules that a company has been mismanaged, the discussions on personal liability of board members usually are held in private and end with an agreement between the insurer and the party that intends to initiate liability proceedings before the civil courts. It may be expected that such proceedings will more often be initiated immediately given the increase of threshold for proceedings at the Enterprise Court.

f) Long-termism and Institutional Investors

The Dutch government has been considering the introduction of instruments enhancing the creation of long-term shareholder commitment by offering share-

---

[396] See, *inter alia*, L. Timmerman in *Mok-aria: collection of articles offered to M.R. Mok* (2002); J.W. Winter in *LT, collection of articles offered to Vino Timmerman*, Serie IvO Vol. 44 (2003).

holders more dividend or voting rights when they keep their shares for a longer time ('slow capital'). In 2009, the Lower House adopted a resolution requesting the Government to incorporate the instruments of extra voting rights or extra dividend rights (*loyaliteitsdividend*) in the law.[397] A majority of interviewed board members, however, stated that their companies would not use an option to introduce extra voting rights or extra dividend rights.[398] In June 2012, the Minister of Finance abolished the idea on the basis of the general conclusion that these instruments are not an effective means to enhance long-termism.[399]

Most Dutch institutional investors are members of Eumedion, which represents their interests and acts as proxy of many investors at shareholders' meetings.[400] In 2011, Eumedion issued a set of *Best practices for engaged share ownership*. The Best Practices recommend that participants monitor their investee companies' activities including environmental and social aspects;[401] and cast informed votes at shareholder meetings and disclose quarterly the way they voted. The recommendation to monitor the investee companies' activities may include the maintaining of an ongoing dialogue with these companies. If pension funds have mandated management over all investments to an external asset manager, they are encouraged to request the asset manager to monitor the investee companies' activities on their behalf. The recommendation to cast informed votes will probably (further) reduce the influence of voting agencies. The Best Practices further recommend that participants have an intervention policy, which may include issuing public statements, intervening jointly with other institutional investors, using the right to put items on the agenda, nominating directors for appointment and initiating a proceeding with the Enterprise Court. All these recommendations are expected to enhance shareholder engagement and long-termism.

The most important category of long-term investors are institutional investors (pension funds, insurers, investment funds and asset managers). In 2010, institutional investors (foreign and Dutch) together held 84% of the shares in AEX companies.[402] It has been pointed out in literature that the investment horizon for

---

[397] TK 2008/2009, 31 371, no. 197. See for a discussion of the pros and cons of multiple dividend rights: M. de Jongh, 'Reactie: loyaal aan duurzame waarde creatie', *Ondernemingsrecht* 2010/152. Those who are against it often argue that is contrary to the principle of equality of shareholders.

[398] TK 2009/2010, 32 014, no. 8, p. 2.

[399] TK 2011/2012, 32 014, no. 30, pp. 4–5.

[400] See extensively sec. 3.1.4.

[401] The recommendation to also monitor environmental and social aspects reflects a trend that is also becoming visible by the growing practice to incorporate sustainability criteria in bonus plans.

[402] See R. Abma and R. Munsters in S.C. Peij et al (ed.), *Handboek Corporate Governance* (2010).

these long-term investors is becoming shorter.[403] This paradox is difficult to explain.[404] But the observation is in line with developments elsewhere, such as in the US, where 70% of the listed shares are held by institutional investors and the average holding term of shares in listed companies decreased from 57 months in 1980 to 5 months in 2009.[405] Almost all Dutch pension funds have mandated their investments to one or more asset management funds. The term for mandates with asset managers is three years on average. The pension funds decide whether or not to renew the mandate on the basis of the benchmarked performance of the asset manager. This encourages asset managers to have shorter investment horizons than their clients.[406] However, a recent study commissioned by Eumedion and published in November 2012, seems to contradict these observations.[407] The study, analysing the holdings of four large pension funds and two asset managers between 2003 and 2011, discovered that more than 80% of their portfolio (core portfolio) was held for five years or more.

6. Selection of Literature in English

Articles

Boot, A.M. and Labeur, R.E., 'The Dutch Banking Code', *Journal of International Banking Law and Regulation* 2010, 25, p. 363.

Burbidge, P., '"How can you be sure of Shell?" Is Corporate Governance better served by unitary or two-tier boards?', *International Company and Commercial Law Review* 2005, 16, p. 291.

---

[403] See further on this issue: Abma and Munsters in S.C. Peij et al (ed.), *Handboek Corporate Governance* (2010).

[404] More precise research instruments are needed to distinguish different types of investments. The AEX company Philips distinguishes between growth investors, index investors, value investors and growth-against a reasonable-price investors; the first two types of investors may be considered long term investors, the latter two may be activist shareholders. See further R. Abma, 'De verander(en)de rol van de private aandeelhouder binnen de vennootschap', in Faber et al (eds.), *De kredietcrisis*, Serie OO&R Vol. 54 (2010).

[405] See J.C. Brogle, 'Restoring Faith in Financial Markets', in *Wall Street Journal Europe*, 18 January 2010.

[406] See for this and other possible explanations: R. Abma and R. Munsters in S.C. Peij et al (ed.), *Handboek Corporate Governance* (2010).

[407] F. de Roon and A. Slagter, *The Duration and Turnover of Dutch Equity Ownership. A Case Study of Dutch Institutional Investors*. See <www.eumedion.nl/nl/public/kennisbank/publicaties/2012_research_report_duration_and_turnover_dutch_equities.pdf?utm_source=Eumedion+Nieuwsbrief+%7C+NL&utm_campaign=4a7a776a0b-Nieuwsbrief_Januari_20121_31_2012&utm_medium=email>.

Castermans, A.G., 'Corporations for human rights', *European Company Law* 2010, 7, p. 217.

de Groot, C., 'The Level and Composition of Executive Remuneration: a View from the Netherlands', *European Company Law* 2006, 1, p. 11.

Eumedion reports on corporate governance of Dutch listed companies, available at: <www.eumedion.nl>.

Garcia, J., 'Shareholders seize the agenda', *European Lawyer* 2007, 69, p. 15.

Groenewald, E., 'Corporate Governance in the Netherlands: from the Verdam Report of 1964 to the Tabaksblat Code of 2003', *European Business Organization Law Review* 2005, 6, p. 291.

Groenewald, Th. and & Bouchez, L.C., 'The Tabaksblat Report – Audit, remuneration and nomination committees in international Perspective', *Ondernemingsrecht* 2003, p. 423.

Hament, J.S., 'Hedge funds and private equity under scrutiny in the Netherlands', *Maastricht Journal of European and Comparative Law* 2009, 16, p. 225.

Jacobs, J.B., 'The role of specialized courts in resolving corporate governance disputes in the United States and in the EU: an American judge's perpective', *Ondernemingsrecht* 2007, 28.

Koster, H., 'Independent non-executive directors: the way forward', *Ondernemingsrecht* 2006, p. 133.

Kroeze, M.J., 'The Companies and Business Court as a specialized court', *Ondernemingsrecht* 2007, p. 29.

Lambooy, T., '30 per cent of women on boards: new law in the Netherlands', *European Company Law* 2012, 9, p. 53.

Lambooy, T., 'A Model on co-determination and CSR, the Netherlands: a bottom-up approach', *European Company Law* 2011, 8, p. 74.

Lokin, E., Timmerman, L. and Kroeze, M., 'The credit crisis and Dutch company law', *Ondernemingsrecht* 2009, p. 135.

Mason, F. and Waalkes, J., 'IPOs of Dutch Public Companies: Practical Notes', *In-House Lawyer,* October 2010, p. 44.

Olden, P., 'The company citadel', *European Lawyer* 2006, 63, p. 44.

Ramanna, A., 'The Netherlands', *International Financial Law Review* – supplement: 'The 2006 Guide to Corporate Governance', 2006, 10, pp. 29–31.

Schuit, S.R., 'New governance code sets the Netherlands on track', *International Financial Law Review* February 2004, p. 50.

Schwarz, K. and Bisschop, B.S., 'Shareholders democracy; a comparitative perspective', *Tijdschrift voor Ondernemingsbestuur* 2008-6, p. 141.

van den Muijsenbergh, W., 'Corporate Governance: The Dutch Experience', 16 *Transnational Law* 2002–2003, p. 63.

Verhoeff, L.J., 'Corporate Governance in the Netherlands', *International Business Lawyer* 2004, 32, p. 110.

Wegman, H., 'Report from the Netherlands', *European Company Law* 2007, 4, p. 86.

Books

Calkoen, W.J.L., *The One-tier Board in the Changing and Converging World of Corporate Governance: a Comparative Study of Boards in the UK, the US and the Netherlands*, Uitgaven vanwege het Instituut voor Ondernemings-recht, Rijksuniversiteit Groningen, 2012.

van Ees, H. and Marra, T., 'Corporate Governance and Initial Public Offerings – An International Perspective', *Corporate Governance and Initial Public Offerings in the Netherlands*, Chapter 13, p. 306–329, Cambridge University Press, 2012.

Frentrop P., translated from the Dutch by T. Alkins, *A History of Corporate Governance, 1602–2002*, Deminor, 2003.

de Groot, C., *Corporate Governance as a Limited Legal Concept*, Kluwer Law International, 2009.

Corporate Boards in Poland

STANISŁAW SOŁTYSIŃSKI

1. General Introduction

1.1. Legal and Business Environment in which Boards Operate

1.1.1. The Code of Commercial Companies: Sources of Inspiration and Scope of Application

Polish company law adopted a two-tier board model both for joint stock and private limited liability companies. The management board is the most important organ of the commercial company. Its competencies include management and representation of the company while the supervisory board is responsible for supervision over all activities of the company. The latter board meets from time to time, usually 3–4 times during a fiscal year.

German and Austrian company laws were models for the Polish Commercial Code of 1934[1] which survived until the end of 2000 when the Code of Commercial Companies of 2000 (CCC)[2] entered into force. The Commercial Code played a minimal role between 1948–1989 when State-owned enterprises and socialist cooperations replaced commercial companies as the main vehicles of business activity. German company law constituted the main source of foreign

---

[1] *Rozporządzenie Prezydenta Rzeczypospolitej* of 27 June 1934 r. *Kodeks handlowy*, as published in Dziennik Ustaw of 1934, No. 57, Item 502.

[2] *Kodeks spółek handlowych* of 15 September 2000, as published in Dziennik Ustaw 2000, No. 94, item 1037.

inspiration for drafters of the current CCC. However, the CCC is not an example of slavish imitation of the German model. The main difference is that the Polish code rejected the dichotomy of civil and commercial law. In principle, according to Article 2 of the CCC its lacunae shall be governed by pertinent provisions of the Civil Code.[3] However, where the nature of the legal relationship of a commercial company so requires, the latter rules shall be applied *mutatis mutandis* which may lead even to the exclusion of the application of a given rule of the Civil Code rule. The general principle incorporated in Article 2 of the CCC constitutes a legal basis for the doctrine of limited autonomy of company law in the broader context of civil law. Some company law solutions have been borrowed from other legal systems (eg. the limited liability partnership has been patterned after the US model).

The CCC constitutes a comprehensive regulation of capital companies and commercial partnerships, including their restructurings (ie. mergers, split-offs and transformations).[4] Stock corporations (*spółki akcyjne*) are regulated in the CCC. The Code distinguishes between public and private capital companies.[5] The majority of the Code rules apply to both forms of corporations. But there are a growing number of special rules that apply only to public companies. Sometimes, especially in the process of implementation of EU directives which govern public companies, the Polish Parliament extends European rules to private companies (ie. companies whose shares are not traded on stock exchanges). For instance, after the implementation of the EU Directive of 11 July 2007 on the exercise of certain rights of shareholders in listed companies,[6] shareholders of private corporations have gained from the implementation of many rules of the Directive, although some of these norms, especially those regarding different voting from each share or formalities for proxy holder, seem to be too complicated and expensive in practical application for non-listed companies.

[3] *Kodeks cywilny* of 23 April 1964, as published in Dziennik Ustaw of 1964, No. 16, item 93.

[4] St. Sołtysiński, 'Sources of Foreign Inspirations in the Draft of the Polish Company Law', 1999, in: Th. Baums, K.J. Hopt and N. Horn (eds.), *Corporations, Capital Markets and Business in the Law* (Hamburg, Aspen Pub 2000), at 533 et seq.

[5] The Polish stock corporation (*spółka akcyjna*) is a close equivalent of the German and Austrian *Aktiengesellschaft*, whilst the limited liability company (*spółka z ograniczoną odpowiedzialnością*) is modelled after the German *Gesellschaft mit beschränkter Haftung* (GmbH). No bearer shares, registered shares or endorsable documents may be issued in respect of shares or rights to participate in profit of the limited liability company. I use the terms 'limited liability company' and 'private company' as interchangeable denominations. It is worth mentioning that those stock companies whose shares are not admitted on a stock exchange or alternative markets are also 'private' *sensu largo*.

[6] Directive No. 2007/36/EC, Official Journal, p. 0017-0024.

This paper deals almost exclusively with stock companies (*spółki akcyjne*), including private companies *sensu largo* whose shares are not traded on the stock exchanges or alternative markets.

There is a dispute regarding the classification of companies whose shares are traded on alternative markets outside the regulated market (ie. outside the stock exchanges). The view prevails that, subject to a few exceptions, the latter companies shall be subject to the same rules as those applicable to stock exchange companies because shares traded on regulated and alternative markets are offered to an unlimited number of potential investors. Recently, the Government has adopted a draft law defining the concept of 'public company', so that it embraces stock companies whose shares have been admitted either on the regulated market or alternative markets. The broadening of the concept of 'public company' is in line with the view that it should cover all companies whose shares are traded on 'some form market or publicly accessible trading facility, including Multilateral Trading Facilities (...)'.[7]

1.1.2. General Characteristics of the Best Practices Code Adopted by the Warsaw Stock Exchange

The Best Practices Code adopted by the Warsaw Stock Exchange (*Dobre Praktyki Spółek Notowanych na GPW*) on 19 May 2010[8] constitute a voluntary code that companies apply individually on the basis of the principle of comply-or-explain. They sometimes mirror Polish law[9] and good usages (*dobre obyczaje*) to which the CCC refers. The majority of these soft rules are practical recommendations with the aim of maintaining corporate order in companies such that decision-making takes into account certain values for the common corporate mission. The *ultima ratio* of the creation of the Best Practices Code then stands on the shaping of decisions of corporate organs beyond the invoking of values whose adherence one cannot, and should not, force by law (*non omne licitum honestum*). The first version of the Best Practices Code was adopted following a bottom–up approach with wide market participation from executives of listed companies to organisations of investors, business groups and academics. The current version of 2010 is the fifth edition of the original version adopted jointly by the market regulator and the Warsaw Stock Exchange in 2002. The new document is divided into recommendations addressed to listed companies generally, their management boards, members of supervisory boards and shareholders.

---

[7] *Report on the Reflection Group on the Future of EU Company Law*, Brussels, 5 April 2011, p. 9.

[8] Hereinafter referred to as the 'Best Practices Code' or 'Best Practices'.

[9] For instance, the dualistic division of competencies into supervisory and management boards.

It shares certain aspects with Western European best practices codes, and also incorporates recommendations of the European Commission.

The Best Practices Code aims at increased transparency of listed companies and addresses those areas where its application may have a positive impact on the market valuation of companies. It strengthens the protection of shareholders' rights, including those not regulated by legislation and improves communication between companies and investors. It is implemented using the English concept of comply-or-explain, ie. a company must publicly state which of the recommendations it follows and which it does not follow, giving an explanation. In practice, companies have complied with this informative obligation and corporate standards have improved. The independence of supervisory board members and publicly available by-laws relating to management and supervisory boards are becoming a recognised guideline for public companies, which have become more transparent towards investors and have recognised the value of good corporate governance. The Warsaw Stock Exchange, which was privatised in 2010, has always been interested in creating and maintaining a proper corporate culture; as such it is active in educating market participants and the general public about corporate governance through a series of conferences and seminars on the topic.

1.1.3. The Interplay between Hard and Soft Company Law Rules

Aside from reputational effects, the legal consequences of the Best Practices are not entirely clear. Since the duty to declare observance of the Best Practices does not come from law but from the rules of the Stock Exchange, there are doubts as to whether they can have any meaning in the sphere of civil responsibility of the company and members of its organs.[10] Domański[11] argues that if publication regarding adherence to the Best Practices is misleading, then this constitutes a breach of law. It also means that the members of the management and supervisory boards did not properly fulfil their functions and may be subject to personal liability for causing loss to the company. Shareholders may then claim for the loss incurred by relying on the declaration made by the company directors. They ensure observance of the Best Practices through the general law, ie. by claims against the company or members of the boards for loss before a court or an arbitration tribunal, and liability will have a tortious character (Art. 415 of the Civil Code). There are two possible situations: First of all, if a company declares adherence to the Best Practices, then its articles of association should implement

---

[10] M. Furtek, Witold Jurcewicz, *Corporate Governance – Ład Korporacyjny w Spółkach Akcyjnych*, Przegląd Prawa Handlowego, 2002, No. 6, at 29.

[11] G. Domański: 'Znaczenie dobrych praktyk ładu korporacyjnego dla odpowiedzialności cywilnej spółek publicznych i członków ich organów', in A. Nowicka (ed.), *Prawo prywatne czasu przemian*, Poznań 2004, Księga Pamiątkowa dedykowana Profesorowi Stanisławowi Sołtysińskiemu at 407.

some of those rules.[12] If they are incorporated, then non–adherence to the Best Practices will be an independent basis of liability for loss, vis à vis the company[13] or vis-à-vis the shareholders.[14] Secondly, if they are not incorporated into the constitution of the listed company (eg. Best Practices regarding the minimum number of independent directors), then these may constitute additional grounds for liability for loss when determining whether members of both boards have given the required effort in fulfilling their function, but they are not responsible if the general meeting of shareholders rejects their proposals regarding incorporation of the recommended Best Practices.[15]

It remains contentious whether the behaviour of board members in contravention of publicly declared standards constitutes an illegal act. The Best Practices also include recommendations directed solely to shareholders. It is an unresolved issue whether in Polish civil law it is possible to construct tortious liability of companies vis-à-vis their shareholders for losses incurred through the violation of the Best Practices by shareholders in contravention of a positive declaration that the company would follow them.[16] Due to the frequent prominence of dominant shareholders, conflicts often arise between the strategic shareholder and minority shareholders.[17] Whether or not such liability exists, in practice it would often be very difficult to satisfy the burden of proof establishing the necessary causal link between the violation of the Best Practices and the decline in the market value of the company's shares.

An apparent paradox is that a firm declaring to adhere to the Best Practices may find itself in a legally weaker position than a firm declaring that it does not comply. If the market does not honour 'fair play' with the premium of higher demand from investors, then self-regulation will have limited effect and will not reach the envisaged goal. So far the empirical data available in Poland does not indicate that investors are capable of and interested in evaluating the quality of articles of association and observance of the Best Practices by listed companies. However, it is worth mentioning that the Warsaw Stock Exchange is growing faster than other regulated markets in the Central European region. Also, the

---

[12] It does not mean a duty of incorporation of all Best Practices rules, but some must be incorporated for this comprises an instance of adherence to them, eg. Rule 20 applying to the composition of the supervisory board.

[13] Art. 483 § 1 of the CCC.

[14] Art. 490 of the CCC.

[15] Art. 483 § 2 of the CCC.

[16] Domański (see n. 11), at p. 408.

[17] Cf. the current complaint by Staten Pensjonsfond of Norway (holding €270 million in VW shares) that Ferdinand Piëch is not acting primarily qua President of VW's supervisory board but qua major shareholder of Porsche when assisting VW's purchase of Porsche assets; *Die Presse*, 8 October 2009. Similar conflicts have arisen in Polish public companies.

reporting obligation on the observance of the Best Practices seems to mobilise the directors to respect the adopted rules.

1.1.4. Regulation of Capital Markets

Whilst the majority of governance rules applicable to public companies are found in the CCC, there is a growing body of additional norms aimed specifically at regulating companies that trade their shares and other financial instruments on regulated markets. The following acts regulate trading in financial instruments on the Warsaw Stock Exchange and other regulated markets: the Act on Trading in Financial Instruments of 29 July 2005,[18] the Act on Public Offer, Conditions Governing the Introduction of Financial Instruments to Organised Trading and Public Companies of 29 July 2005,[19] the Act on Investment Funds of 27 May 2004,[20] and the Act on Financial Instruments of 29 July 2005.[21]

The Act on Public Offer regulates public tenders and rights and obligations of shareholders in public companies. It provides, *inter alia,* that a majority share-holder who owns shares representing at least 90% of the total vote in the public company shall be entitled to demand that the remaining minority shareholders sell all their shares held in the company (mandatory buy-out). Such a squeeze-out was introduced for the first time by the CCC with respect to all corporations in 2000.[22] The Act also regulates the legal framework of public offers, including 'poison pills' that are basically permitted, unless the articles of association provide other-wise.

1.1.5. The Role of Case Law

There are a growing number of legal disputes involving both private and public companies. The jurisprudence of the Supreme Court (*Sąd Najwyższy*) and lower courts shapes the final ramifications of statutory law. The Supreme Court has rendered dozens of judgments applying the CCC rules. The case law is significant in such areas, for instance, as challenging the resolutions of the general assembly of stock companies by shareholders and the right of standing of board members in case of their dismissal and ratification of void and voidable resolutions of com-pany organs.

The CCC distinguishes between void and voidable resolutions of the meetings of shareholders (Arts. 422 and 425 of the CCC). The Code rules provide that a

---

[18] As published in the Dziennik Ustaw 2005, No. 183, item 1538, as amended (hereinafter 'Act on Public Offer').

[19] Dziennik Ustaw 2005, No. 184, item 1539, as amended.

[20] Dziennik Ustaw 2004, No. 146, item 1546, as amended.

[21] Dziennik Ustaw 2010, No. 211, item 1384.

[22] Art. 418 of the CCC.

resolution is null and void in case of violation of the law (eg. statutory rules or EU regulations), but the right to challenge such resolutions is subject to a statutory period for filing a court action (statutes of limitation). By contrast, a resolution that violates the company charter (articles of association) or *bona mores* and is contrary to the interests of the company or detrimental to a shareholder is voidable (ie. it may be challenged in courts but it is effective until declared invalid by the court). However, after a period of judgments consistent with the letter of the CCC and the statements found in the legislative history, the Supreme Court has ruled that all the challenged resolutions of the general meeting of shareholders remain effective until finally adjudicated to be null and void by the court.[23] This dynamic law-making precedent of the Supreme Court is very controversial because it enables a group of shareholders, who have managed to pass a resolution that is flagrantly contrary to law to change the management and/or the supervisory board, and to 'empty' the assets of the company during a period of sometimes several years that usually passes until the case is finally adjudicated. Hence, there are proposals to amend the Code by establishing a list of gross violations of the law that would entail a sanction of invalidity *ex tunc* and *ex lege* and breaches of less important statutory rules and articles of associations that would entail such resolutions as voidable and ineffective until so finally proclaimed by a court of law.

The Supreme Court has also rendered a judgment that allows the appropriate company organ to ratify a voidable resolution of its predecessor (ie. a resolution or a contract made by a truncated board).[24] The Court applied by way of *analogia legis* Article 103 of the Civil Code which provides that a principal may ratify a defective act of an attorney-in-fact who acted without or by exceeding their mandate. The latter precedent has been approved by the majority of commentators.

Conflicts involving company law have reached the Constitutional Court of Poland (*Trybunał Konstytucyjny*). First, the Court ruled that a specific provision of the Commercial Code (a predecessor of the CCC), which required a statutory minimum of votes for challenging resolutions of a general meeting of shareholders, was unconstitutional. The Court explained that each shareholder shall have a right of standing in such disputes. More recently, the Constitutional Court has ruled that the squeeze-out (a compulsory buy-out) of minority shareholders provided for in Article 418 of the CCC is not unconstitutional, but that the

---

[23] Judgment of 16 March 2006, III CSK 32/06, Orzecznictwo Sądów Polskich 2007, No. 3, item 7.

[24] Decision of the Supreme Court of 14 September 2007, III CZP 31/07, OSP 2008, No. 5, item 56.

majority shareholders must justify their resolutions.[25] The decision has been criticised. Its Salomon-style judgment has watered down the squeeze-out which was subsequently also adopted in the Act on Public Offering as a step of implementation of the EU Directive.

More recently, the Constitutional Court approved the Supreme Court's construction of Article 422 § 2(1) of the CCC.[26] The challenge involved the Supreme Court's narrow interpretation of Article 422 § 2 of the CCC refusing dismissed members of the management and supervisory board a right to challenge their removal even where such challenged resolutions have been taken by shareholders in violation of mandatory rules.

1.2. The Role of Private Equity Funds and Foreign Investors

Unlike in Germany, banks do not play a significant role as major shareholders in Polish listed companies. However, the majority of large Polish banks are listed on the Warsaw Stock Exchange. Foreign investors such as Citi, Uni Credit, Commerzbank, Rabobank, Deutsche Bank, and ING are strategic investors in Polish privatised banks. During the process of privatisation, the Government has demanded that the foreign strategic investors should promise to sell at least 25% of their total shares in the acquired banks and that their Polish local banking subsidiaries should remain listed on the Warsaw Stock Exchange. The Polish Treasury remains a majority shareholder in only one major Polish bank, which has been partially privatised (Bank PKO BP SA). Surprisingly, the market position and performance of this bank has remained strong. Similarly, the position of PZU SA—a partially privatised insurance company—has remained equally strong, despite payment of huge compensation to Eureco, a consortium of foreign firms which acquired a substantial part of the shareholding of that partially privatised company along with an option to buy additional shares during the IPO.[27] The critics of privatisation of the majority of strategically important financial institutions in Poland argue that the examples of Bank Pekao BP SA and PZU SA illustrate that the State should not rush to privatise such companies, and especially that such companies should not be sold to foreign strategic investors.

Polish banks have performed unexpectedly well during the recent financial crisis. Effective supervision by the market regulator, limited exposure to toxic

---

[25] Decision of the Constitution Court of 21 June, 2005, P-25/02, Orzecznictwo Trybunału Konstytucyjnego A-2005, No. 6, item 65.

[26] Decision of 2 June 2009, *Journal of Laws of 2009*, No. 91, item 752.

[27] Eureco sued Poland for violation of the Dutch-Polish Bilateral Investment Treaty because Poland had refused to sell a majority package of shares in PZU SA. The dispute was settled after the arbitral tribunal issued a preliminary award in favour of the claimant.

financial instruments, minimal scale of subprime loans, and strong performance of the Polish economy in 2008 and 2009, were the main factors credited for the healthy situation of the local financial sector. However, the budgetary deficit remains a serious problem.

Private equity companies and hedge funds are present on the Polish market. There are no restrictions in this field, except for rules of prudential regulation that are consistent with the EU law. However, the role of private equity funds and hedge funds is rather limited although by no means negligible at present. The legal of foreign investment remains high and stable. It amounted to more than USD 18 billion in 2011.

1.3. Ownership Structure

Despite the significant growth of the Warsaw Stock Exchange (WSE), which constitutes the largest regulated market in the region, the majority of Polish listed companies are dominated by block-holdings. Even the twenty largest corporations at the WSE are controlled by private or Treasury holdings, resulting mainly from privatisation strategies. The largest and most attractive Polish companies—banks, insurance companies, telecom companies, etc.—have been acquired by foreign investors who were interested only in the acquisition of full ownership or majority shareholdings. Only in a few cases has the Government successfully persuaded bidders to acquire their shares through the WSE and abstain from squeezing out minority shareholders.

The role of institutional investors remains rather limited. Some analysts have hoped that private retirement funds patterned after the Chilean model introduced during the Pinochet era would gradually contribute to the increase of the dispersed ownership structure of listed companies once they are permitted to invest freely on the regulated market.[28] However, in 2011 the Government presented a bill which substantially reduces the amount of payments to the retirement funds and the European Commission brought a complaint against Poland alleging that the funds should be free to invest in all EU countries. The Bill was adopted by Parliament and entered into force on 1 May 2011. It provides that only 2.3% instead of 7.3% of social security payments will be administered by the private retirement funds. This limitation will remain in force until 2012 and will grow gradually but only up to 3.5% in 2017. Hence, as a result, the retirement funds will invest much less in the companies listed on the WSE. It should be also mentioned that all except three such funds are owned directly or indirectly by foreign financial institutions. The retirement funds have been criticised by the

---

[28] So far, these funds must invest 40% of their resources in Polish listed companies and 60% in Government bonds.

Government and some economists for charging very high fees,[29] contributing to the growing deficit of the Treasury, avoiding competition and spending too much on misleading advertising. Some top economists criticise the Government for sabotaging the retirement funds reform and doing too little to reduce the budgetary deficit. The critics argue that the Parliament has *de facto* partially nationalised retirement assets that are the property of the beneficiaries of the retirement funds. This seems to be an overstatement because the beneficiaries of the retirement funds have not owned assets administered by the funds but have merely expectation rights which have been substituted by similar inheritable and inchoate entitlements once the part of the social security funds has been transferred from the retirement funds to *Zakład Ubezpieczeń Społecznych*, the State controlled social security fund. The new law limiting the role of private retirement funds may have a negative impact on the Warsaw Stock Exchange (WSE) because they will invest less on the regulated markets.[30]

Since foreign strategic investors were interested in the acquisition of whole privatised companies in Poland, the many local privatised blue chips function as private companies and members of transnational groups. Some listed companies are fully controlled by the Treasury, which has retained blocks of shares permitting the Government to dominate such entities, including PKO BP (the largest Polish bank), PKN Orlen SA (the largest regional petrochemical *Konzern*) or KGHM (the largest European copper company).

The role of foreign investors in private and public companies is growing steadily. Recently, Warsaw Stock Exchange has witnessed IPOs of companies from the region (ie. Czech Republic, Ukraine and Baltic States).

1.4. Dominant Company and Controlled Company

The structure of the ownership in the Polish listed companies triggers difficult agency costs problems. In companies controlled by foreign strategic investors conflicts arise between the group having its centre abroad and minority shareholders in their Polish subsidiaries, who allege transfer pricing and dominance of the interest of the parent company.[31] In State-dominated companies the agency costs are frequently very high due to incompetence, frequent changes of board members, political favouritism and close relations existing between board mem-

---

[29] At the outset it was 10%, now 3.5%.

[30] The private retirement funds have been subject to similar or even more drastic measures in many Central/Eastern European countries (eg. in Hungary, Slovakia and the Baltic states).

[31] Compare A. Opalski, *Rada nadzorcza w spółce akcyjnej* (C.H. Beck, Warsaw 2006), at pp. 16–18.

bers and their political 'principals'. There is no perfect panacea for such problems in the arsenals of Western best corporate practices either.

Numerous provisions of the CCC apply to 'dominant (majority)' companies (*spółka dominująca*) and 'controlled' (dependent) companies (*spółka zależna*). Thus, for instance, a dominant company is obliged to inform the dependent company of the establishment of a relationship of dominance within two weeks of the date of such event (Art. 6 § 1): the conclusion of a 'Konzern' agreement (eg. a contract concerning the management of a company) requires approval from the general meeting of the managed company (Art. 392 Subs. 7); and voting rights held by a dominant and controlled company in a third joint company, whose articles of association provide for a voting ceiling, may be subject to cumulation (ie. the articles of association may provide that all voting rights belonging to a dominant company (A) and its controlled companies (a_1, a_2 and a_3) in company B shall be calculated jointly, thus preventing the group circumventing voting ceilings.

To avoid problems associated with the interpretation of the notions of control and dependence, the CCC has introduced a comprehensive definition of the concepts of dominant and controlled companies. The pertinent definitions read as follows:

'4) a dominant company – a commercial company in the case where:
  a) it controls, indirectly or directly, a majority of the votes at the general meeting or the general assembly, also as pledge or usufructuary, or in the management board of another capital company (a dependent company), also under agreements with other parties, or
  b) it is entitled to appoint or dismiss a majority of the members of the management board of another capital company (a dependent company) or a cooperative (a dependent cooperative), also under agreements with other parties, or
  c) it is entitled to appoint or dismiss a majority of the members of the supervisory board of another capital company (a dependent company) or a cooperative (a dependent cooperative), also under agreements with other parties, or
  d) the members of its management board constitute more than half of the members of the management board of another capital company (the dependent company) or of a cooperative (the dependent cooperative), or
  e) it controls, indirectly or directly, a majority of the votes in the dependent partnership or at the general meeting of the dependent cooperative, also under agreements with other parties, or
  f) it exerts a decisive influence on the operations of the dependent capital company or dependent cooperative, in particular based on the agreements referred to in Article 7.[32]

§ 3. Where two commercial companies mutually control a majority of the votes, calculated in accordance with § point 4 letter a), the commercial company which holds a larger percentage of the votes at the general meeting or the general assembly of the other company (the dependent company) shall be deemed to be the dominant company. Where

---

[32] Art. 4 § 1(4) of the CCC (author's translation).

each of the commercial companies holds the same percentage of the votes at the general meeting or the general assembly of the other company, that company which exerts an influence on the dependent company also on the basis of the link provided for in § 1 point 4 letters b)-f) shall be deemed to be dominant company.

§ 4. Where the relationship of dominance and dependence between two commercial companies cannot be established under the criteria provided for in § 3, that commercial company which may exert an influence on another company on the basis of a larger number of links referred to in § 1 point 4 letters b)-f) shall be deemed to be the dominant company.

§ 5. Where it is impossible to establish in accordance with § 3 and 4 which of the companies is the dominant company, both companies shall be mutually dominant and dependent companies.'

The foregoing definitions reduce the risk of disputes whether a given company is controlled' or whether it shall be considered a dominant entity in most cases. However, in a company with dispersed shareholding, an entity holding 15–18% of the votes may exercise a controlling influence over the activities of a company within the meaning of Article 4 § 1 Subs. 4(f) of the CCC. The statutory definitions of a controlled and dominant company require further qualifications for the purpose of regulation of groups of companies.[33]

In principle, transgression of statutory powers by the management board that require approval of the general meeting of shareholders triggers invalidity of an unauthorised legal act (eg. a disposal of the business of the company or entering into a contract subjecting the company to the management powers of the dominant entity). However, Article 17 § 2 of the CCC offers a two months *cure period* during which a legal act executed without the statutory consent may be ratified by the competent organ (ie. the general meeting of shareholders or the supervisory board). In 2007, the Supreme Court has offered yet another route of ratification of the *ultra vires* acts executed by the management board. It ruled that the ratification of such acts should be permitted also after the lapse of the two months period pursuant to Article 103 § of the Civil Code.[34]

The latter provision deals with the issue of ratification of defective acts of an attorney-in-fact (*falsus procurator*). Thus, in fact, the judicial law-making precedent of the Supreme Court transformed the consequences of the acts without authority into voidable legal acts. The Supreme Court applied Article 103 of the Civil Code by way of *analogia legis*. On ratification, the management board's acts produce the same effects as if they had been performed with all legal powers from the outset of the transaction (*ex tunc* effects).

---

[33] See further sec. 5.2. below.

[34] Resolution of the Supreme Court of 14 September, 2007, III CZP 31.07, OSP 2008, No. 5, item 56.

1.5. Available Board Models

In joint stock companies the two-tier board is mandatory (Art. 381).

In limited liability companies whose share capital exceeds 500,000 zlotys (about €110,000) and there are more than 25 shareholders, the supervisory board or auditors' committee shall also be established (Art. 213 § 1 of the CCC). In the other limited liability companies, the articles of association may provide the formation of a supervisory board or auditors' committee, or both these organs. Thus the establishment of a two or three-tier board in the limited liability company is, in principle, optional.

The choice between a unitary board and a two-tier board is available only in Societas Europea (SE). In the latter company a one-tier board distinguishes between executive and non-executive directors. The former may be members of the board or function as officers of the company outside the board. So far, only three SE companies have been formed in Poland.

At present, the CCC provides that shareholders may establish only such organs that are expressly provided in the law. Thus, the joint stock company may not have an auditors' committee but supervisory boards in both types of capital companies may set up audit committees and other advisory bodies that do not constitute company organs.[35] This principle of *numerus clausus* is widely approved. However, several commentators propose that the legislators should permit the shareholders to choose between a unitary and two-tier board. Also, the articles of association should provide for establishing permanent and *ad hoc* committees functioning as advisory bodies of the boards (eg. audit or remuneration committees of the supervisory board).

2. Functions and Powers of the Two-Tier Board

2.1. Management Board

The management board shall represent the company and manage its affairs (Art. 201 § 1 and 368 § 1 of the CCC). The functions and powers of management board of joint stock and limited liability companies are largely identical. Members of the management board enjoy broadly defined powers of representation. The right of a member of the management board to represent the company may not be restricted with a legal effect to third parties.

In principle, the management board and supervisory board of a joint stock company are collegial organs. The majority of their decisions require a resolution. Delegation of specific powers to a board member is permitted only in cases

---

[35] See further, sec. 2.6 below.

provided by law and/or the articles of association. The management board is the only permanent organ of the company. For this and other reasons, jurisprudence has developed the principle of presumption of competence of the management board in all matters when the law does not empower the general meeting of shareholders or the supervisory board to perform a given function.

In a joint stock company the general meeting of shareholders and supervisory board may not issue binding instructions to the management board in the area of management of the company (Art. 375[1] of the CCC). This prohibition is derived from German law and does not apply to limited liability companies. Furthermore, given the fact that the general meeting of shareholders and supervisory board may dismiss members of the management board any time (dismissal *ad nutum*), management board members rarely disregard non-binding recommendations or advice issued by these bodies. It is also worth mentioning that the management board needs a prior approval of the general meeting of shareholders for several important decisions. Pursuant to Article 393 of the CCC, the following transactions require the approval of the general meeting of shareholders:

'In addition to other matters stipulated in this Division or in the statutes, the following matters shall require a resolution of the general assembly:

1) consideration and approval of the report of the management board on the operations of the company and the financial report for the previous financial year and the granting of approval of the performance by the members of the company governing bodies of their duties,
2) decisions concerning claims for redress of damage caused upon formation of the company or in the course of management or supervision,
3) transfer or tenancy of the enterprise or its organised part and the creation of a limited right in rem on them,
4) acquisition and transfer or real estate, the right of perpetual usufruct, or a share in real estate, unless the statutes provide otherwise,
5) issue of convertible bonds or bonds with the right of priority, and issue of subscription warrants referred to in Article 453 § 2,
6) acquisition of the company's own shares in the case referred to in Article 362 § 1 point 2 and authorisation to acquire them in the case referred to in Article 362 § 1 point 8,
7) conclusion of a contract referred to in Article 7.'[36]

2.2. Supervisory Board

The main function of the supervisory board consists of permanent supervision over the company's activities in all aspects of its business (Art. 382 § 1 of the CCC). The Code also lists specific statutory duties of the board: (i) Evaluation of

---

[36] Art. 7 of the CCC defines the concept of a so-called *Konzern* agreements, for instance, management or transfer of profit contracts.

the reports presented by the management board to the general meeting, their consistency with the books of the company and the facts, and (ii) evaluation of the motions of the management board concerning distribution of profits and coverage of losses (Art. 382 § 3 of the CCC).

The Code mandates strict separation of the competencies of the management and the supervisory functions in joint stock companies and limited liability companies. The supervisory board may not issue binding directives to the management board. In practice, however, supervisory boards quite frequently pass resolutions advising the management board to consider a concrete project or express opinions on a project presented by the management board.

Although, a strict construction of the above mentioned provisions implies that the supervisory board performs a merely *ex post* monitoring function, commentators argue that supervision should include participation in devising the company's strategy, as well as *an ante* evaluation of risk.[37] It is argued that supervision involves initial, current and *ex post* monitoring. A growing number of supervisory boards of listed companies participate in setting strategy. The articles of association frequently provide for the approval of annual and long term business plans of the company by the supervisory board.

The Best Practices Code recommends that the supervisory board should also evaluate the internal risk management mechanism (eg. internal audit). A recent empirical study shows that about 40% of the listed companies report that their supervisory boards evaluate corporate mechanisms of risk control. However, less than 10% of the respondents describe concrete forms and instruments of risk evaluation.[38] It is also worth noting that risk committees have been established in almost all financial institutions. They are directly supervised by supervisory boards.

The supervisory board may also be empowered to approve major transactions and other decisions pursuant to the charter of the company (Art. 384 of the CCC). As already mentioned, the list of decisions requiring prior approval of the supervisory board frequently includes granting consent to annual and long term business plans. The charter may not, however, shift the management responsibilities from the management board to the supervisory board. An overly long (comprehensive) list of approvals required from the supervisory board may be challenged and held invalid as contrary to the statutory division of powers between the two organs. The registration court may also refuse to register a charter that would muzzle the management board by too broadly defined powers of the supervisory board.

---

[37] Opalski (see n. 31), at pp. 339–343; St. Sołtysiński in *System prawa prywatnego. Prawo spółek kapitałowych*, v. 17B (Warsaw, C.H. Beck 2010), pp. 500–501.

[38] A. Skitek and A. Kostrzyca, 'System kontroli i zarządzania ryzykiem – praktyka spółek notowanych na Giełdzie Papierów Wartościowych. Wyniki badań Edycja 2011', *Przegląd Corporate Governance*, 2011, No. 2(26), pp. 59–62.

The third important competence of the supervisory board involves appointment, removal and suspension of management board members (Art. 368 § 4 and Art. 383 of the CCC).[39]

In practice, the supervisory boards frequently employ their own experts. The company shall conclude contracts and pay remuneration of such advisors.

2.3. The Size and Composition of the Two Boards

The size of the management board is left to the discretion of the shareholders' meeting. The minimum number of seats in the supervisory board is three for a private company, and five members in listed companies. There are no statutory maxima with respect to the size of both boards. The maximum duration of the office term of a management board member in a joint stock company is five years, but there are no restrictions regarding the number of renewals of the term (Art. 369 of the CCC). Staggered boards are permitted, but not frequently adopted in articles of association, except in a few listed companies. There is no statutory maximum of management or supervisory board members.

An empirical study shows that the average management board of a listed company has between 3–4 directors, whilst supervisory boards consist of 6–13 members.[40] Women account for slightly more than 13% of the members of the supervisory board and about 10% of members of the management board in listed companies (2008).[41] Foreigners represent about 15% of the supervisory boards of companies listed on the WSE. Less than 10% of management board members are foreigners.

2.4. The Role of the President of the Management Board and the Chairman of the Supervisory Board

In principle, members of the two boards perform their duties collectively and enjoy equal competencies. The president of the management board is only *primus inter pares*. However, the CCC, unlike the Commercial Code of 1934, has allowed the shareholders' meeting to upgrade the role of the chief executive officer (CEO). The president of the management board may have the right of exercising a casting vote and be granted other special competencies by the articles

---

[39] See further, sec. 3.1. below.

[40] Leszek Bohdanowicz, 'Liczebność i struktura organów statutowych polskich spółek publicznych w 2008', *Przegląd Corporate Governance*, No. 3(19) 2009, at 113.

[41] *Ibid.*, at 114.

of association, which may also grant similar prerogatives to the chairman of the supervisory board.

Day-to-day 'cohabitation' of the two boards is more and more similar to that of executive and non-executive directors in a one-tier board. As a rule, the supervisory board meets in the presence of the management board members, who are requested to leave the board room only in case of discussing their dismissal, evaluation of executive directors or similar matters. It is also worth mentioning that according to a statutory model, the members of the management board are appointed, dismissed and suspended by the supervisory board. The articles of association may, however, provide otherwise. The right of appointment of members of both boards may be shifted to the general meeting of shareholders. It may also be granted by the articles of association to individual shareholders or even third parties.

2.5. Independent Directors

The definition of independence is modelled on the EU guidelines. Articles of association frequently deviate from these guidelines, especially in private companies. The Best Practices Code of 2002 required that the majority of supervisory board members shall be independent directors. This requirement has been gradually diluted due to the opposition of the majority of the listed companies that are controlled by strategic investors. At present, the Best Practices Code of 2010 provides that at least two members of the supervisory board should meet the criteria of independence under Annex II to the Commission Recommendation of 15 February 2005 on the role of non-executive or supervisory directors of listed companies and on the committees of the (supervisory) board (Rule III.6).

There are diverging stances relating to the institution of the independent director. The critics opine that their independence is doubtful given the process of their selection and that there is a risk of forming a constituency of independent directors in the board, leading to a split within this body.[42] In the author's opinion, the latter criticism is exaggerated, although it is true that independent directors are frequently recruited from friends and good acquaintances of the majority shareholder or president of the management board. However, a person who meets the criteria of independence is more likely to have their own opinion and to take difficult personal decisions than, for instance, an employee of the majority shareholder or their business client. The strong opposition of many majority shareholders controlling listing companies, who prefer to appoint their agents to supervisory boards, speaks for itself. Although, independent directors

---

[42] A. Opalski, 'Obowiązek lojalności w spółkach kapitałowych', *Kwartalnik Prawa Prywatnego* 2008, vol. 2, p. 467.

are frequently congeneric to the majority shareholders and insufficiently autonomous, the proposition that an agent, partner or person financially dependent can effectively supervise his principal's or partner's company and will be impartial acting in the interest of minority shareholders and stakeholders is much less persuasive.

2.6. Special Committees

The CCC has adopted the German concept of *Satzungsstrenge* (the strict application of the statutory rules and the compliance of the articles of association with the law). According to this principle, the rules governing stock corporations are mandatory, except as expressly provided otherwise. Hence, for instance, the shareholders may only establish organs permitted by the law. However, the charter may provide for establishing advisory bodies assisting the management board and the supervisory board in performing their duties. In particular, the supervisory board is now frequently assisted by such advisory bodies as the audit committee, the remuneration committee, the strategy committee, the risk committee, and the nomination committee. As a rule, such committees consist of board members but outside persons are not prohibited. It should be stressed that resolutions and recommendations of the advisory committees are not binding on the board. The Best Practices require that at least two members of the audit company should be independent and Annex I of the European Commission Recommendation of 15 February 2010 on the role of non-executive or supervisory directors should apply to the operation of the committees of the board.[43]

The Law of 7 May, 2009 on Expert Auditors and their Self-government[44] provides that, subject to a few statutory exceptions, in the so-called entities of public interest the supervisory council shall establish an audit committee composed of at least three members. The term 'entity of public interest' covers, for instance, companies issuing financial instruments on regulated markets, domestic banks, insurance companies, retirement funds, and investment funds. Such companies meet the criteria of public interest entities within the meaning of the Eighth Directive (Art. 41–42) and Recommendation of the European Commission on the Role of Executive and Non-Executive Directors.[45] At least one member of the audit company must meet the criteria of being an independent board member.

The statutory tasks of the audit committee comprise, *inter alia*, (i) monitoring the process of the financial reporting of the company, (ii) monitoring the effectiveness of the internal system of supervision, internal audit and risk

---

[43] The Best Practices, Rule III. 7–8.

[44] Dziennik Ustaw 2009, No. 77, item 649.

[45] Recommendation 2005/162/EC, Official Journal of the European Union L 52/51.

management, and (iii) monitoring the independence of the professional auditor and the firm auditing the company.

2.7. Decision-Making Process

As already mentioned, in principle, both management board and supervisory board perform their duties collectively. There are statutory exceptions to this principle. For instance, in a joint stock company the articles may provide otherwise. However, certain important decisions shall be made only by way of a resolution (eg. a decision on payment of an advance dividend or convocation of a meeting of shareholders). The principle of collective performance of powers or duties speaks against granting a board member a veto right. However, the requirement of supermajority or unanimity may amount to granting each member a veto power. The unanimity requirement may be justified only in special situations (eg. in a private company owned by two or three shareholders). A member of the supervisory board in a joint stock company may be empowered by resolution of the board to perform specific supervisory tasks (Art. 390 § 1 of the CCC).

2.8. Special Rights of Minority Shareholders

A salient feature of the Polish joint stock company (ie. *spółka akcyjna*) is the cumulative vote in electing members of the supervisory board. At the request of shareholders representing at least one-fifth of the share capital, members of the supervisory board shall be elected at the next general meeting by voting in separate groups, even if the articles of association provide for a different manner of appointing the board (Art. 385 § 3 of the CCC). Shareholders representing the portion of shares which constitutes the number of votes necessary to elect one member of the supervisory board form a separate group and may not participate in the election of the other members of the board. During the election of board members by groups of shareholders, one share shall give the right to one vote only, without any multi-vote privileges or restrictions (eg. ceiling votes).

The provisions of the CCC on electing supervisory board members are mandatory. They apply to both listed and non-listed joint stock companies. Where members of the supervisory board were elected by a vote in separate groups of shareholders (ie. in the case of cumulative vote), each group shall have the right to delegate one of the elected members to perform supervisory tasks individually on a permanent basis. Members so delegated shall have the right to attend meetings of the management board and provide advisory functions at such meetings (Art. 390 § 2 of the CCC). Cumulative voting during the election of supervisory board members constitutes a powerful right of minority shareholders and may not be opted out by the majority. The right of the elected members to perform the supervisory tasks individually is an effective deterrent against the abuse of power by the majority but it may also be abused by a minority shareholder. In principle, the majority may dismiss a supervisory board member elected by a group. Several commentators are of the opinion that although, in principle, the dismissal of a board member may be effected without cause, in the absence of justified circumstances recalling a minority representative shortly after the election performed by groups of shareholders may be challenged as null and void.[46] The Supreme Court has ruled that, in principle, the general meeting may recall a supervisory board member elected by a group of shareholders.[47] Since the minority shareholders may respond by immediately requesting yet another round of board elections by groups of shareholders, majority shareholders usually try to avoid such confrontations by negotiating a balanced composition of the supervisory board, including persons recommended by minority shareholders. In case of a serious conflict, the majority shareholders frequently offer minority shareholders the right of exit.

Whilst Code provisions on cumulative voting and election of supervisory board members by groups of shareholders protect a single shareholder or a group of shareholders representing jointly at least one-fifth of the outstanding share capital, a small shareholder or shareholders representing no more than 5% of the share capital may exercise the right of compulsory sell-out (Art. 418[1] of the CCC).

2.9. Information Streams

The asymmetry of information controlled by the management board and filtered before it reaches the supervisory board also raises problems in Polish companies. The situation is slightly improved by the audit and risk committees where supervisory board members may meet company officers and rank-and-file employees without the presence of the management board members. However, rapidly growing responsibilities of supervisors cannot be realistically performed as long as the supervisory board members meet only four times a year. The gap between statutory duties of supervisory board members and their part-time corporate jobs is growing in both two-tier and one-tier systems. Auditing firms offer little help. They also rely on information received from the management board. The contents of their long disclaimers presented at the end of the reports indicate that the value of such external inspection is very limited indeed. A realistic solution would be either limiting the scope of the supervisory board duties or requiring that internal

---

[46] St. Sołtysiński, 'Nieważne i wzruszalne uchwały zgromadzeń spółek kapitałowych', *Przegląd Prawa Handlowego* 2006, No 1, pp. 11–12; W. Popiołek in J. Strzępka (ed.) *Kodeks spółek handlowych. Komentarz* (Warsaw, C.H. Beck 2009), p. 877.

[47] Decision of 21 January 2005, 1 CK 505/04, OSNCP 2006, No. 1, item 10.

supervisors perform their duties on a permanent or almost permanent basis.[48] This, in turn, would trigger additional costs.

Polish corporate practice shows that some supervisory board members elected by minority shareholders perform their duties only for the benefit of their constituencies. Some commentators argue that the management board may refuse to disclose sensitive information to such supervisors, raising the shield of abuse of right.[49] Pursuant to Article 382 § 4 of the CCC, the supervisory board may inspect all documents of the company, request reports and explanations from the management board and employees. In practice, however, the supervisory board requests the management board or the CEO to provide specific documents. Recently, however, committees established by the supervisory board—in particular, audit committees—issue orders for the production of documents to supervisory board members and employees concerned. For reasons of courtesy and avoidance of conflict between the two boards, requests for sensitive documents are handled by the chairman of the supervisory board and the CEO.

3. Accountability

3.1. Boards and Shareholders

3.1.1. *Appointment, Suspension and Removal*

Management board members in limited liability companies are appointed by shareholders' resolution, unless the articles provide otherwise (Art. 201 § 4 of the CCC). The same body removes directors. In joint stock companies, in principle, members of the management board are elected, suspended and dismissed by a resolution of the supervisory board, unless the articles provide otherwise (Art. 368 § 4 of the CCC). However, the general meeting of shareholders retains the powers of dismissal and suspension of executives (ie. the management board members).

In principle, the management board members of limited liability and joint stock companies may be removed without cause. In 2007, the Supreme Court has further weakened the position of managers, ruling that a removed management board member has no right of standing to challenge such a resolution of the shareholders meeting even if they allege that it has been passed in violation of law (eg. if it has been passed without the required quorum or majority of votes).[50]

---

[48] Opalski (see n. 31), at p. 340, 361.

[49] A. Szumański, 'Ten obcy', *Rzeczpospolita* of March 2001, pp. 3–4.

[50] Resolution of the Supreme Court of 1 March, 2007, III CZP 94/06, OSNC 2007, No. 7–8, item 95.

The removal from office shall not deprive the dismissed board member of the right to raise claims under their employment or other contract concerning the performance of the function of a management board member (Art. 370 § 1).

Members of the supervisory board in joint stock companies are appointed and dismissed by the shareholders meeting. As indicated above, a peculiar feature of the Polish CCC consists in a cumulative voting by groups of shareholders organised during the general meeting of shareholders.[51] Persons representing at the general meeting of shareholders the portion of shares which is the aggregate number of shares represented at the meeting divided by the number of members of the supervisory board form a separate group authorised to elect one member of the board. For instance, where the supervisory board consists of 5 members and the general meeting of shareholders consists of 100 shareholders each having 100 shares, each group comprising 10 shareholders may elect one board member.

The powers of the supervisory board of the joint stock company (both listed and private companies) includes suspending, for important reasons, individual and even all management board members (Art. 383 § 1 of the CCC). In such a case the supervisory board may delegate its member(s) to temporarily perform the executive duties of the suspended member(s) of the management organ. Such delegation shall not exceed three months. As can be seen, the separation of the statutory functions of the executive and non-executive members of the two boards is less strict in Polish law than, for instance, under the German Stock Corporation Act (*Aktiengesetz*).

3.1.2. *Division of Powers between the Management Board and Shareholders*

Generally, the powers to manage (administer) and represent the company in limited liability and joint stock companies is vested in the management board. As already mentioned,[52] in a joint stock company neither the general meeting of shareholders nor the supervisory board may issue binding instructions to the management board relating to the management of the company (Art. 375¹ of the CCC). However, the CCC provides a list of fundamental management matters which require prior approval of the general meeting of shareholders. They include, *inter alia*, disposal or lease of the business enterprise or an organised part thereof, or establishment of a limited right *in rem* thereon; acquisition and disposal of a real property or of an interest therein, unless the articles provide otherwise; issuance of convertible bonds; acquisition of company own shares; and execution of management and other *Konzern* agreements. If a management board enters into a contract without a prior approval of the general meeting of shareholders, such legal act is null and void unless it is ratified by the share-

---

[51] See sec. 2.8 above.
[52] See sec. 2.1 above.

holders no later than two months following the date of execution of the transaction by the board (Art. 17 § 2 of the CCC).[53]

The list of transactions requiring prior approval of the general meeting of
shareholders may be extended in the articles of association. However, a breach of
such stipulation by the management board does not trigger invalidity of the legal
act. The directors may only be subject to a claim for damages, if at all.

3.1.3. Special Issues

a) Conflict of Interest and Related-Party Transactions

The CCC contains two twin rules regulating conflict of interest in the context of
related-party transactions with participation of management board members.
Pursuant to Article 377, in case of a conflict of interest between a joint stock
company and its management board member, his spouse, relatives up to the
second degree of kinship, as well as persons with whom the director has a
personal relationship, the board member shall refrain from participating in the
resolution of such matters. He/she may request that the minutes of the board
meeting should record the fact that the executive director has not participated in
the resolution of such matter (Art. 377 of the CCC). A substantially identical rule
applies to board members of limited liability companies (Art. 209 of the CCC).

The sanction in case of violation of the above rule is subject to diverging
interpretation. A single Supreme Court decision provides that the transaction
binds the company but a culpable director may be held liable for damages.[54] The
decision has been criticised by commentators.[55]

b) Duty of Non-Competition

The scope of a duty of non-competition of management board members in capital
companies is set out in Article 211 and Article 380 of the Code. These twin rules
provide that a director of the management board shall not, without the company's
consent, engage in competitive business or participate in competitive companies
or partnership. The prohibition covers all competitive entities, including civil law
partnerships. Participation means equity participation, except below the level of
10% of the outstanding shares of a competitive company, being a member of the

---

[53] The statutory requirements of prior approval of certain material transactions by the
shareholders resemble the assumptions of the German *Holzmüller* doctrine developed by
BGHZ. See further, F.G. Semler in: *Münchener Handbuch des Gesellschaftsrechts*, v. 4,
Aktiengesellschaft (München, C.H. Beck 2007), p. 502 et seq.

[54] Decision of the Supreme Court of 11 January 2002, IV CKN 1903/00, Orzecznictwo
Sądu Najwyższego, No. 11, item 137.

[55] See further Popiołek (see n. 47), at p. 860.

supervisory board or management board of a competing entity, or having the right to appoint a management board in such a company.

Unless the articles provide otherwise, the consent to engage in a competitive business by a management board member shall be granted by the body that appointed a director (ie. a board member). As a rule, such consent shall be bestowed upon a management board member by the supervisory board.

The duty of non-competition covers actual competitors of the company. It is debatable whether it embraces potential competitors (eg. entities whose activities may compete with such areas of business which are merely listed among the objects of activities of the company but not conducted by the company).

c) Corporate Opportunity

Corporate opportunity doctrine is neither enshrined in the CCC nor developed by case law. However, recent legal doctrine maintains that directors should refrain from taking advantage of corporate opportunities because of the requirements of the duty of loyalty (Art. 2 of the CCC in conjunction of Art. 354 of the Civil Code).[56]

d) Duties of Loyalty of Supervisory Board Member

Loyalty obligations of members of the management and supervisory boards are different from those of shareholders. Board members must do their utmost to administer the company's assets and to further its envisaged goals set in the articles. The strength of such obligations correlates directly with the trust and powers given to members of the boards. Polish law regulates these duties exclusively with regard to the management board by establishing: (i) A ban on competitive activities;[57] (ii) a prohibition to participate in a decision in matters where there is a conflict of interest; even voicing of one's opinion in such matters can contravene the law;[58] (iii) a requirement of the alignment of their own personal interest with that of the company;[59] and (iv) that there is a general duty to act in accordance with *bona mores* (usages).[60] These duties are not a new concern: In 1936, T. Dziurzyński argued that management should refrain from any activity in conflict with the company's interests.[61]

---

[56] Stanisław Sołtysiński in *Sołtysiński, Szajkowski, Szwaja, Kodeks handlowy* (Warsaw, C.H.Beck 2001), v. 1, p. 72 and 193; Opalski (see n. 31), at p. 194–199.

[57] Code of Commercial Companies Arts. 211 and 380.

[58] *Ibid.*, Arts. 209 & 377.

[59] *Ibid.*, Art. 15, Art. 210 § 1, Art. 228(2), Art. 379 § 1, Art. 393(2).

[60] Civil Code Art. 354.

[61] T. Dziurzyński, Z. Fenichel and M. Honzatko, *Kodeks Handlowy. Komentarz*, Cracow 1936, Księgarnia Powszechna, Art. 204 (1) of the Commercial Code (1934).

Recently, some commentators have argued that the aforementioned Code loyalty rules should be applicable *mutatis mutandis* to members of the supervisory board.[62] For instance, a prohibition to participate in matters where there is a conflict of interest and the duty to disclose a conflict of interest by a supervisory board member can be argued by way of *analogia legis* interpretation of Article 377 of the CCC.[63] Of course, duties of supervisory board members are less intensive than those of managers because they participate in administering the company principally only in the matters bestowed on the supervisory board by the articles of association.

e) Insider Information

Members of the two boards must refrain from exploiting and disclosing confidential information where disclosure may affect the price of the company shares or other securities. The Act on Public Offer[64] provides that a public company may disclose confidential information only to providers of financial, tax, business and legal advisors, as well as other persons listed in Article 66 of that law. The recipients of such information become insiders bound by a duty to keep the received data confidential. The breach of the insider's duty is subject to criminal and civil law sanctions set forth in the Act on Public Offer and other laws. Of course, members of the management board and supervisory board are also insiders within the meaning of those laws.

Public prosecutors are not well prepared to deal with violation of insiders' duties and the enforcement of these laws is sluggish. Dozens of investigations have been initiated by but there have been only two successful prosecutions ending in judicial decisions.

f) Takeover Situations

Pursuant to Article 80 of the Act on Public Offer, the management board of a public company is required to publish its opinion regarding a takeover bid aimed at acquisition of more than 33% of all shares of the company. The opinion shall express the management's evaluation of a potential impact of such takeover bids in the interest of the company, including its employment, strategic plans of the bidder vis-à-vis the company, etc. Moreover, the opinion shall state whether the offered price constitutes a fair value of the shares.

---

[62] *Ibid.*, at 176 et seq.

[63] St. Sołtysiński, 'Przepisy ogólne kodeksu spółek handlowych', *Państwo i Prawo* 2001, No. 7, pp. 8–9.

[64] *Ustawa o ofercie publicznej i warunkach wprowadzania instrumentów finansowych do zorganizowanego systemu obrotu oraz o spółkach publicznych z dnia* 29.7.2005 r., as published in Dziennik Ustaw No. 184, item 1539, as amended.

The articles of association of a listed company may contain poison pills aimed at protecting the target entity against hostile takeovers. The constitution of such company may also provide that the management board and the supervisory board may not undertake acts aimed at frustrating a public offer without a prior consent of the general meeting of shareholders. In such a case poisonpills stipulated in the articles of association are ineffective.[65] Such opt-in rules are rarely found in practice.

3.1.4. Institutional Investors; Shareholders' Apathy

Institutional investors sometimes form ad-hoc coalitions aimed at electing supervisory board members by way of cumulative voting or passing resolutions regarding payment of dividend, acquisition of the company's own shares by the corporation, etc. Generally, however, shareholder activism is rare. Shareholders' attitudes are characterised by apathy rather than activism. Institutional investors in listed companies are reluctant to form *ad hoc* coalitions because they are obligated to publicly disclose such agreements and may be subject to other onerous obligations.

3.1.5. Remuneration

The Code leaves the issue of remuneration of management board and supervisory board members largely to the discretion of the organ responsible for the appointment of directors. Thus, remuneration of the management board members is usually in the hands of the supervisory board, whilst members of the latter body are remunerated by the general meeting of shareholders. The amount of such remuneration must be set forth in the articles of association or a resolution of the general meeting. They may also participate in the company's profit for a given financial year (Art. 392 § 2 of the CCC) but the shareholders rarely pass such resolutions. The prevailing view is that non-executive directors' remuneration should not be linked to the economic performance of the company.

Remuneration of management board directors of a joint stock company usually consists of fixed and variable components. Members of the supervisory board receive fixed remuneration established by way of a resolution of the general meeting of shareholders. Recently, several public companies have introduced new remuneration policies based upon guidelines of the European Commission. New variable remuneration schemes provide for deferred bonuses and, less frequently, for claw back stipulations. The vested periods are usually 2–3 years. Polish public companies generally publish their remuneration policies and earnings of their directors in the company's annual reports.

---

[65] Art. 80a of the *Act on Public Offer.*

Bonuses paid to executives of controlled companies are usually fully or predominantly aligned with the economic performance of the group, which may increase the conflict between their companies and the holding entity.

3.2. Boards and Stakeholders; the Notion of Company's Interest

Several provisions of the CCC and other laws indicate that member of the management board and the supervisory board shall act in the interest of the company.[66] Whilst the shareholders are the principal economic beneficiaries of the company, they are not the legal owners of its assets. The statutory concept of the company's interest is the subject of doctrinal controversy. Some authors maintain that it is reduced to a residue of shareholders' interests.[67]

Although, the interests of the shareholders remain predominant, the organs of the company must take into account the interest of stakeholders within the limits established by specific rules of the law and in light of the concept of the company's interest. It is interesting to note that leading Polish pre-war commentators stressed that a legal person is a real social phenomenon (an entity) legally distinct from its shareholders that may have 'its own interests separate and diverging from those of its members or organs'.[68] To sum up, the concept of the company's interest in Polish company law is very close to the Dutch idea of 'enlightened shareholder value'. While I share this view, I admit that the line between the predominant shareholders' interest and the interests of the stakeholders is frequently unclear and offers the company organs a wide discretion. However, the boards may not avoid their social responsibilities.

Employees and creditors are the main and only stakeholders whose interests are expressly recognised by Polish law. Employees' interests are acknowledged and protected, for instance, in the Statute on Commercialisation and Privatisation of State Enterprises.[69] The said act provides for employee 'representatives' participation in the management board and supervisory board of capital companies owned exclusively or partially by the State Treasury. The employee 'repre-

---

[66] Art. 249 § 1, 422 § 1, 481–485 of the Code.

[67] A. Stokłosa, 'Interes spółki a interes akcjonariuszy', *Przegląd Corporate Governance* 2011, No. 2, pp. 19–24.

[68] R Longshamps de Berier, *Wstęp do nauki prawa cywilnego* (Lublin, Nakładem Uniwersytetu Lubelskiego 1922), p. 111–112; F. Zoll, *Prawo cywilne* (Poznań, Nakładem Wojewódzkiego Instytutu Wydawniczego w Poznaniu 1931), pp. 161–165. These views have been quoted with approval by a leading contemporary author. Compare J. Frąckowiak in M. Safjan (ed.) *System prawa prywatnego. Prawo cywilne-część ogólna* (Warsaw, C.H. Beck 2007), pp. 1012–1013.

[69] Ustawa o komercjalizacji i prywatyzacji przedsiębiorstw of 30 August 1996, as published in *Dziennik Ustaw* No. 118, item 561.

sentatives' are elected by the workforce of the company. In theory, they should represent the interests of the company rather than only those of its employees. It is not settled whether they may be dismissed by the general meeting of shareholders or only by their electorate.

In case of privatisation of State-owned companies, employees are entitled to receive free of charge up to 15% of the outstanding shares. Furthermore, as already indicated, the Act on Public Offer provides that in case of a public offer the opinion of the management board must publish an opinion evaluating, *inter alia*, the impact of the bid on employment.

Creditors' interests are protected by numerous Code rules on protection of the capitalisation of the company. The Code mentions creditors and bestows upon them specific rights in the event of reduction of the share capital (Art. 456 § 1–2), liquidation (Art. 474 § 1), and cross-border merger (Art. 516[10]).

Polish public and private companies frequently make charitable contributions and conduct other activities for the benefit of local communities. There are no statutory rules defining the scope of management's discretion in this field.

3.3. Changing Roles in Financial Distress

The foregoing, principally normative description of the division of powers and competencies of the two boards under Polish law, requires an admission that, as in other jurisdictions, supervisory boards rarely perform their statutory functions will full independence. CEOs and strategic investors have *de facto* powers of selection and control of the members of supervisory boards. Presidents of the management board usually determine what supervisory boards do. The asymmetry of business and other information between management board and supervisory board members limits the non-executive board members' ability to exercise their principal duty of permanent supervision over the company's activities. Frequently, prestigious supervisory board members serve on too many boards and are too busy to perform their duties.[70]

There are striking similarities between the weaknesses of non-executive directors in one-tier board systems and two-tier board models. However, my practical experience indicates that the role of Polish supervisory boards usually changes in the event of a crisis. Supervisory board members are ready to devote more time and frequently make difficult decisions in such situations. It seems to me that the organisational separation of the supervisory board makes it easier for

---

[70] My evaluation of the situation in Poland based on my personal experience is almost identical with that described by O.E. Williamson: 'Corporate Boards of Directors: In Principle and in Practice', *The Journal of Law, Economics & Organization*, 2007, vol. 24, No. 2, p. 251 et seq.

supervisors to act more independently from the executive directors in a crisis situation. The undesirable effects of the buddy system seem to be less visible in the two-tier system in emergency situations.

4. Enforcement

4.1. Civil and Criminal Law Sanctions

4.1.1. Civil Law Sanctions Generally

The duties and civil law responsibilities of members of management and supervisory board of a Polish joint stock company are regulated in the CCC. According to Article 483 § 1 of the CCC, a member of a management board or a supervisory board and a liquidator are responsible vis-à-vis the company for damage contrary to law or the articles of the company, unless the director proves that there was no fault on his/her part. Furthermore, pursuant to § 2 of that provision, a director shall perform his/her duties taking into account the professional character of his/her activity.

The rules presented above establish a very high standard of liability not only in comparison with the prevailing US standards but also the applicable rules in leading Western European jurisdictions. First, the appurtenant CCC rules are of mandatory character and may not be modified as often permitted by many US state laws. Second, the provisions of Article 483 of the CCC establish a presumption of the board member's liability, so that the burden of proof is on the defendant. Third, the applicable measure of duty of care refers to the standard required from a professional business actor, rather than to that of ordinary negligence. Fourth, the appurtenant rules do not expressly provide for the application of the business judgment rule although some commentators are of the opinion that such standard is permitted under the applicable rules. On the other hand, a recent Supreme Court Decision has narrowed the scope of the defendant's liability, maintaining that the claimant has to prove a specific legal provision or a charter rule violated by a member of the board for the purpose of proving the breach of Article 483 § 1 of the CCC.[71] This makes the task of the claimant difficult because there are frequent cases of gross negligence that are not associated with a violation of a specific statutory or articles of association rule, except the general duty of professional care under Article 483 § 2 of the CCC.

There are not too many instances of civil law claims brought against board members. The majority of claims have been brought against management board members and not against members of supervisory boards. Recently, however, an

---

[71] Decision of the Supreme Court of 9 February 2006, V CSK 128/05, TPP 2006, No. 2, p. 134.

amendment to the Accounting Law[72] has introduced a joint and several liability of management and supervisory board members for the correctness and accuracy of the books of the company. This amendment has triggered a flurry of comments on this subject. It is being argued that it is an illusion to expect that supervisory board members can effectively control the accuracy of the accounts of the company. Members of the supervisory board, like non-executive directors in monistic legal systems, usually meet four to ten times a year. The newly established responsibilities, however, have led to the establishment of audit committees, an advisory body to the supervisory board. Also, company auditors are more frequently invited to report to the supervisory board and the audit committee.

In principle, members of each of the two boards are jointly and severally liable for the damage done to the company. The CCC rules on duties of the management and supervisory boards provide that members of each of the two organs must perform their duties jointly, except in some cases when the law or the charter provides otherwise. It does not mean, however, that all board members are always jointly responsible for wrongs committed by a single member of a given organ. For instance, a board member who voted against an illegal project supported by his peers will have a solid defence if an action is brought against all members of the management board.

4.1.2. *The Significance of a Vote of Acceptance of Performance of Duties by a Board Member*

A feature of Polish company law is a vote of the general assembly on accepting the performance of duties by each member of the two boards. Such vote of confidence or no-confidence takes place during the annual meeting of shareholders. Obtaining an approval by the general meeting of shareholders does not automatically excuse a given board member from all civil liability, but the company is barred from bringing an action against a director when the management board or supervisory board report presented during the annual meeting gives a sufficient description of essential aspects of the activities of the board, including those which have resulted in a loss to the company. However, if the general assembly of shareholders was not informed of an excessively risky project or a breach of the law, an action may also be brought against a board member who received the approval of the general assembly. A vote of no-confidence has both moral and economic consequences. A board member who has not received an annual approval of his duties has diminished chances of finding a new job, especially in public companies.

---

[72] *Ustawa o rachunkowości* of 29 September 1994 (Dziennik Ustaw of 1994, No. 121, item 591, as amended.

It is worth mentioning again that the general assembly has broad competencies; they include, *inter alia,* a decision concerning bringing an action against a board member and approving a settlement between the company and a board member.

4.1.3. Derivative Actions

Where the company has failed to bring an action for relief within one year from the disclosure of the injurious act, any shareholder or person otherwise entitled to participate in profits or in the distribution of assets of the company may file a complaint for making good the damage inflicted to the company (Art. 486 § 1 of the CCC). In case of a dispute between the company and a management board member, the former shall be represented by the supervisory board or by an attorney appointed by way of a resolution of the general meeting (Art. 379 § 1 of the CCC). In the event such derivative action is brought by a shareholder against a board member, the defendant may request the court to order a security deposit to be provided by the plaintiff. The court shall determine the amount and form of security deposit at its discretion. Failing timely provision of the security deposit ordered by the judge, the complaint shall be dismissed (Art. 486 § 2 of the Code). Where the action has proven groundless and, by bringing the action, the plaintiff acted in bad faith or was flagrantly negligent, the plaintiff shall make good the damage brought upon the defendant (Art. 486 § 4 of the Code). According to a decision of the Court of Appeal in Katowice *actio pro socio* may not be brought against third parties (eg. a licensor who has breached a license contract concluded with the company).[73] Thus, *actio pro socio* may be brought mainly against members of the two boards.

The derivative action provisions are not widely used because in most cases the shareholder does not have an incentive to bring such a claim. First, it is not settled whether he/she may recover the cost of bringing such claim even in the event of success. Second, the successful shareholder may not participate directly in the benefits resulting from a judicial award. According to the prevailing view, a shareholder is not entitled to claim indirect damages in this way. Pursuant to a minority view, a shareholder may bring an action against the wrongdoer (ie. a board member) only in exceptional cases where the wrong committed by a board member results in a direct loss to the shareholder—for instance when the board has illegally stopped paying a dividend due to a shareholder.

4.1.4. Criminal Law Sanctions and Disqualification of Board Members

Until very recently, the CCC provided for stiff criminal law sanctions directed against board members. Two sanctions are worth mentioning. Pursuant to Article 585 § 1 of the Code, a person participating in the creation of a commercial

---

[73] Decision of 28 September 2005, I ACa 597/05, Lex No. 164621.

company or being a member of the management board, supervisory board or the audit board, or a liquidator thereof, who has acted to the detriment of the company was liable for a penalty of imprisonment of up to five years and a fine. Pursuant to § 2 of Article 585, a person aiding or abetting an illegal act set forth in § 1 was liable for the same penalty. It is worth stressing that the sanctions set forth in Article 585 § 1 and 2 of the CCC were directed not only at board members but also to promoters and valuers of in-kind contributions during the process of formation of a company. In 2011 Article 585 of the CCC was repealed. The recent modifications of penal sanctions are discussed in Section 5.1 (below).

Disqualification of an executive or non-executive board member results from a criminal law sanction. Pursuant to Article 18 § 2 of the CCC a person convicted in a final judicial verdict that may not be appealed under specific Criminal Code and other statutory sanction (eg. in cases of theft, fraud or embezzlement) may not serve as a board members, liquidator or member of an auditors' committee. The disqualification occurs by operation of law. However, the convicted person may appeal within three months of the date on which the judgment became final and non-appealable. This special appeal applies exclusively to the sanction of disqualification of holding a position in a commercial company. The sanction ceases *ipso iure* when five years have lapsed. The foregoing provisions do not address the consequences of disqualification resulting from foreign judgments.

4.1.5. The Role of Insurance

Local and foreign insurance companies provide insurance instruments aimed at protecting members of management board and supervisory board. Transnational groups benefit from contracts covering top managers in all member companies. The D&O insurance policies may not cover criminal law liability. Polish tax authorities treat D&O benefits as taxable income. There are disputes as to how to measure a given taxable benefit.

4.2. Nullification of Resolutions of the Management Board and the Supervisory Board

The issue of challenging resolutions of the shareholders meeting has been discussed at section 1.1.5. (above). It is debatable whether such disputes may be resolved by way of arbitration. There are frequent court disputes relating to the nullification and repeal of shareholder resolutions.

There are conflicting precedents of the Supreme Court regarding the grounds for challenging resolutions of the supervisory board. Recently, however, the view prevailed that the provisions of the CCC on challenging the resolutions of the shareholdings meeting shall not be applied to resolutions of the supervisory board.

According to a recent decision of the Supreme Court 'Resolutions of the supervisory board of a joint stock company may be challenged in case they violate legal rules pursuant to Article 189 of the Code of Civil Procedure. The court may decide the dispute by way of a declaratory judgment (*Feststellungs-klage*).[74] The foregoing precedent has been approved by commentators who are of the opinion that it applies *mutatis mutandis* to challenges of management board resolutions.[75]

5. The Dynamics of Change

5.1. Modification of Criminal Sanctions in 2011

The sanctions provided for in Article 585 of the CCC were quite harsh. A board member was liable if the defendant has acted 'to the detriment of the company.' The proof of actual damage was not necessary. It was enough if the defendant has caused a concrete and real danger of causing detriment by his/her negligent acts or omissions. The foregoing basis of action was quite frequently used by public prosecutors against board members but there were not too many successful pro-secutions. However, the mere risk of long criminal proceedings was an effective deterrent. The majority of commentators were of the opinion that Article 585 of the CCC failed to meet the constitutional grounds of specificity of punishable acts under criminal law. Hence it was argued that this provision should be modified. Dozens of criminal investigations were conducted *ex officio* against board mem-bers even in private companies. Several cases were brought in courts. Frequent *ex officio* investigations conducted by public prosecutors against board members of private companies alleging defendants acted 'to the detriment of the company' prompted business organisations to petition the Government to repeal Article 585 of the CCC. As a result, the Government presented a bill aimed at repealing Article 585 of the CCC and regulating the responsibility of board members in the Penal Code (PC).[76] The modified Article 296 of the PC provides criminal sanctions for abusing competencies or non-performing of duties by, *inter alia*, board members. At present, the prosecutor must prove that the defendant's deed was a source of direct danger of causing the company a serious loss. The prosecution must be initiated at the petition of the company or other injured per-son, except when the loss is suffered by the Treasury. In the latter case, the prosecutor may act *ex officio*. The amendments also provide enhanced sanctions

---

[74] Decision of the Supreme Court of 20 January 2009 II CSK 449/09, BSN 2010, No. 4.

[75] The pertinent provision of the Code of Civil Procedure reads as follows: 'Claimant may demand that the court shall render a declaratory judgment regarding existence or non-existence of a legal relationship or right, if [the claimant] has an interest therein'.

[76] *Kodeks karny* of 6 June 1997, as published in Dziennik Ustaw of 1997, No. 88, item 553, as amended.

up to eight years' imprisonment in the event the defendant acted with the intent of obtaining material benefits.

Moderation of criminal sanctions can be explained by two factors. First, prosecutors have conducted many dubious persecutions against board members in private companies, thereby causing a reaction from the business community and underestimating the risk of doing business. Second, there were no reported major corporate scandals during the first decade of this century in Poland, in contrast to other jurisdictions.

5.2. Groups of Companies

The Codification Commission (*Komisja Kodyfikacyjna Prawa Cywilnego*) has prepared a draft aimed at an explicit recognition of the group interest. The draft has been modelled after the *Rozenblum* doctrine. The draft gives the parent company privileged access to the business information of its subsidiaries. On the other hand, it requires the disclosure of the participation of the subsidiary in a group and gives the minority shareholders the right to demand the appointment of a special auditor to evaluate business and legal correctness of the transactions between the parent and subsidiary. If the general meeting of shareholders refuses to pass the pertinent resolution, the minority shareholders may petition the registration court.

The draft has been accepted by Confederation of the Private Employers and majority of ministers but met with criticism of some Polish and foreign company groups that demanded an express recognition of the primacy of the group interest and the majority block-holder's right to issue binding instructions. By contrast, the Central Bank of Poland, the Treasury and the Commission of Financial Supervision (*Komisja Nadzoru Finansowego*) opposed the draft arguing that even the *Rozenblum* doctrine constitutes an excessive risk to the Polish financial sector and other strategic branches of the national economy because majority shareholders in leading Polish companies are foreign shareholders. The Government had decided not to send the draft to the Parliament before the General Election on 10 October 2011. Thus, it is clear from the above that whilst the dominant groups would like to have the best of the both worlds, namely, the right to issue binding orders treating board members of their subsidiaries as servants without liability for the damage resulting from such orders, the other critics of the draft also refuse to recognise the business reality of permitting board members to weigh the company's interest with the interests of the group. The prospect of a compromise is uncertain.

In two unpublished court decisions, Polish courts absolved board members of holding companies and subsidiaries (ie. controlled companies) from criminal liability. The courts followed the line of reasoning which recognises to some extent the interest of the group. In one case, the court expressly followed the *Rozenblum* precedent.[77]

In 2011 a group of government advisors proposed that members of the supervisory boards of State controlled companies shall be appointed and removed by a committee of well-known personalities (experts) named by the Prime Minister. This would diminish the role of branch ministers, who now exercise the power of appointment of board members and are exposed to the pressure of members of the Parliament belonging to the party in power, as well as other lobbyists. The final decision regarding the proposal after the Parliamentary Election of 10 October 2011 is still uncertain. The Minister of Treasury has been arguing that he is responsible for the performance of State companies. Hence, he may not remain powerless and replaced by members of the proposed Council appointed by the Prime Minister whose responsibilities would be very unclear.

5.3. Concluding Remarks

There are growing examples of approximation of the two board models (ie. one-tier and two-tier board systems). Meetings of the supervisory boards are usually held with participation of all members of the management board, except for those items on the agenda that deal, for instance, with evaluation of managers' performance, remuneration or dismissal. On the other hand, supervisory board members may participate in management board meetings (Art. 390 § 2 of the CCC). Moreover, supervisory board members may be delegated to perform managerial functions for a limited period, if necessary (Art. 383 of the CCC). Recommendations of special committees established in the field of appointment, remuneration, auditing and risk assessment are addressed to both boards, thus contributing to the convergence of the two models.

It is worth mentioning that the powers of the supervisory board in Poland are wider in scope than those in Germany. First, the supervisory board is usually equipped with the competence of approval of business plans and other major transactions (Art. 383 of the CCC). Secondly, the powers of the supervisory board also include the right to suspend individual members of the management board for important reasons and delegate members of the former board to temporarily perform executive functions.

---

[77] Decision of the District Court in Szczecin of 2 April 2008, III K 288/03 (unpublished). An extraordinary appeal was rejected by the Supreme Court on 5 October 2010, V KK 22/10 (unpublished).

Finally, the growing role of the advisory committees of the supervisory board constitutes a *de facto* platform of frequent cooperation between executive and non-executive members of the two legally separate boards.

It is expected that the CCC will be modified enabling the shareholders' meeting to choose between the current two-tier board and one-tier board. However, the phenomenon of 'path dependence' will most likely lead to limited deviations from the existed corporate governance structure of the two-tier board. The Codification Commission has commenced deliberations on this issue.

6. Selection of Literature

Aluchna, M., Dzierżanowski, M., Przybyłowski, M., Zamojska-Adamczak, A., Analiza empiryczna relacji między strukturami nadzoru korporacyjnego (corporate governance) a wskaźnikami ekonomicznymi i wyceną spółek notowanych na Giełdzie Papierów Wartościowych (*Empirical Analysis of Relations Between Corporate Governance Structures and Economic Indexes and Valuation of Companies Listed on the Warsaw Stock Exchange*), Gdansk 2005.

Chojecka, J., Przestrzeganie zasad dobrych praktyk a występowanie naruszeń na rynku giełdowym (*Observance of the Good Practice Principles and Occurrence of Infringements on the Capital Market*), Polski Instytut Dyrektorów, Przegląd Corporate Governance No 2/2011, p. 69 et seq.

Domański G., Znaczenie Dobrych Praktyk Ładu Korporacyjnego dla Odpowiedzialności Cywilnej Spółek Publicznych i Członków ich Organów (*The Meaning of Best Practices of Corporate Governance for the Civil Liability of Listed Companies and Members of their Bodies)*, in: Nowicka A. Prawo prywatne czasu przemian (*The Private Law of the Time of Changes)*, Poznan: Wydawnictwo Naukowe UAM 2004, p. 405 et seq.

Dzierżanowski, M., Ewolucja struktury własności i kontroli polskiej korporacji – obraz modelu polskiego rynku kapitałowego (*Evolution of Ownership and Control Structures of Polish Corporation – Picture of Polish Capital Market and Corporate Governance System)*, Gdansk 2002.

Furtek, M., Jurcewicz, W., Corporate Governance – ład korporacyjny w spółkach akcyjnych (*'Corporate Governance' – Corporate Governance in Joint-Stock Companies)*, Przegląd Prawa Handlowego No 6/2002, p. 24 et seq.

Jeżak, J., Czynniki determinujące efektywność nadzoru właścicielskiego – doświadczenia zachodnie i krajowe (*Factors Determining the Effectiveness of Ownership Supervision – Western and National Experience)*, Nasz Rynek Kapitałowy No 3/2002, p. 25 et seq.

Karasek, I., Wacławik, A., Polski kodeks corporate governance – mechanizmy wdrażania i egzekwowania (*Polish Code of Corporate Governance – Implementation and Enforcement Mechanisms)*, Przegląd Prawa Handlowego No 7/2002, p. 24 et seq.

Korus, M., Corporate Compliance jako metoda zarządzania zgodnością prawną oraz etyczną korporacji (*'Corporate Compliance' as a Method of Management of Legal and Ethical Corporate Compliance)*, Polski Instytut Dyrektorów, Przegląd Corporate Governance No 2/2012, p.15 et seq.

Kulesza, T., Nadzór korporacyjny a zarządzanie spółką kapitałową (*Corporate Governance and Management of the Capital Company)*, Warsaw 2002.

Lis, A., Sterniczuk, H., Nadzór korporacyjny (*Corporate Governance)*, Warsaw 2005.

Mazars Team, *Analysis of legal and market aspects concerning annual reports published by companies listed on the stock exchanges in the United Kingdom, France, Germany and Poland*, Polski Instytut Dyrektorów, Przegląd Corporate Governance, No 2/2012, p. 27 et seq.

Opalski, A., Rada Nadzorcza w spółce akcyjnej (*The Supervisory Board of the Joint-Stock Company)*, Warsaw 2006.

Oplustil, K., Corporate Governance – Komitet audytu w radzie nadzorczej spółki publicznej (*Corporate Governance – Audit Committee of the Supervisory Board of Public Company)*, Prawo Spółek No 7-8/2005, p. 11 et seq.

Rudolf, S., Partycypacja pracownicza. Echa przeszłości czy perspektywa rozwoju (*Employee Participation. Echo of the Past or Prospect of Development)*, Lodz 2001.

Studziński, J., Ewolucja systemów nadzoru korporacyjnego (*Evolution of Corporate Governance Systems),* Polski Instytut Dyrektorów, Przegląd Corporate Governance No 1/2012, p. 65 et seq.

Wiktorowicz M., Dobre Praktyki w Spółkach (Corporate Governance) (*Best Practices of Joint-Stock Companies (Corporate Governance)),* Prawo Spółek No 10/2003, p. 17–26.

Corporate Boards in Spain

ANDRÉS RECALDE CASTELLS, FRANCISCO LEÓN SANZ
and NURIA LATORRE CHINER[*]

[*] 'General Introduction', 'Authority functions', 'Institutional investors', 'Enforcement and Dynamics of change', by Andrés Recalde Castells, Of counsel CMS-Albiñana&Suárez de Lezo', Research Project P1-1B2011-51 supported by *Fundación Bancaixa Castellón*. 'Organisation/internal functioning', 'Information streams' by Nuria Latorre Chiner, Research Project *Los derechos de los socios ante los nuevos retos del derecho de sociedades* (DGCYT DER2010-17798/JURI); 'Accountability' (except 3.1.4 Institutional Investors), by Francisco León Sanz, Of counsel Pérez-Llorca; Research Project *Principales instituciones del derecho de la insolvencia. la reforma concursal. Sociedades y reintegración* (DER2011-29417-C02-02 DGCYT). Thanks to Elizabeth Mulready, Javier Gomar and Larry Lillue for their assistance in the translation.

1. General Introduction

1.1. Legal Environment

a) Spanish Company Law

The Spanish legal framework relating to public companies and, specifically, stock listed companies has seen many developments since the approval of the Securities Markets Act (*Ley 24/1988, del Mercado de Valores*, LMV), and the extensive reform of the Public Companies Act (*Texto Refundido de la Ley de Sociedades Anónimas, aprobado por RD Legislativo 1564/1989, de 22 de diciembre*). Soon after the adoption of the Act relating to Limited Liability Companies (*Ley 2/1995, de 23 de marzo, de Sociedades de Responsabilidad Limitada*), a radical change took place in the choice of company types by the business community. In contrast to what had hitherto been the case, where the public company was the most common company type, Spanish corporations began to be largely configured as limited liability companies.[1]

In the last ten years, many partial legal reforms have enhanced the Public Companies Act and the Securities Markets Act. Milestones include the Disclosure Act 26/2003,[2] which amends both laws in relation to the corporate governance of public companies, with specific rules applicable to listed companies. As regards company law, changes included an in-depth determination of directors' duties in terms of diligent management of the company and fiduciary and loyalty duties.[3] It was also established that liability for infringement of these duties would apply to the de facto directors of the company.[4] Information rights of the shareholder were changed, as

---

[1] According to the statistics published by the Official Central Mercantile Register (*Registro Mercantil Central*), between 2005 and 2011 the number of Public Companies newly incurporated reached 7,359, while in the same period the number of Limited Liability Companies rose to 61,1427, and the number of other companies was 27,803. Due to the crisis, in the period 2009–2011, the incorporation of new companies under any of these forms has experienced a steep decrease, available at <www.rmc.es/documentacion/publico/ContenedorDocumentoPublico.aspx?arch=Estadisticas\ESTADISTICAS-2011.pdf>.

[2] Ley 26/2003, de 17 de julio, por la que se modifican la Ley 24/1998, de 28 de julio, del Mercado de Valores y el Texto Refundido de la Ley de Sociedades Anónimas, aprobado por RD Legislativo 1564/1989, de 22 de diciembre, con el fin de reforzar la transparencia de las sociedades anónimas cotizadas (hereinafter, Ley 26/2003, de transparencia).

[3] Quijano and Mambrilla, 'Los deberes fiduciarios de diligencia y lealtad. En particular los conflictos de interés y las operaciones vinculadas', in Rodríguez Artigas et al (eds.), *Derecho de sociedades anónimas cotizadas*, 2006, II, 915; Embid, 'Apuntes sobre los deberes de fidelidad y lealtad de los administradores de las Sociedades Anónimas', *CDC* n° 46, 2006, 304; Ribas, 'Deberes de los administradores en la ley de sociedades de capital', *RdS* 38, 2012,75.

[4] Latorre, 'El concepto de administrador de hecho en el nuevo Art. 133.2 LSA', *RDM* 253, 2004, 853.

was shareholder attendance, and it became possible to exercise voting rights remotely, including by electronic media.[5] The Disclosure Act also introduced changes to the Securities Markets Act by including certain rules for stock listed companies on proxy rights of shareholders at the general meeting, particularly when representation is designated to directors, or by making the publishing of shareholders' agreements of these companies mandatory.[6] It also established the obligation to prepare an annual corporate governance report wherein listed companies must publish their degree of compliance with the recommendations set out in good governance codes (Art. 61.bis.4.b LMV, in the text stipulated by the Sustainable Economy Act[7] 2/2011). This would lay the foundation for a special listed public company law,[8] which had already been anticipated a year previously (Act on Financial System Reform[9]) when the LMV obliged security issuing companies to create an audit committee.

The law on public companies has continued to be subject to further reform. Act 19/2005[10] recognised minorities' rights to participate in the drafting of the agenda and present proposals in the general meeting.[11] Act 3/2009[12] regulated all types of

---

[5] Recalde, 'Incidencia de las Tecnologías de la Información y Comunicación en el desarrollo de las juntas generales de las sociedades anónimas españolas', *Indret* nº 3, July 2007, available at <www.indret.com>; Muñoz Paredes, *Nuevas tecnologías en el funcionamiento de las juntas generales y de los consejos de administración*, 2005.

[6] León, 'La publicación de los pactos parasociales por las sociedades cotizadas', in *Derecho de sociedades anónimas cotizadas*, II (see n. 3) 1167; Recalde and De Dios, 'Los pactos parasociales en la ley de transparencia', *La Ley* 5929, 2004, 1 ff.

[7] Ley 2/2011, de 5 de marzo, de Economía Sostenible; that has been modified recently by Orden ECC/461/2013, of 20 March, por la que se determinan el contenido y la estructura del informe annual de gobierno corporativo, del informe annual sobre remuneraciones y de otros instrumentos de información de las sociedades anónimas cotizadas y otras entidades

[8] Sánchez Calero, *La sociedad cotizada en bolsa en la evolución del Derecho de sociedades*, 2001; Tapia, *Sociedades anónimas cotizadas y ofertas públicas de adquisición*, 2012. This trend has not been followed by the necessary reflections on the fundaments of a special regulation applicable to listed companies, as was the case in Germany (eg. Spindler, 'Los derechos de los accionistas en relación con el Derecho europeo. La Directiva sobre los derechos de los accionistas y sus implicaciones para el Derecho alemán', in Embid, Abriani, Boquera and Emparanza (eds.), *Los derechos de los accionistas en las sociedades cotizadas*, 2011, 15, n. 15).

[9] Ley 44/2002, de 22 de noviembre, de Medidas de Reforma del Sistema Financiero.

[10] Ley 19/2005, de 14 de noviembre, sobre la Sociedad Anónima Europea domiciliada en España.

[11] Roncero, 'Ampliación del orden del día y solicitud pública de representación', *RdS* 26, 2006, 59; Latorre, 'Convocatoria de la Junta y derecho de información en la Directiva de derechos y en el Proyecto de Ley', in *Los derechos de los accionistas en las sociedades cotizadas* (see n. 8), 117. These rules were then modified by Act 25/2011, of 1 August (Boquera, 'El derecho a completar el orden del día y a presentar nuevas propuestas de acuerdos en las sociedades cotizadas', *RDM* 282, 2011, 29; Escuin Ibáñez, 'El derecho de la minoría a ampliar el orden del día', *RDM* nº 284, 2012, 293).

[12] Ley 3/2009, de 3 de abril, sobre modificaciones estructurales de las sociedades mercantiles.

structural changes (merger, split-off, global assignment of assets and debts) that were applicable to all types of companies and partnerships, not just public companies.[13]

But the most relevant reform has been the enhancement of the Consolidated Spanish Corporations Act (*Texto Refundido de la Ley de Sociedades de Capital, LSC*[14]). This gathers in one single Act the law applying to all 'capital companies': public companies (*sociedades anónimas*), including *the European public company (sociedad anónima europea)*, limited liability companies (*sociedades de responsabilidad limitada*), and partnerships limited by shares (*sociedad comanditaria por acciones*). The Act provides a common regulation for all capital companies, together with specific rules for each company type and, lastly, a section dedicated to public listed companies.[15] New reforms have subsequently introduced changes in the Corporations Act in order for it to adhere to the European Directive on shareholder rights.[16] Most recently, new reforms included a framework purporting to simplify mergers and split-offs, the regulation on restrictions on voting rights and the neutralisation of any measures concerning preventive takeover bids, rules for websites of public limited companies, and facilitation of e-communication between the company and shareholders.[17]

When analysing the legal framework of boards in Spain and control systems over their performance, the regulation applicable to takeover bids, which was

[13] Rodríguez Artigas et al (eds.), *Modificaciones estructurales de las sociedades mercantiles*, 2009.

[14] RD Legislativo 1/2010, of 2 July, Two days prior to the approval of Act 12/2010, of 30 June, which amended the Accounts Audit Act and certain rules of the Corporation Law; in particular, the right to introduce restrictions on voting rights in public listed companies was repealed. This rule was changed once again the Act 1/2012, of 22 June, which reintroduced the possibility of establishing this type of clause in articles of association (Recalde, 'Limitación del número de votos de los accionistas y neutralización de las cláusulas estatutarias de limitación de voto', in Rodríguez Artigas, Farrando and González Castilla (eds.), *Las reformas de la Ley de Sociedades de Capital*, 2nd ed, 2012, 691 f).

[15] The LSC contains certain rules for listed companies concerning the representation of shareholders and redeemable shares, another speciality in relation to the exercise of preferential rights and limits on treasury shares, a partial regulation of bonds, and rules concerning the functioning of the general meeting, the board, the disclosure obligation for shareholders agreements and the information these companies must publish, as well as instruments for the disclosure of such information.

[16] Act 25/2011, of 1 August, which incorporates Directive 2007/36/CE, on shareholder rights in listed companies, but which also introduced other reforms, fundamentally in relation to the call to the general meeting.

[17] On simplifying information and documentation obligations for mergers and split-offs of corporations which has also ruled on company websites, Farrando, 'La página web de la sociedad y el régimen de comunicaciones electrónicas entre socios y sociedad', in *Las reformas de la Ley de Sociedades de Capital* (see n. 14), 55.

modified in 2007 (Arts. 60 et seq. LMV) to include the European Directive must be taken into account. This constitutes greater assimilation with the more extensive legislation in other European countries, and attempts to harmonise shareholders' protection with a single legal structure that would ease the performance of such operations with regard to the degree of trust placed in the market of corporate control by acting as an external supervisory tool of company management.[18]

b) Self-Regulation

In the last 15 years, the regulation of public listed companies and, in particular, their boards, can also be found in 'good governance codes'. Three codes have been approved in Spain, always under the guidance of the National Commission on Securities Markets (*Comisión Nacional del Mercado de Valores*, CNMV), the independent agency in charge of supervising and inspecting Spanish securities markets. These codes reflect developments with respect to considered areas, targets to satisfy or, even, interests that public companies should pursue, and also how corporate practices should be disclosed.

The first of these 'soft law' codes was the Olivencia Code, approved in 1997.[19] It envisaged a radical option for voluntary compliance with its provisions and confidence in spontaneous disclosure. The Code also reflects scepticism concerning the effectiveness of internal control instruments provided by corporate law for management of the general meeting and shareholders' rights. The Code put an almost exclusive focus on the structure and composition of boards and on directors' duties. It provided for the creation of internal advisory committees (audit, remuneration, appointments) within the board of directors and the distinction between different types of directors (executive, non-executive, or representatives of more important and independent shareholders). Reference is also made to directors' obligations with the company. In short, the scheme fully trusted in the efficiency of information and self-regulation in order to improve corporate governance.[20] The Olivencia Code did not set a specific format, which meant that the small amount of information trickling through to the markets was aggregated and untested. Therefore, Spanish listed companies almost unanimously declared their compliance with most of the recommendations, although it did not take long for questions to arise about the sincerity of these declarations.

---

[18]   Act 6/2007 of 12 April. This Act was developed by Royal Decree 1066/2007 (Sánchez Calero, *Ofertas públicas de adquisición de acciones*, 2009, 460; García de Enterria and Zurita (eds.), *La regulación de las OPAs*, 2009; Juste and Recalde (eds.), *Derecho de OPAs*, 2010).

[19]   Manuel Olivencia was the president of the commission designed by the government in charge of drafting a report on boards in Spanish listed companies and the code on corporate governance. For this code, see Esteban Velasco (ed.), *El gobierno de las sociedades cotizadas*, 1999.

[20]   Paz-Ares, 'El gobierno corporativo como estrategia de creación de valor', *RDM* 251, 2004, 7.

The feeling of certain failure reverberating from the application of the Code, acknowledged even by its advocates, led the eventual publication in 2003 of a new document—the Aldama Code.[21] This new Corporate Governance Code must be analysed alongside the approval of the Disclosure Act (*Ley 26/2003, de transparencia*) just a few months later, which forced listed companies to prepare an annual corporate governance report in which the degree of compliance with the recommendations of the good governance code should be published or, as the case may be, an explanation should be given for the reasons why such recommendations were not followed, once again following the comply-or-explain principle.[22] The market on its own was not able to guarantee the efficiency of strategies based on self-regulation. As was warned by critics of the good governance process, at times the approach proved to be no more than window dressing in an attempt to conceal or camouflage the lack of material change in the conduct of executives and in the organisational structure of large corporations.[23] Moreover, whilst the first Code was almost exclusively board-focused, the Aldama Code attempted to breathe new life into the general meeting and the exercise of shareholder rights as monitoring and control tools in the relations between executive directors and shareholders.

Even though the process continues to rely on self-regulation and transparency, similar concerns as those expressed with regard to the 2003 code persist in the changes brought by the Uniform Good Corporate Governance Code 2006 (*Código Unificado de Buen Gobierno*, CUBG), which is still in force today. It maintains the model of voluntary fulfilment of recommendations, documented in the annual

[21] Special Committee for Greater Transparency and Security in Markets and Listed Companies created by resolution of the Council of Ministers on 19 July 2002. All good governance codes quoted can be consulted on the CNMV website at <www.cnmv.es/portal/Legislacion/COBG/COBG.aspx>.

[22] The comments of a participant in the three committees that prepared the successive codes is interesting, since he acknowledges certain 'optimism' in the hypothesis that markets would evaluate governance structures of listed companies (Paz-Ares, *RDM* nº 251, 2004, 7 ff.; Paz-Ares, 'El gobierno de las sociedades: un apunte de política legislative', *Estudios Homenaje Sánchez Calero*, II, 2002, 1805. Here it was recognised that there was a reverse correlation between the extent of supervision of the boards and the mandatory nature of the rules, although it also recognised the option for legal intervention in conduct rules). A much more sceptical approach to the capacity of markets to discipline officers' conduct and lead the way to the creation of internal control systems (Gondra, 'La teoría contractual de la sociedad anónima: una aproximación a sus fundamentos teórico-económicos', *RDM* 278, 2010, 1171, 1194).

[23] Gondra, *RDM* 278, 2010, 1214; Recalde, 'Del 'Código Olivencia' a la aplicación de la Ley de Transparencia (un balance provisional – y decepcionante – sobre la reforma del 'gobierno corporativo' en las sociedades cotizadas españolas)', *RCDI* 692, 2005, 1861. As is widely known, this concern is not limited to Spain, but throughout Europe: 'Green Paper The EU corporate governance framework> of the European Commission <http://ec.europa.eu/internal_market/consultations/2011/corporate-governance-framework_en.htm>, cites in note 11 sceptical studies on the effectiveness of the comply-or-explain model.

corporate governance report in compliance with the law. However, in order to prevent these reports being purely cosmetic, the CUBG established that definitions given therein would be binding, a move that fundamentally affected the conditions for classifying directors as independent and the use of this term. It also recommended removing the most common voting restrictions in Spain, enabling the general meeting to handle particularly pertinent matters such as company equity (eg. sale of substantial amounts of company equity), the separate voting in the general meeting of different corporate resolutions, and imposing the publication of directors' remuneration or related-party transactions in greater detail.

The formal declaration of a high level of compliance with these good governance rules by the majority of listed companies[24] did not prevent a degree of disappointment in view of the expectations of improved agency controls, very tellingly, in relation to the target of moderating directors' remuneration or the establishment of effective controls by way of the general meeting. This would explain a noted trend of returning to the original legislation as a corporation regulatory tool. Such a moment came in conjunction with reforms of the LSC and the LMV in 2011 and 2012, as mentioned previously.

1.2. Shareholders v. Stakeholders Model

Despite the imperative nature of the matter, Spanish law does not take a clear position on the purpose that a company should adopt. No rule that refers to 'corporate interest' actually defines the actual term. Article 204 LSC certainly does not; it allows resolutions which 'damage corporate interest' to be challenged. Even less support is provided by Article 226 LSC, which provides— tautologically—that directors are obliged to perform their duties 'as loyal representatives in defence of the corporate interest, understood to be the interest of the company'.

---

[24] This is stated as such in the *Report on Corporate Governance of IBEX 35 Companies*, in which the CNMV analyses the *Annual Report of Corporate Governance* prepared by leading listed companies included in the IBEX 35 index; see <www.cnmv.es/DocPortal/Publicaciones/In formes/IAGC_IBEX35_2011.pdf>). This report indicates that 'On average, 90.2% of IBEX companies comply with the Code (87.8% in 2010) with an additional 5.1% partially complying (6.2% in 2010). Thus at aggregate level, 4.7% of companies did not even partially meet the Code (6% in 2010)'. Traditionally, the recommendation concerning directors' remuneration in good governance codes is that which is least picked up by listed companies. The obligation for listed companies to prepare and publish an annual report on remuneration eventually came from a legislative rule (Art. 61.*ter* LMV, in the text approved by the Ley 2/2011, de Economía Sostenible).

The IBEX 35 is the main benchmark index of the Spanish stock market which is formed by the companies with greatest liquidity included in the Stock Exchange Interconnection System which includes the four Spanish stock exchanges (Madrid, Barcelona, Bilbao and Valencia)).

Corporate governance codes reveal changes with respect to the definition of 'corporate interest'. The initial position was clearly contractually focused, although this was subsequently consolidated into a more balanced standpoint, such as those contained in the present CUBG. Effectively, for the Olivencia Code, the sole objective of company administration was to maximise the company's value, which was aligned with the defence of shareholders' interests to increase share value. However, the Aldama Code (2003) already proposed also taking into account stakeholders' interests, given that the interests of the company should also be assimilated with the 'good of the company as a whole and its long term continuity'. This formula opens the door to pluralist approaches which look beyond the interests of shareholders.[25] In 2006, the Uniform Good Corporate Governance Code also insisted on this more eclectic vision.[26]

In general, case law has upheld that the corporate interest must be considered as the common interest of shareholders.[27] However, in view of the difficulty in determining what would be the element to group varying and often conflicting interests, legislators appreciate the contrast between those who uphold that directors should limit themselves to the target of maximising company value,[28] and those who deny that corporate interest is merely boosting the share price. The creation of value must be harmonious with the long term continuity of the company, insofar as decision-making in consideration of interests that may be affected by the management of directors must overrule the distribution of value.[29]

---

[25] Company management must focus on 'creation of value for the company, yet neither solely or principally considered to be share price at any given time'; specifically, strategy must focus on the 'long term continuity of the company, which entails the creation of sufficient profits by way of a positively competitive position in markets, in compliance with the law and in avoidance of all unfair conduct, beyond even the scope of the law'.

[26] The CUBG declares the company interest must be understood as 'maximising its value overtime'. It immediately indicates that directors 'shall ensure that in relation with interest groups, the company respect laws and regulations; that it fulfils its obligations and contracts in good faith; that it respects the uses and best practices of the sectors and geographical areas where is carries out its activity; and that it observes additional corporate social responsibility rules accepted voluntarily.' Accordingly, recommendation seven thereof states that 'the company abides by the law and regulations; fulfils its obligations and contracts in good faith; respects the customs and good practices of the sector and territories where it does business; and upholds any additional social responsibility principles it has subscribed voluntarily'.

[27] Supreme Court Judgments (Sentencias del Tribunal Supremo – STS) of 5 July 1986, 19 February 1991, 4 March 2000.

[28] Paz-Ares, 'El gobierno corporativo como estrategia de creación de valor', *RDM* 251, 2004, 7; Alfaro, *Interés social y derecho de suscripción preferente*, 1996, 51.

[29] Esteban Velasco, 'Interés social, buen gobierno y responsabilidad social corporativa (algunas consideraciones desde una perspectiva jurídico-societaria)', in *Responsabilidad social corporativa aspectos jurídico-económicos*, 2005, 13; Sánchez-Calero Guilarte, 'El interés social y los varios intereses presentes en la sociedad anónima cotizada', *RDM* 246, 2002, 1653;

cont. ...

In particular, the nuances to the contractualist vision originate from policies for the promotion of corporate social responsibility.[30] Conversely, insolvency law provides for a certain obligation of directors to appropriately capitalise the company in consideration of creditors' interests (below section 3.3), which is of particular interest for corporate groups.

1.3. Available Board Models

When analysing models of boards, once again a distinction must be made between those offered by corporation law for public companies (with a few nuances for listed companies) and the model which, in practice, listed companies select in order to comply with Corporate Governance Codes and the law regulating securities markets.

In accordance with the law applicable to both limited liability companies and public companies, corporate by-laws must set out the company's form of management. This may be in the form of a sole director, various directors operating jointly or separately, or a board of directors (Art. 210 LSC). Statistics show that the dominant form of management is that of sole directorship.[31] This endures in the continued use of the public company form in Spain by small enterprises, despite being the prevalent model also for corporate groups. That said, the use of the board of directors in public companies as a body of governance represents a similar proportion, whilst being virtually unheard of in limited liability companies. In any event, in public listed companies, the board of directors is the sole administration model used.

The legal layout of the board of directors in Spain is a one-tier board model. The option of choosing between a one-tier and a two-tier model is only available to European public companies incorporated in Spain (Art. 476 LSC), with a specific regulation being provided for the two-tier model (Arts. 478 et seq.

Sánchez-Calero Guilarte, 'Creación de valor, interés social y responsabilidad social corporativa', in *Derecho de sociedades anónimas cotizadas*) (see n. 3), 866 ff.

[30] Sánchez-Calero, Fuentes and Fernández, 'La primacía de los accionistas y la RSC: ¿Una compatibilidad posible?', available at <http://eprints.ucm.es/11962/1/Primac%C3%ADa_share holders_y_RSC.pdf>.

[31] According to statistics from the Central Mercantile Register for companies incorporated in 2011, 47% of public companies opted for a sole directorship structure, whilst boards of directors featured in 40% of cases, joint and several directors in 11% and joint directors in 2% of cases. Also in 2011, administration models in limited liability companies are 71% sole shareholdings, 20% joint and several directors, 5% joint directors and 4% board of directors available at <www.rmc.es/documentacion/publico/ContenedorDocumentoPublico.aspx?arch=Es tadisticas\ESTADISTICAS-2011.pdf>.

LSC).[32] Given that this corporate structure is of negligible importance in Spain, a more in-depth analysis is not necessary.

However, the difference between the Spanish management model for public companies and the models that make a distinction between two types of governance bodies (that in charge of management and that which holds a supervisory role) has become barely detectable, due to a number of reasons. On the one hand, this is due to the freedom given to the board to configure its own *modus operandi* (Art. 245.2 LSC);[33] on the other, because the board of directors can delegate some of its functions to an executive committee and/or to one or more delegated directors. Above all it is due to the creation of internal committees that, in pursuit of fulfilment of good governance recommendations, has given way to a certain distribution of powers and capabilities of the directors within the board.

1.4. Ownership Structure

Historically capital ownership has been very concentrated in the majority of Spanish listed companies. This commonly leads to conflicts between majority and minority shareholders to a much greater extent that those occurring between shareholders and management, which is more common to those with separate ownership and management and most common among companies with a more scattered distribution of capital. Effectively, in Spain agency costs that arise between block-holders and minority shareholders are at the core of most regulatory developments. This is demonstrated where there is election of directors by minority shareholders, who according to Spanish law can appoint some board members, a point which has caused a great judicial dispute in some listed stock companies.

This high concentration of capital, with a controlling shareholder or with various linked by agreement is seen in the majority of companies incorporated in Spain, including the 149 admitted to trading on official stock markets.[34]

---

[32] Quijano, 'Administración y control: el sistema monista', 689 and Esteban Velasco, 'Administración y control: el sistema dualista', 763, both in Fernández del Pozo and Esteban Velasco (eds.), *La sociedad anónima europea: régimen societario, fiscal y laboral*, 2004, 689.

[33] Salelles, in Ángel Rojo and Emilio Beltrán (eds.), *Comentario de la ley de sociedades de capital*, 2011, Art. 245, 1765.

[34] Statistics on all companies date back to 2011 and were obtained from the *Corporate Governance Report of Entities with Securities Admitted to Trading on Regulated Markets 2011*, published in December 2012 by the CNMV <www.cnmv.es/DocPortal/Publicaciones/Informes/IAGC2011_ENen.pdf>. For 35 companies listed in IBEX, the CNMV specific report that analyses the Annual Corporate Governance Report includes data for 2010. Therefore, these are the data that should be taken into account for them <www.cnmv.es/DocPortal/Publicaciones/Informes/IAGC_IBEX35_2011.pdf>, given the lack of a specific reference with respect to

cont. ...

The overall distribution of capital in all entities with securities admitted to trading on regulated markets was: Non-director significant shareholders controlling 32.5% of share capital; boards of directors', including significant shareholders being members of the board, owned 28.3%; treasury stock was 1.7% (although this rises to 2.2% when taking into account that only 115 companies declared treasury stock); and free-floating equity stood at 37.5%. In 102 companies free float is in excess of 25%, whilst in 7 companies it is below 5%. The number of companies where the sum of significant shareholdings and the stakes held by the board of directors exceeded 50% of share capital amounted to 110 companies. In 24.8% of listed companies there is an individual or entity that holds the majority of voting rights or that exercises or may exercise control.

The high degree of ownership concentration does not alter noticeably in the data of the 35 companies included in the select IBEX 35. There is a certain increase in free float, reaching 50.7% on average of capital of all companies listed in this index, whilst board directors owned 13.1% of capital[35] and non-director significant shareholders owned 34.2% of capital. In this last group, the weight of financial institutions and collective investment institutions is important, as these are often tacit allies of managers.[36] However, this point should not be misunderstood, as they are aggregated statistics for all IBEX 35 companies. In fact, for the majority of the 35 Ibex companies, free float continues to be fairly negligible. In only 15 companies does free float exceed 50% of capital, and in two it does not even exceed 21%. Privatisation and merger processes of certain banking institutions carried out during the 1980s and 1990s boosted the growth of free float in some companies, climbing until it represented the majority of capital. This is certainly true of the five largest and most solvent companies in Spain (Banco Santander, BBVA, Telefónica, Repsol and Iberdrola[37]), although in each

---

ownership structure of IBEX 35 companies in the *Corporate Governance Report of Entities with Securities Admitted to Trading on Regulated Markets 2011*.

[35] Sixty-five executive directors held an average capital interest of 0.23%; two executive directors has holdings in excess of 20%; and one director held an interest of over 10%. In the case of independent directors, their average capital interest is 0.04%, although there is record of the existence of two independent directors that declare an interest in excess of 1%.

[36] Yet 60% of shareholders with significant interests that are not directors proposed the appointment of a director to represent them on the board. The remaining 40% of holders of significant interests with no board representation are largely non-residents (86.5%). Of the aggregate interest of significant shareholders (34.2%), 5.9% correspond to shareholders with no board representation. By type of investors, the distribution of significant shareholders lacking representation on the board is as follows: 10% are financial institutions, 4% belong to resident private entities, 25% are agents, international investment funds or international public sector investors, and the remaining 1% corresponds to non-resident private entities.

[37] ENDESA was another listed company with highly dispersed capital. However, in 2009 it was subject to a takeover bid by the Italian company ENEL in conjunction with Acciona.

cont. ...

case with its own particular characteristics. Effectively, whilst in Banco Santander and BBVA no shareholder (alone or via a shareholder agreement) owns an interest in excess of 5% of share capital, Telefónica has two financial institutions holding stakes slightly above this figure.[38] In Iberdrola there is a significant shareholder (ACS, by way of a subsidiary), which has been waging a confrontation for some time with the company's senior management team as a result of its aspirations to have a seat on the board of directors.[39] In 2012 a similar scenario occurred in Repsol, although it was subsequently normalised.[40]

In short, strong control is being consolidated via agreements between executive directors and financial institutions, traditionally important shareholders (above all *cajas de ahorro* – savings banks) of Spanish listed companies, via cross holdings and abundant shareholder agreements. Effectively, in IBEX 35 companies a total of 19 shareholder agreements were declared, affecting 17 of the companies listed therein, and which represented an average of 29.4% of capital per agreement.

The acute concentration of capital poses obstacles to changes in control via hostile bids. Moreover, internal control tools implemented via corporate governance procedures often prove to be ineffective. Indeed, the creation of effective systems to control executive directors has not come to fruition via shareholders' exercise of their supervisions rights at general meetings, which are often dominated by managers, via their proxies, nor by the control structures and committees within the board, whose members are adversely influenced by appointment and termination committees, or remuneration of the members thereof.

Subsequent agreements between the two entities led to the current situation wherein the ENEL owns 92% of share capital.

[38] BBVA owns 6.9% and CaixaBank 5%.

[39] ACS (via its subsidiary) owns 7% of Iberdrola, but holds further voting rights (4%) via an equity swap with Natixix. The confrontation of ACS with Iberdrola management has caused numerous corporate disputes that have been resolved before the courts. There is also another shareholder in Iberdrola with a 4% interest (Bancaja, a savings bank now merged into Bankia), which in this case was an ally of the management team.

[40] CaixaBank owns 12.99%, Pemex owns 9.7% and Sacyr 9.7%. In 2012 there was an agreement between Pemex and Sacyr, who took a contrary stand to the current management team, through which they purported to execute a change of control in Repsol. However, financial problems in Sacyr (also a listed company) gave rise to a change in its power structure as the result of an agreement between a number of its significant shareholders, which in turn positively changed the nature of relations of the new control group with Repsol's management team.

2. Authority

2.1. Functions/Powers

a) General Description of Functions and Powers in the Board of Directors

The distribution of functions and powers of the various bodies of the public company is closely linked to the structural administration model adopted (above section 1.3). The model designed by law still reflects the classic view given by public companies law, which gives the shareholders' general meeting a superior position in the hierarchy than the board of directors. This has the effect of recognising the meeting a supervisory role over the board.

In this model, directors must all take care of the company's administration and representation before third parties, whilst control of this administration lies with the shareholders. This distribution of functions and powers can be seen in the annual obligation imposed on directors to be accountable before the general meeting, or in the meeting's power to appoint or terminate directors with no need for justification. This is also seen in other regulations on directors, such as remuneration, liability or acknowledgement of the general meeting's powers to instruct the board in terms of specific company administration issues.

The model of a board whose powers and capacities are subordinated to those of shareholders is highly unsuitable for an effective and streamlined management of large companies. A common remedy to counteract this is the tendency to accentuate autonomy and discretion of the board of directors. This remedy first came about due to the difficulties encountered by the general meeting in constituting an efficient governance body in which shareholders met and debated matters of interest, and through which the management carried out by directors was supervised. Moreover, the process towards strengthening the power of executive directors has gone hand in hand with Spanish listed companies' adaptation to the structure set out in Corporate Governance Codes. These highlighted the working difficulties of the general meeting, which had become no more than a cosmetic act of representation with no real supervisory role. Yet these failings in the general meeting did not remove the need to establish supervision mechanisms for executive directors. Corporate governance codes advocate organisational models adapted to models usually found in the United States, wherein within the board of directors a distinction began to be made between executive directors (those effectively in charge of company management), and other directors, who perform a purely advisory, supervisory or monitoring role.

The *de facto* changes in the structure of boards have not always been accompanied by legal reforms that make a record of the double role given to directors according to whether they are executive director or advisors and supervisors. This has caused a certain degree of uncertainty with respect to the contents and scope of the legal regulation applicable to directors. Doubts have arisen in a number of areas, most pertinently in terms of remuneration, appointment and liability for damages that may be occasioned onto the company by its own activities.

b) Delegation within the Board of Directors

A full board effectively set up as a body in charge of the permanent and ongoing management of the company is an extremely difficult feat to accomplish, partly due to its size and the lack of expertise of some members. The CUBG assumes that there is a trend towards smaller sized boards and that would entail the disappearance of executive committees.

On the other hand it appears to be necessary to assign effective control tasks to the board due to the ineffectiveness of the general meeting. In order for a board to hold both functions (business management and supervision) different directors must be bestowed with specialised powers.

The traditional set-up under Spanish public companies law was based on the possibility of the board of directors delegating some of its duties to an executive committee and/or to one or more delegated directors (Art. 249 LSC). The members of the executive committee or the delegated directors thus form the nucleus of the executive directors. These individuals must be chosen from full board members.[41] With respect to the executive committee, the CUBG recommends the adoption of the same structure for the board:[42] The breakdown of the executive committee's members by director category should be similar to that of the board itself. This is one of the less-followed recommendations by Ibex companies. Those that do not follow the recommendation understand that the executive committee is a delegate organ of an entirely executive nature and they regard efficiency criteria as having priority, therefore incorporating a higher proportion of executive directors. Most of the board's Regulations taken into consideration establish that it is incumbent upon the chairman of the board to chair the committee.

But, when determining directors' obligation, the law does not distinguish the criteria on which the board would delegate different powers (or not as the case may be). Effectively, all board members are bound to manage and represent the company and under no circumstances may the delegation of powers exonerate any of them from these obligations. However, as the specialty of duties carried as a consequence of the delegation it is understood that the delegated directors undertake the executive management of the company, whilst the remaining board members are appointed to supervise this management. This amounts to their liability for damages occasioned as a result of non-compliance with the obligations of each of these roles, which will depend on the tasks effectively carried out.

---

[41] Salelles, in *Comentario de la ley de sociedades de capital* (see n. 33), Art. 249, 1794.

[42] On variations experienced by the functionality of the executive committee, Alonso Ureba, 'El modelo de administración de la SA cotizada en el Código Unificado de Buen Gobierno', in *Estudios de derecho de sociedades y derecho concursal: Libro Homenaje al profesor Rafael García Villaverde*, 2007, I, 177 f.

On the other hand the delegation of powers cannot be a channel by which non-executive directors attempt to free themselves of any duties. As such, certain board powers cannot be delegated. Specifically, the duty of management accountability to the general meeting cannot be delegated, nor can the duty to prepare balance sheets and other accounts. The powers established in the company by-laws are also non-delegable.

By virtue of the delegation of powers, the full board assumes a monitoring role of the effective management of the executive directors. This monitoring role of non-delegated directors in executive management is strictly mandatory. The law expressly includes in directors' obligations the duty of reporting on the ongoing progress of the company, another obligation that cannot be delegated (Art. 225.2 LSC).

The CUBG also makes clear that delegation may not be a channel by which directors may be freed of any obligations. At the same time it is given ample freedom in delegating such powers, it is recommended that a clear distinction must be made of the different fields of powers of the full board and the delegated directors and, above all, the duties that must be reserved for the board of directors.

CUBG recommends that board members have full and direct knowledge about matters discussed by the executive committee. To this end, all board members should receive a copy of the committee's minutes. But directors would not only be entitled to ask the delegated organs to provide specific information about the company's management but, in case of delegation of powers, would be legally obliged to supervise the management carried out by the executive or delegated directors.[43]

c) Creation of Internal Control Systems

The successive Corporate Governance Codes recommend creating internal committees on executive management matters be set up within the board of directors. Specifically, the first of these codes (Olivencia Code) advised creating an internal control committee, a remunerations committee[44] and an appointments committee within the full board of directors.[45] They are not executive, but merely perform a consultation or advisory role, and may be created by company by-laws and by the board of directors itself. In order to guarantee independence in the fulfilment or assistance and advisory duties, these committees should be entirely composed of external directors, although in fact the CUBG's recommendation

---

[43] Ribas, in *Comentario de la ley de sociedades de capital* (see n. 33), Art. 225, 1618. For the provisions of the Olivencia Code, Velasco San Pedro, 'La información en el consejo de administración: derechos y deberes del consejo y de los consejeros', in *El gobierno de las sociedades cotizadas* (see n. 19), 305.

[44] Juste, 'Retribución de consejeros', in *El gobierno de las sociedades cotizadas* (see n. 19), 497.

[45] Alonso Ureba and Roncero, 'Sistema de elección de los consejeros, comité de nombramiento', in *El gobierno de las sociedades cotizadas* (see n. 19), 213.

only requires that the majority of their members should be independent directors. These committees have an important impact on liability for breach of duties.[46]

The creation of the audit and internal control committee has been recommended since the first good governance code. It would be charged with setting up the risk management and internal control system and supervising the performance of external entities instructed to carry out the company's accounts audit. In view of the structural difficulties in the way of full board members directly carrying out their duties, it was considered that the creation of the internal audit committee would help to establish efficient risk prevention systems for listed companies, as well as guaranteeing control on the fulfilment of obligation by executive directors. Definitively, in terms of general surveillance of accounting verification, this committee would help the full board to effectively complete the generic supervision and monitoring tasks of the company's executive management.

The importance of functions assigned to the internal audit committee in the corporate governance system led to its legal recognition. Effectively, since 2002 the final provision 18 LMV has obliged all securities-issuing companies admitted to trading on an official secondary market to create an internal audit committee.[47]

The number of members and operative rules of the audit committee can be set out in the corporate by-laws or, where appropriate, in the board regulations, which is the more common scenario. There is a logical concern as to ensuring that the various elements of the board carry out their duties independently, since managers can undervalue risk. However, the law does not require all these to be non-executive directors, but merely a majority and that at least one of these is an independent director. This flexible option brings up quite a lot of doubts, since there is a risk that their decisions could be adversely influenced by the will of the executive directors. The members of the audit committee should be professionals with some particular financial expertise and/or a knowledge base with relevance to the activity of the company, although experience has shown that this require-

---

[46] Alonso Ureba, 'Diferenciación de funciones (supervisión y dirección) y tipología de consejeros (ejecutivos y no ejecutivos) en la perspectiva de los artículos 133.3 responsabilidad de administradores) y 141.1 (autoorganización del consejo) del TRLSA', *RdS* 25, 2005, 19; Sánchez-Calero Guilarte, 'Autonomía y responsabilidad de las Comisiones del Consejo (Auditoría y Nombramientos y Retribuciones)', *RDBB* 127, 2012, 237 ff.

[47] This rule was amended by Act 62/2003 to impose the creation of an audit committee upon securities issuing companies and not just companies in general (Velasco San Pedro, 'El comité de auditoria', in *Derecho de sociedades anónimas cotizadas*, II (see n. 3), 1087 ff.; Farrando, 'Evolution and Deregulation in the Spanish Corporate Law', in Ventoruzzo (ed.), *Nuovo diritto societario e analisi economica del diritto*, Milano 2005, 34, 66). Subsequently, the rule was amended once again, by Act 12/2010 (Emparanza, 'Los comités de auditoría y control interno', in Albiñana (ed.), *Cuadernos de Derecho para ingenieros Iberdrola*, 2012, 2). The importance of internal control systems was heightened with the reform of the criminal code (Act 5/2010) which provisioned for criminal liability of legal entities. In order to avoid such a result, companies establish formal procedures aimed at preventing criminally relevant conduct.

ment is not always met in Spain. Occasional scandals affecting financial corporations have questioned the independence and training of the audit committees' members, and their effectiveness as a tool to prevent risk that should operate in close collaboration with external auditors.

The CUBG recommends also the constitution of the remuneration and appointment committees within the board. Given that director duties in these areas are reserved to the full board, with full delegation not being admissible, the existence of these committees provides an advisory role, more than just mere surveillance or supervision of the decisions of the executive committee or of the delegated executive directors (below section 2.2.2(d)). Once again, the good fulfilment of these duties will depend on the independence of its members, which often is by no means certain in listed companies.

d) External Auditors

Control of accounting in public companies is carried out by external auditors. Their legal regime corresponds to certain provisions of the LSC[48] and to the Accounts Auditing Act, the most recent version of which is from 2011.[49] This function is instructed to individuals or audit companies comprising specialised professionals (accounts auditors) who must prove their impartiality and technical preparation. These must be registered with an appropriate registry and subject to control by the Institute of Accounting and Account Auditing (Instituto de Contabilidad y Auditoría de Cuentas, ICAC. They shall be appointed by the general meeting before the end of the financial year to be audited for an initial period that may be no less than three and no more than nine years, without prejudice to a possible extension. The general meeting may not dismiss auditors without just cause before the end of the period for which they were appointed. Exceptionally, they may be appointed by the Mercantile Register or the Court. Should they breach any technical rules applicable to the preparation of their reports, auditors will be subject to sanctions by the ICAC, and they could also be liable to the company for the damages occasioned.[50]

This external control exclusively refers to annual and consolidated accounts, and the purpose of the audit is to verify that the accounts reflect the true and fair view of the net worth, financial position and earnings of the company, and as appropriate, the consistency between the management report and the financial statements for the financial year. The technical opinion of the auditors must be

---

[48]   Amended by Act 25/2011 (Amesti, 'Reformas del régimen de los auditores y en materia de cuentas anuales', in *Las reformas de la Ley de sociedades de Capital* (see n. 14), 279).

[49]   Royal legislative Decree 1/2011, of 1 July.

[50]   The crisis of a leading financial institution (Bankia) during 2012 has bought the onset of numerous legal complaints against the company that prepared its auditor's report (Deloitte), which failed to include caveats therein until just weeks before the entity was bailed out.

recorded in a report, which may be favourable, unfavourable or may contain caveats or reserves. Companies that are entitled to issue abridged balance sheets shall be released from the obligation.

2.2. Organisation/Internal Functioning

2.2.1. *Composition of Boards*

a) *Size of the Boards*

The LSC contains two references to size of the board. The first one is to be found in the Article 242.2 LSC referring to limited liability companies; in this instance, the number of board members cannot exceed twelve. The last one, regarding those European public companies resident in Spain opting for the two-tier board model. Article 481 LSC establishes that the 'board of directors will comprise a minimum of three members and a maximum of seven'.

The articles of association state the number of board members, either specifically, or establishing a minimum and a maximum. When opting for this second option, it falls to the general meeting to establish the specific number of members.

In the interests of maximum effectiveness and participation, for public listed companies, the CUBG recommends (Rec. 9) that the board of directors should comprise no fewer than five and no more than fifteen members. The Annual Report on Corporate Governance elaborated in 2011 by the Spanish Commission on Securities Markets shows that for IBEX 35 Companies the board of director's average size is 14.4 members, and at least 11 of those companies surpassed the amount of 15 members, reaching 22 members in some cases (Mapfre).

Irrespective of the size, companies must strike an optimal balance between external and executive directors. The board must be able to appraise managers' performance with a degree of distance and impartiality. Therefore it is recommended that a majority of board places be held by external directors. Executive appointments should be the minimum necessary for informational and co-ordination purposes, especially considering that informational requirements can be addressed in other ways than by executive director appointments, for instance by having managers participate in meetings and have speaking rights but no vote. For those reasons, external directors (proprietary and independent) should occupy an ample majority of board places.

The relation between proprietary members of the board and independent directors should match the proportion between the capital represented on the board by proprietary directors and the remainder of the company's capital.[51]

---

[51] Listed companies can freely decide to comply or not with the CUBG recommendations, but their reporting on the same must follow invariably the definitions given by the Code. In this
cont. ...

However this proportional criterion can be relaxed in favour of proprietary directors: (a) in large cap companies where few or no equity stakes attain the legal threshold for significant shareholdings, despite the considerable sums actually invested; and (b) in companies with a plurality of shareholders represented on the board but not otherwise related.

b) Labour Representatives

Employee co-determination is only regulated when dealing with European Public Companies and European Cooperative Societies resident in Spain.[52]

Neither LSC nor CUBG contemplate co-determination in public listed companies. CUBG's sole reference to such concept is made on occasion of the Code's recommended mechanisms for denouncing irregularities within listed companies. The Code takes from the European Commission Recommendation and other countries the recommendation (Rec. 50.1°.d) that the audit committee should establish and supervise a mechanism whereby employees can report confidentially—and anonymously, if necessary—any irregularities with potentially serious implications for the firm that they detect in the course of their duties, in particular financial or accounting irregularities.

The CNMV Annual Report 2011 shows that, for the first time, all Ibex companies follow the recommendation to establish and communicate a mechanism that will enable employees to report on irregularities of significant relevance. The fulfilment of this recommendation has gone up from 94.3% in 2010 to 100% in 2011.

c) Special Qualification Requirements

The request for special qualifications to become a director falls within the self-organising capacity of every company, which will establish such rules depending

---

respect, proprietary directors are 'a) directors who own an equity stake above or equal to the legally determined threshold for significant holdings, or otherwise appointed due to their status as shareholders; and b) those representing the shareholders stated in a)'; independent directors are 'directors appointed for their personal or professional qualities who are in a position to perform their duties without being influenced by any connection with the company, its shareholders or its management'.

[52] Ley 31/2006, de 18 de octubre, sobre implicación de los trabajadores en las sociedades anónimas y cooperativas europeas. Arufe Varela, 'La implicación de los trabajadores en la Sociedad Anónima Europea: puntos críticos sobre la Ley 31/2006, de 18 de octubre', *Actualidad laboral* 21, 2009, 2 ff.; Casas Baamonde, 'La implicación de los trabajadores en la Sociedad Anónima Europea (Procedimientos de negociación colectiva y diferentes modelos de implicación convenica', *Revista Española de Derecho del Trabajo* 117, 2003, 355 ff.; Aguilar Gonzáles, 'La aplicación en España de las normas comunitarias sobre la participación de los trabajadores en la SAE', *Justicia laboral: revista de derecho del trabajo y seguridad social* 32, 2007, 89 ff.

on a variety of factors (business sector, activity, public funding, etc.). Regarding the legal framework, Spanish legislation follows the approach of other legal systems: The requirements that the law demands to become a director focus on issues of legal capacity, and list a number of prohibitions and incompatibilities for exercising such position.

The LSC allows for directors to be legal persons, although it is necessary in this case that a sole natural person be designated to exercise in a permanent fashion the duties of the office (Art. 212 *bis* LSC). The possibility is also considered that articles of association may request a shareholder to become a director (Art. 212.2 LSC), but this is obviously a measure most likely aimed at limited liability companies or, at any rate, public non-listed companies.

To become a director it is necessary to have reached adulthood (or emancipation) and have the right to freely dispose of one's own goods. The LSC does not impose these requirements specifically—it does so by establishing a list of 'prohibitions' that really are instances of legal incapacity. Thus, it is not possible for non-emancipated minors, the judicially incapacitated, or persons disqualified according to the Insolvency Law to become directors (*Ley Concursal* – LC) as long as the disqualification period has not ended, and those guilty of crimes against freedom, against the property or the socio-economic order, against collective security, against the judicial system or due to false statements of any nature, as well as those who are prevented from carrying out commercial activities due to the nature of their office. The list of instances of legal inabilities is completed by a series of legal prohibitions against being a director that affect public servants with duties related to the inherent activities of the companies in question, judges and magistrates and other persons affected by a legal prohibition (Art. 213.2 LSC). The legal prohibitions in the LSC must be applied to the natural person who represents the director-legal person.

Specific requirements to become administrator are usually set and evaluated by the nomination committee. It falls to the nomination committee to evaluate the balance of skills, knowledge and experience of the board, define the roles and capabilities required of the candidates to fill each vacancy, and decide the time and dedication necessary for them to properly perform their duties. Transparency enhancing in the candidates' selection process is the final goal of Recommendation 28, which suggests that the companies make public the directors' professional experience and background on their websites.

Public listed companies do not usually incorporate specific requisites to become director in their articles of association or their board regulations, besides the maximum age, and this is not even a generalised provision. The CNMV Annual Report shows that only eleven companies set an age limit for board members, of around 71 as an average, with a maximum of 80 years and a minimum of 65 years.

d) Requirements for Chairman/CEO

The chairman or the CEO does not have any special duties regarding applicable requirements for the performance of their duties. The legal capacity and legal prohibitions and incompatibilities established in the LSC have already been discussed above.

Board regulations consider the chairman's regulatory framework, stressing its function and its dual chairman-CEO status. Of all the companies listed in the IBEX 35, the chairman assumes the role of chief executive officer in 25 companies.[53]

e) Restrictions with Respect to Similar Positions in Other Companies

Based on the formula obtained from the European Recommendation dated 15 February 2005 about independent directors and committees, Recommendation 26 of the CUBG demands that companies request their directors to devote sufficient time and effort to perform their duties effectively, an expression of the traditional duty of care of directors in performing their duties.[54]

It is desirable that companies should ensure that other professional obligations of the directors do not detract from performance of their functions, so it is recommended that the companies establish the rules about the number of directorships the board members can hold.

This leads to the obligation of directors to inform the nomination committee about any other professional obligations, in case such positions might detract from the necessary dedication required for their duties. Communicating only those that could interfere is not deemed sufficient; the recommendation is to compulsorily communicate any and all, without exception, lest they could interfere with the office held, and such is to be considered by the nomination committee.

The CNMV Annual Report shows that this is one of the least fulfilled recommendations. Only 57.1% of Ibex Companies have established the number of board positions their directors may hold. Companies that do not observe this recommendation argue that control on this matter is sufficiently assured by the nomination committee, whose functions include the review of the professional commitments of every director.

When the activity of directors may conflict with the interests of the company in a permanent way,[55] the LSC provides a special mechanism of removal, which allows any shareholder to request the removal of the director in question by the general meeting. This is reflected in the shareholder's right to make a removal

---

[53] See below sec. 2.2.2(c).

[54] Quijano, 'Estatuto de los administradores (selección, nombramiento y cese de consejeros. Información y dedicación de los consejeros)', *RdS* 27, 2006, 122.

[55] The situations of conflict of interest are regulated in Art. 229 LSC and will be further discussed below.

proposition at any time of the meeting; in this particular case, the limitation in Art. 519.2 LSC, which regulates the right of proposal conditional on having 5% of capital, would not be applied.

The LSC provides that any shareholder may apply to the general meeting for the removal of the director who had any form of opposed interests to those of the company (Art. 224.2 LSC) or who is a director of a concurrent company (Art. 230.3 LSC).[56] This is considered by the majority doctrine as a case of discretionary appreciation by the general meeting; it is up to the general meeting to decide if the factual situation occurs (conflict of interest or concurrent activity), but also to decide, if such was the case, whether or not to remove the director.[57] The general meeting's agreement against removal (despite there being a situation of conflicting interests) may also be challenged if it is considered detrimental to the company's interests.

f)   Expertise Requirements and Gender Diversity

The CUBG recommends sufficient accounting, financial and even managerial skills but only regarding audit committee members (Rec. 46). The audit committee's regulation set by LMV (D.A. 18ª 2) establishes that at least one of the members of the said committee should be independent and appointed according to accounting or auditing (or both) knowledge and experience.

Regarding the members of remuneration committee it is requested that they have the right expertise and judgment for the complex task of designing a fair and efficient remuneration system. However this has not been turned into a specific recommendation.

The power to request and assess further requisites to become a director falls to the nomination committee.

The CUBG calls on listed companies with few women on their boards to actively seek out female candidates whenever a board vacancy needs to be filled, especially for independent directorships. It is recommended (Rec. 15) that the nomination committee should take steps to ensure that: (a) the process of filling board vacancies has no implicit bias against women candidates; and (b) the company makes a conscious effort to include women with the target profile among the candidates for board places.

---

[56] In case of concurrent activities, and as a manifestation of the duty of loyalty, LSC expressly provides for the directors the obligation of seeking the general meeting's authorisation (Art. 230.1 LSC). This is a cautionary measure to guarantee the discharge of the duty of loyalty, whose neglect will only be considered for liability's purposes.

[57] On the opposite, STS June 12, 2008 poses that, once the conflict of interests is deemed to exist, adopting the removal agreement is no longer discretionary for the general meeting, and considers it can be challenged on grounds of nullity.

The CNMV's 2011 Annual Report shows the scarce presence of women on Ibex 35 boards of directors. Out of 63 appointments made during the year, only 8 were women. Nevertheless, this represents a 8.5% increase on the previous year, which shows a sustained increasing trend observed since 2007. In 2007, the relative weight of women in the boards of directors was a 12.1% average of the members' total number. By typology, the relative weight of executives and independents goes down, whereas there is an increase in the proportion of proprietary directors and the so-called 'other externals'.

Slight progress has been made concerning the legal framework. Act 3/2007 (*Ley Orgánica 3/2007, de 22 de marzo, para la igualdad efectiva de hombres y mujeres*) regarding the effective equality between women and men, establishes in its Article 75 'Companies under the obligation to present unabridged profit and loss accounts will strive to include a number of women in their boards of directors that will make it possible to achieve a balanced presence of men and women in the term of eight years from the time this laws becomes effective'.[58] By including this provision in such a relevant law, the legislature has chosen to lend as much transcendence as possible to the regulation contained in Article 75. However, the imprecise delimitation of the companies affected by the rule, the lack of sanctions for non-compliance and its rather obtuse wording tend to obscure the legislative purpose.[59] In conclusion, the norm has not gone far enough in its goal of promoting equality, since there are no punitive consequences for non-compliance, and it limits itself to impose on the companies under its scope the observance of a specific degree of diligence.

The LSC also assumes the growing concerns regarding the need for companies' governing bodies to incorporate gender diversity but, as is the case with the Act, it has not been turned into an obligation to achieve specific results, the non-compliance of which would entail some kind of sanctions. The legislature only demands that the notes to the annual accounts include the company's

---

[58] Balanced presence means the presence of men and women so that, in all that relates to the people of each sex did not exceed 60% or be less than 40% (D.A.1ª).

[59] Campuzano, 'La presencia equilibrada de hombres y mujeres en los consejos de administración de las sociedades mercantiles', in Mercader Uguina (ed.), *Comentarios laborales de la ley de igualdad entre mujeres y hombres*, 2007, 440 ff.; Embid, 'Los aspectos mercantiles de la Ley orgánica para la igualdad efectiva de mujeres y hombres' in Sala Franco (ed.) *Comentarios a la Ley Orgánica 3/2007, de 22 de marzo, para la igualdad efectiva de mujeres y hombres*, 2008, 324 ff.; Huerta Viesca, *Las mujeres en la nueva regulación de los consejos de administración de las sociedades mercantiles españolas*, 2009; Leciñena, 'La participación de la mujer en los consejos de administración de las sociedades corporativas', *RDM* 278, 2012, 1233 ff.; Senent, 'La aplicación del principio de presencia equilibrada de mujeres y hombres en las sociedades cotizadas', en *Estudios del Derecho del Mercado Financiero. Homenaje al profesor Vicente Cuñat Edo*, 2012, 235 ff.; Perdices, 'Apuntes sobre el género del Consejo de Administración de las sociedades mercantiles' in Sierra Hernáiz (ed.), *Eficiencia, igualdad y empresa. La aplicabilidad real a la empresa de la Ley Orgánica de igualdad*, 2011, 201 ff.

employee breakdown by gender, itemised by categories and levels, including senior officers and directors (Art. 260.8ª LSC).

g) Evaluation of Board Performance

A major part of the board's workings is subject to self-evaluation. One of the recommendations of the CUBG is to establish some mechanism to scrutinise its own performance and that of its Committees with a certain regularity, using its own resources or seeking the help of an external expert. Although the Code makes no reference to appraising directors individually, it makes sense that evaluations should at least extend to the chairman and the chief executive. Thus Recommendation 22 establishes that on a annual basis, the full board should evaluate: (a) the quality and efficiency of the board's operation; (b) starting from a report submitted by the nomination committee, how well the chairman and the chief executive have carried out their duties; and (c) the performance of its committees on the basis of the reports furnished by the same.

There is a sustained growing trend in the number of Ibex companies that evaluate every year the quality and efficiency of boards, chairmen and executive committees, which have increased from 68.6% in 2007 to 88.6% in 2010.

2.2.2. Decision-Making

a) Veto/Approval Rights for Non-Executives

According to Art. 247 LSC, a meeting of the board of directors is validly held when a majority of its members concur, whether in person or by proxy. The majority required for the adoption of agreements is the absolute majority of the board members concurring at the meeting (Art. 248.1 LSC), but the affirmative vote of two-thirds of the members of the board (Art. 249.3 LSC) is required for the permanent delegation of faculties in the executive commission or in the CEO, and the designations of specific persons (Art. 249.3). Majorities established by law cannot be increased by the articles of association, but it does seem possible to provide in them for a casting vote attributed to the chairman of the board.

The law also allows for the adoption of agreements in writing without a meeting, which will only be accepted if no board member objects to this procedure. Some board regulations include this possibility, as well as holding meetings in several rooms simultaneously, as long as intercommunication and interacting in real time among them is guaranteed by audio-visual or telephonic means, and therefore, the proceedings can be considered as a single act.

b) Delegation of Tasks within the Board

Spanish law assigns to the board full corporate organisational and management faculties, as well as a broad delegation capacity, with no more limitations than those established by law (Art. 249.2 LSC): The accountability of corporate management, the presentation of balance sheets at the general meeting, and the faculties delegated by the general meeting to the board, unless it is expressly authorised by the meeting.

In such a legal framework companies may embrace a wide array of organisational and performance patterns, but should avoid the board being prevented from fulfilling its most essential function, which is that of general supervision, by excessive delegation. The monitoring function splits into three key responsibilities, which should therefore not be subject to delegation: To guide and promote the company's policy (strategic responsibility), control its management echelons (stewardship) and liaise with its shareholders (disclosure). The CUBG therefore recommends (Rec. 8) that the full board should reserve the right to approve: (a) the company's general policies and strategies; (b) decisions such as the proposal of the CEO, the appointment and removal of senior officers, and their compensation clauses, directors' remuneration, the financial information listed companies must disclose, investments or operations considered strategic by virtue of their amount or special characteristics, and the creation or acquisition of shares in special purpose vehicles or entities resident in jurisdictions considered tax havens, and any other similar transactions whose complexity may impair the transparency of the group; and (c) the 'related-party transactions'. The Code establishes that ideally the above powers should not be delegated, with the exception of those mentioned in (b) and (c) which in urgent cases may be delegated to the executive committee and later ratified by the full board.

In 2011, the boards of seven Ibex companies declined to retain the faculties to approve the company's overall policies and strategies, transactions with related parties or appointments and removals of senior officers. These companies argue that, for expediency, effectiveness and operational reasons, the board had delegated the faculty to approve this decision to the executive committee or the Chief Executive.

c) Role of the Chairman of the Board

The chairman plays a key role regarding the board's adequate functioning. He is in charge of calling the board, drawing up the agenda and chairing the session itself. He has to ensure that the information reaches the board members in a timely fashion and promote the active participation of all members in the board's decision-making process.

The chairman is often also the CEO. In fact, the CNMV 2011 Annual Report shows that out of the 35 companies that comprise the Ibex 35 index, 25 of them concentrate the roles of chairman and CEO in a single person.

The CUBG follows the Olivencia Code by allowing for a chairman/CEO, but also stressing the need for checks and balances to prevent an excessive concentration of power. In this respect, Recommendation 17 establishes: 'When a company's chairman is also its chief executive, an independent director should be empowered to request the calling of board meetings or the inclusion of new business on the agenda, to coordinate and give voice to the concerns of external directors; and to lead the board's evaluation of the chairman'.[60] Special faculties have been delegated to one of the independent directors in 18 of the Ibex 35 companies, because the roles of chairman and CEO were concentrated in a single person. As in previous years, some of the companies which do not follow this recommendation argue that they adopted some measures as a check on the overconcentration of power, such as the establishment of executive committees. Other measures are: ratification by the general meeting of relevant agreements made by the board, bestowing day-to-day management in a different person from the chairman, delegation of faculties in committees with a significant presence of independent directors, or the specification of the chairman's functions by the board's regulation.

According to the LSC, the board may be called by one-third of its members if the chairman had not attended the petition to call it without justification (Art. 246.2 LSC)

d) Committees

The constitution of committees within the board of directors has been one of the recurrent recommendations included in the Corporate Governance Codes. The CUBG recommends (Rec. 44) the establishment of either one or two separate committees, and commissions regarding appointments and remunerations on top of the audit committee, an obligation which is derived from D.A. 18ª of the Securities Market Act (LMV). It is not necessary to create a separate corporate governance committee; the job of supervising compliance with internal codes of conduct and corporate governance rules should be entrusted to the audit committee or the nomination committee.[61]

The rules governing the committees should be set forth in the board regulations and include the following: (a) The board should appoint the members of such committees; discuss their proposals and reports; and be responsible for overseeing and evaluating their work, which should be reported to the first board plenary following each meeting; (b) these committees should be formed exclusively of external directors and have a minimum of three members; (c) committees should be chaired by independent directors; (d) they may engage

---

[60] Critisised by Alonso Ureba, 'El modelo de administración de la SA cotizada en el Código Unificado de Buen Gobierno' (see n. 42), 181, as an unrealistic solution, since the independent directors will hardly have the requisite information that will enable them to call the meeting.

[61] For such committees Fernández de la Gándara, 'Las comisiones de supervisión y control del Consejo de Administración (Recomendaciones 44 a 58)', *RdS* 27, 2006, 149 ff.

external advisors; and (e) meeting proceedings should be minuted and a copy sent to all board members.

The observance of this recommendation regarding control committees functions and make-up among Ibex companies has increased from 68.8% in 2010 to 71.4% 2011. Companies that do not follow this recommendation explain that in the process of designating the members of the control committees the director's capabilities, experience and qualification have been taken into account, factors that have prevailed over typology.

The obligation for public listed companies to have an audit committee was introduced by Act 44/2002, (*Ley 44/2002, de 22 de noviembre, de Medidas de Reforma del Sistema Financiero*) and is regulated by Additional Provision 18 LMV, which sets the basic rules for its composition and competences. The chairman, who should be non-executive (and, desirably, independent according to Recommendation 44 CUBG), will be substituted every four years, and may become re-elected for the chairmanship a year after stepping down.

The number of members, its working regulations and the competencies of the audit committee should be established in the articles of association. The minimum competencies will be the following (D.A. $18^{a}.4$ LMV): (1) Informing the general meeting about the issues discussed in it falling under the scope of the audit committee. To promote a more fluid communication between the audit committee and the shareholders, the Code proposes that its chairman should address the general meeting directly concerning any reservations or qualifications in external auditors' reports; (2) Supervising the company's control system, the internal audit function and the risk management systems. The CUBG further elaborates the faculties related to the reporting and internal control systems, and as a new item, recommends establishing a whistleblowing mechanism whereby staff can report confidentially and anonymously any irregularities they detect in the course of their duties, in particular, financial or accounting irregularities, with potentially serious implications for the firm. All the Ibex companies but one comply with this recommendation; (3) Supervising the process of making and reporting the financial information that all listed companies must periodically disclose. The CUBG demands that the audit committee prepares information for input to the board decision-making process on the following points: The financial information that all listed companies must periodically disclose; the creation or acquisition of shares in special purpose vehicles or entities resident in tax havens, and any other operations of a comparable nature whose complexity might impair the transparency of the group;[62] and the related-party transactions, except when their scrutiny has been entrusted to some other supervision and control committee; (4) Proposing to the board, to be submitted to the general meeting, the appoint-

---

[62] According to the CNMV report on Corporate Governance Annual Reports of listed companies the audit committee of three IBEX companies do not have among its functions this one.

ment of the external auditors; (5) Establishing adequate relationships with the external auditors and receiving from them the disclosure related to their status of independence from the company; and (6) Issuing every year a report stating their opinion on the external auditors' independence.

Related to the last three faculties, the CUBG recommends: (a) Making recommendations to the board for the selection, appointment and removal of the auditor; (b) receiving regular information from the external auditor on the progress and findings of the audit programme and checking that senior management are acting on its recommendations; (c) monitoring independence, specifically by notifying any change of the auditor to the CNMV as a significant event, ensuring that the company and the auditor adhere to current regulations on the provisions designed to safeguard auditors' independence, and investigating the issues giving rise to the resignation of any external auditor.

Getting the right director appointed is of capital importance for an efficiently performing board. The nomination committee, whose role is merely advisory, assists the board in achieving this objective and can help forestall conflicts of interest among board members in connection with directorships appointments. The nomination committee acts at two levels: (a) Submitting the directors' nomination or re-election proposals to the board, so it will elevate them, in its stead, to the general meeting; and (b) submitting the nomination proposals that the board makes effective through co-optation.[63]

The Committee's intervention differs in nature if it concerns independent or other type of directors. If it regards independent directors, the Committee has to submit the proposal to the board. Without such proposal, the board can neither propose that nomination before the general meeting nor nominate a different director from the one proposed by the Committee.[64] And it is so to such an extent that the definition of independent director makes it impossible to consider as independent those directors whose nomination or re-election had not been proposed by the nomination committee. The committee is also in charge of verifying every year that each independent director continues to fulfil the requirements that allow him to be so considered, and expressly stating it in the corporate governance Annual Report. As regards the rest of the directors (proprietary and executive), the committee's intervention is limited to the elaboration of a preliminary report which is obligatory in its issuing but not in its contents.

The CUBG recommends that the majority of nomination committee members should be independent directors: 25.7% of Ibex 35 companies do not follow this recommendation, arguing that they give priority to directors' skills, experience and qualifications, in order to contribute to a better performance of the committee's duties and faculties.

---

[63] Quijano, 'Estatuto de los administradores...' (see n. 54), 124.

[64] Quijano, 'Estatuto de los administradores...' (see n. 54), 125.

The CUBG lists the committee's duties as follows: (a) Evaluate the balance of skills, knowledge and experience on the board, define the roles and capabilities required of the candidates to fill each vacancy, and decide the time and dedication necessary for them to properly perform their duties; (b) examine or organise the succession of the chairman and CEO; (c) report on the senior officer appointment and removals with the CEO proposes to the board; and (d) report to the board on gender diversity. Up to ten companies have failed to assign all these functions to the nomination committee, especially the review or organising of the chairman's succession and gender diversity reporting. The causes for this omission remain unexplained.

The requirements regarding the remunerations committee have become more flexible in comparison to the previous Good Governance Code (Aldama Report 2003). It is still necessary that the committee is comprised of external directors and chaired by an independent director, but it is no longer necessary for it to comprise a majority of independents.

The remuneration committee must have the right expertise and judgment for the complex task of designing a remuneration system for directors and senior officers that manages to be both fair and efficient. The board should bear these requirements in mind when appointing committee members. The board should also provide the committee members with any advisory resources they need. The remuneration committee should consult with the chairman and chief executive, especially on matters relating to executive directors and senior officers.

The Remuneration Committee should have the following functions: (a) Make proposals to the board regarding the remuneration policy for directors and senior officers, the individual remuneration and other contractual conditions of executive director, and the standard conditions for senior officer employment contracts; and (b) oversee compliance with the remuneration policy set by the company.

2.2.3. Independent Directors

After the reform carried out by Law 2/2011 *(Ley de Economía Sostenible)*, Article 61 bis.7 LMV, establishes that information on the board's composition, its delegated committees and the directors' qualifications that must be included in the public listed companies' Annual Report on Corporate Governance, must be elaborated according to the definitions set by the CNMV. It will be considered— for the definition of independent director, among other issues—that designations must be made at the proposal of the nomination committee, considering their personal and professional characteristics, and that the discharge of their duties will not affect their relations to the company, its significant shareholders or its directors. The CNMV will determine the conditions that a director must fulfil so he can be qualified as independent, as well as the grounds for exclusion: Past employees or executive directors of group companies; partners, now or in the past three years, in the external auditor or the firm responsible for the audit report; spouses, or partners maintaining an analogous affective relationship, or close relatives of one of the company's executive director or senior officers.

The provisions included in the CUBG are thus legal status that remains the CNMV's document of reference regarding definitions and conditions. The CUBG establishes—as now does the LMV, but in a more detailed form—a general clause defining the independent director, and a list of instances that exclude some persons from attaining the condition of suitable candidate for independent director or staying on as such.[65] This general clause considers as independent directors the 'directors appointed for their personal or professional qualities who are in a position to perform their duties without being influenced by any connection with the company, its shareholders or its management'. Heading 5 of part III (Definitions) of the CUBG establishes the cases that shall under no circumstances qualify as independent directors. Such instances may be completed for every company because, as previously noted by EC Recommendation 2005/162/CE, it is impossible to make an exhaustive list of everything that threatens the administrators' independence. Those instances are: (a) Past employees or executive directors of group companies; (b) people who have received some payment or other form of compensation from the company or its group; (c) partners in the external auditor or the firm responsible for the audit report; (d) executive directors or senior officers of another company where an executive director or senior officer of the company is an external director; (e) people having material business dealings with the company, which includes the provision of goods or services, including financial services, as well as advisory or consultancy relationships; (f) significant shareholders, executive directors or seniors officers of an entity that receive significant donations from the company or its group; (g) spouses or analogous or close relatives of one of the company's executive directors or senior officers; (h) any person not proposed for appointment or renewal by the nomination committee; or (i) those standing in some of the situations listed in (a), (e), (f) or (g) above in relation to a significant shareholder or a shareholder with board representation. Finally the 'definition' establishes: 'Proprietary directors disqualified as such and obliged to resign due to the disposal of shares by the shareholder they represent may only be re-elected as independents once the said shareholder has sold all remaining shares in the company'; and 'A director with shares in the company may qualify as independent, provides he or she meets all the conditions stated in this recommendation and the holding in question is not significant'.

In contrast to the Aldama Code, the CUBG suppresses the 12-year limit as an independency defining element for an independent director, although it maintains the recommendation not to hold the office for a longer term. Companies that follow this recommendation have increased from 68.6% in 2010 to 77.1% in 2011. Com-

---

[65] Esteban Velasco, 'Consejeros independientes: función y criterios de independencia en el Código Unificado de Buen Gobierno', in *Estudios de derecho de sociedades y derecho concursal*, I (see n. 42), 499 ff.

panies that do not comply argue that the permanence of independent directors should be based on their contribution, experience and qualification; and that independence is not affected by the length of the period the directors hold their office.

Finally, the removal of the independent is contemplated in a specific recommendation: the board of directors should not propose it before the expiry of their tenure as mandated by the articles of association, except where just cause is found by the board, based on a proposal from the nomination committee. Two Ibex companies do not fulfil this recommendation and argue that its compliance would entail granting a different treatment to this sort of directors and it would be contrary to the principle whereby all directors must act in the interests of the company and the shareholders.

2.3. Information Streams

The Disclosure Act (*Ley 26/2003, de transparencia*) modified the LMV by introducing two obligations regarding corporate information. The first was the obligation that the public listed companies had to publish an Annual Report on corporate governance. The second was to fulfil the obligations regarding the reporting to the shareholders by any information technology and technical means. To this end, listed companies should have a website to facilitate the shareholders' right of information and to disseminate relevant information. This second obligation is contemplated in Article 539 LSC. Recently, the LSC has been modified by RDL 9/2012[66] to introduce the general regulation applicable to websites in Articles 11 *bis*, 11 ter and 11 quáter, and to state that the website is an obligation for public listed companies and a facility for non-listed ones.[67]

As a development of the Disclosure Act, the Order 3722/2003 (*Orden del Ministerio de Economía, de 26 de diciembre*) established the structure of the Annual Report on corporate governance and the obligation to make it accessible to the shareholders through the company's website. The webpage, according to the said Order, must include: The articles of association; the regulations of the general meeting and the board; the notes to the annual accounts; the regulation of good governance; the documents regarding the general meeting (agenda, proposals, information to the shareholders, composition, shareholders agreements); and significant events. It was also established that the directors have

---

[66] Real Decreto – Ley 91/2012, de 16 de marzo, de simplificación de las obligaciones de información y documentación de fusiones y escisiones de sociedades de capital.

[67] Recalde and Apilánez, 'La Reforma de la Ley de Sociedades de Capital y de la Ley sobre modificaciones estructurales de las sociedades mercantiles', *La Ley*, 7853, 2012. Álvarez Royo-Villanova, S., 'La web corporativa y otras modificaciones al régimen general de las sociedades de capital en la ley 25/2011, de 1 de agosto', *CDC*, 56, 2011, 13 ff.

responsibility in keeping the information on the web updated and in coordinating its contents with the documents presented to the relevant public Registries.

In Circular 1/2004[68] the CNMV specified different aspects concerning the minimum content of webpages and the period during which they must remain available (Annex III), as well as certain legal and technical specifications regarding this information tool (rules 7, 8 and 9).

3. Accountability

3.1. Board and Shareholders

3.1.1. *Appointment and Removal*

The rules on appointment and removal of directors are similar for a public limited company and a private limited company. There are, nevertheless, specific measures for the public limited company and recommendations in the CUBG. The most important differences between publicly traded companies and all other business corporations is the way the regulatory framework is applied to the different types of companies. Whereas in listed companies the normal procedure for appointing directors is co-option by the board of directors itself, in other companies those decisions are normally made in the general meeting.

Holding a directorship in a corporation does not require status as shareholder, and both natural and legal persons may be appointed to seats on the board of directors. Where a legal entity is appointed to hold a directorship, a natural person must be designated as representative of the legal entity (Art. 212bis LSC).[69] The directorship is held directly by the legal person. In listed companies it is relatively common to find that entities with significant shareholdings in the company are appointed to sit on the board as proprietary directors. Executive directors, on the other hand, are normally natural persons. The law makes express provision for the possibility of appointing alternates in the event the appointed directors leave office before the end of their term (Art. 216 LSC).[70]

[68] Circular 1/2004, de 17 de marzo, de la CNMV, sobre el Informe anual de gobierno corporativo de las sociedades anónimas cotizadas y otras entidades emisoras de valores admitidos a negociación en mercados secundarios oficiales de valores y otros instrumentos de información de las sociedades anónimas cotizadas.

[69] Salelles and Castañer, 'Reformas en materia del órgano de administración', in *Las Reformas de la Ley de Sociedades de Capital* (see n. 14), 227 ff.

[70] Esteban Velasco, 'La administración de las sociedades de capital', *RdS* 36, 2011-2012, 155.

In general terms, the power to appoint directors rests with the shareholders in general meeting as a basic and non-delegable function[71] (Art. 214 LSC). For public limited companies, moreover, two special procedures are envisaged: appointment by proportional representation (Art. 243 LSC) and appointment by co-option (Art. 244 LSC).

The appointment takes effect as from the time the appointee accepts and agrees to serve as director. Once accepted, the appointment to the directorship is registered in the company's page of the Mercantile Register

a) Appointment by Co-Option and CUBG Recommendations

Appointment of directors by co-option rests with the board of directors itself. The LSC establishes this procedure as a temporary form of covering vacancies.[72] Appointment by co-option is only undertaken if a director leaves or is removed from office before the end of his or her term of office. The new appointee must be a shareholder. The appointee will hold the directorship until the first general meeting held after the vacancy arose.

In listed companies, however, appointment by co-option is more than a provisional measure and in practice is the customary means for entering the board. This system of appointments gives executive directors decisive influence in the composition of the board and, indirectly, also in the general meeting's approval of the director appointment and ratification resolution. Co-option[73] thus emerges as one of the key manifestations of the board's *de facto* preeminence over the general meeting in listed companies and of the real control over said companies wielded by their executive directors.

The importance of co-option is heightened by its combination with the use of certain control-enhancing mechanisms (CEM),[74] especially, the proxies issued directly or indirectly by shareholders to the board of directors.[75] Issuing proxies

---

[71] Gallego, in *Comentario de la ley de sociedades de capital* (see n. 33), 1526; Martínez Sanz and Navarro Máñez in Arroyo, Embid and Górriz (eds.), *Comentarios a la Ley de Sociedades Anónimas*, 2009, 1375; ff.; Sánchez Calero, *Los administradores de las sociedades de capital*, 2005, 81, drawing on the STS of 19 September 1986.

[72] Martínez Sanz, *Provisión de vacantes en el consejo de administración de la sociedad anónima (la cooptación)*, 1994; Martínez Sanz and Navarro Máñez in *Comentarios a la Ley de Sociedades Anónimas* (see n. 71), 1596 ff.

[73] Sánchez Calero, *Los administradores de las sociedades de capital* (see n. 71), 517.

[74] León, 'Los mecanismos de control reforzados en las sociedades cotizadas Control-Enhancing Mechanisms, CEM' *La Ley*, 7463, 2010, 1 ff.

[75] In the companies in Spain's select IBEX 35 index, over 40% of total shareholder attendance at general meetings was by proxy in 2011. Average general meeting attendance was 72.9% (*Annual Corporate Governance Report of the IBEX 35*, 57). On the other hand, in publicly traded companies as a whole, physical attendance is higher than for the IBEX 35; in 2011 participation reached 73% with 42.3% attendance in person. However, the smaller the
cont. ...

to directors is expressly allowed, although specific rules are established in relation to conflicts of interest for such proxies (Art. 526 LSC).[76]

Spanish law does not allow shares with plural voting rights. However, limitations on voting rights are allowed at present, after a series of reforms and counter-reforms, (Art. 527 LSC).[77] Obviously, this measure favours greater control of the company by its directors and requires that a tender offer be presented for practically the entire share capital —a threshold of 70% must be met to withdraw the voting restriction from the articles of association— by whomever seeks to acquire control of the company.

With the aim of giving greater legitimacy to and cleaning up the director-appointment procedure, a series of recommendations have been made in the CUBG.[78] The most important one is for the creation of a nomination committee.[79]

company's market cap, the higher the average equity stake held by the board of directors (*Corporate Governance Report of issuers of securities admitted to trading in secondary securities markets*, 14 and 78). León, 'La adaptación del Derecho español a la Directiva sobre derechos de socios en materia de solicitud pública de representación', in *Los derechos de los accionistas en las sociedades cotizadas* (see n. 8), 213 ff.

[76] The rules on proxies in publicly traded companies are quite detailed as a result of the implementation in Spain of Directive 2007/36/EC of the European Parliament and of the Council of 11 July 2007 on the exercise of certain rights of shareholders in listed companies. The reform associated with the Directive's transposition sought to make it easier for investors to exercise their attendance and voting rights regardless of their location. The regulatory framework addresses the question of conflicts of interest and dedicates special attention to relations between financial intermediaries and their clients. In this respect, the transposition of article 13 of Directive 2007/36/EC on the exercise of voting rights by global custodians was done in unequivocal terms through article 524 LSC. The possibility of a financial intermediary with standing as shareholder being able to cast split votes as nominee for different shareholders is expressly addressed in CUBG Recommendation 6; for a detailed discussion of this issue, see Martínez Martínez, 'La Directiva sobre el ejercicio de los derechos de los accionistas en la Junta general de las sociedades cotizadas, y su impacto sobre el Derecho español', *RdS* 29, 2008, 74 to 80); Rodríguez Artigas, 'Participación en la Junta por medio de representante', in *Las reformas de la Ley de sociedades de Capital* (see n. 14), 631 ff.

[77] Recalde, 'Limitación del número de votos de los accionistas y neutralización de las cláusulas estatutarias de limitación de voto', in *Las reformas de la Ley de sociedades de Capital* (see n. 14), 691 ff.

[78] Alonso Ureba and Roncero, 'Sistema de elección de los consejeros. Comité de Nombramiento', in *El gobierno de las sociedades cotizadas* (see n. 19), 213 ff.; Martínez Sanz and Navarro Máñez in *Comentarios a la ley de sociedades anónimas* (see n. 71), 1375 ff.; Quijano, 'Estatuto de los administradores (Selección, nombramiento y cese de consejeros. Información y dedicación de los consejeros) (Recomendaciones 23 a 34)', *RdS* 27, 2007, 115 ff.

[79] In 2011, all companies in the IBEX 35 had a nomination and remuneration committee; the figure for all publicly traded companies as a whole was 89.13% (*Corporate Governance Report of issuers of securities admitted to trading in secondary securities markets*, 46). Torrent, 'Reflexiones sobre el gobierno corporativo: la comisión de nombramientos (Apuntes críticos al proyecto de código Conthe)', *RdS* 26, 2006, 219 ff.

The majority of the members of this committee should be independent directors.[80] The nomination committee is responsible for assessing the competence, knowledge and experience of candidates, and for defining their functions, the skills they must have and the time and dedication needed for them to perform their duties (Recommendation 55). Companies should determine the number of directorships their directors may hold and require directors to disclose any other professional obligations to the nomination committee so that it can check for possible interference with their duties as directors (Recommendation 26).[81]

Appointment of directors requires a prior report from the nomination committee.[82] In relation to independent directors, the involvement of the nomination committee is more intense, as the committee must recognise the candidate's competence to serve as director before making the nomination (Recommendation 27).

It is also required that for board of directors to bring a report before the general meeting on each of the directors up for appointment or ratification and, where applicable, on the rationale for appointing proprietary directors at the initiatives of shareholders with an equity stake of less 5% accompanied by the reasons for rejecting any other formal requests from holders of similar or larger shareholdings (Recommendation 13). Listed companies must publicly publish on their website and keep up to date the salient information on the professional experience and background of each director, the other directorships they hold, their classification as executive, proprietary or independent director and—in the case of proprietary directors—the ties to the significant shareholder represented by the director, the date of their first and subsequent appointments as directors of the company, and on the shares or stock options they hold in the company (Recommendation 28).

---

[80] In 2011, some 25.7% of the IBEX 35 companies did not have a nomination and remuneration committee with a majority of independent directors (*Annual Corporate Governance Report of the IBEX 35*, 71).

[81] This recommendation to set a limit on the number of directorships that can be held by board members is the one that is most frequently goes unheeded. It was complied with by 57.1% of the IBEX 35 companies in 2011 (*Annual Corporate Governance Report of the IBEX 35*, 66) and by 36.2% of listed companies as a whole (*Corporate Governance Report of issuers of securities admitted to trading in secondary securities markets*, 89). Non-fulfilment of the recommendation is explained by arguing that the directors' dedication is sufficiently assured by the nomination and remuneration committee's involvement in the nominating process and by the general duty of diligence that applies to directors.

[82] Some 82.7% of directorship appointments made in 2011 in all listed companies were at the proposal of or upon prior report from the nomination and remuneration committee. And 71.5% of the re-elections were done at the proposal of or upon prior report from that committee (*Corporate Governance Report of issuers of securities admitted to trading in secondary securities markets*, 46–47).

The information on directors must be made public at the time the notice is published of the call of the general meeting that is to resolve on their appointment or ratification (Recommendation 4). At the general meeting, voting on appointment or ratification of directors should be carried out separately from the rest of the resolutions put to vote (Recommendation 5).

b) *Proportional Representation System*

The appointment of directors by a system of proportional representation is established as a means of protecting minority shareholders. This system makes it easier for minority shareholders to place a number of directors on the board proportional to their overall equity stake in the company. The proportional representation election procedure is regulated in detail in Royal Decree 821/1991.[83]

Appointment of a director using this procedure presupposes that there are vacant seats on the board. The pooling of shares in order to name a director must be notified to the company at least five days before the general meeting is held. The election is executed *in* the general meeting, but not *by* the general meeting. The shares which have been voluntarily pooled to appoint a board member under this procedure cannot participate in the appointment of the rest of the directors.

The rules on proportional representation raise many questions[84] which hinder exercise of this right. One of the biggest obstacles is the majority case-law trend to recognise the right of the general meeting to also resolve to instantly remove the directors appointed via this procedure.[85] As a result, since the majority thus retains the possibility of removing directors appointed by the proportional representation system, the impact of this right is to a large extent diluted. In listed companies, exercise of the right to name a director by this system can arise in connection with a battle to control the company between shareholders with significant holdings who seek to acquire control or, at the least, to be represented on the board of directors.

---

[83] Real Decreto 821/1991, de 17 de mayo, por el que se desarrolla el Art. 137 del Texto Refundido de la Ley de Sociedades Anónimas, en materia de nombramiento de miembros del Consejo de Administración por el sistema proporcional. Martínez Sanz, *La representación proporcional de la minoría en el consejo de administración de la sociedad anónima*, 1992.

[84] Juste, 'Algunas cuestiones relativas al nombramiento de consejeros mediante el sistema de representación proporcional', in *II Foro de encuentro de Jueces y profesores de Derecho mercantil*, 2010, 11 ff.; Martínez-Gijón Machuca, 'El derecho de representación proporcional en las sociedades de capital: cuestiones prácticas', *RdS* 37, 2011, 47 ff.; Roncero, 'La cobertura de vacantes en el consejo de administración de una sociedad anónima por el sistema de cooptación y el ejercicio del derecho de representación proporcional', *RdS* 31, 2008, 187 ff.

[85] Martínez Sanz and Navarro Mañez in *Comentarios a la ley de sociedades anónimas* (see n. 71), 1507–1509; Salelles in *Comentarios de la ley de sociedades de capital* (see n. 33), 1751; conversely, Sánchez Calero, *Los Administradores de las sociedades de capital* (see n. 71), 516–517.

c) Appointment of Executive Directors, Chairman and Secretary

The delegation of powers and appointment of directors as executives rests with the board of directors. The CUBG refers to such managing directors as executive directors. The delegation of powers and election of managing directors requires the favourable vote of two-thirds of the board of directors (Art. 249.3 LSC). The delegation of powers has no effect until entered in the company's page of the Mercantile Register, ie. registration of the managing directors renders their powers effective. The legal scope of the representation of managing directors is the same as for the board of directors (Art. 149.3 of the Mercantile Register Regulation[86] in relation to Art. 234 LSC).

The chairman of the board must be appointed by the board of directors by an absolute majority of the attending directors (Art. 248.1 LSC). The CEO of listed companies may be the managing director or the chairman of the board of directors. Where the chairman also serves as chief executive, his or her election requires the favourable vote of two-thirds of the board members. The CUBG recommends that the nomination committee should examine and organise the succession of the chairman and of the chief executive and make proposals to the board, where applicable, so the succession is carried out in an orderly fashion (Recommendation 55-b).[87]

The secretary of the board of directors may (but need not) hold a directorship. In any event, regardless of whether or not the secretary is a director, the CUBG recommends the involvement of the nomination committee[88] by reporting on the secretary's appointment or removal and that the board regulations should spell out an appointment and removal procedure that guarantees the independence, professionalism and impartiality of the secretary (Recommendation 18).

d) Removal

The term of office for directors of public limited companies must be specified in the company's articles of association, subject to a maximum of six years (Art. 221 LSC). At the end of that term, the appointment will be considered to lapse at the next general meeting or at the expiry of the time limit for holding the general meeting called to approve the annual financial statements and allocation of the preceding year's profit or loss (Art. 222 LSC). In relation to independent directors, the CUBG advocates encouraging rotation. Pursuant to the European

---

[86] Real Decreto 1784/1996, de 19 de julio, por el que se aprueba el Reglamento del Registro Mercantil.

[87] This Recommendation went unfulfilled in a majority of IBEX 35 companies in 2011 (*Annual Corporate Governance Report of the IBEX 35*, 57).

[88] Some 79.8% of listed companies complied with this recommendation in 2011 (*Corporate Governance Report of issuers of securities admitted to trading in secondary securities markets*, 38).

Commission Recommendation of 15 February 2005, the code recommends that independent directorships may only be held for two consecutive terms of office, that is, no independent director should stay on for more than 12 continuous years (Recommendation 29).[89]

The removal of directors may be resolved by the general meeting instantly without the need to state any justified cause. In general terms, the LSC provides that directors may be dismissed at any time by the general meeting, even if the dismissal was not included on the meeting agenda (Art. 223 LSC). For public limited companies, moreover, it is provided that directors must be dismissed immediately, at the request of any shareholder, if they run afoul of any legal prohibition on holding the directorship or if they have any interest contrary to the interests of the company (Art. 224 LSC).[90]

The CUBG introduced several recommendations on removal and resignation depending on the category of the directorship. The Code recommends that proprietary directors tender their resignation when the shareholders they represent sells all of their shares in the company or that the number of such directors be reduced proportionately when the represented shareholders sells part of their shares (Recommendation 30).

The stability and independence of independent directors is fostered by the recommendation that they remain in office until the end of their term of office as fixed in the articles of association. Removal should only be allowable on justified grounds and upon prior report from the nomination committee. Justified cause is considered to exist if the independent director is in breach or fails to perform his or her duties or is involved in any circumstance that disqualifies him or her from being classified as independent director (Recommendation 31, by reference to section III.5). Removal of independent directors is also allowed in the event of a change of control as a result of a takeover, a merger or any other corporate operation, if the operation implies a change in the composition of the board of directors that affects the proportional relation between the different categories of directors according to the proportion of capital represented by the proprietary directors and the rest of the company's capital (Recommendation 12).

In order to safeguard the company's name and reputation, it is recommended that directors should resign if their continuance would otherwise harm it. Specifically, directors should be obliged to disclose if criminal charges are brought against them and report on any subsequent trial for criminal offences against basic rights, property or the socio-economic order, against collective security, against the administration of justice or for falsehoods of any kind. The board of directors should pronounce itself as soon as possible on the continuance

---

[89] In 2011, 77.1% of the IBEX 35 companies complied with this recommendation (*Annual Corporate Governance Report of the IBEX 35*, 67).

[90] Esteban Velasco, 'La administración de las sociedades de capital' (see n. 70), 157.

in their directorships of directors who are indicted or brought to trial (Recommendation 32).

Whenever a director resigns before the end of his or her term of office, it is recommended that the director must state the reasons for said decision in a letter (Recommendation 34). Disclosure of the reasons for resigning is especially important when the resignation is tendered because the director believes the board of directors has adopted significant or reiterated decisions contrary to the company's interest and on which the director expressed reservations (Recommendation 33).

3.1.2. *Division of Powers between Board and Shareholders*

In business corporations the general meeting is the sovereign body in which the company's members meet to decide the express the company's will and make the most important decisions for it. In listed companies,[91] however, the preeminent body in practice is the board of directors, due to the lack of interest of investors in taking part in managing the company's business and to the mechanisms used to tighten control by executive directors and controlling shareholders. The successive reforms seen in the last 15 years in connection with the corporate governance movement have sought to strengthen the legitimacy and control of directors, reinvigorate general meetings and provide incentives for investors to participate. Those measures have introduced great complexity into the corporate structure of publicly traded companies, but their real impact has been rather limited when viewed by the light of the objectives they pursue.

The powers of the general meeting are set out in Article 160 LSC: The approval of the financial statements, the distribution of earnings and the approval of the management performance; the appointment and dismissal of directors, liquidators and, where necessary, the statutory auditors, and the bringing of a company action for liability against said persons; the amendment of the articles of association; capital increases and decreases; disapplication or limitation of pre-emptive share purchase or subscription rights; structural changes such as alteration of corporate status, merger, spin-off or global assignment of assets and liabilities and relocation of the registered office abroad; the winding-up of the company and approval of the final balance sheet for liquidation and other matters determined by law or by the articles of association.

Powers for managing and representing the company rest with the directors. The board of a listed company also holds all powers not expressly attributed to the shareholders in general meeting.

---

[91] Alonso Ledesma, 'El papel de la Junta general en el gobierno corporativo de las sociedades de capital', in *El gobierno de las sociedades cotizadas* (see n. 19), 624 ff.; Sánchez Calero, *La Junta General*, 2007, 631 ff.

Within listed companies, the possibility of the general meeting taking part in management matters is considered technically, and in practice, rather limited. The involvement of the general meeting in such matters is regarded as possible and advisable in relation to the fundamental decisions that affect the company's business. On those questions the general meeting may authorise certain operations of special magnitude or give general instructions on how the pursuit of the basic corporate object is to be conducted in practice.

Along these lines, the CUBG has sought to buttress the powers of the general meeting of listed companies to ensure that the shareholders pronounce themselves on the most salient matters for the life of the company (Recommendation 3).[92] In this regard the Code recommends that the general meeting be expressly recognised as the competent body to decide on any type of corporate restructuring, such as the conversion of a listed company into a holding company, the 'subsidiarisation',[93] ie. the spinning off to a subsidiary of core businesses that were previously carried on directly by the company, even where the listed company maintains full ownership of the new subsidiary. The general meeting may also be competent to authorise the acquisition or disposal of essential operating assets of such magnitude as may involve a *de facto* modification of the company's registered corporate objects. The general meeting should also decide on any operations that effectively imply the company's liquidation.

3.1.3. *Special Issues*

The directors' duty of care is expressly regulated in the LSC in article 225. The scope of this duty is broadly delimited by a general clause: Directors are obliged to discharge their functions with the diligence of an orderly businessman.[94]

The orderly businessman test expresses the director's duty to perform his or her functions in such way that the basic corporate activity is pursued in the company's best interests in accordance with reasonable business management practices. This standard of care should be understood in relation to the specific type of company and to the specific type of business it carries on. The director

---

[92] This recommendation was followed by 80% of IBEX 35 companies in 2011 (*Annual Corporate Governance Report of the IBEX 35*, 63) and by 75.2% of all listed companies (*Corporate Governance Report of issuers of securities admitted to trading in secondary securities markets*, 85).

[93] This recommendation was not followed by the majority of IBEX 35 companies in 2011, on the grounds that it diminished the operational effectiveness of the board of directors (*Annual Corporate Governance Report of the IBEX 35*, 63).

[94] Quijano and Mambrilla, 'Los deberes fiduciarios de diligencia y lealtad. En particular, los conflictos de intereses y las operaciones vinculadas', in *Derecho de sociedades anónimas cotizadas* (see n. 3), 935 ff.; Sánchez Calero, *Los administradores de las sociedades de capital* (see n. 71), 166 ff.

must at all times act according to reasonable criteria based on the type of business conducted by the company.

In publicly traded companies, the CUBG underscores that it is the board of directors as a whole that must act with diligent care in the company's interests, irrespective of the origin, of the nature or of the functions discharged within the board (Recommendation 7). All directors, whether they are proprietary or independent, or perform executive or oversight functions, have the obligation to act with unity of purpose in the service of the company's best interest.

The business judgment rule is not expressly written into Spanish law, although the successive reforms of the duties of directors are moving in that direction.[95] In Spanish law, this rule may be useful for assessing the reasonable margin of business discretion and determining if the duty of care has been properly observed in a specific case. But it would not operate to exempt the director from liability in the strict objective sense, given that the events by which directors are released from liability are specifically defined and regulated. To be released from liability directors must show that they did not participate in approving or executing the decision in question, were not aware of its existence or, if aware, did everything possible to avert the harm (Art. 237 LSC).[96]

The director's duty to keep informed as an essential element of the duty of care is expressly regulated (Art. 225 LSC). It is posited as a duty of each director irrespective of the structure and composition of the company's governing body. Directors must remain diligently abreast of the matters relating to the company's performance.[97] One manifestation of the division of functions inside the board of directors is the existence of different levels of information, especially between the executive and non-executive directors. However, the fact that daily management must inescapably be left in the hands of the executive directors is no justification for passivity on the part of the other board members. The obligation to keep informed of the company's development applies to all directors regardless of their functions within the board and of their status as executive, proprietary or independent directors.

The CUBG recommends that the necessary measures be implemented so that directors are kept appropriately informed. In this regard, the Code provides that directors should be able to request the additional information they deem fit on

---

[95] Font Galán, 'El deber de diligente administración en el nuevo sistema de deberes de los administradores sociales', *RdS* 25, 2005, 94 ff.; Quijano and Mambrilla, 'Los deberes fiduciarios de diligencia y lealtad. En particular, los conflictos de intereses y las operaciones vinculadas', in *Derecho de sociedades anónimas cotizadas* (see n. 3), 938.

[96] Rodríguez Artigas, 'El deber de diligencia', in *El gobierno de las sociedades cotizadas* (see n. 19), 428.

[97] Quijano and Mambrilla, 'Los deberes fiduciarios de diligencia y lealtad. En particular, los conflictos de intereses y las operaciones vinculadas', in *Derecho de sociedades anónimas cotizadas* (see n. 3), 941 ff.

matters within the board's competence (Recommendation 23). Suitable channels should be established by the company so that directors can seek out any advice they need, including from external advisors at the company's expense where appropriate (Recommendation 24). Companies should set up induction programmes so that new directors can quickly become fully versed on the company's workings, and refresher programmes for incumbent directors when circumstances so warrant (Recommendation 25).[98]

The quality and efficiency of the board's operation and the performance of its chairman and chief executive should be examined on an annual basis by the board in full upon prior report from the nomination committee (Recommendation 22).

The director duty of care is intensified in those cases in which the company undergoes economic difficulties. Insolvency Act (*Ley Concursal*, LC) provides that the insolvency is to be classified as culpable if it was generated or aggravated as a result of wilful misconduct or gross fault (Art. 164), or in the presence of any of the conducts that by law lead to such classification or that give rise to a presumption of wilful misconduct or gross fault, such as breach of the duty to file for insolvency proceedings (Art. 165.1). If the insolvency is classified as culpable, the judge in the insolvency proceedings may order the directors of the insolvent company to cover all or part of the deficit (Art. 172bis). The attribution of liability extends to the persons who held directorships during the two years preceding the declaration of insolvency.

a) Conflicts of Interest

The directors' duty of loyalty is expressly defined in Spanish law in article 226 LSC.[99] Directors are obliged to discharge their office as loyal representatives in the defence of the company's interests. This duty is repeated and underscored in the CUBG for listed companies (Recommendation 7).

---

[98] This recommendation was followed by all but one of the IBEX 35 companies in 2011 (*Annual Corporate Governance Report of the IBEX 35*, 66) and by 76.5% of all listed companies (*Corporate Governance Report of issuers of securities admitted to trading in secondary securities markets*, 89).

[99] Embid, 'Apuntes sobre los deberes de fidelidad y lealtad de los administradores en las sociedades anónimas', *CDC* 46, 2006, 9 ff.; Emparanza, 'Los conflictos de interés de los administradores en la gestión de las sociedades de capital', *RDM* 281, 2011, 13 ff.; Gorriz, 'El deber de lealtad de los administradores de las sociedades de capital (Arts. 226 and 231 LSC)' in *Estudios en Homenaje a Anibal Sánchez Andrés*, 2010, 665 ff. Ribas Ferrer, *El deber de lealtad del administrador de sociedades*, 2010; id, in *Comentarios a la ley de sociedades anónimas* (see n. 71), 1620 ff.; Serrano Cañas, *El conflicto de intereses en la administración de las sociedades mercantiles*, 2008.

The successive Corporate Governance Codes published in Spain have highlighted the importance of this duty in publicly traded companies.[100] Pursuant to the proposals put forth in those reports, in 2003 a reform was carried out of the general regulations governing business corporations, and listed companies in particular, with the aim of providing precise definitions of specific conducts considered contrary to the duty of loyalty, establishing the procedures to be followed when a conflict of interests arises and enhancing transparency.

The standard of loyalty obliges directors to act in the company's best interests in the performance of their duties. According to the CUBG, in publicly traded companies the corporate interest consists in maximising the value of the business on a sustained basis (Recommendation 7).[101] This conception of the corporate interest takes in respect for all applicable laws and regulations by listed companies in their dealings with all stakeholders, good faith compliance with contracts, customs and good practices of the sectors and territories where they operate and with other additional principles of corporate social responsibility freely embraced by the companies.

The raison d'être of the duty of loyalty is to safeguard the company's interests in situations where they may enter into conflict with those of its directors so as to ensure that no director obtains undue advantage or causes harm to the corporate interest. Application of this duty means directors cannot engage in any activity that is identical, similar or supplementary to the basic business pursued by the company, whether for their own account or in the employment of others, without the express authorisation of the company in the form of a general meeting resolution (Art. 230 LSC). Any director with interests opposed to the company's must give up the directorship. The LSC stipulates in this regard that any shareholder may bring a request before the general meeting to resolve to dismiss a director on these grounds (Art. 224.2).

In order to ensure proper compliance with the duty of loyalty, the law sets out a fairly detailed definition of related persons of directors (Art. 231 LSC).[102]

---

[100] Alcalá, 'El deber de fidelidad de los administradores', in *El gobierno de las sociedades cotizadas* (see n. 19), 483 ff.; Paz-Ares, 'Deber de lealtad y gobierno corporativo' in Bacigalupo Saggese, Gómez-Jara and Bajo Fernández (eds.), *Gobierno Corporativo y Derecho Penal*, 2008, 13 ff.; Quijano and Mambrilla 'Los deberes fiduciarios de diligencia y lealtad. En particular, los conflictos de intereses y las operaciones vinculadas', in *Derecho de sociedades anónimas cotizadas*(see n. 3), 915 ff., 948 ff.

[101] Sánchez-Calero Guilarte, 'Creación de valor, interés social y responsabilidad social corporativa', in *Derecho de sociedades anónimas cotizadas* (see n. 3), 866 ff.

[102] According to Article 231 LSC, such related persons of directors include their spouses or persons with a comparable sentimental relationship; ascendants, descendants and siblings of directors or of their spouses; spouses of the ascendants, descendants and siblings of directors; companies in relation to which the director, either directly or through a nominee person, has any of the ties set out in Article 42 of the Spanish Commercial Code on the definition of corporate groups. In the case of directorships held by a legal person, the related persons are those who bear

cont. ...

There is also a public disclosure obligation for the interests held by the director in other companies.[103] The notes to the annual financial statements of the company (Art. 229 LSC) and the corporate governance report of listed companies must indicate the ownership interests held by members of the board of directors and their related persons in companies that carry on the same, analogous or supplementary type of activity as the registered corporate object, both of the company and of its group, as well as the offices and functions they discharge in those companies (see the model corporate governance report drawn up by the CNMV pursuant to Article 61bis LMV, included as schedule to CNMV Circular 4/2007, which amended the model annual corporate governance report for listed companies[104]). The disclosure duty has a broader sweep with respect to the Annual Corporate Governance Report, as it must also include the list of proprietary directors, the board members who hold directorships or executive offices in other companies that form part of the listed company's group, and the directors of the company who sit on the boards of other non-group companies traded on official securities markets in Spain, as notified to the company.

With respect to conflicts of interests between the company and directors, a procedure has been established to safeguard the company's interests (Art. 229 LSC). The law provides that a director with a conflict of interest has the obligation to report the conflict to the board. The director concerned is subject to a duty of abstention[105] so that he or she cannot take part in resolutions or decisions in relation to the conflicted situation or operations.

---

any of the relations provided for in said Article 42 of the Spanish Commercial Code with respect to the entity; the de jure or de facto directors, liquidators and representatives with general powers of attorney of the legal person director; companies forming part of the same group and their partners; the persons who according to the preceding paragraph qualify as related persons of directors in relation to the representative of the legal person director. Quijano and Mambrilla, 'Los deberes fiduciarios de diligencia y lealtad. En particular, los conflictos de intereses y las operaciones vinculadas', in *Derecho de sociedades anónimas cotizadas* (see n. 3), 970.

[103] Quijano and Mambrilla, 'Los deberes fiduciarios de diligencia y lealtad. En particular, los conflictos de intereses y las operaciones vinculadas', in *Derecho de sociedades anónimas cotizadas* (see n. 3), 967 ff.

[104] Circular 4/2007, de 27 de diciembre, por la que se modifica el modelo de informe anual de gobierno corporativo de las sociedades anónimas cotizadas. Recently modified by Orden ECC/461/2013, of 20 March, por la que se determina el contenido y la estructura del informe anual de gobierno corporativo, del informe anual sobre remuneraciones y de otros instrumentos de información de las sociedades anónimas cotizadas, de las cajas de ahorros y de otras entidades que emitan valores admitidos a negociación en mercados oficiales de valores.

[105] Embid and Górriz in *Comentarios a la Ley de Sociedades Anónimas* (see n. 71) 1437– 1439; Quijano and Mambrilla, 'Los deberes fiduciarios de diligencia y lealtad. En particular, los conflictos de intereses y las operaciones vinculadas', in *Derecho de sociedades anónimas cotizadas*(see n. 3), 963 ff.

For listed companies,[106] it is recommended that the company set up the necessary mechanisms to detect, determine and resolve such conflicted situations. The board of directors in plenum should have a non-delegable power to authorise operations in which a conflict of interest exists (Recommendation 8), after first hearing from the audit committee (Recommendation 52, c).

The notes to the annual financial statements of companies (Art. 229.3 LSC) and the corporate governance report of listed companies should include precise information on situations involving a conflict of interest.[107]

b) Related-party Transactions and Self-dealing

The regulatory treatment of related-party transactions mainly consists in imposing the obligation to make a relatively detailed disclosure in the notes to the annual financial statements of companies and in the annual corporate governance report of listed companies. The CUBG recommends that a prior check and authorisation procedure be established for board authorisation of related-party transactions (Recommendation 8).

The regulation of the duties of loyalty is confined to directors. No such duty of loyalty regulation exists for shareholders with significant holdings that afford them control over publicly traded companies, unless they have been appointed to the board or can be considered *de facto* directors. Naming a proprietary director does not operate to extend the standard of loyalty to the shareholder who nominated the director. The regulation of related-party transactions is broader, however, and extends to the company's transactions with its directors as well as to operations between the company and its significant shareholders.

Spanish GAAP (hereinafter referred to as PGC – *Plan General de Contabilidad*, General Chart of Accounts) delimits related-party transactions by reference to the relation between the parties who engage in the operation. The PGC establishes a general provision whereby persons are considered related parties if one of them, or a group of them acting in unison, exercise or have the possibility to exercise, directly or indirectly or by means of agreements or other arrangements between shareholders, control over the other or significant influence in the financial and operating decisions of the other. It then goes on to list the situations that must in all events be considered to involve related parties:

---

[106] In 2011, most publicly traded companies had procedures in place to facilitate director disclosure of conflicts of interest (*Corporate Governance Report of issuers of securities admitted to trading in secondary securities markets*, 76).

[107] In 2011, some 28 listed companies identified conflicts of interest affecting 135 directors. Those conflicts involved, for example, the approval of contract and remuneration terms and conditions of sizable operations that entailed a transfer of resources or recognition of obligations between the company and parties related to the director (*Corporate Governance Report of issuers of securities admitted to trading in secondary securities markets*, 75).

Companies belonging to the same group, natural persons having an equity stake such as allows them to wield significant influence, the executives, etc. (General Standard 15 on the formulation of annual financial statements).

With respect to the notes to a company's annual financial statements, the PGC establishes the obligation to report the related-party transactions carried out during the year, broken down by type of related persons involved (parent company, other group affiliates, joint ventures, etc.). It includes a list of related-party transactions for which such disclosure is mandatory (purchases and sales, provision of services, licensing agreements, finance agreements, etc.). It also provides that the operations should be described in detail, although allowing the information to be presented in aggregate for operations of a similar nature.

In publicly traded companies, the CUBG recommends that mechanisms be put in place to safeguard the company's interests in related-party transactions (Recommendation 8). According to the Code, approval of such transactions should rest with the board of directors on a non-delegable basis, upon prior report from the audit committee or, if applicable, the supervision and control committee (Recommendation 52, c). Prior board authorisation of a related-party transaction is not considered necessary for mass contracts with standard terms, with prices or fees that are established in general terms by the party that provides the service or supplies the product, and when the transaction is not in excess of 1% of the company's annual turnover.

The disclosure of the related-party transactions carried out during the year and a description of the safeguards implemented in relation to such operations and their fulfilment are part of the essential content of the annual corporate governance report of listed companies (Art. 61bis.4-d) LMV).[108]

c) Corporate Opportunities

Express regulatory treatment of director appropriation of corporate opportunities was first introduced in the 2003 reform (*Ley de transparencia*) of the former Spanish Public Limited Companies Act, likewise in connection with the better corporate governance movement. Until that time the question had been considered as included in the general duty of loyalty of directors. A distinction is made between two main types of appropriation of corporate opportunities: Use of the corporate name (Art. 227 LSC) and exploitation of business opportunities in the strict sense (Art. 228 LSC).

Under the LSC directors are subject to a general prohibition on taking advantage of corporate opportunities. It is considered a breach of the duty of

---

[108] In relation to the volume of related-party transactions in IBEX 35 companies, see *Annual Corporate Governance Report of the IBEX 35*, 53-55, and, for listed companies as a whole, *Corporate Governance Report of issuers of securities admitted to trading in secondary securities markets*, 73-75.

loyalty for a director to carry out for his or her own benefit, or for that of a related-party, any operation affecting the company's assets of which they become aware by reason of their office, if the investment or operations was offered to the company or the company has an interest therein, unless the company declined to pursue the investment or operation in a decision not influenced by the director.[109]

The LSC also expressly prohibits directors of companies from using the name of the company or invoking their directorship in the company—and thereby capitalising on its reputation and standing—to carry out operations for their own account or the account of a related person.[110]

No specific consequences have been stipulated for director breach of these specific duties encompassed by the standard of loyalty. Failure to comply with these duties by taking advantage of corporate opportunities is considered unlawful conduct that will be subject to application of the rules on director liability, provided the relevant conditions laid down in the LSC for claiming that liability are met (articles 236 and ff).

d) Inside Information

The duty of secrecy of company directors is expressly regulated in Spanish company law subsequent to the Disclosure Act reform (*Ley 26/2003, de transparencia*) (Art. 232 LSC). That duty is considered a correlate to the director's duty to be informed in the discharge of his or her office and to the access to the accounting, documents, data and pertinent information on the life of the company.[111]

The scope of this duty is delimited by a series of considerations. The information covered by the secrecy obligation must be confidential, ie. information which by its nature should not be known by or shared with third parties. The duty of secrecy takes in those matters that a director learns of as a result of his or her directorship. Lastly, the law provides that the purpose of the

---

[109] Embid and Górriz, in*Comentarios a la ley de sociedades anónimas* (see n. 71)), 1436 and 1437; Quijano and Mambrilla, 'Los deberes fiduciarios de diligencia y lealtad. En particular, los conflictos de intereses y las operaciones vinculadas', in *Derecho de sociedades anónimas cotizadas* (see n. 3), 961 ff.

[110] Embid and Górriz, in *Comentarios a la ley de sociedades anónimas*(see n. 71), 1435 and 1436; Quijano and Mambrilla, 'Los deberes fiduciarios de diligencia y lealtad. En particular, los conflictos de intereses y las operaciones vinculadas', in *Derecho de sociedades anónimas cotizadas* (see n. 3), 959–960.

[111] Sánchez Calero, *Los administradores de las sociedades de capital* (see n. 71), 198. Castellano Ramírez, 'El deber de secreto de los administradores a la luz de la Ley de Transparencia (Análisis de las novedades introducidas por el artículo 127 quáter de la Ley de Sociedades Anónimas)', *RdS* 23, 2004, 117 ff.; Gallego Sánchez, 'El deber de secreto de los administradores tras la reforma de la Ley de Sociedades Anónimas por la Ley de Transparencia' in *Derecho de las sociedades anónimas cotizadas* (see n. 3), 1005 ff.

duty is to avoid the harm that might be caused to the company by the disclosure of the information.

Directors in publicly traded companies[112] are subject to the prohibition on using inside information established in the Spanish Securities Market Act (LMV) in Article 81, on similar terms to the EU regulations. Inside information is defined as:

'all information of a concrete nature that refers directly or indirectly to one or more negotiable securities or financial instruments of those covered by this Act, or to an issuer or issuers of those negotiable securities or financial instruments, that has not been made public and which, if made public, could appreciably influence or could have appreciably influenced their price in an organised trading market or system.'

The prohibition on use of inside information by directors of a listed company takes in the preparation or execution of any type of operation with negotiable securities or financial instruments or any other type of security or contract, unless it is the existence of said operations which *per se* constitutes the inside information. The prohibition also applies to mere disclosure of inside information to third parties except in the normal and ordinary exercise of the office. And it also bans directors from making any recommendation to third parties to carry out operations with financial instruments or securities on the basis of the inside information.

e) Takeovers

Directive 2004/25/EC of 21 April 2004 of the European Parliament and Council on takeover bids was written into Spanish law by means of the 2007 reform of the LMV and Royal Decree 1066/2007 of 27 July 2007. Said reform modified the rules on the duty of directors in connection with takeover bids. Before then, directors were required to abstain from carrying out or arranging operations outside the company's ordinary business or primarily intended to disturb the development of the bid. They were at all times obliged to place priority on the interests of the shareholders over their own interests (Art. 14 Royal Decree 1197/1991, repealed by Royal Decree 1066/2007).[113] The current provisions now reflect the terms of the EU Directive (articles 61bis LMV and 28 RD 1066/2007).

[112] Martínez Flórez, 'Sobre los destinatarios de la prohibición de usar información privilegiada', *RDM* 240, 2001, 495 ff.

[113] Real Decreto 1197/1991, de 26 de julio, sobre régimen de las Ofertas Públicas de Adquisición de Valores, and Real Decreto 1066/2007, de 27 de julio. Fernández de la Gándara and Sánchez Álvarez, 'Limitación de la actuación del órgano de administración de sociedad afectada por el lanzamiento de una oferta pública de adquisición', *RdS* 18, 2002, 231 ff.

When a takeover bid is presented, directors cannot act at their own initiative to frustrate its successful outcome.[114] They are obliged to respect the will of the shareholders on the matter as expressed in the general meeting. The only exception to this duty of abstention is where directors seek alternative bids. The involvement of the general meeting is in all events indispensable before any securities are issued that could block the offer or from acquiring control of the offeree company. The general meeting resolutions on the matter must necessarily be approved with the legally stipulated quorum and majorities for amending the company's articles of association. In relation to decisions that have already been adopted, directors cannot put in motion or pursue actions outside the company's normal course of business whose implementation could frustrate the bid.

Spanish law envisages the possibility of companies introducing mechanisms of reciprocity if the company that issues the takeover bid does not have its registered office in Spain. The general meeting, subject to the quorum and majorities required for amending the articles of association, may decide that no decisions may be adopted that prevent the takeover bid from being presented if made by an entity with registered office outside of Spain and not subject to equivalent provisions. Such decision will have a maximum valid term of 18 months.

Spanish law-makers also provided for the opposite possibility when transposing the EU rules, ie. that the company may adopt measures to break through any barriers that may exist for the presentation of a takeover bid.[115] Specifically, during the term for accepting the bid the company may decide to suspend the application of restrictions on transferability of securities that exist in any agreements between shareholders of the company, and of limitations on voting rights provided for in the articles of association or in shareholders' agreements. In any event, no limitations on voting rights in the articles shall apply if the takeover bid achieves 70% acceptance or higher, unless the offeror does not have an equivalent breakthrough measure. In all other cases, the general meeting may decide whether the breakthrough measure applies in all cases or only if the bid achieves acceptance of 70% or more. The implementation of breakthrough measures and their elimination must be approved by the general meeting subject to the quorums and majorities required for amending the articles of association. The measures adopted must be notified to the CNMV and to the supervisors where the

---

[114]   Garrido, 'El deber de neutralidad' in *Derecho de OPAs* (see n. 18), 496 ff.

[115]   Díaz Moreno, 'La neutralización de las medidas de defensa Anti-OPA', in *Derecho de OPAs* (see n. 18), 519 ff. New regulation on the neutralisation of preventive measures against takeover bids was adopted by Act 1/2012, of 22 June (Recalde, 'Limitación del número de votos de los accionistas y neutralización de las cláusulas estatutarias de limitación de voto', in *Las reformas de la Ley de sociedades de capital* (see n. 14), 691 ff.; Díaz Moreno and Juste Mencía, 'Apuntes de urgencia sobre la Ley 11/2012 de 22 de junio, de simplificación de las obligaciones de información y documentación de fusiones y escisiones de sociedades de capital', *RdS* 39, 2012, 199, 225 f.

company's securities are admitted to trading. Exceptions are also introduced in relation to breakthrough measures for reasons of reciprocity on the basis of the rules applicable to an offeror with registered office outside of Spain.

Furthermore, as a means of favouring disclosure to investors so that they are in a better position to decide on whether or not to accept the takeover bid, the offeree company's board of directors must draw up and publicly release a detailed report on the bid.[116]

3.1.4. *Institutional Investors*

In Spain, a continuous rise in investments in the capital of listed companies by institutional investors is appreciated, in particular via foreign collective investment institutions. Although these investors cannot invoke the traditional justification for the rationality of shareholders apathy in listed companies, until now their attitude has been reticent with regard to participating and voting in the general meeting. The reasons for the passivity of collective investors are varied. The first is the feeling that their voting is largely irrelevant, which is debatable; the argument of the high cost of analysing the information necessary in order to cast a vote is also alleged, above all taking into account that the holding of the general meeting of all listed companies is condensed into a small period of time.[117]

Spanish law has attempted to foster participation in corporate decision-making of institutional investors, in consideration of the potentially positive role they may play. It thus established legal rules that force them to vote in the general meeting of the listed companies in which they have holdings.[118] This measure has not always been effective, partly because the obligation to attend and vote so far only affects agents of collective investment institutions incorporated and resident in Spain, and those authorised to operate in Spain. It is not applicable to foreign collective investors which operate from their country of origin. Furthermore, there is no effective sanctions system in case of non-compliance with these attendance and voting obligations.[119]

---

[116] Garcia de Enterría, 'El informe sobre la OPA del órgano de administración de la sociedad afectada', *RdS* 30, 2008, 33 ff.; Recalde and De Dios, 'El informe del órgano de administración de la sociedad afectada por la OPA', in *Derecho de OPAs* (see n. 18), 425 ff.

[117] Questionnaire on the participation of Spanish institutional investors in general shareholders' meeting, *Funds People*, December 2012, 4.

[118] Art. 46.1 Act 35/2003, on Collective Investment Institutions (Ley 35/2003, de 4 de noviembre, de Instituciones de Inversión Colectiva) and Art. 81.1 of Royal Decree 1309/2005.

[119] Roncero and Valmaña, 'El alcance de la imposición por la LIIC a las instituciones de inversión colectiva del deber de asistencia y voto en las juntas generales', *RdS* nº 25, 2005, 283 ff.; Roncero, 'El deber de ejercicio de los derechos inherentes a los valores integrados en la cartera de un investor institucional', *NotUE* 283, 2008, 101 f.

3.1.5. Remuneration (as an Incentive)

Director remuneration, particularly in publicly traded companies, is one of the issues that evokes the greatest controversy in Spanish law, due to deficiencies of the widely criticised regulatory provisions this regard.[120] Corporate governance rules have sought to improve the regulatory framework by introducing duties of disclosure and recommending the implementation of measures aimed at resolving conflicts of interests. Specific measures have been put in place for banks in the wake of the financial crisis that call for intervention by the banking supervisor and limits on the compensation payable to directors and executives of banks that have been bailed out.

A key provision, and one that has also provoked great debate, is Article 217 LSC, which provides in its first sentence that 'Directorships are unremunerated, unless the articles of association otherwise provide, specifying the remuneration scheme.' Company law experts and practitioners agree in criticising the short-comings of this provision. Writing the remuneration scheme into the articles of association is unnecessarily rigorous and, precisely due to that excessive safeguard, perverts the treatment of the material issues raised by director compensation. The discussion of this question concentrates on the possibilities and limits of the interpretative scope of this rule. This raises numerous questions, some of considerable weight, such as the competence to determine the specific remuneration of directors, the nature of the relation between the director and the company and its implications for the compensation scheme, and the submission of executive director compensation to the articles of association in general and with respect to listed companies in particular.

With the aim of rendering the regulation more flexible, there is broad agreement that there is no need for the articles to specify the concrete amounts to be received by each board member. That compensation need not be determined in the articles of association, it being sufficient for the remuneration to be

---

[120] Domínguez García, 'Retribución de los administradores de las sociedades cotizadas. La comisión de retribuciones', in *Derecho de sociedades anónimas cotizadas* (see n. 3), 1055 ff.; Duque, 'Situación actual del problema de la remuneración de los administradores', in *Estudios en Homenaje a Anibal Sánchez Andrés* (see n. 99), 719 ff.; Farrando, 'La remuneración de los administradores y la doctrina jurisprudencial del doble vínculo', *RdS* 32, 2009, 99 ff.; Juste, 'Retribución de consejeros', in *El gobierno de las sociedades cotizadas* (see n. 19) 497 ff.; León, 'La previsión en los estatutos de la retribución de los administradores de la sociedad anónima. El estado de la cuestión en la doctrina española', *I Foro de encuentro de jueces y profesores de Derecho mercantil*, 2010, 13 ff.; Paz-Ares, 'La retribución de los consejeros ejecutivos' *AAMN* 47, 2006–2007, 269 ff.; '*Ad imposibilia nemo tenetur* (o por qué recelar de la novísima jurisprudencia sobre retribución de administradores)', *Indret*, 1, 2009, 1 ff., available at <www.indret.com>; Sánchez-Calero Guilarte, 'La retribución de los administradores de las sociedades cotizadas (la información societaria como solución)', *RdS* 28, 2007, 19 ff.; Vela, 'Criterios judiciales sobre retribución de administradores sociales', *I Foro de encuentro de jueces y profesores de Derecho mercantil*, 2010, 33 ff.

determinable based on the provisions of the articles. In exploring this question account must be taken of the particularity of the corporate structure of the public company and the legal nature of its articles of association. The articles must regulate at least two questions in this regard: the system of remuneration[121]—fixed, variable, profit share—and the procedure for exact calculation and allocation of the remuneration to each director.

A special rule is established in the event the variable compensation consists of a share in profits (Art. 218.2 LSC). The remuneration can only be drawn from the net profits obtained by the company after having covered the legal reserve and the reserves provided for in the articles of association and after declaring a shareholder dividend of at least 4%.[122]

There is likewise a specific rule if the director compensation takes the form of shares or options on shares (Art. 219 LSC).[123] This type of compensation must be explicitly mentioned in the articles of association and be approved in a general meeting resolution specifying the number of shares, the option exercise price, the share price taken as reference and the term of this remuneration scheme.

With respect to the procedure for determining the concrete compensation receivable by each director, the law allows the articles to regulate different corporate procedures, such that the general meeting can delegate certain specified questions to the board of directors, the board can be authorised to specify the terms of the resolution adopted at the general meeting or even for the board to have full authority to fix the director remuneration by applying the provisions of the articles without the need for a general meeting decision. The latter is the solution most commonly seen in listed companies.

The board's authority to determine the remuneration of directors within the framework laid down in the articles is expressly recognised in the CUBG (see Recommendation 8). The remuneration committee or nomination and remuneration committee, the majority of which should consist of independent directors, is responsible for proposing the policy on remuneration of board members and senior officers, the individual remuneration and other contractual terms of executive directors and the standard conditions for senior officers (Recommendation 57). To draw up the proposal, they should consult the chairman of the board of directors and the chief executive of the company in relation to matters regarding executive directors and senior officers (Recommendation 58). The

---

[121] Roncero, 'Grado de concreción del sistema retributivo de los administradores en los estatutos sociales de una sociedad', *RdS* 32, 2009, 82 ff.

[122] Olivencia and Sancho Mendizábel, 'Sobre la base de cálculo del dividendo de los accionistas precio a la retribución de los administradores consistente en participación en beneficios', *RDM* 271, 2009, 7 ff.

[123] Montero García-Noblejas, *Las opciones sobre acciones como sistema de retribución de administradores de S.A. cotizadas*, 2009.

remuneration committee is charged with overseeing compliance with the agreed remuneration policy.

The CUBG[124] gives a detailed description of the minimum content of the remuneration policy to be approved by the board of directors: The amount of the fixed components, with an itemisation of the per diems for participating on the board and its committees and an estimate of the annual remuneration they originate. In relation to the variable remuneration, it is recommended that the board should make pronouncements as regards the following: The category of directorships to which the variable components apply; the relative weight of variable remuneration to fixed amounts; the criteria for assessing performance used to award remuneration based on shares, options or any other variable component; the essential parameters and grounds for annual bonuses or other non-cash components; the estimated total amount of the variable remuneration; the main characteristics of supplementary pension plans, life insurance or similar benefits, including an estimate of their amount; and the basic terms of the contracts of directors with executive functions, such as the duration, advance notice requirements and clauses on hiring bonuses, indemnities or 'golden parachutes' in case of early termination.

With respect to how the remuneration of each individual director is deter-mined, the CUBG recommends that remuneration based on shares, options or similar instruments should be confined to the executive directors; non-executive directors should receive appropriate remuneration commensurate with the dedication, qualification and responsibility entailed by the post. Performance-based remuneration should take into account any qualifications that may be set out in the audit report and the necessary measures should be put in place to ensure that the variable remuneration is based on the director's performance and not on the evolution of the markets or sector in which the company does business.

The CNMV has issued a proposal to update the CUBG to comply with the European Commission Recommendation of 30 April 2009 complementing Rec-ommendations 2004/913/EC and 2005/162/EC as regards the regime for the re-muneration of directors of listed companies. The proposed revision of the CUBG is pending final approval.

With regard to the European Commission's new guidance on director remuneration, the IBEX 35 companies comply with the recommendation that the variable components of remuneration should be linked to predetermined and measurable performance criteria. The variable used most frequently refers to the annual profit before tax adjusted for current and future risks and for the cost of capital. In share-based remuneration, the key parameter is total return for the shareholder, measured as a function of the variation in the trading price plus

---

[124] Velasco San Pedro, 'Retribuciones de los consejeros y altos directivos (Recomenda-ciones 35 a 41)', *RdS* 27, 2007, 137 ff.

dividends. On the other hand, no deferment is normally envisaged for remuneration based on shares, options or similar instruments, except for the case of the financial institutions that are required to defer a substantial part of the variable remuneration for three years. IBEX 35 companies do not report the inclusion of limits in their remuneration policies and, in those that have such caps, they only apply to non-executive directors. Nor do they indicate whether limits have been set on indemnities. In some cases what they have stated is that the indemnity payable to the chairman and to the managing director is equal to three years' remuneration, including the fixed and variable components. Very few IBEX 35 companies have implemented clauses or formulas that allow the company to claim return of the variable part of remuneration packages when it has been paid without achievement of the performance targets or on the basis of data subsequently shown to be inaccurate.[125]

As regards disclosure issues, the LMV requires the boards of directors of listed companies to issue an annual report on the remuneration of their directors together with the annual corporate governance report (Art. 61ter LMV, recently developed by Order ECC/461/2013, de 20 de marzo, por la que se determinan el contenido y la estructura del informe annual de gobierno corporativo, del informe annual sobre remuneraciones y de otros instrumentos de información de las sociedades anónimas cotizadas, de las cajas de ahorros y de otras entidades que emitan valores admitidos a negociación en mercados oficiales de valores). That annual report must make full, clear and comprehensible disclosure of the company's remuneration policy and give a comprehensive summary of how the remuneration policy was applied during the year, along with an itemisation of each director's individual remuneration. The model director remuneration report has not yet been approved and the information released by listed companies is therefore fairly disparate and not always complete.[126]

The annual report on director's remuneration is to be disseminated to the shareholders. It must express the remuneration policy approved by the board of directors for the year in progress and envisaged for the ensuing years, the remuneration policy's application during the year, and the itemised individual remuneration of each director must be brought before the annual general meeting,

---

[125] *Annual Corporate Governance Report of the IBEX 35*, 35–37. For detailed information on the amount of director and senior officer remuneration in IBEX 35 companies by type of directorship and by remuneration component, see *Annual Corporate Governance Report of the IBEX 35*, 37 ff. and *Corporate Governance Report of issuers of securities admitted to trading in secondary securities markets*, 51 ff.

[126] Some IBEX 35 companies do not include information on the remuneration received by directors who gave up their directorship during the year or on the pay received by directors for holding directorships in subsidiaries (*Annual Corporate Governance Report of the IBEX 35*, 35).

and be put to a consultative vote as a separate point on the meeting agenda.[127] The legal status of this general meeting resolution is a rather contentious question.

In the wake of the financial crisis,[128] a series of specific measures have been adopted on director and executive pay in banks, given that one of the causes of the crisis was precisely the establishment of inappropriate compensation systems that encouraged excessive risk taking in financial institutions. In this regard, the Bank of Spain has been given authority to require banks to embrace corporate governance rules that include remuneration policies and practices that are consistent with the promotion of solid and effective risk management (Art. 10bis.1-d Act 13/1985—*Ley 13/1985, de 25 de mayo, de Coeficientes de Inversión, Recursos Propios y Obligaciones de Información de los Intermediarios Financieros*, as implemented by Articles 76*quater* to 76*septies* of Royal Decree 216/2008—*Real Decreto 216/2008, de 15 de febrero, de recursos propios de las entidades financieras*). In relation to credit institutions that have received financial assistance from Spain's Fund for Orderly Bank Restructuring (*Fondo de Reestructuración Ordenada Bancaria*, FROB), a number of restrictions have been placed on director and executive pay, based on the functions they perform in the bank, with a cap of €500,000 for the chairman, managing director and executives (Art. 5 Royal Decree Law 2/2012—*Real Decreto–ley 2/2012, de 3 de febrero, de saneamiento del sector financier*).

3.2. Board and Stakeholders

3.2.1. Board and Employees

Spanish law does not provide for employee representation on corporate boards of directors. Nor have any co-management schemes formed part of the successive reforms undertaken of the regulation of public limited companies since 1989. Employment legislation provides for systems of collective representation of employees through personnel 'delegates' and the works council (the *comité de empresa* of Article 62 et seq. of Legislative Royal Decree 1/1995 (*Real Decreto legislative 1/1994, de 24 de marzo, por el que se aprueba el Texto Refundido del*

---

[127] In IBEX 35 companies in 2011, the average percentage approval of the director remuneration policy was 90.06% and was in all cases higher than 60%. The average vote against approval was 6.9%, with abstentions of 2.3%, although in three companies the abstention percentage did exceed 10% (*Corporate Governance Report of issuers of securities admitted to trading in secondary securities markets*, 50–51).

[128] On the impact of the financial crisis on board remuneration, see Aparicio Gonzáles and Cuscó, 'La retribución de los consejeros en periodo de crisis financiera', in *Estudios en Homenaje a Anibal Sánchez Andrés* (see n. 99), 765 ff. León, 'La retribución de los administradores y de los ejecutivos en caso de crisis de empresa', in *Estudios en homenaje a Anibal Sánchez Andrés* (see n. 99), 737 ff.

Estatuto de los Trabajadores). The function of the works council is to defend the interests of the employees of the company, or of the specific workplace, vis-à-vis the employer.

3.2.2. Board and Creditors

Creditors may pursue individual actions against directors to claim liability for acts that have caused direct harm to their interests (Art. 241 LSC; see section 4.1 of this report).

3.2.3. Board and Other Stakeholders

The LSC recognises the right of any third-party to bring individual direct action for liability as a result of acts that have caused direct harm to their interests (Art. 241 LSC; see section 4.1 of this report). Apart from this provision, neither the LSC nor the LMV contains any other specific measure aimed at protecting stakeholders. Given the plurality of interests brought together within the framework of corporate social responsibility, the function of corporations in that context is fraught with indeterminacy.[129]

The Spanish Parliament has drawn up a White Paper on Corporate Social Responsibility (published in the official gazette of the Parliament on 31 July 2006). That publication was later followed up with the creation of the State Council on the Social Responsibility of Enterprises by Royal Decree 221/2008 – *Real Decreto 221/2008, de 15 de febrero, por el que se crea y regula el Consejo Estatal de Responsabilidad Social de las Empresas*. The White Paper recommends that publicly traded companies prepare and release a report on corporate social responsibility (Recommendation 6). This recommendation has as yet not been included in the CUBG. It is common practice, however, for IBEX 35 companies to voluntarily release information on their policies and actions in the area of corporate social responsibility and sustainability on their websites.

3.3. Changing Roles in Financial Distress

The duties of directors to the company's creditors intensify when the company runs into economic difficulties. We may distinguish between two basic situations in this regard: when the company is recording major losses and when it becomes insolvent. Directors are obliged to move to reduce the share capital of a public limited company if it records losses that lower its equity to less than two-thirds of the share capital figure for a full financial year without recovery (Art. 327 LSC).

---

[129] Sánchez-Calero Guilarte, 'Creación de valor, interés social y responsabilidad social corporativa', in *Derecho de Sociedades Anónimas Cotizadas* (see n. 3), 895 ff.

If the losses reduce equity to less than half of the share capital, the directors of the public limited company are obliged to move to wind up the company (Art. 363 LSC).[130] Failure to comply with this obligation renders the directors jointly and severally liable for the company's debts incurred after the legal grounds for winding-up arose (Art. 367 LSC).

If the company becomes insolvent, the directors are bound to apply for the declaration of insolvency within two months after the date on which they knew or should have known of the situation of insolvency (Art. 5 LC). Breach of this duty operates to classify the company's insolvency as culpable (Art. 165 LC). When insolvencies are held to be culpable, the directors and holders of general powers of attorney of the company may be ordered by the courts to cover all or part of the deficit (Art. 172bis LC). To inject flexibility into the obligation to seek a declaration of insolvency and make it easier to arrive at a solution to the company's financial distress that avoids such declaration, a procedure has been established that allows the deadline for filing for insolvency proceedings to be extended (Art. 5bis). The directors may give formal notice to the competent commercial court that the company is in a state of insolvency and in the process of negotiating with its creditors to reach an agreement on a solution to the economic difficulties. Submission of that notice initiates a three-month period in which the obligation to file for insolvency proceedings is lifted and during which no requests for declaration of insolvency will be accepted from parties other than the debtor (Art. 15.3 LC).

4. Enforcement

4.1. Courts

4.1.1. Personal Liability Claims

The effectiveness of supervision not only depends on minority shareholders recognising rights to control directors.[131] It is also linked to establishing tools that will help these rights to be upheld before the courts. However, analysis of the Spanish enforcement system and control rights over directors does not appear to be homogenous for all public companies. Data shows a reverse link between the size and subjective structure of the company, and the exercise of instruments to defend shareholders' interests before the courts, and even the likelihood of success of such legal action. Effectively, whilst it is common for small and medium-sized enterprises to resort to court action to resolve disputes between minority and

---

[130] Bataller, 'La Disolución', in Rojo and Beltrán (eds.), *La Liquidación de las Sociedades mercantiles*, 2012, 74 ff.

[131] Spanish companies law does not recognise class actions.

majority shareholders via nullification of general meeting resolutions, in large—and particularly in listed companies, which hold a significant part of free float capital—court proceedings are rare, and the likelihood of success for shareholders is even more remote.[132] Procedural obstacles often undermine the acknowledgement of legal defence resources for minority shareholders.

But this difference not only affects legal action for the nullification of resolutions of the general meeting or the board of directors, but also claims for damages occasioned by directors upon the company or shareholder, which is much less common in listed companies than in small and medium-sized public companies as an instrument to clarify disputes between the majority and the minority.

There are a number of reasons for these difficulties in the enforcement of internal control mechanisms. Firstly, obstacles that hinder the exercise of shareholders rights must be mentioned as they concern the rigorous legal requirement for qualification, a requirement difficult for minority shareholders to reach. Specifically, at times the filing of legal action can only be admitted when a certain level of capital holding can be proven, a requirement which poses quite an obstacle in companies with a disperse shareholdings. In other cases, the barriers suppose the duration of proceedings[133] or costs which are borne by the claimant should the claim be dismissed, whilst if the claim is successful, the proceedings arising from the award are given to the company. This all poses a disincentive to pursuing such actions.

4.1.2. Nullification of Resolutions

Spanish law provides the possibility of challenging the resolutions of the general meeting (Art. 204 LSC) and the board of directors (Art. 251 LSC), both before the court and by arbitration should this option be provided for in the company by-laws.[134] In both cases, the grounds for the challenge are identical and entail making a distinction between *void* resolutions, which are contrary to the law, and

---

[132] Based on Westlaw data for the period spanning 1 January and 31 December 2011, up to 413 Supreme Court or Appeal Court judgments concerned nullification of resolutions. However, for listed companies this figure is much lower (De Juan, 'Landesbericht: Spanien', in Fleischer (ed.), *Anfechtungsklagen in Europa* (to be published), (fn. 23 and 27).

[133] A period of 30 months to first instance ruling, 17 further months to appeal and another 74 months to final appeal judgment of the Supreme Court (*Sánchez-Calero Guilarte, Juan,* 'Propuesta de revisión de la impugnación de acuerdos, especial referencia a las sociedades cotizadas', in Rodríguez Artigas/Farrando/González Castilla/Tena (eds.) *La junta general de las sociedades de capital. Cuestiones actuales,* 2009, S. 395; De Juan, 'Landesbericht: Spanien', in *Anfechtungsklagen in Europa* (tbp) (see n. 132)(fn. 29).

[134] Act 11/2011, introduced article 11.bis into Act 60/2003, on arbitration *(Ley 60/2003, de 23 de diciembre, de Arbitraje)*, which allows company by-laws to set out that disputes and, in particular the challenge of corporate resolutions, will be subject to arbitration. To do so, at least two thirds of shareholder votes of the limited liability company must be cast in favour.

voidable resolutions, which are contrary to by-laws or which harm corporate interest to the benefit of one or several shareholders or third parties. Although the issue is subject to debate, courts have understood that these grounds for challenge are a closed list and, consequently, no challenges outside of these are admissible (such as violation of the shareholders agreement by the general meeting, even when signed unanimously by all shareholders).[135]

With respect to the resolutions of the general meeting, the difference between the two types of resolution lies in the term in which to sue for nullification, which is one year in void resolutions (except when contrary to public order, which have no time limit), whilst the claim against voidable resolutions must be filed within 40 days from the date of approval of the resolution or, where appropriate, from the date of its publishing in the Mercantile Register Official Gazette (*Boletín Oficial del Registro Mercantil*). Moreover, legal actions challenging void resolutions of the general meeting can be filed by all shareholders, directors and any third party that can prove legitimate interest. Conversely, challenge of a voidable resolution can only be filed by the shareholders in attendance at the general meeting who expressly opposed the resolution, absentees and those who had been unlawfully refused their vote, as well as directors.

In the case of resolutions of the board of directors, the term for challenge is 30 days from adoption thereof if the challenge is filed by a director. However, if the claim originates from shareholders, this term begins upon their knowledge of the agreement and provided a year has not passed since adoption thereof. In any event, when the legal action is filed by shareholders, these must hold at least a 5% stake in capital.[136] Practice shows how scarcely this mechanism for defence of shareholder is used.

In listed companies there is no real problem of so-called predatory shareholders' actions. The rarity of action for nullification of resolutions is not linked to qualification requirements to sue; in the case of the resolutions of the general meeting, any shareholder may sue. Their justification would lie more in procedural costs (both those of the claimant and the respondent company) which are borne by the petitioner of nullification if the courts dismiss the suit, whilst if successful, the positive effects would only be felt indirectly. On the other hand, formal faults, which are the most common and simple recourse used by judges to void resolutions for a general meeting in public companies, are by no means common in such complex and institutionalised structures as those adopted by listed companies. Courts know well of the disputes that can occur in power struggles between managers and certain shareholders with significant capital holdings.

---

[135] Critics to that decission Pérez Millán, 'Presupuestos y fundamento jurídico de la impugnación de acuerdos sociales por incumplimiento de pactos parasociales', *RDBB*, 2010, 231 ff.

[136] Alclá Día, *El derecho de impugnación del socio en la sociedad anónima cotizada*, 2006.

Nullification of resolutions of the general meeting is only exceptionally the aim of court action. Much more common is the legality of general meeting resolutions (for procedural faults in the running of the general meeting, aspects regarding content, and oppressive situations between minorities and majorities) in small and medium-sized entities.[137]

4.1.3. Special Procedures and Issues

The members of the board respond jointly to damages occasioned by the company in non-compliance of its obligations of due administration or its fiduciary duties (misconduct against loyalty duties in the company's interest). Exercise of liability actions theoretically corresponds to the company itself and, as such, the corresponding resolution must be approved by the general meeting. If the general meeting does not file the action, there is a derivative action that may be lodged by shareholders (provided that these hold at least 5% of share capital); exceptionally creditors also have the capacity to institute action for liability (Art. 240 LSC).[138] However, in cases of derivative action, the recovery obtained as a result of the sanction on directors goes to the company and shareholders would only benefit indirectly, either from the company's increase in equity or by creditors, as a result of their improved fulfilment of obligations. This is what Spanish law call 'corporate liability action' (Arts. 238 and 239 LSC).

However, if the loss suffered by the individual shareholder is separate from the loss suffered by the company and if there is also a breach of a separate duty owed by the directors to the individual shareholders, direct action by the shareholders of third parties is permitted. In this case, the shareholders or third parties (eg. creditors) may benefit directly from the claim. This would be a case of 'individual action for liability' (Art. 241 LSC).[139]

In large public companies the pursuit of actions against directors is uncommon. Yet this is not the case for small and medium-sized public companies, wherein

---

[137] De Juan, 'Landesbericht: Spanien', in *Anfechtungsklagen in Europa* (tbp) (see n. 132; Hernando Cebria, 'Del socio de control al socio tirano y al abuso de la mayoría en las sociedades de capital', *RdS* 37, 2012, 173 ff.

138 Indirect protection channel for credits are most commonly applicable to bankruptcy scenarios (Marín de la Bárcena, 'La Derivative Action como medio de tutela de la posición jurídica de socio en las sociedades cotizadas', RDBB 116, 2009, 143 ff.).

[139] The nature and qualifying scenarios for these actions are subject to debate. See Esteban Velasco,'La acción individual de responsabilidad', in Rojo and Beltrán (eds.) *La responsabilidad de los administradores de las sociedades mercantiles*, 2nd ed, 2008, 211; Marín de la Bárcena, *La acción individual de responsabilidad frente a los adminsitradores de sociedades de capital (Art. 135 LSA)*, 2005; Alfaro, 'La llamada acción individual de responsabilidad contra los administradores sociales', *RdS* 18, 2002, 45 f.; Alfaro, 'La llamada acción individual de responsabilidad o 'responsabilidad externa contra los administradores sociales', *InDret*, 413, 2007, available at <www.indret.com>.

creditors often use individual actions in order to ensure that directors satisfy their obligations to the company. It is also relatively common for a liability action to be filed against members of the board in cases of abuse of majority, when concerning senior management posts in the company. Lastly are those legal actions filed at times following changes in control of a company, resulting from the introduction of a new shareholder acquiring a majority shareholding. In these cases, the new majority shareholder may drive through approval by the general meeting of a liability action against the directors of the previous board for damages occasioned to the company. This is not uncommon in instances of company sale. For these purposes, the repercussions for a shareholder release resolution adopted in the annual general meeting are very limited (Art. 238.4 LSC). Conversely, in a purely contractual sphere, it would be contrary to good faith for the purchasers that voted to pursue corporate liability actions against prior directors, when the due diligence carried out prior to the purchase included, as is common, the exemption of the seller's liability for 'faults' in the company that may be revealed after effective handover. However, these clauses in company transfer agreements would not be challengeable before other shareholders that were not party thereto.

In listed companies, the exercise of liability actions against directors is exceptional, even in the event of changes of control. This could be due to the rarity of hostile takeovers successfully executed in Spain. In the few takeovers that were originally proposed against the will of the board and which ended in a change of control, this was the result of an agreement between the bidder and the executive directors, which ensured an exit for the latter under good economic conditions and with no risk with respect to prior management.

Furthermore, under Spanish law D&O insurance—paid for by the company—is generally accepted to protect the director against liability of breach of duty, yet there is some discussion as to the limits of such insurance. Under no circumstances does such insurance cover criminal liability or civil liability for intentional wrongdoing.[140] Neither the law nor the CUBG sets out an obligation for executive directors and managers to pay part of the insurance premium out of their own pockets. Likewise, there are no specific disclosure duties when the company takes out such insurance.

In the civil scope, greater importance has been given in recent years to imposing upon directors' insolvency prevention duties, as well as certain rigorous consequences in terms of personal liability arising from insolvency declarations. In both cases, it is provided that all or some of the company's debts will extent to the equity of director, in some cases due to non-compliance with their obligations (above section 3.3).

---

[140] Roncero, *El seguro de responsabilidad civil de administradores de una sociedad anónima (sujetos, interés y riesgo)*, 2002; Guerrero Lebrón, *El seguro de responsabilidad civil de administradores y directivos*, Madrid 2004; Iribarren, *El seguro de responsabilidad civil de los administradores y altos directivos de sociedades de capital (D&O)*, 2005.

4.1.4. Criminal Litigation

The Spanish Criminal Code (*Ley Orgánica 10/1995, de 23 de noviembre, del Código Penal*) contains specific provisions aimed to penalise conduct of *de facto* or *de jure* directors of commercial companies that violate the legal provisions governing their operations (Title XIII, Chapter XIII, 'On corporate offences'). Sanctions are in place for falsification of corporate documents, imposition of abusive or damaging agreements, hindering the exercise of shareholders rights, hindering inspection or supervision activities and, in particular, fraudulent corporate administration, ie. unfair management conduct carried out for own benefit or that of a third party and in abuse of office (Arts. 290, 291, 292, 293, 294 and 295 of the Criminal Code). Legislators declare their concern for the similar definition of the standard of conduct required of directors and, in particular, tension arises between the criminal and the civil approaches to breaches of fiduciary duties. It seems to be accepted that the criminal approach should be exceptional and reserved for the most serious conduct. Yet the effectiveness of coercion in the criminal approach cannot be unknown. In any event, this is the structure that has been used with the onset of the financial crisis and, in particular, the crisis of Spanish savings banks in 2011 and 2012, in order to bring numerous directors of savings banks subject to nationalisation before the criminal courts.

4.2. Regulators

Listed companies are subject to supervision by the CNMV, which is a public agency in charge of supervising and inspecting the Spanish Stock Markets and the activities of all the participants in those markets. It was created in 1998 by the Securities Market Law (LMV), which instituted in-depth reforms of this segment of the Spanish financial system.

Its mandate is to ensure the correct functioning of securities markets, via 'transparency of the securities markets, the correct formulation of pricing in these, and the protection of investors' (Art. 13 Securities Markets Act). It is in charge of detecting and pursuing illegal activities by unregistered intermediaries. The CNMV also holds control powers for takeovers. The CNMV focus particularly on improving the quality of information disclosure to the market, and particular efforts are made in the area of auditing and in developing new disclosure requirements relating to remuneration schemes for directors and executives that are linked to the price of the shares of the company where they work. Regarding the annual corporate governance reports that listed companies should develop and publish, and pursuant to Article *bis* LMV, the CNMV is the institution responsible for monitoring corporate governance rules. To this effect, it can collect all information needed and make public the information it considers relevant regarding the actual degree of compliance. It also corresponds to the CNMV to impose sanctions on companies referred by the lack of submission of the documentation or annual report on corporate governance, or the existence of omissions or misleading or erroneous data (Art. 61 *bis*. 5 LMV).

The CNMV is thus equipped to instruct or even impose sanctions in case of infringement of securities regulations.

4.3. Self-Regulation

Since 1997, three codes including mere recommendations related to corporate good governance practices codes have been published, all with the backing of the CNMV which monitors fulfilment with the declaration of compliance of the recommendations of the code by listed companies in accordance with the comply-or-explain principle. The premise for all three codes is to leave it up to each company as to whether or not it will heed the good governance recommendations contained therein.

The first code envisaged one option for voluntary compliance of its provisions and confidence in spontaneous disclosure. The feeling of scepticism in relating to the application of the code, led to the legal recognition of the comply-or-explain principle. The Disclosure Act (*Ley 26/2003, de transparencia*)established the obligation to produce an annual report on corporate governance to make public the extent of compliance with the recommendations set out in the codes of good governance or, where appropriate, the reasons for its non-compliance. This obligation is contained in Article 61 bis LMV, modified by Law of Sustainable Economy (*Ley 2/2011, de Economía Sostenible*). This Law has also imposed the duty to produce an annual report on remuneration of directors (Art. 61 ter LMV).

The CUBG of 2006 undertakes the task of harmonising and updating the recommendations of the Olivencia and Aldama reports, and makes some additional recommendations, relative to competencies and functional structure of the board, its composition and typology of directors (eg. requisites of independent directors), greater transparency in their remunerations, gender diversity and implementation of special mechanisms for employees to report irregularities.

The high level of compliance shown by listed companies could call for optimism. However, the on-going development of self-regulation does give way to certain scepticism as to the quality of explanations for compliance or non-compliance. Effectively, there have been some suspicions that annual reports indications on compliance with the good governance codes contain merely cosmetic window-dressing rather than an improvement in real corporate ethics. On the other hand, in the case of declarations of non-compliance, explanations offered by companies are often insufficient. The annual monitoring of the reports by the CNMV could be a useful instrument in implementing better practices, although as far this has not been proven.

Some recent legal reforms (eg. *Ley 2/2011, de Economía Sostenible*) in the uncertain fulfilment of the CUBG recommendations have included certain requirements that previously were only contained in these codes. This has been the case for remuneration of officers, for which, in the name of transparency, an annual report must be prepared and agreement of the general meeting must be sought, although in a purely consultative capacity. Likewise, guarantees of the independence of independent executives are established by legal regulation.

5. The Dynamics of Change

An important reform of companies regulation is currently underway in Spain, yet the drivers of change in relation to the configuration of the board in public companies remain unclear. Effectively, the Ministry of Justice has pushed forward a significant legislative change which should eventually lead to a new code of commerce being passed, to then be included in companies law. From proposals for the new regulation it appears that a return to the 2010 Corporations Act will be made, once again including differential treatment for partnerships and each company type. This will entail a return to separation of rules applicable to limited liability companies, public companies (with specific rules for listed companies) and partnerships limited by shares. In any event, the reform is basically limited to collecting the current regulation and thus, no fundamental changes are expected.

Furthermore, some of the most recent reforms (eg. those approved under the 2011 Sustainable Economy Act) have entailed the inclusion in legislation of recommendations of the Corporate Governance Codes. This could perhaps be considered a change of pace with regard to the trust placed in self-regulation. However, this favourable stance towards statutory regulation of corporate governance must be tempered. The scope of change is rather limited. In fact, more significant reforms in corporate governance regulation in listed company have commonly been the result of a need to adapt to EU rules or demands put in place by the international financial markets. A fine example of this would be the detailed demands on defining related-party transactions in accounting 'rules' compared to the more limited and generic scope of companies law or the securities regulation.

Moreover, significant reforms have been brought in as a result of the economic crisis, which fundamentally affect the financial sector. Improving corporate governance of financial entities is one of the most pertinent trends currently in Spanish law. The significant downscaling of savings banks (*cajas de ahorro*) is a major feature of this, and goes hand in hand with the loss of trust in corporate governance systems. The reform of banking institutions embraces more rigorous corporate governance rules, including remuneration policies and practices that are consistent with the promotion of solid and effective risk management.

6. Selection of Literature

Alonso Ureba, 'El modelo de administración de la SA cotizada en el Código Unificado de Buen Gobierno', in *Estudios de derecho de sociedades y derecho concursal: Libro Homenaje al profesor Rafael García Villaverde*, 2007, I, 177.

Embid, Abriani, Boquera and Emparanza (eds.), *Los derechos de los accionistas en las sociedades cotizadas*, 2011.

Esteban Velasco (ed.), *El gobierno de las sociedades cotizadas*, 1999.

Esteban Velasco, 'El gobierno de las sociedades cotizadas. La experiencia española', *CDC* 35, 2001, 11.

Esteban Velasco, 'Interés social, buen gobierno y responsabilidad social corporativa (algunas consideraciones desde una perspectiva jurídico-societaria)', in *Responsabilidad social corporativa aspectos jurídico-económicos*, 2005, 13.

Farrando, 'Evolution and Deregulation in the Spanish Corporate Law', in Ventoruzzo (ed.), *Nuovo diritto societario e analisi economica del diritto*, 2005, 66.

García Castro, Aguilera, 'A Decade of Corporate Governance Reforms in Spain (2000–10)', http://papers.ssrn.com/sol3/papers.cfm?abstract_id=2025893.

García de Enterría, Zurita (eds.), *La regulación de las OPAs*, 2009.

Garrido, 'Corporate Governance in Spain. Company Law and Corporate Governance Code', in Hopt et al, *European Corporate Governance in Company Law and Codes*, 2003.

Garrido, Rojo, 'Institutional Investors and Corporate Governance: Solution or Problem', in Hopt, Wymeersch (eds.), *Capital Markets and Company Law*, 2002.

Gondra, 'El control del poder de los directivos de las grandes corporaciones', *RDM* 269, 2008, 841.

Gondra, 'La teoría contractual de la sociedad anónima. Una aproximación a sus fundamentos teórico-económicos', *RDM* 278, 2010, 1215.

Iglesias Rodríguez, 'The Role of Corporate Governance Recommendations in the Creation of Mandatory Law: The Case of Spain', *Journal of Corporate Ownership and Control*, Vol. 5, No. 3, 2008, 291.

Juste, Recalde (eds.), *Derecho de OPAs*, 2010.

Leech, Manjon, 'Corporate Governance in Spain (with an Application of the Power Indices Approach)', *EJLE* 13, 2002, 157.

León, 'Los mecanismos de control reforzados en las sociedades cotizadas Control-Enhancing Mechanisms, CEM', *La Ley* 7463, 2010, 1.

Paz-Ares, 'Spain', Grefory, Millstein (eds.), *Comparative Corporate Governance*, 2002.

Paz-Ares, 'El gobierno corporativo como estrategia de creación de valor', *RDM* 251, 2004, 7.

Peña, Mínguez, 'Spain', *Corporate Governance 2010 A practical insight to cross-border Corporate Governance*, 2010.

Quijano, 'Estatuto de los administradores (selección, nombramiento y cese de consejeros. Información y dedicación de los consejeros)', *RdS* 27, 2006, 122.

Recalde, 'Del "Código Olivencia" a la aplicación de la Ley de Transparencia (un balance provisional – y decepcionante – sobre la reforma del "gobierno corporativo" en las sociedades cotizadas españolas)', *RCDI* 692, 2005, 1861.

Rodríguez Artigas et al (eds.), *Derecho de sociedades anónimas cotizadas,* 2006.

Rodríguez Artigas, Farrando Miguel, González Castilla (eds.), *Las reformas de la Ley de Sociedades de Capital,* 2nd ed, 2012.

Rojo, Beltrán (eds.), *Comentario de la ley de sociedades de capital,* 2011.

Rojo, Beltrán (eds.) *La responsabilidad de los administradores de las sociedades mercantiles,* 4nd ed., 2011.

Sánchez Calero, *Los administradores de las sociedades de capital,* 2005.

Sánchez-Calero Guilarte, 'El interés social y los varios intereses presentes en la sociedad anónima cotizada', *RDM* 246, 2002, 1653.

Tapia Hermida, *Sociedades anónimas cotizadas y ofertas públicas de adquisición,* 2012.

Corporate Boards in Sweden

ROLF SKOG and ERIK SJÖMAN

1. General Introduction

1.1. Environment in which Boards Operate

a) *Private, Public, and Listed Companies*

In Sweden, there are at present some 425,000 limited liability companies (*aktiebolag, AB*). The Swedish Companies Act 2005 (*aktiebolagslagen*) divides limited companies into two categories: private companies and public companies. Of the 425,000 companies registered in the Companies Register some 424,000 are private companies and approximately 1,000 are public companies.

The fundamental difference between private and public companies is that public companies, but not private companies, raise capital from the general public. The fact that a company is public entails nothing other than that the company is entitled to invite the general public to acquire shares and other securities issued by the company. A private company, on the other hand, is prohibited from seeking to distribute shares, subscription rights or other securities issued by the company to the general public. It is also forbidden for a securities exchange or other organised market place to trade such securities.

There are at present 230 Swedish public companies whose shares are traded on Swedish regulated markets (ie., the main markets of NASDAQ OMX Stockholm and Nordic Growth Market NGM*).* These companies are hereinafter referred to as listed companies.

The companies listed on the NGM main market (NGM Equity) are typically smaller than the companies listed on the NASDAQ OMX Stockholm main market. However, as shown in Table 1 even amongst the latter companies there are significant variances in terms of size. Approximately 90% of the NASDAQ OMX Stockholm companies' total market capitalisation is attributable to less than 50 Large Cap companies.

Table 1: Swedish listed companies (June 2012)

List	Number of companies	Percentage of total market capitalisation
Small Cap	111	1.8
Mid Cap	71	8.1
Large Cap	48	90.1
Total	230	100.0

Source: SIS

There are also some 250 companies, most of them even smaller, whose shares are traded on multilateral trading facilities (MTFs) such as NASDAQ OMX First North, Nordic MTF and AktieTorget. These companies and the listed companies are sometimes jointly referred to as publicly traded companies.

b)   The Structure of Ownership of Listed Companies

From a historical perspective, private owners have dominated the ownership of Swedish listed companies. In the early 1950s, nearly 75% of the market capitalisation of the Stockholm Stock Exchange (now, NASDAQ OMX Stockholm) was directly held by individual investors. The remaining 25% or so was owned in part by family-controlled foundations, holding companies and (closed end) investment companies, and in part by listed companies themselves, which had significant holdings in other companies. Institutional portfolio investors were practically non-existent at the time.

Two decades later, in the mid-1970s, direct holdings by individual investors had declined to around 50% of the market's capitalisation, and by the mid-1980s it had dropped to 25%. Today less than 15% of the total market capitalisation of the NASADAQ OMX Stockholm market is attributable to direct shareholdings by individuals. Institutional investors account for more than 85%.[1]

The reasons behind the institutionalisation of shareholder structures are well known. Due to, among other things, changes in savings, pension and tax legislation, capital accumulation has been collectivised and increasingly channeled to institutional investors. These institutions, in turn, have invested more of their assets in the stock market. Over a number of years, pension funds, insurance companies, mutual funds and other institutional portfolio investors have been net buyers of shares, while individuals have been net sellers. Moreover, institutions have been over-represented in new share issues, whereas individuals have been equally under-represented.

Despite this institutionalisation of the ownership structure, many listed companies still have a single or limited number of major shareholders. Recent data shows that approximately 64% of Swedish listed companies had one shareholder with at least a 25% shareholding (by comparison, in Italy it was 65% and Germany 82%). Further, in 26% of the listed companies the block-holder had a majority holding of at least 50% (Italy 56% and Germany 64%). These large shareholders often play an active ownership role and take particular responsibility for the company, for example through board representation.

The structure of ownership is fully transparent. All companies must maintain a register of their shares and shareholders. Share registers are maintained by a central securities depository, the only Swedish one being Euroclear Sweden AB. The register is public, so that anyone can gain access at any time to information on the ownership structure of a company.

The institutionalisation of share ownership has been a lengthy process. That is not the case, however, with another change in the shareholder structure of listed companies: internationalisation.

---

[1] As regards the distribution of the stock market's capitalisation by shareholder categories, see, for example, M. Henrekson and U. Jakobsson, 'The Swedish Model of Corporate Ownership and Control in Transition', *SSE/EFI Working Paper Series in Economics and Finance*, No. 521, 2003. See also by the same author, in Swedish, 'Ägarpolitik och ägarstruktur i efterkrigstidens Sverige' [Ownership policies and ownership structures in post-war Sweden], in Jonung, L. (ed.), *Vem skall äga Sverige? 2002* [Who will own Sweden? 2002]. See also, for example, *Ägande och inflytande i svenskt näringsliv* [Ownership and influence in Swedish business] (SOU 1988:38), *Ägande i det privata näringslivet* [Ownership in private business] (SIND 1980:5), and *Ägande och inflytande i det privata näringslivet* [Ownership and influence in private business] (SOU 1968:7). As regards the ownership structures of listed Swedish companies, especially during the 1950s and 60s, refer also to, among others, Lindgren, H., *Aktivt ägande. Investor under växlande konjunkturer* [Active ownership: Investor under changing economic conditions], 1994, p. 100 et seq.; J. Glete, *Nätverk i näringslivet* [Business networks], 1994; and, by the same author, *Ägande och industriell omvandling* [Ownership and industrial transformation], 1987.

In order to protect Sweden's natural resources and Swedish businesses from excessive foreign ownership, special legislation was introduced in the early 1900s whereby practically every purchase of real property and large shareholdings in Swedish limited liability companies by foreigners required the approval of the Swedish state.

This control legislation effectively held foreign ownership of limited liability companies in check for almost a century. A slight change was noted in the 1980s, when US pension funds were among those to see the potential in undervalued shares in Swedish-based, internationally recognised public companies. The share of the market capitalisation of the Stockholm Stock Exchange owned by foreign investors rose slightly, but even in the late 1980s only around 5% of total capitalisation of the Stockholm Stock Exchange was in the hands of foreign investors.

A significant change came about when Sweden joined the EU in the mid-1990s, which required Sweden to adapt its legislation to the non-discrimination principle of the EC Treaty and to eliminate restrictions on capital flows and investments by investors from other Member States. Sweden decided to take the opportunity to abolish all restrictions on acquisitions of shares in Swedish companies.[2]

The results were almost immediate. There was a dramatic rise in direct foreign investments in the form of, among other things, corporate takeovers and portfolio investments in Swedish listed companies. Less than ten years after the abolition of the control legislation, 37 of the 100 largest Swedish companies were 100% foreign-owned,[3] and foreign ownership of Swedish listed shares now ranges between 30% and 40%.[4]

Not surprisingly, the main reason for the increase in foreign ownership of Swedish listed shares is that foreign institutional investors with global portfolios have adjusted their holdings to include Swedish equities. Similarly, due to more liberal investment regulations, Swedish institutions have reduced the portion of Swedish shares in their portfolios during the same period.[5]

---

[2] See, for example, *Bundna aktier* [Restricted shares] (SOU 1992:13) p. 77, and R. Skog, 'Foreign Acquisitions of Shares in Swedish Companies', *International Company and Commercial Law Review*, April 1992.

[3] Figures relate to 2001; see the report entitled 'Med utländska flaggor i topp och konjunkturen i botten – Hur går det för Sverige?' [With foreign flags flying high and the economy declining, how is Sweden doing?], *ISA* 2003 s. 64.

[4] See, for example, Statistics Sweden, *Ägandet av aktier i bolag noterade på svensk marknadsplats, åren 1983–2003* [Ownership of shares in companies listed on Swedish marketplaces, 1983–2003].

[5] See, for example, Henrekson and Jakobson (see n. 1) p. 26.

c) Sources of Board Rules

Corporate governance in Swedish listed companies is regulated by a combination of written rules and generally accepted practices. The framework includes the Companies Act, the Swedish Corporate Governance Code (as amended in February 2010) (*Svensk kod för bolagsstyrning*) and the rules of the market places on which shares are admitted to trading, as well as statements by the Securities Council (*Aktiemarknadsnämnden*) on what constitutes best practices in the Swedish securities market. Finally, for companies becoming the object of a takeover bid, key provisions are included in the Takeovers Act 2006 (*lagen om offentliga uppköpserbjudanden på aktiemarknaden*) and applicable Takeover Rules (*Regler rörande offentliga uppköpserbjudanden på aktiemarknaden*).

The Companies Act applies to both private and public companies, unless otherwise expressly stated in specific provisions. In some instances, there are certain provisions of the Act that only apply to listed companies. These rules, many of which emanate from EU directives are— with some exceptions—stricter than the rules applying to non-listed companies.

The Companies Act contains general rules regarding the governance of the company. The Act specifies which governance bodies must exist in a company, the tasks of each body and the responsibilities of the people in each of these positions.

The Companies Act and the Corporate Governance Code do not conflict with each other. However, the Code covers many issues not covered by the Companies Act. The Corporate Governance Code complements the Act by placing more stringent demands on listed companies in certain respects, while simultaneously allowing them to deviate from rules in individual cases (the comply-or-explain principle).[6]

The Swedish Securities Council is a self-regulatory body that promotes best practices in the Swedish securities market through statements, advice and information. During the 25 years of its existence, the Council has published more than 600 statements.

d) The Corporate Governance System of Listed Companies in Brief

Swedish corporate governance is primarily based on the shareholder value theory, although restrictions apply with a view to protecting creditors and minority shareholders.[7] The preparatory works relating to the Swedish Companies Act emphasise the importance of active ownership. Shareholders provide the business sector with risk capital, but they also contribute to the efficiency and dynamism of individual companies and the business sector in general by buying and selling

---

[6] See further sec. 4.3.1 below.

[7] See further sec. 3.2 for a description of the regulation concerning the interests of shareholders and other stakeholders.

shares, as well as by participating in and exercising influence at shareholders' meetings. Active shareholder participation promotes a healthy balance of power between owners, the board and the executive management.

As a general rule, resolutions at shareholders' meetings are adopted by simple majority vote. However, certain resolutions—such as amendments to the articles of association—require a qualified majority.

The presumption in the Companies Act is that each share confers the same right in the company. However, the articles of association may provide that shares of different classes with different rights in the company may be issued. This means that a Swedish company can, for example, issue shares of different classes that are distinguished by their voting power. However, the maximum voting ratio between high vote and low vote shares may not exceed 1:10.

The system of dual class common stock is widely used among Swedish listed companies. In the beginning of the 1990s, around 85% of these companies had multiple classes of shares carrying different voting rights. Due mainly to initial public offerings by companies having only one class of shares, the system is less frequent today. Nevertheless, more than half of the listed companies have issued two or more classes of common shares with different voting rights. Almost without exception, the voting ratio is 1:10.

1.2. Financial Institutions

As regards the governance of financial institutions, Sweden has implemented the EU-driven initiatives in this field and will continue to do so. Leaving national implementation of EU initiatives aside, there are no Sweden-specific rules of material relevance for the analysis set forth in this paper.

1.3. Available Board Models

From a structural point of view, corporate governance of Swedish listed companies can be described as a third alternative to the so-called unitary board system, predominantly used in the US and UK and other countries with an Anglo-American legal tradition and the dual board system, used in many European continental countries. Compared with those, the Swedish Companies Act provides for a unitary board system but with entirely or predominantly non-executive boards and the executive duties statutorily delegated to a separate, one-person, CEO function. The main governance decision bodies—the shareholders' meeting, the board and the CEO—make up a strictly hierarchical chain of command, where each body is fully subordinate to the next higher body.

In practice, the board of directors' main responsibilities are: To elect a chief executive officer (CEO); to supervise the CEO's day-to-day running of the company; and to make strategic decisions. As such, the board has potentially greater powers than a traditional supervisory board, but not necessarily the same extent of executive power usually exercised by a unitary board. In addition, the only executive member of the board, if any, is typically the CEO (and only slightly more than half of the listed companies have the CEO on its board), which means that external and independent members dominate. The CEO has the responsibility of appointing the remainder of the executive management, which is at a level below the CEO. They report only to the CEO. Hence, their position is quite different from the members of the management boards in operation in continental Europe.

For a Societas Europaea (SE) company governed by Swedish law, both the unitary and the dual board models are available. If the unitary board model is chosen, the administrative organ will to a large extent have the same function as the board of a Swedish limited liability company. In matters not regulated or covered by the SE Regulation, the administrative organ and its members are governed by the same laws and regulations as the Swedish board and its members, with the exception of the Board Representation (Private Employees) Act 1987 (*lagen om styrelserepresentation för de privatanställda*). The same applies to the management organ and its members, in case a company has opted for the dual board model, whereas the supervisory organ and its members will only be governed to a limited extent by the same provisions as a Swedish board and its members. It should be noted in particular that under Swedish law the supervisory organ not only supervises the management organ but also the CEO's management of the company.

2. Authority

2.1. Functions and Division of Powers

The Companies Act stipulates that companies must have three decision-making bodies in a hierarchical relationship to one another: The shareholders' meeting, the board of directors and the chief executive officer (CEO). There must also be a controlling body, the statutory auditor, which is appointed by the shareholders' meeting.

a) The Board

The board has a general obligation to ensure that the company's organisation is appropriate. This means, among other things, that the organisation must include routines and functions that ensure quality. This includes having in place sensible administrative procedures and a good choice of employees. Naturally, the board must also be a forum for planning and assessment of the company's development. The board will discuss the company's strategic issues and make the appropriate strategic decisions.

The board is also responsible for *management of the company's affairs.* This includes responsibility for, in principle, all duties where the shareholders' meeting is not the exclusive decision-maker. This includes long-term decisions regarding the company's future policy and focus, measures relating to organisation and planning, measures regarding day-to-day operations and management as well as necessary bookkeeping, accounting and funds management. The board's responsibility for these duties does not, however, mean that the board must actively take part in all measures. The board can delegate duties. If a CEO has been appointed, he or she will be in charge of the day-to-day management. However, the board retains, however, overall responsibility for the management of the company.

The board is required to clarify the allocation of work between the board and the CEO through written instructions. Through such instructions, the board can clarify which measures may be undertaken by the CEO independently, for example with respect to representing the company vis-à-vis third parties or the investment of the company's funds. The instructions are adopted by the board pursuant to an ordinary board resolution.

Furthermore, according to the Companies Act, the board must ensure that the company's organisation is structured so that accounting, management of funds and the company's finances in general are monitored in a satisfactory manner. By virtue of this provision, emphasis is placed on the board's responsibility for the company's organisation in light of the economic issues of significance for the company. Depending on the structure of the organisation, the need for control may, however, vary from company to company. Naturally, it is up to the board of directors to ensure that the company's control functions are structured in a manner which meets the needs of the individual case.

The board is also required to ensure that the company has adequate internal controls and formalised routines to ensure that approved principles for financial reporting and internal controls are applied, and that the company's financial reports are produced in accordance with legislation, applicable accounting standards and other requirements for listed companies.

Under the Companies Act, the board of a listed company is required to appoint an audit committee from among its members to supervise the activities of the management and the board with respect to, among other things, the operation of the internal risk management and control systems, the provision of financial information by the company, and compliance with recommendations of internal and external auditors. The audit committee must consist of least three board members, the majority of whom have to be independent of the company and its executive management. At least one of the committee members who are independent of the company and its executive management must also be independent of the company's major shareholders (>10% of the shares or votes in the company). This independent member must possess special auditing or accounting competence. The company may resolve that the board of directors will not have an audit committee, provided that the board itself performs the above tasks and at least one independent board member satisfies the requirement for special auditing or accounting competence.

Each year, the board must adopt written rules of procedure regarding its own work. This normally takes place at the initial (constituent) board meeting which is held after the shareholders' meeting at which the board is elected.

If the board delegates certain responsibilities to particular board members, the rules of procedure must state the work allocation as between the members. This may, for example, involve a particular member being responsible for monitoring a certain operation or for undertaking special controls or preparatory measures. Further, if the board establishes special committees to prepare its decisions on specific issues, the Corporate Governance Code stipulates that the rules of procedure must specify the duties and decision-making powers that the board has delegated to these committees and how the committees are to report to the board.

Pursuant to the Companies Act, the employee representatives on the board of directors are equated with other board members, unless otherwise stated in the Board Representation (Private Employees) Act or the Companies Act. Thus, as a general rule, the employee representatives on the board have the same rights, obligations and responsibilities as other board members.

b) The Chairman of the Board

The task of the chairman is to preside over the work of the board and to ensure that the board performs the duties as prescribed in the Companies Act and other legislation.

Under the Corporate Governance Code, the chairman is required to ensure that the work of the board is conducted efficiently and that the board fulfils its obligations. In particular, the chairman has to:

- organise and lead the work of the board, creating the best possible conditions for the board's activities;
- ensure that new board members receive the necessary introductory training, as well as any other training that the chairman and member agree is appropriate;
- ensure that the board regularly updates and develops its knowledge of the company and its operations;
- be responsible for contacts with the shareholders regarding ownership issues and communicate shareholders' views to the board;
- ensure that the board receives sufficient information and documentation to enable it to conduct its work;
- in consultation with the CEO, draw up proposed agendas for board meetings;
  verify that the board's decisions are implemented; and
- ensure that the work of the board is evaluated annually.

If the chairman is an employee of the company or has duties assigned by the company in addition to his or her responsibilities as chairman, the division of work and responsibilities between the chairman and the CEO is to be clearly stated in the board's rules of procedure and its instructions to the CEO.

c) The CEO

The CEO is responsible for the day-to-day management of the company's affairs. According to the Companies Act, the day-to-day management of the company includes all measures that, taking into consideration the scope and nature of the company's business, are not of an unusual nature or major significance. For example, this may include agreements with customers and suppliers, employment agreements, etc. Any agreements which appear to be uncommon or of major significance for the company, when viewed in light of their content, long-term nature, or the values at stake, do not fall within the scope of day-to-day management. The board must, through instructions, state the allocation of work between the board and the CEO.

The CEO is responsible for the operation of the company and the execution of the board's decisions. Furthermore, he or she must take the measures required to ensure that the company's accounts are maintained in accordance with the law and that the management of funds is conducted in a satisfactory manner. The CEO may also take measures that fall outside day-to-day management if the board's decision cannot be awaited without material detriment to the company's operations. In such case, the board must be notified of the measure as soon as possible.

The CEO is subordinate to the board of directors. The board may instruct the CEO on how day-to-day management issues are to be handled or decided. Within the framework defined by the Companies Act and the company's articles of association, the CEO is obliged to follow instructions given by the board. The board itself may also decide on matters that are part of day-to-day management.

The CEO may be a member of the board but not its chairman.[8] Irrespective of whether the CEO is a member of the board, he or she has the right to attend and speak at board meetings provided that the board does not decide otherwise in a particular circumstance.

d) The Company's Representatives

The duty to represent the company externally falls primarily on the board. The Companies Act provides that 'the board of directors represents the company and signs its name'. The CEO may also represent the company and sign its name, but only within the scope of the day-to-day management.

The board may also appoint a board member, the CEO, or another person to represent the company and sign its name (special company signatory). A special

---

[8] In 60% of the 230 listed Swedish companies the CEO is not a member of the board.

company signatory has no independent right of decision-making or any right to exercise managerial functions in the company.

If the board of directors or a special company signatory has performed a legal act on behalf of the company and thereby acted in violation of the provisions of the Companies Act regarding the authority of the company's organs, such legal act is not enforceable against the company. This is also the case if a CEO, when performing a legal act, exceeds his day-to-day management authority and the company demonstrates that the other party realised or should have realised that the authority had been exceeded.

Nor is a legal act enforceable against the company if the board of directors, the CEO or an individual company signatory has exceeded their authority and the company demonstrates that the other party realised or should have realised that the authority was exceeded. However, this does not apply if the board or the CEO has violated a provision regarding the company's objects or other provisions in the articles of association or issued by another company organ. If, for example, the articles of association state that the board may not purchase or sell real property without the approval of a shareholders' meeting, the company will nevertheless be bound by a property transaction carried out by the board without the requisite approval from a shareholders' meeting.

e) Company Secretary

The company secretary is not a position which is recognised in the Companies Act or in the Corporate Governance Code. The various functions of a company secretary would instead be carried out by the board, individual board members, the CEO or another member of the executive management, or any other individual so appointed, pursuant to delegation by the board of directors, if required. As mentioned under (d) above, the day-to-day management of the company, and the entry into agreements within the scope thereof falls within the responsibility and competence of the CEO. Thus, in such a case no further delegation from the board of directors would be required.

f) Auditor

Certain small private companies may decide not to have an auditor. Such deviation must be stated in the articles of association in order to be effective. All other companies must have at least one auditor. While it is possible to state in the articles of association that an external party shall be entitled to appoint one or more auditors, at least one auditor must be appointed by the shareholders' meeting.

The primary task of the auditor is to examine the company's annual report and accounting practices as well as the management of the board of directors and the CEO. In the case of a parent company, the auditor will also examine the consolidated accounts.

The auditor is appointed by, and is obliged to report to, the shareholders' meeting. The work of the auditor must not be influenced by the board of directors or the executive management. The auditor will submit an auditor's report to the shareholders' meeting following each financial year. Part of the auditor's mandate is to recommend whether or not the annual shareholders' meeting should adopt the balance sheet and the profit and loss account and whether the company's results should be appropriated in accordance with the board's proposal.

The auditor constitutes an important part of the shareholders' monitoring of the board and the management of the company. However, the auditor also plays an important role in safeguarding the interests of other stakeholders, primarily creditors.

In addition to the statutory auditor, a minority representing 10% of all shares in a company or one-third of the shares represented at the shareholders' meeting may submit a request to the County Administrative Board (*länsstyrelsen*) to appoint a minority auditor who will participate in the audit together with the other auditor(s).

2.2. Organisation/Internal Functioning

2.2.1. Composition

a) Number of Board Members

The board of directors of a public company must comprise at least three members. Legal persons may not be board members.

The board may also include employee representatives, either voluntarily through a resolution by the shareholders' meeting or pursuant to mandatory provisions contained in the Board Representation (Private Employees) Act.[9]

Among the 230 listed companies the average number of board members (excluding employee representatives) is 6.6 members. Dividing the companies into different categories according to size shows that there is a positive correlation between size and the number of board members (Table 2). Among the 48 Large Cap companies, representing 90.1% of the total market value, the average number of board members (excluding employee representatives) is 8.3 members.

Table 2: Average number of board members in listed companies (June 2012)

List	Percentage of total market cap	Average number of board members
Small Cap	1.8	5.7
Mid Cap	8.1	6.6
Large Cap	90.1	8.3

Source: SIS

---

[9] See sec. 3.2.1. below.

Alternate members may be appointed for board members. An alternate member takes the place of an ordinary member when the latter resigns, is removed, dies or loses his competence to be a board member. An alternate member also takes the place of an ordinary member when the latter is unable to participate in the work of the board. The board's rules of procedure will govern the extent to which the alternate member is to participate in the work of the board.

b) Chairman of the Board

The Companies Act prescribes that the board is to elect a chairman from among its members. However, nothing prevents the shareholders' meeting, in its capacity as the company's highest decision-making body, from appointing the chairman of the board. According to the Corporate Governance Code, the chairman is to be elected by the shareholders' meeting.

c) Restrictions with Respect to Similar Positions in Other Companies

There are no explicit restrictions in the Companies Act or the Corporate Governance Code with respect to board members holding similar positions in other companies. This is a matter which is left to the shareholders to consider when electing members of the board. Hence, for public companies the Companies Act states that before board elections are held the chairman of the shareholders' meeting must inform the meeting about the appointments in other companies held by the person to whom the election relates.

In the 230 listed companies there are at present a total of 1,511 board positions held by 1,155 individuals. In other words, almost 25% of the positions are held by individuals who are members of two or more boards. There are 15 individuals holding board positions in five or more listed companies. Together these 'board professionals' hold 83 board positions.

d) Qualification Requirements for Board Members

With the exception of the general principles for board composition in the Corporate Governance Code (see under (e) below) and certain formal requirements contained in the Companies Act—for example that a legal person, child, undischarged bankrupt or a person who is subject to an injunction against trading, etc. may not be a board member, and that at least half of the board members must be resident in the European Economic Area (unless otherwise approved by the Companies Registration Office (*Bolagsverket*))—there are no explicit rules in the Companies Act or in the Corporate Governance Code governing the composition of the board or the qualifications to be possessed by its members.[10] The election of board members has been left to the discretion of the shareholders' meeting. However, specific rules apply to certain types of companies. As regards credit institutions, ie. banks and financing companies, a board member (including alternate board members) and the CEO (including deputy CEO) must possess sufficient insight and experience to participate in the management of a credit institution and otherwise be suitable to perform such duties. In many cases, the management assessment procedure is a mere formality. However, quite recently a former board member of the financial holding company HQ AB (the former parent company of the troubled HQ Bank AB which was put into liquidation shortly after its licences to engage in banking business and fund management were revoked in August 2010) was not approved by the Swedish Financial Supervisory Authority to take a seat on the board of a Swedish fund management company.

As regards state-owned companies, the Swedish government has stated that each nomination to the board must be based on the competence required on the board of that company. The board members must possess industrial expertise or other knowledge which is directly relevant for the company in question. A member must have a high level of general competence in relation to current business activities, business development sector knowledge, financial issues or other relevant areas as well as a high degree of integrity and he or she must have the ability to understand and act in the best interests of the company. Except for the competence requirements, it is stated that each board must achieve a balance as regards the background, sphere of competence and experience of its members. The aim is that, in order to achieve a balanced gender distribution, the proportion of each sex shall be at least 40%.

e) Overall Principles for Composition

According to the Corporate Governance Code, the board must have a size and composition that enables it to manage the company's affairs efficiently and with integrity. The composition must be appropriate to the company's operations, phase of development and other relevant circumstances.

According to the Code, the board members elected by the shareholders' meeting are collectively to exhibit diversity and breadth of qualifications, experience and background.

During the last couple of years gender distribution on the board has been a recurring theme in public debate. Legislative proposals have been put forward but so far the Government has resisted any form of legislative intervention and left

---

[10] However, qualification requirements apply to the audit committee and the remuneration committee, see further sec. 2.1(a) above and sec. 3.1.5(b) below.

the matter to the business sector to regulate internally.[11] According to the Corporate Governance Code, companies are to 'strive for equal gender distribution on the board'. Statistics show, however, that there is still a long way to go. Currently, 22% of the 1,155 board members in listed companies are women. Together, women hold 24% of the 1,511 board positions.

The average age of board members in the listed companies is 56 years with little differences between companies of different size. Five per cent of the board members are 70 years old or more.

The composition of the boards also reflects to some extent the general internationalisation of business and the increased foreign ownership of Swedish listed shares; 197 of the 1,511 board positions are held by foreigners. In 17 companies half or more of the board members are foreigners.

f) Evaluation of Board Performance

The Companies Act does not contain any provisions concerning evaluation of the board's performance. Under the Corporate Governance Code, however, the board of directors and the CEO will be regularly and systematically evaluated. The board is to evaluate its work annually, using a systematic and structured process, with the aim of developing its working methods and efficiency. The results of the evaluation will be made available to the nomination committee, if relevant.

At present, there are few guidelines governing how the evaluation will be performed. However, the preferred course of action is that the board participates in the evaluation even if it is performed by an external party since one of the main purposes of the evaluation is to provide a basis for the development of the board's work. The chairman bears the ultimate responsibility for the evaluation of the board and the nomination committee is informed of the results.

2.2.2. Decision-making

The Companies Act does not require a certain minimum number of board meetings be held each year. The chairman of the board must ensure that meetings are held as required. The rules of procedure are to state how often meetings are to be held. The board members and the CEO may, however, submit a request that a board meeting be convened at any time. If, following such a request, the chairman, intentionally or negligently fails to convene a meeting he or she may be subject to imprisonment or fines.

The CEO is entitled to be present and speak at board meetings. In fact, it is usually he or she who is best acquainted with the company's business.

---

[11] This would of course change in the event of an EU directive on gender balance, as proposed by the Commission in November 2012, being adopted.

According to the Companies Act, the board is quorate if more than one half of the total number of board members, including employee representatives, or such higher number as prescribed in the articles of association, are present.

If any board member has a conflict of interest with respect to any issue or issues to be considered at the meeting, such member is deemed to be absent. If this results in the meeting not being quorate with respect to the issue or issues on which the member has a conflict of interest, an alternate member who does not have a conflict of interest can be required to attend the meeting instead.

In order for board members to make decisions on different issues, they must have received satisfactory information as a basis for the decision. Such information may include written material as well as an oral presentation. The information must be easy to understand and informative. Everything that is of importance for consideration of the matter must be stated in the material. The chairman bears the ultimate responsibility for ensuring that this is the case.

Board resolutions are adopted by a simple majority. Thus, in a board comprising six members, if all members are present a decision must be supported by four members. If not all members are present, at least one-third of the entire number of board members must support the resolution in order for the resolution to be valid. In the event of a tied vote, the chairman has a casting vote. The articles of association may prescribe either stricter or more lenient majority requirements than stated in the Companies Act.

Is it possible for a board member to abstain from voting? The answer is probably no. As a consequence of the fiduciary position held by board members, a board member is deemed obliged to vote on all issues—except in the case of a conflict of interests—and there is no scope for a member to abstain from voting.

Under the Corporate Governance Code, all listed companies must have a nomination committee, a remuneration committee and an audit committee.[12] The nomination committee differs from the remuneration committee and the audit committee in that, unlike in many other countries, it is not a board committee. The shareholders' meeting will either appoint members of the nomination committee or specify how they are to be appointed.

Delegation of work from the board of directors, or the establishment of board committees to prepare its decisions on certain issues, does not relieve the board from the ultimate responsibility for the company's organisation and management or the responsibility to ensure satisfactory control of the company's accounting, funds management and finances. The responsibility lies with the board, which must demonstrate care when assigning a task to another party and must regularly monitor that the party which has assumed certain duties is indeed carrying them

---

[12] See further sec. 3.1.1(a) as regards the nomination committee, sec. 3.1.5(b) as regards the remuneration committee and sec. 2.1(a) as regards the audit committee.

out. Accordingly, most board committees of Swedish companies are given mainly preparatory tasks, leaving the important decisions to the board itself.

2.2.3. Independent Directors

There are no provisions in the Companies Act concerning independent directors, with the exception that in a public company the CEO may not be chairman of the board.[13]

However, the independence concept plays an important role in the Corporate Governance Code, under which the majority of the directors elected by the shareholders' meeting are to be independent of the company and its executive management. Employee representatives would generally not be considered as independent from the company.[14] However, since the independence requirement only applies to directors elected by the shareholders' meeting, employee representatives are excluded.

A director's independence is to be determined by a general assessment of all factors that may give cause to question the individual's independence of the company or its executive management. Factors that should be considered include:

- whether the individual is the CEO or has been the CEO of the company or a closely related company within the last five years;
- whether the individual is employed or has been employed by the company or a closely related company within the last three years;
- whether the individual receives a not insignificant amount of remuneration for advice or other services beyond the remit of the board position from the company, a closely related company or a person in the executive management of the company;
- whether the individual has or has within the last year had a significant business relationship or other significant financial dealings with the company or a closely related company as a client, supplier or partner, either individually or as a member of the executive management, a member of the board or a major shareholder in a company with such a business relationship with the company;
- whether the individual is or has within the last three years been a partner at, or has as an employee participated in an audit of the company conducted by, the company's or a closely related company's current or then auditor;

---

[13] See further sec. 2.1(c) above.

[14] Where applicable, employee representatives are appointed by the labour union(s), see further sec. 3.2.1. Under section 9 of the Board Representation (Private Employees) Act, an employee representative ought to be appointed from among the employees of the relevant company or, if such company is a parent company, from among the employees of the group companies.

- whether the individual is a member of the executive management of another company where a member of the board of that company is a member of the executive management of the company; or
- whether the individual has a close family relationship with a person in the executive management or with another person named in the points above if that person's direct or indirect business with the company is of such magnitude or significance as to justify the opinion that the board member is not to be regarded as independent.

Furthermore, at least two of the members of the board who are independent of the company and its executive management must also be independent in relation to the company's major shareholders (>10% of the shares or votes in the company). Hence, in most companies it is possible for major shareholders of Swedish companies to appoint a majority of members with whom they have close ties. This is in line with the positive view of active and responsible ownership expressed in the preparatory works relating to the Companies Act.

Accordingly, two types of independence may be distinguished in the Corporate Governance Code: Independence in relation to the company and its executive management, and independence in relation to the company's major shareholders.

2.3. Information Streams

According to the Companies Act, the board must regularly assess the company's financial situation. This requires that the board keeps itself informed of the company's financial position. Thus, the board must establish a reporting system within the company including instructions as to when and how information is to be compiled. In order for the board to obtain adequate information, the reporting must contain information on the company's order stock, financing situation, liquidity and other economic circumstances, such as particular risks. The reporting system should be linked to board routines whereby the board convenes in connection with the presentation of reports in order to consider the contents thereof, discuss the company's development and decide upon measures required as a consequence of the reports. Normally, the reporting is made by the CEO, who has better direct access to information regarding the company as a consequence of his or her involvement in the day-to-day management. Thus, in practice the board's access to information is almost exclusively indirect as the information flow is filtered by the CEO. The potential problems from a corporate governance perspective are apparent, in particular considering the fact that board members may have board and/or other management positions in several other companies.[15]

Nevertheless, it is the board's responsibility to obtain all information required and state, in relation to the CEO, what is to be reported, when this is to take place and the form in which information is to be provided. The CEO is obliged to provide the board with the required information.[16] The board of directors may not reach a decision on a matter if it has not been provided with satisfactory information. Although the chairman of the board has an overall responsibility in this regard, each of the board members has a responsibility to ensure that the information provided is sufficient. Failure to comply with this may result in criminal liability.

3. Accountability

3.1. Board and Shareholders

3.1.1. Appointment and Dismissal of Board Members and CEO

a) Board Members

The principal rule of the Companies Act is that the board of directors is appointed by the shareholders' meeting. In a public company, more than half of the board members must be appointed by the shareholders' meeting. The articles of association may provide that one or more board members shall be appointed in some other manner but that is virtually never the case among listed companies.

Board members are elected by 'plurality vote', ie. the person who has received the largest number of votes is elected. There is no requirement that the winner gain an absolute majority of votes. If two candidates receive the same number of votes, the election is determined by the drawing of lots. The meeting has, however, the possibility before the election to decide that in the event of a tie a new vote will be carried out instead of the drawing of lots.

While the Companies Act explicitly regulates the election of board members it is silent on the process of nominating the candidates for board positions. On the

---

[15] As stated in sec. 2.2.1(a) there are no explicit restrictions as to board members holding similar positions in other companies.

[16] It has been discussed whether the CEO, in case of a board member's conflict of interest, may refuse to provide such board member with certain information. On the one hand, the company's interest must be protected from a disloyal board member's misuse of information. On the other hand, the board member has been appointed by the shareholders and must receive the information required in order to perform his or her obligations under mandatory law. If the CEO considers that a certain board member should be denied access to certain information, he may request the board in its entirety to decide on the matter.

other hand this is probably the most well developed and important area in the Corporate Governance Code.

In general terms the Code states that the shareholders' meeting's decisions on election and remuneration of the board of directors (and auditor) are to be prepared in a structured, clearly stated process governed by the shareholders that provides conditions for well-informed decision-making. Hence, listed companies are to have a nomination committee, the task of which is to propose candidates for the post of chairman and other members of the board, as well as fees and other remuneration to each member of the board. The nomination committee is also required to make proposals on the election and remuneration of the statutory auditor.

There are presently nomination committees in 224 of the 230 listed companies. The nomination committee must consist of at least three members, one of whom is to be appointed committee chairman. The majority of the members of the nomination committee are to be independent of the company and its executive management. Neither the CEO nor other members of the executive management may be members of the nomination committee. Typically, representatives of the four largest shareholders in the company are appointed as members of the committee. However, at least one member of the committee must be independent of the company's largest shareholder or group of shareholders that act in concert in the governance of the company.

Members of the board of directors may be members of the nomination committee but may not constitute a majority thereof. Typically only one (the chairman of the board) is a member of the nomination committee. Neither the chairman of the board nor any other member of the board may be the chairman of the nomination committee.

The nomination committee is required to submit a proposal to the annual shareholders' meeting regarding the size of the board and nominates a corresponding number of candidates for election for a one-year term. Any shareholder may (at or prior to the meeting) propose additional candidates for consideration or suggest an alternative board size, but this is rare in practice. Where the board size and the number of candidates are identical, a single vote in favour is sufficient to elect a candidate to the board. Technically each director is elected individually, although it may appear to some observers as if the proposal is a bundled resolution.

A board member's term of office is one year, unless otherwise prescribed in the articles of association. The term applies from the date that the member is elected to the board until the end of the first annual shareholders' meeting which is held after the meeting at which the member was appointed.

A board member is always entitled to resign early. He or she does so by giving notice of resignation to the board of directors. No reason needs to be stated for the resignation.

A board member may also be removed from his or her appointment at any time by the party that appointed the board member. This is due to the fact that an appointment as board member is an appointment based on trust. If the shareholders no longer have confidence in one or more board members, an extraordinary shareholders' meeting can be held at any time in order to resolve on termination of the appointment of the member concerned. The dismissal can take place without cause and the dismissed member is not entitled to pursue any claim for compensation.

If a board member resigns early or is removed and there is no alternate member who can take his or her place, the other board members must convene an extraordinary shareholders' meeting for the appointment of a new member. Where the board member is to be elected by the shareholders' meeting, the election may, however, be deferred until the next annual shareholders' meeting, provided the board of directors is quorate with the remaining members and alternate members.

b) The CEO

The Companies Act does not state any specific term of office for the CEO. He or she is normally appointed as an employee until further notice.

Among the large listed companies, the average tenure of an executive director is less than four years (OECD). The 'turnover rate' for CEOs in listed companies rose from 8% in 1994 to 29% in 2005. It has since been declining. Approximately 17% (39 companies) of the present 230 listed companies appointed a new CEO during the period June 2011–May 2012.

3.1.2. Division of Powers Between the Board and the Shareholders

The board holds a fiduciary position in relation to the company. Hence, the board is obliged to demonstrate care regarding the company and to act in the company's interests. The board is also obliged to comply with the provisions of the Companies Act[17] and the articles of association in relation to individual shareholders, the company's creditors and other third parties. However, as described above,[18] the board of directors has an extensive decision-making authority which is primarily limited by the shareholders' meeting's exclusive decision-making powers on certain matters, for example amendments to the articles of association, election of board members and auditor and adoption of the balance sheet and profit and loss account. However, in its capacity as the company's highest decision-making body, the shareholders' meeting may decide on any company issue which does not expressly fall within the exclusive competence of another corporate body, for example resolutions on the company's organisation and the preparation of guidelines for the administration of the company's affairs. In other

[17] For example, the principal rule of the Companies Act pursuant to which the operations of a limited company are to be conducted in order to generate a profit for distribution to the shareholders.

[18] See sec. 2.2.2.

words, the shareholders' meeting has a sovereign role over the board and the CEO and the board is obliged to follow any specific directives passed by the shareholders' meeting, providing these do not contravene the Companies Act, the Annual Reports Act 1995 (*årsredovisningslagen*) or the company's articles of association. Such directives may also be included in the articles of association.

3.1.3. Special Issues

a) Conflict of Interest

According to the Companies Act, a board member or CEO may not address a question regarding:

1. an agreement between the board member or the CEO and the company;
2. an agreement between the company and a third party, where the board member or the CEO in question has a material interest which may conflict with that of the company; or
3. an agreement between the company and a legal person which the board member or CEO alone or together with a third person may represent.

Point 1 covers, for example, questions regarding the entry into supply contracts or compensation for own work performed. Point 2 covers situations involving an agreement between, for example, a person closely related to the board member (or CEO) and the company. Point 3 entails, for example, that a member of the board of a bank, who is also a member of the board of an industrial company, cannot participate in a decision by the industrial company's board to take up a loan with the bank in question. It is irrelevant whether he or she has had anything to do with the matter in the capacity of member of the board of the bank.

A board member or CEO can also be deemed to have a conflict of interest in situations other than those directly covered by the Companies Act. In such situations involving the 'appearance of propriety', he or she should not participate in the handling of the matter in question.

The purpose of the conflict of interest rules is to protect the company's interests, ie. ultimately the shareholders' interests. Accordingly, such rules may be set aside if all shareholders agree thereto.

b) Related-party Transactions

Except for the conflict of interest rules described above, there are no rules in the Companies Act regarding related-party transactions. Nor are there any such rules in the Corporate Governance Code. This is an area where the Swedish legislator has chosen a general approach and there are no ongoing or forthcoming national legislative reforms in this field.

However, according to the statement 2012:05 by the Swedish Securities Council, in the event that a listed company decides to transfer shares in a subsidiary or a business or other assets to an officer of the company—provided the transfer is not insignificant to the company—a resolution concerning the transfer must be adopted or approved by a shareholders' meeting of the parent company. Before the proposed resolution is presented to the shareholders' meeting, the board of directors must obtain an appraisal opinion from an independent expert and prepare a report regarding the proposed transfer. The appraisal opinion and report must be made available by the company and posted on the company's website prior to the shareholders' meeting that will address the issue. The appraisal opinion and report must also be presented at the shareholders' meeting. The aforementioned will also apply where the company or its subsidiary adopts a resolution to acquire assets from an officer of the company.

c) Corporate Opportunities

There is no explicit prohibition under Swedish law against board members making use of corporate opportunities. Since case law is also very limited, it is difficult to determine the contents of Swedish law in this regard. Nevertheless, arguably, the board's fiduciary duties place restrictions on the board members' flexibility in terms of engaging in competing business activities to the detriment of the company. For example, it could be argued that a board member is prohibited from making use of a business opportunity if, taking into consideration the company's business objects, financial means and legal possibilities as well as the other party's interest, it could be anticipated that the company would make use of the opportunity in question.

d) Inside Information

The Companies Act does not contain any explicit provisions concerning a board member's duty of confidentiality.[19] However, such a duty may be derived from the board's fiduciary duties under which, if required in order to avoid harm to the company, the board may be obliged to take appropriate measures to prevent insider trading and to prevent inadvertent disclosure of sensitive information. If a board member or the CEO causes the company to incur damage as a consequence of sensitive information being disclosed, such board member may be liable in damages.

Further, disclosing inside information may in certain circumstances constitute a criminal act under the Financial Instruments Trading (Market Abuse Penalties) Act 2005 (*lagen om straff för marknadsmissbruk vid handel med finansiella instrument*). However, in many cases it may be legitimate to disclose inside information. For example, disclosures made as a normal part of the performance

---

[19] Although it could be argued that such a duty could be derived from chapter 7 section 34 of the Companies Act, under which a shareholder at a shareholders' meeting may only require the provision of information by the board of directors if such may take place without causing significant harm to the company.

of a service, activities or obligations is exempted from the criminalised area. The question of whether, and to whom, certain information may be disclosed must be resolved on a case-by-case basis.

Under the rules of NASDAQ OMX Stockholm and Nordic Growth Market NGM (and underlying statutory provisions and EU legislation), a listed company is under a general obligation to disclose price sensitive information as soon as possible.

e) Takeover Situations

The role of the board in a takeover situation is derived from its fiduciary duties, according to which it must act in the best interests of the company and all shareholders. In the context of takeovers, this principle is reflected in section II.17 of the Takeover Rules issued by NASDAQ OMX Stockholm and Nordic Growth Market NGM, respectively. Furthermore, under chapter 5, section 1 of the Takeovers Act, the board of directors is only entitled to take measures likely to impair the prerequisites for making or implementing a takeover bid with prior shareholder approval. The board may, however, seek alternative bids without shareholder approval.

Pursuant to section II.20 of the Takeover Rules, the board of a target company is required to express its opinion regarding a takeover bid. However, this does not mean that the board must recommend either acceptance or rejection of the offer. The board may also adopt a neutral attitude towards the offer, in which case it must provide an explanation as to the reasons.

3.1.4. Institutional Investors

As mentioned under 1.1(b), the shareholding of institutional investors has increased during the last few decades and currently accounts for more than 85% of the total shareholding in listed companies. Since the aim for institutional investors is not to engage in the long-term management of a company in which it holds shares, but to generate as much (immediate) profit as possible for its owners, critics claim that institutional investors do not exercise their voting rights and do not act in the long-term interests of the company but, rather, focus on short-term share price increases.

Even though Sweden has had its fair share of corporate scandals that could partly be attributable to passive shareholdings and lack of corporate governance responsibility,[20] Swedish law does not impose any corporate governance obliga-

---

[20] A noteworthy example in this regard is the case concerning the insurance company Skandia, subsequently a subsidiary of Old Mutual plc but at the time listed on the Stockholm Stock Exchange. The case raised several corporate governance issues, for example as regards passive shareholders in the hands of a strong management, the shortage of financial information from the management and the lack of internal controls and resolution procedure. The Skandia

cont. ...

tions on shareholders (institutional or otherwise), thus granting absolute discretion to the shareholders whether to exercise their voting rights. The issue of passive shareholding has been addressed in the Corporate Governance Code, which contains several provisions aimed at creating favourable conditions for active and responsible shareholding. There are no rules comparable to the UK Stewardship Code.

Although common practice among investors, neither the Companies Act nor the Corporate Governance Code impose any obligation for investors to publicly account for their voting policy. Furthermore, Swedish law does not contain any special provisions concerning road shows, etc. The persons involved in a road show must, however, comply with applicable laws on insider dealing,[21] and the rules of the relevant stock exchange regarding selective disclosure of price sensitive information.

3.1.5. Remuneration

Directors and executive remuneration is addressed both in the Companies Act and the Corporate Governance Code. The provisions of the Code have been significantly expanded with new rules in the February 2010 version. Generally, the Code states that 'remuneration and other terms of employment of members of the board and the executive management are to be designed with the aim of ensuring that the company has access to the competence required at a cost appropriate to the company, and so that they have the intended effects for the company's operations'.

a) Remuneration of the Board

Remuneration of the board in a Swedish limited liability company is, and has always been, a matter for the shareholders' meeting to decide upon. Hence, on the basis of the proposal from the nomination committee, it is for the shareholders' meeting to decide on fees and other compensation in respect of the board duties of each of the board members. It is not permissible for the meeting to determine a lump sum which the board can allocate between its members as it sees fit.

b) Remuneration of the CEO and Executive Management

Ten years ago, executive remuneration was largely the province of the chairman and the CEO, with little or no involvement by institutional investors (controlling investors being the exception as they are able to provide input on executive remuneration through their membership on the board). Since 2006, Swedish com-

---

case highlighted the need for a new corporate governance regulation, which led to the adoption of the Swedish Corporate Governance Code.

[21] See further sec. 3.1.3.4.

panies are required to include a binding resolution on the remuneration policy on the agenda of the annual shareholders' meeting. In addition, all equity issuances that would dilute the percentage holding of existing shareholders—such as share schemes for executives and other employees—must be presented to the shareholders' meeting and garner the support of 90% of the votes casted as well as the share capital present to be approved. Today, owing to these approval provisions and the increasing use of share-based incentive schemes (particularly at large listed companies), it is common for Swedish companies to consult their shareholders on executive remuneration matters in advance of shareholders' meetings.

While Swedish boards have always decided the CEO's remuneration package, their involvement in setting overall remuneration policy in listed companies has expanded in recent years. This trend is driven by the increasing use of equity-based incentive schemes, which must be presented to shareholders for approval.

Pursuant to the Code the board is required to establish a *remuneration committee*, the main tasks of which include to:

- prepare the board's decisions on issues concerning principles for remuneration as well as the remuneration and other terms of employment for the executive management;
- monitor and evaluate programmes or schemes governing variable remuneration, both ongoing and those that have ended during the year, for the executive management; and
- monitor and evaluate the application of the guidelines for remuneration that the shareholders' meeting is to establish, as well as the current remuneration structures and levels in the company.

The chairman of the board may chair the remuneration committee. The other shareholders' meeting-elected members of the committee must be independent of the company and its executive management. The members of the committee must possess the appropriate level of knowledge and experience of executive remuneration issues. If the board considers it is more appropriate, the entire board may perform the remuneration committee's tasks provided of course no board member who is also a member of the executive management participates in this work.

If the remuneration committee or the board uses the services of an external consultant, the committee must ensure that there is no conflict of interest regarding other assignments which this consultant may have for the company or its executive management.

Variable remuneration is to be linked to predetermined and measurable performance criteria aimed at promoting the company's long-term value creation. Variable remuneration paid in cash is to be subject to predetermined limits regarding the total outcome.

When designing systems for variable remuneration of the executive management that is to be paid in cash, the board must consider imposing restrictions:

- which make payment of a certain proportion of the remuneration conditional on whether the performance on which compensation is based proves to be sustainable over time; and

– which allow the company to reclaim components of remuneration that have been paid on the basis of information which subsequently proves to be manifestly misstated.

The shareholders' meeting will decide on all share and share-price related incentive schemes for the executive management. The decision of the shareholders' meeting will include all the principal conditions of the scheme. Background material and documentation pertaining to the proposed scheme must be made available to shareholders in due time prior to the shareholders' meeting. The material has to be clear and simple enough to allow shareholders to form an opinion on the reasons for the scheme, the principal conditions of the scheme and any dilution of the share capital that may result from it, as well as the total cost to the company of different conceivable outcomes.

Share-related and share-price-related incentive schemes are to be designed with the aim of achieving increased alignment between the interests of the participating individual and the company's shareholders. Schemes that involve acquisition of shares should be designed so that a personal holding of shares in the company is promoted. The vesting period or the period from the commencement of an agreement to the date for acquisition of shares must be no less than three years.

Non-executive members of the board are prohibited from participating in schemes designed for the executive management or other employees. The remuneration of non-executive board members must not include share options.

Fixed salary during a period of notice and severance pay must not on aggregate exceed an amount equivalent to the individual's fixed salary for two years.

3.2. Board and Stakeholders

The Swedish Corporate Governance Code is shareholder-oriented, almost exclusively concerned with the relationship between the shareholders and the company's management and thus excludes the relationship between the company and other stakeholders. Most of the regulation concerning the relationship between the board and other stakeholders can be found in the Companies Act, which may be considered as a compromise aimed at resolving conflicts of interests between different stakeholders, the fundamental ones being management versus shareholders, majority versus minority and shareholders versus creditors.

3.2.1. Board and Employees

Employment representation in the board of directors is governed by the Board Representation (Private Employees) Act, under which the employees' right to be represented in the board of directors depends on (i) the number of employees of the company in question (or in case the company is the ultimate parent of a group, the number of employees in the whole group) and (ii) whether the company is bound by a collective agreement.

If the company, or the group as applicable, has more than 25 employees, two employee representatives may be appointed and, if the company has more than 1,000 employees and is engaged in different lines of businesses, three representatives may be appointed.

The employee representatives are appointed by the trade union to which the company is bound by a collective bargaining agreement. Hence, if the company is not bound by a collective agreement, employee representatives need not be appointed. The number of employee representatives in a board may not exceed the number of other board members.

3.2.2. Board and Creditors

The minimum share capital requirement for private companies was recently decreased from SEK 100,000 to SEK 50,000, whilst the SEK 500,000 requirement for public companies remains unaltered.

The Companies Act contains a quite comprehensive set of provisions aiming to protect a company's creditors. Most of the creditor protection rules concern actions relating to the company's capital, mainly the contributing of capital in connection with the formation and subsequent maintenance of the share capital in the form of, for example, restrictions on value transfers (for example dividends) and loans to shareholders or management made not for purely commercial reasons. In addition, the objects of the company's business, as stated in its articles of association, and the purpose to generate profit (which may only be derogated from through provisions in the articles of association) act as a restraint on the company's business operations.

In relation to the company's creditors, the board of directors is responsible for supervising and managing the company's compliance with applicable creditor protection provisions. If a board member has, intentionally or through negligence, been involved in an action on behalf of the company (for example, in the decision-making procedure) in breach of any rule governing the protection of creditors, he or she may be liable in damages towards a creditor.

3.2.3. Board and Other Stakeholders

The Companies Act does not, in principle, contain any provisions concerning a company's business operations and its business decisions (except for the obligation to comply with the purpose to generate profit and the provisions of the articles of association). There are no specific provisions on corporate social responsibility in Sweden and no known Swedish legislative initiatives are under way. Nevertheless, specific legislation in different segments together form a comprehensive network for the protection of other stakeholders, for example employment law, work environmental law, environmental law, competition law, marketing law, tax law, etc, which a company—supervised and managed by the board of directors—must comply with.

3.3. Changing Roles in Financial Distress/Wrongful Trading

The board must regularly assess the company's financial situation. Accordingly, the board has to continually keep itself up to date with the company's financial situation. In times of financial distress, the board is required to play a more active role in order to avoid personal liability. If there is reason to believe that the company's shareholders' equity is less than half of the registered share capital or if it is shown that the company lacks distrainable assets, this triggers a chain of actions that must be taken by the board. Firstly, the board has to immediately prepare and cause the auditor to examine a balance sheet for liquidation purposes. Special rules apply with respect to the preparation of the aforementioned balance sheet, including, among other things, extraordinary methods for valuation of assets and liabilities. If the balance sheet shows that the company's shareholders' equity is less than one-half of the registered share capital, the board is required to convene a shareholders' meeting as soon as possible which shall consider whether the company should go into liquidation. If the meeting does not resolve to liquidate the company, the company must cure the impaired balance sheet within eight months. If, at the end of the eight month period, the shareholders' equity does not equal the registered share capital and a second shareholders' meeting has not resolved that the company shall be liquidated, the board must petition the court for a liquidation order.

Failure to comply with the aforementioned obligations may result in personal liability for the members of the board in respect of obligations incurred by the company.

In addition, a board member may also be personally liable if he or she, with intent or gross negligence, fails to pay the company's taxes in due time or to withhold such taxes.

4. Enforcement

4.1. Courts

4.1.1. Personal Liability Claims

The degree of litigiousness in Sweden is generally low. This also applies to personal liability claims against members of the board of directors.

The principal rule is that the person claiming to have suffered damage has the burden of proof in personal liability cases, both as regards the objective conditions (the actual damage sustained, causality between the act and the damage, etc.) and the subjective conditions (negligence, intent, etc., as applicable).

a) Liability in Damages

A board member or CEO must perform his or her duties with the care and good faith required of an advisor or provider of services in general. If a board member or the CEO disregards his duties and intentionally or negligently causes the *company* damage, he or she may be liable to compensate the damage.

The liability in damages is individual. It may, for example, result in one board member being liable but not another. In this context, various factors may also play a role in the assessment of liability. For example, a member who has been elected as an expert on certain issues assumes a stricter form of liability than his or her board colleagues. Consideration must also be given to the allocation of work that has taken place between the members of the board. The board's rules of procedure and the instructions that clarify the allocation of work between the board and the CEO may be of significance in the liability assessment.

Board members and the CEO are also liable to third parties that may be affected by their activities in the company. Such persons may be *individual shareholders, creditors, employees* or *other third parties.* However, the liability to such persons is not as strict as the liability to the company and is incurred only if the Companies Act, the Annual Accounts Act, certain other regulations or the company's articles of association have been breached, either intentionally or through negligence. There may be liability for damages if, for example, a creditor has provided credit or failed to secure his claim as a consequence of an incorrect annual report. A shareholder may also be entitled to damages if he or she has missed out on the opportunity to participate in a new issue of shares as a consequence of the board's failure to give them due notice thereof.

b) Discharge from Liability

At the annual shareholders' meeting, a resolution must be adopted whether to grant the members of the board and the CEO discharge from liability vis-à-vis the company. The issue of discharge from liability relates to each person individually. The meeting can thus grant discharge from liability to certain persons and refuse to grant it to others.

The consequences of a person being granted discharge from liability are that the company approves his or her management and refrains from bringing any claims in damages against him or her. If the annual shareholders' meeting has decided on discharge from liability for the board and the CEO then, as a general rule, this precludes an action in damages. A minority shareholder may, however, prevent the adoption of a resolution regarding discharge from liability at the annual shareholders' meeting. If shareholders holding at least 10% of the shares in the company vote against a proposal regarding discharge from liability, an action in damages may nevertheless be brought.

A refusal to grant discharge from liability does not necessarily have to result in an action in damages; the refusal itself may also be an expression of the wishes of the majority at the meeting to 'reprimand' the outgoing board without raising any financial claims.

Nor does a resolution regarding discharge from liability entirely rule out an action in damages. Even if the shareholders' meeting has decided to grant discharge from liability, an action in damages may be brought if, in the annual report or the auditor's report or otherwise, true and complete information has not been provided to the shareholders' meeting regarding important matters with respect to the decision or measure on which the action is based. In other words, in order for the person affected by the resolution regarding discharge from liability to be absolved from liability in damages to the company, the shareholders' meeting must have been correctly and fully informed in all respects regarding the incorrect decision or the incorrect measure which may form the basis for an action in damages. Thus, a resolution regarding discharge from liability is irrelevant if the shareholders' meeting based a decision on incorrect and incomplete information. Finally, an action in damages as a result of criminal behaviour may always be brought, irrespective of whether or not discharge from liability has been granted.

c) Actions in Damages

An action against a board member or CEO regarding damages to the company may be brought only if the shareholders' meeting decides that such an action shall be brought, or has at least resolved that discharge from liability shall not be granted. If an action in damages becomes relevant despite the fact that discharge from liability has been granted, the issue need not be addressed again at the shareholders' meeting. If the action relates to damages as a consequence of a criminal act, the board of the company may at all times bring proceedings, even if the issue has not been addressed by the shareholders' meeting.

A shareholder may also bring an action in damages on his own behalf. According to the Companies Act, shareholders with at least one-tenth of all shares in the company may bring an action in their own name regarding damage to the company (derivative action). An action brought by a minority shareholder in his own name is also conditional on the issue of damages having been addressed at the relevant shareholders' meeting.

4.1.2. Nullification of Resolutions

If a board resolution has not been adopted in the correct manner or if it exceeds the board's authority, the resolution is per se not valid. There is no possibility to formally challenge board decisions in court as there is with resolutions adopted by the shareholders' meeting.

4.1.3. Disqualification of Board Members

As mentioned under section 2.2.1(d) above, with the exception of general principles for board composition in the Corporate Governance Code, some limited formal requirements in the Companies Act and special rules applicable to certain types of companies, including credit institutions and state-owned companies, there are no provisions governing the qualifications of board members.[22] The appointment and dismissal of board members has been left to the discretion of the shareholders, and the public authorities have, as a general rule, no power to disqualify a board member. However, if a board member does not satisfy the formal requirements of the Act, such board member shall be removed from the board and de-registered from the Companies Register. This would apply only in exceptional circumstances, for example if a board member is declared bankrupt or becomes subject to an injunction against trading. An injunction against trading may be issued, for example, against a person (including a board member) who has grossly neglected his obligations in the conduct of business and thereby committed a criminal act which is not insignificant or failed to pay taxes.

In addition, certain types of companies, for example securities companies and credit institutions, are subject to special legislation entailing, among other things, that the board members and CEO must possess sufficient insight and experience. If this requirement is not satisfied, the Financial Supervisory Authority (*Finans-inspektionen*) may revoke the company's authorisation.

4.2. Regulators

The Swedish Financial Supervisory Authority has the power to intervene in respect of issues relating to the governance of financial institutions. Outside the area of firms under the supervision of the FSA, the FSA has no enforcement powers directly relating to the corporate governance of listed companies. The Companies Registration Office (*Bolagsverket*) is assigned with the task of ensuring that corporate resolutions passed and filed for registration with the Registration Office comply with the requirements of the Companies Act, other applicable statutory requirements and the articles of association of the company in question.

---

[22] However, qualification requirements apply to the audit committee and the remuneration committee, see further sec. 2.1(a) and sec. 3.1.5(b), respectively.

4.3. Self-Regulation

4.3.1. The Swedish Corporate Governance Code

As mentioned above, the Swedish Corporate Governance Code was introduced in 2005 and last revised effective (with a few exceptions) as from 1 February 2010. The Code is based on the comply-or-explain principle. Thus, companies obliged to apply the Code are not required to comply with every rule of the Code. However, companies must provide an account of their application of the Code in an annual corporate governance report, which must include, where applicable, the reasons for any deviations from the Code and what solutions have been selected in their place.

The Code applies to all Swedish companies with shares traded on a regulated market in Sweden. At present, these markets are the main markets of NASDAQ OMX Stockholm and Nordic Growth Market NGM (currently 230 companies).

4.3.2. Does the Comply-or-explain System Produce Effective Results?

The Corporate Governance Code has received general acceptance on the Swedish market and the experiences have so far been positive. The listed companies obliged to apply the Code generally do so and demonstrate an ambitious attitude towards complying with it. The majority of companies report no or only minor deviations from the Code. In fact, the general reluctance to deviate from the Code and the prospects of having to explain such a deviation, may well produce ineffective results in cases where there really is valid cause for a deviation.

5. The Dynamics of Change

No major reforms relating to corporate governance are expected in Swedish company law in the foreseeable future. Most of the ongoing or future reform movements are EU driven, including the April 2011 Commission Green Paper on Corporate Governance and the ensuing 2012 Action Plan on European company law and corporate governance, and are thus not specific to Swedish company law and corporate governance. Being considered largely ill-founded and inadequately thought-through, as well as too detailed and poorly suited for the Swedish corporate governance system, the Commission Green Paper was strongly criticised in Sweden. The general opinion was that, although a discussion concerning potential improvements of the corporate governance system is welcomed, regulation based on the Green Paper's overall approach and proposals would be too detailed and inflexible and impose unnecessary administrative burdens on the companies affected.

In April 2009, an Official Report proposing simplifications to the Companies Act was presented.[23] The report mainly concerns private limited liability companies and is aimed at reducing the administrative burden on such companies.[24]

Taking into account that the current Corporate Governance Code is still relatively new (February 2010), there are no current proposals for material amendments to the Code.

6. Selection of Literature in English

The Swedish Corporate Governance Code, February 2010, available at <www.corporategovernanceboard.se>.

Annual reports 2006-2012 of the Swedish Corporate Governance Board, available at <www.corporategovernanceboard.se>.

Corporate Governance in the Nordic Countries, The working group of the self-regulatory corporate governance bodies of the five Nordic countries, April 2009.

Dent, G.W. Jr., *Corporate Governance: The Swedish Solution*, Working Paper, Case Western University, Feb. 2012, <http://ssrn.com/abstract=1999454>.

Henrekson, M. and Jakobsson, U. 'The Swedish Model of Corporate Ownership and Control in Transition' in Huizinga, H. and L. Jonung, (eds)., *Who Will Own Europe? The Internationalisation of Asset Ownership in Europe*, Cambridge: Cambridge University Press, September 2005.

Henrekson, M. and Jakobsson, U., 'The Swedish Corporate Control Model – Convergence, Persistence or Decline?' *Corporate Governance: An International Review*, Vol. 20, No 2, 2012.

Isaksson, M. and Skog, R., *Aspects of Corporate Governance*, Corporate Governance Forum, 1994.

Isaksson, M. and Skog, R., *The Future of Corporate Governance – The Stockholm Symposium*, Corporate Governance Forum, 2004.

Lekvall, P., 'Board Committees in Nordic Corporate Governance – A Road to Increased Efficiency or Diluted Accountability?', *Nordisk Tidsskrift for Selskabsret*, 2012:1.

Lekvall, P., 'Nomination Committees in Swedish Listed Companies', International Corporate Governance Network (ICGN) 2008 Yearbook.

---

[23] *Förenklingar i aktiebolagslagen m.m.* [Simplifications to the Companies Act] (SOU 2009:34).

[24] The proposal includes abolishing the requirement to adopt rules of procedure for the board of directors and the requirement for written instructions on the allocation of work between company organs.

Lekvall, P., 'The Swedish Corporate Governance Model', *The International Corporate Governance Handbook*, 2009, chapter 6.14.

Lekvall, P., *Future EU regulation of corporate governance in financial institutions – A criticial review from a Swedish point of view*. Report to the Swedish Financial Markets Committee, Stockholm, June 2011.

Lekvall, P., *Say on Pay – pro or con good governance? Some reflections based on the Swedish experience:* Boardview 4/2012, pp. 47–50, Directors' Institute of Finland, Helsinki, Finland.

Skog, R. and Fäger, C., *The Swedish Companies Act – An introduction*, 2007.

Svernlöv, C., *Discharge from liability in the Swedish listed company*, The Swedish Corporate Governance Board, November 2007.

Swedish Code of Corporate Governance – Report of the Code Group, Swedish Government Official Reports SOU 2004:130.

Tomorrow's Corporate Governance: Bridging the UK engagement gap through Swedish-style nomination committees, Centre for Tomorrow's Company, London, March 2010.

Unger, S., *Special features of Swedish corporate governance*, The Swedish Corporate Governance Board, December 2006.

Corporate Boards in Switzerland

PETER BÖCKLI

1. General Introduction

1.1. Environment in which Swiss Boards Operate

a) *Ownership Structure*

The present report focuses on approximately 300 Swiss public companies which are listed on the Swiss Stock Exchange (SIX) in Zurich.[1] All Swiss public companies are organised as *Aktiengesellschaften* (AG, corporations) pursuant to Article 620 ff. of the Swiss Code of Obligations (*Schweizerisches Obligationenrecht*; CO or Corporation Law).

The largest public companies (such as Nestlé, Novartis, UBS, Credit Suisse, Swiss Re, Zurich Financial Services etc.) have a very broadly diversified ownership, with a majority of non-Swiss and predominantly institutional share-holders.[2] There is a constantly shrinking core of local individuals holding shares, and sometimes a small remnant of family shareholders descending from the 19th century founders, but with an equity interest rarely exceeding 2% of total voting rights. These companies are genuinely publicly held.

The exceptions in this tier of the largest public companies are companies with concentrated shareholding, such as Roche, where due to a privileged voting structure the founding families still hold a controlling 45% voting interest, though this represents less than 10% of total capital,[3] and ABB where the Swedish

---

[1] See www.six-swiss-exchange.com/shares/companies/issuer_list_de.html. The author is indebted to his partner, Christoph B. Bühler, to Daniel Häring, his younger partner, and to Anne-Sophie Buchs, his associate, for valuable help in the preparation of this text and numerous suggestions.

[2] Nearly 60% of all portfolio holdings in Swiss public companies are held by institutional investors, see C. Wälti, *Investitionspolitik von institutionellen Investoren*, Dissertation in Corporate Finance, University of Zurich 2007, Executive Summary 1; T. Spillmann, *Institutionelle Investoren im Recht der (echten) Publikumsgesellschaften*, Zurich, Schulthess (2004), 227 ff.; eg. *Nestlé*: 63.5% of registered shares held by non-Swiss and more than 70% (61.2% of the total share capital) by institutional shareholders (see Annual Report of Nestlé 2010, 45, available at <http://www.nestle.com/asset-library/Documents/Library/Documents/Annual_Reports/2010-Annual-Report-EN.pdf>); Novartis: 56.82% of registered shares (excluding 6.33% as treasury shares) held by non-Swiss, 40.21% by legal entities and 46.63% by nominees and fiduciaries (see Annual Report of Novartis 2010, 89, available at <http://www.novartis.com/downloads/newsroom/corporate-publications/novartis-annual-report-2010-en.pdf>); UBS: 78.1% of registered shares held by non-Swiss, 18.7 by legal entities and 32.7 by nominees and fiduciaries (see Annual Report of UBS 2010, 214, available at <http://www.ubs.com>); Credit Suisse: 45% of registered shares held by non-Swiss and 55% by institutional investors (see Annual Report of Credit Suisse 2010, 149, available at <https://www.credit-suisse.com/investors/doc/ar10/csg_ar_2010_en.pdf>).

[3] See *Financial Report of Roche 2010*, 145 and 171, available at <http://www.roche.com/investors/annual_reports/annual_reports_archive.htm>.

Wallenberg family and related interests hold a significant minority stake,[4] as well as Schindler (the lift maker), where the founding families still control the company through a shareholders' pool.[5] Holcim (the cement maker) is another example of a public company with factual family control.[6]

Institutional shareholding is playing an ever more important part in the twenty largest Swiss public companies.[7] In a typical general shareholder's meeting with a 50% or so presence of all votes registered, institutional shareholders—provided they do exercise their voting rights—may easily command one-third or more of the actual vote. In contentions situations they may more often than not determine the outcome of the matter to be voted upon.

In middle-sized and smaller public companies, in almost one-half of all cases there are permanent or core shareholders with 20% to 60% of all shares, sometimes with a publicly declared long-term engagement.[8] Switzerland has a comparatively strong *Mittelstand* of entrepreneurs and entrepreneurial families who run mostly non-listed companies of various sizes. There are about 300,000 non-listed private companies, incorporated either as limited liability companies (*GmbH*) or, traditionally, even more often in the form of corporations (*AG*).[9] The segment of small and middle-sized non-listed enterprises (*SMEs*) plays a very significant part in the Swiss domestic economy, comparable in this respect to Germany.[10]

While at a time before and after the Second World War there was interlocking stock ownership among listed companies, this always was a minor phenomenon in Switzerland, and it has almost disappeared. Large Swiss Banks (as a result of several mergers, Credit Suisse and UBS today) never held the kind of major stock interests that were typical for Germany until about ten years ago. There is one important exception: Novartis, the pharmaceutical company, has acquired and still holds a stake of 33% of privileged voting stock (but only a small part of the

---

[4] See *Annual Report of ABB Group* 2010, 17, available at < http://www.abb.ch>.

[5] See *Annual Report of Schindler 2010*, 61, available at <http://www.schindler.com/com/internet/en/investor-relations/reports/reports-2011-2008.html>.

[6] See *Annual Report of Holcim 2010*, 212, available at <http://www.holcim.com/fileadmin/templates/CORP/doc/e-reports/AR_2010/>.

[7] See n. 2 above.

[8] Eg, *Annual Report of Schindler 2010* (fn. 5) 61.

[9] There are a total of 312,861 registered enterprises (listed and not listed): 142,546 individual businesses and trades (Einzelfirmen), 86,965 corporations (Aktiengesellschaften, AG), 58,017 limited liability companies (Gesellschaften mit beschränkter Haftung, GmbH), 8,006 unlimited commercial partnerships (Kollektivgesellschaften), 1,821 cooperatives (Genossenschaften), 1,318 limited commercial partnerships (Kommanditgesellschaften) and 14,188 others (see Swiss Federal Statistical Office, establishment census 2008, data as of 29 March 2010).

[10] See M. Habersaat, A. Schönenberger and W. Weber, *Die KMU in der Schweiz und in Europa*, Berne (State Secretariat for Economic Affairs) 2001, modification in 2006, 4 ff. and 12.

equity capital) in its competitor Roche.[11] The large banks today have almost no shareholdings in Swiss industry.

b) 'Shareholder' versus 'Stakeholder' Model

Switzerland never fully adopted the shareholder value doctrine;[12] the country has traditionally followed the enterprise ideology which comprises both the shareholder and stakeholder approaches[13] by stressing enterprise value as a sound basis for the long-term well-being of providers of equity capital, credit and labour alike, as well as for the tax-collecting government. While the stakeholder approach—where the shareholders are even not specifically mentioned but are seen as one of several groups having claims to the enterprise—has its defenders[14] the prevailing view is quite pragmatic. As long as the directors and managers recognise that an enterprise pursues its profit-oriented activities imbedded in a network of stakeholders, the long-term pursuit of shareholders' interest and stakeholders' interest tend to converge when the laws and regulations are complied with and there is a good balance of direction and control at the top of the corporation.[15]

Therefore, while the discussion of the shareholder vs. the stakeholder model is being noticed, actual internal debates are focusing much more on other issues, such as shareholder's rights,[16] minority protection and, particularly, excessive pay for managers. This latter issue is, in fact, the only one where the specific pattern of thought expressed in the term 'principal and agent conflict' can be said to be in the focus of the national debate—but in this instance very much so, to the extent that a popular initiative was adopted by the Swiss people on 3 March 2013, transferring, by an Amendment to the Swiss Constitution, 'say on pay' to the

---

[11] See Annual Report of *Novartis* 2010 (fn. 2) 107 and Annual Report of *Roche* 2010, 171, available at < http://www.roche.com/investors/annual_reports/annual_reports_archive.htm>.

[12] See P. Böckli, *Schweizer Aktienrecht*, 4th edn, Zurich, Schulthess (2009) § 14 N. 36; K. Schildknecht, *Corporate Governance, Das subtile Spiel um Geld und Macht*, 2nd edn, Zurich, Neue Zürcher Zeitung (2009) 25 ff.; C.B. Bühler, *Regulierung im Bereich der Corporate Governance*, habilitation thesis, Zurich, Dike (2009) N. 343 ff.

[13] See P. Forstmoser, A. Meier-Hayoz and P. Nobel, *Schweizerisches Aktienrecht*, Berne, Staempfli (1996) § 3 N. 27; G. Giger, *Corporate Governance als neues Element im Schweizerischen Aktienrecht*, Thesis, Zurich, Schulthess (2003) 12; C.B. Bühler (fn. 12) N. 362 ff.

[14] C.B. Bühler (fn. 12) N. 365.

[15] See the *Swiss Code of Best Practice for Corporate Governance*, Zurich 2002 (as amended in 2007).—P. Böckli, 'Corporate Governance: The "Cadbury Report" and the Swiss Board Concept of 1991', *Schweizerische Zeitschrift für Wirtschaftsrecht* 68 (1996), 149; P. Böckli (fn. 12), § 14 N. 247 ff.; C.B. Bühler (fn. 12) N. 36.

[16] Bill on the Revision of Corporation Law, issued by the Federal Council (Government) on 21 December 2007, *Federal Monitor 2008*, 1751, with a Government Report ('*Message to Parliament*') Bill of 21 December 2007 on the revision of corporation law and accounting rules, *Federal Monitor 2007*, 1589.

Shareholders' Meeting. It covers not only board compensation, but particularly also annual compensation for managers.[17]

c) Little Government Interference in Switzerland

Switzerland never followed the French tendency of significant industrial holdings of the State and overt (or covert) interventions of the head of State or key politicians in corporate matters. It also refrained from going down the road of German *Mitbestimmung* (equal representation of workers and other employees on the highest corporate body).[18] Workers and other employees traditionally exercise influence through collective bargaining agreements which provide for representation of workers and other employees with consultative functions within the company, but practically never on the highest corporate body (the *Verwaltungsrat, conseil d'administration* or board of directors[19]). Workers and other employees do participate with equal voting power in the administration of the firm-specific pension plan entities[20] which are run on a fully funded basis for each Swiss enterprise, contrary to both the French and the German systems. The total shareholdings of these pension plan entities are significant, but these entities have, so far, exercised little noticeable influence on voting practices in general Shareholders' Meetings of Swiss companies.[21] This may change (see section 3.1.4 below).

d) Influences and Tendencies

While Swiss corporation law and practice, for more than a century, had been subject to the influence of French and German laws,[22] British and US American

---

[17] Popular Initiative 'Thomas Minder' from 26 February 2008 to fight against 'excessive pay' of Directors and Managers of Swiss public companies, see *Federal Monitor 2008*, 341, adopted by popular vote on 3 March 2013, with a detailed Amendment to the Federal Constitution by a new Article 95 para. 3, including a series of compulsory measures to fight against excessive pay of Directors and Managers in public Swiss companies.

[18] Negative popular vote of 21 March 1976, on the introduction of an equivalent of the German *Mitbestimmung*, see P. Böckli, 'Konvergenz: Annäherung des monistischen und des dualistischen Führungs- und Aufsichtssystems', in P. Hommelhoff, K.J. Hopt and A. v. Werder (eds.), *Handbuch Corporate Governance*, 2nd edn, Stuttgart/Cologne, Otto Schmidt/Schaefer-Poeschel (2009), 255, 264.

[19] Art. 707 Corporation Law ('CO').

[20] Art. 89a Civil Code (*Schweizerisches Zivilgesetzbuch*) of 10 December 1907 and Federal Law of 25 June 1982 (*Bundesgesetz über die berufliche Alters-, Hinterlassenen- und Invalidenvorsorge*) as amended.

[21] *Federal Monitor 2010*, 8295, Art. 71a.

[22] P. Böckli, 'Osmosis of Anglo-Saxon Concepts in Swiss Business Law', in N.P. Vogt (ed.), *Liber amicorum Thomas Bär and Robert Karrer, The International Practice of Law*, The Hague/Zurich, Kluwer/Helbing & Lichtenhahn (1997) 9.

ideas had the strongest impact from about 1992. The Cadbury Report opened an ever-increasing corporate governance discussion[23] which led to the *Swiss Code of Best Practice for Corporate Governance* in 2002[24] and improved disclosure of compensation of directors and managers in the same year[25] and a follow-up of the legislature in 2005.[26] In the meantime, a consultative shareholders' vote on compensation matters (say on pay) has been introduced by many—but still not all—public companies.[27] As from 1998, Swiss Boards had a marked tendency to shrink in size. Their functioning has been improved, and generally speaking the UK corporate governance ideas of the 1990s, as expressed in the UK reports from Cadbury to Walker, were implemented to an astonishing extent. A Swiss public company without an Audit Committee[28] would be unthinkable today, and the functions of Chairman and CEO have—at least in the large public companies—been separated in most cases.[29] Remuneration Committees[30] have been introduced almost universally, Nominating and corporate governance Committees are almost as ubiquitous. Great emphasis is set on a functioning system of internal control.

The Swiss corporate environment cannot be properly described without a reference to the lively market for corporate control, which has developed particularly since the introduction of the Stock Exchange Act (SESTA) in 1995.[31] Switzerland has essentially adopted the London *City Code on Takeovers and Mergers*, including the compulsory bid requirement for any shareholder acquiring a large minority position (33⅓% in the case of Switzerland).[32] The Merger Act[33] has also been

---

[23] P. Böckli (fn. 15) 149.

[24] See C.B. Bühler (fn. 12) N. 1250 ff.

[25] Directive of the Swiss Stock Exchange on Disclosure in Corporate Governance Matters (*Richtlinie der Schweizer Börse betr. Informationen zur Corporate Governance*) of 17 April 2002, Zurich (as amended in 2006 and 2008).

[26] Federal Law of 7 October 2005 (*Bundesgesetz zur Transparenz betreffend Vergütungen an Mitglieder des Verwaltungsrates und der Geschäftsleitung*), introducing Art. 663b^bis and 663c para. 3 into the Corporation Law (CO).

[27] About 80% of them (estimation).

[28] Corporate Governance Code (fn. 15) para. 23 and 24.

[29] Nestlé separated the functions in 2005, Novartis in 2010; the others had separate CEO and Chair functions already introduced in the period after 2001. For all banks separation has been mandatory since 1971; See P. Böckli (fn. 12) § 14 N. 283.

[30] P. Böckli (fn. 15) 167; C.B. Bühler (fn. 12) N. 1300 ff.

[31] SESTA, Federal Law of 24 March 1995 (*Bundesgesetz über die Börsen und den Effektenhandel*), with substantial Implementing Ordinances from 1996/97 (all as amended) and the far-reaching Listing Requirements of the Stock Exchange (in the current version of 2009) providing for ad hoc disclosure procedure and management transaction disclosure.

[32] Art. 32 SESTA (fn. 31).

[33] Merger Law (*Bundesgesetz über Fusion, Spaltung, Umwandlung und Vermögensübertragung*) of 3 October 2003.—See P. Böckli (fn. 12) § 3 N. 15 ff.

totally revised in 2003 and offers a wide range of restructuring mechanics. In the meantime, a great number of both friendly and hostile takeover procedures have been successfully completed in Switzerland,[34] under the tight supervision and guidance of the Swiss Takeover Board (*Übernahmekommission*).[35]

Corporation law today is one of the most debated topics in Switzerland—but primarily due to the 'say on pay' issue which goes very close to the innermost democratic feelings of the public. It is also one of the best covered areas of the law, being the subject of extensive academic debate in publications and seminars, in doctoral theses and comprehensive handbooks. There is a disproportionately large body of court cases where the academic discussion is echoed regularly by references to the opinions expressed in academia.

Increasingly the law distinguishes between listed and non-listed corporations.[36] The present Bill before Parliament will enhance this dissociation but a very large area of common rules remain. While there are about 300 public companies, there are almost 300,000 non-listed companies, of which about 10,000 are operative stand-alone companies, of small and middle-size. The rest are micro-corporations, real estate companies, holding companies of all kinds, special purpose vehicles and subsidiaries of groups—often foreign groups—of companies.[37]

1.2. Financial Institutions

The financial sector plays an important role in Switzerland[38]—relatively much more than in France, Germany and Italy. The financial industry is tightly

---

[34] See the list of all transactions in Switzerland since 1997, divided into the respective transaction properties (ie. initially friendly/hostile, friendly/hostile completion, etc.): http://www.takeover.ch/transactions/list/reset/filter/lang/en.

[35] Art. 23 SESTA (fn. 31).

[36] See H.C. von der Crone, 'Ein Aktienrecht für das 21. Jahrhundert', *Schweizerische Zeitschrift für Wirtschaftsrecht* 70 (1998) 157 ff.; G. Krneta, *Praxiskommentar Verwaltungsrat*, 2nd edn, Berne, Staempfli (2005) N. 1534; P. Böckli (fn. 12) § 7 N. 3; C.B. Bühler (fn. 12) N. 390 and 790 ff.; P. Nobel, *Schweizerisches Finanzmarktrecht und internationale Standards*, 3rd edn, Berne, Staempfli (2010) § 10 N. 2 and 345 ff.

[37] There are a total of 312,861 registered enterprises (listed and not listed). 99.6% of these companies are SMEs (kleinere und mittlere Unternehmen, KMU; up to 249 employers), 0.4% are large companies. Within these 99.6% of SMEs, 87.1% are micro-enterprises, 10.6% are small enterprises and 2.0% are middle-sized companies (see Swiss Federal Statistical Office, establishment census 2008, data as of 29 March 2010).

[38] About 14% of the total fiscal revenue results in Switzerland from the financial sector, see BAK Basel economic research & consultancy, *Finanzplatz Schweiz, Volkswirtschaftliche Bedeutung und Wechselwirkungen mit dem Werkplatz, Eine Analyse im Auftrag der Schweizerischen Bankiervereinigung und economiesuisse*, March 2011, 1 ff. From 1999 to 2009, about one-third of macroeconomic GDP-growth was generated by the financial sector; an EVA of

cont. ...

regulated under the stewardship of FINMA (Swiss Financial Market Supervisory Authority—*Eidgenössische Finanzmarktaufsicht*),[39] which supervises both the banking and the insurance industries. The Banking Law imposes a 'German' type two-tier Board structure on all regulated financial institutions, the Board being excluded from day-to-day management which vests in the Management Board. No member of the Bank's top management can sit on the board of directors; a combination of chairman and CEO functions is barred by the statute.[40]

There is a slow but noticeable spill-over effect from bank regulation to the realm of larger non-financial corporations,[41] although a myriad of detailed regulatory rules remain strictly limited to financial operations. A spill-over is to be seen in the following areas:

- internal control system[42] (where the regulatory directives of the FINMA[43] are often used as a model);
- internal audit procedures independent from management;
- risk evaluation management and control (an approach which was first developed in financial institutions although the basic function as such had always been known in almost every enterprise);
- compliance[44] (a function which was mentioned in corporation law since 1936, but was first distinctly developed in financial institutions);
- top management compensation practices (where, again, the Federal Financial Regulator's directives[45] are used as a sort of guidance);

CHF 88 billion is related to economic activity, ie. nearly one-fifth of macroeconomic EVA in Switzerland; along with that about 12% of all jobs are in the financial sector.

[39] Art. 98 of the Federal Constitution (*Bundesverfassung der Schweizerischen Eidgenossenschaft*) of 18 April 1999 and Federal Act on the Swiss Financial Market Supervisory Authority FINMAG (*Bundesgesetz über die Eidgenössische Finanzmarktaufsicht* – Financial Supervision Act) of 22 June 2007.

[40] Art. 3 para. 2(a) of the Swiss Federal Banking Act (*Bundesgesetz über die Banken und Sparkassen*) of 8 November 1934 and Art. 8 para. 2 of the Implementing Ordinance (*Verordnung über die Banken und Sparkassen*) of 17 May 1972.

[41] See H.C. von der Crone, 'Auf dem Weg zu einem Recht der Publikumsgesellschaft', *Zeitschrift des Bernischen Juristenvereins* 133 (1997) 73, 83; C.B. Bühler (fn. 12) N. 792 ff.

[42] Art. 728a para. 1 no. 3 of the Federal Law of 16 December 2005 revising the Audit Procedures (*Bundesgesetz vom 16. Dez. 2005, GmbH-Recht sowie Anpassungen im Aktien-, Genossenschafts-, Handelsregister- und Firmenrecht*).

[43] Swiss Financial Market Supervisory Authority (*FINMA*), formerly Federal Banking Commission, Circular 06/6, Supervision and Internal Control in Banks (as revised on 20 November 2008).

[44] Compliance as a concept was indeed already part of the Swiss Corporation Law of 1936, Art. 722 para. 2 no. 3 CO 1936, but the function was not really developed until the financial institutions took the lead as from about 1985.

[45] FINMA (fn. 43), Circular 2010/1, Remuneration schemes for financial institutions, 21 October 2009.

- asset and liability management (first formalised in banks), and
- separation of CEO and Chairman functions[46] (which is not mandatory in non-financial companies, but increasingly seen as good practice).

The intensity of interventions by FINMA in the financial industry has greatly increased as a consequence of the financial crisis of 2008/2009 which started early in Switzerland (in October 2007) and led, a year later, to financial assistance[47] of the Government and the Central Bank to the largest Swiss Bank, UBS. FINMA has a variety of possibilities of intervening in banks' corporate matters, but steers clear of becoming a shadow director.[48]

1.3. Available Board Models

From the outset Switzerland introduced a flexible structure for Boards in its corporate law.[49] The law permits each company to implement its own preferences between the extremes of a classical one-tier board (where the directors are themselves the highest executives), and something very close to a two-tier board, where the entire executive management is permanently delegated to a management board (*Geschäftsleitung* or *direction générale*), similar to a German *Vorstand* or a French *directoire*).[50] In such a case, the Board—while still called a board of directors—in essence assumes the functions of a Supervisory Board. A remaining difference with the Supervisory Board of the German, French and *Societas Europaea* type of company (SE) consists in the determination of the company's ultimate direction (strategy), which always and by law vests in the highest corporate body (and not the management board).[51]

---

[46] See n. 40 above.—A rather timid reference to the problem is to be found in the Corporate Governance Code (fn. 15) para. 18 subpara. 2.

[47] See *UBS News* of 12 August 2008, available at <http://www.ubs.com/global/de/about_ubs/about_us/news/news.html/de/2008/08/12/2008_8_14b.html>; Federal Act (*Bundesbeschluss über einen Kredit für die Rekapitalisierung der UBS AG*) of 15 December 2008 and *Federal Monitor 2008*, 8944 ff. and 8960 ff.

[48] See D. Gericke, 'Funktioniert der Rechtsstaat im Kapitalmarkt?', in H.C. von der Crone (eds.), *Liber amicorum Dieter Zobel, Aktuelle Fragen des Bank- und Finanzmarktrechts*, Zurich, Schulthess (2004) 359, 364; J.-B. Zufferey and F. Contratto, *FINMA—The New Supervisory Authority for the Swiss Financial Market, A First Overview for Practitioners*, Basel, Helbing & Lichtenhahn (2009) 1 ff.; C.B. Bühler, 'Finanzmarktregulierung im Spannungsfeld von Recht und Politik', *Schweizerische Juristen-Zeitung* 106 (2010) 469, 474 ff.

[49] Original Swiss Corporation Law of 1881, Art. 650 para. 1, today Art. 716b para. 1 CO.

[50] Art. 716b CO.—See P. Böckli (fn. 18) 264.

[51] Art. 716a para. 1 numbered subpara. 1 CO.

Practically all Swiss public companies have adopted the equivalent of a two-tier model[52] which is flexible enough to permit a company, if it is deemed appropriate, to elect the CEO to the Board (*administrateur-délégué*, or managing director[53]), or even for some time to combine the CEO and Chairman functions.[54] Still, almost all members of Boards of public companies in Switzerland are non-executive[55] and most of them fulfil the criteria of independence;[56] in fact, executive directors are rare.

2. Authority

2.1. Functions, Powers

a) Functions

The board of directors (*Conseil d'administration, Verwaltungsrat*) is elected by the shareholders and is the highest-ranking body in all matters of both management and control. As mentioned above, practically all listed companies have used the possibility offered by the Swiss Corporation Law to create a separate Management Body below the board of directors. This leads to a certain

---

[52] Of all examined Swiss public companies, 5% have a unitary board, 60% a two-tier board and 35% adopted a mixed system (Heidrick & Struggles, *European Corporate Governance Report 2011*, 'Challenging board performance', 11, figure 7). See P. Forstmoser, 'Monistische oder dualistische Unternehmensverfassung? Das Schweizer Konzept', *Zeitschrift für Unternehmens- und Gesellschaftsrecht* 32 (2003) 688, 688 ff.; M. Wegmüller, *Die Ausgestaltung der Führungs- und Aufsichtsaufgaben des schweizerischen Verwaltungsrates*, Thesis, Berne, Staempfli (2008) 234; P. Böckli (fn. 12) § 13 N. 948; C.B. Bühler (fn. 12) N. 451.

[53] Art. 716b para. 1 CO.—G. Krneta (fn. 36) N. 1668; D. Daeniker, 'Vergütung von Verwaltungsrat und Geschäftsleitung schweizerisches Publikumsgesellschaften', *Schweizerische Juristen-Zeitung* 101 (2005) 381, 384; P. Böckli (fn. 12) § 13 N. 282; C.B. Bühler (fn. 12) N. 638.

[54] Corporate Governance Code (fn. 15) para. 18. See 2.1(b)(i), (ii) and (iii) below. See P. Böckli (fn. 15) 170.

[55] In 2011, on the boards of the examined Swiss listed companies, 1% are executive directors, 8% are former executive directors, 62% are independent non-executive directors, 7% are reference shareholders, 1% are employee representatives and 17% are other non-independent directors (see Heidrick & Struggle (fn. 52), 42, figure 35).—In 2003 already, 89% of all board members of the examined Swiss listed companies were non-executive (see C. Meyer, *Studie zur praktischen Umsetzung der Corporate Governance-Richtlinie vom 1. Dezember 2003*, 35, figure 17).

[56] See 2.2.3 below.

degree of convergence with the classical two-tier system.[57] Yet, there remain a number of differences.

The board of directors, even after having created a management board with extensive managerial powers, always retains non-transferable and inalienable duties and powers in accordance with the so-called 'seven-points' catalogue:[58]

(1) the determination of the strategy of the company and the giving of necessary directions;

(2) the establishment of the company's organisation;

(3) the structuring of the accounting system and of financial controls as well as financial planning;

(4) the appointment and the removal of top managers;

(5) the ultimate supervision of management, in particular with regard to compliance with the law, the articles of Association, regulations and directions;

(6) the preparation of the Annual Statement and Report as well as of the General Meeting of Shareholders, and the implementation of its resolutions, and

(7) the notification to the Bankruptcy Court in the case of insolvency (defined as excess of total indebtedness over total assets).

Furthermore, the board of directors has the right to withdraw delegated powers from the management level at all times and exercise them on its own,[59] especially in crises situations or an emergency.

Swiss Boards, in practice acting as a 'Supervisory Board plus', have structured their work process in Board Committees[60] and are the stewards of the

---

[57] See P. Forstmoser (fn. 52) 688; P. Böcklij (fn. 18, 1st edn 2003) 201; M.D. Amstutz, *Macht und Ohnmacht des Aktionärs, Möglichkeiten und Grenzen der Corporate Governance bei der Wahrung der Aktionärsinteressen*, Zurich, Neue Zürcher Zeitung (2007) 157; P. Böckli (fn. 12) § 13 N. 948 ff.

[58] Art. 716a para. 1 CO *Oberleitung* (or 'ultimate direction') is rendered here as 'strategy' in English.—See G. Krneta (fn. 36) N. 1177; P. Böckli (fn. 12) § 13 N. 282 and n. 303; C.B. Bühler, *Corporate Governance* (fn. 12) N. 616; M.F. Rüdisser, *Boards of Directors at Work: An Integral Analysis of Nontransferable Duties under Swiss Company Law from an Economic Perspective,* Thesis, St. Gallen, Bamberg, 2009, 25, 118 and 149; R. Watter and K. Roth Pellanda, 'Commentary on Art. 716–716b CO', in *Basler Kommentar zum Obligationenrecht II*, H. Honsell, N.P. Vogt and R. Watter (eds.), 3rd edn, Basel, Helbing & Lichtenhahn (2012) Art. 716a N. 4.

[59] Art. 716b CO, which allows for a revocation of any delegation by simple board resolution.

[60] Art. 716a para. 2 CO. See G. Krneta (fn. 36) N. 1652; T. Jutzi, *Verwaltungsratsausschüsse im schweizerischen Aktienrecht, unter besonderer Berücksichtigung der Verhältnisse in den USA, Deutschland und England,* Thesis, Berne, Staempfli (2008) 13; P. Böckli (fn. 12) § 13 N. 405; C.B. Bühler (fn. 12) N. 630 and N. 1292; M.F. Rüdisser (fn. 58) 95.

Internal Control System[61] as well as the overseers of the auditing process. They closely cooperate with the management board, whose members participate in most Board meetings. Yet the Board retains the final decision on strategy and the means of its implementation. A core duty of Boards, stressed by the Corporate Governance Code,[62] is the responsibility to see to well-planned and orderly succession at the top (of both its own body and the management), and on-going close scrutiny of management's performance.[63]

The law permits, and the Corporate Governance Code encourages, the Board to subject certain important decisions of the management board to its formal approval.[64] In practice, this is an important element of Swiss corporate life.

b) Division of Powers

In financial institutions, as mentioned above, the two-tier structure is mandatory.[65] In other listed companies a separation of day-to-day management on the one hand, and strategic direction, supervision and control on the other is in almost all cases adopted on a voluntary basis (closely, but not entirely, converging to the classical two-tier system).[66]

Outside financial institutions, the Board is usually empowered by the Articles to tailor details of the separation of powers through the Organisational Regulations to meet the particular company's needs.[67] In practice, three models have emerged:

(i) More and more companies have a double-headed top. The Chairman is not simultaneously CEO, and the CEO, being the head of the management board, is not a member of the board of directors, although he is invited to assist at most board meetings.

(ii) The combination of Chairman and CEO functions in one person (emulating the classical French model of *PDG, président directeur-général*, Chairman and CEO) is legal, but it is the exception today. The Swiss Code for corporate governance deals with this as follows: 'If, for

---

[61] Art. 728a para. 1 numbered subpara. 3 CO indirectly obliges the Board to have a system of internal control implemented (in all companies above the SME level as defined by Art. 728 para. 1 no. 2 CO).

[62] Corporate Governance Code (fn. 15) para. 12 and 13.

[63] Art. 716a para. 1 numbered subpara. 5 CO.

[64] Art. 716b CO; Art. 716c para. 2 numbered subpara. 4 of the Bill on revision of the Swiss Corporation Law of 21 December 2007. Corporate Governance Code (fn. 15) para. 11 subpara. 2.

[65] Art. 3 para. 2 (b) Swiss Federal Banking Act (fn. 40) and Art. 8 Swiss Federal Banking Ordinance (fn. 40).

[66] See P. Böckli (fn. 57) 201 and P. Böckli (fn. 12) § 13 N. 948.

[67] Art. 716b CO.—See P. Forstmoser, *Organisation und Organisationsreglement der Aktiengesellschaft*, Zurich, Schulthess (2011) § 14 N. 12 and 14.

reasons specific to the company or because the circumstances relating to availability of senior management makes it appropriate, the board of directors decides that a single individual should assume joint responsibility at the top of the company, it should provide for adequate control mechanisms. The board of directors may appoint an experienced non-executive member (lead director) to perform this task. Such person should be entitled to convene on his own and chair meetings of the Board when necessary.'[68]

(iii) Some Boards, though rarely outside a start-up or crisis situation, entrust top management functions to another director (*administrateur-délégué*, or managing director).[69] The *administratuer-délégué* system has widely fallen out of favour, with the important and quite unique exception of Nestlé.

A company adopting either the *PDG* or the *administrateur délégué* model is under pressure from the public and the media to institute a likeness of the British concept of an independent lead director on the board of directors in conformity with the Swiss Code for corporate governance,[70] although neither company law nor the pending bills require such an arrangement.[71]

Division of powers between the Board and management is generally well structured by Organisational Regulations[72] and also fairly well complied with, following the dividing red line drawn by the law in its seven-points catalogue for the Board's core powers (as mentioned above). However, in practice there is a tendency of strong top managers to pre-empt[73] many decisions that belong to the Board's reserved turf by indirect and informal exertion of power in the preparatory stages of decision-making.

c) *Strategy*

While the 'ultimate direction of the Company', or strategy, is reserved by law to the full board of directors,[74] it is determined in a process of interaction between the Directors and the management board. In practice, the exchange of views

---

[68] Corporate Governance Code (fn. 15) para. 18 subpara. 2.

[69] Specifically permitted by Art. 716b para. 1 CO.

[70] Corporate Governance Code (fn. 15) para. 18 subpara. 2.

[71] See M. Wegmüller (fn. 52) 208; P. Böckli (fn. 12) § 13 N. 554, with further references, and § 13 N. 557; C.B. Bühler (fn. 12) N. 1289.

[72] Art. 716b CO.—See K. Roth Pellanda, *Organisation des Verwaltungsrates: Zusammensetzung, Arbeitsteilung, Information und Verantwortlichkeit*, Thesis, Zurich, Dike (2007) 100; P. Böckli (fn. 12) § 13 N. 321 ff., N. 437 and N. 518; P. Forstmoser (fn. 67) § 16 N. 4.

[73] See P. Böckli (fn. 15) 164 and P. Böckli (fn. 12) § 13 N. 555.

[74] Art. 716a para. 1 numbered subpara. 1 CO; M.F. Rüdisser (fn. 58) 138.

between the two top persons, the Chairman and the CEO, and the influence they exert often largely determine the strategy (decision shaping), subject to the thorough discussion and usually adoption by the full Board (decision taking). The determination of strategy (literally, in the law, 'ultimate direction') always comprises the final say on what the Company's main objectives are, how they are in general to be pursued, and what matters the company shall not pursue. Basic decisions on the appointment of top personnel, their pay and their demotion always vest in the full Board.[75] The Board is responsible for the follow-up on strategy and timely adjustments or changes whenever the earlier strategic decision proves a failure internally or in the market.

d) *Supervision*

No genuine one-tier Board has survived in Swiss public companies. Today, ultimate direction (strategy) and ultimate supervision vest in the Board, and execution in the management body. The exact separation of functions is a hot subject in the 'quasi two-tier' arrangement prevalent in Swiss listed companies. Supervision comprises two quite different functions. The first is the duty of the Board to closely follow-up on the company's business and especially the acts and omissions of management in its day-to-day management. This function is usually entrusted, in the first place, to the Chairman who attends meetings of top management and maintains close contact with the business. The second area of supervision is more formal and tends to be entrusted to Board committees: A duty of care as regards implementation of a sound, risk-oriented internal control system with a robust compliance function, and an internal audit independent from management.[76] While risk management is a genuine task of the management board,[77] direction and supervision of this activity vest in the Board. There are a variety of structural approaches to organising the supervision function, usually centering on the Board's Audit Committee. As this committee in its main function necessarily is more or less backward-looking, quite frequently a Risk Committee is created which follows a decidedly real-time and forward-looking view of company matters. If a Risk Committee or a Strategic Committee is established, Swiss experience shows that special care must be taken to avoid interferences between the management's prime responsibility for risk management and the Board committee's supervision-oriented activities.

---

[75] Art. 716a para. 1 numbered subpara. 4 CO.

[76] Corporate Governance Code (fn. 15) para. 19 and 20.

[77] R. Müller, L. Lipp and A. Plüss, *Der Verwaltungsrat—Ein Handbuch für die Praxis*, 3rd edn, Zurich, Schulthess (2007) 201; P. Böckli (fn. 12) § 13 N. 307; R. Watter and K. Roth Pellanda (fn. 58) Art. 716a N. 6.

Swiss Boards being almost exclusively composed of non-executive persons[78] (except in the cases mentioned above where a *PDG* or *administrateur-délégué* model is adopted, or when a former executive is elected to the Boards with more active involvement in management questions), all supervisory tasks on the Board are taken care of by non-executive and indeed independent Directors.

e) Internal Control System

The Corporate Governance Code recommended to all public companies in 2002 what the more conscientious among them had implemented for a long time: establishing a robust internal control system.[79] This practically comprises a large number of organisational measures to increase security and reliability of internal streams of relevant information, but, more visible to the outside, the organisation of an internal audit department independent from management, and a professional compliance function. Swiss public companies followed the initiatives taken by the Turnbull committee in the UK at an early stage. At the same time, the interdependence of risk evaluation, risk management as a whole, and risk-oriented internal audit was recognised and led to a much more risk-conscious approach of the supervisory function. The Swiss Corporation Law contains an indirect reference to this important area of corporate practice (Art. 716a, 'seven core points catalogue') and a direct one in the provision on statutory auditing which requires the annual Auditor's Report to confirm that an internal control system is in place within the company.[80]

f) External Auditors

Subsequent to the Sarbanes-Oxley legislation in the US, Switzerland introduced an independent State supervisory body, the Federal Audit Supervisory Board (*Eidgenössische Revisionsaufsichtsbehörde*).[81] The substantive law on external audit was modernised and adapted to current international requirements. The external auditors are subject to the Federal Audit Supervisory Board's controls and regulations. While the supervision of auditors active in private companies is largely limited to a tight admission procedure, firms auditing public companies

---

[78] About 90%, see n. 55 above.

[79] Corporate Governance Code (fn. 15) para. 19, a late emanation of the Cadbury Code of 1992. See M. Peyer, *Das interne Kontrollsystem als Aufgabe des Verwaltungsrats und der Revisionsstelle*, Zurich, Dike (2009) 67 ff.

[80] Art. 728a para. 1 numbered subpara. 3 CO.

[81] *RAB.*—Federal Law on the Supervision of Auditing (*Bundesgesetz über die Zulassung und Beaufsichtigung der Revisorinnen und Revisoren*) of 16 December 2005 (*RAG*). See P. Böckli (fn. 12) § 15 N. 7.

are subject to strict on-going scrutiny.[82] External auditors are elected by the Shareholders' Meeting;[83] it is, however, a fact that the Board's proposal is adopted in almost all cases. The auditors of public companies must follow international auditing procedures,[84] and their lead auditor engaged in the company must be replaced after seven years.[85] Contrary to practices of other countries, the Company's external auditors are also required by law to formulate a recommendation to the Shareholders' Meeting[86] (i) on whether to adopt or reject the annual statement as prepared and proposed by the board of directors and (ii) on whether the Board's dividend proposal is in compliance with the law and the Articles of Association.[87]

2.2. Organisation/Internal Functioning

2.2.1. *Composition*

a) *In General*

The size of Boards in large listed companies was reduced to a significant extent from 1998 to 2002 in Switzerland but is now increasing again to some extent.[88] Still, under the influence of the corporate governance movement, the typical board size declined from between 12–24 members to between 7–13 (or at the most 15) members.[89] As has been pointed out, in almost all cases a very large majority of members are non-executive (80% to 90% as an indication), and most of them qualify as independent from the company and its management. Labour representatives are not required either by the law or self-regulatory codes[90] and,

---

[82] Art. 12, 13 and 14 RAG (fn. 81).

[83] Art. 698 para. 2 numbered para. 2 CO.

[84] Art. 12 para. 3(c) RAG (fn. 81).

[85] Art. 730a para. 2 CO.

[86] Art. 728b para. 2 numbered subpara. 4 CO.

[87] Art. 728a para. 1 numbered subpara. 2 CO.

[88] In 2003, in the Swiss public companies under review, there were 7 directors per board on the average, in 2005 7.7 and in 2011, there were 10.4 (see C. Meyer (fn. 55) 32, figure 13; Ethos, Corporate Governance der Schweizer Unternehmen, November 2005 26, table 7; M.F. Rüdisser (fn. 58) 150; Heidrick & Struggles (fn. 52) 37, figure 27.

[89] P. Böckli (fn. 15) 170 and P. Böckli (fn. 12) § 13 N. 19.—The largest public companies still tend to have the largest Boards in comparison; Ethos (fn. 88) 27, figure 13.

[90] A popular initiative to introduce a German-type *Mitbestimmung* of labour representatives at Board level by an amendment to the constitution was narrowly rejected in 1976.—Original language in *Federal Monitor 1971*, 780.

in practice, such arrangements are only likely to be found in State-controlled corporations (public service corporations or public utilities).[91]

There are no specific legal qualification requirements for board membership, except in financial institutions where a *non obstat* of the regulatory authority is required.[92] The recommendations of the Corporate Governance Code are being followed almost everywhere to the letter: Non-executive, preferably independent directors, a majority of whom (and always the chairman) must be financially literate, should make up the Audit Committee.[93] Only independent directors should sit on Remuneration Committees.[94] In financial institutions and very large international companies the presence of a financial expert on the Board and its Audit Committee is widely believed to be a quasi-mandatory good practice.

The Corporation Law contains no provisions for the composition of Boards of Directors or a minimum number of members. The Board with all its members is elected by majority vote in the Shareholders' Meeting, and the law does not provide for any kind of compulsory minority representation on the Board. While the law contains a provision allowing the courts to order the election of a minority representative,[95] the preconditions for such an act of authority are extremely strict, and no court case to this effect has become known to date. The Corporate Governance Code, however, encourages Boards to strive for a well-balanced membership, small enough in numbers for efficient decision-making and large enough for its members to contribute with experience and knowledge from different fields and to allocate leadership and control functions among themselves. Directors should be persons with abilities necessary to ensure an independent decision-making process in a critical exchange of ideas with the executive management.[96] In practice, the Board has to select its members especially with a view to staffing the several Committees of the Board, some of which require special knowledge or experience.

---

[91] Based upon Art. 762 CO or special federal legislation, such as the Federal Railway Act (*Bundesgesetz über die Schweizerischen Bundesbahnen*) of 20 March 1998, or the Telecommunication Act (*Fernmeldegesetz*) of 30 April 1997. Similar public law institutions also exist on the level of the 26 Cantons.

[92] Swiss Federal Banking Act as amended in 1971, Art. 3 para. 2(c) (fn. 40) and regulatory papers issued by FINMA (fn. 43).

[93] Corporate Governance Code (fn. 15) para. 23 subpara. 1. For some time already, it has been common practice to have exclusively independent directors participate in Audit Committees of public companies.

[94] Corporate Governance Code (fn. 15) as amended on 6 September 2007 (para. 2 of the amendment).

[95] Art. 736 numbered para. 4 CO.

[96] Corporate Governance Code (fn. 15) para. 12 subpara. 2.

There are no political appointees, either in financial institutions or in other companies, except in state-controlled companies (which are rarely listed on the Stock Exchange).[97]

Almost all listed companies have an age limit in their Articles of Association or the Board Regulations, putting an automatic end to the Board membership at the age of 70 or, in some cases, 72.[98]

b) Chairman

Parliament has rejected proposals to outlaw or restrict multiple board memberships,[99] and the Corporate Governance Code is silent as to this issue. Companies are expected to set their own rules in their Organisational Regulations, and some of them do, usually setting limits at three public company board memberships. In practice, greatly increased demand on time to be devoted to board and committee work has put an effective limit to multiple board memberships. Symmetrical interlocking functions (Vice-Chairman of Company A serving as Chairman in Company B, and vice-versa), well known in earlier Swiss practice, are considered to be absolutely out of the question today, although the law is silent on this point. The Corporate Governance Code limits its recommendations to shed doubt on the independence of persons in an interlocking board position.[100] A bill pending in Parliament is to outlaw any influence of directors in an interlocking position regarding their own compensation.[101]

The Chairman of the Board, except in the relatively rare event of a Chairman and CEO arrangement, is non-executive, but there is great reluctance to stress this point as an active Chairman with a half or full-time job tends to become 'executive' to some extent by the mere logic of his intense activity within the company. In good practice, a Board Chairman is not considered to be

---

[97] With the exception eg. of the Government-controlled Swiss Telecommunication company Swisscom Corporation (para. 6.1.4 of the articles of incorporation of *Swisscom*, available at https://www.swisscom.ch/content/dam/swisscom/en/ghq/corporate_governance/documents/ Statuten_2011_A5_en.pdf.dl.res/Statuten_2011_A5_en.pdf) and RUAG, the supplier of the Swiss Armed Forces (Art. 4 of the Swiss Federal Act on Swiss Armed Forces (*Bundesgesetz über die Rüstungsunternehmen des Bundes*) of 10 October 1997).

[98] G. Krneta (fn. 36) N. 61; K. Roth Pellanda (fn. 72) 204 ff.; P. Böckli (fn. 12) § 13 N. 43.

[99] Specifically rejected by Parliament in 1985, and pointedly left out of the Bill on revision of the Corporation Law of 21 December 2007 (fn. 16) (rejecting a parliamentary initiative of 20 June 2001).

[100] Corporate Governance Code (fn. 15) para. 22, subpara. 2.

[101] Bill on the revision of the Corporation Law of 21 December 2007 (fn. 16), Art. 717b.

independent, and he should not sit on the Audit Committee[102] although there presently is no legal text setting this rule.

c) Gender Diversity

Gender diversity on Boards is an unwritten rule in Switzerland. The percentage of women has steadily increased over the last decade, to reach 10% to 15% in typical cases, but rarely more and quite frequently less.[103] At the management board level, however, there are still few women, no more than 3–5% in total,[104] and more often than not their presence is limited to human resources departments. There have been initiatives to introduce a binding quota.[105]

d) Foreigners as Directors

Swiss public companies have a large number of foreigners serving on their Boards, much more than in France, Germany or the UK.[106] The Corporate Governance Code deals with the matter as follows:[107]

'If a significant part of the company's operations is abroad, the Board of Directors should also include members having long-standing international experience or members from abroad.'

In a company with significant transnational business activities, the percentage tends to exceed one-third or may reach one-half of all members.[108] An increasing

---

[102] See I.W. Hungerbühler, *Der Verwaltungsratspräsident*, Thesis, Zurich, Schulthess (2003) 29; Expertenkommission Revisionswesen, *Bericht zuhanden der Eidgenössischen Bankenkommission*, December 2000, 18.

[103] Of all board members of the examined Swiss listed companies, 4% were women in 2003, 6% in 2005 and 11% in 2011, see C. Meyer (fn. 55) 36, figure 19; Ethos (fn. 88) 26, table 7; M.F. Rüdisser (fn. 58) 159 and Heidrick & Struggles (fn. 52) 39, figure 31.

[104] See C. Meyer (fn. 55) 36, figure 19.

[105] See Question in the Federal Parliament Nr. 11.5026: *Frauen in Führungspositionen von bundesnahen Unternehmen* of 7 March 2011; State Secretariat for Economic Affairs SECO, 'Frauen in Führungspositionen: so gelingt's!', Media release of 3 March 2011 and Publication of December 2010.

[106] In Switzerland today, 53% of all board members of the Swiss listed companies under review are non-Swiss. In France, there are 27% and in Germany 11% non-national directors, see Heidrick & Struggles (fn. 52) 37, figure 28; see also M. Romer, *Der Einfluss des Internationalisierungsgrades von Verwaltungsräten auf den Unternehmenserfolg: Eine empirische Untersuchung börsenkotierter Unternehmen mit Sitz in der Schweiz*, Thesis, St. Gallen, Schaan (2009) 4.

[107] Corporate Governance Code (fn. 15) para. 12 subpara. 4.

[108] Non-Swiss board members in companies with significant transnational business activities, eg. Nestlé: 42.9% (see Corporate Governance Report of Nestlé 2010, 6, available at <http://www.nestle.com/asset-library/Documents/Library/Documents/Corporate_Governance/Corp_Governance_Report_2010_EN.pdf>); Novartis: 58.3%, see Annual Report of Novartis 2010 (fn.

cont. ...

number of foreigners serve as Chairmen or CEOs of Swiss public companies (eg. Nestlé, where the Chairman is an Austrian and the CEO is a Belgian national, or Novartis, where the Chairman is Swiss and the CEO an American, or Roche, where both functions are held by Austrians, although one of them has also Swiss nationality).

e) Performance Evaluation

All Boards of Swiss listed companies hold a performance evaluation at least once a year, following established procedures, as a consequence of a recommendation of the Corporate Governance Code.[109]

2.2.2. Decision-Making

a) General Rules

Swiss Boards adopt resolutions by a simple majority vote[110] although the Articles of Association or the Organisational Regulations may provide for a supermajority for important matters (mostly two-thirds of all votes cast, or of all Board members).[111] The Chairman leading the process has a casting vote, unless otherwise provided by the Articles of Association.[112]

Matters belonging to the legal 'seven-points' list mentioned above can only be decided upon by the full Board, and not by a Committee or a special group such as the non-executive Board members amongst themselves.[113] Casting of votes by an absent Director by letter or by electronic means is not deemed to be valid, nor according to the prevailing view is the granting of a written proxy to another Board member resulting in the casting of two votes by the latter.

Preparatory, compliance or control matters outside the 'seven-points' area may be assigned to a Committee of the Board.[114]

---

2), 96; UBS: 63.6%, see Annual Report of UBS 2010 (fn. 2), 218 ff.; Credit Suisse: 60.0%, see Annual Report of Credit Suisse 2010 (fn. 2), 175; ABB: 87.5%, see Annual Report of ABB 2010 (fn. 4), 20.

[109] Corporate Governance Code (fn. 15) para. 14 subpara. 4.

[110] Art. 713 para. 1 CO.

[111] P. Forstmoser (fn. 67) § 11 N. 80.

[112] Art. 713 para. 1 (second sentence) CO.

[113] Art. 716a para. 1 CO; A. Meier-Hayoz and P. Forstmoser, *Schweizerisches Gesellschaftsrecht*, 10th edn, Berne, Staempfli (2007) § 16 N. 408; R. Müller, L. Lipp and A. Plüss (fn. 77) 58; P. Böckli (fn. 12) § 13 N. 405 and 423; C.B. Bühler (fn. 12) N. 630; R.Watter and K. Roth Pellanda (fn. 58) Art. 716a N. 37.

[114] Art. 716a para. 2 CO.—T. Jutzi (fn. 60) 51 ff.; P. Forstmoser (fn. 67) § 5 N. 10 ff.

According to the prevailing view, veto rights of certain Board members (such as the Chairman or a representative of the founding family) are not considered to be legally sustainable, nor are multiple voting rights of certain Board members: In a Swiss Board, there is a one seat–one vote principle.[115] It is a widely held belief that this rule is mandatory as a correlative element of the strict individual liability of each Board member.[116] Although rarely seen, a Company might have the idea to subject certain substantial decisions (of course, outside the legal 'seven-core-points' list) to the approval by a majority vote of non-executive independent directors alone, but this arrangement is in an obvious conflict with the one seat-one vote principle. The case would be different if there was a specific conflict of interest matter to be resolved (see below).[117]

Although the law is silent on this point, Swiss Boards regularly hold separate meetings of independent directors, particularly to discuss delicate issues where executives (or those non-executives on the Board who are not independent) are concerned and to proceed to the evaluation of the Board's own work and effectiveness.[118]

While the law deals only to a limited extent with the person presiding over the Board, the Chairman plays a paramount role in Swiss Boards, he 'makes or

---

[115] See W.F. Bürgi, 'Commentary on Art. 660-697 CO', in *Züricher Kommentar zum Obligationenrecht, 5. Teil: Die Aktiengesellschaft, Teilband V 5b/1: Rechte und Pflichten der Aktionäre*, Zurich, Schulthess (1957), 'Commentary on Art. 698-738 CO', in *Züricher Kommentar zum Obligationenrecht, 5. Teil: Die Aktiengesellschaft, Teilband V 5b/2*, Zurich, Schulthess (1969) Art. 708 N. 41; C. von Greyerz, 'Die Aktiengesellschaft', in *Schweiz. Privatrecht, Bd. VIII/2*, Basel, Helbing & Lichtenhahn (1982) 206; B. Tanner, *Quoren für die Beschlussfassung in der Aktiengesellschaft*, Thesis, Zurich, Schulthess (1987) 48; M. Weber, *Vertretung im Verwaltungsrat, Qualifikation—Zulässigkeit—Schranken*, Thesis, Zurich, Schulthess (1994) 159 ff.; I. von Moos-Busch, *Das Organisationsreglement des Verwaltungsrats*, Thesis, Zurich (1995) 92; P. Forstmoser, A. Meier-Hayoz and P. Nobel (fn. 13) § 31 N. 22; E. Homburger, 'Commentary on Art. 707–726 CO', in *Zürcher Kommentar zum Obligationenrecht, 5. Teil: Die Aktiengesellschaft, Teilband V 5b: Der Verwaltungsrat*, Zurich, Schulthess (1997) Art. 713 N. 293; G. Krneta (fn. 36) N. 284; R. Müller, L. Lipp and A. Plüss (fn. 77) 127 ff.; P. Böckli (fn. 12) § 13 N. 127; P. Forstmoser (fn. 67) N. 83/84; M. Wernli and M.A. Rizzi, 'Commentary on Art. 707–715a and 762–763 CO', in *Basler Kommentar zum Obligationenrecht II*, H. Honsell, N.P. Vogt and R. Watter (eds.), 3rd edn, Basel, Helbing & Lichtenhahn (2012) Art. 713 n. 8; see also Swiss Supreme Court (*Schweizerisches Bundesgericht*), BGE 71 I 187 (1945) and BGE 71 II 279 (1945).

[116] See P. Böckli (fn. 12) § 13 N. 126; P. Forstmoser (fn. 67) N. 83.

[117] See below 3.1.3.3.

[118] Eg. Novartis (see Organizational Rules of Novartis, para. 14 subpara. 5, available at <http://www.novartis.com/downloads/investors/corporate-governance/regulations-en.pdf>), UBS (see Organizational Rules of UBS, para. 6 subpara. 7, available at <http://www.ubs.com>) and Holcim (see Organizational Rules of Holcim, para. 5 subpara. 3 and 4, available at <http://www.holcim.com/fileadmin/templates/CORP/doc/Organizational_ Rules_110505.pdf>).

breaks' the board.[119] The General Shareholders' Meeting traditionally is directed by the Chairman of the Board (not a member of the management board, or the Chief Executive Officer). The Chairman not only largely shapes the image and the public recognition of the company and its leaders, he also sets the tone, and influences the Board's effectiveness and integrity in a great variety of formal and informal ways. He is the guarantor of the flow of information to the Board[120] and represents the Board vis-à-vis the management during the whole year. His personal clout, his flair for developing problems, his power to initiate and his determination to follow-up on matters are irreplaceable.

There are no legal constraints on the election of a former CEO to the function of Chairman of the Board, and the Corporate Governance Code does not address this specific issue. It is entirely a matter for the Board to form an opinion on the pros and cons of such a co-opting succession, and up to the shareholders to decide implicitly by a refusal to elect the former CEO to the Board.

b) Board Consent Requirement for Certain Managerial Decisions

The Corporate Governance Code recommended from its inception—and practically all listed companies followed—the recommendation to subject certain important decisions of the management to prior Board consent.[121] The establishment of the consent requirement list, which is to be embodied in the Organisational Regulation,[122] is entirely up to the Board's judgment. It usually comprises the investments not contained in the annual budget and going beyond a certain limit, entry into (or exit out of) substantial areas of corporate activity, commencement of substantial legal proceedings, issuance of large amounts of corporate debt not included in the financial planning, and remuneration guidelines for managers below the Board of Managers.

c) Board Committees

Board Committees are specifically provided for under corporation law as a tool of efficient structuring.[123] In accordance with the Corporate Governance Code,[124] all listed companies have an Audit Committee, a Remuneration Committee and a Nomination Committee, where most members are independent directors (in the

---

[119] To quote the title of a book on this subject.—See G. Krneta (fn. 36) N. 481; P. Böckli (fn. 12) § 13 N. 105, 314; C.B. Bühler (fn. 12) N. 627.

[120] Corporate Governance Code (fn. 15) para 15.

[121] Corporate Governance Code (fn. 15) para. 11 subpara. 2.

[122] Art. 716a para. 2 CO; such a list would be mandatory according to the Bill of 21 December 2007 (fn. 16).

[123] Art. 716a para. 2 CO (actually, introduced already in Art. 650 para. 2 CO 1881).

[124] Corporate Governance Code (fn. 15) para. 21 ff.

Audit and Remuneration Committees, all members[125]). From the beginning, Board candidates are chosen with a view to a later function in the various committees, especially the Audit Committee. Many companies form additional committees, such as an *ad hoc* committee for a specific task, or a Risk Committee, a Strategic Committee, a Financial Committee or a Corporate Governance Committee, although these functions usually are combined with one or the other of the three 'classical' committees. A number of companies combine the nomination and the compensation functions in one Board Committee. Creation of an Executive Committee, which was quite usual in the past and often pre-empted the functioning of the whole Board,[126] has fallen more and more out of favour.

Usually, the Committees of the Board are composed of three members, all of them, including their Chair, being designated by the full Board. The Committee Charters, sometimes integrated in the Organisational Regulations, are established by the full Board. In some rare cases there are Committees of four or even five members.

Committees are, by law, required to report regularly on their activities to the full Board.[127] Most tasks of the Committees are confined to special analysis and generally the preparation of Board decisions, or, in the case of the Audit Committee in particular, to forming a solid view of, and following up on, matters of accounting and auditing. Outside the law's 'seven-points' list of core full board matters, [128] the Committees may be assigned specific decisionary powers, although in the field of management compensation such a practice is increasingly frowned upon. The Audit Committee may be granted sole decision-making power only in relatively limited areas, such as regarding internal auditing, the assumption of non-audit tasks by the external auditors,[129] or the confirmation of the external auditors' independence.[130]

---

[125] Regarding Audit Committees, the original version of the Corporate Governance Code of 2002 had not had the courage to say as much, but the current practice goes beyond the letter of its para. 23. The Amendment of the Code of 6 September 2007 excluded, in its para. 2, all non-independent directors from the Remuneration Committee, and having executive directors or the Chairman of the Board elected to the Audit Committee is deemed to be inappropriate these days.

[126] P. Böckli (fn. 12) § 13 N. 420.

[127] Art. 716a para. 2 and, where decision powers are delegated to the committee, Art. 716b para. 2 CO.

[128] See above 2.1.1.; Art. 716a para. 1 CO.

[129] Corporate Governance Code (fn. 15) para. 24 subpara. 5.

[130] The criteria are embedded in the corporation law, Art. 728 CO.

d) Typical Assignments of Board Committees

The following may be mentioned as typical areas of committee work in Swiss public companies.[131]

(1) It is the task of the Board's Audit Committee to form an independent judgment of the quality of the External Auditors, the internal control system and the annual financial statements. The Audit Committee should assess the quality of the risk management and of the state of compliance with laws, regulations and other binding provisions within the company. The Committee is to examine the individual and consolidated financial statements as well as to review the interim statements intended for publication and thoroughly discuss these with the Chief Financial Officer (CFO) and the head of Internal Audit and, separately, with the head of the External Auditors.[132] The Audit Committee has the task annually to decide whether the financial statement should be recommended to the board of directors for presentation to the Shareholders' Meeting. The Audit Committee also assesses the performance and the fees charged by the External Auditors; it pre-approves 'parallel' consulting work to be performed by the Auditors.[133]

(2) The role of the Compensation Committee[134] was considerably upgraded in Switzerland by the 2007 amendment of the Corporate Governance Code[135] although the Swiss Parliament appears to consider such committees to be basically unable to cope with the 'fact cats'[136] issue. According to the Code, it is the responsibility of this Committee to draft the compensation system for the Management and the Board itself, to have it discussed, amended and approved by the full Board, to have it implemented during the business year and to take all detailed compensation decisions assigned to it. The Compensation Committees also monitor the delicate subject of

---

[131] See among many others: K. Roth Pellanda (fn. 72) 288 ff.; P. Böckli (fn. 12) § 13 N. 411 ff.; C.B. Bühler (fn. 12) N. 1292 ff.; P. Forstmoser (fn. 67) § 5 N. 75 ff.; A. Meier-Hayoz and P. Forstmoser (fn. 113) § 16 N. 392e ff.—R. Watter and K. Roth Pellanda (fn. 58) Art. 716a N. 41; Corporate Governance Code (fn. 15) para. 21 ff.

[132] Corporate Governance Code (fn. 15) para. 24 subpara. 3.

[133] Corporate Governance Code (fn. 15) para. 24 subpara. 4.

[134] Corporate Governance Code (fn. 15) para. 25 and 26.

[135] Amendment of 6 September 2007 to the 2002 Code, with Basis for Conclusions dated 26 September 2007; see K. Hofstetter, *Fünf Jahre Swiss Code of Best Practice: Special Report on the question of compensation of directors and managers in public companies*, Berne, SwissHoldings (2007) 65.

[136] Report of the *Ständerat* (Upper House) of 25 October 2010, *Federal Monitor 2010*, 8299.

company credits extended to members of the Board or the Management,[137] and they supervise the extensive legal transparency requirements [138] regarding compensation paid and credits extended to the board of directors or management board members.

(3) The Nomination Committee primarily lays down the principles for the selection of candidates for election or re-election to the Board.[139] It prepares a selection of candidates in accordance with these criteria and monitors the replacement process. It often also functions as Corporate Governance Committee and may be assigned the task to look more deeply into conflict of interest or related persons issues.

(4) If there is a Risk Committee, the Board has to carefully determine its assignments and limits as regards risk management which, according to Swiss practice, is a substantial task of the Management.[140] The Board has to take similar decisions if it assigns specific supervisory functions to a Finance Committee or an Executive Committee created from amongst its members.

e) Drawbacks of a Highly Structured Board

Organisation of practical board activities in small committees is part of the corporate culture in Switzerland today. Even middle-sized enterprises which are not listed on the Stock Exchange have adopted this system with good results. However, a Board structured in a series of Committees is not without drawbacks. Committees like the ones for Audit and Remuneration matters, but also Risk Committees tend to develop a distinct factual knowledge and professional expertise in their fields, so that the full Board is less and less in a position to effectively question or challenge their findings and their proposals to the full Board. This has the secondary effect that directors who are not serving on the respective committee tend to lean back, studying the issues less carefully than they would do had there been no such committee. This leads to an ever-increasing specialisation and splitting of relevant knowledge within the full Board, and favours a 'rubberstamping' ritual at the end of the presentation of most committee proposals to the full Board. Generally speaking, there is a certain tendency to

---

[137] Credits to directors or officers must be extensively disclosed by public companies in accordance with Art. 663b^bis CO.—See P. Böckli (fn. 12) § 8 N. 631 ff.

[138] Art. 663b^bis and Art. 663c para. 3 CO.

[139] Corporate Governance Code (fn. 15) para. 27.

[140] See *Federal Monitor 2004*, 4023, point 2.1.3.2.1; P. Böckli (fn. 12) § 13 N. 307 and § 15 N. 192; P. Forstmoser (fn. 67) § 8 N. 27 and N. 126.

increasingly subdivide Board work and to make the Chairman's coordination and leadership function more difficult.[141]

2.2.3. *Independent Directors*

The specific kind of 'independence' requires from persons performing the tasks of the statutory audit is painstakingly defined by the law.[142] 'Independence' of Board members is not a notion of corporation law, and even less a requirement. A political decision has been made that it will not be embodied in the ongoing reform of the law but it continues to play an important role in the Corporate Governance Code.[143]

In Switzerland, Boards of public companies are composed almost exclusively (with the exceptions mentioned above) of non-executive directors, and those coming largely from outside the company,[144] generally speaking, but the issue of independence is less of a fascinating issue than in certain Anglo-Saxon jurisdictions. Still, the matter is being taken under consideration.

a) Independence Defined

'Independence' as regards directors, is understood to mean independence from the Company, its business and its management. The definition of the Corporate Governance Code is as follows:[145]

'...Independent members shall mean non-executive members of the Board of Directors who never were or were more than three years ago a member of the executive management and who have no or comparatively minor business relations with the company.

Where there is a cross membership in Boards of Directors, the independence of the respective member should be carefully examined case by case.'

Independence can be and often is defined more precisely in the Board Regulations, following for example the precept of the New York Stock Exchange Rules. In prevailing Swiss practice

– a representative of a large shareholder on the Board does not, by that fact alone, lose 'independence' from the Company, its business and its management. On the contrary (and based upon practical experience), such a configuration tends to contribute to independent supervision of manage-

---

[141] See G. Giger (fn. 13) 331; P. Böckli (fn. 12) § 14 N. 368; C.B. Bühler (fn. 12) N. 458.

[142] Art. 728 CO.

[143] Corporate Governance Code (fn. 15) para. 22, and Amendment of 6 September 2007, para. 2.

[144] In 2011, 62% of all board members of the Swiss public companies under review were independent and non-executive—see Heidrick & Struggles (fn. 52) 42, figure 35.

[145] *Loc. cit.* para. 22.

ment practices.[146] When there is a conflict of interest between the Company and its significant shareholder, the rules dealing with conflicted board members are to be applied on a case-by-case basis;[147]

- an employee of the Company, especially a member of the company's management, should not be deemed to be 'independent', as he or she is in a major business relationship with the company and the Management, or the Board in any event, holds sway over his or her working existence.[148]

b) The Role of Independent Directors

The appropriate role for independent directors is to take care of specific committee work,[149] especially where the potential of material conflicts of interest with top management is looming, ie. on the Audit, Nomination and Compensation Committees. Their view is sought in the ongoing evaluation of the performance of the management board.[150] Generally speaking, independent directors should— and in practically all cases do in Switzerland—make up a large majority of the Board to counterbalance the omnipresent influence of full-time managers in board affairs.[151]

In public companies living up to higher standards of good governance, independent directors, under the guidance of one of their senior figures (often formally designated as 'lead director'), hold meetings amongst themselves, separate from executive directors and management, to take care of specific issues where executives' personal position or interests are put into question.[152]

Independence on the one hand and expertise on the other are qualifications which generally should be combined and cannot be weighed against each other meaningfully. In any event, a qualified director's views carry more weight when

---

[146] See K. Hofstetter (fn. 135) 19 and 20, n. 86.

[147] Corporate Governance Code (fn. 15) para. 16 and Bill on the revision of Swiss Corporation Law of 21 December 2007 (fn. 16), Art. 717a.—P. Böckli, 'Insichgeschäfte und Interessenkonflikte im Verwaltungsrat: Heutige Rechtslage und Blick auf den kommenden Art. 717a E-OR', *Gesellschafts- und Kapitalmarktrecht*, 7 (2012) 365 ff.

[148] Switzerland does not know the dilemma of the German practice, where the 50% representation of employees and other representatives of the labour side on Supervisory Boards make truly independent boards impossible in practice.

[149] Corporate Governance Code (fn. 15) para. 18 subpara. 22.

[150] Art. 716a para. 1 numbered subpara. 5 CO.

[151] See C.B. Bühler, *US Corporate Governance Reform: Impact on NYSE-Listed Swiss Companies*, 2nd edn, Zurich, Schulthess (2004) 32, and C.B. Bühler (fn. 12) N. 1279 and N. 1424. In 2011, 62% of all board members of Swiss public companies reviewed were independent and non-executive — see Heidrick & Struggles (fn. 52) 42, figure 35.

[152] Corporate Governance Code (fn. 15) para. 18 subpara. 3 (third sentence); see also n. 118.

he or she is unquestionably independent. An unqualified member of the Board finds himself marginalised whether he is independent or not.

c) 'Independent' versus 'Not-conflicted' Directors

While an independent director should, by definition, be free from personal interests that tie him to the management or the business as such, he or she may, from time to time, still be seriously conflicted for other specific reasons.[153] The terms have to be clearly differentiated in Swiss practice, and usually are.

d) A Sceptical Assessment

The fact that a person fulfils all criteria of independence from the Company and its management does not in itself guarantee that shareholders' interests are better protected in practical clashes with top management who pursue their agenda. Expectations in this respect of regulators, the media and corporate government experts are exaggerated. An independent director may still prefer not to speak up and not to thwart certain initiatives cherished by the CEO and his colleagues, in order not to endanger his standing and indeed popularity with top management and other directors who are known to steadfastly back management. In unwritten Board practice, a director who has seriously upset top management without being able to oust the management should not be surprised to find his name lacking on the slate for the next Board re-election.

The prevalent tendency to go along with management's proposals tends to be enhanced by the fear of imminent loss of Board fees (which in Switzerland doubled or tripled in the last fifteen years, so as to often make up for a significant portion of a director's total personal income). Factual financial dependence of a well remunerated 'independent' director is rarely discussed openly.

2.2.4. Board Secretary

Two decades ago Swiss law introduced the compulsory function of a Board Secretary.[154] In public companies, the Secretary has proved to be quite indispensable as the requirements of an orderly information and decision-making process has constantly been expanded. Today the Secretary, who usually is not a member of the Board or the management, plays an important role as a 'corporate memory' and an advisor of the Chairman regarding a variety of legal, procedural and indeed compliance issues. He often assists the chairs of the Board Committees and also the individual Board members on corporate affairs. In public companies, he is the watchdog in the enforcement of internal measures

---

[153] See 3.1.3.3 below.
[154] Art. 712 para. 1 CO.

(such as 'close periods'), enforcing proper conduct in the area of insider dealings and fair disclosure.

2.3. Information Streams

The Board's functioning essentially depends on a continuing information stream from management to the Board level.[155] In Swiss practice, this is a thorny issue.

a) Right to Obtain Information

On the positive side is the right of each director, stressed in the corporation law and unconditional, to be informed on all business matters in the Company.[156] With the consent of the Chairman, which shall not be unreasonably withheld, each director can inspect accounting entries, contracts and business correspondence.[157] Companies must introduce a system of regular board information, dealing both with periodical routine information on the course of business and various particular subjects, including finances. The Board as an entity has to ask the management for all information necessary to fulfil its duties. It is responsible for organising the flow of information in its Organisational Regulations.[158] The Board must require management to immediately inform it comprehensively on unforeseen major events and on all issues important to the Company.

The timely providing of appropriate information to the Board is one of the Chairman's key responsibilities. While the law is parsimonious in this field, the Corporate Governance Code contains the necessary guidance.[159] It is up to the Chairman to ensure that procedures related to preparatory work, deliberation, passing resolutions and implementation of decisions are carried out properly. According to Swiss practice, it is the distinct responsibility of the Chairman to ensure that, on a timely basis, information is made available on all aspects of the company which are relevant for decision-making and supervision. It is up to the Chairman to ensure that persons responsible for a particular business are present at the Board meetings to answer questions in greater depth.[160]

---

[155] See P. Böckli (fn. 12) § 13 N. 190a and N. 197; P. Forstmoser (fn. 67) § 4 N. 56.

[156] Art. 715a CO.

[157] Art. 715a para. 4 CO.

[158] See P. Böckli (fn. 12) § 13 N. 189 ff.; P. Forstmoser (fn. 67) § 4 N. 93 and N. 94.

[159] Corporate Governance Code (fn. 15) para. 15.

[160] *Loc. cit.* para. 15 subpara. 3.

b) Information Deficits

On the negative side the directors, who on average show up at the Company's headquarters only every two months or so, and depend on the very persons they should supervise as an almost exclusive source of information, in practice suffer from a serious information deficit with respect to the management.[161] The problem is enhanced by the substantial gap between the sheer physical presence, knowledge and he business know-how of the Management and non-executive members of the Board. A solid basis of knowledge is a precondition to the asking of pertinent questions. It is even more important for a critical assessment of the answer received and when an independent Board member ventures onto the slippery ground of targeted follow-up questions, which are in reality indispensable to reach a clear judgment.

According to a special legal provision, a Board member may go out to actively request relevant information from rank and file employees only based upon special approval granted by the Chairman.[162] Even inquiries with top managers outside formal Board meetings are subject to a specific authorisation of the Chairman, except when limited to general questions regarding the course of business.[163]

The Statutory Auditors are the only truly independent source of information of the Board. The Board Members sitting on the Audit Committees have a privileged position in this respect as they get together about every three months with the head of the external auditors for the review of intermediate statements, or even more often, as Audit Committee meetings have become more frequent over time. Still, the other non-executive Board members do not have this easy access to the external auditors. And more often than not it turns out that very serious problems developing in the company are not on the Statutory Auditors' radar, or at least not early enough to allow for effective Board intervention. The Internal Audit, while a valuable institution, is likewise only readily accessible to Board members who serve on the Audit Committee. The internal auditors' independence from management is not always assured in practice and quite frequently they turn out to be an unreliable source of information in the very early stage of things, going awry at middle management level.

In Swiss practice it has been established quite clearly that managers have an 'agent's' basic interest not to charge themselves by feeding negative news to their 'principal', the Board. This natural though regrettable tendency leads to asymmetric Board information. Good news goes up fast and undistorted, bad news go up slowly and in a filtered form—or even not at all. Those Board

---

[161] P. Böckli (fn. 15) 21 and P. Böckli (fn. 12) § 13 N. 164a and N. 197.

[162] Art. 715a para. 3 (second sentence) CO.

[163] Art. 715a para. 3 (first sentence) CO.

members who call themselves 'independent' do not have a major independent internal source of information. The problem is resolved neither in Swiss corporate law nor in practice.

3. Accountability

3.1. Board and Shareholders

While sceptical perception of Boards of Directors has, in the end, varied very little in the eyes of the Swiss public, the image of the *shareholder* is about to change. Even the most idealistic shareholder activists have to accept the fact of 'depersonalisation'. The shareholder being an individual, investing his own savings, has become the exception, and the legal entity whose voting decisions are made by an obscure body of persons acting in a fiduciary capacity for collective savings, following standardised outside advice, is becoming fast the typical shareholder.[164] 'Short-termism' (the average holding period of shares has gone down from many years to close to one year and recently even less) is a very visible phenomenon. Still, in Switzerland few have drawn the consequences of this slow but inexorable change of facts behind the term 'the shareholder' which, in the ongoing discussion, is still used with an excessively romantic and conservative undertone based on the strong belief that shareholders act like an 'owner' of the company, primarily seeking long-term development.

3.1.1. Task and Powers of the Board and the Shareholders

a) Election, Term, Revocation

Directors, whether executive or non-executive, dependent or independent, are always and exclusively elected by the General Meeting of Shareholders.[165]

While in almost all cases the proposals for the election of a candidate is brought forth by the Board, each shareholder individually has the right to validly propose a candidate, even as late as during the General Shareholders' Meeting.[166] Directors are usually elected for a term of office of three years,[167] although the Articles

---

[164] See n. 2 above.

[165] Art. 698 para. 2 numbered subpara. 2 and Art. 710 para. 1 CO.

[166] Art. 700 para. 4 CO.—Subject to the condition that the topic of the election of directors is to be found on the Agenda presented to the shareholders 20 days before the day of the shareholders' meeting.

[167] The Corporate Governance Code (fn. 15) para. 13 subpara. 1 recommends not to go beyond a term of four years, while the law still permits six years at the most, Art. 710 CO. A

cont. ...

of Association can provide for a shorter term (one year is not so rare any more) or a longer term (of up to six years, which has mostly fallen out of usage). Re-election is possible and there is no legal limit to subsequent re-elections. The Board itself has no right to appoint a new director or provisionally to replace a position that has become vacant during the term of office.[168]

The appointment of each Board member can be revoked without cause during his or her term by the General Shareholders' Meeting,[169] and the board of directors may at any time remove from office any member of a Board Committee and all officers, including the Managing Director, if any, and the members of the Board of Management.[170] The Board may do so even without cause if it so decides in the interest of the company, subject to civil liability for damages in the event of a breach of contract.

There are no 'Dutch type' arrangements of the law or practice to impede free decisions of shareholders regarding elections of Directors or—with one exception—to prevent the revocation of a Director.[171] There is a possibility to set out in the Articles of Association a rule against simultaneous removal of more than one-third of all Board members in one Shareholders' Meeting, in order to engender board stability.[172] The Shareholders' Meeting, conversely, is absolutely not empowered to designate or dismiss members of the management board (or managers in general), this being one of the legal 'seven points' reserved to the Board absolutely.[173]

b) No Mandatory Minority Representation

While the law permits for a provision of the Articles of Association instituting minority shareholders to be represented on the Board,[174] such clauses are practically never seen in listed companies. Cumulative voting is permitted by law, but practically never instituted in public companies.[175] The minority shareholders have no right to ask for the introduction of such a system.

---

popular initiative on 3 March 2013 adopted by the Swiss people introduced a compulsory one year term of office for public companies.

[168] Contrary to French law, for example.

[169] Art. 705 para. 1 CO.

[170] Art. 726 CO.

[171] Shareholders' Agreements are valid under Swiss Law; however, in voting matters they are not binding on the Company as a legal entity but they are enforceable as contracts between the parties.

[172] Swiss Supreme Court (*Schweizerisches Bundesgericht*), BGE 117 II 314 (1991).

[173] Art. 716a para. 1 numbered para. 4 CO.

[174] Art. 709 para. 2 CO.

[175] See R. Watter and K. Maizar, 'Aktionärsdemokratie, über erweiterte Zuständigkeiten der Generalversammlung und Erleichterungen bei der Stimmrechtsausübung in schweizerischen

cont. ...

There are no rights of appointment in listed companies under Swiss corporation or Stock Exchange law. Contrary to a certain French practice, in Switzerland the Government also refrains from using direct or indirect pressure to be represented on the Boards of certain companies. Only in mixed economy companies (*Gemischtwirtschaftliche Unternehmen*) or companies organised under specific federal laws (where federal or local State entities hold a significant equity interest) is there a system of State-appointed representatives on the Board.[176]

There is no legal *guillotine* provision limiting total board service time to—by way of example—nine or twelve years, although some public companies have adopted such limits in their Organisational Regulations.[177]

3.1.2. Division of Power between Board and Shareholders

a) Shareholders

Swiss law consequently separates the powers of the Board and the Shareholders' Meeting. The latter is not empowered to engage in management or supervision matters, but is called upon primarily to enact and modify the Articles, increase or reduce stated capital, elect directors and external auditors, and to approve the annual statement and declare a dividend in matters where the Board is confined to a preparatory role.[178] The shareholders alone have the power to increase or decrease the capital,[179] to put the company in liquidation,[180] to change its purpose, clause and its name[181] as well as some other basic acts. The shareholders have the exclusive right to issue non-voting stock or to limit voting rights of voting stock in certain matters.[182]

The Shareholders' Meeting cannot give binding instructions to the Board, but its range of empowerment has been extended by an Amendment to the Federal

---

Aktiengesellschaften', in P. Breitschmid et al (eds.), *Liber amicorum Hans Michael Riemer, Grundfragen der juristischen Person*, Berne, Staempfli (2007) 403, 429; P. Böckli (fn. 12) § 13 N. 80 and N. 81; C.B. Bühler (fn. 12) N. 692; M. Wernli and M.A. Rizzi (fn. 115) Art. 709 N. 27 and N. 28.

[176] Art. 762 CO and specific federal laws, such as the Swisscom Law (*Bundesgesetz über die Organisation der Telekommunikationsunternehmung des Bundes*) of 30 April 1997 and the Federal Railway Act (*Bundesgesetz über die Schweizerischen Bundesbahnen*) of 20 March 1998.

[177] Such provisions in the Regulations do not limit the powers of shareholders, but they prevent the Board from proposing a further re-election beyond the ninth or twelfth year. To be binding on shareholders, the limit must be inserted into the Articles of Association, Art. 626 numbered para. 6 CO.

[178] Art. 698 and 716a para. 1 numbered subpara. 6 CO.

[179] Art. 650 ff. and Art. 632 CO.

[180] Art. 736 CO.

[181] Art. 704 and Art. 626 numbered paragraph 1 CO.

[182] Art. 656a para. 1, Art. 685a and Art. 692 para. 2 (second sentence) CO.

Constitution adopted by the Swiss people on 3 March 2013, requiring share-holders' approval for both Board and Management remuneration. Say-on-pay is one of the hottest issues of Swiss politics at the moment.[183]

Under Swiss law shareholders enjoy a relatively strong legal position as they are able to individually propose election or revocation of directors,[184] to propose a larger distribution then what the Board wishes, and also, individually, to chal-lenge shareholders' resolutions in court.[185] In Shareholders' Meetings they have a right of information vis-à-vis the Board.[186] Shareholders can, with certain repre-sentation thresholds, call for a matter to be put on the Agenda or require the Board to convene an extraordinary Shareholders' Meeting,[187] or ask for a special inquiry into purported misdeeds or negligent omissions of the Board or top management.[188] Shareholders representing 10% of share capital can require the court, for cause and *in extremis*, to dissolve the company or to take other appro-priate remedial measures.[189]

b) Board

Directors are obligated to direct the company in good faith and with due care, respecting the rule of equal treatment of shareholders.[190] All these requirements, sounding self-evident, are construed quite severely by the courts, apparently more severe in most respects than by the Delaware Court of Chancery, for example. The Board is responsible for carrying out its core duties of the legal 'seven-points' catalogue mentioned above,[191] including oversight of financial planning, legal compliance and introduction and maintenance of an appropriate Internal

---

[183] For an overview, see P. Forstmoser, 'Die Entschädigung der Mitglieder von Verwal-tungsrat und Topmanagement—Binsenwahrheiten, Missverständnisse und ein konkreter Vor-schlag', in R.T. Trindade, H. Peter and C. Bovet (eds.), *Liber amicorum Anne Petitpierre-Sauvain, Economie Environnement Ethique*, Zurich, Schulthess (2009) 145; C.B. Bühler, 'Vergütungen an Verwaltungsrat und Geschäftsleitung: Volksinitiative 'gegen die Abzockerei' und Gegenentwürfe', in R. Watter (ed.), *Die 'grosse' Schweizer Aktienrechtsrevision, Eine Standortbestimmung per Ende 2010*, Zurich Dike (2010) 247—The *Parliamentary Amendment* on Board and Top Management remuneration rules, of 16 March 2012, was, on 3 March 2013, rejected in favour of the so-called „*Minder Amendment*", see n. 17.

[184] Subject to the Agenda providing for such an election or revocation which only a substantial minority of shareholders can force upon the Board. Art. 699 para. 3 CO.

[185] Art. 706 CO.

[186] Art. 697 CO.

[187] Art. 699 para. 3 CO.

[188] Art. 697a CO.

[189] Art. 736 numbered para. 4 CO.

[190] Art. 717 CO.

[191] Art. 716a para. 1 CO. See above sec. 2.1.1.

Control System (ICS),[192] and is required to monitor its functioning.[193] It is held unanimously that the Board, although the law does not specifically say so, has to see to it that the ICS is supervised and properly documented, either in a special Regulation or as an annex to the Board Regulations.

One of the main tasks of directors is to closely supervise management[194] and to timely and forcefully intervene when things start to go awry.[195] In financially dire times, the Board has the responsibility to prevent the company from indulging in unlawful trading;[196] a large number of Swiss bankruptcy cases end up with the directors being made liable for damages on the theory that the declaration of insolvency should have been filed with the Courts earlier.

As pointed out at the outset, there is a slow spill-over from certain aspects of financial market law into corporation law, mostly as regards compliance and internal control requirements, but this effect is practically limited to the 300 listed companies,[197] while the several hundred thousand unlisted Swiss corporations and limited liability companies remain mostly outside of this specific trickle-down effect.

3.1.3. Special Issues

a) 'Dormant' Voting Rights in Public Companies

One of the most serious special issues regarding the functioning of Swiss public companies is the phenomenon of dormant voting rights, locally and euphemistically referred to as *Dispo-Aktien*.[198] Almost all public companies have issued registered shares which can only be voted if the acquirer has duly filed for registration in the stock ledger—something that an increasingly large part of investors do not do. The dividend is paid, conversely, to non-registered stock purchasers. For different reasons—one of them the lack of interest in exercising voting rights—in most companies 20% to 40% (or even more) of all shares have

---

[192] Indirect consequences of a provision on the auditing of larger companies (those above the SME-level) in Art. 728a para. 1 numbered subpara. 3 CO. See M. Peyer (fn. 79) 67 ff.

[193] Art. 716a para. 1 numbered subpara. 5 CO.

[194] Art. 716a para. no. 5 and Art. 754 para. 2 CO.

[195] 'Duty to intervene' or *Eingriffspflicht*, based upon court practice, Swiss Supreme Court (*Schweizerisches Bundesgericht*), BGE 97 II 411 (1971, leading case); also BGE 113 IV 74 (1987); BGE 114 IV 224 (1988); BGE 122 III 199 (1995) and BGE 128 III 133 (2002).— P.R. Isler, 'Sorgfalt und Haftung des Verwaltungsrates', in R.H. Weber (ed.), *Verantwortlichkeit im Unternehmensrecht I*, Europa Institut Zürich, Zurich, Schulthess (2003) 1, 13.

[196] Art. 725 para. 2 CO.

[197] See n. 41 above.

[198] See the Government Report accompanying the Bill of 21 December 2007 (fn. 16), 1619.

no registered owner [199] and are, therefore, excluded from voting in the shareholders' meeting. By that token, those who do register have a position somehow equivalent to an increased or, in the case of 50% dormant voting rights, double voting rights although this is not what the law says and the Articles of association appear to provide for. Therefore, in a typical case of a Swiss public company, decisions are taken by a minority or 17.6% of all shares, if there are 30% dormant voting rights and a customary 50% presence of all registered shares. No solution to this problem appears to find the necessary political support in Parliament.[200]

b) Privileges for Long-term Shareholders or for Those who Participate in Voting at Shareholders' Meetings

The idea of granting more voting rights ('double voting rights' in the French model) to long-term shareholders has never been seriously discussed in Switzerland, although awareness of the drawbacks of shareholder 'short-termism' is increasing slowly and steadily. The present corporation law, due to certain of its mechanisms,[201] would probably not permit a system of privileged voting rights dependant on a certain time span of registration in the stock ledger.

Conversely, the proposal to grant defined special advantages to shareholders who actively participate in shareholders' meetings (eg. an add-on to the dividend) has been discussed for quite some time, but has always been discarded in the end.

---

[199] See K. Hofstetter, *Corporate Governance in der Schweiz, Bericht im Zusammenhang mit den Arbeiten der Expertengruppe 'Corporate Governance' vom 1. Juli 2002*, 22; H.C. von der Crone, 'Stimmrechtsvertretung und Dispoaktien, Bericht zu einer Teilrevision des Aktienrechts', *Zeitschrift zur Rechtsetzung und Praxis im Gesellschafts- und Handelsregisterrecht* 5 (2003) 12; P. Böckli, 'Zum Vorentwurf für eine Revision des Aktien- und Rechnungslegungsrechts. Eine kritische Übersicht', *Gesellschafts- und Kapitalmarktrecht* 1 (2006) 4, 15; P. Böckli, 'Nachbesserungen und Fehlleistungen in der Revision des Aktienrechts. Zum Gesetzesentwurf vom 21. Dezember 2007', *Schweizerische Juristen-Zeitung* 104 (2008) 333, 363; P. Böckli (fn. 12) § 6 N. 166 ff.; P. Böckli and J. Bangert, 'Lösung der Dispoaktienproblematik: Gesetzesvorschlag und Erläuterungen', Berne 2008, passim, available at <www.swissholdings.ch/vernehmlassung/kapitalmarkt-und-gesellschaftsrecht.html>; U. Brügger, 'Transparenz im Aktionariat von Publikumsgesellschaften: der tatsächliche Aktionär ist und bleibt ein Phantom', in N.P. Vogt, E. Stupp and D. Dubs (eds.), *Liber amicorum Rolf Watter, Unternehmen—Transaktion—Recht*, Zurich, Dike (2008) 83, 102; H.C. von der Crone and P.R. Isler, 'Dispoaktien', *Gesellschafts- und Kapitalmarktrecht* 3 (2008) Sondernummer, Die grosse Aktienrechtsrevision, 76.

[200] See Government Report accompanying the Bill of 21 December 2007 (fn. 16) 1621; P. Böckli (fn. 12) § 6 N. 152 ff.

[201] Art. 693 CO ties the voting privilege to par value of a class of shares.

No bill or serious amendment in the present revision of corporate law[202] provides for such a solution.

c) Conflict of Interest and Related-parties' Transactions

While the reform bill pending in Parliament introduces a specific legal provision dealing with conflict of interest situations, [203] currently the respective recommendation—which is widely followed—is to be found in the Corporate Governance Code only.[204] It reads:

'Each member of the Board of Directors and Executive Board should arrange his personal and business affairs so as to avoid, as far as possible, conflicts of interest with the company.
– Should a conflict of interest arise, the member of the Board of Directors or Executive Management concerned should inform the Chairman of the Board. The Chairman, or Vice-Chairman, should request a decision by the Board of Directors which reflects the seriousness of the conflict of interest. The Board shall decide without participation of the person concerned.
– Anyone who has an interest in conflict with the company or is obligated to represent such interests on behalf of third parties should not participate to that extent in decision-making. Anyone having a permanent conflict of interest should not be a member of the Board of Directors or the Executive Management.
– Transactions between the company and members of corporate bodies or related persons should be carried out 'at arm's length' and should be approved without participation of the party concerned. If necessary, a neutral opinion should be obtained.'

A bill pending in Parliament embodies these rules, with some few modifications, in the Corporation Law.[205]

There is a body of court cases[206] and literature[207] dealing with the handling and resolution of conflicts of interest. Most listed companies have embodied

---

[202] See Government Report to the Bill of 21 December 2007 (fn. 16). The *Amendment* to the Corporation Law of 16 March 2012was rejected by the Swiss people on 3 March 2013, in favour of the so-called "*Minder Amendment*", see n. 17.

[203] Art. 717a of the Bill on the revision of Corporation Law of 21 December 2007 (fn. 16).

[204] See Corporate Governance Code (fn. 15) para. 16.

[205] Art. 717a of the Bill on the revision of Corporation Law of 21 December 2007 (fn. 16).

[206] Swiss Supreme Court (*Schweizerisches Bundesgericht*), BGE 99 Ia 9 (1973) and BGE 113 II 57 (1987), leading cases; BGE 126 III 366 (2000) and BGE 127 III 332 (2001); non-published judgment of the Swiss Federal Supreme Court 4A_462/2009 of 16 March 2010, consideration 6.3.

[207] Eg. H.C. von der Crone, 'Interessenkonflikte im Aktienrecht', *Schweizerische Zeitschrift für Wirtschafts- und Finanzmarktrecht* 66 (1994) 1; A. Schott, *Insichgeschäft und Interessenkonflikt*, Thesis, Zurich, Schulthess (2002) 259; P. Forstmoser, 'Interessenkonflikte von Verwaltungsratsmitgliedern', in N.P. Vogt and P. Zobel (eds.), *Liber amicorum Hermann Schulin,* Basel, Helbing & Lichtenhahn (2002) 9; L. Handschin, 'Treuepflicht des Verwaltungsrates bei der gesellschaftsinternen Entscheidfindung', in H.C. von der Crone et al (eds.), *Liber*

cont. ...

these or similar rules in their Organisational Regulations.[208] The Chairman, or if he is conflicted the Vice-Chairman, plays a leading role in dealing with conflicts of interest. When a conflict of interest affects the board of directors or the management board, it is up to the Chairman or the Vice-Chairman to recommend to the Board a resolution reflecting the specific nature and the seriousness of the conflict. The decision, according to prevailing Swiss practice, is taken without participation of the person who is directly concerned by a substantial conflict, through a majority decision of the rest of the Board.[209]

According to the present state of legal development, one of the following remedial measures (or a combination of them) may be considered to be appropriate in a conflict of interest situation:

(i) exclusion of the conflicted member from the substantive decision;[210]

(ii) creation of a specific Board Committee[211] composed of non-conflicted and independent directors to analyse the situation and recommend a solution;

(iii) obtaining an independent expert's opinion[212] on the 'at arm's length' conditions for a specific transaction between the company and the conflicted person;

(iv) specific approval of the respective transaction by a majority vote of all non-conflicted directors;[213]

---

amicorum Peter Forstmoser, Zurich, Schulthess (2003) 169, 171; M. Lazopoulos, 'Massnahmen zur Bewältigung von Interessenkonflikten im Verwaltungsrat', *Aktuelle Juristische Praxis* 15 (2006) 139; M. Kissling, *Der Mehrfachverwaltungsrat*, Thesis, Zurich, Schulthess (2006) 47; K. Roth Pellanda (fn. 72) 175; R. Müller, L. Lipp and A. Plüss (fn. 77) 233; N. Zürcher Fausch, *Konkurrenzverbote in Konzernverhältnissen*, Thesis, St. Gallen, Berne, Staempfli (2007) 268 and 303; P. Böckli (fn. 12) § 13 N. 633 ff.; C.B. Bühler (fn. 12) N. 643; M. Blanc, *Corporate Governance dans les groups de sociétiés*, Thesis, Zurich, Dike (2010) 167 ff.; C. Sommer, *Die Treuepflicht des Verwaltungsrats gemäss Art. 717 Abs. 1 OR*, Thesis, Zurich, Dike (2010) 85 ff.; P. Forstmoser (fn. 67) N. 102; P. Böckli (fn. 147) 354 ff.

[208] Art. 716b para. 2 CO.—See P. Böckli (fn. 12) § 13 N. 33 (9); P. Forstmoser (fn. 67) § 11 N. 102.

[209] See Art. 717a of the Bill on the revision of Corporation Law of 21 December 2007 (fn. 16) and P. Böckli (fn. 147) 365 ff.

[210] Corporate Governance Code (fn. 15) para. 16 subpara. 2; Art. 717a para. 3 (second sentence) of the Bill of 21 December 2007 (fn. 16); P. Böckli (fn. 147) 368.

[211] Eg. P. Forstmoser (fn. 207) 19; M. Lazopoulos (fn. 207) 143; P. Böckli (fn. 147) 368.

[212] Corporate Governance Code (fn. 15) para. 16 subpara. 3 (second sentence).

[213] According to court practice the contract concluded in self-dealing may be authorised by at least one non-conflicted board member entitled to bind the company by his signature, based upon his or her own diligent analysis, Swiss Supreme Court (*Schweizerisches Bundesgericht*), BGE 127 III 334 (2001).

(v) presentation of the problem-fraught transaction to the shareholders' meeting[214] for approval (this is considered to be quite unworkable in the case of a listed company, except in the event of a merger or demerger).

While there is no established legal doctrine, it is generally held that a member of the Board cannot at the same time serve another company which is a substantial and direct competitor. Anyone having a permanent and serious conflict of interest should put an end to his or her membership on the board of directors or the management board.[215]

The Chairman is to ascertain that related-party transactions[216] are properly dealt with according to the rules on conflicts of interest.

d) *Grasping of Corporate Opportunities*

Grasping of corporate opportunities is considered to be a breach of loyalty owed to the Company. While such events are not always clear-cut, nor easy to discover, in an obvious case both civil action and criminal prosecution are possible.[217] The director or officer involved may be required to hand the product of his disloyal activity over to the Company.[218]

e) *Inside Information*

Switzerland introduced insider trading legislation relatively early (in 1987), but failed to organise appropriate enforcement measures in this area so that in almost a quarter century there were few convictions. Moreover, taking advantage of a profit warning information and similar situations was declared unlawful only a few years ago[219] so that the most likely insider dealings were not punishable in

---

[214] Swiss Supreme Court (*Schweizerisches Bundesgericht*), BGE 99 Ia 9 (1973); BGE 126 III 366 (2000) and BGE 127 III 332 (2001).

[215] Specific recommendation in the Corporate Governance Code (fn. 15) para. 16 subpara. 2 (second sentence).

[216] This is good practice. The law today in force and effect specifically mentions related party transactions only at scattered occasions, in Art. 663a para. 4; Art. 663b^bis para. 1 numbered subpara. 5; Art. 663c para. 2 and Art. 678 para. 1 CO.

[217] Art. 158 para. 1 of the Swiss Penal Code (*Schweizerisches Strafgesetzbuch vom 21. Dezember 1937*, neu gefasst am 17. Juni 1994).

[218] Art. 423 para. 1 CO.

[219] See L. Marolda Martinez, *Information der Aktionäre nach schweizerischem Aktien- und Kapitalmarktrecht*, Thesis, Zurich, Schulthess (2006) 293; P. Böckli (fn. 12) § 13 N. 614; C.B. Bühler (fn. 12) N. 1124; R. Mabillard and M. Ammann, 'Kursrelevanz zwischen ökonomischer Beobachtung und rechtlicher Steuerung', *Gesellschafts- und Kapitalmarktrecht* 6 (2011) 155.

Switzerland for two decades. The role that the Board has to play in preventing insider dealing is clearly recognised.[220]

This matter is addressed in the Corporate Governance Code as follows:[221]

'The Board of Directors should regulate the principles governing ad hoc publicity in more detail and take measures to prevent insider-dealing offences.

The Board of Directors should consider in particular whether appropriate action (eg. "close periods") should be taken with regard to purchasing and selling securities of the company or other sensitive assets during critical periods, eg. in connection with take-over projects, before media conferences or prior to announcing corporate results.'

The Board has a general task, derived from its duty of care, to take appropriate measures preventing prohibited insider dealings by Board members, managers and other key employees close to the source of the privileged information. In the context of a special event falling within the legal definition of the Penal Code (*Schweizerisches Strafgesetzbuch*) (eg. profit warning, forthcoming merger or acquisition, surprise resignation of the CEO etc.), the flow of inside information to third parties, including in particular a major shareholder, is a punishable act.[222]

Even outside of the context of a special event, the corporation law itself (equal treatment rule[223]) and capital market law (level playing field and fair disclosure rules) do not allow selective and privileged information to flow to a major shareholder. While in practice there is a grey area (top managers assert they must be allowed to further explain and detail generally known facts to substantial shareholders who specifically inquire, and major shareholders often forcefully insist on getting more and earlier information), the rules quite clearly prohibit privileged information.[224]

In a situation where the company practically depends on a prior approval by major shareholders to go ahead with an important project (such as a takeover or a merger plan), prevailing practice requires the company to make the respective

---

[220] The provision of the Swiss Penal Code (*Schweizerisches Strafgesetzbuch*) of 21 December 1937, as amended in 1987/2007 on *Insider Dealing* (Art. 161). The provision has been largely harmonised with the EU format on 28 September 2012, enforcement has been strengthened, and the penal provision has been transferred to Art. 40 of the Stock Exchange Law (*Bundesgesetz über die Börsen und den Effektenhandel*, SESTA, n. 31).

[221] Corporate Governance Code (fn. 15) para. 17.

[222] Art. 161 of the Swiss Penal Code (*Schweizerisches Strafgesetzbuch*), as amended in 2007, replaced by Art. 40 of the Law of 28 September 2012 (implementing the penal provision in the Stock Exchange Law, SESTA, n. 31).

[223] Art. 717 para. 2 CO.

[224] See P. Böckli and C.B. Bühler, 'Vorabinformation an Grossaktionäre: Möglichkeiten und Grenzen nach Gesellschafts- und Kapitalmarktrecht', *Schweizerische Zeitschrift für Wirtschafts- und Finanzmarktrecht* 77 (2005) 101; D. Daeniker and E. Dettwiler, 'Selektive Information von Grossaktionären', in R. Sethe et al (eds.), *Liber amicorum Rolf H. Weber, Kommunikation*, Berne, Staempfli (2011) 19.

person or persons a qualified insider by means of signing a confidentiality and no-action agreement.

f) Takeover Situations

Takeover law, practically inexistent in Switzerland until 1985, has been developed to an astonishing degree in the last quarter century. The starting point was soft law, worked out and written down in a set of rules by the Swiss Stock Exchange Association (which borrowed heavily from the London City Code of that period of time). In the meantime, the rules have been replaced by binding regulation on the basis of the 1995 Stock Exchange Law (*Bundesgesetz über die Börsen und den Effektenhandel*) [225] which introduced the Takeover Commission, whose powers and duties were extended in the meantime (partially by the law and regulations, partially through the sheer weight of the body of rulings that have emanated from it). The system is based on mandatory disclosure of holdings of 3% (or more) in public companies,[226] a 33⅓% threshold for the legal duty to make a tender offer for all remaining shares, [227] and detailed rules on the procedure to be followed (including the best price rule).

The role of a Board of a company which is the target in a takeover procedure is precisely described by the rules of both the Swiss Stock Exchange Act and the implementation regulations and specific rulings of the Takeover Commission.[228] These rules today form quite a comprehensive body of law, enforcing equal treatment, fairness and transparency in all public tender proceedings. Of particular relevance for Swiss Boards are the following points:

(i)   While general corporate duties continue to be relevant in a takeover situation, the Board's powers to take certain resolutions which may endanger a smooth auction process and its fairness are severely restrained by law.[229] The Board has to fulfil a series of additional duties imposed by the takeover rules. It can, however, decide freely on whether to recommend acceptance of the tender offer to its shareholders, or to resist it, or to take a non-involved, properly 'neutral' attitude (without making a positive or negative recommendation to the shareholders).

(ii) In the event of a decision to resist the tender offer, under Swiss law the Board is allowed to take a partial—ie. basically hostile—general attitude,

---

[225] Art. 22 ff. of that Law (SESTA, n. 31) and the extensive Regulations of 1997 (as amended).

[226] Art. 20 SESTA (fn. 31) and corresponding Regulations.

[227] Art. 28 SESTA (fn. 31).

[228] Art. 33a ff. SESTA (fn. 31) and Takeover Regulation (*Übernahmeverordnung vom 21. August 2008*).

[229] Art. 29 SESTA (fn. 31) and Art. 36 of the Takeover Regulation.

fighting the offer with legal means, but it must painstakingly refrain from any unfair practices which tend to thwart the offeror's chances. This 'duty of fairness' in a strategy of defense is frequently (and wrongly) referred to as 'duty of neutrality'. As in all takeover proceedings, the Board cannot (without either shareholder or Takeover Commission approval) indulge in specific defensive measures which are prohibited by law.

g) Legal Strings on Collective Shareholder Actions

While corporation law clearly favours attempts of shareholders to coordinate and bundle their initiatives,[230] by way of rules such as the ones requiring several shareholders to act together to reach a certain minimum quota as a precondition for the exercise of certain shareholders rights,[231] the Stock Exchange Act tends to derive serious adverse legal consequences from such collective actions. The Takeover Commission went so far as to announce its determination to prosecute certain targeted behaviours as an unannounced concerted action (or 'group-building')[232] even though the collective action does not result in a specific organisation holding the various shareholders together to ensure and enforce predetermined use of voting rights. Even professional proxy advisors' services may be concerned by this concept, which forces them to stick to stringent preconditions in order to stay clear of the extremely heavy fines for intentional non-disclosure of concerted voting behaviour.[233]

3.1.4. Institutional Investors

a) In General

Institutional investors (pension funds, investment funds, hedge funds, private equity vehicles, sovereign investment funds, insurance companies, and also nominee companies often related to large banks) have become the most important group of shareholders in the top tier of Swiss listed companies.[234] An ever larger part or a majority are based outside Switzerland. As in other countries, it has become obvious that the term 'institutional shareholders' comprises such a variety of different players and situations that it should be used, as a general notion, with great care. Activist private equity vehicles have almost nothing in common

---

[230] Often referred to by corporation lawyers as the 'right to associate' of shareholders.

[231] Among others, Art. 699 para. 3 (first sentence) CO (minimum shareholding necessary to force the convening of an extraordinary shareholders' meeting); Art. 699 para. 3 CO.

[232] 'Concerted action' or 'group' concept in Art. 20 para. 3 SESTA (fn. 31) and Art. 10 para. 1 of the Stock Exchange Ordinance FINMA (fn. 43).

[233] Art. 40 SESTA (fn. 31).

[234] See n. 2 above.

with a life insurance company holding the same number of shares, and open-end investment funds have a totally different attitude towards the companies whose shares have been included in their portfolio than sovereign funds. Nominee companies are totally different again, inasmuch as they are not even 'investors' themselves.

In any event, whatever the specificity of any such 'institutional investor', many among them have little understanding or even interest regarding specific issues coming up in Swiss listed companies; they tend to rely on voting recommendations issued by special proxy advisor services in their country, sometimes in cooperation with Swiss-based services.

b) Pension Funds as Shareholders of Swiss Companies

As mentioned at the outset, in contrast to Germany and France, Switzerland maintains an important privately run Occupational Pension System above and beyond the Government's compulsory minimum social security system which is based on funding separate from the employer's balance sheet.[235] This has necessarily led to an increasing portion of shares being held by Swiss Occupational Pension Entities. The way to vote shares has to be decided by the Board of Trustees of each such entity, which is composed of an equal number of employer's and employees' representatives.[236]

Experience shows, however, that Pension Funds and other institutional investors—which are obligated by law to invest only a part of their assets in shares and, if doing so, to spread out their equity investments over a large number of issuing companies (eg. 12 or 20)—have for years shown relatively little interest or incentive to exercise their voting rights in a specific company as long as matters in the company follow a certain routine. Regularly, they only wake up in the event of a corporate crisis or a highly mediatised special issue coming before the shareholders' meeting. Then, institutional shareholders—mostly following recommendations of proxy services—may be found to have the casting vote. They are, in such an event, the target of intense lobbying efforts of the board of directors and Management in the critical phase before the meeting.[237]

---

[235] Based upon the 'Three Pillars' provision of the Swiss Federal Constitution, Art. 111 para. 1, where the compulsory government-run system is the first pillar, the occupational pension system composed of independently funded pension plans of firms is the second, and individual saving and insurance the third pillar.

[236] Art. 89a Swiss Civil Code (*Schweizerisches Zivilgesetzbuch*).

[237] One public Swiss company (Lonza Inc.), after having seen its Remuneration Report rejected by its shareholders due to a negative recommendation of a US shareholder service institution, publicly promised in 2011 to more intensively lobby that institution in the future (sic).

The Corporate Governance Code puts store by a contact between shareholders and the Board also outside of the shareholders' meeting.[238] There is no government policy to push an 'engagement' attitude, or to expect more from institutional shareholders than—hopefully—the exercise of voting rights at the Shareholders' Meeting[239] and a certain degree of transparency on voting policy. The government confines its efforts in this area to a Bill, pending in Parliament, which requires Swiss pension funds to exercise the voting rights of shares in their portfolio and to disclose in their annual reports the fact that and the way how they voted.[240] A constitutional amendment requiring all incorporated pension plans (*Pensionskassen*) to exercise voting rights attached to shares they own has been adopted by popular vote on 3 March 2013.

In the aftermath of the British Stewardship Code, a non-government initiative established Guidance (*Richtlinie*) containing recommendations on governance of institutional shareholders with respect to the exercise of their voting and other shareholder rights as well as regarding professional proxy advisors.[241]

Switzerland has no specific policy on road shows.

3.1.5. Remuneration (as Incentive)

In Switzerland, fees of non-executive directors (who represent almost all board members in listed companies) have risen considerably, but remained at a level very much below the sometimes astronomical salaries and bonuses paid to top managers, especially in the financial and pharmaceutical industries. In 2010, one CEO of a Swiss bank received a special bonus and an 'ordinary' salary equivalent to CHF 90 million. The problem perceived by the people has led to the popular vote of 3 March 2013 amending the Federal Constitution quoted above.[242] The problem of excessive pay is, in any event, very much one of the top managers, not of the outside directors.

The problem with top management pay,[243] especially in the financial and pharmaceutical industries, is twofold:

---

[238] Corporate Governance Code (fn. 15) para. 8.

[239] See P. Böckli (fn. 12) § 12 N. 134.

[240] *Federal Monitor 2010*, 8295, Art. 71a.

[241] Swiss Employers' Association Economiesuisse and others, Initiative of 2011, *Guidance* published in early 2013 (*Richtlinien für Institutionelle Investoren zur Ausübung ihrer Mitwirkungsrechte bei Aktiengesellschaften vom 21. Januar 2013*).

[242] Popular Initiative 'Thomas Minder' (fn. 17), *Federal Monitor 2008*, 341, adopted by popular vote on 3 March 2013.

[243] See K. Hofstetter (fn. 135) 9; P. Forstmoser (fn. 183) 145; P. Böckli, 'Zum neuen Schweizer Vergütungsrecht: Entlöhnung der Unternehmensspitze zwischen Lohndirigismus, Populismus und Aktienrecht', in S. Grundmann et al (eds.), *Liber amicorum Klaus J. Hopt, Unternehmen, Markt und Verantwortung*, Berlin, De Gruyter (2010) II, 3003; C.B. Bühler
cont. ...

Firstly, the mere absolute figures of salary and bonus combined are just 'too high' in the eyes of practically the entire public opinion in Switzerland. Secondly, it has proven impossible to effectively align manager interest with shareholder interest (in spite of the American-generated alignment theory). The basic idea that a person who will be paid increasingly large amounts will fulfil their duties with an ever increasing degree of effort and success, and that the amount finally paid can then rationally be traced back to such effort and success, appears to be a fallacy.[244]

The hope set in the action of Compensation Committees was—in the view of the Swiss public—in vain: these selected independent directors chosen by large companies' Boards may have prevented irregularities as such and certainly improved procedures, but they did not prevent two big problems from continuing and even getting worse. While the obvious self-dealing risk in pay-setting for top management can formally be taken care of through the institution of a Compensation Committee, factual developments in Switzerland tend to show that such Committees, for reasons of group dynamics and consent-driven attitudes at the top of companies, probably do not withstand upward pressure in top management pay. No way to effectively deal with this phenomenon has yet been found.

3.2. Boards and Stakeholders

3.2.1. Boards and Employees

While the phenomenon of path dependence appears to induce Germany forever to hold on to the institution of 50:50 '*Mitbestimmung*' in Supervisory Boards, Switzerland has an equally deeply engraved track-record of refraining from such a structural constraint. Even the trade unions have not come forward with any plans in this respect.[245] Switzerland has, however, a long-standing tradition of collective bargaining agreements. Those often contain consultation mechanisms on a level distinctly below the board of directors and top management.

(fn. 183) 248; H.C. von der Crone and B. Burg, 'Salärgovernance und Markt für Führungs-kräfte', in R. Sethe et al (eds.), *Liber amicorum Rolf H. Weber, Kommunikation*, Zurich, Staempfli (2011) 331; P. Forstmoser, "Say-on-Pay": Die Volksinitiative „gegen die Abzo-ckerei" und der Gegenvorschlag des Parlaments', *Schweizerische Juristen-Zeitung*, 108 (2012) 337 ff.—Popular Initiative 'Thomas Minder' (fn. 17) which was adopted as an Amendment to the Federal Constitution by popular vote on 3 March 2013.

[244] P. Böckli (fn. 243) 3003.

[245] Initiative of the Swiss Trade Unions of 25 August, 1971, *Federal Monitor 1971*, 780 was rejected by popular vote, and the later Initiative Urs Hofmann of December 2001 was rejected in Parliament in 2003.

3.2.2. Boards and Creditors

Corporate Law instituted a comprehensive system of creditor and stakeholder protection through a limitation of withdrawals of equity capital from the company (by ways of excessive dividends,[246] constructive dividends,[247] unsecured loans to shareholders etc.). The Boards have a watchdog function in this respect.[248] It is liable to creditors in the event of bankruptcy whenever its duties have not been properly fulfilled (see section 4.1.1 below), but the Board is not subject to specifically enforceable duties towards the creditors.[249]

Creditors no longer sit on Boards, except for exceptional situations. In a long period of time ending about 1995, representatives of large Banks—often their Chairman or CEO—could be found sitting on the Boards of industrial and commercial companies, providing the largest creditor with an easy access to the bill of health of their major debtor. This system has been given up completely, as it was connected with the idea of one privileged bank relationship (*Hausbank* system) and was a source of serious conflicts of interest.

3.2.3. Board and Other Stakeholders

Switzerland has a tight and very comprehensive network of industrial labour, environmental protection, sustainability and money laundering laws and regulations which the companies, supervised by the Board, have to comply with. The same thing holds true as to human rights, child labour and generally labour protection measures. Many companies have adopted codes of ethics and corporate social responsibility guidelines[250] defining the company's attitudes vis-à-vis the society at large and human rights, above and beyond legal requirements.

---

[246] Art. 660, Art. 675 para. 2, Art. 678, Art. 728b para. 2 numbered subpara. 4, Art. 731 CO.

[247] Art. 678 para. 2 CO.—See P. Böckli (fn. 12) § 1 N. 168 ff.

[248] See L. Glanzmann, 'Die Pflicht zur angemessenen Kapitalausstattung der Aktiengesellschaft', *Aktuelle Juristische Praxis* 6 (1997) 51 and L. Glanzmann, *Der Darlehensvertrag mit einer Aktiengesellschaft aus gesellschaftsrechtlicher Sicht*, Thesis, St. Gallen, Berne, Haupt (1996) 122; P. Böckli (fn. 12) § 1 N. 273 and § 13 N. 729; C.B. Bühler, *Sanierung nach Aktienrecht de lege lata et ferenda*, Zurich, Schulthess (2010) 4.

[249] Except, of course, in the case of insolvency, when the Board loses control by operation of the law (Art. 725 para. 2 and Art. 725a CO), and has a difficult role in the last phase of financial decline, see 3.3 below.

[250] There is no recommendation as to this point in the Corporate Governance Code, and even less in the Law.

3.3. Changing Roles in Financial Distress

As mentioned above, under Swiss law providing for flexibility in the organisation at the top, the board of directors may, if need be, quickly concentrate the entire leadership functions in one person (Chairman/CEO). [251] This arrangement, adopted under extraordinary circumstances, facilitates the flow of information, shortens the lines of command, increases the negotiating capacity with banks and other important creditors, and generally permits a faster decision-making and implementation. It also protects the company from the ever-looming risk of a rift between the two top personalities at the company's helm. [252]

The Board will, during times of distress, simplify its procedure and, where appropriate, create a Steering and Restructuring Committee with relative extensive powers to closely follow events.

In the last phase of financial decline, one of the unresolved problems in Switzerland is the influence of strict creditor protection and equality rules (as embodied in the Bankruptcy Act [253]) on the guidelines to be followed by the Board. While the pursuit of the 'going concern' model is mandatory as long as there is a reasonable chance of a successful reorganisation and recapitalisation, after a definitive failure, a variety of decisions of the Board suddenly look highly questionable in hindsight. Board members run the risk, if things go awry, of being accused of having favoured some creditors or classes of creditors over others. [254]

---

[251] Art. 716b CO.—See above 1.3 and 2.1(b) (ii).

[252] Corporate Governance Code (fn. 15) para. 18.—See P. Böckli (fn. 15) and P. Böckli (fn. 12) § 14 N 284/85.

[253] The Swiss Bankruptcy Law (*Bundesgesetz über Schuldbetreibung und Konkurs*) of 11 April 1889, restated on 16 December 1994, providing for quite extensive 'claw-back' measures as regards constructive fraudulent conveyance prior to insolvency, is based on strict equal treatment rules with respect to creditors.

[254] P. Forstmoser, 'Paulianische Anfechtung und aktienrechtliche Verantwortlichkeit', in M. Oertle et al (eds.), *Festschrift für Rudolf Tschäni, M&A—Recht und Wirtschaft in der Praxis*, Zurich, Dike (2010) 432, 447 f.

4. Enforcement

4.1. Courts

4.1.1. *Personal Liability Claims*

a) General Traits of Board Liability Litigation in Switzerland

Swiss law provides for a strict personal, unlimited and joint and several liability of each Board member, each manager and the auditors, for damage caused to the company by his or her intentional or negligent violation of corporate duties.[255]

(i) In practice, this liability provision has traditionally had little impact as long as the company which was damaged remains solvent. In such a case, the right to sue vests in the company itself (which in practice rarely sues) and any one of its shareholders (who also rarely sue, as the proceeds of the judgment against a director, an executive or an auditor exclusively belong to the company).[256]

(ii) Conversely, directors' and officers' liability is a serious matter as soon as the company has become insolvent, ie. is declared bankrupt by a court ruling[257] or becomes subject to the equivalent of a 'Chapter 11' procedure.[258] In that case the right, and indeed the obligation, to sue directors or managers and especially auditors, provided it appears they have failed in the fulfilment of their duties, vests in the Receiver.[259] In practice, in an insolvency claims are regularly brought against directors and, even more frequently, against auditors based on the grounds of negligence and, in particular, wrongful trading (ie. failure to commence an insolvency procedure in a timely manner by the required filing with the Bankruptcy

---

[255] Art. 754 and 755 CO.—The literature is very broad, for an overview, see P. Forstmoser, Th. Sprecher and G.A. Töndury, *Personal Liability [under] Swiss Corporation Law*, Zurich, Schulthess (2005) and D. Gericke and S. Waller, 'Commentary on Art. 754-761 CO', in *Basler Kommentar zum Obligationenrecht II*, in H. Honsell, N.P. Vogt and R. Watter (eds.), 4th edn., Basel, Helbing & Lichtenhahn (2012), Art. 754 and 755. There are a cohort of Swiss Supreme Court cases, amongst the most consequential ones: Swiss Supreme Court (*Schweizerisches Bundesgericht*), BGE 117 II 439 (1991); BGE 122 III 198 (1996); BGE 131 III 311 (2004) and BGE 132 III 523 (2005).

[256] Art. 756 CO.

[257] Art. 725 para. 2 CO, and Art. 171 of the Swiss Bankruptcy Law (*Bundesgesetz über Schuldbetreibung und Konkurs*, n. 253).

[258] Art. 317 of the Swiss Bankruptcy Law (fn. 253).

[259] Art. 757 para. 1 (second sentence) CO.

Court[260]). Claims for liability in cases of insolvency are a frequent and serious matter in Switzerland. They are almost customarily launched by Receivers in insolvency procedures of larger companies. As much as 90% of these claims are settled, in court or out of court.[261]

Swiss law provides for an annual vote of release to the members of the board of directors.[262] The legal effect of such a shareholders' resolution is limited as it only covers causes for action known by the shareholders, and only those rather rare liability suits lodged while the company is solvent. Release granted by shareholders does not prevent or restrain action by a Receiver on behalf of the creditors in the event of insolvency.

According to prevailing opinion,[263] the Company may indemnify its directors and managers against liability claims, but only in the event of suits based upon simple negligence. The company cannot hold a director or officer harmless against his own reckless misbehaviour or wilful misconduct, and in any event an indemnification commitment undertaken by a company is worthless in the most perilous situation, ie. once the company has become bankrupt.

The Shareholders' Meeting acting either through a special resolution or the Articles of Association adopted by it cannot limit directors' liability or subject it to conditions.[264]

Wrongful trading, as mentioned above, is a major cause of directors' liability in Switzerland.[265]

b) Burden of Proof

The burden of proof in a liability action is on the claimant regarding the actual damage sustained, the specific wrongful act or omission of the director or officer at the origin of the damage, and the causality relationship between the act or omission and the relevant damage. In principle, in a liability suit brought by the

---

[260] Liability claims based on a concept quite close to British 'wrongful trading' are frequent in Swiss practice, Swiss Supreme Court (*Schweizerisches Bundesgericht*), leading case BGE I 16 II 541 (1990); see P. Böckli (fn. 12) § 18 N. 369.

[261] This figure is not available in reliable statistics, but is based upon the experience of Swiss liability insurers most familiar with the events.

[262] Art. 698 para. 2 numbered subpara. 5 and Art. 758 CO.

[263] More reluctant D. Daeniker, 'Versicherung, Prozesskostenersatz und Freistellung (Indemnification) von Organpersonen. Vergleich des Delaware-Rechts mit dem schweizerischen Aktienrecht', in H.C. von der Crone et al (eds.), *Liber amicorum Peter Forstmoser, Neue Tendenzen im Gesellschaftsrecht*, Zurich, Schulthess (2003) 523, 534; P. Forstmoser et al (fn. 255) N. 247; Y. Schneller, *Die Organe der Aktiengesellschaft bei einer ordentlichen Fusion*, Thesis St. Gallen, Zurich, Dike (2006) 394.

[264] Practically unanimous opinion in Switzerland.

[265] See 4.1.1(a) above.

Receiver in bankruptcy, the burden of proof for negligence or wilfulness lies with the Receiver, but once the first three objective conditions of liability are established (damage, wrongful act, and causality), the subjective element of negligence or wilfulness is presumed by the judge to be fulfilled, and there is practically no chance to avoid liability on subjective grounds. Still, the Receiver must overcome quite a difficult basic hurdle in proving both the specific wrongful act (breach of a duty of care in most cases), and the amount of damage specifically attributable to it.[266]

c) *Statute of Limitations*

Claims for directors' or officers' liability are barred by the statute of limitations five years following the day when the damaged person has sufficient knowledge both of the damage and the liable person.[267] The final deadline is ten years subsequent to the day of the act or omission having caused the damage. The statute of limitations is interrupted by the filing of a suit against, or a written declaration of waiver by, the liable person. While the liability as such is personal, unlimited and joint and several, to some extent particular legal provisions limit the obligation to cover an unpaid amount owed by another liable person.[268]

d) *Business Judgment Rule*

The business judgment rule[269] has not so far been formally introduced by law or adopted by a specific court decision, but an equivalent has at all times been used by Swiss courts as a basic guideline for *ex post* evaluations of Board behaviour: The judge does not substitute his own judgment for that of the corporate directors or officers, but observes an attitude of general restraint as regards all acts of business.[270] But the reception by legal writers of the more specific business judgment rule developed in certain US state laws[271] has led to a stronger

---

[266] See D. Zobl, 'Haftung der Gesellschaft für die Vertretungshandlungen ihrer Organe in der bundesgerichtlichen Rechtsprechung', in R. von Büren (ed.), *Liber amicorum Rolf Bär, Aktienrecht 1992–1997*, Berne, Staempfli (1998) 435, 443; P. Forstmoser et al (fn. 255) 157; G. Krneta (fn. 36) N. 2035; D. Gericke and S. Waller (fn. 255) Art. 754 N. 13 ff.

[267] Art. 760 CO.

[268] Art. 759 CO, whose exact limitative meaning is still subject to considerable controversy twenty years after its enactment.

[269] See P. Böckli (fn. 12) § 13 N. 581 ff.; D. Gericke and S. Waller (fn. 255) Art. 754 N. 31a.

[270] Leading case appears to be an unpublished decision from 1981, accessible in *Semaine Judiciaire* 104 (1982) 225: 'Les personnes chargées de la gestion conservent néanmoins *un large pouvoir d'appréciation* dans l'examen de l'opportunité d'une affaire ...'.

[271] While many Swiss practitioners look at Delaware law and practice in the first place, others stress the limits of such a methodology under Swiss corporate law, see H.C. von der

cont. ...

insistence on procedural correctness in reaching a corporate decision. The theory, however, that in the absence of illegal acts procedural correctness in the preparation of a decision and good faith would ward off personal liability[272] has never been confirmed by a Swiss court. The courts will not entirely refrain from looking—albeit with due restraint—at the material decision itself to verify its basic sustainability from a legal point of view. One of the shortcomings of the business judgment rule is, in any event, its focus on active decision-taking; most Swiss board liability cases turn, however, around omissions to apply due care in preventing certain damaging events, not corporate decisions adopted and properly minuted.[273] Mostly for these reasons, those who hoped the introduction of the business judgment rule of the Delaware type would protect board members from some excessive consequences of the severe Swiss liability provisions have largely been disappointed.

e) The Crucial Switch: Solvency or Insolvency

Liability claims brought by a solvent company (or, on its behalf, by a shareholder) are quite rare, but suits commenced by Receivers in bankruptcy are frequent. The main focus is in fact often aimed at external auditors who are considered to be solvent or well insured, or both, and due to their reputational problem and driven by their insurers, are known to tend to settle.[274] Claims in bankruptcy against non-executive and independent directors are not rare at all. Although the degree of litigiousness in Switzerland is lower than in the US, propensity to sue is increasing. Trigger-happy filing of claims is hindered to some extent by the claimant's obligation to advance costs to the court and the general procedural rule 'the loser bears all costs'. Bankruptcy Receivers traditionally have a high degree of litigiousness, while usually being ready to settle substantially below the 50:50 level with respect to the original complaint.

f) Insurance

Directors' and Officers' liability insurance (D&O) can be taken out by Swiss companies, and almost all listed companies have done so, with a great variation of amounts, special conditions and exceptions in the small print of the policies.[275]

Crone, A. Carbonara and S. Hunziker, 'Aktienrechtliche Verantwortlichkeit und Geschäftsführung', *Zeitschrift für Schweizerisches Recht*, Supplement 43 (2006) 3, 46.

[272] Advanced by D. Gericke and S. Waller (fn. 255) Art. 754 N. 31a.

[273] P. Böckli (fn. 12) § 13 N. 594a ff. and § 18 N. 403a.

[274] P. Böckli and C.B. Bühler, 'Ausklammerung der Revisionsstelle aus der Solidarhaftung mit den geschäftsführenden Organen', in *Liber amicorum Max Boemle*, Zurich, SKV (2008) 235.

[275] See P. Forstmoser et al (fn. 255) 200 ff.; P. Böckli (fn. 12) § 13 N. 876 ff.; M. Haller, 'Die D&O-Versicherung für KMU-Unternehmen', in G.G. Zindel, P.R. Peyer and B.G. Schott
cont. ...

One of the delicate points is the possibility to also cover liability suits brought by a solvent company against its own director, and another is the destiny of the insurance policy in the event of bankruptcy, when the Receiver in bankruptcy refuses to pay any further premiums, causing the policy to lapse.[276] The law or the Corporate Governance Code do not provide for a compulsory deductible in a D&O insurance, but virtually all policies actually contain such an arrangement.

D&O insurers tend to settle as many cases as possible, and also claims against uninsured directors mostly end up being settled.[277]

4.1.2. Nullification of Resolutions

Under Swiss law, nullification of Board resolutions and decisions of the Shareholders' Meeting are treated in a totally different manner.

Board resolutions—Resolutions of the board of directors cannot be ordinarily challenged in court.[278] While the option to set a Board resolution aside in court due to its unconscionable content or very serious formal mistakes is indeed provided for by law,[279] so far there have apparently been no cases where such an extraordinary 'nullification' procedure would have been successfully completed against a Board resolution.[280]

Shareholders' resolutions—Decisions of the General Shareholders' Meeting, may within two months subsequent to the meeting be challenged in court by any one of the shareholders based on the grounds of violation of corporation law or serious formal mistakes.[281] Such claims are quite frequent in practice, commenced by dissatisfied minority shareholders. The Board itself is entitled to challenge shareholders' resolution in court[282] but such cases are extremely rare as the Board is elected by the same majority that is supposed to have adopted the questionable resolution.

(eds.), *Liber amicorum Peter Forstmoser, Wirtschaftsrecht in Bewegung*, Zurich, Schulthess (2008) 249, 250 ff.

[276] See M. Haller, *Organhaftung und Versicherung*, Thesis, Zurich, Dike (2008) 174 and M. Haller (fn. 275) 251.

[277] Frequently on a substantially reduced basis (20% to 40% of the amount originally claimed, as an indication).

[278] Art. 706 and 714 CO; almost unanimous opinion in Switzerland, and confirmed by the Bill on revision of Corporation Law of 21 December 2007 (fn. 16).

[279] Art. 714 and Art. 706b CO.

[280] P. Forstmoser (fn. 67) 57; see n. 145 also.

[281] Art. 706 CO.

[282] Art. 706a para. 2 CO.

4.1.3. Claw-back of Constructive Dividends

Swiss law specifically allows for a claim for restitution ('claw-back') of constructive dividends.[283] Not only the Company, but also a single shareholder acting on behalf of the Company, may sue recipient shareholders or directors (or persons close to them) for repayment to the Company.[284] The scope of the law is presently being expanded to comprise excessive remuneration to managers (or persons close to them).[285]

4.1.4. Whistleblowing

One measure to improve the practical chances of obtaining knowledge of deviations from laws and regulations, and thereby to strengthen enforcement, is whistleblowing. Earlier Swiss tradition, still very strong and even prevalent today, was scornful of any delation or denunciation in a business environment. Yet the initiative taken by the Sarbanes-Oxley Act[286] with regard to whistle-blowing in 2002 has begun to trickle down through the Swiss corporate world.[287] Some companies, although still a minority, have set up an internal information point where employees can complain about specific assumed breaches of laws and regulations by superior managers (or even colleagues on the same level). Experience and results, as everywhere, are mixed. The law-makers still ponder on the adoption of whistleblowing provisions in Swiss Labour Law, with an uncertain prognosis.

4.2. Regulators

There is no *regulator* for corporations and their boards outside specific areas (ie. financial institutions, airlines, railways, telecommunication, nuclear power plants etc.).

---

[283] Art. 678 CO.

[284] Art. 678 para. 3 CO.

[285] Bill on the revision of corporation law of 21 December 2007 (fn. 16) Art. 678 (to be revised); popular initiative 'Thomas Minder' (fn. 17), adopted by popular vote on 3 March 2013.

[286] Sarbanes-Oxley Act (2002) Section 806.

[287] See Z. Ledergerber, *Whistleblowing unter dem Aspekt der Korruptionsbekämpfung*, Thesis Zurich, Berne, Staempfli (2005) 7; C.B. Bühler (fn. 12) N. 505 and N. 777; R. Sethe, 'Compliance, Whistleblowing and Critical Incident Reporting' in R. Sethe et al (eds.), *Liber amicorum Rolf H. Weber, Kommunikation*, Zurich, Staempfli (2011) 189, 195.

4.3. Self-Regulation

In 2002 Switzerland introduced, as mentioned above, the Swiss Code of Best Practice for corporate governance which in 30 articles contains concise recommendations on the main topics regarding the good functioning of the General Meeting of Shareholders, the board of directors, and External Auditing. The Code is totally independent from Government input, but, conversely, the legislature has tended to embody Code rules into the law. This was the case in such matters as disclosure of top management remuneration, the internal control system and conflicts of interest. The Corporate Governance Code painstakingly avoids repeating provisions contained in corporation law[288] and also refrains from reaching out into the field of more general recommendations on good business administration. The twenty rules of the Code were amended in 2007 by ten rules on good practice regarding matters of Board and top management compensation. The Corporate Governance Code is largely followed today by all listed companies (about 300)[289] although, technically, it does not even contain an explicit comply-or-explain provision.

All disclosure matters in the area of corporate governance are dealt with in a Directive of the Swiss Stock Exchange ('Directive on Transparency in corporate governance Matters'[290]) which, from the beginning, contained a comply-or-explain provision.[291]

The 'Code' and the 'Directive' form one single set of rules on corporate governance. In practice, Swiss listed companies, after some initial difficulties after introduction, rarely deviate from the respective recommendations.[292] Compliance with the Stock Exchange's Directive (and its implementing regulation) on

---

[288] With one exception: the 'seven core points' definition (Art. 716a para. 1 CO) of inalienable 'Full Board' duties and powers, is to be found in para. 10 of the Corporate Governance Code (fn. 15).

[289] Eg. Roche, see Annual Report of Roche 2010 (fn. 3), 87; Novartis, see Annual Report of Novartis 2010 (fn. 2), 87; UBS, see Annual Report of UBS 2010 (fn. 2), 210; Credit Suisse, see Annual Report of Credit Suisse 2010 (fn. 2), 166, Nobel Biocare, see Annual Report of Nobel Biocare 2010, 58, available at <http://corporate.nobelbiocare.com/Images/en/83299_RL21_NB_AR2010_E_final_web_tcm269-38731.pdf>).—Concerning the adherence to the Directive on Corporate Governance see n. 292 below.

[290] Directive on Corporate Governance and respective Regulation of the Swiss Stock Exchange (fn. 25).

[291] See SWX Swiss Exchange, *Kommentar zur Corporate Governance-Richtlinie*, 18 November 2002, as amended on 20 September 2007, 6; P. Böckli (fn. 12) § 7 N. 37 and § 14 N. 230; C.B. Bühler (fn. 12) N. 1122.

[292] One year after the Directive's entering into force, the average degree of compliance of Swiss listed companies was 85%; 110 companies reached 90%, see C. Meyer (fn. 55) VI, and 94% in 2005, C. Meyer and P. Staub, 'Umsetzung der Corporate-Governance-Richtlinie', *Der Schweizer Treuhänder* 79 (2005) 27, 32.

disclosure is quite strictly enforced by the supervisory body of the Swiss Stock Exchange.

So far there is no code similar to the UK Stewardship Code which would deal with the engagement of institutional investors in public companies. However, there is an initiative and a draft document to also introduce recommendations in this area.[293]

In the last ten years, the system of self-regulation (in the case of the Corporate Governance Code, even without a formal requirement to comply-or-explain) has produced substantial positive results, as both the general impression in the public suggests and specific fact-finding surveys have established.[294] In international perception, Swiss public companies are to be found in the upper echelon as regards corporate governance.

5. The Dynamics of Change

a) Reform Movements

A series of initiatives is the object of Bills pending in Parliament:

A popular initiative (as described above[295]) lodged in 2008 by the Swiss citizen Thomas Minder, subjecting not only Board compensation, but all remuneration of Executives to a binding vote of the General Shareholders' Meeting, was adopted by popular vote on 3 March 2013. It reduces, among many other points, the term of office of all directors in public companies to one year (renewable), absolutely prohibits golden parachutes and severance payments, and subjects directors and executives to imprisonment (of up to three years) and heavy finds in the event of a violation of the law.[296]

The bill before Parliament[297] on the revision of Corporation Law contains a thorough review and revision of extant corporate law with many modernisations (electronic shareholders' vote etc.), updates (flexibility in the procedures of share issuances and buy-backs) and improvements of individual shareholders' rights. The bill increases considerably the number of special rules for public companies.

While there is no formal Bill pending, Parliament has expressed its willingness to empower both the General Shareholders' Meeting as a body and each

---

[293] Release of the text of the recommendations by Economiesuisse, the Swiss employers' association, is forthcoming in early 2013.

[294] See C. Meyer (fn. 55); C. Meyer and P. Staub (fn. 292) 32; Ethos (fn. 88).

[295] *Federal Monitor 2008*, 341; adopted by popular vote on 3 March 2013; above 3.1.5.

[296] *Federal Monitor 2008*, 342, Art. 95 para. 3 subpara. d; adopted by popular vote on 3 March 2013.—For a succinct rendering of the initiative, see C.B. Bühler (fn. 183) 247.

[297] Bill on the revision of Corporation Law of 21 December 2007 (see n. 16), *Federal Monitor 2008*, 1589.

shareholder individually to have directors or executives compelled by courts to repay to the company any part of their remuneration deemed by the judge to be 'out of balance' with the performance of the respective director or executive. It is, moreover, determined to make directors personally liable for any compensation allocated to an executive that has (again with hindsight) not been determined with the necessary care and diligence, especially if the Board provides for a compensation which is not in an 'adequate' relation to the task, performance and responsibility of the recipient.[298]

A law of 23 December 2011 completely restated the corporate accounting rules[299] especially for small and mid-size companies which do not use either the domestic Swiss GAAP FER rules (which implement a 'true and fair view' concept) or the International Financial Reporting Standards (IFRS). The IFRS standards, due to Stock Exchange requirements, are compulsory for the consolidated statements of all public companies.

b) Summary of Main Findings and List of Key Issues in Switzerland

Swiss corporation law, as lived in practice and enforced by the Courts, functions well in a middle band width, steering clear of both overregulation and laxism. While Switzerland is not a member of the European Community, it is connected with the EU by a very large and tight network of special treaties and it is economically integrated into the Common Market. For more than twenty years the declared intention of the Federal Government has been to align Swiss corporation law and Stock Exchange Law with EU standards. As a result, there are relatively few idiosyncrasies of Swiss corporation law or even less provisions that could be deemed to be incompatible with requirements of European law.

Key issues in Swiss corporations, as regards Boards and their governance, may be summarised in brief as follows:

Information issue—Boards have practically no source of information within the company which is not under the control of the very people the Board should supervise—the top management. The Board tends to receive unfavourable information late and 'asymmetrically' (good info goes up fast, bad info goes up slowly, filtered and sometimes not at all). Corporate governance recommendations are toothless in this respect, and none of the pending bills effectively addresses the problem.

A disintegration tendency due to proliferating committees—While Board committees (Audit, Remuneration, Nomination, and more) are a good thing as such,

---

[298] Vote of both Houses of Parliament of 16 March 2012, *Federal Monitor 2012*, Art. 678.

[299] Art. 957 ff. of the Law of 23 December 2011 (*Bundesgesetz vom 23. Dezember 2011, Rechnungslegungsrecht*), *Federal Monitor* 2012, 63 ff., based upon the Bill of 21 December 2007 (fn. 16), *Federal Monitor 2007*, 1705.

there tends to be too many of them. Special knowledge areas develop fast within committees so that the entire Board tends to lean back and automatically rely on committee recommendations ('rubber stamping').[300]

Excessive duties and obligations being burdened on Boards—While the Boards have been conceived essentially as a deliberating and decision-taking body of (a few) full-time insiders and (many) part-time outsiders, laws and regulations make Board members increasingly responsible for matters which go clearly beyond the time available, the manageable workload and the knowledge potential of outsiders. Swiss corporation law developments are, more than ever, scandal-induced and crisis-driven,[301] and an obvious regulatory target of most such drives is the Board which is perceived by many as a full-time guarantor of economic success of the company.

Delimitation of powers between the Board and top management—The typical Board of a Swiss public company has powers and duties quite similar to those of a German *Aufsichtsrat* or French *Conseil de surveillance*. Still, the power to finally determine enterprise strategy and the basic business direction, according to the law, vests exclusively in the Board. The delimitation is difficult in practice and top management tends to have enormous factual power in almost all respects, independently of what the law provides for.

Compensation issues—In large companies, particularly of the financial and pharmaceutical sectors, there is an unresolved clash between US-inspired 'mega' (or even 'giga') compensation-packages and public opinion. The protest attitude of a very large majority of the Swiss voters against the sheer absolute level of certain remuneration packages in the financial and pharmaceutical industries has reached unusual intensity in Switzerland. For many years already, it has dominated the public debate on corporation law. There is a distinct risk it will result in inadequate, burdensome and restrictive legislation.[302]

Distortion of the majority principle—The fact that acquirers of Swiss public company stock automatically receive their dividend while being excluded from voting rights (unless they complete the registration paperwork), has brought about a large volume of 'dormant' voting rights (20% to 40% of all shares in a typical case).[303] This phenomenon tends to seriously distort the functioning of majority-based decision-making in Swiss public companies.[304]

---

[300] See above 2.2.2(e).

[301] P. Forstmoser, 'Wirtschaftsrecht im Wandel, Erfahrungen aus vier Jahrzehnten', *Schweizerische Juristen-Zeitung* 104 (2008) 133, 138; C.B. Bühler (fn. 48) 472.

[302] See above 3.1.5.

[303] See above 3.1.3.1 and n. 199.

[304] See above 3.1.3.1.

Personal liability issue—Swiss law and long-standing jurisprudence hold Board members and auditors personally liable in case of bankruptcy or forced receivership, based upon a strict diligence test.[305] In a solvent company this happens only rarely. The dichotomy inherent in this almost exclusively bankruptcy-based accountability system, but also the severity as such of the personal liability, creates a variety of problems which have only partially been solved so far.

6. Selection of Literature in English

Bauen, M., *Swiss board of directors: Organisation, Powers, Liability, Corporate Governance,* Zurich, Schulthess (2009).

Bauen, M. and Bernet R., *Swiss Company Limited by Shares,* Zurich, Schulthess (2007).

Böckli, P., 'Corporate Governance and "Swiss Code of Best Practice"', *Neuere Tendenzen im Gesellschaftsrecht,* Zurich, Schulthess (2003) 257 ff.

— 'Osmosis of Anglo-Saxon Concepts in Swiss Business Law', in: *Liber amicorum für Thomas Bär und Robert Karrer,* Basel, Helbing & Lichtenhahn (1997) 9 ff.

— 'Corporate Governance: The "Cadbury Report" and the Swiss Board Concept of 1991', *Schweizerische Zeitschrift für Wirtschaftsrecht* 68 (1996) 149 ff.

Bohrer, A., *Corporate Governance and Capital Market Transactions in Switzerland,* Habilitation Thesis, Zürich, Schulthess (2004).

— 'Takeover Legislation in the European Community and Switzerland', *Der Schweizer Treuhänder* 68 (1994) 729 ff.

Brunner, C., *Liability of Publicly Held Corporations for a Violation of a Duty to Disclose, in Particular the 'Ad Hoc Publicity',* Berne, Staempfli (1998)

Bühler, C.B., *US Corporate Governance Reform: Impact on NYSE-Listed Swiss Companies,* 2nd edn., Zurich, Schulthess (2004).

Glatthaar, M, Bernet, R. and Luginbühl, J., *Swiss Takeover Law in a Nutshell,* Zurich, Dike (2013).

Gnos, U.P. and Vischer, M., *Swiss Merger Act,* Zurich, Schulthess (2004).

Gnos, U.P., Vischer, M. and Caleff, D., *Swiss Law on Limited Liability Companies,* Zurich, Schulthess (2010).

Handschin, L., *Swiss Company Law,* Zurich, Dike (2008).

Hänni, L., 'Fiduciary Duty of a Shareholder's Representative in the Board of Directors of a Swiss Listed Company', *Gesellschafts- und Kapitalmarktrecht* 6 (2011) 66 ff.

---

[305] Art. 754 and 755 CO. See above 4.1.1(a) (ii).

Harris, C.A., *Informing offeree shareholders, A comparative analysis of the circulars issued in England and Switzerland by the Offeree Board of Directors in response to a hostile takeover offer,* Thesis, St. Gallen (2005).

Hofstetter, K., *Corporate Governance in Switzerland,* Zurich (2002).

Hopfmüller, L.K.R., *The role of the board of directors in turnaround situations,* Thesis, St. Gallen (2010).

Kopta-Stutz, B., Pfister, L. and von der Crone, H.C., 'Some Theses Concerning Modern Swiss Reorganisation Law Going Concern and Corporate Governance', *Der Schweizer Treuhänder* 12 (2005) 1028 ff.

Lengauer, D. et al, *Company Law in Switzerland,* Zurich, Schulthess (2009).

Nobel P., *Swiss Finance Law and International Standards,* Berne, Staempfli (2002).

Nobel, P., Krehan, K. and Tanner, A. (eds.), *Law and Economics of Global Financial Institutions,* St. Gallen, Schulthess (2010).

Maestretti, M. and Peter, H., 'Corporate Governance and Special Purpose Vehicles, Understanding the Enron Case, Use and Abuse of Enron's Own Stock under the Prospective of Swiss Law', *Der Schweizer Treuhänder* 12 (2002) 1131 ff.

Monnier, J., *Integrity-based corporate governance: an empirical study in four Swiss transnational companies,* Thesis, St. Gallen (2012).

Rüdisser, M., *Boards of directors at work: an integral analysis of nontransferable duties under Swiss company law from an economic perspective,* Thesis, St. Gallen, Bamberg, Difo-Druck (2009).

Zufferey, J.P. and Contratto, F., *Finma, The Swiss Financial Market Supervisory Authority,* Basel, Helbing & Lichtenhahn (2009).

Corporate Boards in the United Kingdom

PAUL DAVIES

1. General Introduction

1.1. Environment in which Boards Operate

a) Ownership Structure and Governmental Policy on Shareholder Engagement

Two stylised facts about the shareholders of UK listed companies are important in explaining the applicable board rules. First, shareholdings are not normally concentrated. Becht and Mayer put the median size of the largest voting block in UK listed companies at 9.9% at the beginning of the 1990s, smaller than any other country in Europe (though somewhat larger than in the case of NYSE or Nasdaq companies). Second, a large proportion of the total issued capital of listed companies is held by institutional shareholders, especially pension funds and insurance companies. The table below shows the chronic decline in the proportion of the market held by retail investors directly but also in recent years the growing important of non-UK institutional investors.

Two developments can be linked to this shareholding pattern. First, the institutional shareholders have been influential over the past half century in setting the 'rules of the game' as far as corporate governance is concerned, including therefore board rules. They exercise this influence mainly through their industry associations, of which the two most important are the British Bankers Association and the National Association of Pension Funds. They have influenced legislation but they have been even more influential in relation to those rules which are set by bodies with statutory powers.[1] Particularly important are the Financial Reporting Council (FRC), which has responsibility for the UK Corporate Governance Code (CGC); the UK Listing Authority (formerly part of the Financial Services Authority (FSA), but from April 2013 part of the Financial Conduct Authority (FCA)) which sets the listing rules; and the Takeover Panel and its associated Code Committee, which sets the takeover rules. Because these bodies lie somewhat outside the mainstream of political debate about legislation

---

[1] At an earlier stage the Takeover Panel and the body responsible for the CGC did not have statutory powers but were wholly constructs of various associations representative of 'City' interests, which, if anything, made them more open to institutional shareholder influence. At present, the FSA/FCA is (and always has been) a body created by statute, whilst the Takeover Panel and the FRC are private bodies upon which statutory functions have been conferred.

and claim legitimacy on the basis of expertise rather than democratic representativeness, they are more open to lobbying by interest groups, which can themselves claim to be more expert than might have been the case had these board rules been set through general legislation.[2] In consequence, these rules, including board rules, are heavily pro-shareholder.

Table 1: Ownership of listed UK equities

Beneficial Owner	1963	1969	1975	1981	1989	1993	1997	2001	2004	2008	2010
Individuals	54	47.4	37.5	28.2	20.6	17.7	16.5	14.8	12.8	10.2	11.5
Insurance companies	10	12.2	15.9	20.5	18.6	20	23.6	20.0	17.2	13.4	8.6
Pension funds	6.4	9.0	16.8	26.7	30.6	31.7	22.1	16.1	15.7	12.8	5.1
Other financial institutions*	n/a	n/a	n/a	n/a	1.1	0.6	1.3	7.2	8.2	10.0	16
Unit and investment trusts	n/a	n/a	n/a	n/a	7.5	9.1	5.4	2.9	3.9	3.7	8.8
Banks	1.3	1.7	0.7	0.3	0.7	0.6	0.1	1.3	2.7	3.5	2.5
Rest of the world	7.0	6.6	5.6	3.6	12.8	16.3	8.0	35.7	36.3	41.5	41.2

*For example, securities dealers, but also includes bank holding companies, which may not be classified as banks.
Source: Office of National Statistics, *Share Ownership Survey 2008* (January 2010) and *Share Ownership Survey 2010* (January 2012).

Second, there is potential for the institutional shareholders to influence the policies of the companies in which they invest ('portfolio' companies), *provided* a small number of the biggest institutional shareholders in a particular portfolio company are able to form and sustain a coalition for this purpose. In fact, this potential is not fully realised because of free-rider issues (generated by competition among institutions) and conflicts of interest (generated by the multiple activities of financial conglomerates, only one of whose activities is fund management). Thus, the full potential for shareholder engagement with portfolio companies via institutional shareholder coalitions (ie. intervention whenever this

---

[2] For an application of this argument to rule-making by the Takeover Panel, see J. Armour and D. Skeel, 'Who Writes the Rules for Hostile Takeovers and Why?', (2007) 95 *Georgetown Law Journal* 1727. Of course, mainstream politics may intervene even in the rule-setting by these bodies if those rules, unusually, become salient for the marginal voter. In the area of banking regulation this has been a feature of the recent crisis. Even with board rules, this phenomenon can sometimes be detected as, for example, with quotas for women on the board, as we discuss below.

is likely to promote shareholder value) has probably never been realised, even though it is a strong feature of the UK set-up.

However, the situation is not simply that the 'supply' of shareholder engagement increased in the UK with the growth of institutional shareholding. It is also the case that over the past two decades the 'demand' from government for such intervention has increased. Governmental policy has been to pressurise the institutions to engage more actively with portfolio companies, seeing that as a more attractive form of regulation than direct regulation of companies by legislation. This policy underlies the recently created 'Stewardship Code' which sits alongside the CGC under the auspices of the FRC. In other words, one can identify an implicit 'deal' in the corporate governance area (including in relation to boards). The institutional investors have been allowed considerable freedom to shape the corporate governance rules, but in return the government expects them to engage as shareholders with their portfolio companies. This is discussed further in section 3.1.4.

However, Table 1 also reveals that the ownership underpinnings of the influence of institutional shareholders have changed significantly in recent years. In the 1980s and 1990s UK pension funds and insurance companies routinely held well over 40% of the total market in UK equities. In the new millennium the equity holdings of both these types of shareholder began to decline, so that by 2010 their holdings were lower than they were in the early 1960s. It is likely that this change has been driven by a decline in the coverage of occupational pension schemes (especially defined benefit schemes) and the growing attractiveness of bonds in a low-inflation environment. The place occupied by UK insurance companies and pension funds has not been taken up by individual investors (though individual holdings seem to have stabilised in the 21st century) but by overseas investors, mainly institutions. Whether the foreign institutions have the same objectives as domestic ones is not clear. We will return to this topic at the end of the chapter.

b) Sources of Rules and Board Structure: From an Advisory to a Monitoring Board

Thus, it can be said that the influence which institutional shareholders have been able to exercise over corporate governance rules in the UK and the rules relating to boards in particular flows very substantially from the size of the institutional holdings in large British companies and from the way these rules are made in the UK. In particular, rules made by statutory bodies are much more important in the corporate governance area than rules made by Parliament and taking the form of legislation. However, it is important to note that these bodies have been able to occupy the area of board rules in part because the companies' legislation has *not* sought to regulate the area. The lack of interest shown by the Companies Acts in issues of *board structure, composition and function* is a long-standing feature of British corporate law, a characteristic it displayed when it took its modern form in the middle of the nineteenth century. Those matters traditionally have been regarded in the UK as a matter for companies themselves to decide on. The division of powers between the shareholders and the board and between the board and management is not determined by legislation. Although the legislation assumes a single-tier board, it does not mandate it, so that the flexibility in relation to the division of powers among shareholders, board and management allows a variety of patterns to emerge concerning the allocation of decision-making within the company.

Today, however, the UK Corporate Governance Code, for which the FRC is responsible, substantially qualifies the policy of leaving it to the company to decide its board arrangements on a wholly autonomous basis. In effect, the CGC imposes on companies with a Premium Listing on the Main Market of the London Stock Exchange[3] a particular default model of the single-tier board, ie. one which applies unless the company can show good reasons why it should depart from that model. As we shall see below, the UK CGC recommends a strong set of rules about the composition of the board of directors (recommendation for half the board to be independent directors and for the positions of chair of the board and chief executive officer of the company to be split) and about the functioning of the board (role of board committees; allocation of tasks as between the board and the management). Overall, the model of the board embodied in the CGC (that of the 'monitoring' board) is very different from the governance system that was commonly found in practice in, for example, the 1950s. Then the governance system was heavily managerialist (though qualified by strong trade unions), ie. the board was typically dominated by the management of the company and performed largely an advisory role vis-à-vis management. The shift from an advisory to a monitoring model of the board occurred even though the formal board rules in the companies legislation did not change significantly in the latter half of the twentieth century.[4]

The CGC has been through several iterations since its adoption in 1992. These need not be analysed in detail but they are set out briefly in Table 2. References in this chapter are to the 2012 version of the CGC.

---

[3] Commercial companies issuing equity shares have a choice between a 'premium' and a 'standard' listing. See Listing Rule (LR) 1.5.1. The standard listing requires compliance only with the minimum EU requirements, whilst premium listing brings in additional requirements. The UK CGC is applicable only to companies with a premium listing: LR 9.1 and 9.8.6. However, the EU minima require all companies to report their response to any corporate governance code to which they may be subject (see Disclosure and Transparency Rule (DTR) 7.2). This may be the UK CGC, if the issuer has chosen voluntarily to subject itself to the Code, but is more likely to be the code of another jurisdiction. However, there are reputational incentives to obtain a premium listing. For example, only companies with such a listing form part of the FTSE Indexes. Companies with a premium listing probably also benefit from a lower cost of capital than companies with a standard listing.

[4] P. Davies, 'Shareholder Value, Company Law and Securities Markets' in K. Hopt and E. Wymeersch (eds.), *Capital Markets and Company Law* (OUP, 2003) ch. 11.

Table 2: Brief History of the UK Corporate Governance Code

Date	Review/Report	Name of Resulting Document
1992	The Financial Aspects of Corporate Governance (Cadbury Report)	Code of Best Practice
1995	Directors' Remuneration (Greenbury Report)	Code of Best Practice (on remuneration)
1998	Committee on Corporate Governance (Hampel Report)	The Combined Code on Corporate Governance
2003	Review of the Role and Effectiveness of Non-executive Directors (Higgs Report)	The Combined Code on Corporate Governance (revised)
2003	Audit Committees (Smith Report)	
2005	Financial Reporting Council Review	Guidance on Audit Committees
2006	Financial Report Council Review	The Combined Code on Corporate Governance (revised)
2008	Financial Reporting Council Review	The Combined Code on Corporate Governance (revised)
2008	Financial Reporting Council Review	Guidance on Audit Committees (revised)
2010	Financial Reporting Council Review	UK Corporate Governance Code UK Stewardship Code
2012		UK CGC and SC reviewed

The CGC operates on a comply-or-explain basis, ie. the company must either comply with the recommendations of the CGC or explain in its annual report to the shareholders any areas of divergence, justifying those divergences. The Code is sometimes referred to as 'soft' law. However, at the heart of the CGC is a genuinely 'hard' obligation, ie. an obligation to comply-or-explain, imposed on companies with a premium listing on the Main Market of the London Stock Exchange by the rules of the FCA. In fact, such companies can escape the provisions of the CGC less easily than is sometimes thought. The UK Corporate Governance Code consists of three types of provision: Main Principles, Supporting Principles and Provisions. The Listing Rules[5] require a company with a premium listing to state annually how it has complied with the Main Principles and whether it has complied with 'all relevant provisions', giving reasons for non-compliance. Thus, compliance with the high-level Main Principles is obligatory; only the Supporting Principles and the Provisions are subject to the comply-or-explain flexibility.

A similar development can be seen in relation to the more recent Stewardship Code (SC), which was promulgated by the FRC in 2010, replacing and expanding

---

[5] Rule 9.8.6.

upon that part of the CGC which deals with shareholder/company relations. However, in this case the emphasis is on the duties rather than the powers of long-term institutional shareholders. Traditionally, it was a matter of shareholder autonomy how and whether to exercise governance rights over the company. Today, the Stewardship Code generates pressure on institutional shareholders to 'engage' with portfolio companies, unless they can show good reasons not to do so. Both sets of rules apply on a comply-or-explain principle rather than being mandatory rules.

Thus, on the one hand, the institutional shareholders have been in a better position to influence the CGC and SC rules than would have been the case had those rules been embodied in legislation. On the other hand, the existence of the Codes, even though they operate on a comply-or-explain basis, implies a restriction of company and shareholder autonomy which classical UK company law would not have contemplated.

Legislative abstention from specifying the composition of the board has meant the absence of rules requiring *representatives of the employees* on the board. On the other hand, the Act does not require directors to be chosen by the share-holders. It simply requires private companies to have one director and public companies two.[6] However, since the Act gives the shareholders the power to remove directors at any time by ordinary majority,[7] it can be said that the assumption of the legislation is that directors will be either be appointed by the shareholders or remain in office with their consent. The appointment of directors is normally dealt with in the articles of association.

c) The Role of the Companies' Legislation

Classical company law did develop an important set of rules designed to constrain to some degree the exercise by the directors of the powers which are typically invested in them. This is the law of *directors' duties*. These rules, originally in the common law but now in the Companies Act 2006, lay down general standards aimed at inducing the directors to act competently and to avoid conflicts of interest. These rules thus aim to regulate the principal/agent problems between dispersed shareholders and the board, though they can also be used to address controlling/non-controlling shareholder conflicts if the controlling share-holder is also a de jure, de facto or shadow director of the company. As is well known, these rules were derived historically from the rules regulating the relationship of trustees and beneficiaries. They were applied by analogy to directors and shareholders. Thus, in classical British company law, the focus of

---

[6] Companies Act 2006, s. 154.

[7] CA 2006, s. 172. Subject to shareholders' removal rights it is thus easy to give creditors board appointment rights, for example, though there may be very good reasons for the creditors not to take them up.

regulation of the board was not on board structure and composition but on the development of standards, by which the court might review the exercise of the broad powers which, it was assumed, would be conferred on the board.

Thus, the rules on directors' duties were designed to constrain the way in which directors exercised the powers in fact conferred upon them under the company's constitution (ie. by or with the consent of the shareholders) rather than to determine which powers should be allocated to the board. However, at the margin this is a difficult line to draw. For example, the standards on directors' competence—initially very weak but now somewhat stronger—do have an impact on the relationship between non-executive and executive directors and between board and management, by setting limits on the freedom of non-executive to delegate matters to executive directors and the freedom of the board to delegate matters to non-board managers.

The rules on directors' duties and the shareholders' power to remove directors constitute the principal elements of the Act which addresses the subject matter of this chapter. For all other matters, the most important rules are to be found in the Corporate Governance Code or the Stewardship Code (made by the FRC), the Listing Rules (made by the FCA) or the Takeover Code (made by the Takeover Panel). This division in the sources of the rules also means that some of the most important board rules apply, either formally or in practice, only to a small, but important, sub-set of the total population of companies registered under the Companies Act 2006 and earlier legislation, ie. those which are listed on the Main Market of the London Stock Exchange and often only to those which have chosen a premium listing.

d) Public and Private Companies

The Companies Act 2006 divides companies into two categories, public and private, in a rather traditional way. A public company may offer its shares to the public (but need not have done so), whilst a private company is forbidden to do so.[8] However, the public offering prohibition is taken in the Act as a proxy for a distinction between companies which should be more heavily regulated (public companies) and those which should be less heavily regulated (private). Thus, public companies are more heavily regulated in many ways (for example, in relation to legal capital) which have nothing *directly* to do with offering shares to the public. Thus, within the single Companies Act 2006 a functional equivalent to having separate Acts for public and private companies is achieved.

As of July 2012 there were about 7600 public companies on the 'active' register of companies (ie. ignoring those in liquidation or in course of removal) out of a total number of over 2.6m registered companies (ie. public companies were 0.3% of the total on the UK register).

---

[8] CA 2006, s. 755.

e) Publicly Traded Companies

This is not a term used in the companies' legislation. Here it is used to refer to companies whose securities are traded on a public market. Such companies are necessarily public companies, as the Act defines them (but not all public companies have publicly traded securities). There are some rules which apply to all publicly traded companies, for example, the rules on market abuse, but not to companies which are simply public in the Companies Act sense of the term. For our purposes, however, two crucial divisions *within* the category of publicly traded companies need to be noticed. First, there is the division between '*listed*' companies and those which are not 'listed' but whose securities are nevertheless publicly traded. Listed companies are those which have chosen to be subject to the Listing Rules produced by the Financial Conduct Authority (FCA)[9] and whose securities can in consequence be traded on a regulated market (as defined by the Markets in Financial Instruments Directive). In the UK the most prominent regulated market is the Main Market of the London Stock Exchange (though there are others) and, of course, listed securities may also be traded on multilateral trading facilities. There were just over 1000 UK companies on the Main Market as of July 2011.

As already noted, the category of listed companies is further divided into those which have chosen to have a *premium* listing and those which have chosen a *standard* listing. A company with a standard listing is subject only to the rules required by Community law to be imposed on companies traded on a regulated market. A company with a premium listing is also subject to the additional rules which the listing authority has traditionally imposed on UK listed companies (referred to as 'super equivalent' rules). Before 2009 standard listing was available only to listed companies not incorporated in the UK; the choice of listing formats is now available to UK-incorporated companies as well.[10] It is a distinctive feature of the UK arrangements that the listing rules are extensively used to address governance issues and do not confine themselves to ensuring the efficiency of capital markets. Within the category of listed companies, the division between premium and standard listing is particularly important for corporate governance purposes, since many corporate governance provisions contained in the Listing Rules apply only to companies with premium listing.

Companies which have chosen not to subject themselves to the Listing Rules may nevertheless be traded on non-regulated markets, of which the most prom-

---

[9] The functions of the Financial Services Authority considered in this report were transferred to the Financial Conduct Authority in April 2013. At the time of writing, however, this transition had not been effected fully, so that many of the sources cited refer to FSA documents (which are likely to be taken over as they stand by the FCA).

[10] FSA, *Listing Rules*, 1.5. For a discussion of the policy considerations which led to this development, see FSA, *A Review of the Structure of the Listing Regime*, DP 08/1, January 2008.

inent market in the UK is the Alternative Investment Market (AIM)—also run by the London Stock Exchange. Coincidentally, there were also just over 1000 UK companies on AIM as of July 2011 (down from a high of about 1300 in 2006). It can thus be seen that a substantial number of public companies (around 7000) appear not to have their securities traded on a public market.

1.2. Financial Institutions

Until the recent financial crisis, the corporate governance rules discussed in this paper applied equally to publicly-traded financial and non-financial companies. The crisis caused the corporate governance of financial institutions to be examined in the UK as a separate issue, in particular in the Walker review of corporate governance in financial institutions.[11] That report was rather ambiguous on the central question of whether a strengthening of traditional, shareholder-focused corporate governance in the financial sector is needed or whether one should re-orient the focus of the governance system towards the protection of creditors (and, by extension, taxpayers) in the light of the highly leveraged positions of banks and other financial institutions. This issue arose in the light of research findings that banks more responsive to shareholder (especially institutional shareholder) interests took greater risks in the run up to the crisis and performed less well than banks with less shareholder-oriented governance systems.[12]

Most of the Walker recommendations[13] simply aimed to strengthen the existing provisions of the Corporate Governance Code as they apply to financial companies, for example recommendations about the amount of time non-executive directors should devote to their duties in financial institutions. Some are new and could be seen as creditor-focused. Examples are recommendations:

(a) that financial institutions have a board risk committee which is separate from the audit committee, with a corporate risk director reporting to it,

(b) that executive director bonuses be subject to retention and deferral provisions

---

[11] D. Walker, *A review of corporate governance in UK banks and other financial industry entities*, November 2009—a report commissioned by the UK government.

[12] D. Erkins, H. Mingyi and P. Mators, 'Corporate Governance in the 2007–2008 Financial Crisis: Evidence from Financial Institutions Worldwide' (Electronic copy available at <http://ssrn.com/abstract=1397685>); D. Ferreira, D. Kershaw, T. Kirchmaier, E. Schuster, 'Shareholder Empowerment and Bank Bailouts' (2012) (Electronic copy available at <http://ssrn.com/abstract=2170392>).

[13] These are usefully summarised at the beginning of the report.

(c) that the bank regulator should use its 'fit and proper person' power to
scrutinise not only the honesty but also the competence of proposed
directors and their understanding of the regulatory framework.[14]

Other new recommendations seem to focus on accountability of boards to shareholders, as with the recommendations on shareholder engagement.

The Walker recommendations were confined to financial institutions, but
there has been some 'spill over' effect into the non-financial area. The leading
examples are that the Walker recommendations for greater shareholder engagement were extended by the FRC to all companies (via in the Stewardship Code)
as was the proposal that all directors be subject to annual election (now in the
CGC). In addition, the Walker recommendations on remuneration in financial
institutions were overtaken by the provisions of Directive 2010/76/EU (CRD 3)[15]
and further provisions on remuneration are likely to make their way into CRD 4.

For the purposes of this paper, the special rules for banks and other financial
institutions will not be analysed in detail, but full attention will be paid to them
where they have 'spilled over' into the corporate governance rules for companies
in general.

1.3. Available Board Models

It follows from what has been said above about the abstentionist nature of British
company law that the legislation does not structure the board. The Act does not
require a *single-tier* or a *two-tier board*; it says nothing about the issue. In
practice, UK companies operate with one-tier boards and this is the system the
Act assumes to be in place in companies, even if it does not mandate it.
Consequently, when the British legislature came to implement the SE Regulation,
which requires SEs incorporated in the UK to be given the choice of a one-tier or
a two-tier board structure, relatively little legislative adaption of domestic
company law was thought to be required.[16] In essence, the Companies Act rules
on directors are applied, with limited exceptions, to the directors of both boards
of a two-tier board. Equally, the non-legislative provisions, such as the UK CGC,
do not refer to the two-tier board. This is more surprising, given the Code's more
rigorous approach to board composition and structure. So, the working assump-

---

[14] This latter proposal has been implemented by the FSA (see FSA, *Effective Corporate
Governance*, Consultation Paper 10/03, ch. 4) which even interviews proposed directors. The
FSA's practice proved controversial and, apparently, has become somewhat relaxed recently:
Financial Times, 'FSA relaxes vetting process for top jobs', 15 October 2012.

[15] Capital Requirements Directive (CRD)—though the contents of the Directive go beyond
required capital for banks. See FSA, *Revising the Remuneration Code*, Consultation Paper 10/19.

[16] See European Public Limited Company Regulations 2004/2326, regs. 78–80C.

tion is that the company uses a one-tier board structure, even if the company takes the form of an SE incorporated and listed in the UK. However, the lack of legal regulation of the board means that companies have considerable flexibility as to how that single tier board is structured, at least as far as the companies' legislation is concerned.

2. Authority

2.1. Functions and Powers

As will be expected from what has been said in section 1.1, the Companies Act 2006 is virtually silent on the functions and powers of the board. As far as the general run of companies is concerned, these matters are left to be determined in the company's articles of association (statutes). The traditional approach of leaving these matters to the company is reflected in the *'model' articles* for companies which the legislature suggests. The production of model articles goes back to the beginnings of modern company law in the middle of the nineteenth century. Their aim is to save on transaction costs for the incorporators of companies by producing a default set of articles. However, the model rules can easily be amended or replaced, if a particular company so wishes, by filing a (wholly or partially) different set of articles when the company is formed or by altering the articles subsequently by shareholder resolution.[17]

The current model articles contain a broad grant of powers to the board: 'Subject to the articles, the directors are responsible for the management of the company, for which purpose they may exercise all the powers of the company.'[18] Thus, the efficiency arguments for giving broad powers to the board are recognised to the fullest extent in the default rule. Two further points about this formulation should be noted. First, the wording leaves it entirely open how far the board conducts the management itself and how far it delegates to others. Thus, the dividing line between board powers and management powers is for the board to define,[19] except that the board cannot divest itself of overall responsibility for management by delegating particular functions. Thus, the board must be in a position to monitor the performance of delegated tasks (see the discussion of negligence liability below.) Second, the shareholders can qualify this broad grant

---

[17] CA 2006, s. 21. Post formation amendment requires a 'special' resolution, ie. a three-quarters majority of those voting.

[18] Model Articles for Public Companies, Art 3 (SI 2008/3229, sched. 3). See also FRC, *Guidance on Board Effectiveness*, March 2011, which gives supplementary guidance on many of the CGC's provisions relating to boards.

[19] *Ibid.*, Art 5.

of powers to the board by adopting articles which keep certain powers in their hands, and this is frequently done in private companies. In addition, the model articles permit shareholders to give ad hoc instructions to the board as to how they exercise the powers conferred on them, provided such instructions are given by the same majority as would be required to alter the articles (ie. three quarters of those voting).[20]

The model articles are thus mainly directed at the division of powers between the shareholders and the board. The question of how the board should exercise the powers given to it is addressed in part by the rules in the Act on directors' duties (discussed in section 3.1.3), but these duties do not specify the objectives the board should set itself, only that, when exercising their powers, the directors should act competently and loyally and avoid conflicts of interest. The CGC does, however, address in a substantive sense the role of the board in the company. It states:

'The board's role is to provide entrepreneurial leadership of the company within a framework of prudent and effective controls which enables risk to be assessed and managed. The board should set the company's strategic aims, ensure that the necessary financial and human resources are in place for the company to meet its objectives and review management performance. The board should set the company's values and standards and ensure that its obligations to its shareholders and others are understood and met.'[21]

The Code also addresses, at least at a procedural level, the issue which the model articles leave open, ie. the division of powers between the board and the management. In large companies it is to be expected that there will be substantial delegation to the management (with sub-delegation beyond them). However, the Code says that 'there should be a formal schedule of matters specifically reserved for [the board's] decision.'[22] This at least requires the board to consider the question of how matters are to be divided up between itself and the management of the company and, in making the division, the board must presumably have regard to the statement of its role quoted above.

The upshot of the Code's provisions is thus that the board (rather than the management) sets the company's 'strategic aims' and should ensure that it has retained in its hands a sufficient range of decision-making powers to achieve that objective. However, it is doubtful whether this is what happens in large public companies, other than in a formal sense. Although the board approves corporate strategy, it will do so on the basis of proposals put forward by the management of

---

[20] *Ibid.*, Art 4. It is doubtful whether this specific provision in the articles is strictly necessary, in that at common law shareholders have the power to give instructions to the board by special resolution, whether the articles say so or not. The purpose of Article 4 is to make it clear that article 3 is not designed to confer an exclusive set of powers on the board: the shareholders can take decisions provided they act by special resolution.

[21] CGC, A.1, Supporting Principles.

[22] CGC, A.1.1 (Code Provision).

the company. The input of the board into strategy thus depends on the rigor and extent of the review of the management's proposals by the board—on which, in the one-tier system, the senior managers will be present as directors. Although the recommendations for independent directors on the board (see section 2.2.2) are designed to promote board scrutiny of the company's strategy, non-executive directors may not have the knowledge or incentives to undertake this task at a high level. A study by Acharya, Kehoe and Reyner is instructive in this regard.[23] Although based on only a small number of interviews with board members of British public companies and equivalent British companies held by private equity owners, it found contrasting views from the directors in the two types of company about their role in setting corporate strategy. The private equity directors regarded themselves as 'leading' the strategy-setting process, whilst the public company directors saw the management of company as leading the strategy-setting process, while the board 'challenged and moulded' the management's proposals. In the case of public companies the board 'accompanied' management in setting the company's strategy rather than leading the strategy-setting process. This distinction might be explained on the basis that public company boards have more governance duties and duties towards the securities markets to perform than private equity companies (to which the CGC and the FCA's disclosure rules do not apply). However, it seems more likely that the difference is due to the closer linkages between the directors and (concentrated) shareholders in a private equity company than in a public company, where the shareholdings are relatively dispersed. Indeed, in a company held by a private equity fund the shareholders' strategy towards the company is likely to have been set by the future shareholders, at least initially, during the due diligence process which occurred before the company was acquired.

The same analysis is probably applicable to the other elements in the high level statement of the board's functions quoted above from the CGC. Of course, there will be times in the company's history when leadership in the full sense of the term falls to the board. These are normally exceptional situations, such as a bid for the company in which the senior management are involved or the sudden and unexpected departure of the CEO and perhaps other senior managers.

Internal controls have been regarded as tasks of the board (rather than just management) since the earliest versions of the British CGC. However, the Code was not explicit on the board's responsibilities in relation to the risks inherent in the company's business model until the 2010 revision. The 2010 version of the

---

[23] V. Acharya, C. Kehoe and M. Reyner, *Private Equity vs PLC Boards: A Comparison of Practices and Effectiveness*, Centre for Economic Policy Research, Discussion Paper 7148, 2009. See also T. Long, V. Dulevicz and K. Gay, 'The Role of the Non-Executive Director: findings of an empirical investigation into the differences between listed and unlisted UK boards' (2005) 13 *Corporate Governance* 667.

Code stated the board's responsibilities as follows, with the first sentence of the Principle being new.

'The board is responsible for determining the nature and extent of the significant risks it is willing to take in achieving its strategic objectives. The board should maintain sound risk management and internal control systems.'[24]

Guidance on what the internal control responsibilities of the board entail has been provided since 1999. It is usually referred to as the 'Turnbull' guidance, after the name of its original author. It was revised in 2005 and is currently under further review, in the light of the addition made to the Principle.[25] This assigns to the board the function of setting risk policy and of obtaining assurance that the systems put in place are functioning effectively. The task of management is to implement the board's policies.[26]

UK company law knows no system of internal auditors who have a formal role in the corporate governance system. However, the Corporate Governance Code puts special responsibilities on the *company secretary*, whom the Companies Act requires all public companies to appoint.[27] As might be expected of the British legislation, having required such a person to be appointed, it fails to specify the functions of the secretary. Initially, in practice the function was to ensure that the company conducted its business in accordance with company legislation and, more important, the articles of association and any by-laws laid down by the board. Building on this latter aspect of the secretary's work, the CGC states that 'the company secretary should be responsible for advising the board through the chairman on all governance matters.'[28] Thus, although the company secretary does not decide on the company's corporate governance arrangements, that person's role is to ensure that the company (board or shareholders) take the necessary decisions about those arrangements and that those decisions and the CGC are properly implemented within the company.

---

[24] CGC, C.2 (Main Principle). This formulation is repeated in the 2012 version of the CGC. In the consultation leading up to the adoption of the 2010 version of the CGC, the FRC remarked that the first sentence is one 'which with hindsight the FRC considers to have been a significant omission from previous versions of the Code.' (FRC, *Revisions to the UK Corporate Governance Code*, May 2010, para 29).

[25] The 2005 guidance is available at <www.frc.org.uk/Our-Work/Publications/Corporate-Governance/Turnbull-guidance-October-2005.aspx >.

[26] *Ibid.*, paras 15–17.

[27] Section 271.

[28] B.5 – supporting principle.

2.2. Organisation and Internal Functioning

2.2.1. Composition

The Companies Act rules on board composition are, of course, exiguous. Most of the important issues, to the extent that they are dealt with at all, are considered in the CGC.

Size of the board—However, even the CGC contains no recommendations on the overall size of the board, other than the general requirement that the board be 'effective'.[29] In 2000 the average size of a large company board was 9.[30] The Walker Review reported in 2009 that the average size of a FTSE 100 non-financial company was 10, though the average size of a bank board was 16. The Walker Review took the view that the ideal size for a board was in the range of 10–12 members.[31]

Executive and non-executive directors—Although the early versions of the CGC, for example the initial Cadbury Code of Best Practice of 1992, recommended that boards have at least three non-executive directors, the modern versions of the Code are expressed entirely in terms of the number of *independent* non-executive directors. There are now no recommendations relating to non-executive directors who are not independent. Consequently, these provisions of the Code are taken up in section 2.2.3 below. Of course, the board may contain non-executive directors who do not meet the independence criteria, since such persons are not prohibited from being members of the board, but their presence is not required by the CGC or, indeed, any other set of applicable rules.

However, as we see below, since the CGC recommends that boards of all but small listed companies should be composed of at least 50% independent non-executive directors, it follows that the Code recommends implicitly that at least half the board should be non-executive directors. The important point here is perhaps that the Code has also sought to cap the number of non-executive directors. In its various iterations, the Code has always recommended an 'appropriate combination of executive and non-executive directors'.[32] Consequently, a typical US board comprising only a single executive director (usually the CEO) would not be in compliance with the recommendations of the UK CGC. The thought here appears to be that the flow of information to the non-executive members of

---

[29] Main Principle A.1. Nor does the FRC Guidance (above n. 18) address this issue.

[30] PIRC, *Corporate Governance Annual Review*, 2000.

[31] Walker, above n. 11, para 3.1 and Annex 4.

[32] CGC, B.1 (Supporting Principles).

the board will be enhanced if all the top executives of the company are members of the board.[33]

Labour representatives—There are no general requirements for employee representation at board level, though companies are free to make provision for such representatives in their articles. It is thought that no listed UK companies do so. Mandatory provisions for employee representation at board level in large companies were in fact recommended by a government-appointed committee in the 1970s, but the proposals never secured sufficient political support to be enacted and are currently nowhere near the live political agenda.[34]

Special qualification requirements—The Companies Act used to contain some not very effective rules restricting those over the age of 70 from continuing as directors. In line with current mores these have disappeared from the 2006 Act. They have been replaced by rules aimed at the opposite end of the age spectrum which require directors to be at least 16 years' old.[35] The purpose of this requirement is to safeguard the efficiency of enforcement of the rules against directors, since a person under the age of 16 is de jure or de facto immune from prosecution for Companies Act offences (and a private company need have only one director). For the same reason a company is now required to have at least one director who is a natural person.[36] Corporate directors are not forbidden, but since the 2006 Act they cannot constitute the whole of the board.

As we shall see in section 2.2.2, the allocation of certain types of decision to a committee of the board is a notable characteristic of modern board decision-making. A competence qualification is now applied to one of those committees, namely the audit committee. The CGC recommends that at least one member of the audit committee should have recent and relevant financial experience.[37] This provision has probably been largely overtaken today by a requirement of the Listing Rules, made by the FCA in order to implement in the UK the requirement

---

[33] Thus, whereas the board of a large US company may appear to be analogous to a supervisory board (without employee representatives) in a two-tier structure, the CGC seeks to avoid that result.

[34] See P. Davies and M. Freedland, *Labour Legislation and Public Policy* (OUP, 1993), ch. 8.4. A watered down version of this proposal recently re-emerged in relation to the constitution of the company's remuneration committee, but in the end it was not taken up by the government. See Department for Business Innovation and Skills (BIS), *Directors' Pay*, 2012, URN 12/888, para 55. Of course, an SE incorporated in the UK may be required to have employee representatives at board level if one of the founding companies was subject to such a requirement, but it is not believed that such an SE currently exists.

[35] Section 157.

[36] Section 155.

[37] Provision C.3.1.

of Art. 41 of the Audit Directive (2006/43/EC), that at least one member of the audit committee 'have competence in accounting and/or auditing.'[38]

There are no other *ex ante* competence qualifications applied generally to the members of boards.[39] The *ex post* duty of care is discussed in section 3.1.2 and the statutory provisions on the disqualification of directors in section 4.2. These provisions may feed back into the process of appointing directors. The *ex post* obligation of the board to review its effectiveness is discussed below.

CEO and chair of the board—A notable feature of the development of the CGC in the UK has been the strengthening of its requirements for a separation of the positions of CEO and chair of the board. This is not a feature of the equivalent requirements in the US. In a US board it is common for the same person to perform both roles, though in that system some of the functions performed by the chair are then taken by the lead independent director. The initial Cadbury Report stated that 'given the importance and particular nature of the chairman's role, it should in principle be separate from that of the chief executive.'[40] The accompanying Code of Best Practice, however, did not actually recommend such a division, simply recommending that 'there should be a clearly accepted division of responsibilities at the head of the company, which will ensure a balance of power and authority, such that no one individual has unfettered powers of decision. Where the chairman is also the chief executive, it is essential that there should be a strong and independent element on the board, with a recognised senior member.'[41] By 1998, in the 'Combined Code' which emerged from a review of the Cadbury Code by the Hampel Committee,[42] a decision to combine the posts of chair of the board and CEO was stated to be one which required public justification.[43] In a comply-or-explain system of enforcement, this was in effect a recommendation that the posts should not be combined, though the Combined Code stopped short of formally making this recommendation. The formal recommendation came with the post-Enron Higgs Review of the Code.[44] The recommendation is stated straightforwardly in the current version of the CGC.[45]

Thus, separation of the roles of CEO and chair of the board has become a central feature of the recommended governance structure in the UK. The chair

---

[38] FSA, Disclosure and Transparency Rule (DTR) 7.1.1.

[39] The special provisions relating to banks were mentioned in 1.2.

[40] *Report on the Financial Aspects of Corporate Governance*, December 1992, para 4.9.

[41] Code of Best Practice 1992, para 1.2.

[42] Committee on Corporate Governance, *Final Report*, 1998.

[43] Combined Code, 1998, A.2.1.

[44] D. Higgs, *Review of the Role and Effectiveness of Non-Executive* Directors, Department of Trade and Industry, January 2003, para 5.3.

[45] A.2.1.

runs the board; the CEO the company, it is often said—though the exact division of responsibilities between them is not obvious and is a matter for agreement between them.[46] Separation is seen as a crucial mechanism for the implementation of the notion of the board as a monitor of the management of the company. The fear is that, if the CEO ran the board, s/he would be able to downgrade the board's monitoring function. The chair is recommended to be independent on appointment, so that the previously common practice of the retiring CEO moving on to be chair of the board is contrary to the CGC. However, in the light of the burden and significance of the chair's role, the chair is not required to remain independent thereafter.[47] This enables the chair to act as an 'executive chair' after appointment.[48] More important, it enables even a non-executive chair to receive substantial rewards for his/her work without running up against the requirement that independent directors should not have a 'substantial business relationship' with the company.[49]

Two things can be said about the CEO/chair split. First, the recommendation is widely, but not universally, followed. At the end of the 1990s research found that 87% of all listed companies had a separate CEO and chair of the board.[50] A study looking at the period 1998–2004 found that the level of non-compliance with the separation recommendation was about 10%.[51] Sometimes the explanation offered to the shareholders for the former CEO becoming chair of the board has been accepted, notably where deep knowledge of the company's business was thought to be needed by the chair.[52] In other cases, it has been a cause of friction in the company's relations with its shareholders.[53]

---

[46] G. Owen and T. Kirchmaier, 'The Changing Role of the Chairman', (2008) 9 *European Business Organization Law Review* 187 at 198–9.

[47] Code Provision A.3.1.

[48] Some 20% of chairs of boards (where there is a separate CEO) described themselves in a survey as having 'executive' as well as 'non-executive' functions (Owen and Kirchmaier, above n. 46 at 199).

[49] Owen and Kirchmaier found that chairs were paid up to £500,000 (in 2006) in large companies: *ibid.*, p. 200. The criteria for independence are discussed below at sec. 2.2.3.

[50] Pensions and Investments Research Consultants Ltd (PIRC), *Compliance with the Combined Code*, September 1999, Table 3.

[51] S. Arcot and V. Bruno, 'In Letter but not in Spirit: An Analysis of Corporate Governance in the UK', 2006 (available at <http://ssrn.com/abstract=819784>) Table 8.

[52] Owen and Kirchmaier, above n. 46, pp. 196 f., citing HSBC bank and a high tech company.

[53] As in the case of the combination of the two roles by Sir Stuart Rose at Marks & Spencer between 2008 and 2010, though he was re-appointed by the shareholders as director of the company in 2008 after he had assumed the two roles.

Second, the empirical evidence is at best only weakly supportive of the proposition that the split contributes to the financial performance of the company.[54] This may be because the creation of a duopoly at the top of the company will enhance corporate performance if the two people develop a cooperative relationship but not if they develop a competitive one.[55] Since it is as likely that chair and CEO will compete as that they will cooperate, the overall effect of the recommendation may be nil.

Multiple directorships—The CGC recommends that the board should not agree to a full-time executive director of the company taking on more than one non-executive directorship of a FTSE 100 company and should not agree at all to such a director taking on the chair of such a company.[56] Other than in relation to executive directors, however, no restrictions are imposed on the number of directorships a person may hold. The limited nature of the CGC provisions on multiple directorships probably reflects the unwillingness of the drafters of the Code to lay down precise rules in this area. The issue is instead addressed through general provisions, covering both independent directors and the chair, that the time commitment expected should be made clear at the time of appointment, the director should undertake to make that time available and the director's other commitments should be disclosed to the board and, in the case of the chair, to the general meeting in the annual report.[57]

Expertise requirements—Apart from the specific expertise requirements noted above, at a general level the CGC emphasises the need for boards to contain appropriate levels of experience, skill and knowledge. This is discussed further below in relation to the independence requirement, with which the requirement for expertise has recently been seen to be in conflict.

Gender requirements—This is an issue which has only recently come onto the corporate governance agenda and is an example of a concern which has been pushed by political forces from outside the groups which have been accustomed to setting the corporate governance rules. For the first time in 2010 the CGC made a (single) reference, albeit in somewhat lukewarm terms, to 'the benefits of

---

[54] J. Dahya, L. Garcia and J van Bommel, 'One Man Two Hats: What's All the Commotion!'(2009) 44 *The Financial Review* 179; P. McKnight, N. Milonas, N. Travlos and C. Weir, 'The Cadbury Code Reforms and Corporate Performance', 2005 (available at <http://ssrn.com/abstract=675627>) at p. 18; M. Benz and B.S. Frey, 'Corporate Governance: What Can We Learn from Public Governance?', (2007) 32 *Academy of Management Review* 92.

[55] J. Roberts and P. Stiles, 'The Relationship between Chairmen and Chief Executives: Competitive or Complementary Roles?', (1999) 32 *Long Range Planning* 36.

[56] Code Provision B.3.3.

[57] *Ibid.*, B.3.1 and 2.

diversity on the board, including gender'.[58] The issue was then considered in a report by Lord Davies of Abersoch in 2011, whose report was commissioned by the government.[59] This report noted that at that time only 12.5% of FTSE 100 directors were women and that only 5.5% of executive directors of FTSE 100 companies were women. Its recommendations as to how to move forward from this position are a classic example of self-regulation in the shadow of the law. First, the Report stated that 'gender diverse' boards have a positive impact on performance (though robust academic evidence to this effect is not quoted) and then that appointment to board positions must always be on merit. Difficult questions about positive discrimination and board effectiveness were thus avoided. Second, it noted that some governments are considering quotas for women on the board, but suggested that in the UK voluntary action would be preferable to government-imposed quotas. To that end it recommended that all FTSE 350 companies should 'aim' for 25% women on the board by 2015; that each company should set out its own aims for the proportion of female directors it wishes to have by 2013 and 2015; that these goals should be disclosed; that the CGC should be amended to require companies to adopt and make public a diversity policy for board appointments; and, finally, that government should reserve the power to legislate for quotas if sufficient progress was not made.

In response to the Davies report, the FRC, after consultation, amended the CGC so as to add a provision on the disclosure by boards of their diversity policy (and by implication a recommendation to have one), but without specifying any goals for the proportion of women on the board.[60] The main pressure on companies to increase the number of female board members comes from proposed legislative action. The UK government expects to alter the reporting requirements in 2013 so as to require companies to disclose annually the number persons of each sex who are (a) directors of the company (b) managers of the company and (c) employees of the company.[61] Stronger pressure comes from the EU level where a target of 40% for female tenure of board seats by 2020 may be set—though, curiously, only for non-executive directors.[62] Not surprisingly, the threat of legislation is having some impact on the proportion of women on boards of UK companies. In 2012 26% of FTSE 100 board appointments (2011: 18.5%) and 30.6% of FTSE 250 (11.9%) appointments were women. The impact of this increased flow of female appointments was to increase the stock of female directors (executive and non-executive) of FTSE 100 companies to 17.4% (2011: 14.2%) and of FTSE 250

[58] Supporting Principles B.2.

[59] Lord Davies of Abersoch, *Women on Boards*, February 2011, URN 11/745.

[60] See FRC, *Consultation Document: Gender Diversity on Boards*, May 2011 and CGC, B.2.4 and B.6.

[61] Proposed new s. 414C(5) of the Companies Act 2006.

[62] COM(2012) 614 final.

companies to 11.8% (8.4%). However, the number of female executive directors remained low at 6.6% (FTSE 100) and 4.9% (FTSE 250).[63]

Evaluation of board performance—The CGC has always attached considerable importance to evaluation of the board on a continuing basis. Main Principle B.6 states that 'the board should undertake a formal and rigorous annual evaluation of its own performance and that of its committees and individual directors.' The CGC also recommends external facilitation of the annual evaluation in FTSE 350 companies at least once every three years. It is made clear that one result of the evaluation might be the replacement of individual directors. The chairman's performance should be evaluated by the non-executive directors, led by the Senior Independent Director (SID). Recent data suggests that in 2011/12 one-third of FTSE 350 companies undertook externally facilitated reviews, which—scaled up for a three year period—suggests a high rate of compliance.[64]

2.2.2. Decision-making

Voting on boards—In principle, this is a matter to be regulated in the company's articles. The model articles for public companies provide that, unless stipulated elsewhere in the articles, decision-making is by a simple majority of those voting and each director has one vote.[65] It is thought that this pattern is followed widely in practice, though in some cases (notably in private companies) the consent of a particular director or directors may be required in order to give effect to a shareholder agreement or to protect a creditor's interests. There is thus normally no formal division between the voting rights of executive, non-executive and independent directors. However, as we see below in discussing board committees, a veto or even an initiation right is given to independent directors in certain areas because of their dominance of these committees.

Separate meetings—Separate meetings of executive and non-executive directors undoubtedly take place. Indeed, the CGC recommends that the chairman meet the non-executive directors without the executives being present.[66] The frequency of such meetings is not specified. Such meetings would not constitute formal meetings of the board. It seems likely that such meetings occur routinely in many

---

[63] Association of British Insurers, *Report on Board Effectiveness*, 2012, p. 6.

[64] See Supporting Principles B.6 and Provisions B 6.2 and .3 and FRC, *Developments in Corporate Governance in 2012*, p. 14.

[65] Article 13. Decisions may be taken either at meetings or by means of written resolutions: art 7. The model articles set the quorum for the board at two, but allow the directors to decide on a different number. Quorum requirements in the articles are often used in private companies when it is desired to give a particular shareholder a veto over a board decision by making that shareholder's board representative a mandatory part of the quorum for the decision in question.

[66] Code Provision A.4.2.

companies before each meeting of the full board, but it is not clear how effectively the non-executives co-ordinate their positions in such pre-meetings.

Informally, the top management of the company may form themselves into an 'executive committee' or some similarly titled body. In some companies the chair routinely attends meetings of the executive committee, thus conferring a somewhat enhanced status on it, though the practice risks compromising the willingness of the chairman to encourage questioning of the management's proposals at board meetings.[67] At these informal executive meetings no resolutions binding the company in matters which require board approval may be taken, but, given the hierarchical structure of management, it is likely that the executives co-ordinate their positions in advance of a full board meeting more effectively than the non-executives.

The chair—Given the CGC's insistence on the separation of the role of CEO and chair of the board, it is not surprising that the Code attaches great importance to the role of the chair.[68] 'The chair is responsible for leadership of the board and ensuring its effectiveness on all aspects of its role.'[69] The chair has control of the board's agenda and of progress through the agenda at the meeting. The pivotal role of the chair as between the non-executives and the executives is highlighted: 'The chairman should also promote a culture of openness and debate by facilitating the effective contribution of non-executive directors in particular and ensuring constructive relations between executive and non-executive directors.'[70] Owen and Kirchmaier[71] conclude that the task of the chair of a listed company is 'complex and demanding', primarily as a result of the need to manage two potentially conflicting relationships, that between the chair and the CEO and that between the executive and non-executive directors. Establishing those two relationships on a fruitful basis is the task which sits at the core of UK corporate governance and thus with the chair. However, there is no single way of managing those relationships successfully and the rules on corporate governance, having set up the problem, do not and probably cannot determine how it is best solved.

Board committees—The model articles have always given the board a broad power to delegate any of its powers to a committee of the board (or, indeed, to any person).[72] Board committees are a long-standing feature of board operation in

---

[67] Owen and Kirchmaier, above n. 46, at p. 198.

[68] The Act, however, makes no reference to the chair of the board or the role attached to this position, and even the model articles refer to 'the chairman or other director chairing the meeting' only for the purpose of conferring a casting vote on the chair: art 14.

[69] Main Principle A.3.

[70] Supporting Principle A.3.

[71] Owen and Kirchmaier, above n. 46 at p. 208.

[72] Art 5.

the UK. However, with the emergence of the corporate governance code in the UK, they have become more important, both in terms of their number and the position of independent directors on them. The Cadbury Code of Best Practice recommended the creation of an audit committee of at least three independent directors. The current CGC recommends the creation of three committees (audit, remuneration and nomination), all dominated by independent directors. In the case of banks and insurance companies the Walker report recommended the creation of a further committee of the board: the risk committee.[73]

The audit committee should consist of at least three independent directors, though in smaller companies the recommended number is two and, in addition, in those companies the chair of the board may be a member of the committee, though not its chair.[74]

The remuneration committee is also recommended to consist of at least three independent directors (two in smaller companies), but the chair of the board is routinely permitted to be a member of the committee (provided the chair was independent on appointment).[75] The chair used to be excluded from membership of the remuneration committee, but this was changed in the 2006 iteration of the Combined Code, apparently on the grounds that setting the remuneration of the executives, especially of the CEO, was a crucial element in the chair's management of the relationship with the CEO.

The nomination committee is the committee least dominated by independent directors. Only a majority of its members need be independent directors and the chair of the board may chair this committee (except when it is dealing with the chair's successor).[76] Consequently, a five-person nomination committee of which both the chair and the CEO were members would comply with the CGC's recommendations. The Code would appear to take the view that the executives' conflicts of interest in board appointments are less than in relation to audit and remuneration and/or that the need to secure directors who are effective as well as independent justifies greater executive input into this committee.

The risk committee in banks and insurance companies is also less dominated by independent directors. The Walker review seemed to be as much concerned with making risk an issue of greater concern for the board as with viewing risk as a matter of potential conflict between executive and independent directors. Expertise on the risk committee is as important as independence. Consequently, although the recommendation is for the risk committee to be chaired by a non-

---

[73] Above n. 11, ch. 6. These recommendations have been implemented by the FSA, notably in its Rules on Senior Management Arrangements, Systems and Controls (SYSC) 21.

[74] Code Provision C.3.1.

[75] Code Provision D.2.1. Thus, for a former CEO who becomes chair of the board to be a member of the remuneration committee would be contrary to the recommendations of the Code.

[76] Code Provision B.2.1.

executive and to have a majority of non-executive members, it is anticipated that the chief financial officer (CFO) will be a member of the committee and the membership of the CEO is not excluded.[77] It is interesting in this regard that there is no recommendation that the non-executives on the risk committee should be independent; more important is that they should have 'substantial financial experience'.[78]

The committees recommended by the CGC operate in principle by making recommendations to the full board. However, the remuneration committee is recommended to have 'delegated responsibility' (ie. it decides on behalf of the company) for setting the remuneration of the executive directors and the chair (including pension payments and compensation for loss of office).[79] However, as we see in section 3.1.5, there is now also significant shareholder input into the setting of directors' remuneration. The CGC does not require the audit committee to be given any particular level of delegated authority, but some of its functions will be more easily and speedily discharged if it does have such delegated authority.[80]

Even where the audit committee operates by way of recommendation to the full board, there is formal pressure on the full board to accept its recommendations in some cases. Thus, if the audit committee's recommendations on the appointment, reappointment or removal of the statutory auditor are not accepted by the full board, the division of opinion and the reasons for it are to be revealed to the shareholders (with whom the final decision lies).[81] In relation to all three committees, a certain pressure on the board to accept the committees' recommendations is generated by the recommendations that the terms of reference of the committee should be publicly available and a section of the company's annual report should be devoted to describing the work of the committee.[82] These provisions increase the chances of committee and board disagreements becoming known to shareholders and thus, ex ante, put pressure on board and committee to reach an agreement.

[77] FSA Handbook, SYSC 21.1.5. The provisions of this part of the Handbook provide 'guidance' rather than lay down firm rules.

[78] Walker Report, above n. 11, para 6.17.

[79] Code Provision D.2.2. The remuneration committee makes recommendations to the full board on level and structure of the remuneration of senior, but non directorial, managers. The remuneration of the non-executive directors is decided on by the full board or by a committee to which this task has been delegated, which committee may include the chair of the board. Thus, the chair is at the centre of all remuneration decisions.

[80] Code Provision C.3.2 and 3.

[81] Code Provision C.3.7.

[82] Code Provisions B.2.1, B.2.4, C.3.3 and C.3.8 for the nomination and audit committees. Disclosure of the activities of the remuneration committee is now part of the directors' remuneration report (DRR) required by the Act, and so is mandatory. See below.

2.2.3. *Independent Directors*

The Code's recommendations about independent directors have strengthened steadily over the years—but have recently been expressed in a more qualified way. The original Cadbury Code of 1992 recommended that 'the board should include non-executive directors of sufficient calibre and number to carry significant weight in the board's decisions' and that the majority of the non-executives should be independent.[83] There was no specific requirement for a particular proportion of the board to be non-executive, and only in the body of the report which led to the promulgation of the Code was there mention of a minimum number of three non-executive directors, which would be approaching one-third of a typical board.[84] By the time of the 2006 revision of the Code—put in place in the light of the Enron scandal—the recommendation was that, except in smaller listed companies, half the members of the board should consist of independent non-executive directors (henceforward just 'independent' directors), so a merely non-executive director no longer counted towards meeting the Code's recommendations.

In the light of what are sometimes seen as the corporate governance failures in the lead-up to the financial crisis, it is interesting to note that the balance between independence and expertise in the wording of the Code has changed somewhat. Although the recommendation that half the board be independent directors has been retained in the Code, the overarching Main Principle on board composition changed in a potentially significant way between 2006 and 2010. In 2006 it read as follows:

'The board should include a balance of executive and non-executive directors (and in particular independent non-executive directors) such that no individual or small group of individuals can dominate the board's decision taking.' (Main Principle A3, 2006)

It now reads as follows:

'The board and its committees should have the appropriate balance of skills, experience, independence and knowledge of the company to enable them to discharge their respective duties and responsibilities effectively.' (Main Principle B1, 2012—change introduced in 2010.)

The underlying goal has changed from avoiding dominance by a small group to emphasising the characteristics (of which independences is only one) for the effective discharge of the responsibilities of the board. Indeed, the Walker Review recommended that a financial company should not feel inhibited from departing from the 50% recommendation of the CGC in relation to independent directors if it needed to increase the number of non-independent directors in order

---

[83] *Report on the Financial Aspects of Corporate Governance – Code of Best Practice*, paras 1.3 and 2.1.

[84] *Ibid.*, p. 22.

to obtain the required level of board expertise.[85] In other words, if the need for expertise caused a financial company to have to choose between an unwieldy large board and departure from the 50% recommendation, it should take the latter course. This is quite a good illustration of the way in which competence is beginning to rise up the scale of required virtues in a director and independence is beginning to move down.[86]

There is some empirical support for the proposition that there is a trade-off between independence and expertise as far as corporate performance is concerned. McKnight et al found that a small proportion of independent directors on the board was associated with worse corporate performance, whilst larger proportions were neutral in their impact on firm performance.[87] One possible explanation is that a small proportion of independent directors has no impact on the reduction of shareholders' agency costs, whilst lowering the overall expertise of the board, whereas with a larger proportion of independent directors, shareholders' agency costs are addressed effectively and this benefit counterbalances the cost of a less expert board. On the other hand, a study by Dahya and McConnell found that an increase in the number of non-executive directors, in accordance with the recommendations of the Cadbury Report, was associated with improved firm performance.[88] This suggests a greater gain from the reduction of shareholder agency costs associated with the increase in non-executive directors or a smaller loss in terms of expertise than other studies had suggested. Whichever set of findings is more persuasive, it is far from clear that the problem can be finessed in the way the 2010 Code attempted.

---

[85] Walker, above n. 11, para 3.3. The Review even contemplated, though somewhat guardedly, that the need for expertise might drive the financial company to explain to shareholders a departure from the recommendation of a 'balance' of executive and non-executive directors in favour of a non-executive dominated board, presumably so as to create space for more non-independent non-executive directors: *ibid.*, para 3.4.

[86] This may also go some way to explain the fact that the recommendation for 50% independent directors is the least observed in practice of the Code's recommendations. One in five companies did not comply with it in 2011, compared with one in ten or one in twenty for the other controversial recommendations. See FRC, *Developments in Corporate Governance in 2012*, p. 12.

[87] P. McKnight, N. Milonas, N. Travlos and C. Weir, 'The Cadbury Code Reforms and Corporate Performance', (2009) 8 *ICFAI Journal of Corporate Governance* 22 at pp. 37–38. See also H. Hsu and Y. Wu, 'Board Composition, Audit Committee Structure, "Grey" Directors and the Incidences of Corporate Failure in the UK' (available at <http://ssrn.com/abstract=153 2997>) showing that a lower failure rate of companies is associated with a higher proportion of non-independent non-executive ('grey') directors on the board but negatively associated with a higher proportion of independent directors.

[88] J. Dahya and J. McConnell, 'Board Composition, Corporate Performance and the Cadbury Committee Recommendation', (2007) 42 *Journal of Financial and Quantitative Analysis* 535.

The approach of the CGC to the definition of 'independence' is to put that task in the hands of the board itself, which must state in its annual report which of the non-executive directors it has determined to be independent.[89] Independence includes independence in character and judgment as well as in relationships with the company. However, the board is required to give an explanation of its determination that a non-executive director is independent if any of the following relationships between that person and the company exist:

- the director has been an employee of the company or group within the last five years;
- has, or has had within the last three years, a material business relationship with the company either directly, or as a partner, shareholder, director or senior employee of a body that has such a relationship with the company;
- has received or receives additional remuneration from the company apart from a director's fee, participates in the company's share option or a performance-related pay scheme, or is a member of the company's pension scheme;
- has close family ties with any of the company's advisors, directors or senior employees;
- holds cross-directorships or has significant links with other directors through involvement in other companies or bodies;
- represents a significant shareholder; or
- has served on the board for more than nine years from the date of their first election.

It should be noted that a representative of a significant shareholder is not treated as independent.

The role of the independent director plays into the agency theory of company law in a very direct way. Dispersed shareholders, having necessarily delegated substantial powers to the board, incur the potential cost that the directors may act in their own interests rather than those of the shareholders. These costs, it is argued, can be reduced by independent directors who monitor the actions of the management on behalf of dispersed shareholders. However, this concept of independent directors as monitors is often argued to be an incomplete analysis of the role of independent directors, because they are also expected to contribute to the effectiveness of board decision-making.[90] The events leading up to the financial crisis have served to emphasise the role of independent directors in ensuring board effectiveness.

---

[89] Code Provision B.1.1.

[90] J. Roberts, T. McNulty and P. Stiles, 'Beyond Agency Conceptions of the Work of the Non-executive Director: Creating Accountability in the Board Room', (2005) 16 *British Journal of Management* S5.

It is clear that, if the executive directors perceive the role of the non-executives to be solely that of monitoring their performance, the executive directors will seek to minimise the role of the board as a whole in corporate decision-making. This could be by minimising the matters which go to the board for approval or reducing the information made available to the board when referred items are discussed. Although neither of these issues is in the gift of the executive directors—indeed it is the role of the chair to ensure that an appropriate range of matters goes to the board and that range is fully discussed—the executive directors de facto can have a substantial influence on these issues. Consequently, a contribution on the part of the independent directors to the board's decision-making is probably a pre-condition for the effective discharge of their monitoring role. If the executive directors perceive that full board discussion of particular issues adds to the quality of the decisions reached, they will be more inclined to take the independent directors into their confidence.

Monitoring is a central role for the independent directors when the board is engaging in activities where the executive directors have a high level of self-interest (such as setting remuneration or compiling the company's annual financial statements), whilst it could be said that enhancing effectiveness is the role they should perform in relation to the setting of corporate strategy. The committee structure recommended by the CGC gives strong support for this view (see section 2.2.2 above) because it gives the independent directors a dominant role in three areas where conflicts of interest can be expected to be present. However, it is doubtful whether monitoring and contributing to decision-making map onto the issues before the board in quite such a simple way. For example, a corporate strategy proposal may be an expression of the executives' self-interest, as is where the executives propose an expansion of the company for 'empire building' reasons. Or it may be that the executives come up with a flawed strategy because of limited competence (honestly exercised) and not because of any self-seeking. If it is further assumed that limited competence (bounded rationality) is an inherent feature of the human condition, it will be in the interests of the shareholders that the independent directors not only control self-seeking by the executives but also 'guide' the executives in the setting of corporate strategy.[91]

What form, however, can this guidance be expected to take? The usual phrase used to describe what the independent directors should do is 'constructive challenge'.[92] The independent directors should sceptically examine the foundations upon which the strategy proposal is built and be mindful of areas of risk which the executives have not taken into account. It is clear that, for independent

---

[91] J. Hendry, 'Beyond Self-interest: Agency Theory and the Board in a Satisficing World', (2005) 16 *British Journal of Management* 55.

[92] CGC, Main Principle A.4: independent directors 'should constructively challenge and help develop proposals on strategy'.

directors to do this effectively, they will need a good knowledge of the industry in which the company operates and of the company itself—its capabilities and weaknesses. Some provisions of the CGC help in this direction, such as the time commitments discussed above, the recommendation for formal induction of new board members and subsequent up-dating,[93] and the recommendations on information flow to the board, as discussed below. However, it should be remembered that even the setting of corporate strategy is something which needs to take place on the basis of incomplete information and strong time constraints. It is not like a piece of academic research. Thus, there is likely to be a fine line between executives' perception that the independent directors are helping to improve corporate strategy and their perception, especially on the part of the CEO, that business opportunities are being lost through delay and unwillingness to take risks. It may be that independent directors flourish best where the production of strategic proposals is a collegiate and deliberative exercise on the part of executive management (probably not the case in large UK companies), ie. precisely the situation in which the executives are least likely to misjudge corporate strategy. It may even be that the directors' monitoring function and their 'improvement' function are in conflict, in the sense that it may be in the interests of dispersed and diversified shareholders that the company should take a higher level of risk than is implicit in the notion of getting the corporate strategy right.[94]

2.3. Information Streams

The common law of companies provides that a director has a legal entitlement to see any document or record of the company. Practically, this is of little use unless the director knows what he is looking for. The point is put rather more fully in the CGC: 'The board should be supplied in a timely manner with information in a form and of a quality appropriate to enable it to discharge its duties.'[95] The CGC throws the ultimate duty of obtaining the relevant information on the chair: 'The chairman is responsible for ensuring that the directors receive accurate, timely and clear information.'[96] The day-to-day duty of seeing that this recommendation is fulfilled falls on the company secretary.

If an independent director believes that s/he is not obtaining the information needed, this is something which could be brought up in the board evaluation process (above). If the director wishes to take individual action to obtain more information than is provided by the executives under the guidance of the chair,

---

[93] Code Provisions B.4.1 and 2.

[94] This argument has been advance most convincingly in relation to financial institutions.

[95] Main Principle B.5.

[96] Supporting Principles A.3 and B.5.

then the CGC gives some support to that director. 'To function effectively, all directors need [...] access to its operations and staff.'[97] All directors should also have access to professional advice at the company's expense when they judge it necessary for the discharge of their responsibilities.[98] In the first instance, the director will probably raise the issues of the lack of information or the need for professional advice with the company secretary.[99] There is little doubt that for an independent director to talk to company staff without at least the tacit consent of the executive directors or to seek outside professional advice for the purpose of challenging an executive proposal would be regarded as an unfriendly act by the executives. The independent director's standing on the board would be reduced if these extraordinary steps did not reveal something amiss in the company.

The terms of reference of the audit, nomination and remuneration committees will imply that extensive corporate information should be supplied to them. In the case of the audit committee this is spelled out in the FRC's guidance, which recommends access to the company's secretariat for the purposes of collecting and distributing information and access to outside professional advice, including legal and accounting advice.[100] Only in the case of the risk committee recommended for banks and insurance companies is a specialist executive director (company risk officer) given the task of servicing the committee.[101] However, in the light of the sections in the annual report contributed by the three general committees, it seems unlikely that the management would refuse access to information sought by any of these three committees.

3. Accountability

This section discusses the various mechanisms and techniques deployed in the UK to render directors accountable in relation to the exercise of the extensive powers normally conferred on them.

---

[97] Supporting Principle B.4.

[98] Code Provision B.5.1.

[99] Code Provision B.5.2. However, in the case of a conflict of view between the chair and the independent directors as to the provision of information or access to independent advice, the secretary cannot be relied upon to act contrary to the views of the chair.

[100] FRC, *Guidance on Audit Committees*, 2010, paras 2.11–2.14.

[101] Above n. 77.

3.1. Board and Shareholders

3.1.1. *Appointment and Removal*

Appointment of directors is essentially a matter governed by the articles of association. Typically these will provide for appointment by the shareholders as a body by ordinary resolution, though appointment rights can be allocated elsewhere, eg. to particular shareholders or creditors.[102] Between shareholder meetings the board normally has the power to fill casual vacancies but with the board appointee being subject to ratification at the next shareholder meeting. Any person may stand for election, assuming it is lawful for them to do so (eg. they are not currently disqualified).[103] In practice, the board determines its own composition in the normal run of things through the exercise of its power to make nominations to the shareholders for appointment to the board. This explains the importance attached by the CGC the composition of the nomination committee of the board, since the board's proposals normally carry the day. Occasionally, activist shareholders seek to put pressure on the company by advancing their own nominees against those nominated by the board.[104] The problems which shareholders often face in the US in getting their nominees before the shareholder body are not replicated in the UK system. The articles normally provide a reasonably shareholder-friendly process for the nomination of candidates other than by the board. In the light of the shareholders' statutory removal powers, described below, it may be ultimately ineffective for the articles to block shareholder nominations.

For the general run of companies, reappointment is also a matter left to the articles and the articles normally provide for re-election every three years.[105] However, in a controversial move the CGC in 2010 recommended annual re-election of all members of the boards of FTSE 350 companies.[106]

By contrast, in relation to removal, the Companies Act law contains a tough mandatory rule: the shareholders, by ordinary resolution, can at any time remove any director (or, indeed, all of them) without having to assign a reason for so doing.[107] This power overrides anything to the contrary in the company's articles or in any contract with the director, and so removal may occur at any time and not

---

[102] A company could adopt cumulative voting. It is not mandatory and its adoption voluntarily is very rare. However, see the recent FSA proposals about director elections in controlled companies, below, text attached to n. 229.

[103] Model articles 20 and 21. On disqualification see sec. 4.2 below.

[104] As in the case of the recent board battle in National Express; see *Financial Times*, 27 April 2011.

[105] Model article 21.

[106] Code Provision B.7.1.

[107] Section 168.

just when the director comes up for re-appointment at the end of his or her term of office. The rule applies even to directors not appointed by the shareholders, though if a director appointed by the creditors is removed, that may put the company in breach of its loan covenants and so removal in that case may carry undesirable consequences for the company, such as an obligation to re-pay the loan.

There are qualifications to the effectiveness of this rule, one formal, the other behavioural. First, the Act specifically preserves for the dismissed director the right to 'compensation or damages payable to him in respect of the termination of his appointment as director or of any appointment terminating with that as director'. This clearly permits an executive director who has a service contract with the company [108] to claim damages if dismissed by the shareholders under their statutory powers but in breach of the service contract. The newspapers are full of reports of dismissed directors receiving sums running into several million pounds as compensation for loss of office, even where the cause of their removal seems to have been the poor performance of the company. Whether such payments do in fact serve as a check on the shareholders' use of their powers in the case of companies with multi-billion pound turnovers is not clear. However, large payments may blunt the *ex ante* impact of the removal power on the director: why bother to avoid a situation in which the shareholders wish to remove you if the financial consequences of removal are attractive? The matter of large cash payoffs to directors raises issues which relate to the rewards strategy which is discussed below.

Second, there is the question of whether the institutional shareholders' coordination problems (free riding and conflicts of interest) are so strong as to discourage effective exercise of the removal power. The Act makes it relatively easy for shareholders to convene a shareholders' meeting or to add a removal resolution to an annual general meeting (AGM)—5% of the voting shares being required in either case. [109] Nevertheless, a successful removal resolution requires 50% of those voting. So, the coordination problems referred to in section 1.1 resurface here.

It is unclear what effect the recent change in the Corporate Governance Code will have in the companies to which it applies. On the one hand, it will remove the need to add a removal resolution to the AGM agenda. The shareholders will

---

[108] Whist any director may have a formal contract by which (s)he is appointed director, the management or 'service' contract which an executive director has with the company as a senior manager and which is separate from the directorial contract, if any, will be far more important in financial terms. It is normal to provide in the articles that the executive position will terminate if the manager is removed from the board. Whether such termination is a breach of the service contract is a matter of construction of the agreement, but the contract will normally be worded so that it is. Hence the importance of the final words of s. 168: 'or of any appointment terminating with that as director'.

[109] Sections 303 and 338—for adding a resolution at least 100 shareholders with voting rights upon whose shares an average of £100 has been paid up will also suffice.

routinely have an opportunity not to re-appoint (in effect, to remove) all the directors without effort on their part. On the other hand, the coordination problems of the shareholders are not addressed by this change. It may still appear more attractive and cost effective for an institution to sell out of a holding in a company in whose management it has lost faith than to organise a vote against the board.

The underlying question thus turns on the willingness of the large shareholders in British listed companies to form coalitions with other large shareholders to remove managers, remembering that a large shareholder in a listed British company can be regarded as any shareholder with more than 3% of the voting rights. The difficulty with measuring this propensity empirically is that such coalitions are normally ad hoc (ie. simply for the purpose of replacing members of the board; not to run the company on a continuing basis) and that their existence becomes public knowledge only rarely. Nevertheless, Crespi and Renneboog[110] found in a study of UK listed companies in the period 1998–2003 (ie. before the Cadbury Code became fully effective) that there was an association between shareholder voting power, using Shaply values, and CEO and executive director turnover. Companies in the lowest decile of share price performance had a rate of CEO and executive director turnover that was three times higher than companies in the top decile of performance. Director turnover in the poorly performing companies was then associated with voting power, negatively in the case of voting power in the hands of the executives themselves and positively in the case of voting power in the hands of other industrial companies or insurance companies.

3.1.2. Division of Powers

As noted in section 1.1 the Companies Act leaves matters of board function to the company itself. In consequence, the division of powers between board and shareholders is formally determined in the company's articles of association. The powers of the directors derive from the company's constitution, not from legislation. The initial division of powers is set by the articles when the company is formed and may be altered subsequently by majority shareholder vote. In practice, of course, for reasons of efficiency the powers conferred upon the board of a publicly-traded British company are no different from those conferred on the boards of such companies by legislation in other countries. That is, there is a very broad grant of power to the board in the articles. In non-listed and private companies, however, use may be made of the freedom to assign management powers to the shareholders.

The fact that the articles constitute the source of the directors' powers could have one practical consequence. Just as the shareholders can alter the division of

---

[110] R. Crespi and L. Renneboog, 'Is (Institutional) Shareholder Activism New? Evidence from UK Shareholder Coalitions in the Pre-Cadbury Era', (2010) *Corporate Governance: An International Review* 274.

powers through a supermajority vote, they can give ad hoc instructions to the board on a particular matter by a similar supermajority. This view is now reflected in the model articles.[111] However, as we have just seen, since the shareholders can remove a director at any time by ordinary resolution, if the shareholders' views are not followed, the shareholders are likely to deploy a threat to remove (if they choose to intervene) rather than a direction to the board.

It should be noted that provisions in the articles conferring extensive powers on the board cannot override provisions in the Act which require shareholder approval for certain corporate actions. These are particularly prominent when what is proposed is a variation of the rights of the shareholders under the company's articles or action likely to affect the interests of the shareholders as financiers of the company (for example, the issuance of further shares in the company). The list of matters for which the Companies Act requires shareholder approval does not differ significantly from the list likely to be found in any other European jurisdiction. The central point is that it is possible (and usual) for the articles to give the board very broad powers to formulate and implement the business strategy of the company.

3.1.3. Liability Rules

The exercise of the management powers granted to the board is constrained by the standards normally referred to as 'directors' duties'. These are liability rules, which attach to the directors individually, and which not only make the director liable to the company for damages but also, in some cases, for the disgorgement of profit made in breach of duty or for the restoration to the company of assets obtained by the director in breach of the duty. Directors' duties are thus 'hard law'. They were developed initially wholly as a matter of the common law of companies (ie. by the courts) but today the duties are set out in Part 10 of the 2006 Companies Act.

Duty of care—A duty of care on directors has long been part of UK company law, but it was, until recently, of little practical importance because the standard of care required was set initially at a subjective level: The director was required to be no more competent that s/he was personally capable of being. Whilst it was not completely impossible to demonstrate a breach of this standard of care, it was extremely difficult to do so. A lengthy and slow process of evolution of that standard of care into an objective standard was eventually finalised in the 2006 Act,[112] which requires the director to achieve the level of competence to which a reasonable person in the director's position would adhere. Any subjective capabilities serve only to raise the standard of care required. In many jurisdictions

---

[111] Model article 4. See n. 20 above.

[112] Section 174. This is modelled on s. 214 of the Insolvency Act 1986, discussed below.

the adoption of an objective test for the standard of care has been accompanied by the deployment of a business judgment rule, in order to guard against hindsight bias on the part of the courts in the application of the standard. The British legislature did not take that second step, apparently on the grounds that the British courts could be expected to avoid hindsight bias. Whether that confidence is justified remains to be seen.

Conflicts of interest—Conflicts of interest are dealt with extensively in the Companies Act;[113] the CGC hardly touches on this matter at all. There are some rules in the Takeover Code in this area, but this section will focus on the Companies Act rules because they are of general application.

An important preliminary remark concerns the general approach of the Act and the prior common law to conflict situations. British law has a very broad approach to what may constitute a conflict of interest, bringing in situations which some other systems may not regard as giving rise to conflicts. However, the concern of the law is then to identify a procedure within the company through which such conflicts can be handled. British law does not ask the courts to opine on the fairness of the transaction in the manner of Delaware law, at least in principle. Initially, that internal procedural approach on the part of British law involved *ex ante* ('authorisation') or *ex post* ('ratification') approval of the conflicted transaction by the shareholders.[114] Over the years the law moved to allow authorisation by the independent members of the board, or even simple disclosure to the board, as an additional mechanism to supplement shareholder authorisation. This was achieved initially by provisions in the articles of association but the 2006 Act endorsed this approach, at least as a starting point. However, if authorisation of the conflicted transaction is not obtained, then ratification remains a matter for the shareholders alone. In fact, the 2006 Act tightened the rules on ratification by excluding interested directors from voting on the ratification of their own breach of duty, something which the common law (surprisingly) allowed.[115] So, the incentives generated by the Act operate so as to induce directors to seek authorisation of conflicted transaction because authorisation is generally a less onerous procedure than ratification.

Self-dealing transactions—In the case of a director dealing (directly or indirectly) with his own company, it is difficult to say whether the dominant rule is disclosure to the board of the proposed transaction or authorisation by the share-

---

[113] Principally ss. 175–177, though also Chapter 4 of Part 10 of the Act.

[114] There is some complex law—not explored here—about when not even shareholder approval will absolve the director from breach of duty.

[115] Section 239. The previous rule was an expression of the classical view that fiduciary duties should be imposed on directors but not shareholders because the latter hold the powers attached to the shares in their own right.

holders (the traditional common law rule). The former appears to be the dominant rule when one looks at s 177 of the Act, which requires only disclosure of the proposed self-dealing transaction to the board.[116] This is a relatively weak rule and is open to the risk of 'mutual back scratching',[117] though it has the obvious attraction of providing a low-cost method of handling low-level and routine self-dealing transactions. However, the disclosure rule is replaced by a shareholder authorisation requirement in four cases, as laid down in Chapter 4 of Part 10 of the 2006 Act. These are areas where experience has shown that the risks of directorial abuse are high. The most important of the four relates to substantial property transactions between the director and the company, 'substantial' being widely defined. Shareholder authorisation is also required for loans to directors and a number of analogous transactions, and for two situations involving directors' remuneration, which are mentioned below. These rules apply to all public companies and most also apply to private companies.

Further, for listed companies with a premium listing, the Act's requirement of disclosure to the board, qualified in specific cases by a requirement for shareholder authorisation, is virtually reversed. The Listing Rules impose a shareholder authorisation requirement for all related party transactions, subject to some *de minimis* exceptions, and apply the authorisation requirement strictly, eg. by excluding the director and his associates from voting on the authorisation resolution—something the Act permits.[118] The provisions of the Listing Rules dealing with related-party transactions are a good example of (a) the role of the Listing Rules in setting corporate governance standards for companies with a premium listing and (b) the shareholder orientation of the Rules.

Corporate opportunities—These are not transactions with the company and so do not fall within the previous paragraph. Indeed, the whole notion of a corporate opportunity is that it is a business opportunity from which the company has been excluded in favour of the director taking the opportunity personally, directly or indirectly. The essence of the directors' breach of duty is that the exclusion of the company from the opportunity was wrongful because the company had a legitimate prior claim on the opportunity. Only if the company decides to forgo the opportunity is the director free to take it personally.

The typical mechanism for giving corporate approval for the taking of the opportunity by a director personally is board approval by the independent mem-

---

[116] The Act also requires disclosure in relation to past transactions, but the sanctions here are only criminal, whereas for proposed transactions the sanctions are civil.

[117] That is, directors taking no action in relation to the disclosure of each other's self-dealing transactions.

[118] Listing Rule 11. Under the Act, where it requires shareholder authorisation, it appears the interested director can vote his or her shares in favour of a transaction in which s/he is interested. Section 239 (above n. 115) applies only to shareholder ratification.

bers of the board, provided—in the case of public companies—the articles permit the board to give approval.[119] Thus, shareholder approval of the taking is the default rule for public companies, but companies can add board approval via an appropriate provision in the articles.[120] In this case, the 'independent' members of the board are not those who satisfy the independence requirements of the CGC (section 2.2.3 above), but those not involved in the transaction which requires approval. In general, independence under the statute excludes fewer directors from voting on the opportunity than the CGC requirements would.[121]

The Listing Rules on related party transactions will also pick up a few examples of corporate opportunities, but in the main the Listing Rules do not seek to make the Act's provisions more demanding in this area.

The Act does not deal with the definition of a corporate opportunity. This has been left to the courts, which have taken a quite strict line—stricter than that of the US courts on this particular issue.[122] One might hazard the view that as the definition of a corporate opportunity has become stricter, the machinery for obtaining corporate approval for the taking of the opportunity by the director personally has become easier, at least where the articles of public companies permit board approval of the taking of the opportunity.

Inside information—The rules discussed in the previous paragraph also apply to the personal use by a director of corporate information where that use gives rise to a conflict of interest between the director and the company. Trading by a director on the basis of information confidential to the company would probably give rise to such a conflict, because of the risk that the market will then be able to identify the existence of the inside information, if not its precise content. In practice, however, the general Companies Act rules on conflicts of interest are not extensively relied upon in the area of insider dealing. This seems to be so for three reasons. First, a director of a company with a premium listing is prohibited by the Listing Rules from dealing in the shares of the company during sensitive periods whether or not s/he is in possession of any inside information.[123] This regulatory technique thus consists of banning trading by directors where it is

---

[119] Section 175. This is also the residual rule for all conflicts of interest where no other specific procedure is imposed by the Act. Anecdotal evidence suggests that the articles of new public companies routinely give power to the board to authorise the taking of corporate opportunities and other conflicts of interest.

[120] For private companies the default rule embraces both board and shareholder approval, but the articles may remove board approval.

[121] Thus, an executive director will be independent for the purposes of the conflict rules, if not involved in the proposed taking of the opportunity, whilst a director who is independent under the CGC will be excluded from voting if he or she is involved in the proposed taking.

[122] See, for example, *Bhullar v Bhullar* [2003] 2 BCLC 241, CA.

[123] Listing Rule 9.2 and Annex 1.

highly likely the director will be in possession of price-sensitive information, whether that is in fact the case or not. Second, insider trading, whether by a director or anyone else, is a criminal offence under Part V of the Criminal Justice Act 1993 and an administrative offence under the Financial Services and Markets Act 2000. Although enforcement of these rules has traditionally been weak, in the wake of the financial crisis the FSA/FCA devoted significantly more enforcement resources to them. Third, failure to make full disclosure to the market of significant events as they occur is a breach by the company (and probably its directors) of the Disclosure and Transparency Rules. All these obligations are enforced by the FSA/FCA and are considered in the UK to be part of market regulation, not corporate governance.

However, there is one corporate governance implication of the market rules on disclosure and insider information: The company is at risk of breaching the market rules if it discloses information which is relevant to the market price to some shareholders only and equally the recipients of that information are at risk if they trade in the shares whilst in possession of information not available to the market as a whole. This puts some regulatory hurdles in the way of the policy of shareholder 'engagement', which is discussed below.

Takeovers—Takeovers, especially hostile takeovers, are generally regarded as having two functions: Providing an incentive to directors to act in the interests of the shareholders (a corporate governance consideration) [124] and providing a mechanism for re-drawing the boundaries of the firm (an industrial structure consideration, which is not further discussed here). In terms of board responsiveness to shareholders, the pervasive threat of a hostile takeover offer is more effective in securing board responsiveness to shareholder interests than the directors' duties discussed (which depend upon litigation for their effect) or the power of the majority shareholder to easily remove all incumbent directors (which requires shareholder coordination). However, the removal power clearly helps a bidder who has acquired a majority of the voting rights to assert management control immediately. In effect, a staggered board cannot be effectively implemented in the UK.

Hostile takeovers in the UK are facilitated by the incorporation of a board neutrality rule (BNR) in the Takeover Code.[125] This has been part of the Code since its adoption in the late 1960s. In effect, it achieves a mandatory reversal of the division of powers as between the board and the shareholders when a bid has

---

[124] However, the intensity of this threat varies across companies according to the attractiveness of the company as a target. Ironically, some very poorly performing companies may be unattractive takeover targets because the risks involved in attempting to turn them around may be judged too great. See J. Franks and C. Mayer, 'Hostile takeovers and the correction of managerial failure', (1996) 40 *Journal of Financial Economics* 163.

[125] The Takeover Code, r. 21.

been made or is known by the target board to be imminent. The board may not take action which would frustrate the bid without the approval of the share-holders, even if that action would normally be within the power of the board. The rule is a strong one because it requires shareholder approval after the bid is made or is imminent (*ex ante* shareholder approval does not satisfy the rule) and because approval is required for action which has the effect of frustrating the bid, no matter what the reasons the board has for taking the defensive action. The BNR is not qualified in the UK by a reciprocity exception (as is permitted under the Takeover Directive) nor can the shareholders opt out of the BNR generally by shareholder resolution. It is a mandatory, not a default, rule, though of course the shareholders can permit defensive action in the face of a particular offer.

Perhaps surprisingly, UK law does not contain a breakthrough rule (BTR). The absence of a BTR would seem to give the management of British companies an incentive to put defensive measures in place before a bid emerges, for exam-ple, through weighted or non-voting classes of share or through entering into joint ventures which give the venture partner a buy-out right on favourable terms if a bid is made for one of the partners. Although some action of this type can be seen, it is not widespread. A combination of the difficulty of identifying action which will be effective but not hobble the company's business in the period before the bid emerges, the need for shareholder approval under the Companies Act for some types of pre-bid defensive action (for example, the issue of share warrants), and the opposition of the institutional shareholders to non-voting or weighted-voting shares seem to explain the low level of pre-bid defensive action.

Other conflict situations—The Act contains additional rules on conflicts of interest not so far mentioned. There is a duty to exercise independent judgment[126] and a duty not to accept benefits from third parties in exchange for exercising directorial powers in a particular way ('bribes'). [127] In these two cases the procedure to be followed if a breach of these provisions is contemplated is the traditional common law rule of authorisation by the shareholders. Board author-isation in these cases does not suffice.

3.1.4. Institutional Investors and Stewardship

As noted above, the commonly accepted view is that British company law is shareholder centred, and thus the make-up of the shareholder body becomes cru-cial when examining the impact in practice of board rules. We have noted the power of the shareholders to remove directors easily and to give instructions to the board, and the inability of the board to take frustrating action in relation to hostile takeovers. Has this orientation of the law been altered by the statutory

---

[126] Section 173.
[127] Section 176.

codification of the directors' core duty of loyalty? That core duty is to 'promote the success of the company for the benefit of its members' (ie. normally the shareholders). This is clearly a shareholder-centred statement of the rule. However, the Company Law Review, which proposed the principle currently to be found in the Act, saw itself promoting 'enlightened shareholder value' (ESV).[128] The 'enlightenment' consists of recognising that the interests of the shareholders can be adversely affected if the interests of other stakeholder groups are not taken into account in appropriate ways by the directors. Thus, section 172 requires directors, whilst acting to promote the success of the company for the benefit of its members, to 'have regard' to a number of stakeholder interests, such as those of the company's employees, suppliers and customers, as well as the impact of the company's activities on the community and the environment. This formulation constitutes enlightened shareholder value rather than a stakeholder approach because non-shareholder interests are required to be taken into account only in so far as they have an impact on the directors' goal of achieving business success for the benefit of the members (shareholders). The directors are not required to 'balance' the interests of shareholders and other stakeholders so as, for example, to maximise the joint utility of all the stakeholders where this would involve a diminution in shareholder utility.

As noted in section 1.1, the strong legal rights of the shareholders have led to pressure on those shareholders thought to be capable of taking such action (ie. the institutional shareholders) (i) to exercise those rights and (ii) less clearly, but implicitly, to do so in a socially responsible way—despite the difficulty of defining what constitutes social responsibility. A particularly important example of the governmental 'demand' for shareholder engagement can be found in the Myners Report of 2001.[129] Although this report did not focus solely on engagement—indeed the impetus for the inquiry seems to have been the government's view that the investment strategies of institutions were too narrow, focusing on listed securities and ignoring small companies and private equity funds—the report devoted a chapter to making out the case that the level of institutional investor intervention in portfolio companies was sub-optimal.

In response to the Myners Report, institutional investors produced a set of Principles committing themselves to engagement with portfolio companies.[130] The institutions lost formal control of those Principles in the wake of the current crisis when the Principles were replaced by a Stewardship Code, for whose content the

---

[128] CLR, *Developing the Framework*, March 2000, ch. 3; *Completing the Structure*, November 2000, ch. 3

[129] P. Myners, *Institutional Investment in the United Kingdom: A Review*, H M Treasury, 2001, especially ch. 5.

[130] Institutional Shareholders Committee, *The Responsibilities of Institutional Shareholders and Agents – Statement of Principles*, 2002.

Financial Reporting Council is responsible (ie. the same body as is now responsible for the Corporate Governance Code).[131] However, the substantive content of the new Code is not (yet) much different from the former statement of Principles.

The Stewardship Code (SC) is binding on a comply-or-explain basis. However, unlike the situation in relation to the CGC, it is not obvious that any agency has authority impose a comply-or-explain obligation on shareholders in relation to the SC. Recognising this, the Stewardship Code stated in its initial 2010 version that it was addressed 'in the first instance to firms who manage assets on behalf of institutional shareholders'.[132] Such asset managers need FSA/FCA approval to conduct their business. The FSA introduced the necessary 'hard' comply-or-explain requirement for UK-authorised firms managing investments on behalf of professional clients. However, the requirement imposed on asset managers is less precise than that imposed on companies in relation to the CGC. It requires an authorised asset manager simply to disclose on its website '(1) the nature of its commitment to the FRC's Stewardship Code; or (2) where it does not commit to the Code, its alternative investment strategy.'[133] This shows that it is permissible for an asset manager to operate an investment strategy which involves no engagement with portfolio companies (for example, certain sorts of hedge fund strategies). By contrast a listed company always has an obligation to comply with the Main Principles of the CGC.[134]

In relation to the institutions themselves, the 2010 version of the SC 'strongly encouraged' institutional shareholders to adopt the Code, ie. it recognised that it had no power to require adoption of the Code.[135] However, the FRC had some success in encouraging them to adopt the SC voluntarily.[136] Perhaps for this reason the 2012 version of the SC states that is addressed to both institutional shareholders ('asset owners') and asset managers but it remains the case, as the SC recognises, that there is there is no rule underpinning of the comply-or-explain basis of the SC, except in relation to asset managers.[137]

As with most implicit and political deals there is some uncertainty about the precise terms of the exchange underlying the SC. In particular, are the institutions (or their asset managers) encouraged to intervene only when it is in the interests

---

[131] The current version of the Stewardship Code is available at <www.frc.org.uk/Our-Work/Codes-Standards/Corporate-governance/UK-Stewardship-Code.aspx>.

[132] FRC, *The UK Stewardship Code*, 2010, p. 2.

[133] FSA, *Conduct of Business Sourcebook*, 2.2.3.

[134] See sec. 1.1 above.

[135] Above n. 132, p. 2.

[136] In 2012 there were 259 signatories of the Code, of which 187 were asset managers (ie. covered by the FSA rule) and 58 asset owners (of which 40 were pension funds), so that asset managers still predominate. See FRC, *Developments in Corporate Governance in 2012*, p. 22.

[137] Above n. 131, p. 4.

of the shareholders to do so, or is the duty broader? For example, if the costs of intervention exceed the benefits to shareholders, or if greater benefits are to be gained for shareholders not from engagement but from exit, are the institutions still expected to intervene? Whilst the formal statements of what is required of institutional shareholders are usually formulated in terms of the benefits to shareholders of engagement,[138] the difficulty of identifying the costs and benefits of intervention can result in the institutions coming under pressure to engage more closely, even when they do not believe such engagement is in the interests of the shareholders. There is thus some ambiguity about whether the Stewardship Code enhances or modifies the shareholder-centric nature of British corporate governance.

The Stewardship Code recommends the following steps. Institutional investors should:

- develop a policy on intervention in portfolio companies and publicly disclose it;
- have a robust policy on managing conflicts of interest in relation to intervention (for example in financial conglomerates) and this policy too should be publicly disclosed;
- monitor their investee companies;
- establish clear guidelines on when and how they will intervene and how they will escalate their intervention if it is not initially successful (up to and including summoning a general meeting of the shareholders with the goal of replacing board members);
- be willing to act collectively with other investors where appropriate;
- have a clear policy on voting and disclosure of voting activity;
- report periodically on their stewardship and voting activities.[139]

In relation to voting policies and decisions, it should be noted that the Companies Act 2006[140] contains a 'reserve power' for the government to require disclosure. It is a reserve power because the government has said it will not exercise its statutory powers if disclosure develops voluntarily in the desired direction.

The recent emphasis on stewardship has led also to a re-examination of the role of the oldest and most traditional technique for directorial accountability, namely the annual report and accounts laid before the shareholders by the board. Two developments in particular have been significant. First, the Companies Act 2006 (s 417) took a form of reporting developed in the market, the 'business

---

[138] 'Institutional shareholders are free to choose whether or not to engage but their choice should be a considered one based on their investment approach.' (Financial Reporting Council (FRC), *The UK Stewardship Code*, July 2010, p. 1.

[139] Above n. 131, p. 5. The FRC, above n. 136 at p. 25, has stated that such disclosure is currently confined to large institutions.

[140] Sections 1277–1280.

review' (BR), and made it mandatory for all companies, but in a particularly strong way for publicly traded companies. The BR supplements the hard, backward-looking, financial data about the company with softer, forward-looking, non-financial data which is nevertheless crucial for an assessment of the company's prospects. This form of reporting is usually referred to as 'narrative reporting'. The additional data concerns, for example, the risks and opportunities facing the company and the quality of its relationships with the suppliers of key inputs. The current government plans to strengthen and somewhat re-orient the BR and to re-name it the Strategic Report.[141]

Second, the notion of board reporting to the shareholders has been extended to reporting by the main committees of the board, through dedicated sections of the annual report. As we have already noted, this has been a development brought about by the CGC (see section 2.2.2). This reporting requirement not only strengthens the position of the committees, dominated by independent directors, against the board as a whole but also strengthens the accountability of the committees to the shareholders. However, in relation to the audit committees, which have the most wide-ranging remit of the three committees recommended by the CGC and whose interactions with executive management are potentially adversarial, their reports have been criticised as bland and uninformative. The FRC made proposals for an up-grading of reporting by audit committees and these were reflected in the 2012 version of the Code.[142]

It is clear that the development of policies of intervention entails fairly significant costs for institutional shareholders. Thus, even if long-term shareholders still have sufficient critical mass to intervene effectively, the costs of so doing may make alternative courses of action (such as selling the shares) more attractive. The costs of intervention can be categorised as follows:[143]

- The cost of developing expertise and the expenditure of time on engagement is borne by the activist, while the benefits are shared by unaffiliated investors who are able to free ride on the efforts of the activist.

---

[141] BIS, *The Future of Narrative Reporting*, September 2011, URN 11/945. The proposed reforms, expected to be implemented in October 2013, are set out in BIS, *The Future of Narrative Reporting: A New Structure for Narrative Reporting in the UK*, October 2012, URN 12/979.

[142] FRC, *Effective Company Stewardship: Enhanced Corporate Reporting and Audit*, 2011. The main change is to be found in Provision 3.7 of the Code, requiring the audit committee to report on all the significant issues it considered in relation to the financial statements and on the effectiveness of the external auditor.

[143] M. Becht, J. Franks and S. Rossi, 'Returns to Shareholder Activism: Evidence from a Clinical Study of the Hermes UK Focus Fund', (2008) 22 *Review of Financial Studies* 3098. The study also shows that in specific circumstance intervention can be profitable for the fund, despite its costs.

- Regulation may discourage institutions from becoming insiders in the portfolio company (because they will forfeit the ability to trade the security) or may impose additional disclosure requirements on parties acting in concert or even require them to make a bid for all the outstanding shares in the portfolio company.[144]
- The risk that engagement will highlight the deficiencies of the portfolio company and trigger a fall in the value of its shares as other investors exit in response.
- The risk that portfolio companies will react negatively to engagement and reduce their degree of communication with activist investors.

It should be noted that these costs are not simply costs that a passive fund manager (ie. one who tracks an index) may be unwilling to incur, on the grounds that the tracking mandate will be met no matter how well or badly the particular companies composing the index fare. 'Active' fund managers (ie. managers who select companies for investment on the basis of detailed analysis of their likely future performance) may also be unwilling to do so, because engagement involves the additional, and potentially expensive, step beyond analysis of seeking to change the strategy or management (or both) of the portfolio company. The first bullet point above (the free-rider point) may be particularly discouraging even to an activist manager, whilst the fact that investors as a whole—and society in general—may benefit from improved corporate performance is probably at the heart of governmental encouragement of engagement. In the language often used in the investment field, it is not clear that the incentives of investors, even activist ones, and the public authorities are aligned.

Despite these obstacles to effective institutional engagement with portfolio companies, it would be wrong to leave the impression that shareholder engagement is something which the government is aiming to impose on wholly reluctant institutional investors. Engagement is a technique which institutional investors have made use of over the past half century as their weight in the largest British companies has increased. It is difficult, however, to measure the level of this engagement, because it typically occurs in private. The issue is only likely to emerge into the public arena if the management of the company is not responsive to a private approach made by the institutional shareholders and the institutional shareholders decide not to accept their rebuff by management but to seek to exercise their governance powers to secure a solution more acceptable to them. We have referred above[145] to the study by Crespi and Renneboog, which attempts to calibrate the significance of institutional shareholder intervention statistically,

---

[144] In response to governmental concerns the Takeover Panel took steps to give comfort to institutional investors that they would not be caught by the mandatory bid rule unless their intervention can be classified as 'board control seeking': Takeover Code, Rule 9.1, Note 2.

[145] Above n. 110.

and other more qualitative studies have concluded that institutional shareholder engagement has been a significant feature of the British corporate governance system for some time.[146] In the past, however, the level of such engagement was left to the institutions themselves to determine. Currently, the institutions face governmental pressure to be more active, but it is unclear whether the rationale for that pressure is the view that the institutions have misconceived their own best interests or whether greater institutional engagement is encouraged because it is seen as solving the government's problems (ie. government wishing to address public concerns about corporate governance without legislating in the area).

3.1.5. Remuneration

Remuneration deserves separate consideration because of its dual nature. On the one hand, a director dealing with the company over terms and conditions of employment is the clearest example of a self-dealing transaction; on the other hand, remuneration systems can be designed—at least in principle—so as to align the interests of the director with those of the shareholders (or some other stakeholder group), thus counteracting the conflict of interest. The legislation in the UK tends to focus on the self-dealing aspect of remuneration; the CGC also addresses the incentive issues.

The companies' legislation has long required two areas of directors' remuneration to be subject to shareholder approval (as noted in section 3.1.3 above): These are gratuitous payments to directors made in connection with their loss of office or under contracts for compensation entered into in the face of the loss of office.[147] These provisions thus address only one aspect of the 'rewards for failure' problem. Second, a company cannot enter into a service contract with a director which lasts for more than two years without shareholder approval.[148] This provision was introduced in 1980 because long-term service contracts were thought to undermine the effectiveness of the shareholders' removal power.

Where the variable remuneration consists of a share option scheme, the introduction of that scheme (but not individual grants under it) requires shareholder approval because it implies the issuance by the company of new shares.[149] This is not so much a provision aimed at controlling directors' remuneration as protecting shareholders against dilution. With the decline in share option schemes

---

[146] G. Stapledon, *Institutional Shareholders and Corporate Governance* (Oxford, OUP, 1996); B. Black and J. Coffee, 'Hail Britannia? Institutional Investor Behaviour under Limited Regulation', (1994) 92 *Michigan Law Review* 1997.

[147] Companies Act 2006, ss. 215–226.

[148] *Ibid.*, ss. 188 f. Originally, shareholder approval was required for contracts over five years.

[149] Companies Act 2006, s. 551.

and the growth of long-term incentive plans (LTIPs), the Listing Rules extended the shareholder approval rule to schemes for LTIPs.[150]

However, the major extension of shareholder approval requirements came in 2002, with the introduction of statutory say-on-pay provisions in favour of shareholders. The extension of legislation in this area indicates a failure of non-legislative rule-making. The legislation was a response by government to what it saw as the failure of the Combined Code (as the UK CGC was then called) to deal adequately with public disquiet about directors' and senior managers' remuneration, which was becoming an increasingly large multiple of the average pay of workers as a whole. Whilst the Code focused on the structure of remuneration packages, public disquiet was probably driven by the size of those packages. Although the government was not prepared to move to a position in which it regulated the size of executive remuneration packages, it did respond to public concern by involving shareholders more fully in the setting of remuneration. Whilst shareholders can be expected to be opposed to certain types of remuneration packages (for example, where variable pay is not subject to demanding performance conditions), it is not clear that shareholders have an interesting in applying a general downward pressure on executive remuneration.[151] So, the tension between the public and corporate views of the appropriate level and design of executive remuneration has not been fully resolved.

Under the 2002 reforms, as re-stated in the 2006 Act,[152] the board (or the remuneration committee) was required to draw up a Directors Remuneration Report (DRR) if the company was a quoted company. The DRR discloses to the AGM the details of directors' service contracts on an individual basis, the amounts paid to each director in the previous financial year and the board's policy on remuneration issues, including its choice of performance criteria. The DRR was subject to a mandatory but advisory vote of the shareholders, which encouraged companies to discuss proposed significant changes in remuneration arrangements with their major shareholders in advance of the AGM. However, listed companies still occasionally lose these resolutions or suffer significant votes against. There was a notable spate of such losses in the 'shareholder Spring' of 2012. In this way, the Act fosters institutional shareholder engagement with companies.

Despite this reform, the level of directors' pay continued to be salient for politicians. In 2011 the relevant government department floated a series of

---

[150] LR 13.8. An LTIP is based on grants of actual shares in the future, not of options to acquire shares.

[151] B. Cheffins and R. Thomas, 'Should Shareholders Have Greater Say over Executive Pay? Learning from US Experience', (2001) 1 *Journal of Corporate Law Studies* 277.

[152] Companies Act 2006 ss. 420–422 and 439–440. A 'quoted company' is one whose equity is officially listed in any EEA state or quoted on the NYSE or Nasdaq. The DRR provisions are thus not confined to companies with a premium listing.

potentially radical proposals in this area, such as greater controls over the structure of executive remuneration and the presence of employees on remuneration committees. In the end the government opted for more limited reforms, notably splitting the shareholder vote on the DRR in two. The vote on the company's remuneration policy (to be held at least at three-yearly intervals) becomes a binding vote, whilst the vote on its implementation within the policy (including the amounts paid to directors) remains non-binding, though the second vote is based on enhanced disclosure.[153]

As we have seen, the CGC recommends the establishment of a remuneration committee, dominated by the independent directors, something the Act does not require. It also contains recommendations about the design of remuneration packages. In particular, the Code recommends that 'a significant proportion of executive directors' remuneration should be structured so as to link rewards to corporate and individual performance.'[154] However, independent directors' remuneration should not contain performance-related elements for fear of jeopardizing their independence.[155] The performance criteria attached to the executives' pay should be flexible and designed to promote the long-term success of the company.[156]

The empirical data suggests that the Code recommendations on the involvement of independent directors in setting executive remuneration have had little success in making executive compensation more sensitive to firm performance.[157] The 'say-on-pay' reforms have been assessed somewhat more optimistically. The following conclusions seem to have been established.

- The statutory reforms had no impact on the overall level of remuneration but high levels of shareholder dissent do lead to changes in the structure of the remuneration.

---

[153] Department for Business Innovation and Skills, *Executive Remuneration: Discussion Paper*, September 2011 and *ibid.*, *Directors' Pay: Guide to Government Reforms*, June 2012. The reforms are contained in the Enterprise and Regulatory Reform Act 2013, likely to be implemented from October 2013. A director who receives a payment in breach of the policy is liable to restore to the company the excess received, unless the non-conforming payment is approved ad hoc by the shareholders, and the directors approving the payment are liable to make good to the company any loss suffered.

[154] Main Principle D.1. Schedule A gives some general guidance on the design of performance-related remuneration, but recommends claw-back of awards already made only in cases of 'misstatement or misconduct'.

[155] Provision D.1.3.

[156] Supporting Principle D.1.

[157] S. Girma, S. Thompson and P. Wright, 'Corporate Governance Reforms and Executive Compensation Determination: Evidence from the UK', (2007) 75 *The Manchester School* 65; S. Thompson, 'The Impact of Corporate Governance Reforms on the Remuneration of Executives in the UK', (2005) 13 *Corporate Governance* 19.

- There is greater sensitivity to poor corporate performance in setting the pay of CEOs where there are high levels of shareholder dissent over pay.
- The say-on-pay provisions have produced greater consultation of institutional shareholders over pay issues in advance of the AGM.[158]

Overall, public and government dissatisfaction with the overall lack of relation between corporate performance and executive remuneration and the growing gap between executive and senior management remuneration and levels of earnings elsewhere in the labour force continues to manifest itself.

3.2. Board and Stakeholders

3.2.1. Board and Employees

There is little to say here: There is no mandatory requirement for employee representatives on the board. An attempt to introduce such a system in the 1970s was stoutly resisted—and not just by the corporate world.[159] There is no well-grounded system of works councils which might functionally substitute for some aspects of board representation. Traditionally, the function of employee representation has been performed in the UK by trade unions through the mechanism of collective bargaining. Up until the 1980s there was a strong collective bargaining system in place which in some (probably not many) cases did reach into areas of corporate strategy. However, over the past thirty years the number of union members and the coverage (in terms of workers) and scope (in terms of subject matter) of collective bargaining have shrunk dramatically, so that it can no longer claim any significant impact on board decision-making, except in isolated cases where the company provides a perishable product, such as transportation.

3.2.2. Creditors

In contrast to employees creditors have always been a central concern of British corporate law: This is because of their exposure to opportunistic conduct by or on behalf of shareholders as a result of the doctrine of limited liability. However, the mechanisms for giving effect to creditor protection so long as the company is a going concern have not been located in the area of corporate governance and the

---

[158] F. Ferri and D. Maber, 'Say on Pay Votes and Executive Compensation: Evidence from the UK', (2013) 17 *Review of Finance* 527; M. Conyon and G. Sadler, 'Shareholder Voting and Directors' Remuneration Report Legislation: Say on Pay in the UK', (2010) 18 *Corporate Governance: An International Review* 296 (less positive); J. Gordon, '"Say on Pay": Cautionary Notes on the UK Experience and the Case for Shareholder Opt-in', (2009) 46 *Harvard Journal on Legislation* 323.

[159] See n. 34 above.

board. The two principal protective mechanisms for creditors upon which British law relies are (a) private contracting, for example through loan covenants, possibly including board seats for creditors, and (b) the doctrine of legal capital, in so far as it constrains distributions to shareholders.[160]

However, when a company approaches insolvency, corporate governance rules become relevant, in particular the duties of directors. Section 214 of the Insolvency Act 1986 imposes an objective duty of care on directors towards creditors once they realise or ought to have realised that the company has no reasonable prospect of avoiding insolvent liquidation. This is the 'wrongful trading' provision, introduced in the middle of the 1980s to supplement the long-standing fraudulent trading remedy.[161] This means that the directors must take all reasonable steps to avoid further loss to the creditors of the company. Breach of the duty is enforceable by the liquidator if the company does enter insolvent liquidation, and the director can then be made liable to contribute to the assets of the company for distribution to the creditors to the extent that the director's breach of duty reduced the assets available for distribution. In short, the directors' duty of care to the shareholders is supplemented by a duty of care owed to creditors when the company approaches insolvency and in practice the creditor-oriented duty of care often becomes the dominant one, because the shareholders are no longer exposed to the downside risk of corporate decisions.

It seems too that there is a parallel common law duty owed by directors to creditors as the company approaches insolvency. The nature and extent of this duty are still obscure, mainly because the ground the common law duty might occupy is already held by s. 214 and other provisions of the Insolvency Act, which protect creditors from opportunistic conduct by directors in the period before insolvency

3.2.3. Other Groups and Objectives

Beyond creditors, other groups do not appear as major players in the corporate governance area in general or in relation to boards in particular. These interests may be protected by regulation external to the company but not within the system of corporate governance. However, these groups and interests are not entirely missing. They appear in the core duty of loyalty of directors (see section 3.1.4) and the associated duty of the board to produce a business review.

The core duty of loyalty in s. 172 requires directors to have regard, when promoting the success of the company for the benefit of its members, to (i) the

---

[160] As is well known, the minimum capital doctrine is very weak in the UK, but capital maintenance as a constraint on distributions has always been there, albeit varying in intensity over time.

[161] Section 213 of the Insolvency Act 1986. Sections 213 and 214 provide the second main technique, along with disqualification (see sec. 4.2), used by UK to combat opportunism in small companies arising out of the absence of a minimum capital requirement.

interests of the company's employees, (ii) its business relations with customers and suppliers, (iii) the impact of the company's operations on the community and the environment, and (iv) the company's reputation. None of these groups has standing to enforce the duty and, even if they did, proving breach of the duty would be extremely difficult because the duty is cast on the director in very subjective terms. Further, as noted above, these non-shareholder interests have no independent value except in so far as they contribute to the success of the business for the benefit of the shareholders. Nevertheless, directors cannot discharge their core duty of loyalty without thinking about the impact of their decisions on these non-shareholder constituencies and the potential impact of the reaction of these constituencies on the operations of the company.

This approach to the core duty of loyalty was reinforced in the Companies Act 2006 by the new obligation upon the board to produce a business review (BR) as part of the annual report to the shareholders.[162] As from 2013 the BR is re-named the 'strategic report' (SR). In the case of a quoted company, the SR must include information about (i) environmental matters, (ii) the company's employees, and (iii) social, community and human rights matters.[163] The information must normally be presented using key performance indicators, ie. there must be some attempt to inject quantitative rigour into the analysis. Although the purpose of the disclosure obligation under the SR is 'to inform members of the company and help them assess how the directors have performed their duty under section 172 (duty to promote the success of the company)',[164] nevertheless it is a public document and may contain information of use to non-shareholder groups which they can use in their separate interactions with the company.

3.3. Changing Roles in Financial Distress

This has been dealt with under section 3.2.2. Except in relation to creditors, the role of the board does not change as the company nears insolvency.

If we put into tabular form the information given in sections 2 and 3, the result is as follows.

---

[162] Companies Act 2006, s. 417 (now repealed).
[163] Section 414C(4)—replacing the former s. 417.
[164] Section 414C(1).

Table 3: Sources of board rules in the UK

Structure, composition and role of the board	Corporate Governance Code (listed companies with premium listing) Company's articles (all companies)
Division of powers between board and management	Ditto
Division of powers between shareholders and the board	Ditto
Accountability of board to shareholders	Companies Act (setting out directors' duties, shareholders' right to remove directors, say-on-pay) and Takeover Code (containing BNR)
Accountability of board to creditors	Insolvency Act 1986 esp. s. 214; common law on directors' duties to creditors
Accountability to other stakeholder groups	Companies Act (Strategic Review reporting requirements for quoted companies) Non-companies legislation
Shareholder engagement duties	Stewardship Code

4. Enforcement

4.1. The Courts

4.1.1. *Personal Liability Claims*

The role of the courts is most important in relation to breaches of the duties of directors (now) laid down in the Companies Act 2006 and discussed in section 3.1.3 above. Directors are personally liable in principle to the company for breaches of these duties. Breaches of the CGC or Stewardship Code do not generate personal liability directly, though their provisions may be used by the courts indirectly to fill out the standards which the law of directors' duties create.[165]

The liabilities created by the law on directors' duties give rise primarily to civil remedies, though in some cases there is criminal liability as well. The burden of proving breach of duty will fall on the claimant and will be proof 'on the balance of probabilities' (not 'beyond reasonable doubt' as in criminal cases). The main civil remedies available to the company against the director are:

- Damages to compensate the company for the loss inflicted on the company as a result of the breach of duty.

---

[165] S. Goulding, L. Miles and A. Schall, 'Judicial Enforcement of Extra-legal Codes in UK and German Company Law', (2005) 2 *European Company and Financial Law Review* 20.

— A claim that the director account to the company for the profit made or other assets acquired as a result of the breach of duty (even if the company has suffered no loss). This head of recovery is especially important in corporate opportunity cases, where the director has made a substantial profit out of the opportunity but the company would have been unlikely to obtain the opportunity or exploit it profitably. In most cases the duty to account gives rise to a personal claim, but in some cases the claim is proprietary. In the latter situation the company's claim will prevail over the claims of the directors' other creditors (because the asset is not part of the insolvent director's estate) and the company will be able claim, at least in some instances, any increase in value of the asset after it came into the hands of the director.

— The transaction entered into is not binding on the company (subject to the protection of the rights of innocent third parties).

In addition to the director, third parties may be liable to the company in the first two ways described above where either the third party has assisted the director in the breach of duty or the third party receives corporate assets knowing that they came to him as a result of a breach of duty by the director.

Since the law of directors' duties is stated in terms of principles, the role of the courts is, and always has been, very important in developing those principles. The important cases are dealt with by the Chancery Division of the High Court, which handles a range of other matters but company law constitutes an important part of its workload. The Chancery court can thus be regarded as a semi-specialised court as far as company law is concerned. The Chancery division currently has 17 judges attached to it. Appeals lie to the generalist Court of Appeal and then to the Supreme Court, which consist of relatively small numbers of judges (about 40 in the Court of Appeal and about 12 in the Supreme Court). There will always be some former Chancery judges among the judges in the Court of Appeal and Supreme Court.

As we have already noted, actions that would otherwise be a breach of the duties of directors may be authorised (*ex ante*) or ratified (*ex post*) by the shareholders (by ordinary resolution).[166] Since directors' duties are owed to the company,[167] they can be waived by the company (ie. the shareholders). This does not apply, however, to duties owed to the company for the protection of the creditors, ie. in the vicinity of insolvency, where the shareholders and creditors' interests are likely to be in opposition to each other.

---

[166] In a limited and ill-defined category of cases waiver of the breach of duty may require unanimous shareholder agreement, ie. where the breach involves the transfer of a corporate asset to the controlling shareholders.

[167] Companies Act 2006, s. 170.

Authorisation and ratification refer to the approval of specific breaches of directors' duties, either proposed or committed. In principle, where general authorisation is given in the articles in relation to *categories* of proposed breaches of duty, these provisions ought also to be effective to relieve directors of liability, since the shareholders are consenting to the breaches through the articles. This was the common law position. However, since the 1920s legislation has controlled the extent to which authorisation of breaches of categories of duty can be given in the articles (or any other contract with the company). The starting point is that such authorisation is ineffective,[168] although the scope of this provision has been the subject of considerable controversy. In recent years reforms to the legislation have made it clear that a company may buy insurance for a director against liability for breach of duty to the company without infringing the prohibition.[169]

4.1.2. *Special Procedures and Enforcement*

Despite the well-developed substantive law on directors' duties, the extensive remedies which support the substantive law and the availability of a set of semi-specialised judges to enforce the rules, the level of formal enforcement activity by shareholders is low. Thus, if the overall impact of a legal rule is a function of the scope of the rule and likelihood of a sanction being imposed for breach of the rule, the UK rules on directors' duties are in fact much less effective than they seem at first sight. This is certainly true of enforcement of directors' duties in the case of publicly traded companies. Directors' duties are somewhat more strongly enforced in the case of private companies, but even here the level of enforcement is low.[170]

Why should this be? First, the normal civil procedure rules do not encourage litigation, since the costs rules put the litigant at risk of not only his or her own costs but also those of a successful opponent. Second, the specific company law rules relating to the enforcement of directors' duties are much less favourable to non-controlling shareholders than is the substantive law creating those duties. If the board itself or a controlling shareholder or a liquidator in the company's insolvency wishes to sue, there are no company law hurdles to litigation, but the non-controlling shareholder may face significant problems in establishing standing to sue. Given the dispersed nature of shareholdings in UK publicly traded companies, the incentives for non-controlling shareholders to sue directors who are in breach of duty are crucial to the overall level of enforcement of directors' duties in such companies, at least while the company is a going concern.

There are two methods by which non-controlling shareholders may enforce the law on directors' duties: one is through the derivative claim; the other is the

---

[168] Section 232.

[169] Section 233.

[170] See J. Armour, *Enforcement Strategies in UK Corporate Governance: A Road Map and Empirical Assessment*, ECGI Working Paper 106/2008, upon which I draw heavily.

unfair prejudice remedy. In a derivative claim a shareholder seeks to enforce the company's rights (ie. acts on behalf of the company) against the director. At common law two restrictive rules made derivative claims rarely available. First, if the breach could be ratified by the shareholders by ordinary resolution (as most breaches could), the derivative action was not available (even if the actual breach in question had not been ratified). Second, even if the breach were not ratifiable, the individual shareholder could not sue unless the directors responsible for the alleged wrongdoing were in control of the company, meaning in control of the general meeting.[171] The effect of both these rules was to push the decision on whether litigation against the director should proceed into the hands of the general meeting and away from the hands of individual shareholders. It was thus a rule well designed for companies with concentrated shareholding structures, but not for those with dispersed shareholding structures, where the general meeting might never get around to considering litigation. Institutional shareholders sought to challenge the common law rules on derivative actions in a famous case in the early 1980s, *Prudential Assurance Co Ltd v. Newman Industries (No 2)*.[172] They were successful at first instance but were roundly rebuffed in the Court of Appeal.

After an investigation by the Law Commission, however, the rules on derivative claims were changed in a more shareholder-friendly direction by Part 11 of the Companies Act 2006, effective from 1 October 2007. In essence, the exclusionary rules have been replaced by a judicial filter, the court being asked to determine whether it is in the interests of the company that the litigation should be brought. A derivative claim against directors for breach of duty may proceed only if the court decides to permit it and the court is required to take into account a wide range of factors in reaching that decision. It remains to be seen whether and how quickly judicial attitudes, formed by the common law and restrictive of the derivative action, will change under the new procedure.[173]

Unlike the derivative claim, which dates back to the early days of company law, the unfair prejudice petition was introduced into British company law only in 1980. Its aim was to improve the protection available to non-controlling shareholders against opportunistic conduct of controlling shareholders, regardless of whether that opportunism arose out of the controllers' exercise of their powers as shareholders or as directors. In contrast to the derivative action, its aim is to provide relief to minority shareholders personally in response to unfairness by the

---

[171] In the US, where derivative actions are more easily available, an important doctrinal reform was that the 'wrongdoer control' concept became applied to the board (which the defendant directors might often control, at least de facto) rather than the general meeting. This step was not taken in the UK.

[172] [1980] 2 All ER 841 (first instance); [1982] 1 All ER 354 (Court of Appeal).

[173] Some authors take a very pessimistic—arguably an overly pessimistic—view of the prospects of Part 11. See A. Reisberg, 'Shadows of the Past and Back to the Future: Part 11 of the UK Companies Act (in)action', (2009) 6 *ECFR* 219.

controllers.[174] It was quickly established that unfair prejudice petitions could be based on breaches of directors' duties committed by company controllers.[175] The typical remedy is an order that the controllers purchase the petitioner's shares at a fair price (ie. one which takes account of the harm done to the company by the unfairly prejudicial conduct).[176] Thus, in a successful unfair prejudice claim the minority shareholder is compensated directly by the controllers for the harm done by them to the company in their capacity as directors, whereas in a successful derivative-based claim the recovery is by the company, from which the minority shareholder benefits only indirectly via an increase in the value of the shares. However, the remedy is regarded by the courts as available only in the case of boards controlled by majority shareholders, ie. where the shareholdings are concentrated, not dispersed. Consequently, the unfair prejudice route to the enforcement of directors' duties has not raised the level of litigation over directors' duties in the case of listed companies.

Armour reports the average number of reported judgments per year in directors' duties claims, in both the derivative and unfair prejudice form, in relation to publicly and non-publicly traded companies over the period 1990 to 2006 to be as follows:

Table 4: Reported judgments where breach of duty alleged[177]

All Companies		Publicly Traded Companies	
Derivative	Unfair prejudice	Derivative	Unfair Prejudice
1.5	1.5	0.0	0.2

This table suggests that the incidence of claims is low for all companies, and very low in the case of publicly traded companies. In the case of listed companies Armour reports further than none of the three unfair prejudice claims brought in the period was successful. The data in Table 4 refers only to reported judgments. It is conceivable that many more claims are made and are settled short of judgment, but the available data does not support this contention. Thus, in another

---

[174] Whether and in what circumstances corporate relief can be obtained through the unfair prejudice petition is currently a highly debated topic and one which is not further elaborated here. See *Gower and Davies Principles of Modern Company Law*, 9th edition, 2012, 20–26 to 20–32.

[175] The concept of 'unfairness' extends well beyond breaches of duty (see *Gower and Davies*, previous note, 20–10 ff.) but unfairness claims where no breach of directors' duties is alleged fall outside the scope of this chapter.

[176] The court is not bound to order the minority to be bought out. Sometimes, the minority buys out the majority or some other order is made. But the minority buy-out is the standard remedy.

[177] Derived from Armour, above n. 170, p. 14.

study, Armour et al found in relation to public companies (ie. excluding private companies in the Companies Act sense of the term) that in the period 2004 to 2006 four claims per year were brought of which only one per year concerned a director of a publicly traded company.[178]

Turning to actions not brought by minority shareholders, there are some reported cases where litigation is brought by a board on behalf of the company or by a controlling shareholder against directors for breach of duty. Although precise numbers are not available, it is clear that such cases are very few in number. Enforcement of directors' duties by liquidators of insolvent companies is a little more common. Liquidators may allege either breaches of the directors' general duties or fraudulent or wrongful trading in the period prior to insolvency (see section 3.2.2). Special provision for both types of claim is made in ss. 212–214 of the Insolvency Act 1986. In 2006 judgments were rendered in 11 cases brought by liquidators against directors (of all types of company), a year in which there were only three judgments in cases brought by shareholders. This suggests that claims brought by liquidators are more important in enforcing directors' duties than claims brought by shareholders (but even the number of judgments rendered in cases brought by liquidators was not high). However, in the whole period 1990–2006 only one judgment was given in a case brought by a liquidator and involving a publicly traded company, a fact probably explained by the rarity of the insolvency of a publicly traded company.

The overall conclusion is that the law of directors' duties is not extensively enforced in the UK by private enforcement action and such action as exists focuses predominantly on non-publicly traded companies.

4.2. Regulators

a) Insolvency Service

In this section I deal with formal enforcement by the public authorities, in contrast with enforcement by shareholders. I do not thus confine myself to regulators *stricto sensu*.

The public authorities have long had powers to disqualify directors of failed companies from acting in the future as either de jure or de facto directors of companies (or in various other corporate roles). This is one of the main techniques used by British law to combat the opportunism which is encouraged by the absence of minimum capital requirements for private companies. In the insolvency reforms of the 1980s, these powers were substantially revised and ex-

---

[178] J. Armour, B. Black, B. Cheffins and R. Nolan, 'Private Enforcement of Corporate Law: An Empirical Comparison of the UK and the US', (2009) 6 *Journal of Empirical Legal Studies* 687.

tended. In particular, section 6 of the Company Directors Disqualification Act 1986 empowers the public authorities to seek disqualification of directors of insolvent companies[179] where the insolvency practitioner's investigations into the affairs of the insolvent company suggest that the director is 'unfit' to be a director of a company. Initially, disqualification could be imposed only by a court (on the application of the public authorities) but it is now possible for the director to offer, and the public authorities to accept, a disqualification 'undertaking' which has a similar effect to a court order but does not involve a court hearing.

The Insolvency Service (an 'executive agency' of the relevant governmental department) has been reasonably active in securing disqualification orders or undertakings. In 2011/12 the Service secured 1151 disqualifications (on all grounds, not just unfitness, though this is the most common), of which 80% were on the basis of undertakings. This was a decrease from 1437 in the previous year (likely a result of restrictions on governmental expenditure—always a risk with public enforcement).[180] The average disqualification period was 5.9 years. The test for disqualification under s. 6 is unfitness, which is not identical with breach of duty as a director. However, the courts have interpreted unfitness widely enough to embrace incompetence, at least of the grosser kind, and major breaches of fiduciary duties. In fact, the grounds upon which unfitness disqualifications were obtained suggest, as is to be expected, that the principal sufferers of the disqualified directors' conduct were the company's creditors (often the state itself in its capacity as collector of taxes or social security contributions) rather than its shareholders, so that disqualification is principally a way of enforcing directors' creditor-oriented duties.

However, although the disqualification procedure is an important way of enforcing directors' duties in the case of non-publicly traded companies which fail, it has only occasional impact on publicly traded companies, because these infrequently become insolvent. Nevertheless, when this does occur, disqualification of the directors thought to be responsible for the collapse can operate as a way of 'naming and shaming' directors for broader corporate governance failures, as well as limiting their future participation in corporate activities.[181] The disqualification

---

[179] A company is 'insolvent' not only if it goes into insolvent liquidation but also where the company enters into administration, so that the disqualification provisions have a wider scope than the wrongful trading provisions which apply only in insolvent liquidations.

[180] Insolvency Service, *Annual Report and Accounts 2011-2012*, p. 30. Some 200 further disqualification orders are made annually by courts on their own initiative in criminal proceedings, often involving fraud, against directors. See Companies House, *Statistical Tables on Companies Registration Activities 2011/12*, Table D 1.

[181] One of the most important reported cases on unfitness (in fact, directors' failure to put in place proper internal control systems) concerned the failure of Barings Bank (a large listed company) in 1995 (see *Re Barings plc (No 5)* [2000] 1 BCLC 523, CA). More recently, the directors of MG Rover Group Ltd, a large but not publicly traded company, gave disquali-
cont. ...

laws thus have the greater impact on non-publicly traded companies. Even in relation to non-publicly traded companies, the disqualification provisions cannot be invoked in relation to companies which remain solvent, though the fear of disqualification may have some *ex ante* impact on the directors of such companies.

The Insolvency Service has a range of other enforcement powers. It may carry out a (public) inspection of a company, though this power has fallen virtually into desuetude, with inspectors being appointed only once in the last decade.[182] Private investigations happen more often, but typically on the basis of a request made to the Service rather than of its own motion. In 2011/12 it received nearly 3523 within-scope requests but commenced only 165 investigations.[183] When agreeing to a request for an investigation, the Service looks for some public (as opposed to private) interest in having the company's affairs investigated. Generally, this means that the Service thinks there are credible allegations of fraud or strongly opportunistic conduct on the part of the controllers of the company. Given the total number of companies registered in the UK (over 2.5m – see section 1.1), fewer than 200 investigations annually is not a high rate of investigation. Further, the investigation power is unlikely to be used at all if the controllers have inflicted harm only on the shareholders of the company.

The investigation is essentially a fact-finding exercise, though it may help those affected to proceed with litigation on their own account. The Service may respond to the findings of the investigators by seeking the disqualification of the directors involved,[184] bring an unfair prejudice petition on behalf of the share-holders (rarely done)[185] or seek to have the company wound up by the court in the public interest.[186] In 2011/12, 355 companies were wound up as a result of

fication undertakings on the basis they had manipulated the assets and income streams of the company for their own benefit and to the detriment of the company's creditors. See Insolvency Service, *Press Notice*, 9 May 2011. In January 2011 the Insolvency Service commenced disqualification proceedings in respect of directors European Home Retail, a publicly traded company whose collapse in October 2006 left many consumers who had been saving through the company for Christmas out of pocket just before the festive season. The disqualification proceedings collapsed amid strong criticism from the judge about how the Service had handled the proceedings. The Service later published a somewhat defensive report on this failure: Insolvency Service, *Review of Disqualification Proceedings Taken in the case of European Home Retail plc and Farepak Food and Gifts Ltd*, December 2012.

[182] Though in a highly politically charged case: the final collapse of MG Rover Ltd. See previous note.

[183] The Insolvency Service, above n. 180, p. 32. The Report in the previous year noted the impact of governmental expenditure cuts on its ability to carry out a larger number of investigations.

[184] This is under s. 8 (not 6) of the Company Directors Disqualification Act 1986.

[185] Companies Act 2006, s. 995.

[186] Insolvency Act 1986, s. 124A.

Insolvency Service investigations[187]—an unusually large number because two investigations led to multiple winding up orders—and six disqualifications order were obtained.[188]

Overall, one can conclude that the formal enforcement activity of the Insolvency Service is larger than the formal enforcement activity by shareholders, but its focus is on non-publicly traded companies and on the protection of creditors and the public interest rather than the routine enforcement of the duties of directors.

b) FCA and Other Regulators

Beyond the Insolvency Service (which is part of the Department for Business, Innovation and Skills) the important regulatory bodies for the purposes of this paper are the Financial Conduct Authority, the Takeover Panel and the Financial Reporting Council. Two things can be said about the exercise by these bodies of their enforcement powers. First, they have traditionally relied on informal enforcement (via private or public warnings or censure) rather than the impositions of formal sanctions by way of monetary penalties or disqualification.[189] Second, in the light of the financial crisis, this approach has changed in a number of areas (for example, the FCA now pursues a much more vigorous policy of formal enforcement of the market abuse provisions) but this new approach seems to have spread less strongly into the areas which concern the enforcement of board rules.

In some cases the predilection of the regulatory bodies for informal enforcement is understandable historically. Thus, for most of the period since it was established in the late 1960s the Takeover Panel had no formal legal status and thus no formal enforcement powers. When this situation changed with the transposition of the Takeover Directive in the United Kingdom, the Panel was placed on a statutory basis and obtained formal enforcement powers. Nevertheless, it is perhaps not surprising that it prefers to operate—at least for the time being—with the informal enforcement powers which it developed during its non-statutory existence. Why do (or did) boards of target companies in the UK observe the board neutrality rule (BNR) even though the directors of the target could not be sanctioned formally by the Panel for breaching the rule? Part of the answer is given in section 4.3 below, but another part is that the FCA rules require financial advisors (mainly investment banks) not to act for (ie. to 'cold shoulder') com-

---

[187] Insolvency Service, above n. 180, p. 32.

[188] Companies House, above n. 180, Table D 1.

[189] As has been pointed out, the reputational cost to a company of informal public censure may well exceed the cost to it of any fine imposed: J. Armour, C. Mayer and A. Polo, *Regulatory Sanctions and Reputational Damage in Financial Markets*, ECGI Finance Working Paper 300/2010.

panies which act in breach of the Takeover Rules.[190] A target board seeking to defend itself against an unwelcome bid by breaking the BNR was thus likely to lose its advisors if it acted in this way. No direct formal enforcement of the rules against the target board was thus required—though such enforcement is now provided for in the Companies Act[191]—because the threat of indirect enforcement via advisors acted as a substitute.

For the purpose of board rules, the FCA is probably the most important of these regulators because, as we have seen, the Listing Rules contain a number of central corporate governance rules and the comply-or-explain obligation underlying the Corporate Governance and Stewardship Codes is also to be found there. The FSA (the predecessor of the FCA) traditionally devoted a relatively low level of resources to enforcement.[192] Unlike the Takeover Panel, an historical explanation of this preference is not available, since the FSA was always a statutory body with potentially wide-ranging enforcement powers.[193] Its traditional preference for informal enforcement is probably to be explained by broader considerations about regulatory style in the UK.

Although the FCA has a wide range of enforcement responsibilities, our main concern is with its enforcement of the listing rules, which contain the comply-or-explain obligation in relation to the CGC and, as indicated above, various other board-related rules for companies with a premium listing. In the 2002–2007 period, Armour reports[194] that the FSA (as the FCA then was) undertook an average of only six investigations in relation to breaches of the listing rules, which led to an average of two enforcement actions each year. Although the resources devoted to enforcement have increased after the financial crisis, this increase in effort has not focussed particularly on the Listing Rule. In 2009/10 the FSA initiated three new investigations in relation to the Listing Rules, two in 2010/11 and four in 2011/12.[195]

A somewhat older study focused particularly on the enforcement of the comply-or-explain obligation in relation to the CGC. A study covering the period 1998 to 2004 showed that over this period as a whole companies chose on

---

[190] FSA, Code of Market Conduct, 4.3.

[191] Sections 952 ff.

[192] J.C. Coffee, Jr, 'Law and the Market: The Impact of Enforcement', (2007) 156 *University of Pennsylvania Law Review* 229.

[193] Though human rights considerations led to these powers being more hedged around than the government would have wished when the Financial Services and Markets Act 2000 was enacted. See G. Walker, 'Penalties for Market Abuse' in M Blair QC et al, *The Financial Services and Markets Act 2000* (London, Blackstone, 2001) ch. 8.

[194] Above n. 170, Table 5.

[195] FSA, *Annual Report 2009/10*, App 5, *Annual Report 2010/11*, App 2, *Annual Report 2011/12*, App 2. And it is by no means certain that any of these enforcement actions concerned board rules rather than, for example, breach of the Listing Rules relating to public offerings.

average not to follow 1.57 of the eight Code recommendations studied but provided, in the authors' assessment, adequate explanations for their conduct only in relation to 1.38 of the recommendations not followed, thus leaving a group of unexplained departures and, arguably, breaches of the Listing Rules.[196] As far as the authors could establish, the FSA never took formal action to enforce the comply-or-explain obligation. Despite this finding, the FRC stated as follows in its 2009 review of the CGC:

'There was little enthusiasm among commentators for the FRC or FSA to take on a more formal role in monitoring and enforcing reporting against the Code. There were concerns among both companies and investors that this might have the effect of reducing the flexibility of "comply-or-explain", and that regulatory activity might get in the way of, or be seen as an alternative to, engagement between boards and shareholders. The FRC understands these concerns and does not intend to extend its formal activities. However, it will continue informally to monitor standards of disclosure.'[197]

However, this somewhat complacent attitude altered when the European Commission raised the issue of inadequate explanations in its Green Paper, *The EU Corporate Governance Framework*.[198] In consequence, the FRC, as the body responsible for the Codes, generated a public debate on the implementation of the comply-or-explain principle.[199] Although the FRC is by no means in the clear on the quality of the explanations, the potential Achilles' heel of comply-or-explain, its lobbying seems to have been successful to the extent that the Commission's 2012 Action Plan inclined towards a Commission Recommendation concerning explanations for non-compliance rather than any more interventionist response.[200]

Of course, the number of formal enforcement actions taken by the FSA in relation to breaches of the Listing Rules does not tell the whole story. The FSA/ FCA may take informal enforcement action which will not show up in the statistics for enforcement. Presumably, however, such informal enforcement action occurs only as a result of an investigation begun by the regulator, ie. the number of investigations sets an outer bound to the level of informal enforcement

[196] S. Arcot and V. Bruno, 'In Letter but not in Spirit: An Analysis of Corporate Governance in the UK', (May 2006), Table 7. Available on SSRN at: <http://ssrn.com/abstract=819784>.

[197] FRC, *2009 Review of the Combined Code: Final Report*, December 2009, 2.11.

[198] COM(2011) 164 final, especially section 3.

[199] See, in particular, FRC, *What Constitutes an Explanation under Comply-or-Explain?* February 2012 and the 2012 version of the CGC, p. 4, expanded para 3 on comply-or-explain. See also FRC, *Developments in Corporate Governance 2011*, pp. 15–16, *ibid., Comply or Explain: 20th Anniversary of the UK Corporate Governance Code*, 2012. Quite apart from EU pressure, better explanations fit well into the FRC's post-financial crisis concern with stewardship and better reporting by boards to shareholders. See above, n. 142.

[200] European Commission, *Action Plan: European company law and corporate governance* COM 2012 740/2, esp. 2.2.

action by that body. If this is so, then the figure reported by Armour of an average of six investigations per year into breaches of the Listing Rules suggests that informal enforcement does not make up for the apparent low level of formal enforcement action by the FSA/FCA.

4.3. Self-Regulation

The picture which emerges so far is one of rare private enforcement of the board rules, together with low levels of formal (and informal) enforcement by the public authorities (with the possible exception of action by the Insolvency Service against the 'unfit' directors of failed companies, predominantly in the non-publicly traded sphere). Does this mean that the shareholder-centric system of UK board rules is a sham because it is not enforced? It is suggested that this is not the case. Precisely because of the pro-shareholder orientation of the basic rules of the system, *informal* private enforcement is facilitated. Because the structure of the governance system, coupled with the structure of shareholdings in large British companies, facilitates the communication of shareholder views directly to the board on matters which the institutional shareholders regard as important, low levels of public and private formal enforcement of board rules are much less important than they might be. It might be said that the exercise of governance powers by the institutional shareholders (coupled with their traditionally dominant market position) is a substitute for high levels of enforcement of the formal board rules, at least in the case of publicly traded companies.

The sources of the strong governance powers of the institutional shareholders have already been set out above. Here they are summarised in tabular form.

Table 5: Principal Sources of Governance Powers of Shareholders

Governance Power	Source
Right to remove directors by ordinary resolution and to call shareholder meetings	Companies Act 2006
Annual Re-election of Directors	Corporate Governance Code
Board Neutrality Rule	Takeover Code
One Share One Vote	Market Power of Institutional Shareholders
Major Transaction Approval	Listing Rules

Three points can be made about these rules. First, only the removal power stems from the Companies Act. The other contributors to the powers of the shareholders are found outside the companies' legislation in sources of rules which the institutional shareholders have been well-placed to influence. Second, all five categories of (institutional shareholder) power are located in different sources, which shows the self-reinforcing nature of these sources and the widespread nature of institutional shareholder influence. Third, and most important for the topic of self-regulation, these governance rights are self-enforcing, ie. they do not need extensive resort to the courts or other enforcement bodies to be effective. For example, whilst the shareholders' right to remove directors under the Companies Act has generated some litigation,[201] it is predominantly a right the shareholders can enforce without resort to the courts. Five per cent of the shareholders have the right to requisition a meeting to put a removal resolution; if the directors do not respond to the requisition, the shareholders can convene the meeting themselves and the shareholders' costs of convening it fall on the errant directors.[202] If the resolution is passed, the law will no longer treat the removed persons as directors of the company.

5. The Dynamics of Change

The picture presented above is one in which board rules in the UK are shareholder friendly and are enforced by shareholders through use of their governance rights rather than through extensive resort to litigation or enforcement by the public authorities. The most important of the shareholders' legal rights appears to be their right to remove directors at any time by simple majority vote (and the associated right to convene shareholder meetings at a 5% threshold), coupled with their veto over defensive measures against hostile takeovers. These core legal rights are then supplemented by CGC recommendations which are designed to enhance board effectiveness (in controlling management) and accountability (to shareholders) through the central roles assigned to independent directors (and the committees which they dominate) and the role of the chairman in ensuring the board operates according to this prescription. Clearly, it is crucial to the effective functioning of such a system that the shareholders should be in a position to enforce their governance rights and to apply pressure on companies (either through the exercise of those rights or by exiting the company) if the explanations for non-compliance with CGC recommendations seem to them unsatisfactory. If, because of collective action problems, those shareholder-friendly rights were unenforceable, or if exit from the shareholder register had little impact on the market price of the shares because the actions of the largest shareholders were not correlated, the governance system would be expected to operate very differently. The British system would probably take on a managerialist manner of operation, ie. the formal structures, whatever their ostensible goals, would be dominated in

---

[201] *Bushell v. Faith* [1970] A C 1099, HL; *Monnington v Easier plc* [2006] 1 BCLC 283.

[202] Companies Act 2006 ss. 303–306. Of course, even this set of rules will not be effective if companies are free to ignore them, so that even self-enforcing rules suppose some minimum level of the rule of law. However, self-enforcing rules do not require courts to make complicated assessments of the merits of managerial action but only a willingness to enforce procedural rules.

fact by executive management. The board would be unchallenged and in un-challengeable control of the company, subject possibly to external state regulation and strong trade unions. There is good evidence that this is how the British system operated in the 1950s.[203]

The change in later decades towards a system working in the shareholder-friendly way indicated by the substantive rules was the result of the rise of the long-only institutional shareholders (especially pension funds and insurance company). As an increasing proportion of the total equity market came to be held by the institutions (see Table 1, above), the institutions came to have an increasing influence on the setting of the corporate governance rules in the UK[204] and, just as important, they acquired some ability to exercise the rights conferred upon them at portfolio company level. Although never able to enforce governance rights as easily as a single majority shareholder, the institutions were at times able to form coalitions with each other to take advantage of their governance potential.[205]

Finally, from the beginning of this century onwards, the institutions discovered that, having helped to create a strong pro-shareholder structure in which there was little 'public interest' regulation, they were subject to pressure from government to engage with portfolio companies so as to redress deficiencies as perceived by the government in the operation of companies. At the current time, 'shareholder engagement' is probably the most significant element of the public authorities' policy towards the governance of large non-financial corporations, as exemplified above all in the new Stewardship Code of the FRC (see section 3.1.4 above). The Kay Review of UK equity markets, which reported in 2012, enshrined 'stewardship' as the central pillar in governmental policy towards the relationship between companies and those who invest in them.[206] Stewardship is presented as the way of reconciling private ownership of the productive economy with the societal interest in long-term economic growth, together with the jobs and tax revenues such growth is expected to provide.

How stable is this pattern of governance of large UK public companies? The history of its change over the past 60 years or so would suggest that the drivers of future change will be (a) the investment strategies of the traditional long-only shareholders, (b) changes in the character of the substantial shareholders in large companies in the UK, and (c) the willingness of government (at both national and Community levels) to rely on a shareholder-centred corporate governance system for large UK companies.

---

[203] Davies, above n. 4; C.A.R. Crossland, *The Future of Socialism* (London, 1956) ch. XV.

[204] See sec. 1.1 above.

[205] See n. 146 above.

[206] *The Kay Review of UK Equity Markets and Long-Term Decision Making: Final Report,* July 2012, URN 12/917. See also BIS, *Ensuring Equity Markets Support Long-term Growth: the Government Response to the Kay Review,* November 2012, URN 12/1188.

a) *Intervention Incentives of Traditional Long-Only Shareholders*

The current desire of long-only institutional shareholders to have strong
governance rights over their portfolio companies and their willingness to exercise
those rights might be thought to depend, at least as a first cut, upon a cost/benefit
analysis of intervention. The costs of intervention are clear: They are principally
the immediate resource costs of intervention, which may be substantial. The
benefits are the proportion of the gains to the company resulting from changed
management or policies which the intervening institutions capture through their
shareholdings. [207] Intervention will be indicated not only where the benefits
exceed the costs but also when the benefit/cost ratio of intervention appears more
attractive than that of the alternative course of action, ie. selling the holding in the
market. Even if the benefits of intervention exceed the costs, if the ratio between
the two is more favourable in the case of a sale of the holding, the indicated
course of action would be sale of the holding. Where the holding can be disposed
of at current market prices, the costs of exit are low, but equally the benefits of
intervention are foregone. Where the institution's holding is large, it may not be
able to dispose of its holding without driving down the market price and so the
costs of exit increase, whilst the benefits of intervention increase as a function of
the size of the institution's shareholding. Assessing the immediate costs and
likely benefits of the two main courses of action open to any institutional shareholder may not be an easy task for them, especially in relation to intervention, the
costs and benefits of which may be difficult to predict, since they depend in part
on the (partially unknown) reactions of incumbent management and other shareholders to the intervention. The traditional institutions, in consequence, have been
concerned to keep both courses of action open to them.[208]

However, the cost/benefit analysis is more complex than the above account
suggests, because of the 'free-rider' and conflicts of interest issues. Because of
competition among asset managers, a manager will always prefer the intervention
to be the result of other institutions' actions. In that case the non-intervening
institution will capture (some of) the benefits of intervention without incurring
(any of) the costs. If all the institutions take this view, none will join the coalition
of institutional investors which is normally necessary to produce change. This
argument applies most strongly to 'expensive' forms of intervention: for example,

---

[207] There is a further collective benefit to the institutions from intervention. This is the maintenance of the shareholder-friendly system of corporate governance. Without intervention by
shareholders to replace failing management, government might less willing to maintain that system. However, it is difficult to know how much weight this carries when an institution is assessing the costs and benefits of intervention in a particular case.

[208] Thus, the SC, Principle 1, requires those who sign up to it to have a policy on intervention, but it does not dictate the content of that policy. There is no doubt, however, that the
existence of the SC puts pressure on institutions to shift the balance of their activity to some
degree in favour of engagement.

shareholder coalitions to vote against management remuneration proposals may not suffer from the free-rider problem, but a plan to remove existing management in order to implement a new strategy which the incumbent management resists is likely to require a high level of resources from the intervening shareholders, including investment manager time. The Kay Review proposes a non-governmental 'investor forum' in order to address institutional investors collective action problems, but it is far from clear how effective such a body could be.[209]

However, even if the free-rider problem can be overcome, institutional shareholders may face significant conflicts of interest when contemplating intervention at the portfolio company level. If the fund manager is part of a financial conglomerate which supplies other services—for example, corporate finance services—to portfolio companies, the manager may be disincentivised to take any action towards the portfolio company which its management perceives as hostile. The Kay Review proposals to address this issue seem either imprecise or weak.[210] The main justification for government pressure on the institutions towards greater intervention in the interests of the institutions' beneficiaries[211] is that it may help to counteract sub-optimal levels of institutional intervention caused by free-rider issues and conflicts of interest.

So far, it has been assumed that the goal of institutional intervention (and of institutional shareholding in general) is to maximise the long-run value of their portfolios. However, there is some evidence that the time horizon of long-only shareholders is shortening, which suggests that their investment strategies are becoming less long-term. This may be the result of the development of high-frequency trading strategies by hedge funds but it seems to be in substantial part due to shorter investment periods by institutional shareholders themselves.

This is a puzzle. It is difficult to think of an investor with a longer time horizon than a pension fund and so it is unclear why they should be interested in maximising the value of their holdings in the short-term. A possible explanation relates to the way that institutional investors make their investment decisions, ie. often by outsourcing the fund management to a third party. That third party asset manager is then monitored, usually on a quarterly basis, thus generating an incentive for the asset manager to perform on a short-term basis. However, this explanation simply pushes the question one stage back: Why do institutional shareholders assess their managers on a short-term basis if their interest is in long-term performance? One answer might be that the 'prudence' obligations

---

[209] Kay Review, above n. 206, paras 7.1 ff.

[210] A non-binding 'Statement of Good Practice for Asset Managers' is proposed which would require them to avoid conflicts of interest 'wherever possible' (*ibid.* 53), whilst a so far imprecise duty of care/fiduciary duty would be imposed on all those in the investment chain (*ibid.*, ch. 9). It is not clear that either proposal adds much that is significant to existing regulation.

[211] Which the SC says is the basis of its encouragement of intervention: see Guidance to Principle 2.

imposed on institutional investors mean that they are safe from criticism if the returns of any one institution mimic the market but are exposed to criticism, and possibly litigation, if they follow a strategy which entails departure from the market view of the value of investments for any significant period of time.[212] This suggests that the adoption of a long-term investment focus by institutions and their fund managers would require some relaxation of the regulation to which they are subject.

An alternative explanation suggests a short-term bias in securities markets as a whole, not in institutional investors' investment decisions specifically. In other words, it has been suggested that the market fails to value long-term investments by companies accurately, thus inducing an emphasis within companies on short-term pay-offs. The causes of such inefficiencies in market valuations of companies have not been clearly identified. Nevertheless, if this criticism can be sustained, it raises a very fundamental question about the value of institutional shareholder intervention. Not having the inside knowledge which a controlling shareholder has, institutional shareholders are dependent on the market price as a signal about when it is appropriate to intervene and about the gains from intervention. If the market price is misleading, then the underlying rationale for institutional shareholder intervention becomes suspect.[213] On this hypothesis, a low share price no longer signals necessarily that it is appropriate for shareholders to be concerned about management's strategy whilst a high share price no longer necessarily indicates that inaction is appropriate. However, in the absence of reliable signals from the share price, it is unclear how outside shareholders are to formulate a policy on intervention, short of designing a commercial strategy for each of their portfolio companies. Yet, the SC assigns the 'primary responsibility' for managing the company to the board, not the shareholders.[214]

Overall, the strength of the commitment of long-only shareholders to high levels of engagement with portfolio companies is open to question, as is the extent to which it can be bolstered by governmental pressure in favour of engagement.

---

[212] See *European Company Law Experts' Response to the European Commission's Green Paper, 'The EU Corporate Governance Framework'* (22 July 2011). Available on SSRN at: <http://ssrn.com/abstract=1912548>. There is some support for this analysis in the Kay Review (above n. 206, paras 5.22 ff.), where regulation is said to lead to 'closet indexation'.

[213] See A. Haldane and R. Davies, *The Short Long* (speech to 29th Société Universitaire Européenne de Recherches Financières Colloquium, *New Paradigms in Money and Finance*, Brussels, May 2011). For a traditional defence of shareholders against short-termism see P Marsh, *Short-termism on Trial*, Institutional Fund Managers' Association, 1990.

[214] SC, p. 1, para 2.

b) Changes in the Character of Dominant Shareholders

Decline of UK long-only institutions—The primary data about the dominant shareholders in large British companies is that provided by the Office of National Statistics (see Table 1 above). However, that data is not constructed in the most helpful way for present purposes. The first six categories (Individuals, Insurance Companies, Pension Funds, Other Financial Institutions, Unit and Investment Trusts and Banks) describe different types of investor which are, though this is less clear, resident in the UK or owned by UK interests. The final category—Rest of the World (RoW)—refers to non-UK residence or ownership of investors and tells one nothing about their category. So long as the 'Rest of the World' category was a residual one, this did not matter very much, but with the globalisation of investment management, the utility of the data is reduced by this approach.[215]

At first sight, the latest ONS data presents a picture which is negative for the stewardship project because the holdings of UK insurance companies and pension funds (traditionally the largest of the long-only investors) have declined to the level last seen before the 20th century growth of engagement by the institutions. This pessimism can be somewhat overdone, however, because a UK asset manager which falls under foreign ownership will move to the RoW category even if it continues to be based in and managed from London and to act for UK clients.[216] Nevertheless, even if it is true, as the Kay Review asserts,[217] that 'the dominant players in UK equity markets are London-based asset managers', it is not clear that foreign-owned asset managers are subject to the same incentives to follow the preferences of the UK government as domestically owned ones, whilst more rules designed to produce such behaviour might simply lead them to re-locate to other centres for investment management and/or to reduce their allocations to the UK equity market.[218]

Hedge funds and tracking funds—Recent data suggests there is a wide variety of different types of fund operating within the UK market, not just pension funds and insurance companies. Thus, it may be an error to distinguish simply between the traditional long-only funds and short-term traders. There might be a variety of

---

[215] Further research into the composition of shareholdings is under way in a joint project between the Cass Business School (City University, London) and Junction RDS, an independent shareholder analysis house, but it has not yet produced significantly more granular data which is publicly available. See Kay Review (above n. 206), Figure 7.

[216] Kay Review (above n. 206) para 3.16.

[217] *Ibid.*, para 3.17.

[218] This point has recently been made by the government itself in relation to shareholder engagement on the issue of executive remuneration: 'However, this is increasingly challenging as a growing proportion of the diverse UK shareholder base comprises overseas or short-term investors.' (Department for Business Innovation and Skills, *Executive Remuneration: Discussion Paper*, September 2011, para 58.)

investment strategies being pursued. Although the SC fully allows for this, by requiring funds to only disclose their policy on engagement rather than requiring them to have a policy of a particular type, it may be that the policy of maximising the long-term value of portfolio companies will not be the dominant investment strategy of the funds operating in the UK market.[219]

Hedge funds, both 'event-driven' and 'activist', are among the new types of fund operating in the UK. Activist hedge funds acquire shares in a target company in order to promote a particular change of direction and to sell out shortly after that change of direction is adopted and has been reflected in the share price. Event-driven hedge funds typically seek to ride on a change of direction which has been proposed but which they have not generated—for example, a hostile takeover bid—but which they anticipate will increase the value of the company if it is adopted. They join the share register in a bet that the change of direction will occur and also in order to do what they can to encourage it to take place. Research shows that they hold only a very small percentage of the overall market (0.5%) but that they may be significant in particular situations.[220] Activist hedge funds will certainly engage with the company, but may have short-term goals which diverge from the government's model of shareholder engagement based on the promotion of long-term value.[221] It is true that both types of hedge fund can be effective only if, in the case of activist shareholders, their proposals for change are supported by the long-only shareholders or, in the case of event-driven hedge funds, only if some long-only shareholders are prepared to sell out to them.[222] The point may be that both types of hedge fund provide lost-cost strategies to long-only shareholders by which long-only investors can reap short-term profits on at least parts of their shareholdings. This is an opportunity which fund managers and asset owners find difficult to resist so long as their own performance is judged on a relatively short-term basis by reference to an explicit or implicit benchmark. Overall, the notion of intervention by institutional shareholders may acquire a more ambiguous reputation, at least in the eyes of govern-

---

[219] This is not to suggest that non-traditional institutions are necessarily less long term. To date, many sovereign wealth funds have adopted a conspicuously long strategy towards investment.

[220] J. Armour and B. Cheffins, *The Rise and Fall (?) of Activism by Hedge Funds*, ECGI Law Working Paper 136/2009; E. Rock and M. Kahan, *Hedge Funds in Corporate Governance and Corporate Control*, ECGI Law Working Paper 76/2006.

[221] The Kay Review is ambiguous about how activist hedge funds fit into its categorisation of shareholders between investors ('good') and traders ('bad'). See above n. 206, para 5.4.

[222] In the case of the successful bid by Kraft for Cadbury, hedge fund holdings in Cadbury moved from 5% before the deal was announced to 30% during the course of the bid period.

ment, if it ceases to be identified with intervention to promote the long-term value of the company.[223]

An unrelated development, at the opposite end of the range of investment strategies, is the growth of 'tracking funds', which may reduce incentives to engage. Although funds which track a market are by definition locked into that market and might be thought to have an incentive to improve performance in that market, their business model is based on low fees and so they will not have the resources to support engagement beyond the most minimal level. What they offer is a low-cost way of holding an index, not a promise to improve the performance of the companies constituting that index. The Kay Review states that 'Passive managers should recognise a special responsibility to improve the performance of the index they track.'[224] However, it is very unclear how the normative basis of this 'special responsibility' is constructed. It seems to contradict the terms upon which they contract with investors.

Controlling shareholders—Finally, from a completely different perspective, there is evidence of growth, albeit from a small base, in the number of Main Market companies where there is a dominant shareholder, ie. the opposite of the commonly found dispersed shareholding pattern. These majority-controlled companies are typically foreign-incorporated resources companies which have carried out IPOs in London in recent years and some of them are large enough to be included in the FTSE 100 index.[225] Two particular problems arise in respect of such companies. First, the comply-or-explain principle underlying the CGC does not work well in this context, since the board, appointed by the controlling shareholder, explains any divergence from the Code in effect to itself. Second, the CGC and the Listing Rules do not contain well developed protection for minority shareholders, since they assume the established pattern of dispersed ownership.

In an initial consultation over the issue, the FSA seemed lukewarm about significant reform,[226] but consultation showed that investors had significant con-

---

[223] See also *Financial Times*, 'Activist Investors Toast a Banner Year', 23 December 2012, referring mainly to North America. It is very difficult, of course, to determine whether any particular change is driven by short-term or long-term considerations.

[224] Above n. 206, p. 50. The Review doubts the value of index tracking for investors, but makes no proposals to control it, perhaps not surprisingly given its popularity with investors, large and small. See *ibid.*, paras 7.26–7.30.

[225] Examples are Eurasian Natural Resources Corporation, Kazakhyms, Fresnillo, Vedenta and Essar Energy. See the *Financial Times*, 17 June 2011. For a detailed analysis see B. Cheffins, *The Undermining of UK Corporate Governance(?)*, 2012 (available at <ssrn.com/abstract=2129686>).

[226] FSA, *Amendments to the Listing Rules etc*, cp 12/02, paras 1.18–1.23.

cerns in the area and a Consultation Paper[227] published in October 2012 proposed to make a number of important changes—a recent example of investors' continuing power to influence the making of board rules in the UK. To address the argument that comply-or-explain does not work well where there is a controlling shareholder, the FSA favoured making the CGC recommendation concerning the proportion of independent members on the board mandatory for premium-listed companies with a controlling shareholder (ie. one holding at least 30% of the voting rights).[228] This was a significant recognition of the limits of comply-or-explain in the presence of a controlling shareholder. To make this suggestion fully effective, it was further proposed that the election of independent directors should be subject to a dual-approval requirement, ie. approval by both the controlling shareholder and a majority of the non-controlling shareholders.[229]

Going beyond the election of independent directors, the FSA proposed to reinstate a requirement for premium-listed companies which had been part of the Listing Rules until 2004: This was that the company should be capable of acting independently of its controlling shareholder. The purpose of the requirement for independence is to ensure that the controlling shareholder does not have a commercial stranglehold over the listed company's business, to the point where it has little alternative but to do what that shareholder asks—for example, where the company has no access to financing but that provided by the controlling shareholder. The independence requirement would be supported by a further requirement that the company enter into a (disclosed) 'relationship agreement' with the controlling shareholder. The content of that agreement would be to some extent for the parties to determine, but it would be required to contain a commitment from the controlling shareholder to abstain from influencing the day-to-day running of the company and to conduct all transactions with the company at arm's length and on a commercial basis. Significant amendments to the relationship agreement would require the consent of the non-controlling shareholders.[230]

The FSA thus sought to address the governance issues of controlled companies directly rather than indirectly by strengthening the free float rules for premium-listed companies. Indeed, it proposed to relax the free float requirements for standard listing in order to maintain the attractiveness of London as a place for foreign companies to launch IPOs.[231] The problems this might cause for

---

[227] FSA, *Enhancing the Effectiveness of the Listing Regime and Feedback on CP 12-02*, cp 12–25, 2012.

[228] Paras 7.85 ff.—two slightly different ways of implementing the principle would be offered to companies.

[229] Paras 7.93 ff. In the case of deadlock there would be a second (or further) vote within 90 days.

[230] Paras 7.58 ff.

[231] Paras. 7.107 ff.

funds which track one of the FTSE UK indices were partially addressed by FTSE itself, a commercial organisation. In December 2011 FTSE raised its free float requirement for admission to the main UK indices from 15% to 25%, but important institutional investors were reported as thinking the figure should be 50%—ie. a majority-controlled company would not have access to the indices and so tracking funds would not be required to invest in them.[232]

Overall, one can say that the simple picture of UK companies having dispersed shareholdings but where long-only shareholders (only) have the capacity to form coalitions which may engage with the management of portfolio companies in some circumstances is incomplete. The pension funds and insurance companies, whilst still very important, are less dominant than they were a decade ago, whilst we see the emergence of other types of non-passive investor whose incentives are not as yet well understood.

c) Changes in Governmental Policy

The shareholder-centred orientation of UK company law depends upon, as a minimum, governmental tolerance of this policy and probably requires some governmental support—for example, in setting appropriate governance rules in the Companies Acts. Over the past 50 years that toleration and support have usually been forthcoming. There are obviously alternative theories of how company law should be organised and from time to time these alternatives have gained some purchase in policy debates—for example, mandatory employee representation at board level in the 1970s[233] and 'stakeholderism' more recently. The shareholder-friendly policy, although well entrenched, is not incapable of change and would be under threat of change if government concluded that shareholders' interests were not sufficiently well aligned with those of society as a whole. It cannot therefore be assumed that the shareholder-centred focus of UK company law will continue as a matter of right for the indefinite future.

However, at both national and European Union levels the UK system has been able to see off fundamental challenge to date. Currently, at domestic level, the notion of stewardship, coupled with the 'enlightened shareholder value' restatement of directors' duties,[234] appears to be doing the job of downgrading more interventionist governmental policies, even while stewardship itself implies some constraints on investors' freedom to pursue whatever policies they please towards portfolio companies. At Union level, the adoption of more interventionist policies is always a greater risk, because the Union contains a wide range of company law systems whose historical development has been very different from that of the

---

[232] *Financial Times*, 'FTSE pushed on investor rights', 15 December 2011.

[233] See text attached to n. 34 above.

[234] Above sec. 3.1.4.

British system. Recently, the comply-or-explain approach has been viewed
sceptically by the European Commission,[235] possibly because the market conditions for its effective operation do not exist across the Community. However,
the current corporate law and corporate governance action plan proposes only a
non-binding Recommendation on the specific issue of non-compliance explanations and generally bases its policies on a stewardship or engagement approach
which is well aligned with the domestic UK rules.[236]

6. Conclusion

The formal rules of British company law, including therefore its board rules, have
retained into the twenty-first century the characteristic which they were given in
the formative period of modern company law in the middle of the nineteenth
century. This principal characteristic was control by the members (ie. the shareholders) of the company, which was viewed primarily as a private association.
The structure of the company, including the role and structure of the board, were
thus perceived mainly as matters for those members, not for the legislature. The
actual level of control shareholders were able to exercise over companies
depended, however, partly on the structure of shareholdings and partly on
features of the external environment in which companies had to operate. In the
period immediately after the Second World War the increasing dispersion of
shareholdings, coupled with state policies of nationalisation of the 'commanding
heights' of the economy and strong trade unions, meant that the actual level of
shareholder control was much less than the formal company law rules would have
suggested. Managers dominated boards and there was little accountability to
shareholders. With the partial re-concentration of shareholdings in the hands of
the long-only institutions (notably insurance companies and pension funds), the
retreat of the state from ownership of UK industry and the decline in the strength
of trade unions, a resurgence of investor influence over companies took place in
the last decades of the twentieth century. Investors exercised a new-found degree
of influence over the setting of board rules and over the strategies of portfolio
companies. Over the past decade, whilst this pattern of investor influence has
continued to be the established norm, government has been somewhat less ready
to assume a complete alignment between investor and societal interests. Stewardship is the modern way of asserting a public interest in the strategic decisions of
management, but it has come to the fore just at a time when the continuing

---

[235] European Commission, Green Paper on EU Corporate Governance, COM(2011) 164
final, § 3.

[236] Communication from the Commission on an Action Plan on European company law and
corporate governance, COM(2012) 740/2, esp 2.2 and 3.

evolution of patterns of share ownership has placed a question mark over the capacity of the long-only shareholders to exercise the influence over corporate management which they had so recently acquired.

7. Selection of Literature

Books

Cheffins, B., *Corporate Ownership and Control: British Business Transformed,* 2008.

Conaglen, M., *Fiduciary Loyalty,* 2010.

Davies, P., *Introduction to Company Law,* 2nd edn., 2010, ch. 6.

Davies, P. and Worthington, S., *Gower and Davies' Principles of Modern Company Law,* 9th edn., 2012, Part Three.

Kershaw, D., *Company Law in Context,* 2009, Part II.

Reisberg, A., *Derivative Actions and Corporate Governance,* 2007.

Worthington, S., *Sealy's Cases and Materials on Company Law,* 9th edn., 2010, ch. 5, 6 and 12.

Articles and chapters in books

Acharya,V., Kehoe, C., Reyner, M., *Private Equity vs PLC Boards: A Comparison of Practices and Effectiveness,* Centre for Economic Policy Research, Discussion Paper 7148, 2009.

Arcot, S, Bruno, V., Faure-Grimaud, A., 'Corporate governance in the UK: Is the comply or explain approach working?', (2010) 30 *International Review of Law and Economics,* 193.

Conyon, M., Sadler, G., 'Shareholder Voting and Directors' Remuneration Report Legislation', (2010) 18 *Corporate Governance: an International Review* 296.

Davies, P., 'Board Structure in the UK and Germany: Convergence or Continuing Divergence?', (2001) 2 *International and Comparative Corporate Law Journal* 435.

Hill, J., 'The Rising Tension between Shareholder and Director Power in the Common Law World', (2010) 18 *Corporate Governance: an International Review* 344.

Hood, P., 'Directors' Duties under the Companies Act 2006: Clarity or Confusion', (2013) 13 *Journal of Corporate Law Studies* 1.

Moore, M., 'The Evolving Contours of the Board's Risk Management Function in UK Corporate Governance', 10 *Journal of Corporate Law Studies* 279 (2010).

Owen, G., Kirchmaier, T., 'The Changing Role of the Chairman', (2008) 9 *European Business Organization Law Review* 187

Roach, L., 'The UK Stewarship Code', (2011) 11 *Journal of Corporate Law Studies* 463.

Index